Official Product Documentation from Macromedia

Powerful design and development tools require authoritative technical documentation. With the release of Macromedia Studio 8, there is no more authoritative source than the development and writing teams who created the product. Now their official documentation is available to you in printed book form, to help you evaluate the software or to advance your capabilities as you take advantage of the powerful features in this release.

Developing Extensions for Macromedia Flash 8
Learn firsthand how to extend the capabilities of the Web's most popular authoring platform, using JavaScript. Create commands and extensible tools for use in this authoring environment.
0-321-39416-X, $44.99

Using ActionScript 2.0 Components with Macromedia Flash 8
The resource for developers and ActionScript users who want to use components to speed development.
0-321-39539-5, $54.99

Learning Actionscript 2.0 for Macromedia Flash 8
A detailed introduction to coding with ActionScript to add interactivity and produce high-impact Web experiences. Includes extensive reusable code examples.
0-321-39415-1, $49.99

Macromedia Flash 8: A Tutorial Guide
A collection of step-by-step tutorials that teach both beginning and advanced Flash techniques.
0-321-39414-3, $29.99

ActionScript 2.0 Language Reference for Macromedia Flash 8
Dictionary-style reference covers valuable syntax and usage information; detailed descriptions of classes, functions, properties, and events; and code samples for every element in the ActionScript language.
0-321-38404-0, $39.99

Developing Extensions for Macromedia Dreamweaver 8
Extend the capabilities of Dreamweaver 8 using JavaScript. Write your own objects, behavior actions, and commands that affect Dreamweaver 8 documents and the elements within them.
0-321-39540-9, $54.99

macromedia®
PRESS
www.macromediapress.com

ActionScript 2.0 Language Reference for Macromedia® FLASH® 8

Francis Cheng, Jen deHaan,
Robert L. Dixon, Shimul Rahim

macromedia®
PRESS

ActionScript 2.0 Language Reference for Macromedia Flash 8

Francis Cheng, Jen deHaan, Robert L. Dixon, Shimul Rahim

Macromedia Press books are published by:
Peachpit
1249 Eighth Street
Berkeley, CA 94710
510/524-2178 510/524-2221 (fax)
Find us on the World Wide Web at:
www.peachpit.com   www.macromedia.com

To report errors, please send a note to errata@peachpit.com

ISBN 0-321-38404-0

9 8 7 6 5 4 3 2 1

Printed and bound in the United States of America

Credits

Macromedia

Project Management: JuLee Burdekin

Lead Writers: Francis Cheng, Robert Dixon, Shimul Rahim

Additional Writers: Jen deHaan, Thais Derich, Guy Haas, David Jacowitz, Jeff Swartz

Samples Developers: Luke Bayes, Francis Cheng, Robert Dixon, Ali Mills, Jeff Swartz

Editing: Linda Adler, Geta Carlson, Evelyn Eldridge, John Hammett, Noreen Maher, Mark Nigara, Lisa Stanziano, Anne Szabla, Jessie Wood

Production Management: Patrice O'Neill

Media Design and Production: Adam Barnett, John Francis, Brett Jarvis, Mario Reynoso

Special thanks to: Peter deHaan, Gary Grossman, Lee Thomason, and The Flash Player Core Team

Macromedia Press

Macromedia Press Editor: Angela C. Kozlowski

Production Editor: Pat Christenson

Product Marketing Manager: Zigi Lowenberg

Cover Design: Charlene Charles Will

Dedication

The Studio 8 Documentation Team recognizes and honors Patrice O'Neill, who inspires all of us with her dedication and commitment.

Contents

CHAPTER 1

ActionScript language elements

1

This section provides syntax, usage information, and code samples for global functions and properties (those elements that do not belong to an ActionScript class); compiler directives; and for the constants, operators, statements, and keywords used in ActionScript and defined in the ECMAScript (ECMA-262) edition 4 draft language specification.

Compiler Directives

This section contains the directives to include in your ActionScript file to direct the compiler to preprocess certain instructions. Do not place a semicolon (;) at the end of the line that contains the directive.

Compiler Directives summary

Directive	Description
`#endinitclip`	Indicates the end of a block of initialization actions.
`#include`	Includes the contents of the specified file, as if the commands in the file are part of the calling script.
`#initclip`	Indicates the beginning of a block of initialization actions.

#endinitclip directive

`#endinitclip`

Indicates the end of a block of initialization actions.

Do not place a semicolon (;) at the end of the line that contains the #endinitclip directive.

Availability: ActionScript 1.0; Flash Player 6.0

Example

```
#initclip
...initialization actions go here...
#endinitclip
```

#include directive

`#include "[path]filename.as":String`

Includes the contents of the specified file, as if the commands in the file are part of the calling script. The `#include` directive is invoked at compile time. Therefore, if you make any changes to an external file, you must save the file and recompile any FLA files that use it.

If you use the Check Syntax button for a script that contains `#include` statements, the syntax of the included files is also checked.

You can use `#include` in FLA files and in external script files, but not in ActionScript 2.0 class files.

You can specify no path, a relative path, or an absolute path for the file to be included. If you don't specify a path, the AS file must be in one of the following locations:

- The same directory as the FLA file. The same directory as the script containing the `#include` statement

- The global Include directory, which is one of the following:
  --Windows 2000 or Windows XP: C:\Documents and Settings*user* \Local Settings\ Application Data\Macromedia\Flash 8*language*\Configuration\Include

  --Macintosh OS X: Hard Drive/Users/Library/Application Support/Macromedia/Flash 8/*language*/Configuration/Include

- The *Flash 8 program\language*\First Run\Include directory; if you save a file here, it is copied to the global Include directory the next time you start Flash.

To specify a relative path for the AS file, use a single dot (.) to indicate the current directory, two dots (..) to indicate a parent directory, and forward slashes (/) to indicate subdirectories. See the following example section.

To specify an absolute path for the AS file, use the format supported by your platform (Macintosh or Windows). See the following example section. (This usage is not recommended because it requires the directory structure to be the same on any computer that you use to compile the script.)

If you place files in the First Run/Include directory or in the global Include directory, back up these files. If you ever need to uninstall and reinstall Flash, these directories might be deleted and overwritten.

Do not place a semicolon (;) at the end of the line that contains the #include directive.

Availability: ActionScript 1.0; Flash Player 4.0

Parameters

`[path]filename.as`: `String` - *filename.as* The filename and optional path for the script to add to the Actions panel or to the current script; *.as* is the recommended filename extension.

Example

The following examples show various ways of specifying a path for a file to be included in your script:

```
// Note that #include statements do not end with a semicolon (;)
// AS file is in same directory as FLA file or script
// or is in the global Include directory or the First Run/Include directory
#include "init_script.as"

// AS file is in a subdirectory of one of the above directories
// The subdirectory is named "FLA_includes"
#include "FLA_includes/init_script.as"
// AS file is in a subdirectory of the script file directory
// The subdirectory is named "SCRIPT_includes"
#include "SCRIPT_includes/init_script.as"
// AS file is in a directory at the same level as one of the above
    directories
// AS file is in a directory at the same level as the directory
// that contains the script file
// The directory is named "ALL_includes"
#include "../ALL_includes/init_script.as"

// AS file is specified by an absolute path in Windows
// Note use of forward slashes, not backslashes
#include "C:/Flash_scripts/init_script.as"

// AS file is specified by an absolute path on Macintosh
#include "Mac HD:Flash_scripts:init_script.as"
```

#initclip directive

`#initclip [order:Number]`

Indicates the beginning of a block of initialization actions. When multiple clips are initialized at the same time, you can use the `order` parameter to specify which initialization occurs first. Initialization actions are executed when a movie clip symbol is defined. If the movie clip is an exported symbol, the initialization actions are executed before the actions on Frame 1 of the SWF file. Otherwise, they are executed immediately before the actions of the frame that contains the first instance of the associated movie clip symbol.

Initialization actions are executed only once when a SWF file is played. Use them for one-time initializations, such as class definition and registration.

Do not place a semicolon (;) at the end of the line that contains the #initclip directive.

Availability: ActionScript 1.0; Flash Player 6.0

Parameters

`order:Number` [optional] - A non-negative integer that specifies the execution order of blocks of #initclip code. This is an optional parameter. You must specify the value by using an integer literal (only decimal values are allowed, not hexadecimal), and not by using a variable. If you include multiple #initclip blocks in a single movie clip symbol, then the compiler uses the last `order` value specified in that movie clip symbol for all #initclip blocks in that symbol.

Example

In the following example, ActionScript is placed on Frame 1 in a movie clip instance. A variables.txt text file is placed in the same directory.

```
#initclip

trace("initializing app");

var variables:LoadVars = new LoadVars();

variables.load("variables.txt");

variables.onLoad = function(success:Boolean) {

  trace("variables loaded:"+success);

  if (success) {
  for (i in variables) {
  trace("variables."+i+" = "+variables[i]);
  }
  }
};

#endinitclip
```

Constants

A constant is a variable used to represent a property whose value never changes. This section describes global constants that are available to every script.

Constants summary

Modifiers	Constant	Description
	false	A unique Boolean value that represents the opposite of true.
	Infinity	Specifies the IEEE-754 value representing positive infinity.
	-Infinity	Specifies the IEEE-754 value representing negative infinity.
	NaN	A predefined variable with the IEEE-754 value for NaN (not a number).
	newline	Inserts a carriage return character ($\backslash$r) that generates a blank line in text output generated by your code.
	null	A special value that can be assigned to variables or returned by a function if no data was provided.
	true	A unique Boolean value that represents the opposite of false.
	undefined	A special value, usually used to indicate that a variable has not yet been assigned a value.

false constant

A unique Boolean value that represents the opposite of true.

When automatic data typing converts false to a number, it becomes 0; when it converts false to a string, it becomes "false".

Availability: ActionScript 1.0; Flash Player 5

Example

This example shows how automatic data typing converts false to a number and to a string:

```
var bool1:Boolean = Boolean(false);

// converts it to the number 0
trace(1 + bool1); // outputs 1
```

```
// converts it to a string
trace("String: " + bool1); // outputs String: false
```

Infinity constant

Specifies the IEEE-754 value representing positive infinity. The value of this constant is the same as `Number.POSITIVE_INFINITY`.

Availability: ActionScript 1.0; Flash Player 5

See also

`POSITIVE_INFINITY (Number.POSITIVE_INFINITY property)`

-Infinity constant

Specifies the IEEE-754 value representing negative infinity. The value of this constant is the same as `Number.NEGATIVE_INFINITY`.

Availability: ActionScript 1.0; Flash Player 5

See also

`NEGATIVE_INFINITY (Number.NEGATIVE_INFINITY property)`

NaN constant

A predefined variable with the IEEE-754 value for NaN (not a number). To determine whether a number is NaN, use `isNaN()`.

Availability: ActionScript 1.0; Flash Player 5

See also

`isNaN function, NaN (Number.NaN property)`

newline constant

Inserts a carriage return character (\r) that generates a blank line in text output generated by your code. Use `newline` to make space for information that is retrieved by a function or statement in your code.

Availability: ActionScript 1.0; Flash Player 4

Example

The following example shows how `newline` displays output from the `trace()` statement on multiple lines.

```
var myName:String = "Lisa", myAge:Number = 30;
trace(myName+myAge);
trace("-----");
trace(myName+newline+myAge);
// output:
Lisa30
-----
Lisa
30
```

See also

`trace function`

null constant

A special value that can be assigned to variables or returned by a function if no data was provided. You can use `null` to represent values that are missing or that do not have a defined data type.

Availability: ActionScript 1.0; Flash Player 5

Example

The following example checks the first six values of an indexed array and outputs a message if no value is set (if the value == `null`):

```
var testArray:Array = new Array();
testArray[0] = "fee";
testArray[1] = "fi";
testArray[4] = "foo";

for (i = 0; i < 6; i++) {
  if (testArray[i] == null) {
  trace("testArray[" + i + "] == null");
  }
}
```

The output is the following:

```
testArray[2] == null
testArray[3] == null
testArray[5] == null
```

true constant

A unique Boolean value that represents the opposite of `false`. When automatic data typing converts `true` to a number, it becomes 1; when it converts `true` to a string, it becomes `"true"`.

Availability: ActionScript 1.0; Flash Player 5

Example

The following example shows the use of `true` in an `if` statement:

```
var shouldExecute:Boolean;
// ...
// code that sets shouldExecute to either true or false goes here
// shouldExecute is set to true for this example:

shouldExecute = true;

if (shouldExecute == true) {
 trace("your statements here");
}

// true is also implied, so the if statement could also be written:
// if (shouldExecute) {
// trace("your statements here");
// }
```

The following example shows how automatic data typing converts `true` to the number 1:

```
var myNum:Number;
myNum = 1 + true;
trace(myNum); // output: 2
```

See also

`false constant`, `Boolean`

undefined constant

A special value, usually used to indicate that a variable has not yet been assigned a value. A reference to an undefined value returns the special value `undefined`. The ActionScript code `typeof(undefined)` returns the string `"undefined"`. The only value of type `undefined` is `undefined`.

In files published for Flash Player 6 or earlier, the value of `String(undefined)` is "" (an empty string). In files published for Flash Player 7 or later, the value of `String(undefined)` is `"undefined"` (undefined is converted to a string).

In files published for Flash Player 6 or earlier, the value of Number(undefined) is 0. In files published for Flash Player 7 or later, the value of Number(undefined) is NaN.

The value undefined is similar to the special value null. When null and undefined are compared with the equality (==) operator, they compare as equal. However, when null and undefined are compared with the strict equality (===) operator, they compare as not equal.

Availability: ActionScript 1.0; Flash Player 5

Example

In the following example, the variable x has not been declared and therefore has the value undefined.

In the first section of code, the equality operator (==) compares the value of x to the value undefined, and the appropriate result is sent to the Output panel.

In the second section of code, the equality (==) operator compares the values null and undefined.

```
// x has not been declared
trace("The value of x is "+x);

if (x == undefined) {
 trace("x is undefined");
} else {
 trace("x is not undefined");
}

trace("typeof (x) is "+typeof (x));

if (null == undefined) {
 trace("null and undefined are equal");
} else {
 trace("null and undefined are not equal");
}
```

The following result is displayed in the Output panel.

```
The value of x is undefined
x is undefined
typeof (x) is undefined
null and undefined are equal
```

Global Functions

This section contains a set of built-in functions that are available in any part of a SWF file where ActionScript is used. These global functions cover a wide variety of common programming tasks such as working with data types (`Boolean()`, `int()`, and so on), producing debugging information (`trace()`), and communicating with Flash Player or the browser (`fscommand()`).

Global Functions summary

Modifiers	Signature	Description
	`Array([numElements:N umber], [elementN:Object])`	Creates a new, empty array or converts specified elements to an array.
	`asfunction(function: String, parameter:String)`	A special protocol for URLs in HTML text fields that allows an HREF link to call an ActionScript function.
	`Boolean(expression:O bject)`	Converts the parameter *expression* to a Boolean value and returns `true` or `false`.
	`call(frame:Object)`	**Deprecated** since Flash Player 5. This action was deprecated in favor of the `function` statement. Executes the script in the called frame without moving the playhead to that frame.
	`chr(number:Number)`	**Deprecated** since Flash Player 5. This function was deprecated in favor of `String.fromCharCode()`. Converts ASCII code numbers to characters.
	`clearInterval(interv alID:Number)`	Stops the `setInterval()` call.
	`duplicateMovieClip(t arget:Object, newname:String, depth:Number)`	Creates an instance of a movie clip while the SWF file is playing.
	`escape(expression:St ring)`	Converts the parameter to a string and encodes it in a URL-encoded format, where all nonalphanumeric characters are replaced with % hexadecimal sequences.
	`eval(expression:Obje ct)`	Accesses variables, properties, objects, or movie clips by name.
	`fscommand(command:St ring, parameters:String)`	Lets the SWF file communicate with either Flash Player or the program hosting Flash Player, such as a web browser.

Modifiers	Signature	Description
	`getProperty(my_mc:St ring, property)`	Returns the value of the specified property for the movie clip *my_mc*.
	`getTimer()`	Returns the number of milliseconds that have elapsed since the SWF file started playing.
	`getURL(url:String, [window:String], [method:String])`	Loads a document from a specific URL into a window or passes variables to another application at a defined URL.
	`getVersion()`	Returns a string containing Flash Player version and platform information.
	`gotoAndPlay([scene:S tring], frame:Object)`	Sends the playhead to the specified frame in a scene and plays from that frame.
	`gotoAndStop([scene:S tring], frame:Object)`	Sends the playhead to the specified frame in a scene and stops it.
	`ifFrameLoaded([scene :String], frame:Object)`	**Deprecated** since Flash Player 5. This function has been deprecated. Macromedia recommends that you use the `MovieClip._framesloaded` property. Checks whether the contents of a specific frame are available locally.
	`int(value:Number)`	**Deprecated** since Flash Player 5. This function was deprecated in favor of `Math.round()`. Converts a decimal number to an integer value by truncating the decimal value.
	`isFinite(expression: Object)`	Evaluates *expression* and returns `true` if it is a finite number or `false` if it is infinity or negative infinity.
	`isNaN(expression:Obj ect)`	Evaluates the parameter and returns `true` if the value is `NaN` (not a number).
	`length(expression:St ring, variable:Object)`	**Deprecated** since Flash Player 5. This function, along with all the string functions, has been deprecated. Macromedia recommends that you use the methods of the String class and the `String.length` property to perform the same operations. Returns the length of the specified string or variable.
	`loadMovie(url:String , target:Object, [method:String])`	Loads a SWF or JPEG file into Flash Player while the original SWF file plays.
	`loadMovieNum(url:Str ing, level:Number, [method:String])`	Loads a SWF or JPEG file into a level in Flash Player while the originally loaded SWF file plays.

Modifiers	Signature	Description
	`loadVariables(url:St ring, target:Object, [method:String])`	Reads data from an external file, such as a text file or text generated by ColdFusion, a CGI script, Active Server Pages (ASP), PHP, or Perl script, and sets the values for variables in a target movie clip.
	`loadVariablesNum(url :String, level:Number, [method:String])`	Reads data from an external file, such as a text file or text generated by a ColdFusion, CGI script, ASP, PHP, or Perl script, and sets the values for variables in a Flash Player level.
	`mbchr(number:Number)`	**Deprecated** since Flash Player 5. This function was deprecated in favor of the `String.fromCharCode()` method. Converts an ASCII code number to a multibyte character.
	`mblength(string:Stri ng)`	**Deprecated** since Flash Player 5. This function was deprecated in favor of the methods and properties of the String class. Returns the length of the multibyte character string.
	`mbord(character:Stri ng)`	**Deprecated** since Flash Player 5. This function was deprecated in favor of `String.charCodeAt()`. Converts the specified character to a multibyte number.
	`mbsubstring(value:St ring, index:Number, count:Number)`	**Deprecated** since Flash Player 5. This function was deprecated in favor of `String.substr()`. Extracts a new multibyte character string from a multibyte character string.
	`MMExecute(command:St ring)`	Lets you issue Flash JavaScript API (JSAPI) commands from ActionScript.
	`nextFrame()`	Sends the playhead to the next frame.
	`nextScene()`	Sends the playhead to Frame 1 of the next scene.
	`Number(expression:Ob ject)`	Converts the parameter *expression* to a number.
	`Object([value:Object ])`	Creates a new empty object or converts the specified number, string, or Boolean value to an object.
	`on(mouseEvent:Object )`	Specifies the mouse event or keypress that triggers an action.
	`onClipEvent(movieEve nt:Object)`	Triggers actions defined for a specific instance of a movie clip.

Modifiers	Signature	Description
	`ord(character:String)`	**Deprecated** since Flash Player 5. This function was deprecated in favor of the methods and properties of the String class. Converts characters to ASCII code numbers.
	`parseFloat(string:String)`	Converts a string to a floating-point number.
	`parseInt(expression:String, [radix:Number])`	Converts a string to an integer.
	`play()`	Moves the playhead forward in the Timeline.
	`prevFrame()`	Sends the playhead to the previous frame.
	`prevScene()`	Sends the playhead to Frame 1 of the previous scene.
	`print(target:Object, boundingBox:String)`	Prints the `target` movie clip according to the boundaries specified in the parameter (`bmovie`, `bmax`, or `bframe`).
	`printAsBitmap(target:Object, boundingBox:String)`	Prints the `target` movie clip as a bitmap according to the boundaries specified in the parameter (`bmovie`, `bmax`, or `bframe`).
	`printAsBitmapNum(level:Number, boundingBox:String)`	Prints a level in Flash Player as a bitmap according to the boundaries specified in the parameter (`bmovie`, `bmax`, or `bframe`).
	`printNum(level:Number, boundingBox:String)`	Prints the level in Flash Player according to the boundaries specified in the `boundingBox` parameter (`bmovie`, `bmax`, `bframe`).
	`random(value:Number)`	**Deprecated** since Flash Player 5. This function was deprecated in favor of `Math.random()`. Returns a random integer between 0 and one less than the integer specified in the *value*.
	`removeMovieClip(target:Object)`	Deletes the specified movie clip.
	`setInterval(functionReference:Function, interval:Number, [param:Object], objectReference:Object, methodName:String)`	Calls a function or a method of an object at periodic intervals while a SWF file plays.

Modifiers	Signature	Description
	setProperty(target:0 bject, property:Object, expression:Object)	Changes a property value of a movie clip as the movie clip plays.
	showRedrawRegions(en able:Boolean, [color:Number])	Provides the ability for the debugger player to outline the regions of the screen that are being redrawn.
	startDrag(target:Obj ect, [lock:Boolean], [left,top,right,bott om:Number])	Makes the *target* movie clip draggable while the movie plays.
	stop()	Stops the SWF file that is currently playing.
	stopAllSounds()	Stops all sounds currently playing in a SWF file without stopping the playhead.
	stopDrag()	Stops the current drag operation.
	String(expression:Ob ject)	Returns a string representation of the specified parameter.
	substring(string:Str ing, index:Number, count:Number)	**Deprecated** since Flash Player 5. This function was deprecated in favor of String.substr(). Extracts part of a string.
	targetPath(targetObj ect:Object)	Returns a string containing the target path of *movieClipObject*.
	tellTarget(target:St ring, statement(s))	**Deprecated** since Flash Player 5. Macromedia recommends that you use dot (.) notation and the with statement. Applies the instructions specified in the *statements* parameter to the Timeline specified in the *target* parameter.
	toggleHighQuality()	**Deprecated** since Flash Player 5. This function was deprecated in favor of _quality. Turns anti-aliasing on and off in Flash Player.
	trace(expression:Obj ect)	Evaluates the expression and outputs the result.
	unescape(string:Stri ng)	Evaluates the parameter *x* as a string, decodes the string from URL-encoded format (converting all hexadecimal sequences to ASCII characters), and returns the string.
	unloadMovie(target:0 bject)	Removes a movie clip that was loaded by means of loadMovie() from Flash Player.

Modifiers	Signature	Description
	`unloadMovieNum(level :Number)`	Removes a SWF or image that was loaded by means of `loadMovieNum()` from Flash Player.
	`updateAfterEvent()`	Updates the display when you call it within an handler or using `setInterval()`.

Array function

```
Array() : Array
Array(numElements:Number) : Array
Array(element0:Object, [element1, element2, ...elementN]) : Array
```

Creates a new array of length 0 or more, or an array populated by a list of specified elements, possibly of different data types.

Use `Array()` to create one of the following:

- An empty array
- An array with a specific length but whose elements have undefined values
- An array whose elements have specific values

Using this function is similar to creating an array with the Array constructor (see "Constructor for the Array class").

You can pass a number (`numElements`) or a list of elements containing one or more different types (`element0, element1, ... elementN`).

Parameters that can accept more than one data type are listed in the signature as type `Object`.

Availability: ActionScript 1.0; Flash Player 6

Parameters

`numElements:Number` [optional] - A positive integer that specifies the number of elements in the array. You can specify either `numElements` or the list of elements, but not both.

`elementN:Object` [optional] - One or more parameters, `element0, element1, ...` , `elementN`, the values of which can be of any type. Parameters that can accept more than one data type are listed as type `Object`. You can specify either numElements or the list of elements, but not both.

Returns

`Array` - An array.

Example

```
var myArray:Array = Array();
```

```
myArray.push(12);
trace(myArray); //traces 12
myArray[4] = 7;
trace(myArray); //traces 12,undefined,undefined,undefined,7
```

Usage 2: The following example creates an array of length 4 but with no elements defined:

```
var myArray:Array = Array(4);
trace(myArray.length); // traces 4
trace(myArray); // traces undefined,undefined,undefined,undefined
```

Usage 3: The following example creates an array with three defined elements:

```
var myArray:Array = Array("firstElement", "secondElement", "thirdElement");
trace (myArray); // traces firstElement,secondElement,thirdElement
Unlike the Array class constructor, the Array() function does not use the
  keyword new .
```

See also

`Array`

asfunction protocol

`asfunction:function:Function, parameter:String`

A special protocol for URLs in HTML text fields that allows an HREF link to call an ActionScript function. In HTML text fields, you can create links using the HTML A tag. The HREF attribute of the A tag contains a URL that uses a standard protocol such as HTTP, HTTPS, or FTP. The `asfunction` protocol is an additional protocol that is specific to Flash, which causes the link to invoke an ActionScript function.

Availability: ActionScript 1.0; Flash Player 5

Parameters

`function:String` - An identifier for a function.

`parameter:String` - A string that is passed to the function named in the *function* parameter.

Example

In the following example, the `playMP3()` function is defined. The TextField object list_txt is created and set so HTML text can be rendered. The text Track 1 and Track 2 are links inside the text field. The `playMP3()` function is called when the user clicks either link and plays the MP3 that is passed as a parameter of the asfunction call.

```
var myMP3:Sound = new Sound();
function playMP3(mp3:String) {
 myMP3.loadSound(mp3, true);
```

```
myMP3.onLoad = function(success) {
if (!success) {
// code to handle errors here
}
};
}
this.createTextField("list_txt", this.getNextHighestDepth(), 0, 0, 200,
  100);
list_txt.autoSize = true;
list_txt.html = true;
list_txt.multiline = true;
list_txt.htmlText = "<a href=\"asfunction:playMP3, track1.mp3\">Track 1</
  a><br>";
list_txt.htmlText += "<a href=\"asfunction:playMP3, track2.mp3\">Track 2</
  a><br>";
```

When you click a link, the MP3 sound file streams in Flash Player.

See also

`htmlText (TextField.htmlText property)`

Boolean function

`Boolean(expression:Object) : Boolean`

Converts the `expression` parameter to a Boolean value and returns a value as described in the following list:

- If `expression` is a Boolean value, the return value is `expression`.
- If `expression` is a number, the return value is `true` if the number is not 0; otherwise the return value is `false`.

If `expression` is a string, the return value is as follows:

- In files published for Flash Player 6 and earlier, the string is first converted to a number. The value is `true` if the number is not 0, otherwise the return value is `false`.
- In files published for Flash Player 7 and later, the result is `true` if the string has a length greater than 0; the value is `false` for an empty string.

If `expression` is a string, the result is `true` if the string has a length greater than 0; the value is `false` for an empty string.

- If `expression` is `undefined` or `NaN` (not a number), the return value is `false`.
- If `expression` is a movie clip or an object, the return value is `true`.

Unlike the Boolean class constructor, the `Boolean()` function does not use the keyword new. Moreover, the Boolean class constructor initializes a Boolean object to `false` if no parameter is specified, while the `Boolean()` function returns `undefined` if no parameter is specified.

Availability: ActionScript 1.0; Flash Player 5 - Behavior changed in Flash Player 7.

Parameters

`expression:Object` - An expression to convert to a Boolean value.

Returns

`Boolean` - A Boolean value.

Example

```
trace(Boolean(-1)); // output: true
trace(Boolean(0)); // output: false
trace(Boolean(1)); // output: true


trace(Boolean(true)); // output: true
trace(Boolean(false)); // output: false


trace(Boolean("true")); // output: true
trace(Boolean("false")); // output: true

trace(Boolean("Craiggers")); // output: true
trace(Boolean("")); // output: false
```

If files are published for Flash Player 6 and earlier, the results differ for three of the preceding examples:

```
trace(Boolean("true")); // output: false
trace(Boolean("false")); // output: false
trace(Boolean("Craiggers")); // output: false
```

This example shows a significant difference between use of the `Boolean()` function and the Boolean class. The `Boolean()` function creates a Boolean value, and the Boolean class creates a Boolean object. Boolean values are compared by value, and Boolean objects are compared by reference.

```
// Variables representing Boolean values are compared by value
var a:Boolean = Boolean("a"); // a is true
var b:Boolean = Boolean(1); // b is true
trace(a==b); // true


// Variables representing Boolean objects are compared by reference
var a:Boolean = new Boolean("a"); // a is true
var b:Boolean = new Boolean(1); // b is true
trace(a == b); // false
```

See also

`Boolean`

---

call function

`call(frame)`

Deprecated since Flash Player 5. This action was deprecated in favor of the `function` statement.

Executes the script in the called frame without moving the playhead to that frame. Local variables do not exist after the script executes.

- If variables are not declared inside a block ({ }) but the action list was executed with a call() action, the variables are local and expire at the end of the current list.
- If variables are not declared inside a block and the current action list was not executed with the call() action, the variables are interpreted as Timeline variables.

Availability: ActionScript 1.0; Flash Player 4

Parameters

`frame:Object` - The label or number of a frame in the Timeline.

See also

`function statement, call (Function.call method)`

chr function

`chr(number:Number) : String`

Deprecated since Flash Player 5. This function was deprecated in favor of `String.fromCharCode()`.

Converts ASCII code numbers to characters.

Availability: ActionScript 1.0; Flash Player 4

Parameters

`number:Number` - An ASCII code number.

Returns

`String` - The character value of the specified ASCII code.

Example

The following example converts the number 65 to the letter A and assigns it to the variable myVar: `myVar = chr(65);`

See also
fromCharCode (String.fromCharCode method)

clearInterval function

```
clearInterval(intervalID:Number) : Void
```
Stops the setInterval() call.

Availability: ActionScript 1.0; Flash Player 6

Parameters

intervalID:Number - A numeric (integer) identifier returned from a call to setInterval().

Example

The following example first sets and then clears an interval call:

```
function callback() {
 trace("interval called: "+getTimer()+" ms.");
}

var intervalID:Number = setInterval(callback, 1000);
```
You must clear the interval when you have finished using the function. Create a button called clearInt_btn and use the following ActionScript to clear setInterval():

```
clearInt_btn.onRelease = function(){
 clearInterval( intervalID );
 trace("cleared interval");
};
```

See also
setInterval function

duplicateMovieClip function

```
duplicateMovieClip(target:String, newname:String, depth:Number) : Void
duplicateMovieClip(target:MovieClip, newname:String, depth:Number) : Void
```
Creates an instance of a movie clip while the SWF file is playing. The playhead in duplicate movie clips always starts at Frame 1, regardless of where the playhead is in the original movie clip. Variables in the original movie clip are not copied into the duplicate movie clip. Use the removeMovieClip() function or method to delete a movie clip instance created with duplicateMovieClip().

Availability: ActionScript 1.0; Flash Player 4

Parameters

`target:Object` - The target path of the movie clip to duplicate. This parameter can be either a String (e.g. "my_mc") or a direct reference to the movie clip instance (e.g. my_mc). Parameters that can accept more than one data type are listed as type `Object`.

`newname:String` - A unique identifier for the duplicated movie clip.

`depth:Number` - A unique depth level for the duplicated movie clip. The depth level is a stacking order for duplicated movie clips. This stacking order is similar to the stacking order of layers in the Timeline; movie clips with a lower depth level are hidden under clips with a higher stacking order. You must assign each duplicated movie clip a unique depth level to prevent it from replacing SWF files on occupied depths.

Example

In the following example, a new movie clip instance is created called `img_mc`. An image is loaded into the movie clip, and then the `img_mc` clip is duplicated. The duplicated clip is called `newImg_mc`, and this new clip is moved on the Stage so it does not overlap the original clip, and the same image is loaded into the second clip.

```
this.createEmptyMovieClip("img_mc", this.getNextHighestDepth());
img_mc.loadMovie("http://www.helpexamples.com/flash/images/image1.jpg");
duplicateMovieClip(img_mc, "newImg_mc", this.getNextHighestDepth());
newImg_mc._x = 200;
newImg_mc.loadMovie("http://www.helpexamples.com/flash/images/image1.jpg");
```

To remove the duplicate movie clip, you could add this code for a button called `myButton_btn`.

```
this.myButton_btn.onRelease = function(){
 removeMovieClip(newImg_mc);
};
```

See also

`removeMovieClip` function, `duplicateMovieClip` (MovieClip.duplicateMovieClip method), `removeMovieClip` (MovieClip.removeMovieClip method)

escape function

`escape(expression:String) : String`

Converts the parameter to a string and encodes it in a URL-encoded format, where all nonalphanumeric characters are replaced with % hexadecimal sequences. When used in a URL-encoded string, the percentage symbol (%) is used to introduce escape characters, and is not equivalent to the modulo operator (%).

Availability: ActionScript 1.0; Flash Player 5

Parameters

expression:String - The expression to convert into a string and encode in a URL-encoded format.

Returns

String - URL-encoded string.

Example

The following code produces the result someuser%40somedomain%2Ecom:

```
var email:String = "someuser@somedomain.com";
trace(escape(email));
```

In this example, the at symbol (@) was replaced with %40 and the dot symbol (.) was replaced with %2E. This is useful if you're trying to pass information to a remote server and the data has special characters in it (for example, & or ?), as shown in the following code:

```
var redirectUrl:String = "http://
  www.somedomain.com?loggedin=true&username=Gus";
getURL("http://www.myothersite.com?returnurl="+ escape(redirectUrl));
```

See also

unescape function

eval function

```
eval(expression:Object) : Object
eval(expression:String) : Object
```

Accesses variables, properties, objects, or movie clips by name. If expression is a variable or a property, the value of the variable or property is returned. If expression is an object or movie clip, a reference to the object or movie clip is returned. If the element named in expression cannot be found, undefined is returned.

In Flash 4, eval() was used to simulate arrays; in Flash 5 or later, you should use the Array class to simulate arrays.

In Flash 4, you can also use eval() to dynamically set and retrieve the value of a variable or instance name. However, you can also do this with the array access operator ([]).

In Flash 5 or later, you cannot use eval() to dynamically set and retrieve the value of a variable or instance name, because you cannot useeval() on the left side of an equation. For example, replace the code

```
eval ("var" + i) = "first";
```

with this:

```
this["var"+i] = "first"
```

or this:

```
set ("var" + i, "first");
```

Availability: ActionScript 1.0; Flash Player 5 - Flash Player 5 or later for full functionality. You can use the `eval()` function when exporting to Flash Player 4, but you must use slash notation and can access only variables, not properties or objects.

Parameters

`expression:Object` - The name of a variable, property, object, or movie clip to retrieve. This parameter can be either a String or a direct reference to the object instance (i.e use of quotation marks (" ") is optional.)

Returns

`Object` - A value, reference to an object or movie clip, or `undefined` .

Example

The following example uses `eval()` to set properties for dynamically named movie clips. This ActionScript sets the `_rotation` property for three movie clips, called `square1_mc`, `square2_mc`, and `square3_mc`.

```
for (var i = 1; i <= 3; i++) {
  setProperty(eval("square"+i+"_mc"), _rotation, 5);
}
```

You can also use the following ActionScript:

```
for (var i = 1; i <= 3; i++) {
  this["square"+i+"_mc"]._rotation = -5;
}
```

See also

```
Array, set variable statement
```

fscommand function

```
fscommand(command:String, parameters:String) : Void
```

Lets the SWF file communicate with either Flash Player or the program that is hosting Flash Player, such as a web browser. You can also use the `fscommand()` function to pass messages to Macromedia Director, or to Visual Basic (VB), Visual C++, and other programs that can host ActiveX controls.

The fscommand() function lets a SWF file communicate with a script in a web page. However, script access is controlled by the web page's allowScriptAccess setting. (You set this attribute in the HTML code that embeds the SWF file—for example, in the PARAM tag for Internet Explorer or the EMBED tag for Netscape. When allowScriptAccess is set to "never", a SWF file cannot access web page scripts. With Flash Player 7 and later, when allowScriptAccess is set to "always", a SWF file can always access web page scripts. When allowScriptAccess is set to "sameDomain", scripting is allowed only from SWF files that are in the same domain as the web page; scripting is always allowed with previous versions of Flash Player. If allowScriptAccess is not specified in an HTML page, the attribute is set by default to "sameDomain" for SWF files of version 8 and later, and to "always" for SWF files of version 7 and earlier.

Usage 1: To use fscommand() to send a message to Flash Player, you must use predefined commands and parameters. The following table shows the values that you can specify for the fscommand() function's command and parameters parameters. These values control SWF files that are playing in Flash Player, including projectors. (A *projector* is a SWF file saved in a format that can run as a stand-alone application—that is, without Flash Player.)

Command	Parameter	Purpose
quit	None	Closes the projector.
fullscreen	true or false	Specifying true sets Flash Player to full-screen mode. Specifying false returns the player to normal menu view.
allowscale	true or false	Specifying false sets the player so that the SWF file is always drawn at its original size and never scaled. Specifying true forces the SWF file to scale to 100% of the player.
showmenu	true or false	Specifying true enables the full set of context menu items. Specifying false hides all of the context menu items except About Flash Player and Settings.
exec	Path to application	Executes an application from within the projector.
trapallkeys	true or false	Specifying true sends all key events, including accelerator keys, to the onClipEvent(keyDown/keyUp) handler in Flash Player.

Availability:

- None of the commands described in the table are available in web players.

- All of the commands are available in stand-alone applications, such as projectors.

- Only allowscale and exec are available in test-movie players.

The exec command can contain only the characters A-Z, a-z, 0-9, period (.), and underscore (_). The exec command runs in the subdirectory fscommand only. In other words, if you use the exec command to call an application, the application must reside in a subdirectory named fscommand. The exec command works only from within a Flash projector file.

Usage 2: To use fscommand() to send a message to a scripting language such as JavaScript in a web browser, you can pass any two parameters in the command and parameters parameters. These parameters can be strings or expressions, and they are used in a JavaScript function that handles, or *catches*, the fscommand() function.

In a web browser, fscommand() calls the JavaScript function moviename_DoFScommand, which resides in the webpage that contains the SWF file. For moviename, supply the name of the Flash object that you used for the NAMEattribute of the EMBED tag or the ID property of the OBJECT tag. If you assign the SWF file the name myMovie, the JavaScript function myMovie_DoFScommand is called.

In the web page that contains the SWF file, set the allowScriptAccess attribute to allow or deny the SWF file's ability to access the web page. (You set this attribute in the HTML code that embeds the SWF file—for example, in the PARAM tag for Internet Explorer or the EMBED tag for Netscape.) When allowScriptAccess is set to "never", outbound scripting always fails. When allowScriptAccess is set to "always", outbound scripting always succeeds. When it is set to "sameDomain", scripting is allowed only from SWF files that are in the same domain as the web page. If allowScriptAccess is not specified in a web page, it defaults to "sameDomain" for Flash Player 8, and to "always" for previous versions of Flash Player.

When using this function, consider the Flash Player security model. For Flash Player 8, the fscommand() function is not allowed if the calling SWF file is in the local-with-file-system or local-with-network sandbox and the containing HTML page is in an untrusted sandbox. For more information, see the following:

- Chapter 17, "Understanding Security," in *Learning ActionScript 2.0 in Flash*

- The Flash Player 8 Security white paper at http://www.macromedia.com/go/fp8_security

- The Flash Player 8 Security-Related API white paper at http://www.macromedia.com/go/ fp8_security_apis

Usage 3: The `fscommand()` function can send messages to Macromedia Director. These messages are interpreted by Lingo (the Director scripting language) as strings, events, or executable Lingo code. If a message is a string or an event, you must write the Lingo code to receive the message from the `fscommand()` function and carry out an action in Director. For more information, see the Director Support Center at www.macromedia.com/support/director.

Usage 4: In VisualBasic, Visual C++, and other programs that can host ActiveX controls, `fscommand()` sends a VB event with two strings that can be handled in the environment's programming language. For more information, use the keywords "Flash method" to search the Flash Support Center at www.macromedia.com/support/flash.

Note: If you are publishing for Flash Player 8 or later, the ExternalInterface class provides better functionality for communication between JavaScript and ActionScript (Usage 2) and between ActionScript and VisualBasic, Visual C++, or other programs that can host ActiveX controls (Usage 4). You should continue to use `fscommand()` for sending messages to Flash Player (Usage 1) and Macromedia Director (Usage 3).

Availability: ActionScript 1.0; Flash Player 3

Parameters

`command:String` - A string passed to the host application for any use, or a command passed to Flash Player.

`parameters:String` - A string passed to the host application for any use, or a value passed to Flash Player.

Example

In the following example, `fscommand()` sets Flash Player to scale the SWF file to the full monitor screen size when the `fullscreen_btn` or `unfullscreen_btn` button is released:

```
this.fullscreen_btn.onRelease = function() {
  fscommand("fullscreen", true);
};

this.unfullscreen_btn.onRelease = function() {
  fscommand("fullscreen", false);
};
```

The following example applies `fscommand()` to a button in Flash for the purpose of opening a JavaScript message box in an HTML page. The message itself is sent to JavaScript as the `fscommand` parameter.

You must add a function to the web page that contains the SWF file. This function, `myDocument_DoFSCommand()`, waits for an `fscommand()` call. When `fscommand()` is triggered in Flash (for example, when a user clicks the button), the `command` and `parameter` strings are passed to the `myDocument_DoFSCommand()`function. You can use the passed strings in your JavaScript or VBScript code in any way you like. In this example, the function contains a conditional `if` statement that checks to see if the command string is `"messagebox"`. If it is, a JavaScript alert box displays the contents of the `fscommand()` function's `parameters` string.

```
function myDocument_DoFSCommand(command, args) {
 if (command == "messagebox") {
 alert(args);
 }
}
```

In the Flash document, add `fscommand()` to a button:

```
fscommand("messagebox", "This is a message box called from within Flash.")
```

You can use expressions for the parameters of the `fscommand()` function, as shown in the following example:

```
fscommand("messagebox", "Hello, " + name + ", welcome to our website!")
```

To test the SWF file, select File > Publish Preview > HTML. If you publish your SWF file using the Flash with FSCommand template (in the Publish Settings dialog box, select the HTML tag), Flash inserts the `myDocument_DoFSCommand()` function automatically. The SWF file's `NAME` and `ID` attributes will be the filename. For example, for the file myDocument.fla, the attributes would be set to `myDocument`.

See also

`ExternalInterface (flash.external.ExternalInterface)`

getProperty function

`getProperty(my_mc:Object, property:Object) : Object`

Returns the value of the specified property for the movie clip *my_mc*.

Availability: ActionScript 1.0; Flash Player 4

Parameters

`my_mc:Object` - The instance name of a movie clip for which the property is being retrieved.

`property:Object` - A property of a movie clip.

Returns

`Object` - The value of the specified property.

Example

The following example creates a new movie clip `someClip_mc` and shows the alpha value (`_alpha`) for the movie clip `someClip_mc` in the Output panel:

```
this.createEmptyMovieClip("someClip_mc", 999);
trace("The alpha of "+getProperty(someClip_mc, _name)+" is:
  "+getProperty(someClip_mc, _alpha));
```

getTimer function

`getTimer() : Number`

Returns the number of milliseconds that have elapsed since the SWF file started playing.

Availability: ActionScript 1.0; Flash Player 4

Returns

`Number` - The number of milliseconds that have elapsed since the SWF file started playing.

Example

In the following example, the `getTimer()` and `setInterval()` functions are used to create a simple timer:

```
this.createTextField("timer_txt", this.getNextHighestDepth(), 0, 0, 100,
  22);
function updateTimer():Void {
 timer_txt.text = getTimer();
}

var intervalID:Number = setInterval(updateTimer, 100);
```

getURL function

`getURL(url:String, [window:String, [method:String]]) : Void`

Loads a document from a specific URL into a window or passes variables to another application at a defined URL. To test this function, make sure the file to be loaded is at the specified location. To use an absolute URL (for example, *http://www.myserver.com*), you need a network connection.

Availability: ActionScript 1.0; Flash Player 4 - The `GET` and `POST` options are available only in and later versions.

Parameters

`url:String` - The URL from which to obtain the document.

`window:String` [optional] - Specifies the window or HTML frame into which the document should load. You can enter the name of a specific window or select from the following reserved target names:

- `_self` specifies the current frame in the current window.
- `_blank` specifies a new window.
- `_parent` specifies the parent of the current frame.
- `_top` specifies the top-level frame in the current window.

`method:String` [optional] - A `GET` or `POST` method for sending variables. If there are no variables, omit this parameter. The `GET` method appends the variables to the end of the URL, and is used for small numbers of variables. The `POST` method sends the variables in a separate HTTP header and is used for sending long strings of variables.

Example

This example loads an image into a movie clip. When the image is clicked, a new URL is loaded in a new browser window.

```
var listenerObject:Object = new Object();
listenerObject.onLoadInit = function(target_mc:MovieClip) {
 target_mc.onRelease = function() {
 getURL("http://www.macromedia.com/software/flash/flashpro/", "_blank");
 };
};
var logo:MovieClipLoader = new MovieClipLoader();
logo.addListener(listenerObject);
logo.loadClip("http://www.helpexamples.com/flash/images/image1.jpg",
 this.createEmptyMovieClip("macromedia_mc", this.getNextHighestDepth()));
```

In the following example, `getURL()` is used to send an e-mail message:

```
myBtn_btn.onRelease = function(){
 getURL("mailto:you@somedomain.com");
};
```

In the following ActionScript, JavaScript is used to open an alert window when the SWF file is embedded in a browser window (please note that when calling JavaScript with getURL(), the url parameter is limited to 508 characters):

```
myBtn_btn.onRelease = function(){
 getURL("javascript:alert('you clicked me')");
};
```

You can also use GET or POST for sending variables. The following example uses GET to append variables to a URL:

```
var firstName:String = "Gus";
var lastName:String = "Richardson";
var age:Number = 92;
myBtn_btn.onRelease = function() {
 getURL("http://www.macromedia.com", "_blank", "GET");
};
```

The following ActionScript uses POST to send variables in the HTTP header. Make sure you test your documents in a browser window, because otherwise your variables are sent using GET:

```
var firstName:String = "Gus";
var lastName:String = "Richardson";
var age:Number = 92;
getURL("http://www.macromedia.com", "_blank", "POST");
```

See also

loadVariables function, send (XML.send method), sendAndLoad (XML.sendAndLoad method)

getVersion function

getVersion() : String

Returns a string containing Flash Player version and platform information. The getVersion function returns information only for Flash Player 5 or later versions of Flash Player.

Availability: ActionScript 1.0; Flash Player 5

Returns

String - A string containing Flash Player version and platform information.

Example

The following examples trace the version number of the Flash Player playing the SWF file:

```
var flashVersion:String = getVersion();
trace(flashVersion); // output: WIN 8,0,1,0
trace($version); // output: WIN 8,0,1,0
trace(System.capabilities.version); // output: WIN 8,0,1,0
```

The following string is returned by the getVersion function:

WIN 8,0,1,0

This returned string indicates that the platform is Microsoft Windows, and the version number of Flash Player is major version 8, minor version 1 (8.1).

`os (capabilities.os property), version (capabilities.version property)`

gotoAndPlay function

`gotoAndPlay([scene:String], frame:Object) : Void`

Sends the playhead to the specified frame in a scene and plays from that frame. If no scene is specified, the playhead goes to the specified frame in the current scene. You can use the *scene* parameter only on the root Timeline, not within Timelines for movie clips or other objects in the document.

Availability: ActionScript 1.0; Flash Player 2

Parameters

`scene:String` [optional] - A string specifying the name of the scene to which the playhead is sent.

`frame:Object` - A number representing the frame number, or a string representing the label of the frame, to which the playhead is sent.

Example

In the following example, a document has two scenes: `sceneOne` and `sceneTwo`. Scene one contains a frame label on Frame 10 called `newFrame` and two buttons, `myBtn_btn` and `myOtherBtn_btn`. This ActionScript is placed on Frame 1, Scene 1 of the main Timeline.

```
stop();
myBtn_btn.onRelease = function(){
 gotoAndPlay("newFrame");
};

myOtherBtn_btn.onRelease = function(){
 gotoAndPlay("sceneTwo", 1);
};
```

When the user clicks the buttons, the playhead moves to the specified location and continues playing.

See also

`gotoAndPlay (MovieClip.gotoAndPlay method), nextFrame function, play function, prevFrame function`

gotoAndStop function

`gotoAndStop([scene:String], frame:Object) : Void`

Sends the playhead to the specified frame in a scene and stops it. If no scene is specified, the playhead is sent to the frame in the current scene. You can use the *scene* parameter only on the root Timeline, not within Timelines for movie clips or other objects in the document.

Availability: ActionScript 1.0; Flash Player 2

Parameters

`scene:String` [optional] - A string specifying the name of the scene to which the playhead is sent.

`frame:Object` - A number representing the frame number, or a string representing the label of the frame, to which the playhead is sent.

Example

In the following example, a document has two scenes: `sceneOne` and `sceneTwo`. Scene one contains a frame label on Frame 10 called `newFrame`, and two buttons, `myBtn_btn` and `myOtherBtn_btn`. This ActionScript is placed on Frame 1, Scene 1 of the main Timeline:

```
stop();

myBtn_btn.onRelease = function(){
 gotoAndStop("newFrame");
};

myOtherBtn_btn.onRelease = function(){
 gotoAndStop("sceneTwo", 1);
};
```

When the user clicks the buttons, the playhead moves to the specified location and stops.

See also

`gotoAndStop` (MovieClip.gotoAndStop method), `stop` function, `play` function, `gotoAndPlay` function

ifFrameLoaded function

```
ifFrameLoaded([scene:String], frame) {
statement(s);
}
```

Deprecated since Flash Player 5. This function has been deprecated. Macromedia recommends that you use the `MovieClip._framesloaded` property.

Checks whether the contents of a specific frame are available locally. Use `ifFrameLoaded` to start playing a simple animation while the rest of the SWF file downloads to the local computer. The difference between using `_framesloaded` and `ifFrameLoaded` is that `_framesloaded` lets you add custom `if` or `else` statements.

Availability: ActionScript 1.0; Flash Player 4

Parameters

`scene:String` [optional] - A string that specifies the name of the scene that must be loaded.

`frame:Object` - The frame number or frame label that must be loaded before the next statement is executed.

See also

`, addListener (MovieClipLoader.addListener method)`

int function

`int(value:Number) : Number`

Deprecated since Flash Player 5. This function was deprecated in favor of `Math.round()`.

Converts a decimal number to an integer value by truncating the decimal value. This function is equivalent to `Math.floor()` if the *value* parameter is positive and `Math.ceil()` if the *value* parameter is negative.

Availability: ActionScript 1.0; Flash Player 4

Parameters

`value:Number` - A number to be rounded to an integer.

Returns

`Number` - The truncated integer value.

See also

`round (Math.round method)`, `floor (Math.floor method)`, `ceil (Math.ceil method)`

isFinite function

`isFinite(expression:Object) : Boolean`

Evaluates *expression* and returns `true` if it is a finite number or `false` if it is infinity or negative infinity. The presence of infinity or negative infinity indicates a mathematical error condition such as division by 0.

Availability: ActionScript 1.0; Flash Player 5

Parameters

`expression:Object` - A Boolean value, variable, or other expression to be evaluated.

Returns

`Boolean` - A Boolean value.

Example

The following example shows return values for `isFinite`:

```
isFinite(56)
// returns true

isFinite(Number.POSITIVE_INFINITY)
//returns false
```

isNaN function

`isNaN(expression:Object) : Boolean`

Evaluates the parameter and returns `true` if the value is `NaN`(not a number). This function is useful for checking whether a mathematical expression evaluates successfully to a number.

Availability: ActionScript 1.0; Flash Player 5

Parameters

`expression:Object` - A Boolean, variable, or other expression to be evaluated.

Returns

`Boolean` - A Boolean value.

Example

The following code illustrates return values for the `isNaN()` function:

```
trace( isNaN("Tree") );
// returns true

trace( isNaN(56) );
// returns false

trace( isNaN(Number.POSITIVE_INFINITY) )
// returns false
```

The following example shows how you can use `isNAN()` to check whether a mathematical expression contains an error:

```
var dividend:Number;
var divisor:Number;
divisor = 1;
trace( isNaN(dividend/divisor) );
// output: true
// The output is true because the variable dividend is undefined.
// Do not use isNAN() to check for division by 0 because it will return
  false.
// A positive number divided by 0 equals Infinity
  (Number.POSITIVE_INFINITY).
// A negative number divided by 0 equals -Infinity
  (Number.NEGATIVE_INFINITY).
```

See also

`NaN` constant, `NaN (Number.NaN property)`

length function

`length(expression:String)length(variable)`

Deprecated since Flash Player 5. This function, along with all the string functions, has been deprecated. Macromedia recommends that you use the methods of the String class and the `String.length` property to perform the same operations.

Returns the length of the specified string or variable.

Availability: ActionScript 1.0; Flash Player 4

Parameters

`expression:String` - A string.

`variable:Object` - The name of a variable.

Returns

`Number` - The length of the specified string or variable.

Example

The following example returns the length of the string "Hello": `length("Hello");` The result is 5.

See also

`" string delimiter operator,` `String,` `length (String.length property)`

loadMovie function

`loadMovie(url:String, target:Object, [method:String]) : Void`
`loadMovie(url:String, target:String, [method:String]) : Void`

Loads a SWF, JPEG, GIF, or PNG file into a movie clip in Flash Player while the original SWF file is playing. Support for unanimated GIF files, PNG files, and progressive JPEG files is added in Flash Player 8. If you load an animated GIF, only the first frame is displayed.

 If you want to monitor the progress of the download, use `MovieClipLoader.loadClip()` instead of this function.

The `loadMovie()` function lets you display several SWF files at once and switch among SWF files without loading another HTML document. Without the `loadMovie()` function, Flash Player displays a single SWF file.

If you want to load a SWF or JPEG file into a specific level, use `loadMovieNum()` instead of `loadMovie()`.

When a SWF file is loaded into a target movie clip, you can use the target path of that movie clip to target the loaded SWF file. A SWF file or image loaded into a target inherits the position, rotation, and scale properties of the targeted movie clip. The upper left corner of the loaded image or SWF file aligns with the registration point of the targeted movie clip. Alternatively, if the target is the root Timeline, the upper left corner of the image or SWF file aligns with the upper left corner of the Stage.

Use `unloadMovie()` to remove SWF files that were loaded with `loadMovie()`.

When using this function, consider the Flash Player security model.

For Flash Player 8:

■ Loading is not allowed if the calling movie clip is in the local-with-file-system sandbox and the loaded movie clip is from a network sandbox.

■ Loading is not allowed if the calling SWF file is in a network sandbox and the movie clip to be loaded is local.

■ Network sandbox access from the local-trusted or local-with-networking sandbox requires permission from the website by means of a cross-domain policy file.

■ Movie clips in the local-with-file-system sandbox may not script movie clips in the local-with-networking sandbox (and the reverse is also prevented).

For Flash Player 7 and later:

■ Websites can permit cross-domain access to a resource by means of a cross-domain policy file.

■ Scripting between SWF files is restricted based on the origin domain of the SWF files. Use the `System.security.allowDomain()` method to adjust these restrictions.

For more information, see the following:

■ Chapter 17, "Understanding Security," in *Learning ActionScript 2.0 in Flash*

■ The Flash Player 8 Security white paper at http://www.macromedia.com/go/fp8_security

■ The Flash Player 8 Security-Related API white paper at http://www.macromedia.com/go/fp8_security_apis

Availability: ActionScript 1.0; Flash Player 3 - The ability to load JPEG files is available as of Flash Player 6. The ability to load unanimated GIF files, PNG files, or progressive JPEG files is available as of Flash Player 8.

Parameters

`url:String` - The absolute or relative URL of the SWF or JPEG file to be loaded. A relative path must be relative to the SWF file at level 0. Absolute URLs must include the protocol reference, such as http:// or file:///.

`target:Object` - A reference to a movie clip object or a string representing the path to a target movie clip. The target movie clip is replaced by the loaded SWF file or image.

`method:String` [optional] - Specifies an HTTP method for sending variables. The parameter must be the string GET or POST . If there are no variables to be sent, omit this parameter. The GET method appends the variables to the end of the URL and is used for small numbers of variables. The POST method sends the variables in a separate HTTP header and is used for long strings of variables.

Example

Usage 1: The following example loads the SWF file circle.swf from the same directory and replaces a movie clip called mySquare that already exists on the Stage:

```
loadMovie("circle.swf", mySquare);
// equivalent statement (Usage 1): loadMovie("circle.swf",
  _level0.mySquare);
// equivalent statement (Usage 2): loadMovie("circle.swf", "mySquare");
```

The following example loads the SWF file circle.swf from the same directory, but replaces the main movie clip instead of the mySquare movie clip:

```
loadMovie("circle.swf", this);
// Note that using "this" as a string for the target parameter will not work
// equivalent statement (Usage 2): loadMovie("circle.swf", "_level0");
```

The following loadMovie() statement loads the SWF file sub.swf from the same directory into a new movie clip called logo_mc that's created using createEmptyMovieClip():

```
this.createEmptyMovieClip("logo_mc", 999);
loadMovie("sub.swf", logo_mc);
```

You could add the following code to load a JPEG image called image1.jpg from the same directory as the SWF file loading sub.swf. The JPEG is loaded when you click a button called myBtn_btn. This code loads the JPEG into logo_mc. Therefore, it will replace sub.swf with the JPEG image.

```
myBtn_btn.onRelease = function(){
 loadMovie("image1.jpg", logo_mc);
};
```

Usage 2: The following example loads the SWF file circle.swf from the same directory and replaces a movie clip called mySquare that already exists on the Stage:

```
loadMovie("circle.swf", "mySquare");
```

See also

_level property, loadMovieNum function, loadMovie (MovieClip.loadMovie method), loadClip (MovieClipLoader.loadClip method), unloadMovie function

loadMovieNum function

loadMovieNum(url:String, level:Number, [method:String]) : Void

Loads a SWF, JPEG, GIF, or PNG file into a level while the original SWF file is playing. Support for unanimated GIF files, PNG files, and progressive JPEG files is added in Flash Player 8. If you load an animated GIF, only the first frame is displayed.

 | If you want to monitor the progress of the download, use MovieClipLoader.loadClip() instead of this function.

Normally, Flash Player displays a single SWF file and then closes. The `loadMovieNum()` action lets you display several SWF files at once and switch among SWF files without loading another HTML document.

If you want to specify a target instead of a level, use `loadMovie()` instead of `loadMovieNum()`.

Flash Player has a stacking order of levels starting with level 0. These levels are like layers of acetate; they are transparent except for the objects on each level. When you use `loadMovieNum()`, you must specify a level in Flash Player into which the SWF file will load. When a SWF file is loaded into a level, you can use the syntax, `_level`*N*, where *N* is the level number, to target the SWF file.

When you load a SWF file, you can specify any level number and you can load SWF files into a level that already has a SWF file loaded into it. If you do, the new SWF file will replace the existing SWF file. If you load a SWF file into level 0, every level in Flash Player is unloaded, and level 0 is replaced with the new file. The SWF file in level 0 sets the frame rate, background color, and frame size for all other loaded SWF files.

The `loadMovieNum()` action also lets you load JPEG files into a SWF file while it plays. For images and SWF files, the upper left corner of the image aligns with the upper left corner of the Stage when the file loads. Also in both cases, the loaded file inherits rotation and scaling, and the original content is overwritten in the specified level.

> **NOTE** JPEG files saved in progressive format are not supported.

Use `unloadMovieNum()` to remove SWF files or images that were loaded with `loadMovieNum()`.

When using this method, consider the Flash Player security model.

For Flash Player 8:

- Loading is not allowed if the calling movie clip is in the local-with-file-system sandbox and the loaded movie clip is from a network sandbox.
- Loading is not allowed if the calling SWF file is in a network sandbox and the movie clip to be loaded is local.
- Network sandbox access from the local-trusted or local-with-networking sandbox requires permission from the website by means of a cross-domain policy file.
- Movie clips in the local-with-file-system sandbox may not script movie clips in the local-with-networking sandbox (and the reverse is also prevented).

For Flash Player 7 and later:

- Websites can permit cross-domain access to a resource by means of a cross-domain policy file.

- Scripting between SWF files is restricted based on the origin domain of the SWF files. Use the `System.security.allowDomain()` method to adjust these restrictions.

For more information, see the following:

- Chapter 17, "Understanding Security," in *Learning ActionScript 2.0 in Flash*

- The Flash Player 8 Security white paper at http://www.macromedia.com/go/fp8_security

- The Flash Player 8 Security-Related API white paper at http://www.macromedia.com/go/fp8_security_apis

Availability: ActionScript 1.0; Flash Player 4 - Flash 4 files opened in Flash 5 or later are converted to use the correct syntax. The ability to load JPEG files is available as of Flash Player 6. The ability to load unanimated GIF files, PNG files, or progressive JPEG files is available as of Flash Player 8.

Parameters

`url:String` - The absolute or relative URL of the SWF or JPEG file to be loaded. A relative path must be relative to the SWF file at level 0. For use in the stand-alone Flash Player or for testing in test mode in the Flash authoring application, all SWF files must be stored in the same folder and the filenames cannot include folder or disk drive specifications.

`level:Number` - An integer specifying the level in Flash Player into which the SWF file will load.

`method:String` [optional] - Specifies an HTTP method for sending variables. The parameter must be the string `GET` or `POST`. If there are no variables to be sent, omit this parameter. The `GET` method appends the variables to the end of the URL and is used for small numbers of variables. The `POST` method sends the variables in a separate HTTP header and is used for long strings of variables.

Example

The following example loads the JPEG image tim.jpg into level 2 of Flash Player:

```
loadMovieNum("http://www.helpexamples.com/flash/images/image1.jpg", 2);
```

See also

`unloadMovieNum` function, `loadMovie` function, `loadClip` (MovieClipLoader.loadClip method), `_level` property

loadVariables function

`loadVariables(url:String, target:Object, [method:String]) : Void`

Reads data from an external file, such as a text file or text generated by ColdFusion, a CGI script, Active Server Pages (ASP), PHP, or Perl script, and sets the values for variables in a target movie clip. This action can also be used to update variables in the active SWF file with new values.

The text at the specified URL must be in the standard MIME format *application/x-www-form-urlencoded* (a standard format used by CGI scripts). Any number of variables can be specified. For example, the following phrase defines several variables:

`company=Macromedia&address=600+Townsend&city=San+Francisco&zip=94103`

In SWF files running in a version earlier than Flash Player 7, *url* must be in the same superdomain as the SWF file that is issuing this call. A superdomain is derived by removing the leftmost component of a file's URL. For example, a SWF file at www.someDomain.com can load data from a source at store.someDomain.com because both files are in the same superdomain of someDomain.com.

In SWF files of any version running in Flash Player 7 or later, *url* must be in exactly the same domain as the SWF file that is issuing this call (see "Flash Player security features" in *Using ActionScript in Flash*). For example, a SWF file at www.someDomain.com can load data only from sources that are also at www.someDomain.com. If you want to load data from a different domain, you can place a *cross-domain policy file* on the server hosting the SWF file that is being accessed. For more information, see "About allowing cross-domain data loading" in *Using ActionScript in Flash*.

If you want to load variables into a specific level, use `loadVariablesNum()` instead of `loadVariables()`.

Availability: ActionScript 1.0; Flash Player 4 - Behavior changed in Flash Player 7.

Parameters

`url:String` - An absolute or relative URL where the variables are located. If the SWF file issuing this call is running in a web browser, *url* must be in the same domain as the SWF file; for details, see the Description section.

`target:Object` - The target path to a movie clip that receives the loaded variables.

`method:String` [optional] - Specifies an HTTP method for sending variables. The parameter must be the string `GET` or `POST`. If there are no variables to be sent, omit this parameter. The `GET` method appends the variables to the end of the URL and is used for small numbers of variables. The `POST` method sends the variables in a separate HTTP header and is used for long strings of variables.

Example

The following example loads information from a text file called params.txt into the target_mc movie clip that is created using createEmptyMovieClip(). The setInterval() function is used to check the loading progress. The script checks for a variable in the params.txt file named done.

```
this.createEmptyMovieClip("target_mc", this.getNextHighestDepth());
loadVariables("params.txt", target_mc);
function checkParamsLoaded() {
 if (target_mc.done == undefined) {
 trace("not yet.");
 } else {
 trace("finished loading. killing interval.");
 trace("-------------");
 for (i in target_mc) {
 trace(i+": "+target_mc[i]);
 }
 trace("-------------");
 clearInterval(param_interval);
 }
}
var param_interval:Number = setInterval(checkParamsLoaded, 100);
```

The external file, params.txt, includes the following text:

```
var1="hello"&var2="goodbye"&done="done"
```

See also

loadVariablesNum function, loadMovie function, loadMovieNum function, getURL function, loadMovie (MovieClip.loadMovie method), loadVariables (MovieClip.loadVariables method), load (LoadVars.load method)

loadVariablesNum function

loadVariablesNum(url:String, level:Number, [method:String]) : Void

Reads data from an external file, such as a text file or text generated by ColdFusion, a CGI script, ASP, PHP, or a Perl script, and sets the values for variables in a Flash Player level. You can also use this function to update variables in the active SWF file with new values.

The text at the specified URL must be in the standard MIME format application/x-www-form-urlencoded(a standard format used by CGI scripts). Any number of variables can be specified. For example, the following phrase defines several variables:

```
company=Macromedia&address=601+Townsend&city=San+Francisco&zip=94103
```

In SWF files running in a version of the player earlier than Flash Player 7, *url* must be in the same superdomain as the SWF file that is issuing this call. A superdomain is derived by removing the leftmost component of a file's URL. For example, a SWF file at www.someDomain.com can load data from a source at store.someDomain.com, because both files are in the same superdomain of someDomain.com.

In SWF files of any version running in Flash Player 7 or later, *url* must be in exactly the same domain as the SWF file that is issuing this call (see "Flash Player security features" in *Using ActionScript in Flash*). For example, a SWF file at www.someDomain.com can load data only from sources that are also at www.someDomain.com. If you want to load data from a different domain, you can place a *cross-domain policy file* on the server hosting the SWF file. For more information, see "About allowing cross-domain data loading" in *Using ActionScript in Flash*.

If you want to load variables into a target MovieClip, use `loadVariables()` instead of `loadVariablesNum()`.

Availability: ActionScript 1.0; Flash Player 4 - Behavior changed in Flash Player 7. Flash 4 files opened in Flash 5 or later are converted to use the correct syntax.

Parameters

`url:String` - An absolute or relative URL where the variables are located. If the SWF file issuing this call is running in a web browser, *url* must be in the same domain as the SWF file; for details, see the Description section.

`level:Number` - An integer specifying the level in Flash Player to receive the variables.

`method:String` [optional] - Specifies an HTTP method for sending variables. The parameter must be the string `GET` or `POST` . If there are no variables to be sent, omit this parameter. The `GET` method appends the variables to the end of the URL and is used for small numbers of variables. The `POST` method sends the variables in a separate HTTP header and is used for long strings of variables.

Example

The following example loads information from a text file called params.txt into the main Timeline of the SWF at level 2 in Flash Player. The variable names of the text fields must match the variable names in the params.txt file. The `setInterval()` function is used to check the progress of the data being loaded into the SWF. The script checks for a variable in the params.txt file named `done`.

```
loadVariablesNum("params.txt", 2);
function checkParamsLoaded() {
 if (_level2.done == undefined) {
 trace("not yet.");
 } else {
```

```
trace("finished loading. killing interval.");
trace("-------------");
for (i in _level2) {
trace(i+": "+_level2[i]);
}
trace("-------------");
clearInterval(param_interval);
}
}
var param_interval:Number = setInterval(checkParamsLoaded, 100);

// Params.txt includes the following text
var1="hello"&var2="goodbye"&done="done"
```

See also

getURL function, loadMovie function, loadMovieNum function, loadVariables
function, loadMovie (MovieClip.loadMovie method), loadVariables
(MovieClip.loadVariables method), load (LoadVars.load method)

mbchr function

mbchr(number:Number)

Deprecated since Flash Player 5. This function was deprecated in favor of the
String.fromCharCode() method.

Converts an ASCII code number to a multibyte character.

Availability: ActionScript 1.0; Flash Player 4

Parameters

number:Number - The number to convert to a multibyte character.

See also

fromCharCode (String.fromCharCode method)

mblength function

mblength(string:String) : Number

Deprecated since Flash Player 5. This function was deprecated in favor of the methods and
properties of the String class.

Returns the length of the multibyte character string.

Availability: ActionScript 1.0; Flash Player 4

Parameters

`string:String` - The string to measure.

Returns

`Number` - The length of the multibyte character string.

See also

`String`, `length (String.length property)`

mbord function

`mbord(character:String) : Number`

Deprecated since Flash Player 5. This function was deprecated in favor of `String.charCodeAt()`.

Converts the specified character to a multibyte number.

Availability: ActionScript 1.0; Flash Player 4

Parameters

`character:String` - The character to convert to a multibyte number.

Returns

`Number` - The converted character.

See also

`charCodeAt (String.charCodeAt method)`

mbsubstring function

`mbsubstring(value:String, index:Number, count:Number) : String`

Deprecated since Flash Player 5. This function was deprecated in favor of `String.substr()`.

Extracts a new multibyte character string from a multibyte character string.

Availability: ActionScript 1.0; Flash Player 4

Parameters

`value:String` - The multibyte string from which to extract a new multibyte string.

`index:Number` - The number of the first character to extract.

count:Number - The number of characters to include in the extracted string, not including the index character.

Returns

String - The string extracted from the multibyte character string.

See also

substr (String.substr method)

MMExecute function

MMExecute(*"Flash JavaScript API command;":String*) : String

Lets you issue Flash JavaScript API (JSAPI) commands from ActionScript. In Flash MX2004 the MMExecute function can be called only by a movie that is used as a Flash Panel (file is stored in WindowSWF directory), by an XMLtoUI dialog box, or by the Custom UI of a component. JSAPI commands have no effect in the player, in test movie mode, or outside the authoring environment.

The Flash JSAPI provides several objects, methods, and properties to duplicate or emulate commands that a user can enter in the authoring environment. Using the JSAPI, you can write scripts that extend Flash in several ways: adding commands to menus, manipulating objects on the Stage, repeating sequences of commands, and so on.

In general, a user runs a JSAPI script by selecting Commands > Run Command. However, you can use this function in an ActionScript script to call a JSAPI command directly. If you use MMExecute() in a script on Frame 1 of your file, the command executes when the SWF file is loaded.

For more information on the JSAPI, see www.macromedia.com/go/jsapi_info_en.

Availability: ActionScript 1.0; Flash Player 7

Parameters

command:String - Any command that you can use in a Flash JavaScript (JSFL) file.

Returns

String - A string representation of the result, if any, sent by the JavaScript statement.

Example

The following command will output the number of items in the library of the current document to the trace window. You must run this example as a Flash panel because Flash files can't call `MMExecute` if they are run in either test movie or the browser.

- Place the following code into frame 1 of the main Timeline of an empty Flash document:

```
var numLibItems = MMExecute("fl.getDocumentDOM().library.items.length");

var message = numLibItems + " items in library";

MMExecute('fl.trace("' + message + '");');
```

- Save the FLA file in the WindowSWF directory that is located in your Configuration directory, and then select File > Publish (or save it elsewhere and either publish the SWF file directly to that directory, or move the SWF file to that directory).

- Quit and restart the application (you need to do this step the first time you add your file to the WindowSWF directory).

Now you can select your file from the bottom of the Window > Other Panels menu.

The ActionScript trace function does not work from a Flash panel; this example uses the JavaScript `fl.trace` version to get the output. It might be easier to copy the results of `MMExecute` to a text field that is part of your Flash Panel file.

nextFrame function

```
nextFrame() : Void
```

Sends the playhead to the next frame.

Availability: ActionScript 1.0; Flash Player 2

Example

In the following example, when the user presses the Right or Down arrow key, the playhead goes to the next frame and stops. If the user presses the Left or Up arrow key, the playhead goes to the previous frame and stops. The listener is initialized to wait for the arrow key to be pressed, and the `init` variable is used to prevent the listener from being redefined if the playhead returns to Frame 1.

```
stop();

if (init == undefined) {
 someListener = new Object();
 someListener.onKeyDown = function() {
 if (Key.isDown(Key.LEFT) || Key.isDown(Key.UP)) {
```

```
_level0.prevFrame();
} else if (Key.isDown(Key.RIGHT) || Key.isDown(Key.DOWN)) {
_level0.nextFrame();
}
};
Key.addListener(someListener);
init = 1;
}
```

See also

prevFrame function

nextScene function

nextScene() : Void

Sends the playhead to Frame 1 of the next scene.

Availability: ActionScript 1.0; Flash Player 2

Example

In the following example, when a user clicks the button that is created at runtime, the playhead is sent to Frame 1 of the next scene. Create two scenes, and enter the following ActionScript on Frame 1 of Scene 1.

```
stop();

if (init == undefined) {
 this.createEmptyMovieClip("nextscene_mc", this.getNextHighestDepth());
 nextscene_mc.createTextField("nextscene_txt", this.getNextHighestDepth(),
  200, 0, 100, 22);
 nextscene_mc.nextscene_txt.autoSize = true;
 nextscene_mc.nextscene_txt.border = true;
 nextscene_mc.nextscene_txt.text = "Next Scene";
 this.createEmptyMovieClip("prevscene_mc", this.getNextHighestDepth());
 prevscene_mc.createTextField("prevscene_txt", this.getNextHighestDepth(),
  00, 0, 100, 22);
 prevscene_mc.prevscene_txt.autoSize = true;
 prevscene_mc.prevscene_txt.border = true;
 prevscene_mc.prevscene_txt.text = "Prev Scene";
 nextscene_mc.onRelease = function() {
 nextScene();
 };

 prevscene_mc.onRelease = function() {
 prevScene();
 };

 init = true;
}
```

Make sure you place a `stop()` action on Frame 1 of Scene 2.

See also

prevScene function

Number function

Number(expression) : Number

Converts the parameter *expression* to a number and returns a value as described in the following list:

- If *expression* is a number, the return value is *expression*.
- If *expression* is a Boolean value, the return value is 1 if *expression* is true, 0 if *expression* is false.

- If *expression* is a string, the function attempts to parse *expression* as a decimal number with an optional trailing exponent (that is, 1.57505e-3).
- If *expression* is NaN, the return value is NaN.
- If *expression* is undefined, the return value is as follows:
  - In files published for Flash Player 6 or earlier, the result is 0.

  - In files published for Flash Player 7 or later, the result is NaN.

Availability: ActionScript 1.0; Flash Player 4 - Behavior changed in Flash Player 7.

Parameters

expression:Object - An expression to convert to a number. Numbers or strings that begin with 0x are interpreted as hexadecimal values. Numbers or strings that begin with 0 are interpreted as octal values.

Returns

Number - A number or NaN (not a number).

Example

In the following example, a text field is created on the Stage at runtime:

```
this.createTextField("counter_txt", this.getNextHighestDepth(), 0, 0, 100,
  22);
counter_txt.autoSize = true;
counter_txt.text = 0;
function incrementInterval():Void {
 var counter:Number = counter_txt.text;
 // Without the Number() function, Flash would concatenate the value instead
 // of adding values. You could also use "counter_txt.text++;"
 counter_txt.text = Number(counter) + 1;
}
var intervalID:Number = setInterval(incrementInterval, 1000);
```

See also

NaN constant, Number, parseInt function, parseFloat function

Object function

```
Object([value:Object]) : Object
```

Creates a new empty object or converts the specified number, string, or Boolean value to an object. This command is equivalent to creating an object using the Object constructor (see "Constructor for the Object class").

Availability: ActionScript 1.0; Flash Player 5

Parameters

`value:Object` [optional] - A number, string, or Boolean value.

Returns

`Object` - An object.

Example

In the following example, a new empty object is created, and then the object is populated with values:

```
var company:Object = new Object();
company.name = "Macromedia, Inc.";
company.address = "600 Townsend Street";
company.city = "San Francisco";
company.state = "CA";
company.postal = "94103";
for (var i in company) {
  trace("company."+i+" = "+company[i]);
}
```

See also

`Object`

on handler

```
on(mouseEvent:Object) {
// your statements here
}
```

Specifies the mouse event or keypress that triggers an action.

Availability: ActionScript 1.0; Flash Player 2 - Flash 2. Not all events are supported in Flash 2.

Parameters

mouseEvent:Object - A *mouseEvent* is a trigger called an *event* . When the event occurs, the statements following it within curly braces ({ }) execute. Any of the following values can be specified for the *mouseEvent* parameter:

- press The mouse button is pressed while the pointer is over the button.
- release The mouse button is released while the pointer is over the button.
- releaseOutside While the pointer is over the button, the mouse button is pressed and then rolls outside the button area just before it is released. Both the press and the dragOut events always precede a releaseOutside event.
- rollOut The pointer rolls outside the button area.
- rollOver The mouse pointer rolls over the button.
- dragOut While the pointer is over the button, the mouse button is pressed and then rolls outside the button area.
- dragOver While the pointer is over the button, the mouse button has been pressed, then rolled outside the button, and then rolled back over the button.
- keyPress "*<key>* " The specified keyboard key is pressed. For the *key* portion of the parameter, specify a key constant, as shown in the code hinting in the Actions Panel. You can use this parameter to intercept a key press, that is, to override any built-in behavior for the specified key. The button can be anywhere in your application, on or off the Stage. One limitation of this technique is that you can't apply the on() handler at runtime; you must do it at authoring time. Make sure that you select Control > Disable Keyboard Shortcuts, or certain keys with built-in behavior won't be overridden when you test the application using Control > Test Movie.

For a list of key constants, see the Key class.

Example

In the following script, the startDrag() function executes when the mouse is pressed, and the conditional script is executed when the mouse is released and the object is dropped:

```
on (press) {
 startDrag(this);
}
on (release) {
 trace("X:"+this._x);
 trace("Y:"+this._y);
 stopDrag();
}
```

See also

onClipEvent handler, Key

onClipEvent handler

```
onClipEvent(movieEvent:Object) {
// your statements here
}
```

Triggers actions defined for a specific instance of a movie clip.

Availability: ActionScript 1.0; Flash Player 5

Parameters

`movieEvent:Object` - The *movieEvent* is a trigger called an *event* . When the event occurs, the statements following it within curly braces ({}) are executed. Any of the following values can be specified for the *movieEvent* parameter:

- `load` The action is initiated as soon as the movie clip is instantiated and appears in the Timeline.

- `unload` The action is initiated in the first frame after the movie clip is removed from the Timeline. The actions associated with the `Unload` movie clip event are processed before any actions are attached to the affected frame.

- `enterFrame` The action is triggered continually at the frame rate of the movie clip. The actions associated with the `enterFrame` clip event are processed before any frame actions that are attached to the affected frames.

- `mouseMove` The action is initiated every time the mouse is moved. Use the `_xmouse` and `_ymouse` properties to determine the current mouse position.

- `mouseDown` The action is initiated when the left mouse button is pressed.

- `mouseUp` The action is initiated when the left mouse button is released.

- `keyDown` The action is initiated when a key is pressed. Use `Key.getCode()` to retrieve information about the last key pressed.

- `keyUp` The action is initiated when a key is released. Use the `Key.getCode()` method to retrieve information about the last key pressed.

- `data` The action is initiated when data is received in a `loadVariables()` or `loadMovie()` action. When specified with a `loadVariables()` action, the `data` event occurs only once, when the last variable is loaded. When specified with a `loadMovie()` action, the `data` event occurs repeatedly, as each section of data is retrieved.

Example

The following example uses `onClipEvent()` with the `keyDown` movie event and is designed to be attached to a movie clip or button. The `keyDown` movie event is usually used with one or more methods and properties of the Key object. The following script uses `Key.getCode()` to find out which key the user has pressed; if the pressed key matches the `Key.RIGHT` property, the playhead is sent to the next frame; if the pressed key matches the `Key.LEFT` property, the playhead is sent to the previous frame.

```
onClipEvent (keyDown) {
 if (Key.getCode() == Key.RIGHT) {
 this._parent.nextFrame();
 } else if (Key.getCode() == Key.LEFT) {
 this._parent.prevFrame();
 }
}
```

The following example uses `onClipEvent()` with the `load` and `mouseMove` movie events. The `_xmouse` and `_ymouse` properties track the position of the mouse each time the mouse moves, which appears in the text field that's created at runtime.

```
onClipEvent (load) {
 this.createTextField("coords_txt", this.getNextHighestDepth(), 0, 0, 100,
   22);
 coords_txt.autoSize = true;
 coords_txt.selectable = false;
}
onClipEvent (mouseMove) {
 coords_txt.text = "X:"+_root._xmouse+",Y:"+_root._ymouse;
}
```

See also

`Key`, `_xmouse (MovieClip._xmouse property)`, `_ymouse (MovieClip._ymouse property)`, `on handler`, `updateAfterEvent function`

ord function

`ord(character:String) : Number`

Deprecated since Flash Player 5. This function was deprecated in favor of the methods and properties of the String class.

Converts characters to ASCII code numbers.

Availability: ActionScript 1.0; Flash Player 4

Parameters

`character:String` - The character to convert to an ASCII code number.

Returns

`Number` - The ASCII code number of the specified character.

See also

`String, charCodeAt (String.charCodeAt method)`

parseFloat function

`parseFloat(string:String) : Number`

Converts a string to a floating-point number. The function reads, or *parses*, and returns the numbers in a string until it reaches a character that is not a part of the initial number. If the string does not begin with a number that can be parsed, `parseFloat()` returns `NaN`. White space preceding valid integers is ignored, as are trailing nonnumeric characters.

Availability: ActionScript 1.0; Flash Player 5

Parameters

`string:String` - The string to read and convert to a floating-point number.

Returns

`Number` - A number or `NaN` (not a number).

Example

The following examples use the `parseFloat()` function to evaluate various types of numbers:

```
trace(parseFloat("-2")); // output: -2
trace(parseFloat("2.5")); // output: 2.5
trace(parseFloat(" 2.5")); // output: 2.5
trace(parseFloat("3.5e6")); // output: 3500000
trace(parseFloat("foobar")); // output: NaN
trace(parseFloat("3.75math")); // output: 3.75
trace(parseFloat("0garbage")); // output: 0
```

See also

`NaN constant, parseInt function`

parseInt function

```
parseInt(expression:String, [radix:Number]) : Number
```

Converts a string to an integer. If the specified string in the parameters cannot be converted to a number, the function returns `NaN`. Strings beginning with 0x are interpreted as hexadecimal numbers. Integers beginning with 0 or specifying a radix of 8 are interpreted as octal numbers. White space preceding valid integers is ignored, as are trailing nonnumeric characters.

Availability: ActionScript 1.0; Flash Player 5

Parameters

`expression:String` - A string to convert to an integer.

`radix:Number` [optional] - An integer representing the radix (base) of the number to parse. Legal values are from 2 to 36.

Returns

`Number` - A number or `NaN` (not a number).

Example

The examples in this section use the `parseInt()` function to evaluate various types of numbers.

The following example returns 3:

```
parseInt("3.5")
```

The following example returns `NaN`:

```
parseInt("bar")
```

The following example returns 4:

```
parseInt("4foo")
```

The following example shows a hexadecimal conversion that returns 1016:

```
parseInt("0x3F8")
```

The following example shows a hexadecimal conversion using the optional *radix* parameter that returns 1000:

```
parseInt("3E8", 16)
```

The following example shows a binary conversion and returns 10, which is the decimal representation of the binary 1010:

```
parseInt("1010", 2)
```

The following examples show octal number parsing and return 511, which is the decimal representation of the octal 777:

```
parseInt("0777")
```

```
parseInt("777", 8)
```

See also

```
, parseFloat function
```

play function

```
play() : Void
```
Moves the playhead forward in the Timeline.

Availability: ActionScript 1.0; Flash Player 2

Example

In the following example, there are two movie clip instances on the Stage with the instance names stop_mc and play_mc. The ActionScript stops the SWF file's playback when the stop_mc movie clip instance is clicked. Playback resumes when the play_mc instance is clicked.

```
this.stop_mc.onRelease = function() {
 stop();
};
this.play_mc.onRelease = function() {
 play();
};
trace("frame 1");
```

See also

```
gotoAndPlay function, gotoAndPlay (MovieClip.gotoAndPlay method)
```

prevFrame function

```
prevFrame() : Void
```
Sends the playhead to the previous frame. If the current frame is Frame 1, the playhead does not move.

Availability: ActionScript 1.0; Flash Player 2

Example

When the user clicks a button called myBtn_btn and the following ActionScript is placed on a frame in the Timeline for that button, the playhead is sent to the previous frame:

```
stop();
this.myBtn_btn.onRelease = function(){
 prevFrame();
};
```

See also

nextFrame function, prevFrame (MovieClip.prevFrame method)

prevScene function

prevScene() : Void

Sends the playhead to Frame 1 of the previous scene.

Availability: ActionScript 1.0; Flash Player 2

See also

nextScene function

print function

print(target:Object, boundingBox:String) : Void

Prints the target movie clip according to the boundaries specified in the parameter (bmovie, bmax, or bframe). If you want to print specific frames in the target movie clip, attach a #p frame label to those frames. Although print() results in higher quality prints than printAsBitmap() it cannot be used to print movie clips that use alpha transparencies or special color effects.

If you use bmovie for the boundingBox parameter but do not assign a #b label to a frame, the print area is determined by the Stage size of the loaded movie clip. (The loaded movie clip does not inherit the main movie clip's Stage size.)

All the printable elements in a movie clip must be fully loaded before printing can begin.

The Flash Player printing feature supports PostScript and non-PostScript printers. Non-PostScript printers convert vectors to bitmaps.

Availability: ActionScript 1.0; Flash Player 4 - (4.0.20.0) If you are authoring for Flash Player 7 or later, you can create a PrintJob object, which gives you (and the user) more control over the printing process. For more information, see the PrintJob class entry.

Parameters

`target:Object` - The instance name of a movie clip to print. By default, all of the frames in the target instance can be printed. If you want to print specific frames in the movie clip, assign a *#p* frame label to those frames.

`boundingBox:String` - A modifier that sets the print area of the movie clip. Enclose this parameter in quotation marks (" or '), and specify one of the following values:

- `bmovie` Designates the bounding box of a specific frame in a movie clip as the print area for all printable frames in the movie clip. Assign a *#b* frame label to the frame whose bounding box you want to use as the print area.

- `bmax` Designates a composite of all the bounding boxes of all the printable frames as the print area. Specify `bmax` if the printable frames in your movie clip vary in size.

- `bframe` Indicates that the bounding box of each printable frame should be used as the print area for that frame, which changes the print area for each frame and scales the objects to fit the print area. Use `bframe` if you have objects of different sizes in each frame and want each object to fill the printed page.

Example

The following example prints all of the printable frames in `holder_mc` with a print area defined by the bounding box of each frame:

```
this.createEmptyMovieClip("holder_mc", 999);
holder_mc.loadMovie("http://www.helpexamples.com/flash/images/image1.jpg");

this.myBtn_btn.onRelease = function() {
 print(this._parent.holder_mc, "bframe");
};
```

In the previous ActionScript, you could replace `bframe` with `bmovie` so that the print area is defined by the bounding box of a frame with the *#b* frame label attached.

See also

`printAsBitmap function`, `printAsBitmapNum function`, `PrintJob`, `printNum function`

printAsBitmap function

`printAsBitmap(target:Object, boundingBox:String) : Void`

Prints the `target` movie clip as a bitmap according to the boundaries specified in the parameter (`bmovie`, `bmax`, or `bframe`). Use `printAsBitmap()` to print movie clips that contain frames with objects that use transparency or color effects. The `printAsBitmap()` action prints at the highest available resolution of the printer in order to maintain as much definition and quality as possible.

If your movie clip does not contain alpha transparencies or color effects, Macromedia recommends that you use `print()` for better quality results.

If you use `bmovie` for the `boundingBox` parameter but do not assign a #b label to a frame, the print area is determined by the Stage size of the loaded movie clip. (The loaded movie clip does not inherit the main movie clip's Stage size.)

All the printable elements in a movie clip must be fully loaded before printing can begin.

The Flash Player printing feature supports PostScript and non-PostScript printers. Non-PostScript printers convert vectors to bitmaps.

Availability: ActionScript 1.0; Flash Player 4 - (4.0.20.0) If you are authoring for Flash Player 7 or later, you can create a PrintJob object, which gives you (and the user) more control over the printing process. For more information, see the PrintJob class entry.

Parameters

`target:Object` - The instance name of the movie clip to print. By default, all of the frames in the movie clip are printed. If you want to print specific frames in the movie clip, attach a #p frame label to those frames.

`boundingBox:String` - A modifier that sets the print area of the movie clip. Enclose this parameter in quotation marks (" or '), and specify one of the following values:

- `bmovie` Designates the bounding box of a specific frame in a movie clip as the print area for all printable frames in the movie clip. Assign a #b frame label to the frame whose bounding box you want to use as the print area.

- `bmax` Designates a composite of all the bounding boxes of all the printable frames as the print area. Specify the `bmax` parameter if the printable frames in your movie clip vary in size.

- `bframe` Indicates that the bounding box of each printable frame should be used as the print area for that frame. This changes the print area for each frame and scales the objects to fit the print area. Use `bframe` if you have objects of different sizes in each frame and want each object to fill the printed page.

Example

The following example prints all of the printable frames in `holder_mc` with a print area defined by the bounding box of the frame:

```
this.createEmptyMovieClip("holder_mc", 999);
holder_mc.loadMovie("http://www.helpexamples.com/flash/images/image1.jpg");

this.myBtn_btn.onRelease = function() {
 printAsBitmap(this._parent.holder_mc, "bframe");
};
```

See also

`print` function, `printAsBitmapNum` function, `printNum` function, `PrintJob`

printAsBitmapNum function

`printAsBitmapNum(level:Number, boundingBox:String) : Void`

Prints a level in Flash Player as a bitmap according to the boundaries specified in the parameter (`bmovie`, `bmax`, or `bframe`). Use `printAsBitmapNum()` to print movie clips that contain frames with objects that use transparency or color effects. The `printAsBitmapNum()` action prints at the highest available resolution of the printer in order to maintain the highest possible definition and quality. To calculate the printable file size of a frame designated to be printed as a bitmap, multiply pixel width by pixel height by printer resolution.

If your movie clip does not contain alpha transparencies or color effects, using `printNum()` will give you better quality results.

If you use `bmovie` for the `boundingBox` parameter but do not assign a #b label to a frame, the print area is determined by the Stage size of the loaded movie clip. (The loaded movie clip does not inherit the main movie's Stage size.)

All the printable elements in a movie clip must be fully loaded before printing can start.

The Flash Player printing feature supports PostScript and non-PostScript printers. Non-PostScript printers convert vectors to bitmaps.

Availability: ActionScript 1.0; Flash Player 5 - If you are authoring for Flash Player 7 or later, you can create a PrintJob object, which gives you (and the user) more control over the printing process. For more information, see the PrintJob class entry.

Parameters

`level:Number` - The level in Flash Player to print. By default, all of the frames in the level are printed. If you want to print specific frames in the level, assign a #p frame label to those frames.

boundingBox:String - A modifier that sets the print area of the movie clip. Enclose this parameter in quotation marks (" or '), and specify one of the following values:

- bmovie Designates the bounding box of a specific frame in a movie clip as the print area for all of the printable frames in the movie clip. Assign a #b frame label to the frame whose bounding box you want to use as the print area.

- bmax Designates a composite of all the bounding boxes of all the printable frames as the print area. Specify the bmax parameter if the printable frames in your movie clip vary in size.

- bframe Indicates that the bounding box of each printable frame should be used as the print area for that frame. This changes the print area for each frame and scales the objects to fit the print area. Use bframe if you have objects of different sizes in each frame and you want each object to fill the printed page.

Example

The following example prints the contents of the Stage when the user clicks the button myBtn_btn. The area to print is defined by the bounding box of the frame.

```
myBtn_btn.onRelease = function(){
 printAsBitmapNum(0, "bframe")
};
```

See also

print function, printAsBitmap function, PrintJob, printNum function

printNum function

printNum(level:Number, boundingBox:String) : Void

Prints the level in Flash Player according to the boundaries specified in the boundingBox parameter (bmovie, bmax, bframe). If you want to print specific frames in the target movie clip, attach a #p frame label to those frames. Although using printNum() results in higher quality prints than using printAsBitmapNum(), you cannot use printNum() to print movies with alpha transparencies or special color effects.

If you use bmovie for the boundingBox parameter but do not assign a #b label to a frame, the print area is determined by the Stage size of the loaded movie clip. (The loaded movie clip does not inherit the main movie's Stage size.)

All the printable elements in a movie clip must be fully loaded before printing can begin.

The Flash Player printing feature supports PostScript and non-PostScript printers. Non-PostScript printers convert vectors to bitmaps.

Availability: ActionScript 1.0; Flash Player 5 - If you are authoring for Flash Player 7 or later, you can create a PrintJob object, which gives you (and the user) more control over the printing process. For more information, see the PrintJob class entry.

Parameters

`level`:`Number` - The level in Flash Player to print. By default, all of the frames in the level are printed. If you want to print specific frames in the level, assign a #p frame label to those frames.

`boundingBox`:`String` - A modifier that sets the print area of the movie clip. Enclose this parameter in quotation marks (" or '), and specify one of the following values:

- `bmovie` Designates the bounding box of a specific frame in a movie clip as the print area for all printable frames in the movie clip. Assign a #b frame label to the frame whose bounding box you want to use as the print area.

- `bmax` Designates a composite of all the bounding boxes of all the printable frames as the print area. Specify the `bmax` parameter if the printable frames in your movie clip vary in size.

- `bframe` Indicates that the bounding box of each printable frame should be used as the print area for that frame. This changes the print area for each frame and scales the objects to fit the print area. Use `bframe` if you have objects of different sizes in each frame and want each object to fill the printed page.

See also

`print function`, `printAsBitmap function`, `printAsBitmapNum function`, `PrintJob`

random function

`random(value:Number) : Number`

Deprecated since Flash Player 5. This function was deprecated in favor of `Math.random()`.

Returns a random integer between 0 and one less than the integer specified in the *value* parameter.

Availability: ActionScript 1.0; Flash Player 4

Parameters

`value`:`Number` - An integer.

Returns

`Number` - A random integer.

Example

The following use of `random()` returns a value of 0, 1, 2, 3, or 4: `random(5)`;

See also

`random (Math.random method)`

removeMovieClip function

`removeMovieClip(target:Object)`

Deletes the specified movie clip.

Availability: ActionScript 1.0; Flash Player 4

Parameters

`target:Object` - The target path of a movie clip instance created with `duplicateMovieClip()` or the instance name of a movie clip created with `MovieClip.attachMovie()`, `MovieClip.duplicateMovieClip()`, or `MovieClip.createEmptyMovieClip()`.

Example

The following example creates a new movie clip called `myClip_mc` and duplicates the movie clip. The second movie clip is called `newClip_mc`. Images are loaded into both movie clips. When a button, `button_mc`, is clicked, the duplicated movie clip is removed from the Stage.

```
this.createEmptyMovieClip("myClip_mc", this.getNextHighestDepth());
myClip_mc.loadMovie("http://www.helpexamples.com/flash/images/image1.jpg");
duplicateMovieClip(this.myClip_mc, "newClip_mc",
  this.getNextHighestDepth());
newClip_mc.loadMovie("http://www.helpexamples.com/flash/images/
  image1.jpg");
newClip_mc._x = 200;
this.button_mc.onRelease = function() {
 removeMovieClip(this._parent.newClip_mc);
};
```

See also

`duplicateMovieClip function`, `duplicateMovieClip (MovieClip.duplicateMovieClip method)`, `attachMovie (MovieClip.attachMovie method)`, `removeMovieClip (MovieClip.removeMovieClip method)`, `createEmptyMovieClip (MovieClip.createEmptyMovieClip method)`

setInterval function

```
setInterval(functionReference:Function, interval:Number, [param1:Object,
    param2, ..., paramN]) : Number
setInterval(objectReference:Object, methodName:String, interval:Number,
    [param1:Object, param2, ..., paramN]) : Number
```

Calls a function or a method of an object at periodic intervals while a SWF file plays. You can use `setInterval()` to execute any function repetitively over time.

Use the following tips when working with `setInterval()`:

- Identify the scope of the function being called.

- Identify the scope where the interval ID (the return value of `setInterval()`) was set.

- Clear previously set intervals before starting new ones.

These tips are discussed in further detail in the following paragraphs.

Identify the scope of the function being called. To identify the scope of the function being called, pass the object where the `setInterval()` method can execute (the object scope) as the first parameter and the method name you want to execute as the second parameter (as shown in the second signature). This ensures that the desired method is executed from the scope of the object reference passed in. When the method is executed in this manner, it can reference member variables on the object using the `this` keyword.

Identify the scope where the interval identifier was set. To identify the scope where the interval identifier (`intervalId`) was set, you can assign it to a member variable on the object scope that you pass to `setInterval()`. In this way, the function being called can locate the interval identifier at `this.intervalId`.

Clear previously set intervals. To clear previously set intervals before starting new ones, you should usually call `clearInterval()` *before* calling `setInterval()`. This ensures that you do not overwrite or otherwise destroy your `intervalId` variable, which is the only reference to the currently running interval. To call `clearInterval()` prior to calling `setInterval()`, both the initiating script and the script being executed must have access to the `intervalId`, as shown in the Examples.

> **NOTE**
>
> Always be sure to call `clearinterval()` when you want the script to stop looping.

Availability: ActionScript 1.0; Flash Player 6

Parameters

`functionReference:Function` - A reference to the function to be called.

`interval:Number` - The time in milliseconds between calls to the `functionReference` or `methodName` function passed in.

If `interval` is less than the SWF file's frame rate (for example, 10 frames per second [fps] is equal to 100 millisecond intervals), the interval function is called as close in time to the value of `interval` as possible. Executing long, memory-intensive scripts during an interval causes delays. If the function being called initiates a change to visual elements, you should use the `updateAfterEvent()` function to make sure that the screen refreshes often enough. If `interval` is greater than the SWF file's frame rate, the interval function is called only after `interval` has expired *and* the playhead has entered the next frame; this minimizes the impact each time the screen is refreshed.

`param:Object` [optional] - Parameters passed to the function that was sent to `functionReference` or `methodName`. Multiple parameters should be separated by commas: *param1,param2, ...,paramN*

`objectReference:Object` - An object that contains the method specified by `methodName`.

`methodName:String` - A method that exists in the scope of the object specified by `objectReference`.

Returns

`Number` - An integer that identifies the interval (the interval ID), which you can pass to `clearInterval()` to cancel the interval.

Example

Example 1: The following example traces a message at an interval of 20 milliseconds, up to 10 times, and then clears the interval. The object scope, `this`, is passed in as the first parameter, and the method name, `executeCallback`, as the second. This ensures that `executeCallback()` is executed from the same scope as the calling script.

```
var intervalId:Number;
var count:Number = 0;
var maxCount:Number = 10;
var duration:Number = 20;

function executeCallback():Void {
 trace("executeCallback intervalId: " + intervalId + " count: " + count);
 if(count >= maxCount) {
 clearInterval(intervalId);
 }
 count++;
}

intervalId = setInterval(this, "executeCallback", duration);
```

Example 2: The following example is similar to the first, except that it calls `clearInterval()` before `setInterval()`. This can help prevent unwanted loops and is especially important in event-based systems where the initiating script can be executed multiple times before any particular interval has been cleared.

```
var intervalId:Number;
var count:Number = 0;
var maxCount:Number = 10;
var duration:Number = 20;

function executeCallback():Void {
  trace("executeCallback intervalId: " + intervalId + " count: " + count);
  if(count >= maxCount) {
  clearInterval(intervalId);
  }
  count++;
}

function beginInterval():Void {
  if(intervalId != null) {
  trace("clearInterval");
  clearInterval(intervalId);
  }
  intervalId = setInterval(this, "executeCallback", duration);
}

beginInterval();
beginInterval();
beginInterval();
```

Example 3: The following example shows how to pass a custom argument to the function that is being called.

```
var intervalId:Number;
var count:Number = 0;
var maxCount:Number = 10;
var duration:Number = 20;
var colors:Array = new Array("red",
  "blue",
  "yellow",
  "purple",
  "green",
  "orange",
  "salmon",
  "pink",
  "lilac",
```

```
"powder blue",
"mint");

function executeCallback(param:String) {
 trace("executeCallback intervalId: " + intervalId + " count: " + count + "
  param: " + param);
 clearInterval(intervalId);
 if(count < maxCount) {
 count++;
 intervalId = setInterval(this, "executeCallback", duration,
  colors[count]);
 }
}

if(intervalId != null) {
 clearInterval(intervalId);
}

intervalId = setInterval(this, "executeCallback", duration, colors[count]);
```

Example 4: The following example shows how to use setInterval() correctly from an
ActionScript 2.0 custom class. Note that similar to previous examples, this is passed to the
setInterval() function to ensure that the called method is executed within the correct
scope.

```
class CustomClass {
 private var intervalId:Number;
 private var count:Number = 0;
 private var maxCount:Number = 10;
 private var duration:Number = 20;

 public function CustomClass():Void {
 beginInterval();
 }

 private function beginInterval():Void {
 if(intervalId != null) {
 trace("clearInterval");
 clearInterval(intervalId);
 }
 intervalId = setInterval(this, "executeCallback", duration);
 }

 public function executeCallback():Void {
 trace("executeCallback intervalId: " + intervalId + " count: " + count);
 if(count >= maxCount) {
 clearInterval(intervalId);
 }
```

```
count++;
  }
}
```

In a new document, instantiate a new instance of the new class:

```
var custom:CustomClass = new CustomClass();
```

See also

clearInterval function, updateAfterEvent function, class statement

setProperty function

setProperty(target:Object, property:Object, expression:Object) : Void
Changes a property value of a movie clip as the movie clip plays.
Availability: ActionScript 1.0; Flash Player 4

Parameters

target:Object - The path to the instance name of the movie clip whose property is to be set.

property:Object - The property to be set.

expression:Object - Either the new literal value of the property, or an equation that evaluates to the new value of the property.

Example

The following ActionScript creates a new movie clip and loads an image into it. The _x and _y coordinates are set for the clip using setProperty(). When you click the button called right_btn, the _x coordinate of a movie clip named params_mc is incremented by 20 pixels.

```
this.createEmptyMovieClip("params_mc", 999);
params_mc.loadMovie("http://www.helpexamples.com/flash/images/image1.jpg");
setProperty(this.params_mc, _y, 20);
setProperty(this.params_mc, _x, 20);
this.right_btn.onRelease = function() {
  setProperty(params_mc, _x, getProperty(params_mc, _x)+20);
};
```

See also

getProperty function

showRedrawRegions function

```
showRedrawRegions(enable:Boolean, [color:Number]) : Void
```

Provides the ability for the debugger player to outline the regions of the screen that are being redrawn (that is, dirty regions that are being updated). The outlines can also be turned on with the Show Redraw Regions menu option.

Availability: ActionScript 1.0; Flash Player 8

Parameters

`enable:Boolean` - Specifies whether to enable (`true`) or disable (`false`) redraw regions. When set to `true`, the redraw rectangles are shown. When set to `false`, the redraw rectangles are cleared.

`color:Number` [optional] - The color to draw with. The default is red: 0xFF0000.

Example

The following example demonstrates the `showRedrawRegions` function.

```
var w:Number = 100;
var h:Number = 100;

var shape1:MovieClip = createShape("shape1");
shape1.onEnterFrame = function():Void {
 this._x += 5;
 this._y += 5;
}

var shape2:MovieClip = createShape("shape2");
shape2.onEnterFrame = function():Void {
 this._y += 5;
}

_global.showRedrawRegions(true);

function createShape(name:String):MovieClip {
 var mc:MovieClip = this.createEmptyMovieClip(name,
  this.getNextHighestDepth());
 mc.beginFill(0xFFCC00);
 mc.moveTo(200, 200);
 mc.curveTo(300, 200, 300, 100);
 mc.curveTo(300, 0, 200, 0);
 mc.curveTo(100, 0, 100, 100);
 mc.curveTo(100, 200, 200, 200);
 mc.endFill();
 return mc;
}
```

startDrag function

```
startDrag(target:Object, [lock:Boolean, left:Number, top:Number,
right:Number, bottom:Number]) : Void
```

Makes the *target* movie clip draggable while the movie plays. Only one movie clip can be dragged at a time. After a `startDrag()` operation is executed, the movie clip remains draggable until it is explicitly stopped by `stopDrag()` or until a `startDrag()` action for another movie clip is called.

Availability: ActionScript 1.0; Flash Player 4

Parameters

`target:Object` - The target path of the movie clip to drag.

`lock:Boolean` [optional] - A Boolean value specifying whether the draggable movie clip is locked to the center of the mouse position (`true`) or locked to the point where the user first clicked the movie clip (`false`).

`left,top,right,bottom:Number` [optional] - Values relative to the coordinates of the movie clip's parent that specify a constraint rectangle for the movie clip.

Example

The following example creates a movie clip, `pic_mc`, at runtime that users can drag to any location by attaching the `startDrag()` and `stopDrag()` actions to the movie clip. An image is loaded into `pic_mc` using the MovieClipLoader class.

```
var pic_mcl:MovieClipLoader = new MovieClipLoader();
pic_mcl.loadClip("http://www.helpexamples.com/flash/images/image1.jpg",
 this.createEmptyMovieClip("pic_mc", this.getNextHighestDepth()));
var listenerObject:Object = new Object();
listenerObject.onLoadInit = function(target_mc) {
 target_mc.onPress = function() {
 startDrag(this);
 };
 target_mc.onRelease = function() {
 stopDrag();
 };
};
pic_mcl.addListener(listenerObject);
```

See also

`stopDrag function, _droptarget (MovieClip._droptarget property), startDrag
(MovieClip.startDrag method)`

stop function

`stop() : Void`

Stops the SWF file that is currently playing. The most common use of this action is to control movie clips with buttons.

Availability: ActionScript 1.0; Flash Player 2

See also

`gotoAndStop function, gotoAndStop (MovieClip.gotoAndStop method)`

stopAllSounds function

`stopAllSounds() : Void`

Stops all sounds currently playing in a SWF file without stopping the playhead. Sounds set to stream will resume playing as the playhead moves over the frames in which they are located.

Availability: ActionScript 1.0; Flash Player 3

Example

The following code creates a text field, in which the song's ID3 information appears. A new Sound object instance is created, and your MP3 is loaded into the SWF file. ID3 information is extracted from the sound file. When the user clicks `stop_mc`, the sound is paused. When the user clicks `play_mc`, the song resumes from its paused position.

```
this.createTextField("songinfo_txt", this.getNextHighestDepth, 0, 0,
  Stage.width, 22);
var bg_sound:Sound = new Sound();
bg_sound.loadSound("yourSong.mp3", true);
bg_sound.onID3 = function() {
 songinfo_txt.text = "(" + this.id3.artist + ") " + this.id3.album + " - " +
  this.id3.track + " - "
 + this.id3.songname;
 for (prop in this.id3) {
 trace(prop+" = "+this.id3[prop]);
 }
 trace("ID3 loaded.");
};
this.play_mc.onRelease = function() {
 /* get the current offset. if you stop all sounds and click the play
  button, the MP3 continues from
 where it was stopped, instead of restarting from the beginning. */
 var numSecondsOffset:Number = (bg_sound.position/1000);
 bg_sound.start(numSecondsOffset);
};
this.stop_mc.onRelease = function() {
```

```
stopAllSounds();
};
```

See also

Sound

stopDrag function

```
stopDrag() : Void
```

Stops the current drag operation.

Availability: ActionScript 1.0; Flash Player 4

Example

The following code, placed in the main Timeline, stops the drag action on the movie clip instance my_mc when the user releases the mouse button:

```
my_mc.onPress = function () {
  startDrag(this);
}

my_mc.onRelease = function() {
  stopDrag();
}
```

See also

startDrag function, _droptarget (MovieClip._droptarget property), startDrag (MovieClip.startDrag method), stopDrag (MovieClip.stopDrag method)

String function

```
String(expression:Object) : String
```

Returns a string representation of the specified parameter, as described in the following list:

- If *expression* is a number, the return string is a text representation of the number.
- If *expression* is a string, the return string is *expression*.
- If *expression* is an object, the return value is a string representation of the object generated by calling the string property for the object, or by calling `Object.toString()` if no such property exists.
- If *expression* is a Boolean value, the return string is `"true"` or `"false"`.
- If *expression* is a movie clip, the return value is the target path of the movie clip in slash (/) notation.

If *expression* is `undefined`, the return values are as follows:

- In files published for Flash Player 6 and earlier, the result is an empty string (`""`).
- In files published for Flash Player 7 and later, the result is `undefined`.

Note: Slash notation is not supported by ActionScript 2.0.

Availability: ActionScript 1.0; Flash Player 4 - Behavior changed in Flash Player 7.

Parameters

`expression:Object` - An expression to convert to a string.

Returns

`String` - A string.

Example

In the following example, you use ActionScript to convert specified expressions to a string:

```
var string1:String = String("3");
var string2:String = String("9");
trace(string1+string2); // output: 39
```

Because both parameters are strings, the values are concatenated rather than added.

See also

`toString (Number.toString method)`, `toString (Object.toString method)`, `String,` `" string delimiter operator`

substring function

`substring(string:String, index:Number, count:Number) : String`

Deprecated since Flash Player 5. This function was deprecated in favor of `String.substr()`.

Extracts part of a string. This function is one-based, whereas the String object methods are zero-based.

Availability: ActionScript 1.0; Flash Player 4

Parameters

`string:String` - The string from which to extract the new string.

`index:Number` - The number of the first character to extract.

`count:Number` - The number of characters to include in the extracted string, not including the index character.

Returns

`String` - The extracted substring.

See also

`substr (String.substr method)`

targetPath function

`targetPath(targetObject:Object) : String`

Returns a string containing the target path of a MovieClip, Button, TextField, or Videoobject. The target path is returned in dot (.) notation. To retrieve the target path in slash (/) notation, use the `_target` property.

Availability: ActionScript 1.0; Flash Player 5 - Support for Button, TextField, and Video objects added in Flash Player 6.

Parameters

`targetObject:Object` - Reference (for example, `_root` or `_parent`) to the object for which the target path is being retrieved. This can be a MovieClip, Button, or TextField object.

Returns

`String` - A string containing the target path of the specified object.

Example

The following example traces the target path of a movie clip as soon as it loads:

```
this.createEmptyMovieClip("myClip_mc", this.getNextHighestDepth());
trace(targetPath(myClip_mc)); // _level0.myClip_mc
```

See also

```
eval function
```

tellTarget function

```
tellTarget(target:String) {
statement(s);
}
```

Deprecated since Flash Player 5. Macromedia recommends that you use dot (.) notation and the with statement.

Applies the instructions specified in the *statements* parameter to the Timeline specified in the *target* parameter. The tellTarget action is useful for navigation controls. Assign tellTarget to buttons that stop or start movie clips elsewhere on the Stage. You can also make movie clips go to a particular frame in that clip. For example, you might assign tellTarget to buttons that stop or start movie clips on the Stage or prompt movie clips to jump to a particular frame.

In Flash 5 or later, you can use dot (.) notation instead of the tellTarget action. You can use the with action to issue multiple actions to the same Timeline. You can use the with action to target any object, whereas the tellTarget action can target only movie clips.

Availability: ActionScript 1.0; Flash Player 3

Parameters

target:String - A string that specifies the target path of the Timeline to be controlled.

statement(s) - The instructions to execute if the condition is true.

Example

This tellTarget statement controls the movie clip instance ball on the main Timeline. Frame 1 of the ball instance is blank and has a stop() action so it isn't visible on the Stage. When you click the button with the following action, tellTarget tells the playhead in ball to go to Frame 2, where the animation starts:

```
on(release) {
tellTarget("_parent.ball") {
gotoAndPlay(2);
}
}
```

The following example uses dot (.) notation to achieve the same results:

```
on(release) {
```

```
_parent.ball.gotoAndPlay(2);
}
```

If you need to issue multiple commands to the ball instance, you can use the with action, as shown in the following statement:

```
on(release) {
with(_parent.ball) {
gotoAndPlay(2);
_alpha = 15;
_xscale = 50;
_yscale = 50;
}
}
```

See also

```
with statement
```

toggleHighQuality function

```
toggleHighQuality()
```

Deprecated since Flash Player 5. This function was deprecated in favor of _quality.

Turns anti-aliasing on and off in Flash Player. Anti-aliasing smooths the edges of objects and slows down SWF playback. This action affects all SWF files in Flash Player.

Availability: ActionScript 1.0; Flash Player 2

Example

The following code could be applied to a button that, when clicked, would toggle anti-aliasing on and off:

```
on(release) {
toggleHighQuality();
}
```

See also

```
, _quality property
```

trace function

```
trace(expression:Object)
```

You can use Flash Debug Player to capture output from the trace() function and display the result.

Use this statement to record programming notes or to display messages in the Output panel while testing a SWF file. Use the *expression* parameter to check whether a condition exists, or to display values in the Output panel. The trace() statement is similar to the alert function in JavaScript.

You can use the Omit Trace Actions command in the Publish Settings dialog box to remove trace()actions from the exported SWF file.

Availability: ActionScript 1.0; Flash Player 4

Parameters

expression:Object - An expression to evaluate. When a SWF file is opened in the Flash authoring tool (using the Test Movie command), the value of the *expression* parameter is displayed in the Output panel.

Example

The following example uses a trace() statement to display in the Output panel the methods and properties of the dynamically created text field called error_txt:

```
this.createTextField("error_txt", this.getNextHighestDepth(), 0, 0, 100,
    22);
for (var i in error_txt) {
trace("error_txt."+i+" = "+error_txt[i]);
}
/* output:
error_txt.styleSheet = undefined
error_txt.mouseWheelEnabled = true
error_txt.condenseWhite = false
...
error_txt.maxscroll = 1
error_txt.scroll = 1
*/
```

unescape function

unescape(string:String) : String

Evaluates the parameter *x* as a string, decodes the string from URL-encoded format (converting all hexadecimal sequences to ASCII characters), and returns the string.

Availability: ActionScript 1.0; Flash Player 5

Parameters

string:String - A string with hexadecimal sequences to escape.

Returns

`String` - A string decoded from a URL-encoded parameter.

Example

The following example shows the escape-to-unescape conversion process:

```
var email:String = "user@somedomain.com";
trace(email);
var escapedEmail:String = escape(email);
trace(escapedEmail);
var unescapedEmail:String = unescape(escapedEmail);
trace(unescapedEmail);
```

The following result is displayed in the Output panel.

```
user@somedomain.com
user%40somedomain%2Ecom
user@somedomain.com
```

unloadMovie function

```
unloadMovie(target:MovieClip) : Void
unloadMovie(target:String) : Void
```

Removes a movie clip that was loaded by means of `loadMovie()` from Flash Player. To unload a movie clip that was loaded by means of `loadMovieNum()`, use `unloadMovieNum()` instead of `unloadMovie()`.

Availability: ActionScript 1.0; Flash Player 3

Parameters

`target:Object` - The target path of a movie clip. This parameter can be either a String (e.g. "my_mc") or a direct reference to the movie clip instance (e.g. my_mc). Parameters that can accept more than one data type are listed as type `Object`.

Example

The following example creates a new movie clip called `pic_mc` and loads an image into that clip. It is loaded using the MovieClipLoader class. When you click the image, the movie clip unloads from the SWF file:

```
var pic_mcl:MovieClipLoader = new MovieClipLoader();
pic_mcl.loadClip("http://www.helpexamples.com/flash/images/image1.jpg",
 this.createEmptyMovieClip("pic_mc", this.getNextHighestDepth()));
var listenerObject:Object = new Object();
listenerObject.onLoadInit = function(target_mc) {
 target_mc.onRelease = function() {
```

```
unloadMovie(pic_mc);
/* or you could use the following, which refers to the movie clip
  referenced by 'target_mc'. */
//unloadMovie(this);
};
};
pic_mc1.addListener(listenerObject);
```

See also

loadMovie (MovieClip.loadMovie method), unloadClip
(MovieClipLoader.unloadClip method)

unloadMovieNum function

unloadMovieNum(level:Number) : Void

Removes a SWF or image that was loaded by means of loadMovieNum() from Flash Player.
To unload a SWF or image that was loaded with MovieClip.loadMovie(), use
unloadMovie() instead of unloadMovieNum().

Availability: ActionScript 1.0; Flash Player 3

Parameters

level:Number - The level (_level N) of a loaded movie.

Example

The following example loads an image into a SWF file. When you click unload_btn, the
loaded content is removed.

```
loadMovieNum("yourimage.jpg", 1);
unload_btn.onRelease = function() {
 unloadMovieNum(1);
}
```

See also

loadMovieNum function, unloadMovie function, loadMovie (MovieClip.loadMovie
method)

updateAfterEvent function

updateAfterEvent() : Void

Updates the display (independent of the frames per second set for the movie) when you call it within an `onClipEvent()` handler or as part of a function or method that you pass to setInterval(). Flash ignores calls to `updateAfterEvent` that are not within an `onClipEvent()` handler or part of a function or method passed to setInterval(). This function works only with certain Mouse and MovieClip handlers: the mouseDown, mouseUp, mouseMove, keyDown and keyUp handlers for the Mouse class; the onMouseMove, onMouseDown, onMouseUp, onKeyDown, and onKeyUp handlers for the MovieClip class. It does not work with the Key class.

Availability: ActionScript 1.0; Flash Player 5

Example

The following example show how to create a custom cursor called `cursor_mc`. ActionScript is used to replace the mouse cursor with `cursor_mc`. Then `updateAfterEvent()` is used to continually refresh the Stage to make the cursor's movement appear smooth.

```
Mouse.hide();
cursor_mc.onMouseMove = function() {
  this._x = this._parent._xmouse;
  this._y = this._parent._ymouse;
  updateAfterEvent();
};
```

See also

`onClipEvent handler`, `setInterval function`

Global Properties

Global properties are available in every script, and are visible to every Timeline and scope in your document. For example, global properties allow access to the timelines of other loaded movie clips, both relative (_parent) and absolute (_root). They also let you restrict (this) or expand (super) scope. And, you can use global properties to adjust runtime settings like screen reader accessibility, playback quality, and sound buffer size.

Global Properties summary

Modifiers	Property	Description
	_accProps	Lets you control screen reader accessibility options for SWF files, movie clips, buttons, dynamic text fields, and input text fields at runtime.
	_focusrect	Property (global); specifies whether a yellow rectangle appears around the button or movie clip that has keyboard focus.
	_global	A reference to the global object that holds the core ActionScript classes, such as String, Object, Math, and Array.
	_highquality	**Deprecated** since Flash Player 5. This property was deprecated in favor of _quality. Specifies the level of anti-aliasing applied to the current SWF file.
	_level	A reference to the root Timeline of _level*N*.
	maxscroll	**Deprecated** since Flash Player 5. This property was deprecated in favor of TextField.maxscroll. Indicates the line number of the top line of visible text in a text field when the bottom line in the field is also visible.
	_parent	Specifies or returns a reference to the movie clip or object that contains the current movie clip or object.
	_quality	Sets or retrieves the rendering quality used for a movie clip.
	_root	Specifies or returns a reference to the root movie clip Timeline.
	scroll	**Deprecated** since Flash Player 5. This property was deprecated in favor of TextField.scroll. Controls the display of information in a text field associated with a variable.
	_soundbuftime	Establishes the number of seconds of streaming sound to buffer.
	this	References an object or movie clip instance.

_accProps property

```
_accProps.propertyName
instanceName._accProps.propertyName
```

Lets you control screen reader accessibilityoptions for SWF files, movie clips, buttons, dynamic text fields, and input textfields at runtime. Theseproperties override the corresponding settings available in the Accessibilitypanel during authoring. For changes to these properties to take effect,you must call Accessibility.updateProperties().

For information on the Accessibility panel, see "The Flash Accessibility panel" in *Using Flash*.

To determine whether the player is running in an environment that supports accessibility aids, use the System.capabilities.hasAccessibility() method .

The following table lists the name and data type of each _accProps property , its equivalent setting in the Accessibility panel, and the kinds of objects to which the property can be applied. The term *inverse logic* means that the property setting is the inverse of the corresponding setting in the Accessibility panel. For example, setting the silent property to true is equivalent to deselecting the Make Movie Accessible or Make Object Accessible option.

Property	Data type	Equivalent in Accessibility panel	Applies to
silent	Boolean	Make Movie Accessible/ Make Object Accessible (*inverse logic*)	Whole SWF files Movie clips Buttons Dynamic text Input text
forceSimple	Boolean	Make Child Objects Accessible (*inverse logic*)	Whole SWF files Movie clips
name	String	Name	Whole SWF files Movie clips Buttons Input text
description	String	Description	Whole SWF files Movie clips Buttons Dynamic text Input text
shortcut	String	Shortcut	Movie clips Buttons Input text

For the Shortcut field, use names of the form Control+A. Adding a keyboard shortcut to the Accessibility panel doesn't create a keyboard shortcut; it merely advises screen readers of an existing shortcut. For information on assigninga keyboard shortcut to an accessible object, see Key.addListener().

To specify settings that correspond to the Tab index setting in the Accessibility panel, use the Button.tabIndex, MovieClip.tabIndex, or TextField.tabIndex properties.

There is no way to specify an Auto Label setting at runtime.

To refer to the _accProps object that represents the entire Flash document, omit the instanceName parameter. The value of _accProps must be an object. This means that if no _accProps object already exists, you must create one, as shown in the following example, before you can assign values to the properties of the _accProps object:

```
if ( _accProps == undefined )
{
 _accProps = new Object();
}
_accProps.name = "My SWF file";
```

When _accProps is used without the *instanceName* parameter, changes made to _accProps properties apply to the whole SWF file. For example, the following code sets the Accessibility name property for the whole SWF file to the string "Pet Store" and then calls Accessibility.updateProperties() to cause that change:

```
_accProps.name = "Pet Store";
Accessibility.updateProperties();
```

In contrast, the following code sets the name property for a movie clip with the instance name price_mc to the string "Price":

```
price_mc._accProps.name = "Price";
Accessibility.updateProperties();
```

If you are specifying several accessibility properties, make as many changes as you can before calling Accessibility.updateProperties(), instead of calling it after each property statement, as shown in the following example:

```
_accProps.name = "Pet Store";

animal_mc._accProps.name = "Animal";
animal_mc._accProps.description = "Cat, dog, fish, etc.";

price_mc._accProps.name = "Price";
price_mc._accProps.description = "Cost of a single item";

Accessibility.updateProperties();
```

If you don't specify an accessibility property for a document or an object, any values set in the Accessibility panel are implemented.

After you specify an accessibility property, you can't revert its value to a value set in the Accessibility panel. However, you can set the property to its default value (`false` for Boolean values; empty strings for string values) by deleting the property from the _accProps object, as shown in the following example:

```
my_mc._accProps.silent = true; // set a property
// other code here
delete my_mc._accProps.silent; // revert to default value
```

The value of _accProps must be an object. This means that if no _accProps object already exists, you must create one before you can assign clues to the properties of the _accProps object.

```
if (_accProps == undefined)
{
 _accProps = new Object();
}
_accProps.name = "My movie";
```

Availability: ActionScript 1.0; Flash Player 6,0,65,0

Parameters

`propertyName`:Boolean or String - An accessibility property name (see the following description for valid names). *instanceName*

`instanceName`:String - The instance name assigned to an instance of a movie clip, button, dynamic text field, or input text field. To refer to the _accProps object that represents the entire Flash document, omit *instanceName*.

Example

If you change an image and want to update its accessibility description, you can use the following ActionScript code:

```
my_mc.gotoAndStop(2);

if (my_mc._accProps == undefined ) {
 my_mc._accProps = new Object();
}

my_mc._accProps.name = "Photo of Mount Rushmore";
Accessibility.updateProperties();
```

See also

```
isActive (Accessibility.isActive method), updateProperties
(Accessibility.updateProperties method), hasAccessibility
(capabilities.hasAccessibility property)
```

_focusrect property

_focusrect = *Boolean*;

Specifies whether a yellow rectangle appears around the button or movie clip that has keyboard focus. If _focusrect is set to its default value of true, then a yellow rectangle appears around the currently focused button or movie clip as the user presses the Tab key to navigate through objects in a SWF file. Specify false if you do not want to show the yellow rectangle. This is a global property that can be overridden for specific instances.

If the global _focusrect property is set to false, then the default behavior for all buttons and movieclips is that keyboard navigation is limited to the Tab key. All other keys, including the Enter and arrow keys, are ignored. To restore full keyboard navigation, you must set _focusrect to true. To restore full keyboard functionality for a specific button or movieclip, you can override this global property using either Button._focusrect or MovieClip._focusrect.

 If you use a component, then FocusManager overrides Flash Player's focus handling, including use of this global property.

Availability: ActionScript 1.0; Flash Player 4

Example

The following example demonstrates how to hide the yellow rectangle around any instances in a SWF file when they have focus in a browser window. Create some buttons or movie clips and add the following ActionScript in frame 1 of the Timeline:

_focusrect = false;

Change the publish settings to Flash Player 6, and test the SWF file in a browser window by selecting File > Publish Preview > HTML. Give the SWF focus by clicking it in the browser window, and use the Tab key to focus each instance. Pressing Enter or the Space key when _focusrect is disabled does not invoke the onRelease event handler as it does when _focusrectis enabled or true.

See also

_focusrect (Button._focusrect property), _focusrect (MovieClip._focusrect property)

_global property

`_global.identifier`

A reference to the global object that holds the core ActionScript classes, such as String, Object, Math, and Array. For example, you could create a library that is exposed as a global ActionScript object, similar to the Math or Date object. Unlike Timeline-declared or locally declared variables and functions, global variables and functions are visible to every Timeline and scope in the SWF file, provided they are not obscured by identifiers with the same names in inner scopes.

> **NOTE**
>
> When setting the value of a global variable, you must use the fully qualified name of the variable, e.g. _global.variableName. Failure to do so will create a local variable of the same name that obscures the global variable you are attempting to set.

Returns A reference to the global object that holds the core ActionScript classes, such as String, Object, Math, and Array.

Availability: ActionScript 1.0; Flash Player 6

Example

The following example creates a top-level function, `factorial()`, that is available to every Timeline and scope in a SWF file:

```
_global.factorial = function(n:Number) {
if(n <= 1) {
return 1;
}
else {
return n * factorial(n - 1);
}
}

trace(factorial(1)); // 1
trace(factorial(2)); // 2
trace(factorial(3)); // 6
trace(factorial(4)); // 24
```

The following example shows how the failure to use the fully qualified variable name when setting the value of a global variable leads to unexpected results:

```
_global.myVar = "globalVariable";
trace(_global.myVar); // globalVariable
trace(myVar); // globalVariable

myVar = "localVariable";
trace(_global.myVar); // globalVariable
trace(myVar); // localVariable
```

See also

var statement, set variable statement

_highquality property

`_highquality`

Deprecated since Flash Player 5. This property was deprecated in favor of `_quality`.

Specifies the level of anti-aliasing applied to the current SWF file. Specify 2 (best quality) to apply high quality with bitmap smoothing always on. Specify 1 (high quality) to apply anti-aliasing; this will smooth bitmaps if the SWF file does not contain animation. Specify 0 (low quality) to prevent anti-aliasing.

Availability: ActionScript 1.0; Flash Player 4

Example

The following ActionScript is placed on the main Timeline, and sets the global quality property to always apply bitmap smoothing in non-animated files. `_highquality = 1;`

See also

_quality property

_level property

`_levelN`

A reference to the root Timeline of `_levelN`. You must use `loadMovieNum()` to load SWF files into the Flash Player before you use the `_level` property to target them. You can also use `_levelN` to target a loaded SWF file at the level assigned by *N*.

The initial SWF file loaded into an instance of the Flash Player is automatically loaded into `_level0`. The SWF file in `_level0` sets the frame rate, background color, and frame size for all subsequently loaded SWF files. SWF files are then stacked in higher-numbered levels above the SWF file in `_level0`.

You must assign a level to each SWF file that you load into the Flash Player using `loadMovieNum()`. You can assign levels in any order. If you assign a level that already contains a SWF file (including `_level0`), the SWF file at that level is unloaded and replaced by the new SWF file.

Availability: ActionScript 1.0; Flash Player 4

Example

The following example stops the playhead in the main Timeline of the SWF file sub.swf that is loaded into _level9. The sub.swf file contains animation and is in the same directory as the document that contains the following ActionScript:

```
loadMovieNum("sub.swf", 9);
myBtn_btn.onRelease = function() {
 _level9.stop();
};
```

You could replace _level9.stop() in the previous example with the following code:

```
_level9.gotoAndStop(5);
```

This action sends the playhead in the main Timeline of the SWF file in _level9 to Frame 5 instead of stopping the playhead.

See also

loadMovie function, swapDepths (MovieClip.swapDepths method)

maxscroll property

variable_name.maxscroll

Deprecated since Flash Player 5. This property was deprecated in favor of TextField.maxscroll.

Indicates the line number of the top line of visible text in a text field when the bottom line in the field is also visible. The maxscroll property works with the scroll property to control how information appears in a text field. This property can be retrieved, but not modified.

Availability: ActionScript 1.0; Flash Player 4

See also

maxscroll (TextField.maxscroll property), scroll (TextField.scroll property)

_parent property

_parent.*property*
_parent._parent.*property*

Specifies or returns a reference to the movie clip or object that contains the current movie clip or object. The current object is the object containing the ActionScript code that references _parent. Use _parent to specify a relative path to movie clips or objects that are above the current movie clip or object.

Availability: ActionScript 1.0; Flash Player 5

Example

In the following example, there is a movie clip on the Stage with the instance name square_mc. Within that movie clip is another movie clip with an instance name circle_mc. The following ActionScript lets you modify the circle_mc parent instance (which is square_mc) when the circle is clicked. When you are working with relative addressing (using _parent instead of _root), it might be easier to use the Insert Target Path button in the Actions panel at first.

```
this.square_mc.circle_mc.onRelease = function() {
 this._parent._alpha -= 5;
};
```

See also

_root property, targetPath function

_quality property

_quality:*String*

Sets or retrieves the rendering quality used for a movie clip. Device fonts are always aliased and therefore are unaffected by the _quality property.

The _quality property can be set to the values described in the following table.

Value	Description	Graphic Anti-Aliasing	Bitmap Smoothing
"LOW"	Low rendering quality.	Graphics are not anti-aliased.	Bitmaps are not smoothed.
"MEDIUM"	Medium rendering quality. This setting is suitable for movies that do not contain text.	Graphics are anti-aliased using a 2 x 2 pixel grid.	Flash Player 8: Bitmaps are smoothed based on the smoothing parameter used in MovieClip.attachBitmap() and MovieClip.beginBitmapFill() calls. Flash Player 6 and 7: Bitmaps are not smoothed.

Value	Description	Graphic Anti-Aliasing	Bitmap Smoothing
"HIGH"	High rendering quality. This setting is the default rendering quality setting that Flash uses.	Graphics are anti-aliased using a 4 x 4 pixel grid.	Flash Player 8: Bitmaps are smoothed based on the `smoothing` parameter used in `MovieClip.attachBitmap()` and `MovieClip.beginBitmapFill()` calls. Flash Player 6 and 7: Bitmaps are smoothed if the movie clip is static.
"BEST"	Very high rendering quality.	Graphics are anti-aliased using a 4 x 4 pixel grid.	Flash Player 8: Bitmaps are smoothed based on the `smoothing` parameter used in `MovieClip.attachBitmap()` and `MovieClip.beginBitmapFill()` calls. When `smoothing` is set to "Best", the result is rendered with higher quality when the movie clip is scaled down by the use of an averaging algorithm. This can slow down rendering, but it allows high-quality thumbnails of large images, for example. Flash Player 6 and 7: Bitmaps are always smoothed.

Availability: ActionScript 1.0; Flash Player 5

Example

The following example sets the rendering quality to LOW:

```
_quality = "LOW";
```

_root property

```
_root.movieClip
_root.action
_root.property
```

Specifies or returns a reference to the root movie clip Timeline. If a movie clip has multiple levels, the root movie clip Timeline is on the level containing the currently executing script. For example, if a script in level 1 evaluates _root, _level1 is returned.

Specifying _root is the same as using the deprecated slash notation (/) to specify an absolute path within the current level.

Note: If a movie clip that contains _root is loaded into another movie clip, _root refers to the Timeline of the loading movie clip, not the Timeline that contains _root. If you want to ensure that _root refers to the Timeline of the loaded movie clip even if it is loaded into another movie clip, use MovieClip._lockroot.

Availability: ActionScript 1.0; Flash Player 5

Parameters

movieClip:String - The instance name of a movie clip.

action:String - An action or method.

property:String - A property of the MovieClip object.

Example

The following example stops the Timeline of the level containing the currently executing script:

```
_root.stop();
```

The following example traces variables and instances in the scope of _root:

```
for (prop in _root) {
  trace("_root."+prop+" = "+_root[prop]);
}
```

See also

_lockroot (MovieClip._lockroot property), _parent property, targetPath function

scroll property

textFieldVariableName.scroll = *x*

Deprecated since Flash Player 5. This property was deprecated in favor of TextField.scroll.

Controls the display of information in a text field associated with a variable. The scroll property defines where the text field begins displaying content; after you set it, Flash Player updates it as the user scrolls through the text field. The scroll property is useful for directing users to a specific paragraph in a long passage or creating scrolling text fields. This property can be retrieved and modified.

Availability: ActionScript 1.0; Flash Player 4

Example

The following code is attached to an Up button that scrolls the text field named myText:

```
on (release) {
myText.scroll = myText.scroll + 1;
}
```

See also

maxscroll (TextField.maxscroll property), scroll (TextField.scroll property)

_soundbuftime property

_soundbuftime:*Number* = *integer*

Establishes the number of seconds of streaming sound to buffer. The default value is 5 seconds.

Availability: ActionScript 1.0; Flash Player 4

Parameters

integer:Number - The number of seconds before the SWF file starts to stream.

Example

The following example streams an MP3 file and buffers the sound before it plays for the user. Two text fields are created at runtime to hold a timer and debugging information. The _soundbuftime property is set to buffer the MP3 for 10 seconds. A new Sound object instance is created for the MP3.

```
// create text fields to hold debug information.
this.createTextField("counter_txt", this.getNextHighestDepth(), 0, 0, 100,
    22);
this.createTextField("debug_txt", this.getNextHighestDepth(), 0, 20, 100,
    22);
// set the sound buffer to 10 seconds.
_soundbuftime = 10;
// create the new sound object instance.
var bg_sound:Sound = new Sound();
// load the MP3 sound file and set streaming to true.
bg_sound.loadSound("yourSound.mp3", true);
// function is triggered when the song finishes loading.
bg_sound.onLoad = function() {
  debug_txt.text = "sound loaded";
};
debug_txt.text = "sound init";
function updateCounter() {
  counter_txt.text++;
}
counter_txt.text = 0;
setInterval(updateCounter, 1000);
```

this property

`this`

References an object or movie clip instance. When a script executes, `this` references the movie clip instance that contains the script. When a method is called, `this` contains a reference to the object that contains the called method.

Inside an `on()` event handler attached to a button, `this` refers to the Timeline that contains the button. Inside an `onClipEvent()` event handler attached to a movie clip, `this` refers to the Timeline of the movie clip itself.

Because `this` is evaluated in the context of the script that contains it, you can't use `this` in a script to refer to a variable defined in a class file.

Availability: ActionScript 1.0; Flash Player 5

Example

Create an ActionsScript file named ApplyThis.as and then enter the following code:

```
class ApplyThis {
 var str:String = "Defined in ApplyThis.as";
 function conctStr(x:String):String {
 return x+x;
 }
 function addStr():String {
 return str;
 }
}
```

Then, in a FLA or a separate ActionScript file, add the following code

```
var obj:ApplyThis = new ApplyThis();
var abj:ApplyThis = new ApplyThis();
abj.str = "defined in FLA or AS";
trace(obj.addStr.call(abj, null)); //output: defined in FLA or AS
trace(obj.addStr.call(this, null)); //output: undefined
trace(obj.addStr.call(obj, null)); //output: Defined in applyThis.as
```

Similarly, to call a function defined in a dynamic class, you must use this to invoke the function in the proper scope:

```
// incorrect version of Simple.as
/*
dynamic class Simple {
 function callfunc() {
 trace(func());
 }
}
*/
// correct version of Simple.as
dynamic class simple {
 function callfunc() {
 trace(this.func());
 }
}
```

Inside the FLA or a separate ActionScript file, add the following code:

```
var obj:Simple = new Simple();
obj.num = 0;
obj.func = function() {
 return true;
};
obj.callfunc();
// output: true
```

The above code works when you use this in the callfunc() method. However you would get a syntax error if you used the incorrect version of Simple.as, which was commented out in the above example.

In the following example, the keyword this references the Circle object:

```
function Circle(radius:Number):Void {
 this.radius = radius;
 this.area = Math.PI*Math.pow(radius, 2);
}
var myCircle = new Circle(4);
trace(myCircle.area);
```

In the following statement assigned to a frame inside a movie clip, the keyword this references the current movie clip.

```
// sets the alpha property of the current movie clip to 20
this._alpha = 20;
```

In the following statement inside a MovieClip.onPress handler, the keyword this references the current movie clip:

```
this.square_mc.onPress = function() {
 startDrag(this);
};
this.square_mc.onRelease = function() {
 stopDrag();
};
```

See also

on handler, onClipEvent handler

Operators

Symbolic operators are characters that specify how to combine, compare, or modify the values of an expression.

Operators summary

Operator	Description
+ (addition)	Adds numeric expressions or concatenates (combines) strings.
+= (addition assignment)	Assigns *expression1* the value of *expression1* + *expression2*.
[] (array access)	Initializes a new array or multidimensional array with the specified elements (*a0* , and so on), or accesses elements in an array.
= (assignment)	Assigns the value of *expression2* (the parameter on the right) to the variable, array element, or property in *expression1*.

Operator	Description
`& (bitwise AND)`	Converts *expression1* and *expression2* to 32-bit unsigned integers, and performs a Boolean AND operation on each bit of the integer parameters.
`&= (bitwise AND assignment)`	Assigns *expression1* the value of *expression1*& *expression2*.
`<< (bitwise left shift)`	Converts *expression1* and *expression2* to 32-bit integers, and shifts all the bits in *expression1* to the left by the number of places specified by the integer resulting from the conversion of *expression2*.
`<<= (bitwise left shift and assignment)`	This operator performs a bitwise left shift (`<<=`) operation and stores the contents as a result in *expression1*.
`~ (bitwise NOT)`	Also known as the one's complement operator or the bitwise complement operator.
`| (bitwise OR)`	Converts *expression1* and *expression2* to 32-bit unsigned integers, and returns a 1 in each bit position where the corresponding bits of either *expression1* or *expression2* are 1.
`|= (bitwise OR assignment)`	Assigns *expression1* the value of *expression1* `|` *expression2*.
`>> (bitwise right shift)`	Converts *expression1* and *expression2* to 32-bit integers, and shifts all the bits in *expression1* to the right by the number of places specified by the integer that results from the conversion of *expression2*.
`>>= (bitwise right shift and assignment)`	This operator performs a bitwise right-shift operation and stores the contents as a result in *expression1*.
`>>> (bitwise unsigned right shift)`	The same as the bitwise right shift (`>>`) operator except that it does not preserve the sign of the original *expression* because the bits on the left are always filled with 0. Floating-point numbers are converted to integers by discarding any digits after the decimal point.
`>>>= (bitwise unsigned right shift and assignment)`	Performs an unsigned bitwise right-shift operation and stores the contents as a result in *expression1*.
`^ (bitwise XOR)`	Converts *expression1* and *expression2* to 32-bit unsigned integers, and returns a 1 in each bit position where the corresponding bits in *expression1* or *expression2*, but not both, are 1.
`^= (bitwise XOR assignment)`	Assigns *expression1* the value of *expression1* `^` *expression2*.
`/*..*/ (block comment delimiter)`	Indicates one or more lines of script comments.

Operator	Description
, (comma)	Evaluates *expression1*, then *expression2*, and so on.
add (concatenation (strings))	**Deprecated** since Flash Player 5. Macromedia recommends that you use the add (+) operator when creating content for Flash Player 5 or later. This operator is not supported in Flash Player 8 or later. Concatenates two or more strings.
?: (conditional)	Instructs Flash to evaluate *expression1*, and if the value of *expression1* is true, it returns the value of *expression2*; otherwise it returns the value of *expression3*.
-- (decrement)	A pre-decrement and post-decrement unary operator that subtracts 1 from the *expression*.
/ (division)	Divides *expression1* by *expression2*.
/= (division assignment)	Assigns *expression1* the value of *expression1* / *expression2*.
. (dot)	Used to navigate movie clip hierarchies to access nested (child) movie clips, variables, or properties.
== (equality)	Tests two expressions for equality.
eq (equality (strings))	**Deprecated** since Flash Player 5. This operator was deprecated in favor of the == (equality) operator. Returns true if the string representation of *expression1* is equal to the string representation of *expression2*, false otherwise.
> (greater than)	Compares two expressions and determines whether *expression1* is greater than *expression2*; if it is, the operator returns true.
gt (greater than (strings))	**Deprecated** since Flash Player 5. This operator was deprecated in favor of the > (greater than) operator. Compares the string representation of *expression1* with the string representation of *expression2* and returns true if *expression1* is greater than *expression2*, false otherwise.
>= (greater than or equal to)	Compares two expressions and determines whether *expression1* is greater than or equal to *expression2* (true) or *expression1* is less than *expression2* (false).
ge (greater than or equal to (strings))	**Deprecated** since Flash Player 5. This operator was deprecated in favor of the >= (greater than or equal to) operator. Returns true if *expression1* is greater than or equal to *expression2*, false otherwise.
++ (increment)	A pre-increment and post-increment unary operator that adds 1 to *expression*.
!= (inequality)	Tests for the exact opposite of the equality (==) operator.

Operator	Description
<> (inequality)	**Deprecated** since Flash Player 5. This operator has been deprecated. Macromedia recommends that you use the != (inequality) operator. Tests for the exact opposite of the equality (==) operator.
instanceof	Tests whether object is an instance of classConstructor or a subclass of classConstructor.
< (less than)	Compares two expressions and determines whether *expression1* is less than *expression2*; if so, the operator returns true.
lt (less than (strings))	**Deprecated** since Flash Player 5. This operator was deprecated in favor of the < (less than) operator. Returns true if expression1 is less than expression2, false otherwise.
<= (less than or equal to)	Compares two expressions and determines whether *expression1* is less than or equal to *expression2*; if it is, the operator returns true.
le (less than or equal to (strings))	**Deprecated** since Flash Player 5. This operator was deprecated in Flash 5 in favor of the <= (less than or equal to) operator. Returns true if *expression1* is less than or equal to *expression2*, false otherwise.
// (line comment delimiter)	Indicates the beginning of a script comment.
&& (logical AND)	Performs a Boolean operation on the values of both expressions.
and (logical AND)	**Deprecated** since Flash Player 5. Macromedia recommends that you use the logical AND (&&) operator. Performs a logical AND (&&) operation in Flash Player 4.
! (logical NOT)	Inverts the Boolean value of a variable or expression.
not (logical NOT)	**Deprecated** since Flash Player 5. This operator was deprecated in favor of the! (logical NOT) operator. Performs a logical NOT (!) operation in Flash Player 4.
|| (logical OR)	Evaluates *expression1* (the expression on the left side of the operator) and returns true if the expression evaluates to true.
or (logical OR)	**Deprecated** since Flash Player 5. This operator was deprecated in favor of the || (logical OR) operator. Evaluates *condition1* and *condition2*, and if either expression is true, the whole expression is true.
% (modulo)	Calculates the remainder of *expression1* divided by *expression2*.
%= (modulo assignment)	Assigns *expression1* the value of *expression1* % *expression2*.
* (multiplication)	Multiplies two numerical expressions.

Operator	Description
*= (multiplication assignment)	Assigns *expression1* the value of *expression1 * expression2*.
new	Creates a new, initially anonymous, object and calls the function identified by the `constructor` parameter.
ne (not equal (strings))	**Deprecated** since Flash Player 5. This operator was deprecated in favor of the != (inequality) operator. Returns `true` if *expression1* is not equal to *expression2*; `false` otherwise.
{} (object initializer)	Creates a new object and initializes it with the specified *name* and *value* property pairs.
() (parentheses)	Performs a grouping operation on one or more parameters, performs sequential evaluation of expressions, or surrounds one or more parameters and passes them as parameters to a function outside the parentheses.
=== (strict equality)	Tests two expressions for equality; the strict equality (===)operator performs in the same way as the equality (==) operator, except that data types are not converted.
!== (strict inequality)	Tests for the exact opposite of the strict equality (===) operator.
" (string delimiter)	When used before and after characters, quotation marks (") indicate that the characters have a literal value and are considered a *string*, not a variable, numerical value, or other ActionScript element.
- (subtraction)	Used for negating or subtracting.
-= (subtraction assignment)	Assigns *expression1* the value of *expression1 - expression2*.
: (type)	Used for strict data typing; this operator specifies the variable type, function return type, or function parameter type.
typeof	The `typeof` operator evaluate the `expression` and returns a string specifying whether the expression is a `String`, `MovieClip`, `Object`, `Function`, `Number`, or `Boolean` value.
void	The `void` operator evaluates an expression and then discards its value, returning `undefined`

+ addition operator

expression1 + expression2

Adds numeric expressions or concatenates (combines) strings. If one expression is a string, all other expressions are converted to strings and concatenated. If both expressions are integers, the sum is an integer; if either or both expressions are floating-point numbers, the sum is a floating-point number.

Availability: ActionScript 1.0; Flash Player 4 - In Flash 4, + is only a numeric operator. In Flash Player 5 and later, + is either a numeric operator or a string concatenator depending on the data type of the parameter. Flash 4 files that are brought into the Flash 5 or later authoring environment undergo a conversion process to maintain data type integrity. The following example illustrates the conversion of a Flash 4 file containing a numeric quality comparison:

Flash 4 file: x + y

Converted Flash 5 or later file: Number(x) + Number(y)

Operands

`expression1` - A number or string.

`expression2 : Number` - A number or string.

Returns

`Object` - A string, integer, or floating-point number.

Example

Usage 1: The following example concatenates two strings and displays the result in the Output panel.

```
var name:String = "Cola";
var instrument:String = "Drums";
trace(name + " plays " + instrument); // output: Cola plays Drums
```

Usage 2: This statement adds the integers 2 and 3 and displays the resulting integer, 5, in the Output panel:

```
trace(2 + 3); // output: 5
```

This statement adds the floating-point numbers 2.5 and 3.25 and displays the resulting floating-point number, 5.75, in the Output panel

```
trace(2.5 + 3.25); // output: 5.75
```

Usage 3: Variables associated with dynamic and input text fields have the data type String. In the following example, the variable `deposit` is an input text field on the Stage. After a user enters a deposit amount, the script attempts to add `deposit` to `oldBalance`. However, because `deposit` is a String data type, the script concatenates (combines to form one string) the variable values rather than summing them.

```
var oldBalance:Number = 1345.23;
```

```
var currentBalance = deposit_txt.text + oldBalance;
trace(currentBalance);
```

For example, if a user enters 475 in the deposit text field, the trace() statement sends the value 4751345.23 to the Output panel. To correct this, use the Number() function to convert the string to a number, as in the following:

```
var oldBalance:Number = 1345.23;
var currentBalance:Number = Number(deposit_txt.text) + oldBalance;
trace(currentBalance);
```

The following example shows how numeric sums to the right of a string expression are not calculated:

```
var a:String = 3 + 10 + "asdf";
trace(a); // 13asdf
var b:String = "asdf" + 3 + 10;
trace(b); // asdf310
```

+= addition assignment operator

expression1 += *expression2*

Assigns *expression1* the value of *expression1+ expression2*. For example, the following two statements have the same result:

```
x += y;
x = x + y;
```

This operator also performs string concatenation. All the rules of the addition (+) operator apply to the addition assignment (+=) operator.

Availability: ActionScript 1.0; Flash Player 4

Operands

expression1 : Number - A number or string.

expression2 : Number - A number or string.

Returns

Number - The result of the addition.

Example

Usage 1: This example uses the+= operator with a string expression and sends "My name is Gilbert" to the Output panel.

```
var x1:String = "My name is ";
x1 += "Gilbert";
trace(x1); // output: My name is Gilbert
```

Usage 2: The following example shows a numeric use of the addition assignment (+=) operator:

```
var x:Number = 5;
var y:Number = 10;
x += y;
trace(x); // output: 15
```

See also

```
+ addition operator
```

[] array access operator

```
myArray = [ a0, a1,...aN ]
myArray[ i ] = value
myObject [ propertyName ]
```

Initializes a new array or multidimensional array with the specified elements (*a0*, and so on), or accesses elements in an array. The array access operator lets you dynamically set and retrieve instance, variable, and object names. It also lets you access object properties.

Usage 1: An array is an object whose properties are called *elements*, which are each identified by a number called an *index*. When you create an array, you surround the elements with the array access ([]) operator (or *brackets*). An array can contain elements of various types. For example, the following array, called `employee`, has three elements; the first is a number and the second two are strings (inside quotation marks):

```
var employee:Array = [15, "Barbara", "Jay"];
```

You can nest brackets to simulate multidimensional arrays. You can nest arrays up to 256 levels deep. The following code creates an array called `ticTacToe` with three elements; each element is also an array with three elements:

```
var ticTacToe:Array = [[1, 2, 3], [4, 5, 6], [7, 8, 9]]; // Select Debug >
  List Variables in test mode
// to see a list of the array elements.
```

Usage 2: Surround the index of each element with brackets ([]) to access it directly; you can add a new element to an array, or you can change or retrieve the value of an existing element. The first index in an array is always 0, as shown in the following example:

```
var my_array:Array = new Array();
my_array[0] = 15;
my_array[1] = "Hello";
my_array[2] = true;
```

You can use brackets ([]) to add a fourth element, as shown in the following example:

```
my_array[3] = "George";
```

You can use brackets ([]) to access an element in a multidimensional array. The first set of brackets identifies the element in the original array, and the second set identifies the element in the nested array. The following lines of code send the number 6 to the Output panel.

```
var ticTacToe:Array = [[1, 2, 3], [4, 5, 6], [7, 8, 9]];
trace(ticTacToe[1][2]);// output: 6
```

Usage 3: You can use the array access ([]) operator instead of the eval() function to dynamically set and retrieve values for movie clip names or any property of an object. The following line of code sends the number 6 to the Output panel.

```
name["mc" + i] = "left_corner";
```

Availability: ActionScript 1.0; Flash Player 4

Operands

myArray : Object - *myArray* The name of an array.

a0, a1,...aN : Object - *a0,a1,...aN* Elements in an array; any native type or object instance, including nested arrays.

i : Number - *i* An integer index greater than or equal to 0.

myObject : Object - *myObject* The name of an object.

propertyName : String - *propertyName* A string that names a property of the object.

Returns

Object -

Usage 1: A reference to an array.

Usage 2: A value from the array; either a native type or an object instance (including an Array instance).

Usage 3: A property from the object; either a native type or an object instance (including an Array instance).

Example

The following example shows two ways to create a new empty Array object; the first line uses brackets ([]):

```
var my_array:Array = [];
var my_array:Array = new Array();
```

The following example creates an array called employee_array and uses the trace() statement to send the elements to the Output panel. In the fourth line, an element in the array is changed, and the fifth line sends the newly modified array to the Output panel:

```
var employee_array = ["Barbara", "George", "Mary"];
```

```
trace(employee_array); // output: Barbara,George,Mary
employee_array[2] = "Sam";
trace(employee_array); // output: Barbara,George,Sam
```

In the following example, the expression inside the brackets (`"piece"` + `i`) is evaluated and the result is used as the name of the variable to be retrieved from the my_mc movie clip. In this example, the variable i must live on the same Timeline as the button. If the variable i is equal to 5, for example, the value of the variable piece5 in the my_mc movie clip is displayed in the Output panel:

```
myBtn_btn.onRelease = function() {
  x = my_mc["piece"+i];
  trace(x);
};
```

In the following example, the expression inside the brackets is evaluated, and the result is used as the name of the variable to be retrieved from movie clip name_mc:

```
name_mc["A" + i];
```

If you are familiar with the Flash 4 ActionScript slash syntax, you can use the eval() function to accomplish the same result:

```
eval("name_mc.A" & i);
```

You can use the following ActionScript to loop over all objects in the _root scope, which is useful for debugging:

```
for (i in _root) {
  trace(i+": "+_root[i]);
}
```

You can also use the array access ([]) operator on the left side of an assignment statement to dynamically set instance, variable, and object names:

```
employee_array[2] = "Sam";
```

See also

Array, Object, eval function

= assignment operator

expression1 = expression2

Assigns the value of *expression2* (the parameter on the right) to the variable, array element, or property in *expression1*. Assignment can be either by value or by reference. Assignment by value copies the actual value of *expression2* and stores it in *expression1*. Assignment by value is used when a variable is assigned a number or string literal. Assignment by reference stores a reference to *expression2* in *expression1*. Assignment by reference is commonly used with the `new` operator. Use of the `new` operator creates an object in memory and a reference to that location in memory is assigned to a variable.

Availability: ActionScript 1.0; Flash Player 4 - In Flash 4, = is a numeric equality operator. In Flash 5 or later, = is an assignment operator, and the == operator is used to evaluate equality. Flash 4 files that are brought into the Flash 5 or later authoring environment undergo a conversion process to maintain data type integrity.

Flash 4 file: x = y

Converted Flash 5 or later file: Number(x) == Number(y)

Operands

`expression1` : `Object` - A variable, element of an array, or property of an object.

`expression2` : `Object` - A value of any type.

Returns

`Object` - The assigned value, *expression2* .

Example

The following example uses assignment by value to assign the value of 5 to the variable `x`.

```
var x:Number = 5;
```

The following example uses assignment by value to assign the value `"hello"` to the variable `x`:

```
var x:String;
x = " hello ";
```

The following example uses assignment by reference to create the moonsOfJupiter variable, which contains a reference to a newly created Array object. Assignment by value is then used to copy the value "Callisto" to the first element of the array referenced by the variable `moonsOfJupiter`:

```
var moonsOfJupiter:Array = new Array();
moonsOfJupiter[0] = "Callisto";
```

The following example uses assignment by reference to create a new object, and assign a reference to that object to the variable `mercury`. Assignment by value is then used to assign the value of 3030 to the `diameter` property of the `mercury` object:

```
var mercury:Object = new Object(); mercury.diameter = 3030; // in miles
```

```
trace (mercury.diameter); // output: 3030
```

The following example builds upon the previous example by creating a variable named
merkur (the German word for mercury) and assigning it the value of mercury. This creates
two variables that reference the same object in memory, which means you can use either
variable to access the object's properties. We can then change the diameter property to use
kilometers instead of miles:

```
var merkur:Object = mercury;
merkur.diameter = 4878; // in kilometers
trace (mercury.diameter); // output: 4878
```

See also

```
== equality operator
```

& bitwise AND operator

expression1 & *expression2*

Converts *expression1* and *expression2* to 32-bit unsigned integers, and performs a
Boolean AND operation on each bit of the integer parameters. Floating-point numbers are
converted to integers by discarding any digits after the decimal point. The result is a new 32-
bit integer.

Positive integers are converted to an unsigned hexadecimal value with a maximum value of
4294967295 or 0xFFFFFFFF; values larger than the maximum have their most significant
digits discarded when they are converted, therefore their value is still 32-bit. Negative
numbers are converted to an unsigned hexadecimal value using two's complement notation,
with the minimum being -2147483648 or 0x800000000; numbers less than the minimum
are converted to two's complement with greater precision and then have the most significant
dig its discarded as well.

The return value is interpreted as a two's complement number with sign, so the return is an
integer in the range -2147483648 to 2147483647.

Availability: ActionScript 1.0; Flash Player 5 - In Flash 4, the AND (&) operator was used for
concatenating strings. In Flash 5 and later, the AND (&) operator is a bitwise AND, and you
must use the addition (+) operator to concatenate strings. Flash 4 files that use the AND (&)
operator are automatically updated to use addition (+) operator when imported into the Flash
5 or later authoring environment.

Operands

expression1 : Number - A number.

expression2 : Number - A number.

Returns

`Number` - The result of the bitwise operation.

Example

The following example compares the bit representation of the numbers and returns 1 only if both bits at the same position are 1. In this ActionScript, you add 13 (binary 1101) and 11 (binary 1011) and return 1 only in the position where both numbers have a 1.

```
var insert:Number = 13;
var update:Number = 11;
trace(insert & update); // output : 9 (or 1001 binary)
```

In the numbers 13 and 11 the result is 9 because only the first and last positions in both numbers have the number 1.

The following examples show the behavior of the return value conversion:

```
trace(0xFFFFFFFF); // 4294967295
trace(0xFFFFFFFF & 0xFFFFFFFF); // -1
trace(0xFFFFFFFF & -1); // -1
trace(4294967295 & -1); // -1
trace(4294967295 & 4294967295); // -1
```

See also

`&=` bitwise AND assignment operator, `^` bitwise XOR operator, `^=` bitwise XOR assignment operator, `|` bitwise OR operator, `|=` bitwise OR assignment operator, `~` bitwise NOT operator

&= bitwise AND assignment operator

expression1 `&=` *expression2*

Assigns *expression1* the value of *expression1*`&` *expression2*. For example, the following two expressions are equivalent:

```
x &= y;
x = x & y;
```

Availability: ActionScript 1.0; Flash Player 5

Operands

`expression1` : `Number` - A number.

`expression2` : `Number` - A number.

Returns

`Number` - The value of *expression1* `&` *expression2* .

Example

The following example assigns the value 9 to x:

```
var x:Number = 15;
var y:Number = 9;
trace(x &= y); // output: 9
```

See also

& bitwise AND operator, ^ bitwise XOR operator, ^= bitwise XOR assignment operator, | bitwise OR operator, |= bitwise OR assignment operator, ~ bitwise NOT operator

« bitwise left shift operator

expression1 << expression2

Converts expression1 and expression2 to 32-bit integer values; you can call them V1 and V2. Shifts all bits of the value of V1 to the left by V2 positions. Discards bits shifted off the left end of V1 by this operation, and inserts zeros in the bit positions on the right that are emptied. Shifting a value left by one position is the equivalent of multiplying it by 2.

Floating-point numbers are converted to integers by discarding any digits after the decimal point. Positive integers are converted to an unsigned hexadecimal value with a maximum value of 4294967295 or 0xFFFFFFFF; values larger than the maximum have their most significant digits discarded when they are converted so the value is still 32-bit. Negative numbers are converted to an unsigned hexadecimal value via the two's complement notation, with the minimum being -2147483648 or 0x800000000; numbers less than the minimum are converted to two's complement with greater precision and also have the most significant digits discarded.

The return value is interpreted as a two's complement number with sign, so the return value will be an integer in the range -2147483648 to 2147483647.

Availability: ActionScript 1.0; Flash Player 5

Operands

expression1 : Number - A number or expression to be shifted left.

expression2 : Number - A number or expression that converts to an integer from 0 to 31.

Returns

Number - The result of the bitwise operation.

Example

In the following example, the integer 1 is shifted 10 bits to the left: x = 1 << 10 The result of this operation is x = 1024. This is because 1 decimal equals 1 binary, 1 binary shifted left by 10 is 10000000000 binary, and 10000000000 binary is 1024 decimal. In the following example, the integer 7 is shifted 8 bits to the left: x = 7 << 8 The result of this operation is x = 1792. This is because 7 decimal equals 111 binary, 111 binary shifted left by 8 bits is 11100000000 binary, and 11100000000 binary is 1792 decimal. If you trace the following example, you see that the bits have been pushed two spaces to the left:

```
// 2 binary == 0010
// 8 binary == 1000
trace(2 << 2); // output: 8
```

See also

>>= bitwise right shift and assignment operator, >> bitwise right shift operator, <<= bitwise left shift and assignment operator, >>> bitwise unsigned right shift operator, >>>= bitwise unsigned right shift and assignment operator

<<= bitwise left shift and assignment operator

expression1 <<= *expression2*

This operator performs a bitwise left shift (<<=) operation and stores the contents as a result in *expression1*. The following two expressions are equivalent:

```
A <<= B;
A = (A << B)
```

Availability: ActionScript 1.0; Flash Player 5

Operands

expression1 : Number - A number or expression to be shifted left.

expression2 : Number - A number or expression that converts to an integer from 0 to 31.

Returns

Number - The result of the bitwise operation.

Example

In the following example, you use the bitwise left shift and assignment (<<=) operator to shift all bits one space to the left:

```
var x:Number = 4;
// shift all bits one slot to the left.
```

```
x <<= 1;
trace(x); // output: 8
// 4 decimal = 0100 binary
// 8 decimal = 1000 binary
```

See also

```
<< bitwise left shift operator, >>= bitwise right shift and assignment
operator, >> bitwise right shift operator
```

~ bitwise NOT operator

~expression

Also known as the one's complement operator or the bitwise complement operator. Converts the *expression* to a 32-bit signed integer, and then applies a bitwise one's complement. That is, every bit that is a 0 is set to 1 in the result, and every bit that is a 1 is set to 0 in the result. The result is a signed 32-bit integer.

For example, the hexadecimal value 0x7777 is represented as this binary number: 0111011101110111

The bitwise negation of that hexadecimal value, ~0x7777, is this binary number: 1000100010001000

In hexadecimal, this is 0x8888. Therefore, ~0x7777 is 0x8888.

The most common use of bitwise operators is for representing *flag bits* (Boolean values packed into 1 bit each).

Floating-point numbers are converted to integers by discarding any digits after the decimal point. Positive integers are converted to an unsigned hexadecimal value with a maximum value of 4294967295 or 0xFFFFFFFF; values larger than the maximum have their most significant digits discarded when they are converted so the value is still 32-bit. Negative numbers are converted to an unsigned hexadecimal value via the two's complement notation, with the minimum being -2147483648 or 0x800000000; numbers less than the minimum are converted to two's complement with greater precision and also have the most significant digits discarded.

The return value is interpreted as a two's complement number with sign, so the return value is an integer in the range -2147483648 to 2147483647.

Availability: ActionScript 1.0; Flash Player 5

Operands

```
expression : Number - A number.
```

Returns

`Number` - The result of the bitwise operation.

Example

The following example demonstrates a use of the bitwise NOT (-) operator with flag bits:

```
var ReadOnlyFlag:Number = 0x0001; // defines bit 0 as the read-only flag
var flags:Number = 0;
trace(flags);
/* To set the read-only flag in the flags variable,
 the following code uses the bitwise OR:
*/
flags |= ReadOnlyFlag;
trace(flags);
/* To clear the read-only flag in the flags variable,
 first construct a mask by using bitwise NOT on ReadOnlyFlag.
 In the mask, every bit is a 1 except for the read-only flag.
 Then, use bitwise AND with the mask to clear the read-only flag.
 The following code constructs the mask and performs the bitwise AND:
*/
flags &= ~ReadOnlyFlag;
trace(flags);
// output: 0 1 0
```

See also

`&` bitwise AND operator, `&=` bitwise AND assignment operator, `^` bitwise XOR operator, `^=` bitwise XOR assignment operator, `|` bitwise OR operator, `|=` bitwise OR assignment operator

| bitwise OR operator

expression1 | *expression2*

Converts *expression1* and *expression2* to 32-bit unsigned integers, and returns a 1 in each bit position where the corresponding bits of either *expression1* or *expression2* are 1. Floating-point numbers are converted to integers by discarding any digits after the decimal point. The result is a new 32-bit integer.

Positive integers are converted to an unsigned hexadecimal value with a maximum value of 4294967295 or 0xFFFFFFFF; values larger than the maximum have their most significant digits discarded when they are converted so the value is still 32-bit. Negative numbers are converted to an unsigned hexadecimal value via the two's complement notation, with the minimum being -2147483648 or 0x800000000; numbers less than the minimum are converted to two's complement with greater precision and also have the most significant digits discarded.

The return value is interpreted as a two's complement number with sign, so the return value will be an integer in the range -2147483648 to 2147483647.

Availability: ActionScript 1.0; Flash Player 5

Operands

`expression1 : Number` - A number.

`expression2 : Number` - A number.

Returns

`Number` - The result of the bitwise operation.

Example

The following is an example of a bitwise OR (|) operation:

```
// 15 decimal = 1111 binary
var x:Number = 15;
// 9 decimal = 1001 binary
var y:Number = 9;
// 1111 | 1001 = 1111
trace(x | y); // returns 15 decimal (1111 binary)
```

Don't confuse the single | (bitwise OR) with || (logical OR).

See also

`& bitwise AND operator`, `&= bitwise AND assignment operator`, `^ bitwise XOR operator`, `^= bitwise XOR assignment operator`, `|= bitwise OR assignment operator`, `~ bitwise NOT operator`

|= bitwise OR assignment operator

`expression1 |= expression2`

Assigns `expression1` the value of `expression1 | expression2`. For example, the following two statements are equivalent:

```
x |= y;
x = x | y;
```

Availability: ActionScript 1.0; Flash Player 5

Operands

`expression1 : Number` - A number or variable.

`expression2 : Number` - A number or variable.

Returns

`Number` - The result of the bitwise operation.

Example

The following example uses the bitwise OR assignment (`|=`) operator:

```
// 15 decimal = 1111 binary
var x:Number = 15;
// 9 decimal = 1001 binary
var y:Number = 9;
// 1111 |= 1001 = 1111
trace(x |= y); // returns 15 decimal (1111 binary)
```

See also

`&` bitwise AND operator, `&=` bitwise AND assignment operator, `^` bitwise XOR operator, `^=` bitwise XOR assignment operator, `|` bitwise OR operator, `|=` bitwise OR assignment operator, `~` bitwise NOT operator

» bitwise right shift operator

expression1 `>>` *expression2*

Converts *expression1* and *expression2* to 32-bit integers, and shifts all the bits in *expression1* to the right by the number of places specified by the integer that results from the conversion of *expression2* . Bits that are shifted off the right end are discarded. To preserve the sign of the original *expression* , the bits on the left are filled in with 0 if the most significant bit (the bit farthest to the left) of *expression1* is 0, and filled in with 1 if the most significant bit is 1. Shifting a value right by one position is the equivalent of dividing by 2 and discarding the remainder.

Floating-point numbers are converted to integers by discarding any digits after the decimal point. Positive integers are converted to an unsigned hexadecimal value with a maximum value of 4294967295 or 0xFFFFFFFF; values larger than the maximum have their most significant digits discarded when they are converted so the value is still 32-bit. Negative numbers are converted to an unsigned hexadecimal value via the two's complement notation, with the minimum being -2147483648 or 0x800000000; numbers less than the minimum are converted to two's complement with greater precision and also have the most significant digits discarded.

The return value is interpreted as a two's complement number with sign, so the return value will be an integer in the range -2147483648 to 2147483647.

Availability: ActionScript 1.0; Flash Player 5

Operands

expression1 : Number - A number or expression to be shifted right.

expression2 : Number - A number or expression that converts to an integer from 0 to 31.

Returns

Number - The result of the bitwise operation.

Example

The following example converts 65535 to a 32-bit integer and shifts it 8 bits to the right:

```
var x:Number = 65535 >> 8;
trace(x); // outputs 255
```

The following example shows the result of the previous example:

```
var x:Number = 255;
```

This is because 65535 decimal equals 1111111111111111 binary (sixteen 1s), 1111111111111111 binary shifted right by 8 bits is 11111111 binary, and 11111111 binary is 255 decimal. The most significant bit is 0 because the integers are 32-bit, so the fill bit is 0.

The following example converts -1 to a 32-bit integer and shifts it 1 bit to the right:

```
var x:Number = -1 >> 1;
trace(x); // outputs -1
```

The following example shows the result of the previous example:

```
var x:Number = -1;
```

This is because -1 decimal equals 11111111111111111111111111111111 binary (thirty-two 1s), shifting right by one bit causes the least significant (bit farthest to the right) to be discarded and the most significant bit to be filled in with 1. The result is 11111111111111111111111111111111 (thirty-two 1s) binary, which represents the 32-bit integer -1.

See also

>>= bitwise right shift and assignment operator

>>= bitwise right shift and assignment operator

expression1 >>= expression2

This operator performs a bitwise right-shift operation and stores the contents as a result in *expression1*.

The following two statements are equivalent:

```
A >>= B;
A = (A >> B);
```

Availability: ActionScript 1.0; Flash Player 5

Operands

`expression1 : Number` - A number or expression to be shifted right.

`expression2 : Number` - A number or expression that converts to an integer from 0 to 31.

Returns

`Number` - The result of the bitwise operation.

Example

The following commented code uses the bitwise right shift and assignment (>>=) operator.

```
function convertToBinary(numberToConvert:Number):String {
 var result:String = "";
 for (var i = 0; i<32; i++) {
 // Extract least significant bit using bitwise AND
 var lsb:Number = numberToConvert & 1;
 // Add this bit to the result
 string result = (lsb ? "1" : "0")+result;
 // Shift numberToConvert right by one bit, to see next bit
 numberToConvert >>= 1;
 }
 return result;
}
trace(convertToBinary(479));
// Returns the string 00000000000000000000000111011111
// This string is the binary representation of the decimal
// number 479
```

See also

`>> bitwise right shift operator`

⋙ bitwise unsigned right shift operator

expression1 >>> expression2

The same as the bitwise right shift (>>) operator except that it does not preserve the sign of the original *expression* because the bits on the left are always filled with 0.

Floating-point numbers are converted to integers by discarding any digits after the decimal point. Positive integers are converted to an unsigned hexadecimal value with a maximum value of 4294967295 or 0xFFFFFFFF; values larger than the maximum have their most significant digits discarded when they are converted so the value is still 32-bit. Negative numbers are converted to an unsigned hexadecimal value via the two's complement notation, with the minimum being -2147483648 or 0x800000000; numbers less than the minimum are converted to two's complement with greater precision and also have the most significant digits discarded.

Availability: ActionScript 1.0; Flash Player 5

Operands

`expression1 : Number` - A number or expression to be shifted right.

`expression2 : Number` - A number or expression that converts to an integer between 0 and 31.

Returns

`Number` - The result of the bitwise operation.

Example

The following example converts -1 to a 32-bit integer and shifts it 1 bit to the right:

```
var x:Number = -1 >>> 1;
trace(x); // output: 2147483647
```

This is because -1 decimal is 11111111111111111111111111111111 binary (thirty-two 1s), and when you shift right (unsigned) by 1 bit, the least significant (rightmost) bit is discarded, and the most significant (leftmost) bit is filled with a 0. The result is 01111111111111111111111111111111 binary, which represents the 32-bit integer 2147483647.

See also

`>>= bitwise right shift and assignment operator`

>>>= bitwise unsigned right shift and assignment operator

`expression1 >>>= expression2`

Performs an unsigned bitwise right-shift operation and stores the contents as a result in `expression1`. The following two statements are equivalent:

```
A >>>= B;
```

```
A = (A >>> B);
```
Availability: ActionScript 1.0; Flash Player 5

Operands

`expression1` : `Number` - A number or expression to be shifted right.

`expression2` : `Number` - A number or expression that converts to an integer from 0 to 31.

Returns

`Number` - The result of the bitwise operation.

Example

See also

`>>>` bitwise unsigned right shift operator, `>>=` bitwise right shift and assignment operator

^ bitwise XOR operator

expression1 ^ expression2

Converts *expression1* and *expression2* to 32-bit unsigned integers, and returns a 1 in each bit position where the corresponding bits in *expression1* or *expression2*, but not both, are 1. Floating-point numbers are converted to integers by discarding any digits after the decimal point. The result is a new 32-bit integer.

Positive integers are converted to an unsigned hexadecimal value with a maximum value of 4294967295 or 0xFFFFFFFF; values larger than the maximum have their most significant digits discarded when they are converted so the value is still 32-bit. Negative numbers are converted to an unsigned hexadecimal value via the two's complement notation, with the minimum being -2147483648 or 0x800000000; numbers less than the minimum are converted to two's complement with greater precision and also have the most significant digits discarded.

The return value is interpreted as a two's complement number with sign, so the return value will be an integer in the range -2147483648 to 2147483647.

Availability: ActionScript 1.0; Flash Player 5

Operands

`expression1` : `Number` - A number.

`expression2` : `Number` - A number.

Returns

`Number` - The result of the bitwise operation.

Example

The following example uses the bitwise XOR operator on the decimals 15 and 9, and assigns the result to the variable x:

```
// 15 decimal = 1111 binary
// 9 decimal = 1001 binary
var x:Number = 15 ^ 9;
trace(x);
// 1111 ^ 1001 = 0110
// returns 6 decimal (0110 binary)
```

See also

& bitwise AND operator, &= bitwise AND assignment operator, ^= bitwise XOR assignment operator, | bitwise OR operator, |= bitwise OR assignment operator, ~ bitwise NOT operator

^= bitwise XOR assignment operator

expression1 ^= expression2

Assigns *expression1* the value of *expression1 ^ expression2*. For example, the following two statements are equivalent:

```
x ^= y;
x = x ^ y;
```

Availability: ActionScript 1.0; Flash Player 5

Operands

`expression1` : `Number` - Integers and variables.

`expression2` : `Number` - Integers and variables.

Returns

`Number` - The result of the bitwise operation.

Example

The following example shows a bitwise XOR assignment (^=) operation:

```
// 15 decimal = 1111 binary
var x:Number = 15;
// 9 decimal = 1001 binary
var y:Number = 9;
```

```
trace(x ^= y); // returns 6 decimal (0110 binary)
```

See also

& bitwise AND operator, &= bitwise AND assignment operator, ^ bitwise XOR operator, | bitwise OR operator, |= bitwise OR assignment operator, ~ bitwise NOT operator

/*..*/ block comment delimiter operator

```
/* comment */
/* comment
comment */
```

Indicates one or more lines of script comments. Any characters that appear between the opening comment tag (/*) and the closing comment tag (*/), are interpreted as a comment and ignored by the ActionScript interpreter. Use the // (comment delimiter) to identify single-line comments. Use the /* comment delimiter to identify comments on multiple successive lines. Leaving off the closing tag (*/) when using this form of comment delimiter returns an error message. Attempting to nest comments also returns an error message. After an opening comment tag (/*) is used, the first closing comment tag (*/) will end the comment, regardless of the number of opening comment tags (/*) placed between them.

Availability: ActionScript 1.0; Flash Player 5

Operands

comment - Any characters.

Example

The following script uses comment delimiters at the beginning of the script:

```
/* records the X and Y positions of
the ball and bat movie clips */
var ballX:Number = ball_mc._x;
var ballY:Number = ball_mc._y;
var batX:Number = bat_mc._x;
var batY:Number = bat_mc._y;
```

The following attempt to nest comments will result in an error message:

```
/* this is an attempt to nest comments.
/* But the first closing tag will be paired
with the first opening tag */
and this text will not be interpreted as a comment */
```

See also

// line comment delimiter operator

, comma operator

(expression1 , expression2 [, expressionN...])

Evaluates *expression1*, then *expression2*, and so on. This operator is primarily used with the for loop statement and is often used with the parentheses () operator.

Availability: ActionScript 1.0; Flash Player 4

Operands

expression1 : Number - An expression to be evaluated.

expression2 : Number - An expression to be evaluated.

expressionN : Number - Any number of additional expressions to be evaluated.

Returns

Object - The value of *expression1*, *expression2*, and so on.

Example

The following example uses the comma (,) operator in a for loop:

```
for (i = 0, j = 0; i < 3 && j < 3; i++, j+=2) {
  trace("i = " + i + ", j = " + j);
}
// Output:
// i = 0, j = 0
// i = 1, j = 2
```

The following example uses the comma (,) operator without the parentheses () operator and illustrates that the comma operator returns only the value of the first expression without the parentheses () operator:

```
var v:Number = 0;
v = 4, 5, 6;
trace(v); // output: 4
```

The following example uses the comma (,) operator with the parentheses () operator and illustrates that the comma operator returns the value of the last expression when used with the parentheses () operator:

```
var v:Number = 0;
v = (4, 5, 6);
trace(v); // output: 6
```

The following example uses the comma (,) operator without the parentheses () operator and illustrates that the comma operator sequentially evaluates all of the expressions but returns the value of the first expression. The second expression, z++, is evaluated and z is incremented by one.

```
var v:Number = 0;
var z:Number = 0;
v = v + 4 , z++, v + 6;
trace(v); // output: 4
trace(z); // output: 1
```

The following example is identical to the previous example except for the addition of the parentheses () operator and illustrates once again that, when used with the parentheses () operator, the comma (,) operator returns the value of the last expression in the series:

```
var v:Number = 0;
var z:Number = 0;
v = (v + 4, z++, v + 6);
trace(v); // output: 6
trace(z); // output: 1
```

See also

```
() parentheses operator
```

add concatenation (strings) operator

string1 add *string2*

Deprecated since Flash Player 5. Macromedia recommends that you use the add (+) operator when creating content for Flash Player 5 or later. This operator is not supported in Flash Player 8 or later.

Concatenates two or more strings. The add (+) operator replaces the Flash 4 & operator; Flash Player 4 files that use the & operator are automatically converted to use the add (+) operator for string concatenation when brought into the Flash 5 or later authoring environment. Use the add (+) operator to concatenate strings if you are creating content for Flash Player 4 or earlier versions of the Player.

Availability: ActionScript 1.0; Flash Player 4

Operands

string1 : String - A string.

string2 : String - A string.

Returns

String - The concatenated string.

See also

+ addition operator

?: conditional operator

expression1 ? expression2 : expression3

Instructs Flash to evaluate *expression1*, and if the value of *expression1* is `true`, it returns the value of *expression2*; otherwise it returns the value of *expression3*.

Availability: ActionScript 1.0; Flash Player 4

Operands

expression1 : `Object` - An expression that evaluates to a Boolean value; usually a comparison expression, such as `x < 5`.

expression2 : `Object` - Values of any type.

expression3 : `Object` - Values of any type.

Returns

`Object` - The value of *expression2* or *expression3*.

Example

The following statement assigns the value of variable `x` to variable `z` because `expression1` evaluates to `true`:

```
var x:Number = 5;
var y:Number = 10;
var z = (x < 6) ? x: y;
trace (z); // returns 5
```

The following example shows a conditional statement written in shorthand:

```
var timecode:String = (new Date().getHours() < 11) ? "AM" : "PM";
trace(timecode);
```

The same conditional statement could also be written in longhand, as shown in the following example:

```
if (new Date().getHours() < 11) {
 var timecode:String = "AM";
} else {
 var timecode:String = "PM";
} trace(timecode);
```

-- decrement operator

```
--expression
expression--
```

A pre-decrement and post-decrement unary operator that subtracts 1 from the `expression`. The `expression` can be a variable, element in an array, or property of an object. The pre-decrement form of the operator (`--expression`) subtracts 1 from `expression` and returns the result. The post-decrement form of the operator (`expression--`) subtracts 1 from the `expression` and returns the initial value of `expression` (the value prior to the subtraction).

Availability: ActionScript 1.0; Flash Player 4

Operands

`expression` : `Number` - A number or a variable that evaluates to a number.

Returns

`Number` - The result of the decremented value.

Example

The pre-decrement form of the operator decrements x to 2 (x - 1 = 2) and returns the result as y:

```
var x:Number = 3;
var y:Number = --x; //y is equal to 2
```

The post-decrement form of the operator decrements x to 2 (x - 1 = 2) and returns the original value of x as the result y:

```
var x:Number = 3;
var y:Number = x--; //y is equal to 3
```

The following example loops from 10 to 1, and each iteration of the loop decreases the counter variable i by 1.

```
for (var i = 10; i>0; i--) {
 trace(i);
}
```

/ division operator

```
expression1 / expression2
```

Divides `expression1` by `expression2`. The result of the division operation is a double-precision floating-point number.

Availability: ActionScript 1.0; Flash Player 4

Operands

expression : Number - A number or a variable that evaluates to a number.

Returns

Number - The floating-point result of the operation.

Example

The following statement divides the current width and height of the Stage, and then displays the result in the Output panel.

```
trace(Stage.width/2);
trace(Stage.height/2);
```

For a default Stage width and height of 550 x 400, the output is 275 and 150.

See also

% modulo operator

/= division assignment operator

expression1 /= expression2

Assigns *expression1* the value of *expression1 / expression2*. For example, the following two statements are equivalent:

```
x /= y;
x = x / y;
```

Availability: ActionScript 1.0; Flash Player 4

Operands

expression1 : Number - A number or a variable that evaluates to a number.

expression2 : Number - A number or a variable that evaluates to a number.

Returns

Number - A number.

Example

The following code illustrates using the division assignment (/=) operator with variables and numbers:

```
var x:Number = 10;
var y:Number = 2;
x /= y; trace(x); // output: 5
```

See also

`/ division operator`

. dot operator

`object.property_or_methodinstancename.variable`
`instancename.childinstanceinstancename.childinstance.variable`

Used to navigate movie clip hierarchies to access nested (child) movie clips, variables, or properties. The dot operator is also used to test or set the properties of an object or top-level class, execute a method of an object or top-level class, or create a data structure.

Availability: ActionScript 1.0; Flash Player 4

Operands

`object` : `Object` - An instance of a class. The object can be an instance of any of the built-in ActionScript classes or a custom class. This parameter is always to the left of the dot (.) operator.

`property_or_method` - The name of a property or method associated with an object. All the valid methods and properties for the built-in classes are listed in the method and property summary tables for that class. This parameter is always to the right of the dot (.) operator.

`instancename` : `MovieClip` - The instance name of a movie clip. `variable` — The instance name to the left of the dot (.) operator can also represent a variable on the Timeline of the movie clip.

`childinstance` : `MovieClip` - A movie clip instance that is a child of, or nested in, another movie clip.

Returns

`Object` - The method, property or movie clip named on the right side of the dot.

Example

The following example identifies the current value of the variable `hairColor` in the movie clip `person_mc`:

`person_mc.hairColor`

The Flash 4 authoring environment did not support dot syntax, but Flash MX 2004 or later files published for Flash Player 4 can use the dot operator. The preceding example is equivalent to the following (deprecated) Flash 4 syntax:

`/person_mc:hairColor`

The following example creates a new movie clip within the _root scope. Then a text field is created inside the movie clip called container_mc. The text field's autoSize property is set to true and then populated with the current date.

```
this.createEmptyMovieClip("container_mc", this.getNextHighestDepth());
this.container_mc.createTextField("date_txt", this.getNextHighestDepth(),
    0, 0, 100, 22);
this.container_mc.date_txt.autoSize = true;
this.container_mc.date_txt.text = new Date();
```

The dot (.) operator is used when targeting instances within the SWF file and when you need to set properties and values for those instances.

== equality operator

expression1 == expression2

Tests two expressions for equality. The result is true if the expressions are equal.

The definition of equal depends on the data type of the parameter:

- Numbers and Boolean values are compared by value and are considered equal if they have the same value.
- String expressions are equal if they have the same number of characters and the characters are identical.
- Variables representing objects, arrays, and functions are compared by reference. Two such variables are equal if they refer to the same object, array, or function. Two separate arrays are never considered equal, even if they have the same number of elements.

When comparing by value, if *expression1* and *expression2* are different data types, ActionScript will attempt to convert the data type of *expression2* to match that of *expression1*.

Availability: ActionScript 1.0; Flash Player 5

Operands

expression1 : Object - A number, string, Boolean value, variable, object, array, or function.

expression2 : Object - A number, string, Boolean value, variable, object, array, or function.

Returns

Boolean - The Boolean result of the comparison.

Example

The following example uses the equality (==) operator with an if statement:

```
var a:String = "David", b:String = "David";
if (a == b) {
 trace("David is David");
}
```

The following examples show the results of operations that compare mixed types:

```
var x:Number = 5;
var y:String = "5";
trace(x == y); // output: true
var x:String = "5";
var y:String = "66";
trace(x == y); // output: false
var x:String = "chris";
var y:String = "steve";
trace(x == y); // output: false
```

The following examples show comparison by reference. The first example compares two arrays with identical length and elements. The equality operator will return false for these two arrays. Although the arrays appear equal, comparison by reference requires that they both refer to the same array. The second example creates the thirdArray variable, which points to the same array as the variable firstArray. The equality operator will return true for these two arrays because the two variables refer to the same array.

```
var firstArray:Array = new Array("one", "two", "three");
var secondArray:Array = new Array("one", "two", "three");
trace(firstArray == secondArray);
// will output false
// Arrays are only considered equal
// if the variables refer to the same array.
var thirdArray:Array = firstArray;
trace(firstArray == thirdArray); // will output true
```

See also

! logical NOT operator, != inequality operator, !== strict inequality operator, && logical AND operator, || logical OR operator, === strict equality operator

eq equality (strings) operator

expression1 eq *expression2*

Deprecated since Flash Player 5. This operator was deprecated in favor of the == (equality) operator.

Compares two expressions for equality and returns a value of true if the string representation of *expression1* is equal to the string representation of *expression2*, false otherwise.

Availability: ActionScript 1.0; Flash Player 4

Operands

expression1 : Object - Numbers, strings, or variables.

expression2 : Object - Numbers, strings, or variables.

Returns

Boolean - The result of the comparison.

See also

== equality operator

> greater than operator

expression1 > *expression2*

Compares two expressions and determines whether *expression1* is greater than *expression2*; if it is, the operator returns true. If *expression1* is less than or equal to *expression2*, the operator returns false. String expressions are evaluated using alphabetical order; all capital letters come before lowercase letters.

Availability: ActionScript 1.0; Flash Player 4 - In Flash 4, > is a numeric operator. In Flash 5 or later, the greater-than (>) operator is a comparison operator capable of handling various data types. Flash 4 files that are brought into the Flash 5 or later authoring environment undergo a conversion process to maintain data type integrity. The following illustrates the conversion of a Flash 4 file containing a numeric quality comparison. Flash 4 file: x > y Converted Flash 5 or later file: Number(x) > Number(y)

Operands

expression1 : Object - A number or string.

expression2 : Object - A number or string.

Returns

Boolean - The Boolean result of the comparison.

Example

In the following example, the greater than (>) operator is used to determine whether the value of the text field score_txt is greater than 90:

```
if (score_txt.text>90) {
 trace("Congratulations, you win!");
} else {
 trace("sorry, try again");
}
```

gt greater than (strings) operator

expression1 gt *expression2*

Deprecated since Flash Player 5. This operator was deprecated in favor of the > (greater than) operator.

Compares the string representation of *expression1* with the string representation of *expression2* and returns true if *expression1* is greater than *expression2*, false otherwise.

Availability: ActionScript 1.0; Flash Player 4

Operands

expression1 : Object - Numbers, strings, or variables.

expression2 : Object - Numbers, strings, or variables.

Returns

Boolean - The Boolean result of the comparison.

See also

> greater than operator

>= greater than or equal to operator

expression1 >= *expression2*

Compares two expressions and determines whether *expression1* is greater than or equal to *expression2* (true) or *expression1* is less than *expression2* (false).

Availability: ActionScript 1.0; Flash Player 4 - In Flash 4, > is a numeric operator. In Flash 5 or later, the greater than or equal to (>=) operator is a comparison operator capable of handling various data types. Flash 4 files that are brought into the Flash 5 or later authoring environment undergo a conversion process to maintain data type integrity. The following illustrates the conversion of a Flash 4 file containing a numeric quality comparison. Flash 4 file: x >= y Converted Flash 5 or later file: Number(x) >= Number(y)

Operands

`expression1` : `Object` - A string, integer, or floating-point number.

`expression2` : `Object` - A string, integer, or floating-point number.

Returns

`Boolean` - The Boolean result of the comparison.

Example

In the following example, the greater than or equal to (>=) operator is used to determine whether the current hour is greater than or equal to 12:

```
if (new Date().getHours() >= 12) {
 trace("good afternoon");
} else {
 trace("good morning");
}
```

ge greater than or equal to (strings) operator

expression1 `ge` *expression2*

Deprecated since Flash Player 5. This operator was deprecated in favor of the >= (greater than or equal to) operator.

Compares the string representation of *expression1* with the string representation of *expression2* and returns `true` if *expression1* is greater than or equal to *expression2*, `false` otherwise.

Availability: ActionScript 1.0; Flash Player 4

Operands

`expression1` : `Object` - Numbers, strings, or variables.

`expression2` : `Object` - Numbers, strings, or variables.

Returns

`Boolean` - The result of the comparison.

See also

`>= greater than or equal to operator`

++ increment operator

++expression
expression++

A pre-increment and post-increment unary operator that adds 1 to *expression* . The *expression* can be a variable, element in an array, or property of an object. The pre-increment form of the operator (*++expression*) adds 1 to *expression* and returns the result. The post-increment form of the operator (*expression++*) adds 1 to *expression* and returns the initial value of *expression* (the value prior to the addition).

The pre-increment form of the operator increments x to 2 (x + 1 = 2) and returns the result as y:

```
var x:Number = 1;
var y:Number = ++x;
trace("x:"+x); //traces x:2
trace("y:"+y); //traces y:2
```

The post-increment form of the operator increments x to 2 (x + 1 = 2) and returns the original value of x as the result y:

```
var x:Number = 1;
var y:Number = x++;
trace("x:"+x); //traces x:2
trace("y:"+y); //traces y:1
```

Availability: ActionScript 1.0; Flash Player 4

Operands

expression : Number - A number or a variable that evaluates to a number.

Returns

Number - The result of the increment.

Example

The following example uses ++ as a post-increment operator to make a `while` loop run five times:

```
var i:Number = 0;
while (i++ < 5) {
 trace("this is execution " + i);
}
/* output:
 this is execution 1
 this is execution 2
 this is execution 3
 this is execution 4
 this is execution 5
*/
```

The following example uses ++ as a pre-increment operator:

```
var a:Array = new Array();
var i:Number = 0;
while (i < 10) {
 a.push(++i);
}
trace(a.toString()); //traces: 1,2,3,4,5,6,7,8,9,10
```

This example also uses ++ as a pre-increment operator.

```
var a:Array = [];
for (var i = 1; i <= 10; ++i) {
 a.push(i);
}
trace(a.toString()); //traces: 1,2,3,4,5,6,7,8,9,10
```

This script shows the following result in the Output panel: 1,2,3,4,5,6,7,8,9,10 The following example uses ++ as a post-increment operator in a `while` loop:

```
// using a while loop
var a:Array = new Array();
var i:Number = 0;
while (i < 10) {
 a.push(i++);
}
trace(a.toString()); //traces 0,1,2,3,4,5,6,7,8,9
```

The following example uses ++ as a post-increment operator in a `for` loop:

```
// using a for loop
var a:Array = new Array();
for (var i = 0; i < 10; i++) {
 a.push(i);
}
trace(a.toString()); //traces 0,1,2,3,4,5,6,7,8,9
```

This script displays the following result in the Output panel:

`0,1,2,3,4,5,6,7,8,9`

!= inequality operator

expression1 `!=` *expression2*

Tests for the exact opposite of the equality (`==`) operator. If *expression1* is equal to *expression2* , the result is `false`. As with the equality (`==`) operator, the definition of equal depends on the data types being compared, as illustrated in the following list:

- Numbers, strings, and Boolean values are compared by value.
- Objects, arrays, and functions are compared by reference.
- A variable is compared by value or by reference, depending on its type.

Comparison by value means what most people would expect equals to mean--that two expressions have the same value. For example, the expression (2 + 3) is equal to the expression (1 + 4) when compared by value.

Comparison by reference means that two expressions are equal only if they both refer to the same object, array, or function. Values inside the object, array, or function are not compared.

When comparing by value, if *expression1* and *expression2*are different data types, ActionScript will attempt to convert the data type of *expression2* to match that of *expression1*.

Availability: ActionScript 1.0; Flash Player 5

Operands

expression1 : `Object` - A number, string, Boolean value, variable, object, array, or function.

expression2 : `Object` - A number, string, Boolean value, variable, object, array, or function.

Returns

`Boolean` - The Boolean result of the comparison.

Example

The following example illustrates the result of the inequality (`!=`) operator:

```
trace(5 != 8); // returns true
trace(5 != 5) //returns false
```

The following example illustrates the use of the inequality (!=) operator in an if statement:

```
var a:String = "David";
var b:String = "Fool";
if (a != b) {
 trace("David is not a fool");
}
```

The following example illustrates comparison by reference with two functions:

```
var a:Function = function() { trace("foo"); };
var b:Function = function() { trace("foo"); };
a(); // foo
b(); // foo
trace(a != b); // true
a = b;
a(); // foo
b(); // foo
trace(a != b); // false
// trace statement output: foo foo true foo foo false
```

The following example illustrates comparison by reference with two arrays:

```
var a:Array = [ 1, 2, 3 ];
var b:Array = [ 1, 2, 3 ];
trace(a); // 1, 2, 3
trace(b); // 1, 2, 3
trace(a!=b); // true
a = b;
trace(a); // 1, 2, 3
trace(b); // 1, 2, 3
trace(a != b); // false
// trace statement output: 1,2,3 1,2,3 true 1,2,3 1,2,3 false
```

See also

! logical NOT operator, !== strict inequality operator, && logical AND operator, || logical OR operator, == equality operator, === strict equality operator

<> inequality operator

expression1 <> expression2

Deprecated since Flash Player 5. This operator has been deprecated. Macromedia recommends that you use the != (inequality) operator.

Tests for the exact opposite of the equality (==) operator. If *expression1* is equal to *expression2*, the result is false. As with the equality (==)operator, the definition of equal depends on the data types being compared:

■ Numbers, strings, and Boolean values are compared by value.

- Objects, arrays, and functions are compared by reference.
- Variables are compared by value or by reference depending on their type.

Availability: ActionScript 1.0; Flash Player 2

Operands

expression1 : Object - A number, string, Boolean value, variable, object, array, or function.

expression2 : Object - A number, string, Boolean value, variable, object, array, or function.

Returns

Boolean - The Boolean result of the comparison.

See also

!= inequality operator

instanceof operator

object instanceof *classConstructor*

Tests whether object is an instance of classConstructor or a subclass of classConstructor. The instanceof operator does not convert primitive types to wrapper objects. For example, the following code returns true:

new String("Hello") instanceof String;

Whereas the following code returns false:

"Hello" instanceof String;

Availability: ActionScript 1.0; Flash Player 6

Operands

object : Object - An ActionScript object.

classConstructor : Function - A reference to an ActionScript constructor function, such as String or Date.

Returns

Boolean - If object is an instance of or a subclass of classConstructor, instanceof returns true, otherwise it returns false. Also, _global instanceof Object returns false.

See also

`typeof operator`

‹ less than operator

expression1 ‹ expression2

Compares two expressions and determines whether *expression1* is less than *expression2*; if so, the operator returns `true`. If *expression1* is greater than or equal to *expression2*, the operator returns `false`. String expressions are evaluated using alphabetical order; all capital letters come before lowercase letters.

Availability: ActionScript 1.0; Flash Player 4 - In Flash 4, ‹ is a numeric operator. In Flash 5 and later, the ‹ (less than) operator is a comparison operator capable of handling various data types. Flash 4 files that are brought into the Flash 5 or later authoring environment undergo a conversion process to maintain data type integrity. The following illustrates the conversion of a Flash 4 file containing a numeric quality comparison.

Flash 4 file: `x ‹ y`

Converted Flash 5 or later file: `Number(x) ‹ Number(y)`

Operands

`expression1` : `Number` - A number or string.

`expression2` : `Number` - A number or string.

Returns

`Boolean` - The Boolean result of the comparison.

Example

The following examples show `true` and `false` returns for both numeric and string comparisons:

```
trace(3 ‹ 10); // true
trace(10 ‹ 3); // false
trace("Allen" ‹ "Jack"); // true
trace("Jack" ‹ "Allen"); //false
trace("11" ‹ "3"); // true
trace("11" ‹ 3); // false (numeric comparison)
trace("C" ‹ "abc"); // true
trace("A" ‹ "a"); // true
```

lt less than (strings) operator

expression1 `lt` *expression2*

Deprecated since Flash Player 5. This operator was deprecated in favor of the < (less than) operator.

Compares *expression1* to *expression2* and returns `true` if *expression1* is less than *expression2*, `false` otherwise.

Availability: ActionScript 1.0; Flash Player 4

Operands

`expression1` : `Object` - Numbers, strings, or variables.

`expression2` : `Object` - Numbers, strings, or variables.

Returns

`Boolean` - The result of the comparison.

See also

`<` less than operator

<= less than or equal to operator

expression1 `<=` *expression2*

Compares two expressions and determines whether *expression1* is less than or equal to *expression2*; if it is, the operator returns `true`. If *expression1* is greater than *expression2*, the operator returns `false`. String expressions are evaluated using alphabetical order; all capital letters come before lowercase letters.

Availability: ActionScript 1.0; Flash Player 4 - In Flash 4, <= is a numeric operator. In Flash 5 or later, the less than or equal to (<=) operator is a comparison operator capable of handling various data types. Flash 4 files that are brought into the Flash 5 or later authoring environment undergo a conversion process to maintain data type integrity. The following illustrates the conversion of a Flash 4 file containing a numeric quality comparison.

Flash 4 file: x <= y

Converted Flash 5 or later file: `Number(x) <= Number(y)`

Operands

`expression1` : `Object` - A number or string.

`expression2` : `Object` - A number or string.

Returns

`Boolean` - The Boolean result of the comparison.

Example

The following examples show `true` and `false` results for both numeric and string comparisons:

```
trace(5 <= 10); // true
trace(2 <= 2); // true
trace(10 <= 3); // false
trace("Allen" <= "Jack"); // true
trace("Jack" <= "Allen"); // false
trace("11" <= "3"); // true
trace("11" <= 3); // false (numeric comparison)
trace("C" <= "abc"); // true
trace("A" <= a); // true
```

le less than or equal to (strings) operator

expression1 `le` *expression2*

Deprecated since Flash Player 5. This operator was deprecated in Flash 5 in favor of the `<=` (less than or equal to) operator.

Compares *expression1* to *expression2* and returns a value of `true` if *expression1* is less than or equal to *expression2*, `false` otherwise.

Availability: ActionScript 1.0; Flash Player 4

Operands

`expression1 : Object` - Numbers, strings, or variables.

`expression2 : Object` - Numbers, strings, or variables.

Returns

`Boolean` - The result of the comparison.

See also

`<= less than or equal to operator`

// line comment delimiter operator

// comment

Indicates the beginning of a script comment. Any characters that appear between the comment delimiter (//) and the end-of-line character are interpreted as a comment and ignored by the ActionScript interpreter.

Availability: ActionScript 1.0; Flash Player 1.0

Operands

comment - Any characters.

Example

The following script uses comment delimiters to identify the first, third, fifth, and seventh lines as comments:

```
// record the X position of the ball movie clip
var ballX:Number = ball_mc._x;
// record the Y position of the ball movie clip
var ballY:Number = ball_mc._y;
// record the X position of the bat movie clip
var batX:Number = bat_mc._x;
// record the Y position of the ball movie clip
var batY:Number = bat_mc._y;
```

See also

/*..*/ block comment delimiter operator

&& logical AND operator

expression1 && expression2

Performs a Boolean operation on the values of both expressions. If *expression1* and *expression2* are both true, then true is returned; otherwise, false is returned.

Expression	Evaluates
true&&true	true
true&&false	false
false&&false	false
false&&true	false

Availability: ActionScript 1.0; Flash Player 4

Operands

`expression1` : `Number` - A Boolean value or an expression that converts to a Boolean value.

`expression2` : `Number` - A Boolean value or an expression that converts to a Boolean value.

Returns

`Boolean` - A Boolean result of the logical operation.

Example

The following example uses the logical AND (`&&`) operator to perform a test to determine if a player has won the game. The `turns` variable and the `score` variable are updated when a player takes a turn or scores points during the game. The script shows "You Win the Game!" in the Output panel when the player's score reaches 75 or higher in 3 turns or less.

```
var turns:Number = 2;
var score:Number = 77;
if ((turns <= 3) && (score >= 75)) {
 trace("You Win the Game!");
} else {
 trace("Try Again!");
}
// output: You Win the Game!
```

See also

`!` logical NOT operator, `!=` inequality operator, `!==` strict inequality operator, `||` logical OR operator, `==` equality operator, `===` strict equality operator

and logical AND operator

condition1 and *condition2*

Deprecated since Flash Player 5. Macromedia recommends that you use the logical AND (`&&`) operator.

Performs a logical AND (`&&`) operation in Flash Player 4. If both expressions evaluate to `true`, the entire expression is `true`.

Availability: ActionScript 1.0; Flash Player 4

Operands

`condition1` : `Boolean` - Conditions or expressions that evaluate to `true` or `false`.

`condition2` : `Boolean` - Conditions or expressions that evaluate to `true` or `false`.

Returns

`Boolean` - A Boolean result of the logical operation.

See also

`&& logical AND operator`

! logical NOT operator

`! expression`

Inverts the Boolean value of a variable or expression. If *expression* is a variable with the absolute or converted value `true`, the value of `!expression` is `false`. If the expression `x && y` evaluates to `false`, the expression `!(x && y)` evaluates to `true`.

The following expressions illustrate the result of using the logical NOT (!) operator:

`! true returns false! false returns true`

Availability: ActionScript 1.0; Flash Player 4

Operands

`expression : Boolean` - An expression or a variable that evaluates to a Boolean value.

Returns

`Boolean` - The Boolean result of the logical operation.

Example

In the following example, the variable `happy` is set to `false`. The `if` condition evaluates the condition `!happy`, and if the condition is `true`, the trace() statement sends a string to the Output panel.

```
var happy:Boolean = false;
if (!happy) {
 trace("don't worry, be happy"); //traces don't worry, be happy
}
```

The statement traces because `!false` equals `true`.

See also

`!= inequality operator, !== strict inequality operator, && logical AND operator, || logical OR operator, == equality operator, === strict equality operator`

not logical NOT operator

`not expression`

Deprecated since Flash Player 5. This operator was deprecated in favor of the `!` (`logical NOT`) operator.

Performs a logical NOT (!) operation in Flash Player 4.

Availability: ActionScript 1.0; Flash Player 4

Operands

`expression : Object` - A variable or other expression that converts to a Boolean value.

Returns

`Boolean` - The result of the logical operation.

See also

`! logical NOT operator`

|| logical OR operator

`expression1 || expression2`

Evaluates `expression1` (the expression on the left side of the operator) and returns `true` if the expression evaluates to `true`. If `expression1` evaluates to `false`, `expression2` (the expression on the right side of the operator) is evaluated. If `expression2` evaluates to `false`, the final result is `false`; otherwise, it is `true`.

If you use a function call as `expression2`, the function will not be executed by that call if `expression1` evaluates to true.

The result is `true` if either or both expressions evaluate to `true`; the result is `false` only if both expressions evaluate to `false`. You can use the logical OR operator with any number of operands; if any operand evaluates to `true`, the result is `true`.

Availability: ActionScript 1.0; Flash Player 4

Operands

`expression1 : Number` - A Boolean value or an expression that converts to a Boolean value.

`expression2 : Number` - A Boolean value or an expression that converts to a Boolean value.

Returns

`Boolean` - The result of the logical operation.

Example

The following example uses the logical OR (||) operator in an if statement. The second expression evaluates to true, so the final result is true:

```
var x:Number = 10;
var y:Number = 250;
var start:Boolean = false;
if ((x > 25) || (y > 200) || (start)) {
  trace("the logical OR test passed"); // output: the logical OR test passed
}
```

The message the logical OR test passed appears because one of the conditions in the if statement is true (y>200). Although the other two expressions evaluate to false, as long as one condition evaluates to true, the if block executes.

The following example demonstrates how using a function call as *expression2* can lead to unexpected results. If the expression on the left of the operator evaluates to true, that result is returned without evaluating the expression on the right (the function fx2() is not called).

```
function fx1():Boolean {
  trace("fx1 called");
  return true;
}
function fx2():Boolean {
  trace("fx2 called");
  return true;
}
if (fx1() || fx2()) {
  trace("IF statement entered");
}
```

The following is sent to the Output panel: fx1 called IF statement entered

See also

! logical NOT operator, != inequality operator, !== strict inequality operator, && logical AND operator, == equality operator, === strict equality operator

or logical OR operator

condition1 or *condition2*

Deprecated since Flash Player 5. This operator was deprecated in favor of the || (logical OR) operator.

Evaluates *condition1* and *condition2*, and if either expression is true, the whole expression is true.

Availability: ActionScript 1.0; Flash Player 4

Operands

condition1 : Boolean - An expression that evaluates to true or false.

condition2 : Boolean - An expression that evaluates to true or false.

Returns

Boolean - The result of the logical operation.

See also

|| logical OR operator, | bitwise OR operator

% modulo operator

expression1 % *expression2*

Calculates the remainder of *expression1* divided by *expression2*. If either of the *expression* parameters are non-numeric, the modulo (%) operator attempts to convert them to numbers. The *expression* can be a number or string that converts to a numeric value.

The sign of the result of modulo operation matches the sign of the dividend (the first number). For example, -4 % 3 and -4 % -3 both evaluate to -1.

Availability: ActionScript 1.0; Flash Player 4 - In Flash 4 files, the % operator is expanded in the SWF file as x - int(x/y) * y and may not be as fast or as accurate in later versions of Flash Player.

Operands

expression1 : Number - A number or expression that evaluates to a number.

expression2 : Number - A number or expression that evaluates to a number.

Returns

Number - The result of the arithmetic operation.

Example

The following numeric example uses the modulo (%) operator:

```
trace(12%5); // traces 2
trace(4.3%2.1); // traces 0.0999999999999996
trace(4%4); // traces 0
```

The first trace returns 2, rather than 12/5 or 2.4, because the modulo (%) operator returns only the remainder. The second trace returns 0.0999999999999996 instead of the expected 0.1 because of the limitations of floating-point accuracy in binary computing.

See also

/ division operator, round (Math.round method)

%= modulo assignment operator

expression1 %= expression2

Assigns *expression1* the value of *expression1 % expression2*. The following two
statements are equivalent:

```
x %= y;
x = x % y;
```

Availability: ActionScript 1.0; Flash Player 4 - In Flash 4 files, the % operator is expanded in
the SWF file as x - int(x/y) * y and may not be as fast or as accurate in later versions of
Flash Player.

Operands

expression1 : Number - A number or expression that evaluates to a number.

expression2 : Number - A number or expression that evaluates to a number.

Returns

Number - The result of the arithmetic operation.

Example

The following example assigns the value 4 to the variable x:

```
var x:Number = 14;
var y:Number = 5;
trace(x = y); // output: 4
```

See also

% modulo operator

* multiplication operator

*expression1 * expression2*

Multiplies two numerical expressions. If both expressions are integers, the product is an
integer. If either or both expressions are floating-point numbers, the product is a floating-
point number.

Availability: ActionScript 1.0; Flash Player 4

Operands

`expression1 : Number` - A number or expression that evaluates to a number.

`expression2 : Number` - A number or expression that evaluates to a number.

Returns

`Number` - An integer or floating-point number.

Example

Usage 1: The following statement multiplies the integers 2 and 3:

`trace(2*3); // output: 6`

The result, 6, is an integer. Usage 2: This statement multiplies the floating-point numbers 2.0 and 3.1416:

`trace(2.0 * 3.1416); // output: 6.2832`

The result, 6.2832, is a floating-point number.

*= multiplication assignment operator

*expression1 *= expression2*

Assigns *expression1* the value of *expression1 * expression2*. For example, the following two expressions are equivalent:

```
x *= y;
x = x * y
```

Availability: ActionScript 1.0; Flash Player 4

Operands

`expression1 : Number` - A number or expression that evaluates to a number.

`expression2 : Number` - A number or expression that evaluates to a number.

Returns

`Number` - The value of *expression1 * expression2*. If an expression cannot be converted to a numeric value, it returns `NaN` (not a number).

Example

Usage 1: The following example assigns the value 50 to the variable `x`:

```
var x:Number = 5;
var y:Number = 10;
trace(x *= y); // output: 50
```

Usage 2: The second and third lines of the following example calculate the expressions on the right side of the equal sign and assign the results to `x` and `y`:

```
var i:Number = 5;
var x:Number = 4 - 6;
var y:Number = i + 2;
trace(x *= y); // output: -14
```

See also

```
* multiplication operator
```

new operator

```
new constructor()
```

Creates a new, initially anonymous, object and calls the function identified by the
`constructor` parameter. The `new` operator passes to the function any optional parameters in
parentheses, as well as the newly created object, which is referenced using the keyword `this`.
The `constructor` function can then use `this` to set the variables of the object.

Availability: ActionScript 1.0; Flash Player 5

Operands

`constructor` : `Object` - A function followed by any optional parameters in parentheses.
The function is usually the name of the object type (for example, `Array`, `Number`, or `Object`)
to be constructed.

Example

The following example creates the `Book()` function and then uses the `new` operator to create
the objects `book1` and `book2`.

```
function Book(name, price){
 this.name = name;
 this.price = price;
}

book1 = new Book("Confederacy of Dunces", 19.95);
book2 = new Book("The Floating Opera", 10.95);
```

The following example uses the `new` operator to create an `Array` object with 18 elements:

```
golfCourse_array = new Array(18);
```

See also

```
[] array access operator, {} object initializer operator
```

ne not equal (strings) operator

expression1 ne *expression2*

Deprecated since Flash Player 5. This operator was deprecated in favor of the != (inequality) operator.

Compares *expression1* to *expression2* and returns true if *expression1* is not equal to *expression2*; false otherwise.

Availability: ActionScript 1.0; Flash Player 4

Operands

expression1 : Object - Numbers, strings, or variables.

expression2 : Object - Numbers, strings, or variables.

Returns

Boolean - Returns true if expression1 is not equal to expression2; false otherwise.

See also

!= inequality operator

{} object initializer operator

object = { *name1* : *value1* , *name2* : *value2* ,... *nameN* : *valueN* }
{*expression1*; [...*expressionN*]}

Creates a new object and initializes it with the specified *name* and *value* property pairs. Using this operator is the same as using the new Object syntax and populating the property pairs using the assignment operator. The prototype of the newly created object is generically named the Object object.

This operator is also used to mark blocks of contiguous code associated with flow control statements (for, while, if, else, switch) and functions.

Availability: ActionScript 1.0; Flash Player 5

Operands

object : Object - The object to create. *name1,2,...N* The names of the properties. *value1,2,...N* The corresponding values for each *name* property.

Returns

Object -

Usage 1: An Object object.

Usage 2: Nothing, except when a function has an explicit `return` statement, in which case the return type is specified in the function implementation.

Example

The first line of the following code creates an empty object using the object initializer (`{}`) operator; the second line creates a new object using a constructor function:

```
var object:Object = {};
var object:Object = new Object();
```

The following example creates an object `account` and initializes the properties `name`, `address`, `city`, `state`, `zip`, and `balance` with accompanying values:

```
var account:Object = {name:"Macromedia, Inc.", address:"600 Townsend
  Street", city:"San Francisco", state:"California", zip:"94103",
  balance:"1000"};
for (i in account) {
 trace("account." + i + " = " + account[i]);
}
```

The following example shows how array and object initializers can be nested within each other:

```
var person:Object = {name:"Gina Vechio", children:["Ruby", "Chickie",
  "Puppa"]};
```

The following example uses the information in the previous example and produces the same result using constructor functions:

```
var person:Object = new Object();
person.name = "Gina Vechio";
person.children = new Array();
person.children[0] = "Ruby";
person.children[1] = "Chickie";
person.children[2] = "Puppa";
```

The previous ActionScript example can also be written in the following format:

```
var person:Object = new Object();
person.name = "Gina Vechio";
person.children = new Array("Ruby", "Chickie", "Puppa");
```

See also

Object

() parentheses operator

```
(expression1 [, expression2])
( expression1, expression2 )
function ( parameter1,..., parameterN )
```

Performs a grouping operation on one or more parameters, performs sequential evaluation of expressions, or surrounds one or more parameters and passes them as parameters to a function outside the parentheses.

Usage 1: Controls the order in which the operators execute in the expression. Parentheses override the normal precedence order and cause the expressions within the parentheses to be evaluated first. When parentheses are nested, the contents of the innermost parentheses are evaluated before the contents of the outer ones.

Usage 2: Evaluates a series of expressions, separated by commas, in sequence, and returns the result of the final expression.

Usage 3: Surrounds one or more parameters and passes them as parameters to the function outside the parentheses.

Availability: ActionScript 1.0; Flash Player 4

Operands

`expression1` : `Object` - Numbers, strings, variables, or text.

`expression2` : `Object` - Numbers, strings, variables, or text.

`function` : `Function` - The function to be performed on the contents of the parentheses.

`parameter1...parameterN` : `Object` - A series of parameters to execute before the results are passed as parameters to the function outside the parentheses.

Example

Usage 1: The following statements show the use of parentheses to control the order in which expressions are executed (the value of each expression appears in the Output panel):

```
trace((2 + 3)*(4 + 5)); // Output: 45
trace((2 + 3) * (4 + 5)); // Output: 45trace(2 + (3 * (4 + 5))); // // //
  writes 29
trace(2 + (3 * (4 + 5))); // Output: 29trace(2+(3*4)+5); // writes 19
trace(2 + (3 * 4) + 5); // Output: 19
```

Usage 2: The following example evaluates the function foo(), and then the function bar(), and returns the result of the expression a + b:

```
var a:Number = 1;
var b:Number = 2;
function foo() { a += b; }
function bar() { b *= 10; }
trace((foo(), bar(), a + b)); // outputs 23
```

Usage 3: The following example shows the use of parentheses with functions:

```
var today:Date = new Date();
trace(today.getFullYear()); // traces current year
function traceParameter(param):Void { trace(param); }
traceParameter(2 * 2); //traces 4
```

See also

with statement

=== strict equality operator

expression1 === expression2

Tests two expressions for equality; the strict equality (===)operator performs in the same way as the equality (==) operator, except that data types are not converted. The result is true if both expressions, including their data types, are equal.

The definition of equal depends on the data type of the parameter:

- Numbers and Boolean values are compared by value and are considered equal if they have the same value.

- String expressions are equal if they have the same number of characters and the characters are identical.

- Variables representing objects, arrays, and functions are compared by reference. Two such variables are equal if they refer to the same object, array, or function. Two separate arrays are never considered equal, even if they have the same number of elements.

Availability: ActionScript 1.0; Flash Player 6

Operands

expression1 : Object - A number, string, Boolean value, variable, object, array, or function.

expression2 : Object - A number, string, Boolean value, variable, object, array, or function.

Returns

`Boolean` - The Boolean result of the comparison.

Example

The comments in the following code show the returned value of operations that use the equality and strict equality operators:

```
// Both return true because no conversion is done
var string1:String = "5";
var string2:String = "5";
trace(string1 == string2); // true
trace(string1 === string2); // true
// Automatic data typing in this example converts 5 to "5"
var string1:String = "5";
var num:Number = 5;
trace(string1 == num); // true
trace(string1 === num); // false
// Automatic data typing in this example converts true to "1"
var string1:String = "1";
var bool1:Boolean = true;
trace(string1 == bool1); // true
trace(string1 === bool1); // false
// Automatic data typing in this example converts false to "0"
var string1:String = "0";
var bool2:Boolean = false;
trace(string1 == bool2); // true
trace(string1 === bool2); // false
```

The following examples show how strict equality treats variables that are references differently than it treats variables that contain literal values. This is one reason to consistently use String literals and to avoid the use of the new operator with the String class.

```
// Create a string variable using a literal value
var str:String = "asdf";
// Create a variable that is a reference
var stringRef:String = new String("asdf");
// The equality operator does not distinguish among literals, variables,
// and references
trace(stringRef == "asdf"); // true
trace(stringRef == str); // true
trace("asdf" == str); // true
// The strict equality operator considers variables that are references
// distinct from literals and variables
trace(stringRef === "asdf"); // false
trace(stringRef === str); // false
```

See also

! logical NOT operator, != inequality operator, !== strict inequality operator, && logical AND operator, || logical OR operator, == equality operator

!== strict inequality operator

expression1 !== *expression2*

Tests for the exact opposite of the strict equality (===)operator. The strict inequality operator performs the same as the inequality operator except that data types are not converted.

If *expression1* is equal to *expression2*, and their data types are equal, the result is `false`. As with the strict equality (===) operator, the definition of equal depends on the data types being compared, as illustrated in the following list:

- Numbers, strings, and Boolean values are compared by value.
- Objects, arrays, and functions are compared by reference.
- A variable is compared by value or by reference, depending on its type.

Availability: ActionScript 1.0; Flash Player 6

Operands

`expression1 : Object` - A number, string, Boolean value, variable, object, array, or function.

`expression2 : Object` - A number, string, Boolean value, variable, object, array, or function.

Returns

`Boolean` - The Boolean result of the comparison.

Example

The comments in the following code show the returned value of operations that use the equality (==), strict equality (===), and strict inequality (!==) operators:

```
var s1:String = "5";
var s2:String = "5";
var s3:String = "Hello";
var n:Number = 5;
var b:Boolean = true;
trace(s1 == s2); // true
trace(s1 == s3); // false
trace(s1 == n); // true
trace(s1 == b); // false
trace(s1 === s2); // true
```

```
trace(s1 === s3); // false
trace(s1 === n); // false
trace(s1 === b); // false
trace(s1 !== s2); // false
trace(s1 !== s3); // true
trace(s1 !== n); // true
trace(s1 !== b); // true
```

See also

! logical NOT operator, != inequality operator, && logical AND operator, ||
logical OR operator, == equality operator, === strict equality operator

" string delimiter operator

"*text*"

When used before and after characters, quotation marks (") indicate that the characters have a
literal value and are considered a *string*, not a variable, numerical value, or other ActionScript
element.

Availability: ActionScript 1.0; Flash Player 4

Operands

text : String - A sequence of zero or more characters.

Example

The following example uses quotation marks (") to indicate that the value of the variable
yourGuess is the literal string "Prince Edward Island" and not the name of a variable. The
value of province is a variable, not a literal; to determine the value of province, the value of
yourGuess must be located.

```
var yourGuess:String = "Prince Edward Island";
submit_btn.onRelease = function() { trace(yourGuess); };
// displays Prince Edward Island
```

See also

String, String function

- subtraction operator

(Negation) -*expression*
(Subtraction) *expression1* - *expression2*

Used for negating or subtracting.

Usage 1: When used for negating, it reverses the sign of the numerical *expression*. Usage 2: When used for subtracting, it performs an arithmetic subtraction on two numerical expressions, subtracting *expression2* from *expression1*. When both expressions are integers, the difference is an integer. When either or both expressions are floating-point numbers, the difference is a floating-point number.

Availability: ActionScript 1.0; Flash Player 4

Operands

`expression1` : `Number` - A number or expression that evaluates to a number.

`expression2` : `Number` - A number or expression that evaluates to a number.

Returns

`Number` - An integer or floating-point number.

Example

Usage 1: The following statement reverses the sign of the expression 2 + 3:

`trace(-(2+3)); // output: -5`

Usage 2: The following statement subtracts the integer 2 from the integer 5:

`trace(5-2); // output: 3`

The result, 3, is an integer. Usage 3: The following statement subtracts the floating-point number 1.5 from the floating-point number 3.25:

`trace(3.25-1.5); // output: 1.75`

The result, 1.75, is a floating-point number.

-= subtraction assignment operator

expression1 `-=` *expression2*

Assigns *expression1* the value of *expression1*- *expression2*. For example, the following two statements are equivalent: `x -= y ;x = x - y;`

String expressions must be converted to numbers; otherwise, `NaN` (not a number) is returned.

Availability: ActionScript 1.0; Flash Player 4

Operands

`expression1` : `Number` - A number or expression that evaluates to a number.

`expression2` : `Number` - A number or expression that evaluates to a number.

Returns

`Number` - The result of the arithmetic operation.

Example

The following example uses the subtraction assignment (`-=`) operator to subtract 10 from 5 and assign the result to the variable `x`:

```
var x:Number = 5;
var y:Number = 10;
x -= y; trace(x); // output: -5
```

The following example shows how strings are converted to numbers:

```
var x:String = "5";
var y:String = "10";
x -= y; trace(x); // output: -5
```

See also

`- subtraction operator`

: type operator

```
[ modifiers ] var variableName : type
function functionName () : type { ... }
function functionName ( parameter1:type , ... , parameterN:type ) [ :type ]{
    ... }
```

Used for strict data typing; this operator specifies the variable type, function return type, or function parameter type. When used in a variable declaration or assignment, this operator specifies the variable's type; when used in a function declaration or definition, this operator specifies the function's return type; when used with a function parameter in a function definition, this operator specifies the variable type expected for that parameter.

Types are a compile-time-only feature. All types are checked at compile time, and errors are generated when there is a mismatch. Mismatches can occur during assignment operations, function calls, and class member dereferencing using the dot (`.`) operator. To avoid type mismatch errors, use strict data typing.

Types that you can use include all native object types, classes and interfaces that you define, and Function and Void. The recognized native types are Boolean, Number, and String. All built-in classes are also supported as native types.

Availability: ActionScript 1.0; Flash Player 6

Operands

`variableName : Object` - An identifier for a variable. *type* A native data type, class name that you have defined, or interface name. *functionName* An identifier for a function. *parameter* An identifier for a function parameter.

Example

Usage 1: The following example declares a public variable named `userName` whose type is String and assigns an empty string to it:

```
var userName:String = "";
```

Usage 2: The following example shows how to specify a function's parameter type by defining a function named `randomInt()` that takes a parameter named `integer` of type Number:

```
function randomInt(integer:Number):Number {
 return Math.round(Math.random()*integer);
}
trace(randomInt(8));
```

Usage 3: The following example defines a function named `squareRoot()` that takes a parameter named `val` of the Number type and returns the square root of `val`, also a Number type:

```
function squareRoot(val:Number):Number {
 return Math.sqrt(val);
}
trace(squareRoot(121));
```

See also

`var statement`, `function statement`

typeof operator

`typeof(expression)`

Evaluates the `expression` and returns a string specifying whether the expression is a `String`, `MovieClip`, `Object`, `Function`, `Number`, or `Boolean` value.

Availability: ActionScript 1.0; Flash Player 5

Operands

`expression : Object` - A string, movie clip, button, object, or function.

Returns

`String` - A `String` representation of the type of `expression`. The following table shows the results of the `typeof` operator on each type of `expression`.

Expression Type	Result
String	`string`
Movie clip	`movieclip`
Button	`object`
Text field	`object`
Number	`number`
Boolean	`boolean`
Object	`object`
Function	`function`

See also

`instanceof operator`

void operator

`void expression`

The `void` operator evaluates an expression and then discards its value, returning `undefined`. The `void` operator is often used in comparisons using the `==` operator to test for undefined values.

Availability: ActionScript 1.0; Flash Player 5

Operands

`expression : Object` - An expression to be evaluated.

Statements

Statements are language elements that perform or specify an action. For example, the return statement returns a result as a value of the function in which it executes. The if statement evaluates a condition to determine the next action that should be taken. The switch statement creates a branching structure for ActionScript statements.

Statements summary

Statement	Description
break	Appears within a loop (`for`, `for..in`, `do..while` or `while`) or within a block of statements associated with a particular case within a `switch` statement.
case	Defines a condition for the `switch` statement.
class	Defines a custom class, which lets you instantiate objects that share methods and properties that you define.
continue	Jumps past all remaining statements in the innermost loop and starts the next iteration of the loop as if control had passed through to the end of the loop normally.
default	Defines the default case for a `switch` statement.
delete	Destroys the object reference specified by the *reference* parameter, and returns `true` if the reference is successfully deleted; `false` otherwise.
do..while	Similar to a `while` loop, except that the statements are executed once before the initial evaluation of the condition.
dynamic	Specifies that objects based on the specified class can add and access dynamic properties at runtime.
else	Specifies the statements to run if the condition in the `if` statement returns `false`.
else if	Evaluates a condition and specifies the statements to run if the condition in the initial `if` statement returns `false`.
extends	Defines a class that is a subclass of another class; the latter is the superclass.
for	Evaluates the *init* (initialize) expression once and then starts a looping sequence.
for..in	Iterates over the properties of an object or elements in an array and executes the *statement* for each property or element.

Statement	Description
`function`	Comprises a set of statements that you define to perform a certain task.
`get`	Permits implicit *getting* of properties associated with objects based on classes you have defined in external class files.
`if`	Evaluates a condition to determine the next action in a SWF file.
`implements`	Specifies that a class must define all the methods declared in the interface (or interfaces) being implemented.
`import`	Lets you access classes without specifying their fully qualified names.
`interface`	Defines an interface.
`intrinsic`	Allows compile-time type checking of previously defined classes.
`private`	Specifies that a variable or function is available only to the class that declares or defines it or to subclasses of that class.
`public`	Specifies that a variable or function is available to any caller.
`return`	Specifies the value returned by a function.
`set`	Permits implicit setting of properties associated with objects based on classes you have defined in external class files.
`set variable`	Assigns a value to a variable.
`static`	Specifies that a variable or function is created only once per class rather than being created in every object based on that class.
`super`	Invokes the superclass' version of a method or constructor.
`switch`	Creates a branching structure for ActionScript statements.
`throw`	Generates, or *throws* , an error that can be handled, or *caught* , by a `catch{ }` code block.
`try..catch..finally`	Enclose a block of code in which an error can occur, and then respond to the error.
`var`	Used to declare local or Timeline variables.
`while`	Evaluates a condition and if the condition evaluates to `true` , runs a statement or series of statements before looping back to evaluate the condition again.
`with`	Lets you specify an object (such as a movie clip) with the *object* parameter and evaluate expressions and actions inside that object with the *statement(s)* parameter.

break statement

```
break
```

Appears within a loop (for , for..in, do..while or while) or within a block of statements associated with a particular case within a switch statement. When used in a loop, the break statement instructs Flash to skip the rest of the loop body, stop the looping action, and execute the statement following the loop statement. When used in a switch, the break statement instructs Flash to skip the rest of the statements in that case block and jump to the first statement following the enclosing switch statement.

In nested loops, the break statement only skips the rest of the immediate loop and does not break out of the entire series of nested loops. For breaking out of an entire series of nested loops, see try..catch..finally.

Availability: ActionScript 1.0; Flash Player 4

Example

The following example uses the break statement to exit an otherwise infinite loop:

```
var i:Number = 0;
while (true) {
 trace(i);
 if (i >= 10) {
 break; // this will terminate/exit the loop
 }
 i++;
}
```

which traces the following output:

```
0
1
2
3
4
5
6
7
8
9
10
```

See also

```
for statement
```

case statement

```
case expression : statement(s)
```

Defines a condition for the switch statement. If the *expression* parameter equals the *expression* parameter of the switch statement using strict equality (===), then Flash Player will execute statements in the *statement(s)* parameter until it encounters a break statement or the end of the switch statement.

If you use the case statement outside a switch statement, it produces an error and the script doesn't compile.

Note: You should always end the *statement(s)* parameter with a break statement. If you omit the break statement from the *statement(s)* parameter, it continues executing with the next case statement instead of exiting the switch statement.

Availability: ActionScript 1.0; Flash Player 4

Parameters

expression:String - Any expression.

Example

The following example defines conditions for the switch statement thisMonth. If thisMonth equals the expression in the case statement, the statement executes.

```
var thisMonth:Number = new Date().getMonth();
switch (thisMonth) {
 case 0 :
 trace("January");
 break;
 case 1 :
 trace("February");
 break;
 case 5 :
 case 6 :
 case 7 :
 trace("Some summer month");
 break;
 case 8 :
 trace("September");
 break;
 default :
 trace("some other month");
}
```

See also

break statement

class statement

```
[dynamic] class className [ extends superClass ] [ implements
    interfaceName[, interfaceName... ] ] {
  // class definition here
}
```

Defines a custom class, which lets you instantiate objects that share methods and properties that you define. For example, if you are developing an invoice-tracking system, you could create an invoice class that defines all the methods and properties that each invoice should have. You would then use the `new invoice()` command to create invoice objects.

The name of the class must match the name of the external file that contains the class. The name of the external file must be the name of the class with the file extension .as appended. For example, if you name a class Student, the file that defines the class must be named Student.as.

If a class is within a package, the class declaration must use the fully qualified class name of the form base.sub1.sub2.MyClass. Also, the class's AS file must be stored within the path in a directory structure that reflects the package structure, such as base/sub1/sub2/MyClass.as. If a class definition is of the form "class MyClass," it is in the default package and the MyClass.as file should be in the top level of some directory in the path.

For this reason, it's good practice to plan your directory structure before you begin creating classes. Otherwise, if you decide to move class files after you create them, you have to modify the class declaration statements to reflect their new location.

You cannot nest class definitions; that is, you cannot define additional classes within a class definition.

To indicate that objects can add and access dynamic properties at runtime, precede the class statement with the `dynamic` keyword. To declare that a class implements an interface, use the `implements` keyword. To create subclasses of a class, use the `extends` keyword. (A class can extend only one class, but can implement several interfaces.) You can use `implements` and `extends` in a single statement. The following examples show typical uses of the `implements` and `extends` keywords:

```
class C implements Interface_i, Interface_j // OK
class C extends Class_d implements Interface_i, Interface_j // OK
class C extends Class_d, Class_e // not OK
```

Availability: ActionScript 2.0; Flash Player 6

Parameters

`className:String` - The fully qualified name of the class.

Example

The following example creates a class called Plant. The Plant constructor takes two parameters.

```
// Filename Plant.as
class Plant {
// Define property names and types
var leafType:String;
var bloomSeason:String;
// Following line is constructor
// because it has the same name as the class
function Plant(param_leafType:String, param_bloomSeason:String) {
// Assign passed values to properties when new Plant object is created
this.leafType = param_leafType;
this.bloomSeason = param_bloomSeason;
}
// Create methods to return property values, because best practice
// recommends against directly referencing a property of a class
function getLeafType():String {
return leafType;
}
function getBloomSeason():String {
return bloomSeason;
}
}
```

In an external script file or in the Actions panel, use the new operator to create a Plant object.

```
var pineTree:Plant = new Plant("Evergreen", "N/A");
// Confirm parameters were passed correctly
trace(pineTree.getLeafType());
trace(pineTree.getBloomSeason());
```

The following example creates a class called ImageLoader. The ImageLoader constructor takes three parameters.

```
// Filename ImageLoader.as
class ImageLoader extends MovieClip {
function ImageLoader(image:String, target_mc:MovieClip, init:Object) {
var listenerObject:Object = new Object();
listenerObject.onLoadInit = function(target) {
for (var i in init) {
target[i] = init[i];
}
};
var JPEG_mcl:MovieClipLoader = new MovieClipLoader();
JPEG_mcl.addListener(listenerObject);
JPEG_mcl.loadClip(image, target_mc);
}
}
```

In an external script file or in the Actions panel, use the new operator to create an ImageLoader object.

```
var jakob_mc:MovieClip = this.createEmptyMovieClip("jakob_mc",
   this.getNextHighestDepth());
var jakob:ImageLoader = new ImageLoader("http://www.helpexamples.com/flash/
   images/image1.jpg", jakob_mc, {_x:10, _y:10, _alpha:70, _rotation:-5});
```

See also

`dynamic statement`

continue statement

`continue`

Jumps past all remaining statements in the innermost loop and starts the next iteration of the loop as if control had passed through to the end of the loop normally. It has no effect outside a loop.

Availability: ActionScript 1.0; Flash Player 4

Example

In the following `while` loop, `continue` causes the Flash interpreter to skip the rest of the loop body and jump to the top of the loop, where the condition is tested:

```
trace("example 1");
var i:Number = 0;
while (i < 10) {
 if (i % 3 == 0) {
 i++;
 continue;
 }
 trace(i);
 i++;
}
```

In the following `do..while` loop, `continue` causes the Flash interpreter to skip the rest of the loop body and jump to the bottom of the loop, where the condition is tested:

```
trace("example 2");
var i:Number = 0;
do {
 if (i % 3 == 0) {
 i++;
 continue;
 }
 trace(i);
 i++;
}
while (i < 10);
```

In a `for` loop, `continue` causes the Flash interpreter to skip the rest of the loop body. In the following example, if the i modulo 3 equals 0, then the `trace(i)` statement is skipped:

```
trace("example 3");
for (var i = 0; i < 10; i++) {
 if (i % 3 == 0) {
 continue;
 }
 trace(i);
}
```

In the following `for..in` loop, `continue` causes the Flash interpreter to skip the rest of the loop body and jump back to the top of the loop, where the next value in the enumeration is processed:

```
for (i in _root) {
 if (i == "$version") {
 continue;
 }
 trace(i);
}
```

See also

default statement

```
default: statements
```

Defines the default case for a `switch` statement. The statements execute if the *expression* parameter of the `switch` statement doesn't equal (using the strict equality [===] operation) any of the *expression* parameters that follow the `case` keywords for a given `switch` statement.

A `switch` is not required to have a `default` case statement. A `default` case statement does not have to be last in the list. If you use a `default` statement outside a `switch` statement, it produces an error and the script doesn't compile.

Availability: ActionScript 1.0; Flash Player 6

Parameters

`statements`:`String` - Any statements.

Example

In the following example, the expression A does not equal the expressions B or D, so the statement following the `default` keyword is run and the `trace()` statement is sent to the Output panel.

```
var dayOfWeek:Number = new Date().getDay();
switch (dayOfWeek) {
case 1 :
trace("Monday");
break;
case 2 :
trace("Tuesday");
break;
case 3 :
trace("Wednesday");
break;
case 4 :
trace("Thursday");
break;
case 5 :
trace("Friday");
break;
default :
trace("Weekend");
}
```

See also

`switch statement`

delete statement

`delete reference`

Destroys the object reference specified by the *reference* parameter, and returns `true` if the reference is successfully deleted; `false` otherwise. This operator is useful for freeing memory used by scripts. You can use the `delete` operator to remove references to objects. After all references to an object are removed, Flash Player removes the object and frees the memory used by that object.

Although `delete` is an operator, it is typically used as a statement, as shown in the following example:

`delete x;`

The `delete` operator can fail and return `false` if the *reference* parameter does not exist or cannot be deleted. You cannot delete predefined objects and properties, and you cannot delete variables that are declared within a function with the `var` statement. You cannot use the `delete` operator to remove movie clips.

Availability: ActionScript 1.0; Flash Player 5

Returns

`Boolean` - A Boolean value.

Parameters

`reference:Object` - The name of the variable or object to eliminate.

Example

Usage 1: The following example creates an object, uses it, and deletes it when it is no longer needed:

```
var account:Object = new Object();
account.name = "Jon";
account.balance = 10000;
trace(account.name); //output: Jon
delete account;
trace(account.name); //output: undefined
```

Usage 2: The following example deletes a property of an object:

```
// create the new object "account"
var account:Object = new Object();
// assign property name to the account
account.name = "Jon";
// delete the property
delete account.name;
```

Usage 3: The following example deletes an object property:

```
var my_array:Array = new Array();
my_array[0] = "abc"; // my_array.length == 1
my_array[1] = "def"; // my_array.length == 2
my_array[2] = "ghi"; // my_array.length == 3
// my_array[2] is deleted, but Array.length is not changed
delete my_array[2];
trace(my_array.length); // output: 3
trace(my_array); // output: abc,def,undefined
```

Usage 4: The following example shows the behavior of delete on object references:

```
var ref1:Object = new Object();
ref1.name = "Jody";
// copy the reference variable into a new variable
// and delete ref1
ref2 = ref1;
delete ref1;
trace("ref1.name "+ref1.name); //output: ref1.name undefined
trace("ref2.name "+ref2.name); //output: ref2.name Jody
```

If ref1 had not been copied into ref2, the object would have been deleted when ref1 was deleted because there would be no references to it. If you delete ref2, there are no references to the object; it is destroyed, and the memory it used becomes available.

See also

var statement

do..while statement

`do { statement(s) } while (condition)`

Similar to a while loop, except that the statements are executed once before the initial evaluation of the condition. Subsequently, the statements are executed only if the condition evaluates to true.

A do..while loop ensures that the code inside the loop is executed at least once. Although this can also be done with a while loop by placing a copy of the statements to be executed before the while loop begins, many programmers believe that do..while loops are easier to read.

If the condition always evaluates to true, the do..while loop is infinite. If you enter an infinite loop, you encounter problems with Flash Player and eventually get a warning message or crash the player. Whenever possible, you should use a for loop if you know the number of times that you want to loop. Although for loops are easy to read and debug, they cannot replace do..while loops in all circumstances.

Availability: ActionScript 1.0; Flash Player 4

Parameters

condition:Boolean - The condition to evaluate. The *statement(s)* within the do block of code are executed as long as the *condition* parameter evaluates to true .

Example

The following example uses a do..while loop to evaluate whether a condition is true, and traces myVar until myVar is greater than 5. When myVar is greater than 5, the loop ends.

```
var myVar:Number = 0;
do {
 trace(myVar);
 myVar++;
}
while (myVar < 5);
/* output:
0
1
2
3
4
*/
```

See also

break statement

dynamic statement

```
dynamic class className [ extends superClass ] [ implements interfaceName[,
  interfaceName... ] ] {
 // class definition here
}
```

Specifies that objects based on the specified class can add and access dynamic properties at runtime.

Type checking on dynamic classes is less strict than type checking on nondynamic classes, because members accessed inside the class definition and on class instances are not compared with those defined in the class scope. Class member functions, however, can still be type checked for return type and parameter types. This behavior is especially useful when you work with MovieClip objects, because there are many different ways of adding properties and objects to a movie clip dynamically, such as MovieClip.createEmptyMovieClip() and MovieClip.createTextField().

Subclasses of dynamic classes are also dynamic.

Be sure to specify the type when declaring an object, as in the following:

```
var x:MyClass = new MyClass();
```

If you do *not* specify the type when declaring an object (as in the following) then the object is considered dynamic:

```
var x = new MyClass();
```

Availability: ActionScript 2.0; Flash Player 6

Example

In the following example, class `Person2` has not yet been marked as dynamic, so calling an undeclared function on it generates an error at compile time:

```
class Person2 {
 var name:String;
 var age:Number;
 function Person2(param_name:String, param_age:Number) {
 trace ("anything");
 this.name = param_name;
 this.age = param_age;
 }
}
```

In a FLA or AS file that's in the same directory, add the following ActionScript to Frame 1 on the Timeline:

```
// Before dynamic is added
var craig:Person2 = new Person2("Craiggers", 32);
for (i in craig) {
 trace("craig." + i + " = " + craig[i]);
}
/* output:
craig.age = 32
craig.name = Craiggers */
```

If you add an undeclared function, `dance`, an error is generated, as shown in the following example:

```
trace("");
craig.dance = true;
for (i in craig) {
 trace("craig." + i + " = " + craig[i]);
}
/* output: **Error** Scene=Scene 1, layer=Layer 1, frame=1:Line 14: There is
  no property with the name 'dance'. craig.dance = true; Total ActionScript
  Errors: 1 Reported Errors: 1 */
```

Add the `dynamic` keyword to the Person2 class, so that the first line appears as follows:

```
dynamic class Person2 {
```

Test the code again, and you see the following output:

```
craig.dance = true craig.age = 32 craig.name = Craiggers
```

See also

`class statement`

else statement

```
if (condition){
statement(s);
} else {
statement(s);
}
```

Specifies the statements to run if the condition in the `if` statement returns `false`. The curly braces ({}) used to enclose the block of statements to be executed by the `else` statement are not necessary if only one statement will execute.

Availability: ActionScript 1.0; Flash Player 4

Parameters

`condition:Boolean` - An expression that evaluates to `true` or `false`.

Example

In the following example, the `else` condition is used to check whether the `age_txt` variable is greater than or less than 18:

```
if (age_txt.text>=18) {
 trace("welcome, user");
}
else {
 trace("sorry, junior");
 userObject.minor = true;
 userObject.accessAllowed = false;
}
```

In the following example, curly braces ({}) are not necessary because only one statement follows the `else` statement:

```
if (age_txt.text>18) { trace("welcome, user"); } else trace("sorry,
  junior");
```

See also

`if statement`

else if statement

```
if(condition) {
statement(s);
} else if(condition) {
```

```
statement(s);
}
```

Evaluates a condition and specifies the statements to run if the condition in the initial if statement returns false. If the else if condition returns true, the Flash interpreter runs the statements that follow the condition inside curly braces ({ }). If the else if condition is false, Flash skips the statements inside the curly braces and runs the statements following the curly braces.

Use the elseif statement to create branching logic in your scripts. If there are multiple branches, you should consider using a switch statement.

Availability: ActionScript 1.0; Flash Player 4

Parameters

condition:Boolean - An expression that evaluates to true or false.

Example

The following example uses else if statements to compare score_txt to a specified value:

```
if (score_txt.text>90) {
 trace("A");
}
else if (score_txt.text>75) {
 trace("B");
}
else if (score_txt.text>60) {
 trace("C");
}
else {
 trace("F");
}
```

See also

if statement

extends statement

```
class className extends otherClassName {}
interface interfaceName extends otherInterfaceName {}
```

Defines a class that is a subclass of another class; the latter is the superclass. The subclass inherits all the methods, properties, functions, and so on that are defined in the superclass.

Interfaces can also be extended by using the extends keyword. An interface that extends another interface includes all of the method declarations of the original interface.

Availability: ActionScript 2.0; Flash Player 6

Parameters

`className:String` - The name of the class that you are defining.

Example

In the following example, the Car class extends the Vehicle class so that all of its methods, properties, and functions are inherited. If your script instantiates a Car object, methods from both the Car class and the Vehicle class can be used.

The following example shows the contents of a file called Vehicle.as, which defines the Vehicle class:

```
class Vehicle {
 var numDoors:Number;
 var color:String;
 function Vehicle(param_numDoors:Number, param_color:String) {
 this.numDoors = param_numDoors;
 this.color = param_color;
 }
 function start():Void {
 trace("[Vehicle] start");
 }
 function stop():Void {
 trace("[Vehicle] stop");
 }
 function reverse():Void {
 trace("[Vehicle] reverse");
 }
}
```

The following example shows a second AS file, called Car.as, in the same directory. This class extends the Vehicle class, modifying it in three ways. First, the Car class adds a variable `fullSizeSpare` to track whether the car object has a full-size spare tire. Second, it adds a new method specific to cars, `activateCarAlarm()`, which activates the car's antitheft alarm. Third, it overrides the `stop()` function to add the fact that the Car class uses an antilock braking system to stop.

```
class Car extends Vehicle {
 var fullSizeSpare:Boolean;
 function Car(param_numDoors:Number, param_color:String,
  param_fullSizeSpare:Boolean) {
 this.numDoors = param_numDoors;
 this.color = param_color;
 this.fullSizeSpare = param_fullSizeSpare;
 }
 function activateCarAlarm():Void {
 trace("[Car] activateCarAlarm");
 }
 function stop():Void {
```

```
trace("[Car] stop with anti-lock brakes");
  }
}
```

The following example instantiates a Car object, calls a method that is defined in the Vehicle class (start()), then calls the method that is overridden by the Car class (stop()), and finally calls a method from the Car class (activateCarAlarm()):

```
var myNewCar:Car = new Car(2, "Red", true);
myNewCar.start(); // output: [Vehicle] start
myNewCar.stop(); // output: [Car] stop with anti-lock brakes
myNewCar.activateCarAlarm(); // output: [Car] activateCarAlarm
```

A subclass of the Vehicle class can also be written by using the keyword super, which the subclass can use to access properties and methods of the superclass. The following example shows a third AS file, called Truck.as, again in the same directory. The Truck class uses the super keyword in the constructor and again in the overridden reverse() function.

```
class Truck extends Vehicle {
  var numWheels:Number;
  function Truck(param_numDoors:Number, param_color:String,
    param_numWheels:Number) {
  super(param_numDoors, param_color);
  this.numWheels = param_numWheels;
  }
  function reverse():Void {
  beep();
  super.reverse();
  }
  function beep():Void {
  trace("[Truck] make beeping sound");
  }
}
```

The following example instantiates a Truck object, calls a method overridden by the Truck class (reverse()), and then calls a method defined in the Vehicle class (stop()):

```
var myTruck:Truck = new Truck(2, "White", 18);
myTruck.reverse(); // output: [Truck] make beeping sound [Vehicle] reverse
myTruck.stop(); // output: [Vehicle] stop
```

See also

class statement

for statement

```
for(init; condition; next) {
statement(s);
}
```

Evaluates the *init* (initialize) expression once and then starts a looping sequence. The looping sequence begins by evaluating the *condition* expression. If the *condition* expression evaluates to true, *statement* is executed and the *next* expression is evaluated. The looping sequence then begins again with the evaluation of the *condition* expression.

The curly braces ({ }) used to enclose the block of statements to be executed by the for statement are not necessary if only one statement will execute.

Availability: ActionScript 1.0; Flash Player 5

Parameters

init - An expression to evaluate before beginning the looping sequence; usually an assignment expression. A var statement is also permitted for this parameter.

Example

The following example uses for to add the elements in an array:

```
var my_array:Array = new Array();
for (var i:Number = 0; i < 10; i++) {
 my_array[i] = (i + 5) * 10;
}
trace(my_array); // output: 50,60,70,80,90,100,110,120,130,140
```

The following example uses for to perform the same action repeatedly. In the code, the for loop adds the numbers from 1 to 100.

```
var sum:Number = 0;
for (var i:Number = 1; i <= 100; i++) {
 sum += i;
}
trace(sum); // output: 5050
```

The following example shows that curly braces ({}) are not necessary if only one statement will execute:

```
var sum:Number = 0;
for (var i:Number = 1; i <= 100; i++)
 sum += i;
trace(sum); // output: 5050
```

See also

```
++ increment operator
```

for..in statement

```
for (variableIterant in object) {
statement(s);
}
```

Iterates over the properties of an object or elements in an array and executes the *statement* for each property or element. Methods of an object are not enumerated by the `for..in` action.

Some properties cannot be enumerated by the `for..in` action. For example, movie clip properties, such as _x and _y, are not enumerated. In external class files, static members are not enumerable, unlike instance members.

The `for..in` statement iterates over properties of objects in the iterated object's prototype chain. Properties of the object are enumerated first, then properties of its immediate prototype, then properties of the prototype's prototype, and so on. The `for..in` statement does not enumerate the same property name twice. If the object `child` has prototype `parent` and both contain the property `prop`, the `for..in` statement called on `child` enumerates `prop` from `child` but ignores the one in `parent`.

The curly braces ({ }) that are used to enclose the block of statements to be executed by the `for..in` statement are not necessary if only one statement is executed.

If you write a `for..in` loop in a class file (an external AS file), then instance members are not available for the loop, but static members are. However, if you write a `for..in` loop in a FLA file for an instance of the class, then instance members are available but static ones are not.

Availability: ActionScript 1.0; Flash Player 5

Parameters

`variableIterant:String` - The name of a variable to act as the iterant, referencing each property of an object or element in an array.

Example

The following example uses `for..in` to iterate over the properties of an object:

```
var myObject:Object = {firstName:"Tara", age:27, city:"San Francisco"};
for (var prop in myObject) {
 trace("myObject."+prop+" = "+myObject[prop]);
}
//output
myObject.firstName = Tara
myObject.age = 27
myObject.city = San Francisco
```

The following example uses `for..in` to iterate over the elements of an array:

```
var myArray:Array = new Array("one", "two", "three");
for (var index in myArray)
 trace("myArray["+index+"] = " + myArray[index]);
// output:
myArray[2] = three
myArray[1] = two
myArray[0] = one
```

The following example uses the `typeof` operator with `for..in` to iterate over a particular type of child:

```
for (var name in this) {
 if (typeof (this[name]) == "movieclip") {
 trace("I have a movie clip child named "+name);
 }
}
```

> **NOTE** If you have several movie clips, the output consists of the instance names of those clips.

The following example enumerates the children of a movie clip and sends each to Frame 2 in itsrespective Timeline. The `RadioButtonGroup` movie clip is a parent with three children: `_RedRadioButton_`, `_GreenRadioButton_`,, and `_BlueRadioButton_`.

```
for (var name in RadioButtonGroup) { RadioButtonGroup[name].gotoAndStop(2);
 }
```

function statement

```
Usage 1: (Declares a named function.)
function functionname([parameter0, parameter1,...parameterN]){
statement(s)
}
Usage 2: (Declares an anonymous function and returns a reference to it.)
function ([parameter0, parameter1,...parameterN]){
statement(s)
}
```

Comprises a set of statements that you define to perform a certain task. You can define a function in one location and invoke, or *call*, it from different scripts in a SWF file. When you define a function, you can also specify parameters for the function. Parameters are placeholders for values on which the function operates. You can pass different parameters to a function each time you call it so you can reuse a function in different situations.

Use the `return` statement in a function's *statement(s)* to cause a function to generate, or *return*, a value.

You can use this statement to define a `function` with the specified *functionname*, *parameters*, and *statement(s)*. When a script calls a function, the statements in the function's definition are executed. Forward referencing is permitted; within the same script, a function may be declared after it is called. A function definition replaces any previous definition of the same function. You can use this syntax wherever a statement is permitted.

You can use the function statement to create an anonymous function and return a reference to it. This syntax is used in expressions and is particularly useful for installing methods in objects.

For additional functionality, you can use the `arguments` object in your function definition. Some common uses of the `arguments` object are to create a function that accepts a variable number of parameters and to create a recursive anonymous function.

Availability: ActionScript 1.0; Flash Player 5

Returns

`String` - Usage 1: The declaration form does not return anything. Usage 2: A reference to the anonymous function.

Parameters

`functionname:String` - The name of the declared function.

Example

The following example defines the function `sqr`, which accepts one parameter and returns the `Math.pow(x, 2)` of the parameter:

```
function sqr(x:Number) {
  return Math.pow(x, 2);
}
var y:Number = sqr(3);
trace(y); // output: 9
```

If the function is defined and used in the same script, the function definition may appear after using the function:

```
var y:Number = sqr(3);
trace(y); // output: 9
function sqr(x:Number) {
  return Math.pow(x, 2);
}
```

The following function creates a LoadVars object and loads params.txt into the SWF file. When the file successfully loads, `variables loaded` traces:

```
var myLV:LoadVars = new LoadVars();
myLV.load("params.txt");
myLV.onLoad = function(success:Boolean) {
 trace("variables loaded");
}
```

get statement

```
function get property () {
 // your statements here
}
```

Permits implicit *getting* of properties associated with objects based on classes you have defined in external class files. Using implicit get methods lets you access properties of objects without accessing the property directly. Implicit get/set methods are syntactic shorthand for the `Object.addProperty()` method in ActionScript 1.0.

Availability: ActionScript 2.0; Flash Player 6

Parameters

`property:String` - The word you use to refer to the property that `get` accesses; this value must be the same as the value used in the corresponding `set` command.

Example

In the following example, you define a Team class. The Team class includes get/set methods that let you retrieve and set properties within the class:

```
class Team {
 var teamName:String;
 var teamCode:String;
 var teamPlayers:Array = new Array();
 function Team(param_name:String, param_code:String) {
 this.teamName = param_name;
 this.teamCode = param_code;
 }
 function get name():String {
 return this.teamName;
 }
 function set name(param_name:String):Void {
 this.teamName = param_name;
 }
}
```

Enter the following ActionScript in a frame on the Timeline:

```
var giants:Team = new Team("San Fran", "SFO");
trace(giants.name);
giants.name = "San Francisco";
trace(giants.name);
/* output:
San Fran San Francisco */
```

When you trace giants.name, you use the get method to return the value of the property.

See also

addProperty (Object.addProperty method)

if statement

```
if(condition) {
statement(s);
}
```

Evaluates a condition to determine the next action in a SWF file. If the condition is true, Flash runs the statements that follow the condition inside curly braces ({ }). If the condition is false, Flash skips the statements inside the curly braces and runs the statements following the curly braces. Use the if statement along with the else and else if statements to create branching logic in your scripts.

The curly braces ({ }) used to enclose the block of statements to be executed by the if statement are not necessary if only one statement will execute.

Availability: ActionScript 1.0; Flash Player 4

Parameters

condition:Boolean - An expression that evaluates to true or false.

Example

In the following example, the condition inside the parentheses evaluates the variable name to see if it has the literal value "Erica". If it does, the play() function inside the curly braces runs.

```
if(name == ."Erica"){
 play();
}
```

The following example uses an `if` statement to evaluate how long it takes a user to click the `submit_btn`instance in a SWF file. If a user clicks the button more than 10 seconds after the SWF file plays, the condition evaluates to `true` and the message inside the curly braces (`{ }`) appears in a text field that's created at runtime (using `createTextField()`). If the user clicks the button less than 10 seconds after the SWF file plays, the condition evaluates to `false` and a different message appears.

```
this.createTextField("message_txt", this.getNextHighestDepth, 0, 0, 100,
  22);
message_txt.autoSize = true;
var startTime:Number = getTimer();
this.submit_btn.onRelease = function() {
 var difference:Number = (getTimer() - startTime) / 1000;
 if (difference > 10) {
 this._parent.message_txt.text = "Not very speedy, you took "+difference+"
  seconds.";
 }
 else {
 this._parent.message_txt.text = "Very good, you hit the button in
  "+difference+" seconds.";
 }
};
```

See also

`else statement`

implements statement

myClass implements *interface01* [, *interface02* , ...]

Specifies that a class must define all the methods declared in the interface (or interfaces) being implemented.

Availability: ActionScript 2.0; Flash Player 6

Example

See `interface`.

See also

`class statement`

import statement

```
import className
import packageName.*
```

Lets you access classes without specifying their fully qualified names. For example, if you want to use a custom class macr.util.users.UserClass in a script, you must refer to it by its fully qualified name or import it; if you import it, you can refer to it by the class name:

```
// before importing
var myUser:macr.util.users.UserClass = new macr.util.users.UserClass();
// after importing
import macr.util.users.UserClass;
var myUser:UserClass = new UserClass();
```

If there are several class files in the package (*working_directory*/macr/utils/users) that you want to access, you can import them all in a single statement, as shown in the following example:

```
import macr.util.users.*;
```

You must issue the import statement before you try to access the imported class without fully specifying its name.

If you import a class but don't use it in your script, the class isn't exported as part of the SWF file. This means you can import large packages without being concerned about the size of the SWF file; the bytecode associated with a class is included in a SWF file only if that class is actually used.

The import statement applies only to the current script (frame or object) in which it's called. For example, suppose on Frame 1 of a Flash document you import all the classes in the macr.util package. On that frame, you can reference classes in that package by their simple names:

```
// On Frame 1 of a FLA:
import macr.util.*;
var myFoo:foo = new foo();
```

On another frame script, however, you would need to reference classes in that package by their fully qualified names (var myFoo:foo = new macr.util.foo();) or add an import statement to the other frame that imports the classes in that package.

Availability: ActionScript 2.0; Flash Player 6

Parameters

className:String - The fully qualified name of a class you have defined in an external class file.

interface statement

```
interface InterfaceName [extends InterfaceName ] {}
```

Defines an interface. An interface is similar to a class, with the following important differences:

- Interfaces contain only declarations of methods, not their implementation. That is, every class that implements an interface must provide an implementation for each method declared in the interface.

- Only public members are allowed in an interface definition; instance and class members are not permitted.

- The get and set statements are not allowed in interface definitions.

Availability: ActionScript 2.0; Flash Player 6

Example

The following example shows several ways to define and implement interfaces:

```
(in top-level package .as files Ia, B, C, Ib, D, Ic, E)
// filename Ia.as
interface Ia {
 function k():Number; // method declaration only
 function n(x:Number):Number; // without implementation
}
// filename B.as
class B implements Ia {
 function k():Number {
 return 25;
 }
 function n(x:Number):Number {
 return x + 5;
 }
} // external script or Actions panel // script file
var mvar:B = new B();
trace(mvar.k()); // 25
trace(mvar.n(7)); // 12
// filename c.as
class C implements Ia {
 function k():Number {
 return 25;
 }
} // error: class must implement all interface methods
// filename Ib.as
interface Ib {
 function o():Void;
}
class D implements Ia, Ib {
 function k():Number {
```

```
    return 15;
    }
    function n(x:Number):Number {
    return x * x;
    }
    function o():Void {
    trace("o");
    }
} // external script or Actions panel // script file
mvar = new D();
trace(mvar.k()); // 15
trace(mvar.n(7)); // 49
trace(mvar.o()); // "o"
interface Ic extends Ia {
  function p():Void;
}
class E implements Ib, Ic {
  function k():Number {
  return 25;
  }
  function n(x:Number):Number {
  return x + 5;
  }
  function o():Void {
  trace("o");
  }
  function p():Void {
  trace("p");
  }
}
```

See also

`class statement`

intrinsic statement

```
intrinsic class className [extends superClass] [implements interfaceName [,
    interfaceName...] ] {
  //class definition here
}
```

Allows compile-time type checking of previously defined classes. Flash uses intrinsic class declarations to enable compile-time type checking of built-in classes such as `Array`, `Object`, and `String`. This keyword indicates to the compiler that no function implementation is required, and that no bytecode should be generated for it.

The `intrinsic` keyword can also be used with variable and function declarations. Flash uses this keyword to enable compile-time type checking for global functions and properties.

The intrinsic keyword was created specifically to enable compile-time type checking for built-in classes and objects, and global variables and functions. This keyword was not meant for general purpose use, but may be of some value to developers seeking to enable compile-time type checking with previously defined classes, especially if the classes are defined using ActionScript 1.0.

This keyword is supported only when used in external script files, not in scripts written in the Actions panel.

Availability: ActionScript 2.0; Flash Player 6

Example

The following example shows how to enable compile-time file checking for a previously defined ActionScript 1.0 class. The code will generate a compile-time error because the call myCircle.setRadius() sends a String value as a parameter instead of a Number value. You can avoid the error by changing the parameter to a Number value (for example, by changing "10" to 10).

```
// The following code must be placed in a file named Circle.as
// that resides within your classpath:
intrinsic class Circle {
 var radius:Number;
 function Circle(radius:Number);
 function getArea():Number;
 function getDiameter():Number;
 function setRadius(param_radius:Number):Number;
}

// This ActionScript 1.0 class definition may be placed in your FLA file.
// Circle class is defined using ActionScript 1.0
function Circle(radius) {
 this.radius = radius;
 this.getArea = function(){
 return Math.PI*this.radius*this.radius;
 };
 this.getDiameter = function() {
 return 2*this.radius;
 };
 this.setRadius = function(param_radius) {
 this.radius = param_radius;
 }
}

// ActionScript 2.0 code that uses the Circle class
var myCircle:Circle = new Circle(5);
trace(myCircle.getArea());
trace(myCircle.getDiameter());
myCircle.setRadius("10");
```

```
trace(myCircle.radius);
trace(myCircle.getArea());
trace(myCircle.getDiameter());
```

See also

class statement

private statement

```
class someClassName{
 private var name;
 private function name() {
 // your statements here
 }
}
```

Specifies that a variable or function is available only to the class that declares or defines it or to subclasses of that class. By default, a variable or function is available to any caller. Use this keyword if you want to restrict access to a variable or function. This keyword is intended as a software development aid to facilitate good coding practices such as encapsulation, and not as a security mechanism to obfuscate or secure sensitive data. It does not necessarily prevent access to a variable at runtime.

You can use this keyword only in class definitions, not in interface definitions.

Availability: ActionScript 2.0; Flash Player 6

Parameters

name:String - The name of the variable or function that you want to specify as private.

Example

The following example demonstrates how to restrict access to variables or functions by using the private keyword. Create a new AS file called Alpha.as:

```
class Alpha {
 private var privateProperty = "visible only within class and subclasses";
 public var publicProperty = "visible everywhere";
}
```

In the same directory as Alpha.as, create a new AS file named Beta.as that contains the following code:

```
class Beta extends Alpha {
 function Beta() {
 trace("privateProperty is " + privateProperty);
 }
}
```

As the following code demonstrates, the constructor for the Beta class is able to access the `privateProperty` property that is inherited from the Alpha class:

```
var myBeta:Beta = new Beta(); // Output: privateProperty is visible only
  within class and subclasses
```

Attempts to access the `privateProperty` variable from outside the Alpha class or a class that inherits from the Alpha class result in an error. The following code, which resides outside of any class, causes an error:

```
trace(myBeta.privateProperty); // Error
```

See also
```
public statement
```

public statement
```
class someClassName{
 public var name;
 public function name() {
 // your statements here
 }
}
```

Specifies that a variable or function is available to any caller. Because variables and functions are public by default, this keyword is used primarily for stylistic reasons. For example, you might want to use it for reasons of consistency in a block of code that also contains private or static variables.

Availability: ActionScript 2.0; Flash Player 6

Parameters
`name:String` - The name of the variable or function that you want to specify as public.

Example
The following example shows how you can use public variables in a class file. Create a new class file called User.as and enter the following code:

```
class User {
 public var age:Number;
 public var name:String;
}
```

Then create a new FLA or AS file in the same directory, and enter the following ActionScript in Frame 1 of the Timeline:

```
import User;
var jimmy:User = new User();
```

```
jimmy.age = 27;
jimmy.name = "jimmy";
```

If you change one of the public variables in the User class to a private variable, an error is generated when trying to access the property.

See also

```
private statement
```

return statement

```
return[expression]
```

Specifies the value returned by a function. The return statement evaluates *expression* and returns the result as a value of the function in which it executes. The return statement causes execution to return immediately to the calling function. If the return statement is used alone, it returns undefined.

You can't return multiple values. If you try to do so, only the last value is returned. In the following example, c is returned:

```
return a, b, c ;
```

If you need to return multiple values, you might want to use an array or object instead.

Availability: ActionScript 1.0; Flash Player 5

Returns

String - The evaluated *expression* parameter, if provided.

Parameters

expression - A string, number, Boolean, array, or object to evaluate and return as a value of the function. This parameter is optional.

Example

The following example uses the return statement inside the body of the sum() function to return the added value of the three parameters. The next line of code calls sum() and assigns the returned value to the variable newValue.

```
function sum(a:Number, b:Number, c:Number):Number {
 return (a + b + c);
}
var newValue:Number = sum(4, 32, 78);
trace(newValue); // output: 114
```

See also
function statement

set statement

```
function set property(varName) {
 // your statements here
}
```

Permits implicit setting of properties associated with objects based on classes you have defined
in external class files. Using implicit set methods lets you modify the value of an object's
property without accessing the property directly. Implicit get/set methods are syntactic
shorthand for the Object.addProperty() method in ActionScript 1.0.

Availability: ActionScript 2.0; Flash Player 6

Parameters

property:String - Word that refers to the property that set will access; this value must be
the same as the value used in the corresponding get command.

Example

The following example creates a Login class that demonstrates how the set keyword can be
used to set private variables:

```
class Login {
 private var loginUserName:String;
 private var loginPassword:String;
 public function Login(param_username:String, param_password:String) {
 this.loginUserName = param_username;
 this.loginPassword = param_password;
 }
 public function get username():String {
 return this.loginUserName;
 }
 public function set username(param_username:String):Void {
 this.loginUserName = param_username;
 }
 public function set password(param_password:String):Void {
 this.loginPassword = param_password;
 }
}
```

In a FLA or AS file that is in the same directory as Login.as, enter the following ActionScript
in Frame 1 of the Timeline:

```
var gus:Login = new Login("Gus", "Smith");
trace(gus.username); // output: Gus
gus.username = "Rupert";
```

```
trace(gus.username); // output: Rupert
```
In the following example, the get function executes when the value is traced. The set function triggers only when you pass it a value, as shown in the line:
```
gus.username = "Rupert";
```

See also
get statement

set variable statement

```
set("variableString",expression)
```

Assigns a value to a variable. A *variable* is a container that holds data. The container is always the same, but the contents can change. By changing the value of a variable as the SWF file plays, you can record and save information about what the user has done, record values that change as the SWF file plays, or evaluate whether a condition is true or false.

Variables can hold any data type (for example, String, Number, Boolean, Object, or MovieClip). The Timeline of each SWF file and movie clip has its own set of variables, and each variable has its own value independent of variables on other Timelines.

Strict data typing is not supported inside a set statement. If you use this statement to set a variable to a value whose data type is different from the data type associated with the variable in a class file, no compiler error is generated.

A subtle but important distinction to bear in mind is that the parameter *variableString* is a string, not a variable name. If you pass an existing variable name as the first parameter to set() without enclosing the name in quotation marks (""), the variable is evaluated before the value of *expression* is assigned to it. For example, if you create a string variable named myVariable and assign it the value "Tuesday," and then forget to use quotation marks, you will inadvertently create a new variable named Tuesday that contains the value you intended to assign to myVariable:

```
var myVariable:String = "Tuesday";
set (myVariable, "Saturday");
trace(myVariable); // outputs Tuesday
trace(Tuesday); // outputs Saturday
```

You can avoid this situation by using quotation marks (""):

```
set ("myVariable", "Saturday");
trace(myVariable); //outputs Saturday
```

Availability: ActionScript 1.0; Flash Player 4

Parameters

`variableString:String` - A string that names a variable to hold the value of the *expression* parameter.

Example

In the following example, you assign a value to a variable. You are assigning the value of `"Jakob"` to the `name` variable.

```
set("name", "Jakob");
trace(name);
```

The following code loops three times and creates three new variables, called `caption0`, `caption1`, and `caption2`:

```
for (var i = 0; i < 3; i++) {
  set("caption" + i, "this is caption " + i);
}
trace(caption0);
trace(caption1);
trace(caption2);
```

See also

`var statement`

static statement

```
class someClassName{
  static var name;
  static function name() {
  // your statements here
  }
}
```

Specifies that a variable or function is created only once per class rather than being created in every object based on that class.

You can access a static class member without creating an instance of the class by using the syntax `someClassName.name`. If you do create an instance of the class, you can also access a static member using the instance, but only through a non-static function that accesses the static member.

You can use this keyword in class definitions only, not in interface definitions.

Availability: ActionScript 2.0; Flash Player 6

Parameters

`name:String` - The name of the variable or function that you want to specify as static.

Example

The following example demonstrates how you can use the `static` keyword to create a counter that tracks how many instances of the class have been created. Because the `numInstances` variable is static, it will be created only once for the entire class, not for every single instance. Create a new AS file called Users.as and enter the following code:

```
class Users {
 private static var numInstances:Number = 0;
 function Users() {
 numInstances++;
 }
 static function get instances():Number {
 return numInstances;
 }
}
```

Create a FLA or AS document in the same directory, and enter the following ActionScript in Frame 1 of the Timeline:

```
trace(Users.instances);
var user1:Users = new Users();
trace(Users.instances);
var user2:Users = new Users();
trace(Users.instances);
```

See also

`private statement`

super statement

```
super.method([arg1, ..., argN])
super([arg1, ..., argN])
```

the first syntax style may be used within the body of an object method to invoke the superclass version of a method, and can optionally pass parameters (`arg1 ... argN`) to the superclass method. This is useful for creating subclass methods that add additional behavior to superclass methods, but also invoke the superclass methods to perform their original behavior.

The second syntax style may be used within the body of a constructor function to invoke the superclass version of the constructor function and may optionally pass it parameters. This is useful for creating a subclass that performs additional initialization, but also invokes the superclass constructor to perform superclass initialization.

Availability: ActionScript 1.0; Flash Player 6

Returns

Both forms invoke a function. The function may return any value.

Parameters

`method:Function` - The method to invoke in the superclass.

`argN` - Optional parameters that are passed to the superclass version of the method (syntax 1) or to the constructor function of the superclass (syntax 2).

switch statement

```
switch (expression){
caseClause:
 [defaultClause:]
}
```

Creates a branching structure for ActionScript statements. As with the `if` statement, the `switch` statement tests a condition and executes statements if the condition returns a value of `true`. All switch statements should include a default case. The default case should include a break statement that prevents a fall-through error if another case is added later. When a case falls through, it doesn't have a break statement.

Availability: ActionScript 1.0; Flash Player 4

Parameters

`expression` - Any expression.

Example

In the following example, if the `String.fromCharCode(Key.getAscii())` parameter evaluates to A, the `trace()` statement that follows case `"A"` executes; if the parameter evaluates to a, the `trace()` statement that follows case `"a"` executes; and so on. If no `case` expression matches the `String.fromCharCode(Key.getAscii())` parameter, the `trace()` statement that follows the `default` keyword executes.

```
var listenerObj:Object = new Object();
listenerObj.onKeyDown = function() {
 switch (String.fromCharCode(Key.getAscii())) {
 case "A" :
 trace("you pressed A");
 break;
 case "a" :
 trace("you pressed a");
 break;
 case "E" :
 case "e" :
```

```
trace("you pressed E or e");
break;
case "I" :
case "i" :
trace("you pressed I or i");
break;
default :
trace("you pressed some other key");
break;
}
};
Key.addListener(listenerObj);
```

See also

```
=== strict equality operator
```

throw statement

```
throw expression
```

Generates, or *throws*, an error that can be handled, or *caught*, by a catch{} code block. If an exception is not caught by a catch block, the string representation of the thrown value is sent to the Output panel.

Typically, you throw instances of the Error class or its subclasses (see the Example section).

Availability: ActionScript 1.0; Flash Player 7

Parameters

expression:Object - An ActionScript expression or object.

Example

In this example, a function named checkEmail() checks whether the string that is passed to it is a properly formatted e-mail address. If the string does not contain an @ symbol, the function throws an error.

```
function checkEmail(email:String) {
 if (email.indexOf("@") == -1) {
 throw new Error("Invalid email address");
 }
}
checkEmail("someuser_theirdomain.com");
```

The following code then calls the checkEmail() function within a try code block. If the email_txtstring does not contain a valid e-mail address, the error message appears in a text field (error_txt).

```
try {
```

```
 checkEmail("Joe Smith");
}
catch (e) {
 error_txt.text = e.toString();
}
```

In the following example, a subclass of the Error class is thrown. The checkEmail() function is modified to throw an instance of that subclass.

```
// Define Error subclass InvalidEmailError // In InvalidEmailError.as:
  class InvalidEmailAddress extends Error { var message = "Invalid email
  address."; }
```

In a FLA or AS file, enter the following ActionScript in Frame 1 of the Timeline:

```
import InvalidEmailAddress;
function checkEmail(email:String) {
 if (email.indexOf("@") == -1) {
 throw new InvalidEmailAddress();
 }
}
try {
 checkEmail("Joe Smith");
}
catch (e) {
 this.createTextField("error_txt", this.getNextHighestDepth(), 0, 0, 100,
  22);
 error_txt.autoSize = true;
 error_txt.text = e.toString();
}
```

See also

```
Error
```

try..catch..finally statement

```
try {
// ... try block ...
} finally {
// ... finally block ...
}
try {
// ... try block ...
} catch(error [:ErrorType1]) {
// ... catch block ...
} [catch(error[:ErrorTypeN]) {
// ... catch block ...
}] [finally {
// ... finally block ...
}]
```

Encloses a block of code in which an error can occur, and then respond to the error. If any code in the `try` code block throws an error (using the `throw` statement), control passes to the `catch` block, if one exists, and then to the `finally` code block, if one exists. The `finally` block is always executed, regardless of whether an error was thrown. If code in the `try` block doesn't throw an error (that is, if the `try` block completes normally), then the code in the `finally` block is still executed. The `finally` block is executed even if the `try` block exits using a `return` statement.

A `try` block must be followed by a `catch` block, a `finally` block, or both. A single `try` block can have multiple `catch` blocks but only one `finally` block. You can nest `try` blocks as many levels deep as necessary.

The *error* parameter specified in a `catch` handler must be a simple identifier such as e or theException or x. The variable in a `catch` handler can also be typed. When used with multiple `catch` blocks, typed errors let you catch multiple types of errors thrown from a single `try` block.

If the exception thrown is an object, the type matches if the thrown object is a subclass of the specified type. If an error of a specific type is thrown, the `catch` block that handles the corresponding error is executed. If an exception that is not of the specified type is thrown, the `catch` block is not executed and the exception is automatically thrown out of the `try` block to a `catch` handler that matches it.

If an error is thrown within a function, and the function does not include a `catch` handler, then the ActionScript interpreter exits that function, as well as any caller functions, until a `catch` block is found. During this process, `finally` handlers are called at all levels.

Availability: ActionScript 1.0; Flash Player 7

Parameters

`error:Object` - The expression thrown from a `throw` statement, typically an instance of the Error class or one of its subclasses.

Example

The following example shows how to create a `try..finally` statement. Because code in the `finally` block is guaranteed to be executed, it is typically used to perform any necessary clean-up after a `try` block is executed. In the following example, `setInterval()` calls a function every 1000 millisecond (1 second). If an error occurs, an error is thrown and is caught by the `catch` block. The finally block is always executed whether or not an error occurs. Because `setInterval()` is used, `clearInterval()` must be placed in the `finally` block to ensure that the interval is cleared from memory:

```
myFunction = function () {
```

```
  trace("this is myFunction");
};
try {
 myInterval = setInterval(this, "myFunction", 1000);
 throw new Error("my error");
}
catch (myError:Error) {
 trace("error caught: "+myError);
}
finally {
 clearInterval(myInterval);
 trace("error is cleared");
}
```

In the following example, the `finally` block is used to delete an ActionScript object, regardless of whether or not an error occurred. Create a new AS file called Account.as:

```
class Account {
 var balance:Number = 1000;
 function getAccountInfo():Number {
 return (Math.round(Math.random() * 10) % 2);
 }
}
```

In the same directory as Account.as, create a new AS or FLA document and enter the following ActionScript in Frame 1 of the Timeline:

```
import Account;
var account:Account = new Account();
try {
 var returnVal = account.getAccountInfo();
 if (returnVal != 0) {
 throw new Error("Error getting account information.");
 }
}
finally {
 if (account != null) {
 delete account;
 }
}
```

The following example demonstrates a `try..catch` statement. The code in the `try` block is executed. If an exception is thrown by any code in the `try` block, control passes to the `catch` block, which shows the error message in a text field by using the `Error.toString()` method.

In the same directory as Account.as, create a new FLA document and enter the following ActionScript in Frame 1 of the Timeline:

```
import Account;
var account:Account = new Account();
try {
 var returnVal = account.getAccountInfo();
```

```
    if (returnVal != 0) {
    throw new Error("Error getting account information.");
    }
    trace("success");
}
catch (e) {
  this.createTextField("status_txt", this.getNextHighestDepth(), 0, 0, 100,
    22);
  status_txt.autoSize = true;
  status_txt.text = e.toString();
}
```

The following example shows a try code block with multiple, typed catch code blocks. Depending on the type of error that occurred, the try code block throws a different type of object. In this case, myRecordSet is an instance of a (hypothetical) class named RecordSet whose sortRows() method can throw two types of errors, RecordSetException and MalformedRecord.

In the following example, the RecordSetException and MalformedRecord objects are subclasses of the Error class. Each is defined in its own AS class file.

```
// In RecordSetException.as:
class RecordSetException extends Error {
 var message = "Record set exception occurred.";
}
// In MalformedRecord.as:
class MalformedRecord extends Error {
 var message = "Malformed record exception occurred.";
}
```

Within the RecordSet class's sortRows() method, one of these previously defined error objects is thrown, depending on the type of exception that occurred. The following example shows how this code might look:

```
class RecordSet {
 function sortRows() {
 var returnVal:Number = randomNum();
 if (returnVal == 1) {
 throw new RecordSetException();
 }
 else if (returnVal == 2) {
 throw new MalformedRecord();
 }
 }
 function randomNum():Number {
 return Math.round(Math.random() * 10) % 3;
 }
}
```

Finally, in another AS file or FLA script, the following code invokes the `sortRows()` method on an instance of the RecordSet class. It defines `catch` blocks for each type of error that is thrown by `sortRows()`

```
import RecordSet;
var myRecordSet:RecordSet = new RecordSet();
try {
 myRecordSet.sortRows();
 trace("everything is fine");
}
catch (e:RecordSetException) {
 trace(e.toString());
}
catch (e:MalformedRecord) {
 trace(e.toString());
}
```

See also

Error

var statement

```
var variableName [= value1][...,variableNameN[=valueN]]
```

Used to declare local variables. If you declare variables inside a function, the variables are local. They are defined for the function and expire at the end of the function call. More specifically, a variable defined using `var` is local to the code block containing it. Code blocks are demarcated by curly braces ({}).

If you declare variables outside a function, the variables are available througout the timeline containing the statement.

You cannot declare a variable scoped to another object as a local variable.

```
my_array.length = 25; // ok
var my_array.length = 25; // syntax error
```

When you use `var`, you can strictly type the variable.

You can declare multiple variables in one statement, separating the declarations with commas (although this syntax may reduce clarity in your code):

```
var first:String = "Bart", middle:String = "J.", last:String = "Bartleby";
```

> **NOTE** You must also use `var` when declaring properties inside class definitions in external scripts. Class files also support public, private, and static variable scopes.

Availability: ActionScript 1.0; Flash Player 5

Parameters

`variableName:String` - An identifier.

Example

The following ActionScript creates a new array of product names. `Array.push` adds an element onto the end of the array. If you want to use strict typing, it is essential that you use the `var` keyword. Without `var` before `product_array`, you get errors when you try to use strict typing.

```
var product_array:Array = new Array("MX 2004", "Studio", "Dreamweaver",
    "Flash", "ColdFusion", "Contribute", "Breeze");
product_array.push("Flex");
trace(product_array);
// output: MX
    2004,Studio,Dreamweaver,Flash,ColdFusion,Contribute,Breeze,Flex
```

while statement

```
while(condition) {
statement(s);
}
```

Evaluates a condition and if the condition evaluates to `true`, runs a statement or series of statements before looping back to evaluate the condition again. After the condition evaluates to `false`, the statement or series of statements is skipped and the loop ends.

The `while` statement performs the following series of steps. Each repetition of steps 1 through 4 is called an *iteration* of the loop. The `condition` is retested at the beginning of each iteration, as shown in the following steps:

- The expression `condition` is evaluated.
- If `condition` evaluates to `true` or a value that converts to the Boolean value `true`, such as a nonzero number, go to step 3. Otherwise, the `while` statement is completed and execution resumes at the next statement after the `while` loop.
- Run the statement block `statement(s)`.
- Go to step 1.

Looping is commonly used to perform an action while a counter variable is less than a specified value. At the end of each loop, the counter is incremented until the specified value is reached. At that point, the `condition` is no longer `true`, and the loop ends.

The curly braces ({ }) used to enclose the block of statements to be executed by the `while` statement are not necessary if only one statement will execute.

Availability: ActionScript 1.0; Flash Player 4

Parameters

`condition:Boolean` - An expression that evaluates to `true` or `false`.

Example

In the following example, the `while` statement is used to test an expression. When the value of `i` is less than 20, the value of `i` is traced. When the condition is no longer `true`, the loop exits.

```
var i:Number = 0;
while (i < 20) {
  trace(i);
  i += 3;
}
```

The following result is displayed in the Output panel.

```
0
3
6
9
12
15
18
```

See also

`continue statement`

with statement

```
with (object:Object) {
  statement(s);
}
```

Lets you specify an object (such as a movie clip) with the *object* parameter and evaluate expressions and actions inside that object with the *statement(s)* parameter. This prevents you from having to repeatedly write the object's name or the path to the object.

The *object* parameter becomes the context in which the properties, variables, and functions in the *statement(s)* parameter are read. For example, if *object* is `my_array`, and two of the properties specified are `length` and `concat`, those properties are automatically read as `my_array.length` and `my_array.concat`. In another example, if *object* is `state.california`, any actions or statements inside the `with` statement are called from inside the `california` instance.

To find the value of an identifier in the *statement(s)* parameter, ActionScript starts at the beginning of the scope chain specified by the *object* and searches for the identifier at each level of the scope chain, in a specific order.

The scope chain used by the `with` statement to resolve identifiers starts with the first item in the following list and continues to the last item:

- The object specified in the *object* parameter in the innermost `with` statement.
- The object specified in the *object* parameter in the outermost `with` statement.
- The Activation object. (A temporary object that is automatically created when a function is called that holds the local variables called in the function.)
- The movie clip that contains the currently executing script.
- The Global object (built-in objects such as Math and String).

To set a variable inside a `with` statement, you must have declared the variable outside the `with` statement, or you must enter the full path to the Timeline on which you want the variable to live. If you set a variable in a `with` statement without declaring it, the `with` statement will look for the value according to the scope chain. If the variable doesn't already exist, the new value will be set on the Timeline from which the `with` statement was called.

Instead of using `with()`, you can use direct paths. If you find that paths are long and cumbersome to type, you can create a local variable and store the path in the variable, which you can then reuse in your code, as shown in the following ActionScript:

```
var shortcut = this._parent._parent.name_txt; shortcut.text = "Hank";
   shortcut.autoSize = true;
```

Availability: ActionScript 1.0; Flash Player 5

Parameters

`object:Object` - An instance of an ActionScript object or movie clip.

Example

The following example sets the _x and _y properties of the `someOther_mc` instance, and then instructs `someOther_mc` to go to Frame 3 and stop.

```
with (someOther_mc) {
 _x = 50;
 _y = 100;
 gotoAndStop(3);
}
```

The following code snippet shows how to write the preceding code without using a `with` statement.

```
someOther_mc._x = 50;
someOther_mc._y = 100;
someOther_mc.gotoAndStop(3);
```

The `with` statement is useful for accessing multiple items in a scope chain list simultaneously. In the following example, the built-in `Math` object is placed at the front of the scope chain. Setting `Math` as a default object resolves the identifiers `cos`, `sin`, and `PI` to `Math.cos`, `Math.sin`, and `Math.PI`, respectively. The identifiers `a`, `x`, `y`, and `r` are not methods or properties of the `Math` object, but because they exist in the object activation scope of the function `polar()`, they resolve to the corresponding local variables.

```
function polar(r:Number):Void {
 var a:Number, x:Number, y:Number;
 with (Math) {
 a = PI * pow(r, 2);
 x = r * cos(PI);
 y = r * sin(PI / 2);
 }
 trace("area = " + a);
 trace("x = " + x);
 trace("y = " + y);
} polar(3);
```

The following result is displayed in the Output panel.

```
area = 28.2743338823081
x = -3
y = 3
```

CHAPTER 2

ActionScript classes

Documentation for ActionScript classes includes syntax, usage information, and code samples for methods, properties, and event handlers and listeners that belong to a specific class in ActionScript (as opposed to global functions or properties). The classes are listed alphabetically and include new classes in Flash Player 8 that are found in the flash.* packages. If you are not sure to which class a certain method or property belongs, you can look it up in the Index.

Accessibility

```
Object
  |
  +-Accessibility
```

```
public class Accessibility
extends Object
```

The Accessibility class manages communication with screen readers. Screen readers are a type of assistive technology for visually impaired users that provides an audio version of screen content. The methods of the Accessibility class are static--that is, you don't have to create an instance of the class to use its methods.

To get and set accessible properties for a specific object, such as a button, movie clip, or text field, use the _accProps property. To determine whether the player is running in an environment that supports accessibility aids, use System.capabilities.hasAccessibility.

Availability: ActionScript 1.0; Flash Player 6

See also

hasAccessibility (capabilities.hasAccessibility property), _accProps property

Property summary

Properties inherited from class Object

```
constructor (Object.constructor property), __proto__ (Object.__proto__
property), prototype (Object.prototype property), __resolve
(Object.__resolve property)
```

Method summary

Modifiers	Signature	Description
static	isActive() : Boolean	Indicates whether an accessibility aid is currently active and the player is communicating with it.
static	updateProperties() : Void	Causes all changes to _accProps (accessibility properties) objects to take effect.

Methods inherited from class Object

```
addProperty (Object.addProperty method), hasOwnProperty
(Object.hasOwnProperty method), isPropertyEnumerable
(Object.isPropertyEnumerable method), isPrototypeOf (Object.isPrototypeOf
method), registerClass (Object.registerClass method), toString
(Object.toString method), unwatch (Object.unwatch method), valueOf
(Object.valueOf method), watch (Object.watch method)
```

isActive (Accessibility.isActive method)

```
public static isActive() : Boolean
```

Indicates whether an accessibility aid is currently active and the player is communicating with it. Use this method when you want your application to behave differently in the presence of a screen reader or other accessibility aid.

> **NOTE**
>
> **NOTE** If you call this method within one or two seconds of the first appearance of the Flash window in which your document is playing, you might get a return value of false even if there is an active Microsoft Active Accessibility (MSAA) client. This is because of an asynchronous communication mechanism between Flash and MSAA clients. You can work around this limitation by ensuring a delay of one to two seconds after loading your document before calling this method.

Availability: ActionScript 1.0; Flash Player 6

Returns

Boolean - A Boolean value: `true` if the Flash Player is communicating with an accessibility aid (usually a screen reader); `false` otherwise.

Example

The following example checks whether an accessibility aid is currently active:

```
if (Accessibility.isActive()) {
  trace ("An accessibility aid is currently active");
} else {
  trace ("There is currently no active accessibility aid");
}
```

See also

updateProperties (Accessibility.updateProperties method), _accProps property, hasAccessibility (capabilities.hasAccessibility property)

updateProperties (Accessibility.updateProperties method)

`public static updateProperties() : Void`

Causes all changes to _accProps (accessibility properties) objects to take effect. For information on setting accessibility properties, see _accProps.

If you modify the accessibility properties for multiple objects, only one call to `Accessibility.updateProperties()` is necessary; multiple calls can result in reduced performance and unintelligible screen reader results.

Availability: ActionScript 1.0; Flash Player 6,0,65,0

Example

If you change an image and want to update its accessible description, you could use the following ActionScript code:

```
my_mc.gotoAndStop(2);

if (my_mc._accProps == undefined ) {
  my_mc._accProps = new Object();
}
my_mc._accProps.name = "Photo of Mount Rushmore";
Accessibility.updateProperties();
```

See also

isActive (Accessibility.isActive method), _accProps property,
hasAccessibility (capabilities.hasAccessibility property)

arguments

```
Object
   |
   +-arguments
```

```
public class arguments
extends Object
```

An `arguments` object is used to store and access a function's arguments. While inside the function's body it can be accessed with the local `arguments` variable.

The arguments are stored as array elements, the first is accessed as `arguments[0]`, the second as `arguments[1]`, etc. The `arguments.length` property indicates the number of arguments passed to the function. Note that there may be a different number of arguments passed in than the function declares.

Availability: ActionScript 1.0; Flash Player 5 - As of Flash Player 6 the arguments object supports all methods and properties of the Array class.

See also
Function

Property summary

Modifiers	Property	Description
	callee:Object	A reference to the currently executing function.
	caller:Object	A reference to the function that called the currently executing function, or null if it wasn't called from another function.
	length:Number	The number of arguments passed to the function.

Properties inherited from class Object

```
constructor (Object.constructor property), __proto__ (Object.__proto__
property), prototype (Object.prototype property), __resolve
(Object.__resolve property)
```

Method summary
Methods inherited from class Object

```
addProperty (Object.addProperty method), hasOwnProperty
(Object.hasOwnProperty method), isPropertyEnumerable
(Object.isPropertyEnumerable method), isPrototypeOf (Object.isPrototypeOf
method), registerClass (Object.registerClass method), toString
(Object.toString method), unwatch (Object.unwatch method), valueOf
(Object.valueOf method), watch (Object.watch method)
```

callee (arguments.callee property)

`public callee : Object`

A reference to the currently executing function.

Availability: ActionScript 1.0; Flash Player 5

See also
`caller (arguments.caller property)`

caller (arguments.caller property)

`public caller : Object`

A reference to the function that called the currently executing function, or `null` if it wasn't called from another function.

Availability: ActionScript 1.0; Flash Player 6

See also
`callee (arguments.callee property)`

length (arguments.length property)

`public length : Number`

The number of arguments passed to the function. This may be more or less than the function declares.

Availability: ActionScript 1.0; Flash Player 5

Array

```
Object
  |
  +-Array
```

```
public dynamic class Array
extends Object
```

The Array class lets you access and manipulate indexed arrays. An indexed array is an object whose properties are identified by a number representing their position in the array. This number is referred to as the *index*. All indexed arrays are zero-based, which means that the first element in the array is [0], the second element is [1], and so on. To create an Array object, you use the constructor new Array(). To access the elements of an array, you use the array access ([ ]) operator.

You can store a wide variety of data types in an array element, including numbers, strings, objects, and even other arrays. You can create a *multidimensional* array by creating an indexed array and assigning to each of its elements a different indexed array. Such an array is considered multidimensional because it can be used to represent data in a table.

Array assignment is by reference rather than by value: when you assign one array variable to another array variable, both refer to the same array:

```
var oneArray:Array = new Array("a", "b", "c");
var twoArray:Array = oneArray; // Both array variables refer to the same
    array.
twoArray[0] = "z";
trace(oneArray); // Output: z,b,c.
```

The Array class should not be used to create *associative arrays*, which are different data structures that contain named elements instead of numbered elements. You should use the Object class to create associative arrays (also called *hashes*). Although ActionScript permits you to create associative arrays using the Array class, you can not use any of the Array class methods or properties. At its core, an associative array is an instance of the Object class, and each key-value pair is represented by a property and its value. Another reason to declare an associative array using the Object data type is that you can then use an object literal to populate your associative array (but only at the time you declare it). The following example creates an associative array using an object literal, accesses items using both the dot operator and the array access operator, and then adds a new key-value pair by creating a new property:

```
var myAssocArray:Object = {fname:"John", lname:"Public"};
trace(myAssocArray.fname); // Output: John
trace(myAssocArray["lname"]); // Output: Public
myAssocArray.initial = "Q";
trace(myAssocArray.initial); // Output: Q
```

Availability: ActionScript 1.0; Flash Player 5 - Became a native object in Flash Player 6, which improved performance significantly.

Example

In the following example, my_array contains four months of the year:

```
var my_array:Array = new Array();
my_array[0] = "January";
my_array[1] = "February";
my_array[2] = "March";
my_array[3] = "April";
```

Property summary

Modifiers	Property	Description
static	CASEINSENSITIVE:Number	In the sorting methods, this constant specifies case-insensitive sorting.
static	DESCENDING:Number	In the sorting methods, this constant specifies descending sort order.
	length:Number	A non-negative integer specifying the number of elements in the array.
static	NUMERIC:Number	In the sorting methods, this constant specifies numeric (instead of character-string) sorting.
static	RETURNINDEXEDARRAY:Number	Specifies that a sort returns an indexed array as a result of calling the sort() or sortOn() method.
static	UNIQUESORT:Number	In the sorting methods, this constant specifies the unique sorting requirement.

Properties inherited from class Object

```
constructor (Object.constructor property), __proto__ (Object.__proto__
property), prototype (Object.prototype property), __resolve
(Object.__resolve property)
```

Constructor summary

Signature	Description
Array([value:Object])	Lets you create an array.

Method summary

Modifiers	Signature	Description
	`concat([value:Object ]) : Array`	Concatenates the elements specified in the parameters with the elements in an array and creates a new array.
	`join([delimiter:Stri ng]) : String`	Converts the elements in an array to strings, inserts the specified separator between the elements, concatenates them, and returns the resulting string.
	`pop() : Object`	Removes the last element from an array and returns the value of that element.
	`push(value:Object) : Number`	Adds one or more elements to the end of an array and returns the new length of the array.
	`reverse() : Void`	Reverses the array in place.
	`shift() : Object`	Removes the first element from an array and returns that element.
	`slice([startIndex:Nu mber], [endIndex:Number]) : Array`	Returns a new array that consists of a range of elements from the original array, without modifying the original array.
	`sort([compareFunctio n:Object], [options:Number]) : Array`	Sorts the elements in an array.
	`sortOn(fieldName:Obj ect, [options:Object]) : Array`	Sorts the elements in an array according to one or more fields in the array.
	`splice(startIndex:Nu mber, [deleteCount:Number] , [value:Object]) : Array`	Adds elements to and removes elements from an array.
	`toString() : String`	Returns a string value representing the elements in the specified Array object.
	`unshift(value:Object ) : Number`	Adds one or more elements to the beginning of an array and returns the new length of the array.

Methods inherited from class Object

```
addProperty (Object.addProperty method), hasOwnProperty
(Object.hasOwnProperty method), isPropertyEnumerable
(Object.isPropertyEnumerable method), isPrototypeOf (Object.isPrototypeOf
method), registerClass (Object.registerClass method), toString
(Object.toString method), unwatch (Object.unwatch method), valueOf
(Object.valueOf method), watch (Object.watch method)
```

Array constructor

```
public Array([value:Object])
```

Lets you create an array. You can use the constructor to create different types of arrays: an empty array, an array with a specific length but whose elements have undefined values, or an array whose elements have specific values.

Usage 1: If you don't specify any parameters, an array with a length of 0 is created.

Usage 2: If you specify only a length, an array is created with `length` number of elements. The value of each element is set to `undefined`.

Usage 3: If you use the `element` parameters to specify values, an array is created with specific values.

Availability: ActionScript 1.0; Flash Player 5

Parameters

`value:Object` [optional] - Either:

- An integer that specifies the number of elements in the array.
- A list of two or more arbitrary values. The values can be of type Boolean, Number, String, Object, or Array. The first element in an array always has an index or position of 0.

 If only a single numeric parameter is passed to the Array constructor, it is assumed to be length and it is converted to an integer by using the `integer()` function.

Example

Usage 1: The following example creates a new `Array` object with an initial length of 0:

```
var my_array:Array = new Array();
trace(my_array.length); // Traces 0.
```

Usage 2: The following example creates a new Array object with an initial length of 4:

```
var my_array:Array = new Array(4);
trace(my_array.length); // Returns 4.
trace(my_array[0]); // Returns undefined.
```

```
if (my_array[0] == undefined) { // No quotation marks around undefined.
  trace("undefined is a special value, not a string");
} // Traces: undefined is a special value, not a string.
```

Usage 3: The following example creates the new Array object go_gos_array with an initial length of 5:

```
var go_gos_array:Array = new Array("Belinda", "Gina", "Kathy", "Charlotte",
  "Jane");
trace(go_gos_array.length); // Returns 5.
trace(go_gos_array.join(", ")); // Displays elements.
```

The initial elements of the go_gos_array array are identified, as shown in the following example:

```
go_gos_array[0] = "Belinda";
go_gos_array[1] = "Gina";
go_gos_array[2] = "Kathy";
go_gos_array[3] = "Charlotte";
go_gos_array[4] = "Jane";
```

The following code adds a sixth element to the go_gos_array array and changes the second element:

```
go_gos_array[5] = "Donna";
go_gos_array[1] - "Nina"
trace(go_gos_array.join(" + "));
// Returns Belinda + Nina + Kathy + Charlotte + Jane + Donna.
```

See also

`[] array access operator, length (Array.length property)`

CASEINSENSITIVE (Array.CASEINSENSITIVE property)

`public static CASEINSENSITIVE : Number`

In the sorting methods, this constant specifies case-insensitive sorting. You can use this constant for the `options` parameter in the `sort()` or `sortOn()` method.

The value of this constant is 1.

Availability: ActionScript 1.0; Flash Player 7

See also

`sort (Array.sort method), sortOn (Array.sortOn method)`

concat (Array.concat method)

```
public concat([value:Object]) : Array
```

Concatenates the elements specified in the parameters with the elements in an array and creates a new array. If the `value` parameters specify an array, the elements of that array are concatenated, rather than the array itself. The array `my_array` is left unchanged.

Availability: ActionScript 1.0; Flash Player 5

Parameters

`value:Object` [optional] - Numbers, elements, or strings to be concatenated in a new array. If you don't pass any values, a duplicate of `my_array` is created.

Returns

`Array` - An array that contains the elements from this array followed by elements from the parameters.

Example

The following code concatenates two arrays:

```
var alpha_array:Array = new Array("a","b","c");
var numeric_array:Array = new Array(1,2,3);
var alphaNumeric_array:Array =alpha_array.concat(numeric_array);
trace(alphaNumeric_array);
// Creates array [a,b,c,1,2,3].
```

The following code concatenates three arrays:

```
var num1_array:Array = [1,3,5];
var num2_array:Array = [2,4,6];
var num3_array:Array = [7,8,9];
var nums_array:Array=num1_array.concat(num2_array,num3_array)
trace(nums_array);
// Creates array [1,3,5,2,4,6,7,8,9].
```

Nested arrays are not flattened in the same way as normal arrays. The elements in a nested array are not broken into separate elements in array `x_array`, as shown in the following example:

```
var a_array:Array = new Array ("a","b","c");

// 2 and 3 are elements in a nested array.
var n_array:Array = new Array(1, [2, 3], 4);

var x_array:Array = a_array.concat(n_array);
trace(x_array[0]); // a
trace(x_array[1]); // b
trace(x_array[2]); // c
```

```
trace(x_array[3]); // 1
trace(x_array[4]); // 2, 3
trace(x_array[5]); // 4
```

DESCENDING (Array.DESCENDING property)

`public static DESCENDING : Number`

In the sorting methods, this constant specifies descending sort order. You can use this constant for the `options` parameter in the `sort()` or `sortOn()` method.

The value of this constant is 2.

Availability: ActionScript 1.0; Flash Player 7

See also

`sort (Array.sort method)`, `sortOn (Array.sortOn method)`

join (Array.join method)

`public join([delimiter:String]) : String`

Converts the elements in an array to strings, inserts the specified separator between the elements, concatenates them, and returns the resulting string. A nested array is always separated by a comma (,), not by the separator passed to the `join()` method.

Availability: ActionScript 1.0; Flash Player 5

Parameters

`delimiter:String` [optional] - A character or string that separates array elements in the returned string. If you omit this parameter, a comma (,) is used as the default separator.

Returns

`String` - A string.

Example

The following example creates an array with three elements: Earth, Moon, and Sun. It then joins the array three times—first by using the default separator (a comma [,] and a space), then by using a dash (-), and then by using a plus sign (+).

```
var a_array:Array = new Array("Earth","Moon","Sun")
trace(a_array.join());
// Displays Earth,Moon,Sun.
trace(a_array.join(" - "));
// Displays Earth - Moon - Sun.
```

```
trace(a_array.join(" + "));
// Displays Earth + Moon + Sun.
```

The following example creates a nested array that contains two arrays. The first array has three elements: Europa, Io, and Callisto. The second array has two elements: Titan and Rhea. It joins the array by using a plus sign (+), but the elements within each nested array remain separated by commas (,).

```
var a_nested_array:Array = new Array(["Europa", "Io", "Callisto"],
  ["Titan", "Rhea"]);
trace(a_nested_array.join(" + "));
// Returns Europa,Io,Callisto + Titan,Rhea.
```

See also

split (String.split method)

length (Array.length property)

`public length : Number`

A non-negative integer specifying the number of elements in the array. This property is automatically updated when new elements are added to the array. When you assign a value to an array element (for example, `my_array[index] = value`), if index is a number, and index+1 is greater than the length property, the length property is updated to index+1.

 If you assign a value to the length property that is shorter than the existing length, the array will be truncated.

Availability: ActionScript 1.0; Flash Player 5

Example

The following code explains how the length property is updated. The initial length is 0, and then updated to 1, 2, and 10. If you assign a value to the length property that is shorter than the existing length, the array will be truncated:

```
var my_array:Array = new Array();
trace(my_array.length); // initial length is 0
my_array[0] = "a";
trace(my_array.length); // my_array.length is updated to 1
my_array[1] = "b";
trace(my_array.length); // my_array.length is updated to 2
my_array[9] = "c";
trace(my_array.length); // my_array.length is updated to 10
trace(my_array);
// displays:
```

```
//
  a,b,undefined,undefined,undefined,undefined,undefined,undefined,undefine
  d,c

// if the length property is now set to 5, the array will be truncated
my_array.length = 5;
trace(my_array.length); // my_array.length is updated to 5
trace(my_array); // outputs: a,b,undefined,undefined,undefined
```

NUMERIC (Array.NUMERIC property)

`public static NUMERIC : Number`

In the sorting methods, this constant specifies numeric (instead of character-string) sorting. Including it in the `options` parameter causes the `sort()` and `sortOn()` methods to sort numbers as numeric values, not as strings of numeric characters. Without the NUMERIC constant, sorting treats each array element as a character string and produces the results in Unicode order.

For example, given the Array of values [2005, 7, 35], if the NUMERIC constant is **not** included in the `options` parameter, the sorted Array is [2005, 35, 7], but if the NUMERIC constant **is** included, the sorted Array is [7, 35, 2005].

Note that this constant only applies to numbers in the array; it does not apply to strings that contain numeric data (such as ["23", "5"]).

The value of this constant is 16.

Availability: ActionScript 1.0; Flash Player 7

See also

`sort (Array.sort method)`, `sortOn (Array.sortOn method)`

pop (Array.pop method)

`public pop() : Object`

Removes the last element from an array and returns the value of that element.

Availability: ActionScript 1.0; Flash Player 5

Returns

`Object` - The value of the last element in the specified array.

Example

The following code creates the array myPets_array array containing four elements, and then removes its last element:

```
var myPets_array:Array = new Array("cat", "dog", "bird", "fish");
var popped:Object = myPets_array.pop();
trace(popped); // Displays fish.
trace(myPets_array); // Displays cat,dog,bird.
```

See also

push (Array.push method), shift (Array.shift method), unshift (Array.unshift method)

push (Array.push method)

```
public push(value:Object) : Number
```

Adds one or more elements to the end of an array and returns the new length of the array.

Availability: ActionScript 1.0; Flash Player 5

Parameters

value:Object - One or more values to append to the array.

Returns

Number - An integer representing the length of the new array.

Example

The following example creates the array myPets_array with two elements, cat and dog. The second line adds two elements to the array.

Because the push() method returns the new length of the array, the trace() statement in the last line sends the new length of myPets_array (4) to the Output panel.

```
var myPets_array:Array = new Array("cat", "dog");
var pushed:Number = myPets_array.push("bird", "fish");
trace(pushed); // Displays 4.
```

See also

pop (Array.pop method), shift (Array.shift method), unshift (Array.unshift method)

RETURNINDEXEDARRAY
(Array.RETURNINDEXEDARRAY property)

`public static RETURNINDEXEDARRAY : Number`

Specifies that a sort returns an indexed array as a result of calling the `sort()` or `sortOn()` method. You can use this constant for the `options` parameter in the `sort()` or `sortOn()` method. This provides preview or copy functionality by returning an array that represents the results of the sort and leaves the original array unmodified.

The value of this constant is 8.

Availability: ActionScript 1.0; Flash Player 7

See also

`sort (Array.sort method)`, `sortOn (Array.sortOn method)`

reverse (Array.reverse method)

`public reverse() : Void`

Reverses the array in place.

Availability: ActionScript 1.0; Flash Player 5

Example

The following example uses this method to reverse the array `numbers_array`:

```
var numbers_array:Array = new Array(1, 2, 3, 4, 5, 6);
trace(numbers_array); // Displays 1,2,3,4,5,6.
numbers_array.reverse();
trace(numbers_array); // Displays 6,5,4,3,2,1.
```

shift (Array.shift method)

`public shift() : Object`

Removes the first element from an array and returns that element.

Availability: ActionScript 1.0; Flash Player 5

Returns

`Object` - The first element in an array.

Example

The following code creates the array myPets_array and then removes the first element from the array and assigns it to the variable shifted:

```
var myPets_array:Array = new Array("cat", "dog", "bird", "fish");
var shifted:Object = myPets_array.shift();
trace(shifted); // Displays "cat".
trace(myPets_array); // Displays dog,bird,fish.
```

See also

pop (Array.pop method), push (Array.push method), unshift (Array.unshift method)

slice (Array.slice method)

public slice([startIndex:Number], [endIndex:Number]) : Array

Returns a new array that consists of a range of elements from the original array, without modifying the original array. The returned array includes the startIndex element and all elements up to, but not including, the endIndex element.

If you don't pass any parameters, a duplicate of the original array is created.

Availability: ActionScript 1.0; Flash Player 5

Parameters

startIndex:Number [optional] - A number specifying the index of the starting point for the slice. If *start* is a negative number, the starting point begins at the end of the array, where -1 is the last element.

endIndex:Number [optional] - A number specifying the index of the ending point for the slice. If you omit this parameter, the slice includes all elements from the starting point to the end of the array. If *end* is a negative number, the ending point is specified from the end of the array, where -1 is the last element.

Returns

Array - An array that consists of a range of elements from the original array.

Example

The following example creates an array of five pets and uses `slice()` to populate a new array that contains only four-legged pets:

```
var myPets_array:Array = new Array("cat", "dog", "fish", "canary",
  "parrot");
var myFourLeggedPets_array:Array = new Array();
var myFourLeggedPets_array = myPets_array.slice(0, 2);
trace(myFourLeggedPets_array); // Returns cat,dog.
trace(myPets_array); // Returns cat,dog,fish,canary,parrot.
```

The following example creates an array of five pets, and then uses `slice()` with a negative `start` parameter to copy the last two elements from the array:

```
var myPets_array:Array = new Array("cat", "dog", "fish", "canary",
  "parrot");
var myFlyingPets_array:Array = myPets_array.slice(-2);
trace(myFlyingPets_array); // Traces canary,parrot.
```

The following example creates an array of five pets and uses `slice()` with a negative `end` parameter to copy the middle element from the array:

```
var myPets_array:Array = new Array("cat", "dog", "fish", "canary",
  "parrot");
var myAquaticPets_array:Array = myPets_array.slice(2,-2);
trace(myAquaticPets_array); // Returns fish.
```

sort (Array.sort method)

```
public sort([compareFunction:Object], [options:Number]) : Array
```

Sorts the elements in an array. Flash sorts according to Unicode values. (ASCII is a subset of Unicode.)

By default, `Array.sort()` works as described in the following list:

- Sorting is case-sensitive (*Z* precedes *a*).

- Sorting is ascending (*a* precedes *b*).

- The array is modified to reflect the sort order; multiple elements that have identical sort fields are placed consecutively in the sorted array in no particular order.

- Numeric fields are sorted as if they were strings, so 100 precedes 99, because "1" is a lower string value than "9".

If you want to sort an array by using settings that deviate from the default settings, you can either use one of the sorting options described in the entry for the `options` parameter or you can create your own custom function to do the sorting. If you create a custom function, you can use it by calling the `sort()` method, using the name of your custom function as the first parameter (`compareFunction`).

Availability: ActionScript 1.0; Flash Player 5 - Array sorting option added in Flash Player 7.

Parameters

`compareFunction:Object` [optional] - A comparison function used to determine the sorting order of elements in an array. Given the elements A and B, the result of `compareFunction` can have one of the following three values:

- -1, if A should appear before B in the sorted sequence
- 0, if A equals B
- 1, if A should appear after B in the sorted sequence

`options:Number` [optional] - One or more numbers or names of defined constants, separated by the | (bitwise OR) operator, that change the behavior of the sort from the default. The following values are acceptable for the `options` parameter:

- `Array.CASEINSENSITIVE` or 1
- `Array.DESCENDING` or 2
- `Array.UNIQUESORT` or 4
- `Array.RETURNINDEXEDARRAY` or 8
- `Array.NUMERIC` or 16

For more information about this parameter, see the `Array.sortOn()` method.

> **NOTE** Array.sort() is defined in ECMA-262, but the array sorting options introduced in Flash Player 7 are Flash-specific extensions to the ECMA-262 specification

Returns

`Array` - The return value depends on whether you pass any parameters, as described in the following list:

- If you specify a value of 4 or `Array.UNIQUESORT` for the `options` parameter and two or more elements being sorted have identical sort fields, Flash returns a value of 0 and does not modify the array.
- If you specify a value of 8 or `Array.RETURNINDEXEDARRAY` for the `options` parameter, Flash returns an array that reflects the results of the sort and does not modify the array.
- Otherwise, Flash returns nothing and modifies the array to reflect the sort order.

Example

Usage 1: The following example shows the use of `Array.sort()` with and without a value passed for `options`:

```
var fruits_array:Array = new Array("oranges", "apples", "strawberries",
   "pineapples", "cherries");
trace(fruits_array); // Displays
   oranges,apples,strawberries,pineapples,cherries.
fruits_array.sort();
trace(fruits_array); // Displays
   apples,cherries,oranges,pineapples,strawberries.
trace(fruits_array); // Writes
   apples,cherries,oranges,pineapples,strawberries.
fruits_array.sort(Array.DESCENDING);
trace(fruits_array); // Displays
   strawberries,pineapples,oranges,cherries,apples.
trace(fruits_array); // Writes
   strawberries,pineapples,oranges,cherries,apples.
```

Usage 2: The following example uses `Array.sort()` with a compare function. The entries are sorted in the form name:password. Sort using only the name part of the entry as a key:

```
var passwords_array:Array = new Array("mom:glam", "ana:ring", "jay:mag",
   "anne:home", "regina:silly");
function order(a, b):Number {
   var name1:String = a.split(":")[0];
   var name2:String = b.split(":")[0];
   if (name1<name2) {
   return -1;
   } else if (name1>name2) {
   return 1;
   } else {
   return 0;
   }
}
trace("Unsorted:");
//Displays Unsorted:
trace(passwords_array);
//Displays mom:glam,ana:ring,jay:mag,anne:home,regina:silly.
//Writes mom:glam,ana:ring,jay:mag,anne:home,regina:silly
passwords_array.sort(order);
trace("Sorted:");
//Displays Sorted:
trace(passwords_array);
//Displays ana:ring,anne:home,jay:mag,mom:glam,regina:silly.
//Writes ana:ring,anne:home,jay:mag,mom:glam,regina:silly.
```

See also

| bitwise OR operator, sortOn (Array.sortOn method)

sortOn (Array.sortOn method)

```
public sortOn(fieldName:Object, [options:Object]) : Array
```

Sorts the elements in an array according to one or more fields in the array. The array should have the following characteristics:

- The array is an indexed array, not an associative array.
- Each element of the array holds an object with one or more properties.
- All of the objects have at least one property in common, the values of which can be used to sort the array. Such a property is called a *field*.

If you pass multiple fieldName parameters, the first field represents the primary sort field, the second represents the next sort field, and so on. Flash sorts according to Unicode values. (ASCII is a subset of Unicode.) If either of the elements being compared does not contain the field that is specified in the fieldName parameter, the field is assumed to be undefined, and the elements are placed consecutively in the sorted array in no particular order.

By default, Array.sortOn() works in the following way:

- Sorting is case-sensitive (*Z* precedes *a*).
- Sorting is ascending (*a* precedes *b*).
- The array is modified to reflect the sort order; multiple elements that have identical sort fields are placed consecutively in the sorted array in no particular order.
- Numeric fields are sorted as if they were strings, so 100 precedes 99, because "1" is a lower string value than "9".

Flash Player 7 added the options parameter, which you can use to override the default sort behavior. To sort a simple array (for example, an array with only one field), or to specify a sort order that the options parameter doesn't support, use Array.sort().

To pass multiple flags, separate them with the bitwise OR (|) operator:

```
my_array.sortOn(someFieldName, Array.DESCENDING | Array.NUMERIC);
```

Flash Player 8 added the ability to specify a different sorting option for each field when you sort by more than one field. In Flash Player 8, the options parameter accepts an array of sort options such that each sort option corresponds to a sort field in the fieldName parameter. The following example sorts the primary sort field, a, using a descending sort; the secondary sort field, b, using a numeric sort; and the tertiary sort field, c, using a case-insensitive sort:

```
Array.sortOn (["a", "b", "c"], [Array.DESCENDING, Array.NUMERIC,
    Array.CASEINSENSITIVE]);
```

> **NOTE**
> The fieldName and options arrays must have the same number of elements; otherwise, the options array is ignored. Also, the Array.UNIQUESORT and Array.RETURNINDEXDARRAY options can be used only as the first element in the array; otherwise, they are ignored.

Availability: ActionScript 1.0; Flash Player 6 - The options parameter was added in Flash Player 7. The ability to use different options parameters on multiple sort fields was added in Flash Player 8.

Parameters

`fieldName:Object` - A string that identifies a field to be used as the sort value, or an array in which the first element represents the primary sort field, the second represents the secondary sort field, and so on.

`options:Object` [optional] - One or more numbers or names of defined constants, separated by the `bitwise OR` (`|`) operator, that change the sorting behavior. The following values are acceptable for the `options` parameter:

- `Array.CASEINSENSITIVE` or 1
- `Array.DESCENDING` or 2
- `Array.UNIQUESORT` or 4
- `Array.RETURNINDEXEDARRAY` or 8
- `Array.NUMERIC` or 16

Code hinting is enabled if you use the string form of the flag (for example, `DESCENDING`) rather than the numeric form (2).

Returns

`Array` - The return value depends on whether you pass any parameters:

- If you specify a value of 4 or `Array.UNIQUESORT` for the `options` parameter, and two or more elements being sorted have identical sort fields, a value of 0 is returned and the array is not modified.
- If you specify a value of 8 or `Array.RETURNINDEXEDARRAY` for the `options` parameter, an array is returned that reflects the results of the sort and the array is not modified.
- Otherwise, nothing is returned and the array is modified to reflect the sort order.

Example

The following example creates a new array and sorts it according to the `name` and `city` fields. The first sort uses `name` as the first sort value and `city` as the second. The second sort uses `city` as the first sort value and `name` as the second.

```
var rec_array:Array = new Array();
rec_array.push({name: "john", city: "omaha", zip: 68144});
rec_array.push({name: "john", city: "kansas city", zip: 72345});
rec_array.push({name: "bob", city: "omaha", zip: 94010});
for(i=0; i<rec_array.length; i++){
  trace(rec_array[i].name + ", " + rec_array[i].city);
```

```
}
// Results:
// john, omaha
// john, kansas city
// bob, omaha

rec_array.sortOn(["name", "city"]);
for(i=0; i<rec_array.length; i++){
  trace(rec_array[i].name + ", " + rec_array[i].city);
}
// Results:
// bob, omaha
// john, kansas city
// john, omaha

rec_array.sortOn(["city", "name" ]);
for(i=0; i<rec_array.length; i++){
  trace(rec_array[i].name + ", " + rec_array[i].city);
}
// Results:
// john, kansas city
// bob, omaha
// john, omaha
```

The following array of objects is used by the remaining examples, which show how to use the options parameter:

```
var my_array:Array = new Array();
my_array.push({password: "Bob", age:29});
my_array.push({password: "abcd", age:3});
my_array.push({password: "barb", age:35});
my_array.push({password: "catchy", age:4});
```

Performing a default sort on the password field produces the following results:

```
my_array.sortOn("password");
// Bob
// abcd
// barb
// catchy
```

Performing a case-insensitive sort on the password field produces the following results:

```
my_array.sortOn("password", Array.CASEINSENSITIVE);
// abcd
// barb
// Bob
// catchy
```

Performing a case-insensitive, descending sort on the password field produces the following results:

```
my_array.sortOn("password", Array.CASEINSENSITIVE | Array.DESCENDING);
// catchy
// Bob
// barb
// abcd
```

Performing a default sort on the age field produces the following results:

```
my_array.sortOn("age");
// 29
// 3
// 35
// 4
```

Performing a numeric sort on the age field produces the following results:

```
my_array.sortOn("age", Array.NUMERIC);
// my_array[0].age = 3
// my_array[1].age = 4
// my_array[2].age = 29
// my_array[3].age = 35
```

Performing a descending numeric sort on the age field produces the following results:

```
my_array.sortOn("age", Array.DESCENDING | Array.NUMERIC);
// my_array[0].age = 35
// my_array[1].age = 29
// my_array[2].age = 4
// my_array[3].age = 3
```

When you use the `Array.RETURNEDINDEXARRAY` sorting option, you must assign the return value to a different array. The original array is not modified.

```
var indexArray:Array = my_array.sortOn("age", Array.RETURNINDEXEDARRAY);
```

See also

```
| bitwise OR operator, sort (Array.sort method)
```

splice (Array.splice method)

```
public splice(startIndex:Number, [deleteCount:Number], [value:Object]) :
    Array
```

Adds elements to and removes elements from an array. This method modifies the array without making a copy.

Availability: ActionScript 1.0; Flash Player 5

Parameters

startIndex:Number - An integer that specifies the index of the element in the array where the insertion or deletion begins. You can specify a negative integer to specify a position relative to the end of the array (for example, -1 is the last element of the array).

deleteCount:Number [optional] - An integer that specifies the number of elements to be deleted. This number includes the element specified in the startIndex parameter. If no value is specified for the deleteCount parameter, the method deletes all of the values from the startIndex element to the last element in the array. If the value is 0, no elements are deleted.

value:Object [optional] - Specifies the values to insert into the array at the insertion point specified in the startIndex parameter.

Returns

Array - An array containing the elements that were removed from the original array.

Example

The following example creates an array and splices it by using element index 1 for the startIndex parameter. This removes all elements from the array starting with the second element, leaving only the element at index 0 in the original array:

```
var myPets_array:Array = new Array("cat", "dog", "bird", "fish");
trace( myPets_array.splice(1) ); // Displays dog,bird,fish.
trace( myPets_array ); // cat
```

The following example creates an array and splices it by using element index 1 for the startIndex parameter and the number 2 for the deleteCount parameter. This removes two elements from the array, starting with the second element, leaving the first and last elements in the original array:

```
var myFlowers_array:Array = new Array("roses", "tulips", "lilies",
    "orchids");
trace( myFlowers_array.splice(1,2 ) ); // Displays tulips,lilies.
trace( myFlowers_array ); // roses,orchids
```

The following example creates an array and splices it by using element index 1 for the startIndex parameter, the number 0 for the deleteCount parameter, and the string chair for the value parameter. This does not remove anything from the original array, and adds the string chair at index 1:

```
var myFurniture_array:Array = new Array("couch", "bed", "desk", "lamp");
trace( myFurniture_array.splice(1,0, "chair" ) ); // Displays empty array.
trace( myFurniture_array ); // displays couch,chair,bed,desk,lamp
```

toString (Array.toString method)

`public toString() : String`

Returns a string value representing the elements in the specified Array object. Every element in the array, starting with index 0 and ending with the highest index, is converted to a concatenated string and separated by commas. To specify a custom separator, use the `Array.join()` method.

Availability: ActionScript 1.0; Flash Player 5

Returns

`String` - A string.

Example

The following example creates `my_array` and converts it to a string.

```
var my_array:Array = new Array();
my_array[0] = 1;
my_array[1] = 2;
my_array[2] = 3;
my_array[3] = 4;
my_array[4] = 5;
trace(my_array.toString()); // Displays 1,2,3,4,5.
```

This example outputs 1,2,3,4,5 as a result of the `trace` statement.

See also

`split (String.split method)`, `join (Array.join method)`

UNIQUESORT (Array.UNIQUESORT property)

`public static UNIQUESORT : Number`

In the sorting methods, this constant specifies the unique sorting requirement. You can use this constant for the options parameter in the `sort()` or `sortOn()` method. The unique sorting option aborts the sort if any two elements or fields being sorted have identical values.

The value of this constant is 4.

Availability: ActionScript 1.0; Flash Player 7

See also

`sort (Array.sort method)`, `sortOn (Array.sortOn method)`

unshift (Array.unshift method)

`public unshift(value:Object) : Number`

Adds one or more elements to the beginning of an array and returns the new length of the array.

Availability: ActionScript 1.0; Flash Player 5

Parameters

`value:Object` - One or more numbers, elements, or variables to be inserted at the beginning of the array.

Returns

`Number` - An integer representing the new length of the array.

Example

The following example shows the use of the `Array.unshift()` method:

```
var pets_array:Array = new Array("dog", "cat", "fish");
trace( pets_array ); // Displays dog,cat,fish.
pets_array.unshift("ferrets", "gophers", "engineers");
trace( pets_array ); // Displays ferrets,gophers,engineers,dog,cat,fish.
```

See also

`pop (Array.pop method)`, `push (Array.push method)`, `shift (Array.shift method)`

AsBroadcaster

```
Object
  |
  +-AsBroadcaster
```

`public class AsBroadcaster`
`extends Object`

> **NOTE** A common mistake is to capitalize the second letter of `AsBroadcaster`. When calling the `AsBroadcaster.initialize()` method, ensure that the second letter is lowercase. Any misspelling of `AsBroadcaster` fails silently.

Availability: ActionScript 1.0; Flash Player 6

Property summary

Modifiers	Property	Description
	_listeners:Array [read-only]	A list of references to all registered listener objects.

Properties inherited from class Object

```
constructor (Object.constructor property),__proto__ (Object.__proto__
property),prototype (Object.prototype property),__resolve
(Object.__resolve property)
```

Method summary

Modifiers	Signature	Description
	addListener(listenerObj:Object) : Boolean	Registers an object to receive event notification messages.
	broadcastMessage(eventName:String) : Void	Sends an event message to each object in the list of listeners.
static	initialize(obj:Object) : Void	Adds event notification and listener management functionality to a given object.
	removeListener(listenerObj:Object) : Boolean	Removes an object from the list of objects that receive event notification messages.

Methods inherited from class Object

```
addProperty (Object.addProperty method),hasOwnProperty
(Object.hasOwnProperty method),isPropertyEnumerable
(Object.isPropertyEnumerable method),isPrototypeOf (Object.isPrototypeOf
method),registerClass (Object.registerClass method),toString
(Object.toString method),unwatch (Object.unwatch method),valueOf
(Object.valueOf method),watch (Object.watch method)
```

addListener (AsBroadcaster.addListener method)

```
public addListener(listenerObj:Object) : Boolean
```

Registers an object to receive event notification messages. This method is called on the broadcasting object and the listener object is sent as an argument.

Availability: ActionScript 1.0; Flash Player 6

Parameters

`listenerObj:Object` - The name of the listener object that receives event notification.

Returns

`Boolean` - Although this method technically returns a Boolean value, in practical terms it returns `Void` because it always returns the value `true`.

Example

The following example is an excerpt from the full example provided in the entry for the `AsBroadcaster.initialize()` method.

```
someObject.addListener(myListener1); // Register myListener1 as listener.
someObject.addListener(myListener2); // Register myListener2 as listener.
```

See also

`initialize (AsBroadcaster.initialize method)`, `removeListener (AsBroadcaster.removeListener method)`

broadcastMessage (AsBroadcaster.broadcastMessage method)

`public broadcastMessage(eventName:String) : Void`

Sends an event message to each object in the list of listeners. When the message is received by the listening object, Flash Player attempts to invoke a function of the same name on the listening object. Suppose that your object broadcasts an event message like this:

`obj.broadcastMessage("onAlert");`

When this message is received, Flash Player invokes a method named `onAlert()` on the receiving listener object.

> **NOTE** You can pass arguments to your listener functions by including additional arguments to the `broadcastMessage()` method. Any arguments that appear after the `eventName` parameter are received as arguments by the listener method.

You can call this method only from an object that was initialized by using the `AsBroadcaster.initialize()` method.

Availability: ActionScript 1.0; Flash Player 6

Parameters

`eventName:String` - The name of the event to broadcast. The name of any listener methods must match this parameter in order to receive the broadcast event. You can pass arguments to the listener methods by including additional arguments after `eventName`.

Example

The following example is an excerpt from the first full example provided in the entry for the `AsBroadcaster.initialize()` method:

```
someObject.broadcastMessage("someEvent"); // Broadcast the "someEvent"
    message.
```

The following example is an excerpt from the second full example provided in the entry for the `AsBroadcaster.initialize()` method. It shows how to send arguments to listener methods.

```
someObject.broadcastMessage("someEvent", 3, "arbitrary string");
```

See also

`initialize (AsBroadcaster.initialize method)`, `removeListener (AsBroadcaster.removeListener method)`

initialize (AsBroadcaster.initialize method)

`public static initialize(obj:Object) : Void`

Adds event notification and listener management functionality to a given object. This is a static method; it must be called by using the AsBroadcaster class (where `someObject` is the name of the object to be initialized as an event broadcaster):

```
AsBroadcaster.initialize(someObject);
```

 NOTE A common mistake is to capitalize the second letter of `AsBroadcaster`. When calling the `AsBroadcaster.initialize()` method, ensure that the second letter is lowercase. Any misspelling of `AsBroadcaster` fails silently.

This method adds the `_listeners` property along with the following three methods to the object specified by the `obj` parameter:

- `obj.addListener()`
- `obj.removeListener()`
- `obj.broadcastMessage()`

Availability: ActionScript 1.0; Flash Player 6

Parameters

`obj:Object` - An object to serve as a broadcasting object.

Example

The following example creates a generic object, someObject, and turns it into an event broadcaster. The output should be the strings shown in the two trace() statements:

```
var someObject:Object = new Object(); // Creates broadcast object.

var myListener1:Object = new Object(); // Creates listener object.
var myListener2:Object = new Object(); // Creates listener object.

myListener1.someEvent = function() { // Creates listener method.
  trace("myListener1 received someEvent");
}
myListener2.someEvent = function() { // Createz listener method.
  trace("myListener2 received someEvent");
}

AsBroadcaster.initialize(someObject); // Makes someObject an event
  broadcaster.
someObject.addListener(myListener1); // Registers myListener1 as listener.
someObject.addListener(myListener2); // Registers myListener2 as listener.
someObject.broadcastMessage("someEvent"); // Broadcasts the "someEvent"
  message.
```

The following example shows how to pass extra arguments to a listener method by using the broadcastMessage() method. The output should be the three strings shown in the three trace() statements, which also include the arguments passed in through the broadcastMessage() method.

```
var someObject:Object = new Object();

var myListener:Object = new Object();
myListener.someEvent = function(param1:Number, param2:String) {
  trace("myListener received someEvent");
  trace("param1: " + param1);
  trace("param2: " + param2);
}

AsBroadcaster.initialize(someObject);
someObject.addListener(myListener);
someObject.broadcastMessage("someEvent", 3, "arbitrary string");
```

_listeners (AsBroadcaster._listeners property)

A list of references to all registered listener objects. This property is intended for internal use, and is not intended for direct manipulation. Objects are added to and removed from this array by calls to the addListener() and removelistener() methods.

You can call this property only from an object that was initialized by using the AsBroadcaster.initialize() method.

Availability: ActionScript 1.0; Flash Player 6

Example

The following example shows how to use the length property to ascertain the number of listener objects currently registered to an event broadcaster. The following code works if it is added to the first full example in the Examples section of the AsBroadcaster.initialize() entry:

```
trace(someObject._listeners.length); // Output: 2
```

For advanced users, the following example shows how to use the _listeners property to list all of the listeners registered with an event broadcaster, along with all of the properties of each listener object. The following example creates two different listener methods for the first listener object.

```
var someObject:Object = new Object(); // create broadcast object

var myListener1:Object = new Object(); // create listener object
var myListener2:Object = new Object(); // create listener object

myListener1.someEvent = function() { // create listener method
   trace("myListener1 received someEvent");
}
myListener1.anotherEvent = function() { // create another listener method
   trace("myListener1 received anotherEvent");
}
myListener2.someEvent = function() { // create listener method
   trace("myListener2 received someEvent");
}

AsBroadcaster.initialize(someObject); // make someObject an event
   broadcaster
someObject.addListener(myListener1); // register myListener1 as listener
someObject.addListener(myListener2); // register myListener2 as listener

var numListeners:Number = someObject._listeners.length; // get number of
   registered listeners
```

```
// cycle through all listener objects, listing all properties of each
   listener object
for (var i:Number = 0; i < numListeners; i++) {
  trace("Listener " + i + " listens for these events:");
  for (item in someObject._listeners[i]) {
    trace (" " + item + ": " + someObject._listeners[i][item]);
  }
}
```

See also

initialize (AsBroadcaster.initialize method)

removeListener (AsBroadcaster.removeListener method)

public removeListener(listenerObj:Object) : Boolean

Removes an object from the list of objects that receive event notification messages.

You can call this method only from an object that has been initialized by using the AsBroadcaster.initialize() method.

Availability: ActionScript 1.0; Flash Player 6

Parameters

listenerObj:Object - The name of a listener object that is registered to receive event notification from the broadcasting object.

Returns

Boolean - Returns true if the listener object is removed, and false otherwise.

Example

The following example shows how to remove a listener from the list of registered listeners. The following code works if it is added to the first full example in the Examples section of the AsBroadcaster.initialize() entry. The trace() statements are included only to verify that the number of registered listeners is reduced by one after calling the removeListener() method.

```
trace(someObject._listeners.length); // Output: 2
someObject.removeListener(myListener1);
trace(someObject._listeners.length); // Output: 1
```

See also

addListener (AsBroadcaster.addListener method), initialize
(AsBroadcaster.initialize method)

BevelFilter (flash.filters.BevelFilter)

```
Object
  |
  +-flash.filters.BitmapFilter
    |
    +-flash.filters.BevelFilter
```

public class **BevelFilter**
extends BitmapFilter

The BevelFilter class lets you add a bevel effect to a variety of objects in Flash. A bevel effect gives objects such as buttons a three-dimensional look. You can customize the look of the bevel with different highlight and shadow colors, the amount of blur on the bevel, the angle of the bevel, the placement of the bevel, and a knockout effect.

The use of filters depends on the object to which you apply the filter:

- To apply filters to movie clips, text fields, and buttons at runtime, use the filters property. Setting the filters property of an object does not modify the object, and you can undo the setting by clearing the filters property.

- To apply filters to BitmapData instances, use the BitmapData.applyFilter() method. Calling applyFilter on a BitmapData object takes the source BitmapData object and the filter object and generates a filtered image.

You can also apply filter effects to images and video at authoring time. For more information, see your authoring documentation.

If you apply a filter to a movie clip or button, the cacheAsBitmap property of the movie clip or button is set to true. If you clear all filters, the original value of cacheAsBitmap is restored.

This filter supports stage scaling. However, it does not support general scaling, rotation, and skewing. If the object itself is scaled (if _xscale and _yscale are not 100%), the filter is not scaled. It is scaled only when you zoom in on the Stage.

A filter is not applied if the resulting image exceeds 2880 pixels in width or height. If, for example, you zoom in on a large movie clip with a filter applied, the filter is turned off if the resulting image exceeds the limit of 2880 pixels.

Availability: ActionScript 1.0; Flash Player 8

See also

filters (MovieClip.filters property), cacheAsBitmap (MovieClip.cacheAsBitmap property), filters (Button.filters property), cacheAsBitmap (Button.cacheAsBitmap property), filters (TextField.filters property), applyFilter (BitmapData.applyFilter method), MovieClip

Property summary

Modifiers	Property	Description
	angle:Number	The angle of the bevel.
	blurX:Number	The amount of horizontal blur in pixels.
	blurY:Number	The amount of vertical blur in pixels.
	distance:Number	The offset distance of the bevel.
	highlightAlpha:Number	The alpha transparency value of the highlight color.
	highlightColor:Number	The highlight color of the bevel.
	knockout:Boolean	Applies a knockout effect (true), which effectively makes the object's fill transparent and reveals the background color of the document.
	quality:Number	The number of times to apply the filter.
	shadowAlpha:Number	The alpha transparency value of the shadow color.
	shadowColor:Number	The shadow color of the bevel.
	strength:Number	The strength of the imprint or spread.
	type:String	The type of bevel.

Properties inherited from class Object

constructor (Object.constructor property), __proto__ (Object.__proto__ property), prototype (Object.prototype property), __resolve (Object.__resolve property)

Constructor summary

Signature	Description
BevelFilter([distance:Number], [angle:Number], [highlightColor:Number], [highlightAlpha:Number], [shadowColor:Number], [shadowAlpha:Number], [blurX:Number], [blurY:Number], [strength:Number], [quality:Number], [type:String], [knockout:Boolean])	Initializes a new BevelFilter instance with the specified parameters.

Method summary

Modifiers	Signature	Description
	clone() : BevelFilter	Returns a copy of this filter object.

Methods inherited from class BitmapFilter

```
clone (BitmapFilter.clone method)
```

Methods inherited from class Object

```
addProperty (Object.addProperty method), hasOwnProperty
(Object.hasOwnProperty method), isPropertyEnumerable
(Object.isPropertyEnumerable method), isPrototypeOf (Object.isPrototypeOf
method), registerClass (Object.registerClass method), toString
(Object.toString method), unwatch (Object.unwatch method), valueOf
(Object.valueOf method), watch (Object.watch method)
```

angle (BevelFilter.angle property)

`public angle : Number`

The angle of the bevel. Valid values are from 0 to 360 degrees. The default value is 45.

The angle value represents the angle of the theoretical light source falling on the object and determines the placement of the effect relative to the object. If distance is set to 0, the effect is not offset from the object and, therefore, the angle property has no effect.

Availability: ActionScript 1.0; Flash Player 8

Example

The following example changes the `angle` property on an existing MovieClip instance (`rect`) when a user clicks it:

```
import flash.filters.BevelFilter;

var rect:MovieClip = createBevelRectangle("BevelDistance");
rect.onRelease = function() {
  var filter:BevelFilter = this.filters[0];
  filter.angle = 225;
  this.filters = new Array(filter);
}

function createBevelRectangle(name:String):MovieClip {
  var w:Number = 100;
  var h:Number = 100;
  var bgColor:Number = 0x00CC00;

  var rect:MovieClip = this.createEmptyMovieClip(name,
  this.getNextHighestDepth());
  rect.beginFill(bgColor);
  rect.lineTo(w, 0);
  rect.lineTo(w, h);
  rect.lineTo(0, h);
  rect.lineTo(0, 0);
  rect._x = 20;
  rect._y = 20;

  var filter:BevelFilter = new BevelFilter(5, 45, 0xFFFF00, .8, 0x0000FF,
  .8, 20, 20, 1, 3, "inner", false);
  rect.filters = new Array(filter);
  return rect;
}
```

BevelFilter constructor

```
public BevelFilter([distance:Number], [angle:Number],
  [highlightColor:Number], [highlightAlpha:Number], [shadowColor:Number],
  [shadowAlpha:Number], [blurX:Number], [blurY:Number], [strength:Number],
  [quality:Number], [type:String], [knockout:Boolean])
```

Initializes a new BevelFilter instance with the specified parameters.

Availability: ActionScript 1.0; Flash Player 8

Parameters

distance:Number [optional] - The offset distance of the bevel, in pixels (floating point). The default value is 4.

angle:Number [optional] - The angle of the bevel, from 0 to 360 degrees. The default value is 45.

highlightColor:Number [optional] - The highlight color of the bevel, *0xRRGGBB*. The default value is 0xFFFFFF.

highlightAlpha:Number [optional] - The alpha transparency value of the highlight color. Valid values are 0 to 1. For example, .25 sets a transparency value of 25%. The default value is 1.

shadowColor:Number [optional] - The shadow color of the bevel, *0xRRGGBB*. The default value is 0x000000.

shadowAlpha:Number [optional] - The alpha transparency value of the shadow color. Valid values are 0 to 1. For example, .25 sets a transparency value of 25%. The default value is 1.

blurX:Number [optional] - The amount of horizontal blur in pixels. Valid values are 0 to 255 (floating point). The default value is 4. Values that are a power of 2 (such as 2, 4, 8, 16 and 32) are optimized to render more quickly than other values.

blurY:Number [optional] - The amount of vertical blur in pixels. Valid values are 0 to 255 (floating point). The default value is 4. Values that are a power of 2 (such as 2, 4, 8, 16 and 32) are optimized to render more quickly than other values.

strength:Number [optional] - The strength of the imprint or spread. The larger the value, the more color is imprinted and the stronger the contrast between the bevel and the background. Valid values are 0 to 255. The default value is 1.

quality:Number [optional] - The number of times to apply the filter. The default value is 1, which is equivalent to low quality. A value of 2 is medium quality, and a value of 3 is high quality.

type:String [optional] - The type of bevel. Valid values are "inner", "outer", and "full". The default value is "inner".

knockout:Boolean [optional] - Applies a knockout effect (true), which effectively makes the object's fill transparent and reveals the background color of the document. The default value is false (no knockout).

Example

The following example instantiates a new BevelFilter and applies it to the MovieClip instance (rect):

```
import flash.filters.BevelFilter;

var distance:Number = 5;
var angleInDegrees:Number = 45;
var highlightColor:Number = 0xFFFF00;
var highlightAlpha:Number = .8;
var shadowColor:Number = 0x0000FF;
var shadowAlpha:Number = .8;
var blurX:Number = 5;
var blurY:Number = 5;
var strength:Number = 5;
var quality:Number = 3;
var type:String = "inner";
var knockout:Boolean = false;

var filter:BevelFilter = new BevelFilter(distance,
                         angleInDegrees,
                         highlightColor,
                         highlightAlpha,
                         shadowColor,
                         shadowAlpha,
                         blurX,
                         blurY,
                         strength,
                         quality,
                         type,
                         knockout);

var rect:MovieClip = createRectangle(100, 100, 0x00CC00,
   "bevelFilterExample");
rect.filters = new Array(filter);

function createRectangle(w:Number, h:Number, bgColor:Number,
   name:String):MovieClip {
   var rect:MovieClip = this.createEmptyMovieClip(name,
   this.getNextHighestDepth());
   rect.beginFill(bgColor);
   rect.lineTo(w, 0);
```

```
    rect.lineTo(w, h);
    rect.lineTo(0, h);
    rect.lineTo(0, 0);
    rect._x = 20;
    rect._y = 20;
    return rect;
}
```

blurX (BevelFilter.blurX property)

```
public blurX : Number
```

The amount of horizontal blur in pixels. Valid values are from 0 to 255 (floating point). The default value is 4. Values that are a power of 2 (such as 2, 4, 8, 16, and 32) are optimized to render more quickly than other values.

Availability: ActionScript 1.0; Flash Player 8

Example

The following example changes the blurX property on the existing MovieClip instance (rect) when a user clicks it:

```
import flash.filters.BevelFilter;

var rect:MovieClip = createBevelRectangle("BevelBlurX");
rect.onRelease = function() {
  var filter:BevelFilter = this.filters[0];
  filter.blurX = 10;
  this.filters = new Array(filter);
}

function createBevelRectangle(name:String):MovieClip {
  var w:Number = 100;
  var h:Number = 100;
  var bgColor:Number = 0x00CC00;

  var rect:MovieClip = this.createEmptyMovieClip(name,
  this.getNextHighestDepth());
  rect.beginFill(bgColor);
  rect.lineTo(w, 0);
  rect.lineTo(w, h);
  rect.lineTo(0, h);
  rect.lineTo(0, 0);
  rect._x = 20;
  rect._y = 20;
```

```
var filter:BevelFilter = new BevelFilter(5, 45, 0xFFFF00, .8, 0x0000FF,
.8, 20, 20, 1, 3, "inner", false);
rect.filters = new Array(filter);
return rect;
}
```

blurY (BevelFilter.blurY property)

```
public blurY : Number
```

The amount of vertical blur in pixels. Valid values are from 0 to 255 (floating point). The default value is 4. Values that are a power of 2 (such as 2, 4, 8, 16, and 32) are optimized to render more quickly than other values.

Availability: ActionScript 1.0; Flash Player 8

Example

The following example changes the blurY property on the existing MovieClip instance (rect) when a user clicks it:

```
import flash.filters.BevelFilter;

var rect:MovieClip = createBevelRectangle("BevelBlurY");
rect.onRelease = function() {
  var filter:BevelFilter = this.filters[0];
  filter.blurY = 10;
  this.filters = new Array(filter);
}

function createBevelRectangle(name:String):MovieClip {
  var w:Number = 100;
  var h:Number = 100;
  var bgColor:Number = 0x00CC00;

  var rect:MovieClip = this.createEmptyMovieClip(name,
  this.getNextHighestDepth());
  rect.beginFill(bgColor);
  rect.lineTo(w, 0);
  rect.lineTo(w, h);
  rect.lineTo(0, h);
  rect.lineTo(0, 0);
  rect._x = 20;
  rect._y = 20;
```

```
var filter:BevelFilter = new BevelFilter(5, 45, 0xFFFF00, .8, 0x0000FF,
.8, 20, 20, 1, 3, "inner", false);
rect.filters = new Array(filter);
return rect;
}
```

clone (BevelFilter.clone method)

```
public clone() : BevelFilter
```
Returns a copy of this filter object.

Availability: ActionScript 1.0; Flash Player 8

Returns

`flash.filters.BevelFilter` - A new BevelFilter instance with all the same properties as the original BevelFilter instance.

Example

The following example creates three BevelFilter objects and compares them. You can create the `filter_1` object by using the BevelFilter constructor. You create the `filter_2` object by setting it equal to `filter_1`. You create the `clonedFilter` by cloning `filter_1`. Notice that while `filter_2` evaluates as being equal to `filter_1`, `clonedFilter` does not, even though it contains the same values as `filter_1`.

```
import flash.filters.BevelFilter;

var filter_1:BevelFilter = new BevelFilter(5, 45, 0xFFFF00, .8, 0x0000FF,
    .8, 20, 20, 1, 3, "inner", false);
var filter_2:BevelFilter = filter_1;
var clonedFilter:BevelFilter = filter_1.clone();

trace(filter_1 == filter_2); // true
trace(filter_1 == clonedFilter); // false

for(var i in filter_1) {
   trace(">> " + i + ": " + filter_1[i]);
   // >> clone: [type Function]
   // >> type: inner
   // >> blurY: 20
   // >> blurX: 20
   // >> knockout: false
   // >> strength: 1
   // >> quality: 3
     // >> shadowAlpha: 0.8
   // >> shadowColor: 255
```

```
// >> highlightAlpha: 0.8
// >> highlightColor: 16776960
// >> angle: 45
// >> distance: 5
}

for(var i in clonedFilter) {
    trace(">> " + i + ": " + clonedFilter[i]);
    // >> clone: [type Function]
    // >> type: inner
    // >> blurY: 20
    // >> blurX: 20
    // >> knockout: false
    // >> strength: 1
    // >> quality: 3
    // >> shadowAlpha: 0.8
    // >> shadowColor: 255
    // >> highlightAlpha: 0.8
    // >> highlightColor: 16776960
    // >> angle: 45
    // >> distance: 5
}
```

To further demonstrate the relationships between `filter_1`, `filter_2`, and `clonedFilter`, the following example modifies the `knockout` property of `filter_1`. Modifying `knockout` demonstrates that the `clone()` method creates an instance based on values of the `filter_1` instead of referring to the values.

```
import flash.filters.BevelFilter;

var filter_1:BevelFilter = new BevelFilter(5, 45, 0xFFFF00, .8, 0x0000FF,
    .8, 20, 20, 1, 3, "inner", false);
var filter_2:BevelFilter = filter_1;
var clonedFilter:BevelFilter = filter_1.clone();

trace(filter_1.knockout); // false
trace(filter_2.knockout); // false
trace(clonedFilter.knockout); // false

filter_1.knockout = true;

trace(filter_1.knockout); // true
trace(filter_2.knockout); // true
trace(clonedFilter.knockout); // false
```

distance (BevelFilter.distance property)

`public distance : Number`

The offset distance of the bevel. Valid values are in pixels (floating point). The default value is 4.

Availability: ActionScript 1.0; Flash Player 8

Example

The following example changes the `distance` property on the existing MovieClip instance (`rect`) when a user clicks it:

```
import flash.filters.BevelFilter;

var rect:MovieClip = createBevelRectangle("BevelDistance");
rect.onRelease = function() {
  var filter:BevelFilter = this.filters[0];
  filter.distance = 3;
  this.filters = new Array(filter);
}

function createBevelRectangle(name:String):MovieClip {
  var w:Number = 100;
  var h:Number = 100;
  var bgColor:Number = 0x00CC00;

  var rect:MovieClip = this.createEmptyMovieClip(name,
  this.getNextHighestDepth());
  rect.beginFill(bgColor);
  rect.lineTo(w, 0);
  rect.lineTo(w, h);
  rect.lineTo(0, h);
  rect.lineTo(0, 0);
  rect._x = 20;
  rect._y = 20;

  var filter:BevelFilter = new BevelFilter(5, 45, 0xFFFF00, .8, 0x0000FF,
  .8, 20, 20, 1, 3, "inner", false);
  rect.filters = new Array(filter);
  return rect;
}
```

highlightAlpha (BevelFilter.highlightAlpha property)

`public highlightAlpha : Number`

The alpha transparency value of the highlight color. The value is specified as a normalized value from 0 to 1. For example, .25 sets a transparency value of 25%. The default value is 1.

Availability: ActionScript 1.0; Flash Player 8

Example

The following example changes the `highlightAlpha` property on the existing MovieClip instance (`rect`) when a user clicks it:

```
import flash.filters.BevelFilter;

var rect:MovieClip = createBevelRectangle("BevelHighlightAlpha");
rect.onRelease = function() {
  var filter:BevelFilter = this.filters[0];
  filter.highlightAlpha = .2;
  this.filters = new Array(filter);
}

function createBevelRectangle(name:String):MovieClip {
  var w:Number = 100;
  var h:Number = 100;
  var bgColor:Number = 0x00CC00;

  var rect:MovieClip = this.createEmptyMovieClip(name,
  this.getNextHighestDepth());
  rect.beginFill(bgColor);
  rect.lineTo(w, 0);
  rect.lineTo(w, h);
  rect.lineTo(0, h);
  rect.lineTo(0, 0);
  rect._x = 20;
  rect._y = 20;

  var filter:BevelFilter = new BevelFilter(5, 45, 0xFFFF00, .8, 0x0000FF,
  .8, 20, 20, 1, 3, "inner", false);
  rect.filters = new Array(filter);
  return rect;
}
```

highlightColor (BevelFilter.highlightColor property)

`public highlightColor : Number`

The highlight color of the bevel. Valid values are in hexadecimal format, *0xRRGGBB*. The default value is 0xFFFFFF.

Availability: ActionScript 1.0; Flash Player 8

Example

The following example changes the `highlightColor` property on the existing MovieClip instance (`rect`) when a user clicks it:

```
import flash.filters.BevelFilter;

var rect:MovieClip = createBevelRectangle("BevelHighlightColor");
rect.onRelease = function() {
  var filter:BevelFilter = this.filters[0];
  filter.highlightColor = 0x0000FF;
  this.filters = new Array(filter);
}

function createBevelRectangle(name:String):MovieClip {
  var w:Number = 100;
  var h:Number = 100;
  var bgColor:Number = 0x00CC00;

  var rect:MovieClip = this.createEmptyMovieClip(name,
  this.getNextHighestDepth());
  rect.beginFill(bgColor);
  rect.lineTo(w, 0);
  rect.lineTo(w, h);
  rect.lineTo(0, h);
  rect.lineTo(0, 0);
  rect._x = 20;
  rect._y = 20;

  var filter:BevelFilter = new BevelFilter(5, 45, 0xFFFF00, .8, 0x0000FF,
  .8, 20, 20, 1, 3, "inner", false);
  rect.filters = new Array(filter);
  return rect;
}
```

knockout (BevelFilter.knockout property)

```
public knockout : Boolean
```

Applies a knockout effect (true), which effectively makes the object's fill transparent and reveals the background color of the document. The default value is false (no knockout).

Availability: ActionScript 1.0; Flash Player 8

Example

The following example changes the knockout property on the existing MovieClip instance (rect) when a user clicks it:

```
import flash.filters.BevelFilter;

var rect:MovieClip = createBevelRectangle("BevelKnockout");
rect.onRelease = function() {
  var filter:BevelFilter = this.filters[0];
  filter.knockout = true;
  this.filters = new Array(filter);
}

function createBevelRectangle(name:String):MovieClip {
  var w:Number = 100;
  var h:Number = 100;
  var bgColor:Number = 0x00CC00;

  var rect:MovieClip = this.createEmptyMovieClip(name,
  this.getNextHighestDepth());
  rect.beginFill(bgColor);
  rect.lineTo(w, 0);
  rect.lineTo(w, h);
  rect.lineTo(0, h);
  rect.lineTo(0, 0);
  rect._x = 20;
  rect._y = 20;

  var filter:BevelFilter = new BevelFilter(5, 45, 0xFFFF00, .8, 0x0000FF,
  .8, 20, 20, 1, 3, "inner", false);
  rect.filters = new Array(filter);
  return rect;
}
```

quality (BevelFilter.quality property)

`public quality : Number`

The number of times to apply the filter. The default value is 1, which is equivalent to low quality. A value of 2 is medium quality, and a value of 3 is high quality. Filters with lower values are rendered more quickly.

For most applications, a `quality` value of 1, 2, or 3 is sufficient. Although you can use additional numeric values up to 15 to achieve different effects, larger values are rendered more slowly. Instead of increasing the value of `quality`, you can often get a similar effect, and with faster rendering, by simply increasing the values of `blurX` and `blurY`.

Availability: ActionScript 1.0; Flash Player 8

Example

The following example changes the `quality` property on the existing MovieClip instance (`rect`) when a user clicks it:

```
import flash.filters.BevelFilter;

var rect:MovieClip = createBevelRectangle("BevelQuality");
rect.onRelease = function() {
  var filter:BevelFilter = this.filters[0];
  filter.quality = 1;
  this.filters = new Array(filter);
}

function createBevelRectangle(name:String):MovieClip {
  var w:Number = 100;
  var h:Number = 100;
  var bgColor:Number = 0x00CC00;

  var rect:MovieClip = this.createEmptyMovieClip(name,
  this.getNextHighestDepth());
  rect.beginFill(bgColor);
  rect.lineTo(w, 0);
  rect.lineTo(w, h);
  rect.lineTo(0, h);
  rect.lineTo(0, 0);
  rect._x = 20;
  rect._y = 20;

  var filter:BevelFilter = new BevelFilter(5, 45, 0xFFFF00, .8, 0x0000FF,
  .8, 20, 20, 1, 3, "inner", false);
  rect.filters = new Array(filter);
  return rect;
}
```

shadowAlpha (BevelFilter.shadowAlpha property)

```
public shadowAlpha : Number
```

The alpha transparency value of the shadow color. This value is specified as a normalized value from 0 to 1. For example, .25 sets a transparency value of 25%. The default value is 1.

Availability: ActionScript 1.0; Flash Player 8

Example

The following example changes the shadowAlpha property on the existing MovieClip instance (rect) when a user clicks it:

```
import flash.filters.BevelFilter;

var rect:MovieClip = createBevelRectangle("BevelShadowAlpha");
rect.onRelease = function() {
  var filter:BevelFilter = this.filters[0];
  filter.shadowAlpha = .2;
  this.filters = new Array(filter);
}

function createBevelRectangle(name:String):MovieClip {
  var w:Number = 100;
  var h:Number = 100;
  var bgColor:Number = 0x00CC00;

  var rect:MovieClip = this.createEmptyMovieClip(name,
  this.getNextHighestDepth());
  rect.beginFill(bgColor);
  rect.lineTo(w, 0);
  rect.lineTo(w, h);
  rect.lineTo(0, h);
  rect.lineTo(0, 0);
  rect._x = 20;
  rect._y = 20;

  var filter:BevelFilter = new BevelFilter(5, 45, 0xFFFF00, .8, 0x0000FF,
  .8, 20, 20, 1, 3, "inner", false);
  rect.filters = new Array(filter);
  return rect;
}
```

shadowColor (BevelFilter.shadowColor property)

`public shadowColor : Number`

The shadow color of the bevel. Valid values are in hexadecimal format, *0xRRGGBB*. The default value is 0x000000.

Availability: ActionScript 1.0; Flash Player 8

Example

The following example changes the `shadowColor` property on the existing MovieClip instance (`rect`) when a user clicks it:

```
import flash.filters.BevelFilter;

var rect:MovieClip = createBevelRectangle("BevelShadowColor");
rect.onRelease = function() {
  var filter:BevelFilter = this.filters[0];
  filter.shadowColor = 0xFFFF00;
  this.filters = new Array(filter);
}

function createBevelRectangle(name:String):MovieClip {
  var w:Number = 100;
  var h:Number = 100;
  var bgColor:Number = 0x00CC00;

  var rect:MovieClip = this.createEmptyMovieClip(name,
  this.getNextHighestDepth());
  rect.beginFill(bgColor);
  rect.lineTo(w, 0);
  rect.lineTo(w, h);
  rect.lineTo(0, h);
  rect.lineTo(0, 0);
  rect._x = 20;
  rect._y = 20;

  var filter:BevelFilter = new BevelFilter(5, 45, 0xFFFF00, .8, 0x0000FF,
  .8, 20, 20, 1, 3, "inner", false);
  rect.filters = new Array(filter);
  return rect;
}
```

strength (BevelFilter.strength property)

```
public strength : Number
```

The strength of the imprint or spread. Valid values are from 0 to 255. The larger the value, the more color is imprinted and the stronger the contrast between the bevel and the background. The default value is 1.

Availability: ActionScript 1.0; Flash Player 8

Example

The following example changes the strength property on the existing MovieClip instance (rect) when a user clicks it:

```
import flash.filters.BevelFilter;

var rect:MovieClip = createBevelRectangle("BevelStrength");
rect.onRelease = function() {
  var filter:BevelFilter = this.filters[0];
  filter.strength = 10;
  this.filters = new Array(filter);
}

function createBevelRectangle(name:String):MovieClip {
  var w:Number = 100;
  var h:Number = 100;
  var bgColor:Number = 0x00CC00;

  var rect:MovieClip = this.createEmptyMovieClip(name,
  this.getNextHighestDepth());
  rect.beginFill(bgColor);
  rect.lineTo(w, 0);
  rect.lineTo(w, h);
  rect.lineTo(0, h);
  rect.lineTo(0, 0);
  rect._x = 20;
  rect._y = 20;

  var filter:BevelFilter = new BevelFilter(5, 45, 0xFFFF00, .8, 0x0000FF,
  .8, 20, 20, 1, 3, "inner", false);
  rect.filters = new Array(filter);
  return rect;
}
```

type (BevelFilter.type property)

```
public type : String
```

The type of bevel. Valid values are `"inner"`, `"outer"`, and `"full"`.

Availability: ActionScript 1.0; Flash Player 8

Example

The following example changes the `type` property on the existing MovieClip instance (`rect`) when a user clicks it:

```
import flash.filters.BevelFilter;

var rect:MovieClip = createBevelRectangle("BevelType");
rect.onRelease = function() {
  var filter:BevelFilter = this.filters[0];
  filter.type = "outer";
  this.filters = new Array(filter);
}

function createBevelRectangle(name:String):MovieClip {
  var w:Number = 100;
  var h:Number = 100;
  var bgColor:Number = 0x00CC00;

  var rect:MovieClip = this.createEmptyMovieClip(name,
  this.getNextHighestDepth());
  rect.beginFill(bgColor);
  rect.lineTo(w, 0);
  rect.lineTo(w, h);
  rect.lineTo(0, h);
  rect.lineTo(0, 0);
  rect._x = 20;
  rect._y = 20;

  var filter:BevelFilter = new BevelFilter(5, 45, 0xFFFF00, .8, 0x0000FF,
  .8, 20, 20, 1, 3, "inner", false);
  rect.filters = new Array(filter);
  return rect;
}
```

BitmapData (flash.display.BitmapData)

```
Object
 |
 +-flash.display.BitmapData
```

```
public class BitmapData
extends Object
```

The BitmapData class lets you create arbitrarily sized transparent or opaque bitmap images and manipulate them in various ways at runtime.

This class lets you separate bitmap rendering operations from the Flash Player internal display updating routines. By manipulating a BitmapData object directly, you can create very complex images without incurring the per-frame overhead of constantly redrawing the content from vector data.

The methods of the BitmapData class support a variety of effects that are not available through the generic filter interface.

A BitmapData object contains an array of pixel data. This data can represent either a fully opaque bitmap or a transparent bitmap that contains alpha channel data. Either type of BitmapData object is stored as a buffer of 32-bit integers. Each 32-bit integer determines the properties of a single pixel in the bitmap.

Each 32-bit integer is a combination of four 8-bit channel values (from 0 to 255) that describe the alpha transparency and the red, green, and blue (ARGB) values of the pixel.

The four channels (red, green, blue, and alpha) are represented as numbers when you use them with the `BitmapData.copyChannel()` method or the `DisplacementMapFilter.componentX` and `DisplacementMapFilter.componentY` properties, as follows:

- 1 (red)
- 2 (green)
- 4 (blue)
- 8 (alpha)

You can attach BitmapData objects to a MovieClip object by using the `MovieClip.attachBitmap()` method.

You can use a BitmapData object to fill an area in a movie clip by using the `MovieClip.beginBitmapFill()` method.

The maximum width and maximum height of a BitmapData object is 2880 pixels.

Availability: ActionScript 1.0; Flash Player 8

See also

attachBitmap (MovieClip.attachBitmap method), beginBitmapFill
(MovieClip.beginBitmapFill method)

Property summary

Modifiers	Property	Description
	height:Number [read-only]	The height of the bitmap image in pixels.
	rectangle:Rectangle [read-only]	The rectangle that defines the size and location of the bitmap image.
	transparent:Boolean [read-only]	Defines whether the bitmap image supports per-pixel transparency.
	width:Number [read-only]	The width of the bitmap image in pixels.

Properties inherited from class Object

constructor (Object.constructor property), __proto__ (Object.__proto__
property), prototype (Object.prototype property), __resolve
(Object.__resolve property)

Constructor summary

Signature	Description
BitmapData(width:Number, height:Number, [transparent:Boolean], [fillColor:Number])	Creates a BitmapData object with a specified width and height.

Method summary

Modifiers	Signature	Description
	`applyFilter(sourceBitmap:BitmapData, sourceRect:Rectangle, destPoint:Point, filter:BitmapFilter) : Number`	Takes a source image and a filter object and generates the filtered image.
	`clone() : BitmapData`	Returns a new BitmapData object that is a clone of the original instance with an exact copy of the contained bitmap.
	`colorTransform(rect:Rectangle, colorTransform:ColorTransform) : Void`	Adjusts the color values in a specified area of a bitmap image by using a ColorTransform object.
	`copyChannel(sourceBitmap:BitmapData, sourceRect:Rectangle, destPoint:Point, sourceChannel:Number, destChannel:Number) : Void`	Transfers data from one channel of another BitmapData object or the current BitmapData object into a channel of the current BitmapData object.
	`copyPixels(sourceBitmap:BitmapData, sourceRect:Rectangle, destPoint:Point, [alphaBitmap:BitmapData], [alphaPoint:Point], [mergeAlpha:Boolean]) : Void`	Provides a fast routine to perform pixel manipulation between images with no stretching, rotation, or color effects.
	`dispose() : Void`	Frees memory that is used to store the BitmapData object.
	`draw(source:Object, [matrix:Matrix], [colorTransform:ColorTransform], [blendMode:Object], [clipRect:Rectangle], [smooth:Boolean]) : Void`	Draws a source image or movie clip onto a destination image, using the Flash Player vector renderer.
	`fillRect(rect:Rectangle, color:Number) : Void`	Fills a rectangular area of pixels with a specified ARGB color.

Modifiers	Signature	Description
	`floodFill(x:Number, y:Number, color:Number) : Void`	Performs a flood fill operation on an image starting at an (x, y) coordinate and filling with a certain color.
	`generateFilterRect(sourceRect:Rectangle, filter:BitmapFilter) : Rectangle`	Determines the destination rectangle that the `applyFilter()` method call affects, given a BitmapData object, a source rectangle, and a filter object.
	`getColorBoundsRect(mask:Number, color:Number, [findColor:Boolean]) : Rectangle`	Determines a rectangular region that fully encloses all pixels of a specified color within the bitmap image.
	`getPixel(x:Number, y:Number) : Number`	Returns an integer that reresents an RGB pixel value from a BitmapData object at a specific point (x, y).
	`getPixel32(x:Number, y:Number) : Number`	Returns an ARGB color value that contains alpha channel data and RGB data.
	`hitTest(firstPoint:Point, firstAlphaThreshold:Number, secondObject:Object, [secondBitmapPoint:Point], [secondAlphaThreshold:Number]) : Boolean`	Performs pixel-level hit detection between one bitmap image and a point, rectangle or other bitmap image.
static	`loadBitmap(id:String) : BitmapData`	Returns a new BitmapData object that contains a bitmap image representation of the symbol that is identified by a specified linkage ID in the library.
	`merge(sourceBitmap:BitmapData, sourceRect:Rectangle, destPoint:Point, redMult:Number, greenMult:Number, blueMult:Number, alphaMult:Number) : Void`	Performs per-channel blending from a source image to a destination image.
	`noise(randomSeed:Number, [low:Number], [high:Number], [channelOptions:Number], [grayScale:Boolean]) : Void`	Fills an image with pixels representing random noise.

Modifiers	Signature	Description
	`paletteMap(sourceBitmap:BitmapData, sourceRect:Rectangle, destPoint:Point, [redArray:Array], [greenArray:Array], [blueArray:Array], [alphaArray:Array]) : Void`	Remaps the color channel values in an image that has up to four arrays of color palette data, one for each channel.
	`perlinNoise(baseX:Number, baseY:Number, numOctaves:Number, randomSeed:Number, stitch:Boolean, fractalNoise:Boolean, [channelOptions:Number], [grayScale:Boolean], [offsets:Object]) : Void`	Generates a Perlin noise image.
	`pixelDissolve(sourceBitmap:BitmapData, sourceRect:Rectangle, destPoint:Point, [randomSeed:Number], [numberOfPixels:Number], [fillColor:Number]) : Number`	Performs a pixel dissolve either from a source image to a destination image or by using the same image.
	`scroll(x:Number, y:Number) : Void`	Scrolls an image by a certain (x, y) pixel amount.
	`setPixel(x:Number, y:Number, color:Number) : Void`	Sets the color of a single pixel of a BitmapData object.
	`setPixel32(x:Number, y:Number, color:Number) : Void`	Sets the color and alpha transparency values of a single pixel of a BitmapData object.
	`threshold(sourceBitmap:BitmapData, sourceRect:Rectangle, destPoint:Point, operation:String, threshold:Number, [color:Number], [mask:Number], [copySource:Boolean]) : Number`	Tests pixel values in an image against a specified threshold and sets pixels that pass the test to new color values.

Methods inherited from class Object

addProperty (Object.addProperty method), hasOwnProperty
(Object.hasOwnProperty method), isPropertyEnumerable
(Object.isPropertyEnumerable method), isPrototypeOf (Object.isPrototypeOf
method), registerClass (Object.registerClass method), toString
(Object.toString method), unwatch (Object.unwatch method), valueOf
(Object.valueOf method), watch (Object.watch method)

applyFilter (BitmapData.applyFilter method)

```
public applyFilter(sourceBitmap:BitmapData, sourceRect:Rectangle,
    destPoint:Point, filter:BitmapFilter) : Number
```

Takes a source image and a filter object and generates the filtered image.

This method relies on the behavior of built-in filter objects, which have code to determine the destination rectangle that is affected by an input source rectangle.

After a filter is applied, the resulting image can be larger than the input image. For example, if you use a BlurFilter class to blur a source rectangle of (50,50,100,100) and a destination point of (10,10), the area that changes in the destination image is larger than (10,10,60,60) because of the blurring. This happens internally during the applyFilter() call.

If the sourceRect parameter of the sourceBitmapData parameter is an interior region, such as (50,50,100,100) in a 200 x 200 image, the filter uses the source pixels outside the sourceRect parameter to generate the destination rectangle.

Availability: ActionScript 1.0; Flash Player 8

Parameters

sourceBitmap:flash.display.BitmapData - The input bitmap image to use. The source image can be a different BitmapData object or it can refer to the current BitmapData instance.

sourceRect:flash.geom.Rectangle - A rectangle that defines the area of the source image to use as input.

destPoint:flash.geom.Point - The point within the destination image (the current BitmapData instance) that corresponds to the upper-left corner of the source rectangle.

filter:flash.filters.BitmapFilter - The filter object that you use to perform the filtering operation. Each type of filter has certain requirements, as follows:

■ **BlurFilter** — This filter can use source and destination images that are either opaque or transparent. If the formats of the images do not match, the copy of the source image that is made during the filtering matches the format of the destination image.

- **BevelFilter, DropShadowFilter, GlowFilter** — The destination image of these filters must be a transparent image. Calling DropShadowFilter or GlowFilter creates an image that contains the alpha channel data of the drop shadow or glow. It does not create the drop shadow onto the destination image. If you use any of these filters with an opaque destination image, an error code value of -6 is returned.

- **ConvolutionFilter** — This filter can use source and destination images that are either opaque or transparent.

- **ColorMatrixFilter** — This filter can use source and destination images that are either opaque or transparent.

- **DisplacementMapFilter** — This filter can use source and destination images that are either opaque or transparent, but the source and destination image formats must be the same.

Returns

`Number` - A number that indicates whether the filter was applied successfully. If 0 is returned, the filter was applied successfully. If a negative number is returned, an error occurred during the application of the filter.

Example

The following example shows how to apply a bevel filter to a BitmapData instance:

```
import flash.display.BitmapData;
import flash.filters.BevelFilter;
import flash.geom.Point;

var myBitmapData:BitmapData = new BitmapData(100, 80, true, 0xCCCCCCCC);

var mc:MovieClip = this.createEmptyMovieClip("mc",
  this.getNextHighestDepth());
mc.attachBitmap(myBitmapData, this.getNextHighestDepth());

var filter:BevelFilter = new BevelFilter(5, 45, 0xFFFF00, .8, 0x0000FF, .8,
  20, 20, 1, 3, "inner", false);

mc.onPress = function() {
  myBitmapData.applyFilter(myBitmapData, myBitmapData.rectangle, new
  Point(0, 0), filter);
}
```

See also

BevelFilter (flash.filters.BevelFilter), BlurFilter
(flash.filters.BlurFilter), ColorMatrixFilter
(flash.filters.ColorMatrixFilter), ConvolutionFilter
(flash.filters.ConvolutionFilter), DisplacementMapFilter
(flash.filters.DisplacementMapFilter), DropShadowFilter
(flash.filters.DropShadowFilter), GlowFilter (flash.filters.GlowFilter),
filters (MovieClip.filters property)

BitmapData constructor

public BitmapData(width:Number, height:Number, [transparent:Boolean],
  [fillColor:Number])

Creates a BitmapData object with a specified width and height. If you specify a value for the fillColor parameter, every pixel in the bitmap is set to that color.

By default, the bitmap is created as opaque, unless you pass the value true for the transparent parameter. Once you create an opaque bitmap, you cannot change it to a transparent bitmap. Every pixel in an opaque bitmap uses only 24 bits of color channel information. If you define the bitmap as transparent, every pixel uses 32 bits of color channel information, including an alpha transparency channel.

The maximum width and maximum height of a BitmapData object is 2880 pixels. If you specify a width or height value that is greater than 2880, a new instance is not created.

Availability: ActionScript 1.0; Flash Player 8

Parameters

width:Number - The width of the bitmap image in pixels.

height:Number - The height of the bitmap image in pixels.

transparent:Boolean [optional] - Specifies whether the bitmap image supports per-pixel transparency. The default value is true (transparent). To create a fully transparent bitmap set the value of the transparent parameter to true and the value of the fillColor parameter to 0x00000000 (or to 0).

fillColor:Number [optional] - A 32-bit ARGB color value that you use to fill the bitmap image area. The default value is 0xFFFFFFFF (solid white).

Example

The following example creates a new BitmapData object. The values in this example are the default values for the `transparent` and `fillColor` parameters; you could call the constructor without these parameters and get the same result.

```
import flash.display.BitmapData;

var width:Number = 100;
var height:Number = 80;
var transparent:Boolean = true;
var fillColor:Number = 0xFFFFFFFF;

var bitmap_1:BitmapData = new BitmapData(width, height, transparent,
    fillColor);

trace(bitmap_1.width); // 100
trace(bitmap_1.height); // 80
trace(bitmap_1.transparent); // true

var bitmap_2:BitmapData = new BitmapData(width, height);

trace(bitmap_2.width); // 100
trace(bitmap_2.height); // 80
trace(bitmap_2.transparent); // true
```

clone (BitmapData.clone method)

```
public clone() : BitmapData
```

Returns a new BitmapData object that is a clone of the original instance with an exact copy of the contained bitmap.

Availability: ActionScript 1.0; Flash Player 8

Returns

`flash.display.BitmapData` - A new BitmapData object that is identical to the original.

Example

The following example creates three BitmapData objects and compares them. You can create the `bitmap_1` instance by using the `BitmapData` constructor. You create the `bitmap_2` instance by setting it equal to `bitmap_1`. You create he `clonedBitmap` instance by cloning `bitmap_1`. Notice that although `bitmap_2` evaluates as being equal to `bitmap_1`, `clonedBitmap` does not, even though it contains the same values as `bitmap_1`.

```
import flash.display.BitmapData;

var bitmap_1:BitmapData = new BitmapData(100, 80, false, 0x000000);
```

```
var bitmap_2:BitmapData = bitmap_1;
var clonedBitmap:BitmapData = bitmap_1.clone();

trace(bitmap_1 == bitmap_2); // true
trace(bitmap_1 == clonedBitmap); // false

for(var i in bitmap_1) {
  trace(">> " + i + ": " + bitmap_1[i]);
  // >> generateFilterRect: [type Function]
  // >> dispose: [type Function]
  // >> clone: [type Function]
  // >> copyChannel: [type Function]
  // >> noise: [type Function]
  // >> merge: [type Function]
  // >> paletteMap: [type Function]
  // >> hitTest: [type Function]
  // >> colorTransform: [type Function]
  // >> perlinNoise: [type Function]
  // >> getColorBoundsRect: [type Function]
  // >> floodFill: [type Function]
  // >> setPixel32: [type Function]
  // >> getPixel32: [type Function]
  // >> pixelDissolve: [type Function]
  // >> draw: [type Function]
  // >> threshold: [type Function]
  // >> scroll: [type Function]
  // >> applyFilter: [type Function]
  // >> copyPixels: [type Function]
  // >> fillRect: [type Function]
  // >> setPixel: [type Function]
  // >> getPixel: [type Function]
  // >> transparent: false
  // >> rectangle: (x=0, y=0, w=100, h=80)
  // >> height: 80
  // >> width: 100
}

for(var i in clonedBitmap) {
  trace(">> " + i + ": " + clonedBitmap[i]);
  // >> generateFilterRect: [type Function]
  // >> dispose: [type Function]
  // >> clone: [type Function]
  // >> copyChannel: [type Function]
  // >> noise: [type Function]
  // >> merge: [type Function]
  // >> paletteMap: [type Function]
  // >> hitTest: [type Function]
  // >> colorTransform: [type Function]
  // >> perlinNoise: [type Function]
  // >> getColorBoundsRect: [type Function]
```

```
// >> floodFill: [type Function]
// >> setPixel32: [type Function]
// >> getPixel32: [type Function]
// >> pixelDissolve: [type Function]
// >> draw: [type Function]
// >> threshold: [type Function]
// >> scroll: [type Function]
// >> applyFilter: [type Function]
// >> copyPixels: [type Function]
// >> fillRect: [type Function]
// >> setPixel: [type Function]
// >> getPixel: [type Function]
// >> transparent: false
// >> rectangle: (x=0, y=0, w=100, h=80)
// >> height: 80
// >> width: 100
}
```

To further demonstrate the relationships between `bitmap_1`, `bitmap_2`, and `clonedBitmap` the following example modifies the pixel value at (1, 1) of `bitmap_1`. Modifying pixel value at (1, 1) demonstrates that the `clone()` method creates an instance based on values of the `bitmap_1` instance instead instead of refering to the values.

```
import flash.display.BitmapData;

var bitmap_1:BitmapData = new BitmapData(100, 80, false, 0x000000);
var bitmap_2:BitmapData = bitmap_1;
var clonedBitmap:BitmapData = bitmap_1.clone();

trace(bitmap_1.getPixel32(1, 1)); // -16777216
trace(bitmap_2.getPixel32(1, 1)); // -16777216
trace(clonedBitmap.getPixel32(1, 1)); // -16777216

bitmap_1.setPixel32(1, 1, 0xFFFFFF);

trace(bitmap_1.getPixel32(1, 1)); // -1
trace(bitmap_2.getPixel32(1, 1)); // -1
trace(clonedBitmap.getPixel32(1, 1)); // -16777216
```

colorTransform (BitmapData.colorTransform method)

```
public colorTransform(rect:Rectangle, colorTransform:ColorTransform) : Void
```
Adjusts the color values in a specified area of a bitmap image by using a ColorTransform object. If the rectangle matches the boundaries of the bitmap image, this method transforms the color values of the entire image.

Availability: ActionScript 1.0; Flash Player 8

Parameters

`rect`:`flash.geom.Rectangle` - A Rectangle object that defines the area of the image in which the ColorTransform object is applied.

`colorTransform`:`flash.geom.ColorTransform` - A ColorTransform object that describes the color transformation values to apply.

Example

The following example shows how to apply a color transform operation to a BitmapData instance.

```
import flash.display.BitmapData;
import flash.geom.ColorTransform;

var myBitmapData:BitmapData = new BitmapData(100, 80, false, 0x00CCCCCC);

var mc:MovieClip = this.createEmptyMovieClip("mc",
  this.getNextHighestDepth());
mc.attachBitmap(myBitmapData, this.getNextHighestDepth());

mc.onPress = function() {
  myBitmapData.colorTransform(myBitmapData.rectangle, new
  ColorTransform(1, 0, 0, 1, 255, 0, 0, 0));
}
```

See also

ColorTransform (flash.geom.ColorTransform), Rectangle (flash.geom.Rectangle)

copyChannel (BitmapData.copyChannel method)

```
public copyChannel(sourceBitmap:BitmapData, sourceRect:Rectangle,
  destPoint:Point, sourceChannel:Number, destChannel:Number) : Void
```

Transfers data from one channel of another BitmapData object or the current BitmapData object into a channel of the current BitmapData object. All of the data in the other channels in the destination BitmapData object are preserved.

The source channel value and destination channel value can be one of following values or a sum of any of the values:

- 1 (red)
- 2 (green)
- 4 (blue)
- 8 (alpha)

Availability: ActionScript 1.0; Flash Player 8

Parameters

`sourceBitmap:flash.display.BitmapData` - The input bitmap image to use. The source image can be a different BitmapData object or it can refer to the current BitmapData object.

`sourceRect:flash.geom.Rectangle` - The source Rectangle object. If you only want to copy channel data from a smaller area within the bitmap, specify a source rectangle that is smaller than the overall size of the BitmapData object.

`destPoint:flash.geom.Point` - The destination Point object that represents the upper-left corner of the rectangular area where the new channel data is placed. If you want to copy channel data from one area to a different area in the destination image, specify a point other than (0,0).

`sourceChannel:Number` - The source channel. Use a value from the set (1,2,4,8), which represent red, green, blue, and alpha channels, respectively, or a sum of any of the values.

`destChannel:Number` - The destination channel. Use a value from the set (1,2,4,8), which represent red, green, blue, and alpha channels, respectively, or a sum of any of the values.

Example

The following example shows how to copy a source ARGB channel from a `BitmapData` object back onto itself at a different location:

```
import flash.display.BitmapData;
import flash.geom.Rectangle;
import flash.geom.Point;

var myBitmapData:BitmapData = new BitmapData(100, 80, false, 0x00CCCCCC);

var mc:MovieClip = this.createEmptyMovieClip("mc",
  this.getNextHighestDepth());
mc.attachBitmap(myBitmapData, this.getNextHighestDepth());

mc.onPress = function() {
  myBitmapData.copyChannel(myBitmapData, new Rectangle(0, 0, 50, 80), new
  Point(51, 0), 3, 1);
}
```

See also

`Rectangle (flash.geom.Rectangle)`

copyPixels (BitmapData.copyPixels method)

```
public copyPixels(sourceBitmap:BitmapData, sourceRect:Rectangle,
    destPoint:Point, [alphaBitmap:BitmapData], [alphaPoint:Point],
    [mergeAlpha:Boolean]) : Void
```

Provides a fast routine to perform pixel manipulation between images with no stretching, rotation, or color effects. This method copies a rectangular area of a source image to a rectangular area of the same size at the destination point of the destination BitmapData object.

If include the `alphaBitmap` and `alphaPoint` parameters, you can use a secondary image as an alpha source for the source image. If the source image has alpha data, both sets of alpha data are used to composite pixels from the source image to the destination image. The `alphaPoint` parameter is the point in the alpha image that corresponds to the upper-left corner of the source rectangle. Any pixels outside the intersection of the source image and alpha image are not copied to the destination image.

The `mergeAlpha` property controls whether or not the alpha channel is used when a transparent image is copied onto another transparent image. To simply copy pixels (with no alpha used), set the `mergeAlpha` property to `false`. Then all pixels are copied from source to destination. By default, the `mergeAlpha` property is `true`.

Availability: ActionScript 1.0; Flash Player 8

Parameters

`sourceBitmap:flash.display.BitmapData` - The input bitmap image from which to copy pixels. The source image can be a different BitmapData instance, or it can refer to the current BitmapData instance.

`sourceRect:flash.geom.Rectangle` - A rectangle that defines the area of the source image to use as input.

`destPoint:flash.geom.Point` - The destination point, that represents the upper-left corner of the rectangular area where the new pixels are placed.

`alphaBitmap:flash.display.BitmapData` [optional] - A secondary, alpha BitmapData object source.

`alphaPoint:flash.geom.Point` [optional] - The point in the alpha BitmapData object source that corresponds to the upper-left corner of the `sourceRect` parameter.

`mergeAlpha:Boolean` [optional] - A Boolean value:To use the alpha channel, set the value to `true`. To copy pixels with no alpha channel, set the value to `false`.

Example

The following example shows how to copy pixels from one BitmapData instance to another.

```
import flash.display.BitmapData;
import flash.geom.Rectangle;
import flash.geom.Point;

var bitmapData_1:BitmapData = new BitmapData(100, 80, false, 0x00CCCCCC);
var bitmapData_2:BitmapData = new BitmapData(100, 80, false, 0x00FF0000);

var mc_1:MovieClip = this.createEmptyMovieClip("mc",
    this.getNextHighestDepth());
mc_1.attachBitmap(bitmapData_1, this.getNextHighestDepth());

var mc_2:MovieClip = this.createEmptyMovieClip("mc",
    this.getNextHighestDepth());
mc_2.attachBitmap(bitmapData_2, this.getNextHighestDepth());
mc_2._x = 101;

mc_1.onPress = function() {
   bitmapData_2.copyPixels(bitmapData_1, new Rectangle(0, 0, 50, 80), new
   Point(51, 0));
}

mc_2.onPress = function() {
   bitmapData_1.copyPixels(bitmapData_2, new Rectangle(0, 0, 50, 80), new
   Point(51, 0));
}
```

dispose (BitmapData.dispose method)

```
public dispose() : Void
```

Frees memory that is used to store the BitmapData object.

When this method is called on an image, the width and height of the image are set to 0. After a BitmapData object's memory has been freed, method and property access calls on the instance fail, returning a value of -1.

Availability: ActionScript 1.0; Flash Player 8

Example

The following example shows how to release the memory of a BitmapData instance, which results in a cleared instance.

```
import flash.display.BitmapData;

var myBitmapData:BitmapData = new BitmapData(100, 80, false, 0x00CCCCCC);
```

```
var mc:MovieClip = this.createEmptyMovieClip("mc",
   this.getNextHighestDepth());
mc.attachBitmap(myBitmapData, this.getNextHighestDepth());

mc.onPress = function() {
   myBitmapData.dispose();

   trace(myBitmapData.width); // -1
   trace(myBitmapData.height); // -1
   trace(myBitmapData.transparent); // -1
}
```

draw (BitmapData.draw method)

```
public draw(source:Object, [matrix:Matrix],
   [colorTransform:ColorTransform], [blendMode:Object],
   [clipRect:Rectangle], [smooth:Boolean]) : Void
```

Draws a source image or movie clip onto a destination image, using the Flash Player vector renderer. You can use Matrix, ColorTransform, BlendMode objects, and a destination Rectangle object to control how the rendering performs. Optionally, you can specify whether the bitmap should be smoothed when scaled. This works only if the source object is a BitmapData object.

This method directly corresponds to how objects are drawn using the standard vector renderer for objects in the authoring tool interface.

A source MovieClip object does not use any of its on-stage transformations for this call. It is treated as it exists in the library or file, with no matrix transform, no color transform, and no blend mode. If you want to draw the movie clip by using its own transform properties, you can use its Transform object to pass the various transformation properties.

Availability: ActionScript 1.0; Flash Player 8

Parameters

`source:Object` - The BitmapData object to draw.

`matrix:flash.geom.Matrix` [optional] - A Matrix object used to scale, rotate, or translate the coordinates of the bitmap. If no object is supplied, the bitmap image will not be transformed. Set this parameter to an identity matrix, created using the default `new Matrix()` constructor, if you must pass this parameter but you do not want to transform the image.

colorTransform:flash.geom.ColorTransform [optional] - A ColorTransform object that you use to adjust the color values of the bitmap. If no object is supplied, the bitmap image's colors will not be transformed. Set this parameter to a ColorTransform object created using the default new ColorTransform() constructor, if you must pass this parameter but you do not want to transform the image.

blendMode:Object [optional] - A BlendMode object.

clipRect:flash.geom.Rectangle [optional] - A Rectangle object. If you do not supply this value, no clipping occurs.

smooth:Boolean [optional] - A Boolean value that determines whether a BitmapData object is smoothed when scaled. The default value is false.

Example

The following example shows how to draw from a source MovieClip instance to a BitmapData object.

```
import flash.display.BitmapData;
import flash.geom.Rectangle;
import flash.geom.Matrix;
import flash.geom.ColorTransform;

var myBitmapData:BitmapData = new BitmapData(100, 80, false, 0x00CCCCCC);

var mc_1:MovieClip = this.createEmptyMovieClip("mc",
   this.getNextHighestDepth());
mc_1.attachBitmap(myBitmapData, this.getNextHighestDepth());

var mc_2:MovieClip = createRectangle(50, 40, 0xFF0000);
mc_2._x = 101;

var myMatrix:Matrix = new Matrix();
myMatrix.rotate(Math.PI/2);

var translateMatrix:Matrix = new Matrix();
translateMatrix.translate(70, 15);

myMatrix.concat(translateMatrix);

var myColorTransform:ColorTransform = new ColorTransform(0, 0, 1, 1, 0, 0,
   255, 0);
var blendMode:String = "normal";

var myRectangle:Rectangle = new Rectangle(0, 0, 100, 80);
var smooth:Boolean = true;
```

```
mc_1.onPress = function() {
  myBitmapData.draw(mc_2, myMatrix, myColorTransform, blendMode,
  myRectangle, smooth);
}

function createRectangle(width:Number, height:Number,
  color:Number):MovieClip {
  var depth:Number = this.getNextHighestDepth();
  var mc:MovieClip = this.createEmptyMovieClip("mc_" + depth, depth);
  mc.beginFill(color);
  mc.lineTo(0, height);
  mc.lineTo(width, height);
  mc.lineTo(width, 0);
  mc.lineTo(0, 0);
  return mc;
}
```

fillRect (BitmapData.fillRect method)

```
public fillRect(rect:Rectangle, color:Number) : Void
```
Fills a rectangular area of pixels with a specified ARGB color.

Availability: ActionScript 1.0; Flash Player 8

Parameters

`rect:flash.geom.Rectangle` - The rectangular area to fill.

`color:Number` - The ARGB color value that fills the area. ARGB colors are often specified in hexadecimal format; for example, 0xFF336699.

Example

The following example shows how to fill an area that is defined by a `Rectangle` within a `BitmapData` with a color.

```
import flash.display.BitmapData;
import flash.geom.Rectangle;

var myBitmapData:BitmapData = new BitmapData(100, 80, false, 0x00CCCCCC);

var mc:MovieClip = this.createEmptyMovieClip("mc",
  this.getNextHighestDepth());
mc.attachBitmap(myBitmapData, this.getNextHighestDepth());

mc.onPress = function() {
  myBitmapData.fillRect(new Rectangle(0, 0, 50, 40), 0x00FF0000);
}
```

See also

Rectangle (flash.geom.Rectangle)

floodFill (BitmapData.floodFill method)

```
public floodFill(x:Number, y:Number, color:Number) : Void
```

Performs a flood fill operation on an image starting at an (*x*, *y*) coordinate and filling with a certain color. The `floodFill()` method is similar to the paint bucket tool in various painting programs. The color is an ARGB color that contains alpha information and color information.

Availability: ActionScript 1.0; Flash Player 8

Parameters

`x:Number` - The *x* coordinate of the image.

`y:Number` - The *y* coordinate of the image.

`color:Number` - The ARGB color to use as a fill. ARGB colors are often specified in hexadecimal format, like 0xFF336699.

Example

The following example shows how to apply a flood fill a color into to an image starting at the point where a user clicks the mouse within a BitmapData object.

```
import flash.display.BitmapData;
import flash.geom.Rectangle;

var myBitmapData:BitmapData = new BitmapData(100, 80, false, 0x00CCCCCC);

var mc:MovieClip = this.createEmptyMovieClip("mc",
  this.getNextHighestDepth());
mc.attachBitmap(myBitmapData, this.getNextHighestDepth());

myBitmapData.fillRect(new Rectangle(0, 0, 50, 40), 0x00FF0000);

mc.onPress = function() {
  myBitmapData.floodFill(_xmouse, _ymouse, 0x000000FF);
}
```

generateFilterRect (BitmapData.generateFilterRect method)

```
public generateFilterRect(sourceRect:Rectangle, filter:BitmapFilter) :
  Rectangle
```

Determines the destination rectangle that the `applyFilter()` method call affects, given a BitmapData object, a source rectangle, and a filter object.

For example, a blur filter normally affects an area larger than the size of the original image. A 100 x 200 pixel image that is being filtered by a default BlurFilter instance, where `blurX` = `blurY` = 4 generates a destination rectangle of (`-2,-2,104,204`). The `generateFilterRect()` method lets you find out the size of this destination rectangle in advance so that you can size the destination image appropriately before performing a filter operation.

Some filters clip their destination rectangle based on the source image size. For example, an inner `DropShadow` does not generate a larger result than its source image. In this API, the BitmapData object is used as the source bounds and not the source `rect` parameter.

Availability: ActionScript 1.0; Flash Player 8

Parameters

`sourceRect:flash.geom.Rectangle` - A rectangle defining the area of the source image to use as input.

`filter:flash.filters.BitmapFilter` - A filter object that you use to calculate the destination rectangle.

Returns

`flash.geom.Rectangle` - A destination rectangle computed by using an image, the `sourceRect` parameter, and a filter.

Example

The following example shows how to determine the destination rectangle that the `applyfilter()` method affects:

```
import flash.display.BitmapData;
import flash.filters.BevelFilter;
import flash.geom.Rectangle;

var myBitmapData:BitmapData = new BitmapData(100, 80, true, 0xCCCCCCCC);

var filter:BevelFilter = new BevelFilter(5, 45, 0xFFFF00, .8, 0x0000FF, .8,
  20, 20, 1, 3, "outer", false);
```

```
var filterRect:Rectangle =
  myBitmapData.generateFilterRect(myBitmapData.rectangle, filter);

trace(filterRect); // (x=-31, y=-31, w=162, h=142)
```

getColorBoundsRect (BitmapData.getColorBoundsRect method)

```
public getColorBoundsRect(mask:Number, color:Number, [findColor:Boolean]) :
  Rectangle
```

Determines a rectangular region that fully encloses all pixels of a specified color within the bitmap image.

For example, if you have a source image and you want to determine the rectangle of the image that contains a nonzero alpha channel, you pass {mask: 0xFF000000, color: 0x00000000} as parameters. The entire image is searched for the bounds of pixels whose (value & mask) != color. To determine white space around an image, you pass {mask: 0xFFFFFFFF, color: 0xFFFFFFFF} to find the bounds of nonwhite pixels.

Availability: ActionScript 1.0; Flash Player 8

Parameters

mask:Number - A hexadecimal color value.

color:Number - A hexadecimal color value.

findColor:Boolean [optional] - If the value is set to true, returns the bounds of a color value in an image. If the value is set to false, returns the bounds of where this color doesn't exist in an image. The default value is true.

Returns

flash.geom.Rectangle - The region of the image that is the specified color.

Example

The following example shows how to determine a rectangular region that fully encloses all pixels of a specified color within the bitmap image:

```
import flash.display.BitmapData;
import flash.geom.Rectangle;

var myBitmapData:BitmapData = new BitmapData(100, 80, false, 0x00CCCCCC);

var mc:MovieClip = this.createEmptyMovieClip("mc",
  this.getNextHighestDepth());
```

```
mc.attachBitmap(myBitmapData, this.getNextHighestDepth());
myBitmapData.fillRect(new Rectangle(0, 0, 50, 40), 0x00FF0000);

mc.onPress = function() {
  var colorBoundsRect:Rectangle =
  myBitmapData.getColorBoundsRect(0x00FFFFFF, 0x00FF0000, true);
  trace(colorBoundsRect); // (x=0, y=0, w=50, h=40)
}
```

getPixel (BitmapData.getPixel method)

```
public getPixel(x:Number, y:Number) : Number
```

Returns an integer that reresents an RGB pixel value from a BitmapData object at a specific point (*x*, *y*). The getPixel() method returns an unmultiplied pixel value. No alpha information is returned.

All pixels in a BitmapData object are stored as premultiplied color values. A premultiplied image pixel has the red, green, and blue color channel values already multiplied by the alpha data. For example, if the alpha value is 0, the values for the RGB channels are also 0, independent of their unmultiplied values.

This loss of data can cause some problems when you are performing operations. All Flash Player methods take and return unmultiplied values. The internal pixel representation is unmultiplied before it is returned as a value. During a set operation, the pixel value is premultiplied before setting the raw image pixel.

Availability: ActionScript 1.0; Flash Player 8

Parameters

x:Number - The *x* position of the pixel.

y:Number - The *y* position of the pixel.

Returns

Number - A number that represents an RGB pixel value. If the (*x*, *y*) coordinates are outside the bounds of the image, 0 is returned.

Example

The following example uses the getPixel() method to retrieve the RGB value of a pixel at a specific *x* and *y* position.

```
import flash.display.BitmapData;

var myBitmapData:BitmapData = new BitmapData(100, 80, false, 0x00CCCCCC);
```

```
var mc:MovieClip = this.createEmptyMovieClip("mc",
  this.getNextHighestDepth());
mc.attachBitmap(myBitmapData, this.getNextHighestDepth());
trace("0x" + myBitmapData.getPixel(0, 0).toString(16)); // 0xcccccc
```

See also

getPixel32 (BitmapData.getPixel32 method)

getPixel32 (BitmapData.getPixel32 method)

`public getPixel32(x:Number, y:Number) : Number`

Returns an ARGB color value that contains alpha channel data and RGB data. This method is similar to the getPixel() method, which returns an RGB color without alpha channel data.

Availability: ActionScript 1.0; Flash Player 8

Parameters

x:Number - The *x* position of the pixel.

y:Number - The *y* position of the pixel.

Returns

Number - A number that represent an ARGB pixel value. If the (*x, y*) coordinates are outside the bounds of the image, 0 is returned. If the bitmap was created as an opaque bitmap and not a transparent one, then this method will return an error code of -1.

Example

The following example uses the getPixel32() method to retrieve the ARGB value of a pixel at a specific *x* and *y* position:

```
import flash.display.BitmapData;

var myBitmapData:BitmapData = new BitmapData(100, 80, true, 0xFFAACCEE);

var mc:MovieClip = this.createEmptyMovieClip("mc",
  this.getNextHighestDepth());
mc.attachBitmap(myBitmapData, this.getNextHighestDepth());

var alpha:String = (myBitmapData.getPixel32(0, 0) >> 24 &
  0xFF).toString(16);
trace(">> alpha: " + alpha); // ff

var red:String = (myBitmapData.getPixel32(0, 0) >> 16 & 0xFF).toString(16);
trace(">> red: " + red); // aa
```

```
var green:String = (myBitmapData.getPixel32(0, 0) >> 8 &
  0xFF).toString(16);
trace(">> green: " + green); // cc

var blue:String = (myBitmapData.getPixel32(0, 0) & 0xFF).toString(16);
trace(">> blue: " + blue); // ee

trace("0x" + alpha + red + green + blue); // 0xffaaccee
```

See also

```
getPixel (BitmapData.getPixel method)
```

height (BitmapData.height property)

```
public height : Number [read-only]
```

The height of the bitmap image in pixels.

Availability: ActionScript 1.0; Flash Player 8

Example

The following example shows that the height property of the BitmapData instance is read-only by trying to set it and failing:

```
import flash.display.BitmapData;

var myBitmapData:BitmapData = new BitmapData(100, 80, false, 0x00CCCCCC);

var mc:MovieClip = this.createEmptyMovieClip("mc",
  this.getNextHighestDepth());
mc.attachBitmap(myBitmapData, this.getNextHighestDepth());
trace(myBitmapData.height); // 80

myBitmapData.height = 999;
trace(myBitmapData.height); // 80
```

hitTest (BitmapData.hitTest method)

```
public hitTest(firstPoint:Point, firstAlphaThreshold:Number,
  secondObject:Object, [secondBitmapPoint:Point],
  [secondAlphaThreshold:Number]) : Boolean
```

Performs pixel-level hit detection between one bitmap image and a point, rectangle or other bitmap image. No stretching, rotation, or other transformation of either object is considered when doing the hit test.

If an image is an opaque image, it is considered a fully opaque rectangle for this method. Both images must be transparent images to perform pixel-level hit testing that considers transparency. When you are testing two transparent images, the alpha threshold parameters control what alpha channel values, from 0 to 255, are considered opaque.

Availability: ActionScript 1.0; Flash Player 8

Parameters

`firstPoint:flash.geom.Point` - A point that defines a pixel location in the current BitmapData instance.

`firstAlphaThreshold:Number` - The highest alpha channel value that is considered opaque for this hit test.

`secondObject:Object` - A Rectangle, Point, or BitmapData object.

`secondBitmapPoint:flash.geom.Point` [optional] - A point that defines a pixel location in the second BitmapData object. Use this parameter only when the value of `secondObject` is a BitmapData object.

`secondAlphaThreshold:Number` [optional] - The highest alpha channel value that is considered opaque in the second BitmapData object. Use this parameter only when the value of `secondObject` is a BitmapData object and both BitmapData objects are transparent.

Returns

`Boolean` - A Boolean value. If there is a hit, returns a value of `true`; otherwise, `false`.

Example

The following example shows how to determine if a BitmapData object is colliding with a `MovieClip`.

```
import flash.display.BitmapData;
import flash.geom.Point;

var myBitmapData:BitmapData = new BitmapData(100, 80, false, 0x00CCCCCC);

var mc_1:MovieClip = this.createEmptyMovieClip("mc",
  this.getNextHighestDepth());
mc_1.attachBitmap(myBitmapData, this.getNextHighestDepth());

var mc_2:MovieClip = createRectangle(20, 20, 0xFF0000);

var destPoint:Point = new Point(myBitmapData.rectangle.x,
  myBitmapData.rectangle.y);
var currPoint:Point = new Point();

mc_1.onEnterFrame = function() {
```

```
    currPoint.x = mc_2._x;
    currPoint.y = mc_2._y;
    if(myBitmapData.hitTest(destPoint, 255, currPoint)) {
      trace(">> Collision at x:" + currPoint.x + " and y:" + currPoint.y);
    }
}

mc_2.startDrag(true);

function createRectangle(width:Number, height:Number,
  color:Number):MovieClip {
  var depth:Number = this.getNextHighestDepth();
  var mc:MovieClip = this.createEmptyMovieClip("mc_" + depth, depth);
  mc.beginFill(color);
  mc.lineTo(0, height);
  mc.lineTo(width, height);
  mc.lineTo(width, 0);
  mc.lineTo(0, 0);
  return mc;
}
```

loadBitmap (BitmapData.loadBitmap method)

`public static loadBitmap(id:String) : BitmapData`

Returns a new BitmapData object that contains a bitmap image representation of the symbol that is identified by a specified linkage ID in the library.

Availability: ActionScript 1.0; Flash Player 8

Parameters

`id:String` - A linkage ID of a symbol in the library.

Returns

`flash.display.BitmapData` - A bitmap image representation of the symbol.

Example

The following example loads a bitmap with the linkageId `libraryBitmap` from your library. You must attach it to a `MovieClip` object to give it a visual representation.

```
import flash.display.BitmapData;

var linkageId:String = "libraryBitmap";
var myBitmapData:BitmapData = BitmapData.loadBitmap(linkageId);
trace(myBitmapData instanceof BitmapData); // true
```

```
var mc:MovieClip = this.createEmptyMovieClip("mc",
  this.getNextHighestDepth());
mc.attachBitmap(myBitmapData, this.getNextHighestDepth());
```

merge (BitmapData.merge method)

```
public merge(sourceBitmap:BitmapData, sourceRect:Rectangle,
  destPoint:Point, redMult:Number, greenMult:Number, blueMult:Number,
  alphaMult:Number) : Void
```

Performs per-channel blending from a source image to a destination image. The following formula is used for each channel:

```
new red dest = (red source * redMult) + (red dest * (256 - redMult) / 256;
```

The redMult, greenMult, blueMult, and alphaMult values are the multipliers used for each color channel. Their valid range is from 0 to 256.

Availability: ActionScript 1.0; Flash Player 8

Parameters

sourceBitmap:flash.display.BitmapData - The input bitmap image to use. The source image can be a different BitmapData object, or it can refer to the current BitmapData object.

sourceRect:flash.geom.Rectangle - A rectangle that defines the area of the source image to use as input.

destPoint:flash.geom.Point - The point within the destination image (the current BitmapData instance) that corresponds to the upper-left corner of the source rectangle.

redMult:Number - A number by which to multiply the red channel value.

greenMult:Number - A number by which to multiply the green channel value.

blueMult:Number - A number by which to multiply the blue channel value.

alphaMult:Number - A number by which to multiply the alpha transparency value.

Example

The following example shows how to merge part of one BitmapData with another.

```
import flash.display.BitmapData;
import flash.geom.Rectangle;
import flash.geom.Point;

var bitmapData_1:BitmapData = new BitmapData(100, 80, false, 0x00CCCCCC);
var bitmapData_2:BitmapData = new BitmapData(100, 80, false, 0x00FF0000);

var mc_1:MovieClip = this.createEmptyMovieClip("mc",
  this.getNextHighestDepth());
mc_1.attachBitmap(bitmapData_1, this.getNextHighestDepth());
```

```
var mc_2:MovieClip = this.createEmptyMovieClip("mc",
    this.getNextHighestDepth());
mc_2.attachBitmap(bitmapData_2, this.getNextHighestDepth());
mc_2._x = 101;

mc_1.onPress = function() {
    bitmapData_1.merge(bitmapData_2, new Rectangle(0, 0, 50, 40), new
    Point(25, 20), 128, 0, 0, 0);
}
```

noise (BitmapData.noise method)

```
public noise(randomSeed:Number, [low:Number], [high:Number],
    [channelOptions:Number], [grayScale:Boolean]) : Void
```

Fills an image with pixels representing random noise.

Availability: ActionScript 1.0; Flash Player 8

Parameters

randomSeed:Number - The random seed to use.

low:Number [optional] - The lowest value to generate for each channel (0 to 255). The default is 0.

high:Number [optional] - The highest value to generate for each channel (0 to 255). The default is 255.

channelOptions:Number [optional] - A number that can be a combination of any of the four color channel values: 1 (red), 2 (green), 4 (blue), and 8(alpha). You can use the logical OR operator | to combine channel values. The default value is (1 | 2 | 4).

grayScale:Boolean [optional] - A Boolean value. If the value is true, a grayscale image is created by setting all of the color channels to the same value. The alpha channel selection is not affected by setting this parameter to true. The default value is false.

Example

The following example shows how to apply pixel noise to a BitmapData object for both a color and black-and-white bitmap.

```
import flash.display.BitmapData;
import flash.geom.Rectangle;
import flash.geom.Point;

var bitmapData_1:BitmapData = new BitmapData(100, 80, false, 0x00CCCCCC);
var bitmapData_2:BitmapData = new BitmapData(100, 80, false, 0x00FF0000);
```

```
var mc_1:MovieClip = this.createEmptyMovieClip("mc",
    this.getNextHighestDepth());
mc_1.attachBitmap(bitmapData_1, this.getNextHighestDepth());

var mc_2:MovieClip = this.createEmptyMovieClip("mc",
    this.getNextHighestDepth());
mc_2.attachBitmap(bitmapData_2, this.getNextHighestDepth());
mc_2._x = 101;

mc_1.onPress = function() {
    bitmapData_1.merge(bitmapData_2, new Rectangle(0, 0, 50, 40), new
    Point(25, 20), 128, 0, 0, 0);
}

mc_1.onPress = function() {
    bitmapData_1.noise(128, 0, 255, 1, true);
}

mc_2.onPress = function() {
    bitmapData_2.noise(128);
}
```

paletteMap (BitmapData.paletteMap method)

```
public paletteMap(sourceBitmap:BitmapData, sourceRect:Rectangle,
    destPoint:Point, [redArray:Array], [greenArray:Array], [blueArray:Array],
    [alphaArray:Array]) : Void
```

Remaps the color channel values in an image that has up to four arrays of color palette data, one for each channel.

Flash Player uses the following formula to generate the resulting image.

After the red, green, blue, and alpha values are computed, they are added together using standard 32-bit-integer arithmetic. The red, green, blue, and alpha channel values of each pixel are is extracted into a separate 0 to 255 value. These values are used to look up new color values in the appropriate array: redArray, greenArray, blueArray, and alphaArray. Each of these four arrays should contain 256 values. After all four of the new channel values are retrieved, they are combined into a standard ARGB value, which is applied to the pixel.

Cross-channel effects can be supported with this method. Each input array can contain full 32-bit values, and there is no shifting when the values are added together. This routine does not support per-channel clamping.

If no array is specified for a channel, the color channel is simply copied from the source image to the destination image.

You can use this method for a variety of effects such as general palette mapping (taking one channel and converting it to a false color image). You can also use this method for a variety of advanced color manipulation algorithms, such as gamma, curves, levels, and quantizing.

Availability: ActionScript 1.0; Flash Player 8

Parameters

sourceBitmap:flash.display.BitmapData - The input bitmap image to use. The source image can be a different BitmapData object, or it can refer to the current BitmapData object.

sourceRect:flash.geom.Rectangle - A rectangle that defines the area of the source image to use as input.

destPoint:flash.geom.Point - The point within the destination image (the current BitmapData object) that corresponds to upper-left corner of the source rectangle.

redArray:Array [optional] - If redArray is not null, red = redArray[source red value] else red = source rect value.

greenArray:Array [optional] - If greenArray is not null, green = greenArray[source green value] else green = source green value.

blueArray:Array [optional] - If blueArray is not null, blue = blueArray[source blue value] else blue = source blue value.

alphaArray:Array [optional] - If alphaArray is not null, alpha = alphaArray[source alpha value] else alpha = source alpha value.

Example

The following example shows how to use a palette map to convert solid red to green, and solid green to red in a single BitmapData object.

```
import flash.display.BitmapData;
import flash.geom.Rectangle;
import flash.geom.Point;

var myBitmapData:BitmapData = new BitmapData(100, 80, false, 0x00FF0000);

var mc:MovieClip = this.createEmptyMovieClip("mc",
  this.getNextHighestDepth()); mc.attachBitmap(myBitmapData,
  this.getNextHighestDepth());

myBitmapData.fillRect(new Rectangle(51, 0, 50, 80), 0x0000FF00);

mc.onPress = function() {
  var redArray:Array = new Array(256);
  var greenArray:Array = new Array(256);

  for(var i = 0; i < 255; i++) {
```

```
    redArray[i] = 0x00000000;
    greenArray[i] = 0x00000000;
  }

  redArray[0xFF] = 0x0000FF00;
  greenArray[0xFF] = 0x00FF0000;

  myBitmapData.paletteMap(myBitmapData, new Rectangle(0, 0, 100, 40), new
    Point(0, 0), redArray, greenArray, null, null);
}
```

perlinNoise (BitmapData.perlinNoise method)

```
public perlinNoise(baseX:Number, baseY:Number, numOctaves:Number,
  randomSeed:Number, stitch:Boolean, fractalNoise:Boolean,
  [channelOptions:Number], [grayScale:Boolean], [offsets:Object]) : Void
```

Generates a Perlin noise image.

The Perlin noise generation algorithm interpolates and combines individual random noise functions (called octaves) into a single function that generates more natural-seeming random noise. Like musical octaves, each octave function is twice the frequency of the one before it. Perlin noise has been described as a "fractal sum of noise" because it combines multiple sets of noise data with different levels of detail.

You can use Perlin noise functions to simulate natural phenomena and landscapes, such as wood grain, clouds, and mountain ranges. In most cases, the output of a Perlin noise function is not displayed directly but is used to enhance other images and give them pseudo-random variations.

Simple digital random noise functions often produce images with harsh, contrasting points. This kind of harsh contrast is not often found in nature. The Perlin noise algorithm blends multiple noise functions that operate at different levels of detail. This algorithm results in smaller variations among neighboring pixel values.

> **NOTE** The Perlin noise algorithm is named for Ken Perlin, who developed it after generating computer graphics for the 1982 film *Tron*. Perlin received an Academy Award for Technical Achievement for the Perlin Noise function in 1997.

Availability: ActionScript 1.0; Flash Player 8

Parameters

baseX:Number - Frequency to use in the *x* direction. For example, to generate a noise that is sized for a 64 x 128 image, pass 64 for the baseX value.

baseY:Number - Frequency to use in the *y* direction. For example, to generate a noise that is sized for a 64 x 128 image, pass 128 for the baseY value.

`numOctaves:Number` - Number of octaves or individual noise functions to combine to create this noise. Larger numbers of octaves create images with greater detail. Larger numbers of octaves also require more processing time.

`randomSeed:Number` - The random seed number to use. If you keep all other parameters the same, you can generate different pseudo-random results by varying the random seed value. The Perlin noise function is a mapping function, not a true random-number generation function, so it creates the same results each time from the same random seed.

`stitch:Boolean` - A Boolean value. If the value is `true`, the method attempts to smooth the transition edges of the image to create seamless textures for tiling as a bitmap fill.

`fractalNoise:Boolean` - A Boolean value. If the value is `true`, the method generates fractal noise; otherwise, it generates turbulence. An image with turbulence has visible discontinuities in the gradient that can make it better approximate sharper visual effects, like flames and ocean waves.

`channelOptions:Number` [optional] - A number that indicates one or more color channels. To create this value, you can use or combine any of the four color channel values: 1 (red), 2 (green), 4 (blue), and 8 (alpha). You can combine the channel values by using the logical OR operator; for example, you can combine the red and green channels by using the following code: 1 | 2.

`grayScale:Boolean` [optional] - A Boolean value. If the value is `true`, a grayscale image is created by setting each of the red, green, and blue color channels to identical values. The alpha channel value is not affected if this value is set to `true`. The default value is `false`.

`offsets:Object` [optional] - An array of points that correspond to *x* and *y* offsets for each octave. By manipulating the offset values you can smoothly scroll the layers of a perlinNoise image. Each point in the offset array affects a specific octave noise function.

Example

The following example shows how to apply Perlin noise to to a BitmapData object.

```
import flash.display.BitmapData;

var bitmapData_1:BitmapData = new BitmapData(100, 80, false, 0x00CCCCCC);
var bitmapData_2:BitmapData = new BitmapData(100, 80, false, 0x00FF0000);

var mc_1:MovieClip = this.createEmptyMovieClip("mc",
  this.getNextHighestDepth());
mc_1.attachBitmap(bitmapData_1, this.getNextHighestDepth());

var mc_2:MovieClip = this.createEmptyMovieClip("mc",
  this.getNextHighestDepth());
mc_2.attachBitmap(bitmapData_2, this.getNextHighestDepth());
mc_2._x = 101;
```

```
mc_1.onPress = function() {
  var randomNum:Number = Math.floor(Math.random() * 10);
    bitmapData_1.perlinNoise(100, 80, 6, randomNum, false, true, 1, true,
  null);
}

mc_2.onPress = function() {
  var randomNum:Number = Math.floor(Math.random() * 10);
    bitmapData_2.perlinNoise(100, 80, 4, randomNum, false, false, 15,
  false, null);
}
```

pixelDissolve (BitmapData.pixelDissolve method)

```
public pixelDissolve(sourceBitmap:BitmapData, sourceRect:Rectangle,
  destPoint:Point, [randomSeed:Number], [numberOfPixels:Number],
  [fillColor:Number]) : Number
```

Performs a pixel dissolve either from a source image to a destination image or by using the same image. Flash Player uses a `randomSeed` value to generate a random pixel dissolve. The return value of the function must be passed in on subsequent calls to continue the pixel dissolve until it is finished.

If the source image does not equal the destination image, pixels are copied from the source to the destination using all of the properties. This allows dissolving from a blank image into a fully populated image.

If the source and destination images are equal, pixels are filled with the `color` parameter. This allows dissolving away from a fully populated image. In this mode, the destination `point` parameter is ignored.

Availability: ActionScript 1.0; Flash Player 8

Parameters

`sourceBitmap:flash.display.BitmapData` - The input bitmap image to use. The source image can be a different BitmapData object or it can refer to the current BitmapData instance.

`sourceRect:flash.geom.Rectangle` - A rectangle that defines the area of the source image to use as input.

`destPoint:flash.geom.Point` - The point within the destination image (the current BitmapData instance) that corresponds to the upper-left corner of the source rectangle.

`randomSeed:Number` [optional] - The random seed to use to start the pixel dissolve. The default value is 0.

numberOfPixels:Number [optional] - The default is 1/30 of the source area (width x height).

fillColor:Number [optional] - An ARGB color value that you use to fill pixels whose source value equals its destination value. The default value is 0.

Returns

Number - The new random seed value to use for subsequent calls.

Example

The following example uses `pixelDissolve()` to convert a grey `BitmapData` object to a red one by dissolving 40 pixels at a time until all 8000 pixels have changed colors:

```
import flash.display.BitmapData;
import flash.geom.Point;

var myBitmapData:BitmapData = new BitmapData(100, 80, false, 0x00CCCCCC);

var mc:MovieClip = this.createEmptyMovieClip("mc",
  this.getNextHighestDepth());
mc.attachBitmap(myBitmapData, this.getNextHighestDepth());

mc.onPress = function() {
  var randomNum:Number = Math.floor(Math.random() * 10);
  dissolve(randomNum);
}

var intervalId:Number;
var totalDissolved:Number = 0;
var totalPixels:Number = 8000;

function dissolve(randomNum:Number) {
  var newNum:Number = myBitmapData.pixelDissolve(myBitmapData,
  myBitmapData.rectangle, new Point(0, 0), randomNum, 40, 0x00FF0000);
  clearInterval(intervalId);
  if(totalDissolved < totalPixels) {
    intervalId = setInterval(dissolve, 10, newNum);
  }
  totalDissolved += 40;
}
```

rectangle (BitmapData.rectangle property)

`public rectangle : Rectangle [read-only]`

The rectangle that defines the size and location of the bitmap image. The top and left of the rectangle are 0; the width and height are equal to the width and height in pixels of the BitmapData object.

Availability: ActionScript 1.0; Flash Player 8

Example

The following example shows that the `rectangle` property of the `Bitmap` instance is read-only by trying to set it and failing:

```
import flash.display.BitmapData;
import flash.geom.Rectangle;

var myBitmapData:BitmapData = new BitmapData(100, 80, false, 0x00CCCCCC);

var mc:MovieClip = this.createEmptyMovieClip("mc",
  this.getNextHighestDepth());
mc.attachBitmap(myBitmapData, this.getNextHighestDepth());
trace(myBitmapData.rectangle); // (x=0, y=0, w=100, h=80)

myBitmapData.rectangle = new Rectangle(1, 2, 4, 8);
trace(myBitmapData.rectangle); // (x=0, y=0, w=100, h=80)
```

scroll (BitmapData.scroll method)

```
public scroll(x:Number, y:Number) : Void
```

Scrolls an image by a certain (*x, y*) pixel amount. Edge regions outside the scrolling area are left unchanged.

Availability: ActionScript 1.0; Flash Player 8

Parameters

`x:Number` - The amount by which to scroll horizontally.

`y:Number` - The amount by which to scroll vertically.

Example

The following example shows how to scroll a BitmapData object.

```
import flash.display.BitmapData;
import flash.geom.Rectangle;

var myBitmapData:BitmapData = new BitmapData(100, 80, false, 0x00CCCCCC);

var mc:MovieClip = this.createEmptyMovieClip("mc",
  this.getNextHighestDepth());
mc.attachBitmap(myBitmapData, this.getNextHighestDepth());

myBitmapData.fillRect(new Rectangle(0, 0, 25, 80), 0x00FF0000);

mc.onPress = function() {
```

```
  myBitmapData.scroll(25, 0);
}
```

setPixel (BitmapData.setPixel method)

```
public setPixel(x:Number, y:Number, color:Number) : Void
```

Sets the color of a single pixel of a BitmapData object. The current alpha channel value of the image pixel is preserved during this operation. The value of the RGB color parameter is treated as an unmultiplied color value.

Availability: ActionScript 1.0; Flash Player 8

Parameters

x:Number - The *x* position of the pixel whose value changes.

y:Number - The *y* position of the pixel whose value changes.

color:Number - The RGB color to which to set the pixel.

Example

The following example uses the setPixel() method to assign a RGB value to a pixel at a specific *x* and *y* position. You can draw on the created bitmap in 0x000000 by dragging.

```
import flash.display.BitmapData;

var myBitmapData:BitmapData = new BitmapData(100, 80, false, 0x00CCCCCC);

var mc:MovieClip = this.createEmptyMovieClip("mc",
  this.getNextHighestDepth());
mc.attachBitmap(myBitmapData, this.getNextHighestDepth());

mc.onPress = function() {
  this.onEnterFrame = sketch;
}

mc.onRelease = function() {
  delete this.onEnterFrame;
}

function sketch() {
  myBitmapData.setPixel(_xmouse, _ymouse, 0x000000);
}
```

See also

getPixel (BitmapData.getPixel method), setPixel32 (BitmapData.setPixel32 method)

---

setPixel32 (BitmapData.setPixel32 method)

`public setPixel32(x:Number, y:Number, color:Number) : Void`

Sets the color and alpha transparency values of a single pixel of a BitmapData object. This method is similar to the `setPixel()` method; the main difference is that the `setPixel32()` method takes an ARGB color value that contains alpha channel information.

Availability: ActionScript 1.0; Flash Player 8

Parameters

`x:Number` - The *x* position of the pixel whose value changes.

`y:Number` - The *y* position of the pixel whose value changes.

`color:Number` - The ARGB color to which to set the pixel. If you created an opaque (not a transparent) bitmap, the alpha transparency portion of this color value is ignored.

Example

The following example uses the `setPixel32()` method to assign an ARGB value to a pixel at a specific x and y position. You can draw on the created bitmap in 0x000000 without an alpha value by pressing you mouse button and dragging.

```
import flash.display.BitmapData;

var myBitmapData:BitmapData = new BitmapData(100, 80, true, 0xFFCCCCCC);

var mc:MovieClip = this.createEmptyMovieClip("mc",
    this.getNextHighestDepth());
mc.attachBitmap(myBitmapData, this.getNextHighestDepth());

mc.onPress = function() {
    this.onEnterFrame = sketch;
}

mc.onRelease = function() {
    delete this.onEnterFrame;
}

function sketch() {
    myBitmapData.setPixel32(_xmouse, _ymouse, 0x00000000);
}
```

See also

`getPixel32 (BitmapData.getPixel32 method)`, `setPixel (BitmapData.setPixel method)`

threshold (BitmapData.threshold method)

```
public threshold(sourceBitmap:BitmapData, sourceRect:Rectangle,
    destPoint:Point, operation:String, threshold:Number, [color:Number],
    [mask:Number], [copySource:Boolean]) : Number
```

Tests pixel values in an image against a specified threshold and sets pixels that pass the test to new color values. Using the threshold() method, you can isolate and replace color ranges in an image and perform other logical operations on image pixels.

The threshold test's logic is as follows:

```
if ((pixelValue & mask) operation (threshold & mask)) then

    set pixel to color

 else

    if (copySource) then

        set pixel to corresponding pixel value from sourceBitmap
```

The operation parameter specifies the comparison operator to use for the threshold test. For example, by using "==", you can isolate a specific color value in an image. Or by using {operation: "<", mask: 0xFF000000, threshold: 0x7f000000, color: 0x00000000}, you can set all destination pixels to be fully transparent when the source image pixel's alpha is less than 0x7F. You can use this technique for animated transitions and other effects.

Availability: ActionScript 1.0; Flash Player 8

Parameters

sourceBitmap:flash.display.BitmapData - The input bitmap image to use. The source image can be a different BitmapData object or it can refer to the current BitmapData instance.

sourceRect:flash.geom.Rectangle - A rectangle that defnes the area of the source image to use as input.

destPoint:flash.geom.Point - The point within the destination image (the current BitmapData instance) that corresponds to upper-left corner of the source rectangle.

operation:String - One of the following comparison operators, passed as a String: "<", "<=", ">", ">=", "==", "!="

threshold:Number - The value that each pixel is tested against to see if it meets or exceeds the threshhold.

`color`: Number [optional] - The color value that a pixel is set to if the threshold test succeeds. The default is 0x00000000.

`mask`: Number [optional] - The mask to use to isolate a color component. The default value is 0xFFFFFFFF.

`copySource`: Boolean [optional] - A Boolean value. If the value is `true`, pixel values from the source image are copied to the destination when the threshold test fails. If the value is `false`, the source image is not copied when the threshold test fails. The default value is `false`.

Returns

`Number` - The number of pixels that were changed.

Example

The following example shows how to change the color value of pixels whose color value is greater than or equal to a certain threshold.

```
import flash.display.BitmapData;
import flash.geom.Rectangle;
import flash.geom.Point;

var myBitmapData:BitmapData = new BitmapData(100, 80, false, 0x00CCCCCC);

var mc:MovieClip = this.createEmptyMovieClip("mc",
  this.getNextHighestDepth());
mc.attachBitmap(myBitmapData, this.getNextHighestDepth());

myBitmapData.fillRect(new Rectangle(0, 0, 50, 80), 0x00FF0000);

mc.onPress = function() {
  myBitmapData.threshold(myBitmapData, new Rectangle(0, 0, 100, 40), new
  Point(0, 0), ">=", 0x00CCCCCC, 0x000000FF, 0x00FF0000, false);
}
```

transparent (BitmapData.transparent property)

`public transparent : Boolean [read-only]`

Defines whether the bitmap image supports per-pixel transparency. You can set this value only when you construct a BitmapData object by passing in `true` for the `transparent` parameter. After you create a BitmapData object, you can check whether it supports per-pixel transparency by seeing if the value of the `transparent` property is `true`.

Availability: ActionScript 1.0; Flash Player 8

Example

The following example shows that the `transparent` property of the `Bitmap` instance is read-only by trying to set it and failing:

```
import flash.display.BitmapData;

var myBitmapData:BitmapData = new BitmapData(100, 80, false, 0x00CCCCCC);

var mc:MovieClip = this.createEmptyMovieClip("mc",
  this.getNextHighestDepth());
mc.attachBitmap(myBitmapData, this.getNextHighestDepth());
trace(myBitmapData.transparent); // false

myBitmapData.transparent = true;
trace(myBitmapData.transparent); // false
```

width (BitmapData.width property)

```
public width : Number [read-only]
```

The width of the bitmap image in pixels.

Availability: ActionScript 1.0; Flash Player 8

Example

The following example shows that the `width` property of the `Bitmap` instance is read-only by trying to set it and failing:

```
import flash.display.BitmapData;

var myBitmapData:BitmapData = new BitmapData(100, 80, false, 0x00CCCCCC);

var mc:MovieClip = this.createEmptyMovieClip("mc",
  this.getNextHighestDepth());
mc.attachBitmap(myBitmapData, this.getNextHighestDepth());
trace(myBitmapData.width); // 100

myBitmapData.width = 999;
trace(myBitmapData.width); // 100
```

BitmapFilter (flash.filters.BitmapFilter)

```
Object
  |
  +-flash.filters.BitmapFilter
```

public class **BitmapFilter**
extends Object

The BitmapFilter base class for all image filter effects.

The BevelFilter, BlurFilter, ColorMatrixFilter, ConvolutionFilter, DisplacementMapFilter, DropShadowFilter, GlowFilter, GradientBevelFilter, and GradientGlowFilter classes all extend the BitmapFilter class. You can apply these filter effects to bitmaps or MovieClip instances.

You can create subclasses only for the preceding subclasses of the BitmapFilter class.

Availability: ActionScript 1.0; Flash Player 8

Property summary

Properties inherited from class Object

```
constructor (Object.constructor property), __proto__ (Object.__proto__
property), prototype (Object.prototype property), __resolve
(Object.__resolve property)
```

Method summary

Modifiers	Signature	Description
	`clone() : BitmapFilter`	Returns a BitmapFilter object that is an exact copy of the original BitmapFilter object.

Methods inherited from class Object

```
addProperty (Object.addProperty method), hasOwnProperty
(Object.hasOwnProperty method), isPropertyEnumerable
(Object.isPropertyEnumerable method), isPrototypeOf (Object.isPrototypeOf
method), registerClass (Object.registerClass method), toString
(Object.toString method), unwatch (Object.unwatch method), valueOf
(Object.valueOf method), watch (Object.watch method)
```

clone (BitmapFilter.clone method)

`public clone() : BitmapFilter`

Returns a BitmapFilter object that is an exact copy of the original BitmapFilter object.

Availability: ActionScript 1.0; Flash Player 8

Returns

`flash.filters.BitmapFilter` - A BitmapFilter object.

BlurFilter (flash.filters.BlurFilter)

```
Object
  |
  +-flash.filters.BitmapFilter
    |
    +-flash.filters.BlurFilter
```

`public class BlurFilter`
`extends BitmapFilter`

The BlurFilter class lets you apply a blur visual effect to a variety of objects in Flash. A blur effect softens the details of an image. You can produce blurs that range from a softly unfocused look to a Gaussian blur, a hazy appearance like viewing an image through semi-opaque glass. When the `quality` property of this filter is set to 1, the result is a softly unfocused look. When the `quality` property is set to 3, it approximates a Gaussian blur filter.

The use of filters depends on the object to which you apply the filter:

- To apply filters to movie clips, text fields, and buttons at runtime, use the `filters` property. Setting the `filters` property of an object does not modify the object, and you can undo the setting by clearing the `filters` property.

- To apply filters to BitmapData instances, use the `BitmapData.applyFilter()` method. Calling `applyFilter` on a BitmapData object takes the source BitmapData object and the filter object and generates a filtered image as a result.

You can also apply filter effects to images and video at authoring time. For more information, see your authoring documentation.

If you apply a filter to a movie clip or button, the `cacheAsBitmap` property of the movie clip or button is set to `true`. If you clear all filters, the original value of `cacheAsBitmap` is restored.

This filter supports stage scaling. However, it does not support general scaling, rotation, and skewing. If the object itself is scaled (`_xscale` and `_yscale` are not 100%), the filter effect is not scaled. It is scaled only when you zoom in on the Stage.

A filter is not applied if the resulting image exceeds 2880 pixels in width or height. If, for example, you zoom in on a large movie clip with a filter applied, the filter is turned off if the resulting image exceeds the limit of 2880 pixels.

Availability: ActionScript 1.0; Flash Player 8

See also

```
filters (MovieClip.filters property), cacheAsBitmap (MovieClip.cacheAsBitmap
property), filters (Button.filters property), cacheAsBitmap
(Button.cacheAsBitmap property), filters (TextField.filters property),
applyFilter (BitmapData.applyFilter method)
```

Property summary

Modifiers	Property	Description
	blurX:Number	The amount of horizontal blur.
	blurY:Number	The amount of vertical blur.
	quality:Number	The number of times to perform the blur.

Properties inherited from class Object

```
constructor (Object.constructor property), __proto__ (Object.__proto__
property), prototype (Object.prototype property), __resolve
(Object.__resolve property)
```

Constructor summary

Signature	Description
BlurFilter([blurX:Number], [blurY:Number], [quality:Number])	Initializes the filter with the specified parameters.

Method summary

Modifiers	Signature	Description
	clone() : BlurFilter	Returns a copy of this filter object.

Methods inherited from class BitmapFilter

```
clone (BitmapFilter.clone method)
```

Methods inherited from class Object

```
addProperty (Object.addProperty method), hasOwnProperty
(Object.hasOwnProperty method), isPropertyEnumerable
(Object.isPropertyEnumerable method), isPrototypeOf (Object.isPrototypeOf
method), registerClass (Object.registerClass method), toString
(Object.toString method), unwatch (Object.unwatch method), valueOf
(Object.valueOf method), watch (Object.watch method)
```

BlurFilter constructor

```
public BlurFilter([blurX:Number], [blurY:Number], [quality:Number])
```
Initializes the filter with the specified parameters. The default values create a soft, unfocused image.

Availability: ActionScript 1.0; Flash Player 8

Parameters

blurX:Number [optional] - The amount to blur horizontally. Valid values are from 0 to 255 (floating-point value). The default value is 4. Values that are a power of 2 (such as 2, 4, 8, 16 and 32) are optimized to render more quickly than other values.

blurY:Number [optional] - The amount to blur vertically. Valid values are from 0 to 255 (floating-point value). The default value is 4. Values that are a power of 2 (such as 2, 4, 8, 16 and 32) are optimized to render more quickly than other values.

quality:Number [optional] - The number of times to apply the filter. The default value is 1, which is equivalent to low quality. A value of 2 is medium quality, and a value of 3 is high quality and approximates a Gaussian blur.

Example

The following example instantiates a new `BlurFilter` constructor and applies it to a flat, rectangular shape:

```
import flash.filters.BlurFilter;
var rect:MovieClip = createRectangle(100, 100, 0x003366,
   "BlurFilterExample");

var blurX:Number = 30;
var blurY:Number = 30;
var quality:Number = 3;

var filter:BlurFilter = new BlurFilter(blurX, blurY, quality);
var filterArray:Array = new Array();
filterArray.push(filter);
rect.filters = filterArray;

function createRectangle(w:Number, h:Number, bgColor:Number,
   name:String):MovieClip {
   var mc:MovieClip = this.createEmptyMovieClip(name,
   this.getNextHighestDepth());
   mc.beginFill(bgColor);
   mc.lineTo(w, 0);
   mc.lineTo(w, h);
   mc.lineTo(0, h);
   mc.lineTo(0, 0);
   mc._x = 20;
   mc._y = 20;
   return mc;
}
```

blurX (BlurFilter.blurX property)

```
public blurX : Number
```

The amount of horizontal blur. Valid values are from 0 to 255 (floating point). The default value is 4. Values that are a power of 2 (such as 2, 4, 8, 16 and 32) are optimized to render more quickly than other values.

Availability: ActionScript 1.0; Flash Player 8

Example

The following example changes the `blurX` property on an existing MovieClip instance when a user clicks it.

```
import flash.filters.BlurFilter;
var mc:MovieClip = createBlurFilterRectangle("BlurFilterBlurX");
mc.onRelease = function() {
   var filter:BlurFilter = this.filters[0];
```

```
  filter.blurX = 200;
  this.filters = new Array(filter);
}

function createBlurFilterRectangle(name:String):MovieClip {
  var rect:MovieClip = this.createEmptyMovieClip(name,
  this.getNextHighestDepth());
  var w:Number = 100;
  var h:Number = 100;
  rect.beginFill(0x003366);
  rect.lineTo(w, 0);
  rect.lineTo(w, h);
  rect.lineTo(0, h);
  rect.lineTo(0, 0);
  rect._x = 20;
  rect._y = 20;

  var filter:BlurFilter = new BlurFilter(30, 30, 2);
  var filterArray:Array = new Array();
  filterArray.push(filter);
  rect.filters = filterArray;
  return rect;
}
```

blurY (BlurFilter.blurY property)

```
public blurY : Number
```

The amount of vertical blur. Valid values are from 0 to 255 (floating point). The default value is 4. Values that are a power of 2 (such as 2, 4, 8, 16 and 32) are optimized to render more quickly than other values.

Availability: ActionScript 1.0; Flash Player 8

Example

The following example changes the blurY property on an existing MovieClip instance when a user clicks it.

```
import flash.filters.BlurFilter;
var mc:MovieClip = createBlurFilterRectangle("BlurFilterBlurY");
mc.onRelease = function() {
  var filter:BlurFilter = this.filters[0];
  filter.blurY = 200;
  this.filters = new Array(filter);
}

function createBlurFilterRectangle(name:String):MovieClip {
  var rect:MovieClip = this.createEmptyMovieClip(name,
  this.getNextHighestDepth());
```

```
var w:Number = 100;
var h:Number = 100;
rect.beginFill(0x003366);
rect.lineTo(w, 0);
rect.lineTo(w, h);
rect.lineTo(0, h);
rect.lineTo(0, 0);
rect._x = 20;
rect._y = 20;

var filter:BlurFilter = new BlurFilter(30, 30, 2);
var filterArray:Array = new Array();
filterArray.push(filter);
rect.filters = filterArray;
return rect;
}
```

clone (BlurFilter.clone method)

```
public clone() : BlurFilter
```

Returns a copy of this filter object.

Availability: ActionScript 1.0; Flash Player 8

Returns

`flash.filters.BlurFilter` - A new BlurFilter instance with all the same properties as the original BlurFilter instance.

Example

The following example creates three BlurFilter objects and compares them. You can create the `filter_1` object by using the `BlurFilter` constructor. You can create the `filter_2` object by setting it equal to `filter_1`. You can create the `clonedFilter` object by cloning `filter_1`. Notice that although `filter_2` evaluates as being equal to `filter_1`, `clonedFilter` does not, even though it contains the same values as `filter_1`.

```
import flash.filters.BlurFilter;

var filter_1:BlurFilter = new BlurFilter(30, 30, 2);
var filter_2:BlurFilter = filter_1;
var clonedFilter:BlurFilter = filter_1.clone();

trace(filter_1 == filter_2); // true
trace(filter_1 == clonedFilter); // false

for(var i in filter_1) {
    trace(">> " + i + ": " + filter_1[i]);
```

```
    // >> clone: [type Function]
    // >> quality: 2
    // >> blurY: 30
    // >> blurX: 30
}

for(var i in clonedFilter) {
    trace(">> " + i + ": " + clonedFilter[i]);
    // >> clone: [type Function]
    // >> quality: 2
    // >> blurY: 30
    // >> blurX: 30
}
```

To further demonstrate the relationships between filter_1, filter_2, and clonedFilter, the following example modifies the quality property of filter_1. Modifying quality demonstrates that the clone() method creates a new instance based on values of the filter_1 instead of referring to the values.

```
import flash.filters.BlurFilter;

var filter_1:BlurFilter = new BlurFilter(30, 30, 2);
var filter_2:BlurFilter = filter_1;
var clonedFilter:BlurFilter = filter_1.clone();

trace(filter_1.quality); // 2
trace(filter_2.quality); // 2
trace(clonedFilter.quality); // 2

filter_1.quality = 1;

trace(filter_1.quality); // 1
trace(filter_2.quality); // 1
trace(clonedFilter.quality); // 2
```

quality (BlurFilter.quality property)

`public quality : Number`

The number of times to perform the blur. Valid values are from 0-15. The default value is 1, which is equivalent to low quality. A value of 2 is medium quality. A value of 3 is high quality and approximates a Gaussian blur.

For most applications, a `quality` value of 1, 2, or 3 is sufficient. Although you can use additional numeric values up to 15 to increase the number of times the blur is applied, thus getting a more blurred effect, be aware that higher values are rendered more slowly. Instead of increasing the value of `quality`, you can often get a similar effect, and with faster rendering, by simply increasing the values of `blurX` and `blurY`.

Availability: ActionScript 1.0; Flash Player 8

Example

The following example creates a rectangle and applies a blur filter with a `quality` value of 1 to the rectangle. When you click the rectangle, the `quality` increases to 3, and the rectangle becomes more blurry.

```
import flash.filters.BlurFilter;
var mc:MovieClip = createBlurFilterRectangle("BlurFilterQuality");
mc.onRelease = function() {
  var filter:BlurFilter = this.filters[0];
  filter.quality = 3;
  this.filters = new Array(filter);
}

function createBlurFilterRectangle(name:String):MovieClip {
  var rect:MovieClip = this.createEmptyMovieClip(name,
  this.getNextHighestDepth());
  var w:Number = 100;
  var h:Number = 100;
  rect.beginFill(0x003366);
  rect.lineTo(w, 0);
  rect.lineTo(w, h);
  rect.lineTo(0, h);
  rect.lineTo(0, 0);
  rect._x = 20;
  rect._y = 20;

  var filter:BlurFilter = new BlurFilter(30, 30, 1);
  var filterArray:Array = new Array();
  filterArray.push(filter);
  rect.filters = filterArray;
  return rect;
}
```

Boolean

```
Object
  |
  +-Boolean
```

```
public class Boolean
extends Object
```

The Boolean class is a wrapper object with the same functionality as the standard JavaScript Boolean object. Use the Boolean class to retrieve the primitive data type or string representation of a Boolean object.

You must use the constructor new `Boolean()` to create a Boolean object before calling its methods.

Availability: ActionScript 1.0; Flash Player 5 - (became a native object in Flash Player 6, which improved performance significantly)

Property summary

Properties inherited from class Object

```
constructor (Object.constructor property), __proto__ (Object.__proto__
property), prototype (Object.prototype property), __resolve
(Object.__resolve property)
```

Constructor summary

Signature	Description
`Boolean([value:Object])`	Creates a Boolean object.

Method summary

Modifiers	Signature	Description
	`toString() : String`	Returns the string representation (`"true"` or `"false"`) of the Boolean object.
	`valueOf() : Boolean`	Returns `true` if the primitive value type of the specified Boolean object is true; `false` otherwise.

Methods inherited from class Object

```
addProperty (Object.addProperty method), hasOwnProperty
(Object.hasOwnProperty method), isPropertyEnumerable
(Object.isPropertyEnumerable method), isPrototypeOf (Object.isPrototypeOf
method), registerClass (Object.registerClass method), toString
(Object.toString method), unwatch (Object.unwatch method), valueOf
(Object.valueOf method), watch (Object.watch method)
```

Boolean constructor

`public Boolean([value:Object])`

Creates a Boolean object. If you omit the `value` parameter, the Boolean object is initialized with a value of `false`. If you specify a value for the `value` parameter, the method evaluates it and returns the result as a Boolean value according to the rules in the global `Boolean()` function.

Availability: ActionScript 1.0; Flash Player 5

Parameters

`value:Object` [optional] - Any expression. The default value is `false`.

Example

The following code creates a new empty Boolean object called `myBoolean`:

```
var myBoolean:Boolean = new Boolean();
```

toString (Boolean.toString method)

`public toString() : String`

Returns the string representation (`"true"` or `"false"`) of the Boolean object.

Availability: ActionScript 1.0; Flash Player 5

Returns

`String` - A string; `"true"` or `"false"`.

Example

This example creates a variable of type Boolean and uses `toString()` to convert the value to a string for use in the trace statement:

```
var myBool:Boolean = true;
trace("The value of the Boolean myBool is: " + myBool.toString());
myBool = false;
trace("The value of the Boolean myBool is: " + myBool.toString());
```

valueOf (Boolean.valueOf method)

`public valueOf() : Boolean`

Returns `true` if the primitive value type of the specified Boolean object is true; `false` otherwise.

Availability: ActionScript 1.0; Flash Player 5

Returns

`Boolean` - A Boolean value.

Example

The following example shows how this method works, and also shows that the primitive value type of a new Boolean object is `false`:

```
var x:Boolean = new Boolean();
trace(x.valueOf());   // false
x = (6==3+3);
trace(x.valueOf());   // true
```

Button

```
Object
  |
  +-Button
```

```
public class Button
extends Object
```

All button symbols in a SWF file are instances of the Button object. You can give a button an instance name in the Property inspector, and use the methods and properties of the Button class to manipulate buttons with ActionScript. Button instance names are displayed in the Movie Explorer and in the Insert Target Path dialog box in the Actions panel.

The Button class inherits from the Object class.

Availability: ActionScript 1.0; Flash Player 6

See also

Object

Property summary

Modifiers	Property	Description
	`_alpha:Number`	The alpha transparency value of the button specified by `my_btn`.
	`blendMode:Object`	The blend mode for the button.
	`cacheAsBitmap:Boolean`	If set to `true`, Flash Player caches an internal bitmap representation of the button.
	`enabled:Boolean`	A Boolean value that specifies whether a button is enabled.
	`filters:Array`	An indexed array containing each filter object currently associated with the button.
	`_focusrect:Boolean`	A Boolean value that specifies whether a button has a yellow rectangle around it when it has keyboard focus.
	`_height:Number`	The height of the button, in pixels.
	`_highquality:Number`	**Deprecated** since Flash Player 7. This property was deprecated in favor of `Button._quality`. Specifies the level of anti-aliasing applied to the current SWF file.
	`menu:ContextMenu`	Associates the `ContextMenu` object `contextMenu` with the button object `my_button`.
	`_name:String`	Instance name of the button specified by `my_btn`.
	`_parent:MovieClip`	A reference to the movie clip or object that contains the current movie clip or object.
	`_quality:String`	Property (global); sets or retrieves the rendering quality used for a SWF file.

Modifiers	Property	Description
	`_rotation:Number`	The rotation of the button, in degrees, from its original orientation.
	`scale9Grid:Rectangle`	The rectangular region that defines the nine scaling regions for the button.
	`_soundbuftime:Number`	The property that specifies the number of seconds a sound prebuffers before it starts to stream.
	`tabEnabled:Boolean`	Specifies whether `my_btn` is included in automatic tab ordering.
	`tabIndex:Number`	Lets you customize the tab ordering of objects in a SWF file.
	`_target:String` [read-only]	Returns the target path of the button instance specified by `my_btn`.
	`trackAsMenu:Boolean`	A Boolean value that indicates whether other buttons or movie clips can receive mouse release events.
	`_url:String` [read-only]	Retrieves the URL of the SWF file that created the button.
	`useHandCursor:Boolean`	A Boolean value that, when set to `true` (the default), indicates whether a pointing hand (hand cursor) displays when the mouse rolls over a button.
	`_visible:Boolean`	A Boolean value that indicates whether the button specified by `my_btn` is visible.
	`_width:Number`	The width of the button, in pixels.
	`_x:Number`	An integer that sets the x coordinate of a button relative to the local coordinates of the parent movie clip.
	`_xmouse:Number` [read-only]	Returns the x coordinate of the mouse position relative to the button.
	`_xscale:Number`	The horizontal scale of the button as applied from the registration point of the button, expressed as a percentage.
	`_y:Number`	The y coordinate of the button relative to the local coordinates of the parent movie clip.

Modifiers	Property	Description
	_ymouse:Number [read-only]	Indicates the y coordinate of the mouse position relative to the button.
	_yscale:Number	The vertical scale of the button as applied from the registration point of the button, expressed as a percentage.

Properties inherited from class Object

```
constructor (Object.constructor property),__proto__ (Object.__proto__
property),prototype (Object.prototype property),__resolve
(Object.__resolve property)
```

Event summary

Event	Description
onDragOut = function() {}	Invoked when the mouse button is clicked over the button and the pointer then dragged outside of the button.
onDragOver = function() {}	Invoked when the user presses and drags the mouse button outside and then over the button.
onKeyDown = function() {}	Invoked when a button has keyboard focus and a key is pressed.
onKeyUp = function() {}	Invoked when a button has input focus and a key is released.
onKillFocus = function(newFocus:Object) {}	Invoked when a button loses keyboard focus.
onPress = function() {}	Invoked when a button is pressed.
onRelease = function() {}	Invoked when a button is released.
onReleaseOutside = function() {}	Invoked when the mouse is released while the pointer is outside the button after the button is pressed while the pointer is inside the button.
onRollOut = function() {}	Invoked when the pointer moves outside a button area.
onRollOver = function() {}	Invoked when the pointer moves over a button area.
onSetFocus = function(oldFocus:Object) {}	Invoked when a button receives keyboard focus.

Method summary

Modifiers	Signature	Description
	`getDepth() : Number`	Returns the depth of the button instance.

Methods inherited from class Object

```
addProperty (Object.addProperty method), hasOwnProperty
(Object.hasOwnProperty method), isPropertyEnumerable
(Object.isPropertyEnumerable method), isPrototypeOf (Object.isPrototypeOf
method), registerClass (Object.registerClass method), toString
(Object.toString method), unwatch (Object.unwatch method), valueOf
(Object.valueOf method), watch (Object.watch method)
```

_alpha (Button._alpha property)

`public _alpha : Number`

The alpha transparency value of the button specified by `my_btn`. Valid values are 0 (fully transparent) to 100 (fully opaque). The default value is 100. Objects in a button with `_alpha` set to 0 are active, even though they are invisible.

Availability: ActionScript 1.0; Flash Player 6

Example

The following code sets the `_alpha` property of a button named myBtn_btn to 50% when the user clicks the button. First, add a Button instance on the Stage. Second, give it an instance name of myBtn_btn. Lastly, with frame 1 selected, place the following code into the Actions panel:

```
myBtn_btn.onRelease = function(){
  this._alpha = 50;
};
```

See also

`_alpha (MovieClip._alpha property)`, `_alpha (TextField._alpha property)`

blendMode (Button.blendMode property)

`public blendMode : Object`

The blend mode for the button. The blend mode affects the appearance of the button when it is in a layer above another object onscreen.

Flash Player applies the `blendMode` property on each pixel of the button. Each pixel is composed of three constituent colors (red, green, and blue), and each constituent color has a value between 0x00 and 0xFF. Flash Player compares each constituent color of one pixel in the button with the corresponding color of the pixel in the background. For example, if `blendMode` is set to `"lighten"`, Flash Player compares the red value of the button with the red value of the background, and uses the lighter of the two as the value for the red component of the displayed color.

The following table describes the `blendMode` settings. To set the `blendMode` property, you can use either an integer from 1 to 14 or a string. The illustrations in the table show `blendMode` applied to a button (2) when superimposed on another onscreen object (1).

Integer value	String value	Illustration	Description
1	`"normal"`		The button appears in front of the background. Pixel values of the button override those of the background. Where the button is transparent, the background is visible.
2	`"layer"`		Forces the creation of a temporary buffer for precomposition for the button. This is done automatically if there is more than one child object in a button and a `blendMode` setting other than `"normal"` is selected for the child.

Integer value	String value	Illustration	Description
3	`"multiply"`		Multiplies the values of the button constituent colors by those of the background color, and then normalizes by dividing by 0xFF, resulting in darker colors. This is commonly used for shadows and depth effects. For example, if a constituent color (such as red) of one pixel in the button and the corresponding color of the pixel in the background both have the value 0x88, the multiplied result is 0x4840. Dividing by 0xFF yields a value of 0x48 for that constituent color, which is a darker shade than that of the button or that of the background.
4	`"screen"`		Multiplies the complement (inverse) of the button color by the complement of the background color, resulting in a bleaching effect. This setting is commonly used for highlights or to remove black areas of the button.
5	`"lighten"`		Selects the lighter of the constituent colors of the button and those of the background (the ones with the larger values). This setting is commonly used for superimposing type. For example, if the button has a pixel with an RGB value of 0xFFCC33, and the background pixel has an RGB value of 0xDDF800, then the resulting RGB value for the displayed pixel is 0xFFF833 (because 0xFF › 0xDD, 0xCC ‹ 0xF8, and 0x33 › 0x00 = 33).

Integer value	String value	Illustration	Description
6	`"darken"`		Selects the darker of the constituent colors of the button and those of the background (the ones with the smaller values). This setting is commonly used for superimposing type. For example, if the button has a pixel with an RGB value of 0xFFCC33, and the background pixel has an RGB value of 0xDDF800, the resulting RGB value for the displayed pixel is 0xDDCC00 (because 0xFF › 0xDD, 0xCC ‹ 0xF8, and 0x33 › 0x00 = 33).
7	`"difference"`		Compares the constituent colors of the button with those of its background, and subtracts the darker of the two constituent colors from the lighter one. This setting is commonly used for more vibrant colors. For example, if the button has a pixel with an RGB value of 0xFFCC33, and the background pixel has an RGB value of 0xDDF800, the resulting RGB value for the displayed pixel is 0x222C33 (because 0xFF - 0xDD = 0x22, 0xF8 - 0xCC = 0x2C, and 0x33 - 0x00 = 0x33).

Integer value	String value	Illustration	Description
8	`"add"`		Adds the values of the constituent colors of the button to those of its background, and applies a ceiling of 0xFF. This setting is commonly used for animating a lightening dissolve between two objects. For example, if the button has a pixel with an RGB value of 0xAAA633, and the background pixel has an RGB value of 0xDD2200, the resulting RGB value for the displayed pixel is 0xFFC833 (because 0xAA + 0xDD › 0xFF, 0xA6 + 0x22 = 0xC8, and 0x33 + 0x00 = 0x33).
9	`"subtract"`		Subtracts the value of the constituent colors in the button from those of the background, and applies a floor of 0. This setting is commonly used for animating a darkening dissolve between two objects. For example, if the button has a pixel with an RGB value of 0xAA2233, and the background pixel has an RGB value of 0xDDA600, the resulting RGB value for the displayed pixel is 0x338400 (because 0xDD - 0xAA = 0x33, 0xA6 - 0x22 = 0x84, and 0x00 - 0x33 ‹ 0x00).
10	`"invert"`		Inverts the background.

Integer value	String value	Illustration	Description
11	`"alpha"`		Applies the alpha value of each pixel of the button to the background. This requires the "layer" `blendMode` to be applied to a parent button. For example, in the illustration, the parent button, which is a white background, has `blendMode = "layer"`.
12	`"erase"`		Erases the background based on the alpha value of the button. This requires the `"layer"` `blendMode` setting to be applied to a parent button. For example, in the illustration, the parent button, which is a white background, has `blendMode = "layer"`.
13	`"overlay"`		Adjusts the color of each bitmap based on the darkness of the background. If the background is lighter than 50% gray, the button and background colors are screened, which results in a lighter color. If the background is darker than 50% gray, the colors are multiplied, which results in a darker color. This setting is commonly used for shading effects.
14	`"hardlight"`		Adjusts the color of each bitmap based on the darkness of the button. If the button is lighter than 50% gray, the button and background colors are screened, which results in a lighter color. If the button is darker than 50% gray, the colors are multiplied, which results in a darker color. This setting is commonly used for shading effects.

If you attempt to set the blendMode property to any other value, Flash Player sets it to "normal".

Availability: ActionScript 1.0; Flash Player 8

Example

In the following example you can see that if you set the property to an integer, Flash Player converts the value to the corresponding string version:

```
my_button.blendMode = 8;
trace (my_button.blendMode) // add
```

For a related example, see the description of the blendMode property of the MovieClip class.

See also

blendMode (MovieClip.blendMode property)

cacheAsBitmap (Button.cacheAsBitmap property)

```
public cacheAsBitmap : Boolean
```

If set to true, Flash Player caches an internal bitmap representation of the button. This can increase performance for buttons that contain complex vector content.

For a button that has cacheAsBitmap set to true, Flash Player stores a bitmap representation for each of the four button states.

All vector data for a button that has a cached bitmap is drawn to the bitmap instead of the main stage. The bitmap is then copied to the main stage as unstretched, unrotated pixels snapped to the nearest pixel boundaries. Pixels are mapped one to one with the parent object. If the bounds of the bitmap change, the bitmap is recreated instead of being stretched.

No internal bitmap is created unless the cacheAsBitmap property is set to true.

After you set a button's cacheAsBitmap property to true, the rendering does not change; however, the button performs pixel snapping automatically. The animation speed can be significantly faster depending on the complexity of the vector content.

The cacheAsBitmap property is automatically set to true whenever you apply a filter to a button (when its filter array is not empty), and if a button has a filter applied to it, cacheAsBitmap is reported as true for that button, even if you set the property to false. If you clear all filters for a button, the cacheAsBitmap setting changes to what it was last set to.

In the following cases a button does not use a bitmap, even if the `cacheAsBitmap` property is set to `true` and instead renders from vector data:

- When the bitmap is too large, that is, greater than 2880 pixels in either direction
- When the bitmap fails to allocate memory (due to an out of memory error)

The `cacheAsBitmap` property is best used with buttons that have mostly static content and that do not scale and rotate frequently. With such buttons, `cacheAsBitmap` can lead to performance increases when the button is translated (when its *x* and *y* position is changed).

Availability: ActionScript 1.0; Flash Player 8

Example

The following example applies a drop shadow to an existing Button instance named `myButton`. It then traces out the value of `cacheAsBitmap`, which is set to `true` when a filter is applied.

```
import flash.filters.DropShadowFilter;
trace(myButton.cacheAsBitmap); // false
var dropShadow:DropShadowFilter = new DropShadowFilter(6, 45, 0x000000, 50,
    5, 5, 1, 2, false, false, false);
myButton.filters = new Array(dropShadow);
trace(myButton.cacheAsBitmap); // true
```

enabled (Button.enabled property)

```
public enabled : Boolean
```

A Boolean value that specifies whether a button is enabled. When a button is disabled (the enabled property is set to `false`), the button is visible but cannot be clicked. The default value is `true`. This property is useful if you want to disable part of your navigation; for example, you may want to disable a button in the currently displayed page so that it can't be clicked and the page cannot be reloaded.

Availability: ActionScript 1.0; Flash Player 6

Example

The following example demonstrates how you can disable and enable buttons from being clicked. Two buttons, `myBtn1_btn` and `myBtn2_btn`, are on the Stage and the following ActionScript is added so that the `myBtn2_btn` button cannot be clicked. First, add two button instances on the Stage. Second, give them instance names of `myBtn1_btn` and `myBtn2_btn`. Lastly, place the following code on frame 1 to enable or disable buttons.

```
myBtn1_btn.enabled = true;
myBtn2_btn.enabled = false;
```

```
//button code
// the following function will not get called
// because myBtn2_btn.enabled was set to false
myBtn1_btn.onRelease = function() {
  trace( "you clicked : " + this._name );
};
myBtn2_btn.onRelease = function() {
  trace( "you clicked : " + this._name );
};
```

filters (Button.filters property)

```
public filters : Array
```

An indexed array containing each filter object currently associated with the button. The flash.filters package contains several classes that define specific filters that you can use.

Filters can be applied in the Flash authoring tool at design-time, or at runtime using ActionScript code. To apply a filter using ActionScript, you must make a temporary copy of the entire Button.filters array, modify the temporary array, and then assign the value of the temporary array back to the Button.filters array. You cannot directly add a new filter object to the Button.filters array. The following code has no effect on the target button, named myButton:

```
myButton.filters[0].push(myDropShadow);
```

To add a filter using ActionScript, you must follow these steps (assume that the target button is named myButton):

- Create a new filter object using the constructor function of your chosen filter class.
- Assign the value of the myButton.filters array to a temporary array, such as one named myFilters.
- Add the new filter object to the temporary array, myFilters.
- Assign the value of the temporary array to the myButton.filters array.

If the filters array is empty, you need not use a temporary array. Instead, you can directly assign an array literal that contains one or more filter objects that you have created.

To modify an existing filter object, whether it was created at design-time or at runtime, you must use the technique of modifying a copy of the filters array:

- Assign the value of the myButton.filters array to a temporary array, such as one named myFilters.
- Modify the property using the temporary array, myFilters. For example, if you want to set the quality property of the first filter in the array, you could use the following code: myList[0].quality = 1;
- Assign the value of the temporary array to the myButton.filters array.

To clear the filters for a button, set `filters` to an empty array (`[]`).

At load time, if a button has an associated filter, it is marked to cache itself as a transparent bitmap. From this point forward, as long as the button has a valid filter list, the player caches the button as a bitmap. This bitmap is used as a source image for the filter effects. Each button usually has two sets of bitmaps: one with the original unfiltered source button and another for the final images (in each of the four button states) after filtering. The final image set is used when rendering. As long as the button does not change, the final image does not need updating.

If you are working with a `filters` array that contains multiple filters and you need to track the type of filter assigned to each array index, you can maintain your own `filters` array and use a separate data structure to track the type of filter associated with each array index. There is no simple way to determine the type of filter associated with each `filters` array index.

Availability: ActionScript 1.0; Flash Player 8

Example

The following example adds a drop shadow filter to a button named `myButton`.

```
import flash.filters.DropShadowFilter;
var myDropFilter:DropShadowFilter = new DropShadowFilter(6, 45, 0x000000,
    50, 5, 5, 1, 2, false, false, false);
var myFilters:Array = myButton.filters;
myFilters.push(myDropFilter);
myButton.filters = myFilters;
```

The following example changes the `quality` setting of the first filter in the array to 15 (this example works only if at least one filter object has been associated with the `myButton` text field).

```
var myList:Array = myButton.filters;
myList[0].quality = 15;
myButton.filters = myList;
```

See also

, cacheAsBitmap (Button.cacheAsBitmap property)

_focusrect (Button._focusrect property)

`public _focusrect : Boolean`

A Boolean value that specifies whether a button has a yellow rectangle around it when it has keyboard focus. This property can override the global `_focusrect` property. By default, the `_focusrect` property of a button instance is null; meaning, the button instance does not override the global `_focusrect` property. If the `_focusrect` property of a button instance is set to `true` or `false`, it overrides the setting of the global `_focusrect` property for the single button instance.

In Flash Player 4 or Flash Player 5 SWF files, the `_focusrect` property controls the global `_focusrect` property. It is a Boolean value. This behavior was changed in Flash Player 6 and later to permit customizing the `_focusrect` property on an individual movie clip.

If the `_focusrect` property is set to `false`, then keyboard navigation for that button is limited to the Tab key. All other keys, including the Enter and arrow keys, are ignored. To restore full keyboard navigation, you must set `_focusrect` to `true`.

Availability: ActionScript 1.0; Flash Player 6

Example

This example demonstrates how to hide the yellow rectangle around a specified button instance in a SWF file when it has focus in a browser window. Create three buttons called `myBtn1_btn`, `myBtn2_btn`, and `myBtn3_btn`, and add the following ActionScript to Frame 1 of the Timeline:

```
myBtn2_btn._focusrect = false;
```

Change the publish settings to Flash Player 6, and test the SWF file in a browser window by selecting File > Publish Preview > HTML. Give the SWF focus by clicking it in the browser window, and use the Tab key to focus each instance. You will not be able to execute code for this button by pressing Enter or the Space key when `_focusrect` is disabled.

getDepth (Button.getDepth method)

`public getDepth() : Number`

Returns the depth of the button instance.

Each movie clip, button, and text field has a unique depth associated with it that determines how the object appears in front of or in back of other objects. Objects with higher depths appear in front.

Availability: ActionScript 1.0; Flash Player 6

Returns

`Number` - The depth of the button instance.

Example

If you create `myBtn1_btn` and `myBtn2_btn` on the Stage, you can trace their depth using the following ActionScript:

```
trace(myBtn1_btn.getDepth());
trace(myBtn2_btn.getDepth());
```

If you load a SWF file called buttonMovie.swf into this document, you could trace the depth of a button, `myBtn4_btn`, inside that SWF file using another button in the main SWF file:

```
this.createEmptyMovieClip("myClip_mc", 999);
myClip_mc.loadMovie("buttonMovie.swf");
myBtn3_btn.onRelease = function(){
  trace(myClip_mc.myBtn4_btn.getDepth());
};
```

You might notice that two of these buttons, one in the main SWF file and one in the loaded SWF file, have the same depth value. This is misleading because buttonMovie.swf was loaded at depth 999, which means that the button it contains will also have a depth of 999 relative to the buttons in the main SWF file. You should keep in mind that each movie clip has its own internal z-order, which means that each movie clip has its own set of depth values. The two buttons may have the same depth value, but the values only have meaning in relation to other objects in the same z-order. In this case, the buttons have the same depth value, but the values relate to different movie clips. For example, the depth value of the button in the main SWF file relates to the z-order of the main timeline, while the depth value of the button in the loaded SWF file relates to the internal z-order of the `myClip_mc` movie clip.

See also

`getDepth (MovieClip.getDepth method)`, `getDepth (TextField.getDepth method)`,

_height (Button._height property)

`public _height : Number`

The height of the button, in pixels.

Availability: ActionScript 1.0; Flash Player 6

Example

The following example sets the height and width of a button called `my_btn` to a specified width and height.

```
my_btn._width = 500;
my_btn._height = 200;
```

_highquality (Button._highquality property)

`public _highquality : Number`

Deprecated since Flash Player 7. This property was deprecated in favor of `Button._quality`.

Specifies the level of anti-aliasing applied to the current SWF file. Specify 2 (best quality) to apply high quality with bitmap smoothing always on. Specify 1 (high quality) to apply anti-aliasing; this smooths bitmaps if the SWF file does not contain animation and is the default value. Specify 0 (low quality) to prevent anti-aliasing.

Availability: ActionScript 1.0; Flash Player 6

Example

Add a button instance on the Stage and name it myBtn_btn. Draw an oval on the Stage using the Oval tool that has a stroke and fill color. Select Frame 1 and add the following ActionScript using the Actions panel:

```
myBtn_btn.onRelease = function() {
 myBtn_btn._highquality = 0;
};
```

When you click myBtn_btn, the circle's stroke will look jagged. You could add the following ActionScript instead to affect the SWF globally:

```
_quality = 0;
```

See also

`_quality (Button._quality property)`, `_quality` property

menu (Button.menu property)

`public menu : ContextMenu`

Associates the `ContextMenu` object `contextMenu` with the button object `my_button`. The ContextMenu class lets you modify the context menu that appears when the user right-clicks (Windows) or Control-clicks (Macintosh) in Flash Player.

Availability: ActionScript 1.0; Flash Player 7

Example

The following example assigns a ContextMenu object to a button instance named myBtn_btn. The ContextMenu object contains a single menu item (labeled "Save...") with an associated callback handler function named doSave.

Add the button instance to the Stage and name it myBtn_btn.

```
var menu_cm:ContextMenu = new ContextMenu();
menu_cm.customItems.push(new ContextMenuItem("Save...", doSave));
function doSave(menu:Object, obj:Object):Void {
  trace( " You selected the 'Save...' menu item ");
}
myBtn_btn.menu = menu_cm;
```

Select Control > Test Movie to test the SWF file. With the pointer over myBtn_btn, right-click or Control-click. The context menu appears with Save in the menu. When you select Save from the menu, the Output panel appears.

See also

ContextMenu, ContextMenuItem, menu (MovieClip.menu property), menu (TextField.menu property)

_name (Button._name property)

```
public _name : String
```

Instance name of the button specified by my_btn.

Availability: ActionScript 1.0; Flash Player 6

Example

The following example traces all instance names of any Button instances within the current Timeline of a SWF file.

```
for (i in this) {
  if (this[i] instanceof Button) {
  trace(this[i]._name);
  }
}
```

onDragOut (Button.onDragOut handler)

`onDragOut = function() {}`

Invoked when the mouse button is clicked over the button and the pointer then dragged outside of the button. You must define a function that executes when the event handler is invoked.

Availability: ActionScript 1.0; Flash Player 6

Example

The following example demonstrates how you can execute statements when the pointer is dragged off a button. Create a button called `my_btn` on the Stage and enter the following ActionScript in a frame on the Timeline:

```
my_btn.onDragOut = function() {
  trace("onDragOut: "+this._name);
};
my_btn.onDragOver = function() {
  trace("onDragOver: "+this._name);
};
```

onDragOver (Button.onDragOver handler)

`onDragOver = function() {}`

Invoked when the user presses and drags the mouse button outside and then over the button. You must define a function that executes when the event handler is invoked.

Availability: ActionScript 1.0; Flash Player 6

Example

The following example defines a function for the onDragOver handler that sends a `trace()` statement to the Output panel. Create a button called `my_btn` on the Stage and enter the following ActionScript on the Timeline:

```
my_btn.onDragOut = function() {
  trace("onDragOut: "+this._name);
};
my_btn.onDragOver = function() {
  trace("onDragOver: "+this._name);
};
```

When you test the SWF file, drag the pointer off the button instance. Then, while holding the mouse button, drag onto the button instance again. Notice that the Output panel tracks your movements.

See also

onDragOut (Button.onDragOut handler)

onKeyDown (Button.onKeyDown handler)

```
onKeyDown = function() {}
```

Invoked when a button has keyboard focus and a key is pressed. The onKeyDown event handler is invoked with no parameters. You can use the Key.getAscii() and Key.getCode() methods to determine which key was pressed. You must define a function that executes when the event handler is invoked.

Availability: ActionScript 1.0; Flash Player 6

Example

In the following example, a function that sends text to the Output panel is defined for the onKeyDown handler. Create a button called my_btn on the Stage, and enter the following ActionScript in a frame on the Timeline:

```
my_btn.onKeyDown = function() {
  trace("onKeyDown: "+this._name+" (Key: "+getKeyPressed()+")");
};
function getKeyPressed():String {
  var theKey:String;
  switch (Key.getAscii()) {
  case Key.BACKSPACE :
    theKey = "BACKSPACE";
    break;
  case Key.SPACE :
    theKey = "SPACE";
    break;
  default :
    theKey = chr(Key.getAscii());
  }
  return theKey;
}
```

Select Control > Test Movie to test the SWF file. Make sure you select Control > Disable Keyboard Shortcuts in the test environment. Then press the Tab key until the button has focus (a yellow rectangle appears around the my_btn instance) and start pressing keys on your keyboard. When you press keys, they are displayed in the Output panel.

See also

onKeyUp (Button.onKeyUp handler), getAscii (Key.getAscii method), getCode (Key.getCode method)

onKeyUp (Button.onKeyUp handler)

```
onKeyUp = function() {}
```

Invoked when a button has input focus and a key is released. The onKeyUp event handler is invoked with no parameters. You can use the Key.getAscii() and Key.getCode() methods to determine which key was pressed.

Availability: ActionScript 1.0; Flash Player 6

Example

In the following example, a function that sends text to the Output panel is defined for the onKeyDown handler. Create a button called my_btn on the Stage, and enter the following ActionScript in a frame on the Timeline:

```
my_btn.onKeyDown = function() {
  trace("onKeyDown: "+this._name+" (Key: "+getKeyPressed()+")");
};
my_btn.onKeyUp = function() {
  trace("onKeyUp: "+this._name+" (Key: "+getKeyPressed()+")");
};
function getKeyPressed():String {
  var theKey:String;
  switch (Key.getAscii()) {
  case Key.BACKSPACE :
    theKey = "BACKSPACE";
    break;
  case Key.SPACE :
    theKey = "SPACE";
    break;
  default :
    theKey = chr(Key.getAscii());
  }
  return theKey;
}
```

Press Control+Enter to test the SWF file. Make sure you select Control > Disable Keyboard Shortcuts in the test environment. Then press the Tab key until the button has focus (a yellow rectangle appears around the my_btn instance) and start pressing keys on your keyboard. When you press keys, they are displayed in the Output panel.

See also

onKeyDown (Button.onKeyDown handler), getAscii (Key.getAscii method), getCode (Key.getCode method)

onKillFocus (Button.onKillFocus handler)

`onKillFocus = function(newFocus:Object) {}`

Invoked when a button loses keyboard focus. The `onKillFocus` handler receives one parameter, `newFocus`, which is an object representing the new object receiving the focus. If no object receives the focus, `newFocus` contains the value `null`.

Availability: ActionScript 1.0; Flash Player 6

Parameters

`newFocus:Object` - The object that is receiving the focus.

Example

The following example demonstrates how statements can be executed when a button loses focus. Create a button instance on the Stage called `my_btn` and add the following ActionScript to Frame 1 of the Timeline:

```
this.createTextField("output_txt", this.getNextHighestDepth(), 0, 0, 300,
    200);
output_txt.wordWrap = true;
output_txt.multiline = true;
output_txt.border = true;
my_btn.onKillFocus = function() {
    output_txt.text = "onKillFocus: "+this._name+newline+output_txt.text;
};
```

Test the SWF file in a browser window, and try using the Tab key to move through the elements in the window. When the button instance loses focus, text is sent to the `output_txt` text field.

The `MovieClip.getNextHighestDepth()` method used in this example requires Flash Player 7 or later. If your SWF file includes a version 2 component, use the version 2 components DepthManager class instead of the `MovieClip.getNextHighestDepth()` method.

onPress (Button.onPress handler)

`onPress = function() {}`

Invoked when a button is pressed. You must define a function that executes when the event handler is invoked.

Availability: ActionScript 1.0; Flash Player 6

Example

In the following example, a function that sends a trace() statement to the Output panel is defined for the onPress handler:

```
my_btn.onPress = function () {
  trace ("onPress called");
};
```

onRelease (Button.onRelease handler)

```
onRelease = function() {}
```

Invoked when a button is released. You must define a function that executes when the event handler is invoked.

Availability: ActionScript 1.0; Flash Player 6

Example

In the following example, a function that sends a trace() statement to the Output panel is defined for the onRelease handler:

```
my_btn.onRelease = function () {
  trace ("onRelease called");
};
```

onReleaseOutside (Button.onReleaseOutside handler)

```
onReleaseOutside = function() {}
```

Invoked when the mouse is released while the pointer is outside the button after the button is pressed while the pointer is inside the button. You must define a function that executes when the event handler is invoked.

Availability: ActionScript 1.0; Flash Player 6

Example

In the following example, a function that sends a trace() statement to the Output panel is defined for the onReleaseOutside handler:

```
my_btn.onReleaseOutside = function () {
  trace ("onReleaseOutside called");
};
```

onRollOut (Button.onRollOut handler)

`onRollOut = function() {}`

Invoked when the pointer moves outside a button area. You must define a function that executes when the event handler is invoked.

Availability: ActionScript 1.0; Flash Player 6

Example

In the following example, a function that sends a trace() statement to the Output panel is defined for the `onRollOut` handler:

```
my_btn.onRollOut = function () {
  trace ("onRollOut called");
};
```

onRollOver (Button.onRollOver handler)

`onRollOver = function() {}`

Invoked when the pointer moves over a button area. You must define a function that executes when the event handler is invoked.

Availability: ActionScript 1.0; Flash Player 6

Example

In the following example, a function that sends a trace() statement to the Output panel is defined for the `onRollOver` handler:

```
my_btn.onRollOver = function () {
  trace ("onRollOver called");
};
```

onSetFocus (Button.onSetFocus handler)

`onSetFocus = function(oldFocus:Object) {}`

Invoked when a button receives keyboard focus. The `oldFocus` parameter is the object that loses the focus. For example, if the user presses the Tab key to move the input focus from a text field to a button, oldFocus contains the text field instance.

If there is no previously focused object, `oldFocus` contains a null value.

Availability: ActionScript 1.0; Flash Player 6

Parameters

`oldFocus:Object` - The object to lose keyboard focus.

Example

The following example demonstrates how you can execute statements when the user of a SWF file moves focus from one button to another. Create two buttons, btn1_btn and btn2_btn, and enter the following ActionScript in Frame 1 of the Timeline:

```
Selection.setFocus(btn1_btn);
trace(Selection.getFocus());
btn2_btn.onSetFocus = function(oldFocus) {
  trace(oldFocus._name + "lost focus");
};
```

Test the SWF file by pressing Control+Enter. Make sure you select Control > Disable Keyboard Shortcuts if it is not already selected. Focus is set on btn1_btn. When btn1_btn loses focus and btn2_btn gains focus, information is displayed in the Output panel.

_parent (Button._parent property)

```
public _parent : MovieClip
```

A reference to the movie clip or object that contains the current movie clip or object. The current object is the one containing the ActionScript code that references _parent.

Use _parent to specify a relative path to movie clips or objects that are above the current movie clip or object. You can use _parent to move up multiple levels in the display list as in the following:

```
this._parent._parent._alpha = 20;
```

Availability: ActionScript 1.0; Flash Player 6

Example

In the following example, a button named my_btn is placed inside a movie clip called my_mc. The following code shows how to use the _parent property to get a reference to the movie clip my_mc:

```
trace(my_mc.my_btn._parent);
```

The Output panel displays the following:

```
_level0.my_mc
```

See also

_parent (MovieClip._parent property), _target (MovieClip._target property), _root property

---

_quality (Button._quality property)

`public _quality : String`

Property (global); sets or retrieves the rendering quality used for a SWF file. Device fonts are always aliased and therefore are unaffected by the `_quality` property.

The `_quality` property can be set to the following values:

- `"LOW"` Low rendering quality. Graphics are not anti-aliased, and bitmaps are not smoothed.
- `"MEDIUM"` Medium rendering quality. Graphics are anti-aliased using a 2 x 2 pixel grid, but bitmaps are not smoothed. This is suitable for movies that do not contain text.
- `"HIGH"` High rendering quality. Graphics are anti-aliased using a 4 x 4 pixel grid, and bitmaps are smoothed if the movie is static. This is the default rendering quality setting used by Flash.
- `"BEST"` Very high rendering quality. Graphics are anti-aliased using a 4 x 4 pixel grid and bitmaps are always smoothed.

> **NOTE** Although you can specify this property for a Button object, it is actually a global property, and you can specify its value simply as `_quality`.

Availability: ActionScript 1.0; Flash Player 6

Example

This example sets the rendering quality of a button named `my_btn` to `LOW`:

```
my_btn._quality = "LOW";
```

_rotation (Button._rotation property)

`public _rotation : Number`

The rotation of the button, in degrees, from its original orientation. Values from 0 to 180 represent clockwise rotation; values from 0 to -180 represent counterclockwise rotation. Values outside this range are added to or subtracted from 360 to obtain a value within the range. For example, the statement `my_btn._rotation = 450` is the same as `my_btn._rotation = 90`.

Availability: ActionScript 1.0; Flash Player 6

Example

The following example rotates two buttons on the Stage. Create two buttons on the Stage called `control_btn` and `my_btn`. Make sure that `my_btn` is not perfectly round, so you can see it rotating. Then enter the following ActionScript in Frame 1 of the Timeline:

```
var control_btn:Button;
var my_btn:Button;
control_btn.onRelease = function() {
  my_btn._rotation += 10;
};
```

Now create another button on the Stage called `myOther_btn`, making sure it isn't perfectly round (so you can see it rotate). Enter the following ActionScript in Frame 1 of the Timeline.

```
var myOther_btn:Button;
this.createEmptyMovieClip("rotater_mc", this.getNextHighestDepth());
rotater_mc.onEnterFrame = function() {
  myOther_btn._rotation += 2;
};
```

The `MovieClip.getNextHighestDepth()` method used in this example requires Flash Player 7 or later. If your SWF file includes a version 2 component, use the version 2 components DepthManager class instead of the `MovieClip.getNextHighestDepth()` method.

See also

`_rotation (MovieClip._rotation property)`, `_rotation (TextField._rotation property)`

scale9Grid (Button.scale9Grid property)

`public scale9Grid : Rectangle`

The rectangular region that defines the nine scaling regions for the button. If set to `null`, the entire button is scaled normally when any scale transformation is applied.

When you define a `scale9Grid` property for a button, the button is divided into a grid with nine regions based on the `scale9Grid` rectangle, which defines the center region of the grid. There are eight other regions of the grid, as follows:

- The area in the upper-left corner outside of the rectangle
- The area above the rectangle
- The area in the upper-right corner outside the rectangle
- The area to the left of the rectangle
- The area to the right of the rectangle
- The area in the lower-left corner outside the rectangle
- The area below the rectangle

- The area in the lower-right corner outside the rectangle

You can think of the eight regions outside of the center (defined by the rectangle) as a picture frame that has special rules applied to it when the button is scaled.

When the scale9Grid property is set and a button is scaled, all text and gradients are scaled normally; however, for other types of objects the following rules apply:

- Content in the center region is scaled normally.
- Content in the corners is not scaled.
- Content in the top and bottom regions is scaled only horizontally. Content in the left and right regions is scaled only vertically.

If a button is rotated, all subsequent scaling is normal, and the scale9Grid property is ignored.

A common use for the scale9Grid property is to set up a button in which edge lines retain the same width when the button is scaled.

For more information, including illustrations and a related example, see MovieClip.scale9Grid.

Availability: ActionScript 1.0; Flash Player 8

See also

Rectangle (flash.geom.Rectangle), scale9Grid (MovieClip.scale9Grid property)

_soundbuftime (Button._soundbuftime property)

public _soundbuftime : Number

The property that specifies the number of seconds a sound prebuffers before it starts to stream.

 Although you can specify this property for a Button object, it is actually a global property that applies to all loaded sounds, and you can specify its value simply as _soundbuftime. Setting this property for a Button actually sets global property.

For more information and an example, see the _soundbuftime global property.

Availability: ActionScript 1.0; Flash Player 6

See also

_soundbuftime property

tabEnabled (Button.tabEnabled property)

`public tabEnabled : Boolean`

Specifies whether my_btn is included in automatic tab ordering. It is `undefined` by default.

If the `tabEnabled` property is `undefined` or `true`, the object is included in automatic tab ordering. If the `tabIndex` property is also set to a value, the object is included in custom tab ordering as well. If `tabEnabled` is `false`, the object is not included in automatic or custom tab ordering, even if the `tabIndex` property is set.

Availability: ActionScript 1.0; Flash Player 6

Example

The following ActionScript is used to set the `tabEnabled` property for one of four buttons to `false`. However, all four buttons (one_btn, two_btn, three_btn, and four_btn) are placed in a custom tab order using `tabIndex`. Although `tabIndex` is set for three_btn, three_btn is not included in a custom or automatic tab order because `tabEnabled` is set to `false` for that instance. To set the tab ordering for the four buttons, add the following ActionScript to Frame 1 of the Timeline:

```
three_btn.tabEnabled = false;
two_btn.tabIndex = 1;
four_btn.tabIndex = 2;
three_btn.tabIndex = 3;
one_btn.tabIndex = 4;
```

Make sure that you disable keyboard shortcuts when you test the SWF file by selecting Control > Disable Keyboard Shortcuts in the test environment.

See also

tabIndex (Button.tabIndex property), tabEnabled (MovieClip.tabEnabled property), tabEnabled (TextField.tabEnabled property)

tabIndex (Button.tabIndex property)

`public tabIndex : Number`

Lets you customize the tab ordering of objects in a SWF file. You can set the `tabIndex` property on a button, movie clip, or text field instance; it is `undefined` by default.

If any currently displayed object in the SWF file contains a `tabIndex` property, automatic tab ordering is disabled, and the tab ordering is calculated from the `tabIndex` properties of objects in the SWF file. The custom tab ordering only includes objects that have `tabIndex` properties.

The tabIndex property may be a non-negative integer. The objects are ordered according to their tabIndex properties, in ascending order. An object with a tabIndex value of 1 precedes an object with a tabIndex value of 2. If two objects have the same tabIndex value, the one that precedes the other in the tab ordering is undefined.

The custom tab ordering defined by the tabIndex property is *flat*. This means that no attention is paid to the hierarchical relationships of objects in the SWF file. All objects in the SWF file with tabIndex properties are placed in the tab order, and the tab order is determined by the order of the tabIndex values. If two objects have the same tabIndex value, the one that goes first is undefined. You shouldn't use the same tabIndex value for multiple objects.

Availability: ActionScript 1.0; Flash Player 6

Example

The following ActionScript is used to set the tabEnabled property for one of four buttons to false. However, all four buttons (one_btn, two_btn, three_btn, and four_btn) are placed in a custom tab order using tabIndex. Although tabIndex is set for three_btn, three_btn is not included in a custom or automatic tab order because tabEnabled is set to false for that instance. To set the tab ordering for the four buttons, add the following ActionScript to Frame 1 of the Timeline:

```
three_btn.tabEnabled = false;
two_btn.tabIndex = 1;
four_btn.tabIndex = 2;
three_btn.tabIndex = 3;
one_btn.tabIndex = 4;
```

Make sure that you disable keyboard shortcuts when you test the SWF file by selecting Control > Disable Keyboard Shortcuts in the test environment.

See also

tabEnabled (Button.tabEnabled property), tabChildren (MovieClip.tabChildren property), tabEnabled (MovieClip.tabEnabled property), tabIndex (MovieClip.tabIndex property), tabIndex (TextField.tabIndex property)

_target (Button._target property)

public _target : String [read-only]

Returns the target path of the button instance specified by my_btn.

Availability: ActionScript 1.0; Flash Player 6

Example

Add a button instance to the Stage with an instance name `my_btn` and add the following code to Frame 1 of the Timeline:

```
trace(my_btn._target); //displays /my_btn
```

Select my_btn and convert it to a movie clip. Give the new movie clip an instance name my_mc. Delete the existing ActionScript in Frame 1 of the Timeline and replace it with:

```
my_mc.my_btn.onRelease = function(){
  trace(this._target); //displays /my_mc/my_btn
};
```

To convert the notation from slash notation to dot notation, modify the previous code example to the following:

```
my_mc.my_btn.onRelease = function(){
  trace(eval(this._target)); //displays _level0.my_mc.my_btn
};
```

This lets you access methods and parameters of the target object, such as:

```
my_mc.my_btn.onRelease = function(){
  var target_btn:Button = eval(this._target);
trace(target_btn._name); //displays my_btn
};
```

See also

`_target (MovieClip._target property)`

trackAsMenu (Button.trackAsMenu property)

`public trackAsMenu : Boolean`

A Boolean value that indicates whether other buttons or movie clips can receive mouse release events. If you drag a button and then release on a second button, the `onRelease` event is registered for the second button. This allows you to create menus. You can set the `trackAsMenu` property on any button or movie clip object. If the `trackAsMenu` property has not been defined, the default behavior is `false`.

You can change the `trackAsMenu` property at any time; the modified button immediately takes on the new behavior.

Availability: ActionScript 1.0; Flash Player 6

Example

The following example demonstrates how to track two buttons as a menu. Place two button instances on the Stage called one_btn and two_btn. Enter the following ActionScript in the Timeline:

```
var one_btn:Button;
var two_btn:Button;
one_btn.trackAsMenu = true;
two_btn.trackAsMenu = true
one_btn.onRelease = function() {
  trace("clicked one_btn");
};
two_btn.onRelease = function() {
  trace("clicked two_btn");
};
```

Test the SWF file by clicking the Stage over one_btn, holding the mouse button down and releasing it over two_btn. Then try commenting out the two lines of ActionScript that contain trackAsMenu and test the SWF file again to see the difference in button behavior.

See also

trackAsMenu (MovieClip.trackAsMenu property)

_url (Button._url property)

public _url : String [read-only]

Retrieves the URL of the SWF file that created the button.

Availability: ActionScript 1.0; Flash Player 6

Example

Create two button instances on the Stage called one_btn and two_btn. Enter the following ActionScript in Frame 1 of the Timeline:

```
var one_btn:Button;
var two_btn:Button;
this.createTextField("output_txt", 999, 0, 0, 100, 22);
output_txt.autoSize = true;
one_btn.onRelease = function() {
  trace("clicked one_btn");
  trace(this._url);
};
two_btn.onRelease = function() {
  trace("clicked "+this._name);
  var url_array:Array = this._url.split("/");
```

```
var my_str:String = String(url_array.pop());
output_txt.text = unescape(my_str);
};
```

When you click each button, the file name of the SWF containing the buttons displays in the Output panel.

useHandCursor (Button.useHandCursor property)

`public useHandCursor : Boolean`

A Boolean value that, when set to `true` (the default), indicates whether a pointing hand (hand cursor) displays when the mouse rolls over a button. If this property is set to `false`, the arrow pointer is used instead.

You can change the `useHandCursor` property at any time; the modified button immediately takes on the new cursor behavior. The `useHandCursor` property can be read out of a prototype object.

Availability: ActionScript 1.0; Flash Player 6

Example

Create two buttons on the Stage with the instance names `myBtn1_btn` and `myBtn2_btn`. Enter the following ActionScript in Frame 1 of the Timeline:

```
myBtn1_btn.useHandCursor = false;
myBtn1_btn.onRelease = buttonClick;
myBtn2_btn.onRelease = buttonClick;
function buttonClick() {
  trace(this._name);
}
```

When the mouse is over and clicks `myBtn1_btn`, there is no pointing hand. However, you see the pointing hand when the button is over and clicks `myBtn2_btn`.

_visible (Button._visible property)

`public _visible : Boolean`

A Boolean value that indicates whether the button specified by `my_btn` is visible. Buttons that are not visible (`_visible` property set to `false`) are disabled.

Availability: ActionScript 1.0; Flash Player 6

Example

Create two buttons on the Stage with the instance names myBtn1_btn and myBtn2_btn.
Enter the following ActionScript in Frame 1 of the Timeline:

```
myBtn1_btn.onRelease = function() {
  this._visible = false;
  trace("clicked "+this._name);
};
myBtn2_btn.onRelease = function() {
  this._alpha = 0;
  trace("clicked "+this._name);
};
```

Notice how you can still click myBtn2_btn after the alpha is set to 0.

See also

_visible (MovieClip._visible property), _visible (TextField._visible
property)

_width (Button._width property)

```
public _width : Number
```

The width of the button, in pixels.

Availability: ActionScript 1.0; Flash Player 6

Example

The following example increases the width property of a button called my_btn, and displays
the width in the Output panel. Enter the following ActionScript in Frame 1 of the Timeline:

```
my_btn.onRelease = function() {
  trace(this._width);
  this._width ~= 1.1;
};
```

See also

_width (MovieClip._width property)

_x (Button._x property)

`public _x : Number`

An integer that sets the x coordinate of a button relative to the local coordinates of the parent movie clip. If a button is on the main Timeline, then its coordinate system refers to the upper left corner of the Stage as (0, 0). If the button is inside a movie clip that has transformations, the button is in the local coordinate system of the enclosing movie clip. Thus, for a movie clip rotated 90 degrees counterclockwise, the enclosed button inherits a coordinate system that is rotated 90 degrees counterclockwise. The button's coordinates refer to the registration point position.

Availability: ActionScript 1.0; Flash Player 6

Example

The following example sets the coordinates of `my_btn` to 0 on the Stage. Create a button called `my_btn` and enter the following ActionScript in Frame 1 of the Timeline:

```
my_btn._x = 0;
my_btn._y = 0;
```

See also

`_xscale (Button._xscale property), _y (Button._y property), _yscale (Button._yscale property)`

_xmouse (Button._xmouse property)

`public _xmouse : Number [read-only]`

Returns the *x* coordinate of the mouse position relative to the button.

Availability: ActionScript 1.0; Flash Player 6

Example

The following example displays the xmouse position for the Stage and a button called `my_btn` that is placed on the Stage. Enter the following ActionScript in Frame 1 of the Timeline:

```
this.createTextField("mouse_txt", 999, 5, 5, 150, 40);
mouse_txt.html = true;
mouse_txt.wordWrap = true;
mouse_txt.border = true;
mouse_txt.autoSize = true;
mouse_txt.selectable = false;
//
var mouseListener:Object = new Object();
mouseListener.onMouseMove = function() {
    var table_str:String = "<textformat tabstops='[50,100]'>";
```

```
table_str += "<b>Stage</b>\t"+"x:"+_xmouse+"\t"+"y:"+_ymouse+newline;
table_str += "<b>Button</
b>\t"+"x:"+my_btn._xmouse+"\t"+"y:"+my_btn._ymouse+newline;
table_str += "</textformat>";
mouse_txt.htmlText = table_str;
};
Mouse.addListener(mouseListener);
```

See also

_ymouse (Button._ymouse property)

_xscale (Button._xscale property)

`public _xscale : Number`

The horizontal scale of the button as applied from the registration point of the button, expressed as a percentage. The default registration point is (0,0).

Scaling the local coordinate system affects the _x and _y property settings, which are defined in pixels. For example, if the parent movie clip is scaled to 50%, setting the _x property moves an object in the button by half the number of pixels that it would if the SWF file were at 100%.

Availability: ActionScript 1.0; Flash Player 6

Example

The following example scales a button called my_btn. When you click and release the button, it grows 10% on the *x* and *y* axis. Enter the following ActionScript in Frame 1 of the Timeline:

```
my_btn.onRelease = function(){
    this._xscale ~= 1.1;
    this._yscale ~= 1.1;
};
```

See also

_x (Button._x property), _y (Button._y property), _yscale (Button._yscale property)

_y (Button._y property)

`public _y : Number`

The *y* coordinate of the button relative to the local coordinates of the parent movie clip. If a button is in the main Timeline, its coordinate system refers to the upper left corner of the Stage as (0, 0). If the button is inside another movie clip that has transformations, the button is in the local coordinate system of the enclosing movie clip. Thus, for a movie clip rotated 90 degrees counterclockwise, the enclosed button inherits a coordinate system that is rotated 90 degrees counterclockwise. The button's coordinates refer to the registration point position.

Availability: ActionScript 1.0; Flash Player 6

Example

The following example sets the coordinates of `my_btn` to 0 on the Stage. Create a button called `my_btn` and enter the following ActionScript in Frame 1 of the Timeline:

```
my_btn._x = 0;
my_btn._y = 0;
```

See also

_x (Button._x property), _xscale (Button._xscale property), _yscale (Button._yscale property)

_ymouse (Button._ymouse property)

`public _ymouse : Number [read-only]`

Indicates the *y* coordinate of the mouse position relative to the button.

Availability: ActionScript 1.0; Flash Player 6

Example

The following example displays the ymouse position for the Stage and a button called `my_btn` that is placed on the Stage. Enter the following ActionScript in Frame 1 of the Timeline:

```
this.createTextField("mouse_txt", 999, 5, 5, 150, 40);
mouse_txt.html = true;
mouse_txt.wordWrap = true;
mouse_txt.border = true;
mouse_txt.autoSize = true;
mouse_txt.selectable = false;
//
var mouseListener:Object = new Object();
mouseListener.onMouseMove = function() {
  var table_str:String = "<textformat tabstops='[50,100]'>";
  table_str += "<b>Stage</b>\t"+"x:"+_xmouse+"\t"+"y:"+_ymouse+newline;
  table_str += "<b>Button</
b>\t"+"x:"+my_btn._xmouse+"\t"+"y:"+my_btn._ymouse+newline;
  table_str += "</textformat>";
```

```
  mouse_txt.htmlText = table_str;
};
Mouse.addListener(mouseListener);
```

See also

_xmouse (Button._xmouse property)

_yscale (Button._yscale property)

`public _yscale : Number`

The vertical scale of the button as applied from the registration point of the button, expressed as a percentage. The default registration point is (0,0).

Availability: ActionScript 1.0; Flash Player 6

Example

The following example scales a button called `my_btn`. When you click and release the button, it grows 10% on the *x* and *y* axis. Enter the following ActionScript in Frame 1 of the Timeline:

```
my_btn.onRelease = function(){
  this._xscale ~= 1.1;
  this._yscale ~ 1.1;
};
```

See also

_y (Button._y property), _x (Button._x property), _xscale (Button._xscale property)

Camera

```
Object
  |
  +-Camera
```

public class **Camera**
extends Object

The Camera class is primarily for use with Macromedia Flash Communication Server, but can be used in a limited way without the server.

The Camera class lets you capture video from a video camera attached to the computer that is running Macromedia Flash Player—for example, to monitor a video feed from a web camera attached to your local system. (Flash provides similar audio capabilities; for more information, see the Microphone class entry.)

Warning: When a SWF file tries to access the camera returned by `Camera.get()`, Flash Player displays a Privacy dialog box that lets the user choose whether to allow or deny access to the camera. (Make sure your Stage size is at least 215 x 138 pixels for the Camera class examples; this is the minimum size Flash requires to display the dialog box.) End users and administrative users may also disable camera access on a per-site or global basis.

To create or reference a Camera object, use the `Camera.get()` method.

Availability: ActionScript 1.0; Flash Player 6

Property summary

Modifiers	Property	Description
	`activityLevel:Number` [read-only]	A numeric value that specifies the amount of motion the camera is detecting.
	`bandwidth:Number` [read-only]	An integer that specifies the maximum amount of bandwidth the current outgoing video feed can use, in bytes.
	`currentFps:Number` [read-only]	The rate at which the camera is capturing data, in frames per second.
	`fps:Number` [read-only]	The maximum rate at which you want the camera to capture data, in frames per second.
	`height:Number` [read-only]	The current capture height, in pixels.
	`index:Number` [read-only]	A zero-based integer that specifies the index of the camera, as reflected in the array returned by `Camera.names`.

Modifiers	Property	Description
	`motionLevel:Number` [read-only]	A numeric value that specifies the amount of motion required to invoke `Camera.onActivity(true)`.
	`motionTimeOut:Number` [read-only]	The number of milliseconds between the time the camera stops detecting motion and the time `Camera.onActivity (false)` is invoked.
	`muted:Boolean` [read-only]	A Boolean value that specifies whether the user has denied access to the camera (`true`) or allowed access (`false`) in the Flash Player Privacy Settings panel.
	`name:String` [read-only]	A string that specifies the name of the current camera, as returned by the camera hardware.
`static`	`names:Array` [read-only]	Retrieves an array of strings reflecting the names of all available cameras without displaying the Flash Player Privacy Settings panel.
	`quality:Number` [read-only]	An integer specifying the required level of picture quality, as determined by the amount of compression being applied to each video frame.
	`width:Number` [read-only]	The current capture width, in pixels.

Properties inherited from class Object

```
constructor (Object.constructor property), __proto__ (Object.__proto__
property), prototype (Object.prototype property), __resolve
(Object.__resolve property)
```

Event summary

Event	Description
`onActivity = function(active: Boolean) {}`	Invoked when the camera starts or stops detecting motion.
`onStatus = function(infoObj ect:Object) {}`	Invoked when the user allows or denies access to the camera.

Method summary

Modifiers	Signature	Description
static	`get([index:Number])` `: Camera`	Returns a reference to a Camera object for capturing video.

	`setMode([width:Numbe`
	`r], [height:Number],`
	`[fps:Number],`
	`[favorArea:Boolean])`
	`: Void`
		Sets the camera capture mode to the native mode that best meets the specified requirements.

	`setMotionLevel([moti`
	`onLevel:Number],`
	`[timeOut:Number]) :`
	`Void`
		Specifies how much motion is required to invoke `Camera.onActivity(true)`.

	`setQuality([bandwidt`
	`h:Number],`
	`[quality:Number]) :`
	`Void`
		Sets the maximum amount of bandwidth per second or the required picture quality of the current outgoing video feed.

Methods inherited from class Object

```
addProperty (Object.addProperty method), hasOwnProperty
(Object.hasOwnProperty method), isPropertyEnumerable
(Object.isPropertyEnumerable method), isPrototypeOf (Object.isPrototypeOf
method), registerClass (Object.registerClass method), toString
(Object.toString method), unwatch (Object.unwatch method), valueOf
(Object.valueOf method), watch (Object.watch method)
```

activityLevel (Camera.activityLevel property)

`public activityLevel : Number [read-only]`

A numeric value that specifies the amount of motion the camera is detecting. Values range from 0 (no motion is being detected) to 100 (a large amount of motion is being detected). The value of this property can help you determine if you need to pass a setting to `Camera.setMotionLevel()`.

If the camera is available but is not yet being used because `Video.attachVideo()` has not been called, this property is set to -1.

If you are streaming only uncompressed local video, this property is set only if you have assigned a function to the `Camera.onActivity` event handler. Otherwise, it is undefined.

Availability: ActionScript 1.0; Flash Player 6

Example

This example detects the amount of motion the camera detects using the `activityLevel` property and a ProgressBar instance. Create a new video instance by selecting New Video from the Library options menu. Add an instance to the Stage and give it the instance name `my_video`. Add a ProgressBar component instance to the Stage and give it the instance name `activity_pb`. Then add the following ActionScript to Frame 1 of the Timeline:

```
// video instance on the Stage.
var my_video:Video;
var activity_pb:mx.controls.ProgressBar;
var my_cam:Camera = Camera.get();
my_video.attachVideo(my_cam);
activity_pb.mode = "manual";
activity_pb.label = "Activity %3%%";

this.onEnterFrame = function() {
  activity_pb.setProgress(my_cam.activityLevel, 100);
};
my_cam.onActivity = function(isActive:Boolean) {
  var themeColor:String = (isActive) ? "haloGreen" : "haloOrange";
  activity_pb.setStyle("themeColor", themeColor);
};
```

See also

`motionLevel (Camera.motionLevel property)`, `setMotionLevel (Camera.setMotionLevel method)`

bandwidth (Camera.bandwidth property)

`public bandwidth : Number [read-only]`

An integer that specifies the maximum amount of bandwidth the current outgoing video feed can use, in bytes. A value of 0 means that Flash video can use as much bandwidth as needed to maintain the desired frame quality.

To set this property, use `Camera.setQuality()`.

Availability: ActionScript 1.0; Flash Player 6

Example

The following example changes the maximum amount of bandwidth used by the camera feed. Create a new video instance by selecting New Video from the Library options menu. Add an instance to the Stage and give it the instance name my_video. Add a NumericStepper component instance to the Stage and give it the instance name bandwidth_nstep. Then add the following ActionScript to Frame 1 of the Timeline:

```
var bandwidth_nstep:mx.controls.NumericStepper;
var my_video:Video;
var my_cam:Camera = Camera.get();
my_video.attachVideo(my_cam);
this.createTextField("bandwidth_txt", this.getNextHighestDepth(), 0, 0,
   100, 22);
bandwidth_txt.autoSize = true;
this.onEnterFrame = function() {
   bandwidth_txt.text = "Camera is currently using "+my_cam.bandwidth+"
   bytes ("+Math.round(my_cam.bandwidth/1024)+" KB) bandwidth.";
};
//
bandwidth_nstep.minimum = 0;
bandwidth_nstep.maximum = 128;
bandwidth_nstep.stepSize = 16;
bandwidth_nstep.value = my_cam.bandwidth/1024;
function changeBandwidth(evt:Object) {
   my_cam.setQuality(evt.target.value 1024, 0);
}
bandwidth_nstep.addEventListener("change", changeBandwidth);
```

The MovieClip.getNextHighestDepth() method used in this example requires Flash Player 7 or later. If your SWF file includes a version 2 component, use the version 2 components DepthManager class instead of the MovieClip.getNextHighestDepth() method.

See also

setQuality (Camera.setQuality method)

currentFps (Camera.currentFps property)

public currentFps : Number [read-only]

The rate at which the camera is capturing data, in frames per second. This property cannot be set; however, you can use the Camera.setMode() method to set a related property-- Camera.fps--which specifies the maximum frame rate at which you would like the camera to capture data.

Availability: ActionScript 1.0; Flash Player 6

Example

The following example detects the rate in frames per second that the camera captures data, using the `currentFps` property and a ProgressBar instance. Create a new video instance by selecting New Video from the Library options menu. Add an instance to the Stage and give it the instance name `my_video`. Add a ProgressBar component instance to the Stage and give it the instance name `fps_pb`. Then add the following ActionScript to Frame 1 of the Timeline:

```
var my_video:Video;
var fps_pb:mx.controls.ProgressBar;
var my_cam:Camera = Camera.get();
my_video.attachVideo(my_cam);
this.onEnterFrame = function() {
  fps_pb.setProgress(my_cam.fps-my_cam.currentFps, my_cam.fps);
};

fps_pb.setStyle("fontSize", 10);
fps_pb.setStyle("themeColor", "haloOrange");
fps_pb.labelPlacement = "top";
fps_pb.mode = "manual";
fps_pb.label = "FPS: %2 (%3%% dropped)";
```

See also

setMode (Camera.setMode method), fps (Camera.fps property)

fps (Camera.fps property)

`public fps : Number [read-only]`

The maximum rate at which you want the camera to capture data, in frames per second. The maximum rate possible depends on the capabilities of the camera; that is, if the camera doesn't support the value you set here, this frame rate will not be achieved.

- To set a desired value for this property, use `Camera.setMode()`.

- To determine the rate at which the camera is currently capturing data, use the `Camera.currentFps` property.

Availability: ActionScript 1.0; Flash Player 6

Example

The following example detects the rate in frames per second that the camera captures data, using the currentFps property and a ProgressBar instance. Create a new video instance by selecting New Video from the Library options menu. Add an instance to the Stage and give it the instance name my_video. Add a ProgressBar component instance to the Stage and give it the instance name fps_pb. Then add the following ActionScript to Frame 1 of the Timeline:

```
var my_video:Video;
var fps_pb:mx.controls.ProgressBar;
var my_cam:Camera = Camera.get();
my_video.attachVideo(my_cam);
this.onEnterFrame = function() {
  fps_pb.setProgress(my_cam.fps-my_cam.currentFps, my_cam.fps);
};

fps_pb.setStyle("fontSize", 10);
fps_pb.setStyle("themeColor", "haloOrange");
fps_pb.labelPlacement = "top";
fps_pb.mode = "manual";
fps_pb.label = "FPS: %2 (%3%% dropped)";
```

> **NOTE**
> This setMode() function does not guarentee the requested fps setting; it sets the fps you requested ot the fastest fps available.

See also

currentFps (Camera.currentFps property), setMode (Camera.setMode method)

get (Camera.get method)

```
public static get([index:Number]) : Camera
```

Returns a reference to a Camera object for capturing video. To actually begin capturing the video, you must attach the Camera object to a Video object (see Video.attachVideo()).

Unlike objects that you create using the new constructor, multiple calls to Camera.get() reference the same camera. Thus, if your script contains the lines first_cam = Camera.get() and second_cam = Camera.get(), both first_cam and second_cam reference the same (default) camera.

In general, you shouldn't pass a value for *index*; simply use Camera.get() to return a reference to the default camera. By means of the Camera settings panel (discussed later in this section), the user can specify the default camera Flash should use. If you pass a value for *index*, you might be trying to reference a camera other than the one the user prefers. You might use *index* in rare cases--for example, if your application is capturing video from two cameras at the same time.

When a SWF file tries to access the camera returned by `Camera.get()`, Flash Player displays a Privacy dialog box that lets the user choose whether to allow or deny access to the camera. (Make sure your Stage size is at least 215 x 138 pixels; this is the minimum size Flash requires to display the dialog box.)

When the user responds to this dialog box, the `Camera.onStatus` event handler returns an information object that indicates the user's response. To determine whether the user has denied or allowed access to the camera without processing this event handler, use the `Camera.muted` property.

The user can also specify permanent privacy settings for a particular domain by right-clicking (Windows) or Control-clicking (Macintosh) while a SWF file is playing, selecting Settings, opening the Privacy panel, and selecting Remember.

You can't use ActionScript to set the Allow or Deny value for a user, but you can display the Privacy panel for the user by using `System.showSettings(0)`. If the user selects Remember, Flash Player no longer displays the Privacy dialog box for SWF files from this domain.

If `Camera.get` returns `null`, either the camera is in use by another application, or there are no cameras installed on the system. To determine whether any cameras are installed, use `Camera.names.length`. To display the Flash Player Camera Settings panel, which lets the user choose the camera to be referenced by `Camera.get()`, use `System.showSettings(3)`.

Scanning the hardware for cameras takes time. When Flash finds at least one camera, the hardware is not scanned again for the lifetime of the player instance. However, if Flash doesn't find any cameras, it will scan each time `Camera.get` is called. This is helpful if a user has forgotten to connect the camera; if your SWF file provides a Try Again button that calls `Camera.get`, Flash can find the camera without the user having to restart the SWF file.

 The correct syntax is `Camera.get()`. To assign the `Camera` object to a variable, use syntax like `active_cam - Camera.get()`.

Availability: ActionScript 1.0; Flash Player 6

Parameters

`index:Number` [optional] - A zero-based integer that specifies which camera to get, as determined from the array returned by the `Camera.names` property. To get the default camera (which is recommended for most applications), omit this parameter.

Returns

`Camera` - If `index` is not specified, this method returns a reference to the default camera or, if it is in use by another application, to the first available camera. (If there is more than one camera installed, the user may specify the default camera in the Flash Player Camera Settings panel.) If no cameras are available or installed, the method returns `null`. If `index` is specified, this method returns a reference to the requested camera, or `null` if it is not available.

Example

The following example lets you select an active camera to use from a ComboBox instance. The current active camera is displayed in a Label instance. Create a new video instance by selecting New Video from the Library options menu. Add an instance to the Stage and give it the instance name `my_video`. Add a Label component instance to the Stage and give it the instance name camera_lbl, and a ComboBox component instance and give it the instance name `cameras_cb`. Then add the following ActionScript to Frame 1 of the Timeline:

```
var my_cam:Camera = Camera.get();
var my_video:Video;
my_video.attachVideo(my_cam);
var camera_lbl:mx.controls.Label;
var cameras_cb:mx.controls.ComboBox;
camera_lbl.text = my_cam.name;
cameras_cb.dataProvider = Camera.names;
function changeCamera():Void {
  my_cam = Camera.get(cameras_cb.selectedIndex);
  my_video.attachVideo(my_cam);
  camera_lbl.text = my_cam.name;
}
cameras_cb.addEventListener("change", changeCamera);
camera_lbl.setStyle("fontSize", 9);
cameras_cb.setStyle("fontSize", 9);
```

See also

index (Camera.index property), muted (Camera.muted property), names (Camera.names property), onStatus (Camera.onStatus handler), setMode (Camera.setMode method), showSettings (System.showSettings method), attachVideo (Video.attachVideo method)

height (Camera.height property)

`public height : Number [read-only]`

The current capture height, in pixels. To set a value for this property, use `Camera.setMode()`.

Availability: ActionScript 1.0; Flash Player 6

Example

The following code displays the current width, height and FPS of a video instance in a Label component instance on the Stage. Create a new video instance by selecting New Video from the Library options menu. Add an instance to the Stage and give it the instance name `my_video`. Add a Label component instance to the Stage and give it the instance name dimensions_lbl. Then add the following ActionScript to Frame 1 of the Timeline:

```
var my_cam:Camera = Camera.get();
var my_video:Video;
my_video.attachVideo(my_cam);
var dimensions_lbl:mx.controls.Label;
dimensions_lbl.setStyle("fontSize", 9);
dimensions_lbl.setStyle("fontWeight", "bold");
dimensions_lbl.setStyle("textAlign", "center");
dimensions_lbl.text = "width: "+my_cam.width+", height: "+my_cam.height+",
  FPS: "+my_cam.fps;
```

See also the example for `Camera.setMode()`.

See also

`width (Camera.width property)`, `setMode (Camera.setMode method)`

index (Camera.index property)

`public index : Number [read-only]`

A zero-based integer that specifies the index of the camera, as reflected in the array returned by `Camera.names`.

Availability: ActionScript 1.0; Flash Player 6

Example

The following example displays an array of cameras in a text field that is created at runtime, and tells you which camera you are currently using. Create a new video instance by selecting New Video from the Library options menu. Add an instance to the Stage and give it the instance name `my_video`. Add a Label component instance to the Stage and give it the instance name camera_lbl. Then add the following ActionScript to Frame 1 of the Timeline:

```
var camera_lbl:mx.controls.Label;
var my_cam:Camera = Camera.get();
var my_video:Video;
my_video.attachVideo(my_cam);

camera_lbl.text = my_cam.index+". "+my_cam.name;
this.createTextField("cameras_txt", this.getNextHighestDepth(), 25, 160,
  160, 80);
```

```
cameras_txt.html = true;
cameras_txt.border = true;
cameras_txt.wordWrap = true;
cameras_txt.multiline = true;
for (var i = 0; i<Camera.names.length; i++) {
   cameras_txt.htmlText += "<li><u><a
   href=\"asfunction:changeCamera,"+i+"\">"+Camera.names[i]+"</a></u></
   li>";
}
function changeCamera(index:Number) {
   my_cam = Camera.get(index);
   my_video.attachVideo(my_cam);
   camera_lbl.text = my_cam.index+". "+my_cam.name;
}
```

The `MovieClip.getNextHighestDepth()` method used in this example requires Flash Player 7 or later. If your SWF file includes a version 2 component, use the version 2 components DepthManager class instead of the `MovieClip.getNextHighestDepth()` method.

See also

`names (Camera.names property)`, `get (Camera.get method)`

motionLevel (Camera.motionLevel property)

`public motionLevel : Number [read-only]`

A numeric value that specifies the amount of motion required to invoke `Camera.onActivity(true)`. Acceptable values range from 0 to 100. The default value is 50.

Video can be displayed regardless of the value of the `motionLevel` property. For more information, see `Camera.setMotionLevel()`.

Availability: ActionScript 1.0; Flash Player 6

Example

The following example continually detects the motion level of a camera feed. Create a new video instance by selecting New Video from the Library options menu. Add an instance to the Stage and give it the instance name `my_video`. Add a Label component instance to the Stage and give it the instance name motionLevel_lbl, a NumericStepper with the instance name `motionLevel_nstep`, and a ProgressBar with the instance name motion_pb. Then add the following ActionScript to Frame 1 of the Timeline:

```
var my_cam:Camera = Camera.get();
var my_video:Video;
my_video.attachVideo(my_cam);

// configure the ProgressBar component instance
```

```
var motion_pb:mx.controls.ProgressBar;
motion_pb.mode = "manual";
motion_pb.label = "Motion: %3%%";

var motionLevel_lbl:mx.controls.Label;
// configure the NumericStepper component instance
var motionLevel_nstep:mx.controls.NumericStepper;
motionLevel_nstep.minimum = 0;
motionLevel_nstep.maximum = 100;
motionLevel_nstep.stepSize = 5;
motionLevel_nstep.value = my_cam.motionLevel;

// Continuously update the progress of the ProgressBar component instance to
    the activityLevel
// of the current Camera instance, which is defined in my_cam
this.onEnterFrame = function() {
    motion_pb.setProgress(my_cam.activityLevel, 100);
};

// When the level of activity goes above or below the number defined in
    Camera.motionLevel,
// trigger the onActivity event handler.
my_cam.onActivity = function(isActive:Boolean) {
    // If isActive equals true, set the themeColor variable to "haloGreen".
    // Otherwise set the themeColor to "haloOrange".
    var themeColor:String = (isActive) ? "haloGreen" : "haloOrange";
    motion_pb.setStyle("themeColor", themeColor);
};

function changeMotionLevel() {
    // Set the motionLevel property for my_cam Camera instance to the value
    of the NumericStepper
    // component instance. Maintain the current motionTimeOut value of the
    my_cam Camera instance.
    my_cam.setMotionLevel(motionLevel_nstep.value, my_cam.motionTimeOut);
}
motionLevel_nstep.addEventListener("change", changeMotionLevel);
```

See also

onActivity (Camera.onActivity handler), onStatus (Camera.onStatus handler),
setMotionLevel (Camera.setMotionLevel method), activityLevel
(Camera.activityLevel property)

motionTimeOut (Camera.motionTimeOut property)

`public motionTimeOut : Number [read-only]`

The number of milliseconds between the time the camera stops detecting motion and the time `Camera.onActivity (false)` is invoked. The default value is 2000 (2 seconds).

To set this value, use `Camera.setMotionLevel()`.

Availability: ActionScript 1.0; Flash Player 6

Example

In the following example, the ProgressBar instance changes its halo theme color when the activity level falls below the motion level. You can set the number of seconds for the `motionTimeout` property using a NumericStepper instance. Create a new video instance by selecting New Video from the Library options menu. Add an instance to the Stage and give it the instance name `my_video`. Add a Label component instance to the Stage and give it the instance name motionLevel_lbl, a NumericStepper with the instance name motionTimeOut_nstep, and a ProgressBar with the instance name motion_pb. Then add the following ActionScript to Frame 1 of the Timeline:

```
var motionLevel_lbl:mx.controls.Label;
var motion_pb:mx.controls.ProgressBar;
var motionTimeOut_nstep:mx.controls.NumericStepper;
var my_cam:Camera = Camera.get();
var my_video:Video;
my_video.attachVideo(my_cam);

this.onEnterFrame = function() {
  motionLevel_lbl.text = "activityLevel: "+my_cam.activityLevel;
};

motion_pb.indeterminate = true;
my_cam.onActivity = function(isActive:Boolean) {
  if (isActive) {
  motion_pb.setStyle("themeColor", "haloGreen");
  motion_pb.label = "Motion is above "+my_cam.motionLevel;
  } else {
  motion_pb.setStyle("themeColor", "haloOrange");
  motion_pb.label = "Motion is below "+my_cam.motionLevel;
  }
};
function changeMotionTimeOut() {
  my_cam.setMotionLevel(my_cam.motionLevel, motionTimeOut_nstep.value
  1000);
}
motionTimeOut_nstep.addEventListener("change", changeMotionTimeOut);
motionTimeOut_nstep.value = my_cam.motionTimeOut/1000;
```

See also

setMotionLevel (Camera.setMotionLevel method), onActivity (Camera.onActivity handler)

muted (Camera.muted property)

public muted : Boolean [read-only]

A Boolean value that specifies whether the user has denied access to the camera (true) or allowed access (false) in the Flash Player Privacy Settings panel. When this value changes, Camera.onStatus is invoked. For more information, see Camera.get().

Availability: ActionScript 1.0; Flash Player 6

Example

In the following example, an error message could be displayed if my_cam.muted evaluates to true. Create a new video instance by selecting New Video from the Library options menu. Add an instance to the Stage and give it the instance name my_video. Then add the following ActionScript to Frame 1 of the Timeline:

```
var my_cam:Camera = Camera.get();
var my_video:Video;
my_video.attachVideo(my_cam);
my_cam.onStatus = function(infoObj:Object) {
    if (my_cam.muted) {
    // If user is denied access to their Camera, you can display an error
    message here. You can display the user's Camera/Privacy settings again
    using System.showSettings(0);
    trace("User denied access to Camera");
    System.showSettings(0);
    }
};
```

See also

get (Camera.get method), onStatus (Camera.onStatus handler)

name (Camera.name property)

```
public name : String [read-only]
```

A string that specifies the name of the current camera, as returned by the camera hardware.

Availability: ActionScript 1.0; Flash Player 6

Example

The following example displays the name of the default camera in a text field. In Windows, this name is the same as the device name listed in the Scanners and Cameras Control Panel. Create a new video instance by selecting New Video from the Library options menu. Add an instance to the Stage and give it the instance name my_video. Then add the following ActionScript to Frame 1 of the Timeline:

```
var my_cam:Camera = Camera.get();
var my_video:Video;
my_video.attachVideo(my_cam);

this.createTextField("name_txt", this.getNextHighestDepth(), 0, 0, 100,
    22);
name_txt.autoSize = true;
name_txt.text = my_cam.name;
```

The MovieClip.getNextHighestDepth() method used in this example requires Flash Player 7 or later. If your SWF file includes a version 2 component, use the version 2 components DepthManager class instead of the MovieClip.getNextHighestDepth() method.

See also

get (Camera.get method), names (Camera.names property)

names (Camera.names property)

```
public static names : Array [read-only]
```

Retrieves an array of strings reflecting the names of all available cameras without displaying the Flash Player Privacy Settings panel. This array behaves in the same way as any other ActionScript array, implicitly providing the zero-based index of each camera and the number of cameras on the system (by means of Camera.names.length). For more information, see the Camera.names Array class entry.

Calling the `Camera.names` property requires an extensive examination of the hardware, and it may take several seconds to build the array. In most cases, you can just use the default camera.

Availability: ActionScript 1.0; Flash Player 6

Example

The following example uses the default camera unless more than one camera is available, in which case the user can choose which camera to set as the default camera. If only one camera is present, then the default camera is used. Create a new video instance by selecting New Video from the Library options menu. Add an instance to the Stage and give it the instance name `my_video`. Then add the following ActionScript to Frame 1 of the Timeline:

```
var my_video:Video;
var cam_array:Array = Camera.names;
if (cam_array.length>1) {
   System.showSettings(3);
}
var my_cam:Camera = Camera.get();
my_video.attachVideo(my_cam);
```

See also

`get (Camera.get method)`, `index (Camera.index property)`, `name (Camera.name property)`

onActivity (Camera.onActivity handler)

`onActivity = function(active:Boolean) {}`

Invoked when the camera starts or stops detecting motion. If you want to respond to this event handler, you must create a function to process its activity value.

To specify the amount of motion required to invoke `Camera.onActivity(true)` and the amount of time that must elapse without activity before invoking `Camera.onActivity(false)`, use `Camera.setMotionLevel()`.

Availability: ActionScript 1.0; Flash Player 6

Parameters

`active:Boolean` - A Boolean value set to true when the camera starts detecting motion, false when the motion stops.

Example

The following example displays true or false in the Output panel when the camera starts or stops detecting motion:

```
// Assumes a Video object named "myVideoObject" is on the Stage
active_cam = Camera.get();
myVideoObject.attachVideo(active_cam);
active_cam.setMotionLevel(10, 500);
active_cam.onActivity = function(mode)
{
   trace(mode);
}
```

See also

setMotionLevel (Camera.setMotionLevel method)

onStatus (Camera.onStatus handler)

onStatus = function(infoObject:Object) {}

Invoked when the user allows or denies access to the camera. If you want to respond to this event handler, you must create a function to process the information object generated by the camera.

When a SWF file tries to access the camera, Flash Player displays a Privacy dialog box that lets the user choose whether to allow or deny access.

- If the user allows access, the Camera.muted property is set to false, and this handler is invoked with an information object whose code property is "Camera.Unmuted" and whose level property is "Status".

- If the user denies access, the Camera.muted property is set to true, and this handler is invoked with an information object whose code property is "Camera.Muted" and whose level property is "Status".

To determine whether the user has denied or allowed access to the camera without processing this event handler, use the Camera.muted property.

Note: If the user chooses to permanently allow or deny access for all SWF files from a specified domain, this handler is not invoked for SWF files from that domain unless the user later changes the privacy setting. For more information, see Camera.get().

Availability: ActionScript 1.0; Flash Player 6

Parameters

infoObject:Object - A parameter defined according to the status message.

Example

The following ActionScript is used to display a message whenever the user allows or denies access to the camera:

```
var my_cam:Camera = Camera.get();
var my_video:Video;
my_video.attachVideo(my_cam);
my_cam.onStatus = function(infoObj:Object) {
  switch (infoObj.code) {
  case 'Camera.Muted' :
  trace("Camera access is denied");
  break;
  case 'Camera.Unmuted' :
  trace("Camera access granted");
  break;
  }
}
```

See also

get (Camera.get method), muted (Camera.muted property), showSettings (System.showSettings method), onStatus (System.onStatus handler)

quality (Camera.quality property)

```
public quality : Number [read-only]
```

An integer specifying the required level of picture quality, as determined by the amount of compression being applied to each video frame. Acceptable quality values range from 1 (lowest quality, maximum compression) to 100 (highest quality, no compression). The default value is 0, which means that picture quality can vary as needed to avoid exceeding available bandwidth.

Availability: ActionScript 1.0; Flash Player 6

Example

The following example uses a NumericStepper instance to specify the amount of compression applied to the camera feed. Create a new video instance by selecting New Video from the Library options menu. Add an instance to the Stage and give it the instance name my_video. Add a NumericStepper with the instance name quality_nstep. Then add the following ActionScript to Frame 1 of the Timeline:

```
var quality_nstep:mx.controls.NumericStepper;

var my_cam:Camera = Camera.get();
var my_video:Video;
my_video.attachVideo(my_cam);
```

```
quality_nstep.minimum = 0;
quality_nstep.maximum = 100;
quality_nstep.stepSize = 5;
quality_nstep.value = my_cam.quality;

function changeQuality() {
  my_cam.setQuality(my_cam.bandwidth, quality_nstep.value);
}
quality_nstep.addEventListener("change", changeQuality);
```

See also

setQuality (Camera.setQuality method)

setMode (Camera.setMode method)

```
public setMode([width:Number], [height:Number], [fps:Number],
  [favorArea:Boolean]) : Void
```

Sets the camera capture mode to the native mode that best meets the specified requirements. If the camera does not have a native mode that matches all the parameters you pass, Flash selects a capture mode that most closely synthesizes the requested mode. This manipulation may involve cropping the image and dropping frames.

By default, Flash drops frames as needed to maintain image size. To minimize the number of dropped frames, even if this means reducing the size of the image, pass false for the favorArea parameter.

When choosing a native mode, Flash tries to maintain the requested aspect ratio whenever possible. For example, if you issue the command *active_cam*.setMode(400, 400, 30), and the maximum width and height values available on the camera are 320 and 288, Flash sets both the width and height at 288; by setting these properties to the same value, Flash maintains the 1:1 aspect ratio you requested.

To determine the values assigned to these properties after Flash selects the mode that most closely matches your requested values, use Camera.width, Camera.height, and Camera.fps.

Availability: ActionScript 1.0; Flash Player 6

Parameters

width:Number [optional] - The requested capture width, in pixels. The default value is 160.

height:Number [optional] - The requested capture height, in pixels. The default value is 120.

fps:Number [optional] - The requested rate at which the camera should capture data, in frames per second. The default value is 15.

favorArea:Boolean [optional] - A Boolean value that specifies how to manipulate the width, height, and frame rate if the camera does not have a native mode that meets the specified requirements. The default value is true, which means that maintaining capture size is favored; using this parameter selects the mode that most closely matches *width* and *height* values, even if doing so adversely affects performance by reducing the frame rate. To maximize frame rate at the expense of camera height and width, pass false for the favorArea parameter.

Example

The following example sets the camera capture mode. You can type a frame rate into a TextInput instance and press Enter or Return to apply the frame rate. Create a new video instance by selecting New Video from the Library options menu. Add an instance to the Stage and give it the instance name my_video. Add a TextInput component instance with the instance name fps_ti. Then add the following ActionScript to Frame 1 of the Timeline:

```
var my_cam:Camera = Camera.get();
var my_video:Video;
my_video.attachVideo(my_cam);

fps_ti.maxChars = 2;
fps_ti.restrict = [0-9];
fps_lbl.text = "Current: "+my_cam.fps+" fps";

function changeFps():Void {
    my_cam.setMode(my_cam.width, my_cam.height, fps_ti.text);
    fps_lbl.text = "Current: "+my_cam.fps+" fps";
    fps_ti.text = my_cam.fps;
    Selection.setSelection(0,2);
}
fps_ti.addEventListener("enter", changeFps);
```

See also

fps (Camera.fps property), height (Camera.height property), width (Camera.width property), currentFps (Camera.currentFps property)

setMotionLevel (Camera.setMotionLevel method)

`public setMotionLevel([motionLevel:Number], [timeOut:Number]) : Void`

Specifies how much motion is required to invoke `Camera.onActivity(true)`. Optionally sets the number of milliseconds that must elapse without activity before Flash considers motion to have stopped and invokes `Camera.onActivity(false)`.

 NOTE Video can be displayed regardless of the value of the sensitivity parameter. This parameter determines only when and under waht circumstances `Camera.onActivity` is invoked -- not whether video is actually being captured or displayed.

- To prevent the camera from detecting motion at all, pass a value of 100 for *sensitivity*; `Camera.onActivity` is never invoked. (You would probably use this value only for testing purposes--for example, to temporarily disable any actions set to occur when `Camera.onActivity` is invoked.)

- To determine the amount of motion the camera is currently detecting, use the `Camera.activityLevel` property.

  Motion sensitivity values correspond directly to activity values. Complete lack of motion is an activity value of 0. Constant motion is an activity value of 100. Your activity value is less than your motion sensitivity value when you're not moving; when you are moving, activity values frequently exceed your motion sensitivity value.

  This method is similar in purpose to `Microphone.setSilenceLevel()`; both methods are used to specify when the `onActivity` event handler should be invoked. However, these methods have a significantly different impact on publishing streams:

- `Microphone.setSilenceLevel()` is designed to optimize bandwidth. When an audio stream is considered silent, no audio data is sent. Instead, a single message is sent, indicating that silence has started.

- `Camera.setMotionLevel()` is designed to detect motion and does not affect bandwidth usage. Even if a video stream does not detect motion, video is still sent.

Availability: ActionScript 1.0; Flash Player 6

Parameters

`motionLevel:Number` [optional] - A numeric value that specifies the amount of motion required to invoke `Camera.onActivity(true)`. Acceptable values range from 0 to 100. The default value is 50.

`timeOut:Number` [optional] - A numeric parameter that specifies how many milliseconds must elapse without activity before Flash considers activity to have stopped and invokes the `Camera.onActivity(false)` event handler. The default value is 2000 (2 seconds).

Example

The following example sends messages to the Output panel when video activity starts or stops. Change the motion sensitivity value of 30 to a higher or lower number to see how different values affect motion detection.

```
// Assumes a Video object named "myVideoObject" is on the Stage
active_cam = Camera.get();
x = 0;
function motion(mode) {
  trace(x + ": " + mode);
  x++;
}
active_cam.onActivity = function(mode) {
  motion(mode);
}
active_cam.setMotionLevel(30, 500);
myVideoObject.attachVideo(active_cam);
```

See also

motionLevel (Camera.motionLevel property), motionTimeOut
(Camera.motionTimeOut property), onActivity (Camera.onActivity handler),
activityLevel (Camera.activityLevel property)

setQuality (Camera.setQuality method)

public setQuality([bandwidth:Number], [quality:Number]) : Void

Sets the maximum amount of bandwidth per second or the required picture quality of the current outgoing video feed. This method is generally applicable only if you are transmitting video using Flash Communication Server.

Use this method to specify which element of the outgoing video feed is more important to your application--bandwidth use or picture quality.

- To indicate that bandwidth use takes precedence, pass a value for *bandwidth* and 0 for *frameQuality*. Flash will transmit video at the highest quality possible within the specified bandwidth. If necessary, Flash will reduce picture quality to avoid exceeding the specified bandwidth. In general, as motion increases, quality decreases.

- To indicate that quality takes precedence, pass 0 for *bandwidth* and a numeric value for *frameQuality*. Flash will use as much bandwidth as required to maintain the specified quality. If necessary, Flash will reduce the frame rate to maintain picture quality. In general, as motion increases, bandwidth use also increases.

- To specify that both bandwidth and quality are equally important, pass numeric values for both parameters. Flash will transmit video that achieves the specified quality and that doesn't exceed the specified bandwidth. If necessary, Flash will reduce the frame rate to maintain picture quality without exceeding the specified bandwidth.

Availability: ActionScript 1.0; Flash Player 6

Parameters

`bandwidth:Number` [optional] - An integer that specifies the maximum amount of bandwidth that the current outgoing video feed can use, in bytes per second. To specify that Flash video can use as much bandwidth as needed to maintain the value of *frameQuality*, pass 0 for *bandwidth*. The default value is 16384.

`quality:Number` [optional] - An integer that specifies the required level of picture quality, as determined by the amount of compression being applied to each video frame. Acceptable values range from 1 (lowest quality, maximum compression) to 100 (highest quality, no compression). To specify that picture quality can vary as needed to avoid exceeding bandwidth, pass 0 for *quality*. The default value is 0.

Example

The following examples illustrate how to use this method to control bandwidth use and picture quality.

```
// Ensure that no more than 8192 (8K/second) is used to send video
active_cam.setQuality(8192,0);

// Ensure that no more than 8192 (8K/second) is used to send video
// with a minimum quality of 50
active_cam.setQuality(8192,50);

// Ensure a minimum quality of 50, no matter how much bandwidth it takes
active_cam.setQuality(0,50);
```

See also

`get (Camera.get method)`, `quality (Camera.quality property)`, `bandwidth (Camera.bandwidth property)`

width (Camera.width property)

`public width : Number [read-only]`

The current capture width, in pixels. To set a desired value for this property, use `Camera.setMode()`.

Availability: ActionScript 1.0; Flash Player 6

Example

The following code displays the current width, height and FPS of a video instance in a Label component instance on the Stage. Create a new video instance by selecting New Video from the Library options menu. Add an instance to the Stage and give it the instance name `my_video`. Add a Label component instance to the Stage and give it the instance name `dimensions_lbl`. Then add the following ActionScript to Frame 1 of the Timeline:

```
var my_cam:Camera = Camera.get();
var my_video:Video;
my_video.attachVideo(my_cam);
var dimensions_lbl:mx.controls.Label;
dimensions_lbl.setStyle("fontSize", 9);
dimensions_lbl.setStyle("fontWeight", "bold");
dimensions_lbl.setStyle("textAlign", "center");
dimensions_lbl.text = "width: "+my_cam.width+", height: "+my_cam.height+",
   FPS: "+my_cam.fps;
```

See also the example for `Camera.setMode()`.

See also

`height (Camera.height property)`, `setMode (Camera.setMode method)`

capabilities (System.capabilities)

```
Object
  |
  +-System.capabilities
```

```
public class capabilities
extends Object
```

The Capabilities class determines the abilities of the system and player hosting a SWF file, which lets you tailor content for different formats. For example, the screen of a cell phone (black and white, 100 square pixels) is different than the 1000-square-pixel color PC screen. To provide appropriate content to as many users as possible, you can use the `System.capabilities` object to determine the type of device a user has. You can then either specify to the server to send different SWF files based on the device capabilities or tell the SWF file to alter its presentation based on the capabilities of the device.

You can send capabilities information using a `GET` or `POST` HTTP method. The following example shows a server string for a computer that has MP3 support, 1600 x 1200 pixel resolution, is running Windows XP, and Flash Player 8 (8.0.0.0):

```
A=t&SA=t&SV=t&EV=t&MP3=t&AE=t&VE=t&ACC=f&PR=t&SP=t&

SB=f&DEB=t&V=WIN%208%2C0%2C0%2C0&M=Macromedia%20Windows&
```

```
R=1600x1200&DP=72&COL=color&AR=1.0&OS=Windows%20XP&

L=en&PT=External&AVD=f&LFD=f&WD=f"
```

All properties of the System.capabilities object are read-only.

Availability: ActionScript 1.0; Flash Player 6

Property summary

Modifiers	Property	Description
static	avHardwareDisable:Bo olean [read-only]	A Boolean value that specifies whether access to the user's camera and microphone has been administratively prohibited (true) or allowed (false).
static	hasAccessibility:Boo lean [read-only]	A Boolean value that is true if the player is running in an environment that supports communication between Flash Player and accessibility aids; false otherwise.
static	hasAudio:Boolean [read-only]	Specifies if the system has audio capabilities.
static	hasAudioEncoder:Bool ean [read-only]	Specifies if the Flash Player can encode an audio stream.
static	hasEmbeddedVideo:Boo lean [read-only]	A Boolean value that is true if the player is running on a system that supports embedded video; false otherwise.
static	hasIME:Boolean [read-only]	Indicates whether the system has an input method editor (IME) installed.
static	hasMP3:Boolean [read-only]	Specifies if the system has a MP3 decoder.
static	hasPrinting:Boolean [read-only]	A Boolean value that is true if the player is running on a system that supports printing; false otherwise.
static	hasScreenBroadcast:B oolean [read-only]	A Boolean value that is true if the player supports the development of screen broadcast applications to be run through the Flash Communication Server; false otherwise.
static	hasScreenPlayback:Bo olean [read-only]	A Boolean value that is true if the player supports the playback of screen broadcast applications that are being run through the Flash Communication Server; false otherwise.

Modifiers	Property	Description
static	`hasStreamingAudio:Bo olean` [read-only]	A Boolean value that is `true` if the player can play streaming audio; `false` otherwise.
static	`hasStreamingVideo:Bo olean` [read-only]	A Boolean value that is `true` if the player can play streaming video; `false` otherwise.
static	`hasVideoEncoder:Bool ean` [read-only]	Specifies if the Flash Player can encode a video stream.
static	`isDebugger:Boolean` [read-only]	A Boolean value that indicates whether the player is an officially released version (`false`) or a special debugging version (`true`).
static	`language:String` [read-only]	Indicates the language of the system on which the player is running.
static	`localFileReadDisable :Boolean` [read-only]	A Boolean value that indicates whether read access to the user's hard disk has been administratively prohibited (`true`) or allowed (`false`).
static	`manufacturer:String` [read-only]	A string that indicates the manufacturer of Flash Player, in the format "`Macromedia OSName`" (`OSName` could be "`Windows`", "`Macintosh`", "`Linux`", or "`Other OS Name`").
static	`os:String` [read-only]	A string that indicates the current operating system.
static	`pixelAspectRatio:Num ber` [read-only]	An integer that indicates the pixel aspect ratio of the screen.
static	`playerType:String` [read-only]	A string that indicates the type of player.
static	`screenColor:String` [read-only]	A string that indicates the screen color.
static	`screenDPI:Number` [read-only]	A number that indicates the dots-per-inch (dpi) resolution of the screen, in pixels.
static	`screenResolutionX:Nu mber` [read-only]	An integer that indicates the maximum horizontal resolution of the screen.
static	`screenResolutionY:Nu mber` [read-only]	An integer that indicates the maximum vertical resolution of the screen.
static	`serverString:String` [read-only]	A URL-encoded string that specifies values for each `System.capabilities` property.
static	`version:String` [read-only]	A string containing the Flash Player platform and version information (for example, "`WIN 8,0,0,0`").

Properties inherited from class Object

```
constructor (Object.constructor property),__proto__ (Object.__proto__
property),prototype (Object.prototype property),__resolve
(Object.__resolve property)
```

Method summary
Methods inherited from class Object

```
addProperty (Object.addProperty method),hasOwnProperty
(Object.hasOwnProperty method),isPropertyEnumerable
(Object.isPropertyEnumerable method),isPrototypeOf (Object.isPrototypeOf
method),registerClass (Object.registerClass method),toString
(Object.toString method),unwatch (Object.unwatch method),valueOf
(Object.valueOf method),watch (Object.watch method)
```

avHardwareDisable (capabilities.avHardwareDisable property)

`public static avHardwareDisable : Boolean [read-only]`

A Boolean value that specifies whether access to the user's camera and microphone has been administratively prohibited (`true`) or allowed (`false`). The server string is `AVD`.

Availability: ActionScript 1.0; Flash Player 7

Example
The following example traces the value of this read-only property:

`trace(System.capabilities.avHardwareDisable);`

See also
`get (Camera.get method),get (Microphone.get method),showSettings (System.showSettings method)`

hasAccessibility (capabilities.hasAccessibility property)

`public static hasAccessibility : Boolean [read-only]`

A Boolean value that is `true` if the player is running in an environment that supports communication between Flash Player and accessibility aids; `false` otherwise. The server string is `ACC`.

Availability: ActionScript 1.0; Flash Player 6

Example

The following example traces the value of this read-only property:

```
trace(System.capabilities.hasAccessibility);
```

See also

isActive (Accessibility.isActive method), updateProperties
(Accessibility.updateProperties method),

hasAudio (capabilities.hasAudio property)

```
public static hasAudio : Boolean [read-only]
```

Specifies if the system has audio capabilities. A Boolean value that is `true` if the player is
running on a system that has audio capabilities; `false` otherwise. The server string is `A`.

Availability: ActionScript 1.0; Flash Player 6

Example

The following example traces the value of this read-only property:

```
trace(System.capabilities.hasAudio);
```

hasAudioEncoder (capabilities.hasAudioEncoder property)

```
public static hasAudioEncoder : Boolean [read-only]
```

Specifies if the Flash Player can encode an audio stream. A Boolean value that is `true` if the
player can encode an audio stream, such as that coming from a microphone; `false` otherwise.
The server string is `AE`.

Availability: ActionScript 1.0; Flash Player 6

Example

The following example traces the value of this read-only property:

```
trace(System.capabilities.hasAudioEncoder);
```

hasEmbeddedVideo
(capabilities.hasEmbeddedVideo property)

```
public static hasEmbeddedVideo : Boolean [read-only]
```

A Boolean value that is `true` if the player is running on a system that supports embedded video; `false` otherwise. The server string is `EV`.

Availability: ActionScript 1.0; Flash Player 6,0,65,0

Example

The following example traces the value of this read-only property:

```
trace(System.capabilities.hasEmbeddedVideo);
```

hasIME (capabilities.hasIME property)

```
public static hasIME : Boolean [read-only]
```

Indicates whether the system has an input method editor (IME) installed. A value of `true` indicates that the player is running on a system that has an IME installed; a value of `false` indicates that no IME is installed. The server string is `IME`.

Availability: ActionScript 1.0; Flash Player 8

Example

The following example sets the IME to `ALPHANUMERIC_FULL` if the player is running on a system that has an IME installed.

```
if(System.capabilities.hasIME) {
  trace(System.IME.getConversionMode());
  System.IME.setConversionMode(System.IME.ALPHANUMERIC_FULL);
  trace(System.IME.getConversionMode());
}
```

hasMP3 (capabilities.hasMP3 property)

```
public static hasMP3 : Boolean [read-only]
```

Specifies if the system has a MP3 decoder. A Boolean value that is `true` if the player is running on a system that has an MP3 decoder; `false` otherwise. The server string is `MP3`.

Availability: ActionScript 1.0; Flash Player 6

Example

The following example traces the value of this read-only property:

```
trace(System.capabilities.hasMP3);
```

hasPrinting (capabilities.hasPrinting property)

```
public static hasPrinting : Boolean [read-only]
```

A Boolean value that is `true` if the player is running on a system that supports printing; `false` otherwise. The server string is PR.

Availability: ActionScript 1.0; Flash Player 6,0,65,0

Example

The following example traces the value of this read-only property:

```
trace(System.capabilities.hasPrinting);
```

hasScreenBroadcast (capabilities.hasScreenBroadcast property)

```
public static hasScreenBroadcast : Boolean [read-only]
```

A Boolean value that is `true` if the player supports the development of screen broadcast applications to be run through the Flash Communication Server; `false` otherwise. The server string is SB.

Availability: ActionScript 1.0; Flash Player 6,0,79,0

Example

The following example traces the value of this read-only property:

```
trace(System.capabilities.hasScreenBroadcast);
```

hasScreenPlayback (capabilities.hasScreenPlayback property)

```
public static hasScreenPlayback : Boolean [read-only]
```

A Boolean value that is `true` if the player supports the playback of screen broadcast applications that are being run through the Flash Communication Server; `false` otherwise. The server string is SP.

Availability: ActionScript 1.0; Flash Player 6,0,79,0

Example

The following example traces the value of this read-only property:

```
trace(System.capabilities.hasScreenPlayback);
```

hasStreamingAudio (capabilities.hasStreamingAudio property)

```
public static hasStreamingAudio : Boolean [read-only]
```

A Boolean value that is true if the player can play streaming audio; false otherwise. The server string is SA.

Availability: ActionScript 1.0; Flash Player 6,0,65,0

Example

The following example traces the value of this read-only property:

```
trace(System.capabilities.hasStreamingAudio);
```

hasStreamingVideo (capabilities.hasStreamingVideo property)

```
public static hasStreamingVideo : Boolean [read-only]
```

A Boolean value that is true if the player can play streaming video; false otherwise. The server string is SV.

Availability: ActionScript 1.0; Flash Player 6,0,65,0

Example

The following example traces the value of this read-only property:

```
trace(System.capabilities.hasStreamingVideo);
```

hasVideoEncoder (capabilities.hasVideoEncoder property)

```
public static hasVideoEncoder : Boolean [read-only]
```

Specifies if the Flash Player can encode a video stream. A Boolean value that is true if the player can encode a video stream, such as that coming from a web camera; false otherwise. The server string is VE.

Availability: ActionScript 1.0; Flash Player 6

Example

The following example traces the value of this read-only property:

```
trace(System.capabilities.hasVideoEncoder);
```

isDebugger (capabilities.isDebugger property)

`public static isDebugger : Boolean [read-only]`

A Boolean value that indicates whether the player is an officially released version (`false`) or a special debugging version (`true`). The server string is `DEB`.

Availability: ActionScript 1.0; Flash Player 6

Example

The following example traces the value of this read-only property:

`trace(System.capabilities.isDebugger);`

language (capabilities.language property)

`public static language : String [read-only]`

Indicates the language of the system on which the player is running. This property is specified as a lowercase two-letter language code from ISO 639-1. For Chinese, an additional uppercase two-letter country code subtag from ISO 3166 distinguishes between Simplified and Traditional Chinese. The languages themselves are named with the English tags. For example, `fr` specifies French.

This property changed in two ways for Flash Player 7. First, the language code for English systems no longer includes the country code. In Flash Player 6, all English systems return the language code and the two-letter country code subtag (`en-US`). In Flash Player 7, English systems return only the language code (`en`). Second, on Microsoft Windows systems this property now returns the User Interface (UI) Language. In Flash Player 6 on the Microsoft Windows platform, `System.capabilities.language` returns the User Locale, which controls settings for formatting dates, times, currency and large numbers. In Flash Player 7 on the Microsoft Windows platform, this property now returns the UI Language, which refers to the language used for all menus, dialog boxes, error messages and help files. The following table lists the possible values:

Language	Tag
Czech	cs
Danish	da
Dutch	nl
English	en
Finnish	fi
French	fr

Language	Tag
German	de
Hungarian	hu
Italian	it
Japanese	ja
Korean	ko
Norwegian	no
Other/unknown	xu
Polish	pl
Portuguese	pt
Russian	ru
Simplified Chinese	zh-CN
Spanish	es
Swedish	sv
Traditional Chinese	zh-TW
Turkish	tr

Availability: ActionScript 1.0; Flash Player 6 - Behavior changed in Flash Player 7.

Example

The following example traces the value of this read-only property:

```
trace(System.capabilities.language);
```

localFileReadDisable (capabilities.localFileReadDisable property)

```
public static localFileReadDisable : Boolean [read-only]
```

A Boolean value that indicates whether read access to the user's hard disk has been administratively prohibited (`true`) or allowed (`false`). If set to `true`, Flash Player will be unable to read files (including the first SWF file that Flash Player launches with) from the user's hard disk. For example, attempts to read a file on the user's hard disk using `XML.load()`, `LoadMovie()`, or `LoadVars.load()` will fail if this property is set to `true`.

Reading runtime shared libraries will also be blocked if this property is set to `true`, but reading local shared objects is allowed without regard to the value of this property. The server string is `LFD`.

Availability: ActionScript 1.0; Flash Player 7

Example

The following example traces the value of this read-only property:

```
trace(System.capabilities.localFileReadDisable);
```

manufacturer (capabilities.manufacturer property)

```
public static manufacturer : String [read-only]
```

A string that indicates the manufacturer of Flash Player, in the format "Macromedia *OSName*" (*OSName* could be "Windows", "Macintosh", "Linux", or "Other OS Name"). The server string is M.

Availability: ActionScript 1.0; Flash Player 6

Example

The following example traces the value of this read-only property:

```
trace(System.capabilities.manufacturer);
```

os (capabilities.os property)

```
public static os : String [read-only]
```

A string that indicates the current operating system. The os property can return the following strings: "Windows XP", "Windows 2000", "Windows NT", "Windows 98/ME", "Windows 95", "Windows CE" (available only in Flash Player SDK, not in the desktop version), "Linux", and "MacOS". The server string is OS.

Availability: ActionScript 1.0; Flash Player 6

Example

The following example traces the value of this read-only property:

```
trace(System.capabilities.os);
```

pixelAspectRatio (capabilities.pixelAspectRatio property)

```
public static pixelAspectRatio : Number [read-only]
```

An integer that indicates the pixel aspect ratio of the screen. The server string is AR.

Availability: ActionScript 1.0; Flash Player 6

Example

The following example traces the value of this read-only property:

```
trace(System.capabilities.pixelAspectRatio);
```

playerType (capabilities.playerType property)

```
public static playerType : String [read-only]
```

A string that indicates the type of player. This property can have one of the following values:

- `"StandAlone"` for the Flash StandAlone Player
- `"External"` for the Flash Player version used by the external player, or test movie mode..
- `"PlugIn"` for the Flash Player browser plug-in
- `"ActiveX"` for the Flash Player ActiveX Control used by Microsoft Internet Explorer

The server string is PT.

Availability: ActionScript 1.0; Flash Player 7

Example

The following example traces the value of this read-only property:

```
trace(System.capabilities.playerType);
```

screenColor (capabilities.screenColor property)

```
public static screenColor : String [read-only]
```

A string that indicates the screen color. This property can have the value `"color"`, `"gray"` or `"bw"`, which represents color, grayscale, and black and white, respectively. The server string is COL.

Availability: ActionScript 1.0; Flash Player 6

Example

The following example traces the value of this read-only property:

```
trace(System.capabilities.screenColor);
```

screenDPI (capabilities.screenDPI property)

```
public static screenDPI : Number [read-only]
```

A number that indicates the dots-per-inch (dpi) resolution of the screen, in pixels. The server string is DP.

Availability: ActionScript 1.0; Flash Player 6

Example

The following example traces the value of this read-only property:

```
trace(System.capabilities.screenDPI);
```

screenResolutionX (capabilities.screenResolutionX property)

```
public static screenResolutionX : Number [read-only]
```

An integer that indicates the maximum horizontal resolution of the screen. The server string is R (which returns both the width and height of the screen).

Availability: ActionScript 1.0; Flash Player 6

Example

The following example traces the value of this read-only property:

```
trace(System.capabilities.screenResolutionX);
```

screenResolutionY (capabilities.screenResolutionY property)

```
public static screenResolutionY : Number [read-only]
```

An integer that indicates the maximum vertical resolution of the screen. The server string is R (which returns both the width and height of the screen).

Availability: ActionScript 1.0; Flash Player 6

Example

The following example traces the value of this read-only property:

```
trace(System.capabilities.screenResolutionY);
```

serverString (capabilities.serverString property)

```
public static serverString : String [read-only]
```

A URL-encoded string that specifies values for each System.capabilities property.

The following example shows a URL-encoded string:

```
A=t&SA=t&SV=t&EV=t&MP3=t&AE=t&VE=t&ACC=f&PR=t&SP=t&

SB=f&DEB=t&V=WIN%208%2C0%2C0%2C0&M=Macromedia%20Windows&

R=1600x1200&DP=72&COL=color&AR=1.0&OS=Windows%20XP&
```

```
L=en&PT=External&AVD=f&LFD=f&WD=f
```
Availability: ActionScript 1.0; Flash Player 6

Example

The following example traces the value of this read-only property:

```
trace(System.capabilities.serverString);
```

version (capabilities.version property)

```
public static version : String [read-only]
```

A string containing the Flash Player platform and version information (for example, "WIN 8,0,0,0"). The server string is V.

Availability: ActionScript 1.0; Flash Player 6

Example

The following example traces the value of this read-only property:

```
trace(System.capabilities.version);
```

Color

```
Object
  |
  +-Color
```

```
public class Color
extends Object
```

Deprecated since Flash Player 8. The Color class has been deprecated in favor of the flash.geom.ColorTransform class.

The Color class lets you set the RGB color value and color transform of movie clips and retrieve those values once they have been set.

You must use the constructor new Color() to create a Color object before calling its methods.

Availability: ActionScript 1.0; Flash Player 5

Property summary

Properties inherited from class Object

```
constructor (Object.constructor property), __proto__ (Object.__proto__
property), prototype (Object.prototype property), __resolve
(Object.__resolve property)
```

Constructor summary

Signature	Description
Color(target:Object)	**Class Deprecated.** Creates a Color object for the movie clip specified by the *target_mc* parameter.

Method summary

Modifiers	Signature	Description
	getRGB() : Number	**Class Deprecated.** Returns the R+G+B combination currently in use by the color object.
	getTransform() : Object	**Class Deprecated.** Returns the transform value set by the last `Color.setTransform()` call.
	setRGB(offset:Number) : Void	**Class Deprecated.** Specifies an RGB color for a Color object.
	setTransform(transformObject:Object) : Void	**Class Deprecated.** Sets color transform information for a Color object.

Methods inherited from class Object

```
addProperty (Object.addProperty method), hasOwnProperty
(Object.hasOwnProperty method), isPropertyEnumerable
(Object.isPropertyEnumerable method), isPrototypeOf (Object.isPrototypeOf
method), registerClass (Object.registerClass method), toString
(Object.toString method), unwatch (Object.unwatch method), valueOf
(Object.valueOf method), watch (Object.watch method)
```

Color constructor

`public Color(target:Object)`

Deprecated since Flash Player 8. The Color class has been deprecated in favor of the flash.geom.ColorTransform class.

Creates a Color object for the movie clip specified by the *target_mc* parameter. You can then use the methods of that Color object to change the color of the entire target movie clip.

Availability: ActionScript 1.0; Flash Player 5

Parameters

`target:Object` - The instance name of a movie clip.

Example

The following example creates a Color object called `my_color` for the movie clip `my_mc` and sets its RGB value to orange:

```
var my_color:Color = new Color(my_mc);
my_color.setRGB(0xff9933);
```

getRGB (Color.getRGB method)

`public getRGB() : Number`

Deprecated since Flash Player 8. The Color class has been deprecated in favor of the flash.geom.ColorTransform class.

Returns the R+G+B combination currently in use by the color object.

Availability: ActionScript 1.0; Flash Player 5

Returns

`Number` - A number that represents the RGB numeric value for the color specified.

Example

The following code retrieves the RGB value for the Color object `my_color`, converts the value to a hexadecimal string, and assigns it to the `myValue` variable. To see this code work, add a movie clip instance to the Stage, and give it the instance name `my_mc`:

```
var my_color:Color = new Color(my_mc);
// set the color
my_color.setRGB(0xff9933);
var myValue:String = my_color.getRGB().toString(16);
// trace the color value
trace(myValue); // traces ff9933
```

See also

`setRGB` (Color.setRGB method), `rgb` (ColorTransform.rgb property)

getTransform (Color.getTransform method)

```
public getTransform() : Object
```

Deprecated since Flash Player 8. The Color class has been deprecated in favor of the flash.geom.ColorTransform class.

Returns the transform value set by the last `Color.setTransform()` call.

Availability: ActionScript 1.0; Flash Player 5

Returns

`Object` - An object whose properties contain the current offset and percentage values for the specified color.

Example

The following example gets the transform object, and then sets new percentages for colors and alpha of `my_mc` relative to their current values. To see this code work, place a multicolored movie clip on the Stage with the instance name `my_mc`. Then place the following code on Frame 1 in the main Timeline and select Control > Test Movie:

```
var my_color:Color = new Color(my_mc);
var myTransform:Object = my_color.getTransform();
myTransform = { ra: 50, ba: 50, aa: 30};
my_color.setTransform(myTransform);
```

For descriptions of the parameters for a color transform object, see `Color.setTransform()`.

See also

`setTransform` (Color.setTransform method)

setRGB (Color.setRGB method)

`public setRGB(offset:Number) : Void`

Deprecated since Flash Player 8. The Color class has been deprecated in favor of the flash.geom.ColorTransform class.

Specifies an RGB color for a Color object. Calling this method overrides any previous `Color.setTransform()` settings.

Availability: ActionScript 1.0; Flash Player 5

Parameters

`offset:Number` - `0x`*RRGGBB* The hexadecimal or RGB color to be set. *RR*, *GG*, and *BB* each consist of two hexadecimal digits that specify the offset of each color component. The `0x` tells the ActionScript compiler that the number is a hexadecimal value.

Example

This example sets the RGB color value for the movie clip `my_mc`. To see this code work, place a movie clip on the Stage with the instance name `my_mc`. Then place the following code on Frame 1 in the main Timeline and select Control > Test Movie:

```
var my_color:Color = new Color(my_mc);
my_color.setRGB(0xFF0000); // my_mc turns red
```

See also

`setTransform (Color.setTransform method)`, `rgb (ColorTransform.rgb property)`

setTransform (Color.setTransform method)

`public setTransform(transformObject:Object) : Void`

Deprecated since Flash Player 8. The Color class has been deprecated in favor of the flash.geom.ColorTransform class.

Sets color transform information for a Color object. The *colorTransformObject* parameter is a generic object that you create from the `new Object` constructor. It has parameters specifying the percentage and offset values for the red, green, blue, and alpha (transparency) components of a color, entered in the format 0xRRGGBBAA.

The parameters for a color transform object correspond to the settings in the Advanced Effect dialog box and are defined as follows:

- *ra* is the percentage for the red component (-100 to 100).
- *rb* is the offset for the red component (-255 to 255).
- *ga* is the percentage for the green component (-100 to 100).

- *gb* is the offset for the green component (-255 to 255).
- *ba* is the percentage for the blue component (-100 to 100).
- *bb* is the offset for the blue component (-255 to 255).
- *aa* is the percentage for alpha (-100 to 100).
- *ab* is the offset for alpha (-255 to 255).

You create a *colorTransformObject* parameter as follows:

```
var myColorTransform:Object = new Object();
myColorTransform.ra = 50;
myColorTransform.rb = 244;
myColorTransform.ga = 40;
myColorTransform.gb = 112;
myColorTransform.ba = 12;
myColorTransform.bb = 90;
myColorTransform.aa = 40;
myColorTransform.ab = 70;
```

You can also use the following syntax to create a *colorTransformObject* parameter:

```
var myColorTransform:Object = { ra: 50, rb: 244, ga: 40, gb: 112, ba: 12,
    bb: 90, aa: 40, ab: 70}
```

Availability: ActionScript 1.0; Flash Player 5

Parameters

transformObject:Object - An object created with the new Object constructor. This instance of the Object class must have the following properties that specify color transform values: ra, rb, ga, gb, ba, bb, aa, ab. These properties are explained below.

Example

This example creates a new Color object for a target SWF file, creates a generic object called myColorTransform with the properties defined above, and uses the setTransform() method to pass the *colorTransformObject* to a Color object. To use this code in a Flash (FLA) document, place it on Frame 1 on the main Timeline and place a movie clip on the Stage with the instance name my_mc, as in the following code:

```
// Create a color object called my_color for the target my_mc
var my_color:Color = new Color(my_mc);
// Create a color transform object called myColorTransform using
// Set the values for myColorTransform
var myColorTransform:Object = { ra: 50, rb: 244, ga: 40, gb: 112, ba: 12,
    bb: 90, aa: 40, ab: 70};
// Associate the color transform object with the Color object
// created for my_mc
my_color.setTransform(myColorTransform);
```

See also

Object

ColorMatrixFilter (flash.filters.ColorMatrixFilter)

```
Object
  |
  +-flash.filters.BitmapFilter
     |
     +-flash.filters.ColorMatrixFilter
```

public class ColorMatrixFilter
extends BitmapFilter

The ColorMatrixFilter class lets you apply a 4 x 5 matrix transformation on the RGBA color and alpha values of every pixel on the input image to produce a result with a new set of RGBA color and alpha values. It allows saturation changes, hue rotation, luminance to alpha and various other effects. You can apply this filter to bitmaps and MovieClip instances.

The use of filters depends on the object to which you apply the filter:

- To apply filters to movie clips at runtime, use the filters property. Setting the filters property of an object does not modify the object and can be undone by clearing the filters property.

- To apply filters to BitmapData instances, use the BitmapData.applyFilter() method. Calling applyFilter() on a BitmapData object takes the source BitmapData object and the filter object and generates a filtered image as a result.

You can also apply filter effects to images and video at authoring time. For more information, see your authoring documentation.

If you apply a filter to a movie clip or button, the cacheAsBitmap property of the movie clip or button is set to true. If you clear all filters, the original value of cacheAsBitmap is restored.

The following formulas are used, where a[0] through a[19] correspond to entries 0 through 19 in the 20-element array property matrix:

```
redResult = a[0] * srcR + a[1] * srcG + a[2] * srcB + a[3] * srcA + a[4]
greenResult = a[5] * srcR + a[6] * srcG + a[7] * srcB + a[8] * srcA + a[9]
blueResult = a[10] * srcR + a[11] * srcG + a[12] * srcB + a[13] * srcA +
   a[14]
alphaResult = a[15] * srcR + a[16] * srcG + a[17] * srcB + a[18] * srcA +
   a[19]
```

This filter separates each source pixel into its red, green, blue, and alpha components as srcR, srcG, srcB, srcA. As a final step, it combines each color component back into a single pixel and writes out the result.

The calculations are performed on unmultiplied color values. If the input graphic consists of premultiplied color values, those values are automatically converted into unmultiplied color values for this operation.

The following two optimized modes are available.

Alpha only. When you pass to the filter a matrix that adjusts only the alpha component, as shown here, the filter optimizes its performance:

```
1 0 0 0 0
0 1 0 0 0
0 0 1 0 0
0 0 0 N 0 (where N is between 0.0 and 1.0)
```

Faster version. Available only with SSE/Altivec accelerator-enabled processors such as Pentium 3 and later, and Apple G4 and later). The accelerator is used when the multiplier terms are in the range -15.99 to 15.99 and the adder terms a[4], a[9], a[14], and a[19] are in the range -8000 to 8000.

A filter is not applied if the resulting image would exceed 2880 pixels in width or height. For example, if you zoom in on a large movie clip with a filter applied, the filter is turned off if the resulting image reaches the 2880-pixel limit.

Availability: ActionScript 1.0; Flash Player 8

Example

The following example uses BitmapFilter to manipulate the color saturation of an image based on the location of the mouse pointer. If you position the pointer in the upper-left corner (0,0), the image should be unmodified. As you move the pointer to the right, the green and blue channels together are removed from the image. As you move the pointer down, the red channel is removed. If the pointer is positioned at the lower right of the Stage, the image should be completely black. This example assumes that you have an image in your library with its Linkage Identifier set to "YourImageLinkage".

```
import flash.filters.BitmapFilter;
import flash.filters.ColorMatrixFilter;

var image:MovieClip = this.attachMovie("YourImageLinkage", "YourImage",
  this.getNextHighestDepth());
image.cacheAsBitmap = true;

var listener:Object = new Object();
listener.image = image;
```

```
listener.onMouseMove = function() {
  var xPercent:Number = 1 - (_xmouse/Stage.width);
  var yPercent:Number = 1 - (_ymouse/Stage.height);
  var matrix:Array = new Array();
  matrix = matrix.concat([yPercent, 0, 0, 0, 0]); // red
  matrix = matrix.concat([0, xPercent, 0, 0, 0]); // green
  matrix = matrix.concat([0, 0, xPercent, 0, 0]); // blue
  matrix = matrix.concat([0, 0, 0, 1, 0]); // alpha

  var filter:BitmapFilter = new ColorMatrixFilter(matrix);
  image.filters = new Array(filter);
}

Mouse.addListener(listener);
listener.onMouseMove();
```

See also

getPixel (BitmapData.getPixel method), applyFilter (BitmapData.applyFilter method), filters (MovieClip.filters property), cacheAsBitmap (MovieClip.cacheAsBitmap property)

Property summary

Modifiers	Property	Description
	matrix:Array	An array of 20 elements for 4 x 5 color transform.

Properties inherited from class Object

constructor (Object.constructor property), __proto__ (Object.__proto__ property), prototype (Object.prototype property), __resolve (Object.__resolve property)

Constructor summary

Signature	Description
ColorMatrixFilter(matrix:Array)	Initializes a new ColorMatrixFilter instance with the specified parameters.

Method summary

Modifiers	Signature	Description
	clone() : ColorMatrixFilter	Returns a copy of this filter object.

Methods inherited from class BitmapFilter

```
clone (BitmapFilter.clone method)
```

Methods inherited from class Object

```
addProperty (Object.addProperty method), hasOwnProperty
(Object.hasOwnProperty method), isPropertyEnumerable
(Object.isPropertyEnumerable method), isPrototypeOf (Object.isPrototypeOf
method), registerClass (Object.registerClass method), toString
(Object.toString method), unwatch (Object.unwatch method), valueOf
(Object.valueOf method), watch (Object.watch method)
```

clone (ColorMatrixFilter.clone method)

public clone() : ColorMatrixFilter

Returns a copy of this filter object.

Availability: ActionScript 1.0; Flash Player 8

Returns

flash.filters.ColorMatrixFilter - A new ColorMatrixFilter instance with all the same properties as the original one.

Example

The following example creates a new ColorMatrixFilter instance and then clones it using the clone method. The matrix property cannot be changed directly (for example, clonedFilter.matrix[2] = 1;). Instead, you must get a reference to the array, make the change, and reset the value using clonedFilter.matrix = changedMatrix.

```
import flash.filters.ColorMatrixFilter;

var matrix:Array = new Array();
matrix = matrix.concat([1, 0, 0, 0, 0]); // red
matrix = matrix.concat([0, 1, 0, 0, 0]); // green
matrix = matrix.concat([0, 0, 1, 0, 0]); // blue
matrix = matrix.concat([0, 0, 0, 1, 0]); // alpha
```

```
var filter:ColorMatrixFilter = new ColorMatrixFilter(matrix);
trace("filter: " + filter.matrix);

var clonedFilter:ColorMatrixFilter = filter.clone();
matrix = clonedFilter.matrix;
matrix[2] = 1;
clonedFilter.matrix = matrix;
trace("clonedFilter: " + clonedFilter.matrix);
```

ColorMatrixFilter constructor

`public ColorMatrixFilter(matrix:Array)`

Initializes a new ColorMatrixFilter instance with the specified parameters.

Availability: ActionScript 1.0; Flash Player 8

Parameters

`matrix:Array` - An array of 20 elements arranged in a 4 x 5 matrix.

matrix (ColorMatrixFilter.matrix property)

`public matrix : Array`

An array of 20 elements for 4 x 5 color transform.

Availability: ActionScript 1.0; Flash Player 8

Example

The following example creates a new ColorMatrixFilter instance and then changes its `matrix` property. The `matrix` property cannot be changed by directly modifying its value (for example, `clonedFilter.matrix[2] = 1;`). Instead, you must get a reference to the array, make the change to the reference, and reset the value using `clonedFilter.matrix = changedMatrix`.

```
import flash.filters.ColorMatrixFilter;

var matrix:Array = new Array();
matrix = matrix.concat([1, 0, 0, 0, 0]); // red
matrix = matrix.concat([0, 1, 0, 0, 0]); // green
matrix = matrix.concat([0, 0, 1, 0, 0]); // blue
matrix = matrix.concat([0, 0, 0, 1, 0]); // alpha

var filter:ColorMatrixFilter = new ColorMatrixFilter(matrix);
trace("filter: " + filter.matrix);
var changedMatrix:Array = filter.matrix;
changedMatrix[2] = 1;
filter.matrix = changedMatrix;
trace("filter: " + filter.matrix);
```

ColorTransform
(flash.geom.ColorTransform)

```
Object
  |
  +-flash.geom.ColorTransform
```

```
public class ColorTransform
extends Object
```

The ColorTransform class lets you mathematically adjust all of the color values in a movie clip. The color adjustment function or *color transformation* can be applied to all four channels: red, green, blue, and alpha transparency.

When a ColorTransform object is applied to a movie clip, a new value for each color channel is calculated like this:

- New red value = (old red value * `redMultiplier`) + `redOffset`
- New green value = (old green value * `greenMultiplier`) + `greenOffset`
- New blue value = (old blue value * `blueMultiplier`) + `blueOffset`
- New alpha value = (old alpha value * `alphaMultiplier`) + `alphaOffset`

If any of the color channel values is greater than 255 after the calculation, it is set to 255. If it is less than 0, it is set to 0.

You must use the `new ColorTransform()` constructor to create a ColorTransform object before you can call the methods of the ColorTransform object.

Color transformations do not apply to the background color of a movie clip (such as a loaded SWF object). They apply only to graphics and symbols that are attached to the movie clip.

Availability: ActionScript 1.0; Flash Player 8

See also

`colorTransform (Transform.colorTransform property)`

Property summary

Modifiers	Property	Description
	`alphaMultiplier:Number`	A decimal value that is multiplied by the alpha transparency channel value.
	`alphaOffset:Number`	A number from -255 to 255 that is added to the alpha transparency channel value after it has been multiplied by the `alphaMultiplier` value.
	`blueMultiplier:Number`	A decimal value that is multiplied by the blue channel value.
	`blueOffset:Number`	A number from -255 to 255 that is added to the blue channel value after it has been multiplied by the `blueMultiplier` value.
	`greenMultiplier:Number`	A decimal value that is multiplied by the green channel value.
	`greenOffset:Number`	A number from -255 to 255 that is added to the green channel value after it has been multiplied by the `greenMultiplier` value.
	`redMultiplier:Number`	A decimal value that is multiplied by the red channel value.
	`redOffset:Number`	A number from -255 to 255 that is added to the red channel value after it has been multiplied by the `redMultiplier` value.
	`rgb:Number`	The RGB color value for a ColorTransform object.

Properties inherited from class Object

```
constructor (Object.constructor property),__proto__ (Object.__proto__
property),prototype (Object.prototype property),__resolve
(Object.__resolve property)
```

Constructor summary

Signature	Description
`ColorTransform([redMultiplier:Number], [greenMultiplier:Number], [blueMultiplier:Number], [alphaMultiplier:Number], [redOffset:Number], [greenOffset:Number], [blueOffset:Number], [alphaOffset:Number])`	Creates a ColorTransform object for a display object with the specified color channel values and alpha values.

Method summary

Modifiers	Signature	Description
	`concat(second:ColorTransform) : Void`	Applies a second, additive color transformation to the movie clip.
	`toString() : String`	Formats and returns a string that describes all of the properties of the ColorTransform object.

Methods inherited from class Object

```
addProperty (Object.addProperty method), hasOwnProperty
(Object.hasOwnProperty method), isPropertyEnumerable
(Object.isPropertyEnumerable method), isPrototypeOf (Object.isPrototypeOf
method), registerClass (Object.registerClass method), toString
(Object.toString method), unwatch (Object.unwatch method), valueOf
(Object.valueOf method), watch (Object.watch method)
```

alphaMultiplier (ColorTransform.alphaMultiplier property)

`public alphaMultiplier : Number`

A decimal value that is multiplied by the alpha transparency channel value.

If you set the alpha transparency value of a movie clip directly by using the `MovieClip._alpha` property, it affects the value of the `alphaMultiplier` property of that movie clip's `ColorTransform` object.

Availability: ActionScript 1.0; Flash Player 8

Example

The following example creates the ColorTransform object `colorTrans` and adjusts its `alphaMultiplier` value from 1 to .5.

```
import flash.geom.ColorTransform;
import flash.geom.Transform;

var colorTrans:ColorTransform = new ColorTransform();
trace(colorTrans.alphaMultiplier); // 1

colorTrans.alphaMultiplier = .5;
trace(colorTrans.alphaMultiplier); // .5

var rect:MovieClip = createRectangle(20, 80, 0x000000);
var trans:Transform = new Transform(rect);
trans.colorTransform = colorTrans;

function createRectangle(width:Number, height:Number, color:Number,
  scope:MovieClip):MovieClip {
  scope = (scope == undefined) ? this : scope;
  var depth:Number = scope.getNextHighestDepth();
  var mc:MovieClip = scope.createEmptyMovieClip("mc_" + depth, depth);
  mc.beginFill(color);
  mc.lineTo(0, height);
  mc.lineTo(width, height);
  mc.lineTo(width, 0);
  mc.lineTo(0, 0);
  return mc;
}
```

See also

_alpha (MovieClip._alpha property)

alphaOffset (ColorTransform.alphaOffset property)

```
public alphaOffset : Number
```

A number from -255 to 255 that is added to the alpha transparency channel value after it has been multiplied by the `alphaMultiplier` value.

Availability: ActionScript 1.0; Flash Player 8

Example

The following example creates the ColorTransform object `colorTrans` and adjusts its `alphaOffset` value from 0 to -128.

```
import flash.geom.ColorTransform;
import flash.geom.Transform;
```

```
var colorTrans:ColorTransform = new ColorTransform();
trace(colorTrans.alphaOffset); // 0

colorTrans.alphaOffset = -128;
trace(colorTrans.alphaOffset); // -128

var rect:MovieClip = createRectangle(20, 80, 0x000000);
var trans:Transform = new Transform(rect);
trans.colorTransform = colorTrans;

function createRectangle(width:Number, height:Number, color:Number,
    scope:MovieClip):MovieClip {
    scope = (scope == undefined) ? this : scope;
    var depth:Number = scope.getNextHighestDepth();
    var mc:MovieClip = scope.createEmptyMovieClip("mc_" + depth, depth);
    mc.beginFill(color);
    mc.lineTo(0, height);
    mc.lineTo(width, height);
    mc.lineTo(width, 0);
    mc.lineTo(0, 0);
    return mc;
}
```

blueMultiplier (ColorTransform.blueMultiplier property)

```
public blueMultiplier : Number
```

A decimal value that is multiplied by the blue channel value.

Availability: ActionScript 1.0; Flash Player 8

Example

The following example creates the ColorTransform object `colorTrans` and adjusts its `blueMultiplier` value from 1 to .5.

```
import flash.geom.ColorTransform;
import flash.geom.Transform;

var colorTrans:ColorTransform = new ColorTransform();
trace(colorTrans.blueMultiplier); // 1

colorTrans.blueMultiplier = .5;
trace(colorTrans.blueMultiplier); // .5

var rect:MovieClip = createRectangle(20, 80, 0x0000FF);
var trans:Transform = new Transform(rect);
trans.colorTransform = colorTrans;
```

```
function createRectangle(width:Number, height:Number, color:Number,
   scope:MovieClip):MovieClip {
   scope = (scope == undefined) ? this : scope;
   var depth:Number = scope.getNextHighestDepth();
   var mc:MovieClip = scope.createEmptyMovieClip("mc_" + depth, depth);
   mc.beginFill(color);
   mc.lineTo(0, height);
   mc.lineTo(width, height);
   mc.lineTo(width, 0);
   mc.lineTo(0, 0);
   return mc;
}
```

blueOffset (ColorTransform.blueOffset property)

```
public blueOffset : Number
```

A number from -255 to 255 that is added to the blue channel value after it has been multiplied by the `blueMultiplier` value.

Availability: ActionScript 1.0; Flash Player 8

Example

The following example creates the ColorTransform object `colorTrans` and adjusts its `blueOffset` value from 0 to 255.

```
import flash.geom.ColorTransform;
import flash.geom.Transform;

var colorTrans:ColorTransform = new ColorTransform();
trace(colorTrans.blueOffset); // 0

colorTrans.blueOffset = 255;
trace(colorTrans.blueOffset); // 255

var rect:MovieClip = createRectangle(20, 80, 0x000000);
var trans:Transform = new Transform(rect);
trans.colorTransform = colorTrans;

function createRectangle(width:Number, height:Number, color:Number,
   scope:MovieClip):MovieClip {
   scope = (scope == undefined) ? this : scope;
   var depth:Number = scope.getNextHighestDepth();
   var mc:MovieClip = scope.createEmptyMovieClip("mc_" + depth, depth);
   mc.beginFill(color);
   mc.lineTo(0, height);
   mc.lineTo(width, height);
   mc.lineTo(width, 0);
```

```
mc.lineTo(0, 0);
return mc;
}
```

ColorTransform constructor

```
public ColorTransform([redMultiplier:Number], [greenMultiplier:Number],
   [blueMultiplier:Number], [alphaMultiplier:Number], [redOffset:Number],
   [greenOffset:Number], [blueOffset:Number], [alphaOffset:Number])
```

Creates a ColorTransform object for a display object with the specified color channel values and alpha values.

Availability: ActionScript 1.0; Flash Player 8

Parameters

`redMultiplier:Number` [optional] - The value for the red multiplier, in the range from 0 to 1. The default value is 1.

`greenMultiplier:Number` [optional] - The value for the green multiplier, in the range from 0 to 1. The default value is 1.

`blueMultiplier:Number` [optional] - The value for the blue multiplier, in the range from 0 to 1. The default value is 1.

`alphaMultiplier:Number` [optional] - The value for the alpha transparency multiplier, in the range from 0 to 1. The default value is 1.

`redOffset:Number` [optional] - The offset for the red color channel value (-255 to 255). The default value is 0.

`greenOffset:Number` [optional] - The offset for the green color channel value (-255 to 255). The default value is 0.

`blueOffset:Number` [optional] - The offset for the blue color channel value (-255 to 255). The default value is 0.

`alphaOffset:Number` [optional] - The offset for alpha transparency channel value (-255 to 255). The default value is 0.

Example

The following example creates a ColorTransform object called `greenTransform`:

```
var greenTransform:flash.geom.ColorTransform = new
   flash.geom.ColorTransform(0.5, 1.0, 0.5, 0.5, 10, 10, 10, 0);
```

The following example creates the ColorTransfrom object colorTrans_1 with the default constructor values. The fact that colorTrans_1 and colorTrans_2 trace the same values is evidence that the default constructor values are used.

```
import flash.geom.ColorTransform;

var colorTrans_1:ColorTransform = new ColorTransform(1, 1, 1, 1, 0, 0, 0,
  0);
trace(colorTrans_1);
//(redMultiplier=1, greenMultiplier=1, blueMultiplier=1, alphaMultiplier=1,
  redOffset=0, greenOffset=0, blueOffset=0, alphaOffset=0)

var colorTrans_2:ColorTransform = new ColorTransform();
trace(colorTrans_2);
//(redMultiplier=1, greenMultiplier=1, blueMultiplier=1, alphaMultiplier=1,
  redOffset=0, greenOffset=0, blueOffset=0, alphaOffset=0)
```

concat (ColorTransform.concat method)

```
public concat(second:ColorTransform) : Void
```

Applies a second, additive color transformation to the movie clip. The second set of transformation parameters is applied to the colors of the movie clip after the first transformation has been completed.

Availability: ActionScript 1.0; Flash Player 8

Parameters

second:flash.geom.ColorTransform - A second ColorTransform object to be combined with the current ColorTransform object.

Example

The following example concatenates the ColorTransform object colorTrans_2 to colorTrans_1 resulting in a full red offset combined with a .5 alpha multiplier.

```
import flash.geom.ColorTransform;
import flash.geom.Transform;

var colorTrans_1:ColorTransform = new ColorTransform(1, 1, 1, 1, 255, 0, 0,
  0);
trace(colorTrans_1);
// (redMultiplier=1, greenMultiplier=1, blueMultiplier=1,
  alphaMultiplier=1, redOffset=255, greenOffset=0, blueOffset=0,
  alphaOffset=0)

var colorTrans_2:ColorTransform = new ColorTransform(1, 1, 1, .5, 0, 0, 0,
  0);
```

```
trace(colorTrans_2);
// (redMultiplier=1, greenMultiplier=1, blueMultiplier=1,
   alphaMultiplier=0.5, redOffset=0, greenOffset=0, blueOffset=0,
   alphaOffset=0)

colorTrans_1.concat(colorTrans_2);
trace(colorTrans_1);
// (redMultiplier=1, greenMultiplier=1, blueMultiplier=1,
   alphaMultiplier=0.5, redOffset=255, greenOffset=0, blueOffset=0,
   alphaOffset=0)

var rect:MovieClip = createRectangle(20, 80, 0x000000);
var trans:Transform = new Transform(rect);
trans.colorTransform = colorTrans_1;

function createRectangle(width:Number, height:Number, color:Number,
   scope:MovieClip):MovieClip {
   scope = (scope == undefined) ? this : scope;
   var depth:Number = scope.getNextHighestDepth();
   var mc:MovieClip = scope.createEmptyMovieClip("mc_" + depth, depth);
   mc.beginFill(color);
   mc.lineTo(0, height);
   mc.lineTo(width, height);
   mc.lineTo(width, 0);
   mc.lineTo(0, 0);
   return mc;
}
```

greenMultiplier (ColorTransform.greenMultiplier property)

```
public greenMultiplier : Number
```

A decimal value that is multiplied by the green channel value.

Availability: ActionScript 1.0; Flash Player 8

Example

The following example creates the ColorTransform object `colorTrans` and adjusts its `greenMultiplier` from 1 to .5.

```
import flash.geom.ColorTransform;
import flash.geom.Transform;

var colorTrans:ColorTransform = new ColorTransform();
trace(colorTrans.greenMultiplier); // 1

colorTrans.greenMultiplier = .5;
trace(colorTrans.greenMultiplier); // .5
```

```
var rect:MovieClip = createRectangle(20, 80, 0x00FF00);
var trans:Transform = new Transform(rect);
trans.colorTransform = colorTrans;

function createRectangle(width:Number, height:Number, color:Number,
  scope:MovieClip):MovieClip {
  scope = (scope == undefined) ? this : scope;
  var depth:Number = scope.getNextHighestDepth();
  var mc:MovieClip = scope.createEmptyMovieClip("mc_" + depth, depth);
  mc.beginFill(color);
  mc.lineTo(0, height);
  mc.lineTo(width, height);
  mc.lineTo(width, 0);
  mc.lineTo(0, 0);
  return mc;
}
```

greenOffset (ColorTransform.greenOffset property)

`public greenOffset : Number`

A number from -255 to 255 that is added to the green channel value after it has been multiplied by the `greenMultiplier` value.

Availability: ActionScript 1.0; Flash Player 8

Example

The following example creates the ColorTransform object `colorTrans` and adjusts its `greenOffset` value from 0 to 255.

```
import flash.geom.ColorTransform;
import flash.geom.Transform;

var colorTrans:ColorTransform = new ColorTransform();
trace(colorTrans.greenOffset); // 0

colorTrans.greenOffset = 255;
trace(colorTrans.greenOffset); // 255

var rect:MovieClip = createRectangle(20, 80, 0x000000);
var trans:Transform = new Transform(rect);
trans.colorTransform = colorTrans;

function createRectangle(width:Number, height:Number, color:Number,
  scope:MovieClip):MovieClip {
  scope = (scope == undefined) ? this : scope;
  var depth:Number = scope.getNextHighestDepth();
  var mc:MovieClip = scope.createEmptyMovieClip("mc_" + depth, depth);
```

```
    mc.beginFill(color);
    mc.lineTo(0, height);
    mc.lineTo(width, height);
    mc.lineTo(width, 0);
    mc.lineTo(0, 0);
    return mc;
}
```

redMultiplier (ColorTransform.redMultiplier property)

```
public redMultiplier : Number
```

A decimal value that is multiplied by the red channel value.

Availability: ActionScript 1.0; Flash Player 8

Example

The following example creates the ColorTransform object `colorTrans` and adjusts its `redMultiplier` value from 1 to .5.

```
import flash.geom.ColorTransform;
import flash.geom.Transform;

var colorTrans:ColorTransform = new ColorTransform();
trace(colorTrans.redMultiplier); // 1

colorTrans.redMultiplier = .5;
trace(colorTrans.redMultiplier); // .5

var rect:MovieClip = createRectangle(20, 80, 0xFF0000);
var trans:Transform = new Transform(rect);
trans.colorTransform = colorTrans;

function createRectangle(width:Number, height:Number, color:Number,
    scope:MovieClip):MovieClip {
    scope = (scope == undefined) ? this : scope;
    var depth:Number = scope.getNextHighestDepth();
    var mc:MovieClip = scope.createEmptyMovieClip("mc_" + depth, depth);
    mc.beginFill(color);
    mc.lineTo(0, height);
    mc.lineTo(width, height);
    mc.lineTo(width, 0);
    mc.lineTo(0, 0);
    return mc;
}
```

redOffset (ColorTransform.redOffset property)

```
public redOffset : Number
```

A number from -255 to 255 that is added to the red channel value after it has been multiplied by the redMultiplier value.

Availability: ActionScript 1.0; Flash Player 8

Example

The following example creates the ColorTransform object colorTrans and adjusts its redOffset value from 0 to 255.

```
import flash.geom.ColorTransform;
import flash.geom.Transform;

var colorTrans:ColorTransform = new ColorTransform();
trace(colorTrans.redOffset); // 0

colorTrans.redOffset = 255;
trace(colorTrans.redOffset); // 255

var rect:MovieClip = createRectangle(20, 80, 0x000000);
var trans:Transform = new Transform(rect);
trans.colorTransform = colorTrans;

function createRectangle(width:Number, height:Number, color:Number,
    scope:MovieClip):MovieClip {
  scope = (scope == undefined) ? this : scope;
  var depth:Number = scope.getNextHighestDepth();
  var mc:MovieClip = scope.createEmptyMovieClip("mc_" + depth, depth);
  mc.beginFill(color);
  mc.lineTo(0, height);
  mc.lineTo(width, height);
  mc.lineTo(width, 0);
  mc.lineTo(0, 0);
  return mc;
}
```

rgb (ColorTransform.rgb property)

```
public rgb : Number
```

The RGB color value for a ColorTransform object.

When you set this property, it changes the three color offset values (redOffset, greenOffset, and blueOffset) accordingly, and it sets the three color multiplier values (redMultiplier, greenMultiplier, and blueMultiplier) to 0. The alpha transparency multiplier and offset values do not change.

Pass a value for this property in the format: 0x*RRGGBB*. *RR*, *GG*, and *BB* each consist of two hexadecimal digits that specify the offset of each color component. The 0x tells the ActionScript compiler that the number is a hexadecimal value.

Availability: ActionScript 1.0; Flash Player 8

Example

The following example creates the ColorTransform object `colorTrans` and adjusts its `rgb` value to 0xFF0000.

```
import flash.geom.ColorTransform;
import flash.geom.Transform;

var colorTrans:ColorTransform = new ColorTransform();
trace(colorTrans.rgb); // 0

colorTrans.rgb = 0xFF0000;
trace(colorTrans.rgb); // 16711680
trace("0x" + colorTrans.rgb.toString(16)); // 0xff0000

var rect:MovieClip = createRectangle(20, 80, 0x000000);
var trans:Transform = new Transform(rect);
trans.colorTransform = colorTrans;

function createRectangle(width:Number, height:Number, color:Number,
  scope:MovieClip):MovieClip {
  scope = (scope == undefined) ? this : scope;
  var depth:Number = scope.getNextHighestDepth();
  var mc:MovieClip = scope.createEmptyMovieClip("mc_" + depth, depth);
  mc.beginFill(color);
  mc.lineTo(0, height);
  mc.lineTo(width, height);
  mc.lineTo(width, 0);
  mc.lineTo(0, 0);
  return mc;
}
```

toString (ColorTransform.toString method)

```
public toString() : String
```

Formats and returns a string that describes all of the properties of the ColorTransform object.

Availability: ActionScript 1.0; Flash Player 8

Returns

`String` - A string that lists all of the properties of the ColorTransform object.

Example

The following example creates the ColorTransform object `colorTrans` and calls its `toSting()` method. This method results in a string with the following format: (redMultiplier=RM, greenMultiplier=GM, blueMultiplier=BM, alphaMultiplier=AM, redOffset=RO, greenOffset=GO, blueOffset=BO, alphaOffset=AO).

```
import flash.geom.ColorTransform;

var colorTrans:ColorTransform = new ColorTransform(1, 2, 3, 4, -255, -128,
    128, 255);
trace(colorTrans.toString());
// (redMultiplier=1, greenMultiplier=2, blueMultiplier=3,
    alphaMultiplier=4, redOffset=-255, greenOffset=-128, blueOffset=128,
    alphaOffset=255)
```

ContextMenu

```
Object
  |
  +-ContextMenu
```

```
public dynamic class ContextMenu
extends Object
```

The ContextMenu class provides runtime control over the items in the Flash Player context menu, which appears when a user right-clicks (Windows) or Control-clicks (Macintosh) on Flash Player. You can use the methods and properties of the ContextMenu class to add custom menu items, control the display of the built-in context menu items (for example, Zoom In and Print), or create copies of menus.

You can attach a ContextMenu object to a specific button, movie clip, or text field object, or to an entire movie level. You use the menu property of the Button, MovieClip, or TextField classes to do this. For more information about the `menu` property, see `Button.menu`, `MovieClip.menu`, and `TextField.menu`.

To add new items to a `ContextMenu` object, you create a `ContextMenuItem` object, and then add that object to the `ContextMenu.customItems` array. For more information about creating context menu items, see the ContextMenuItem class entry.

Flash Player has three types of context menus: the standard menu (which appears when you right-click in Flash Player), the edit menu (which appears when you right-click over a selectable or editable text field), and an error menu (which appears when a SWF file has failed to load into Flash Player.) Only the standard and edit menus can be modified with the ContextMenu class.

Custom menu items always appear at the top of the Flash Player context menu, above any visible built-in menu items; a separator bar distinguishes built-in and custom menu items. You can add no more than 15 custom items to a context menu. You cannot remove the Settings menu item from the context menu. The Settings menu item is required in Flash so users can access the settings that affect privacy and storage on their computers. You also cannot remove the About menu item from the context menu, which is required so users can find out what version of Flash Player they are using.

You must use the constructor new `ContextMenu()` to create a ContextMenu object before calling its methods.

Availability: ActionScript 1.0; Flash Player 7

See also

ContextMenuItem, menu (Button.menu property), menu (MovieClip.menu property), menu (TextField.menu property)

Property summary

Modifiers	Property	Description
	`builtInItems:Object`	An object that has the following Boolean properties: `zoom`, `quality`, `play`, `loop`, `rewind`, `forward_back`, and `print`.
	`customItems:Array`	An array of ContextMenuItem objects.

Properties inherited from class Object

constructor (Object.constructor property), __proto__ (Object.__proto__ property), prototype (Object.prototype property), __resolve (Object.__resolve property)

Event summary

Event	Description
`onSelect = function(item:Object, item_menu:Object) {}`	Called when a user invokes the Flash Player context menu, but before the menu is actually displayed.

Constructor summary

Signature	Description
ContextMenu([callbac kFunction:Function])	Creates a new ContextMenu object.

Method summary

Modifiers	Signature	Description
	copy() : ContextMenu	Creates a copy of the specified ContextMenu object.
	hideBuiltInItems() : Void	Hides all built-in menu items (except Settings) in the specified ContextMenu object.

Methods inherited from class Object

```
addProperty (Object.addProperty method), hasOwnProperty
(Object.hasOwnProperty method), isPropertyEnumerable
(Object.isPropertyEnumerable method), isPrototypeOf (Object.isPrototypeOf
method), registerClass (Object.registerClass method), toString
(Object.toString method), unwatch (Object.unwatch method), valueOf
(Object.valueOf method), watch (Object.watch method)
```

builtInItems (ContextMenu.builtInItems property)

```
public builtInItems : Object
```

An object that has the following Boolean properties: zoom, quality, play, loop, rewind, forward_back, and print. Setting these variables to false removes the corresponding menu items from the specified ContextMenu object. These properties are enumerable and are set to true by default.

Availability: ActionScript 1.0; Flash Player 7

Example

In this example, the built-in Quality and Print menu items are disabled for the ContextMenu object my_cm, which is attached to the current Timeline of the SWF file.

```
var my_cm:ContextMenu = new ContextMenu ();
my_cm.builtInItems.quality=false;
my_cm.builtInItems.print=false;
this.menu = my_cm;
```

> **NOTE** You cannot disable the Settings or About menu items from the context menu.

In the next example, a `for..in` loop enumerates through all names and values of the built-in menu items of the ContextMenu object, `my_cm`.

```
var my_cm:ContextMenu = new ContextMenu();
for(eachProp in my_cm.builtInItems) {
  var propName = eachProp;
  var propValue = my_cm.builtInItems[propName];
  trace(propName + ": " + propValue);
}
```

ContextMenu constructor

```
public ContextMenu([callbackFunction:Function])
```

Creates a new ContextMenu object. You can optionally specify an identifier for an event handler when you create the object. The specified function is called when the user invokes the context menu, but *before* the menu is actually displayed. This is useful for customizing menu contents based on application state or based on the type of object (movie clip, text field, or button) or the Timeline that the user right-clicks or Control-clicks. (For an example of creating an event handler, see `ContextMenu.onSelect`.)

Availability: ActionScript 1.0; Flash Player 7

Parameters

`callbackFunction:Function` [optional] - A reference to a function that is called when the user right-clicks or Control-clicks, before the menu is displayed.

Example

The following example hides all the built-in objects in the Context menu. (However, the Settings and About items still appear, because they cannot be disabled.)

```
var newMenu:ContextMenu = new ContextMenu();
newMenu.hideBuiltInItems();
this.menu = newMenu;
```

In this example, the specified event handler, `menuHandler`, enables or disables a custom menu item (using the `ContextMenu.customItems` array) based on the value of a Boolean variable named `showItem`. If `false`, the custom menu item is disabled; otherwise, it's enabled.

```
var showItem = true; // Change this to false to remove
var my_cm:ContextMenu = new ContextMenu(menuHandler);
my_cm.customItems.push(new ContextMenuItem("Hello", itemHandler));
function menuHandler(obj, menuObj) {
  if (showItem == false) {
  menuObj.customItems[0].enabled = false;
  } else {
  menuObj.customItems[0].enabled = true;
```

```
  }
}
function itemHandler(obj, item) {
  //...put code here...
  trace("selected!");
}
this.menu = my_cm;
```

When the user right-clicks or Control-clicks the Stage, the custom menu is displayed.

See also

menu (Button.menu property), onSelect (ContextMenu.onSelect handler), customItems (ContextMenu.customItems property), hideBuiltInItems (ContextMenu.hideBuiltInItems method), menu (MovieClip.menu property), menu (TextField.menu property)

copy (ContextMenu.copy method)

`public copy() : ContextMenu`

Creates a copy of the specified ContextMenu object. The copy inherits all the properties of the original menu object.

Availability: ActionScript 1.0; Flash Player 7

Returns

`ContextMenu` - A ContextMenu object.

Example

This example creates a copy of the ContextMenu object named `my_cm` whose built-in menu items are hidden, and adds a menu item with the text "Save...". It then creates a copy of `my_cm` and assigns it to the variable `clone_cm`, which inherits all the properties of the original menu.

```
var my_cm:ContextMenu = new ContextMenu();
my_cm.hideBuiltInItems();
var menuItem_cmi:ContextMenuItem = new ContextMenuItem("Save...",
  saveHandler);
my_cm.customItems.push(menuItem_cmi);
function saveHandler(obj, menuItem) {
  // saveDocument();
  // custom function (not shown)
  trace("something");
}
clone_cm = my_cm.copy();
this.menu = my_cm;
for (var i in clone_cm.customItems) {
  trace("clone_cm-> "+clone_cm.customItems[i].caption);
```

```
}
for (var i in my_cm.customItems) {
  trace("my_cm-> "+my_cm.customItems[i].caption);
}
```

customItems (ContextMenu.customItems property)

```
public customItems : Array
```

An array of ContextMenuItem objects. Each object in the array represents a context menu item that you have defined. Use this property to add, remove, or modify these custom menu items.

To add new menu items, you first create a new ContextMenuItem object, and then add it to the *menu_mc*.customItems array (for example, using Array.push()). For more information about creating new menu items, see the ContextMenuItem class entry.

Availability: ActionScript 1.0; Flash Player 7

Example

The following example creates a new custom menu item called menuItem_cmi with a caption of "Send e-mail" and a callback handler named emailHandler. The new menu item is then added to the ContextMenu object, my_cm, using the customItems array. Finally, the new menu is attached to a movie clip named email_mc. To make this example work, create a movie clip instance on your stage, and use the Property Inspector to name the instance email_mc. In Test Movie mode, the new context menu item will appear if you bring up the context menu while your pointer is over the email_mc movie clip.

```
var my_cm:ContextMenu = new ContextMenu();
var menuItem_cmi:ContextMenuItem = new ContextMenuItem("Send e-mail",
  emailHandler);
my_cm.customItems.push(menuItem_cmi);
email_mc.menu = my_cm;
function emailHandler() {
  trace("sending email");
}
```

See also

menu (Button.menu property), menu (MovieClip.menu property), menu (TextField.menu property), push (Array.push method)

hideBuiltInItems (ContextMenu.hideBuiltInItems method)

```
public hideBuiltInItems() : Void
```

Hides all built-in menu items (except Settings) in the specified ContextMenu object. If the Flash Debug Player is running, the Debugging menu item shows, although it is dimmed for SWF files that don't have remote debugging enabled.

This method hides only menu items that appear in the standard context menu; it does not affect items that appear in the edit or error menus.

This method works by setting all the Boolean members of *my_cm*.builtInItems to false. You can selectively make a built-in item visible by setting its corresponding member in *my_cm*.builtInItems to true (as demonstrated in the following example).

Availability: ActionScript 1.0; Flash Player 7

Example

The following example creates a new ContextMenu object named my_cm whose built-in menu items are hidden, except for Print. The menu object is attached to the current Timeline.

```
var my_cm:ContextMenu = new ContextMenu();
my_cm.hideBuiltInItems();
my_cm.builtInItems.print = true;
this.menu = my_cm;
```

onSelect (ContextMenu.onSelect handler)

```
onSelect = function(item:Object, item_menu:Object) {}
```

Called when a user invokes the Flash Player context menu, but before the menu is actually displayed. This event handler allows customization of the contents of the context menu based on the current application state.

It is also possible to specify the callback handler for a ContextMenu object when constructing a new ContextMenu object. For more information, see the ContextMenuItem onSelect entry.

Availability: ActionScript 1.0; Flash Player 7

Parameters

`item:Object` - A reference to the object (movie clip, button, or selectable text field) that was under the mouse pointer when the Flash Player context menu was invoked and whose `menu` property is set to a valid ContextMenu object.

`item_menu:Object` - A reference to the ContextMenu object assigned to the `menu` property of `object`.

Example

The following example determines over what type of object the context menu was invoked.

```
my_cm:ContextMenu = new ContextMenu();
function menuHandler(obj:Object, menu:ContextMenu) {
  if(obj instanceof MovieClip) {
    trace("Movie clip: " + obj);
  }
  if(obj instanceof TextField) {
    trace("Text field: " + obj);
  }
  if(obj instanceof Button) {
    trace("Button: " + obj);
  }
}
my_cm.onSelect = menuHandler;
my_mc.menu = my_cm;
my_btn.menu = my_cm;
```

ContextMenuItem

```
Object
  |
  +-ContextMenuItem
```

`public dynamic class ContextMenuItem`
`extends Object`

The ContextMenuItem class allows you to create custom menu items to display in the Flash Player context menu. Each ContextMenuItem object has a caption (text) that is displayed in the context menu, and a callback handler (a function) that is invoked when the menu item is selected. To add a new context menu item to a context menu, you add it to the customItems array of a ContextMenu object.

You can enable or disable specific menu items, make items visible or invisible, or change the caption or callback handler associated with a menu item.

Custom menu items appear at the top of the context menu, above any built-in items. A separator bar always divides custom menu items from built-in items. You can add no more than 15 custom items to a context menu. Each item must contain at least one visible character; control characters, newlines, and other white space characters are ignored. No item can be more than 100 characters long. Items that are identical to any built-in menu item, or to another custom item, are ignored, whether the matching item is visible or not. Menu items are compared without regard to case, punctuation, or white space.

None of the following words can appear in a custom item: *Macromedia*, *Flash Player*, or *Settings*.

Availability: ActionScript 1.0; Flash Player 7

Property summary

Modifiers	Property	Description
	`caption:String`	A string that specifies the menu item caption (text) displayed in the context menu.
	`enabled:Boolean`	A Boolean value that indicates whether the specified menu item is enabled or disabled.
	`separatorBefore:Boolean`	A Boolean value that indicates whether a separator bar should appear above the specified menu item.
	`visible:Boolean`	A Boolean value that indicates whether the specified menu item is visible when the Flash Player context menu is displayed.

Properties inherited from class Object

```
constructor (Object.constructor property), __proto__ (Object.__proto__
property), prototype (Object.prototype property), __resolve
(Object.__resolve property)
```

Event summary

Event	Description
`onSelect = function(obj:Object, menuItem:Object) {}`	Invoked when the specified menu item is selected from the Flash Player context menu.

Constructor summary

Signature	Description
`ContextMenuItem(caption:String, callbackFunction:Function, [separatorBefore:Boolean], [enabled:Boolean], [visible:Boolean])`	Creates a new ContextMenuItem object that can be added to the `ContextMenu.customItems` array.

Method summary

Modifiers	Signature	Description
	`copy() : ContextMenuItem`	Creates and returns a copy of the specified ContextMenuItem object.

Methods inherited from class Object

```
addProperty (Object.addProperty method),hasOwnProperty
(Object.hasOwnProperty method),isPropertyEnumerable
(Object.isPropertyEnumerable method),isPrototypeOf (Object.isPrototypeOf
method),registerClass (Object.registerClass method),toString
(Object.toString method),unwatch (Object.unwatch method),valueOf
(Object.valueOf method),watch (Object.watch method)
```

caption (ContextMenuItem.caption property)

`public caption : String`

A string that specifies the menu item caption (text) displayed in the context menu.

Availability: ActionScript 1.0; Flash Player 7

Example

The following example displays the caption for the selected menu item (Pause Game) in the Output panel:

```
var my_cm:ContextMenu = new ContextMenu();
var menuItem_cmi:ContextMenuItem = new ContextMenuItem("Pause Game",
   onPause);
my_cm.customItems.push(menuItem_cmi);
function onPause(obj, menuItem) {
   trace("You chose: " + menuItem.caption);
}
this.menu = my_cm;
```

ContextMenuItem constructor

```
public ContextMenuItem(caption:String, callbackFunction:Function,
  [separatorBefore:Boolean], [enabled:Boolean], [visible:Boolean])
```

Creates a new ContextMenuItem object that can be added to the
ContextMenu.customItems array.

Availability: ActionScript 1.0; Flash Player 7

Parameters

`caption:String` - A string that specifies the text associated with the menu item.

`callbackFunction:Function` - A function that you define, which is called when the menu
item is selected.

`separatorBefore:Boolean` [optional] - A Boolean value that indicates whether a separator
bar should appear above the menu item in the context menu. The default value is `false`.

`enabled:Boolean` [optional] - A Boolean value that indicates whether the menu item is
enabled or disabled in the context menu. The default value is `true`.

`visible:Boolean` [optional] - A Boolean value that indicates whether the menu item is
visible or invisible. The default value is `true`.

Example

This example adds Start and Stop menu items, separated by a bar, to the ContextMenu object
my_cm. The `startHandler()` function is called when Start is selected from the context menu;
`stopHandler()` is called when Stop is selected. The ContextMenu object is applied to the
current Timeline.

```
var my_cm:ContextMenu = new ContextMenu();
my_cm.customItems.push(new ContextMenuItem("Start", startHandler));
my_cm.customItems.push(new ContextMenuItem("Stop", stopHandler, true));
function stopHandler(obj, item) {
  trace("Stopping...");
}
function startHandler(obj, item) {
  trace("Starting...");
}
this.menu = my_cm;
```

copy (ContextMenuItem.copy method)

`public copy() : ContextMenuItem`

Creates and returns a copy of the specified ContextMenuItem object. The copy includes all properties of the original object.

Availability: ActionScript 1.0; Flash Player 7

Returns

`ContextMenuItem` - A ContextMenuItem object.

Example

This example creates a new ContextMenuItem object named `original_cmi` with the caption Pause and a callback handler set to the function `onPause`. The example then creates a copy of the ContextMenuItem object and assigns it to the variable `copy_cmi`.

```
var original_cmi:ContextMenuItem = new ContextMenuItem("Pause", onPause);
function onPause(obj:Object, menu:ContextMenu) {
   trace("pause me");
}

var copy_cmi:ContextMenuItem = original_cmi.copy();

var my_cm:ContextMenu = new ContextMenu();
my_cm.customItems.push(original_cmi);
my_cm.customItems.push(copy_cmi);

my_mc.menu = my_cm;
```

enabled (ContextMenuItem.enabled property)

`public enabled : Boolean`

A Boolean value that indicates whether the specified menu item is enabled or disabled. By default, this property is `true`.

Availability: ActionScript 1.0; Flash Player 7

Example

The following example creates two new context menu items: Start and Stop. When the user selects Start, the number of milliseconds from when the SWF file started is traced. Start is then disabled in the menu. When Stop is selected, the number of milliseconds that have elapsed since the SWF file started is traced. The Start menu item is re-enabled and the Stop menu item is disabled.

```
var my_cm:ContextMenu = new ContextMenu();
var startMenuItem:ContextMenuItem = new ContextMenuItem("Start",
   startHandler);
startMenuItem.enabled = true;
my_cm.customItems.push(startMenuItem);
var stopMenuItem:ContextMenuItem = new ContextMenuItem("Stop", stopHandler,
   true);
stopMenuItem.enabled = false;
my_cm.customItems.push(stopMenuItem);
function stopHandler(obj, item) {
   trace("Stopping... "+getTimer()+"ms");
   startMenuItem.enabled = true;
   stopMenuItem.enabled = false;
}
function startHandler(obj, item) {
   trace("Starting... "+getTimer()+"ms");
   startMenuItem.enabled = false;
   stopMenuItem.enabled = true;
}
this.menu = my_cm;
```

onSelect (ContextMenuItem.onSelect handler)

```
onSelect = function(obj:Object, menuItem:Object) {}
```

Invoked when the specified menu item is selected from the Flash Player context menu. The specified callback handler receives two parameters: obj, a reference to the object under the mouse when the user invoked the Flash Player context menu, and item, a reference to the ContextMenuItem object that represents the selected menu item.

Availability: ActionScript 1.0; Flash Player 7

Parameters

`obj:Object` - A reference to the object (movie clip, Timeline, button, or selectable text field) on which the user right or Control clicked.

`menuItem:Object` - A reference to the selected ContextMenuItem object.

Example

The following example determines over what type of object the context menu was invoked.

```
var my_cmi:ContextMenu = new ContextMenu();
var start_cmi:ContextMenuItem = new ContextMenuItem("Start");
start_cmi.onSelect = function(obj, item) {
  trace("You chose: "+item.caption);
};
my_cmi.customItems.push(start_cmi);
my_cmi.customItems.push(new ContextMenuItem("Stop", stopHandler, true));
function stopHandler(obj, item) {
  trace("Stopping...");
}
this.menu = my_cmi;
```

See also

`onSelect (ContextMenu.onSelect handler)`

separatorBefore (ContextMenuItem.separatorBefore property)

`public separatorBefore : Boolean`

A Boolean value that indicates whether a separator bar should appear above the specified menu item. By default, this property is `false`.

 NOTE A separator bar always appears between any custom menu items and the built-in menu items.

Availability: ActionScript 1.0; Flash Player 7

Example

This example creates three menu items, labeled Open, Save, and Print. A separator bar divides the Save and Print items. The menu items are then added to the ContextMenu object's `customItems` array. Finally, the menu is attached to the current Timeline of the SWF file.

```
var my_cm:ContextMenu = new ContextMenu();
var open_cmi:ContextMenuItem = new ContextMenuItem("Open", itemHandler);
var save_cmi:ContextMenuItem = new ContextMenuItem("Save", itemHandler);
var print_cmi:ContextMenuItem = new ContextMenuItem("Print", itemHandler);
print_cmi.separatorBefore = true;
my_cm.customItems.push(open_cmi, save_cmi, print_cmi);
function itemHandler(obj, menuItem) {
  trace("You chose: " + menuItem.caption);
};
this.menu = my_cm;
```

See also

onSelect (ContextMenu.onSelect handler)

visible (ContextMenuItem.visible property)

```
public visible : Boolean
```

A Boolean value that indicates whether the specified menu item is visible when the Flash Player context menu is displayed. By default, this property is `true`.

Availability: ActionScript 1.0; Flash Player 7

Example

The following example creates two new context menu items: Start and Stop. When the user selects Start, the number of milliseconds from when the SWF file started is displayed. Start is then made invisible in the menu. When Stop is selected, the number of milliseconds that have elapsed since the SWF file started is displayed. The Start menu item is made visible and the Stop menu item is made invisible.

```
var my_cm:ContextMenu = new ContextMenu();
var startMenuItem:ContextMenuItem = new ContextMenuItem("Start",
  startHandler);
startMenuItem.visible = true;
my_cm.customItems.push(startMenuItem);
var stopMenuItem:ContextMenuItem = new ContextMenuItem("Stop", stopHandler,
  true);
stopMenuItem.visible = false;
my_cm.customItems.push(stopMenuItem);
function stopHandler(obj, item) {
  trace("Stopping... "+getTimer()+"ms");
  startMenuItem.visible = true;
```

```
   stopMenuItem.visible = false;
}
function startHandler(obj, item) {
   trace("Starting... "+getTimer()+"ms");
   startMenuItem.visible = false;
   stopMenuItem.visible = true;
}
this.menu = my_cm;
```

ConvolutionFilter (flash.filters.ConvolutionFilter)

```
Object
  |
  +-flash.filters.BitmapFilter
     |
     +-flash.filters.ConvolutionFilter
```

```
public class ConvolutionFilter
extends BitmapFilter
```

The ConvolutionFilter class applies a matrix convolution filter effect. A convolution combines pixels in the input image with neighboring pixels to produce an image. A wide variety of imaging operations can be achieved through convolutions, including blurring, edge detection, sharpening, embossing, and beveling. You can apply this effect on bitmaps and MovieClip instances.

The use of filters depends on the object to which you apply the filter:

- To apply filters to movie clips at runtime, use the filters property. Setting the filters property of an object does not modify the object and can be undone by clearing the filters property.

- To apply filters to BitmapData instances, use the BitmapData.applyFilter() method. Calling applyFilter() on a BitmapData object takes the source BitmapData object and the filter object and generates a filtered image as a result.

You can also apply filter effects to images and video at authoring time. For more information, see your authoring documentation.

If you apply a filter to a movie clip or button, the cacheAsBitmap property of the movie clip or button is set to true. If you clear all filters, the original value of cacheAsBitmap is restored.

A matrix convolution is based on an *n* x *m* matrix, which describes how a given pixel value in the input image is combined with its neighboring pixel values to produce a resulting pixel value. Each result pixel is determined by applying the matrix to the corresponding source pixel and its neighboring pixels.

For a 3 x 3 matrix convolution, the following formula is used for each independent color channel:

```
dst (x, y) = ((src (x-1, y-1) * a0 + src(x, y-1) * a1....
src(x, y+1) * a7 + src (x+1,y+1) * a8) / divisor) + bias
```

When run by a processor that offers SSE (Streaming SIMD Extensions), certain filter specifications perform faster.

- The filter must be a 3 x 3 filter.
- All the filter terms must be integers between -127 and +127.
- The sum of all the filter terms must not have an absolute value greater than 127.
- If any filter term is negative, the divisor must be between 2.00001 and 256.
- If all filter terms are positive, the divisor must be between 1.1 and 256.
- The bias must be an integer.

A filter is not applied if the resulting image would exceed 2880 pixels in width or height. For example, if you zoom in on a large movie clip with a filter applied, the filter is turned off if the resulting image reaches the 2880-pixel limit.

Availability: ActionScript 1.0; Flash Player 8

See also

`applyFilter` (`BitmapData.applyFilter` method), `filters` (`MovieClip.filters` property), `cacheAsBitmap` (`MovieClip.cacheAsBitmap` property)

Property summary

Modifiers	Property	Description
	alpha:Number	The alpha transparency value of the substitute color.
	bias:Number	Bias to add to the result of the matrix transformation.
	clamp:Boolean	Indicates whether the image should be clamped.
	color:Number	The hexadecimal color to substitute for pixels that are off the source image.
	divisor:Number	The divisor used during matrix transformation.
	matrix:Array	An array of values used for matrix transformation; returns a copy.
	matrixX:Number	The x dimension of the matrix (the number of columns in the matrix).
	matrixY:Number	The y dimension of the matrix (the number of rows in the matrix).
	preserveAlpha:Boolean	Indicates what the convolution applies to.

Properties inherited from class Object

```
constructor (Object.constructor property),__proto__ (Object.__proto__
property),prototype (Object.prototype property),__resolve
(Object.__resolve property)
```

Constructor summary

Signature	Description
ConvolutionFilter(matrixX:Number, matrixY:Number, matrix:Array, [divisor:Number], [bias:Number], [preserveAlpha:Boolean], [clamp:Boolean], [color:Number], [alpha:Number])	Initializes a ConvolutionFilter instance with the specified parameters.

Method summary

Modifiers	Signature	Description
	`clone() : ConvolutionFilter`	Returns a copy of this filter object.

Methods inherited from class BitmapFilter

```
clone (BitmapFilter.clone method)
```

Methods inherited from class Object

```
addProperty (Object.addProperty method), hasOwnProperty
(Object.hasOwnProperty method), isPropertyEnumerable
(Object.isPropertyEnumerable method), isPrototypeOf (Object.isPrototypeOf
method), registerClass (Object.registerClass method), toString
(Object.toString method), unwatch (Object.unwatch method), valueOf
(Object.valueOf method), watch (Object.watch method)
```

alpha (ConvolutionFilter.alpha property)

`public alpha : Number`

The alpha transparency value of the substitute color. Valid values are 0 to 1.0. The default is 0. For example, .25 sets a transparency value of 25 percent. The default is 1.0.

Availability: ActionScript 1.0; Flash Player 8

Example

The following example changes the `alpha` property of `filter` from its default value of 1 to .35.

```
import flash.filters.ConvolutionFilter;
import flash.display.BitmapData;
import flash.geom.Rectangle;
import flash.geom.Point;

var alpha:Number = .35;
var filter:ConvolutionFilter = new ConvolutionFilter(3, 3, [1, 1, 1, 1, 1,
    1, 1, 1, 1], 9, 0, true, false, 0x0000FF, alpha);

var myBitmapData:BitmapData = new BitmapData(100, 80, true, 0xCCFF0000);

var mc:MovieClip = this.createEmptyMovieClip("mc",
    this.getNextHighestDepth());
mc.attachBitmap(myBitmapData, this.getNextHighestDepth());
myBitmapData.noise(128, 0, 255, 1 | 2 | 4 | 8, false);
```

```
mc.onPress = function() {
  myBitmapData.applyFilter(myBitmapData, new Rectangle(0, 0, 98, 78), new
  Point(2, 2), filter);
}
```

bias (ConvolutionFilter.bias property)

`public bias : Number`

Bias to add to the result of the matrix transformation. The default is 0.

Availability: ActionScript 1.0; Flash Player 8

Example

The following example changes the `bias` property of `filter` from its default value of 0 to 50.

```
import flash.filters.ConvolutionFilter;
import flash.display.BitmapData;

var bias:Number = 50;
var filter:ConvolutionFilter = new ConvolutionFilter(3, 3, [1, 1, 1, 1, 1,
  1, 1, 1, 1], 9, bias);

var myBitmapData:BitmapData = new BitmapData(100, 80, false, 0x00FF0000);

var mc:MovieClip = this.createEmptyMovieClip("mc",
  this.getNextHighestDepth());
mc.attachBitmap(myBitmapData, this.getNextHighestDepth());
myBitmapData.noise(128);

mc.onPress = function() {
  myBitmapData.applyFilter(myBitmapData, myBitmapData.rectangle, new
  Point(0, 0), filter);
}
```

clamp (ConvolutionFilter.clamp property)

`public clamp : Boolean`

Indicates whether the image should be clamped. For pixels that are off the source image, a value of `true` indicates that the input image is extended along each of its borders as necessary by duplicating the color values at the given edge of the input image. A value of `false` indicates that another color should be used, as specified in the `color` and `alpha` properties. The default is `true`.

Availability: ActionScript 1.0; Flash Player 8

Example

The following example changes the clamp property of filter from its default value of true to false.

```
import flash.filters.ConvolutionFilter;
import flash.display.BitmapData;
import flash.geom.Rectangle;
import flash.geom.Point;

var clamp:Boolean = false;
var filter:ConvolutionFilter = new ConvolutionFilter(3, 3, [1, 1, 1, 1, 1,
  1, 1, 1, 1], 9, 0, true, clamp, 0x00FF00, 1);

var myBitmapData:BitmapData = new BitmapData(100, 80, true, 0xCCFF0000);

var mc:MovieClip = this.createEmptyMovieClip("mc",
  this.getNextHighestDepth());
mc.attachBitmap(myBitmapData, this.getNextHighestDepth());
myBitmapData.noise(128, 0, 255, 1 | 2 | 4 | 8, false);

mc.onPress = function() {
  myBitmapData.applyFilter(myBitmapData, new Rectangle(0, 0, 98, 78), new
  Point(2, -2), filter);
}
```

clone (ConvolutionFilter.clone method)

`public clone() : ConvolutionFilter`

Returns a copy of this filter object.

Availability: ActionScript 1.0; Flash Player 8

Returns

`flash.filters.ConvolutionFilter` - A new ConvolutionFilter instance with all the same properties as the original one.

Example

The following example creates three ConvolutionFilter objects and compares them: filter_1 is created by using the ConvolutionFilter constructor; filter_2 is created by setting it equal to filter_1; and clonedFilter is created by cloning filter_1. Notice that although filter_2 evaluates as being equal to filter_1, clonedFilter, even though it contains the same values as filter_1, does not.

```
import flash.filters.ConvolutionFilter;
```

```
var filter_1:ConvolutionFilter = new ConvolutionFilter(3, 3, [1, 1, 1, 1, 1,
    1, 1, 1, 1], 9);
var filter_2:ConvolutionFilter = filter_1;
var clonedFilter:ConvolutionFilter = filter_1.clone();

trace(filter_1 == filter_2); // true
trace(filter_1 == clonedFilter); // false

for(var i in filter_1) {
    trace(">> " + i + ": " + filter_1[i]);
    // >> clone: [type Function]
    // >> alpha: 0
    // >> color: 0
    // >> clamp: true
    // >> preserveAlpha: true
    // >> bias: 0
    // >> divisor: 9
    // >> matrix: 1,1,1,1,1,1,1,1,1
    // >> matrixY: 3
    // >> matrixX: 3
}

for(var i in clonedFilter) {
    trace(">> " + i + ": " + clonedFilter[i]);
    // >> clone: [type Function]
    // >> alpha: 0
    // >> color: 0
    // >> clamp: true
    // >> preserveAlpha: true
    // >> bias: 0
    // >> divisor: 9
    // >> matrix: 1,1,1,1,1,1,1,1,1
    // >> matrixY: 3
    // >> matrixX: 3
}
```

To further demonstrate the relationships between `filter_1`, `filter_2`, and `clonedFilter` the following example modifies the `bias` property of `filter_1`. Modifying `bias` demonstrates that the `clone()` method creates a new instance based on values of `filter_1` instead of pointing to them in reference.

```
import flash.filters.ConvolutionFilter;

var filter_1:ConvolutionFilter = new ConvolutionFilter(3, 3, [1, 1, 1, 1, 1,
    1, 1, 1, 1], 9);
var filter_2:ConvolutionFilter = filter_1;
var clonedFilter:ConvolutionFilter = filter_1.clone();
trace(filter_1.bias); // 0
trace(filter_2.bias); // 0
trace(clonedFilter.bias); // 0
```

```
filter_1.bias = 20;

trace(filter_1.bias); // 20
trace(filter_2.bias); // 20
trace(clonedFilter.bias); // 0
```

color (ConvolutionFilter.color property)

`public color : Number`

The hexadecimal color to substitute for pixels that are off the source image. This is an RGB value with no alpha component. The default is 0.

Availability: ActionScript 1.0; Flash Player 8

Example

The following example changes the `color` property of `filter` from its default value of 0 to 0xFF0000.

```
import flash.filters.ConvolutionFilter;
import flash.display.BitmapData;
import flash.geom.Rectangle;
import flash.geom.Point;

var color:Number = 0x0000FF;
var filter:ConvolutionFilter = new ConvolutionFilter(3, 3, [1, 1, 1, 1, 1,
    1, 1, 1, 1], 9, 0, true, false, color, 1);

var myBitmapData:BitmapData = new BitmapData(100, 80, true, 0xCCFF0000);

var mc:MovieClip = this.createEmptyMovieClip("mc",
    this.getNextHighestDepth());
mc.attachBitmap(myBitmapData, this.getNextHighestDepth());
myBitmapData.noise(128, 0, 255, 1 | 2 | 4 | 8, false);

var height:Number = 100;
var width:Number = 80;
mc.onPress = function() {
  height -= 2;
  width -= 2;
  myBitmapData.applyFilter(myBitmapData, new Rectangle(0, 0, height,
  width), new Point(2, 2), filter);
}
```

ConvolutionFilter constructor

```
public ConvolutionFilter(matrixX:Number, matrixY:Number, matrix:Array,
   [divisor:Number], [bias:Number], [preserveAlpha:Boolean],
   [clamp:Boolean], [color:Number], [alpha:Number])
```

Initializes a ConvolutionFilter instance with the specified parameters.

Availability: ActionScript 1.0; Flash Player 8

Parameters

`matrixX:Number` - The *x* dimension of the matrix (the number of columns in the matrix). The default value is 0.

`matrixY:Number` - The *y* dimension of the matrix (the number of rows in the matrix). The default value is 0.

`matrix:Array` - The array of values used for matrix transformation; returns a copy. The number of items in the array must equal `matrixX*matrixY`.

`divisor:Number` [optional] - The divisor used during matrix transformation. The default value is 1. A divisor that is the sum of all the matrix values evens out the overall color intensity of the result. A value of 0 is ignored and the default is used instead.

`bias:Number` [optional] - The bias to add to the result of the matrix transformation. The default value is 0.

`preserveAlpha:Boolean` [optional] - A value of `false` indicates that the convolution applies to all channels, including the alpha channel. A value of `true` indicates that the convolution applies only to the color channels. The default value is `true`.

`clamp:Boolean` [optional] - For pixels that are off the source image, a value of `true` indicates that the input image is extended along each of its borders as necessary by duplicating the color values at the given edge of the input image. A value of `false` indicates that another color should be used, as specified in the `color` and `alpha` properties. The default is `true`.

`color:Number` [optional] - The hexadecimal color to substitute for pixels that are off the source image.

`alpha:Number` [optional] - The alpha of the substitute color.

Example

The following code creates a 3 x 3 convolution filter with a divisor of 9. The filter would make an image appear blurred:

```
var myArray:Array = [1, 1, 1, 1, 1, 1, 1, 1, 1];
var myFilter:ConvolutionFilter = new flash.filters.ConvolutionFilter (3,
  3, myArray, 9);
```

The following example creates a ConvolutionFilter object with the four required parameters `matrixX`, `matrixY`, `matrix`, and `divisor`.

```
import flash.filters.ConvolutionFilter;
import flash.display.BitmapData;

var matrixX:Number = 3;
var matrixY:Number = 3;
var matrix:Array = [1, 1, 1, 1, 1, 1, 1, 1, 1];
var divisor:Number = 9;

var filter:ConvolutionFilter = new ConvolutionFilter(matrixX, matrixY,
  matrix, divisor);

var myBitmapData:BitmapData = new BitmapData(100, 80, false, 0x00FF0000);

var mc:MovieClip = this.createEmptyMovieClip("mc",
  this.getNextHighestDepth());
mc.attachBitmap(myBitmapData, this.getNextHighestDepth());
myBitmapData.noise(128);

mc.onPress = function() {
  myBitmapData.applyFilter(myBitmapData, myBitmapData.rectangle, new
  Point(0, 0), filter);
}
```

divisor (ConvolutionFilter.divisor property)

```
public divisor : Number
```

The divisor used during matrix transformation. The default value is 1. A divisor that is the sum of all the matrix values evens out the overall color intensity of the result. A value of 0 is ignored and the default is used instead.

Availability: ActionScript 1.0; Flash Player 8

Example

The following example changes the `divisor` property of `filter` to 6.

```
import flash.filters.ConvolutionFilter;
import flash.display.BitmapData;

var filter:ConvolutionFilter = new ConvolutionFilter(3, 3, [1, 1, 1, 1, 1,
  1, 1, 1, 1], 9);

var myBitmapData:BitmapData = new BitmapData(100, 80, false, 0x00FF0000);

var mc:MovieClip = this.createEmptyMovieClip("mc",
  this.getNextHighestDepth());
```

```
mc.attachBitmap(myBitmapData, this.getNextHighestDepth());
myBitmapData.noise(128);

mc.onPress = function() {
  var newDivisor:Number = 6;
  filter.divisor = newDivisor;
    myBitmapData.applyFilter(myBitmapData, myBitmapData.rectangle, new
  Point(0, 0), filter);
}
```

matrix (ConvolutionFilter.matrix property)

```
public matrix : Array
```

An array of values used for matrix transformation; returns a copy. The number of items in the array must equal `matrixX*matrixY`.

The `matrix` property cannot be changed by directly modifying the values (for example, `myFilter.matrix[2] = 1;`). Instead, as shown in the following example, you must get a reference to the array, make the change to the reference, and reset the value using `filter.matrix = newMatrix;`.

Availability: ActionScript 1.0; Flash Player 8

Example

The following example changes the `matrix` property of `filter` from one that blurs a bitmap to one that sharpens it.

```
import flash.filters.ConvolutionFilter;
import flash.display.BitmapData;

var filter:ConvolutionFilter = new ConvolutionFilter(3, 3, [1, 1, 1, 1, 1,
  1, 1, 1, 1], 9);

var myBitmapData:BitmapData = new BitmapData(100, 80, false, 0x00FF0000);

var mc:MovieClip = this.createEmptyMovieClip("mc",
  this.getNextHighestDepth());
mc.attachBitmap(myBitmapData, this.getNextHighestDepth());
myBitmapData.noise(128);

mc.onPress = function() {
  var newMatrix:Array = [0, -1, 0, -1, 8, -1, 0, -1, 0];
  filter.matrix = newMatrix;
  myBitmapData.applyFilter(myBitmapData, myBitmapData.rectangle, new
  Point(0, 0), filter);
}
```

matrixX (ConvolutionFilter.matrixX property)

```
public matrixX : Number
```

The *x* dimension of the matrix (the number of columns in the matrix). The default value is 0.

Availability: ActionScript 1.0; Flash Player 8

Example

The following example displays the `matrixX` property of `filter`.

```
import flash.filters.ConvolutionFilter;

var filter:ConvolutionFilter = new ConvolutionFilter(2, 3, [1, 0, 0, 1, 0,
   0], 6);
trace(filter.matrixX); // 2
```

matrixY (ConvolutionFilter.matrixY property)

```
public matrixY : Number
```

The *y* dimension of the matrix (the number of rows in the matrix). The default value is 0.

Availability: ActionScript 1.0; Flash Player 8

Example

The following example displays the `matrixY` property of `filter`.

```
import flash.filters.ConvolutionFilter;

var filter:ConvolutionFilter = new ConvolutionFilter(2, 3, [1, 0, 0, 1, 0,
   0], 6);
trace(filter.matrixY); // 3
```

preserveAlpha (ConvolutionFilter.preserveAlpha property)

```
public preserveAlpha : Boolean
```

Indicates what the convolution applies to. A value of `false` indicates that the convolution applies to all channels, including the alpha channel. A value of `true` indicates that the convolution applies only to the color channels. The default value is `true`.

Availability: ActionScript 1.0; Flash Player 8

Example

The following example changes the `preserveAlpha` property of `filter` from its default value of `true` to `false`.

```
import flash.filters.ConvolutionFilter;
import flash.display.BitmapData;

var preserveAlpha:Boolean = false;
var filter:ConvolutionFilter = new ConvolutionFilter(3, 3, [1, 1, 1, 1, 1,
    1, 1, 1, 1], 9, 0, preserveAlpha);

var myBitmapData:BitmapData = new BitmapData(100, 80, true, 0xCCFF0000);

var mc:MovieClip = this.createEmptyMovieClip("mc",
    this.getNextHighestDepth());
mc.attachBitmap(myBitmapData, this.getNextHighestDepth());
myBitmapData.noise(128, 0, 255, 1 | 2 | 4 | 8, false);

mc.onPress = function() {
    myBitmapData.applyFilter(myBitmapData, myBitmapData.rectangle, new
    Point(0, 0), filter);
}
```

CustomActions

```
Object
   |
   +-CustomActions
```

```
public class CustomActions
extends Object
```

The methods of the CustomActions class allow a SWF file playing in the Flash authoring tool to manage any custom actions that are registered with the authoring tool. A SWF file can install and uninstall custom actions, retrieve the XML definition of a custom action, and retrieve the list of registered custom actions.

You can use these methods to build SWF files that are extensions of the Flash authoring tool. Such an extension could, for example, use the Flash Application Protocol to navigate a UDDI repository and download web services into the Actions toolbox.

Availability: ActionScript 1.0; Flash Player 6

Property summary

Properties inherited from class Object

```
constructor (Object.constructor property),__proto__ (Object.__proto__
property),prototype (Object.prototype property),__resolve
(Object.__resolve property)
```

Method summary

Modifiers	Signature	Description
static	get(name:String) : String	Reads the contents of the custom action XML definition file named name.
static	install(name:String, data:String) : Boolean	Installs a new custom action XML definition file indicated by the name parameter.
static	list() : Array	Returns an Array object containing the names of all the custom actions that are registered with the Flash authoring tool.
static	uninstall(name:String) : Boolean	Removes the Custom Actions XML definition file named name.

Methods inherited from class Object

```
addProperty (Object.addProperty method),hasOwnProperty
(Object.hasOwnProperty method),isPropertyEnumerable
(Object.isPropertyEnumerable method),isPrototypeOf (Object.isPrototypeOf
method),registerClass (Object.registerClass method),toString
(Object.toString method),unwatch (Object.unwatch method),valueOf
(Object.valueOf method),watch (Object.watch method)
```

get (CustomActions.get method)

```
public static get(name:String) : String
```

Reads the contents of the custom action XML definition file named name.

The name of the definition file must be a simple filename, without the .xml file extension, and without any directory separators (':', '/' or '\').

If the definition file specified by the name cannot be found, a value of undefined is returned. If the custom action XML definition specified by the name parameter is located, it is read in its entirety and returned as a string.

Availability: ActionScript 1.0; Flash Player 6

Parameters

`name:String` - The name of the custom action definition to retrieve.

Returns

`String` - If the custom action XML definition is located, returns a string; otherwise, returns `undefined`.

Example

The following example lists the custom actions in a ComboBox instance, and gets the custom action when a Button instance is clicked. Drag an instance of a ComboBox, Button, and TextArea onto the Stage. Give the ComboBox an instance name of `customActionName_cb`, the TextArea an instance name of `customActionXml_ta`, and the Button an instance name of `view_button`. Enter the following ActionScript on Frame 1 of the Timeline:

```
import mx.controls.*;

var customActionName_cb:ComboBox;
var customActionXml_ta:TextArea;
var view_button:Button;

customActionName_cb.dataProvider = CustomActions.list();

customActionXml_ta.editable = false;

var viewListener:Object = new Object();
viewListener.click = function(evt:Object) {
  var caName:String = String(customActionName_cb.selectedItem);
  customActionXml_ta.text = CustomActions.get(caName);
};
view_button.addEventListener("click", viewListener);
```

install (CustomActions.install method)

`public static install(name:String, data:String) : Boolean`

Installs a new custom action XML definition file indicated by the `name` parameter. The contents of the file is specified by the string *customXML*.

The name of the definition file must be a simple filename, without the .xml file extension, and without any directory separators (':', '/' or '\').

If a custom actions file already exists with the name `name`, it is overwritten.

If the Configuration/ActionsPanel/CustomActions directory does not exist when this method is invoked, the directory is created.

Availability: ActionScript 1.0; Flash Player 6

Parameters

name:String - The name of the custom action definition to install.

data:String - The text of the XML definition to install.

Returns

Boolean - A Boolean value of false if an error occurs during installation; otherwise, a value of true is returned to indicate that the custom action has been successfully installed.

Example

The following example installs information into the Actions panel from an XML file. Open a text editor and save a new document called dogclass.xml. Enter the following code:

```
<?xml version="1.0"?>
<customactions>
  <actionspanel>
  <folder version="7" id="DogClass" index="true" name="Dog" tiptext="Dog
Class">
    <string version="7" id="getFleas" name="getFleas" tiptext="gets number
of fleas" text=".getFleas(% fleas %)" />
  </folder>
  </actionspanel>
  <colorsyntax>
    <identifier text=".getFleas" />
  </colorsyntax>
  <codehints>
    <typeinfo pattern=" _dog" object="Dog"/>
  </codehints>
</customactions>
```

Then open a new FLA file in the same directory and select Frame 1 of the Timeline. Enter the following code into the Actions panel:

```
var my_xml:XML = new XML();
my_xml.ignoreWhite = true;
my_xml.onLoad = function(success:Boolean) {
  trace(success);
  CustomActions.install("dogclass", this.firstChild);
  trace(CustomActions.list());
};
my_xml.load("dogclass.xml");
```

Select Control > Test Movie, and if the XML loads successfully, you will see true, and an array containing the names of all the custom actions that are registered with the Flash authoring tool in the Output panel. Close the SWF file, and open the Actions panel. You will see a new item in the Actions toolbox called Dog, and inside that folder you see getFleas.

list (CustomActions.list method)

```
public static list() : Array
```

Returns an Array object containing the names of all the custom actions that are registered with the Flash authoring tool. The elements of the array are simple names, without the .xml file extension, and without any directory separators (for example, ":", "/", or "\"). If there are no registered custom actions, `list()` returns a zero-length array. If an error occurs, `list()` returns the value `undefined`.

Availability: ActionScript 1.0; Flash Player 6

Returns

`Array` - An array.

Example

The following example lists the custom actions in a ComboBox instance, and gets the custom action when a Button instance is clicked. Drag an instance of a ComboBox, Button, and TextArea onto the Stage. Give the ComboBox an instance name of `customActionName_cb`, the TextArea an instance name of `customActionXml_ta`, and the Button an instance name of `view_button`. Enter the following ActionScript on Frame 1 of the Timeline:

```
import mx.controls.*;

var customActionName_cb:ComboBox;
var customActionXml_ta:TextArea;
var view_button:Button;

customActionName_cb.dataProvider = CustomActions.list();

customActionXml_ta.editable = false;

var viewListener:Object = new Object();
viewListener.click = function(evt:Object) {
  var caName:String = String(customActionName_cb.selectedItem);
  customActionXml_ta.text = CustomActions.get(caName);
};
view_button.addEventListener("click", viewListener);
```

uninstall (CustomActions.uninstall method)

```
public static uninstall(name:String) : Boolean
```

Removes the Custom Actions XML definition file named name.

The name of the definition file must be a simple filename, without the .xml file extension, and without any directory separators (':', '/' or '\').

Availability: ActionScript 1.0; Flash Player 6

Parameters

name:String - The name of the custom action definition to uninstall.

Returns

Boolean - A Boolean value of false if no custom actions are found with the name name. If the custom actions were successfully removed, a value of true is returned.

Example

The following example installs a new custom action and displays an array containing the names of all the custom actions that are registered with the Flash authoring tool in the Output panel. When the uninstall_btn is clicked, the custom action is then uninstalled. An array containing names of the custom actions installed is displayed, and dogclass should then be removed from the array. Create a button called uninstall_btn and then enter the following ActionScript onto Frame 1 of the Timeline:

```
var my_xml:XML = new XML();
my_xml.ignoreWhite = true;
my_xml.onLoad = function(success:Boolean) {
  trace(success);
  CustomActions.install("dogclass", this.firstChild);
  trace(CustomActions.list());
};
my_xml.load("dogclass.xml");

uninstall_btn.onRelease = function() {
  CustomActions.uninstall("dogclass");
  trace(CustomActions.list());
};
```

For information on creating dogclass.xml, see CustomActions.install().

See also

install (CustomActions.install method)

Date

```
Object
  |
  +-Date
```

```
public class Date
extends Object
```

The Date class lets you retrieve date and time values relative to universal time (Greenwich mean time, now called universal time or UTC) or relative to the operating system on which Flash Player is running. The methods of the Date class are not static but apply only to the individual Date object specified when the method is called. The `Date.UTC()` method is an exception; it is a static method.

The Date class handles daylight saving time differently, depending on the operating system and Flash Player version. Flash Player 6 and later versions handle daylight saving time on the following operating systems in these ways:

- Windows - the Date object automatically adjusts its output for daylight saving time. The Date object detects whether daylight saving time is employed in the current locale, and if so, it detects the standard-to-daylight saving time transition date and times. However, the transition dates currently in effect are applied to dates in the past and the future, so the daylight saving time bias might calculate incorrectly for dates in the past when the locale had different transition dates.

- Mac OS X - the Date object automatically adjusts its output for daylight saving time. The time zone information database in Mac OS X is used to determine whether any date or time in the present or past should have a daylight saving time bias applied.

- Mac OS 9 - the operating system provides only enough information to determine whether the current date and time should have a daylight saving time bias applied. Accordingly, the date object assumes that the current daylight saving time bias applies to all dates and times in the past or future.

Flash Player 5 handles daylight saving time on the following operating systems as follows:

- Windows - the U.S. rules for daylight saving time are always applied, which leads to incorrect transitions in Europe and other areas that employ daylight saving time but have different transition times than the U.S. Flash correctly detects whether daylight saving time is used in the current locale.

To call the methods of the Date class, you must first create a Date object using the constructor for the Date class, described later in this section.

Availability: ActionScript 1.0; Flash Player 5

Property summary

Properties inherited from class Object

constructor (Object.constructor property), __proto__ (Object.__proto__ property), prototype (Object.prototype property), __resolve (Object.__resolve property)

Constructor summary

Signature	Description
Date([yearOrTimevalue:Number], [month:Number], [date:Number], [hour:Number], [minute:Number], [second:Number], [millisecond:Number])	Constructs a new Date object that holds the specified date and time.

Method summary

Modifiers	Signature	Description
	`getDate() : Number`	Returns the day of the month (an integer from 1 to 31) of the specified Date object according to local time.
	`getDay() : Number`	Returns the day of the week (0 for Sunday, 1 for Monday, and so on) of the specified Date object according to local time.
	`getFullYear() : Number`	Returns the full year (a four-digit number, such as 2000) of the specified Date object, according to local time.
	`getHours() : Number`	Returns the hour (an integer from 0 to 23) of the specified Date object, according to local time.
	`getMilliseconds() : Number`	Returns the milliseconds (an integer from 0 to 999) of the specified Date object, according to local time.
	`getMinutes() : Number`	Returns the minutes (an integer from 0 to 59) of the specified Date object, according to local time.
	`getMonth() : Number`	Returns the month (0 for January, 1 for February, and so on) of the specified Date object, according to local time.
	`getSeconds() : Number`	Returns the seconds (an integer from 0 to 59) of the specified Date object, according to local time.
	`getTime() : Number`	Returns the number of milliseconds since midnight January 1, 1970, universal time, for the specified Date object.
	`getTimezoneOffset() : Number`	Returns the difference, in minutes, between the computer's local time and universal time.
	`getUTCDate() : Number`	Returns the day of the month (an integer from 1 to 31) in the specified Date object, according to universal time.
	`getUTCDay() : Number`	Returns the day of the week (0 for Sunday, 1 for Monday, and so on) of the specified Date object, according to universal time.
	`getUTCFullYear() : Number`	Returns the four-digit year of the specified Date object, according to universal time.
	`getUTCHours() : Number`	Returns the hour (an integer from 0 to 23) of the specified Date object, according to universal time.
	`getUTCMilliseconds() : Number`	Returns the milliseconds (an integer from 0 to 999) of the specified Date object, according to universal time.

Modifiers	Signature	Description
	`getUTCMinutes() : Number`	Returns the minutes (an integer from 0 to 59) of the specified Date object, according to universal time.
	`getUTCMonth() : Number`	Returns the month (0 [January] to 11 [December]) of the specified Date object, according to universal time.
	`getUTCSeconds() : Number`	Returns the seconds (an integer from 0 to 59) of the specified Date object, according to universal time.
	`getUTCYear() : Number`	Returns the year of this `Date` according to universal time (UTC).
	`getYear() : Number`	Returns the year of the specified Date object, according to local time.
	`setDate(date:Number) : Number`	Sets the day of the month for the specified Date object, according to local time, and returns the new time in milliseconds.
	`setFullYear(year:Number, [month:Number], [date:Number]) : Number`	Sets the year of the specified Date object, according to local time and returns the new time in milliseconds.
	`setHours(hour:Number) : Number`	Sets the hours for the specified Date object according to local time and returns the new time in milliseconds.
	`setMilliseconds(millisecond:Number) : Number`	Sets the milliseconds for the specified Date object according to local time and returns the new time in milliseconds.
	`setMinutes(minute:Number) : Number`	Sets the minutes for a specified Date object according to local time and returns the new time in milliseconds.
	`setMonth(month:Number, [date:Number]) : Number`	Sets the month for the specified Date object in local time and returns the new time in milliseconds.
	`setSeconds(second:Number) : Number`	Sets the seconds for the specified Date object in local time and returns the new time in milliseconds.
	`setTime(millisecond:Number) : Number`	Sets the date for the specified Date object in milliseconds since midnight on January 1, 1970, and returns the new time in milliseconds.
	`setUTCDate(date:Number) : Number`	Sets the date for the specified Date object in universal time and returns the new time in milliseconds.

Modifiers	Signature	Description

	`setUTCFullYear(year:`
	`Number,`
	`[month:Number],`
	`[date:Number]) :`
	`Number`
		Sets the year for the specified Date object (*my_date*) in universal time and returns the new time in milliseconds.

	`setUTCHours(hour:Num`
	`ber,`
	`[minute:Number],`
	`[second:Number],`
	`[millisecond:Number]`
	`) : Number`
		Sets the hour for the specified Date object in universal time and returns the new time in milliseconds.

	`setUTCMilliseconds(m`
	`illisecond:Number) :`
	`Number`
		Sets the milliseconds for the specified Date object in universal time and returns the new time in milliseconds.

	`setUTCMinutes(minute`
	`:Number,`
	`[second:Number],`
	`[millisecond:Number]`
	`) : Number`
		Sets the minute for the specified Date object in universal time and returns the new time in milliseconds.

	`setUTCMonth(month:Nu`
	`mber, [date:Number])`
	`: Number`
		Sets the month, and optionally the day, for the specified Date object in universal time and returns the new time in milliseconds.

	`setUTCSeconds(second`
	`:Number,`
	`[millisecond:Number]`
	`) : Number`
		Sets the seconds for the specified Date object in universal time and returns the new time in milliseconds.

	`setYear(year:Number)` `: Number`	Sets the year for the specified Date object in local time and returns the new time in milliseconds.
	`toString() : String`	Returns a string value for the specified date object in a readable format.

static	`UTC(year:Number,`
	`month:Number,`
	`[date:Number],`
	`[hour:Number],`
	`[minute:Number],`
	`[second:Number],`
	`[millisecond:Number]`
	`) : Number`
		Returns the number of milliseconds between midnight on January 1, 1970, universal time, and the time specified in the parameters.

	`valueOf() : Number`	Returns the number of milliseconds since midnight January 1, 1970, universal time, for this `Date`.

Methods inherited from class Object

```
addProperty (Object.addProperty method), hasOwnProperty
(Object.hasOwnProperty method), isPropertyEnumerable
(Object.isPropertyEnumerable method), isPrototypeOf (Object.isPrototypeOf
method), registerClass (Object.registerClass method), toString
(Object.toString method), unwatch (Object.unwatch method), valueOf
(Object.valueOf method), watch (Object.watch method)
```

Date constructor

```
public Date([yearOrTimevalue:Number], [month:Number], [date:Number],
  [hour:Number], [minute:Number], [second:Number], [millisecond:Number])
```

Constructs a new Date object that holds the specified date and time.

The Date() constructor takes up to seven parameters (year, month, ..., millisecond) to specify a date and time to the millisecond. Alternatively, you can pass a single value to the Date() constructor that indicates a time value based on the number of milliseconds since January 1, 1970 0:00:000 GMT. Or you can specify no parameters, and the Date() date object is assigned the current date and time.

For example, this code shows several different ways to create a Date object:

```
var d1:Date = new Date();
var d3:Date = new Date(2000, 0, 1);
var d4:Date = new Date(65, 2, 6, 9, 30, 15, 0);
var d5:Date = new Date(-14159025000);
```

In the first line of code, a Date object is set to the time when the assignment statement is run.

In the second line, a Date object is created with year, month, and date parameters passed to it, resulting in the time 0:00:00 GMT January 1, 2000.

In the third line, a Date object is created with year, month, and date parameters passed to it, resulting in the time 09:30:15 GMT (+ 0 milliseconds) March 6, 1965. Note that since the year parameter is specified as a two-digit integer, it is interpreted as 1965.

In the fourth line, only one parameter is passed, which is a time value representing the number of milliseconds before or after 0:00:00 GMT January 1, 1970; since the value is negative, it represents a time *before* 0:00:00 GMT January 1, 1970, and in this case the time is 02:56:15 GMT July, 21 1969.

Availability: ActionScript 1.0; Flash Player 5

Parameters

`yearOrTimevalue:Number` [optional] - If other parameters are specified, this number represents a year (such as 1965); otherwise, it represents a time value. If the number represents a year, a value of 0 to 99 indicates 1900 through 1999; otherwise all four digits of the year must be specified. If the number represents a time value (no other parameters are specified), it is the number of milliseconds before or after 0:00:00 GMT January 1, 1970; a negative values represents a time *before* 0:00:00 GMT January 1, 1970, and a positive value represents a time after.

`month:Number` [optional] - An integer from 0 (January) to 11 (December).

`date:Number` [optional] - An integer from 1 to 31.

`hour:Number` [optional] - An integer from 0 (midnight) to 23 (11 p.m.).

`minute:Number` [optional] - An integer from 0 to 59.

`second:Number` [optional] - An integer from 0 to 59.

`millisecond:Number` [optional] - An integer from 0 to 999 of milliseconds.

Example

The following example retrieves the current date and time:

```
var now_date:Date = new Date();
```

The following example creates a new Date object for Mary's birthday, August 12, 1974 (because the month parameter is zero-based, the example uses 7 for the month, not 8):

```
var maryBirthday:Date = new Date (74, 7, 12);
```

The following example creates a new Date object and concatenates the returned values of `Date.getMonth()`, `Date.getDate()`, and `Date.getFullYear()`:

```
var today_date:Date = new Date();
var date_str:String = ((today_date.getMonth()+1)+"/
  "+today_date.getDate()+"/"+today_date.getFullYear());
trace(date_str); // displays current date in United States date format
```

See also

getMonth (Date.getMonth method), getDate (Date.getDate method), getFullYear (Date.getFullYear method)

getDate (Date.getDate method)

`public getDate() : Number`

Returns the day of the month (an integer from 1 to 31) of the specified Date object according to local time. Local time is determined by the operating system on which Flash Player is running.

Availability: ActionScript 1.0; Flash Player 5

Returns

`Number` - An integer.

Example

The following example creates a new Date object and concatenates the returned values of `Date.getMonth()`, `Date.getDate()`, and `Date.getFullYear()`:

```
var today_date:Date = new Date();
var date_str:String = (today_date.getDate()+"/
  "+(today_date.getMonth()+1)+"/"+today_date.getFullYear());
trace(date_str); // displays current date in United States date format
```

See also

`getMonth (Date.getMonth method)`, `getFullYear (Date.getFullYear method)`

getDay (Date.getDay method)

`public getDay() : Number`

Returns the day of the week (0 for Sunday, 1 for Monday, and so on) of the specified Date object according to local time. Local time is determined by the operating system on which Flash Player is running.

Availability: ActionScript 1.0; Flash Player 5

Returns

`Number` - An integer representing the day of the week.

Example

The following example creates a new Date object and uses `getDay()` to determine the current day of the week:

```
var dayOfWeek_array:Array = new Array("Sunday", "Monday", "Tuesday",
  "Wednesday", "Thursday", "Friday", "Saturday");
var today_date:Date = new Date();
var day_str:String = dayOfWeek_array[today_date.getDay()];
trace("Today is "+day_str);
```

getFullYear (Date.getFullYear method)

`public getFullYear() : Number`

Returns the full year (a four-digit number, such as 2000) of the specified Date object, according to local time. Local time is determined by the operating system on which Flash Player is running.

Availability: ActionScript 1.0; Flash Player 5

Returns

`Number` - An integer representing the year.

Example

The following example uses the constructor to create a Date object. The trace statement shows the value returned by the `getFullYear()` method.

```
var my_date:Date = new Date();
trace(my_date.getYear()); // displays 104
trace(my_date.getFullYear()); // displays current year
```

getHours (Date.getHours method)

`public getHours() : Number`

Returns the hour (an integer from 0 to 23) of the specified Date object, according to local time. Local time is determined by the operating system on which Flash Player is running.

Availability: ActionScript 1.0; Flash Player 5

Returns

`Number` - An integer.

Example

The following example uses the constructor to create a Date object based on the current time and uses the `getHours()` method to display hour values from that object:

```
var my_date:Date = new Date();
trace(my_date.getHours());

var my_date:Date = new Date();
var hourObj:Object = getHoursAmPm(my_date.getHours());
trace(hourObj.hours);
trace(hourObj.ampm);

function getHoursAmPm(hour24:Number):Object {
  var returnObj:Object = new Object();
```

```
returnObj.ampm = (hour24<12) ? "AM" : "PM";
var hour12:Number = hour24%12;
if (hour12 == 0) {
hour12 = 12;
}
returnObj.hours = hour12;
return returnObj;
}
```

getMilliseconds (Date.getMilliseconds method)

`public getMilliseconds() : Number`

Returns the milliseconds (an integer from 0 to 999) of the specified Date object, according to local time. Local time is determined by the operating system on which Flash Player is running.

Availability: ActionScript 1.0; Flash Player 5

Returns

Number - An integer.

Example

The following example uses the constructor to create a Date object based on the current time and uses the `getMilliseconds()` method to return the milliseconds value from that object:

```
var my_date:Date = new Date();
trace(my_date.getMilliseconds());
```

getMinutes (Date.getMinutes method)

`public getMinutes() : Number`

Returns the minutes (an integer from 0 to 59) of the specified Date object, according to local time. Local time is determined by the operating system on which Flash Player is running.

Availability: ActionScript 1.0; Flash Player 5

Returns

Number - An integer.

Example

The following example uses the constructor to create a Date object based on the current time, and uses the `getMinutes()` method to return the minutes value from that object:

```
var my_date:Date = new Date();
```

```
trace(my_date.getMinutes());
```

getMonth (Date.getMonth method)

```
public getMonth() : Number
```
Returns the month (0 for January, 1 for February, and so on) of the specified Date object, according to local time. Local time is determined by the operating system on which Flash Player is running.

Availability: ActionScript 1.0; Flash Player 5

Returns

`Number` - An integer.

Example

The following example uses the constructor to create a Date object based on the current time and uses the `getMonth()` method to return the month value from that object:

```
var my_date:Date = new Date();
trace(my_date.getMonth());
```

The following example uses the constructor to create a Date object based on the current time and uses the `getMonth()` method to display the current month as a numeric value, and display the name of the month.

```
var my_date:Date = new Date();
trace(my_date.getMonth());
trace(getMonthAsString(my_date.getMonth()));
function getMonthAsString(month:Number):String {
  var monthNames_array:Array = new Array("January", "February", "March",
  "April", "May", "June", "July", "August", "September", "October",
  "November", "December");
  return monthNames_array[month];
}
```

getSeconds (Date.getSeconds method)

```
public getSeconds() : Number
```
Returns the seconds (an integer from 0 to 59) of the specified Date object, according to local time. Local time is determined by the operating system on which Flash Player is running.

Availability: ActionScript 1.0; Flash Player 5

Returns

`Number` - An integer.

Example

The following example uses the constructor to create a Date object based on the current time and uses the getSeconds() method to return the seconds value from that object:

```
var my_date:Date = new Date();
trace(my_date.getSeconds());
```

getTime (Date.getTime method)

public getTime() : Number

Returns the number of milliseconds since midnight January 1, 1970, universal time, for the specified Date object. Use this method to represent a specific instant in time when comparing two or more Date objects.

Availability: ActionScript 1.0; Flash Player 5

Returns

Number - An integer.

Example

The following example uses the constructor to create a Date object based on the current time, and uses the getTime() method to return the number of milliseconds since midnight January 1, 1970:

```
var my_date:Date = new Date();
trace(my_date.getTime());
```

getTimezoneOffset (Date.getTimezoneOffset method)

public getTimezoneOffset() : Number

Returns the difference, in minutes, between the computer's local time and universal time.

Availability: ActionScript 1.0; Flash Player 5

Returns

Number - An integer.

Example

The following example returns the difference between the local daylight saving time for San Francisco and universal time. Daylight saving time is factored into the returned result only if the date defined in the Date object occurs during daylight saving time. The output in this example is 420 minutes and displays in the Output panel (7 hours * 60 minutes/hour = 420 minutes). This example is Pacific Daylight Time (PDT, GMT-0700). The result varies depending on location and time of year.

```
var my_date:Date = new Date();
trace(my_date.getTimezoneOffset());
```

getUTCDate (Date.getUTCDate method)

`public getUTCDate() : Number`

Returns the day of the month (an integer from 1 to 31) in the specified Date object, according to universal time.

Availability: ActionScript 1.0; Flash Player 5

Returns

`Number` - An integer.

Example

The following example creates a new Date object and uses `Date.getUTCDate()` and `Date.getDate()`. The value returned by `Date.getUTCDate()` can differ from the value returned by `Date.getDate()`, depending on the relationship between your local time zone and universal time.

```
var my_date:Date = new Date(2004,8,25);
trace(my_date.getUTCDate()); // output: 25
```

See also

`getDate (Date.getDate method)`

getUTCDay (Date.getUTCDay method)

`public getUTCDay() : Number`

Returns the day of the week (0 for Sunday, 1 for Monday, and so on) of the specified Date object, according to universal time.

Availability: ActionScript 1.0; Flash Player 5

Returns

Number - An integer.

Example

The following example creates a new Date object and uses `Date.getUTCDay()` and `Date.getDay()`. The value returned by `Date.getUTCDay()` can differ from the value returned by `Date.getDay()`, depending on the relationship between your local time zone and universal time.

```
var today_date:Date = new Date();
trace(today_date.getDay()); // output will be based on local timezone
trace(today_date.getUTCDay()); // output will equal getDay() plus or minus
  one
```

See also

getDay (Date.getDay method)

getUTCFullYear (Date.getUTCFullYear method)

```
public getUTCFullYear() : Number
```

Returns the four-digit year of the specified Date object, according to universal time.

Availability: ActionScript 1.0; Flash Player 5

Returns

Number - An integer.

Example

The following example creates a new Date object and uses `Date.getUTCFullYear()` and `Date.getFullYear()`. The value returned by `Date.getUTCFullYear()` may differ from the value returned by `Date.getFullYear()` if today's date is December 31 or January 1, depending on the relationship between your local time zone and universal time.

```
var today_date:Date = new Date();
trace(today_date.getFullYear()); // display based on local timezone
trace(today_date.getUTCFullYear()); // displays getYear() plus or minus 1
```

See also

getFullYear (Date.getFullYear method)

getUTCHours (Date.getUTCHours method)

```
public getUTCHours() : Number
```

Returns the hour (an integer from 0 to 23) of the specified Date object, according to universal time.

Availability: ActionScript 1.0; Flash Player 5

Returns

Number - An integer.

Example

The following example creates a new Date object and uses Date.getUTCHours() and Date.getHours(). The value returned by Date.getUTCHours() may differ from the value returned by Date.getHours(), depending on the relationship between your local time zone and universal time.

```
var today_date:Date = new Date();
trace(today_date.getHours()); // display based on local timezone
trace(today_date.getUTCHours()); // display equals getHours() plus or minus
    12
```

See also

getHours (Date.getHours method)

getUTCMilliseconds (Date.getUTCMilliseconds method)

public getUTCMilliseconds() : Number

Returns the milliseconds (an integer from 0 to 999) of the specified Date object, according to universal time.

Availability: ActionScript 1.0; Flash Player 5

Returns

Number - An integer.

Example

The following example creates a new Date object and uses getUTCMilliseconds() to return the milliseconds value from the Date object.

```
var today_date:Date = new Date();
trace(today_date.getUTCMilliseconds());
```

getUTCMinutes (Date.getUTCMinutes method)

`public getUTCMinutes() : Number`

Returns the minutes (an integer from 0 to 59) of the specified Date object, according to universal time.

Availability: ActionScript 1.0; Flash Player 5

Returns

`Number` - An integer.

Example

The following example creates a new Date object and uses `getUTCMinutes()` to return the minutes value from the Date object:

```
var today_date:Date = new Date();
trace(today_date.getUTCMinutes());
```

getUTCMonth (Date.getUTCMonth method)

`public getUTCMonth() : Number`

Returns the month (0 [January] to 11 [December]) of the specified Date object, according to universal time.

Availability: ActionScript 1.0; Flash Player 5

Returns

`Number` - An integer.

Example

The following example creates a new Date object and uses `Date.getUTCMonth()` and `Date.getMonth()`. The value returned by `Date.getUTCMonth()` can differ from the value returned by `Date.getMonth()` if today's date is the first or last day of a month, depending on the relationship between your local time zone and universal time.

```
var today_date:Date = new Date();
trace(today_date.getMonth()); // output based on local timezone
trace(today_date.getUTCMonth()); // output equals getMonth() plus or minus
    1
```

See also

`getMonth (Date.getMonth method)`

getUTCSeconds (Date.getUTCSeconds method)

`public getUTCSeconds() : Number`

Returns the seconds (an integer from 0 to 59) of the specified Date object, according to universal time.

Availability: ActionScript 1.0; Flash Player 5

Returns

`Number` - An integer.

Example

The following example creates a new Date object and uses `getUTCSeconds()` to return the seconds value from the Date object:

```
var today_date:Date = new Date();
trace(today_date.getUTCSeconds());
```

getUTCYear (Date.getUTCYear method)

`public getUTCYear() : Number`

Returns the year of this `Date` according to universal time (UTC). The year is the full year minus 1900. For example, the year 2000 is represented as 100.

Availability: ActionScript 1.0; Flash Player 8

Returns

`Number` - An integer.

Example

The following example creates a new Date object and uses `Date.getUTCFullYear()` and `Date.getFullYear()`. The value returned by `Date.getUTCFullYear()` may differ from the value returned by `Date.getFullYear()` if today's date is December 31 or January 1, depending on the relationship between your local time zone and universal time.

```
var today_date:Date = new Date();

trace(today_date.getFullYear()); // display based on local timezone

trace(today_date.getUTCFullYear()); // displays getYear() plus or minus 1
```

getYear (Date.getYear method)

`public getYear() : Number`

Returns the year of the specified Date object, according to local time. Local time is determined by the operating system on which Flash Player is running. The year is the full year minus 1900. For example, the year 2000 is represented as 100.

Availability: ActionScript 1.0; Flash Player 5

Returns

`Number` - An integer.

Example

The following example creates a Date object with the month and year set to May 2004. The `Date.getYear()` method returns 104, and `Date.getFullYear()` returns 2004:

```
var today_date:Date = new Date(2004,4);
trace(today_date.getYear()); // output: 104
trace(today_date.getFullYear()); // output: 2004
```

See also

`getFullYear (Date.getFullYear method)`

setDate (Date.setDate method)

`public setDate(date:Number) : Number`

Sets the day of the month for the specified Date object, according to local time, and returns the new time in milliseconds. Local time is determined by the operating system on which Flash Player is running.

Availability: ActionScript 1.0; Flash Player 5

Parameters

`date:Number` - An integer from 1 to 31.

Returns

`Number` - An integer.

Example

The following example initially creates a new Date object, setting the date to May 15, 2004, and uses `Date.setDate()` to change the date to May 25, 2004:

```
var today_date:Date = new Date(2004,4,15);
```

```
trace(today_date.getDate()); //displays 15
today_date.setDate(25);
trace(today_date.getDate()); //displays 25
```

setFullYear (Date.setFullYear method)

```
public setFullYear(year:Number, [month:Number], [date:Number]) : Number
```

Sets the year of the specified Date object, according to local time and returns the new time in milliseconds. If the `month` and `date` parameters are specified, they are set to local time. Local time is determined by the operating system on which Flash Player is running.

Calling this method does not modify the other fields of the specified Date object but `Date.getUTCDay()` and `Date.getDay()` can report a new value if the day of the week changes as a result of calling this method.

Availability: ActionScript 1.0; Flash Player 5

Parameters

`year:Number` - A four-digit number specifying a year. Two-digit numbers do not represent four-digit years; for example, 99 is not the year 1999, but the year 99.

`month:Number` [optional] - An integer from 0 (January) to 11 (December). If you omit this parameter, the month field of the specified Date object will not be modified.

`date:Number` [optional] - A number from 1 to 31. If you omit this parameter, the date field of the specified Date object will not be modified.

Returns

`Number` - An integer.

Example

The following example initially creates a new Date object, setting the date to May 15, 2004, and uses `Date.setFullYear()` to change the date to May 15, 2002:

```
var my_date:Date = new Date(2004,4,15);
trace(my_date.getFullYear()); //output: 2004
my_date.setFullYear(2002);
trace(my_date.getFullYear()); //output: 2002
```

See also

`getUTCDay (Date.getUTCDay method)`, `getDay (Date.getDay method)`

setHours (Date.setHours method)

`public setHours(hour:Number) : Number`

Sets the hours for the specified Date object according to local time and returns the new time in milliseconds. Local time is determined by the operating system on which Flash Player is running.

Availability: ActionScript 1.0; Flash Player 5

Parameters

`hour:Number` - An integer from 0 (midnight) to 23 (11 p.m.).

Returns

`Number` - An integer.

Example

The following example initially creates a new Date object, setting the time and date to 8:00 a.m. on May 15, 2004, and uses `Date.setHours()` to change the time to 4:00 p.m.:

```
var my_date:Date = new Date(2004,4,15,8);
trace(my_date.getHours()); // output: 8
my_date.setHours(16);
trace(my_date.getHours()); // output: 16
```

setMilliseconds (Date.setMilliseconds method)

`public setMilliseconds(millisecond:Number) : Number`

Sets the milliseconds for the specified Date object according to local time and returns the new time in milliseconds. Local time is determined by the operating system on which Flash Player is running.

Availability: ActionScript 1.0; Flash Player 5

Parameters

`millisecond:Number` - An integer from 0 to 999.

Returns

`Number` - An integer.

Example

The following example initially creates a new Date object, setting the date to 8:30 a.m. on May 15, 2004 with the milliseconds value set to 250, and then uses `Date.setMilliseconds()` to change the milliseconds value to 575:

```
var my_date:Date = new Date(2004,4,15,8,30,0,250);
trace(my_date.getMilliseconds()); // output: 250
my_date.setMilliseconds(575);
trace(my_date.getMilliseconds()); // output: 575
```

setMinutes (Date.setMinutes method)

`public setMinutes(minute:Number) : Number`

Sets the minutes for a specified Date object according to local time and returns the new time in milliseconds. Local time is determined by the operating system on which Flash Player is running.

Availability: ActionScript 1.0; Flash Player 5

Parameters

`minute:Number` - An integer from 0 to 59.

Returns

`Number` - An integer.

Example

The following example initially creates a new Date object, setting the time and date to 8:00 a.m. on May 15, 2004, and then uses `Date.setMinutes()` to change the time to 8:30 a.m.:

```
var my_date:Date = new Date(2004,4,15,8,0);
trace(my_date.getMinutes()); // output: 0
my_date.setMinutes(30);
trace(my_date.getMinutes()); // output: 30
```

setMonth (Date.setMonth method)

`public setMonth(month:Number, [date:Number]) : Number`

Sets the month for the specified Date object in local time and returns the new time in milliseconds. Local time is determined by the operating system on which Flash Player is running.

Availability: ActionScript 1.0; Flash Player 5

Parameters

`month:Number` - An integer from 0 (January) to 11 (December).

`date:Number` [optional] - An integer from 1 to 31. If you omit this parameter, the date field of the specified Date object will not be modified.

Returns

`Number` - An integer.

Example

The following example initially creates a new Date object, setting the date to May 15, 2004, and uses `Date.setMonth()` to change the date to June 15, 2004:

```
var my_date:Date = new Date(2004,4,15);
trace(my_date.getMonth()); //output: 4
my_date.setMonth(5);
trace(my_date.getMonth()); //output: 5
```

setSeconds (Date.setSeconds method)

`public setSeconds(second:Number) : Number`

Sets the seconds for the specified Date object in local time and returns the new time in milliseconds. Local time is determined by the operating system on which Flash Player is running.

Availability: ActionScript 1.0; Flash Player 5

Parameters

`second:Number` - An integer from 0 to 59.

Returns

`Number` - An integer.

Example

The following example initially creates a new Date object, setting the time and date to 8:00:00 a.m. on May 15, 2004, and uses `Date.setSeconds()` to change the time to 8:00:45 a.m.:

```
var my_date:Date = new Date(2004,4,15,8,0,0);
trace(my_date.getSeconds()); // output: 0
my_date.setSeconds(45);
trace(my_date.getSeconds()); // output: 45
```

setTime (Date.setTime method)

`public setTime(millisecond:Number) : Number`

Sets the date for the specified Date object in milliseconds since midnight on January 1, 1970, and returns the new time in milliseconds.

Availability: ActionScript 1.0; Flash Player 5

Parameters

`millisecond:Number` - A number; an integer value where 0 is midnight on January 1, universal time.

Returns

`Number` - An integer.

Example

The following example initially creates a new Date object, setting the time and date to 8:00 a.m. on May 15, 2004, and uses `Date.setTime()` to change the time to 8:30 a.m.:

```
var my_date:Date = new Date(2004,4,15,8,0,0);
var myDate_num:Number = my_date.getTime(); // convert my_date to
  milliseconds
myDate_num += 30 * 60 * 1000; // add 30 minutes in milliseconds
my_date.setTime(myDate_num); // set my_date Date object 30 minutes forward
trace(my_date.getFullYear()); // output: 2004
trace(my_date.getMonth()); // output: 4
trace(my_date.getDate()); // output: 15
trace(my_date.getHours()); // output: 8
trace(my_date.getMinutes()); // output: 30
```

setUTCDate (Date.setUTCDate method)

`public setUTCDate(date:Number) : Number`

Sets the date for the specified Date object in universal time and returns the new time in milliseconds. Calling this method does not modify the other fields of the specified Date object, but `Date.getUTCDay()` and `Date.getDay()` can report a new value if the day of the week changes as a result of calling this method.

Availability: ActionScript 1.0; Flash Player 5

Parameters

`date:Number` - A number; an integer from 1 to 31.

Returns

`Number` - An integer.

Example

The following example initially creates a new Date object with today's date, uses `Date.setUTCDate()` to change the date value to 10, and changes it again to 25:

```
var my_date:Date = new Date();
my_date.setUTCDate(10);
trace(my_date.getUTCDate()); // output: 10
my_date.setUTCDate(25);
trace(my_date.getUTCDate()); // output: 25
```

See also

`getUTCDay (Date.getUTCDay method)`, `getDay (Date.getDay method)`

setUTCFullYear (Date.setUTCFullYear method)

`public setUTCFullYear(year:Number, [month:Number], [date:Number]) : Number`

Sets the year for the specified Date object (*my_date*) in universal time and returns the new time in milliseconds.

Optionally, this method can also set the month and date represented by the specified Date object. Calling this method does not modify the other fields of the specified Date object, but `Date.getUTCDay()` and `Date.getDay()` can report a new value if the day of the week changes as a result of calling this method.

Availability: ActionScript 1.0; Flash Player 5

Parameters

`year:Number` - An integer that represents the year specified as a full four-digit year, such as 2000.

`month:Number` [optional] - An integer from 0 (January) to 11 (December). If you omit this parameter, the month field of the specified Date object will not be modified.

`date:Number` [optional] - An integer from 1 to 31. If you omit this parameter, the date field of the specified Date object will not be modified.

Returns

`Number` - An integer.

Example

The following example initially creates a new Date object with today's date, uses
`Date.setUTCFullYear()` to change the year value to 2001, and changes the date to May 25, 1995:

```
var my_date:Date = new Date();
my_date.setUTCFullYear(2001);
trace(my_date.getUTCFullYear()); // output: 2001
my_date.setUTCFullYear(1995, 4, 25);
trace(my_date.getUTCFullYear()); // output: 1995
trace(my_date.getUTCMonth()); // output: 4
trace(my_date.getUTCDate()); // output: 25
```

See also

getUTCDay (Date.getUTCDay method), getDay (Date.getDay method)

setUTCHours (Date.setUTCHours method)

```
public setUTCHours(hour:Number, [minute:Number], [second:Number],
  [millisecond:Number]) : Number
```

Sets the hour for the specified Date object in universal time and returns the new time in milliseconds.

Availability: ActionScript 1.0; Flash Player 5

Parameters

hour:Number - A number; an integer from 0 (midnight) to 23 (11 p.m.).

minute:Number [optional] - A number; an integer from 0 to 59. If you omit this parameter, the minutes field of the specified Date object will not be modified.

second:Number [optional] - A number; an integer from 0 to 59. If you omit this parameter, the seconds field of the specified Date object will not be modified.

millisecond:Number [optional] - A number; an integer from 0 to 999. If you omit this parameter, the milliseconds field of the specified Date object will not be modified.

Returns

Number - An integer.

Example

The following example initially creates a new Date object with today's date, uses
`Date.setUTCHours()` to change the time to 8:30 a.m., and changes the time again to 5:30:47 p.m.:

```
var my_date:Date = new Date();
my_date.setUTCHours(8,30);
trace(my_date.getUTCHours()); // output: 8
trace(my_date.getUTCMinutes()); // output: 30
my_date.setUTCHours(17,30,47);
trace(my_date.getUTCHours()); // output: 17
trace(my_date.getUTCMinutes()); // output: 30
trace(my_date.getUTCSeconds()); // output: 47
```

setUTCMilliseconds (Date.setUTCMilliseconds method)

`public setUTCMilliseconds(millisecond:Number) : Number`

Sets the milliseconds for the specified Date object in universal time and returns the new time in milliseconds.

Availability: ActionScript 1.0; Flash Player 5

Parameters

`millisecond:Number` - An integer from 0 to 999.

Returns

`Number` - An integer.

Example

The following example initially creates a new Date object, setting the date to 8:30 a.m. on May 15, 2004 with the milliseconds value set to 250, and uses `Date.setUTCMilliseconds()` to change the milliseconds value to 575:

```
var my_date:Date = new Date(2004,4,15,8,30,0,250);
trace(my_date.getUTCMilliseconds()); // output: 250
my_date.setUTCMilliseconds(575);
trace(my_date.getUTCMilliseconds()); // output: 575
```

setUTCMinutes (Date.setUTCMinutes method)

`public setUTCMinutes(minute:Number, [second:Number], [millisecond:Number])`
`  : Number`

Sets the minute for the specified Date object in universal time and returns the new time in milliseconds.

Availability: ActionScript 1.0; Flash Player 5

Parameters

`minute:Number` - An integer from 0 to 59.

`second:Number` [optional] - An integer from 0 to 59. If you omit this parameter, the seconds field of the specified Date object will not be modified.

`millisecond:Number` [optional] - An integer from 0 to 999. If you omit this parameter, the milliseconds field of the specified Date object will not be modified.

Returns

`Number` - An integer.

Example

The following example initially creates a new Date object, setting the time and date to 8:00 a.m. on May 15, 2004, and uses `Date.setUTCMinutes()` to change the time to 8:30 a.m.:

```
var my_date:Date = new Date(2004,4,15,8,0);
trace(my_date.getUTCMinutes()); // output: 0
my_date.setUTCMinutes(30);
trace(my_date.getUTCMinutes()); // output: 30
```

setUTCMonth (Date.setUTCMonth method)

`public setUTCMonth(month:Number, [date:Number]) : Number`

Sets the month, and optionally the day, for the specified Date object in universal time and returns the new time in milliseconds. Calling this method does not modify the other fields of the specified Date object, but `Date.getUTCDay()` and `Date.getDay()` might report a new value if the day of the week changes as a result of specifying a value for the `date` parameter.

Availability: ActionScript 1.0; Flash Player 5

Parameters

`month:Number` - An integer from 0 (January) to 11 (December).

`date:Number` [optional] - An integer from 1 to 31. If you omit this parameter, the date field of the specified Date object will not be modified.

Returns

`Number` - An integer.

Example

The following example initially creates a new Date object, setting the date to May 15, 2004, and uses `Date.setMonth()` to change the date to June 15, 2004:

```
var today_date:Date = new Date(2004,4,15);
trace(today_date.getUTCMonth()); // output: 4
today_date.setUTCMonth(5);
trace(today_date.getUTCMonth()); // output: 5
```

See also

getUTCDay (Date.getUTCDay method), getDay (Date.getDay method)

setUTCSeconds (Date.setUTCSeconds method)

public setUTCSeconds(second:Number, [millisecond:Number]) : Number

Sets the seconds for the specified Date object in universal time and returns the new time in milliseconds.

Availability: ActionScript 1.0; Flash Player 5

Parameters

second:Number - An integer from 0 to 59.

millisecond:Number [optional] - An integer from 0 to 999. If you omit this parameter, the milliseconds field of the specified Date object will not be modified.

Returns

Number - An integer.

Example

The following example initially creates a new Date object, setting the time and date to 8:00:00 a.m. on May 15, 2004, and uses Date.setSeconds() to change the time to 8:30:45 a.m.:

```
var my_date:Date = new Date(2004,4,15,8,0,0);
trace(my_date.getUTCSeconds()); // output: 0
my_date.setUTCSeconds(45);
trace(my_date.getUTCSeconds()); // output: 45
```

setYear (Date.setYear method)

public setYear(year:Number) : Number

Sets the year for the specified Date object in local time and returns the new time in milliseconds. Local time is determined by the operating system on which Flash Player is running.

Availability: ActionScript 1.0; Flash Player 5

Parameters

`year:Number` - A number that represents the year. If `year` is an integer between 0 and 99, `setYear` sets the year at 1900 + `year`; otherwise, the year is the value of the `year` parameter.

Returns

`Number` - An integer.

Example

The following example creates a new Date object with the date set to May 25, 2004, uses `setYear()` to change the year to 1999, and changes the year to 2003:

```
var my_date:Date = new Date(2004,4,25);
trace(my_date.getYear()); // output: 104
trace(my_date.getFullYear()); // output: 2004
my_date.setYear(99);
trace(my_date.getYear()); // output: 99
trace(my_date.getFullYear()); // output: 1999
my_date.setYear(2003);
trace(my_date.getYear()); // output: 103
trace(my_date.getFullYear()); // output: 2003
```

toString (Date.toString method)

`public toString() : String`

Returns a string value for the specified date object in a readable format.

Availability: ActionScript 1.0; Flash Player 5

Returns

`String` - A string.

Example

The following example returns the information in the `dateOfBirth_date` Date object as a string. The output from the trace statements are in local time and vary accordingly. For Pacific Daylight Time the output is seven hours earlier than universal time: Mon Aug 12 18:15:00 GMT-0700 1974.

```
var dateOfBirth_date:Date = new Date(74, 7, 12, 18, 15);
trace (dateOfBirth_date);
trace (dateOfBirth_date.toString());
```

UTC (Date.UTC method)

```
public static UTC(year:Number, month:Number, [date:Number], [hour:Number],
    [minute:Number], [second:Number], [millisecond:Number]) : Number
```

Returns the number of milliseconds between midnight on January 1, 1970, universal time, and the time specified in the parameters. This is a static method that is invoked through the Date object constructor, not through a specific Date object. This method lets you create a Date object that assumes universal time, whereas the Date constructor assumes local time.

Availability: ActionScript 1.0; Flash Player 5

Parameters

`year:Number` - A four-digit integer that represents the year (for example, 2000).

`month:Number` - An integer from 0 (January) to 11 (December).

`date:Number` [optional] - An integer from 1 to 31.

`hour:Number` [optional] - An integer from 0 (midnight) to 23 (11 p.m.).

`minute:Number` [optional] - An integer from 0 to 59.

`second:Number` [optional] - An integer from 0 to 59.

`millisecond:Number` [optional] - An integer from 0 to 999.

Returns

`Number` - An integer.

Example

The following example creates a new `maryBirthday_date` Date object defined in universal time. This is the universal time variation of the example used for the `new Date` constructor method. The output is in local time and varies accordingly. For Pacific Daylight Time the output is seven hours earlier than UTC: Sun Aug 11 17:00:00 GMT-0700 1974.

```
var maryBirthday_date:Date = new Date(Date.UTC(1974, 7, 12));
trace(maryBirthday_date);
```

valueOf (Date.valueOf method)

```
public valueOf() : Number
```

Returns the number of milliseconds since midnight January 1, 1970, universal time, for this Date.

Availability: ActionScript 1.0; Flash Player 5

Returns

`Number` - The number of milliseconds.

DisplacementMapFilter (flash.filters.DisplacementMapFilter)

```
Object
  |
  +-flash.filters.BitmapFilter
     |
     +-flash.filters.DisplacementMapFilter
```

`public class DisplacementMapFilter`
`extends BitmapFilter`

The DisplacementMapFilter class uses the pixel values from the specified BitmapData object (called the *displacement map image*) to perform a displacement of an object on the Stage, such as a MovieClip instance. You can use this filter to achieve a warped or mottled effect on a BitmapData or MovieClip instance.

The use of filters depends on the object to which you apply the filter.

To apply filters to movie clips at runtime, use the `filters` property. Setting the `filters` property of an object does not modify the object and can be undone by clearing the `filters` property.

To apply filters to BitmapData instances, use the `BitmapData.applyFilter()` method. Calling `applyFilter()` on a BitmapData object modifies that BitmapData object and cannot be undone.

You can also apply filter effects to images and video at authoring time. For more information, see your authoring documentation.

If you apply a filter to a movie clip or button, the `cacheAsBitmap` property of the movie clip or button is set to `true`. If you clear all filters, the original value of `cacheAsBitmap` is restored.

The filter uses the following formula:

```
dstPixel[x, y] = srcPixel[x + ((componentX(x, y) - 128) * scaleX) / 256, y +
   ((componentY(x, y) - 128) * scaleY) / 256]
```

where `componentX(x, y)` gets the `componentX` color value from the `mapBitmap` property at `(x - mapPoint.x ,y - mapPoint.y)`.

The map image used by the filter is scaled to match the Stage scaling. It is not scaled in any way when the object itself is scaled.

This filter supports Stage scaling, but not general scaling, rotation, or skewing. If the object itself is scaled (if *x*-scale and *y*-scale are not 100%), the filter effect is not scaled. It is scaled only when the Stage is zoomed in.

Here is how the DisplacementMapFilter class works. For each pixel (x,y) in the *destination* bitmap, the DisplacementMapFilter class does the following:

- Gets the color from (x,y) in the *map* bitmap
- Calculates an offset based on that color
- Looks up that offset location $(x+dx,y+dy)$ in the *source* bitmap
- Writes that pixel to the destination(x,y), if boundary conditions permit

A filter is not applied if the resulting image would exceed 2880 pixels in width or height. For example, if you zoom in on a large movie clip with a filter applied, the filter is turned off if the resulting image reaches the 2880-pixel limit.

Availability: ActionScript 1.0; Flash Player 8

See also

`applyFilter (BitmapData.applyFilter method)`, `filters (MovieClip.filters property)`, `cacheAsBitmap (MovieClip.cacheAsBitmap property)`

Property summary

Modifiers	Property	Description
	alpha:Number	Specifies the alpha transparency value to use for out-of-bounds displacements.
	color:Number	Specifies what color to use for out-of-bounds displacements.
	componentX:Number	Describes which color channel to use in the map image to displace the *x* result.
	componentY:Number	Describes which color channel to use in the map image to displace the *y* result.
	mapBitmap:BitmapData	A BitmapData object containing the displacement map data.
	mapPoint:Point	A flash.geom.Point value that contains the offset of the upper-left corner of the target movie clip from the upper-left corner of the map image.
	mode:String	The mode for the filter.
	scaleX:Number	The multiplier to use to scale the *x* displacement result from the map calculation.
	scaleY:Number	The multiplier to use to scale the *y* displacement result from the map calculation.

Properties inherited from class Object

```
constructor (Object.constructor property), __proto__ (Object.__proto__
property), prototype (Object.prototype property), __resolve
(Object.__resolve property)
```

Constructor summary

Signature	Description
DisplacementMapFilter(mapBitmap:BitmapData, mapPoint:Point, componentX:Number, componentY:Number, scaleX:Number, scaleY:Number, [mode:String], [color:Number], [alpha:Number])	Initializes a DisplacementMapFilter instance with the specified parameters.

Method summary

Modifiers	Signature	Description
	`clone() : DisplacementMapFilter`	Returns a copy of this filter object.

Methods inherited from class BitmapFilter

```
clone (BitmapFilter.clone method)
```

Methods inherited from class Object

```
addProperty (Object.addProperty method), hasOwnProperty
(Object.hasOwnProperty method), isPropertyEnumerable
(Object.isPropertyEnumerable method), isPrototypeOf (Object.isPrototypeOf
method), registerClass (Object.registerClass method), toString
(Object.toString method), unwatch (Object.unwatch method), valueOf
(Object.valueOf method), watch (Object.watch method)
```

alpha (DisplacementMapFilter.alpha property)

```
public alpha : Number
```

Specifies the alpha transparency value to use for out-of-bounds displacements. This is specified as a normalized value from 0.0 to 1.0. For example, .25 sets a transparency value of 25%. The default is 0. Use this property if the mode property is set to 3, COLOR.

Availability: ActionScript 1.0; Flash Player 8

Example

The following example modifies the out-of-range alpha property on the existing MovieClip filteredMc to 0x00FF00 when a user clicks it.

```
import flash.filters.DisplacementMapFilter;
import flash.display.BitmapData;
import flash.geom.Point;
import flash.geom.Matrix;
import flash.geom.ColorTransform;

var filteredMc:MovieClip = createDisplacementMapRectangle();

filteredMc.onPress = function() {
  var filter:DisplacementMapFilter = this.filters[0];
  filter.scaleY = 25;
  filter.mode = "color";
  filter.alpha = .25;
```

```
    this.filters = new Array(filter);
}

function createDisplacementMapRectangle():MovieClip {
  var mapBitmap:BitmapData = createGradientBitmap(300, 80, 0xFF000000,
  "radial");
  var filter:DisplacementMapFilter = new DisplacementMapFilter(mapBitmap,
  new Point(-30, -30), 1, 1, 10, 10, "wrap", 0x000000, 0x000000);

  var txtBlock:MovieClip = createTextBlock();
  txtBlock._x = 30;
  txtBlock._y = 30;

  txtBlock.filters = new Array(filter);

  return txtBlock;
}

function createGradientBitmap(w:Number, h:Number, bgColor:Number,
  type:String, hide:Boolean):BitmapData {
  var mc:MovieClip = this.createEmptyMovieClip("mc", 1);
  var matrix:Matrix = new Matrix();
  matrix.createGradientBox(w, h, 0, 0, 0);

  mc.beginGradientFill(type, [0xFF0000, 0x0000FF], [100, 100], [0x55,
  0x99], matrix, "pad");
  mc.lineTo(w, 0);
  mc.lineTo(w, h);
  mc.lineTo(0, h);
  mc.lineTo(0, 0);
  mc.endFill();
  (hide == true) ? mc._alpha = 0 : mc._alpha = 100;

  var bmp:BitmapData = new BitmapData(w, h, true, bgColor);
    bmp.draw(mc, new Matrix(), new ColorTransform(), "normal",
  bmp.rectangle, true);
  mc.attachBitmap(bmp, this.getNextHighestDepth());

  return bmp;
}

function createTextBlock():MovieClip {
  var txtBlock:MovieClip = this.createEmptyMovieClip("txtBlock",
  this.getNextHighestDepth());
  txtBlock.createTextField("txt", this.getNextHighestDepth(), 0, 0, 300,
  80);
  txtBlock.txt.text = "watch the text bend with the displacement map";
  return txtBlock;
}
```

clone (DisplacementMapFilter.clone method)

`public clone() : DisplacementMapFilter`

Returns a copy of this filter object.

Availability: ActionScript 1.0; Flash Player 8

Returns

`flash.filters.DisplacementMapFilter` - A new DisplacementMapFilter instance with all the same properties as the original one.

Example

The following example creates three DisplacementMapFilter objects and compares them: `filter_1` is created by using the `DisplacementMapFilter` constructor; `filter_2` is created by setting it equal to `filter_1`; and `clonedFilter` is created by cloning `filter_1`. Notice that although `filter_2` evaluates as being equal to `filter_1`, `clonedFilter`, even though it contains the same values as `filter_1`, does not.

```
import flash.filters.DisplacementMapFilter;
import flash.display.BitmapData;
import flash.geom.Point;
import flash.geom.Matrix;
import flash.geom.ColorTransform;

var mapBitmap:BitmapData = createGradientBitmap(300, 80, 0xFF000000,
  "radial", true);

var filter_1:DisplacementMapFilter = new DisplacementMapFilter(mapBitmap,
  new Point(-30, -30), 1, 1, 10, 10, "wrap", 0x000000, 0x000000);
var filter_2:DisplacementMapFilter = filter_1;
var clonedFilter:DisplacementMapFilter = filter_1.clone();

trace(filter_1 == filter_2); // true
trace(filter_1 == clonedFilter); // false

for(var i in filter_1) {
  trace(">> " + i + ": " + filter_1[i]);
  // >> clone: [type Function]
  // >> alpha: 0
  // >> color: 0
  // >> mode: wrap
  // >> scaleY: 10
  // >> scaleX: 10
  // >> componentY: 1
  // >> componentX: 1
  // >> mapPoint: (-30, -30)
  // >> mapBitmap: [object Object]
```

```
}

for(var i in clonedFilter) {
  trace(">> " + i + ": " + clonedFilter[i]);
  // >> clone: [type Function]
  // >> alpha: 0
  // >> color: 0
  // >> mode: wrap
  // >> scaleY: 10
  // >> scaleX: 10
  // >> componentY: 1
  // >> componentX: 1
  // >> mapPoint: (-30, -30)
  // >> mapBitmap: [object Object]
}

function createGradientBitmap(w:Number, h:Number, bgColor:Number,
  type:String, hide:Boolean):BitmapData {
  var mc:MovieClip = this.createEmptyMovieClip("mc", 1);
  var matrix:Matrix = new Matrix();
  matrix.createGradientBox(w, h, 0, 0, 0);

  mc.beginGradientFill(type, [0xFF0000, 0x0000FF], [100, 100], [0x55,
  0x99], matrix, "pad");
  mc.lineTo(w, 0);
  mc.lineTo(w, h);
  mc.lineTo(0, h);
  mc.lineTo(0, 0);
  mc.endFill();
  (hide == true) ? mc._alpha = 0 : mc._alpha = 100;

  var bmp:BitmapData = new BitmapData(w, h, true, bgColor);
    bmp.draw(mc, new Matrix(), new ColorTransform(), "normal",
  bmp.rectangle, true);
  mc.attachBitmap(bmp, this.getNextHighestDepth());

  return bmp;
}
```

To further demonstrate the relationships between filter_1, filter_2, and clonedFilter, the following example modifies the mode property of filter_1. Modifying mode demonstrates that the clone() method creates a new instance based on values of filter_1 instead of pointing to them in reference.

```
import flash.filters.DisplacementMapFilter;
import flash.display.BitmapData;
import flash.geom.Point;
import flash.geom.Matrix;
import flash.geom.ColorTransform;
```

```
var mapBitmap:BitmapData = createGradientBitmap(300, 80, 0xFF000000,
  "radial", true);

var filter_1:DisplacementMapFilter = new DisplacementMapFilter(mapBitmap,
  new Point(-30, -30), 1, 1, 10, 10, "wrap", 0x000000, 0x000000);
var filter_2:DisplacementMapFilter = filter_1;
var clonedFilter:DisplacementMapFilter = filter_1.clone();

trace(filter_1.mode); // wrap
trace(filter_2.mode); // wrap
trace(clonedFilter.mode); // wrap

filter_1.mode = "ignore";

trace(filter_1.mode); // ignore
trace(filter_2.mode); // ignore
trace(clonedFilter.mode); // wrap

function createGradientBitmap(w:Number, h:Number, bgColor:Number,
  type:String, hide:Boolean):BitmapData {
  var mc:MovieClip = this.createEmptyMovieClip("mc", 1);
  var matrix:Matrix = new Matrix();
  matrix.createGradientBox(w, h, 0, 0, 0);

  mc.beginGradientFill(type, [0xFF0000, 0x0000FF], [100, 100], [0x55,
  0x99], matrix, "pad");
  mc.lineTo(w, 0);
  mc.lineTo(w, h);
  mc.lineTo(0, h);
  mc.lineTo(0, 0);
  mc.endFill();
  (hide == true) ? mc._alpha = 0 : mc._alpha = 100;

  var bmp:BitmapData = new BitmapData(w, h, true, bgColor);
    bmp.draw(mc, new Matrix(), new ColorTransform(), "normal",
  bmp.rectangle, true);
  mc.attachBitmap(bmp, this.getNextHighestDepth());

  return bmp;
}
```

color (DisplacementMapFilter.color property)

`public color : Number`

Specifies what color to use for out-of-bounds displacements. The valid range of displacements is 0.0 to 1.0. Values are in hexadecimal format. The default value for `color` is 0. Use this property if the `mode` property is set to `3, COLOR`.

Availability: ActionScript 1.0; Flash Player 8

Example

The following example modifies the out-of-range `color` property on the existing MovieClip
`filteredMc` to `0x00FF00` when a user clicks it.

```
import flash.filters.DisplacementMapFilter;
import flash.display.BitmapData;
import flash.geom.Point;
import flash.geom.Matrix;
import flash.geom.ColorTransform;

var filteredMc:MovieClip = createDisplacementMapRectangle();

filteredMc.onPress = function() {
  var filter:DisplacementMapFilter = this.filters[0];
  filter.scaleY = 25;
  filter.mode = "color";
  filter.alpha = .25;
  filter.color = 0x00FF00;
  this.filters = new Array(filter);
}

function createDisplacementMapRectangle():MovieClip {
  var mapBitmap:BitmapData = createGradientBitmap(300, 80, 0xFF000000,
  "radial");
  var filter:DisplacementMapFilter = new DisplacementMapFilter(mapBitmap,
  new Point(-30, -30), 1, 1, 10, 10, "wrap", 0x000000, 0x000000);

  var txtBlock:MovieClip = createTextBlock();
  txtBlock._x = 30;
  txtBlock._y = 30;

  txtBlock.filters = new Array(filter);

  return txtBlock;
}

function createGradientBitmap(w:Number, h:Number, bgColor:Number,
  type:String, hide:Boolean):BitmapData {
  var mc:MovieClip = this.createEmptyMovieClip("mc", 1);
  var matrix:Matrix = new Matrix();
  matrix.createGradientBox(w, h, 0, 0, 0);

  mc.beginGradientFill(type, [0xFF0000, 0x0000FF], [100, 100], [0x55,
  0x99], matrix, "pad");
  mc.lineTo(w, 0);
  mc.lineTo(w, h);
  mc.lineTo(0, h);
  mc.lineTo(0, 0);
  mc.endFill();
  (hide == true) ? mc._alpha = 0 : mc._alpha = 100;
```

```
  var bmp:BitmapData = new BitmapData(w, h, true, bgColor);
    bmp.draw(mc, new Matrix(), new ColorTransform(), "normal",
  bmp.rectangle, true);
  mc.attachBitmap(bmp, this.getNextHighestDepth());

  return bmp;
}

function createTextBlock():MovieClip {
  var txtBlock:MovieClip = this.createEmptyMovieClip("txtBlock",
  this.getNextHighestDepth());
  txtBlock.createTextField("txt", this.getNextHighestDepth(), 0, 0, 300,
  80);
  txtBlock.txt.text = "watch the text bend with the displacement map";
  return txtBlock;
}
```

componentX (DisplacementMapFilter.componentX property)

`public componentX : Number`

Describes which color channel to use in the map image to displace the *x* result. Possible values are 1 (red), 2 (green), 4 (blue), and 8 (alpha).

Availability: ActionScript 1.0; Flash Player 8

Example

The following example changes the `componentX` property on the existing MovieClip `filteredMc` when a user clicks it. The value changes from 1 to 4, which changes the color channel from red to blue.

```
import flash.filters.DisplacementMapFilter;
import flash.display.BitmapData;
import flash.geom.Point;
import flash.geom.Matrix;
import flash.geom.ColorTransform;

var filteredMc:MovieClip = createDisplacementMapRectangle();

filteredMc.onPress = function() {
  var filter:DisplacementMapFilter = this.filters[0];
  filter.componentX = 4;
  this.filters = new Array(filter);
}
```

```
function createDisplacementMapRectangle():MovieClip {
  var mapBitmap:BitmapData = createGradientBitmap(300, 80, 0xFF000000,
  "radial");
  var filter:DisplacementMapFilter = new DisplacementMapFilter(mapBitmap,
  new Point(-30, -30), 1, 1, 10, 10, "wrap", 0x000000, 0x000000);

  var txtBlock:MovieClip = createTextBlock();
  txtBlock._x = 30;
  txtBlock._y = 30;

  txtBlock.filters = new Array(filter);

  return txtBlock;
}

function createGradientBitmap(w:Number, h:Number, bgColor:Number,
  type:String, hide:Boolean):BitmapData {
  var mc:MovieClip = this.createEmptyMovieClip("mc", 1);
  var matrix:Matrix = new Matrix();
  matrix.createGradientBox(w, h, 0, 0, 0);

  mc.beginGradientFill(type, [0xFF0000, 0x0000FF], [100, 100], [0x55,
  0x99], matrix, "pad");
  mc.lineTo(w, 0);
  mc.lineTo(w, h);
  mc.lineTo(0, h);
  mc.lineTo(0, 0);
  mc.endFill();
  (hide == true) ? mc._alpha = 0 : mc._alpha = 100;

  var bmp:BitmapData = new BitmapData(w, h, true, bgColor);
    bmp.draw(mc, new Matrix(), new ColorTransform(), "normal",
  bmp.rectangle, true);
  mc.attachBitmap(bmp, this.getNextHighestDepth());

  return bmp;
}

function createTextBlock():MovieClip {
  var txtBlock:MovieClip = this.createEmptyMovieClip("txtBlock",
  this.getNextHighestDepth());
  txtBlock.createTextField("txt", this.getNextHighestDepth(), 0, 0, 300,
  80);
  txtBlock.txt.text = "watch the text bend with the displacement map";
  return txtBlock;
}
```

See also

BitmapData (flash.display.BitmapData)

---

componentY (DisplacementMapFilter.componentY property)

`public componentY : Number`

Describes which color channel to use in the map image to displace the *y* result. Possible values are 1 (red), 2 (green), 4 (blue), and 8 (alpha).

Availability: ActionScript 1.0; Flash Player 8

Example

The following example changes the `componentY` property on the existing MovieClip `filteredMc` when a user clicks it. The value changes from 1 to 4, which changes the color channel from red to blue.

```
import flash.filters.DisplacementMapFilter;
import flash.display.BitmapData;
import flash.geom.Point;
import flash.geom.Matrix;
import flash.geom.ColorTransform;

var filteredMc:MovieClip = createDisplacementMapRectangle();

filteredMc.onPress = function() {
  var filter:DisplacementMapFilter = this.filters[0];
  filter.componentY = 4;
  this.filters = new Array(filter);
}

function createDisplacementMapRectangle():MovieClip {
  var mapBitmap:BitmapData = createGradientBitmap(300, 80, 0xFF000000,
  "radial");
  var filter:DisplacementMapFilter = new DisplacementMapFilter(mapBitmap,
  new Point(-30, -30), 1, 1, 10, 10, "wrap", 0x000000, 0x000000);

  var txtBlock:MovieClip = createTextBlock();
  txtBlock._x = 30;
  txtBlock._y = 30;

  txtBlock.filters = new Array(filter);

  return txtBlock;
}

function createGradientBitmap(w:Number, h:Number, bgColor:Number,
  type:String, hide:Boolean):BitmapData {
  var mc:MovieClip = this.createEmptyMovieClip("mc", 1);
  var matrix:Matrix = new Matrix();
  matrix.createGradientBox(w, h, 0, 0, 0);
```

```
mc.beginGradientFill(type, [0xFF0000, 0x0000FF], [100, 100], [0x55,
0x99], matrix, "pad");
mc.lineTo(w, 0);
mc.lineTo(w, h);
mc.lineTo(0, h);
mc.lineTo(0, 0);
mc.endFill();
(hide == true) ? mc._alpha = 0 : mc._alpha = 100;

var bmp:BitmapData = new BitmapData(w, h, true, bgColor);
  bmp.draw(mc, new Matrix(), new ColorTransform(), "normal",
bmp.rectangle, true);
mc.attachBitmap(bmp, this.getNextHighestDepth());

return bmp;
}

function createTextBlock():MovieClip {
  var txtBlock:MovieClip = this.createEmptyMovieClip("txtBlock",
  this.getNextHighestDepth());
  txtBlock.createTextField("txt", this.getNextHighestDepth(), 0, 0, 300,
  80);
  txtBlock.txt.text = "watch the text bend with the displacement map";
  return txtBlock;
}
```

See also

`BitmapData (flash.display.BitmapData)`

DisplacementMapFilter constructor

`public DisplacementMapFilter(mapBitmap:BitmapData, mapPoint:Point,`
`  componentX:Number, componentY:Number, scaleX:Number, scaleY:Number,`
`  [mode:String], [color:Number], [alpha:Number])`

Initializes a DisplacementMapFilter instance with the specified parameters.

Availability: ActionScript 1.0; Flash Player 8

Parameters

`mapBitmap:flash.display.BitmapData` - A BitmapData object containing the
displacement map data.

`mapPoint:flash.geom.Point` - A `flash.geom.Point` value that contains the offset of the
upper-left corner of the target movie clip from the upper-left corner of the map image.

`componentX:Number` - Describes which color channel to use in the map image to displace the
x result. Possible values are the following:

- 1 (red)
- 2 (green)
- 4 (blue)
- 8 (alpha)

componentY:Number - Describes which color channel to use in the map image to displace the *y* result. Possible values are the following:

- 1 (red)
- 2 (green)
- 4 (blue)
- 8 (alpha)

scaleX:Number - The multiplier to use to scale the *x* displacement result from the map calculation.

scaleY:Number - The multiplier to use to scale the *y* displacement result from the map calculation.

mode:String [optional] - The mode of the filter. Possible values are the following:

- "wrap" — Wraps the displacement value to the other side of the source image.
- "clamp" — Clamps the displacement value to the edge of the source image.
- "ignore" — If the displacement value is out of range, ignores the displacement and uses the source pixel.
- "color" — If the displacement value is outside the image, substitutes a pixel value composed of the alpha and color properties of the filter.

color:Number [optional] - Specifies the color to use for out-of-bounds displacements. The valid range of displacements is 0.0 to 1.0. Use this parameter if mode is set to "color".

alpha:Number [optional] - Specifies what alpha value to use for out-of-bounds displacements. This is specified as a normalized value from 0.0 to 1.0. For example, .25 sets a transparency value of 25%. The default is 1.0. Use this parameter if mode is set to "color".

Example

The following constructor function creates a new instance of the filter:

```
myFilter = new flash.filters.DisplacementMapFilter (mapBitmap, mapPoint,
  componentX, componentY, scale, [mode], [color], [alpha])
```

The following example instantiates a new DisplacementMapFilter with a radial gradient bitmap and applies it to the text containing MovieClip object txtBlock.

```
import flash.filters.DisplacementMapFilter;
import flash.display.BitmapData;
import flash.geom.Point;
```

```
import flash.geom.Matrix;
import flash.geom.ColorTransform;

var mapBitmap:BitmapData = createGradientBitmap(300, 80, 0xFF000000,
  "radial");

var mapPoint:Point = new Point(-30, -30);
var componentX:Number = 1;
var componentY:Number = 1;
var scaleX:Number = 10;
var scaleY:Number = 10;
var mode:String = "wrap";
var color:Number = 0x000000;
var alpha:Number = 0x000000;

var filter:DisplacementMapFilter = new DisplacementMapFilter(mapBitmap,
  mapPoint, componentX, componentY, scaleX, scaleY, mode, color, alpha);

var txtBlock:MovieClip = createTextBlock();
txtBlock._x = 30;
txtBlock._y = 30;

txtBlock.filters = new Array(filter);

function createGradientBitmap(w:Number, h:Number, bgColor:Number,
  type:String, hide:Boolean):BitmapData {
  var mc:MovieClip = this.createEmptyMovieClip("mc", 1);
  var matrix:Matrix = new Matrix();
  matrix.createGradientBox(w, h, 0, 0, 0);

  mc.beginGradientFill(type, [0xFF0000, 0x0000FF], [100, 100], [0x55,
  0x99], matrix, "pad");
  mc.lineTo(w, 0);
  mc.lineTo(w, h);
  mc.lineTo(0, h);
  mc.lineTo(0, 0);
  mc.endFill();
  (hide == true) ? mc._alpha = 0 : mc._alpha = 100;

  var bmp:BitmapData = new BitmapData(w, h, true, bgColor);
    bmp.draw(mc, new Matrix(), new ColorTransform(), "normal",
  bmp.rectangle, true);
  mc.attachBitmap(bmp, this.getNextHighestDepth());

  return bmp;
}

function createTextBlock():MovieClip {
  var txtBlock:MovieClip = this.createEmptyMovieClip("txtBlock",
  this.getNextHighestDepth());
```

```
txtBlock.createTextField("txt", this.getNextHighestDepth(), 0, 0, 300,
80);
txtBlock.txt.text = "watch the text bend with the displacement map";
return txtBlock;
}
```

mapBitmap (DisplacementMapFilter.mapBitmap property)

```
public mapBitmap : BitmapData
```

A BitmapData object containing the displacement map data.

The mapBitmap property cannot be changed by directly modifying its value. Instead, you must get a reference to mapBitmap, make the change to the reference, and then set mapBitmap to the reference.

Availability: ActionScript 1.0; Flash Player 8

Example

The following example changes the mapBitmap property on the existing MovieClip filteredMc when a user clicks it.

```
import flash.filters.DisplacementMapFilter;
import flash.display.BitmapData;
import flash.geom.Point;
import flash.geom.Matrix;
import flash.geom.ColorTransform;

var filteredMc:MovieClip = createDisplacementMapRectangle();
var scope:Object = this;

filteredMc.onPress = function() {
  var filter:DisplacementMapFilter = this.filters[0];
  filter.mapBitmap = scope.createGradientBitmap(300, 80, 0xFF000000,
  "linear");
  this.filters = new Array(filter);
}

function createDisplacementMapRectangle():MovieClip {
  var mapBitmap:BitmapData = createGradientBitmap(300, 80, 0xFF000000,
  "radial");
  var filter:DisplacementMapFilter = new DisplacementMapFilter(mapBitmap,
  new Point(-30, -30), 1, 1, 10, 10, "wrap", 0x000000, 0x000000);

  var txtBlock:MovieClip = createTextBlock();
  txtBlock._x = 30;
  txtBlock._y = 30;
```

```
    txtBlock.filters = new Array(filter);

    return txtBlock;
}

function createGradientBitmap(w:Number, h:Number, bgColor:Number,
    type:String, hide:Boolean):BitmapData {
    var mc:MovieClip = this.createEmptyMovieClip("mc", 1);
    var matrix:Matrix = new Matrix();
    matrix.createGradientBox(w, h, 0, 0, 0);

    mc.beginGradientFill(type, [0xFF0000, 0x0000FF], [100, 100], [0x55,
    0x99], matrix, "pad");
    mc.lineTo(w, 0);
    mc.lineTo(w, h);
    mc.lineTo(0, h);
    mc.lineTo(0, 0);
    mc.endFill();
    (hide == true) ? mc._alpha = 0 : mc._alpha = 100;

    var bmp:BitmapData = new BitmapData(w, h, true, bgColor);
        bmp.draw(mc, new Matrix(), new ColorTransform(), "normal",
    bmp.rectangle, true);
    mc.attachBitmap(bmp, this.getNextHighestDepth());

    return bmp;
}

function createTextBlock():MovieClip {
    var txtBlock:MovieClip = this.createEmptyMovieClip("txtBlock",
    this.getNextHighestDepth());
    txtBlock.createTextField("txt", this.getNextHighestDepth(), 0, 0, 300,
    80);
    txtBlock.txt.text = "watch the text bend with the displacement map";
    return txtBlock;
}
```

See also
BitmapData (flash.display.BitmapData)

mapPoint (DisplacementMapFilter.mapPoint property)

public mapPoint : Point

A flash.geom.Point value that contains the offset of the upper-left corner of the target movie clip from the upper-left corner of the map image.

The mapPoint property cannot be changed by directly modifying its value. Instead, you must get a reference to mapPoint, make the change to the reference, and then set mapPoint to the reference.

Availability: ActionScript 1.0; Flash Player 8

Example

The following example changes the mapPoint property on the existing MovieClip filteredMc when a user clicks it.

```
import flash.filters.DisplacementMapFilter;
import flash.display.BitmapData;
import flash.geom.Point;
import flash.geom.Matrix;
import flash.geom.ColorTransform;

var filteredMc:MovieClip = createDisplacementMapRectangle();

filteredMc.onPress = function() {
  var filter:DisplacementMapFilter = this.filters[0];
  filter.mapPoint = new Point(-30, -40);
  this.filters = new Array(filter);
  this._x = 30;
  this._y = 40;
}

function createDisplacementMapRectangle():MovieClip {
  var mapBitmap:BitmapData = createGradientBitmap(300, 80, 0xFF000000,
  "radial");
  var filter:DisplacementMapFilter = new DisplacementMapFilter(mapBitmap,
  new Point(-30, -30), 1, 1, 10, 10, "wrap", 0x000000, 0x000000);

  var txtBlock:MovieClip = createTextBlock();
  txtBlock._x = 30;
  txtBlock._y = 30;

  txtBlock.filters = new Array(filter);

  return txtBlock;
}

function createGradientBitmap(w:Number, h:Number, bgColor:Number,
  type:String, hide:Boolean):BitmapData {
  var mc:MovieClip = this.createEmptyMovieClip("mc", 1);
  var matrix:Matrix = new Matrix();
  matrix.createGradientBox(w, h, 0, 0, 0);

  mc.beginGradientFill(type, [0xFF0000, 0x0000FF], [100, 100], [0x55,
  0x99], matrix, "pad");
```

```
mc.lineTo(w, 0);
mc.lineTo(w, h);
mc.lineTo(0, h);
mc.lineTo(0, 0);
mc.endFill();
(hide == true) ? mc._alpha = 0 : mc._alpha = 100;

var bmp:BitmapData = new BitmapData(w, h, true, bgColor);
    bmp.draw(mc, new Matrix(), new ColorTransform(), "normal",
bmp.rectangle, true);
mc.attachBitmap(bmp, this.getNextHighestDepth());

return bmp;
}

function createTextBlock():MovieClip {
    var txtBlock:MovieClip = this.createEmptyMovieClip("txtBlock",
    this.getNextHighestDepth());
    txtBlock.createTextField("txt", this.getNextHighestDepth(), 0, 0, 300,
    80);
    txtBlock.txt.text = "watch the text bend with the displacement map";
    return txtBlock;
}
```

See also

`Point (flash.geom.Point)`

mode (DisplacementMapFilter.mode property)

`public mode : String`

The mode for the filter. Possible values are the following:

- `"wrap"` — Wraps the displacement value to the other side of the source image. This is the default value.
- `"clamp"` — Clamps the displacement value to the edge of the source image.
- `"ignore"` — If the displacement value is out of range, ignores the displacement and uses the source pixel.
- `"color"` — If the displacement value is outside the image, substitutes a pixel value composed of the `alpha` and `color` properties of the filter.

Availability: ActionScript 1.0; Flash Player 8

Example

The following example modifies scaleY to create a displacement value that is out of range and then changes the mode property on the existing MovieClip filteredMc to ignore when a user clicks it.

```
import flash.filters.DisplacementMapFilter;
import flash.display.BitmapData;
import flash.geom.Point;
import flash.geom.Matrix;
import flash.geom.ColorTransform;

var filteredMc:MovieClip = createDisplacementMapRectangle();

filteredMc.onPress = function() {
  var filter:DisplacementMapFilter = this.filters[0];
  filter.scaleY = 25;
  filter.mode = "ignore";
  this.filters = new Array(filter);
}

function createDisplacementMapRectangle():MovieClip {
  var mapBitmap:BitmapData = createGradientBitmap(300, 80, 0xFF000000,
  "radial");
  var filter:DisplacementMapFilter = new DisplacementMapFilter(mapBitmap,
  new Point(-30, -30), 1, 1, 10, 10, "wrap", 0x000000, 0x000000);

  var txtBlock:MovieClip = createTextBlock();
  txtBlock._x = 30;
  txtBlock._y = 30;

  txtBlock.filters = new Array(filter);

  return txtBlock;
}

function createGradientBitmap(w:Number, h:Number, bgColor:Number,
  type:String, hide:Boolean):BitmapData {
  var mc:MovieClip = this.createEmptyMovieClip("mc", 1);
  var matrix:Matrix = new Matrix();
  matrix.createGradientBox(w, h, 0, 0, 0);

  mc.beginGradientFill(type, [0xFF0000, 0x0000FF], [100, 100], [0x55,
  0x99], matrix, "pad");
  mc.lineTo(w, 0);
  mc.lineTo(w, h);
  mc.lineTo(0, h);
  mc.lineTo(0, 0);
  mc.endFill();
  (hide == true) ? mc._alpha = 0 : mc._alpha = 100;
```

```
var bmp:BitmapData = new BitmapData(w, h, true, bgColor);
   bmp.draw(mc, new Matrix(), new ColorTransform(), "normal",
bmp.rectangle, true);
mc.attachBitmap(bmp, this.getNextHighestDepth());

return bmp;
}

function createTextBlock():MovieClip {
   var txtBlock:MovieClip = this.createEmptyMovieClip("txtBlock",
   this.getNextHighestDepth());
   txtBlock.createTextField("txt", this.getNextHighestDepth(), 0, 0, 300,
   80);
   txtBlock.txt.text = "watch the text bend with the displacement map";
   return txtBlock;
}
```

scaleX (DisplacementMapFilter.scaleX property)

```
public scaleX : Number
```

The multiplier to use to scale the *x* displacement result from the map calculation.

Availability: ActionScript 1.0; Flash Player 8

Example

The following example changes the `scaleX` property on the existing MovieClip `filteredMc` when a user clicks it.

```
import flash.filters.DisplacementMapFilter;
import flash.display.BitmapData;
import flash.geom.Point;
import flash.geom.Matrix;
import flash.geom.ColorTransform;

var filteredMc:MovieClip = createDisplacementMapRectangle();

filteredMc.onPress = function() {
   var filter:DisplacementMapFilter = this.filters[0];
   filter.scaleX = 5;
   this.filters = new Array(filter);
}

function createDisplacementMapRectangle():MovieClip {
   var mapBitmap:BitmapData = createGradientBitmap(300, 80, 0xFF000000,
   "radial");
   var filter:DisplacementMapFilter = new DisplacementMapFilter(mapBitmap,
   new Point(-30, -30), 1, 1, 10, 10, "wrap", 0x000000, 0x000000);
```

```
    var txtBlock:MovieClip = createTextBlock();
    txtBlock._x = 30;
    txtBlock._y = 30;

    txtBlock.filters = new Array(filter);

    return txtBlock;
}

function createGradientBitmap(w:Number, h:Number, bgColor:Number,
    type:String, hide:Boolean):BitmapData {
    var mc:MovieClip = this.createEmptyMovieClip("mc", 1);
    var matrix:Matrix = new Matrix();
    matrix.createGradientBox(w, h, 0, 0, 0);

    mc.beginGradientFill(type, [0xFF0000, 0x0000FF], [100, 100], [0x55,
    0x99], matrix, "pad");
    mc.lineTo(w, 0);
    mc.lineTo(w, h);
    mc.lineTo(0, h);
    mc.lineTo(0, 0);
    mc.endFill();
    (hide == true) ? mc._alpha = 0 : mc._alpha = 100;

    var bmp:BitmapData = new BitmapData(w, h, true, bgColor);
       bmp.draw(mc, new Matrix(), new ColorTransform(), "normal",
    bmp.rectangle, true);
    mc.attachBitmap(bmp, this.getNextHighestDepth());

    return bmp;
}

function createTextBlock():MovieClip {
    var txtBlock:MovieClip = this.createEmptyMovieClip("txtBlock",
    this.getNextHighestDepth());
    txtBlock.createTextField("txt", this.getNextHighestDepth(), 0, 0, 300,
    80);
    txtBlock.txt.text = "watch the text bend with the displacement map";
    return txtBlock;
}
```

scaleY (DisplacementMapFilter.scaleY property)

public scaleY : Number

The multiplier to use to scale the y displacement result from the map calculation.

Availability: ActionScript 1.0; Flash Player 8

Example

The following example changes the scaleY property on the existing MovieClip filteredMc when a user clicks it.

```
import flash.filters.DisplacementMapFilter;
import flash.display.BitmapData;
import flash.geom.Point;
import flash.geom.Matrix;
import flash.geom.ColorTransform;

var filteredMc:MovieClip = createDisplacementMapRectangle();

filteredMc.onPress = function() {
  var filter:DisplacementMapFilter = this.filters[0];
  filter.scaleY = 5;
  this.filters = new Array(filter);
}

function createDisplacementMapRectangle():MovieClip {
  var mapBitmap:BitmapData = createGradientBitmap(300, 80, 0xFF000000,
  "radial");
  var filter:DisplacementMapFilter = new DisplacementMapFilter(mapBitmap,
  new Point(-30, -30), 1, 1, 10, 10, "wrap", 0x000000, 0x000000);

  var txtBlock:MovieClip = createTextBlock();
  txtBlock._x = 30;
  txtBlock._y = 30;

  txtBlock.filters = new Array(filter);

  return txtBlock;
}

function createGradientBitmap(w:Number, h:Number, bgColor:Number,
  type:String, hide:Boolean):BitmapData {
  var mc:MovieClip = this.createEmptyMovieClip("mc", 1);
  var matrix:Matrix = new Matrix();
  matrix.createGradientBox(w, h, 0, 0, 0);

  mc.beginGradientFill(type, [0xFF0000, 0x0000FF], [100, 100], [0x55,
  0x99], matrix, "pad");
  mc.lineTo(w, 0);
  mc.lineTo(w, h);
  mc.lineTo(0, h);
  mc.lineTo(0, 0);
  mc.endFill();
  (hide == true) ? mc._alpha = 0 : mc._alpha = 100;

  var bmp:BitmapData = new BitmapData(w, h, true, bgColor);
```

```
    bmp.draw(mc, new Matrix(), new ColorTransform(), "normal",
  bmp.rectangle, true);
  mc.attachBitmap(bmp, this.getNextHighestDepth());

  return bmp;
}

function createTextBlock():MovieClip {
  var txtBlock:MovieClip = this.createEmptyMovieClip("txtBlock",
  this.getNextHighestDepth());
  txtBlock.createTextField("txt", this.getNextHighestDepth(), 0, 0, 300,
  80);
  txtBlock.txt.text = "watch the text bend with the displacement map";
  return txtBlock;
}
```

DropShadowFilter (flash.filters.DropShadowFilter)

```
Object
  |
  +-flash.filters.BitmapFilter
      |
      +-flash.filters.DropShadowFilter
```

`public class DropShadowFilter`
`extends BitmapFilter`

The DropShadowFilter class lets you add a drop shadow to a variety of objects in Flash. You have several options for the style of the drop shadow, including inner or outer shadow and knockout mode.

The use of filters depends on the object to which you apply the filter:

- To apply filters to movie clips, text fields, and buttons at runtime, use the `filters` property. Setting the `filters` property of an object does not modify the object and can be undone by clearing the `filters` property.

- To apply filters to BitmapData instances, use the `BitmapData.applyFilter()` method. Calling `applyFilter()` on a BitmapData object takes the source BitmapData object and the filter object and generates a filtered image as a result.

You can also apply filter effects to images and video at authoring time. For more information, see your authoring documentation.

If you apply a filter to a movie clip or button, the `cacheAsBitmap` property of the movie clip or button is set to `true`. If you clear all filters, the original value of `cacheAsBitmap` is restored.

This filter supports Stage scaling. However, general scaling, rotation, and skewing are not supported. If the object itself is scaled (if _xscale and _yscale are not 100%), the filter effect is not scaled. It is scaled only when the Stage is zoomed in.

A filter is not applied if the resulting image exceeds 2880 pixels in width or height. For example, if you zoom in on a large movie clip with a filter applied, the filter is turned off if the resulting image exceeds the limit of 2880 pixels.

Availability: ActionScript 1.0; Flash Player 8

See also

filters (MovieClip.filters property), cacheAsBitmap (MovieClip.cacheAsBitmap property), filters (Button.filters property), cacheAsBitmap (Button.cacheAsBitmap property), filters (TextField.filters property), applyFilter (BitmapData.applyFilter method)

Property summary

Modifiers	Property	Description
	alpha:Number	The alpha transparency value for the shadow color.
	angle:Number	The angle of the shadow.
	blurX:Number	The amount of horizontal blur.
	blurY:Number	The amount of vertical blur.
	color:Number	The color of the shadow.
	distance:Number	The offset distance for the shadow, in pixels.
	hideObject:Boolean	Indicates whether or not the object is hidden.
	inner:Boolean	Indicates whether or not the shadow is an inner shadow.
	knockout:Boolean	Applies a knockout effect (true), which effectively makes the object's fill transparent and reveals the background color of the document.
	quality:Number	The number of times to apply the filter.
	strength:Number	The strength of the imprint or spread.

Properties inherited from class Object

constructor (Object.constructor property), __proto__ (Object.__proto__ property), prototype (Object.prototype property), __resolve (Object.__resolve property)

Constructor summary

Signature	Description
`DropShadowFilter([distance:Number], [angle:Number], [color:Number], [alpha:Number], [blurX:Number], [blurY:Number], [strength:Number], [quality:Number], [inner:Boolean], [knockout:Boolean], [hideObject:Boolean])`	Creates a new DropShadowFilter instance with the specified parameters.

Method summary

Modifiers	Signature	Description
	`clone() : DropShadowFilter`	Returns a copy of this filter object.

Methods inherited from class BitmapFilter

```
clone (BitmapFilter.clone method)
```

Methods inherited from class Object

```
addProperty (Object.addProperty method), hasOwnProperty
(Object.hasOwnProperty method), isPropertyEnumerable
(Object.isPropertyEnumerable method), isPrototypeOf (Object.isPrototypeOf
method), registerClass (Object.registerClass method), toString
(Object.toString method), unwatch (Object.unwatch method), valueOf
(Object.valueOf method), watch (Object.watch method)
```

alpha (DropShadowFilter.alpha property)

`public alpha : Number`

The alpha transparency value for the shadow color. Valid values are 0 to 1. For example, .25 sets a transparency value of 25%. The default value is 1.

Availability: ActionScript 1.0; Flash Player 8

Example

The following example changes the `alpha` property on a movie clip when a user clicks it.

```
import flash.filters.DropShadowFilter;
var mc:MovieClip = createDropShadowRectangle("DropShadowAlpha");
mc.onRelease = function() {
  var filter:DropShadowFilter = this.filters[0];
  filter.alpha = .4;
  this.filters = new Array(filter);
}

function createDropShadowRectangle(name:String):MovieClip {
  var art:MovieClip = this.createEmptyMovieClip(name,
  this.getNextHighestDepth());
  var w:Number = 100;
  var h:Number = 100;
  art.beginFill(0x003366);
  art.lineTo(w, 0);
  art.lineTo(w, h);
  art.lineTo(0, h);
  art.lineTo(0, 0);
  art._x = 20;
  art._y = 20;

  var filter:DropShadowFilter = new DropShadowFilter(15, 45, 0x000000, .8,
  16, 16, 1, 3, false, false, false);
  var filterArray:Array = new Array();
  filterArray.push(filter);
  art.filters = filterArray;
  return art;
}
```

angle (DropShadowFilter.angle property)

`public angle : Number`

The angle of the shadow. Valid values are 0 to 360° (floating point). The default value is 45.

The angle value represents the angle of the theoretical light source falling on the object and determines the placement of the effect relative to the object. If distance is set to 0, the effect is not offset from the object, and therefore the angle property has no effect.

Availability: ActionScript 1.0; Flash Player 8

Example

The following example changes the `angle` property on an existing movie clip when a user clicks it.

```
import flash.filters.DropShadowFilter;
var mc:MovieClip = createDropShadowRectangle("DropShadowAngle");
mc.onRelease = function() {
  var filter:DropShadowFilter = this.filters[0];
```

```
    filter.angle = 135;
    this.filters = new Array(filter);
}

function createDropShadowRectangle(name:String):MovieClip {
  var art:MovieClip = this.createEmptyMovieClip(name,
  this.getNextHighestDepth());
  var w:Number = 100;
  var h:Number = 100;
  art.beginFill(0x003366);
  art.lineTo(w, 0);
  art.lineTo(w, h);
  art.lineTo(0, h);
  art.lineTo(0, 0);
  art._x = 20;
  art._y = 20;

  var filter:DropShadowFilter = new DropShadowFilter(15, 45, 0x000000, .8,
  16, 16, 1, 3, false, false, false);
  var filterArray:Array = new Array();
  filterArray.push(filter);
  art.filters = filterArray;
  return art;
}
```

blurX (DropShadowFilter.blurX property)

```
public blurX : Number
```

The amount of horizontal blur. Valid values are 0 to 255 (floating point). The default value is 4. Values that are a power of 2 (such as 2, 4, 8, 16 and 32) are optimized to render more quickly than other values.

Availability: ActionScript 1.0; Flash Player 8

Example

The following example changes the blurX property on an existing movie clip when a user clicks it.

```
import flash.filters.DropShadowFilter;
var mc:MovieClip = createDropShadowRectangle("DropShadowBlurX");
mc.onRelease = function() {
  var filter:DropShadowFilter = this.filters[0];
  filter.blurX = 40;
  this.filters = new Array(filter);
}

function createDropShadowRectangle(name:String):MovieClip {
```

```
var art:MovieClip = this.createEmptyMovieClip(name,
this.getNextHighestDepth());
var w:Number = 100;
var h:Number = 100;
art.beginFill(0x003366);
art.lineTo(w, 0);
art.lineTo(w, h);
art.lineTo(0, h);
art.lineTo(0, 0);
art._x = 20;
art._y = 20;

var filter:DropShadowFilter = new DropShadowFilter(15, 45, 0x000000, .8,
16, 16, 1, 3, false, false, false);
var filterArray:Array = new Array();
filterArray.push(filter);
art.filters = filterArray;
return art;
}
```

blurY (DropShadowFilter.blurY property)

```
public blurY : Number
```

The amount of vertical blur. Valid values are 0 to 255 (floating point). The default value is 4. Values that are a power of 2 (such as 2, 4, 8, 16 and 32) are optimized to render more quickly than other values.

Availability: ActionScript 1.0; Flash Player 8

Example

The following example changes the blurY property on an existing movie clip when a user clicks it.

```
import flash.filters.DropShadowFilter;
var mc:MovieClip = createDropShadowRectangle("DropShadowBlurY");
mc.onRelease = function() {
   var filter:DropShadowFilter = this.filters[0];
   filter.blurY = 40;
   this.filters = new Array(filter);
}

function createDropShadowRectangle(name:String):MovieClip {
   var art:MovieClip = this.createEmptyMovieClip(name,
   this.getNextHighestDepth());
   var w:Number = 100;
   var h:Number = 100;
   art.beginFill(0x003366);
   art.lineTo(w, 0);
```

```
art.lineTo(w, h);
art.lineTo(0, h);
art.lineTo(0, 0);
art._x = 20;
art._y = 20;

var filter:DropShadowFilter = new DropShadowFilter(15, 45, 0x000000, .8,
16, 16, 1, 3, false, false, false);
var filterArray:Array = new Array();
filterArray.push(filter);
art.filters = filterArray;
return art;
}
```

clone (DropShadowFilter.clone method)

```
public clone() : DropShadowFilter
```
Returns a copy of this filter object.

Availability: ActionScript 1.0; Flash Player 8

Returns

`flash.filters.DropShadowFilter` - A new DropShadowFilter instance with all the properties of the original one.

Example

The following example creates three DropShadowFilter objects and compares them; `filter_1` is created by using the DropShadowFilter constructor; `filter_2` is created by setting it equal to `filter_1`; and `clonedFilter` is created by cloning `filter_1`. Notice that although `filter_2` evaluates as being equal to `filter_1`, `clonedFilter`, even though it contains the same values as `filter_1`, does not.

```
import flash.filters.DropShadowFilter;

var filter_1:DropShadowFilter = new DropShadowFilter(15, 45, 0x000000, .8,
    16, 16, 1, 3, false, false, false);
var filter_2:DropShadowFilter = filter_1;
var clonedFilter:DropShadowFilter = filter_1.clone();

trace(filter_1 == filter_2); // true
trace(filter_1 == clonedFilter); // false

for(var i in filter_1) {
  trace(">> " + i + ": " + filter_1[i]);
  // >> clone: [type Function]
  // >> hideObject: false
```

```
// >> strength: 1
// >> blurY: 16
// >> blurX: 16
// >> knockout: false
// >> inner: false
// >> quality: 3
// >> alpha: 0.8
// >> color: 0
// >> angle: 45
// >> distance: 15
}

for(var i in clonedFilter) {
   trace(">> " + i + ": " + clonedFilter[i]);
   // >> clone: [type Function]
   // >> hideObject: false
   // >> strength: 1
   // >> blurY: 16
   // >> blurX: 16
   // >> knockout: false
   // >> inner: false
   // >> quality: 3
   // >> alpha: 0.8
   // >> color: 0
   // >> angle: 45
   // >> distance: 15
}
```

To further demonstrate the relationships between filter_1, filter_2, and clonedFilter, the following example modifies the knockout property of filter_1. Modifying knockout demonstrates that the clone() method creates a new instance based on the values of filter_1 instead of pointing to them in reference.

```
import flash.filters.DropShadowFilter;

var filter_1:DropShadowFilter = new DropShadowFilter(15, 45, 0x000000, .8,
   16, 16, 1, 3, false, false, false);
var filter_2:DropShadowFilter = filter_1;
var clonedFilter:DropShadowFilter = filter_1.clone();

trace(filter_1.knockout); // false
trace(filter_2.knockout); // false
trace(clonedFilter.knockout); // false

filter_1.knockout = true;

trace(filter_1.knockout); // true
trace(filter_2.knockout); // true
trace(clonedFilter.knockout); // false
```

color (DropShadowFilter.color property)

`public color : Number`

The color of the shadow. Valid values are in hexadecimal format *0xRRGGBB*. The default value is 0x000000.

Availability: ActionScript 1.0; Flash Player 8

Example

The following example changes the `color` property on an existing movie clip when a user clicks it.

```
import flash.filters.DropShadowFilter;
var mc:MovieClip = createDropShadowRectangle("DropShadowColor");
mc.onRelease = function() {
  var filter:DropShadowFilter = this.filters[0];
  filter.color = 0xFF0000;
  this.filters = new Array(filter);
}

function createDropShadowRectangle(name:String):MovieClip {
  var art:MovieClip = this.createEmptyMovieClip(name,
  this.getNextHighestDepth());
  var w:Number = 100;
  var h:Number = 100;
  art.beginFill(0x003366);
  art.lineTo(w, 0);
  art.lineTo(w, h);
  art.lineTo(0, h);
  art.lineTo(0, 0);
  art._x = 20;
  art._y = 20;

  var filter:DropShadowFilter = new DropShadowFilter(15, 45, 0x000000, .8,
  16, 16, 1, 3, false, false, false);
  var filterArray:Array = new Array();
  filterArray.push(filter);
  art.filters = filterArray;
  return art;
}
```

distance (DropShadowFilter.distance property)

`public distance : Number`

The offset distance for the shadow, in pixels. The default value is 4 (floating point).

Availability: ActionScript 1.0; Flash Player 8

Example

The following example changes the distance property on an existing movie clip when a user clicks it.

```
import flash.filters.DropShadowFilter;
var mc:MovieClip = createDropShadowRectangle("DropShadowDistance");
mc.onRelease = function() {
   var filter:DropShadowFilter = this.filters[0];
   filter.distance = 40;
   this.filters = new Array(filter);
}

function createDropShadowRectangle(name:String):MovieClip {
   var art:MovieClip = this.createEmptyMovieClip(name,
   this.getNextHighestDepth());
   var w:Number = 100;
   var h:Number = 100;
   art.beginFill(0x003366);
   art.lineTo(w, 0);
   art.lineTo(w, h);
   art.lineTo(0, h);
   art.lineTo(0, 0);
   art._x = 20;
   art._y = 20;

   var filter:DropShadowFilter = new DropShadowFilter(15, 45, 0x000000, .8,
   16, 16, 1, 3, false, false, false);
   var filterArray:Array = new Array();
   filterArray.push(filter);
   art.filters = filterArray;
   return art;
}
```

DropShadowFilter constructor

```
public DropShadowFilter([distance:Number], [angle:Number], [color:Number],
   [alpha:Number], [blurX:Number], [blurY:Number], [strength:Number],
   [quality:Number], [inner:Boolean], [knockout:Boolean],
   [hideObject:Boolean])
```

Creates a new DropShadowFilter instance with the specified parameters.

Availability: ActionScript 1.0; Flash Player 8

Parameters

distance:Number [optional] - The offset distance for the shadow, in pixels. The default value is 4 (floating point).

`angle:Number` [optional] - The angle of the shadow, 0 to 360° (floating point). The default value is 45.

`color:Number` [optional] - The color of the shadow, in hexadecimal format *0xRRGGBB*. The default value is 0x000000.

`alpha:Number` [optional] - The alpha transparency value for the shadow color. Valid values are 0 to 1. For example, .25 sets a transparency value of 25%. The default value is 1.

`blurX:Number` [optional] - The amount of horizontal blur. Valid values are 0 to 255 (floating point). The default value is 4. Values that are a power of 2 (such as 2, 4, 8, 16 and 32) are optimized to render more quickly than other values.

`blurY:Number` [optional] - The amount of vertical blur. Valid values are 0 to 255 (floating point). The default value is 4. Values that are a power of 2 (such as 2, 4, 8, 16 and 32) are optimized to render more quickly than other values.

`strength:Number` [optional] - The strength of the imprint or spread. The higher the value, the more color is imprinted and the stronger the contrast between the shadow and the background. Valid values are 0 to 255. The default is 1.

`quality:Number` [optional] - The number of times to apply the filter. Valid values are 0 to 15. The default value is 1, which is equivalent to low quality. A value of 2 is medium quality, and a value of 3 is high quality.

`inner:Boolean` [optional] - Indicates whether or not the shadow is an inner shadow. A value of `true` specifies an inner shadow. The default is `false`, an outer shadow (a shadow around the outer edges of the object).

`knockout:Boolean` [optional] - Applies a knockout effect (`true`), which effectively makes the object's fill transparent and reveals the background color of the document. The default is `false` (no knockout).

`hideObject:Boolean` [optional] - Indicates whether or not the object is hidden. A value of `true` indicates that the object itself is not drawn; only the shadow is visible. The default is `false` (show the object).

Example

The following example instantiates a new DropShadowFilter instance and applies it to a flat, rectangular shape.

```
import flash.filters.DropShadowFilter;
var art:MovieClip = createRectangle(100, 100, 0x003366,
  "gradientGlowFilterExample");
var distance:Number = 20;
var angleInDegrees:Number = 45;
var color:Number = 0x000000;
var alpha:Number = .8;
```

```
var blurX:Number = 16;
var blurY:Number = 16;
var strength:Number = 1;
var quality:Number = 3;
var inner:Boolean = false;
var knockout:Boolean = false;
var hideObject:Boolean = false;

var filter:DropShadowFilter = new DropShadowFilter(distance,
                              angleInDegrees,
                              color,
                              alpha,
                              blurX,
                              blurY,
                              strength,
                              quality,
                              inner,
                              knockout,
                              hideObject);
var filterArray:Array = new Array();
filterArray.push(filter);
art.filters = filterArray;

function createRectangle(w:Number, h:Number, bgColor:Number,
  name:String):MovieClip {
  var mc:MovieClip = this.createEmptyMovieClip(name,
  this.getNextHighestDepth());
  mc.beginFill(bgColor);
  mc.lineTo(w, 0);
  mc.lineTo(w, h);
  mc.lineTo(0, h);
  mc.lineTo(0, 0);
  mc._x = 20;
  mc._y = 20;
  return mc;
}
```

hideObject (DropShadowFilter.hideObject property)

`public hideObject : Boolean`

Indicates whether or not the object is hidden. The value `true` indicates that the object itself is not drawn; only the shadow is visible. The default is `false` (show the object).

Availability: ActionScript 1.0; Flash Player 8

Example

The following example changes the `hideObject` property on an existing movie clip when a user clicks it.

```
import flash.filters.DropShadowFilter;
var mc:MovieClip = createDropShadowRectangle("DropShadowHideObject");
mc.onRelease = function() {
  var filter:DropShadowFilter = this.filters[0];
  filter.hideObject = true;
  this.filters = new Array(filter);
}

function createDropShadowRectangle(name:String):MovieClip {
  var art:MovieClip = this.createEmptyMovieClip(name,
  this.getNextHighestDepth());
  var w:Number = 100;
  var h:Number = 100;
  art.beginFill(0x003366);
  art.lineTo(w, 0);
  art.lineTo(w, h);
  art.lineTo(0, h);
  art.lineTo(0, 0);
  art._x = 20;
  art._y = 20;

  var filter:DropShadowFilter = new DropShadowFilter(15, 45, 0x000000, .8,
  16, 16, 1, 3, false, false, false);
  var filterArray:Array = new Array();
  filterArray.push(filter);
  art.filters = filterArray;
  return art;
}
```

inner (DropShadowFilter.inner property)

```
public inner : Boolean
```

Indicates whether or not the shadow is an inner shadow. The value true indicates an inner shadow. The default is false, an outer shadow (a shadow around the outer edges of the object).

Availability: ActionScript 1.0; Flash Player 8

Example

The following example changes the inner property on an existing movie clip when a user clicks it.

```
import flash.filters.DropShadowFilter;
var mc:MovieClip = createDropShadowRectangle("DropShadowInner");
mc.onRelease = function() {
  var filter:DropShadowFilter = this.filters[0];
  filter.inner = true;
  this.filters = new Array(filter);
```

```
}

function createDropShadowRectangle(name:String):MovieClip {
  var art:MovieClip = this.createEmptyMovieClip(name,
  this.getNextHighestDepth());
  var w:Number = 100;
  var h:Number = 100;
  art.beginFill(0x003366);
  art.lineTo(w, 0);
  art.lineTo(w, h);
  art.lineTo(0, h);
  art.lineTo(0, 0);
  art._x = 20;
  art._y = 20;

  var filter:DropShadowFilter = new DropShadowFilter(15, 45, 0x000000, .8,
  16, 16, 1, 3, false, false, false);
  var filterArray:Array = new Array();
  filterArray.push(filter);
  art.filters = filterArray;
  return art;
}
```

knockout (DropShadowFilter.knockout property)

```
public knockout : Boolean
```

Applies a knockout effect (true), which effectively makes the object's fill transparent and reveals the background color of the document. The default is false (no knockout).

Availability: ActionScript 1.0; Flash Player 8

Example

The following example changes the knockout property on an existing movie clip when a user clicks it.

```
import flash.filters.DropShadowFilter;
var mc:MovieClip = createDropShadowRectangle("DropShadowKnockout");
mc.onRelease = function() {
  var filter:DropShadowFilter = this.filters[0];
  filter.knockout = true;
  this.filters = new Array(filter);
}

function createDropShadowRectangle(name:String):MovieClip {
  var art:MovieClip = this.createEmptyMovieClip(name,
  this.getNextHighestDepth());
  var w:Number = 100;
  var h:Number = 100;
```

```
art.beginFill(0x003366);
art.lineTo(w, 0);
art.lineTo(w, h);
art.lineTo(0, h);
art.lineTo(0, 0);
art._x = 20;
art._y = 20;

var filter:DropShadowFilter = new DropShadowFilter(15, 45, 0x000000, .8,
16, 16, 1, 3, false, false, false);
var filterArray:Array = new Array();
filterArray.push(filter);
art.filters = filterArray;
return art;
}
```

quality (DropShadowFilter.quality property)

`public quality : Number`

The number of times to apply the filter. Valid values are 0 to 15. The default value is 1, which is equivalent to low quality. A value of 2 is medium quality, and a value of 3 is high quality. Filters with lower values are rendered more quickly.

For most applications, a `quality` value of 1, 2, or 3 is sufficient. Although you can use additional numeric values up to 15 to achieve different effects, higher values are rendered more slowly. Instead of increasing the value of `quality`, you can often get a similar effect, and with faster rendering, by simply increasing the values of `blurX` and `blurY`.

Availability: ActionScript 1.0; Flash Player 8

Example

The following example changes the `quality` property on an existing movie clip when a user clicks it.

```
import flash.filters.DropShadowFilter;
var mc:MovieClip = createDropShadowRectangle("DropShadowQuality");
mc.onRelease = function() {
  var filter:DropShadowFilter = this.filters[0];
  filter.quality = 0;
  this.filters = new Array(filter);
}

function createDropShadowRectangle(name:String):MovieClip {
  var art:MovieClip = this.createEmptyMovieClip(name,
  this.getNextHighestDepth());
  var w:Number = 100;
  var h:Number = 100;
```

```
art.beginFill(0x003366);
art.lineTo(w, 0);
art.lineTo(w, h);
art.lineTo(0, h);
art.lineTo(0, 0);
art._x = 20;
art._y = 20;

var filter:DropShadowFilter = new DropShadowFilter(15, 45, 0x000000, .8,
16, 16, 1, 3, false, false, false);
var filterArray:Array = new Array();
filterArray.push(filter);
art.filters = filterArray;
return art;
}
```

strength (DropShadowFilter.strength property)

```
public strength : Number
```

The strength of the imprint or spread. The higher the value, the more color is imprinted and the stronger the contrast between the shadow and the background. Valid values are from 0 to 255. The default is 1.

Availability: ActionScript 1.0; Flash Player 8

Example

The following example changes the `strength` property on an existing movie clip when a user clicks it.

```
import flash.filters.DropShadowFilter;
var mc:MovieClip = createDropShadowRectangle("DropShadowStrength");
mc.onRelease = function() {
  var filter:DropShadowFilter = this.filters[0];
  filter.strength = .6;
  this.filters = new Array(filter);
}

function createDropShadowRectangle(name:String):MovieClip {
  var art:MovieClip = this.createEmptyMovieClip(name,
  this.getNextHighestDepth());
  var w:Number = 100;
  var h:Number = 100;
  art.beginFill(0x003366);
  art.lineTo(w, 0);
  art.lineTo(w, h);
  art.lineTo(0, h);
  art.lineTo(0, 0);
  art._x = 20;
```

```
art._y = 20;

var filter:DropShadowFilter = new DropShadowFilter(15, 45, 0x000000, .8,
16, 16, 1, 3, false, false, false);
var filterArray:Array = new Array();
filterArray.push(filter);
art.filters = filterArray;
return art;
}
```

Error

```
Object
  |
  +-Error
```

```
public class Error
extends Object
```

Contains information about an error that occurred in a script. You create an Error object
using the `Error` constructor function. Typically, you `throw` a new Error object from within a
`try` code block that is then caught by a `catch` or `finally` code block.

You can also create a subclass of the Error class and throw instances of that subclass.

Availability: ActionScript 1.0; Flash Player 7

Property summary

Modifiers	Property	Description
	message:String	Contains the message associated with the Error object.
	name:String	Contains the name of the Error object.

Properties inherited from class Object

```
constructor (Object.constructor property),__proto__ (Object.__proto__
property),prototype (Object.prototype property),__resolve
(Object.__resolve property)
```

Constructor summary

Signature	Description
Error([message:String])	Creates a new Error object.

Method summary

Modifiers	Signature	Description
	`toString() : String`	Returns the string "Error" by default or the value contained in Error.message, if defined.

Methods inherited from class Object

```
addProperty (Object.addProperty method),hasOwnProperty
(Object.hasOwnProperty method),isPropertyEnumerable
(Object.isPropertyEnumerable method),isPrototypeOf (Object.isPrototypeOf
method),registerClass (Object.registerClass method),toString
(Object.toString method),unwatch (Object.unwatch method),valueOf
(Object.valueOf method),watch (Object.watch method)
```

Error constructor

`public Error([message:String])`

Creates a new Error object. If *message* is specified, its value is assigned to the object's `Error.message` property.

Availability: ActionScript 1.0; Flash Player 7

Parameters

`message:String` [optional] - A string associated with the Error object.

Example

In the following example, a function throws an error (with a specified message) if the two strings that are passed to it are not identical:

```
function compareStrings(str1_str:String, str2_str:String):Void {
   if (str1_str != str2_str) {
   throw new Error("Strings do not match.");
   }
}
try {
   compareStrings("Dog", "dog");
   // output: Strings do not match.
} catch (e_err:Error) {
   trace(e_err.toString());
}
```

See also

`throw statement, try..catch..finally statement`

message (Error.message property)

```
public message : String
```

Contains the message associated with the Error object. By default, the value of this property is "Error". You can specify a message property when you create an Error object by passing the error string to the Error constructor function.

Availability: ActionScript 1.0; Flash Player 7

Example

In the following example, a function throws a specified message depending on the parameters entered into theNum. If two numbers can be divided, SUCCESS and the number are shown. Specific errors are shown if you try to divide by 0 or enter only 1 parameter:

```
function divideNum(num1:Number, num2:Number):Number {
  if (isNaN(num1) || isNaN(num2)) {
  throw new Error("divideNum function requires two numeric parameters.");
  } else if (num2 == 0) {
  throw new Error("cannot divide by zero.");
  }
  return num1/num2;
}
try {
  var theNum:Number = divideNum(1, 0);
  trace("SUCCESS! "+theNum);
} catch (e_err:Error) {
  trace("ERROR! "+e_err.message);
  trace("\t"+e_err.name);
}
```

If you test this ActionScript without any modifications to the numbers you divide, you see an error displayed in the Output panel because you are trying to divide by 0.

See also

throw statement, try..catch..finally statement

name (Error.name property)

```
public name : String
```

Contains the name of the Error object. By default, the value of this property is "Error".

Availability: ActionScript 1.0; Flash Player 7

Example

In the following example, a function throws a specified error depending on the two numbers that you try to divide. Add the following ActionScript to Frame 1 of the Timeline:

```
function divideNumber(numerator:Number, denominator:Number):Number {
   if (isNaN(numerator) || isNaN(denominator)) {
   throw new Error("divideNum function requires two numeric parameters.");
   } else if (denominator == 0) {
   throw new DivideByZeroError();
   }
   return numerator/denominator;
}
try {
   var theNum:Number = divideNumber(1, 0);
   trace("SUCCESS! "+theNum);
   // output: DivideByZeroError -> Unable to divide by zero.
} catch (e_err:DivideByZeroError) {
   // divide by zero error occurred
   trace(e_err.name+" -> "+e_err.toString());
} catch (e_err:Error) {
   // generic error occurred
   trace(e_err.name+" -> "+e_err.toString());
}
```

To add a custom error, add the following code to a .AS file called DivideByZeroError.as and save the class file in the same directory as your FLA document.

```
class DivideByZeroError extends Error {
   var name:String = "DivideByZeroError";
   var message:String = "Unable to divide by zero.";
}
```

See also

`throw statement, try..catch..finally statement`

toString (Error.toString method)

`public toString() : String`

Returns the string "Error" by default or the value contained in Error.message, if defined.

Availability: ActionScript 1.0; Flash Player 7

Returns

`String` - A String

Example

In the following example, a function throws an error (with a specified message) if the two strings that are passed to it are not identical:

```
function compareStrings(str1_str:String, str2_str:String):Void {
if (str1_str != str2_str) {
  throw new Error("Strings do not match.");
  }
}
try {
  compareStrings("Dog", "dog");
  // output: Strings do not match.
} catch (e_err:Error) {
  trace(e_err.toString());
}
```

See also

`message (Error.message property)`, `throw statement`, `try..catch..finally statement`

ExternalInterface (flash.external.ExternalInterface)

```
Object
  |
  +-flash.external.ExternalInterface
```

`public class ExternalInterface`
`extends Object`

The ExternalInterface class is the External API, an application programming interface that enables straightforward communication between ActionScript and the Flash Player container; for example, an HTML page with JavaScript, or a desktop application with Flash Player embedded.

ExternalInterface is similar in functionality to the `fscommand()`, `CallFrame()` and `CallLabel()` methods, but is more flexible and more generally applicable. Use of ExternalInterface is recommended for JavaScript-ActionScript communication.

From ActionScript, you can call any JavaScript function on the HTML page, passing any number of arguments of any data type, and receive a return value from the call.

From JavaScript on the HTML page, you can call an ActionScript function in Flash Player. The ActionScript function can return a value, and JavaScript receives it immediately as the return value of the call.

ExternalInterface is supported in the following combinations of browser and operating system:

Browser	Operating System	
Internet Explorer 5.0 and higher	Windows	
Netscape 8.0 and higher	Windows	Macintosh
Mozilla 1.7.5 and higher	Windows	Macintosh
Firefox 1.0 and higher	Windows	Macintosh
Safari 1.3 and higher		Macintosh

ExternalInterface requires the user's web browser to support either ActiveX or the NPRuntime API that is exposed by some browsers for plugin scripting. See http://www.mozilla.org/projects/plugins/npruntime.html.

Availability: ActionScript 1.0; Flash Player 8

Property summary

Modifiers	Property	Description
static	available:Boolean [read-only]	Indicates whether this player is in a container that offers an external interface.

Properties inherited from class Object

```
constructor (Object.constructor property), __proto__ (Object.__proto__
property), prototype (Object.prototype property), __resolve
(Object.__resolve property)
```

Method summary

Modifiers	Signature	Description
static	addCallback(methodName:String, instance:Object, method:Function) : Boolean	Registers an ActionScript method as callable from the container.
static	call(methodName:String, [parameter1:Object]) : Object	Calls a function exposed by the Flash Player container, passing 0 or more arguments.

Methods inherited from class Object

```
addProperty (Object.addProperty method), hasOwnProperty
(Object.hasOwnProperty method), isPropertyEnumerable
(Object.isPropertyEnumerable method), isPrototypeOf (Object.isPrototypeOf
method), registerClass (Object.registerClass method), toString
(Object.toString method), unwatch (Object.unwatch method), valueOf
(Object.valueOf method), watch (Object.watch method)
```

addCallback (ExternalInterface.addCallback method)

```
public static addCallback(methodName:String, instance:Object,
    method:Function) : Boolean
```

Registers an ActionScript method as callable from the container. After a successful invocation of addCallBack(), the registered function in Flash Player can be called by JavaScript or ActiveX code in the container.

Availability: ActionScript 1.0; Flash Player 8

Parameters

methodName:String - The name by which the ActionScript function can be called from JavaScript. This name does not need to match the actual name of the ActionScript method.

instance:Object - The object to which this resolves in the method. This object is not necessarily the object on which the method can be found — you can specify any object (or null).

method:Function - The ActionScript method to be called from JavaScript.

Returns

`Boolean` - If the call succeeded, returns `true`. If it failed because the instance was not available, a security restriction was encountered, there was no such function object, a recursion occurred, or something similar, returns `false`.

A return value of `false` may also mean that the containing environment belongs to a security sandbox to which the calling code does not have access. You can work around this problem by setting an appropriate value for the `allowScriptAccess` `OBJECT` tag or `EMBED` tag in the HTML of the containing environment.

Example

The following example registers the `goToMacromedia()` function as callable from the container with the name `goHome`.

```
import flash.external.*;

var methodName:String = "goHome";
var instance:Object = null;
var method:Function = goToMacromedia;
var wasSuccessful:Boolean = ExternalInterface.addCallback(methodName,
  instance, method);

var txtField:TextField = this.createTextField("txtField",
  this.getNextHighestDepth(), 0, 0, 200, 50);
txtField.border = true;
txtField.text = wasSuccessful.toString();

function goToMacromedia() {
  txtField.text = "http://www.macromedia.com";
  getURL("http://www.macromedia.com", "_self");
}
```

For the previous example to work properly, you should copy and paste the following code into the containing HTML page. This code relies on the `id` attribute of the `OBJECT` tag and the `name` attribute of the `EMBED` tag to have the value `externalInterfaceExample`. The function `thisMovie` returns the appropriate syntax depending on the browser, since Internet Explorer and Netscape refer to the movie object differently. Unless the HTML page is hosted on a server, your browser may alert you with a security warning.

> **NOTE**
> Avoid using other methods of accessing the plug-in object, such as `document.getElementByID("pluginName")` or `document.all.pluginName`, because these other methods do not work consistantly across all browsers.

```
<form>
  <input type="button" onclick="callExternalInterface()" value="Call
  ExternalInterface" />
```

```
</form>
<script>
function callExternalInterface() {
  thisMovie("externalInterfaceExample").goHome();
}

function thisMovie(movieName) {
  if (navigator.appName.indexOf("Microsoft") != -1) {
    return window[movieName]
  }
  else {
    return document[movieName]
  }
}
</script>
```

available (ExternalInterface.available property)

`public static available : Boolean [read-only]`

Indicates whether this player is in a container that offers an external interface. If the external interface is available, this property is `true`; otherwise, it is `false`.

Availability: ActionScript 1.0; Flash Player 8

Example

The following example uses `ExternalInterface.available` to determine whether the player is in a container that offers an external interface.

```
import flash.external.*;

var isAvailable:Boolean = ExternalInterface.available;
trace(isAvailable);
```

call (ExternalInterface.call method)

`public static call(methodName:String, [parameter1:Object]) : Object`

Calls a function exposed by the Flash Player container, passing 0 or more arguments. If the desired function is not available, the call returns `null`; otherwise it returns the value provided by the function. Recursion is not permitted; a recursive call produces a `null` response.

If the container is an HTML page, this method invokes a JavaScript function in a `<script>` element.

If the container is some other ActiveX container, this method broadcasts an event with the specified name, and the container processes the event.

If the container is hosting the Netscape plug-in, you can either write custom support for the new NPRuntime interface or embed an HTML control and embed Flash Player within the HTML control. If you embed an HTML control, you can communicate with Flash Player through a JavaScript interface that talks to the native container application.

Availability: ActionScript 1.0; Flash Player 8

Parameters

`methodName:String` - The name of the function to call in the container. If the function accepts parameters, they must appear following the `methodName` parameter.

`parameter1:Object` [optional] - Any parameters to be passed to the function. You can specify zero or more parameters, separating them by commas. The parameters can be of any ActionScript data type. When the call is to a JavaScript function, the ActionScript types are automatically marshalled into JavaScript types. When the call is to some other ActiveX container, the parameters are encoded in the request message.

Returns

`Object` - The response received from the container. If the call failed (for example if there is no such function in the container, or the interface was not available, or a recursion occurred, or there was a security issue) `null` is returned.

Example

The following example calls the JavaScript function `sayHello()` in the HTML page that contains the SWF. The call is made by using the `ExternalInterface.call()` method.

```
import flash.external.*;

var greeting:String;
var btn:MovieClip = createButton(100, 30, 0xCCCCCC);
btn.onPress = function() {
   greeting = String(ExternalInterface.call("sayHello", "browser"));
   this.mcTxt.text = greeting; // >> Hi Flash.
}

function createButton(width:Number, height:Number, color:Number):MovieClip
   {
   var depth:Number = this.getNextHighestDepth();
   var mc:MovieClip = this.createEmptyMovieClip("mc_" + depth, depth);
   var mcFmt:TextFormat;

   mc.beginFill(color);
   mc.lineTo(0, height);
   mc.lineTo(width, height);
   mc.lineTo(width, 0);
```

```
mc.lineTo(0, 0);

mcFmt = new TextFormat();
mcFmt.align = "center";
mcFmt.bold = true;

mc.createTextField("mcTxt", depth, 0, 0, width, height);
mc.mcTxt.text = "Call JS Function";
mc.mcTxt.setTextFormat(mcFmt);

return mc;
}
```

For the previous example to work properly, you should be copy and paste the following code into the containing HTML page. Unless the HTML page is hosted on a server, your browser may alert you with a security warning.

```
<script>
   function sayHello(name) {
      alert(">> Hello " + name + ".");
      return ">> Hi Flash.";
   }
</script>
```

FileReference (flash.net.FileReference)

```
Object
 |
 +-flash.net.FileReference
```

```
public class FileReference
extends Object
```

The FileReference class provides a means to upload and download files between a user's computer and a server. An operating-system dialog box prompts the user to select a file to upload or a location for download. Each FileReference object refers to a single file on the user's hard disk and has properties that contain information about the file's size, type, name, creation date, modification date, and creator type (Macintosh only).

FileReference instances are created in two ways:

- When you use the `new` operator with the FileReference constructor: `var myFileReference = new FileReference();`

- When you call `FileReferenceList.browse()`, which creates an array of FileReference objects

During an upload operation, all of the properties of a FileReference object are populated by calls to `FileReference.browse()` or `FileReferenceList.browse()`. During a download operation, the `name` property is populated when `onSelect` has been invoked; all other properties are populated when `onComplete` has been invoked.

The `browse()` method opens an operating-system dialog box which prompts the user to select any local file for upload. The `FileReference.browse()` method lets the user select a single file; the `FileReferenceList.browse()` method lets the user select multiple files. After a successful call to the `browse()` method, call the `FileReference.upload()` method to upload one file at a time. The `FileReference.download()` method prompts the user for a location to save the file and initiates downloading from a remote URL.

The FileReference and FileReferenceList classes do not let you set the default file location for the dialog box generated by `browse()` and `download()` calls. The default location shown in the dialog box is the most recently browsed folder, if that location can be determined, or the desktop. The classes do not allow you to read from or write to the transferred file. They do not allow the SWF file that initiated the upload or download to access the uploaded or downloaded file or the file's location on the user's disk.

The FileReference and FileReferenceList classes also do not provide methods for authentication. With servers that require authentication, you can download files with the Flash Player browser plug-in, but uploading (on all players) and downloading (on the standalone or external player) fails. Use FileReference event listeners to ascertain whether operations have successfully completed and to handle errors.

For uploading and downloading operations, a SWF file can access files only within its own domain, including any domains that are specified by a cross-domain policy file. If the SWF that is initiating the upload or download doesn't come from the same domain as the file server, you must put a policy file on the file server.

While calls to the `FileReference.browse()`, `FileReferenceList.browse()`, or `FileReference.download()` methods are executing, SWF file playback pauses on the following platforms: the Flash Player plug-in for Mac OS X, the external Flash Player for Macintosh, and the stand-alone player for Mac OS X 10.1 and earlier. The SWF file continues to run in all players for Windows and in the stand-alone player for Macintosh on Mac OS X 10.2 and later.

Availability: ActionScript 1.0; Flash Player 8

Example

The following example creates a FileReference object that prompts the user to select an image or text file to be uploaded. It also listens for any possible event.

```
import flash.net.FileReference;

var allTypes:Array = new Array();
var imageTypes:Object = new Object();
imageTypes.description = "Images (*.jpg, *.jpeg, *.gif, *.png)";
imageTypes.extension = "*.jpg; *.jpeg; *.gif; *.png";
allTypes.push(imageTypes);

var textTypes:Object = new Object();
textTypes.description = "Text Files (*.txt, *.rtf)";
textTypes.extension = "*.txt;*.rtf";
allTypes.push(textTypes);

var listener:Object = new Object();

listener.onSelect = function(file:FileReference):Void {
  trace("onSelect: " + file.name);
  if(!file.upload("http://www.yourdomain.com/
  yourUploadHandlerScript.cfm")) {
    trace("Upload dialog failed to open.");
  }
}

listener.onCancel = function(file:FileReference):Void {
  trace("onCancel");
}

listener.onOpen = function(file:FileReference):Void {
  trace("onOpen: " + file.name);
}

listener.onProgress = function(file:FileReference, bytesLoaded:Number,
  bytesTotal:Number):Void {
  trace("onProgress with bytesLoaded: " + bytesLoaded + " bytesTotal: " +
  bytesTotal);
}

listener.onComplete = function(file:FileReference):Void {
  trace("onComplete: " + file.name);
}

listener.onHTTPError = function(file:FileReference):Void {
  trace("onHTTPError: " + file.name);
}

listener.onIOError = function(file:FileReference):Void {
```

```
    trace("onIOError: " + file.name);
}

listener.onSecurityError = function(file:FileReference,
    errorString:String):Void {
    trace("onSecurityError: " + file.name + " errorString: " + errorString);
}

var fileRef:FileReference = new FileReference();
fileRef.addListener(listener);
fileRef.browse(allTypes);
```

See also

`FileReferenceList (flash.net.FileReferenceList)`

Property summary

Modifiers	Property	Description
	`creationDate:Date` [read-only]	The creation date of the file on the local disk.
	`creator:String` [read-only]	The Macintosh creator type of the file.
	`modificationDate:Dat e` [read-only]	The date that the file on the local disk was last modified.
	`name:String` [read-only]	The name of the file on the local disk.
	`size:Number` [read-only]	The size of the file on the local disk, in bytes.
	`type:String` [read-only]	The file type.

Properties inherited from class Object

```
constructor (Object.constructor property),__proto__ (Object.__proto__
property),prototype (Object.prototype property),__resolve
(Object.__resolve property)
```

Event summary

Event	Description
`onCancel = function(fileRef :FileReference) {}`	Invoked when the user dismisses the file-browsing dialog box.
`onComplete = function(fileRef :FileReference) {}`	Invoked when the upload or download operation has successfully completed.
`onHTTPError = function(fileRef :FileReference, httpError:Number ) {}`	Invoked when an upload fails because of an HTTP error.
`onIOError = function(fileRef :FileReference) {}`	Invoked when an input/output error occurs.
`onOpen = function(fileRef :FileReference) {}`	Invoked when an upload or download operation starts.
`onProgress = function(fileRef :FileReference, bytesLoaded:Numb er, bytesTotal:Numbe r) {}`	Invoked periodically during the file upload or download operation.
`onSecurityError = function(fileRef :FileReference, errorString:Stri ng) {}`	Invoked when an upload or download fails because of a security error.
`onSelect = function(fileRef :FileReference) {}`	Invoked when the user selects a file to upload or download from the file-browsing dialog box.

Constructor summary

Signature	Description
`FileReference()`	Creates a new FileReference object.

Method summary

Modifiers	Signature	Description
	`addListener(listener :Object) : Void`	Registers an object to receive notification when a FileReference event listener is invoked.
	`browse([typelist:Arr ay]) : Boolean`	Displays a file-browsing dialog box in which the user can select a local file to upload.
	`cancel() : Void`	Cancels any ongoing upload or download operation on this FileReference object.
	`download(url:String, [defaultFileName:Str ing]) : Boolean`	Displays a dialog box in which the user can download a file from a remote server.
	`removeListener(liste ner:Object) : Boolean`	Removes an object from the list of objects that receive event notification messages.
	`upload(url:String) : Boolean`	Starts the upload of a file selected by a user to a remote server.

Methods inherited from class Object

```
addProperty (Object.addProperty method), hasOwnProperty
(Object.hasOwnProperty method), isPropertyEnumerable
(Object.isPropertyEnumerable method), isPrototypeOf (Object.isPrototypeOf
method), registerClass (Object.registerClass method), toString
(Object.toString method), unwatch (Object.unwatch method), valueOf
(Object.valueOf method), watch (Object.watch method)
```

addListener (FileReference.addListener method)

`public addListener(listener:Object) : Void`

Registers an object to receive notification when a FileReference event listener is invoked.

Availability: ActionScript 1.0; Flash Player 8

Parameters

`listener:Object` - An object that listens for a callback notification from the FileReference event listeners.

Example

The following example adds a listener to an instance of FileReference.

`import flash.net.FileReference;`

```
var listener:Object = new Object();

listener.onProgress = function(file:FileReference, bytesLoaded:Number,
  bytesTotal:Number):Void {
    trace("onProgress with bytesLoaded: " + bytesLoaded + " bytesTotal: " +
    bytesTotal);
}

listener.onComplete = function(file:FileReference):Void {
    trace("onComplete: " + file.name);
}

var fileRef:FileReference = new FileReference();
fileRef.addListener(listener);
var url:String = "http://www.macromedia.com/platform/whitepapers/
  platform_overview.pdf";
fileRef.download(url, "FlashPlatform.pdf");
```

browse (FileReference.browse method)

```
public browse([typelist:Array]) : Boolean
```

Displays a file-browsing dialog box in which the user can select a local file to upload. The dialog box is native to the user's operating system. When you call this method and the user successfully selects a file, the properties of this FileReference object are populated with the properties of that file. Each subsequent time that `FileReference.browse()` is called, the FileReference object's properties are reset to the file selected by the user in the dialog box.

Only one `browse()` or `download()` session can be performed at a time (because only one dialog box can be displayed at a time).

You can pass an array of file types to determine which files the dialog box displays.

Availability: ActionScript 1.0; Flash Player 8

Parameters

`typelist:Array` [optional] - An array of file types used to filter the files displayed in the dialog box. If you omit this parameter, all files are displayed. If you include this parameter, the array must contain one or more elements enclosed in curly braces { }. You can use one of two formats for the array:

- A list of file type descriptions followed by their Windows file extensions only. Each element in the array must contain a string that describes the file type and a semicolon-delimited list of Windows file extensions, with a wildcard character (*) preceding each extension. The syntax for each element is as follows:

```
[{description: "string describing the first set of file types",
extension: "semicolon-delimited list of file extensions"}]
```

  Example:

```
[{description: "Images", extension: "*.jpg;*.gif;*.png"}, {description:
"Flash Movies", extension: "*.swf"}, {description: "Documents",
extension: "*.doc;*.pdf"}]
```

- A list of file type descriptions followed by their Windows file extensions and their Macintosh file types.
  Each element in the array must contain a string that describes the file type; a semicolon-delimited list of Windows file extensions, with a wildcard character (*) preceding each extension; and a semicolon-delimited list of Macintosh file types, with a wildcard character (*) preceding each type. The syntax for each element is as follows:

```
[{description: "string describing the first set of file types",
extension: "semicolon-delimited list of Windows file extensions",
macType: "semicolon-delimited list of Macintosh file types"}]
```

  Example:

```
[{description: "Image files", extension: "*.jpg;*.gif;*.png", macType:
"JPEG;jp2_;GIFF"}, {description: "Flash Movies", extension: "*.swf",
macType: "SWFL"}]
```

The two formats are not interchangeable in a single `browse()` call. You must use one or the other.

The list of extensions is used to filter the files in Windows, depending on the file selected by the user. It is not actually displayed in the dialog box. To display the file types for users, you must list the file types in the description string as well as in the extension list. The description string is displayed in the dialog box in Windows. (It is not used on the Macintosh.) On the Macintosh, if you supply a list of Macintosh file types, that list is used to filter the files. If you don't supply a list of Macintosh file types, the list of Windows extensions is used.

Returns

`Boolean` - Returns `true` if the parameters are valid and the file-browsing dialog box is displayed. Returns `false` if the dialog box is not displayed, if another browse session is already in progress, or if you use the `typelist` parameter but fail to provide a description or extension string in any element in the array.

Example

The following example displays a dialog box in which the user can select an image file to be uploaded.

```
import flash.net.FileReference;

var listener:Object = new Object();
listener.onSelect = function(file:FileReference):Void {
  trace("Opened " + file.name);
}

listener.onCancel = function(file:FileReference):Void {
  trace("User cancelled");
}

var fileRef:FileReference = new FileReference();
fileRef.addListener(listener);
fileRef.browse();
```

See also

`onSelect (FileReferenceList.onSelect event listener)`, `onCancel (FileReference.onCancel event listener)`, `download (FileReference.download method)`, `browse (FileReferenceList.browse method)`

cancel (FileReference.cancel method)

`public cancel() : Void`

Cancels any ongoing upload or download operation on this FileReference object.

Availability: ActionScript 1.0; Flash Player 8

Example

The following example downloads approximately half of the requested file and then cancels the download. This is obviously not a typical usage. You might more often use this method to allow users to click Cancel in a download status dialog box.

```
import flash.net.FileReference;

var listener:Object = new Object();

listener.onProgress = function(file:FileReference, bytesLoaded:Number,
  bytesTotal:Number):Void {
    trace("onProgress with bytesLoaded: " + bytesLoaded + " bytesTotal: " +
    bytesTotal);
    if(bytesLoaded >= (bytesTotal / 2)) {
      file.cancel();
    }
}

var fileRef:FileReference = new FileReference();
fileRef.addListener(listener);
var url:String = "http://www.macromedia.com/platform/whitepapers/
  platform_overview.pdf";
fileRef.download(url, "FlashPlatform.pdf");
```

creationDate (FileReference.creationDate property)

```
public creationDate : Date [read-only]
```

The creation date of the file on the local disk. If the FileReference object has not been populated, a call to get the value of this property returns null.

Availability: ActionScript 1.0; Flash Player 8

Example

The following example retrieves the creation date of a file selected by the user.

```
import flash.net.FileReference;

var listener:Object = new Object();
listener.onSelect = function(file:FileReference):Void {
  trace("creationDate: " + file.creationDate);
}

var fileRef:FileReference = new FileReference();
fileRef.addListener(listener);
fileRef.browse();
```

See also
browse (FileReference.browse method)

creator (FileReference.creator property)

public creator : String [read-only]

The Macintosh creator type of the file. In Windows, this property is null. If the FileReference object has not been populated, a call to get the value of this property returns null.

Availability: ActionScript 1.0; Flash Player 8

Example

The following example retrieves the Macintosh creator type of a file selected by the user.

```
import flash.net.FileReference;

var listener:Object = new Object();
listener.onSelect = function(file:FileReference):Void {
  trace("creator: " + file.creator);
}

var fileRef:FileReference = new FileReference();
fileRef.addListener(listener);
fileRef.browse();
```

See also

browse (FileReference.browse method)

download (FileReference.download method)

public download(url:String, [defaultFileName:String]) : Boolean

Displays a dialog box in which the user can download a file from a remote server. Flash Player can download files of up to 100 MB.

This method first opens an operating-system dialog box that asks the user to enter a filename and select a location on the local computer to save the file. When the user selects a location and confirms the download operation (for example, by clicking Save), the download from the remote server begins. Listeners receive events to indicate the progress, success, or failure of the download. To ascertain the status of the dialog box and the download operation after calling download(), your ActionScript code must listen for events by using event listeners such as onCancel, onOpen, onProgress, and onComplete.

When the file has successfully downloaded, the properties of the FileReference object are populated with the properties of the local file and the `onComplete` listener is invoked.

Only one `browse()` or `download()` session can be performed at a time (because only one dialog box can be displayed at a time).

This method supports downloading of any file type, with either HTTP or HTTPS. You can also send data to the server with the `download()` call by appending parameters to the URL, for the server script to parse.

> **NOTE** If your server requires user authentication, only SWF files that are running in a browser—that is, using the browser plug-in or ActiveX control—can provide a dialog box to prompt the user for a user name and password for authentication, and only for downloads. For uploads using the plug-in or ActiveX control, and for uploads and downloads using the stand-alone or external player, the file transfer fails.

When using this method, consider the Flash Player security model:

- Not allowed if the calling SWF file is in an untrusted local sandbox.
- The default is to deny access between sandboxes. A website can enable access to a resource by adding a cross-domain policy file.

For more information, see the following:

- Chapter 17, "Understanding Security," in *Learning ActionScript 2.0 in Flash*
- The Flash Player 8 Security white paper at http://www.macromedia.com/go/fp8_security
- The Flash Player 8 Security-Related API white paper at http://www.macromedia.com/go/fp8_security_apis

Availability: ActionScript 1.0; Flash Player 8

Parameters

`url:String` - The URL of the file to download to the local computer. You can send data to the server with the `download()` call by appending parameters to the URL, for the server script to parse. For example: `http://www.myserver.com/picture.jpg?userID=jdoe`

On some browsers, URL strings are limited in length. Lengths greater than 256 characters may fail on some browsers or servers.

`defaultFileName:String` [optional] - The default filename displayed in the dialog box, for the file to be downloaded. This string cannot contain the following characters: / \ : * ? " < > | %

If you omit this parameter, the filename of the remote URL is parsed out and used as the default.

Returns

`Boolean` - A value of `true` if the dialog box in which a user can select a file is displayed. If the dialog box is not displayed, the method returns `false`. The dialog box could fail to be displayed for any of the following reasons:

- You did not pass a value for the `url` parameter.
- The parameters passed are of the incorrect type or format.
- The `url` parameter has a length of 0.
- A security violation occurred; that is, your SWF file attempted to access a file from a server that is outside your SWF file's security sandbox.
- Another browse session is already in progress. A browse session can be started by `FileReference.browse()`, `FileReferenceList.browse()`, or `FileReference.download()`.
- The protocol is not HTTP or HTTPS.

Example

The following example attempts to download a file using the `download` method. Notice that there are listeners for all of the events.

```
import flash.net.FileReference;

var listener:Object = new Object();

listener.onSelect = function(file:FileReference):Void {
  trace("onSelect: " + file.name);
}

listener.onCancel = function(file:FileReference):Void {
  trace("onCancel");
}

listener.onOpen = function(file:FileReference):Void {
  trace("onOpen: " + file.name);
}

listener.onProgress = function(file:FileReference, bytesLoaded:Number,
  bytesTotal:Number):Void {
  trace("onProgress with bytesLoaded: " + bytesLoaded + " bytesTotal: " +
  bytesTotal);
}

listener.onComplete = function(file:FileReference):Void {
  trace("onComplete: " + file.name);
}
```

```
listener.onIOError = function(file:FileReference):Void {
  trace("onIOError: " + file.name);
}

var fileRef:FileReference = new FileReference();
fileRef.addListener(listener);
var url:String = "http://www.macromedia.com/platform/whitepapers/
  platform_overview.pdf";
if(!fileRef.download(url, "FlashPlatform.pdf")) {
  trace("dialog box failed to open.");
}
```

See also

```
browse (FileReference.browse method), browse (FileReferenceList.browse
method), upload (FileReference.upload method)
```

FileReference constructor

```
public FileReference()
```

Creates a new FileReference object. When populated, a FileReference object represents a file on the user's local disk.

Availability: ActionScript 1.0; Flash Player 8

Example

The following example creates a new FileReference object and initiates the download of a PDF file.

```
import flash.net.FileReference;

var listener:Object = new Object();
listener.onComplete = function(file:FileReference) {
  trace("onComplete : " + file.name);
}

var url:String = "http://www.macromedia.com/platform/whitepapers/
  platform_overview.pdf";
var fileRef:FileReference = new FileReference();
fileRef.addListener(listener);
fileRef.download(url, "FlashPlatform.pdf");
```

See also

```
browse (FileReference.browse method)
```

modificationDate (FileReference.modificationDate property)

```
public modificationDate : Date [read-only]
```

The date that the file on the local disk was last modified. If the FileReference object has not been populated, a call to get the value of this property returns `null`.

Availability: ActionScript 1.0; Flash Player 8

Example

The following example retrieves the `modificationDate` of a file selected by the user.

```
import flash.net.FileReference;

var listener:Object = new Object();
listener.onSelect = function(file:FileReference):Void {
  trace("modificationDate: " + file.modificationDate);
}

var fileRef:FileReference = new FileReference();
fileRef.addListener(listener);
fileRef.browse();
```

See also

```
browse (FileReference.browse method)
```

name (FileReference.name property)

```
public name : String [read-only]
```

The name of the file on the local disk. If the FileReference object has not been populated, a call to get the value of this property returns `null`.

All the properties of a FileReference object are populated by calling `browse()`. Unlike other FileReference properties, if you call `download()`, the `name` property is populated when `onSelect` is invoked.

Availability: ActionScript 1.0; Flash Player 8

Example

The following example retrieves the name of a file selected by the user.

```
import flash.net.FileReference;

var listener:Object = new Object();
listener.onSelect = function(file:FileReference):Void {
  trace("name: " + file.name);
```

```
}
var fileRef:FileReference = new FileReference();
fileRef.addListener(listener);
fileRef.browse();
```

See also

browse (FileReference.browse method)

onCancel (FileReference.onCancel event listener)

`onCancel = function(fileRef:FileReference) {}`

Invoked when the user dismisses the file-browsing dialog box. This dialog box is displayed
when you call `FileReference.browse()`, `FileReferenceList.browse()`, or
`FileReference.download()`.

Availability: ActionScript 1.0; Flash Player 8

Parameters

`fileRef:flash.net.FileReference` - The FileReference object that initiated the operation.

Example

The following example traces a message if the user dismisses the file-browsing dialog box. This
method is triggered only if the user clicks Cancel or presses the Escape key after the dialog box
is displayed.

```
import flash.net.FileReference;

var listener:Object = new Object();

listener.onCancel = function(file:FileReference):Void {
  trace("onCancel");
}

var fileRef:FileReference = new FileReference();
fileRef.addListener(listener);
var url:String = "http://www.macromedia.com/platform/whitepapers/
  platform_overview.pdf";
if(!fileRef.download(url, "FlashPlatform.pdf")) {
  trace("dialog box failed to open.");
}
```

onComplete (FileReference.onComplete event listener)

```
onComplete = function(fileRef:FileReference) {}
```

Invoked when the upload or download operation has successfully completed. Successful completion means that the entire file has been uploaded or downloaded.

Availability: ActionScript 1.0; Flash Player 8

Parameters

`fileRef:flash.net.FileReference` - The FileReference object that initiated the operation.

Example

The following example traces out a message when the `onComplete` event is triggered.

```
import flash.net.FileReference;

var listener:Object = new Object();

listener.onComplete = function(file:FileReference):Void {
  trace("onComplete: " + file.name);
}

var fileRef:FileReference = new FileReference();
fileRef.addListener(listener);
var url:String = "http://www.macromedia.com/platform/whitepapers/
  platform_overview.pdf";
fileRef.download(url, "FlashPlatform.pdf");
```

onHTTPError (FileReference.onHTTPError event listener)

```
onHTTPError = function(fileRef:FileReference, httpError:Number) {}
```

Invoked when an upload fails because of an HTTP error.

Because of the way that Flash Player relies on the browser stack during file download, this error is not applicable for download failures. If a download fails because of an HTTP error, the error is reported as an I/O error.

Availability: ActionScript 1.0; Flash Player 8

Parameters

`fileRef:flash.net.FileReference` - The File Reference object that initiated the operation.

`httpError:Number` - The HTTP error that caused this upload to fail. For example, an `httpError` of 404 indicates that a page is not found. HTTP error values can be found in sections 10.4 and 10.5 of the HTTP specification at ftp://ftp.isi.edu/in-notes/rfc2616.txt.

Example

The following example creates a FileReference object with a listener for each possible event including `onHttpError`. This listener is triggered only if the upload fails because of an HTTP error.

```
import flash.net.FileReference;

var listener:Object = new Object();

listener.onSelect = function(file:FileReference):Void {
  trace("onSelect: " + file.name);
  if(!file.upload("http://www.yourdomain.com/
  yourUploadHandlerScript.cfm")) {
    trace("Upload dialog failed to open.");
  }
}

listener.onCancel = function(file:FileReference):Void {
  trace("onCancel");
}

listener.onOpen = function(file:FileReference):Void {
  trace("onOpen: " + file.name);
}

listener.onProgress = function(file:FileReference, bytesLoaded:Number,
  bytesTotal:Number):Void {
  trace("onProgress with bytesLoaded: " + bytesLoaded + " bytesTotal: " +
  bytesTotal);
}

listener.onComplete = function(file:FileReference):Void {
  trace("onComplete: " + file.name);
}

listener.onHTTPError = function(file:FileReference):Void {
  trace("onHTTPError: " + file.name);
}

listener.onIOError = function(file:FileReference):Void {
```

```
    trace("onIOError: " + file.name);
}

listener.onSecurityError = function(file:FileReference,
  errorString:String):Void {
    trace("onSecurityError: " + file.name + " errorString: " + errorString);
}

var fileRef:FileReference = new FileReference();
fileRef.addListener(listener);
fileRef.browse();
```

onIOError (FileReference.onIOError event listener)

```
onIOError = function(fileRef:FileReference) {}
```

Invoked when an input/output error occurs.

This listener is invoked when the upload or download fails for any of the following reasons:

- An input/output error occurs while the player is reading, writing, or transmitting the file.

- The SWF file tries to upload a file to a server that requires authentication, such as a user name and password. During upload, Flash Player does not provide a means for users to enter passwords. If a SWF file tries to upload a file to a server that requires authentication, the upload fails.

- The SWF file tries to download a file from a server that requires authentication, in the stand-alone or external player. During download, the stand-alone and external players do not provide a means for users to enter passwords. If a SWF file in these players tries to download a file from a server that requires authentication, the download fails. File download can succeed only in the ActiveX control and browser plug-in players.

- The value passed to the `url` parameter in `upload()` contains an invalid protocol. Valid protocols are HTTP and HTTPS.

Important: Only Flash applications that are running in a browser — that is, using the browser plug-in or ActiveX control — can provide a dialog to prompt the user to enter a user name and password for authentication, and then only for downloads. For uploads that use the plug-in or ActiveX control, or that upload and download using either the standalone or external players, the file transfer fails.

Availability: ActionScript 1.0; Flash Player 8

Parameters

`fileRef:flash.net.FileReference` - The FileReference object that initiated the operation.

Example

The following example traces a message when the `onIOError` event is triggered. For simplicity, none of the other event listeners are included in this example.

```
import flash.net.FileReference;

var listener:Object = new Object();

listener.onIOError = function(file:FileReference):Void {
  trace("onIOError");
}

var fileRef:FileReference = new FileReference();
fileRef.addListener(listener);
fileRef.download("http://www.macromedia.com/NonExistentFile.pdf",
  "NonExistentFile.pdf");
```

onOpen (FileReference.onOpen event listener)

```
onOpen = function(fileRef:FileReference) {}
```

Invoked when an upload or download operation starts.

Availability: ActionScript 1.0; Flash Player 8

Parameters

`fileRef:flash.net.FileReference` - The FileReference object that initiated the operation.

Example

The following example traces a message when the `onOpen` event is triggered.

```
import flash.net.FileReference;

var listener:Object = new Object();

listener.onOpen = function(file:FileReference):Void {
  trace("onOpen: " + file.name);
}

var fileRef:FileReference = new FileReference();
fileRef.addListener(listener);
var url:String = "http://www.macromedia.com/platform/whitepapers/
  platform_overview.pdf";
fileRef.download(url, "FlashPlatform.pdf");
```

onProgress (FileReference.onProgress event listener)

```
onProgress = function(fileRef:FileReference, bytesLoaded:Number,
  bytesTotal:Number) {}
```

Invoked periodically during the file upload or download operation. The `onProgress` listener is invoked while the Flash Player transmits bytes to a server, and it is periodically invoked during the transmission, even if the transmission is ultimately not successful. To determine if and when the file transmission is successful and complete, use `onComplete`.

In some cases, `onProgress` listeners are not invoked; for example, if the file being transmitted is very small, or if the upload or download happens very quickly.

File upload progress cannot be determined on Macintosh platforms earlier than OS X 10.3. The `onProgress` event is called during the upload operation, but the value of the `bytesLoaded` parameter is -1, indicating that the progress cannot be determined.

Availability: ActionScript 1.0; Flash Player 8

Parameters

`fileRef:flash.net.FileReference` - The FileReference object that initiated the operation.

`bytesLoaded:Number` - The number of bytes transmitted so far.

`bytesTotal:Number` - The total size of the file to be transmitted, in bytes. If the size cannot be determined, the value is -1.

Example

The following example traces the progress of a download using the `onProgress` event listener.

```
import flash.net.FileReference;

var listener:Object = new Object();

listener.onProgress = function(file:FileReference, bytesLoaded:Number,
  bytesTotal:Number):Void {
  trace("onProgress: " + file.name + " with bytesLoaded: " + bytesLoaded +
  " bytesTotal: " + bytesTotal);
}

var fileRef:FileReference = new FileReference();
fileRef.addListener(listener);
var url:String = "http://www.macromedia.com/platform/whitepapers/
  platform_overview.pdf";
fileRef.download(url, "FlashPlatform.pdf");
```

See also

onSecurityError (FileReference.onSecurityError event listener)

```
onSecurityError = function(fileRef:FileReference, errorString:String) {}
```
Invoked when an upload or download fails because of a security error. The calling SWF file may have tried to access a SWF file outside its domain and does not have permission to do so. You can try to remedy this error by using a cross-domain policy file.

Availability: ActionScript 1.0; Flash Player 8

Parameters

`fileRef:flash.net.FileReference` - The FileReference object that initiated the operation.

`errorString:String` - Describes the error that caused `onSecurityError` to be called. The value is "securitySandboxError".

Example

The following example creates a FileReference object with a listener for each possible event, including `onSecurityError`. The `onSecurityError` listener is triggered only if the upload fails because of a security error.

```
import flash.net.FileReference;

var listener:Object = new Object();

listener.onSelect = function(file:FileReference):Void {
  trace("onSelect: " + file.name);
  if(!file.upload("http://www.yourdomain.com/
  yourUploadHandlerScript.cfm")) {
    trace("Upload dialog failed to open.");
  }
}

listener.onCancel = function(file:FileReference):Void {
  trace("onCancel");
}

listener.onOpen = function(file:FileReference):Void {
  trace("onOpen: " + file.name);
}

listener.onProgress = function(file:FileReference, bytesLoaded:Number,
  bytesTotal:Number):Void {
```

```
    trace("onProgress with bytesLoaded: " + bytesLoaded + " bytesTotal: " +
    bytesTotal);
}

listener.onComplete = function(file:FileReference):Void {
  trace("onComplete: " + file.name);
}

listener.onHTTPError = function(file:FileReference):Void {
  trace("onHTTPError: " + file.name);
}

listener.onIOError = function(file:FileReference):Void {
  trace("onIOError: " + file.name);
}

listener.onSecurityError = function(file:FileReference,
  errorString:String):Void {
    trace("onSecurityError: " + file.name + " errorString: " + errorString);
}

var fileRef:FileReference = new FileReference();
fileRef.addListener(listener);
fileRef.browse();
```

onSelect (FileReference.onSelect event listener)

```
onSelect = function(fileRef:FileReference) {}
```

Invoked when the user selects a file to upload or download from the file-browsing dialog box. (This dialog box is displayed when you call `FileReference.browse()`, `FileReferenceList.browse()`, or `FileReference.download()`.) When the user selects a file and confirms the operation (for example, by clicking OK), the properties of the FileReference object are populated.

The `onSelect` listener works slightly differently depending on what method invokes it. When `onSelect` is invoked after a `browse()` call, Flash Player can read all of the FileReference object's properties, because the file selected by the user is on the local file system. When `onSelect` is invoked after a `download()` call, Flash Player can read only the `name` property, because the file hasn't yet been downloaded to the local file system at the moment `onSelect` is invoked. When the file has been downloaded and `onComplete` invoked, then Flash Player can read all other properties of the FileReference object.

Availability: ActionScript 1.0; Flash Player 8

Parameters

`fileRef:flash.net.FileReference` - The FileReference object that initiated the operation.

Example

The following example traces a message within the `onSelect` event listener.

```
import flash.net.FileReference;

var listener:Object = new Object();
listener.onSelect = function(file:FileReference):Void {
  trace("onSelect: " + file.name);
  if(!file.upload("http://www.yourdomain.com/
  yourUploadHandlerScript.cfm")) {
    trace("Upload dialog failed to open.");
  }
}

var fileRef:FileReference = new FileReference();
fileRef.addListener(listener);
fileRef.browse();
```

removeListener (FileReference.removeListener method)

`public removeListener(listener:Object) : Boolean`

Removes an object from the list of objects that receive event notification messages.

Availability: ActionScript 1.0; Flash Player 8

Parameters

`listener:Object` - An object that listens for a callback notification from the FileReference event listeners.

Returns

`Boolean` - Returns `true` if the object specified in the `listener` parameter was successfully removed. Otherwise, this method returns `false`.

Example

The following example removes an event listener using the `removeListener` method. If a user cancels the download, the listener is removed so that it no longer receives events from that FileReference object.

```
import flash.net.FileReference;

var listener:Object = new Object();

listener.onCancel = function(file:FileReference):Void {
   trace(file.removeListener(this)); // true
}

var fileRef:FileReference = new FileReference();
fileRef.addListener(listener);
var url:String = "http://www.macromedia.com/platform/whitepapers/
   platform_overview.pdf";
fileRef.download(url, "FlashPlatform.pdf");
```

size (FileReference.size property)

```
public size : Number [read-only]
```

The size of the file on the local disk, in bytes. If the FileReference object has not been populated, a call to get the value of this property returns `null`.

Availability: ActionScript 1.0; Flash Player 8

Example

The following example retrieves the size of a file selected by the user.

```
import flash.net.FileReference;

var listener:Object = new Object();
listener.onSelect = function(file:FileReference):Void {
   trace("size: " + file.size + " bytes");
}

var fileRef:FileReference = new FileReference();
fileRef.addListener(listener);
fileRef.browse();
```

See also

```
browse (FileReference.browse method)
```

type (FileReference.type property)

```
public type : String [read-only]
```

The file type. In Windows, this property is the file extension. On the Macintosh, this property is the four-character file type. If the FileReference object has not been populated, a call to get the value of this property returns `null`.

Availability: ActionScript 1.0; Flash Player 8

Example

The following example retrieves the type of a file selected by the user.

```
import flash.net.FileReference;

var listener:Object = new Object();
listener.onSelect = function(file:FileReference):Void {
  trace("type: " + file.type);
}

var fileRef:FileReference = new FileReference();
fileRef.addListener(listener);
fileRef.browse();
```

See also

```
browse (FileReference.browse method)
```

upload (FileReference.upload method)

```
public upload(url:String) : Boolean
```

Starts the upload of a file selected by a user to a remote server. Flash Player can upload files of up to 100 MB. You must call `FileReference.browse()` or `FileReferenceList.browse()` before calling this method.

Listeners receive events to indicate the progress, success, or failure of the upload. Although you can use the FileReferenceList object to let users select multiple files to upload, you must upload the files one by one. To do so, iterate through the `FileReferenceList.fileList` array of FileReference objects.

The file is uploaded to the URL passed in the url parameter. The URL must be a server script configured to accept uploads. Flash Player uploads files using the HTTP POST method. The server script that handles the upload should expect a POST request with the following elements:

- A Content-Type element of multipart/form-data
- A Content-Disposition element with a name attribute set to "Filedata" and a filename attribute set to the name of the original file
- The binary contents of the file

Here is a sample POST request:

```
Content-Type: multipart/form-data; boundary=AaB03x
--AaB03x
Content-Disposition: form-data; name="Filedata"; filename="example.jpg"
Content-Type: application/octet-stream
... contents of example.jpg ...
--AaB03x--
```

You can send data to the server with the upload() call by appending parameters to the URL.

Note: If your server requires user authentication, only SWF files running in a browser—that is, using the browser plug-in or ActiveX control—can provide a dialog box to prompt the user for a user name and password for authentication, and only for downloads. For uploads that use the plug-in or ActiveX control, and for uploads and downloads that use the stand-alone or external player, the file transfer fails.

When using this method, consider the Flash Player security model:

- Not allowed if the calling SWF file is in an untrusted local sandbox.
- The default is to deny access between sandboxes. A website can enable access to a resource by adding a cross-domain policy file.

For more information, see the following:

- Chapter 17, "Understanding Security," in *Learning ActionScript 2.0 in Flash*
- The Flash Player 8 Security white paper at http://www.macromedia.com/go/fp8_security
- The Flash Player 8 Security-Related API white paper at http://www.macromedia.com/go/fp8_security_apis

Availability: ActionScript 1.0; Flash Player 8

Parameters

url:String - The URL of the server script configured to handle upload through HTTP POST calls. The URL can be HTTP or, for secure uploads, HTTPS.

You can send data to the server with the `upload()` call by appending parameters to the URL; for example, `http://www.myserver.com/upload.cgi?userID=jdoe`

On some browsers, URL strings are limited in length. Lengths greater than 256 characters may fail on some browsers or servers.

Returns

`Boolean` - A value of `false` in any of the following situations:

- `FileReference.browse()` has not yet been successfully called on this object, or if `FileReferenceList.browse()` has not yet been successfully called with this object in its `filelist` array.
- The protocol is not HTTP or HTTPS.
- A security violation occurs; that is, if your SWF file attempts to access a file from a server that is outside your SWF files's security sandbox.
- The `url` parameter is of the incorrect type or format.
- The call does not have the correct number of parameters.

Example

The following example shows an implementation of the `upload()` method by first prompting the user to select a file to upload, then handling the `onSelect` and `onCancel` listeners, and finally handling the results of the actual file upload.

```
import flash.net.FileReference;

var allTypes:Array = new Array();
var imageTypes:Object = new Object();
imageTypes.description = "Images (*.jpg, *.jpeg, *.gif, *.png)";
imageTypes.extension = "*.jpg; *.jpeg; *.gif; *.png";
allTypes.push(imageTypes);

var listener:Object = new Object();

listener.onSelect = function(file:FileReference):Void {
  trace("onSelect: " + file.name);
  if(!file.upload("http://www.yourdomain.com/
  yourUploadHandlerScript.cfm")) {
    trace("Upload dialog failed to open.");
  }
}

listener.onCancel = function(file:FileReference):Void {
  trace("onCancel");
}
```

```
listener.onOpen = function(file:FileReference):Void {
  trace("onOpen: " + file.name);
}

listener.onProgress = function(file:FileReference, bytesLoaded:Number,
  bytesTotal:Number):Void {
    trace("onProgress with bytesLoaded: " + bytesLoaded + " bytesTotal: " +
    bytesTotal);
}

listener.onComplete = function(file:FileReference):Void {
  trace("onComplete: " + file.name);
}

listener.onHTTPError = function(file:FileReference):Void {
  trace("onHTTPError: " + file.name);
}

listener.onIOError = function(file:FileReference):Void {
  trace("onIOError: " + file.name);
}

listener.onSecurityError = function(file:FileReference,
  errorString:String):Void {
    trace("onSecurityError: " + file.name + " errorString: " + errorString);
}

var fileRef:FileReference = new FileReference();
fileRef.addListener(listener);
fileRef.browse(allTypes);
```

See also

browse (FileReference.browse method), browse (FileReferenceList.browse
method), download (FileReference.download method), fileList
(FileReferenceList.fileList property)

FileReferenceList
(flash.net.FileReferenceList)

```
Object
  |
  +-flash.net.FileReferenceList
```

```
public class FileReferenceList
extends Object
```

The FileReferenceList class provides a means to let users select one or more files for uploading. A FileReferenceList object represents a group of one or more local files on the user's disk as an array of FileReference objects. For detailed information and important considerations about FileReference objects and the FileReference class, which you use with FileReferenceList, see the FileReference class.

To work with the FileReferenceList class:

- Instantiate the class: `var myFileRef = new FileReferenceList();`
- Call `FileReferenceList.browse()`, to display a dialog box in which the user can select one or more files to upload: `myFileRef.browse();`
- After `browse()` is successfully called, the `fileList` property of the FileReferenceList object is populated with an array of FileReference objects.
- Call `FileReference.upload()` on each element in the `fileList` array.

The FileReferenceList class includes a `browse()` method and a `fileList` property for working with multiple files.

Availability: ActionScript 1.0; Flash Player 8

Example

The following example allows a user to select multiple files and then uploads each of them to a server.

```
import flash.net.FileReferenceList;
import flash.net.FileReference;

var listener:Object = new Object();

listener.onSelect = function(fileRefList:FileReferenceList) {
  trace("onSelect");
  var list:Array = fileRefList.fileList;
  var item:FileReference;
  for(var i:Number = 0; i < list.length; i++) {
    item = list[i];
    trace("name: " + item.name);
```

```
      trace(item.addListener(this));
      item.upload("http://www.yourdomain.com/");
    }
  }

listener.onCancel = function():Void {
  trace("onCancel");
}

listener.onOpen = function(file:FileReference):Void {
  trace("onOpen: " + file.name);
}

listener.onProgress = function(file:FileReference, bytesLoaded:Number,
  bytesTotal:Number):Void {
  trace("onProgress with bytesLoaded: " + bytesLoaded + " bytesTotal: " +
  bytesTotal);
}

listener.onComplete = function(file:FileReference):Void {
  trace("onComplete: " + file.name);
}

listener.onHTTPError = function(file:FileReference, httpError:Number):Void
  {
  trace("onHTTPError: " + file.name + " httpError: " + httpError);
}

listener.onIOError = function(file:FileReference):Void {
  trace("onIOError: " + file.name);
}

listener.onSecurityError = function(file:FileReference,
  errorString:String):Void {
  trace("onSecurityError: " + file.name + " errorString: " + errorString);
}

var fileRef:FileReferenceList = new FileReferenceList();
fileRef.addListener(listener);
fileRef.browse();
```

See also

```
FileReference (flash.net.FileReference)
```

Property summary

Modifiers	Property	Description
	`fileList:Array`	An array of FileReference objects.

Properties inherited from class Object

```
constructor (Object.constructor property), __proto__ (Object.__proto__
property), prototype (Object.prototype property), __resolve
(Object.__resolve property)
```

Event summary

Event	Description
`onCancel = function(fileRef List:FileReferen ceList) {}`	Invoked when the user dismisses the file-browsing dialog box.
`onSelect = function(fileRef List:FileReferen ceList) {}`	Invoked when the user selects one or more files to upload from the file-browsing dialog box.

Constructor summary

Signature	Description
`FileReferenceList()`	Creates a new FileReferenceList object.

Method summary

Modifiers	Signature	Description
	addListener(listener :Object) : Void	Registers an object to receive notification when a FileReferenceList event listener is invoked.
	browse([typelist:Arr ay]) : Boolean	Displays a file-browsing dialog box in which the user can select one or more local files to upload.
	removeListener(liste ner:Object) : Boolean	Removes an object from the list of objects that receive event notification messages.

Methods inherited from class Object

```
addProperty (Object.addProperty method), hasOwnProperty
(Object.hasOwnProperty method), isPropertyEnumerable
(Object.isPropertyEnumerable method), isPrototypeOf (Object.isPrototypeOf
method), registerClass (Object.registerClass method), toString
(Object.toString method), unwatch (Object.unwatch method), valueOf
(Object.valueOf method), watch (Object.watch method)
```

addListener (FileReferenceList.addListener method)

```
public addListener(listener:Object) : Void
```

Registers an object to receive notification when a FileReferenceList event listener is invoked.

Availability: ActionScript 1.0; Flash Player 8

Parameters

listener:Object - An object that listens for a callback notification from the FileReferenceList event listeners.

Example

The following example demonstrates the addListener() method.

```
import flash.net.FileReferenceList;

var listener:Object = new Object();
listener.onCancel = function(fileRefList:FileReferenceList) {
  trace("onCancel");
}

listener.onSelect = function(fileRefList:FileReferenceList) {
  trace("onSelect: " + fileRefList.fileList.length);
}
```

```
var fileRef:FileReferenceList = new FileReferenceList();
fileRef.addListener(listener);
fileRef.browse();
```

browse (FileReferenceList.browse method)

```
public browse([typelist:Array]) : Boolean
```

Displays a file-browsing dialog box in which the user can select one or more local files to upload. The dialog box is native to the user's operating system. When you call this method and the user successfully selects files, the `fileList` property of this FileReferenceList object is populated with an array of FileReference objects, one for each file selected by the user. Each subsequent time that `FileReferenceList.browse()` is called, the FileReferenceList.fileList property is reset to the file or files selected by the user in the dialog box.

You can pass an array of file types to determine which files the dialog box displays.

Only one `browse()` or `download()` session can be performed at a time on a FileReferenceList object (because only one dialog box can be displayed at a time).

Availability: ActionScript 1.0; Flash Player 8

Parameters

`typelist:Array` [optional] - An array of file types used to filter the files that are displayed in the dialog box. If you omit this parameter, all files are displayed. If you include this parameter, the array must contain one or more elements enclosed in curly braces { }. You can use one of two formats for the array:

- A list of file type descriptions followed by their Windows file extensions only. Each element in the array must contain a string that describes the file type and a semicolon-delimited list of Windows file extensions, with a wildcard (*) character preceding each extension. The syntax for each element is as follows:
  ```
  [{description: "string describing the first set of file types",
  extension: "semicolon-delimited list of file extensions"}]
  ```
  Example:
  ```
  [{description: "Images", extension: "*.jpg;*.gif;*.png"}, {description:
  "Flash Movies", extension: "*.swf"}, {description: "Documents",
  extension: "*.doc;*.pdf"}]
  ```

- A list of file type descriptions followed by their Windows file extensions and their Macintosh file types.

  Each element in the array must contain a string that describes the file type; a semicolon-delimited list of Windows file extensions, with a wildcard (*) character preceding each extension; and a semicolon-delimited list of Macintosh file types, with a wildcard (*) character preceding each type. The syntax for each element is as follows:

  ```
  [{description: "string describing the first set of file types",
  extension: "semicolon-delimited list of Windows file extensions",
  macType: "semicolon-delimited list of Macintosh file types"}]
  ```

  Example:

  ```
  [{description: "Image files", extension: "*.jpg;*.gif;*.png", macType:
  "JPEG;jp2_;GIFf;PNGf"}, {description: "Flash Movies", extension:
  "*.swf", macType: "SWFL"}]
  ```

The two formats are not interchangeable in a single browse() call. You must use one or the other.

The list of extensions is used to filter the files in Windows, depending on the file type the user selects. It is not actually displayed in the dialog box. To display the file types for users, you must list the file types in the description string as well as in the extension list. The description string is displayed in the dialog box in Windows. (It is not used on the Macintosh.) On the Macintosh, if you supply a list of Macintosh file types, that list is used to filter the files. If you don't supply a list of Macintosh file types the list of Windows extensions is used.

Returns

Boolean - Returns true if the parameters are valid and the file-browsing dialog box is displayed. Returns false if the dialog box is not displayed, if another browse session is already in progress, or if you use the typelist parameter but fail to provide a description or extension string in any element in the array.

Example

The following example demonstrates the browse() method.

```
import flash.net.FileReferenceList;

var allTypes:Array = new Array();
var imageTypes:Object = new Object();
imageTypes.description = "Images (*.JPG;*.JPEG;*.JPE;*.GIF;*.PNG;)";
imageTypes.extension = "*.jpg; *.jpeg; *.jpe; *.gif; *.png;";
allTypes.push(imageTypes);

var textTypes:Object = new Object();
textTypes.description = "Text Files (*.TXT;*.RTF;)";
```

```
textTypes.extension = "*.txt; *.rtf";
allTypes.push(textTypes);

var fileRef:FileReferenceList = new FileReferenceList();
fileRef.browse(allTypes);
```

See also

browse (FileReference.browse method), FileReference
(flash.net.FileReference)

fileList (FileReferenceList.fileList property)

public fileList : Array

An array of FileReference objects.

When the FileReferenceList.browse() method has been called and the user has selected one or more files from the dialog box opened by browse(), this property is populated with an array of FileReference objects, each of which represents a file the user selected. You can then use this array to upload the files with FileReference.upload(). You must upload one file at a time.

The fileList property is populated anew each time browse() is called on that FileReferenceList object.

The properties of FileReference objects are described in the FileReference class documentation.

Availability: ActionScript 1.0; Flash Player 8

Example

The following example demonstrates the fileList property.

```
import flash.net.FileReferenceList;
import flash.net.FileReference;

var listener:Object = new Object();
listener.onSelect = function(fileRefList:FileReferenceList) {
  trace("onSelect");
  var list:Array = fileRefList.fileList;
  var item:FileReference;
  for(var i:Number = 0; i < list.length; i++) {
    item = list[i];
    trace("name: " + item.name);
  }
}
```

```
var fileRef:FileReferenceList = new FileReferenceList();
fileRef.addListener(listener);
fileRef.browse();
```

See also

`FileReference (flash.net.FileReference)`, `upload (FileReference.upload method)`, `browse (FileReferenceList.browse method)`

FileReferenceList constructor

`public FileReferenceList()`

Creates a new FileReferenceList object. This object contains nothing until you call `browse()` on it. When you call `browse()` on the FileReference object, the `fileList` property of the object is populated with an array of FileReference objects.

Availability: ActionScript 1.0; Flash Player 8

Example

The following example creates a new `FileReferenceList` object, iterates over each selected file, and outputs their names.

```
import flash.net.FileReferenceList;

var listener:Object = new Object();
listener.onSelect = function(fileRefList:FileReferenceList) {
  trace("onSelect");
  var arr:Array = fileRefList.fileList;
  for(var i:Number = 0; i < arr.length; i++) {
    trace("name: " + arr[i].name);
  }
}

var fileRef:FileReferenceList = new FileReferenceList();
fileRef.addListener(listener);
fileRef.browse();
```

See also

`FileReference (flash.net.FileReference)`, `browse (FileReferenceList.browse method)`

onCancel (FileReferenceList.onCancel event listener)

```
onCancel = function(fileRefList:FileReferenceList) {}
```

Invoked when the user dismisses the file-browsing dialog box. (This dialog box is displayed when you call the `FileReferenceList.browse()`, `FileReference.browse()`, or `FileReference.download()` methods.)

Availability: ActionScript 1.0; Flash Player 8

Parameters

`fileRefList:flash.net.FileReferenceList` - The FileReferenceList object that initiated the operation.

Example

The following example demonstrates the `onCancel` listener.

```
import flash.net.FileReferenceList;

var listener:Object = new Object();
listener.onCancel = function(fileRefList:FileReferenceList) {
    trace("onCancel");
}

var fileRef:FileReferenceList = new FileReferenceList();
fileRef.addListener(listener);
fileRef.browse();
```

See also

`browse (FileReferenceList.browse method)`

onSelect (FileReferenceList.onSelect event listener)

```
onSelect = function(fileRefList:FileReferenceList) {}
```

Invoked when the user selects one or more files to upload from the file-browsing dialog box. (This dialog box is displayed when you call the `FileReferenceList.browse()`, `FileReference.browse()`, or `FileReference.download()` methods.) When the user selects a file and confirms the operation (for example, by clicking Save), the FileReferenceList object is populated with FileReference objects that represent the files selected by the user.

Availability: ActionScript 1.0; Flash Player 8

Parameters

`fileRefList:flash.net.FileReferenceList` - The FileReferenceList object that initiated the operation.

Example

The following example demonstrates the `onSelect` listener.

```
import flash.net.FileReferenceList;
import flash.net.FileReference;

var listener:Object = new Object();

listener.onSelect = function(fileRefList:FileReferenceList) {
  trace("onSelect");
  var list:Array = fileRefList.fileList;
  var item:FileReference;
  for(var i:Number = 0; i < list.length; i++) {
    item = list[i];
    trace("name: " + item.name);
    trace(item.addListener(this));
    item.upload("http://www.yourdomain.com/");
  }
}

listener.onComplete = function(file:FileReference):Void {
  trace("onComplete: " + file.name);
}

var fileRef:FileReferenceList = new FileReferenceList();
fileRef.addListener(listener);
fileRef.browse();
```

See also

`browse (FileReferenceList.browse method)`

removeListener (FileReferenceList.removeListener method)

`public removeListener(listener:Object) : Boolean`

Removes an object from the list of objects that receive event notification messages.

Availability: ActionScript 1.0; Flash Player 8

Parameters

`listener:Object` - An object that listens for a callback notification from the FileReferenceList event listeners.

Returns

`Boolean` - Returns `true` if the object is removed. Otherwise, this method returns `false`.

Example

The following example demonstrates the `removeListener` method.

```
import flash.net.FileReferenceList;

var listener:Object = new Object();
listener.onCancel = function(fileRefList:FileReferenceList) {
  trace("onCancel");
  trace(fileRefList.removeListener(this)); // true
}

listener.onSelect = function(fileRefList:FileReferenceList) {
  trace("onSelect: " + fileRefList.fileList.length);
}

var fileRef:FileReferenceList = new FileReferenceList();
fileRef.addListener(listener);
fileRef.browse();
```

Function

```
Object
  |
  +-Function
```

```
public dynamic class Function
extends Object
```

Both user-defined and built-in functions in ActionScript are represented by Function objects, which are instances of the Function class.

Availability: ActionScript 1.0; Flash Player 6

Property summary

Method summary

Modifiers	Signature	Description
	`apply(thisObject:Obj ect, [argArray:Array]) : Void`	Specifies the value of `thisObject` to be used within any function that ActionScript calls.
	`call(thisObject:Obje ct, [parameter1:Object]) : Object`	Invokes the function represented by a Function object.

apply (Function.apply method)

`public apply(thisObject:Object, [argArray:Array]) : Void`

Specifies the value of `thisObject` to be used within any function that ActionScript calls. This method also specifies the parameters to be passed to any called function. Because `apply()` is a method of the Function class, it is also a method of every Function object in ActionScript.

The parameters are specified as an Array object, unlike `Function.call()`, which specifies parameters as a comma-delimited list. This is often useful when the number of parameters to be passed is not known until the script actually executes.

Returns the value that the called function specifies as the return value.

Availability: ActionScript 1.0; Flash Player 6

Parameters

`thisObject:Object` - The object to which myFunction is applied.

argArray:Array [optional] - An array whose elements are passed to myFunction as parameters.

Example

The following function invocations are equivalent:

```
Math.atan2(1, 0)
Math.atan2.apply(null, [1, 0])
```

The following simple example shows how apply() passes an array of parameters:

```
function theFunction() {
  trace(arguments);
}

// create a new array to pass as a parameter to apply()
var firstArray:Array = new Array(1,2,3);
theFunction.apply(null,firstArray);
// outputs: 1,2,3

// create a second array to pass as a parameter to apply()
var secondArray:Array = new Array("a", "b", "c");
theFunction.apply(null,secondArray);
// outputs a,b,c
```

The following example shows how apply() passes an array of parameters and specifies the value of this:

```
// define a function
function theFunction() {
  trace("this == myObj? " + (this == myObj));
  trace("arguments: " + arguments);
}

// instantiate an object
var myObj:Object = new Object();

// create arrays to pass as a parameter to apply()
var firstArray:Array = new Array(1,2,3);
var secondArray:Array = new Array("a", "b", "c");

// use apply() to set the value of this to be myObj and send firstArray
theFunction.apply(myObj,firstArray);
// output:
// this == myObj? true
// arguments: 1,2,3

// use apply() to set the value of this to be myObj and send secondArray
theFunction.apply(myObj,secondArray);
// output:
// this == myObj? true
```

```
// arguments: a,b,c
```

See also

```
call (Function.call method)
```

call (Function.call method)

```
public call(thisObject:Object, [parameter1:Object]) : Object
```

Invokes the function represented by a Function object. Every function in ActionScript is represented by a Function object, so all functions support this method.

In almost all cases, the function call (( )) operator can be used instead of this method. The function call operator produces code that is concise and readable. This method is primarily useful when the thisObject parameter of the function invocation needs to be explicitly controlled. Normally, if a function is invoked as a method of an object, within the body of the function, thisObject is set to myObject, as shown in the following example:

```
myObject.myMethod(1, 2, 3);
```

In some situations, you might want thisObject to point somewhere else; for example, if a function must be invoked as a method of an object, but is not actually stored as a method of that object:

```
myObject.myMethod.call(myOtherObject, 1, 2, 3);
```

You can pass the value null for the thisObject parameter to invoke a function as a regular function and not as a method of an object. For example, the following function invocations are equivalent:

```
Math.sin(Math.PI / 4)
Math.sin.call(null, Math.PI / 4)
```

Returns the value that the called function specifies as the return value.

Availability: ActionScript 1.0; Flash Player 6

Parameters

thisObject:Object - An object that specifies the value of thisObject within the function body.

parameter1:Object [optional] - A parameter to be passed to the myFunction. You can specify zero or more parameters.

Returns

Object -

Example

The following example uses `Function.call()` to make a function behave as a method of another object, without storing the function in the object:

```
function myObject() {
}
function myMethod(obj) {
  trace("this == obj? " + (this == obj));
}
var obj:Object = new myObject();
myMethod.call(obj, obj);
```

The `trace()` statement displays:

```
this == obj? true
```

See also

`apply (Function.apply method)`

GlowFilter (flash.filters.GlowFilter)

```
Object
  |
  +-flash.filters.BitmapFilter
     |
     +-flash.filters.GlowFilter
```

```
public class GlowFilter
extends BitmapFilter
```

The GlowFilter class lets you apply a glow effect to various objects in Flash. You have several options for the style of the glow, including inner or outer glow and knockout mode. The glow filter is similar to the drop shadow filter with the `distance` and `angle` properties of the drop shadow set to 0.

The use of filters depends on the object to which you apply the filter:

- To apply filters to movie clips, text fields, and buttons at runtime, use the `filters` property. Setting the `filters` property of an object does not modify the object and can be undone by clearing the `filters` property.

- To apply filters to BitmapData instances, use the `BitmapData.applyFilter()` method. Calling `applyFilter()` on a BitmapData object takes the source BitmapData object and the filter object and generates a filtered image as a result.

You can also apply filter effects to images and video during authoring. For more information, see your authoring documentation.

If you apply a filter to a movie clip or button, the `cacheAsBitmap` property of the movie clip or button is set to `true`. If you clear all filters, the original value of `cacheAsBitmap` is restored.

This filter supports Stage scaling. However, it does not support general scaling, rotation, and skewing; if the object itself is scaled (if `_xscale` and `_yscale` are not 100%), the filter effect is not scaled. It is scaled only when the Stage is zoomed.

A filter is not applied if the resulting image exceeds 2880 pixels in width or height. For example, if you zoom in on a large movie clip with a filter applied, the filter is turned off if the resulting image exceeds the limit of 2880 pixels.

Availability: ActionScript 1.0; Flash Player 8

See also

```
applyFilter (BitmapData.applyFilter method), cacheAsBitmap
(Button.cacheAsBitmap property), filters (Button.filters property),
DropShadowFilter (flash.filters.DropShadowFilter), cacheAsBitmap
(MovieClip.cacheAsBitmap property), filters (MovieClip.filters property),
filters (TextField.filters property)
```

Property summary

Modifiers	Property	Description
	`alpha:Number`	The alpha transparency value for the color.
	`blurX:Number`	The amount of horizontal blur.
	`blurY:Number`	The amount of vertical blur.
	`color:Number`	The color of the glow.
	`inner:Boolean`	Specifies whether the glow is an inner glow.
	`knockout:Boolean`	Specifies whether the object has a knockout effect.
	`quality:Number`	The number of times to apply the filter.
	`strength:Number`	The strength of the imprint or spread.

Properties inherited from class Object

```
constructor (Object.constructor property), __proto__ (Object.__proto__
property), prototype (Object.prototype property), __resolve
(Object.__resolve property)
```

Constructor summary

Signature	Description
`GlowFilter([color:Number], [alpha:Number], [blurX:Number], [blurY:Number], [strength:Number], [quality:Number], [inner:Boolean], [knockout:Boolean])`	Initializes a new GlowFilter instance with the specified parameters.

Method summary

Modifiers	Signature	Description
	`clone() : GlowFilter`	Returns a copy of this filter object.

Methods inherited from class BitmapFilter

```
clone (BitmapFilter.clone method)
```

Methods inherited from class Object

```
addProperty (Object.addProperty method),hasOwnProperty
(Object.hasOwnProperty method),isPropertyEnumerable
(Object.isPropertyEnumerable method),isPrototypeOf (Object.isPrototypeOf
method),registerClass (Object.registerClass method),toString
(Object.toString method),unwatch (Object.unwatch method),valueOf
(Object.valueOf method),watch (Object.watch method)
```

alpha (GlowFilter.alpha property)

`public alpha : Number`

The alpha transparency value for the color. Valid values are 0 to 1. For example, .25 sets a transparency value of 25%. The default value is 1.

Availability: ActionScript 1.0; Flash Player 8

Example

The following example changes the `alpha` property on an existing movie clip when a user clicks it.

```
import flash.filters.GlowFilter;
```

```
var mc:MovieClip = createGlowFilterRectangle("GlowFilterAlpha");
mc.onRelease = function() {
  var filter:GlowFilter = this.filters[0];
  filter.alpha = .4;
  this.filters = new Array(filter);
}

function createGlowFilterRectangle(name:String):MovieClip {
  var rect:MovieClip = this.createEmptyMovieClip(name,
  this.getNextHighestDepth());
  var w:Number = 100;
  var h:Number = 100;
  rect.beginFill(0x003366);
  rect.lineTo(w, 0);
  rect.lineTo(w, h);
  rect.lineTo(0, h);
  rect.lineTo(0, 0);
  rect._x = 20;
  rect._y = 20;

  var filter:GlowFilter = new GlowFilter(0x000000, .8, 16, 16, 1, 3, false,
  false);
  var filterArray:Array = new Array();
  filterArray.push(filter);
  rect.filters = filterArray;
  return rect;
}
```

blurX (GlowFilter.blurX property)

```
public blurX : Number
```

The amount of horizontal blur. Valid values are 0 to 255 (floating point). The default value is 6. Values that are a power of 2 (such as 2, 4, 8, 16 and 32) are optimized to render more quickly than other values.

Availability: ActionScript 1.0; Flash Player 8

Example

The following example changes the blurX property on an existing movie clip when a user clicks it.

```
import flash.filters.GlowFilter;

var mc:MovieClip = createGlowFilterRectangle("GlowFilterBlurX");
mc.onRelease = function() {
  var filter:GlowFilter = this.filters[0];
  filter.blurX = 20;
  this.filters = new Array(filter);
```

```
}
function createGlowFilterRectangle(name:String):MovieClip {
  var rect:MovieClip = this.createEmptyMovieClip(name,
  this.getNextHighestDepth());
  var w:Number = 100;
  var h:Number = 100;
  rect.beginFill(0x003366);
  rect.lineTo(w, 0);
  rect.lineTo(w, h);
  rect.lineTo(0, h);
  rect.lineTo(0, 0);
  rect._x = 20;
  rect._y = 20;

  var filter:GlowFilter = new GlowFilter(0x000000, .8, 16, 16, 1, 3, false,
  false);
  var filterArray:Array = new Array();
  filterArray.push(filter);
  rect.filters = filterArray;
  return rect;
}
```

blurY (GlowFilter.blurY property)

```
public blurY : Number
```

The amount of vertical blur. Valid values are 0 to 255 (floating point). The default value is 6. Values that are a power of 2 (such as 2, 4, 8, 16 and 32) are optimized to render more quickly than other values.

Availability: ActionScript 1.0; Flash Player 8

Example

The following example changes the `blurY` property on an existing movie clip when a user clicks it.

```
import flash.filters.GlowFilter;

var mc:MovieClip = createGlowFilterRectangle("GlowFilterBlurY");
mc.onRelease = function() {
  var filter:GlowFilter = this.filters[0];
  filter.blurY = 20;
  this.filters = new Array(filter);
}

function createGlowFilterRectangle(name:String):MovieClip {
  var rect:MovieClip = this.createEmptyMovieClip(name,
  this.getNextHighestDepth());
```

```
var w:Number = 100;
var h:Number = 100;
rect.beginFill(0x003366);
rect.lineTo(w, 0);
rect.lineTo(w, h);
rect.lineTo(0, h);
rect.lineTo(0, 0);
rect._x = 20;
rect._y = 20;

var filter:GlowFilter = new GlowFilter(0x000000, .8, 16, 16, 1, 3, false,
    false);
var filterArray:Array = new Array();
filterArray.push(filter);
rect.filters = filterArray;
return rect;
}
```

clone (GlowFilter.clone method)

```
public clone() : GlowFilter
```

Returns a copy of this filter object.

Availability: ActionScript 1.0; Flash Player 8

Returns

`flash.filters.GlowFilter` - A new GlowFilter instance with all of the properties of the original GlowFilter instance.

Example

The following example creates three GlowFilter objects and compares them: `filter_1` is created by using the GlowFilter constructor; `filter_2` is created by setting it equal to `filter_1`; and `clonedFilter` is created by cloning `filter_1`. Notice that although `filter_2` evaluates as being equal to `filter_1`, `clonedFilter`, even though it contains the same values as `filter_1`, does not.

```
import flash.filters.GlowFilter;

var filter_1:GlowFilter = new GlowFilter(0x33CCFF, .8, 35, 35, 2, 3, false,
    false);
var filter_2:GlowFilter = filter_1;
var clonedFilter:GlowFilter = filter_1.clone();

trace(filter_1 == filter_2); // true
trace(filter_1 == clonedFilter); // false
```

```
for(var i in filter_1) {
  trace(">> " + i + ": " + filter_1[i]);
  // >> clone: [type Function]
  // >> strength: 2
  // >> blurY: 35
  // >> blurX: 35
  // >> knockout: false
  // >> inner: false
  // >> quality: 3
  // >> alpha: 0.8
  // >> color: 3394815
}

for(var i in clonedFilter) {
  trace(">> " + i + ": " + clonedFilter[i]);
  // >> clone: [type Function]
  // >> strength: 2
  // >> blurY: 35
  // >> blurX: 35
  // >> knockout: false
  // >> inner: false
  // >> quality: 3
  // >> alpha: 0.8
  // >> color: 3394815
}
```

To further demonstrate the relationships between filter_1, filter_2, and clonedFilter, the following example modifies the knockout property of filter_1. Modifying knockout demonstrates that the clone() method creates a new instance based on the values of filter_1 instead of pointing to them in reference.

```
import flash.filters.GlowFilter;

var filter_1:GlowFilter = new GlowFilter(0x33CCFF, .8, 35, 35, 2, 3, false,
  false);
var filter_2:GlowFilter = filter_1;
var clonedFilter:GlowFilter = filter_1.clone();

trace(filter_1.knockout); // false
trace(filter_2.knockout); // false
trace(clonedFilter.knockout); // false

filter_1.knockout = true;

trace(filter_1.knockout); // true
trace(filter_2.knockout); // true
trace(clonedFilter.knockout); // false
```

color (GlowFilter.color property)

```
public color : Number
```

The color of the glow. Valid values are in the hexadecimal format 0x*RRGGBB*. The default value is 0xFF0000.

Availability: ActionScript 1.0; Flash Player 8

Example

The following example changes the `color` property on an existing movie clip when a user clicks it.

```
import flash.filters.GlowFilter;

var mc:MovieClip = createGlowFilterRectangle("GlowFilterColor");
mc.onRelease = function() {
  var filter:GlowFilter = this.filters[0];
  filter.color = 0x00FF33;
  this.filters = new Array(filter);
}

function createGlowFilterRectangle(name:String):MovieClip {
  var rect:MovieClip = this.createEmptyMovieClip(name,
  this.getNextHighestDepth());
  var w:Number = 100;
  var h:Number = 100;
  rect.beginFill(0x003366);
  rect.lineTo(w, 0);
  rect.lineTo(w, h);
  rect.lineTo(0, h);
  rect.lineTo(0, 0);
  rect._x = 20;
  rect._y = 20;

  var filter:GlowFilter = new GlowFilter(0x000000, .8, 16, 16, 1, 3, false,
  false);
  var filterArray:Array = new Array();
  filterArray.push(filter);
  rect.filters = filterArray;
  return rect;
}
```

GlowFilter constructor

```
public GlowFilter([color:Number], [alpha:Number], [blurX:Number],
  [blurY:Number], [strength:Number], [quality:Number], [inner:Boolean],
  [knockout:Boolean])
```

Initializes a new GlowFilter instance with the specified parameters.

Availability: ActionScript 1.0; Flash Player 8

Parameters

`color:Number` [optional] - The color of the glow, in the hexadecimal format 0x*RRGGBB*. The default value is 0xFF0000.

`alpha:Number` [optional] - The alpha transparency value for the color. Valid values are 0 to 1. For example, .25 sets a transparency value of 25%. The default value is 1.

`blurX:Number` [optional] - The amount of horizontal blur. Valid values are 0 to 255 (floating point). The default value is 6. Values that are a power of 2 (such as 2, 4, 8, 16 and 32) are optimized to render more quickly than other values.

`blurY:Number` [optional] - The amount of vertical blur. Valid values are 0 to 255 (floating point). The default value is 6. Values that are a power of 2 (such as 2, 4, 8, 16 and 32) are optimized to render more quickly than other values.

`strength:Number` [optional] - The strength of the imprint or spread. The higher the value, the more color is imprinted and the stronger the contrast between the glow and the background. Valid values are 0 to 255. The default is 2.

`quality:Number` [optional] - The number of times to apply the filter. Valid values are 0 to 15. The default value is 1, which is equivalent to low quality. A value of 2 is medium quality, and a value of 3 is high quality.

`inner:Boolean` [optional] - Specifies whether the glow is an inner glow. The value `true` indicates an inner glow. The default is `false`, an outer glow (a glow around the outer edges of the object).

`knockout:Boolean` [optional] - Specifies whether the object has a knockout effect. The value `true` makes the object's fill transparent and reveals the background color of the document. The default is `false` (no knockout effect).

Example

The following example instantiates a new GlowFilter instance and applies it to a flat, rectangular shape.

```
import flash.filters.GlowFilter;

var rect:MovieClip = createRectangle(100, 100, 0x003366,
  "gradientGlowFilterExample");

var color:Number = 0x33CCFF;
var alpha:Number = .8;
var blurX:Number = 35;
var blurY:Number = 35;
var strength:Number = 2;
```

```
var quality:Number = 3;
var inner:Boolean = false;
var knockout:Boolean = false;

var filter:GlowFilter = new GlowFilter(color,
                            alpha,
                            blurX,
                            blurY,
                            strength,
                            quality,
                            inner,
                            knockout);
var filterArray:Array = new Array();
filterArray.push(filter);
rect.filters = filterArray;

function createRectangle(w:Number, h:Number, bgColor:Number,
    name:String):MovieClip {
    var mc:MovieClip = this.createEmptyMovieClip(name,
    this.getNextHighestDepth());
    mc.beginFill(bgColor);
    mc.lineTo(w, 0);
    mc.lineTo(w, h);
    mc.lineTo(0, h);
    mc.lineTo(0, 0);
    mc._x = 20;
    mc._y = 20;
    return mc;
}
```

inner (GlowFilter.inner property)

```
public inner : Boolean
```

Specifies whether the glow is an inner glow. The value `true` indicates an inner glow. The default is `false`, an outer glow (a glow around the outer edges of the object).

Availability: ActionScript 1.0; Flash Player 8

Example

The following example changes the `inner` property on an existing movie clip when a user clicks it.

```
import flash.filters.GlowFilter;

var mc:MovieClip = createGlowFilterRectangle("GlowFilterInner");
mc.onRelease = function() {
    var filter:GlowFilter = this.filters[0];
    filter.inner = true;
```

```
  this.filters = new Array(filter);
}

function createGlowFilterRectangle(name:String):MovieClip {
  var rect:MovieClip = this.createEmptyMovieClip(name,
  this.getNextHighestDepth());
  var w:Number = 100;
  var h:Number = 100;
  rect.beginFill(0x003366);
  rect.lineTo(w, 0);
  rect.lineTo(w, h);
  rect.lineTo(0, h);
  rect.lineTo(0, 0);
  rect._x = 20;
  rect._y = 20;

  var filter:GlowFilter = new GlowFilter(0x000000, .8, 16, 16, 1, 3, false,
  false);
  var filterArray:Array = new Array();
  filterArray.push(filter);
  rect.filters = filterArray;
  return rect;
}
```

knockout (GlowFilter.knockout property)

```
public knockout : Boolean
```

Specifies whether the object has a knockout effect. A value of `true` makes the object's fill transparent and reveals the background color of the document. The default is `false` (no knockout effect).

Availability: ActionScript 1.0; Flash Player 8

Example

The following example changes the `knockout` property on an existing movie clip when a user clicks it.

```
import flash.filters.GlowFilter;

var mc:MovieClip = createGlowFilterRectangle("GlowFilterKnockout");
mc.onRelease = function() {
  var filter:GlowFilter = this.filters[0];
  filter.knockout = true;
  this.filters = new Array(filter);
}
```

```
function createGlowFilterRectangle(name:String):MovieClip {
  var rect:MovieClip = this.createEmptyMovieClip(name,
  this.getNextHighestDepth());
  var w:Number = 100;
  var h:Number = 100;
  rect.beginFill(0x003366);
  rect.lineTo(w, 0);
  rect.lineTo(w, h);
  rect.lineTo(0, h);
  rect.lineTo(0, 0);
  rect._x = 20;
  rect._y = 20;

  var filter:GlowFilter = new GlowFilter(0x000000, .8, 16, 16, 1, 3, false,
  false);
  var filterArray:Array = new Array();
  filterArray.push(filter);
  rect.filters = filterArray;
  return rect;
}
```

quality (GlowFilter.quality property)

```
public quality : Number
```

The number of times to apply the filter. Valid values are 0 to 15. The default value is 1, which is equivalent to low quality. A value of 2 is medium quality, and a value of 3 is high quality. Filters with lower values are rendered more quickly.

For most applications, a `quality` value of 1, 2, or 3 is sufficient. Although you can use additional numeric values up to 15 to achieve different effects, higher values are rendered more slowly. Instead of increasing the value of `quality`, you can often get a similar effect, and with faster rendering, by simply increasing the values of `blurX` and `blurY`.

Availability: ActionScript 1.0; Flash Player 8

Example

The following example changes the `quality` property on an existing movie clip when a user clicks it.

```
import flash.filters.GlowFilter;

var mc:MovieClip = createGlowFilterRectangle("GlowFilterQuality");
mc.onRelease = function() {
  var filter:GlowFilter = this.filters[0];
  filter.quality = 1;
  this.filters = new Array(filter);
```

```
}
function createGlowFilterRectangle(name:String):MovieClip {
  var rect:MovieClip = this.createEmptyMovieClip(name,
  this.getNextHighestDepth());
  var w:Number = 100;
  var h:Number = 100;
  rect.beginFill(0x003366);
  rect.lineTo(w, 0);
  rect.lineTo(w, h);
  rect.lineTo(0, h);
  rect.lineTo(0, 0);
  rect._x = 20;
  rect._y = 20;

  var filter:GlowFilter = new GlowFilter(0x000000, .8, 16, 16, 1, 3, false,
  false);
  var filterArray:Array = new Array();
  filterArray.push(filter);
  rect.filters = filterArray;
  return rect;
}
```

strength (GlowFilter.strength property)

```
public strength : Number
```

The strength of the imprint or spread. The higher the value, the more color is imprinted and the stronger the contrast between the glow and the background. Valid values are 0 to 255. The default is 2.

Availability: ActionScript 1.0; Flash Player 8

Example

The following example changes the `strength` property on an existing movie clip when a user clicks it.

```
import flash.filters.GlowFilter;

var mc:MovieClip = createGlowFilterRectangle("GlowFilterStrength");
mc.onRelease = function() {
  var filter:GlowFilter = this.filters[0];
  filter.strength = .8;
  this.filters = new Array(filter);
}

function createGlowFilterRectangle(name:String):MovieClip {
  var rect:MovieClip = this.createEmptyMovieClip(name,
  this.getNextHighestDepth());
```

```
var w:Number = 100;
var h:Number = 100;
rect.beginFill(0x003366);
rect.lineTo(w, 0);
rect.lineTo(w, h);
rect.lineTo(0, h);
rect.lineTo(0, 0);
rect._x = 20;
rect._y = 20;

var filter:GlowFilter = new GlowFilter(0x000000, .8, 16, 16, 1, 3, false,
false);
var filterArray:Array = new Array();
filterArray.push(filter);
rect.filters = filterArray;
return rect;
}
```

GradientBevelFilter (flash.filters.GradientBevelFilter)

```
Object
  |
  +-flash.filters.BitmapFilter
    |
    +-flash.filters.GradientBevelFilter
```

public class **GradientBevelFilter**
extends BitmapFilter

The GradientBevelFilter class lets you apply a gradient bevel effect to various objects in Flash. A gradient bevel is a beveled edge, enhanced with gradient color, on the outside, inside, or top of an object. Beveled edges make objects look three-dimensional.

The use of filters depends on the object to which you apply the filter:

- To apply filters to movie clips, text fields, and buttons at runtime, use the filters property. Setting the filters property of an object does not modify the object, and you can undo the filter by clearing the filters property.

- To apply filters to BitmapData instances, use the BitmapData.applyFilter() method. Calling applyFilter() on a BitmapData object takes the source BitmapData object and the filter object and generates a filtered image as a result.

You can also apply filter effects to images and video during authoring. For more information, see your authoring documentation.

If you apply a filter to a movie clip or button, the cacheAsBitmap property of the movie clip or button is set to true. If you clear all filters, the original value of cacheAsBitmap is restored.

This filter supports Stage scaling. However, it does not support general scaling, rotation, and skewing; if the object itself is scaled (if _xscale and _yscale are not 100%), the filter effect is not scaled. It is scaled only when the Stage is zoomed.

A filter is not applied if the resulting image exceeds 2880 pixels in width or height. For example, if you zoom in on a large movie clip with a filter applied, the filter is turned off if the resulting image exceeds the limit of 2880 pixels.

Availability: ActionScript 1.0; Flash Player 8

See also

ratios (GradientBevelFilter.ratios property), applyFilter (BitmapData.applyFilter method), BevelFilter (flash.filters.BevelFilter), filters (Button.filters property), cacheAsBitmap (Button.cacheAsBitmap property), cacheAsBitmap (MovieClip.cacheAsBitmap property), filters (MovieClip.filters property), filters (TextField.filters property)

Property summary

Modifiers	Property	Description
	alphas:Array	An array of alpha transparency values for the corresponding colors in the colors array.
	angle:Number	The angle, in degrees.
	blurX:Number	The amount of horizontal blur.
	blurY:Number	The amount of vertical blur.
	colors:Array	An array of RGB hexadecimal color values to use in the gradient.
	distance:Number	The offset distance.
	knockout:Boolean	Specifies whether the object has a knockout effect.
	quality:Number	The number of times to apply the filter.
	ratios:Array	An array of color distribution ratios for the corresponding colors in the colors array.
	strength:Number	The strength of the imprint or spread.
	type:String	The placement of the bevel effect.

Properties inherited from class Object

```
constructor (Object.constructor property),__proto__ (Object.__proto__
property),prototype (Object.prototype property),__resolve
(Object.__resolve property)
```

Constructor summary

Signature	Description
GradientBevelFilter([distance:Number], [angle:Number], [colors:Array], [alphas:Array], [ratios:Array], [blurX:Number], [blurY:Number], [strength:Number], [quality:Number], [type:String], [knockout:Boolean])	Initializes the filter with the specified parameters.

Method summary

Modifiers	Signature	Description
	`clone() : GradientBevelFilter`	Returns a copy of this filter object.

Methods inherited from class BitmapFilter

```
clone (BitmapFilter.clone method)
```

Methods inherited from class Object

```
addProperty (Object.addProperty method), hasOwnProperty
(Object.hasOwnProperty method), isPropertyEnumerable
(Object.isPropertyEnumerable method), isPrototypeOf (Object.isPrototypeOf
method), registerClass (Object.registerClass method), toString
(Object.toString method), unwatch (Object.unwatch method), valueOf
(Object.valueOf method), watch (Object.watch method)
```

alphas (GradientBevelFilter.alphas property)

`public alphas : Array`

An array of alpha transparency values for the corresponding colors in the `colors` array. Valid values for each element in the array are 0 to 1. For example, .25 sets a transparency value of 25%.

The `alphas` property cannot be changed by directly modifying its values. Instead, you must get a reference to `alphas`, make the change to the reference, and then set `alphas` to the reference.

The `colors`, `alphas`, and `ratios` properties are all related. The first element in the `colors` array corresponds to the first element in the `alphas` array and in the `ratios` array, and so on.

Availability: ActionScript 1.0; Flash Player 8

Example

The following example demonstrates how to set the `alphas` property on an existing entity.

```
import flash.filters.GradientBevelFilter;

var mc:MovieClip = setUpFilter("alphasExample");
mc.onPress = function() {
    var arr:Array = this.filters;
    var alphas:Array = [.2, 0, .2];
    arr[0].alphas = alphas;
    this.filters = arr;
```

```
    }
mc.onRelease = function() {
    var arr:Array = this.filters;
    var alphas:Array = [1, 0, 1];
    arr[0].alphas = alphas;
    this.filters = arr;
}

function setUpFilter(name:String):MovieClip {
    var art:MovieClip = this.createEmptyMovieClip(name,
    this.getNextHighestDepth());
    var w:Number = 150;
    var h:Number = 150;
    art.beginFill(0xCCCCCC);
    art.lineTo(w, 0);
    art.lineTo(w, h);
    art.lineTo(0, h);
    art.lineTo(0, 0);

    var colors:Array = [0xFFFFFF, 0xCCCCCC, 0x000000];
    var alphas:Array = [1, 0, 1];
    var ratios:Array = [0, 128, 255];
    var filter:GradientBevelFilter = new GradientBevelFilter(5, 225, colors,
    alphas, ratios, 5, 5, 5, 2, "inner", false);

    art.filters = new Array(filter);
    return art;
}
```

See also

```
colors (GradientBevelFilter.colors property), ratios
(GradientBevelFilter.ratios property)
```

angle (GradientBevelFilter.angle property)

```
public angle : Number
```

The angle, in degrees. Valid values are 0 to 360. The default is 45.

The angle value represents the angle of the theoretical light source falling on the object. The value determines the angle at which the gradient colors are applied to the object: where the highlight and the shadow appear, or where the first color in the array appears. The colors are then applied in the order in which they appear in the array.

Availability: ActionScript 1.0; Flash Player 8

Example

The following example demonstrates how to set the `angle` property on an existing object.

```
import flash.filters.GradientBevelFilter;

var mc:MovieClip = setUpFilter("angleExample");
mc.onRelease = function() {
  var arr:Array = this.filters;
  arr[0].angle = 45;
  this.filters = arr;
}

function setUpFilter(name:String):MovieClip {
  var art:MovieClip = this.createEmptyMovieClip(name,
  this.getNextHighestDepth());
  var w:Number = 150;
  var h:Number = 150;
  art.beginFill(0xCCCCCC);
  art.lineTo(w, 0);
  art.lineTo(w, h);
  art.lineTo(0, h);
  art.lineTo(0, 0);

  var colors:Array = [0xFFFFFF, 0xCCCCCC, 0x000000];
  var alphas:Array = [1, 0, 1];
  var ratios:Array = [0, 128, 255];
  var filter:GradientBevelFilter = new GradientBevelFilter(5, 225, colors,
  alphas, ratios, 5, 5, 5, 3, "inner", false);

  art.filters = new Array(filter);
  return art;
}
```

See also

```
ratios (GradientBevelFilter.ratios property)
```

blurX (GradientBevelFilter.blurX property)

```
public blurX : Number
```

The amount of horizontal blur. Valid values are 0 to 255. A blur of 1 or less means that the original image is copied as is. The default value is 4. Values that are a power of 2 (such as 2, 4, 8, 16 and 32) are optimized to render more quickly than other values.

Availability: ActionScript 1.0; Flash Player 8

Example

The following example demonstrates how to set the blurX property on an existing object.

```
import flash.filters.GradientBevelFilter;

var mc:MovieClip = setUpFilter("blurXExample");
```

```
mc.onRelease = function() {
  var arr:Array = this.filters;
  arr[0].blurX = 16;
  this.filters = arr;
}

function setUpFilter(name:String):MovieClip {
  var art:MovieClip = this.createEmptyMovieClip(name,
  this.getNextHighestDepth());
  var w:Number = 150;
  var h:Number = 150;
  art.beginFill(0xCCCCCC);
  art.lineTo(w, 0);
  art.lineTo(w, h);
  art.lineTo(0, h);
  art.lineTo(0, 0);

  var colors:Array = [0xFFFFFF, 0xCCCCCC, 0x000000];
  var alphas:Array = [1, 0, 1];
  var ratios:Array = [0, 128, 255];
  var filter:GradientBevelFilter = new GradientBevelFilter(5, 225, colors,
  alphas, ratios, 5, 5, 5, 3, "inner", false);

  art.filters = new Array(filter);
  return art;
}
```

blurY (GradientBevelFilter.blurY property)

```
public blurY : Number
```

The amount of vertical blur. Valid values are 0 to 255. A blur of 1 or less means that the original image is copied as is. The default value is 4. Values that are a power of 2 (such as 2, 4, 8, 16 and 32) are optimized to render more quickly than other values.

Availability: ActionScript 1.0; Flash Player 8

Example

The following example demonstrates how to set the blurY property on an existing object.

```
import flash.filters.GradientBevelFilter;

var mc:MovieClip = setUpFilter("blurYExample");
mc.onRelease = function() {
  var arr:Array = this.filters;
  arr[0].blurY = 16;
  this.filters = arr;
}
```

```
function setUpFilter(name:String):MovieClip {
  var art:MovieClip = this.createEmptyMovieClip(name,
  this.getNextHighestDepth());
  var w:Number = 150;
  var h:Number = 150;
  art.beginFill(0xCCCCCC);
  art.lineTo(w, 0);
  art.lineTo(w, h);
  art.lineTo(0, h);
  art.lineTo(0, 0);

  var colors:Array = [0xFFFFFF, 0xCCCCCC, 0x000000];
  var alphas:Array = [1, 0, 1];
  var ratios:Array = [0, 128, 255];
  var filter:GradientBevelFilter = new GradientBevelFilter(5, 225, colors,
  alphas, ratios, 5, 5, 5, 3, "inner", false);

  art.filters = new Array(filter);
  return art;
}
```

clone (GradientBevelFilter.clone method)

```
public clone() : GradientBevelFilter
```

Returns a copy of this filter object.

Availability: ActionScript 1.0; Flash Player 8

Returns

`flash.filters.GradientBevelFilter` - A new GradientBevelFilter instance with all the same properties as the original GradientBevelFilter instance.

Example

The following example creates two rectangle shapes. The first, `sourceClip` has a bevel effect. The second, `resultClip` has no effect until it is clicked.

```
import flash.filters.GradientBevelFilter;

var sourceClip:MovieClip = setUpFlatRectangle(150, 150, 0xCCCCCC,
  "cloneSourceClip");
var resultClip:MovieClip = setUpFlatRectangle(150, 150, 0xCCCCCC,
  "cloneResultClip");

resultClip.source = sourceClip;

var sourceFilter:GradientBevelFilter = getNewFilter();
sourceClip.filters = new Array(sourceFilter);
```

```
resultClip._x = 180;
resultClip.onRelease = function() {
  this.filters = new Array(this.source.filters[0].clone());
}

function setUpFlatRectangle(w:Number, h:Number, bgColor:Number,
  name:String):MovieClip {
  var mc:MovieClip = this.createEmptyMovieClip(name,
  this.getNextHighestDepth());
  mc.beginFill(bgColor);
  mc.lineTo(w, 0);
  mc.lineTo(w, h);
  mc.lineTo(0, h);
  mc.lineTo(0, 0);
  return mc;
}

function getNewFilter():GradientBevelFilter {
  var colors:Array = [0xFFFFFF, 0xCCCCCC, 0x000000];
  var alphas:Array = [1, 0, 1];
  var ratios:Array = [0, 128, 255];
  return new GradientBevelFilter(5, 225, colors, alphas, ratios, 5, 5, 5,
  2, "inner", false);
}
```

colors (GradientBevelFilter.colors property)

`public colors : Array`

An array of RGB hexadecimal color values to use in the gradient. For example, red is 0xFF0000, blue is 0x0000FF, and so on.

The `colors` property cannot be changed by directly modifying its values. Instead, you must get a reference to `colors`, make the change to the reference, and then set `colors` to the reference.

The `colors`, `alphas`, and `ratios` properties are all related. The first element in the `colors` array corresponds to the first element in the `alphas` array and in the `ratios` array, and so on.

Availability: ActionScript 1.0; Flash Player 8

Example

The following example demonstrates how to set the `colors` property on an existing entity.

```
import flash.filters.GradientBevelFilter;

var mc:MovieClip = setUpFilter("colorsExample");
```

```
mc.onPress = function() {
  var arr:Array = this.filters;
  var colors:Array = [0x000000, 0xCCCCCC, 0xFFFFFF];
  arr[0].colors = colors;
  this.filters = arr;
}
mc.onRelease = function() {
  var arr:Array = this.filters;
  var colors:Array = [0xFFFFFF, 0xCCCCCC, 0x000000];
  arr[0].colors = colors;
  this.filters = arr;
}

function setUpFilter(name:String):MovieClip {
  var art:MovieClip = this.createEmptyMovieClip(name,
  this.getNextHighestDepth());
  var w:Number = 150;
  var h:Number = 150;
  art.beginFill(0xCCCCCC);
  art.lineTo(w, 0);
  art.lineTo(w, h);
  art.lineTo(0, h);
  art.lineTo(0, 0);

  var colors:Array = [0xFFFFFF, 0xCCCCCC, 0x000000];
  var alphas:Array = [1, 0, 1];
  var ratios:Array = [0, 128, 255];
  var filter:GradientBevelFilter = new GradientBevelFilter(5, 225, colors,
  alphas, ratios, 5, 5, 5, 2, "inner", false);

  art.filters = new Array(filter);
  return art;
}
```

See also

```
alphas (GradientBevelFilter.alphas property), ratios
(GradientBevelFilter.ratios property)
```

distance (GradientBevelFilter.distance property)

```
public distance : Number
```
The offset distance. The default value is 4.

Availability: ActionScript 1.0; Flash Player 8

Example

The following example demonstrates how to set the `distance` property on an existing object.

```
import flash.filters.GradientBevelFilter;

var mc:MovieClip = setUpFilter("distanceExample");
mc.onRelease = function() {
  var arr:Array = this.filters;
  arr[0].distance = 1;
  this.filters = arr;
}

function setUpFilter(name:String):MovieClip {
  var art:MovieClip = this.createEmptyMovieClip(name,
  this.getNextHighestDepth());
  var w:Number = 150;
  var h:Number = 150;
  art.beginFill(0xCCCCCC);
  art.lineTo(w, 0);
  art.lineTo(w, h);
  art.lineTo(0, h);
  art.lineTo(0, 0);

  var colors:Array = [0xFFFFFF, 0xCCCCCC, 0x000000];
  var alphas:Array = [1, 0, 1];
  var ratios:Array = [0, 128, 255];
  var filter:GradientBevelFilter = new GradientBevelFilter(5, 225, colors,
  alphas, ratios, 5, 5, 5, 3, "inner", false);

  art.filters = new Array(filter);
  return art;
}
```

GradientBevelFilter constructor

```
public GradientBevelFilter([distance:Number], [angle:Number],
  [colors:Array], [alphas:Array], [ratios:Array], [blurX:Number],
  [blurY:Number], [strength:Number], [quality:Number], [type:String],
  [knockout:Boolean])
```

Initializes the filter with the specified parameters.

Availability: ActionScript 1.0; Flash Player 8

Parameters

distance:Number [optional] - The offset distance. Valid values are 0 to 8. The default value is 4.

angle:Number [optional] - The angle, in degrees. Valid values are 0 to 360. The default is 45.

colors:Array [optional] - An array of RGB hexadecimal color values to use in the gradient. For example, red is 0xFF0000, blue is 0x0000FF, and so on.

`alphas:Array` [optional] - An array of alpha transparency values for the corresponding colors in the `colors` array. Valid values for each element in the array are 0 to 1. For example, .25 sets a transparency value of 25%.

`ratios:Array` [optional] - An array of color distribution ratios; valid values are 0 to 255.

`blurX:Number` [optional] - The amount of horizontal blur. Valid values are 0 to 255. A blur of 1 or less means that the original image is copied as is. The default value is 4. Values that are a power of 2 (such as 2, 4, 8, 16 and 32) are optimized to render more quickly than other values.

`blurY:Number` [optional] - The amount of vertical blur. Valid values are 0 to 255. A blur of 1 or less means that the original image is copied as is. The default value is 4. Values that are a power of 2 (such as 2, 4, 8, 16 and 32) are optimized to render more quickly than other values.

`strength:Number` [optional] - The strength of the imprint or spread. The higher the value, the more color is imprinted and the stronger the contrast between the bevel and the background. Valid values are 0 to 255. A value of 0 means that the filter is not applied. The default value is 1.

`quality:Number` [optional] - The quality of the filter. Valid values are 0-15. The default value is 1. In almost all cases, useful values are 1 (low quality), 2 (medium quality), and 3 (high quality). Filters with lower values are rendered more quickly.

`type:String` [optional] - The placement of the bevel effect. Possible values are:

- `"outer"`: Bevel on the outer edge of the object
- `"inner"`: Bevel on the inner edge of the object
- `"full"`: Bevel on top of the object

The default value is `"inner"`.

`knockout:Boolean` [optional] - Specifies whether a knockout effect is applied. The value `true` makes the object's fill transparent and reveals the background color of the document. The default is `false` (no knockout).

Example

The following example creates a new GradientBevelFilter instance, assigns its values, and applies it to a flat rectangle image.

```
import flash.filters.GradientBevelFilter;
import flash.filters.BitmapFilter;
var art:MovieClip = setUpFlatRectangle(150, 150, 0xCCCCCC,
  "gradientBevelFilterExample");
var distance:Number = 5;
var angleInDegrees:Number = 225; // opposite 45 degrees
```

```
var colors:Array = [0xFFFFFF, 0xCCCCCC, 0x000000];
var alphas:Array = [1, 0, 1];
var ratios:Array = [0, 128, 255];
var blurX:Number = 8;
var blurY:Number = 8;
var strength:Number = 2;
var quality:Number = 3;
var type:String = "inner";
var knockout:Boolean = true;

var filter:GradientBevelFilter = new GradientBevelFilter(distance,
                                    angleInDegrees,
                                    colors,
                                    alphas,
                                    ratios,
                                    blurX,
                                    blurY,
                                    strength,
                                    quality,
                                    type,
                                    knockout);
var filterArray:Array = new Array();
filterArray.push(filter);
art.filters = filterArray;

function setUpFlatRectangle(w:Number, h:Number, bgColor:Number,
  name:String):MovieClip {
  var mc:MovieClip = this.createEmptyMovieClip(name,
  this.getNextHighestDepth());
  mc.beginFill(bgColor);
  mc.lineTo(w, 0);
  mc.lineTo(w, h);
  mc.lineTo(0, h);
  mc.lineTo(0, 0);
  return mc;
}
```

See also

ratios (GradientBevelFilter.ratios property)

knockout (GradientBevelFilter.knockout property)

`public knockout : Boolean`

Specifies whether the object has a knockout effect. A knockout effect makes the object's fill transparent and reveals the background color of the document. The value `true` specifies a knockout effect; the default is `false` (no knockout effect).

Availability: ActionScript 1.0; Flash Player 8

Example

The following example demonstrates how to set the knockout property on an existing object.

```
import flash.filters.GradientBevelFilter;

var mc:MovieClip = setUpFilter("knockoutExample");
mc.onRelease = function() {
  var arr:Array = this.filters;
  arr[0].knockout = true;
  this.filters = arr;
}

function setUpFilter(name:String):MovieClip {
  var art:MovieClip = this.createEmptyMovieClip(name,
  this.getNextHighestDepth());
  var w:Number = 150;
  var h:Number = 150;
  art.beginFill(0xCCCCCC);
  art.lineTo(w, 0);
  art.lineTo(w, h);
  art.lineTo(0, h);
  art.lineTo(0, 0);

  var colors:Array = [0xFFFFFF, 0xCCCCCC, 0x000000];
  var alphas:Array = [1, 0, 1];
  var ratios:Array = [0, 128, 255];
  var filter:GradientBevelFilter = new GradientBevelFilter(5, 225, colors,
  alphas, ratios, 5, 5, 5, 3, "inner", false);

  art.filters = new Array(filter);
  return art;
}
```

quality (GradientBevelFilter.quality property)

```
public quality : Number
```

The number of times to apply the filter. Valid values are 0 to 15. The default value is 1, which is equivalent to low quality. A value of 2 is medium quality, and a value of 3 is high quality. Filters with lower values are rendered more quickly.

For most applications, a quality value of 1, 2, or 3 is sufficient. Although you can use additional numeric values up to 15 to achieve different effects, higher values are rendered more slowly. Instead of increasing the value of quality, you can often get a similar effect, and with faster rendering, by simply increasing the values of blurX and blurY.

Availability: ActionScript 1.0; Flash Player 8

Example

The following example demonstrates how to set the `quality` property on an existing object.

```
import flash.filters.GradientBevelFilter;

var mc:MovieClip = setUpFilter("qualityExample");
mc.onRelease = function() {
  var arr:Array = this.filters;
  arr[0].quality = 1; // low quality
  this.filters = arr;
}

function setUpFilter(name:String):MovieClip {
  var art:MovieClip = this.createEmptyMovieClip(name,
  this.getNextHighestDepth());
  var w:Number = 150;
  var h:Number = 150;
  art.beginFill(0xCCCCCC);
  art.lineTo(w, 0);
  art.lineTo(w, h);
  art.lineTo(0, h);
  art.lineTo(0, 0);

  var colors:Array = [0xFFFFFF, 0xCCCCCC, 0x000000];
  var alphas:Array = [1, 0, 1];
  var ratios:Array = [0, 128, 255];
  var filter:GradientBevelFilter = new GradientBevelFilter(5, 225, colors,
  alphas, ratios, 5, 5, 5, 3, "inner", false);

  art.filters = new Array(filter);
  return art;
}
```

See also

`ratios (GradientBevelFilter.ratios property)`

ratios (GradientBevelFilter.ratios property)

`public ratios : Array`

An array of color distribution ratios for the corresponding colors in the `colors` array. Valid values for each element in the array are 0 to 255.

The `ratios` property cannot be changed by directly modifying its values. Instead, you must get a reference to `ratios`, make the change to the reference, and then set `ratios` to the reference.

The `colors`, `alphas`, and `ratios` properties are all related. The first element in the `colors` array corresponds to the first element in the `alphas` array and in the `ratios` array, and so on.

To understand how the colors in a gradient bevel are distributed, think first of the colors that you want in your gradient bevel. Consider that a simple bevel has a highlight color and shadow color; a gradient bevel has a highlight gradient and a shadow gradient. Assume that the highlight appears on the top-left corner, and the shadow appears on the bottom-right corner. Assume that one possible usage of the filter has four colors in the highlight and four in the shadow. In addition to the highlight and shadow, the filter uses a base fill color that appears where the edges of the highlight and shadow meet. Therefore the total number of colors is nine, and the corresponding number of elements in the ratios array is nine.

If you think of a gradient as composed of stripes of various colors, blending into each other, each ratio value sets the position of the color on the radius of the gradient, where 0 represents the outermost point of the gradient and 255 represents the innermost point of the gradient. For a typical usage, the middle value is 128, and that is the base fill value. To get the bevel effect shown in the image below, assign the ratio values as follows, using the example of nine colors:

- The first four colors range from 0-127, increasing in value so that each value is greater than or equal to the previous one. This is the highlight bevel edge.
- The fifth color (the middle color) is the base fill, set to 128. The pixel value of 128 sets the base fill, which appears either outside the shape (and around the bevel edges) if the type is set to outer; or inside the shape, effectively covering the object's own fill, if the type is set to inner.
- The last four colors range from 129-255, increasing in value so that each value is greater than or equal to the previous one. This is the shadow bevel edge.

If you want an equal distribution of colors for each edge, use an odd number of colors, where the middle color is the base fill. Distribute the values between 0-127 and 129-255 equally among your colors, then adjust the value to change the width of each stripe of color in the gradient. For a gradient bevel with nine colors, a possible array is [16, 32, 64, 96, 128, 160, 192, 224, 235]. The following image depicts the gradient bevel as described:

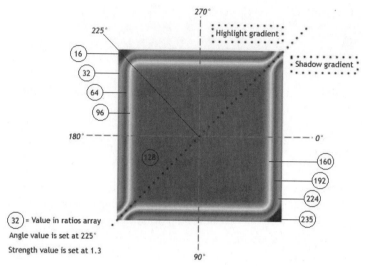

16
32
64
96
128
160
192
224
235

270°

225°

Highlight gradient

Shadow gradient

180° — — —

0°

32 = Value in ratios array
Angle value is set at 225°
Strength value is set at 1.3

90°

Keep in mind that the spread of the colors in the gradient varies based on the values of the blurX, blurY, strength, and quality properties, as well as the ratios values.

Availability: ActionScript 1.0; Flash Player 8

Example

The following example demonstrates how to set the ratios property on an existing entity.

```
import flash.filters.GradientBevelFilter;

var mc:MovieClip = setUpFilter("ratiosExample");
mc.onPress = function() {
  var arr:Array = this.filters;
  var ratios:Array = [127, 128, 129];
  arr[0].ratios = ratios;
  this.filters = arr;
}
mc.onRelease = function() {
  var arr:Array = this.filters;
  var ratios:Array = [0, 128, 255];
  arr[0].ratios = ratios;
  this.filters = arr;
}

function setUpFilter(name:String):MovieClip {
  var art:MovieClip = this.createEmptyMovieClip(name,
  this.getNextHighestDepth());
  var w:Number = 150;
  var h:Number = 150;
```

```
art.beginFill(0xCCCCCC);
art.lineTo(w, 0);
art.lineTo(w, h);
art.lineTo(0, h);
art.lineTo(0, 0);

var colors:Array = [0xFFFFFF, 0xCCCCCC, 0x000000];
var alphas:Array = [1, 0, 1];
var ratios:Array = [0, 128, 255];
var filter:GradientBevelFilter = new GradientBevelFilter(5, 225, colors,
alphas, ratios, 5, 5, 5, 2, "inner", false);

art.filters = new Array(filter);
return art;
}
```

See also

alphas (GradientBevelFilter.alphas property), colors
(GradientBevelFilter.colors property), beginGradientFill
(MovieClip.beginGradientFill method)

strength (GradientBevelFilter.strength property)

public strength : Number

The strength of the imprint or spread. The higher the value, the more color is imprinted and the stronger the contrast between the bevel and the background. Valid values are 0 to 255. A value of 0 means that the filter is not applied. The default value is 1.

Availability: ActionScript 1.0; Flash Player 8

Example

The following example demonstrates how to set the `strength` property on an existing object.

```
import flash.filters.GradientBevelFilter;

var mc:MovieClip = setUpFilter("strengthExample");
mc.onRelease = function() {
  var arr:Array = this.filters;
  arr[0].strength = 1;
  this.filters = arr;
}

function setUpFilter(name:String):MovieClip {
  var art:MovieClip = this.createEmptyMovieClip(name,
  this.getNextHighestDepth());
  var w:Number = 150;
  var h:Number = 150;
  art.beginFill(0xCCCCCC);
  art.lineTo(w, 0);
  art.lineTo(w, h);
  art.lineTo(0, h);
  art.lineTo(0, 0);

  var colors:Array = [0xFFFFFF, 0xCCCCCC, 0x000000];
  var alphas:Array = [1, 0, 1];
  var ratios:Array = [0, 128, 255];
  var filter:GradientBevelFilter = new GradientBevelFilter(5, 225, colors,
  alphas, ratios, 5, 5, 5, 3, "inner", false);

  art.filters = new Array(filter);
  return art;
}
```

See also

`ratios (GradientBevelFilter.ratios property)`

type (GradientBevelFilter.type property)

`public type : String`

The placement of the bevel effect. Possible values are:

- `"outer"`: Bevel on the outer edge of the object
- `"inner"`: Bevel on the inner edge of the object
- `"full"`: Bevel on top of the object

The default value is `"inner"`.

Availability: ActionScript 1.0; Flash Player 8

Example

The following example demonstrates how to set the type property on an existing object.

```
import flash.filters.GradientBevelFilter;

var mc:MovieClip = setUpFilter("typeExample");
mc.onRelease = function() {
  var arr:Array = this.filters;
  arr[0].type = "outer";
  this.filters = arr;
}

function setUpFilter(name:String):MovieClip {
  var art:MovieClip = this.createEmptyMovieClip(name,
  this.getNextHighestDepth());
  var w:Number = 150;
  var h:Number = 150;
  art.beginFill(0xCCCCCC);
  art.lineTo(w, 0);
  art.lineTo(w, h);
  art.lineTo(0, h);
  art.lineTo(0, 0);

  var colors:Array = [0xFFFFFF, 0xCCCCCC, 0x000000];
  var alphas:Array = [1, 0, 1];
  var ratios:Array = [0, 128, 255];
  var filter:GradientBevelFilter = new GradientBevelFilter(5, 225, colors,
  alphas, ratios, 5, 5, 5, 3, "inner", false);

  art.filters = new Array(filter);
  return art;
}
```

GradientGlowFilter (flash.filters.GradientGlowFilter)

```
Object
  |
  +-flash.filters.BitmapFilter
    |
    +-flash.filters.GradientGlowFilter

public class GradientGlowFilter
extends BitmapFilter
```

The GradientGlowFilter class lets you apply a gradient glow effect to a variety of objects in Flash. A gradient glow is a realistic-looking glow with a color gradient that you can control. You can apply a gradient glow around the inner or outer edge of an object or on top of an object.

The use of filters depends on the object to which you apply the filter:

- To apply filters to movie clips, text fields, and buttons at runtime, use the `filters` property. Setting the `filters` property of an object does not modify the object, and you can undo the filter by clearing the `filters` property.

- To apply filters to BitmapData instances, use the `BitmapData.applyFilter()` method. Calling `applyFilter()` on a BitmapData object takes the source BitmapData object and the filter object and generates a filtered image as a result.

You can also apply filter effects to images and video during authoring. For more information, see your authoring documentation.

If you apply a filter to a movie clip or button, the `cacheAsBitmap` property of the movie clip or button is set to `true`. If you clear all filters, the original value of `cacheAsBitmap` is restored.

This filter supports Stage scaling. However, it does not support general scaling, rotation, and skewing; if the object itself is scaled (if `_xscale` and `_yscale` are not 100%), the filter effect is not scaled. It is scaled only when the Stage is zoomed.

A filter is not applied if the resulting image exceeds 2880 pixels in width or height. For example, if you zoom in on a large movie clip with a filter applied, the filter is turned off if the resulting image exceeds the limit of 2880 pixels.

Availability: ActionScript 1.0; Flash Player 8

See also

`ratios (GradientGlowFilter.ratios property)`, `applyFilter (BitmapData.applyFilter method)`, `cacheAsBitmap (Button.cacheAsBitmap property)`, `filters (Button.filters property)`, `GlowFilter (flash.filters.GlowFilter)`, `cacheAsBitmap (MovieClip.cacheAsBitmap property)`, `filters (MovieClip.filters property)`, `filters (TextField.filters property)`

Property summary

Modifiers	Property	Description
	alphas:Array	An array of alpha transparency values for the corresponding colors in the colors array.
	angle:Number	The angle, in degrees.
	blurX:Number	The amount of horizontal blur.
	blurY:Number	The amount of vertical blur.
	colors:Array	An array of colors that defines a gradient.
	distance:Number	The offset distance of the glow.
	knockout:Boolean	Specifies whether the object has a knockout effect.
	quality:Number	The number of times to apply the filter.
	ratios:Array	An array of color distribution ratios for the corresponding colors in the colors array.
	strength:Number	The strength of the imprint or spread.
	type:String	The placement of the filter effect.

Properties inherited from class Object

constructor (Object.constructor property), __proto__ (Object.__proto__ property), prototype (Object.prototype property), __resolve (Object.__resolve property)

Constructor summary

Signature	Description
GradientGlowFilter([distance:Number], [angle:Number], [colors:Array], [alphas:Array], [ratios:Array], [blurX:Number], [blurY:Number], [strength:Number], [quality:Number], [type:String], [knockout:Boolean])	Initializes the filter with the specified parameters.

Method summary

Modifiers	Signature	Description
	`clone() : GradientGlowFilter`	Returns a copy of this filter object.

Methods inherited from class BitmapFilter

```
clone (BitmapFilter.clone method)
```

Methods inherited from class Object

```
addProperty (Object.addProperty method), hasOwnProperty
(Object.hasOwnProperty method), isPropertyEnumerable
(Object.isPropertyEnumerable method), isPrototypeOf (Object.isPrototypeOf
method), registerClass (Object.registerClass method), toString
(Object.toString method), unwatch (Object.unwatch method), valueOf
(Object.valueOf method), watch (Object.watch method)
```

alphas (GradientGlowFilter.alphas property)

`public alphas : Array`

An array of alpha transparency values for the corresponding colors in the `colors` array. Valid values for each element in the array are 0 to 1. For example, .25 sets the alpha transparency value to 25%.

The `alphas` property cannot be changed by directly modifying its values. Instead, you must get a reference to `alphas`, make the change to the reference, and then set `alphas` to the reference.

The `colors`, `alphas`, and `ratios` properties are all related. The first element in the `colors` array corresponds to the first element in the `alphas` array and in the `ratios` array, and so on.

Availability: ActionScript 1.0; Flash Player 8

Example

The following example changes the `alphas` property on an existing movie clip when a user clicks it.

```
import flash.filters.GradientGlowFilter;
var mc:MovieClip = createGradientGlowRectangle("GlowAlphas");
mc.onRelease = function() {
   var filter:GradientGlowFilter = this.filters[0];
   var alphas:Array = filter.alphas;
   alphas.pop();
```

```
    alphas.pop();
    alphas.push(.3);
    alphas.push(1);
    filter.alphas = alphas;
    this.filters = new Array(filter);
}

function createGradientGlowRectangle(name:String):MovieClip {
    var art:MovieClip = this.createEmptyMovieClip(name,
    this.getNextHighestDepth());
    var w:Number = 100;
    var h:Number = 100;
    art.beginFill(0x003366);
    art.lineTo(w, 0);
    art.lineTo(w, h);
    art.lineTo(0, h);
    art.lineTo(0, 0);
    art._x = 20;
    art._y = 20;

    var colors:Array = [0xFFFFFF, 0xFF0000, 0xFFFF00, 0x00CCFF];
    var alphas:Array = [0, 1, 1, 1];
    var ratios:Array = [0, 63, 126, 255];
    var filter:GradientGlowFilter = new GradientGlowFilter(0, 45, colors,
    alphas, ratios, 55, 55, 2.5, 2, "outer", false);
    var filterArray:Array = new Array();
    filterArray.push(filter);
    art.filters = filterArray;
    return art;
}
```

See also

```
colors (GradientGlowFilter.colors property), ratios
(GradientGlowFilter.ratios property)
```

angle (GradientGlowFilter.angle property)

```
public angle : Number
```
The angle, in degrees. Valid values are 0 to 360. The default is 45.

The angle value represents the angle of the theoretical light source falling on the object and determines the placement of the effect relative to the object. If distance is set to 0, the effect is not offset from the object, and therefore the angle property has no effect.

Availability: ActionScript 1.0; Flash Player 8

Example

The following example changes the `angle` property on an existing movie clip when a user clicks it.

```
import flash.filters.GradientGlowFilter;
var mc:MovieClip = createGradientGlowRectangle("GlowAngle");
mc.onRelease = function() {
  var filter:GradientGlowFilter = this.filters[0];
  filter.distance = 50;
  filter.angle = 90;
  this.filters = new Array(filter);
}

function createGradientGlowRectangle(name:String):MovieClip {
  var art:MovieClip = this.createEmptyMovieClip(name,
  this.getNextHighestDepth());
  var w:Number = 100;
  var h:Number = 100;
  art.beginFill(0x003366);
  art.lineTo(w, 0);
  art.lineTo(w, h);
  art.lineTo(0, h);
  art.lineTo(0, 0);
  art._x = 20;
  art._y = 20;

  var colors:Array = [0xFFFFFF, 0xFF0000, 0xFFFF00, 0x00CCFF];
  var alphas:Array = [0, 1, 1, 1];
  var ratios:Array = [0, 63, 126, 255];
  var filter:GradientGlowFilter = new GradientGlowFilter(0, 45, colors,
  alphas, ratios, 55, 55, 2.5, 2, "outer", false);
  var filterArray:Array = new Array();
  filterArray.push(filter);
  art.filters = filterArray;
  return art;
}
```

blurX (GradientGlowFilter.blurX property)

`public blurX : Number`

The amount of horizontal blur. Valid values are 0 to 255. A blur of 1 or less means that the original image is copied as is. The default value is 4. Values that are a power of 2 (such as 2, 4, 8, 16, and 32) are optimized to render more quickly than other values.

Availability: ActionScript 1.0; Flash Player 8

Example

The following example changes the `blurX` property on an existing movie clip when a user clicks it.

```
import flash.filters.GradientGlowFilter;
var mc:MovieClip = createGradientGlowRectangle("GlowBlurX");
mc.onRelease = function() {
  var filter:GradientGlowFilter = this.filters[0];
  filter.blurX = 255;
  this.filters = new Array(filter);
}

function createGradientGlowRectangle(name:String):MovieClip {
  var art:MovieClip = this.createEmptyMovieClip(name,
  this.getNextHighestDepth());
  var w:Number = 100;
  var h:Number = 100;
  art.beginFill(0x003366);
  art.lineTo(w, 0);
  art.lineTo(w, h);
  art.lineTo(0, h);
  art.lineTo(0, 0);
  art._x = 20;
  art._y = 20;

  var colors:Array = [0xFFFFFF, 0xFF0000, 0xFFFF00, 0x00CCFF];
  var alphas:Array = [0, 1, 1, 1];
  var ratios:Array = [0, 63, 126, 255];
  var filter:GradientGlowFilter = new GradientGlowFilter(0, 45, colors,
  alphas, ratios, 55, 55, 2.5, 2, "outer", false);
  var filterArray:Array = new Array();
  filterArray.push(filter);
  art.filters = filterArray;
  return art;
}
```

blurY (GradientGlowFilter.blurY property)

`public blurY : Number`

The amount of vertical blur. Valid values are 0 to 255. A blur of 1 or less means that the original image is copied as is. The default value is 4. Values that are a power of 2 (such as 2, 4, 8, 16, and 32) are optimized to render more quickly than other values.

Availability: ActionScript 1.0; Flash Player 8

Example

The following example changes the `blurY` property on an existing movie clip when a user clicks it.

```
import flash.filters.GradientGlowFilter;
var mc:MovieClip = createGradientGlowRectangle("GlowBlurY");
mc.onRelease = function() {
   var filter:GradientGlowFilter = this.filters[0];
   filter.blurY = 255;
   this.filters = new Array(filter);
}

function createGradientGlowRectangle(name:String):MovieClip {
   var art:MovieClip = this.createEmptyMovieClip(name,
   this.getNextHighestDepth());
   var w:Number = 100;
   var h:Number = 100;
   art.beginFill(0x003366);
   art.lineTo(w, 0);
   art.lineTo(w, h);
   art.lineTo(0, h);
   art.lineTo(0, 0);
   art._x = 20;
   art._y = 20;

   var colors:Array = [0xFFFFFF, 0xFF0000, 0xFFFF00, 0x00CCFF];
   var alphas:Array = [0, 1, 1, 1];
   var ratios:Array = [0, 63, 126, 255];
   var filter:GradientGlowFilter = new GradientGlowFilter(0, 45, colors,
   alphas, ratios, 55, 55, 2.5, 2, "outer", false);
   var filterArray:Array = new Array();
   filterArray.push(filter);
   art.filters = filterArray;
   return art;
}
```

clone (GradientGlowFilter.clone method)

```
public clone() : GradientGlowFilter
```

Returns a copy of this filter object.

Availability: ActionScript 1.0; Flash Player 8

Returns

`flash.filters.GradientGlowFilter` - A new GradientGlowFilter instance with all the same properties as the original GradientGlowFilter instance.

Example

The following example creates three GradientGlowFilter objects and compares them; filter_1 is created by using the GradientGlowFilter construtor; filter_2 is created by setting it equal to filter_1; and, clonedFilter is created by cloning filter_1. Notice that although filter_2 evaluates as being equal to filter_1, clonedFilter, even though it contains the same values as filter_1, does not.

```
import flash.filters.GradientGlowFilter;

var colors:Array = [0xFFFFFF, 0xFF0000, 0xFFFF00, 0x00CCFF];
var alphas:Array = [0, 1, 1, 1];
var ratios:Array = [0, 63, 126, 255];
var filter_1:GradientGlowFilter = new GradientGlowFilter(0, 45, colors,
  alphas, ratios, 55, 55, 2.5, 2, "outer", false);
var filter_2:GradientGlowFilter = filter_1;
var clonedFilter:GradientGlowFilter = filter_1.clone();

trace(filter_1 == filter_2); // true
trace(filter_1 == clonedFilter); // false

for(var i in filter_1) {
  trace(">> " + i + ": " + filter_1[i]);
  // >> clone: [type Function]
  // >> type: outer
  // >> knockout: false
  // >> strength: 2.5
  // >> quality: 2
  // >> blurY: 55
  // >> blurX: 55
  // >> ratios: 0,63,126,255
  // >> alphas: 0,1,1,1
  // >> colors: 16777215,16711680,16776960,52479
  // >> angle: 45
  // >> distance: 0
}

for(var i in clonedFilter) {
  trace(">> " + i + ": " + clonedFilter[i]);
  // >> clone: [type Function]
  // >> type: outer
  // >> knockout: false
  // >> strength: 2.5
  // >> quality: 2
  // >> blurY: 55
  // >> blurX: 55
  // >> ratios: 0,63,126,255
  // >> alphas: 0,1,1,1
  // >> colors: 16777215,16711680,16776960,52479
  // >> angle: 45
```

```
// >> distance: 0
}
```

To further demonstrate the relationships between `filter_1`, `filter_2`, and `clonedFilter`, the following example below modifies the `knockout` property of `filter_1`. Modifying `knockout` demonstrates that the `clone()` method creates a new instance based on the values of `filter_1` instead of pointing to them in reference.

```
import flash.filters.GradientGlowFilter;

var colors:Array = [0xFFFFFF, 0xFF0000, 0xFFFF00, 0x00CCFF];
var alphas:Array = [0, 1, 1, 1];
var ratios:Array = [0, 63, 126, 255];
var filter_1:GradientGlowFilter = new GradientGlowFilter(0, 45, colors,
  alphas, ratios, 55, 55, 2.5, 2, "outer", false);
var filter_2:GradientGlowFilter = filter_1;
var clonedFilter:GradientGlowFilter = filter_1.clone();

trace(filter_1.knockout); // false
trace(filter_2.knockout); // false
trace(clonedFilter.knockout); // false

filter_1.knockout = true;

trace(filter_1.knockout); // true
trace(filter_2.knockout); // true
trace(clonedFilter.knockout); // false
```

colors (GradientGlowFilter.colors property)

`public colors : Array`

An array of colors that defines a gradient. For example, red is 0xFF0000, blue is 0x0000FF, and so on.

The `colors` property cannot be changed by directly modifying its values. Instead, you must get a reference to `colors`, make the change to the reference, and then set `colors` to the reference.

The `colors`, `alphas`, and `ratios` properties are all related. The first element in the `colors` array corresponds to the first element in the `alphas` array and in the `ratios` array, and so on.

Availability: ActionScript 1.0; Flash Player 8

Example

The following example changes the `colors` property on an existing movie clip when a user clicks it.

```
import flash.filters.GradientGlowFilter;
var mc:MovieClip = createGradientGlowRectangle("GlowColors");
mc.onRelease = function() {
  var filter:GradientGlowFilter = this.filters[0];
  var colors:Array = filter.colors;
  colors.pop();
  colors.push(0xFF00FF);
  filter.colors = colors;
  this.filters = new Array(filter);
}

function createGradientGlowRectangle(name:String):MovieClip {
  var art:MovieClip = this.createEmptyMovieClip(name,
  this.getNextHighestDepth());
  var w:Number = 100;
  var h:Number = 100;
  art.beginFill(0x003366);
  art.lineTo(w, 0);
  art.lineTo(w, h);
  art.lineTo(0, h);
  art.lineTo(0, 0);
  art._x = 20;
  art._y = 20;

  var colors:Array = [0xFFFFFF, 0xFF0000, 0xFFFF00, 0x00CCFF];
  var alphas:Array = [0, 1, 1, 1];
  var ratios:Array = [0, 63, 126, 255];
  var filter:GradientGlowFilter = new GradientGlowFilter(0, 45, colors,
  alphas, ratios, 55, 55, 2.5, 2, "outer", false);
  var filterArray:Array = new Array();
  filterArray.push(filter);
  art.filters = filterArray;
  return art;
}
```

See also

`alphas` (GradientGlowFilter.alphas property), `ratios`
(GradientGlowFilter.ratios property)

distance (GradientGlowFilter.distance property)

```
public distance : Number
```

The offset distance of the glow. The default value is 4.

Availability: ActionScript 1.0; Flash Player 8

Example

The following example changes the `distance` property on an existing movie clip when a user clicks it.

```
import flash.filters.GradientGlowFilter;
var mc:MovieClip = createGradientGlowRectangle("GlowDistance");
mc.onRelease = function() {
   var filter:GradientGlowFilter = this.filters[0];
   filter.distance = 20;
   this.filters = new Array(filter);
}

function createGradientGlowRectangle(name:String):MovieClip {
   var art:MovieClip = this.createEmptyMovieClip(name,
   this.getNextHighestDepth());
   var w:Number = 100;
   var h:Number = 100;
   art.beginFill(0x003366);
   art.lineTo(w, 0);
   art.lineTo(w, h);
   art.lineTo(0, h);
   art.lineTo(0, 0);
   art._x = 20;
   art._y = 20;

   var colors:Array = [0xFFFFFF, 0xFF0000, 0xFFFF00, 0x00CCFF];
   var alphas:Array = [0, 1, 1, 1];
   var ratios:Array = [0, 63, 126, 255];
   var filter:GradientGlowFilter = new GradientGlowFilter(0, 45, colors,
   alphas, ratios, 55, 55, 2.5, 2, "outer", false);
   var filterArray:Array = new Array();
   filterArray.push(filter);
   art.filters = filterArray;
   return art;
}
```

GradientGlowFilter constructor

```
public GradientGlowFilter([distance:Number], [angle:Number],
    [colors:Array], [alphas:Array], [ratios:Array], [blurX:Number],
    [blurY:Number], [strength:Number], [quality:Number], [type:String],
    [knockout:Boolean])
```

Initializes the filter with the specified parameters.

Availability: ActionScript 1.0; Flash Player 8

Parameters

`distance:Number` [optional] - The offset distance of the glow. The default is 4.

`angle:Number` [optional] - The angle, in degrees. Valid values are 0 to 360. The default is 45.

`colors:Array` [optional] - An array of colors that defines a gradient. For example, red is 0xFF0000, blue is 0x0000FF, and so on.

`alphas:Array` [optional] - An array of alpha transparency values for the corresponding colors in the `colors` array. Valid values for each element in the array are 0 to 1. For example, a value of .25 sets the alpha transparency value to 25%.

`ratios:Array` [optional] - An array of color distribution ratios. Valid values are 0 to 255. This value defines the percentage of the width where the color is sampled at 100 percent.

`blurX:Number` [optional] - The amount of horizontal blur. Valid values are 0 to 255. A blur of 1 or less means that the original image is copied as is. The default value is 4. Values that are a power of 2 (such as 2, 4, 8, 16 and 32) are optimized to render more quickly than other values.

`blurY:Number` [optional] - The amount of vertical blur. Valid values are 0 to 255. A blur of 1 or less means that the original image is copied as is. The default value is 4. Values that are a power of 2 (such as 2, 4, 8, 16 and 32) are optimized to render more quickly than other values.

`strength:Number` [optional] - The strength of the imprint or spread. The higher the value, the more color is imprinted and the stronger the contrast between the glow and the background. Valid values are 0 to 255. The larger the value, the stronger the imprint. A value of 0 means the filter is not applied. The default value is 1.

`quality:Number` [optional] - The number of times to apply the filter. Valid values are 0 to 15. The default value is 1, which is equivalent to low quality. A value of 2 is medium quality, and a value of 3 is high quality.

`type:String` [optional] - The placement of the filter effect. Possible values are:

- `"outer"`: Glow on the outer edge of the object
- `"inner"`: Glow on the inner edge of the object; the default
- `"full"`: Glow on top of the object

The default value is `"inner"`.

`knockout:Boolean` [optional] - Specifies whether the object has a knockout effect. A knockout effect makes the object's fill transparent and reveals the background color of the document. The value `true` specifies a knockout effect; the default is `false` (no knockout effect).

Example

The following example creates a gradient glow filter, assigns its values, and applies it to a flat rectangle image.

```
import flash.filters.GradientGlowFilter;
var art:MovieClip = createRectangle(100, 100, 0x003366,
  "gradientGlowFilterExample");
var distance:Number = 0;
var angleInDegrees:Number = 45;
var colors:Array = [0xFFFFFF, 0xFF0000, 0xFFFF00, 0x00CCFF];
var alphas:Array = [0, 1, 1, 1];
var ratios:Array = [0, 63, 126, 255];
var blurX:Number = 50;
var blurY:Number = 50;
var strength:Number = 2.5;
var quality:Number = 3;
var type:String = "outer";
var knockout:Boolean = false;

var filter:GradientGlowFilter = new GradientGlowFilter(distance,
                                angleInDegrees,
                                colors,
                                alphas,
                                ratios,
                                blurX,
                                blurY,
                                strength,
                                quality,
                                type,
                                knockout);
var filterArray:Array = new Array();
filterArray.push(filter);
art.filters = filterArray;
```

```
function createRectangle(w:Number, h:Number, bgColor:Number,
    name:String):MovieClip {
    var mc:MovieClip = this.createEmptyMovieClip(name,
    this.getNextHighestDepth());
    mc.beginFill(bgColor);
    mc.lineTo(w, 0);
    mc.lineTo(w, h);
    mc.lineTo(0, h);
    mc.lineTo(0, 0);
    mc._x = 20;
    mc._y = 20;
    return mc;
}
```

knockout (GradientGlowFilter.knockout property)

`public knockout : Boolean`

Specifies whether the object has a knockout effect. A knockout effect makes the object's fill transparent and reveals the background color of the document. The value `true` specifies a knockout effect; the default is `false` (no knockout effect).

Availability: ActionScript 1.0; Flash Player 8

Example

The following example changes the `knockout` property on an existing movie clip when a user clicks it.

```
import flash.filters.GradientGlowFilter;
var mc:MovieClip = createGradientGlowRectangle("GlowKnockout");
mc.onRelease = function() {
    var filter:GradientGlowFilter = this.filters[0];
    filter.knockout = true;
    this.filters = new Array(filter);
}

function createGradientGlowRectangle(name:String):MovieClip {
    var art:MovieClip = this.createEmptyMovieClip(name,
    this.getNextHighestDepth());
    var w:Number = 100;
    var h:Number = 100;
    art.beginFill(0x003366);
    art.lineTo(w, 0);
    art.lineTo(w, h);
    art.lineTo(0, h);
    art.lineTo(0, 0);
    art._x = 20;
    art._y = 20;
```

```
var colors:Array = [0xFFFFFF, 0xFF0000, 0xFFFF00, 0x00CCFF];
var alphas:Array = [0, 1, 1, 1];
var ratios:Array = [0, 63, 126, 255];
var filter:GradientGlowFilter = new GradientGlowFilter(0, 45, colors,
alphas, ratios, 55, 55, 2.5, 2, "outer", false);
var filterArray:Array = new Array();
filterArray.push(filter);
art.filters = filterArray;
return art;
}
```

quality (GradientGlowFilter.quality property)

`public quality : Number`

The number of times to apply the filter. Valid values are 0 to 15. The default value is 1, which is equivalent to low quality. A value of 2 is medium quality, and a value of 3 is high quality. Filters with lower values are rendered more quickly.

For most applications, a `quality` value of 1, 2, or 3 is sufficient. Although you can use additional numeric values up to 15 to achieve different effects, higher values are rendered more slowly. Instead of increasing the value of `quality`, you can often get a similar effect, and with faster rendering, by simply increasing the values of `blurX` and `blurY`.

Availability: ActionScript 1.0; Flash Player 8

Example

The following example changes the `quality` property on an existing movie clip when a user clicks it.

```
import flash.filters.GradientGlowFilter;
var mc:MovieClip = createGradientGlowRectangle("GlowQuality");
mc.onRelease = function() {
  var filter:GradientGlowFilter = this.filters[0];
  filter.quality = 3;
  this.filters = new Array(filter);
}

function createGradientGlowRectangle(name:String):MovieClip {
  var art:MovieClip = this.createEmptyMovieClip(name,
  this.getNextHighestDepth());
  var w:Number = 100;
  var h:Number = 100;
  art.beginFill(0x003366);
  art.lineTo(w, 0);
  art.lineTo(w, h);
```

```
art.lineTo(0, h);
art.lineTo(0, 0);
art._x = 20;
art._y = 20;

var colors:Array = [0xFFFFFF, 0xFF0000, 0xFFFF00, 0x00CCFF];
var alphas:Array = [0, 1, 1, 1];
var ratios:Array = [0, 63, 126, 255];
var filter:GradientGlowFilter = new GradientGlowFilter(0, 45, colors,
alphas, ratios, 55, 55, 2.5, 2, "outer", false);
var filterArray:Array = new Array();
filterArray.push(filter);
art.filters = filterArray;
return art;
}
```

ratios (GradientGlowFilter.ratios property)

`public ratios : Array`

An array of color distribution ratios for the corresponding colors in the `colors` array. Valid values are 0 to 255.

The `ratios` property cannot be changed by directly modifying its values. Instead, you must get a reference to `ratios`, make the change to the reference, and then set `ratios` to the reference.

The `colors`, `alphas`, and `ratios` properties are all related. The first element in the `colors` array corresponds to the first element in the `alphas` array and in the `ratios` array, and so on.

Think of the gradient glow filter as a glow that emanates from the center of the object (if the `distance` value is set to 0), with gradients that are stripes of color blending into each other. The first color in the `colors` array is the outermost color of the glow. The last color is the innermost color of the glow.

Each value in the `ratios` array sets the position of the color on the radius of the gradient, where 0 represents the outermost point of the gradient and 255 represents the innermost point of the gradient. The ratio values can range from 0 to 255 pixels, in increasing value; for example [0, 64, 128, 200, 255]. Values from 0 to 128 appear on the outer edges of the glow. Values from 129 to 255 appear in the inner area of the glow. Depending on the ratio values of the colors and the `type` value of the filter, the filter colors might be obscured by the object to which the filter is applied.

In the following code and image, a filter is applied to a black circle movie clip, with the type set to "full". For instructional purposes, the first color in the colors array, pink, has an alpha value of 1, so it shows against the white document background. (In practice, you probably would not want the first color showing in this way.) Note the last color in the array, yellow, obscures the black circle to which the filter is applied:

```
var colors = [0xFFCCFF, 0x0000FF, 0x9900FF, 0xFF0000, 0xFFFF00];
 var alphas = [1, 1, 1, 1, 1];
 var ratios = [0, 32, 64, 128, 225];
 var myGGF = new GradientGlowFilter(0, 0, colors, alphas, ratios, 50, 50, 1,
  2, "full", false);
```

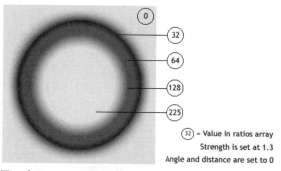

(32) = Value in ratios array
Strength is set at 1.3
Angle and distance are set to 0

To achieve a seamless effect with your document background when you set the type value to "outer" or "full", set the first color in the array to the same color as the document background, or set the alpha value of the first color to 0; either technique makes the filter blend in with the background.

If you make two small changes in the code, the effect of the glow can be very different, even with the same `ratios` and `colors` arrays. Set the alpha value of the first color in the array to 0, to make the filter blend in with the document's white background; and set the `type` property to `"outer"` or `"inner"`. Observe the results, as shown in the following images.

Outer glow

Inner glow

Keep in mind that the spread of the colors in the gradient varies based on the values of the `blurX`, `blurY`, `strength`, and `quality` properties, as well as the `ratios` values.

Availability: ActionScript 1.0; Flash Player 8

Example

The following example changes the `ratios` property on an existing movie clip when a user clicks it.

```
import flash.filters.GradientGlowFilter;
var mc:MovieClip = createGradientGlowRectangle("GlowRatios");
mc.onRelease = function() {
    var filter:GradientGlowFilter = this.filters[0];
    var ratios:Array = filter.ratios;
    ratios.shift();
    ratios.unshift(40);
    filter.ratios = ratios;
    this.filters = new Array(filter);
}
```

```
function createGradientGlowRectangle(name:String):MovieClip {
  var art:MovieClip = this.createEmptyMovieClip(name,
  this.getNextHighestDepth());
  var w:Number = 100;
  var h:Number = 100;
  art.beginFill(0x003366);
  art.lineTo(w, 0);
  art.lineTo(w, h);
  art.lineTo(0, h);
  art.lineTo(0, 0);
  art._x = 20;
  art._y = 20;

  var colors:Array = [0xFFFFFF, 0xFF0000, 0xFFFF00, 0x00CCFF];
  var alphas:Array = [0, 1, 1, 1];
  var ratios:Array = [0, 63, 126, 255];
  var filter:GradientGlowFilter = new GradientGlowFilter(0, 45, colors,
  alphas, ratios, 55, 55, 2.5, 2, "outer", false);
  var filterArray:Array = new Array();
  filterArray.push(filter);
  art.filters = filterArray;
  return art;
}
```

See also

colors (GradientGlowFilter.colors property), alphas
(GradientGlowFilter.alphas property), beginGradientFill
(MovieClip.beginGradientFill method)

strength (GradientGlowFilter.strength property)

public strength : Number

The strength of the imprint or spread. The higher the value, the more color is imprinted and the stronger the contrast between the glow and the background. Valid values are 0 to 255. A value of 0 means that the filter is not applied. The default value is 1.

Availability: ActionScript 1.0; Flash Player 8

Example

The following example changes the `strength` property on an existing movie clip when a user clicks it.

```
import flash.filters.GradientGlowFilter;
var mc:MovieClip = createGradientGlowRectangle("GlowStrength");
mc.onRelease = function() {
   var filter:GradientGlowFilter = this.filters[0];
   filter.strength = 1;
   this.filters = new Array(filter);
}

function createGradientGlowRectangle(name:String):MovieClip {
   var art:MovieClip = this.createEmptyMovieClip(name,
   this.getNextHighestDepth());
   var w:Number = 100;
   var h:Number = 100;
   art.beginFill(0x003366);
   art.lineTo(w, 0);
   art.lineTo(w, h);
   art.lineTo(0, h);
   art.lineTo(0, 0);
   art._x = 20;
   art._y = 20;

   var colors:Array = [0xFFFFFF, 0xFF0000, 0xFFFF00, 0x00CCFF];
   var alphas:Array = [0, 1, 1, 1];
   var ratios:Array = [0, 63, 126, 255];
   var filter:GradientGlowFilter = new GradientGlowFilter(0, 45, colors,
   alphas, ratios, 55, 55, 2.5, 2, "outer", false);
   var filterArray:Array = new Array();
   filterArray.push(filter);
   art.filters = filterArray;
   return art;
}
```

type (GradientGlowFilter.type property)

`public type : String`

The placement of the filter effect. Possible values are:

- `"outer"`: Glow on the outer edge of the object
- `"inner"`: Glow on the inner edge of the object; the default
- `"full"`: Glow on top of the object

The default value is `"inner"`.

Availability: ActionScript 1.0; Flash Player 8

Example

The following example changes the type property on an existing movie clip when a user clicks it.

```
import flash.filters.GradientGlowFilter;
var mc:MovieClip = createGradientGlowRectangle("GlowType");
mc.onRelease = function() {
  var filter:GradientGlowFilter = this.filters[0];
  filter.type = "inner";
  filter.strength = 1;
  this.filters = new Array(filter);
}

function createGradientGlowRectangle(name:String):MovieClip {
  var art:MovieClip = this.createEmptyMovieClip(name,
  this.getNextHighestDepth());
  var w:Number = 100;
  var h:Number = 100;
  art.beginFill(0x003366);
  art.lineTo(w, 0);
  art.lineTo(w, h);
  art.lineTo(0, h);
  art.lineTo(0, 0);
  art._x = 20;
  art._y = 20;

  var colors:Array = [0xFFFFFF, 0xFF0000, 0xFFFF00, 0x00CCFF];
  var alphas:Array = [0, 1, 1, 1];
  var ratios:Array = [0, 63, 126, 255];
  var filter:GradientGlowFilter = new GradientGlowFilter(0, 45, colors,
  alphas, ratios, 55, 55, 2.5, 2, "outer", false);
  var filterArray:Array = new Array();
  filterArray.push(filter);
  art.filters = filterArray;
  return art;
}
```

IME (System.IME)

```
Object
  |
  +-System.IME
```

```
public class IME
extends Object
```

The IME class lets you directly manipulate the operating system's input method editor (IME) in the Flash Player application that is running on a client computer. You can determine whether an IME is installed, whether or not the IME is enabled, and which IME is enabled. You can disable or enable the IME in the Flash Player application, and you can perform other limited functions, depending on the operating system.

Input method editors let users type non-ASCII text characters in Asian languages such as Chinese, Japanese, and Korean. For more information on IMEs, see the operating system documentation for the platform for which you are developing applications. Some additional resources for information about input methods are listed here:

- http://www.microsoft.com/globaldev/default.mspx
- http://developer.apple.com/documentation/
- http://java.sun.com

The following table shows the platform coverage of this class:

Capability	Windows	Macintosh OSX	Macintosh Classic	Linux/Solaris XIM
Determine whether the IME is installed `System.capabilities.hasIME`	Yes	Yes	Yes	Yes
Set IME on or off `System.IME.setEnabled()`	Yes	Yes	Yes	Yes
Find out whether IME is on or off `System.IME.getEnabled()`	Yes	Yes	Yes	Yes
Set IME conversion mode `System.IME.setConversionMode()`	Yes	Yes **	No	Yes

Capability	Windows	Macintosh OSX	Macintosh Classic	Linux/Solaris XIM
Get IME conversion mode `System.IME.getConversionMode()`	Yes	Yes **	No	Yes
Send IME the string to be converted `System.IME.setCompositionString()`	Yes *	No	No	Yes
Get from IME the original string before conversion `System.IME.addListener()` `listener.onIMEComposition()` `System.IME.removeListener()`	Yes *	No	No	Yes
Send request to convert to IME `System.IME.doConversion()`	Yes *	No	No	Yes

* Not all Windows IMEs support all of these operations. So far the only IME that supports them all is the Japanese IME. Every IME differs in its support of the OS calls.

** On Macintosh these methods are supported only for Japanese, and they are not supported for third-party IMEs.

Availability: ActionScript 1.0; Flash Player 8

Property summary

Modifiers	Property	Description
`static`	`ALPHANUMERIC_FULL:String`	A string with the value `"ALPHANUMERIC_FULL"` for use with `setConversionMode()` and `getConversionMode()`.
`static`	`ALPHANUMERIC_HALF:String`	A string with the value `"ALPHANUMERIC_HALF"` for use with `setConversionMode()` and `getConversionMode()`.
`static`	`CHINESE:String`	A string with the value `"CHINESE"` for use with `setConversionMode()` and `getConversionMode()`.
`static`	`JAPANESE_HIRAGANA:String`	A string with the value `"JAPANESE_HIRAGANA"` for use with `setConversionMode()` and `getConversionMode()`.
`static`	`JAPANESE_KATAKANA_FULL:String`	A string with the value `"JAPANESE_KATAKANA_FULL"` for use with `setConversionMode()` and `getConversionMode()`.
`static`	`JAPANESE_KATAKANA_HALF:String`	A string with the value `"JAPANESE_KATAKANA_HALF"` for use with `setConversionMode()` and `getConversionMode()`.
`static`	`KOREAN:String`	A string with the value `"KOREAN"` for use with `setConversionMode()` and `getConversionMode()`.
`static`	`UNKNOWN:String`	A string with the value `"UNKNOWN"` for use with `getConversionMode()`.

Properties inherited from class Object

```
constructor (Object.constructor property),__proto__ (Object.__proto__
property),prototype (Object.prototype property),__resolve
(Object.__resolve property)
```

Event summary

Event	Description
`onIMEComposition = function([readingString:String]){}`	Notified when the IME composition string is being set.

Method summary

Modifiers	Signature	Description
static	addListener(listener :Object) : Void	Registers an object to receive notification when an IME event handler is invoked by the onIMEComposition event.
static	doConversion() : Boolean	Instructs the IME to select the first candidate for the current composition string.
static	getConversionMode() : String	Indicates the conversion mode of the current IME.
static	getEnabled() : Boolean	Indicates whether the system IME is enabled.
static	removeListener(liste ner:Object) : Boolean	Removes a listener object that was previously registered to an IME instance with IME.addListener().
static	setCompositionString (composition:String) : Boolean	Sets the IME composition string.
static	setConversionMode(mo de:String) : Boolean	Sets the conversion mode of the current IME.
static	setEnabled(enabled:B oolean) : Boolean	Enables or disables the system IME.

Methods inherited from class Object

addProperty (Object.addProperty method), hasOwnProperty
(Object.hasOwnProperty method), isPropertyEnumerable
(Object.isPropertyEnumerable method), isPrototypeOf (Object.isPrototypeOf
method), registerClass (Object.registerClass method), toString
(Object.toString method), unwatch (Object.unwatch method), valueOf
(Object.valueOf method), watch (Object.watch method)

addListener (IME.addListener method)

public static addListener(listener:Object) : Void

Registers an object to receive notification when an IME event handler is invoked by the onIMEComposition event.

Availability: ActionScript 1.0; Flash Player 8

Parameters

listener:Object - An object, with an onIMEComposition (readingString) method, that listens for a callback notification from the IME event handlers. The reading string passed to this method is in the composition mode of the IME. For example, if the user enters text in Hiragana and then selects a Kanji candidate, the reading string is the original Hiragana.

Example

The following example shows how to add a listener object to System.IME that outputs notification when a user sets the composition string by clicking in the text field.

```
var IMEListener:Object = new Object();
IMEListener.onIMEComposition = function(str:String) {
  trace(">> onIMEComposition: " + str);
}
System.IME.addListener(IMEListener);
trace(System.IME.length);

var mc:MovieClip = this.createEmptyMovieClip("mc",
  this.getNextHighestDepth());
mc.createTextField("txt", this.getNextHighestDepth(), 0, 0, 0, 0);
mc.txt.border = true;
mc.txt.background = true;
mc.txt.autoSize = "left";
mc.txt.text = "Click this text to add a listener.";

mc.onPress = function() {
  if(System.capabilities.hasIME) {
    Selection.setFocus(mc.txt);
    System.IME.setCompositionString(mc.txt.text);
  }
}
```

ALPHANUMERIC_FULL (IME.ALPHANUMERIC_FULL property)

public static ALPHANUMERIC_FULL : String

A string with the value "ALPHANUMERIC_FULL" for use with setConversionMode() and getConversionMode(). This constant is used with all IMEs.

Availability: ActionScript 1.0; Flash Player 8

Example

The following example sets the IME to `ALPHANUMERIC_FULL` if the system has an Input Method Editor (IME) installed (`System.capabilities.hasIME`).

```
if(System.capabilities.hasIME) {
  trace(System.IME.getConversionMode());

  System.IME.setConversionMode(System.IME.ALPHANUMERIC_FULL);
  trace(System.IME.getConversionMode());
}
```

See also

setConversionMode (IME.setConversionMode method), getConversionMode (IME.getConversionMode method), hasIME (capabilities.hasIME property)

ALPHANUMERIC_HALF (IME.ALPHANUMERIC_HALF property)

`public static ALPHANUMERIC_HALF : String`

A string with the value `"ALPHANUMERIC_HALF"` for use with `setConversionMode()` and `getConversionMode()`. This constant is used with all IMEs.

Availability: ActionScript 1.0; Flash Player 8

Example

The following example sets the IME to `ALPHANUMERIC_HALF` if the system has an Input Method Editor (IME) installed (`System.capabilities.hasIME`).

```
if(System.capabilities.hasIME) {
  trace(System.IME.getConversionMode());

  System.IME.setConversionMode(System.IME.ALPHANUMERIC_HALF);
  trace(System.IME.getConversionMode());
}
```

See also

setConversionMode (IME.setConversionMode method), getConversionMode (IME.getConversionMode method)

CHINESE (IME.CHINESE property)

`public static CHINESE : String`

A string with the value `"CHINESE"` for use with `setConversionMode()` and `getConversionMode()`. This constant is used with simplified and traditional Chinese IMEs.

Availability: ActionScript 1.0; Flash Player 8

Example

The following example sets the IME to `CHINESE` if the system has an Input Method Editor (IME) installed (`System.capabilities.hasIME`).

```
if(System.capabilities.hasIME) {
  trace(System.IME.getConversionMode());

  System.IME.setConversionMode(System.IME.CHINESE);
  trace(System.IME.getConversionMode());
}
```

See also

`setConversionMode (IME.setConversionMode method)`, `getConversionMode (IME.getConversionMode method)`

doConversion (IME.doConversion method)

`public static doConversion() : Boolean`

Instructs the IME to select the first candidate for the current composition string.

Availability: ActionScript 1.0; Flash Player 8

Returns

`Boolean` - Returns `true` if the call is successful; otherwise `false`.

Example

The following example shows how to select the first candidate for the IME composition string. If the user's system has IME, clicking in the text field selects the candidate.

```
var mc:MovieClip = this.createEmptyMovieClip("mc",
  this.getNextHighestDepth());
mc.createTextField("txt", this.getNextHighestDepth(), 0, 0, 0, 0);
mc.txt.border = true;
mc.txt.background = true;
mc.txt.autoSize = "left";
mc.txt.text = "Set this text as the composition string and convert it.";
```

```
mc.onPress = function() {
  if(System.capabilities.hasIME) {
    Selection.setFocus(mc.txt);
    System.IME.setCompositionString(mc.txt.text);
    trace(System.IME.doConversion());
  }
}
```

getConversionMode (IME.getConversionMode method)

```
public static getConversionMode() : String
```
Indicates the conversion mode of the current IME.

Availability: ActionScript 1.0; Flash Player 8

Returns

`String` - The conversion mode. Possible values are IME mode string constants that indicate the conversion mode:

- `ALPHANUMERIC_FULL`
- `ALPHANUMERIC_HALF`
- `CHINESE`
- `JAPANESE_HIRAGANA`
- `JAPANESE_KATAKANA_FULL`
- `JAPANESE_KATAKANA_HALF`
- `KOREAN`
- `UNKNOWN`

Example

The following example gets the IME if the system has an Input Method Editor (IME) installed (`System.capabilities.hasIME`).

```
var mode:String = System.IME.UNKNOWN;
if(System.capabilities.hasIME) {
  mode = System.IME.getConversionMode();
}
trace(mode);
```

See also

ALPHANUMERIC_FULL (IME.ALPHANUMERIC_FULL property), ALPHANUMERIC_HALF
(IME.ALPHANUMERIC_HALF property), CHINESE (IME.CHINESE property),
JAPANESE_HIRAGANA (IME.JAPANESE_HIRAGANA property), JAPANESE_KATAKANA_FULL
(IME.JAPANESE_KATAKANA_FULL property), JAPANESE_KATAKANA_HALF
(IME.JAPANESE_KATAKANA_HALF property), KOREAN (IME.KOREAN property), UNKNOWN
(IME.UNKNOWN property)

getEnabled (IME.getEnabled method)

`public static getEnabled() : Boolean`

Indicates whether the system IME is enabled. An enabled IME performs multibyte input; a disabled IME performs alphanumeric input.

Availability: ActionScript 1.0; Flash Player 8

Returns

`Boolean` - Returns `true` if the system IME is enabled, `false` if it is disabled.

Example

The following example checks to see whether IME is enabled by calling the `isEnabled()` method.

```
if(System.capabilities.hasIME) {
  var isImeEnabled:Boolean = System.IME.getEnabled();
  trace(isImeEnabled);
}
```

JAPANESE_HIRAGANA (IME.JAPANESE_HIRAGANA property)

`public static JAPANESE_HIRAGANA : String`

A string with the value `"JAPANESE_HIRAGANA"` for use with `setConversionMode()` and `getConversionMode()`. This constant is used with Japanese IMEs.

Availability: ActionScript 1.0; Flash Player 8

Example

The following example sets the IME to `JAPANESE_HIRAGANA` if the system has an Input Method Editor (IME) installed (`System.capabilities.hasIME`).

```
if(System.capabilities.hasIME) {
  trace(System.IME.getConversionMode());
```

```
System.IME.setConversionMode(System.IME.JAPANESE_HIRAGANA);
trace(System.IME.getConversionMode());
}
```

See also

setConversionMode (IME.setConversionMode method), getConversionMode
(IME.getConversionMode method)

JAPANESE_KATAKANA_FULL
(IME.JAPANESE_KATAKANA_FULL property)

public static JAPANESE_KATAKANA_FULL : String

A string with the value "JAPANESE_KATAKANA_FULL" for use with setConversionMode()
and getConversionMode(). This constant is used with Japanese IMEs.

Availability: ActionScript 1.0; Flash Player 8

Example

The following example sets the IME to JAPANESE_KATAKANA_FULL if the system has an Input
Method Editor (IME) installed (System.capabilities.hasIME).

```
if(System.capabilities.hasIME) {
  trace(System.IME.getConversionMode());

  System.IME.setConversionMode(System.IME.JAPANESE_KATAKANA_FULL);
  trace(System.IME.getConversionMode());
}
```

See also

setConversionMode (IME.setConversionMode method), getConversionMode
(IME.getConversionMode method)

JAPANESE_KATAKANA_HALF
(IME.JAPANESE_KATAKANA_HALF property)

public static JAPANESE_KATAKANA_HALF : String

A string with the value "JAPANESE_KATAKANA_HALF" for use with setConversionMode()
and getConversionMode(). This constant is used with Japanese IMEs.

Availability: ActionScript 1.0; Flash Player 8

Example

The following example sets the IME to `JAPANESE_KATAKANA_HALF` if the system has an Input Method Editor (IME) installed (`System.capabilities.hasIME`).

```
if(System.capabilities.hasIME) {
  trace(System.IME.getConversionMode());

  System.IME.setConversionMode(System.IME.JAPANESE_KATAKANA_HALF);
  trace(System.IME.getConversionMode());
}
```

See also

setConversionMode (`IME.setConversionMode` method), getConversionMode (`IME.getConversionMode` method)

KOREAN (IME.KOREAN property)

`public static KOREAN : String`

A string with the value `"KOREAN"` for use with `setConversionMode()` and `getConversionMode()`. This constant is used with Korean IMEs.

Availability: ActionScript 1.0; Flash Player 8

Example

The following example sets the IME to `KOREAN` if the system has an Input Method Editor (IME) installed (`System.capabilities.hasIME`).

```
if(System.capabilities.hasIME) {
  trace(System.IME.getConversionMode());

  System.IME.setConversionMode(System.IME.KOREAN);
  trace(System.IME.getConversionMode());
}
```

See also

setConversionMode (`IME.setConversionMode` method), getConversionMode (`IME.getConversionMode` method)

onIMEComposition (IME.onIMEComposition event listener)

`onIMEComposition = function([readingString:String]) {}`

Notified when the IME composition string is being set. To use this listener, you must create a listener object. You can then define a function for this listener and use `IME.addListener()` to register the listener with the IME object, as in the following code:

```
var someListener:Object = new Object();
someListener.onIMEComposition = function () {
  // statements
}
System.IME.addListener(someListener);
```

Listeners enable different pieces of code to cooperate because multiple listeners can receive notification about a single event.

Availability: ActionScript 1.0; Flash Player 8

Parameters

`readingString:String` [optional] - The original text typed into the IME before the user started picking candidates.

Example

The following example shows how to add a listener object with the callback method `onIMEComposition()` to `System.IME`, which outputs notification when a user sets the composition string by clicking in the text field.

```
var IMEListener:Object = new Object();
IMEListener.onIMEComposition = function(str:String) {
  trace(">> onIMEComposition: " + str);
}
System.IME.addListener(IMEListener);
trace(System.IME.length);

var mc:MovieClip = this.createEmptyMovieClip("mc",
  this.getNextHighestDepth());
mc.createTextField("txt", this.getNextHighestDepth(), 0, 0, 0, 0);
mc.txt.border = true;
mc.txt.background = true;
mc.txt.autoSize = "left";
mc.txt.text = "Click this text to add a listener.";

mc.onPress = function() {
  if(System.capabilities.hasIME) {
    Selection.setFocus(mc.txt);
    System.IME.setCompositionString(mc.txt.text);
  }
}
```

See also

addListener (IME.addListener method), setCompositionString
(IME.setCompositionString method)

removeListener (IME.removeListener method)

`public static removeListener(listener:Object) : Boolean`

Removes a listener object that was previously registered to an IME instance with
`IME.addListener()`.

Availability: ActionScript 1.0; Flash Player 8

Parameters

`listener:Object` - The object that no longer receives callback notification from the IME
event handlers.

Returns

`Boolean` - Returns `true` if the listener object is removed; otherwise `false`.

Example

The following example shows how to remove a listener object from `System.IME` when a user
sets the composition string by clicking in the text field.

```
var IMEListener:Object = new Object();
IMEListener.onIMEComposition = function(str:String) {
  trace(">> onIMEComposition: " + str);

  System.IME.removeListener(this);
  trace(System.IME.length); // 0
}
System.IME.addListener(IMEListener);
trace(System.IME.length); // 1

var mc:MovieClip = this.createEmptyMovieClip("mc",
  this.getNextHighestDepth());
mc.createTextField("txt", this.getNextHighestDepth(), 0, 0, 0, 0);
mc.txt.border = true;
mc.txt.background = true;
mc.txt.autoSize = "left";
mc.txt.text = "Click this text to add and remove a listener.";

mc.onPress = function() {
  if(System.capabilities.hasIME) {
    Selection.setFocus(mc.txt);
    System.IME.setCompositionString(mc.txt.text);
```

```
    }
}
```

setCompositionString (IME.setCompositionString method)

```
public static setCompositionString(composition:String) : Boolean
```
Sets the IME composition string. When this string is set, the user can select IME candidates before committing the result to the text field that currently has focus.

Availability: ActionScript 1.0; Flash Player 8

Parameters

`composition:String` - The string to send to the IME.

Returns

`Boolean` - If the IME composition string is successfully set, returns `true`. This method fails and returns `false` if no text field has focus.

Example

The following example shows how to set the IME composition string. If the user's system has IME, clicking in the text field shows the IME options.

```
var mc:MovieClip = this.createEmptyMovieClip("mc",
  this.getNextHighestDepth());
mc.createTextField("txt", this.getNextHighestDepth(), 0, 0, 0, 0);
mc.txt.border = true;
mc.txt.background = true;
mc.txt.autoSize = "left";
mc.txt.text = "Set this text as the composition string.";

mc.onPress = function() {
  if(System.capabilities.hasIME) {
    Selection.setFocus(mc.txt);
    trace(System.IME.setCompositionString(mc.txt.text));
  }
}
```

setConversionMode (IME.setConversionMode method)

```
public static setConversionMode(mode:String) : Boolean
```
Sets the conversion mode of the current IME.

Availability: ActionScript 1.0; Flash Player 8

Parameters

`mode:String` - The conversion mode. Possible values are the IME mode string constants:

- `ALPHANUMERIC_FULL`
- `ALPHANUMERIC_HALF`
- `CHINESE`
- `JAPANESE_HIRAGANA`
- `JAPANESE_KATAKANA_FULL`
- `JAPANESE_KATAKANA_HALF`
- `KOREAN`

Returns

`Boolean` - Returns `true` if the conversion mode was successfully set; otherwise `false`.

Example

The following example gets the IME if the system has an Input Method Editor (IME) installed (`System.capabilities.hasIME`) and sets the variable `mode` to that value.

```
var mode:String = System.IME.UNKNOWN;
if(System.capabilities.hasIME) {
  mode = System.IME.getConversionMode();
}
System.IME.setConversionMode(mode);
trace(System.IME.getConversionMode());
```

See also

`ALPHANUMERIC_FULL` (`IME.ALPHANUMERIC_FULL` property), `ALPHANUMERIC_HALF` (`IME.ALPHANUMERIC_HALF` property), `CHINESE` (`IME.CHINESE` property), `JAPANESE_HIRAGANA` (`IME.JAPANESE_HIRAGANA` property), `JAPANESE_KATAKANA_FULL` (`IME.JAPANESE_KATAKANA_FULL` property), `JAPANESE_KATAKANA_HALF` (`IME.JAPANESE_KATAKANA_HALF` property), `KOREAN` (`IME.KOREAN` property)

setEnabled (IME.setEnabled method)

`public static setEnabled(enabled:Boolean) : Boolean`

Enables or disables the system IME. An enabled IME performs multibyte input; a disabled IME performs alphanumeric input.

Availability: ActionScript 1.0; Flash Player 8

Parameters

`enabled:Boolean` - Set to `true` to enable the system IME, `false` to disable it.

Returns

`Boolean` - If the attempt to enable the system IME is successful, returns `true`; otherwise `false`.

Example

The following example checks to see whether IME is enabled by calling the `isEnabled()` method and then changes its enabled state to the opposite by calling the `setEnabled()` method.

```
if(System.capabilities.hasIME) {
  var isImeEnabled:Boolean = System.IME.getEnabled();
  trace(isImeEnabled);

  if(isImeEnabled) {
    System.IME.setEnabled(false);
  }
  else {
    System.IME.setEnabled(true);
  }

  var isImeEnabled:Boolean = System.IME.getEnabled();
  trace(isImeEnabled);
}
```

UNKNOWN (IME.UNKNOWN property)

`public static UNKNOWN : String`

A string with the value `"UNKNOWN"` for use with `getConversionMode()`. This constant is used with all IMEs.

Availability: ActionScript 1.0; Flash Player 8

Example

The following example sets the IME to `UNKNOWN` if the system has an Input Method Editor (IME) installed (`System.capabilities.hasIME`).

```
if(System.capabilities.hasIME) {
  trace(System.IME.getConversionMode());

  System.IME.setConversionMode(System.IME.UNKNOWN);
  trace(System.IME.getConversionMode());
}
```

getConversionMode (IME.getConversionMode method)

Key

```
Object
  |
  +-Key
```

```
public class Key
extends Object
```

The Key class is a top-level class whose methods and properties you can use without a constructor. Use the methods of the Key class to build an interface that can be controlled by a user with a standard keyboard. The properties of the Key class are constants representing the keys most commonly used to control applications, such as Arrow keys, Page Up, and Page Down.

A Flash application can only monitor keyboard events that occur within its focus. A Flash application cannot detect keyboard events in another application.

Availability: ActionScript 1.0; Flash Player 6

Property summary

Modifiers	Property	Description
static	BACKSPACE:Number	The key code value for the Backspace key (8).
static	CAPSLOCK:Number	The key code value for the Caps Lock key (20).
static	CONTROL:Number	The key code value for the Control key (17).
static	DELETEKEY:Number	The key code value for the Delete key (46).
static	DOWN:Number	The key code value for the Down Arrow key (40).
static	END:Number	The key code value for the End key (35).
static	ENTER:Number	The key code value for the Enter key (13).
static	ESCAPE:Number	The key code value for the Escape key (27).
static	HOME:Number	The key code value for the Home key (36).
static	INSERT:Number	The key code value for the Insert key (45).
static	LEFT:Number	The key code value for the Left Arrow key (37).
static	_listeners:Array [read-only]	A list of references to all listener objects that are registered with the Key object.
static	PGDN:Number	The key code value for the Page Down key (34).
static	PGUP:Number	The key code value for the Page Up key (33).
static	RIGHT:Number	The key code value for the Right Arrow key (39).
static	SHIFT:Number	The key code value for the Shift key (16).
static	SPACE:Number	The key code value for the Spacebar (32).
static	TAB:Number	The key code value for the Tab key (9).
static	UP:Number	The key code value for the Up Arrow key (38).

Properties inherited from class Object

```
constructor (Object.constructor property), __proto__ (Object.__proto__
property), prototype (Object.prototype property), __resolve
(Object.__resolve property)
```

Event summary

Event	Description
`onKeyDown = function() {}`	Notified when a key is pressed.
`onKeyUp = function() {}`	Notified when a key is released.

Method summary

Modifiers	Signature	Description
`static`	`addListener(listener :Object) : Void`	Registers an object to receive `onKeyDown` and `onKeyUp` notification.
`static`	`getAscii() : Number`	Returns the ASCII code of the last key pressed or released.
`static`	`getCode() : Number`	Returns the key code value of the last key pressed.
`static`	`isAccessible() : Boolean`	Returns a Boolean value indicating, depending on security restrictions, whether the last key pressed may be accessed by other SWF files.
`static`	`isDown(code:Number) : Boolean`	Returns `true` if the key specified in *keycode* is pressed; `false` otherwise.
`static`	`isToggled(code:Number) : Boolean`	Returns `true` if the Caps Lock or Num Lock key is activated (toggled to an active state); `false` otherwise.
`static`	`removeListener(listener:Object) : Boolean`	Removes an object previously registered with `Key.addListener()`.

Methods inherited from class Object

```
addProperty (Object.addProperty method), hasOwnProperty
(Object.hasOwnProperty method), isPropertyEnumerable
(Object.isPropertyEnumerable method), isPrototypeOf (Object.isPrototypeOf
method), registerClass (Object.registerClass method), toString
(Object.toString method), unwatch (Object.unwatch method), valueOf
(Object.valueOf method), watch (Object.watch method)
```

addListener (Key.addListener method)

`public static addListener(listener:Object) : Void`

Registers an object to receive `onKeyDown` and `onKeyUp` notification. When a key is pressed or released, regardless of the input focus, all listening objects registered with `addListener()` have either their `onKeyDown` method or `onKeyUp` method invoked. Multiple objects can listen for keyboard notifications. If the listener *newListener* is already registered, no change occurs.

A Flash application can only monitor keyboard events that occur within its focus. A Flash application cannot detect keyboard events in another application.

Availability: ActionScript 1.0; Flash Player 6

Parameters

`listener:Object` - An object with methods `onKeyDown` and `onKeyUp`.

Example

The following example creates a new listener object and defines a function for `onKeyDown` and `onKeyUp`. The last line uses `addListener()` to register the listener with the Key object so that it can receive notification from the key down and key up events.

```
var myListener:Object = new Object();
myListener.onKeyDown = function () {
  trace ("You pressed a key.");
}
myListener.onKeyUp = function () {
  trace ("You released a key.");
}
Key.addListener(myListener);
```

The following example assigns the keyboard shortcut Control+7 to a button with an instance name of `my_btn` and makes information about the shortcut available to screen readers (see `_accProps`). In this example, when you press Control+7 the `myOnPress` function displays the text `hello` in the Output panel.

```
function myOnPress() {
  trace("hello");
}
function myOnKeyDown() {
  // 55 is key code for 7
  if (Key.isDown(Key.CONTROL) && Key.getCode() == 55) {
  Selection.setFocus(my_btn);
  my_btn.onPress();
  }
}
var myListener:Object = new Object();
myListener.onKeyDown = myOnKeyDown;
```

```
Key.addListener(myListener);
my_btn.onPress = myOnPress;
my_btn._accProps.shortcut = "Ctrl+7";
Accessibility.updateProperties();
```

See also

getCode (Key.getCode method), isDown (Key.isDown method), onKeyDown
(Key.onKeyDown event listener), onKeyUp (Key.onKeyUp event listener),
removeListener (Key.removeListener method)

BACKSPACE (Key.BACKSPACE property)

`public static BACKSPACE : Number`

The key code value for the Backspace key (8).

Availability: ActionScript 1.0; Flash Player 5

Example

The following example creates a new listener object and defines a function for onKeyDown.
The last line uses addListener() to register the listener with the Key object so that it can
receive notification from the key down event.

```
var keyListener:Object = new Object();
keyListener.onKeyDown = function() {
  if (Key.isDown(Key.BACKSPACE)) {
  trace("you pressed the Backspace key.");
  } else {
  trace("you DIDN'T press the Backspace key.");
  }
};
Key.addListener(keyListener);
```

When you use this example, be sure to select Control > Disable Keyboard Shortcuts in the test
environment.

CAPSLOCK (Key.CAPSLOCK property)

`public static CAPSLOCK : Number`

The key code value for the Caps Lock key (20).

Availability: ActionScript 1.0; Flash Player 5

Example

The following example creates a new listener object and defines a function for `onKeyDown`. The last line uses `addListener()` to register the listener with the Key object so that it can receive notification from the key down event.

```
var keyListener:Object = new Object();
keyListener.onKeyDown = function() {
  if (Key.isDown(Key.CAPSLOCK)) {
  trace("you pressed the Caps Lock key.");
  trace("\tCaps Lock == "+Key.isToggled(Key.CAPSLOCK));
  }
};
Key.addListener(keyListener);
```

Information is displayed in the Output panel when you press the Caps Lock key. The Output panel displays either `true` or `false`, depending on whether the Caps Lock key is activated using the isToggled method.

CONTROL (Key.CONTROL property)

```
public static CONTROL : Number
```

The key code value for the Control key (17).

Availability: ActionScript 1.0; Flash Player 5

Example

The following example assigns the keyboard shortcut Control+7 to a button with an instance name of `my_btn` and makes information about the shortcut available to screen readers (see `_accProps`). In this example, when you press Control+7 the `myOnPress` function displays the text `hello` in the Output panel.

```
function myOnPress() {
  trace("hello");
}
function myOnKeyDown() {
  // 55 is key code for 7
  if (Key.isDown(Key.CONTROL) && Key.getCode() == 55) {
  Selection.setFocus(my_btn);
  my_btn.onPress();
  }
}
var myListener:Object = new Object();
myListener.onKeyDown = myOnKeyDown;
Key.addListener(myListener);
my_btn.onPress = myOnPress;
my_btn._accProps.shortcut = "Ctrl+7";
Accessibility.updateProperties();
```

DELETEKEY (Key.DELETEKEY property)

`public static DELETEKEY : Number`

The key code value for the Delete key (46).

Availability: ActionScript 1.0; Flash Player 5

Example

The following example lets you draw lines with the mouse pointer using the Drawing API and listener objects. Press the Backspace or Delete key to remove the lines that you draw.

```
this.createEmptyMovieClip("canvas_mc", this.getNextHighestDepth());
var mouseListener:Object = new Object();
mouseListener.onMouseDown = function() {
  this.drawing = true;
  canvas_mc.moveTo(_xmouse, _ymouse);
  canvas_mc.lineStyle(3, 0x99CC00, 100);
};
mouseListener.onMouseUp = function() {
  this.drawing = false;
};
mouseListener.onMouseMove = function() {
  if (this.drawing) {
  canvas_mc.lineTo(_xmouse, _ymouse);
  }
  updateAfterEvent();
};
Mouse.addListener(mouseListener);
//
var keyListener:Object = new Object();
keyListener.onKeyDown = function() {
  if (Key.isDown(Key.DELETEKEY) || Key.isDown(Key.BACKSPACE)) {
  canvas_mc.clear();
  }
};
Key.addListener(keyListener);
```

When you use this example, be sure to select Control > Disable Keyboard Shortcuts in the test environment.

The `MovieClip.getNextHighestDepth()` method used in this example requires Flash Player 7 or later. If your SWF file includes a version 2 component, use the version 2 components DepthManager class instead of the `MovieClip.getNextHighestDepth()` method.

DOWN (Key.DOWN property)

`public static DOWN : Number`

The key code value for the Down Arrow key (40).

Availability: ActionScript 1.0; Flash Player 5

Example

The following example moves a movie clip called `car_mc` a constant distance (10) when you press an arrow key. A sound plays when you press the Spacebar. Give a sound in the library a linkage identifier of `horn_id` for this example.

```
var DISTANCE:Number = 10;
var horn_sound:Sound = new Sound();
horn_sound.attachSound("horn_id");
var keyListener_obj:Object = new Object();
keyListener_obj.onKeyDown = function() {
  switch (Key.getCode()) {
  case Key.SPACE :
  horn_sound.start();
  break;
  case Key.LEFT :
  car_mc._x -= DISTANCE;
  break;
  case Key.UP :
  car_mc._y -= DISTANCE;
  break;
  case Key.RIGHT :
  car_mc._x += DISTANCE;
  break;
  case Key.DOWN :
  car_mc._y += DISTANCE;
  break;
  }
};
Key.addListener(keyListener_obj);
```

END (Key.END property)

`public static END : Number`

The key code value for the End key (35).

Availability: ActionScript 1.0; Flash Player 5

ENTER (Key.ENTER property)

```
public static ENTER : Number
```

The key code value for the Enter key (13).

Availability: ActionScript 1.0; Flash Player 5

Example

The following example moves a movie clip called `car_mc` a constant distance (10) when you press an arrow key. The `car_mc` instance stops when you press Enter and deletes the `onEnterFrame` event.

```
var DISTANCE:Number = 5;
var keyListener:Object = new Object();
keyListener.onKeyDown = function() {
  switch (Key.getCode()) {
  case Key.LEFT :
  car_mc.onEnterFrame = function() {
    this._x -= DISTANCE;
  };
  break;
  case Key.UP :
  car_mc.onEnterFrame = function() {
    this._y -= DISTANCE;
  };
  break;
  case Key.RIGHT :
  car_mc.onEnterFrame = function() {
    this._x += DISTANCE;
  };
  break;
  case Key.DOWN :
  car_mc.onEnterFrame = function() {
    this._y += DISTANCE;
  };
  break;
  case Key.ENTER :
  delete car_mc.onEnterFrame;
  break;
  }
};
Key.addListener(keyListener);
```

When you use this example, be sure to select Control > Disable Keyboard Shortcuts in the test environment.

ESCAPE (Key.ESCAPE property)

`public static ESCAPE : Number`

The key code value for the Escape key (27).

Availability: ActionScript 1.0; Flash Player 5

Example

The following example sets a timer. When you press Escape, the Output panel displays information that includes how long it took you to press the key.

```
var keyListener:Object = new Object();
keyListener.onKeyDown = function() {
  if (Key.isDown(Key.ESCAPE)) {
  // Get the current timer, convert the value to seconds and round it to two
  decimal places.
  var timer:Number = Math.round(getTimer()/10)/100;
  trace("you pressed the Esc key: "+getTimer()+" ms ("+timer+" s)");
  }
};
Key.addListener(keyListener);
```

When you use this example, be sure to select Control > Disable Keyboard Shortcuts in the test environment.

getAscii (Key.getAscii method)

`public static getAscii() : Number`

Returns the ASCII code of the last key pressed or released. The ASCII values returned are English keyboard values. For example, if you press Shift+2, `Key.getAscii()` returns @ on a Japanese keyboard, which is the same as it does on an English keyboard.

A Flash application can only monitor keyboard events that occur within its focus. A Flash application cannot detect keyboard events in another application.

Availability: ActionScript 1.0; Flash Player 5

Returns

`Number` - The ASCII value of the last key pressed. This method returns 0 if no key was pressed or released, or if the key code is not accessible for security reasons.

Example

The following example calls the `getAscii()` method any time a key is pressed. The example creates a listener object named `keyListener` and defines a function that responds to the `onKeyDown` event by calling `Key.getAscii()`. The `keyListener` object is then registered to the `Key` object, which broadcasts the `onKeyDown` message whenever a key is pressed while the SWF file plays.

```
var keyListener:Object = new Object();
keyListener.onKeyDown = function() {
  trace("The ASCII code for the last key typed is: "+Key.getAscii());
};
Key.addListener(keyListener);
```

When you use this example, be sure to select Control > Disable Keyboard Shortcuts in the test environment.

The following example adds a call to `Key.getAscii()` to show how the two methods differ. The main difference is that `Key.getAscii()` differentiates between uppercase and lowercase letters, and `Key.getCode()` does not.

```
var keyListener:Object = new Object();
keyListener.onKeyDown = function() {
  trace("For the last key typed:");
  trace("\tThe Key code is: "+Key.getCode());
  trace("\tThe ASCII value is: "+Key.getAscii());
  trace("");
};
Key.addListener(keyListener);
```

When you use this example, be sure to select Control > Disable Keyboard Shortcuts in the test environment.

See also

`isAccessible (Key.isAccessible method)`

getCode (Key.getCode method)

`public static getCode() : Number`

Returns the key code value of the last key pressed.

Note: The Flash Lite implementation of this method returns a string or a number, depending on the key code passed in by the platform. The only valid key codes are the standard key codes accepted by this class and the special key codes listed as properties of the `ExtendedKey` class.

A Flash application can only monitor keyboard events that occur within its focus. A Flash application cannot detect keyboard events in another application.

Availability: ActionScript 1.0; Flash Player 5

Returns

Number - The key code of the last key pressed. This method returns 0 if no key was pressed or released, or if the key code is not accessible for security reasons.

Example

The following example calls the getCode() method any time a key is pressed. The example creates a listener object named keyListener and defines a function that responds to the onKeyDown event by calling Key.getCode(). The keyListener object is then registered to the Key object, which broadcasts the onKeyDown message whenever a key is pressed while the SWF file plays.

```
var keyListener:Object = new Object();
keyListener.onKeyDown = function() {
  // compare return value of getCode() to constant
  if (Key.getCode() == Key.ENTER) {
    trace ("Virtual key code: "+Key.getCode()+" (ENTER key)");
  }
  else {
    trace("Virtual key code: "+Key.getCode());
  }
};
Key.addListener(keyListener);
```

When you use this example, be sure to select Control > Disable Keyboard Shortcuts in the test environment.

The following example adds a call to Key.getAscii() to show how the two methods differ. The main difference is that Key.getAscii() differentiates between uppercase and lowercase letters, and Key.getCode() does not.

```
var keyListener:Object = new Object();
keyListener.onKeyDown = function() {
  trace("For the last key typed:");
  trace("\tThe Key code is: "+Key.getCode());
  trace("\tThe ASCII value is: "+Key.getAscii());
  trace("");
};
Key.addListener(keyListener);
```

When you use this example, be sure to select Control > Disable Keyboard Shortcuts in the test environment.

See also

getAscii (Key.getAscii method), isAccessible (Key.isAccessible method)

HOME (Key.HOME property)

```
public static HOME : Number
```

The key code value for the Home key (36).

Availability: ActionScript 1.0; Flash Player 5

Example

The following example attaches a draggable movie clip called `car_mc` at the *x* and *y* coordinates of 0,0. When you press the Home key, `car_mc` returns to 0,0. Create a movie clip that has a linkage ID `car_id`, and add the following ActionScript to Frame 1 of the Timeline:

```
this.attachMovie("car_id", "car_mc", this.getNextHighestDepth(), {_x:0,
  _y:0});
car_mc.onPress = function() {
  this.startDrag();
};
car_mc.onRelease = function() {
  this.stopDrag();
};
var keyListener:Object = new Object();
keyListener.onKeyDown = function() {
  if (Key.isDown(Key.HOME)) {
  car_mc._x = 0;
  car_mc._y = 0;
  }
};
Key.addListener(keyListener);
```

The `MovieClip.getNextHighestDepth()` method used in this example requires Flash Player 7 or later. If your SWF file includes a version 2 component, use the version 2 components DepthManager class instead of the `MovieClip.getNextHighestDepth()` method.

INSERT (Key.INSERT property)

```
public static INSERT : Number
```

The key code value for the Insert key (45).

Availability: ActionScript 1.0; Flash Player 5

Example

The following example creates a new listener object and defines a function for `onKeyDown`. The last line uses `addListener()` to register the listener with the Key object so that it can receive notification from the key down event and display information in the Output panel.

```
var keyListener:Object = new Object();
keyListener.onKeyDown = function() {
  if (Key.isDown(Key.INSERT)) {
  trace("You pressed the Insert key.");
  }
};
Key.addListener(keyListener);
```

isAccessible (Key.isAccessible method)

`public static isAccessible() : Boolean`

Returns a Boolean value indicating, depending on security restrictions, whether the last key pressed may be accessed by other SWF files. By default code from a SWF file in one domain may not access a keystroke generated from a SWF file in another domain. For more information on cross-domain security, see "Understanding Security" in *Learning ActionScript 2.0 in Flash*.

Availability: ActionScript 1.0; Flash Player 8

Returns

`Boolean` - The value `true` if the last key pressed may be accessed. If access is not permitted, this method returns `false`.

isDown (Key.isDown method)

`public static isDown(code:Number) : Boolean`

Returns `true` if the key specified in *keycode* is pressed; `false` otherwise. On the Macintosh, the key code values for the Caps Lock and Num Lock keys are identical.

A Flash application can only monitor keyboard events that occur within its focus. A Flash application cannot detect keyboard events in another application.

Availability: ActionScript 1.0; Flash Player 5

Parameters

`code:Number` - The key code value assigned to a specific key or a Key class property associated with a specific key.

Returns

Boolean - The value `true` if the key specified in *keycode* is pressed; `false` otherwise.

Example

The following script lets the user control a movie clip's (car_mc) location:

```
car_mc.onEnterFrame = function() {
 if (Key.isDown(Key.RIGHT)) {
 this._x += 10;
 } else if (Key.isDown(Key.LEFT)) {
 this._x -= 10;
 }
};
```

isToggled (Key.isToggled method)

`public static isToggled(code:Number) : Boolean`

Returns `true` if the Caps Lock or Num Lock key is activated (toggled to an active state); `false` otherwise. Although the term *toggled* usually means that something is switched between two options, the method Key.isToggled() will only return `true` if the key is toggled to an active state. On the Macintosh, the key code values for the Caps Lock and Num Lock keys are identical.

A Flash application can only monitor keyboard events that occur within its focus. A Flash application cannot detect keyboard events in another application.

Availability: ActionScript 1.0; Flash Player 5

Parameters

`code:Number` - The key code for the Caps Lock key (20) or the Num Lock key (144).

Returns

Boolean - The value `true` if the Caps Lock or Num Lock key is activated (toggled to an active state); `false` otherwise.

Example

The following example calls the `isToggled()` method any time a key is pressed and executes a trace statement any time the Caps Lock key is toggled to an active state. The example creates a listener object named `keyListener` and defines a function that responds to the `onKeyDown` event by calling `Key.isToggled()`. The `keyListener` object is then registered to the `Key` object, which broadcasts the `onKeyDown` message whenever a key is pressed while the SWF file plays.

```
var keyListener:Object = new Object();
keyListener.onKeyDown = function() {
  if (Key.isDown(Key.CAPSLOCK)) {
  trace("you pressed the Caps Lock key.");
  trace("\tCaps Lock == "+Key.isToggled(Key.CAPSLOCK));
  }
};
Key.addListener(keyListener);
```

Information displays in the Output panel when you press the Caps Lock key. The Output panel displays either `true` or `false`, depending on whether the Caps Lock is activated using the isToggled method.

The following example creates two text fields that update when the Caps Lock and Num Lock keys are toggled. Each text field displays true when the key is activated, and false when the key is deactivated.

```
this.createTextField("capsLock_txt", this.getNextHighestDepth(), 0, 0, 100,
  22);
capsLock_txt.autoSize = true;
capsLock_txt.html = true;
this.createTextField("numLock_txt", this.getNextHighestDepth(), 0, 22, 100,
  22);
numLock_txt.autoSize = true;
numLock_txt.html = true;
//
var keyListener:Object = new Object();
keyListener.onKeyDown = function() {
  capsLock_txt.htmlText = "<b>Caps Lock:</b> "+Key.isToggled(Key.CAPSLOCK);
  numLock_txt.htmlText = "<b>Num Lock:</b> "+Key.isToggled(144);
};
Key.addListener(keyListener);
```

The `MovieClip.getNextHighestDepth()` method used in this example requires Flash Player 7 or later. If your SWF file includes a version 2 component, use the version 2 components DepthManager class instead of the `MovieClip.getNextHighestDepth()` method.

LEFT (Key.LEFT property)

`public static LEFT : Number`

The key code value for the Left Arrow key (37).

Availability: ActionScript 1.0; Flash Player 5

Example

The following example moves a movie clip called `car_mc` a constant distance (10) when you press an arrow key. A sound plays when you press the Spacebar. Give a sound in the library a linkage identifier of `horn_id` for this example.

```
var DISTANCE:Number = 10;
var horn_sound:Sound = new Sound();
horn_sound.attachSound("horn_id");
var keyListener_obj:Object = new Object();
keyListener_obj.onKeyDown = function() {
  switch (Key.getCode()) {
  case Key.SPACE :
  horn_sound.start();
  break;
  case Key.LEFT :
  car_mc._x -= DISTANCE;
  break;
  case Key.UP :
  car_mc._y -= DISTANCE;
  break;
  case Key.RIGHT :
  car_mc._x += DISTANCE;
  break;
  case Key.DOWN :
  car_mc._y += DISTANCE;
  break;
  }
};
Key.addListener(keyListener_obj);
```

_listeners (Key._listeners property)

`public static _listeners : Array [read-only]`

A list of references to all listener objects that are registered with the Key object. This property is intended for internal use, but it may be useful if you want to ascertain the number of listeners currently registered with the Key object. Objects are added to and removed from this array by calls to the `addListener()` and `removelistener()` methods.

Availability: ActionScript 1.0; Flash Player 6

Example

The following example shows how to use the `length` property to ascertain the number of listener objects currently registered to the Key object.

```
var myListener:Object = new Object();
myListener.onKeyDown = function () {
trace ("You pressed a key.");
}
Key.addListener(myListener);

trace(Key._listeners.length); // Output: 1
```

onKeyDown (Key.onKeyDown event listener)

`onKeyDown = function() {}`

Notified when a key is pressed. To use `onKeyDown`, you must create a listener object. You can then define a function for `onKeyDown` and use `addListener()` to register the listener with the Key object, as shown in the following example:

```
var keyListener:Object = new Object();
keyListener.onKeyDown = function() {
  trace("DOWN -> Code: "+Key.getCode()+"\tACSII: "+Key.getAscii()+"\tKey:
  "+chr(Key.getAscii()));
};
keyListener.onKeyUp = function() {
  trace("UP -> Code: "+Key.getCode()+"\tACSII: "+Key.getAscii()+"\tKey:
  "+chr(Key.getAscii()));
};
Key.addListener(keyListener);
```

Listeners enable different pieces of code to cooperate because multiple listeners can receive notification about a single event.

A Flash application can only monitor keyboard events that occur within its focus. A Flash application cannot detect keyboard events in another application.

Availability: ActionScript 1.0; Flash Player 6

See also

`addListener (Key.addListener method)`

onKeyUp (Key.onKeyUp event listener)

`onKeyUp = function() {}`

Notified when a key is released. To use `onKeyUp`, you must create a listener object. You can then define a function for `onKeyUp` and use `addListener()` to register the listener with the Key object, as shown in the following example:

```
var keyListener:Object = new Object();
keyListener.onKeyDown = function() {
  trace("DOWN -> Code: "+Key.getCode()+"\tACSII: "+Key.getAscii()+"\tKey:
  "+chr(Key.getAscii()));
};
keyListener.onKeyUp = function() {
  trace("UP -> Code: "+Key.getCode()+"\tACSII: "+Key.getAscii()+"\tKey:
  "+chr(Key.getAscii()));
};
Key.addListener(keyListener);
```

Listeners enable different pieces of code to cooperate because multiple listeners can receive notification about a single event.

A Flash application can only monitor keyboard events that occur within its focus. A Flash application cannot detect keyboard events in another application.

Availability: ActionScript 1.0; Flash Player 6

See also
```
addListener (Key.addListener method)
```

PGDN (Key.PGDN property)

```
public static PGDN : Number
```
The key code value for the Page Down key (34).

Availability: ActionScript 1.0; Flash Player 5

Example
The following example rotates a movie clip called car_mc when you press the Page Down or Page Up key.

```
var keyListener:Object = new Object();
keyListener.onKeyDown = function() {
  if (Key.isDown(Key.PGDN)) {
  car_mc._rotation += 5;
  } else if (Key.isDown(Key.PGUP)) {
  car_mc._rotation -= 5;
  }
};
Key.addListener(keyListener);
```

PGUP (Key.PGUP property)

```
public static PGUP : Number
```
The key code value for the Page Up key (33).

Availability: ActionScript 1.0; Flash Player 5

Example

The following example rotates a movie clip called `car_mc` when you press the Page Down or Page Up key.

```
var keyListener:Object = new Object();
keyListener.onKeyDown = function() {
  if (Key.isDown(Key.PGDN)) {
  car_mc._rotation += 5;
  } else if (Key.isDown(Key.PGUP)) {
  car_mc._rotation -= 5;
  }
};
Key.addListener(keyListener);
```

removeListener (Key.removeListener method)

```
public static removeListener(listener:Object) : Boolean
```

Removes an object previously registered with `Key.addListener()`.

Availability: ActionScript 1.0; Flash Player 6

Parameters

`listener:Object` - An object.

Returns

`Boolean` - If the *listener* was successfully removed, the method returns `true`. If the *listener* was not successfully removed (for example, because the *listener* was not on the Key object's listener list), the method returns `false`.

Example

The following example moves a movie clip called `car_mc` using the Left and Right arrow keys. The listener is removed when you press Escape, and `car_mc` no longer moves.

```
var keyListener:Object = new Object();
keyListener.onKeyDown = function() {
  switch (Key.getCode()) {
  case Key.LEFT :
  car_mc._x -= 10;
  break;
  case Key.RIGHT :
  car_mc._x += 10;
  break;
  case Key.ESCAPE :
  Key.removeListener(keyListener);
  }
};
```

```
Key.addListener(keyListener);
```

RIGHT (Key.RIGHT property)

```
public static RIGHT : Number
```

The key code value for the Right Arrow key (39).

Availability: ActionScript 1.0; Flash Player 5

Example

The following example moves a movie clip called `car_mc` a constant distance (10) when you press an arrow key. A sound plays when you press the Spacebar. For this example, give a sound in the library a linkage identifier of `horn_id`.

```
var DISTANCE:Number = 10;
var horn_sound:Sound = new Sound();
horn_sound.attachSound("horn_id");
var keyListener_obj:Object = new Object();
keyListener_obj.onKeyDown = function() {
  switch (Key.getCode()) {
  case Key.SPACE :
  horn_sound.start();
  break;
  case Key.LEFT :
  car_mc._x -= DISTANCE;
  break;
  case Key.UP :
  car_mc._y -= DISTANCE;
  break;
  case Key.RIGHT :
  car_mc._x += DISTANCE;
  break;
  case Key.DOWN :
  car_mc._y += DISTANCE;
  break;
  }
};
Key.addListener(keyListener_obj);
```

SHIFT (Key.SHIFT property)

```
public static SHIFT : Number
```

The key code value for the Shift key (16).

Availability: ActionScript 1.0; Flash Player 5

Example

The following example scales `car_mc` when you press Shift.

```
var keyListener:Object = new Object();
keyListener.onKeyDown = function() {
  if (Key.isDown(Key.SHIFT)) {
  car_mc._xscale = 2;
  car_mc._yscale = 2;
  } else if (Key.isDown(Key.CONTROL)) {
  car_mc._xscale /= 2;
  car_mc._yscale /= 2;
  }
};
Key.addListener(keyListener);
```

SPACE (Key.SPACE property)

```
public static SPACE : Number
```

The key code value for the Spacebar (32).

Availability: ActionScript 1.0; Flash Player 5

Example

The following example moves a movie clip called `car_mc` a constant distance (10) when you press an arrow key. A sound plays when you press the Spacebar. For this example, give a sound in the library a linkage identifier of `horn_id`.

```
var DISTANCE:Number = 10;
var horn_sound:Sound = new Sound();
horn_sound.attachSound("horn_id");
var keyListener_obj:Object = new Object();
keyListener_obj.onKeyDown = function() {
  switch (Key.getCode()) {
  case Key.SPACE :
  horn_sound.start();
  break;
  case Key.LEFT :
  car_mc._x -= DISTANCE;
  break;
  case Key.UP :
  car_mc._y -= DISTANCE;
  break;
  case Key.RIGHT :
  car_mc._x += DISTANCE;
  break;
  case Key.DOWN :
  car_mc._y += DISTANCE;
  break;
```

```
    }
};
Key.addListener(keyListener_obj);
```

TAB (Key.TAB property)

`public static TAB : Number`

The key code value for the Tab key (9).

Availability: ActionScript 1.0; Flash Player 5

Example

The following example creates a text field, and displays the date in the text field when you press Tab.

```
this.createTextField("date_txt", this.getNextHighestDepth(), 0, 0, 100,
    22);
date_txt.autoSize = true;
var keyListener:Object = new Object();
keyListener.onKeyDown = function() {
  if (Key.isDown(Key.TAB)) {
  var today_date:Date = new Date();
  date_txt.text = today_date.toString();
  }
};
Key.addListener(keyListener);
```

When you use this example, be sure to select Control > Disable Keyboard Shortcuts in the test environment.

The `MovieClip.getNextHighestDepth()` method used in this example requires Flash Player 7 or later. If your SWF file includes a version 2 component, use the version 2 components DepthManager class instead of the `MovieClip.getNextHighestDepth()` method.

UP (Key.UP property)

`public static UP : Number`

The key code value for the Up Arrow key (38).

Availability: ActionScript 1.0; Flash Player 5

Example

The following example moves a movie clip called car_mc a constant distance (10) when you
press an arrow key. A sound plays when you press the Spacebar. For this example, give a sound
in the library a linkage identifier of horn_id.

```
var DISTANCE:Number = 10;
var horn_sound:Sound = new Sound();
horn_sound.attachSound("horn_id");
var keyListener_obj:Object = new Object();
keyListener_obj.onKeyDown = function() {
   switch (Key.getCode()) {
   case Key.SPACE :
   horn_sound.start();
   break;
   case Key.LEFT :
   car_mc._x -= DISTANCE;
   break;
   case Key.UP :
   car_mc._y -= DISTANCE;
   break;
   case Key.RIGHT :
   car_mc._x += DISTANCE;
   break;
   case Key.DOWN :
   car_mc._y += DISTANCE;
   break;
   }
};
Key.addListener(keyListener_obj);
```

LoadVars

```
Object
  |
  +-LoadVars
```

```
public dynamic class LoadVars
extends Object
```

You can use the LoadVars class to obtain verification of successful data loading and to monitor
download progress. The LoadVars class is an alternative to the loadVariables() function for
transferring variables between a Flash application and a server.

The LoadVars class lets you send all the variables in an object to a specified URL and to load all the variables at a specified URL into an object. It also lets you send specific variables, rather than all variables, which can make your application more efficient. You can use the `LoadVars.onLoad` handler to ensure that your application runs when data is loaded, and not before.

The LoadVars class works much like the XML class; it uses the `load()`, `send()`, and `sendAndLoad()` methods to communicate with a server. The main difference between the LoadVars class and the XML class is that LoadVars transfers ActionScript name and value pairs, rather than an XML Document Object Model (DOM) tree stored in the XML object. The LoadVars class follows the same security restrictions as the XML class.

Availability: ActionScript 1.0; Flash Player 6

See also

`loadVariables function`, `onLoad (LoadVars.onLoad handler)`, `XML`

Property summary

Modifiers	Property	Description
	`contentType:String`	The MIME type that is sent to the server when you call `LoadVars.send()` or `LoadVars.sendAndLoad()`.
	`loaded:Boolean`	A Boolean value that indicates whether a `load` or `sendAndLoad` operation has completed, `undefined` by default.

Properties inherited from class Object

```
constructor (Object.constructor property), __proto__ (Object.__proto__
property), prototype (Object.prototype property), __resolve
(Object.__resolve property)
```

Event summary

Event	Description
`onData = function(src:String) {}`	Invoked when data has completely downloaded from the server or when an error occurs while data is downloading from a server.
`onHTTPStatus = function(httpStatus:Number) {}`	Invoked when Flash Player receives an HTTP status code from the server.
`onLoad = function(success:Boolean) {}`	Invoked when a `LoadVars.load()` or `LoadVars.sendAndLoad()` operation has ended.

Constructor summary

Signature	Description
`LoadVars()`	Creates a LoadVars object.

Method summary

Modifiers	Signature	Description
	`addRequestHeader(header:Object, headerValue:String) : Void`	Adds or changes HTTP request headers (such as `Content-Type` or `SOAPAction`) sent with `POST` actions.
	`decode(queryString:String) : Void`	Converts the variable string to properties of the specified LoadVars object.
	`getBytesLoaded() : Number`	Returns the number of bytes downloaded by `LoadVars.load()` or `LoadVars.sendAndLoad()`.
	`getBytesTotal() : Number`	Returns the total number of bytes downloaded by `LoadVars.load()` or `LoadVars.sendAndLoad()`.
	`load(url:String) : Boolean`	Downloads variables from the specified URL, parses the variable data, and places the resulting variables in *my_lv*.
	`send(url:String, target:String, [method:String]) : Boolean`	Sends the variables in the *my_lv* object to the specified URL.
	`sendAndLoad(url:String, target:Object, [method:String]) : Boolean`	Posts variables in the *my_lv* object to the specified URL.
	`toString() : String`	Returns a string containing all enumerable variables in *my_lv*, in the MIME content encoding *application/x-www-form-urlencoded*.

Methods inherited from class Object

```
addProperty (Object.addProperty method), hasOwnProperty
(Object.hasOwnProperty method), isPropertyEnumerable
(Object.isPropertyEnumerable method), isPrototypeOf (Object.isPrototypeOf
method), registerClass (Object.registerClass method), toString
(Object.toString method), unwatch (Object.unwatch method), valueOf
(Object.valueOf method), watch (Object.watch method)
```

addRequestHeader (LoadVars.addRequestHeader method)

```
public addRequestHeader(header:Object, headerValue:String) : Void
```

Adds or changes HTTP request headers (such as `Content-Type` or `SOAPAction`) sent with `POST` actions. In the first usage, you pass two strings to the method: `header` and `headerValue`. In the second usage, you pass an array of strings, alternating header names and header values.

If multiple calls are made to set the same header name, each successive value will replace the value set in the previous call.

The following standard HTTP headers *cannot* be added or changed with this method: `Accept-Ranges`, `Age`, `Allow`, `Allowed`, `Connection`, `Content-Length`, `Content-Location`, `Content-Range`, `ETag`, `Host`, `Last-Modified`, `Locations`, `Max-Forwards`, `Proxy-Authenticate`, `Proxy-Authorization`, `Public`, `Range`, `Retry-After`, `Server`, `TE`, `Trailer`, `Transfer-Encoding`, `Upgrade`, `URI`, `Vary`, `Via`, `Warning`, and `WWW-Authenticate`.

Availability: ActionScript 1.0; Flash Player 6

Parameters

`header:Object` - A string or array of strings that represents an HTTP request header name.

`headerValue:String` - A string that represents the value associated with `header`.

Example

The following example adds a custom HTTP header named `SOAPAction` with a value of `Foo` to the `my_lv` object:

```
my_lv.addRequestHeader("SOAPAction", "'Foo'");
```

The following example creates an array named `headers` that contains two alternating HTTP headers and their associated values. The array is passed as an argument to `addRequestHeader()`.

```
var headers = ["Content-Type", "text/plain", "X-ClientAppVersion", "2.0"];
my_lv.addRequestHeader(headers);
```

The following example creates a new LoadVars object that adds a request header called `FLASH-UUID`. The header contains a variable that can be checked by the server.

```
var my_lv:LoadVars = new LoadVars();
my_lv.addRequestHeader("FLASH-UUID", "41472");
my_lv.name = "Mort";
my_lv.age = 26;
my_lv.send("http://flash-mx.com/mm/cgivars.cfm", "_blank", "POST");
```

See also
addRequestHeader (XML.addRequestHeader method)

contentType (LoadVars.contentType property)

`public contentType : String`

The MIME type that is sent to the server when you call `LoadVars.send()` or
`LoadVars.sendAndLoad()`. The default is *application/x-www-form-urlencoded*.

Availability: ActionScript 1.0; Flash Player 6

Example

The following example creates a LoadVars object and displays the default content type of the
data that is sent to the server.

```
var my_lv:LoadVars = new LoadVars();
trace(my_lv.contentType); // output: application/x-www-form-urlencoded
```

See also

`send (LoadVars.send method)`, `sendAndLoad (LoadVars.sendAndLoad method)`

decode (LoadVars.decode method)

`public decode(queryString:String) : Void`

Converts the variable string to properties of the specified LoadVars object.

This method is used internally by the `LoadVars.onData` event handler. Most users do not
need to call this method directly. If you override the `LoadVars.onData` event handler, you
can explicitly call `LoadVars.decode()` to parse a string of variables.

Availability: ActionScript 1.0; Flash Player 7

Parameters

`queryString:String` - A URL-encoded query string containing name/value pairs.

Example

The following example traces the three variables:

```
// Create a new LoadVars object
var my_lv:LoadVars = new LoadVars();
//Convert the variable string to properties
my_lv.decode("name=Mort&score=250000");
trace(my_lv.toString());
// Iterate over properties in my_lv
```

```
for (var prop in my_lv) {
  trace(prop+" -> "+my_lv[prop]);
}
```

See also

onData (LoadVars.onData handler), parseXML (XML.parseXML method)

getBytesLoaded (LoadVars.getBytesLoaded method)

public getBytesLoaded() : Number

Returns the number of bytes downloaded by LoadVars.load() or
LoadVars.sendAndLoad(). This method returns undefined if no load operation is in
progress or if a load operation has not yet begun.

Availability: ActionScript 1.0; Flash Player 6

Returns

Number - An integer.

Example

The following example uses a ProgressBar instance and a LoadVars object to download a text
file. When you test the file, two things are displayed in the Output panel: whether the file
loads successfully and how much data loads into the SWF file. You must replace the URL
parameter of the LoadVars.load() command so that the parameter refers to a valid text file
using HTTP. If you attempt to use this example to load a local file that resides on your hard
disk, this example will not work properly because in Test Movie mode Flash Player loads local
files in their entirety. To see this code work, add a ProgressBar instance called loadvars_pb to
the Stage. Then add the following ActionScript to Frame 1 of the Timeline:

```
var loadvars_pb:mx.controls.ProgressBar;
var my_lv:LoadVars = new LoadVars();
loadvars_pb.mode = "manual";
this.createEmptyMovieClip("timer_mc", 999);
timer_mc.onEnterFrame = function() {
  var lvBytesLoaded:Number = my_lv.getBytesLoaded();
  var lvBytesTotal:Number = my_lv.getBytesTotal();
  if (lvBytesTotal != undefined) {
    trace("Loaded "+lvBytesLoaded+" of "+lvBytesTotal+" bytes.");
    loadvars_pb.setProgress(lvBytesLoaded, lvBytesTotal);
  }
};
my_lv.onLoad = function(success:Boolean) {
```

```
loadvars_pb.setProgress(my_lv.getBytesLoaded(), my_lv.getBytesTotal());
delete timer_mc.onEnterFrame;
if (success) {
trace("LoadVars loaded successfully.");
} else {
trace("An error occurred while loading variables.");
}
};
my_lv.load("[place a valid URL pointing to a text file here]");
```

See also

`load` (LoadVars.load method), `sendAndLoad` (LoadVars.sendAndLoad method)

getBytesTotal (LoadVars.getBytesTotal method)

`public getBytesTotal() : Number`

Returns the total number of bytes downloaded by `LoadVars.load()` or
`LoadVars.sendAndLoad()`. This method returns `undefined` if no load operation is in
progress or if a load operation has not started. This method also returns `undefined` if the
number of total bytes can't be determined (for example, if the download was initiated but the
server did not transmit an HTTP content-length).

Availability: ActionScript 1.0; Flash Player 6

Returns

`Number` - An integer.

Example

The following example uses a ProgressBar instance and a LoadVars object to download a text
file. When you test the file, two things are displayed in the Output panel: whether the file
loads successfully and how much data loads into the SWF file. You must replace the URL
parameter of the `LoadVars.load()` command so that the parameter refers to a valid text file
using HTTP. If you attempt to use this example to load a local file that resides on your hard
disk, this example will not work properly because in test movie mode Flash Player loads local
files in their entirety. To see this code work, add a ProgressBar instance called `loadvars_pb` to
the Stage. Then add the following ActionScript to Frame 1 of the Timeline:

```
var loadvars_pb:mx.controls.ProgressBar;
var my_lv:LoadVars = new LoadVars();
loadvars_pb.mode = "manual";
this.createEmptyMovieClip("timer_mc", 999);
timer_mc.onEnterFrame = function() {
  var lvBytesLoaded:Number = my_lv.getBytesLoaded();
  var lvBytesTotal:Number = my_lv.getBytesTotal();
```

```
    if (lvBytesTotal != undefined) {
    trace("Loaded "+lvBytesLoaded+" of "+lvBytesTotal+" bytes.");
    loadvars_pb.setProgress(lvBytesLoaded, lvBytesTotal);
    }
};
my_lv.onLoad = function(success:Boolean) {
  loadvars_pb.setProgress(my_lv.getBytesLoaded(), my_lv.getBytesTotal());
  delete timer_mc.onEnterFrame;
  if (success) {
  trace("LoadVars loaded successfully.");
  } else {
  trace("An error occurred while loading variables.");
  }
};
my_lv.load("[place a valid URL pointing to a text file here]");
```

See also

load (LoadVars.load method), sendAndLoad (LoadVars.sendAndLoad method)

load (LoadVars.load method)

```
public load(url:String) : Boolean
```

Downloads variables from the specified URL, parses the variable data, and places the resulting variables in my_lv. Any properties in my_lv with the same names as downloaded variables are overwritten. Any properties in my_lv with different names than downloaded variables are not deleted. This is an asynchronous action.

The downloaded data must be in the MIME content type *application/x-www-form-urlencoded*.

This is the same format that is used by loadVariables().

Also, in files published for Flash Player 7, case-sensitivity is supported for external variables that are loaded with LoadVars.load().

This method is similar to XML.load().

 | If a file being loaded contains non-ASCII characters (as found in many non-English languages), it is recommended that you save the file with UTF-8 or UTF-16 encoding as opposed to a non-Unicode format like ASCII.

When using this method, consider the Flash Player security model:

For Flash Player 8:

- Data loading is not allowed if the calling SWF file is in the local-with-file-system sandbox and the target resource is from a network sandbox.

- Data loading is also not allowed if the calling SWF file is from a network sandbox and the target resource is local.

For more information, see the following:

- Chapter 17, "Understanding Security," in *Learning ActionScript 2.0 in Flash*
- The Flash Player 8 Security white paper at http://www.macromedia.com/go/fp8_security
- The Flash Player 8 Security-Related API white paper at http://www.macromedia.com/go/fp8_security_apis

For Flash Player 7 and later websites can permit cross-domain access to a resource via a cross-domain policy file. In SWF files of any version running in Flash Player 7 and later, url must be in exactly the same domain. For example, a SWF file at www.someDomain.com can load data only from sources that are also at www.someDomain.com.

In SWF files that are running in a version of the player earlier than Flash Player 7, url must be in the same superdomain as the SWF file that is issuing this call. A superdomain is derived by removing the left-most component of a file's URL. For example, a SWF file at www.someDomain.com can load data from sources at store.someDomain.com because both files are in the same superdomain of someDomain.com.

Availability: ActionScript 1.0; Flash Player 6 - Behavior changed in Flash Player 7.

Parameters

`url:String` - A string; the URL from which to download the variables. If the SWF file issuing this call is running in a web browser, `url` must be in the same domain as the SWF file.

Returns

`Boolean` - `false` if no parameter (null) is passed; `true` otherwise. Use the `onLoad()` event handler to check the success of loaded data.

Example

The following code defines an `onLoad` handler function that signals when data is returned to the Flash application from a server-side PHP script, and then loads the data in passvars.php.

```
var my_lv:LoadVars = new LoadVars();
my_lv.onLoad = function(success:Boolean) {
  if (success) {
  trace(this.toString());
  } else {
  trace("Error loading/parsing LoadVars.");
  }
};
my_lv.load("http://www.helpexamples.com/flash/params.txt");
```

For another example, see the guestbook.fla file in the ActionScript samples folder. Here are some typical paths to this folder:

- Windows: *boot drive*\Program Files\Macromedia\Flash 8\Samples and Tutorials\Samples\ActionScript
- Macintosh: *Macintosh HD*/Applications/Macromedia Flash 8/Samples and Tutorials/ Samples/ActionScript

See also

```
load (XML.load method), loaded (LoadVars.loaded property), onLoad
(LoadVars.onLoad handler), useCodepage (System.useCodepage property)
```

loaded (LoadVars.loaded property)

```
public loaded : Boolean
```

A Boolean value that indicates whether a `load` or `sendAndLoad` operation has completed, `undefined` by default. When a `LoadVars.load()` or `LoadVars.sendAndLoad()` operation is started, the `loaded` property is set to `false`; when the operation completes, the `loaded` property is set to `true`. If the operation has not completed or has failed with an error, the `loaded` property remains set to `false`.

This property is similar to the `XML.loaded` property.

Availability: ActionScript 1.0; Flash Player 6

Example

The following example loads a text file and displays information in the Output panel when the operation completes.

```
var my_lv:LoadVars = new LoadVars();
my_lv.onLoad = function(success:Boolean) {
  trace("LoadVars loaded successfully: "+this.loaded);
};
my_lv.load("http://www.helpexamples.com/flash/params.txt");
```

See also

```
load (LoadVars.load method), sendAndLoad (LoadVars.sendAndLoad method), load
(XML.load method)
```

LoadVars constructor

```
public LoadVars()
```

Creates a LoadVars object. You can then use the methods of that LoadVars object to send and load data.

Availability: ActionScript 1.0; Flash Player 6

Example

The following example creates a LoadVars object called `my_lv`:

```
var my_lv:LoadVars = new LoadVars();
```

onData (LoadVars.onData handler)

```
onData = function(src:String) {}
```

Invoked when data has completely downloaded from the server or when an error occurs while data is downloading from a server. This handler is invoked before the data is parsed and can be used to call a custom parsing routine instead of the one built in to Flash Player. The value of the `src` parameter passed to the function assigned to `LoadVars.onData` can be either `undefined` or a string that contains the URL-encoded name-value pairs downloaded from the server. If the `src` parameter is `undefined`, an error occurred while downloading the data from the server.

The default implementation of `LoadVars.onData` invokes `LoadVars.onLoad`. You can override this default implementation by assigning a custom function to `LoadVars.onData`, but `LoadVars.onLoad` is not called unless you call it in your implementation of `LoadVars.onData`.

Availability: ActionScript 1.0; Flash Player 6

Parameters

`src:String` - A string or `undefined`; the raw (unparsed) data from a `LoadVars.load()` or `LoadVars.sendAndLoad()` method call.

Example

The following example loads a text file and displays content in a TextArea instance called `content_ta` when the operation completes. If an error occurs, then information displays in the Output panel.

```
var my_lv:LoadVars = new LoadVars();
my_lv.onData = function(src:String) {
  if (src == undefined) {
    trace("Error loading content.");
```

```
    return;
  }
  content_ta.text = src;
};
my_lv.load("content.txt", my_lv, "GET");
```

See also

onLoad (LoadVars.onLoad handler), onLoad (LoadVars.onLoad handler), load
(LoadVars.load method), sendAndLoad (LoadVars.sendAndLoad method)

onHTTPStatus (LoadVars.onHTTPStatus handler)

onHTTPStatus = function(httpStatus:Number) {}

Invoked when Flash Player receives an HTTP status code from the server. This handler lets
you capture and act on HTTP status codes.

The onHTTPStatus handler is invoked before onData, which triggers calls to onLoad with a
value of undefined if the load fails. After onHTTPStatus is triggered, onData is *always*
triggered, whether or not you override onHTTPStatus. To best use the onHTTPStatus
handler, you should write a function to catch the result of the onHTTPStatus call; you can
then use the result in your onData and onLoad handlers. If onHTTPStatus is not invoked, this
indicates that the player did not try to make the URL request. This can happen because the
request violates security sandbox rules for the SWF file.

If Flash Player cannot get a status code from the server, or if it cannot communicate with the
server, the default value of 0 is passed to your ActionScript code. A value of 0 can be generated
in any player (for example, if a malformed URL is requested), and a value of 0 is always
generated by the Flash Player plug-in when it is run in the following browsers, which do not
pass HTTP status codes to the player: Netscape, Mozilla, Safari, Opera, and Internet Explorer
for the Macintosh.

Availability: ActionScript 1.0; Flash Player 8

Parameters

httpStatus:Number - The HTTP status code returned by the server. For example, a value of
404 indicates that the server has not found a match for the requested URI. HTTP status
codes can be found in sections 10.4 and 10.5 of the HTTP specification at ftp://ftp.isi.edu/
in-notes/rfc2616.txt.

Example

The following example shows how to use `onHTTPStatus()` to help with debugging. The example collects HTTP status codes and assigns their value and type to an instance of the LoadVars object. (Notice that this example creates the instance members `this.httpStatus` and `this.httpStatusType` at runtime.) The `onData` method uses these instance members to trace information about the HTTP response that can be useful in debugging.

```
var myLoadVars:LoadVars = new LoadVars();

myLoadVars.onHTTPStatus = function(httpStatus:Number) {
  this.httpStatus = httpStatus;
  if(httpStatus < 100) {
    this.httpStatusType = "flashError";
  }
  else if(httpStatus < 200) {
    this.httpStatusType = "informational";
  }
  else if(httpStatus < 300) {
    this.httpStatusType = "successful";
  }
  else if(httpStatus < 400) {
    this.httpStatusType = "redirection";
  }
  else if(httpStatus < 500) {
    this.httpStatusType = "clientError";
  }
  else if(httpStatus < 600) {
    this.httpStatusType = "serverError";
  }
}

myLoadVars.onData = function(src:String) {
  trace(">> " + this.httpStatusType + ": " + this.httpStatus);
  if(src != undefined) {
    this.decode(src);
    this.loaded = true;
    this.onLoad(true);
  }
  else {
    this.onLoad(false);
  }
}

myLoadVars.onLoad = function(success:Boolean) {
}

myLoadVars.load("http://weblogs.macromedia.com/mxna/flashservices/
  getMostRecentPosts.cfm");
```

See also

onHTTPStatus (XML.onHTTPStatus handler), load (LoadVars.load method),
sendAndLoad (LoadVars.sendAndLoad method)

onLoad (LoadVars.onLoad handler)

onLoad = function(success:Boolean) {}

Invoked when a LoadVars.load() or LoadVars.sendAndLoad() operation has ended. If the
operation was successful, my_lv is populated with variables downloaded by the operation, and
these variables are available when this handler is invoked.

This handler is undefined by default.

This event handler is similar to XML.onLoad.

Availability: ActionScript 1.0; Flash Player 6

Parameters

success:Boolean - A Boolean value that indicates whether the load operation ended in
success (true) or failure (false).

Example

The following example adds a TextInput instance called name_ti, a TextArea instance called
result_ta, and a Button instance called submit_button to the Stage. When the user clicks
the Login button instance, two LoadVars objects are created: send_lv and result_lv. The
send_lv object copies the name from the name_ti instance and sends the data to
greeting.cfm. The result from this script loads into the result_lv object, and the server
response is displayed in the TextArea instance (result_ta). Add the following ActionScript
on Frame 1 of the Timeline:

```
var submitListener:Object = new Object();
submitListener.click = function(evt:Object) {
  var result_lv:LoadVars = new LoadVars();
  result_lv.onLoad = function(success:Boolean) {
    if (success) {
      result_ta.text = result_lv.welcomeMessage;
    } else {
      result_ta.text = "Error connecting to server.";
    }
  };
  var send_lv:LoadVars = new LoadVars();
  send_lv.name = name_ti.text;
  send_lv.sendAndLoad("http://www.flash-mx.com/mm/greeting.cfm",
  result_lv, "POST");
};
submit_button.addEventListener("click", submitListener);
```

To view a more robust example, see the login.fla file in the ActionScript samples folder. Here are some typical paths to this folder:

- Windows: *boot drive*\Program Files\Macromedia\Flash 8\Samples and Tutorials\Samples\ActionScript
- Macintosh: *Macintosh HD*/Applications/Macromedia Flash 8/Samples and Tutorials/ Samples/ActionScript

See also

`onLoad (XML.onLoad handler)`, `loaded (LoadVars.loaded property)`, `load (LoadVars.load method)`, `sendAndLoad (LoadVars.sendAndLoad method)`

send (LoadVars.send method)

`public send(url:String, target:String, [method:String]) : Boolean`

Sends the variables in the *my_lv* object to the specified URL. All enumerable variables in *my_lv* are concatenated into a string in the *application/x-www-form-urlencoded* format by default, and the string is posted to the URL using the HTTP `POST` method. This is the same format used by `loadVariables()`. The MIME content type sent in the HTTP request headers is the value of `my_lv.contentType` or the default *application/x-www-form-urlencoded*. The `POST` method is used unless `GET` is specified.

You must specify the `target` parameter to ensure that the script or application at the specified URL will be executed. If you omit the `target` parameter, the function will return `true`, but the script or application will not be executed.

The `send()` method is useful if you want the server response to:

- Replace the SWF content (use "_self" as the `target` parameter);
- Appear in a new window (use "_blank" as the `target` parameter);
- Appear in the parent or top-level frame (use "_parent" or "_top" as the `target` parameter);
- Appear in a named frame (use the frame's name as a string for the `target` parameter).

A successful `send()` method call will always open a new browser window or replace content in an existing window or frame. If you would rather send information to a server and continue playing your SWF file without opening a new window or replacing content in a window or frame, then you should use `LoadVars.sendAndLoad()`.

This method is similar to `XML.send()`.

The Flash test environment always uses the GET method. To test using the POST method, be sure you are attempting to use it from within a browser.

When using this method, consider the Flash Player security model:

- For Flash Player 8, the method is not allowed if the calling SWF file is in an untrusted local sandbox.
- For Flash Player 7 and later, the method is not allowed if the calling SWF file is a local file.

For more information, see the following:

- Chapter 17, "Understanding Security," in *Learning ActionScript 2.0 in Flash*
- The Flash Player 8 Security white paper at http://www.macromedia.com/go/fp8_security
- The Flash Player 8 Security-Related API white paper at http://www.macromedia.com/go/fp8_security_apis

Availability: ActionScript 1.0; Flash Player 6

Parameters

`url:String` - A string; the URL to which to upload variables.

`target:String` - A string; the browser window or frame in which any response will appear. You can enter the name of a specific window or select from the following reserved target names:

- `"_self"` specifies the current frame in the current window.
- `"_blank"` specifies a new window.
- `"_parent"` specifies the parent of the current frame.
- `"_top"` specifies the top-level frame in the current window.

`method:String` [optional] - A string; the `GET` or `POST` method of the HTTP protocol. The default value is `POST`.

Returns

`Boolean` - A Boolean value; `false` if no parameters are specified, `true` otherwise.

Example

The following example copies two values from text fields and sends the data to a CFM script, which is used to handle the information. For example, the script might check if the user got a high score and then insert that data into a database table.

```
var my_lv:LoadVars = new LoadVars();
my_lv.playerName = playerName_txt.text;
my_lv.playerScore = playerScore_txt.text;
my_lv.send("setscore.cfm", "_blank", "POST");
```

See also

sendAndLoad (LoadVars.sendAndLoad method), send (XML.send method)

sendAndLoad (LoadVars.sendAndLoad method)

public sendAndLoad(url:String, target:Object, [method:String]) : Boolean

Posts variables in the my_lv object to the specified URL. The server response is downloaded, parsed as variable data, and the resulting variables are placed in the target object.

Variables are posted in the same manner as LoadVars.send(). Variables are downloaded into target in the same manner as LoadVars.load().

When using this method, consider the Flash Player security model:

For Flash Player 8:

- Data loading is not allowed if the calling SWF file is in the local-with-file-system sandbox and the target resource is from a network sandbox.

- Data loading is also not allowed if the calling SWF file is from a network sandbox and the target resource is local.

For more information, see the following:

- Chapter 17, "Understanding Security," in *Learning ActionScript 2.0 in Flash*

- The Flash Player 8 Security white paper at http://www.macromedia.com/go/fp8_security

- The Flash Player 8 Security-Related API white paper at http://www.macromedia.com/go/fp8_security_apis

For Flash Player 7 and later:

- Websites can permit cross-domain access to a resource via a cross-domain policy file.

- In SWF files of any version running in Flash Player 7 and later, url must be in exactly the same domain. For example, a SWF file at www.someDomain.com can load data only from sources that are also at www.someDomain.com.

In SWF files that are running in a version of the player earlier than Flash Player 7, url must be in the same superdomain as the SWF file that is issuing this call. A superdomain is derived by removing the left-most component of a file's URL. For example, a SWF file at www.someDomain.com can load data from sources at store.someDomain.com because both files are in the same superdomain named someDomain.com.

This method is similar to XML.sendAndLoad().

Availability: ActionScript 1.0; Flash Player 6 - Behavior changed in Flash Player 7.

Parameters

`url:String` - A string; the URL to which to upload variables. If the SWF file issuing this call is running in a web browser, `url` must be in the same domain as the SWF file.

`target:Object` - The LoadVars or XML object that receives the downloaded variables.

`method:String` [optional] - A string; the `GET` or `POST` method of the HTTP protocol. The default value is `POST`.

Returns

`Boolean` - A Boolean value.

Example

For the following example, add a TextInput instance called `name_ti`, a TextArea instance called `result_ta`, and a Button instance called `submit_button` to the Stage. When the user clicks the Login button instance in the following example, two LoadVars objects are created: `send_lv` and `result_lv`. The `send_lv` object copies the name from the `name_ti` instance and sends the data to greeting.cfm. The result from this script loads into the `result_lv` object, and the server response displays in the TextArea instance (`result_ta`). Add the following ActionScript to Frame 1 of the Timeline:

```
var submitListener:Object = new Object();
submitListener.click = function(evt:Object) {
  var result_lv:LoadVars = new LoadVars();
  result_lv.onLoad = function(success:Boolean) {
  if (success) {
    result_ta.text = result_lv.welcomeMessage;
  } else {
    result_ta.text = "Error connecting to server.";
  }
  };
  var send_lv:LoadVars = new LoadVars();
  send_lv.name = name_ti.text;
  send_lv.sendAndLoad("http://www.flash-mx.com/mm/greeting.cfm",
  result_lv, "POST");
};
submit_button.addEventListener("click", submitListener);
```

To view a more robust example, see the login.fla file in the ActionScript samples folder. Typical paths to the ActionScript samples folder are:

- Windows: *boot drive*\Program Files\Macromedia\Flash 8\Samples and Tutorials\Samples\ActionScript

- Macintosh: *Macintosh HD*/Applications/Macromedia Flash 8/Samples and Tutorials/Samples/ActionScript

See also

send (LoadVars.send method), load (LoadVars.load method), sendAndLoad (XML.sendAndLoad method)

toString (LoadVars.toString method)

`public toString() : String`

Returns a string containing all enumerable variables in *my_lv*, in the MIME content encoding *application/x-www-form-urlencoded.*

Availability: ActionScript 1.0; Flash Player 6

Returns

`String` - A string.

Example

The following example instantiates a new `LoadVars()` object, creates two properties, and uses `toString()` to return a string containing both properties in URL encoded format:

```
var my_lv:LoadVars = new LoadVars();
my_lv.name = "Gary";
my_lv.age = 26;
trace (my_lv.toString()); //output: age=26&name=Gary
```

LocalConnection

```
Object
  |
  +-LocalConnection
```

```
public dynamic class LocalConnection
extends Object
```

The LocalConnection class lets you develop SWF files that can send instructions to each other without the use of `fscommand()` or JavaScript. LocalConnection objects can communicate only among SWF files that are running on the same client computer, but they can be running in different applications--for example, a SWF file running in a browser and a SWF file running in a projector. You can use LocalConnection objects to send and receive data within a single SWF file, but this is not a standard implementation; all the examples in this section illustrate communication between different SWF files.

The primary methods used to send and receive data are `LocalConnection.send()` and `LocalConnection.connect()`. At its most basic, your code will implement the following commands; notice that both the `LocalConnection.send()` and `LocalConnection.connect()` commands specify the same connection name, `lc_name`:

```
// Code in the receiving SWF file
this.createTextField("result_txt", 1, 10, 10, 100, 22);
result_txt.border = true;
var receiving_lc:LocalConnection = new LocalConnection();
receiving_lc.methodToExecute = function(param1:Number, param2:Number) {
result_txt.text = param1+param2;
};
receiving_lc.connect("lc_name");

// Code in the sending SWF file
var sending_lc:LocalConnection = new LocalConnection();
sending_lc.send("lc_name", "methodToExecute", 5, 7);
```

The simplest way to use a LocalConnection object is to allow communication only between LocalConnection objects located in the same domain because you won't have security issues. However, if you need to allow communication between domains, you have several ways to implement security measures. For more information, see the discussion of the `connectionName` parameter in `LocalConnection.send()` and the `LocalConnection.allowDomain` and `LocalConnection.domain()` entries.

Availability: ActionScript 1.0; Flash Player 6

Property summary

Properties inherited from class Object

```
constructor (Object.constructor property),__proto__ (Object.__proto__
property),prototype (Object.prototype property),__resolve
(Object.__resolve property)
```

Event summary

Event	Description
`allowDomain = function([sendin gDomain:String]) {}`	Invoked whenever receiving_lc receives a request to invoke a method from a sending LocalConnection object.

Event	Description
`allowInsecureDomain = function([sendingDomain:String]) {}`	Invoked whenever receiving_lc, which is in a SWF file hosted at a domain using a secure protocol (HTTPS), receives a request to invoke a method from a sending LocalConnection object that is in a SWF file hosted at a nonsecure protocol.
`onStatus = function(infoObject:Object) {}`	Invoked after a sending LocalConnection object tries to send a command to a receiving LocalConnection object.

Constructor summary

Signature	Description
`LocalConnection()`	Creates a LocalConnection object.

Method summary

Modifiers	Signature	Description
	`close() : Void`	Closes (disconnects) a LocalConnection object.
	`connect(connectionName:String) : Boolean`	Prepares a LocalConnection object to receive commands from a `LocalConnection.send()` command (called the *sending LocalConnection object*).
	`domain() : String`	Returns a string representing the domain of the location of the current SWF file.
	`send(connectionName: String, methodName:String, [args:Object]) : Boolean`	Invokes the method named `method` on a connection opened with the `LocalConnection.connect(connectionName)` command (the receiving LocalConnection object).

Methods inherited from class Object

```
addProperty (Object.addProperty method), hasOwnProperty
(Object.hasOwnProperty method), isPropertyEnumerable
(Object.isPropertyEnumerable method), isPrototypeOf (Object.isPrototypeOf
method), registerClass (Object.registerClass method), toString
(Object.toString method), unwatch (Object.unwatch method), valueOf
(Object.valueOf method), watch (Object.watch method)
```

allowDomain (LocalConnection.allowDomain handler)

```
allowDomain = function([sendingDomain:String]) {}
```

Invoked whenever receiving_lc receives a request to invoke a method from a sending LocalConnection object. Flash expects the code you implement in this handler to return a Boolean value of true or false. If the handler doesn't return true, the request from the sending object is ignored, and the method is not invoked.

When this event handler is absent, Flash Player applies a default security policy, which is equivalent to the following code:

```
my_lc.allowDomain = function (sendingDomain)
{
    return (sendingDomain == this.domain());
}
```

Use `LocalConnection.allowDomain` to explicitly permit LocalConnection objects from specified domains, or from any domain, to execute methods of the receiving LocalConnection object. If you don't declare the sendingDomain parameter, you probably want to accept commands from any domain, and the code in your handler would be simply return true. If you do declare sendingDomain, you probably want to compare the value of sendingDomain with domains from which you want to accept commands. The following examples show both implementations.

In files authored for Flash Player 6, the `sendingDomain` parameter contains the superdomain of the caller. In files authored for Flash Player 7 or later, the `sendingDomain` parameter contains the exact domain of the caller. In the latter case, to allow access by SWF files hosted at either www.domain.com or store.domain.com, you must explicitly allow access from both domains.

```
// For Flash Player 6
receiving_lc.allowDomain = function(sendingDomain) {
    return(sendingDomain=="domain.com");
}
// For Flash Player 7 or later
receiving_lc.allowDomain = function(sendingDomain) {
    return(sendingDomain=="www.domain.com" ||
        sendingDomain=="store.domain.com");
}
```

Also, for files authored for Flash Player 7 or later, you can't use this method to let SWF files hosted using a secure protocol (HTTPS) allow access from SWF files hosted in nonsecure protocols; you must use the `LocalConnection.allowInsecureDomain` event handler instead.

Occasionally, you might encounter the following situation. Suppose you load a child SWF file from a different domain. You want to implement this method so that the child SWF file can make LocalConnection calls to the parent SWF file, but you don't know the final domain from which the child SWF file will come. This can happen, for example, when you use load-balancing redirects or third-party servers.

In this situation, you can use the `MovieClip._url` property in your implementation of this method. For example, if you load a SWF file into my_mc, you can then implement this method by checking whether the domain argument matches the domain of `my_mc._url`. (You must parse the domain out of the full URL contained in `my_mc._url`.)

If you do this, make sure that you wait until the SWF file in my_mc is loaded, because the _url property will not have its final, correct value until the file is completely loaded. The best way to determine when a child SWF file finishes loading is to use `MovieClipLoader.onLoadComplete`.

The opposite situation can also occur: You might create a child SWF file that wants to accept LocalConnection calls from its parent but doesn't know the domain of its parent. In this situation, implement this method by checking whether the domain argument matches the domain of _parent._url. Again, you must parse the domain out of the full URL from _parent._url. In this situation, you don't have to wait for the parent SWF file to load; the parent will already be loaded by the time the child loads.

Availability: ActionScript 1.0; Flash Player 7

Parameters

`sendingDomain:String` [optional] - A string that specifies the domain of the SWF file that contains the sending LocalConnection object.

Example

The following example shows how a LocalConnection object in a receiving SWF file can permit SWF files from any domain to invoke its methods. Compare this to the example in `LocalConnection.connect()`, in which only SWF files from the same domain can invoke the `trace()` method in the receiving SWF file. For a discussion of the use of the underscore (_) in the connection name, see `LocalConnection.send()`.

```
this.createTextField("welcome_txt", this.getNextHighestDepth(), 10, 10,
    100, 20);
var my_lc:LocalConnection = new LocalConnection();
my_lc.allowDomain = function(sendingDomain:String) {
  domain_txt.text = sendingDomain;
  return true;
};
my_lc.allowInsecureDomain = function(sendingDomain:String) {
  return (sendingDomain == this.domain());
}
my_lc.sayHello = function(name:String) {
  welcome_txt.text = "Hello, "+name;
};
my_lc.connect("_mylc");
```

The following example sends a string to the previous SWF file and displays a status message about whether the local connection was able to connect to the file. A TextInput component called `name_ti`, a TextArea instance called `status_ta` and a Button instance called `send_button` are used to display content.

```
var sending_lc:LocalConnection;
var sendListener:Object = new Object();
sendListener.click = function(evt:Object) {
  sending_lc = new LocalConnection();
  sending_lc.onStatus = function(infoObject:Object) {
  switch (infoObject.level) {
  case 'status' :
    status_ta.text = "LocalConnection connected successfully.";
    break;
  case 'error' :
    status_ta.text = "LocalConnection encountered an error.";
    break;
  }
  };
  sending_lc.send("_mylc", "sayHello", name_ti.text);
};
send_button.addEventListener("click", sendListener);
```

If your SWF file includes a version 2 component, use the version 2 components DepthManager class instead of the `MovieClip.getNextHighestDepth()` method used in the previous example.

In the following example, the receiving SWF file, which resides in `thisDomain.com`, accepts commands only from SWF files located in `thisDomain.com` or `thatDomain.com`:

```
var aLocalConn:LocalConnection = new LocalConnection();
aLocalConn.Trace = function(aString) {
  aTextField += aString+newline;
};
aLocalConn.allowDomain = function(sendingDomain) {
  return (sendingDomain == this.domain() || sendingDomain ==
  "www.macromedia.com");
};
aLocalConn.connect("_mylc");
```

When published for Flash Player 7 or later, exact domain matching is used. This means that the example will fail if the SWF files are located at www.thatDomain.com but will work if the files are located at thatDomain.com.

See also

```
connect (LocalConnection.connect method), domain (LocalConnection.domain
method), send (LocalConnection.send method), _url (MovieClip._url property),
onLoadComplete (MovieClipLoader.onLoadComplete event listener), _parent
property
```

allowInsecureDomain (LocalConnection.allowInsecureDomain handler)

```
allowInsecureDomain = function([sendingDomain:String]) {}
```

Invoked whenever receiving_lc, which is in a SWF file hosted at a domain using a secure protocol (HTTPS), receives a request to invoke a method from a sending LocalConnection object that is in a SWF file hosted at a nonsecure protocol. Flash expects the code you implement in this handler to return a Boolean value of `true` or `false`. If the handler doesn't return true, the request from the sending object is ignored, and the method is not invoked.

By default, SWF files hosted using the HTTPS protocol can be accessed only by other SWF files hosted using the HTTPS protocol. This implementation maintains the integrity provided by the HTTPS protocol.

Using this method to override the default behavior is not recommended, as it compromises HTTPS security. However, you might need to do so, for example, if you need to permit access to HTTPS files published for Flash Player 7 or later from HTTP files published for Flash Player 6.

A SWF file published for Flash Player 6 can use the `LocalConnection.allowDomain` event handler to permit HTTP to HTTPS access. However, because security is implemented differently in Flash Player 7, you must use the `LocalConnection.allowInsecureDomain()` method to permit such access in SWF files published for Flash Player 7 or later.

Availability: ActionScript 1.0; Flash Player 7

Parameters

`sendingDomain:String` [optional] - A string that specifies the domain of the SWF file that contains the sending LocalConnection object.

Example

The following example allows connections from the current domain or from www.macromedia.com, or allows insecure connections only from the current domain.

```
this.createTextField("welcome_txt", this.getNextHighestDepth(), 10, 10,
    100, 20);
var my_lc:LocalConnection = new LocalConnection();
```

```
my_lc.allowDomain = function(sendingDomain:String) {
  domain_txt.text = sendingDomain;
  return (sendingDomain == this.domain() || sendingDomain ==
  "www.macromedia.com");
};
my_lc.allowInsecureDomain = function(sendingDomain:String) {
  return (sendingDomain == this.domain());
}
my_lc.sayHello = function(name:String) {
  welcome_txt.text = "Hello, "+name;
};
my_lc.connect("lc_name");
```

If your SWF file includes a version 2 component, use the version 2 components DepthManager class instead of the `MovieClip.getNextHighestDepth()` method used in this example.

See also

`allowDomain (LocalConnection.allowDomain handler)`, `connect (LocalConnection.connect method)`

close (LocalConnection.close method)

`public close() : Void`

Closes (disconnects) a LocalConnection object. Issue this command when you no longer want the object to accept commands—for example, when you want to issue a `LocalConnection.connect()` command using the same `connectionName` parameter in another SWF file.

Availability: ActionScript 1.0; Flash Player 6

Example

The following example closes a connection called `receiving_lc` when you click a Button component instance called `close_button`:

```
this.createTextField("welcome_txt", this.getNextHighestDepth(), 10, 10,
  100, 22);
this.createTextField("status_txt", this.getNextHighestDepth(), 10, 42,
  100,44);

var receiving_lc:LocalConnection = new LocalConnection();
receiving_lc.sayHello = function(name:String) {
  welcome_txt.text = "Hello, "+name;
};
receiving_lc.connect("lc_name");
var closeListener:Object = new Object();
```

```
closeListener.click = function(evt:Object) {
  receiving_lc.close();
  status_txt.text = "connection closed";
};
close_button.addEventListener("click", closeListener);
```

The `MovieClip.getNextHighestDepth()` method used in this example requires Flash Player 7 or later. If your SWF file includes a version 2 component, use the version 2 components DepthManager class instead of the `MovieClip.getNextHighestDepth()` method.

See also

connect (LocalConnection.connect method)

connect (LocalConnection.connect method)

`public connect(connectionName:String) : Boolean`

Prepares a LocalConnection object to receive commands from a `LocalConnection.send()` command (called the *sending LocalConnection object*). The object used with this command is called the *receiving LocalConnection object*. The receiving and sending objects must be running on the same client computer.

Make sure you define the methods attached to *receiving_lc* before calling this method, as shown in all the examples in this section.

By default, Flash Player resolves `connectionName` into a value of "*superdomain*:connectionName", where *superdomain* is the superdomain of the SWF file containing the `LocalConnection.connect()` command. For example, if the SWF file containing the receiving LocalConnection object is located at www.someDomain.com, `connectionName` resolves to "someDomain.com:connectionName". (If a SWF file is located on the client computer, the value assigned to `superdomain` is "localhost".)

Also by default, Flash Player lets the receiving LocalConnection object accept commands only from sending LocalConnection objects whose connection name also resolves into a value of "*superdomain*:connectionName". In this way, Flash makes it simple for SWF files located in the same domain to communicate with each other.

If you are implementing communication only between SWF files in the same domain, specify a string for `connectionName` that does not begin with an underscore (_) and that does not specify a domain name (for example, "myDomain:connectionName"). Use the same string in the `LocalConnection.connect(connectionName)` command.

If you are implementing communication between SWF files in different domains, specifying a string for *connectionName* that begins with an underscore (_) will make the SWF with the receiving LocalConnection object more portable between domains. Here are the two possible cases:

- If the string for *connectionName* does not begin with an underscore (_), Flash Player adds a prefix with the superdomain and a colon (for example, "myDomain:connectionName"). Although this ensures that your connection does not conflict with connections of the same name from other domains, any sending LocalConnection objects must specify this superdomain (for example, "myDomain:connectionName"). If the SWF with the receiving LocalConnection object is moved to another domain, the player changes the prefix to reflect the new superdomain (for example, "anotherDomain:connectionName"). All sending LocalConnection objects would have to be manually edited to point to the new superdomain.
- If the string for *connectionName* begins with an underscore (for example, "_connectionName"), Flash Player does not add a prefix to the string. This means that the receiving and sending LocalConnection objects will use identical strings for connectionName. If the receiving object uses LocalConnection.allowDomain to specify that connections from any domain will be accepted, the SWF with the receiving LocalConnection object can be moved to another domain without altering any sending LocalConnection objects.

For more information, see the discussion of connectionName in LocalConnection.send() and also the LocalConnection.allowDomain and LocalConnection.domain() entries.

 NOTE Colons are used as special characters to separate the superdomain from the connectionName string. A string for connectionName that contains a colon is not valid.

Availability: ActionScript 1.0; Flash Player 6

Parameters
connectionName:String - A string that corresponds to the connection name specified in the LocalConnection.send() command that wants to communicate with *receiving_lc*.

Returns
Boolean - A Boolean value: true if no other process running on the same client computer has already issued this command using the same value for the *connectionName* parameter; false otherwise.

Example

The following example shows how a SWF file in a particular domain can invoke a method named `printOut` in a receiving SWF file in the same domain.

First, create one SWF file with the following code:

```
this.createTextField("tf", this.getNextHighestDepth(), 10, 10, 300, 100);
var aLocalConnection:LocalConnection = new LocalConnection();
aLocalConnection.connect("demoConnection");
aLocalConnection.printOut = function(aString:String):Void{
  tf.text += aString;
}
```

Then create a second with the following code:

```
var sending_lc:LocalConnection = new LocalConnection();
sending_lc.send("demoConnection", "printOut", "This is a message from file
  B. Hello.");
```

To test this example, run the first SWF file, and then run the second one.

Here is another example. SWF 1 contains the following code, which creates a new Sound object that plays back an MP3 file at runtime. A ProgressBar called `playback_pb` displays the playback progress of the MP3 file. A Label component instance called `song_lbl` displays the name of the MP3 file. Buttons in different SWF files will be used to control the playback using a LocalConnection object.

```
var playback_pb:mx.controls.ProgressBar;
var my_sound:Sound;
playback_pb.setStyle("themeColor", "haloBlue");
this.createEmptyMovieClip("timer_mc", this.getNextHighestDepth());
var receiving_lc:LocalConnection = new LocalConnection();
receiving_lc.playMP3 = function(mp3Path:String, mp3Name:String) {
  song_lbl.text = mp3Name;
  playback_pb.indeterminate = true;
  my_sound = new Sound();
  my_sound.onLoad = function(success:Boolean) {
  playback_pb.indeterminate = false;
  };
  my_sound.onSoundComplete = function() {
  delete timer_mc.onEnterFrame;
  };
  timer_mc.onEnterFrame = function() {
  playback_pb.setProgress(my_sound.position, my_sound.duration);
  };
  my_sound.loadSound(mp3Path, true);
};
receiving_lc.connect("lc_name");
```

SWF 2 contains a button called play_btn. When you click the button, it connects to SWF 1 and passes two variables. The first variable contains the MP3 file to stream, and the second variable is the filename that you display in the Label component instance in SWF 1.

```
play_btn.onRelease = function() {
    var sending_lc:LocalConnection = new LocalConnection();
    sending_lc.send("lc_name", "playMP3", "song1.mp3", "Album - 01 - Song");
};
```

SWF 3 contains a button called play_btn. When you click the button, it connects to SWF 1 and passes two variables. The first variable contains the MP3 file to stream, and the second variable is the filename that you display in the Label component instance in SWF 1.

```
play_btn.onRelease = function() {
    var sending_lc:LocalConnection = new LocalConnection();
    sending_lc.send("lc_name", "playMP3", "song2.mp3", "Album - 02 - Another
    Song");
};
```

The MovieClip.getNextHighestDepth() method used in these examples requires Flash Player 7 or later. If your SWF file includes a version 2 component, use the version 2 components DepthManager class instead of the MovieClip.getNextHighestDepth() method.

See also

send (LocalConnection.send method), allowDomain (LocalConnection.allowDomain handler), domain (LocalConnection.domain method)

domain (LocalConnection.domain method)

public domain() : String

Returns a string representing the domain of the location of the current SWF file.

In SWF files published for Flash Player 6, the returned string is the superdomain of the current SWF file. For example, if the SWF file is located at www.macromedia.com, this command returns "macromedia.com".

In SWF files published for Flash Player 7 or later, the returned string is the exact domain of the current SWF file. For example, if the SWF file is located at www.macromedia.com, this command returns "www.macromedia.com".

If the current SWF file is a local file residing on the client computer, this command returns "localhost".

The most common way to use this command is to include the domain name of the sending LocalConnection object as a parameter to the method you plan to invoke in the receiving LocalConnection object or with `LocalConnection.allowDomain` to accept commands from a specified domain. If you are enabling communication only between LocalConnection objects that are located in the same domain, you probably don't need to use this command.

Availability: ActionScript 1.0; Flash Player 6 - Behavior changed in Flash Player 7.

Returns

`String` - A string representing the domain of the location of the current SWF file; for more information, see the Description section.

Example

In the following example, a receiving SWF file accepts commands only from SWF files located in the same domain or at macromedia.com:

```
// If both the sending and receiving SWF files are Flash Player 6,
// then use the superdomain
var my_lc:LocalConnection = new LocalConnection();
my_lc.allowDomain = function(sendingDomain):String{
    return (sendingDomain==this.domain() || sendingDomain=="macromedia.com");
}

// If either the sending or receiving SWF file is Flash Player 7 or later,
// then use the exact domain. In this case, commands from a SWF file posted
// at www.macromedia.com will be accepted, but those from one posted at
// a different subdomain, e.g. livedocs.macromedia.com, will not.
var my_lc:LocalConnection = new LocalConnection();
my_lc.allowDomain = function(sendingDomain):String{
    return (sendingDomain==this.domain() ||
    sendingDomain=="www.macromedia.com");
}
```

In the following example, a sending SWF file located at www.yourdomain.com invokes a method in a receiving SWF file located at www.mydomain.com. The sending SWF file includes its domain name as a parameter to the method it invokes, so the receiving SWF file can return a reply value to a LocalConnection object in the correct domain. The sending SWF file also specifies that it will accept commands only from SWF files at mydomain.com.

Line numbers are included for reference purposes. The sequence of events is described in the following list:

- The receiving SWF file prepares to receive commands on a connection named `"sum"` (line 11). The Flash Player resolves the name of this connection to `"mydomain.com:sum"` (see `LocalConnection.connect()`).

- The sending SWF file prepares to receive a reply on the LocalConnection object named `"result"` (line 67). It also specifies that it will accept commands only from SWF files at mydomain.com (lines 51 to 53).

- The sending SWF file invokes the `aSum` method of a connection named `"mydomain.com:sum"` (line 68) and passes the following parameters: its superdomain, the name of the connection to receive the reply (`"result"`), and the values to be used by `aSum` (123 and 456).

- The `aSum` method (line 6) is invoked with the following values: sender = `"mydomain.com:result"`, replyMethod = `"aResult"`, n1 = 123, and n2 = 456. It then executes the following line of code:
  ```
  this.send("mydomain.com:result", "aResult", (123 + 456));
  ```
- The `aResult` method (line 54) shows the value returned by `aSum` (579).
  ```
  // The receiving SWF at http://www.mydomain.com/folder/movie.swf
  // contains the following code

  1 var aLocalConnection:LocalConnection = new LocalConnection();
  2 aLocalConnection.allowDomain = function()
  3 {
     // Allow connections from any domain
  4 return true;
  5 }
  6 aLocalConnection.aSum = function(sender, replyMethod, n1, n2)
  7 {
  8 this.send(sender, replyMethod, (n1 + n2));
  9 }
  10
  11 aLocalConnection.connect("sum");

  // The sending SWF at http://www.yourdomain.com/folder/movie.swf
  // contains the following code

  50 var lc:LocalConnection = new LocalConnection();
  51 lc.allowDomain = function(aDomain) {
      // Allow connections only from mydomain.com
  52 return (aDomain == "mydomain.com");
  53 }
  54 lc.aResult = function(aParam) {
  55 trace("The sum is " + aParam);
  56 }
  ```

```
     // determine our domain and see if we need to truncate it
57 var channelDomain:String = lc.domain();
58 if (getVersion() >= 7 && this.getSWFVersion() >= 7)
59 {
     // split domain name into elements
60 var domainArray:Array = channelDomain.split(".");

     // if more than two elements are found,
     // chop off first element to create superdomain
61 if (domainArray.length > 2)
62 {
63 domainArray.shift();
64 channelDomain = domainArray.join(".");
65 }
66 }

67 lc.connect("result");
68 lc.send("mydomain.com:sum", "aSum", channelDomain + ':' + "result",
"aResult", 123, 456);
```

See also

allowDomain (LocalConnection.allowDomain handler), connect
(LocalConnection.connect method)

LocalConnection constructor

`public LocalConnection()`

Creates a LocalConnection object.

Availability: ActionScript 1.0; Flash Player 6

Example

The following example shows how receiving and sending SWF files create LocalConnnection objects. The two SWF files can use the same name or different names for their respective LocalConnection objects. In this example they use different names.

```
// Code in the receiving SWF file
this.createTextField("result_txt", 1, 10, 10, 100, 22);
result_txt.border = true;
var receiving_lc:LocalConnection = new LocalConnection();
receiving_lc.methodToExecute = function(param1:Number, param2:Number) {
  result_txt.text = param1+param2;
};
receiving_lc.connect("lc_name");
```

The following SWF file sends the request to the first SWF file.

```
// Code in the sending SWF file
var sending_lc:LocalConnection = new LocalConnection();
sending_lc.send("lc_name", "methodToExecute", 5, 7);
```

See also

connect (LocalConnection.connect method), send (LocalConnection.send method)

onStatus (LocalConnection.onStatus handler)

onStatus = function(infoObject:Object) {}

Invoked after a sending LocalConnection object tries to send a command to a receiving LocalConnection object. If you want to respond to this event handler, you must create a function to process the information object sent by the LocalConnection object.

If the information object returned by this event handler contains a level value of status, Flash successfully sent the command to a receiving LocalConnection object. This does not mean that Flash successfully invoked the specified method of the receiving LocalConnection object; it means only that Flash could send the command. For example, the method is not invoked if the receiving LocalConnection object doesn't allow connections from the sending domain or if the method does not exist. The only way to know for sure if the method was invoked is to have the receiving object send a reply to the sending object.

If the information object returned by this event handler contains a level value of error, Flash cannot send the command to a receiving LocalConnection object, most likely because there is no receiving LocalConnection object connected whose name corresponds to the name specified in the sending_lc.send() command that invoked this handler.

In addition to this onStatus handler, Flash also provides a "super" function called System.onStatus. If onStatus is invoked for a particular object and there is no function assigned to respond to it, Flash processes a function assigned to System.onStatus if it exists.

In most cases, you implement this handler only to respond to error conditions, as shown in the following example.

Availability: ActionScript 1.0; Flash Player 6

Parameters

infoObject:Object - A parameter defined according to the status message. For details about this parameter, see the Description section.

Example

The following example displays a status message about whether the SWF file connects to another local connection object called `lc_name`. A TextInput component called `name_ti`, a TextArea instance called `status_ta` and a Button instance called `send_button` are used to display content.

```
var sending_lc:LocalConnection;
var sendListener:Object = new Object();
sendListener.click = function(evt:Object) {
    sending_lc = new LocalConnection();
    sending_lc.onStatus = function(infoObject:Object) {
        switch (infoObject.level) {
        case 'status' :
            status_ta.text = "LocalConnection connected successfully.";
            break;
        case 'error' :
            status_ta.text = "LocalConnection encountered an error.";
            break;
        }
    };
    sending_lc.send("lc_name", "sayHello", name_ti.text);
};
send_button.addEventListener("click", sendListener);
```

See also

send (LocalConnection.send method), onStatus (System.onStatus handler)

send (LocalConnection.send method)

`public send(connectionName:String, methodName:String, [args:Object]) : Boolean`

Invokes the method named `method` on a connection opened with the `LocalConnection.connect(connectionName)` command (the receiving LocalConnection object). The object used with this command is called the sending LocalConnection object. The SWF files that contain the sending and receiving objects must be running on the same client computer.

There is a 40 kilobyte limit to the amount of data you can pass as parameters to this command. If the command returns `false` but your syntax is correct, try dividing the `LocalConnection.send()` requests into multiple commands, each with less than 40K of data.

As discussed in the entry `LocalConnection.connect()`, Flash adds the current superdomain to `connectionName` by default. If you are implementing communication between different domains, you need to define `connectionName` in both the sending and receiving LocalConnection objects in such a way that Flash does not add the current superdomain to `connectionName`. You can do this in one of the following two ways:

- Use an underscore (_) at the beginning of `connectionName` in both the sending and receiving LocalConnection objects. In the SWF file containing the receiving object, use `LocalConnection.allowDomain` to specify that connections from any domain will be accepted. This implementation lets you store your sending and receiving SWF files in any domain.

- Include the superdomain in `connectionName` in the sending LocalConnection object--for example, `myDomain.com:myConnectionName`. In the receiving object, use `LocalConnection.allowDomain` to specify that connections from the specified superdomain will be accepted (in this case, myDomain.com) or that connections from any domain will be accepted.

> **NOTE** You cannot specify a superdomain in `connectionName` in the receiving `LocalConnection` object-- you can only do this in the sending `LocalConnection` object.

When using this method, consider the Flash Player security model. By default, a LocalConnection object is associated with the sandbox of the SWF file that created it, and cross-domain calls to LocalConnection objects are not allowed unless the `LocalConnection.allowDomain()` method has been invoked.

For more information, see the following:

- Chapter 17, "Understanding Security," in *Learning ActionScript 2.0 in Flash*
- The Flash Player 8 Security white paper at http://www.macromedia.com/go/fp8_security
- The Flash Player 8 Security-Related API white paper at http://www.macromedia.com/go/fp8_security_apis

Availability: ActionScript 1.0; Flash Player 6

Parameters

`connectionName:String` - A string that corresponds to the connection name specified in the `LocalConnection.connect()` command that wants to communicate with *sending_lc*.

`methodName:String` - A string specifying the name of the method to be invoked in the receiving LocalConnection object. The following method names cause the command to fail: `send`, `connect`, `close`, `domain`, `onStatus`, and `allowDomain`.

`args:Object` [optional] - Arguments to be passed to the specified method.

Returns

Boolean - A Boolean value: `true` if Flash can carry out the request; `false` otherwise.

> **NOTE** A return value of true does not necessarily mean that Flash successfully connected to a receiving `LocalConnection` object; It means only that the command us syntactically correct. To determine whether the connection succeeded, see `LocalConnection.onStatus`.

Example

For an example of communicating between LocalConnection objects located in the same domain, see `LocalConnection.connect()`. For an example of communicating between LocalConnection objects located in any domain, see `LocalConnection.allowDomain`. For an example of communicating between LocalConnection objects located in specified domains, see `LocalConnection.allowDomain` and `LocalConnection.domain()`.

See also

allowDomain (`LocalConnection.allowDomain handler`), connect (`LocalConnection.connect method`), domain (`LocalConnection.domain method`), onStatus (`LocalConnection.onStatus handler`)

Locale (mx.lang.Locale)

```
Object
  |
  +-mx.lang.Locale
```

```
public class Locale
extends Object
```

The mx.lang.Locale class allows you to control how multilanguage text is displayed in a SWF file. The Flash Strings panel allows you to use string IDs instead of string literals in dynamic text fields. This allows you to create a SWF file that displays text loaded from a language-specific XML file. The XML file must use the XML Localization Interchange File Format(XLIFF). There are three ways to display the language-specific strings contained in the XLIFF files:

- `"automatically at runtime"`—Flash Player replaces string IDs with strings from the XML file matching the default system language code returned by System.capabilities.language.

- `"manually using stage language"`—String IDs are replaced by strings at compile time and cannot be changed by Flash Player.

- `"via ActionScript at runtime"`—String ID replacement is controlled using ActionScript at runtime. This option gives you control over both the timing and language of string ID replacement.

You can use the properties and methods of this class when you want to replace the string IDs "via ActionScript at runtime."

All of the properties and methods available are static, which means that they are accessed through the mx.lang.Locale class itself rather than through an instance of the class.

Note: The Locale class is different from the other classes in the ActionScript 2.0 Language Reference, since it is not part of the Flash Player. Since this class installed in the Flash Authoring classpath it is automatically compiled into your SWF files. Using the Locale class increases the SWF size slightly since the class is compiled into the SWF.

Availability: ActionScript 2.0; Flash Player 7

Property summary

Modifiers	Property	Description
static	`autoReplace:Boolean`	Determines whether strings are replaced automatically after loading the XML file.
static	`languageCodeArray:Array` [read-only]	An array containing language codes for the languages that have been specified or loaded into the FLA file.
static	`stringIDArray:Array` [read-only]	An array containing all the string IDs in the FLA file.

Properties inherited from class Object

`constructor` (Object.constructor property), `__proto__` (Object.__proto__ property), `prototype` (Object.prototype property), `__resolve` (Object.__resolve property)

Method summary

Modifiers	Signature	Description
static	addDelayedInstance(instance:Object, stringID:String) : Void	Adds the {instance, string ID} pair into the internal array for later use.
static	addXMLPath(langCode:String, path:String) : Void	Adds the {languageCode and languagePath} pair into the internal array for later use.
static	checkXMLStatus() : Boolean	Returns true if the XML file is loaded; false otherwise.
static	getDefaultLang() : String	The default language code as set in the Strings panel dialog box or by calling the setDefaultLang() method.
static	initialize() : Void	Automatically determines the language to use and loads the XML language file.
static	loadLanguageXML(xmlLanguageCode:String, customXmlCompleteCallback:Function) : Void	Loads the specified XML language file.
static	loadString(id:String) : String	Returns the string value associated with the given string ID in the current language.
static	loadStringEx(stringID:String, languageCode:String) : String	Returns the string value associated with the given string ID and language code.
static	setDefaultLang(langCode:String) : Void	Sets the default language code.
static	setLoadCallback(loadCallback:Function) : Void	Sets the callback function that is called after the XML file is loaded.
static	setString(stringID:String, languageCode:String, stringValue:String) : Void	Sets the new string value of a given string ID and language code.

Methods inherited from class Object

```
addProperty (Object.addProperty method),hasOwnProperty
(Object.hasOwnProperty method),isPropertyEnumerable
(Object.isPropertyEnumerable method),isPrototypeOf (Object.isPrototypeOf
method),registerClass (Object.registerClass method),toString
(Object.toString method),unwatch (Object.unwatch method),valueOf
(Object.valueOf method),watch (Object.watch method)
```

addDelayedInstance (Locale.addDelayedInstance method)

`public static addDelayedInstance(instance:Object, stringID:String) : Void`

Adds the {instance, string ID} pair into the internal array for later use. This is primarily used by Flash when the strings replacement method is `"automatically at runtime"`.

Availability: ActionScript 2.0; Flash Player 7

Parameters

`instance:Object` - Instance name of the text field to populate.

`stringID:String` - Language string ID.

Example

The following example uses the `autoReplace` property and `addDelayedInstance()` method to populate a text field on the Stage with the `IDS_GREETING` string from the English XML language file.

```
import mx.lang.Locale;
greeting_txt.autoSize = "left";
Locale.autoReplace = true;
Locale.addDelayedInstance(greeting_txt, "IDS_GREETING");
Locale.loadLanguageXML("en");
```

addXMLPath (Locale.addXMLPath method)

`public static addXMLPath(langCode:String, path:String) : Void`

Adds the {languageCode and languagePath} pair into the internal array for later use. This is primarily used by Flash when the strings replacement method is `"automatically at runtime"` or `"via ActionScript at runtime"`.

Availability: ActionScript 2.0; Flash Player 7

Parameters

`langCode:String` - The language code.

`path:String` - The XML path to add.

Example

The following example uses the `setInterval()` method to check whether the language XML file has successfully loaded.

```
import mx.lang.Locale;
Locale.setLoadCallback(localeCallback);
Locale.loadLanguageXML("en");
// create interval to check if language XML file is loaded
var locale_int:Number = setInterval(checkLocaleStatus, 10);
function checkLocaleStatus():Void {
   if (Locale.checkXMLStatus()) {
     clearInterval(locale_int);
     trace("clearing interval @ " + getTimer() + " ms");
   }
}
// callback function for Locale.setLoadCallback()
function localeCallback(success:Boolean):Void {
   greeting_txt.text = Locale.loadString("IDS_GREETING");
}
```

autoReplace (Locale.autoReplace property)

`public static autoReplace : Boolean`

Determines whether strings are replaced automatically after loading the XML file. If set to `true`, the text replacement method is equivalent to the Strings panel setting `"automatically at runtime"`. This means that Flash Player will determine the default language of the host environment and automatically display the text in that language. If set to `false`, the text replacement method is equivalent to the Strings panel setting `"via ActionScript at runtime"`. This means that you are responsible for loading the appropriate XML file to display the text.

The default value of this property reflects the setting that you select for Replace strings in the Strings panel dialog box: `true` for `"automatically at runtime"` (the default setting) and `false` for "via ActionScript at runtime".

Availability: ActionScript 2.0; Flash Player 8

Example

The following example uses the `Locale.autoReplace` property to populate the dynamically created `greeting_txt` text field on the Stage with the contents of the `IDS_GREETING` string in the English XML file. In the Strings panel, click the Settings button to open the Settings dialog box. You can add two active languages using the Settings dialog box: English (en) and French (fr), set the replacement strings radio option to `"via ActionScript at runtime"`, and click OK. Finally, enter a string ID of **IDS_GREETING** in the Strings panel, and add text for each active language.

```
import mx.lang.Locale;
this.createTextField("greeting_txt", 10, 40, 40, 200, 20);
greeting_txt.autoSize = "left";
Locale.autoReplace = true;
Locale.addDelayedInstance(greeting_txt, "IDS_GREETING");
Locale.loadLanguageXML("en");
```

checkXMLStatus (Locale.checkXMLStatus method)

```
public static checkXMLStatus() : Boolean
```

Returns `true` if the XML file is loaded; `false` otherwise.

Availability: ActionScript 2.0; Flash Player 7

Returns

`Boolean` - Returns `true` if the XML file is loaded; `false` otherwise.

Example

The following example uses an interval to check every 10 milliseconds to see if the language file has successfully loaded. Once the XML file has loaded, the `greeting_txt` text field instance on the Stage is populated with the `IDS_GREETING` string from the language XML file.

```
import mx.lang.Locale;
Locale.setLoadCallback(localeCallback);
Locale.loadLanguageXML("en");
// create interval to check if language XML file is loaded
var locale_int:Number = setInterval(checkLocaleStatus, 10);
function checkLocaleStatus():Void {
  if (Locale.checkXMLStatus()) {
    clearInterval(locale_int);
    trace("clearing interval @ " + getTimer() + " ms");
  }
}
// callback function for Locale.setLoadCallback()
function localeCallback(success:Boolean):Void {
  greeting_txt.text = Locale.loadString("IDS_GREETING");
```

}

getDefaultLang (Locale.getDefaultLang method)

`public static getDefaultLang() : String`

The default language code as set in the Strings panel dialog box or by calling the
`setDefaultLang()` method.

Availability: ActionScript 2.0; Flash Player 8

Returns

`String` - Returns the default language code.

Example

The following example creates a variable called `defLang`, which is used to hold the initial
default language for the Flash document. You click the Settings button in the Strings panel to
launch the Settings dialog box. Then you add two active languages: English (en) and French
(fr), set the replace strings radio control to `"via ActionScript at runtime"`, and click OK.
In the Strings panel, you add a string ID of **IDS_GREETING**, and then add text for each
active language.

```
import mx.lang.Locale;
var defLang:String = "fr";
Locale.setDefaultLang(defLang);
Locale.setLoadCallback(localeCallback);
Locale.loadLanguageXML(Locale.getDefaultLang());
function localeCallback(success:Boolean) {
  if (success) {
    trace(Locale.stringIDArray); // IDS_GREETING
    trace(Locale.loadString("IDS_GREETING"));
  } else {
    trace("unable to load XML");
  }
}
```

See also

`setDefaultLang (Locale.setDefaultLang method)`

initialize (Locale.initialize method)

`public static initialize() : Void`

Automatically determines the language to use and loads the XML language file. This is
primarily used by Flash when the strings replacement method is `"automatically at
runtime"`.

Availability: ActionScript 2.0; Flash Player 7

Example

This example shows how to use the `initialize()` method to automatically populate the `greeting_txt` text field on the Stage with the user's current OS language. Instead of using the `initialize()` method directly, use the string replacement method of `"automatically at runtime"`.

```
import mx.lang.Locale;
trace(System.capabilities.language);
Locale.autoReplace = true;
Locale.addDelayedInstance(greeting_txt, "IDS_GREETING");
Locale.initialize();
```

languageCodeArray (Locale.languageCodeArray property)

`public static languageCodeArray : Array [read-only]`

An array containing language codes for the languages that have been specified or loaded into the FLA file. The language codes are not sorted alphabetically.

Availability: ActionScript 2.0; Flash Player 8

Example

The following example loads a language XML file based on the current value of a ComboBox component. You drag a ComboBox component onto the Stage and give it an instance name of `lang_cb`. Using the Text tool, you create a dynamic text field and give it an instance name of `greeting_txt`. In the Strings panel, you add at least two active languages, set the replace strings radio option to `"via ActionScript at runtime"`, and click OK. Next, you add a string ID of **IDS_GREETING** and enter text for each active language. Finally, you add the following ActionScript code to Frame 1 of the main Timeline:

```
import mx.lang.Locale;
Locale.setLoadCallback(localeListener);
lang_cb.dataProvider = Locale.languageCodeArray.sort();
lang_cb.addEventListener("change", langListener);

function langListener(eventObj:Object):Void {
  Locale.loadLanguageXML(eventObj.target.value);
}
function localeListener(success:Boolean):Void {
  if (success) {
    greeting_txt.text = Locale.loadString("IDS_GREETING");
  } else {
    greeting_txt.text = "unable to load language XML file.";
  }
}
```

loadLanguageXML (Locale.loadLanguageXML method)

```
public static loadLanguageXML(xmlLanguageCode:String,
  customXmlCompleteCallback:Function) : Void
```

Loads the specified XML language file.

Availability: ActionScript 2.0; Flash Player 8

Parameters

`xmlLanguageCode:String` - The language code for the XML language file that you want to load.

`customXmlCompleteCallback:Function` - Custom callback function to call when XML language file loads.

Example

The following example uses the `loadLanguageXML()` method to load the English (en) XML language file. Once the language file loads, the `localeCallback()` method is called and populates the `greeting_txt` text field on the Stage with the contents of the `IDS_GREETING` string in the XML file.

```
import mx.lang.Locale;
Locale.setLoadCallback(localeCallback);
Locale.loadLanguageXML("en");
// create interval to check if language XML file is loaded
var locale_int:Number = setInterval(checkLocaleStatus, 10);
function checkLocaleStatus():Void {
  if (Locale.checkXMLStatus()) {
    clearInterval(locale_int);
    trace("clearing interval @ " + getTimer() + " ms");
  }
}
// callback function for Locale.setLoadCallback()
function localeCallback(success:Boolean):Void {
  greeting_txt.text = Locale.loadString("IDS_GREETING");
}
```

loadString (Locale.loadString method)

```
public static loadString(id:String) : String
```

Returns the string value associated with the given string ID in the current language.

Availability: ActionScript 2.0; Flash Player 7

Parameters

`id:String` - The identification (ID) number of the string to load.

Returns

`String` - The string value associated with the given string ID in the current language.

Example

The following example uses an interval to check every 10 milliseconds to see if the language file has successfully loaded. Once the XML file has loaded, the `greeting_txt` text field instance on the Stage is populated with the `IDS_GREETING` string from the XML language file.

```
import mx.lang.Locale;
Locale.setLoadCallback(localeCallback);
Locale.loadLanguageXML("en");
// create interval to check if language XML file is loaded
var locale_int:Number = setInterval(checkLocaleStatus, 10);
```

```
function checkLocaleStatus():Void {
  if (Locale.checkXMLStatus()) {
    clearInterval(locale_int);
    trace("clearing interval @ " + getTimer() + " ms");
  }
}
// callback function for Locale.setLoadCallback()
function localeCallback(success:Boolean):Void {
  greeting_txt.text = Locale.loadString("IDS_GREETING");
}
```

See also

loadStringEx (Locale.loadStringEx method)

loadStringEx (Locale.loadStringEx method)

`public static loadStringEx(stringID:String, languageCode:String) : String`

Returns the string value associated with the given string ID and language code. To avoid unexpected XML file loading, loadStringEx() does not load the XML language file if the XML file is not already loaded. You should decide on the right time to call the loadLanguageXML() method if you want to load a XML language file.

Availability: ActionScript 2.0; Flash Player 8

Parameters

stringID:String - The identification (ID) number of the string to load.

languageCode:String - The language code.

Returns

String - The string value associated with the given string ID in the language specified by the languageCode parameter.

Example

The following example uses the loadStringEx() method to trace the value of the IDS_GREETING string for the currently loaded French language XML file.

```
import mx.lang.Locale;
Locale.setLoadCallback(localeCallback);
Locale.loadLanguageXML("fr");
function localeCallback(success:Boolean) {
  trace(success);
  trace(Locale.stringIDArray); // IDS_GREETING
  trace(Locale.loadStringEx("IDS_GREETING", "fr")); // bonjour
}
```

See also

loadString (Locale.loadString method)

setDefaultLang (Locale.setDefaultLang method)

```
public static setDefaultLang(langCode:String) : Void
```
Sets the default language code.

Availability: ActionScript 2.0; Flash Player 7

Parameters

langCode:String - A string representing a language code.

Example

The following example creates a variable called defLang, which is used to hold the initial default language for the Flash document. You click the Settings button in the Strings panel to open the Settings dialog box. Then you add two active languages: English (en) and French (fr), set the replace strings radio control to "via ActionScript at runtime", and click OK. In the Strings panel, you add a string ID of **IDS_GREETING**, and then add text for each active language.

```
import mx.lang.Locale;
var defLang:String = "fr";
Locale.setDefaultLang(defLang);
Locale.setLoadCallback(localeCallback);
Locale.loadLanguageXML(Locale.getDefaultLang());
function localeCallback(success:Boolean) {
  if (success) {
    trace(Locale.stringIDArray); // IDS_GREETING
    trace(Locale.loadString("IDS_GREETING"));
  } else {
    trace("unable to load XML");
  }
}
```

See also

getDefaultLang (Locale.getDefaultLang method)

setLoadCallback (Locale.setLoadCallback method)

```
public static setLoadCallback(loadCallback:Function) : Void
```
Sets the callback function that is called after the XML file is loaded.

Availability: ActionScript 2.0; Flash Player 7

Parameters

`loadCallback:Function` - The function to call when the XML language file loads.

Example

The following example uses an interval to check every 10 milliseconds to see if the language file has successfully loaded. Once the XML file has loaded, the `greeting_txt` text field instance on the Stage is populated with the `IDS_GREETING` string from the XML language file.

```
import mx.lang.Locale;
Locale.setLoadCallback(localeCallback);
Locale.loadLanguageXML("en");
// create interval to check if language XML file is loaded
var locale_int:Number = setInterval(checkLocaleStatus, 10);
function checkLocaleStatus():Void {
  if (Locale.checkXMLStatus()) {
    clearInterval(locale_int);
    trace("clearing interval @ " + getTimer() + " ms");
  }
}
// callback function for Locale.setLoadCallback()
function localeCallback(success:Boolean):Void {
  greeting_txt.text = Locale.loadString("IDS_GREETING");
}
```

setString (Locale.setString method)

```
public static setString(stringID:String, languageCode:String,
  stringValue:String) : Void
```

Sets the new string value of a given string ID and language code.

Availability: ActionScript 2.0; Flash Player 8

Parameters

`stringID:String` - The identification (ID) number of the string to set.

`languageCode:String` - The language code.

`stringValue:String` - A string value.

Example

The following example uses the `setString()` method to set the `IDS_WELCOME` string for both English (en) and French (fr).

```
import mx.lang.Locale;
Locale.setString("IDS_WELCOME", "en", "hello");
Locale.setString("IDS_WELCOME", "fr", "bonjour");
trace(Locale.loadStringEx("IDS_WELCOME", "en")); // hello
```

stringIDArray (Locale.stringIDArray property)

```
public static stringIDArray : Array [read-only]
```

An array containing all the string IDs in the FLA file. The string IDs are not sorted alphabetically.

Availability: ActionScript 2.0; Flash Player 8

Example

The following example traces the `Locale.stringIDArray` property for the currently loaded language XML file. Click the Settings button in the Strings panel to open the Settings dialog box. Next, you add two active languages: English (en) and French (fr), set the replace strings radio control to `"via ActionScript at runtime"`, and click OK. In the Strings panel, you add a string ID of **IDS_GREETING**, and then add text for each active language.

```
import mx.lang.Locale;
Locale.setLoadCallback(localeCallback);
Locale.loadLanguageXML("fr");
function localeCallback(success:Boolean) {
  trace(success);
  trace(Locale.stringIDArray); // IDS_GREETING
  trace(Locale.loadStringEx("IDS_GREETING", "fr")); // bonjour
}
```

Math

```
Object
  |
  +-Math
```

```
public class Math
extends Object
```

The Math class is a top-level class whose methods and properties you can use without using a constructor.

Use the methods and properties of this class to access and manipulate mathematical constants and functions. All the properties and methods of the Math class are static and must be called using the syntax `Math.method(parameter)` or `Math.constant`. In ActionScript, constants are defined with the maximum precision of double-precision IEEE-754 floating-point numbers.

Several Math class methods use the measure of an angle in radians as a parameter. You can use the following equation to calculate radian values before calling the method and then provide the calculated value as the parameter, or you can provide the entire right side of the equation (with the angle's measure in degrees in place of `degrees`) as the radian parameter.

To calculate a radian value, use the following formula:

```
radians = degrees * Math.PI/180
```

The following is an example of passing the equation as a parameter to calculate the sine of a 45° angle:

```
Math.sin(45 * Math.PI/180)
```
is the same as
```
Math.sin(.7854)
```

Availability: ActionScript 1.0; Flash Player 5 - In Flash Player 4, the methods and properties of the Math class are emulated using approximations and might not be as accurate as the non-emulated math functions that Flash Player 5 supports.

Property summary

Modifiers	Property	Description
static	E:Number	A mathematical constant for the base of natural logarithms, expressed as e.
static	LN10:Number	A mathematical constant for the natural logarithm of 10, expressed as loge10, with an approximate value of 2.302585092994046.
static	LN2:Number	A mathematical constant for the natural logarithm of 2, expressed as loge2, with an approximate value of 0.6931471805599453.
static	LOG10E:Number	A mathematical constant for the base-10 logarithm of the constant e (Math.E), expressed as log10e, with an approximate value of 0.4342944819032518.
static	LOG2E:Number	A mathematical constant for the base-2 logarithm of the constant e (Math.E), expressed as log2e, with an approximate value of 1.442695040888963387.
static	PI:Number	A mathematical constant for the ratio of the circumference of a circle to its diameter, expressed as pi, with a value of 3.141592653589793.
static	SQRT1_2:Number	A mathematical constant for the square root of one-half, with an approximate value of 0.7071067811865476.
static	SQRT2:Number	A mathematical constant for the square root of 2, with an approximate value of 1.4142135623730951.

Properties inherited from class Object

```
constructor (Object.constructor property), __proto__ (Object.__proto__
property), prototype (Object.prototype property), __resolve
(Object.__resolve property)
```

Method summary

Modifiers	Signature	Description
static	`abs(x:Number) : Number`	Computes and returns an absolute value for the number specified by the parameter x.
static	`acos(x:Number) : Number`	Computes and returns the arc cosine of the number specified in the parameter x, in radians.
static	`asin(x:Number) : Number`	Computes and returns the arc sine for the number specified in the parameter x, in radians.
static	`atan(tangent:Number) : Number`	Computes and returns the value, in radians, of the angle whose tangent is specified in the parameter `tangent`.
static	`atan2(y:Number, x:Number) : Number`	Computes and returns the angle of the point y/x in radians, when measured counterclockwise from a circle's x axis (where 0,0 represents the center of the circle).
static	`ceil(x:Number) : Number`	Returns the ceiling of the specified number or expression.
static	`cos(x:Number) : Number`	Computes and returns the cosine of the specified angle in radians.
static	`exp(x:Number) : Number`	Returns the value of the base of the natural logarithm (e), to the power of the exponent specified in the parameter x.
static	`floor(x:Number) : Number`	Returns the floor of the number or expression specified in the parameter x.
static	`log(x:Number) : Number`	Returns the natural logarithm of parameter x.
static	`max(x:Number, y:Number) : Number`	Evaluates x and y and returns the larger value.
static	`min(x:Number, y:Number) : Number`	Evaluates x and y and returns the smaller value.
static	`pow(x:Number, y:Number) : Number`	Computes and returns x to the power of y.
static	`random() : Number`	Returns a pseudo-random number n, where 0 <= n < 1.

Modifiers	Signature	Description
static	round(x:Number) : Number	Rounds the value of the parameter x up or down to the nearest integer and returns the value.
static	sin(x:Number) : Number	Computes and returns the sine of the specified angle in radians.
static	sqrt(x:Number) : Number	Computes and returns the square root of the specified number.
static	tan(x:Number) : Number	Computes and returns the tangent of the specified angle.

Methods inherited from class Object

```
addProperty (Object.addProperty method),hasOwnProperty
(Object.hasOwnProperty method),isPropertyEnumerable
(Object.isPropertyEnumerable method),isPrototypeOf (Object.isPrototypeOf
method),registerClass (Object.registerClass method),toString
(Object.toString method),unwatch (Object.unwatch method),valueOf
(Object.valueOf method),watch (Object.watch method)
```

abs (Math.abs method)

```
public static abs(x:Number) : Number
```

Computes and returns an absolute value for the number specified by the parameter x.

Availability: ActionScript 1.0; Flash Player 5 - In Flash Player 4, the methods and properties of the Math class are emulated using approximations and might not be as accurate as the non-emulated math functions that Flash Player 5 supports.

Parameters

x:Number - A number.

Returns

Number - A number.

Example

The following example shows how Math.abs() returns the absolute value of a number and does not affect the value of the x parameter (called num in this example):

```
var num:Number = -12;
var numAbsolute:Number = Math.abs(num);
trace(num); // output: -12
```

```
trace(numAbsolute); // output: 12
```

acos (Math.acos method)

```
public static acos(x:Number) : Number
```

Computes and returns the arc cosine of the number specified in the parameter x, in radians.

Availability: ActionScript 1.0; Flash Player 5 - In Flash Player 4, the methods and properties of the Math class are emulated using approximations and might not be as accurate as the non-emulated math functions that Flash Player 5 supports.

Parameters

x:Number - A number from -1.0 to 1.0.

Returns

Number - A number; the arc cosine of the parameter x.

Example

The following example displays the arc cosine for several values.

```
trace(Math.acos(-1)); // output: 3.14159265358979
trace(Math.acos(0)); // output: 1.5707963267949
trace(Math.acos(1)); // output: 0
```

See also

asin (Math.asin method), atan (Math.atan method), atan2 (Math.atan2 method), cos (Math.cos method), sin (Math.sin method), tan (Math.tan method)

asin (Math.asin method)

```
public static asin(x:Number) : Number
```

Computes and returns the arc sine for the number specified in the parameter x, in radians.

Availability: ActionScript 1.0; Flash Player 5 - In Flash Player 4, the methods and properties of the Math class are emulated using approximations and might not be as accurate as the non-emulated math functions that Flash Player 5 supports.

Parameters

x:Number - A number from -1.0 to 1.0.

Returns

`Number` - A number between negative pi divided by 2 and positive pi divided by 2.

Example

The following example displays the arc sine for several values.

```
trace(Math.asin(-1)); // output: -1.5707963267949
trace(Math.asin(0)); // output: 0
trace(Math.asin(1)); // output: 1.5707963267949
```

See also

`acos (Math.acos method)`, `atan (Math.atan method)`, `atan2 (Math.atan2 method)`, `cos (Math.cos method)`, `sin (Math.sin method)`, `tan (Math.tan method)`

atan (Math.atan method)

`public static atan(tangent:Number) : Number`

Computes and returns the value, in radians, of the angle whose tangent is specified in the parameter `tangent`. The return value is between negative pi divided by 2 and positive pi divided by 2.

Availability: ActionScript 1.0; Flash Player 5 - In Flash Player 4, the methods and properties of the Math class are emulated using approximations and might not be as accurate as the non-emulated math functions that Flash Player 5 supports.

Parameters

`tangent:Number` - A number that represents the tangent of an angle.

Returns

`Number` - A number between negative pi divided by 2 and positive pi divided by 2.

Example

The following example displays the angle value for several tangents.

```
trace(Math.atan(-1)); // output: -0.785398163397448
trace(Math.atan(0)); // output: 0
trace(Math.atan(1)); // output: 0.785398163397448
```

See also

`acos (Math.acos method)`, `asin (Math.asin method)`, `atan2 (Math.atan2 method)`, `cos (Math.cos method)`, `sin (Math.sin method)`, `tan (Math.tan method)`

atan2 (Math.atan2 method)

`public static atan2(y:Number, x:Number) : Number`

Computes and returns the angle of the point y/x in radians, when measured counterclockwise from a circle's *x* axis (where 0,0 represents the center of the circle). The return value is between positive pi and negative pi.

Availability: ActionScript 1.0; Flash Player 5 - In Flash Player 4, the methods and properties of the Math class are emulated using approximations and might not be as accurate as the non-emulated math functions that Flash Player 5 supports.

Parameters

`y:Number` - A number specifying the *y* coordinate of the point.

`x:Number` - A number specifying the *x* coordinate of the point.

Returns

`Number` - A number.

Example

The following example returns the angle, in radians, of the point specified by the coordinates (0, 10), such that x = 0 and y = 10. Note that the first parameter to atan2 is always the y coordinate.

`trace(Math.atan2(10, 0)); // output: 1.5707963267949`

See also

`acos (Math.acos method)`, `asin (Math.asin method)`, `atan (Math.atan method)`, `cos (Math.cos method)`, `sin (Math.sin method)`, `tan (Math.tan method)`

ceil (Math.ceil method)

`public static ceil(x:Number) : Number`

Returns the ceiling of the specified number or expression. The ceiling of a number is the closest integer that is greater than or equal to the number.

Availability: ActionScript 1.0; Flash Player 5 - In Flash Player 4, the methods and properties of the Math class are emulated using approximations and might not be as accurate as the non-emulated math functions that Flash Player 5 supports.

Parameters

`x:Number` - A number or expression.

Returns

`Number` - An integer that is both closest to, and greater than or equal to, parameter x.

Example

The following code returns a value of 13:

```
Math.ceil(12.5);
```

See also

`floor (Math.floor method)`, `round (Math.round method)`

cos (Math.cos method)

`public static cos(x:Number) : Number`

Computes and returns the cosine of the specified angle in radians. To calculate a radian, see the description of the Math class entry.

Availability: ActionScript 1.0; Flash Player 5 - In Flash Player 4, the methods and properties of the Math class are emulated using approximations and might not be as accurate as the non-emulated math functions that Flash Player 5 supports.

Parameters

`x:Number` - A number that represents an angle measured in radians.

Returns

`Number` - A number from -1.0 to 1.0.

Example

The following example displays the cosine for several different angles.

```
trace (Math.cos(0)); // 0 degree angle. Output: 1
trace (Math.cos(Math.PI/2)); // 90 degree angle. Output: 6.12303176911189e-
  17
trace (Math.cos(Math.PI)); // 180 degree angle. Output: -1
trace (Math.cos(Math.PI*2)); // 360 degree angle. Output: 1
```

Note: The cosine of a 90 degree angle is zero, but because of the inherent inaccuracy of decimal calculations using binary numbers, Flash Player will report a number extremely close to, but not exactly equal to, zero.

`acos (Math.acos method)`, `asin (Math.asin method)`, `atan (Math.atan method)`, `atan2 (Math.atan2 method)`, `sin (Math.sin method)`, `tan (Math.tan method)`

E (Math.E property)

`public static E : Number`

A mathematical constant for the base of natural logarithms, expressed as *e*. The approximate value of *e* is 2.71828182845905.

Availability: ActionScript 1.0; Flash Player 5 - In Flash Player 4, the methods and properties of the Math class are emulated using approximations and might not be as accurate as the non-emulated math functions that Flash Player 5 supports.

Example

This example shows how `Math.E` is used to compute continuously compounded interest for a simple case of 100 percent interest over a one-year period.

```
var principal:Number = 100;
var simpleInterest:Number = 100;
var continuouslyCompoundedInterest:Number = (100 * Math.E) - principal;

trace ("Beginning principal: $" + principal);
trace ("Simple interest after one year: $" + simpleInterest);
trace ("Continuously compounded interest after one year: $" +
  continuouslyCompoundedInterest);

//
Output:
Beginning principal: $100
Simple interest after one year: $100
Continuously compounded interest after one year: $171.828182845905
```

exp (Math.exp method)

`public static exp(x:Number) : Number`

Returns the value of the base of the natural logarithm (*e*), to the power of the exponent specified in the parameter x. The constant `Math.E` can provide the value of *e*.

Availability: ActionScript 1.0; Flash Player 5 - In Flash Player 4, the methods and properties of the Math class are emulated using approximations and might not be as accurate as the non-emulated math functions that Flash Player 5 supports.

Parameters

`x:Number` - The exponent; a number or expression.

Returns

`Number` - A number.

Example

The following example displays the logarithm for two number values.

```
trace(Math.exp(1)); // output: 2.71828182845905
trace(Math.exp(2)); // output: 7.38905609893065
```

See also

`E (Math.E property)`

floor (Math.floor method)

```
public static floor(x:Number) : Number
```

Returns the floor of the number or expression specified in the parameter `x`. The floor is the closest integer that is less than or equal to the specified number or expression.

Availability: ActionScript 1.0; Flash Player 5 - In Flash Player 4, the methods and properties of the Math class are emulated using approximations and might not be as accurate as the non-emulated math functions that Flash Player 5 supports.

Parameters

`x:Number` - A number or expression.

Returns

`Number` - The integer that is both closest to, and less than or equal to, parameter `x`.

Example

The following code returns a value of 12:

```
Math.floor(12.5);
```

The following code returns a value of -7:

```
Math.floor(-6.5);
```

LN10 (Math.LN10 property)

`public static LN10 : Number`

A mathematical constant for the natural logarithm of 10, expressed as loge10, with an approximate value of 2.302585092994046.

Availability: ActionScript 1.0; Flash Player 5 - In Flash Player 4, the methods and properties of the Math class are emulated using approximations and might not be as accurate as the non-emulated math functions that Flash Player 5 supports.

Example

This example traces the value of `Math.LN10`.

```
trace(Math.LN10);
// output: 2.30258509299405
```

LN2 (Math.LN2 property)

`public static LN2 : Number`

A mathematical constant for the natural logarithm of 2, expressed as loge2, with an approximate value of 0.6931471805599453.

Availability: ActionScript 1.0; Flash Player 5 - In Flash Player 4, the methods and properties of the Math class are emulated using approximations and might not be as accurate as the non-emulated math functions that Flash Player 5 supports.

log (Math.log method)

`public static log(x:Number) : Number`

Returns the natural logarithm of parameter x.

Availability: ActionScript 1.0; Flash Player 5 - In Flash Player 4, the methods and properties of the Math class are emulated using approximations and might not be as accurate as the non-emulated math functions that Flash Player 5 supports.

Parameters

`x:Number` - A number or expression with a value greater than 0.

Returns

`Number` - The natural logarithm of parameter x.

Example

The following example displays the logarithm for three numerical values.

```
trace(Math.log(0)); // output: -Infinity
trace(Math.log(1)); // output: 0
trace(Math.log(2)); // output: 0.693147180559945
trace(Math.log(Math.E)); // output: 1
```

LOG10E (Math.LOG10E property)

`public static LOG10E : Number`

A mathematical constant for the base-10 logarithm of the constant e (`Math.E`), expressed as log10e, with an approximate value of 0.4342944819032518.

The `Math.log()` method computes the natural logarithm of a number. Multiply the result of `Math.log()` by `Math.LOG10E` obtain the base-10 logarithm.

Availability: ActionScript 1.0; Flash Player 5 - In Flash Player 4, the methods and properties of the Math class are emulated using approximations and might not be as accurate as the non-emulated math functions that Flash Player 5 supports.

Example

This example shows how to obtain the base-10 logarithm of a number:

```
trace(Math.log(1000) * Math.LOG10E);
// Output: 3
```

LOG2E (Math.LOG2E property)

`public static LOG2E : Number`

A mathematical constant for the base-2 logarithm of the constant e (`Math.E`), expressed as log2e, with an approximate value of 1.442695040888963387.

The `Math.log` method computes the natural logarithm of a number. Multiply the result of `Math.log()` by `Math.LOG2E` obtain the base-2 logarithm.

Availability: ActionScript 1.0; Flash Player 5 - In Flash Player 4, the methods and properties of the Math class are emulated using approximations and might not be as accurate as the non-emulated math functions that Flash Player 5 supports.

Example

This example shows how to obtain the base-2 logarithm of a number:

```
trace(Math.log(16) * Math.LOG2E);
// Output: 4
```

max (Math.max method)

```
public static max(x:Number, y:Number) : Number
```

Evaluates x and y and returns the larger value.

Availability: ActionScript 1.0; Flash Player 5 - In Flash Player 4, the methods and properties of the Math class are emulated using approximations and might not be as accurate as the non-emulated math functions that Flash Player 5 supports.

Parameters

x:Number - A number or expression.

y:Number - A number or expression.

Returns

Number - A number.

Example

The following example displays Thu Dec 30 00:00:00 GMT-0700 2004, which is the larger of the evaluated expressions.

```
var date1:Date = new Date(2004, 11, 25);
var date2:Date = new Date(2004, 11, 30);
var maxDate:Number = Math.max(date1.getTime(), date2.getTime());
trace(new Date(maxDate).toString());
```

See also

min (Math.min method), Date

min (Math.min method)

```
public static min(x:Number, y:Number) : Number
```

Evaluates x and y and returns the smaller value.

Availability: ActionScript 1.0; Flash Player 5 - In Flash Player 4, the methods and properties of the Math class are emulated using approximations and might not be as accurate as the non-emulated math functions that Flash Player 5 supports.

Parameters

x:Number - A number or expression.

y:Number - A number or expression.

Returns

`Number` - A number.

Example

The following example displays `Sat Dec 25 00:00:00 GMT-0700 2004`, which is the smaller of the evaluated expressions.

```
var date1:Date = new Date(2004, 11, 25);
var date2:Date = new Date(2004, 11, 30);
var minDate:Number = Math.min(date1.getTime(), date2.getTime());
trace(new Date(minDate).toString());
```

See also

`max (Math.max method)`

PI (Math.PI property)

`public static PI : Number`

A mathematical constant for the ratio of the circumference of a circle to its diameter, expressed as pi, with a value of 3.141592653589793.

Availability: ActionScript 1.0; Flash Player 5 - In Flash Player 4, the methods and properties of the Math class are emulated using approximations and might not be as accurate as the non-emulated math functions that Flash Player 5 supports.

Example

The following example draws a circle using the mathematical constant pi and the Drawing API.

```
drawCircle(this, 100, 100, 50);
//
function drawCircle(mc:MovieClip, x:Number, y:Number, r:Number):Void {
  mc.lineStyle(2, 0xFF0000, 100);
  mc.moveTo(x+r, y);
  mc.curveTo(r+x, Math.tan(Math.PI/8)*r+y, Math.sin(Math.PI/4)*r+x,
  Math.sin(Math.PI/4)*r+y);
  mc.curveTo(Math.tan(Math.PI/8)*r+x, r+y, x, r+y);
  mc.curveTo(-Math.tan(Math.PI/8)*r+x, r+y, -Math.sin(Math.PI/4)*r+x,
  Math.sin(Math.PI/4)*r+y);
  mc.curveTo(-r+x, Math.tan(Math.PI/8)*r+y, -r+x, y);
  mc.curveTo(-r+x, -Math.tan(Math.PI/8)*r+y, -Math.sin(Math.PI/4)*r+x, -
  Math.sin(Math.PI/4)*r+y);
  mc.curveTo(-Math.tan(Math.PI/8)*r+x, -r+y, x, -r+y);
  mc.curveTo(Math.tan(Math.PI/8)*r+x, -r+y, Math.sin(Math.PI/4)*r+x, -
  Math.sin(Math.PI/4)*r+y);
  mc.curveTo(r+x, -Math.tan(Math.PI/8)*r+y, r+x, y);
```

}

pow (Math.pow method)

`public static pow(x:Number, y:Number) : Number`

Computes and returns x to the power of y.

Availability: ActionScript 1.0; Flash Player 5 - In Flash Player 4, the methods and properties of the Math class are emulated using approximations and might not be as accurate as the non-emulated math functions that Flash Player 5 supports.

Parameters

`x:Number` - A number to be raised to a power.

`y:Number` - A number specifying a power the parameter x is raised to.

Returns

`Number` - A number.

Example

The following example uses `Math.pow` and `Math.sqrt` to calculate the length of a line.

```
this.createEmptyMovieClip("canvas_mc", this.getNextHighestDepth());
var mouseListener:Object = new Object();
mouseListener.onMouseDown = function() {
  this.origX = _xmouse;
  this.origY = _ymouse;
};
mouseListener.onMouseUp = function() {
  this.newX = _xmouse;
  this.newY = _ymouse;
  var minY = Math.min(this.origY, this.newY);
  var nextDepth:Number = canvas_mc.getNextHighestDepth();
  var line_mc:MovieClip =
  canvas_mc.createEmptyMovieClip("line"+nextDepth+"_mc", nextDepth);
  line_mc.moveTo(this.origX, this.origY);
  line_mc.lineStyle(2, 0x000000, 100);
  line_mc.lineTo(this.newX, this.newY);
  var hypLen:Number = Math.sqrt(Math.pow(line_mc._width,
  2)+Math.pow(line_mc._height, 2));
  line_mc.createTextField("length"+nextDepth+"_txt",
  canvas_mc.getNextHighestDepth(), this.origX, this.origY-22, 100, 22);
  line_mc['length'+nextDepth+'_txt'].text = Math.round(hypLen) +" pixels";
};
Mouse.addListener(mouseListener);
```

The `MovieClip.getNextHighestDepth()` method used in this example requires Flash Player 7 or later. If your SWF file includes a version 2 component, use the version 2 components DepthManager class instead of the `MovieClip.getNextHighestDepth()` method.

random (Math.random method)

`public static random() : Number`

Returns a pseudo-random number n, where 0 <= n < 1. The number returned is a pseudo-random number because it is not generated by a truly random natural phenomenon such as radioactive decay.

Availability: ActionScript 1.0; Flash Player 5 - In Flash Player 4, the methods and properties of the Math class are emulated using approximations and might not be as accurate as the non-emulated math functions that Flash Player 5 supports.

Returns

`Number` - A number.

Example

The following example outputs 100 random integers between 4 and 11 (inclusively):

```
function randRange(min:Number, max:Number):Number {
   var randomNum:Number = Math.floor(Math.random() * (max - min + 1)) + min;
   return randomNum;
}
for (var i = 0; i < 100; i++) {
   var n:Number = randRange(4, 11)
   trace(n);
}
```

round (Math.round method)

`public static round(x:Number) : Number`

Rounds the value of the parameter x up or down to the nearest integer and returns the value. If parameter x is equidistant from its two nearest integers (that is, the number ends in .5), the value is rounded up to the next higher integer.

Availability: ActionScript 1.0; Flash Player 5 - In Flash Player 4, the methods and properties of the Math class are emulated using approximations and might not be as accurate as the non-emulated math functions that Flash Player 5 supports.

Parameters

`x:Number` - A number.

Returns

`Number` - A number; an integer.

Example

The following example returns a random number between two specified integers.

```
function randRange(min:Number, max:Number):Number {
  var randomNum:Number = Math.round(Math.random() * (max-min+1) + (min-
  .5));
  return randomNum;
}
for (var i = 0; i<25; i++) {
  trace(randRange(4, 11));
}
```

See also

`ceil (Math.ceil method)`, `floor (Math.floor method)`

sin (Math.sin method)

`public static sin(x:Number) : Number`

Computes and returns the sine of the specified angle in radians. To calculate a radian, see the description of the Math class entry.

Availability: ActionScript 1.0; Flash Player 5 - In Flash Player 4, the methods and properties of the Math class are emulated using approximations and might not be as accurate as the non-emulated math functions that Flash Player 5 supports.

Parameters

`x:Number` - A number that represents an angle measured in radians.

Returns

`Number` - A number; the sine of the specified angle (between -1.0 and 1.0).

Example

The following example draws a circle using the mathematical constant pi, the sine of an angle, and the Drawing API.

```
drawCircle(this, 100, 100, 50);
//
function drawCircle(mc:MovieClip, x:Number, y:Number, r:Number):Void {
  mc.lineStyle(2, 0xFF0000, 100);
  mc.moveTo(x+r, y);
```

```
mc.curveTo(r+x, Math.tan(Math.PI/8)*r+y, Math.sin(Math.PI/4)*r+x,
  Math.sin(Math.PI/4)*r+y);
mc.curveTo(Math.tan(Math.PI/8)*r+x, r+y, x, r+y);
mc.curveTo(-Math.tan(Math.PI/8)*r+x, r+y, -Math.sin(Math.PI/4)*r+x,
  Math.sin(Math.PI/4)*r+y);
mc.curveTo(-r+x, Math.tan(Math.PI/8)*r+y, -r+x, y);
mc.curveTo(-r+x, -Math.tan(Math.PI/8)*r+y, -Math.sin(Math.PI/4)*r+x, -
  Math.sin(Math.PI/4)*r+y);
mc.curveTo(-Math.tan(Math.PI/8)*r+x, -r+y, x, -r+y);
mc.curveTo(Math.tan(Math.PI/8)*r+x, -r+y, Math.sin(Math.PI/4)*r+x, -
  Math.sin(Math.PI/4)*r+y);
mc.curveTo(r+x, -Math.tan(Math.PI/8)*r+y, r+x, y);
}
```

See also

acos (Math.acos method), asin (Math.asin method), atan (Math.atan method),
atan2 (Math.atan2 method), cos (Math.cos method), tan (Math.tan method)

sqrt (Math.sqrt method)

`public static sqrt(x:Number) : Number`

Computes and returns the square root of the specified number.

Availability: ActionScript 1.0; Flash Player 5 - In Flash Player 4, the methods and properties of the Math class are emulated using approximations and might not be as accurate as the non-emulated math functions that Flash Player 5 supports.

Parameters

x:Number - A number or expression greater than or equal to 0.

Returns

Number - A number if parameter *x* is greater than or equal to zero; NaN (not a number) otherwise.

Example

The following example uses Math.pow and Math.sqrt to calculate the length of a line.

```
this.createEmptyMovieClip("canvas_mc", this.getNextHighestDepth());
var mouseListener:Object = new Object();
mouseListener.onMouseDown = function() {
  this.origX = _xmouse;
  this.origY = _ymouse;
};
mouseListener.onMouseUp = function() {
  this.newX = _xmouse;
```

```
this.newY = _ymouse;
var minY = Math.min(this.origY, this.newY);
var nextDepth:Number = canvas_mc.getNextHighestDepth();
var line_mc:MovieClip =
canvas_mc.createEmptyMovieClip("line"+nextDepth+"_mc", nextDepth);
line_mc.moveTo(this.origX, this.origY);
line_mc.lineStyle(2, 0x000000, 100);
line_mc.lineTo(this.newX, this.newY);
var hypLen:Number = Math.sqrt(Math.pow(line_mc._width,
2)+Math.pow(line_mc._height, 2));
line_mc.createTextField("length"+nextDepth+"_txt",
canvas_mc.getNextHighestDepth(), this.origX, this.origY-22, 100, 22);
line_mc['length'+nextDepth+'_txt'].text = Math.round(hypLen) +" pixels";
};
Mouse.addListener(mouseListener);
```

SQRT1_2 (Math.SQRT1_2 property)

`public static SQRT1_2 : Number`

A mathematical constant for the square root of one-half, with an approximate value of 0.7071067811865476.

Availability: ActionScript 1.0; Flash Player 5 - In Flash Player 4, the methods and properties of the Math class are emulated using approximations and might not be as accurate as the non-emulated math functions that Flash Player 5 supports.

Example

This example traces the value of `Math.SQRT1_2`.

```
trace(Math.SQRT1_2);
// Output: 0.707106781186548
```

SQRT2 (Math.SQRT2 property)

`public static SQRT2 : Number`

A mathematical constant for the square root of 2, with an approximate value of 1.4142135623730951.

Availability: ActionScript 1.0; Flash Player 5 - In Flash Player 4, the methods and properties of the Math class are emulated using approximations and might not be as accurate as the non-emulated math functions that Flash Player 5 supports.

Example

This example traces the value of `Math.SQRT2`.

```
trace(Math.SQRT2);
// Output: 1.4142135623731
```

tan (Math.tan method)

```
public static tan(x:Number) : Number
```

Computes and returns the tangent of the specified angle. To calculate a radian, use the information outlined in the introduction to the Math class.

Availability: ActionScript 1.0; Flash Player 5 - In Flash Player 4, the methods and properties of the Math class are emulated using approximations and might not be as accurate as the non-emulated math functions that Flash Player 5 supports.

Parameters

`x:Number` - A number that represents an angle measured in radians.

Returns

`Number` - A number; tangent of parameter x.

Example

The following example draws a circle using the mathematical constant pi, the tangent of an angle, and the Drawing API.

```
drawCircle(this, 100, 100, 50);
//
function drawCircle(mc:MovieClip, x:Number, y:Number, r:Number):Void {
  mc.lineStyle(2, 0xFF0000, 100);
  mc.moveTo(x+r, y);
  mc.curveTo(r+x, Math.tan(Math.PI/8)*r+y, Math.sin(Math.PI/4)*r+x,
  Math.sin(Math.PI/4)*r+y);
  mc.curveTo(Math.tan(Math.PI/8)*r+x, r+y, x, r+y);
  mc.curveTo(-Math.tan(Math.PI/8)*r+x, r+y, -Math.sin(Math.PI/4)*r+x,
  Math.sin(Math.PI/4)*r+y);
  mc.curveTo(-r+x, Math.tan(Math.PI/8)*r+y, -r+x, y);
  mc.curveTo(-r+x, -Math.tan(Math.PI/8)*r+y, -Math.sin(Math.PI/4)*r+x, -
  Math.sin(Math.PI/4)*r+y);
  mc.curveTo(-Math.tan(Math.PI/8)*r+x, -r+y, x, -r+y);
  mc.curveTo(Math.tan(Math.PI/8)*r+x, -r+y, Math.sin(Math.PI/4)*r+x, -
  Math.sin(Math.PI/4)*r+y);
  mc.curveTo(r+x, -Math.tan(Math.PI/8)*r+y, r+x, y);
}
```

See also

`acos (Math.acos method)`, `asin (Math.asin method)`, `atan (Math.atan method)`, `atan2 (Math.atan2 method)`, `cos (Math.cos method)`, `sin (Math.sin method)`

Matrix (flash.geom.Matrix)

```
Object
  |
  +-flash.geom.Matrix
```

public class **Matrix**
extends Object

The flash.geom.Matrix class represents a transformation matrix that determines how to map points from one coordinate space to another. By setting the properties of a Matrix object and applying it to a MovieClip or BitmapData object you can perform various graphical transformations on the object. These transformation functions include translation (x and y repositioning), rotation, scaling, and skewing.

Together these types of transformations are knows as *affine transformations*. Affine transformations preserve the straightness of lines while transforming, and parallel lines stay parallel.

To apply a transformation matrix to a movie clip, you create a flash.geom.Transform object, and set its Matrix property to the transformation matrix. Matrix objects are also used as parameters of some methods, such as the draw() method of the flash.display.BitmapData class.

A transformation matrix object is considered a 3 x 3 matrix with the following contents:

$$\begin{bmatrix} a & b & t_x \\ c & d & t_y \\ u & v & w \end{bmatrix}$$

In traditional transformation matrixes the u, v, and w properties provide extra capabilities. The Matrix class can only operate in two-dimensional space so it always assumes that the property values u and v are 0.0, and that the property value w is 1.0. In other words the effective values of the matrix are as follows:

$$\begin{bmatrix} a & b & t_x \\ c & d & t_y \\ 0 & 0 & 1 \end{bmatrix}$$

You can get and set the values of all six of the other properties in a Matrix object: a, b, c, d, tx, and ty.

The Matrix class supports the four major types of transformation functions: translation, scaling, rotation, and skewing. There are specialized methods for three of these functions, as described in the following table.

Transformation	Method	Matrix values	Display result	Description
Translation (displacement)	`translate(tx, ty)`	$$\begin{bmatrix} 1 & 0 & t_x \\ 0 & 1 & t_y \\ 0 & 0 & 1 \end{bmatrix}$$		Moves the image `tx` pixels to the right and `ty` pixels down.
Scaling	`scale(sx, sy)`	$$\begin{bmatrix} s_x & 0 & 0 \\ 0 & s_y & 0 \\ 0 & 0 & 1 \end{bmatrix}$$		Resizes the image, multiplying the location of each pixel by `sx` on the *x* axis and `sy` on the *y* axis.
Rotation	`rotate(q)`	$$\begin{bmatrix} \cos(q) & \sin(q) & 0 \\ -\sin(q) & \cos(q) & 0 \\ 0 & 0 & 1 \end{bmatrix}$$		Rotates the image by an angle `q`, which is measured in radians
Skewing or shearing	None; must set the properties `b` and `c`.	$$\begin{bmatrix} 0 & sk_y & 0 \\ sk_x & 0 & 0 \\ 0 & 0 & 1 \end{bmatrix}$$		Progressively slides the image in a direction parallel to the *x* or *y* axis. The value `skx` acts as a multiplier controlling the sliding distance along the *x* axis; `sky` controls the sliding distance along the *y* axis.

Each transformation function alters the current matrix properties so that you can effectively combine multiple transformations. To do this, you call more than one transformation function before applying the matrix to its movie clip or bitmap target.

Availability: ActionScript 1.0; Flash Player 8

See also

`transform` (`MovieClip.transform` property), `Transform` (`flash.geom.Transform`),
`draw` (`BitmapData.draw` method), `a` (`Matrix.a` property), `b` (`Matrix.b` property), `c`
(`Matrix.c` property), `d` (`Matrix.d` property), `tx` (`Matrix.tx` property), `ty`
(`Matrix.ty` property), `translate` (`Matrix.translate` method), `scale`
(`Matrix.scale` method), `rotate` (`Matrix.rotate` method)

Property summary

Modifiers	Property	Description
	`a:Number`	The value in the first row and first column of the Matrix object, which affects the positioning of pixels along the x axis when scaling or rotating an image.
	`b:Number`	The value in the first row and second column of the Matrix object, which affects the positioning of pixels along the y axis when rotating or skewing an image.
	`c:Number`	The value in the second row and first column of the Matrix object, which affects the positioning of pixels along the x axis when rotating or skewing an image.
	`d:Number`	The value in the second row and second column of the Matrix object, which affects the positioning of pixels along the y axis when scaling or rotating an image.
	`tx:Number`	The distance by which to translate each point along the x axis.
	`ty:Number`	The distance by which to translate each point along the y axis.

Properties inherited from class Object

`constructor` (`Object.constructor` property), `__proto__` (`Object.__proto__`
property), `prototype` (`Object.prototype` property), `__resolve`
(`Object.__resolve` property)

Constructor summary

Signature	Description
`Matrix([a:Number], [b:Number], [c:Number], [d:Number], [tx:Number], [ty:Number])`	Creates a new Matrix object with the specified parameters.

Method summary

Modifiers	Signature	Description
	`clone() : Matrix`	Returns a new Matrix object that is a clone of this matrix, with an exact copy of the contained object.
	`concat(m:Matrix) : Void`	Concatenates a matrix with the current matrix, effectively combining the geometric effects of the two.
	`createBox(scaleX:Number, scaleY:Number, [rotation:Number], [tx:Number], [ty:Number]) : Void`	Includes parameters for scaling, rotation, and translation.
	`createGradientBox(width:Number, height:Number, [rotation:Number], [tx:Number], [ty:Number]) : Void`	Creates the specific style of matrix expected by the `MovieClip.beginGradientFill()` method.
	`deltaTransformPoint(pt:Point) : Point`	Given a point in the pretransform coordinate space, returns the coordinates of that point after the transformation occurs.
	`identity() : Void`	Sets each matrix property to a value that cause a transformed movie clip or geometric construct to be identical to the original.
	`invert() : Void`	Performs the opposite transformation of the original matrix.
	`rotate(angle:Number) : Void`	Sets the values in the current matrix so that the matrix can be used to apply a rotation transformation.
	`scale(sx:Number, sy:Number) : Void`	Modifies a matrix so that its effect, when applied, is to resize an image.
	`toString() : String`	Returns a text value listing the properties of the Matrix object.

Modifiers	Signature	Description
	`transformPoint(pt:Po int) : Point`	Applies the geometric transformation represented by the Matrix object to the specified point.
	`translate(tx:Number, ty:Number) : Void`	Modifies a Matrix object so that the effect of its transformation is to move an object along the x and y axes.

Methods inherited from class Object

```
addProperty (Object.addProperty method), hasOwnProperty
(Object.hasOwnProperty method), isPropertyEnumerable
(Object.isPropertyEnumerable method), isPrototypeOf (Object.isPrototypeOf
method), registerClass (Object.registerClass method), toString
(Object.toString method), unwatch (Object.unwatch method), valueOf
(Object.valueOf method), watch (Object.watch method)
```

a (Matrix.a property)

`public a : Number`

The value in the first row and first column of the Matrix object, which affects the positioning of pixels along the x axis when scaling or rotating an image.

Availability: ActionScript 1.0; Flash Player 8

Example

The following example creates the Matrix object `myMatrix` and sets its a value.

```
import flash.geom.Matrix;

var myMatrix:Matrix = new Matrix();
trace(myMatrix.a); // 1

myMatrix.a = 2;
trace(myMatrix.a); // 2
```

b (Matrix.b property)

`public b : Number`

The value in the first row and second column of the Matrix object, which affects the positioning of pixels along the y axis when rotating or skewing an image.

Availability: ActionScript 1.0; Flash Player 8

Example

The following example creates the Matrix object myMatrix and sets its b value.

```
import flash.geom.Matrix;

var myMatrix:Matrix = new Matrix();
trace(myMatrix.b); // 0

var degrees:Number = 45;
var radians:Number = (degrees/180) Math.PI;
myMatrix.b = radians;
trace(myMatrix.b); // 0.785398163397448
```

c (Matrix.c property)

```
public c : Number
```

The value in the second row and first column of the Matrix object, which affects the positioning of pixels along the *x* axis when rotating or skewing an image.

Availability: ActionScript 1.0; Flash Player 8

Example

The following example creates the Matrix object myMatrix and sets its c value.

```
import flash.geom.Matrix;

var myMatrix:Matrix = new Matrix();
trace(myMatrix.c); // 0

var degrees:Number = 45;
var radians:Number = (degrees/180) Math.PI;
myMatrix.c = radians;
trace(myMatrix.c); // 0.785398163397448
```

clone (Matrix.clone method)

```
public clone() : Matrix
```

Returns a new Matrix object that is a clone of this matrix, with an exact copy of the contained object.

Availability: ActionScript 1.0; Flash Player 8

Returns

```
flash.geom.Matrix
``` - A Matrix object.

Example

The following example creates the `clonedMatrix` variable from the `myMatrix` variable. The Matrix class does not have an `equals` method, so the following example uses a custom written function to test the equality of two matrixes.

```
import flash.geom.Matrix;

var myMatrix:Matrix = new Matrix(2, 0, 0, 2, 0, 0);
var clonedMatrix:Matrix = new Matrix();

trace(myMatrix); // (a=2, b=0, c=0, d=2, tx=0, ty=0)
trace(clonedMatrix); // (a=1, b=0, c=0, d=1, tx=0, ty=0)
trace(equals(myMatrix, clonedMatrix)); // false

clonedMatrix = myMatrix.clone();

trace(myMatrix); // (a=2, b=0, c=0, d=2, tx=0, ty=0)
trace(clonedMatrix); // (a=2, b=0, c=0, d=2, tx=0, ty=0)
trace(equals(myMatrix, clonedMatrix)); // true

function equals(m1:Matrix, m2:Matrix):Boolean {
   return m1.toString() == m2.toString();
}
```

concat (Matrix.concat method)

`public concat(m:Matrix) : Void`

Concatenates a matrix with the current matrix, effectively combining the geometric effects of the two. In mathematical terms, concatenating two matrixes is the same as combining them using matrix multiplication.

For example, if matrix `m1` scales an object by a factor of four, and matrix `m2` rotates an object by 1.5707963267949 radians (`Math.PI/2`), `m1.concat(m2)` transforms `m1` into a matrix that scales an object by a factor of four and rotates the object by `Math.PI/2` radians.

This method replaces the source matrix with the concatenated matrix. If you want to concatenate two matrixes without altering either of the two source matrixes, you can first copy the source matrix the clone() method, as shown in the Example section.

Availability: ActionScript 1.0; Flash Player 8

Parameters

`m:flash.geom.Matrix` - The matrix to be concatenated to the source matrix.

Example

The following example creates three matrixes that define transformations for three rectangle movie clips. The first two matrixes `rotate45Matrix` and `doubleScaleMatrix` are applied to the two rectangles `rectangleMc_1` and `rectangleMc_2`. Then the third matrix is created using the `concat()` method on `rotate45Matrix` and `doubleScaleMatrix` to create `scaleAndRotateMatrix`. This matrix is then applied to `rectangleMc_3` to scale and rotate it.

```
import flash.geom.Matrix;
import flash.geom.Transform;

var rectangleMc_0:MovieClip = createRectangle(20, 80, 0x000000);
var rectangleMc_1:MovieClip = createRectangle(20, 80, 0xFF0000);
var rectangleMc_2:MovieClip = createRectangle(20, 80, 0x00FF00);
var rectangleMc_3:MovieClip = createRectangle(20, 80, 0x0000FF);

var rectangleTrans_1:Transform = new Transform(rectangleMc_1);
var rectangleTrans_2:Transform = new Transform(rectangleMc_2);
var rectangleTrans_3:Transform = new Transform(rectangleMc_3);

var rotate45Matrix:Matrix = new Matrix();
rotate45Matrix.rotate(Math.PI/4);
rectangleTrans_1.matrix = rotate45Matrix;
rectangleMc_1._x = 100;
trace(rotate45Matrix.toString()); // (a=0.707106781186548,
   b=0.707106781186547, c=-0.707106781186547, d=0.707106781186548, tx=0,
   ty=0)

var doubleScaleMatrix:Matrix = new Matrix();
doubleScaleMatrix.scale(2, 2);
rectangleTrans_2.matrix = doubleScaleMatrix;
rectangleMc_2._x = 200;
trace(doubleScaleMatrix.toString()); // (a=2, b=0, c=0, d=2, tx=0, ty=0)

var scaleAndRotateMatrix:Matrix = doubleScaleMatrix.clone();
scaleAndRotateMatrix.concat(rotate45Matrix);
rectangleTrans_3.matrix = scaleAndRotateMatrix;
rectangleMc_3._x = 300;
trace(scaleAndRotateMatrix.toString()); // (a=1.4142135623731,
   b=1.41421356237309, c=-1.41421356237309, d=1.4142135623731, tx=0, ty=0)
```

```
function createRectangle(width:Number, height:Number,
  color:Number):MovieClip {
  var depth:Number = this.getNextHighestDepth();
  var mc:MovieClip = this.createEmptyMovieClip("mc_" + depth, depth);
  mc.beginFill(color);
  mc.lineTo(0, height);
  mc.lineTo(width, height);
  mc.lineTo(width, 0);
  mc.lineTo(0, 0);
  return mc;
}
```

createBox (Matrix.createBox method)

```
public createBox(scaleX:Number, scaleY:Number, [rotation:Number],
  [tx:Number], [ty:Number]) : Void
```

Includes parameters for scaling, rotation, and translation. When applied to a matrix it sets the matrix's values based on those parameters.

Using the createBox() method lets you obtain the same matrix as you would if you were to apply the identity(), rotate(), scale(), and translate() methods in succession. For example, mat1.createBox(2,2,Math.PI/5, 100, 100) has the same effect as the following:

```
import flash.geom.Matrix;

var mat1:Matrix = new Matrix();
mat1.identity();
mat1.rotate(Math.PI/4);
mat1.scale(2,2);
mat1.translate(10,20);
```

Availability: ActionScript 1.0; Flash Player 8

Parameters

scaleX:Number - The factor by which to scale horizontally.

scaleY:Number - The factor by which scale vertically.

rotation:Number [optional] - The amount to rotate, in radians. The default value is 0.

tx:Number [optional] - The number of pixels to translate (move) to the right along the *x* axis. The default value is 0.

ty:Number [optional] - The number of pixels to translate (move) down along the *y* axis. The default value is 0.

Example

The following example sets the `scaleX`, `scaleY` scale, rotation, *x* location, and *y* location of `myMatrix` by calling its `createBox()` method.

```
import flash.geom.Matrix;
import flash.geom.Transform;

var myMatrix:Matrix = new Matrix();
trace(myMatrix.toString()); // (a=1, b=0, c=0, d=1, tx=0, ty=0)

myMatrix.createBox(1, 2, Math.PI/4, 100, 200);
trace(myMatrix.toString()); // (a=0.707106781186548, b=1.41421356237309,
    c=-0.707106781186547, d=1.4142135623731, tx=100, ty=200)

var rectangleMc:MovieClip = createRectangle(20, 80, 0xFF0000);
var rectangleTrans:Transform = new Transform(rectangleMc);
rectangleTrans.matrix = myMatrix;
```

See also

createGradientBox (Matrix.createGradientBox method)

```
public createGradientBox(width:Number, height:Number, [rotation:Number],
    [tx:Number], [ty:Number]) : Void
```

Creates the specific style of matrix expected by the `MovieClip.beginGradientFill()` method. Width and height are scaled to a `scaleX`/`scaleY` pair and the `tx`/`ty` values are offset by half the width and height.

Availability: ActionScript 1.0; Flash Player 8

Parameters

`width:Number` - The width of the gradient box.

`height:Number` - The height of the gradient box.

`rotation:Number` [optional] - The amount to rotate, in radians. The default value is 0.

`tx:Number` [optional] - The distance in pixels to translate to the right along the *x* axis. This value will be offset by half of the width parameter. The default value is 0.

`ty:Number` [optional] - The distance in pixels to translate down along the *y* axis. This value will be offset by half of the height parameter. The default value is 0.

Example

The following example uses myMatrix as a parameter for the MovieClip object's beginGradientFill() method.

```
import flash.geom.Matrix;

var myMatrix:Matrix = new Matrix();
trace(myMatrix.toString()); // (a=1, b=0, c=0, d=1, tx=0, ty=0)

myMatrix.createGradientBox(200, 200, 0, 50, 50);
trace(myMatrix.toString()); // (a=0.1220703125, b=0, c=0, d=0.1220703125,
   tx=150, ty=150)

var depth:Number = this.getNextHighestDepth();
var mc:MovieClip = this.createEmptyMovieClip("mc_" + depth, depth);
var colors:Array = [0xFF0000, 0x0000FF];
var alphas:Array = [100, 100];
var ratios:Array = [0, 0xFF];
mc.beginGradientFill("linear", colors, alphas, ratios, myMatrix);
mc.lineTo(0, 300);
mc.lineTo(300, 300);
mc.lineTo(300, 0);
mc.lineTo(0, 0);
```

See also

beginGradientFill (MovieClip.beginGradientFill method)

d (Matrix.d property)

public d : Number

The value in the second row and second column of the Matrix object, which affects the positioning of pixels along the *y* axis when scaling or rotating an image.

Availability: ActionScript 1.0; Flash Player 8

Example

The following example creates the Matrix object myMatrix and sets its d value.

```
import flash.geom.Matrix;

var myMatrix:Matrix = new Matrix();
trace(myMatrix.d); // 1

myMatrix.d = 2;
trace(myMatrix.d); // 2
```

deltaTransformPoint (Matrix.deltaTransformPoint method)

```
public deltaTransformPoint(pt:Point) : Point
```

Given a point in the pretransform coordinate space, returns the coordinates of that point after the transformation occurs. Unlike the standard transformation applied using the transformPoint() method, the deltaTransformPoint() method's transformation does not consider the translation parameters tx and ty.

Availability: ActionScript 1.0; Flash Player 8

Parameters

pt:flash.geom.Point - A Point object.

Returns

flash.geom.Point - The new Point object.

Example

The following example uses the deltaTransformPoint() method to create deltaTransformedPoint from myPoint. In the example, the translate() method does not alter the position of the point named deltaTransformedPoint. However, the scale() method does affect that point's position. It increases the point's x value by a factor of three from 50 to 150.

```
import flash.geom.Matrix;
import flash.geom.Point;

var myMatrix:Matrix = new Matrix();
trace(myMatrix); // (a=1, b=0, c=0, d=1, tx=0, ty=0)

myMatrix.translate(100, 0);
trace(myMatrix); // (a=1, b=0, c=0, d=1, tx=100, ty=0)

myMatrix.scale(3, 3);
trace(myMatrix); // (a=3, b=0, c=0, d=3, tx=300, ty=0)

var myPoint:Point = new Point(50,0);
trace(myPoint); // (50, 0)

var deltaTransformedPoint:Point = myMatrix.deltaTransformPoint(myPoint);
trace(deltaTransformedPoint); // (150, 0)

var pointMc_0:MovieClip = createRectangle(10, 10, 0xFF0000);
pointMc_0._x = myPoint.x;
```

```
var pointMc_1:MovieClip = createRectangle(10, 10, 0x00FF00);
pointMc_1._x = deltaTransformedPoint.x;

function createRectangle(width:Number, height:Number,
  color:Number):MovieClip {
  var depth:Number = this.getNextHighestDepth();
  var mc:MovieClip = this.createEmptyMovieClip("mc_" + depth, depth);
  mc.beginFill(color);
  mc.lineTo(0, height);
  mc.lineTo(width, height);
  mc.lineTo(width, 0);
  mc.lineTo(0, 0);
  return mc;
}
```

identity (Matrix.identity method)

```
public identity() : Void
```

Sets each matrix property to a value that cause a transformed movie clip or geometric construct to be identical to the original.

After calling the `identity()` method, the resulting matrix has the following properties: a=1, b=0, c=0, d=1, tx=0, ty=0.

In matrix notation the identity matrix looks like this:

$$\begin{bmatrix} 1 & 0 & 0 \\ 0 & 1 & 0 \\ 0 & 0 & 1 \end{bmatrix}$$

Availability: ActionScript 1.0; Flash Player 8

Example

The following example demonstrates that calling the `identity()` method converts the calling Matrix object to an identity Matrix object. The number and types of transformations applied to the original Matrix object beforehand are irrelevant. If `identity()` is called, the Matrix values are converted to (a=1, b=0, c=0, d=1, tx=0, ty=0).

```
import flash.geom.Matrix;

var myMatrix:Matrix = new Matrix(2, 0, 0, 2, 0 ,0);
trace(myMatrix.toString()); // (a=2, b=0, c=0, d=2, tx=0, ty=0)

myMatrix.rotate(Math.atan(3/4));
trace(myMatrix.toString()); // (a=1.6, b=1.2, c=-1.2, d=1.6, tx=0, ty=0)
```

```
myMatrix.translate(100,200);
trace(myMatrix.toString()); // (a=1.6, b=1.2, c=-1.2, d=1.6, tx=100,
   ty=200)

myMatrix.scale(2, 2);
trace(myMatrix.toString()); // (a=3.2, b=2.4, c=-2.4, d=3.2, tx=200,
   ty=400)

myMatrix.identity();
trace(myMatrix.toString()); // (a=1, b=0, c=0, d=1, tx=0, ty=0)
```

invert (Matrix.invert method)

```
public invert() : Void
```

Performs the opposite transformation of the original matrix. You can apply an inverted matrix to an object to undo the transformation performed when applying the original matrix.

Availability: ActionScript 1.0; Flash Player 8

Example

The following example creates `halfScaleMatrix` by calling the `invert()` method of `doubleScaleMatrix`, and then demonstrates that the two are Matrix inverses of one another, that is, matrixes that undo any transformations performed by the other. The example shows this inversion by creating `originalAndInverseMatrix`, which is equal to `noScaleMatrix`.

```
import flash.geom.Matrix;
import flash.geom.Transform;

var rectangleMc_0:MovieClip = createRectangle(20, 80, 0xFF0000);
var rectangleMc_1:MovieClip = createRectangle(20, 80, 0x00FF00);
var rectangleMc_2:MovieClip = createRectangle(20, 80, 0x0000FF);
var rectangleMc_3:MovieClip = createRectangle(20, 80, 0x000000);

var rectangleTrans_0:Transform = new Transform(rectangleMc_0);
var rectangleTrans_1:Transform = new Transform(rectangleMc_1);
var rectangleTrans_2:Transform = new Transform(rectangleMc_2);
var rectangleTrans_3:Transform = new Transform(rectangleMc_3);

var doubleScaleMatrix:Matrix = new Matrix(2, 0, 0, 2, 0, 0);
rectangleTrans_0.matrix = doubleScaleMatrix;
trace(doubleScaleMatrix.toString()); // (a=2, b=0, c=0, d=2, tx=0, ty=0)

var noScaleMatrix:Matrix = new Matrix(1, 0, 0, 1, 0, 0);
rectangleTrans_1.matrix = noScaleMatrix;
rectangleMc_1._x = 100;
trace(noScaleMatrix.toString()); // (a=1, b=0, c=0, d=1, tx=0, ty=0)

var halfScaleMatrix:Matrix = doubleScaleMatrix.clone();
```

```
halfScaleMatrix.invert();
rectangleTrans_2.matrix = halfScaleMatrix;
rectangleMc_2._x = 200;
trace(halfScaleMatrix.toString()); // (a=0.5, b=0, c=0, d=0.5, tx=0, ty=0)

var originalAndInverseMatrix:Matrix = doubleScaleMatrix.clone();
originalAndInverseMatrix.concat(halfScaleMatrix);
rectangleTrans_3.matrix = originalAndInverseMatrix;
rectangleMc_3._x = 300;
trace(originalAndInverseMatrix.toString()); // (a=1, b=0, c=0, d=1, tx=0,
  ty=0)

function createRectangle(width:Number, height:Number,
  color:Number):MovieClip {
  var depth:Number = this.getNextHighestDepth();
  var mc:MovieClip = this.createEmptyMovieClip("mc_" + depth, depth);
  mc.beginFill(color);
  mc.lineTo(0, height);
  mc.lineTo(width, height);
  mc.lineTo(width, 0);
  mc.lineTo(0, 0);
  return mc;
}
```

Matrix constructor

```
public Matrix([a:Number], [b:Number], [c:Number], [d:Number], [tx:Number],
  [ty:Number])
```

Creates a new Matrix object with the specified parameters. In matrix notation the properties will be organized like this:

$$\begin{bmatrix} a & b & t_x \\ c & d & t_y \\ 0 & 0 & 1 \end{bmatrix}$$

If you do not provide any parameters to the new Matrix() constructor it creates an "identity matrix" with the following values:

a = 1	b = 0
c = 0	d = 1
tx = 0	ty = 0

In matrix notation the identity matrix looks like this:

$$\begin{bmatrix} 1 & 0 & 0 \\ 0 & 1 & 0 \\ 0 & 0 & 1 \end{bmatrix}$$

Availability: ActionScript 1.0; Flash Player 8

Parameters

`a`:`Number` [optional] - The value in the first row and first column of the new Matrix object.

`b`:`Number` [optional] - The value in the first row and second column of the new Matrix object.

`c`:`Number` [optional] - The value in the second row and first column of the new Matrix object.

`d`:`Number` [optional] - The value in the second row and second column of the new Matrix object.

`tx`:`Number` [optional] - The value in the third row and first column of the new Matrix object.

`ty`:`Number` [optional] - The value in the third row and second column of the new Matrix object.

Example

The following example creates `matrix_1` by sending no parameters to the `Matrix` constructor and `matrix_2` by sending parameters to it. The Matrix object `matrix_1`, which is created with no parameters, is an identity Matrix with the values (a=1, b=0, c=0, d=1, tx=0, ty=0).

```
import flash.geom.Matrix;

var matrix_1:Matrix = new Matrix();
trace(matrix_1); // (a=1, b=0, c=0, d=1, tx=0, ty=0)

var matrix_2:Matrix = new Matrix(1, 2, 3, 4, 5, 6);
trace(matrix_2); // (a=1, b=2, c=3, d=4, tx=5, ty=6)
```

rotate (Matrix.rotate method)

`public rotate(angle:Number) : Void`

Sets the values in the current matrix so that the matrix can be used to apply a rotation transformation.

The `rotate()` method alters the a and d properties of the Matrix object. In matrix notation this is shown as follows:

$$\begin{bmatrix} \cos(q) & \sin(q) & 0 \\ -\sin(q) & \cos(q) & 0 \\ 0 & 0 & 1 \end{bmatrix}$$

Availability: ActionScript 1.0; Flash Player 8

Parameters

`angle:Number` - The rotation angle in radians.

Example

The following example shows how the `rotate()` method rotates `rectangleMc` 30° clockwise. Applying `myMatrix` to `rectangleMc` resets its _x value, leaving you to reset it to 100 manually.

```
import flash.geom.Matrix;
import flash.geom.Transform;

var myMatrix:Matrix = new Matrix();
trace(myMatrix.toString()); // (a=1, b=0, c=0, d=1, tx=0, ty=0)

var degrees:Number = 30;
var radians:Number = (degrees/180) Math.PI;
myMatrix.rotate(radians);
trace(myMatrix.toString()); // (a=0.866025403784439, b=0.5, c=-0.5,
  d=0.866025403784439, tx=0, ty=0)

var rectangleMc:MovieClip = createRectangle(20, 80, 0xFF0000);
trace(rectangleMc._x); // 0
rectangleMc._x = 100;
trace(rectangleMc._x); // 100

var rectangleTrans:Transform = new Transform(rectangleMc);
rectangleTrans.matrix = myMatrix;
trace(rectangleMc._x); // 0
rectangleMc._x = 100;
trace(rectangleMc._x); // 100

function createRectangle(width:Number, height:Number,
  color:Number):MovieClip {
  var depth:Number = this.getNextHighestDepth();
  var mc:MovieClip = this.createEmptyMovieClip("mc_" + depth, depth);
  mc.beginFill(color);
  mc.lineTo(0, height);
```

```
mc.lineTo(width, height);
mc.lineTo(width, 0);
mc.lineTo(0, 0);
return mc;
}
```

The previous example uses the `_x` property of the MovieClip object to position `rectangleMc`. Generally, when dealing with Matrix object positioning, mixing positioning techniques is considered poor format. The previous example written in correct syntax would concatenate a translation Matrix to `myMatrix` to change the horizontal location of `rectangleMc`. The following example demonstrates this.

```
import flash.geom.Matrix;
import flash.geom.Transform;

var myMatrix:Matrix = new Matrix();
trace(myMatrix.toString()); // (a=1, b=0, c=0, d=1, tx=0, ty=0)

var degrees:Number = 30;
var radians:Number = (degrees/180) * Math.PI;
myMatrix.rotate(radians);
trace(myMatrix.toString()); // (a=0.866025403784439, b=0.5, c=-0.5,
  d=0.866025403784439, tx=0, ty=0)

var translateMatrix:Matrix = new Matrix();
translateMatrix.translate(100, 0);
myMatrix.concat(translateMatrix);
trace(myMatrix.toString()); // (a=0.866025403784439, b=0.5, c=-0.5,
  d=0.866025403784439, tx=100, ty=0)

var rectangleMc:MovieClip = createRectangle(20, 80, 0xFF0000);
trace(rectangleMc._x); // 0
rectangleMc._x = 100;
trace(rectangleMc._x); // 100

var rectangleTrans:Transform = new Transform(rectangleMc);
rectangleTrans.matrix = myMatrix;
trace(rectangleMc._x); // 100

function createRectangle(width:Number, height:Number,
  color:Number):MovieClip {
  var depth:Number = this.getNextHighestDepth();
  var mc:MovieClip = this.createEmptyMovieClip("mc_" + depth, depth);
  mc.beginFill(color);
  mc.lineTo(0, height);
  mc.lineTo(width, height);
  mc.lineTo(width, 0);
  mc.lineTo(0, 0);
  return mc;
}
```

scale (Matrix.scale method)

```
public scale(sx:Number, sy:Number) : Void
```

Modifies a matrix so that its effect, when applied, is to resize an image. In the resized image, the location of each pixel on the *x* axis is multiplied by `sx`; and on the *y* axis it is multiplied by `sy`.

The `scale()` method alters the `a` and `d` properties of the matrix object. In matrix notation this is shown as follows:

$$\begin{bmatrix} s_x & 0 & 0 \\ 0 & s_y & 0 \\ 0 & 0 & 1 \end{bmatrix}$$

Availability: ActionScript 1.0; Flash Player 8

Parameters

`sx:Number` - A multiplier used to scale the object along the *x* axis.

`sy:Number` - A multiplier used to scale the object along the *y* axis.

Example

The following example uses the `scale()` method to scale `myMatrix` by a factor of three horizontally and a factor of four vertically.

```
import flash.geom.Matrix;

var myMatrix:Matrix = new Matrix(2, 0, 0, 2, 100, 100);
trace(myMatrix.toString()); // (a=2, b=0, c=0, d=2, tx=100, ty=100)

myMatrix.scale(3, 4);
trace(myMatrix.toString()); // (a=6, b=0, c=0, d=8, tx=300, ty=400)
```

toString (Matrix.toString method)

```
public toString() : String
```

Returns a text value listing the properties of the Matrix object.

Availability: ActionScript 1.0; Flash Player 8

Returns

`String` - A string containing the values of the properties of the Matrix object: `a`, `b`, `c`, `d`, `tx`, and `ty`.

Example

The following example creates `myMatrix` and converts its values to a string in the format of (a=A, b=B, c=C, d=D, tx=TX, ty=TY).

```
import flash.geom.Matrix;

var myMatrix:Matrix = new Matrix();
trace("myMatrix: " + myMatrix.toString()); // (a=1, b=0, c=0, d=1, tx=0,
    ty=0)
```

transformPoint (Matrix.transformPoint method)

```
public transformPoint(pt:Point) : Point
```

Applies the geometric transformation represented by the Matrix object to the specified point.

Availability: ActionScript 1.0; Flash Player 8

Parameters

`pt:flash.geom.Point` - The Point (*x,y*) to be transformed.

Returns

`flash.geom.Point` - The new Point object.

Example

The following example uses the `transformPoint()` method to create `transformedPoint` from `myPoint`. The `translate()` method does have an affect on the position of `transformedPoint`. In the example, `scale()` increases the original x value by a factor of three from 50 to 150, and the `translate()` method increases x by 300 for a total value of 450.

```
import flash.geom.Matrix;
import flash.geom.Point;

var myMatrix:Matrix = new Matrix();
trace(myMatrix); // (a=1, b=0, c=0, d=1, tx=0, ty=0)

myMatrix.translate(100, 0);
trace(myMatrix); // (a=1, b=0, c=0, d=1, tx=100, ty=0)

myMatrix.scale(3, 3);
trace(myMatrix); // (a=3, b=0, c=0, d=3, tx=300, ty=0)

var myPoint:Point = new Point(50,0);
trace(myPoint); // (50, 0)
```

```
var transformedPoint:Point = myMatrix.transformPoint(myPoint);
trace(transformedPoint); // (450, 0)

var pointMc_0:MovieClip = createRectangle(10, 10, 0xFF0000);
pointMc_0._x = myPoint.x;

var pointMc_1:MovieClip = createRectangle(10, 10, 0x00FF00);
pointMc_1._x = transformedPoint.x;

function createRectangle(width:Number, height:Number,
  color:Number):MovieClip {
  var depth:Number = this.getNextHighestDepth();
  var mc:MovieClip = this.createEmptyMovieClip("mc_" + depth, depth);
  mc.beginFill(color);
  mc.lineTo(0, height);
  mc.lineTo(width, height);
  mc.lineTo(width, 0);
  mc.lineTo(0, 0);
  return mc;
}
```

translate (Matrix.translate method)

```
public translate(tx:Number, ty:Number) : Void
```

Modifies a Matrix object so that the effect of its transformation is to move an object along the x and y axes.

The translate() method alters the tx and ty properties of the matrix object. In matrix notation, this is shown as follows:

$$\begin{bmatrix} 1 & 0 & t_x \\ 0 & 1 & t_y \\ 0 & 0 & 1 \end{bmatrix}$$

Availability: ActionScript 1.0; Flash Player 8

Parameters

tx:Number - The amount of movement along the x axis to the right, in pixels.

ty:Number - The amount of movement down along the y axis, in pixels.

Example

The following example uses the `translate()` method to position `rectangleMc` x:100 and y:50. The `translate()` method affects the translation properties `tx` and `ty`, but it doesn't affect the a, b, c, or d properties.

```
import flash.geom.Matrix;

var myMatrix:Matrix = new Matrix(2, 0, 0, 2, 100, 100);
trace(myMatrix.toString()); // (a=2, b=0, c=0, d=2, tx=100, ty=100)

myMatrix.translate(100, 50);
trace(myMatrix.toString()); // (a=2, b=0, c=0, d=2, tx=200, ty=150)
```

tx (Matrix.tx property)

```
public tx : Number
```

The distance by which to translate each point along the *x* axis. This represents the value in the third row and first column of the Matrix object.

Availability: ActionScript 1.0; Flash Player 8

Example

The following example creates the Matrix object `myMatrix` and sets its `tx` value.

```
import flash.geom.Matrix;

var myMatrix:Matrix = new Matrix();
trace(myMatrix.tx); // 0

myMatrix.tx = 50; // 50
trace(myMatrix.tx);
```

ty (Matrix.ty property)

```
public ty : Number
```

The distance by which to translate each point along the *y* axis. This represents the value in the third row and second column of the Matrix object.

Availability: ActionScript 1.0; Flash Player 8

Example

The following example creates the Matrix object `myMatrix` and sets its `ty` value.

```
import flash.geom.Matrix;

var myMatrix:Matrix = new Matrix();
```

```
trace(myMatrix.ty); // 0

myMatrix.ty = 50;
trace(myMatrix.ty); // 50
```

Microphone

```
Object
  |
  +-Microphone
```

```
public class Microphone
extends Object
```

The Microphone class lets you capture audio from a microphone attached to the computer that is running Flash Player.

The Microphone class is primarily for use with Flash Communication Server but can be used in a limited fashion without the server, for example, to transmit sound from your microphone through the speakers on your local system.

Caution: Flash Player displays a Privacy dialog box that lets the user choose whether to allow or deny access to the microphone. Make sure your Stage size is at least 215 x 138 pixels; this is the minimum size Flash requires to display the dialog box.

Users and Administrative users may also disable microphone access on a per-site or global basis.

To create or reference a Microphone object, use the `Microphone.get()` method.

Availability: ActionScript 1.0; Flash Player 6

Property summary

Modifiers	Property	Description
	`activityLevel:Number` [read-only]	A numeric value that specifies the amount of sound the microphone is detecting.
	`gain:Number` [read-only]	The amount by which the microphone boosts the signal.
	`index:Number` [read-only]	A zero-based integer that specifies the index of the microphone, as reflected in the array returned by `Microphone.names`.
	`muted:Boolean` [read-only]	A Boolean value that specifies whether the user has denied access to the microphone (`true`) or allowed access (`false`).

Modifiers	Property	Description
	`name:String` [read-only]	A string that specifies the name of the current sound capture device, as returned by the sound capture hardware.
`static`	`names:Array` [read-only]	Retrieves an array of strings reflecting the names of all available sound capture devices without displaying the Flash Player Privacy Settings panel.
	`rate:Number` [read-only]	The rate at which the microphone is capturing sound, in kHz.
	`silenceLevel:Number` [read-only]	An integer that specifies the amount of sound required to activate the microphone and invoke `Microphone.onActivity(true)`.
	`silenceTimeOut:Number` [read-only]	A numeric value representing the number of milliseconds between the time the microphone stops detecting sound and the time `Microphone.onActivity(false)` is invoked.
	`useEchoSuppression:Boolean` [read-only]	Property (read-only); a Boolean value of `true` if echo suppression is enabled, `false` otherwise.

Properties inherited from class Object

```
constructor (Object.constructor property), __proto__ (Object.__proto__
property), prototype (Object.prototype property), __resolve
(Object.__resolve property)
```

Event summary

Event	Description
`onActivity = function(active: Boolean) {}`	Invoked when the microphone starts or stops detecting sound.
`onStatus = function(infoObject:Object) {}`	Invoked when the user allows or denies access to the microphone.

Method summary

Modifiers	Signature	Description
static	`get([index:Number]) : Microphone`	Returns a reference to a Microphone object for capturing audio.
	`setGain(gain:Number) : Void`	Sets the microphone gain--that is, the amount by which the microphone should multiply the signal before transmitting it.
	`setRate(rate:Number) : Void`	Sets the rate, in kHz, at which the microphone should capture sound.
	`setSilenceLevel(sile nceLevel:Number, [timeOut:Number]) : Void`	Sets the minimum input level that should be considered sound and (optionally) the amount of silent time signifying that silence has actually begun.
	`setUseEchoSuppressio n(useEchoSuppression :Boolean) : Void`	Specifies whether to use the echo suppression feature of the audio codec.

Methods inherited from class Object

```
addProperty (Object.addProperty method), hasOwnProperty
(Object.hasOwnProperty method), isPropertyEnumerable
(Object.isPropertyEnumerable method), isPrototypeOf (Object.isPrototypeOf
method), registerClass (Object.registerClass method), toString
(Object.toString method), unwatch (Object.unwatch method), valueOf
(Object.valueOf method), watch (Object.watch method)
```

activityLevel (Microphone.activityLevel property)

`public activityLevel : Number [read-only]`

A numeric value that specifies the amount of sound the microphone is detecting. Values range from 0 (no sound is being detected) to 100 (very loud sound is being detected). The value of this property can help you determine a good value to pass to the `Microphone.setSilenceLevel()` method.

If the microphone is available but is not yet being used because `Microphone.get()` has not been called, this property is set to -1.

Availability: ActionScript 1.0; Flash Player 6

Example

The following example displays the activity level of the current microphone in a ProgressBar instance called `activityLevel_pb`.

```
var activityLevel_pb:mx.controls.ProgressBar;
activityLevel_pb.mode = "manual";
activityLevel_pb.label = "Activity Level: %3%%";
activityLevel_pb.setStyle("themeColor", "0xFF0000");
this.createEmptyMovieClip("sound_mc", this.getNextHighestDepth());
var active_mic:Microphone = Microphone.get();
sound_mc.attachAudio(active_mic);
this.onEnterFrame = function() {
    activityLevel_pb.setProgress(active_mic.activityLevel, 100);
};
active_mic.onActivity = function(active:Boolean) {
    if (active) {
    var haloTheme_str:String = "haloGreen";
    } else {
    var haloTheme_str:String = "0xFF0000";
    }
    activityLevel_pb.setStyle("themeColor", haloTheme_str);
};
```

The `MovieClip.getNextHighestDepth()` method used in this example requires Flash Player 7 or later. If your SWF file includes a version 2 component, use the version 2 components DepthManager class instead of the `MovieClip.getNextHighestDepth()` method.

See also

`get` (Microphone.get method), `setSilenceLevel` (Microphone.setSilenceLevel method), `setGain` (Microphone.setGain method)

gain (Microphone.gain property)

`public gain : Number [read-only]`

The amount by which the microphone boosts the signal. Valid values are 0 to 100. The default value is 50.

Availability: ActionScript 1.0; Flash Player 6

Example

The following example uses a ProgressBar instance called `gain_pb` to display and a NumericStepper instance called `gain_nstep` to set the microphone's gain value.

```
this.createEmptyMovieClip("sound_mc", this.getNextHighestDepth());
var active_mic:Microphone = Microphone.get();
sound_mc.attachAudio(active_mic);

gain_pb.label = "Gain: %3";
gain_pb.mode = "manual";
gain_pb.setProgress(active_mic.gain, 100);
gain_nstep.value = active_mic.gain;
```

```
function changeGain() {
  active_mic.setGain(gain_nstep.value);
  gain_pb.setProgress(active_mic.gain, 100);
}
gain_nstep.addEventListener("change", changeGain);
```

The `MovieClip.getNextHighestDepth()` method used in this example requires Flash Player 7 or later. If your SWF file includes a version 2 component, use the version 2 components DepthManager class instead of the `MovieClip.getNextHighestDepth()` method.

See also

`setGain (Microphone.setGain method)`

get (Microphone.get method)

`public static get([index:Number]) : Microphone`

Returns a reference to a Microphone object for capturing audio. To actually begin capturing the audio, you must attach the Microphone object to a MovieClip object (see `MovieClip.attachAudio()`).

Unlike objects that you create using the `new` constructor, multiple calls to `Microphone.get()` reference the same microphone. Thus, if your script contains the lines `mic1 = Microphone.get()` and `mic2 = Microphone.get()`, both `mic1` and `mic2` reference the same (default) microphone.

In general, you shouldn't pass a value for *index*; simply use the `Microphone.get()` method to return a reference to the default microphone. By means of the Microphone settings panel (discussed later in this section), the user can specify the default microphone Flash should use. If you pass a value for *index*, you might be trying to reference a microphone other than the one the user prefers. You might use *index* in rare cases--for example, if your application is capturing audio from two microphones at the same time.

When a SWF file tries to access the microphone returned by the `Microphone.get()` method--for example, when you issue `MovieClip.attachAudio()`--Flash Player displays a Privacy dialog box that lets the user choose whether to allow or deny access to the microphone. (Make sure your Stage size is at least 215 x 138 pixels; this is the minimum size Flash requires to display the dialog box.)

When the user responds to this dialog box, the `Microphone.onStatus` event handler returns an information object that indicates the user's response. To determine whether the user has denied or allowed access to the camera without processing this event handler, use `Microphone.muted`.

The user can also specify permanent privacy settings for a particular domain by right-clicking (Windows) or Control-clicking (Macintosh) while a SWF file is playing, choosing Settings, opening the Privacy panel, and selecting Remember.

You can't use ActionScript to set the Allow or Deny value for a user, but you can display the Privacy panel for the user by using `System.showSettings(0)`. If the user selects Remember, Flash Player no longer displays the Privacy dialog box for SWF files from this domain.

If `Microphone.get()` returns `null`, either the microphone is in use by another application, or there are no microphones installed on the system. To determine whether any microphones are installed, use `Microphones.names.length`. To display the Flash Player Microphone Settings panel, which lets the user choose the microphone to be referenced by `Microphone.get()`, use `System.showSettings(2)`.

Availability: ActionScript 1.0; Flash Player 6 - Note: The correct syntax is Microphone.get(). To assign the Microphone object to a variable, use syntax like active_mic = Microphone.get().

Parameters

`index:Number` [optional] - A zero-based integer that specifies which microphone to get, as determined from the array that `Microphone.names` contains. To get the default microphone (which is recommended for most applications), omit this parameter.

Returns

`Microphone` -

- If *index* is not specified, this method returns a reference to the default microphone or, if it is not available, to the first available microphone. If no microphones are available or installed, the method returns `null`.

- If *index* is specified, this method returns a reference to the requested microphone, or `null` if it is not available.

Example

The following example lets the user specify the default microphone, and then captures audio and plays it back locally. To avoid feedback, you may want to test this code while wearing headphones.

```
this.createEmptyMovieClip("sound_mc", this.getNextHighestDepth());
System.showSettings(2);
var active_mic:Microphone = Microphone.get();
sound_mc.attachAudio(active_mic);
```

The `MovieClip.getNextHighestDepth()` method used in this example requires Flash Player 7 or later. If your SWF file includes a version 2 component, use the version 2 components DepthManager class instead of the `MovieClip.getNextHighestDepth()` method.

See also

get (Microphone.get method), index (Microphone.index property), muted (Microphone.muted property), names (Microphone.names property), onStatus (Microphone.onStatus handler), attachAudio (MovieClip.attachAudio method), showSettings (System.showSettings method)

index (Microphone.index property)

`public index : Number [read-only]`

A zero-based integer that specifies the index of the microphone, as reflected in the array returned by `Microphone.names`.

Availability: ActionScript 1.0; Flash Player 6

Example

The following example displays the names of the sound capturing devices available on your computer system in a ComboBox instance called `mic_cb`. An instance of the Label component, called `mic_lbl`, displays the index microphone. You can use the ComboBox to switch between the devices.

```
var mic_lbl:mx.controls.Label;
var mic_cb:mx.controls.ComboBox;

this.createEmptyMovieClip("sound_mc", this.getNextHighestDepth());
var active_mic:Microphone = Microphone.get();
sound_mc.attachAudio(active_mic);
mic_lbl.text = "["+active_mic.index+"] "+active_mic.name;
mic_cb.dataProvider = Microphone.names;
mic_cb.selectedIndex = active_mic.index;

var cbListener:Object = new Object();
cbListener.change = function(evt:Object) {
   active_mic = Microphone.get(evt.target.selectedIndex);
   sound_mc.attachAudio(active_mic);
   mic_lbl.text = "["+active_mic.index+"] "+active_mic.name;
};
mic_cb.addEventListener("change", cbListener);
```

The `MovieClip.getNextHighestDepth()` method used in this example requires Flash Player 7 or later. If your SWF file includes a version 2 component, use the version 2 components DepthManager class instead of the `MovieClip.getNextHighestDepth()` method.

See also

get (Microphone.get method), names (Microphone.names property)

muted (Microphone.muted property)

`public muted : Boolean [read-only]`

A Boolean value that specifies whether the user has denied access to the microphone (`true`) or allowed access (`false`). When this value changes, `Microphone.onStatus` is invoked. For more information, see `Microphone.get()`.

Availability: ActionScript 1.0; Flash Player 6

Example

This example gets the default microphone and checks whether it is muted.

```
var active_mic:Microphone = Microphone.get();
trace(active_mic.muted);
```

See also

`get (Microphone.get method)`, `onStatus (Microphone.onStatus handler)`

name (Microphone.name property)

`public name : String [read-only]`

A string that specifies the name of the current sound capture device, as returned by the sound capture hardware.

Availability: ActionScript 1.0; Flash Player 6

Example

The following example displays information about the sound capturing device(s) on your computer system, including an array of names and the default device.

```
var status_ta:mx.controls.TextArea;
status_ta.html = false;
status_ta.setStyle("fontSize", 9);
var microphone_array:Array = Microphone.names;
var active_mic:Microphone = Microphone.get();
status_ta.text = "The default device is: "+active_mic.name+newline+newline;
status_ta.text += "You have "+microphone_array.length+" device(s)
   installed."+newline+newline;
for (var i = 0; i<microphone_array.length; i++) {
   status_ta.text += "["+i+"] "+microphone_array[i]+newline;
}
```

See also

`get (Microphone.get method)`, `names (Microphone.names property)`

names (Microphone.names property)

```
public static names : Array [read-only]
```

Retrieves an array of strings reflecting the names of all available sound capture devices without displaying the Flash Player Privacy Settings panel. This array behaves the same as any other ActionScript array, implicitly providing the zero-based index of each sound capture device and the number of sound capture devices on the system (by means of `Microphone.names.length`). For more information, see the Microphone.names Array class entry.

Calling `Microphone.names` requires an extensive examination of the hardware, and it may take several seconds to build the array. In most cases, you can just use the default microphone.

Availability: ActionScript 1.0; Flash Player 6 - Note: The correct syntax is Microphone.names. To assign the return value to a variable, use syntax like mic_array=Microphone.names. To determine the name of the current microphone, use active_mic.name.

Example

The following example displays information about the sound capturing device(s) on your computer system, including an array of names and the default device.

```
var status_ta:mx.controls.TextArea;
status_ta.html = false;
status_ta.setStyle("fontSize", 9);
var microphone_array:Array = Microphone.names;
var active_mic:Microphone = Microphone.get();
status_ta.text = "The default device is: "+active_mic.name+newline+newline;
status_ta.text += "You have "+microphone_array.length+" device(s)
  installed."+newline+newline;
for (var i = 0; i<microphone_array.length; i++) {
  status_ta.text += "["+i+"] "+microphone_array[i]+newline;
}
```

For example, the following information could be displayed:

```
The default device is: Logitech USB Headset
You have 2 device(s) installed.
[0] Logitech USB Headset
[1] YAMAHA AC-XG WDM Audio
```

See also

```
name (Microphone.name property), get (Microphone.get method)
```

onActivity (Microphone.onActivity handler)

```
onActivity = function(active:Boolean) {}
```

Invoked when the microphone starts or stops detecting sound. If you want to respond to this event handler, you must create a function to process its activity value.

To specify the amount of sound required to invoke `Microphone.onActivity(true)`, and the amount of time that must elapse without sound before `Microphone.onActivity(false)` is invoked, use `Microphone.setSilenceLevel()`.

Availability: ActionScript 1.0; Flash Player 6

Parameters

`active:Boolean` - A Boolean value set to true when the microphone starts detecting sound, and false when it stops.

Example

The following example displays the amount of activity level in a ProgressBar instance called `activityLevel_pb`. When the microphone detects sound, it invokes the `onActivity` function, which modifies the ProgressBar instance.

```
var activityLevel_pb:mx.controls.ProgressBar;
activityLevel_pb.mode = "manual";
activityLevel_pb.label = "Activity Level: %3%%";
this.createEmptyMovieClip("sound_mc", this.getNextHighestDepth());
var active_mic:Microphone = Microphone.get();
sound_mc.attachAudio(active_mic);
active_mic.onActivity = function(active:Boolean) {
  if (active) {
    activityLevel_pb.indeterminate = false;
    activityLevel_pb.label = "Activity Level: %3%%";
  } else {
    activityLevel_pb.indeterminate = true;
    activityLevel_pb.label = "Activity Level: (inactive)";
  }
};
this.onEnterFrame = function() {
  activityLevel_pb.setProgress(active_mic.activityLevel, 100);
};
```

The `MovieClip.getNextHighestDepth()` method used in this example requires Flash Player 7 or later. If your SWF file includes a version 2 component, use the version 2 components DepthManager class instead of the `MovieClip.getNextHighestDepth()` method.

See also

setSilenceLevel (Microphone.setSilenceLevel method)

onStatus (Microphone.onStatus handler)

```
onStatus = function(infoObject:Object) {}
```

Invoked when the user allows or denies access to the microphone. If you want to respond to this event handler, you must create a function to process the information object generated by the microphone.

When a SWF file tries to access the microphone, Flash Player displays a Privacy dialog box that lets the user choose whether to allow or deny access.

- If the user allows access, the Microphone.muted property is set to false, and this event handler is invoked with an information object whose code property is "Microphone.Unmuted" and whose level property is "Status".

- If the user denies access, the Microphone.muted property is set to true, and this event handler is invoked with an information object whose code property is "Microphone.Muted" and whose level property is "Status".

To determine whether the user has denied or allowed access to the microphone without processing this event handler, use `Microphone.muted`.

Note: If the user chooses to permanently allow or deny access to all SWF files from a specified domain, this method is not invoked for SWF files from that domain unless the user later changes the privacy setting.

For more information, see `Microphone.get()`.

Availability: ActionScript 1.0; Flash Player 6

Parameters

`infoObject:Object` - A parameter defined according to the status message.

Example

The following example launches the Privacy dialog box that lets the user choose whether to allow or deny access to the microphone when they click a hyperlink. If the user chooses to deny access, *muted* is displayed in large red text. If microphone access is allowed, the user does not see this text.

```
this.createTextField("muted_txt", this.getNextHighestDepth(), 10, 10, 100,
    22);
muted_txt.autoSize = true;
muted_txt.html = true;
muted_txt.selectable = false;
muted_txt.htmlText = "<a href=\"asfunction:System.showSettings\"><u>Click
    Here</u></a> to Allow/Deny access.";
this.createEmptyMovieClip("sound_mc", this.getNextHighestDepth());
var active_mic:Microphone = Microphone.get();
```

```
sound_mc.attachAudio(active_mic);
active_mic.onStatus = function(infoObj:Object) {
   status_txt._visible = active_mic.muted;
   muted_txt.htmlText = "Status: <a
   href=\"asfunction:System.showSettings\"><u>"+infoObj.code+"</u></a>";
};
this.createTextField("status_txt", this.getNextHighestDepth(), 0, 0, 100,
   22);
status_txt.html = true;
status_txt.autoSize = true;
status_txt.htmlText = "<font size='72' color='#FF0000'>muted</font>";
status_txt._x = (Stage.width-status_txt._width)/2;
status_txt._y = (Stage.height-status_txt._height)/2;
status_txt._visible = active_mic.muted;
```

The `MovieClip.getNextHighestDepth()` method used in this example requires Flash Player 7 or later. If your SWF file includes a version 2 component, use the version 2 components DepthManager class instead of the `MovieClip.getNextHighestDepth()` method.

See also

get (Microphone.get method), muted (Microphone.muted property), showSettings (System.showSettings method), onStatus (System.onStatus handler)

rate (Microphone.rate property)

public rate : Number [read-only]

The rate at which the microphone is capturing sound, in kHz. The default value is 8 kHz if your sound capture device supports this value. Otherwise, the default value is the next available capture level above 8 kHz that your sound capture device supports, usually 11 kHz.

To set this value, use `Microphone.setRate()`.

Availability: ActionScript 1.0; Flash Player 6

Example

The following code lets you use a ComboBox instance, called rate_cb, to change the rate at which your microphone captures sound. The current rate displays in a Label instance called rate_lbl.

```
this.createEmptyMovieClip("sound_mc", this.getNextHighestDepth());
var active_mic:Microphone = Microphone.get();
sound_mc.attachAudio(active_mic);
var rate_array:Array = new Array(5, 8, 11, 22, 44);
rate_cb.dataProvider = rate_array;
rate_cb.labelFunction = function(item:Object) {
   return (item+" kHz");
};
```

```
for (var i = 0; i<rate_array.length; i++) {
  if (rate_cb.getItemAt(i) == active_mic.rate) {
  rate_cb.selectedIndex = i;
  break;
  }
}
function changeRate() {
  active_mic.setRate(rate_cb.selectedItem);
  rate_lbl.text = "Current rate: "+active_mic.rate+" kHz";
}
rate_cb.addEventListener("change", changeRate);
rate_lbl.text = "Current rate: "+active_mic.rate+" kHz";
```

The `MovieClip.getNextHighestDepth()` method used in this example requires Flash Player 7 or later. If your SWF file includes a version 2 component, use the version 2 components DepthManager class instead of the `MovieClip.getNextHighestDepth()` method.

See also

setRate (Microphone.setRate method)

setGain (Microphone.setGain method)

public setGain(gain:Number) : Void

Sets the microphone gain--that is, the amount by which the microphone should multiply the signal before transmitting it. A value of 0 tells Flash to multiply by 0; that is, the microphone transmits no sound.

You can think of this setting like a volume knob on a stereo: 0 is no volume and 50 is normal volume; numbers below 50 specify lower than normal volume, while numbers above 50 specify higher than normal volume.

Availability: ActionScript 1.0; Flash Player 6

Parameters

gain:Number - An integer that specifies the amount by which the microphone should boost the signal. Valid values are 0 to 100. The default value is 50; however, the user may change this value in the Flash Player Microphone Settings panel.

Example

The following example uses a ProgressBar instance called gain_pb to display and a NumericStepper instance called gain_nstep to set the microphone's gain value.

```
this.createEmptyMovieClip("sound_mc", this.getNextHighestDepth());
var active_mic:Microphone = Microphone.get();
sound_mc.attachAudio(active_mic);
```

```
gain_pb.label = "Gain: %3";
gain_pb.mode = "manual";
gain_pb.setProgress(active_mic.gain, 100);
gain_nstep.value = active_mic.gain;

function changeGain() {
  active_mic.setGain(gain_nstep.value);
  gain_pb.setProgress(active_mic.gain, 100);
}
gain_nstep.addEventListener("change", changeGain);
```

The `MovieClip.getNextHighestDepth()` method used in this example requires Flash Player 7 or later. If your SWF file includes a version 2 component, use the version 2 components DepthManager class instead of the `MovieClip.getNextHighestDepth()` method.

See also

`gain (Microphone.gain property)`, `setUseEchoSuppression` `(Microphone.setUseEchoSuppression method)`

setRate (Microphone.setRate method)

```
public setRate(rate:Number) : Void
```

Sets the rate, in kHz, at which the microphone should capture sound.

Availability: ActionScript 1.0; Flash Player 6

Parameters

`rate:Number` - The rate at which the microphone should capture sound, in kHz. Acceptable values are 5, 8, 11, 22, and 44. The default value is 8 kHz if your sound capture device supports this value. Otherwise, the default value is the next available capture level above 8 kHz that your sound capture device supports, usually 11 kHz.

Example

The following example sets the microphone rate to the user's preference (which you have assigned to the `userRate` variable) if it is one of the following values: 5, 8, 11, 22, or 44. If it is not, the value is rounded to the nearest acceptable value that the sound capture device supports.

```
active_mic.setRate(userRate);
```

The following example lets you use a ComboBox instance, called `rate_cb`, to change the rate at which your microphone captures sound. The current rate displays in a Label instance called `rate_lbl`.

```
this.createEmptyMovieClip("sound_mc", this.getNextHighestDepth());
var active_mic:Microphone = Microphone.get();
sound_mc.attachAudio(active_mic);
var rate_array:Array = new Array(5, 8, 11, 22, 44);
rate_cb.dataProvider = rate_array;
rate_cb.labelFunction = function(item:Object) {
  return (item+" kHz");
};
for (var i = 0; i<rate_array.length; i++) {
  if (rate_cb.getItemAt(i) == active_mic.rate) {
  rate_cb.selectedIndex = i;
  break;
  }
}
function changeRate() {
  active_mic.setRate(rate_cb.selectedItem);
  rate_lbl.text = "Current rate: "+active_mic.rate+" kHz";
}
rate_cb.addEventListener("change", changeRate);
rate_lbl.text = "Current rate: "+active_mic.rate+" kHz";
```

The `MovieClip.getNextHighestDepth()` method used in this example requires Flash Player 7 or later. If your SWF file includes a version 2 component, use the version 2 components DepthManager class instead of the `MovieClip.getNextHighestDepth()` method.

See also

`rate (Microphone.rate property)`

setSilenceLevel (Microphone.setSilenceLevel method)

`public setSilenceLevel(silenceLevel:Number, [timeOut:Number]) : Void`

Sets the minimum input level that should be considered sound and (optionally) the amount of silent time signifying that silence has actually begun.

■ To prevent the microphone from detecting sound at all, pass a value of 100 for *level*; `Microphone.onActivity` is never invoked.

■ To determine the amount of sound the microphone is currently detecting, use `Microphone.activityLevel`.

Activity detection is the ability to detect when audio levels suggest that a person is talking. When someone is not talking, bandwidth can be saved because there is no need to send the associated audio stream. This information can also be used for visual feedback so that users know they (or others) are silent.

Silence values correspond directly to activity values. Complete silence is an activity value of 0. Constant loud noise (as loud as can be registered based on the current gain setting) is an activity value of 100. After gain is appropriately adjusted, your activity value is less than your silence value when you're not talking; when you are talking, the activity value exceeds your silence value.

This method is similar in purpose to `Camera.setMotionLevel()`; both methods are used to specify when the `onActivity` event handler should be invoked. However, these methods have a significantly different impact on publishing streams:

- `Camera.setMotionLevel()` is designed to detect motion and does not affect bandwidth usage. Even if a video stream does not detect motion, video is still sent.
- `Microphone.setSilenceLevel()` is designed to optimize bandwidth. When an audio stream is considered silent, no audio data is sent. Instead, a single message is sent, indicating that silence has started.

Availability: ActionScript 1.0; Flash Player 6

Parameters

`silenceLevel:Number` - An integer that specifies the amount of sound required to activate the microphone and invoke `Microphone.onActivity(true)`. Acceptable values range from 0 to 100. The default value is 10.

`timeOut:Number` [optional] - An integer that specifies how many milliseconds must elapse without activity before Flash considers sound to have stopped and invokes `Microphone.onActivity(false)`. The default value is 2000 (2 seconds).

Example

The following example changes the silence level based on the user's input in a NumericStepper instance called `silenceLevel_nstep`. The ProgressBar instance called `silenceLevel_pb` modifies its appearance depending on whether the audio stream is considered silent. Otherwise, it displays the activity level of the audio stream.

```
var silenceLevel_pb:mx.controls.ProgressBar;
var silenceLevel_nstep:mx.controls.NumericStepper;

this.createEmptyMovieClip("sound_mc", this.getNextHighestDepth());
var active_mic:Microphone = Microphone.get();
sound_mc.attachAudio(active_mic);

silenceLevel_pb.label = "Activity level: %3";
silenceLevel_pb.mode = "manual";
silenceLevel_nstep.minimum = 0;
silenceLevel_nstep.maximum = 100;
silenceLevel_nstep.value = active_mic.silenceLevel;
```

```
var nstepListener:Object = new Object();
nstepListener.change = function(evt:Object) {
  active_mic.setSilenceLevel(evt.target.value, active_mic.silenceTimeOut);
};
silenceLevel_nstep.addEventListener("change", nstepListener);

this.onEnterFrame = function() {
  silenceLevel_pb.setProgress(active_mic.activityLevel, 100);
};
active_mic.onActivity = function(active:Boolean) {
  if (active) {
  silenceLevel_pb.indeterminate = false;
  silenceLevel_pb.setStyle("themeColor", "haloGreen");
  silenceLevel_pb.label = "Activity level: %3";
  } else {
  silenceLevel_pb.indeterminate = true;
  silenceLevel_pb.setStyle("themeColor", "0xFF0000");
  silenceLevel_pb.label = "Activity level: (inactive)";
  }
};
```

The `MovieClip.getNextHighestDepth()` method used in this example requires Flash Player 7 or later. If your SWF file includes a version 2 component, use the version 2 components DepthManager class instead of the `MovieClip.getNextHighestDepth()` method.

See also

`setMotionLevel (Camera.setMotionLevel method)`, `activityLevel (Microphone.activityLevel property)`, `onActivity (Microphone.onActivity handler)`, `setGain (Microphone.setGain method)`, `silenceLevel (Microphone.silenceLevel property)`, `silenceTimeOut (Microphone.silenceTimeOut property)`

setUseEchoSuppression (Microphone.setUseEchoSuppression method)

`public setUseEchoSuppression(useEchoSuppression:Boolean) : Void`

Specifies whether to use the echo suppression feature of the audio codec. The default value is `false` unless the user has selected Reduce Echo in the Flash Player Microphone Settings panel.

Echo suppression is an effort to reduce the effects of audio feedback, which is caused when sound going out the speaker is picked up by the microphone on the same computer. (This is different from echo cancellation, which completely removes the feedback.)

Generally, echo suppression is advisable when the sound being captured is played through speakers--instead of a headset--on the same computer. If your SWF file allows users to specify the sound output device, you may want to call `Microphone.setUseEchoSuppression(true)` if they indicate they are using speakers and will be using the microphone as well.

Users can also adjust these settings in the Flash Player Microphone Settings panel.

Availability: ActionScript 1.0; Flash Player 6

Parameters

`useEchoSuppression:Boolean` - A Boolean value indicating whether echo suppression should be used (`true`) or not(`false`).

Example

The following example turns on echo suppression if the user selects a CheckBox instance called `useEchoSuppression_ch`. The ProgressBar instance called `activityLevel_pb` displays the current activity level of the audio stream.

```
var useEchoSuppression_ch:mx.controls.CheckBox;
var activityLevel_pb:mx.controls.ProgressBar;

this.createEmptyMovieClip("sound_mc", this.getNextHighestDepth());
var active_mic:Microphone = Microphone.get();
sound_mc.attachAudio(active_mic);

activityLevel_pb.mode = "manual";
activityLevel_pb.label = "Activity Level: %3";
useEchoSuppression_ch.selected = active_mic.useEchoSuppression;
this.onEnterFrame = function() {
  activityLevel_pb.setProgress(active_mic.activityLevel, 100);
};
var chListener:Object = new Object();
chListener.click = function(evt:Object) {
  active_mic.setUseEchoSuppression(evt.target.selected);
};
useEchoSuppression_ch.addEventListener("click", chListener);
```

The `MovieClip.getNextHighestDepth()` method used in this example requires Flash Player 7 or later. If your SWF file includes a version 2 component, use the version 2 components DepthManager class instead of the `MovieClip.getNextHighestDepth()` method.

See also

`setUseEchoSuppression` (Microphone.setUseEchoSuppression method), `useEchoSuppression` (Microphone.useEchoSuppression property)

silenceLevel (Microphone.silenceLevel property)

```
public silenceLevel : Number [read-only]
```

An integer that specifies the amount of sound required to activate the microphone and invoke `Microphone.onActivity(true)`. The default value is 10.

Availability: ActionScript 1.0; Flash Player 6

Example

The following example changes the silence level based on the user's input in a NumericStepper instance called `silenceLevel_nstep`. The ProgressBar instance called `silenceLevel_pb` modifies its appearance depending on whether the audio stream is considered silent. Otherwise, it displays the activity level of the audio stream.

```
var silenceLevel_pb:mx.controls.ProgressBar;
var silenceLevel_nstep:mx.controls.NumericStepper;

this.createEmptyMovieClip("sound_mc", this.getNextHighestDepth());
var active_mic:Microphone = Microphone.get();
sound_mc.attachAudio(active_mic);

silenceLevel_pb.label = "Activity level: %3";
silenceLevel_pb.mode = "manual";
silenceLevel_nstep.minimum = 0;
silenceLevel_nstep.maximum = 100;
silenceLevel_nstep.value = active_mic.silenceLevel;

var nstepListener:Object = new Object();
nstepListener.change = function(evt:Object) {
   active_mic.setSilenceLevel(evt.target.value, active_mic.silenceTimeOut);
};
silenceLevel_nstep.addEventListener("change", nstepListener);

this.onEnterFrame = function() {
   silenceLevel_pb.setProgress(active_mic.activityLevel, 100);
};
active_mic.onActivity = function(active:Boolean) {
   if (active) {
   silenceLevel_pb.indeterminate = false;
   silenceLevel_pb.setStyle("themeColor", "haloGreen");
   silenceLevel_pb.label = "Activity level: %3";
   } else {
   silenceLevel_pb.indeterminate = true;
   silenceLevel_pb.setStyle("themeColor", "0xFF0000");
   silenceLevel_pb.label = "Activity level: (inactive)";
   }
};
```

The `MovieClip.getNextHighestDepth()` method used in this example requires Flash Player 7 or later. If your SWF file includes a version 2 component, use the version 2 components DepthManager class instead of the `MovieClip.getNextHighestDepth()` method.

See also

gain (Microphone.gain property), setSilenceLevel (Microphone.setSilenceLevel method)

silenceTimeOut (Microphone.silenceTimeOut property)

public silenceTimeOut : Number [read-only]

A numeric value representing the number of milliseconds between the time the microphone stops detecting sound and the time `Microphone.onActivity(false)` is invoked. The default value is 2000 (2 seconds).

To set this value, use `Microphone.setSilenceLevel()`.

Availability: ActionScript 1.0; Flash Player 6

Example

The following example enables the user to control the amount of time between when the microphone stops detecting sound and when `Microphone.onActivity(false)` is invoked. The user controls this value using a NumericStepper instance called silenceTimeOut_nstep. The ProgressBar instance called `silenceLevel_pb` modifies its appearance depending on whether the audio stream is considered silent. Otherwise, it displays the activity level of the audio stream.

```
var silenceLevel_pb:mx.controls.ProgressBar;
var silenceTimeOut_nstep:mx.controls.NumericStepper;

this.createEmptyMovieClip("sound_mc", this.getNextHighestDepth());
var active_mic:Microphone = Microphone.get();
sound_mc.attachAudio(active_mic);

silenceLevel_pb.label = "Activity level: %3";
silenceLevel_pb.mode = "manual";
silenceTimeOut_nstep.minimum = 0;
silenceTimeOut_nstep.maximum = 10;
silenceTimeOut_nstep.value = active_mic.silenceTimeOut/1000;

var nstepListener:Object = new Object();
nstepListener.change = function(evt:Object) {
```

```
    active_mic.setSilenceLevel(active_mic.silenceLevel, evt.target.value
    1000);
};
silenceTimeOut_nstep.addEventListener("change", nstepListener);

this.onEnterFrame = function() {
    silenceLevel_pb.setProgress(active_mic.activityLevel, 100);
};
active_mic.onActivity = function(active:Boolean) {
    if (active) {
    silenceLevel_pb.indeterminate = false;
    silenceLevel_pb.setStyle("themeColor", "haloGreen");
    silenceLevel_pb.label = "Activity level: %3";
    } else {
    silenceLevel_pb.indeterminate = true;
    silenceLevel_pb.setStyle("themeColor", "0xFF0000");
    silenceLevel_pb.label = "Activity level: (inactive)";
    }
};
```

The `MovieClip.getNextHighestDepth()` method used in this example requires Flash Player 7 or later. If your SWF file includes a version 2 component, use the version 2 components DepthManager class instead of the `MovieClip.getNextHighestDepth()` method.

See also

`setSilenceLevel (Microphone.setSilenceLevel method)`

useEchoSuppression (Microphone.useEchoSuppression property)

`public useEchoSuppression : Boolean [read-only]`

Property (read-only); a Boolean value of `true` if echo suppression is enabled, `false` otherwise. The default value is `false` unless the user has selected Reduce Echo in the Flash Player Microphone Settings panel.

Availability: ActionScript 1.0; Flash Player 6

Example

The following example turns on echo suppression if the user selects a CheckBox instance called `useEchoSuppression_ch`. The ProgressBar instance called `activityLevel_pb` displays the current activity level of the audio stream.

```
var useEchoSuppression_ch:mx.controls.CheckBox;
var activityLevel_pb:mx.controls.ProgressBar;

this.createEmptyMovieClip("sound_mc", this.getNextHighestDepth());
```

```
var active_mic:Microphone = Microphone.get();
sound_mc.attachAudio(active_mic);

activityLevel_pb.mode = "manual";
activityLevel_pb.label = "Activity Level: %3";
useEchoSuppression_ch.selected = active_mic.useEchoSuppression;
this.onEnterFrame = function() {
   activityLevel_pb.setProgress(active_mic.activityLevel, 100);
};
var chListener:Object = new Object();
chListener.click = function(evt:Object) {
   active_mic.setUseEchoSuppression(evt.target.selected);
};
useEchoSuppression_ch.addEventListener("click", chListener);
```

The `MovieClip.getNextHighestDepth()` method used in this example requires Flash Player 7 or later. If your SWF file includes a version 2 component, use the version 2 components DepthManager class instead of the `MovieClip.getNextHighestDepth()` method.

See also

setUseEchoSuppression (Microphone.setUseEchoSuppression method)

Mouse

```
Object
  |
  +-Mouse
```

```
public class Mouse
extends Object
```

The Mouse class is a top-level class whose properties and methods you can access without using a constructor. You can use the methods of the Mouse class to hide and show the mouse pointer (cursor) in the SWF file. The mouse pointer is visible by default, but you can hide it and implement a custom pointer that you create using a movie clip .

A Flash application can only monitor mouse events that occur within its focus. A Flash application cannot detect mouse events in another application.

Availability: ActionScript 1.0; Flash Player 5

Property summary

Properties inherited from class Object

```
constructor (Object.constructor property), __proto__ (Object.__proto__
property), prototype (Object.prototype property), __resolve
(Object.__resolve property)
```

Event summary

Event	Description
`onMouseDown =` `function() {}`	Notified when the mouse is pressed.
`onMouseMove =` `function() {}`	Notified when the mouse moves.
`onMouseUp =` `function() {}`	Notified when the mouse is released.

`onMouseWheel =`
`function([delta:`
`Number],`
`[scrollTarget:St`
`ring]) {}`
	Notified when the user rolls the mouse wheel.

Method summary

Modifiers	Signature	Description
`static`	`addListener(listener` `:Object) : Void`	Registers an object to receive notifications of the `onMouseDown`, `onMouseMove`, `onMouseUp`, and `onMouseWheel` listeners.
`static`	`hide() : Number`	Hides the pointer in a SWF file.

`static`	`removeListener(liste`
	`ner:Object) :`
	`Boolean`
		Removes an object that was previously registered with `addListener()`.

`static`	`show() : Number`	Displays the mouse pointer in a SWF file.

Methods inherited from class Object

```
addProperty (Object.addProperty method), hasOwnProperty
(Object.hasOwnProperty method), isPropertyEnumerable
(Object.isPropertyEnumerable method), isPrototypeOf (Object.isPrototypeOf
method), registerClass (Object.registerClass method), toString
(Object.toString method), unwatch (Object.unwatch method), valueOf
(Object.valueOf method), watch (Object.watch method)
```

addListener (Mouse.addListener method)

`public static addListener(listener:Object) : Void`

Registers an object to receive notifications of the `onMouseDown`, `onMouseMove`, `onMouseUp`, and `onMouseWheel` listeners. (The `onMouseWheel` listener is supported only in Windows.)

The `listener` parameter should contain an object that has a defined method for at least one of the listeners.

When the mouse is pressed, moved, released, or used to scroll, regardless of the input focus, all listening objects that are registered with this method have their `onMouseDown`, `onMouseMove`, `onMouseUp`, or `onMouseWheel` method invoked. Multiple objects can listen for mouse notifications. If the `listener` is already registered, no change occurs.

Availability: ActionScript 1.0; Flash Player 6

Parameters

`listener:Object` - An object.

Example

This example is excerpted from the *animation.fla* file in the ActionScript samples folder.

```
// Create a mouse listener object
var mouseListener:Object = new Object();

// Every time the mouse cursor moves within the SWF file,
   update the position of the crosshair movie clip
   instance on the Stage.
mouseListener.onMouseMove = function() {
   crosshair_mc._x = _xmouse;
   crosshair_mc._y = _ymouse;
};

// When you click the mouse, check to see if the cursor is within the
   boundaries of the Stage. If so, increment the number of shots.
mouseListener.onMouseDown = function() {
   if (bg_mc.hitTest(_xmouse, _ymouse, false)) {
   _global.shots++;
   }
};
Mouse.addListener(mouseListener);
```

To view the entire script, see the *animation.fla* file in the ActionScript samples Folder. The following list shows typical paths to the ActionScript samples Folder:

- Windows: *boot drive*\Program Files\Macromedia\Flash 8\Samples and Tutorials\Samples\ActionScript

- Macintosh: *Macintosh HD*/Applications/Macromedia Flash 8/Samples and Tutorials/ Samples/ActionScript

See also

onMouseDown (Mouse.onMouseDown event listener), onMouseMove
(Mouse.onMouseMove event listener), onMouseUp (Mouse.onMouseUp event
listener), onMouseWheel (Mouse.onMouseWheel event listener)

hide (Mouse.hide method)

```
public static hide() : Number
```
Hides the pointer in a SWF file. The pointer is visible by default.

Availability: ActionScript 1.0; Flash Player 5

Returns

`Number` - An integer; either 0 or 1. If the mouse pointer was hidden before the call to `Mouse.hide()`, then the return value is 0. If the mouse pointer was visible before the call to `Mouse.hide()`, then the return value is 1.

Example

The following code hides the standard mouse pointer, and sets the *x* and *y* positions of the `pointer_mc` movie clip instance to the *x* and *y* pointer position. Create a movie clip and set its Linkage identifier to `pointer_id`. Add the following ActionScript to Frame 1 of the Timeline:

```
// to use this script you need a symbol
// in your library with a Linkage Identifier of "pointer_id".
this.attachMovie("pointer_id", "pointer_mc", this.getNextHighestDepth());
Mouse.hide();
var mouseListener:Object = new Object();
mouseListener.onMouseMove = function() {
  pointer_mc._x = _xmouse;
  pointer_mc._y = _ymouse;
  updateAfterEvent();
};
Mouse.addListener(mouseListener);
```

The `MovieClip.getNextHighestDepth()` method used in this example requires Flash Player 7 or later. If your SWF file includes a version 2 component, use the version 2 components DepthManager class instead of the `MovieClip.getNextHighestDepth()` method.

See also

show (Mouse.show method), _xmouse (MovieClip._xmouse property), _ymouse
(MovieClip._ymouse property)

onMouseDown (Mouse.onMouseDown event listener)

```
onMouseDown = function() {}
```

Notified when the mouse is pressed. To use the `onMouseDown` listener, you must create a listener object. You can then define a function for `onMouseDown` and use `addListener()` to register the listener with the Mouse object, as shown in the following code:

```
var someListener:Object = new Object();
someListener.onMouseDown = function () { ... };
Mouse.addListener(someListener);
```

Listeners enable different pieces of code to cooperate because multiple listeners can receive notification about a single event.

A Flash application can only monitor mouse events that occur within its focus. A Flash application cannot detect mouse events in another application.

Availability: ActionScript 1.0; Flash Player 6

Example

The following example uses the Drawing API to draw a rectangle whenever the user clicks, drags and releases the mouse at runtime.

```
this.createEmptyMovieClip("canvas_mc", this.getNextHighestDepth());
var mouseListener:Object = new Object();
mouseListener.onMouseDown = function() {
   this.isDrawing = true;
   this.orig_x = _xmouse;
   this.orig_y = _ymouse;
   this.target_mc = canvas_mc.createEmptyMovieClip("",
   canvas_mc.getNextHighestDepth());
};
mouseListener.onMouseMove = function() {
   if (this.isDrawing) {
      this.target_mc.clear();
      this.target_mc.lineStyle(1, 0xFF0000, 100);
      this.target_mc.moveTo(this.orig_x, this.orig_y);
      this.target_mc.lineTo(_xmouse, this.orig_y);
      this.target_mc.lineTo(_xmouse, _ymouse);
      this.target_mc.lineTo(this.orig_x, _ymouse);
      this.target_mc.lineTo(this.orig_x, this.orig_y);
   }
   updateAfterEvent();
};
mouseListener.onMouseUp = function() {
   this.isDrawing = false;
};
Mouse.addListener(mouseListener);
```

The `MovieClip.getNextHighestDepth()` method used in this example requires Flash Player 7 or later. If your SWF file includes a version 2 component, use the version 2 components DepthManager class instead of the `MovieClip.getNextHighestDepth()` method.

See also

addListener (Mouse.addListener method)

onMouseMove (Mouse.onMouseMove event listener)

```
onMouseMove = function() {}
```

Notified when the mouse moves. To use the `onMouseMove` listener, you must create a listener object. You can then define a function for `onMouseMove` and use `addListener()` to register the listener with the Mouse object, as shown in the following code:

```
var someListener:Object = new Object();
someListener.onMouseMove = function () { ... };
Mouse.addListener(someListener);
```

Listeners enable different pieces of code to cooperate because multiple listeners can receive notification about a single event.

A Flash application can only monitor mouse events that occur within its focus. A Flash application cannot detect mouse events in another application.

Availability: ActionScript 1.0; Flash Player 6

Example

The following example uses the mouse pointer as a tool to draw lines using `onMouseMove` and the Drawing API. The user draws a line when they drag the mouse pointer.

```
this.createEmptyMovieClip("canvas_mc", this.getNextHighestDepth());
var mouseListener:Object = new Object();
mouseListener.onMouseDown = function() {
   this.isDrawing = true;
   canvas_mc.lineStyle(2, 0xFF0000, 100);
   canvas_mc.moveTo(_xmouse, _ymouse);
};
mouseListener.onMouseMove = function() {
   if (this.isDrawing) {
      canvas_mc.lineTo(_xmouse, _ymouse);
   }
   updateAfterEvent();
};
mouseListener.onMouseUp = function() {
   this.isDrawing = false;
};
```

```
Mouse.addListener(mouseListener);
```

The `MovieClip.getNextHighestDepth()` method used in this example requires Flash Player 7 or later. If your SWF file includes a version 2 component, use the version 2 components DepthManager class instead of the `MovieClip.getNextHighestDepth()` method.

The following example hides the standard mouse pointer, and sets the *x* and *y* positions of the `pointer_mc` movie clip instance to the *x* and *y* pointer position. Create a movie clip and set its Linkage identifier to `pointer_id`. Add the following ActionScript to Frame 1 of the Timeline:

```
// to use this script you need a symbol
// in your library with a Linkage Identifier of "pointer_id".
this.attachMovie("pointer_id", "pointer_mc", this.getNextHighestDepth());
Mouse.hide();
var mouseListener:Object = new Object();
mouseListener.onMouseMove = function() {
    pointer_mc._x = _xmouse;
    pointer_mc._y = _ymouse;
    updateAfterEvent();
};
Mouse.addListener(mouseListener);
```

The `MovieClip.getNextHighestDepth()` method used in this example requires Flash Player 7 or later. If your SWF file includes a version 2 component, use the version 2 components DepthManager class instead of the `MovieClip.getNextHighestDepth()` method.

See also

`addListener (Mouse.addListener method)`

onMouseUp (Mouse.onMouseUp event listener)

```
onMouseUp = function() {}
```

Notified when the mouse is released. To use the `onMouseUp` listener, you must create a listener object. You can then define a function for `onMouseUp` and use `addListener()` to register the listener with the Mouse object, as shown in the following code:

```
var someListener:Object = new Object();
someListener.onMouseUp = function () { ... };
Mouse.addListener(someListener);
```

Listeners enable different pieces of code to cooperate because multiple listeners can receive notification about a single event.

A Flash application can only monitor mouse events that occur within its focus. A Flash application cannot detect mouse events in another application.

Availability: ActionScript 1.0; Flash Player 6

Example

The following example uses the mouse pointer as a tool to draw lines using `onMouseMove` and the Drawing API. The user draws a line when they drag the mouse pointer. The user stops drawing the line when they release the mouse button.

```
this.createEmptyMovieClip("canvas_mc", this.getNextHighestDepth());
var mouseListener:Object = new Object();
mouseListener.onMouseDown = function() {
  this.isDrawing = true;
  canvas_mc.lineStyle(2, 0xFF0000, 100);
  canvas_mc.moveTo(_xmouse, _ymouse);
};
mouseListener.onMouseMove = function() {
  if (this.isDrawing) {
    canvas_mc.lineTo(_xmouse, _ymouse);
  }
  updateAfterEvent();
};
mouseListener.onMouseUp = function() {
  this.isDrawing = false;
};
Mouse.addListener(mouseListener);
```

The `MovieClip.getNextHighestDepth()` method used in this example requires Flash Player 7 or later. If your SWF file includes a version 2 component, use the version 2 components DepthManager class instead of the `MovieClip.getNextHighestDepth()` method.

See also

`addListener` (Mouse.addListener method)

onMouseWheel (Mouse.onMouseWheel event listener)

`onMouseWheel = function([delta:Number], [scrollTarget:String]) {}`

Notified when the user rolls the mouse wheel. To use the `onMouseWheel` listener, you must create a listener object. You can then define a function for `onMouseWheel` and use `addListener()` to register the listener with the Mouse object.

Note: Mouse wheel event listeners are available only in Windows versions of Flash Player.

A Flash application can only monitor mouse events that occur within its focus. A Flash application cannot detect mouse events in another application.

Availability: ActionScript 1.0; Flash Player 6 - (Windows only).

Parameters

`delta:Number` [optional] - A number indicating how many lines should be scrolled for each notch the user rolls the mouse wheel. A positive `delta` value indicates an upward scroll; a negative value indicates a downward scroll. Typical values are from 1 to 3; faster scrolling can produce larger values.

`scrollTarget:String` [optional] - A parameter that indicates the topmost movie clip instance under the mouse pointer when the mouse wheel is rolled. If you want to specify a value for `scrollTarget` but don't want to specify a value for `delta`, pass `null` for `delta`.

Example

The following example shows how to create a listener object that responds to mouse wheel events. In this example, the *x* coordinate of a movie clip object named `clip_mc` changes each time the user rotates the mouse wheel:

```
var mouseListener:Object = new Object();
mouseListener.onMouseWheel = function(delta) {
   clip_mc._x += delta;
}
Mouse.addListener(mouseListener);
```

The following example draws a line that rotates when you rotate the mouse wheel. Click the SWF file at runtime and then rotate your mouse wheel to see the movie clip in action.

```
this.createEmptyMovieClip("line_mc", this.getNextHighestDepth());
line_mc.lineStyle(2, 0xFF0000, 100);
line_mc.moveTo(0, 100);
line_mc.lineTo(0, 0);
line_mc._x = 200;
line_mc._y = 200;

var mouseListener:Object = new Object();
mouseListener.onMouseWheel = function(delta:Number) {
   line_mc._rotation += delta;
};
mouseListener.onMouseDown = function() {
   trace("Down");
};
Mouse.addListener(mouseListener);
```

The `MovieClip.getNextHighestDepth()` method used in this example requires Flash Player 7 or later. If your SWF file includes a version 2 component, use the version 2 components DepthManager class instead of the `MovieClip.getNextHighestDepth()` method.

See also

`addListener (Mouse.addListener method)`, `mouseWheelEnabled (TextField.mouseWheelEnabled property)`

---

removeListener (Mouse.removeListener method)

`public static removeListener(listener:Object) : Boolean`

Removes an object that was previously registered with `addListener()`.

Availability: ActionScript 1.0; Flash Player 6

Parameters

`listener:Object` - An object.

Returns

`Boolean` - If the `listener` object is successfully removed, the method returns `true`; if the `listener` is not successfully removed (for example, if the `listener` was not on the Mouse object's listener list), the method returns `false`.

Example

The following example attaches three buttons to the Stage, and lets the user draw lines in the SWF file at runtime, using the mouse pointer. One button clears all of the lines from the SWF file. The second button removes the mouse listener so the user cannot draw lines. The third button adds the mouse listener after it is removed, so the user can draw lines again. Add the following ActionScript to Frame 1 of the Timeline:

```
this.createClassObject(mx.controls.Button, "clear_button",
   this.getNextHighestDepth(), {_x:10, _y:10, label:'clear'});
this.createClassObject(mx.controls.Button, "stopDrawing_button",
   this.getNextHighestDepth(), {_x:120, _y:10, label:'stop drawing'});
this.createClassObject(mx.controls.Button, "startDrawing_button",
   this.getNextHighestDepth(), {_x:230, _y:10, label:'start drawing'});
startDrawing_button.enabled = false;
//
this.createEmptyMovieClip("canvas_mc", this.getNextHighestDepth());
var mouseListener:Object = new Object();
mouseListener.onMouseDown = function() {
   this.isDrawing = true;
   canvas_mc.lineStyle(2, 0xFF0000, 100);
   canvas_mc.moveTo(_xmouse, _ymouse);
};
mouseListener.onMouseMove = function() {
   if (this.isDrawing) {
   canvas_mc.lineTo(_xmouse, _ymouse);
   }
   updateAfterEvent();
};
mouseListener.onMouseUp = function() {
   this.isDrawing = false;
};
```

```
Mouse.addListener(mouseListener);
var clearListener:Object = new Object();
clearListener.click = function() {
  canvas_mc.clear();
};
clear_button.addEventListener("click", clearListener);
//
var stopDrawingListener:Object = new Object();
stopDrawingListener.click = function(evt:Object) {
  Mouse.removeListener(mouseListener);
  evt.target.enabled = false;
  startDrawing_button.enabled = true;
};
stopDrawing_button.addEventListener("click", stopDrawingListener);
var startDrawingListener:Object = new Object();
startDrawingListener.click = function(evt:Object) {
  Mouse.addListener(mouseListener);
  evt.target.enabled = false;
  stopDrawing_button.enabled = true;
};
startDrawing_button.addEventListener("click", startDrawingListener);
```

The `MovieClip.getNextHighestDepth()` method used in this example requires Flash Player 7 or later. If your SWF file includes a version 2 component, use the version 2 components DepthManager class instead of the `MovieClip.getNextHighestDepth()` method.

show (Mouse.show method)

```
public static show() : Number
```

Displays the mouse pointer in a SWF file. The pointer is visible by default.

Availability: ActionScript 1.0; Flash Player 5

Returns

`Number` - An integer; either 0 or 1. If the mouse pointer was hidden before the call to `Mouse.show()`, then the return value is 0. If the mouse pointer was visible before the call to `Mouse.show()`, then the return value is 1.

Example

The following example attaches a custom cursor from the library when it rolls over a movie clip called `my_mc`. Give a movie clip in the Library a Linkage identifier of `cursor_help_id`, and add the following ActionScript to Frame 1 of the Timeline:

```
my_mc.onRollOver = function() {
  Mouse.hide();
```

```
   this.attachMovie("cursor_help_id", "cursor_mc",
   this.getNextHighestDepth(), {_x:this._xmouse, _y:this._ymouse});
};
my_mc.onMouseMove = function() {
   this.cursor_mc._x = this._xmouse;
   this.cursor_mc._y = this._ymouse;
};
my_mc.onRollOut = function() {
   Mouse.show();
   this.cursor_mc.removeMovieClip();
};
```

The `MovieClip.getNextHighestDepth()` method used in this example requires Flash Player 7 or later. If your SWF file includes a version 2 component, use the version 2 components DepthManager class instead of the `MovieClip.getNextHighestDepth()` method.

See also

`hide (Mouse.hide method)`, `_xmouse (MovieClip._xmouse property)`, `_ymouse (MovieClip._ymouse property)`

MovieClip

```
Object
 |
 +-MovieClip
```

```
public dynamic class MovieClip
extends Object
```

The methods for the MovieClip class provide the same functionality as actions that target movie clips. Some additional methods do not have equivalent actions in the Actions toolbox in the Actions panel.

You do not use a constructor method to create a movie clip. You can choose from among three methods to create movie clip instances:

- The `attachMovie()` method allows you to create a movie clip instance based on a movie clip symbol that exists in the library.

- The `createEmptyMovieClip()` method allows you to create an empty movie clip instance as a child based on another movie clip.

- The `duplicateMovieClip()` method allows you to create a movie clip instance based on another movie clip.

To call the methods of the MovieClip class you reference movie clip instances by name, using the following syntax, where *my_mc* is a movie clip instance:

```
my_mc.play();
my_mc.gotoAndPlay(3);
```

You can extend the methods and event handlers of the MovieClip class by creating a subclass.

Availability: ActionScript 1.0; Flash Player 3

Property summary

Modifiers	Property	Description
	`_alpha:Number`	The alpha transparency value of the movie clip.
	`blendMode:Object`	The blend mode for this movie clip.
	`cacheAsBitmap:Boolean`	If set to `true`, Flash Player caches an internal bitmap representation of the movie clip.
	`_currentframe:Number` [read-only]	Returns the number of the frame in which the playhead is located in the movie clip's timeline.
	`_droptarget:String` [read-only]	Returns the absolute path in slash-syntax notation of the movie clip instance on which this movie clip was dropped.

Modifiers	Property	Description
	`enabled:Boolean`	A Boolean value that indicates whether a movie clip is enabled.
	`filters:Array`	An indexed array containing each filter object currently associated with the movie clip.
	`focusEnabled:Boolean`	If the value is `undefined` or `false`, a movie clip cannot receive input focus unless it is a button.
	`_focusrect:Boolean`	A Boolean value that specifies whether a movie clip has a yellow rectangle around it when it has keyboard focus.
	`_framesloaded:Number` [read-only]	The number of frames that are loaded from a streaming SWF file.
	`_height:Number`	The height of the movie clip, in pixels.
	`_highquality:Number`	**Deprecated** since Flash Player 7. This property was deprecated in favor of `MovieClip._quality`. Specifies the level of anti-aliasing applied to the current SWF file.
	`hitArea:Object`	Designates another movie clip to serve as the hit area for a movie clip.
	`_lockroot:Boolean`	A Boolean value that specifies what `_root` refers to when a SWF file is loaded into a movie clip.
	`menu:ContextMenu`	Associates the specified ContextMenu object with the movie clip.
	`_name:String`	The instance name of the movie clip.
	`opaqueBackground:Number`	The color of the movie clip's opaque (not transparent) background of the color specified by the number (an RGB hexadecimal value).
	`_parent:MovieClip`	A reference to the movie clip or object that contains the current movie clip or object.
	`_quality:String`	Sets or retrieves the rendering quality used for a SWF file.
	`_rotation:Number`	Specifies the rotation of the movie clip, in degrees, from its original orientation.
	`scale9Grid:Rectangle`	The rectangular region that defines the nine scaling regions for the movie clip.

Modifiers	Property	Description
	`scrollRect:Object`	The `scrollRect` property allows you to quickly scroll movie clip content and have a window viewing larger content.
	`_soundbuftime:Number`	Specifies the number of seconds a sound prebuffers before it starts to stream.
	`tabChildren:Boolean`	Determines whether the children of a movie clip are included in the automatic tab ordering.
	`tabEnabled:Boolean`	Specifies whether the movie clip is included in automatic tab ordering.
	`tabIndex:Number`	Lets you customize the tab ordering of objects in a movie.
	`_target:String` [read-only]	Returns the target path of the movie clip instance, in slash notation.
	`_totalframes:Number` [read-only]	Returns the total number of frames in the movie clip instance specified in the `MovieClip` parameter.
	`trackAsMenu:Boolean`	A Boolean value that indicates whether other buttons or movie clips can receive mouse release events.
	`transform:Transform`	An object with properties pertaining to a movie clip's matrix, color transform, and pixel bounds.
	`_url:String` [read-only]	Retrieves the URL of the SWF, JPEG, GIF, or PNG file from which the movie clip was downloaded.
	`useHandCursor:Boolean`	A Boolean value that indicates whether the pointing hand (hand cursor) appears when the mouse rolls over a movie clip.
	`_visible:Boolean`	A Boolean value that indicates whether the movie clip is visible.
	`_width:Number`	The width of the movie clip, in pixels.
	`_x:Number`	An integer that sets the x coordinate of a movie clip relative to the local coordinates of the parent movie clip.
	`_xmouse:Number` [read-only]	Returns the x coordinate of the mouse position.
	`_xscale:Number`	Determines the horizontal scale (*percentage*) of the movie clip as applied from the registration point of the movie clip.

Modifiers	Property	Description
	`_y:Number`	Sets the y coordinate of a movie clip relative to the local coordinates of the parent movie clip.
	`_ymouse:Number` [read-only]	Indicates the y coordinate of the mouse position.
	`_yscale:Number`	Sets the vertical scale (*percentage*) of the movie clip as applied from the registration point of the movie clip.

Properties inherited from class Object

```
constructor (Object.constructor property),__proto__ (Object.__proto__
property),prototype (Object.prototype property),__resolve
(Object.__resolve property)
```

Event summary

Event	Description
`onData = function() {}`	Invoked when a movie clip receives data from a `MovieClip.loadVariables()` call or a `MovieClip.loadMovie()` call.
`onDragOut = function() {}`	Invoked when the mouse button is pressed and the pointer rolls outside the object.
`onDragOver = function() {}`	Invoked when the pointer is dragged outside and then over the movie clip.
`onEnterFrame = function() {}`	Invoked repeatedly at the frame rate of the SWF file.
`onKeyDown = function() {}`	Invoked when a movie clip has input focus and user presses a key.
`onKeyUp = function() {}`	Invoked when a key is released.
`onKillFocus = function(newFocus:Object) {}`	Invoked when a movie clip loses keyboard focus.
`onLoad = function() {}`	Invoked when the movie clip is instantiated and appears in the timeline.
`onMouseDown = function() {}`	Invoked when the mouse button is pressed.
`onMouseMove = function() {}`	Invoked when the mouse moves.
`onMouseUp = function() {}`	Invoked when the mouse button is released.

Event	Description
`onPress = function() {}`	Invoked when the user clicks the mouse while the pointer is over a movie clip.
`onRelease = function() {}`	Invoked when a user releases the mouse button over a movie clip.
`onReleaseOutside = function() {}`	Invoked after a user presses the mouse button inside the movie clip area and then releases it outside the movie clip area.
`onRollOut = function() {}`	Invoked when a user moves the pointer outside a movie clip area.
`onRollOver = function() {}`	Invoked when user moves the pointer over a movie clip area.
`onSetFocus = function(oldFocus:Object) {}`	Invoked when a movie clip receives keyboard focus.
`onUnload = function() {}`	Invoked in the first frame after the movie clip is removed from the Timeline.

Method summary

Modifiers	Signature	Description
	`attachAudio(id:Object) : Void`	Specifies the audio source to be played.
	`attachBitmap(bmp:BitmapData, depth:Number, [pixelSnapping:String], [smoothing:Boolean]) : Void`	Attaches a bitmap image to a movie clip.
	`attachMovie(id:String, name:String, depth:Number, [initObject:Object]) : MovieClip`	Takes a symbol from the library and attaches it to the movie clip.
	`beginBitmapFill(bmp:BitmapData, [matrix:Matrix], [repeat:Boolean], [smoothing:Boolean]) : Void`	Fills a drawing area with a bitmap image.
	`beginFill(rgb:Number, [alpha:Number]) : Void`	Indicates the beginning of a new drawing path.

Modifiers	Signature	Description
	`beginGradientFill(fillType:String, colors:Array, alphas:Array, ratios:Array, matrix:Object, [spreadMethod:String], [interpolationMethod:String], [focalPointRatio:Number]) : Void`	Indicates the beginning of a new drawing path.
	`clear() : Void`	Removes all the graphics created during runtime by using the movie clip draw methods, including line styles specified with `MovieClip.lineStyle()`.
	`createEmptyMovieClip (name:String, depth:Number) : MovieClip`	Creates an empty movie clip as a child of an existing movie clip.
	`createTextField(instanceName:String, depth:Number, x:Number, y:Number, width:Number, height:Number) : TextField`	Creates a new, empty text field as a child of the movie clip on which you call this method.
	`curveTo(controlX:Number, controlY:Number, anchorX:Number, anchorY:Number) : Void`	Draws a curve using the current line style from the current drawing position to (`anchorX`, `anchorY`) using the control point that ((`controlX`, `controlY`) specifies.
	`duplicateMovieClip(name:String, depth:Number, [initObject:Object]) : MovieClip`	Creates an instance of the specified movie clip while the SWF file is playing.
	`endFill() : Void`	Applies a fill to the lines and curves that were since the last call to `beginFill()` or `beginGradientFill()`.
	`getBounds(bounds:Object) : Object`	Returns properties that are the minimum and maximum *x* and *y* coordinate values of the movie clip, based on the `bounds` parameter.
	`getBytesLoaded() : Number`	Returns the number of bytes that have already loaded (streamed) for the movie clip.

Modifiers	Signature	Description
	`getBytesTotal() : Number`	Returns the size, in bytes, of the movie clip.
	`getDepth() : Number`	Returns the depth of the movie clip instance.
	`getInstanceAtDepth(depth:Number) : MovieClip`	Determines if a particular depth is already occupied by a movie clip.
	`getNextHighestDepth() : Number`	Determines a depth value that you can pass to `MovieClip.attachMovie()`, `MovieClip.duplicateMovieClip()`, or `MovieClip.createEmptyMovieClip()` to ensure that Flash renders the movie clip in front of all other objects on the same level and layer in the current movie clip.
	`getRect(bounds:Object) : Object`	Returns properties that are the minimum and maximum *x* and *y* coordinate values of the movie clip, based on the `bounds` parameter, excluding any strokes on shapes.
	`getSWFVersion() : Number`	Returns an integer that indicates the Flash Player version for the movie clip was published.
	`getTextSnapshot() : TextSnapshot`	Returns a TextSnapshot object that contains the text in all the static text fields in the specified movie clip; text in child movie clips is not included.
	`getURL(url:String, [window:String], [method:String]) : Void`	Loads a document from the specified URL into the specified window.
	`globalToLocal(pt:Object) : Void`	Converts the `pt` object from Stage (global) coordinates to the movie clip's (local) coordinates.
	`gotoAndPlay(frame:Object) : Void`	Starts playing the SWF file at the specified frame.
	`gotoAndStop(frame:Object) : Void`	Brings the playhead to the specified frame of the movie clip and stops it there.
	`hitTest() : Boolean`	Evaluates the movie clip to see if it overlaps or intersects with the hit area that the `target` or *x* and *y* coordinate parameters identify.

Modifiers	Signature	Description
	lineGradientStyle(fillType:String, colors:Array, alphas:Array, ratios:Array, matrix:Object, [spreadMethod:String], [interpolationMethod:String], [focalPointRatio:Number]) : Void	Specifies a line style that Flash uses for subsequent calls to the lineTo() and curveTo() methods until you call the lineStyle() method or the lineGradientStyle() method with different parameters.
	lineStyle(thickness:Number, rgb:Number, alpha:Number, pixelHinting:Boolean, noScale:String, capsStyle:String, jointStyle:String, miterLimit:Number) : Void	Specifies a line style that Flash uses for subsequent calls to the lineTo() and curveTo() methods until you call the lineStyle() method with different parameters.
	lineTo(x:Number, y:Number) : Void	Draws a line using the current line style from the current drawing position to (x, y); the current drawing position is then set to (x, y).
	loadMovie(url:String, [method:String]) : Void	Loads a SWF, JPEG, GIF, or PNG file into a movie clip in Flash Player while the original SWF file is playing.
	loadVariables(url:String, [method:String]) : Void	Reads data from an external file and sets the values for variables in the movie clip.
	localToGlobal(pt:Object) : Void	Converts the pt object from the movie clip's (local) coordinates to the Stage (global) coordinates.
	moveTo(x:Number, y:Number) : Void	Moves the current drawing position to (x, y).
	nextFrame() : Void	Sends the playhead to the next frame and stops it.
	play() : Void	Moves the playhead in the timeline of the movie clip.
	prevFrame() : Void	Sends the playhead to the previous frame and stops it.
	removeMovieClip() : Void	Removes a movie clip instance created with duplicateMovieClip(), MovieClip.duplicateMovieClip(), MovieClip.createEmptyMovieClip(), or MovieClip.attachMovie().

Modifiers	Signature	Description
	setMask(mc:Object) : Void	Makes the movie clip in the parameter mc a mask that reveals the calling movie clip.
	startDrag([lockCenter:Boolean], [left:Number], [top:Number], [right:Number], [bottom:Number]) : Void	Lets the user drag the specified movie clip.
	stop() : Void	Stops the movie clip that is currently playing.
	stopDrag() : Void	Ends a MovieClip.startDrag() method.
	swapDepths(target:Object) : Void	Swaps the stacking, or depth level (z-order), of this movie clip with the movie clip that is specified by the target parameter, or with the movie clip that currently occupies the depth level that is specified in the target parameter.
	unloadMovie() : Void	Removes the contents of a movie clip instance.

Methods inherited from class Object

```
addProperty (Object.addProperty method), hasOwnProperty
(Object.hasOwnProperty method), isPropertyEnumerable
(Object.isPropertyEnumerable method), isPrototypeOf (Object.isPrototypeOf
method), registerClass (Object.registerClass method), toString
(Object.toString method), unwatch (Object.unwatch method), valueOf
(Object.valueOf method), watch (Object.watch method)
```

_alpha (MovieClip._alpha property)

public _alpha : Number

The alpha transparency value of the movie clip. Valid values are 0 (fully transparent) to 100 (fully opaque). The default value is 100. Objects in a movie clip with _alpha set to 0 are active, even though they are invisible. For example, you can still click a button in a movie clip whose _alpha property is set to 0. To disable the button completely, you can set the movie clip's _visible property to false.

You can extend the methods and event handlers of the MovieClip class by creating a subclass.

Availability: ActionScript 1.0; Flash Player 4

Example

The following code sets the _alpha property of a dynamically created movie clip named triangle to 50% when the mouse rolls over the movie clip. Add the following ActionScript to your FLA or AS file:

```
this.createEmptyMovieClip("triangle", this.getNextHighestDepth());

triangle.beginFill(0x0000FF, 100);
triangle.moveTo(10, 10);
triangle.lineTo(10, 100);
triangle.lineTo(100, 10);
triangle.lineTo(10, 10);

triangle.onRollOver = function() {
  this._alpha = 50;
};
triangle.onRollOut = function() {
  this._alpha = 100;
};
```

The MovieClip.getNextHighestDepth() method used in this example requires Flash Player 7 or later. If your SWF file includes a version 2 component, use the version 2 components DepthManager class instead of the MovieClip.getNextHighestDepth() method.

See also

_alpha (Button._alpha property), _alpha (TextField._alpha property), _visible (MovieClip._visible property)

attachAudio (MovieClip.attachAudio method)

```
public attachAudio(id:Object) : Void
```

Specifies the audio source to be played. To stop playing the audio source, pass the value false for the id.

You can extend the methods and event handlers of the MovieClip class by creating a subclass.

Availability: ActionScript 1.0; Flash Player 6 - The ability to attach audio from Flash Video (FLV) files was added in Flash Player 7.

Parameters

id:Object - The object that contains the audio to play. Valid values are a Microphone object, a NetStream object that is playing an FLV file, and false (stops playing the audio).

Example

The following example creates a new NetStream connection. Add a new Video symbol by opening the Library panel and selecting New Video from the Library options menu. Give the symbol the instance name my_video. Dynamically load the FLV video at runtime. Use the attachAudio() method to attach the audio from the FLV file to a movie clip on the Stage. Then you can control the audio in the movie clip by using the Sound class and two buttons called volUp_btn and volDown_btn.

```
var my_nc:NetConnection = new NetConnection();
my_nc.connect(null);
var my_ns:NetStream = new NetStream(my_nc);
my_video.attachVideo(my_ns);
my_ns.play("yourVideo.flv");
this.createEmptyMovieClip("flv_mc", this.getNextHighestDepth());
flv_mc.attachAudio(my_ns);
var audio_sound:Sound = new Sound(flv_mc);

// Add volume buttons.
volUp_btn.onRelease = function() {
  if (audio_sound.getVolume()<100) {
  audio_sound.setVolume(audio_sound.getVolume()+10);
  updateVolume();
  }
};
volDown_btn.onRelease = function() {
  if (audio_sound.getVolume()>0) {
  audio_sound.setVolume(audio_sound.getVolume()-10);
  updateVolume();
  }
};

// Updates the volume.
this.createTextField("volume_txt", this.getNextHighestDepth(), 0, 0, 100,
  22);
updateVolume();
function updateVolume() {
  volume_txt.text = "Volume: "+audio_sound.getVolume();
}
```

The following example specifies a microphone as the audio source for a dynamically created movie clip instance called audio_mc:

```
var active_mic:Microphone = Microphone.get();
this.createEmptyMovieClip("audio_mc", this.getNextHighestDepth());
audio_mc.attachAudio(active_mic);
```

The MovieClip.getNextHighestDepth() method used in this example requires Flash Player 7 or later. If your SWF file includes a version 2 component, use the version 2 components DepthManager class instead of the MovieClip.getNextHighestDepth() method.

See also

Microphone, play (NetStream.play method), Sound, attachVideo (Video.attachVideo method)

attachBitmap (MovieClip.attachBitmap method)

```
public attachBitmap(bmp:BitmapData, depth:Number, [pixelSnapping:String],
  [smoothing:Boolean]) : Void
```

Attaches a bitmap image to a movie clip.

After the bitmap is attached to the movie clip, a reference is made from the movie clip to the bitmap object. When attaching a bitmap, you can specify pixelSnapping and smoothing parameters to affect the appearance of the bitmap.

After an object is added to the movie clip, it is not an accessible object. The depth, pixelSnapping, and smoothing parameters can only be set during the attachBitmap() method call and cannot be changed later.

First use the createEmptyMovieClip() to create an empty movie clip, then use the attachBitmap() method. This way, you can apply transformations to the movie clip to transform the bitmap; for example, by using the matrix property of the movie clip.

Pixel snapping forces the position of the bitmap to the nearest whole pixel value instead of positioning to be on a partial pixel. There are three pixel snapping modes:

- Auto mode does pixel snapping as long as the bitmap is not stretched or rotated.
- Always mode always does pixel snapping, regardless of stretching and rotation.
- Never mode turns off pixel snapping for the movie clip.

Smoothing mode affects the appearance of the image when it is scaled.

Availability: ActionScript 1.0; Flash Player 8

Parameters

bmp:flash.display.BitmapData - A transparent or opaque bitmap image.

depth:Number - An integer that specifies the depth level within the movie clip where the bitmap image should be placed.

pixelSnapping:String [optional] - The pixel snapping modes are auto, always, and never. The default mode is auto.

smoothing:Boolean [optional] - The smoothing mode is either true for enabled or false for disabled. The default mode is disabled.

Example

The following attaches a very basic bitmap to a movie clip:

```
import flash.display.*;

this.createEmptyMovieClip("bmp1", this.getNextHighestDepth());
var bmpData1:BitmapData = new BitmapData(200, 200, false, 0xaa3344);
bmp1.attachBitmap(bmpData1, 2, "auto", true);
```

If your SWF file includes a version 2 component, use the version 2 components DepthManager class instead of the `MovieClip.getNextHighestDepth()` method, which is used in this example.

attachMovie (MovieClip.attachMovie method)

```
public attachMovie(id:String, name:String, depth:Number,
  [initObject:Object]) : MovieClip
```

Takes a symbol from the library and attaches it to the movie clip. Use `MovieClip.removeMovieClip()` or `MovieClip.unloadMovie()` to remove a SWF file attached with `attachMovie()` method.

You can extend the methods and event handlers of the MovieClip class by creating a subclass.

Availability: ActionScript 1.0; Flash Player 5

Parameters

`id:String` - The linkage name of the movie clip symbol in the library to attach to a movie clip on the Stage. This is the name that you enter in the Identifier field in the Linkage Properties dialog box.

`name:String` - A unique instance name for the movie clip being attached to the movie clip.

`depth:Number` - An integer specifying the depth level where the SWF file is placed.

`initObject:Object` [optional] - (Supported for Flash Player 6 and later) An object that contains properties with which to populate the newly attached movie clip. This parameter allows dynamically created movie clips to receive clip parameters. If `initObject` is not an object, it is ignored. All properties of `initObject` are copied into the new instance. The properties specified with `initObject` are available to the constructor function.

Returns

`MovieClip` - A reference to the newly created instance.

Example

The following example attaches the symbol with the linkage identifier `circle` to the movie clip instance, which is on the Stage in the SWF file:

```
this.attachMovie("circle", "circle1_mc", this.getNextHighestDepth());
this.attachMovie("circle", "circle2_mc", this.getNextHighestDepth(),
  {_x:100, _y:100});
```

The `MovieClip.getNextHighestDepth()` method used in this example requires Flash Player 7 or later. If your SWF file includes a version 2 component, use the version 2 components DepthManager class instead of the `MovieClip.getNextHighestDepth()` method.

See also

`removeMovieClip` (MovieClip.removeMovieClip method), `unloadMovie` (MovieClip.unloadMovie method), `removeMovieClip function`

beginBitmapFill (MovieClip.beginBitmapFill method)

```
public beginBitmapFill(bmp:BitmapData, [matrix:Matrix], [repeat:Boolean],
  [smoothing:Boolean]) : Void
```

Fills a drawing area with a bitmap image. The bitmap can be repeated or tiled to fill the area.

Availability: ActionScript 1.0; Flash Player 8

Parameters

`bmp:flash.display.BitmapData` - A transparent or opaque bitmap image.

`matrix:flash.geom.Matrix` [optional] - A matrix object (of the flash.geom.Matrix class), which you can use to define transformations on the bitmap. For instance, you can use the following matrix to rotate a bitmap by 45 degrees (pi/4 radians):

```
var matrix = new flash.geom.Matrix();
matrix.rotate(Math.PI/4);
```

`repeat:Boolean` [optional] - If `true`, the bitmap image repeats in a tiled pattern. If `false`, the bitmap image does not repeat, and the edges of the bitmap are used for any fill area that extends beyond the bitmap.

For example, consider the following bitmap (a 20 x 20-pixel checkerboard pattern):

When `repeat` is set to `true` (as in the following example), the bitmap fill repeats the bitmap:

When `repeat` is set to `false`, the bitmap fill uses the edge pixels for the fill area outside of the bitmap:

`smoothing:Boolean` [optional] - If `false`, upscaled bitmap images are rendered using a nearest-neighbor algorithm and look pixelated. If `true`, upscaled bitmap images are rendered using a bilinear algorithm. Rendering using the nearest neighbor-algorithm is usually much faster. The default value for this parameter is `false`.

Example

The following code defines a simple bitmap, and then uses `beginBitmapFill()` to fill a movie clip with that bitmap tiled:

```
import flash.display.*;
import flash.geom.*;

var bmpd:BitmapData = new BitmapData(20,20);
var rect1:Rectangle = new Rectangle(0,0,10,10);
var rect2:Rectangle = new Rectangle(0, 10, 10, 20);
var rect3:Rectangle = new Rectangle(10, 0, 20, 10);
var rect4:Rectangle = new Rectangle(10, 10, 20, 20);
bmpd.fillRect(rect1, 0xAA0000FF);
bmpd.fillRect(rect2, 0xAA00FF00);
bmpd.fillRect(rect3, 0xAAFF0000);
bmpd.fillRect(rect4, 0xAA999999);

this.createEmptyMovieClip("bmp_fill_mc", this.getNextHighestDepth());
with (bmp_fill_mc) {
  matrix = new Matrix();
  matrix.rotate(Math.PI/8);
  repeat = true;
  smoothing = true;
  beginBitmapFill(bmpd, matrix, repeat, smoothing);
  moveTo(0, 0);
  lineTo(0, 60);
  lineTo(60, 60);
  lineTo(60, 0);
  lineTo(0, 0);
  endFill();
}

bmp_fill_mc._xscale = 200;
bmp_fill_mc._yscale = 200;
```

If your SWF file includes a version 2 component, use the version 2 components DepthManager class instead of the `MovieClip.getNextHighestDepth()` method, which is used in this example.

beginFill (MovieClip.beginFill method)

`public beginFill(rgb:Number, [alpha:Number]) : Void`

Indicates the beginning of a new drawing path. If an open path exists (that is, if the current drawing position does not equal the previous position that is specified in a `MovieClip.moveTo()` method) and a fill is associated with it, that path is closed with a line and then filled. This is similar to what happens when `MovieClip.endFill()` method is called.

You can extend the methods and event handlers of the MovieClip class by creating a subclass.

Availability: ActionScript 1.0; Flash Player 6

Parameters

`rgb:Number` - A hexadecimal color value; for example, red is 0xFF0000, blue is 0x0000FF. If this value is not provided or is undefined, a fill is not created.

`alpha:Number` [optional] - An integer from 0 to 100 that specifies the alpha value of the fill. If this value is not provided, 100 (solid) is used. If the value is less than 0, Flash uses 0. If the value is greater than 100, Flash uses 100.

Example

The following example creates a square with red fill on the Stage:

```
this.createEmptyMovieClip("square_mc", this.getNextHighestDepth());
square_mc.beginFill(0xFF0000);
square_mc.moveTo(10, 10);
square_mc.lineTo(100, 10);
square_mc.lineTo(100, 100);
square_mc.lineTo(10, 100);
square_mc.lineTo(10, 10);
square_mc.endFill();
```

The `MovieClip.getNextHighestDepth()` method used in this example requires Flash Player 7 or later. If your SWF file includes a version 2 component, use the version 2 components DepthManager class instead of the `MovieClip.getNextHighestDepth()` method.

An example is also in the drawingapi.fla file in the Samples\ActionScript\DrawingAPI. The following list gives typical paths to this folder:

- Windows: \Program Files\Macromedia\Flash 8\Samples and Tutorials\Samples\
- Macintosh: HD/Applications/Macromedia Flash 8/Samples and Tutorials/Samples/

See also

moveTo (MovieClip.moveTo method), endFill (MovieClip.endFill method),
beginGradientFill (MovieClip.beginGradientFill method)

beginGradientFill (MovieClip.beginGradientFill method)

```
public beginGradientFill(fillType:String, colors:Array, alphas:Array,
    ratios:Array, matrix:Object, [spreadMethod:String],
    [interpolationMethod:String], [focalPointRatio:Number]) : Void
```

Indicates the beginning of a new drawing path. If the first parameter is undefined, or if no parameters are passed, the path has no fill. If an open path exists (that is if the current drawing position does not equal the previous position specified in a MovieClip.moveTo() method), and it has a fill associated with it, that path is closed with a line and then filled. This is similar to what happens when you call MovieClip.endFill().

This method fails if any of the following conditions exist:

- The number of items in the colors, alphas, and ratios parameters are not equal.
- The fillType parameter is not "linear" or "radial".
- Any of the fields in the object for the matrix parameter are missing or invalid.

You can extend the methods and event handlers of the MovieClip class by creating a subclass.

Availability: ActionScript 1.0; Flash Player 6 - Additional parameters spreadMethod, interpolationMethod, and focalPointRatio added in Flash Player 8.

Parameters

fillType:String - Valid values are the string "linear" and the string "radial".

colors:Array - An array of RGB hexadecimal color values you can use in the gradient; for example; red is 0xFF0000, blue is 0x0000FF. You can specify up to 15 colors. For each color, ensure to specify a corresponding value in the alphas and ratios parameters.

alphas:Array - An array of alpha values for the corresponding colors in the colors array; valid values are 0 to 100. If the value is less than 0, Flash uses 0. If the value is greater than 100, Flash uses 100.

ratios:Array - An array of color distribution ratios; valid values are 0 to 255. This value defines the percentage of the width where the color is sampled at 100%. Specify a value for each value in the colors parameter.

For example, for a linear gradient that includes two colors, blue and green, the following figure illustrates the placement of the colors in the gradient based on different values in the `ratios` array:

ratios	**Gradient**
[0, 127]	
[0, 255]	
[127, 255]	

The values in the array must increase sequentially; for example, [0, 63, 127, 190, 255].

`matrix:Object` - A transformation matrix that can be in any one of three forms:

- A matrix object (supported by Flash Player 8 and later only), as defined by the flash.geom.Matrix class. The flash.geom.Matrix class includes a `createGradientBox()` method, which lets you conveniently set up the matrix for use with the `beginGradientFill()` method of MovieClip class. Macromedia recommends that you use this form of matrix for Flash Player 8 and later.

  The following example uses the `beginGradientFill()` method with a `matrix` parameter of this type:

```
import flash.geom.*

this.createEmptyMovieClip("gradient_mc",
  this.getNextHighestDepth());
with (gradient_mc)
{
  colors = [0xFF0000, 0x0000FF];
  fillType = "radial"
  alphas = [100, 100];
  ratios = [0, 0xFF];
  spreadMethod = "reflect";
  interpolationMethod = "linearRGB";
  focalPointRatio = 0.9;
  matrix = new Matrix();
  matrix.createGradientBox(100, 100, Math.PI, 0, 0);
  beginGradientFill(fillType, colors, alphas, ratios, matrix,
    spreadMethod, interpolationMethod, focalPointRatio);
  moveTo(100, 100);
  lineTo(100, 300);
  lineTo(300, 300);
  lineTo(300, 100);
  lineTo(100, 100);
  endFill();
}
```

This code draws the following image onscreen:

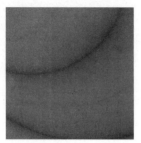

- You can use the properties a, b, c, d, e, f, g, h, and i, which can be used to describe a 3 x 3 matrix of the following form:

```
a b c
d e f
g h i
```

The following example uses the beginGradientFill() method with a matrix parameter of this type:

```
this.createEmptyMovieClip("gradient_mc",
  this.getNextHighestDepth());
with (gradient_mc)
{
  colors = [0xFF0000, 0x0000FF];
  fillType = "radial"
  alphas = [100, 100];
  ratios = [0, 0xFF];
  spreadMethod = "reflect";
  interpolationMethod = "linearRGB";
  focalPointRatio = 0.9;
  matrix = {a:200, b:0, c:0, d:0, e:200, f:0, g:200, h:200, i:1};
  beginGradientFill(fillType, colors, alphas, ratios, matrix,
  spreadMethod,
interpolationMethod, focalPointRatio);
  moveTo(100, 100);
  lineTo(100, 300);
  lineTo(300, 300);
  lineTo(300, 100);
  lineTo(100, 100);
  endFill();
}
```

This code draws the following image onscreen:

- An object with the following properties: matrixType, x, y, w, h, r.

The properties indicate the following: matrixType is the string "box", x is the horizontal position relative to the registration point of the parent clip for the upper-left corner of the gradient, y is the vertical position relative to the registration point of the parent clip for the upper-left corner of the gradient, w is the width of the gradient, h is the height of the gradient, and r is the rotation in radians of the gradient.

> **NOTE**
>
> For Flash Player 8 and later, Macromedia recommends that you define the matrix parameter in the form of a flash.geom.Matrix object (as described in the first item in the list).

The following example uses the beginGradientFill() method with a matrix parameter of this type:

```
this.createEmptyMovieClip("gradient_mc",
  this.getNextHighestDepth());
with (gradient_mc)
{
  colors = [0xFF0000, 0x0000FF];
  fillType = "radial"
  alphas = [100, 100];
  ratios = [0, 0xFF];
  spreadMethod = "reflect";
  interpolationMethod = "linearRGB";
  focalPointRatio = 0.9;
  matrix = {matrixType:"box", x:100, y:100, w:200, h:200, r:(45/
180)*Math.PI};
  beginGradientFill(fillType, colors, alphas, ratios, matrix,
    spreadMethod, interpolationMethod, focalPointRatio);
  moveTo(100, 100);
  lineTo(100, 300);
  lineTo(300, 300);
  lineTo(300, 100);
  lineTo(100, 100);
  endFill();
}
```

This code draws the following image onscreen:

spreadMethod:String [optional] - Added in Flash Player 8. Either "pad", "reflect," or "repeat," which controls the mode of the gradient fill. The default value is "pad".

For example, consider a simple linear gradient between two colors:

```
import flash.geom.*;
var fillType:String = "linear"
var colors:Array = [0xFF0000, 0x0000FF];
var alphas:Array = [100, 100];
var ratios:Array = [0x00, 0xFF];
var matrix:Matrix = new Matrix();
matrix.createGradientBox(20, 20, 0, 0, 0);
var spreadMethod:String = "pad";
this.beginGradientFill(fillType, colors, alphas, ratios, matrix,
    spreadMethod);
this.moveTo(0, 0);
this.lineTo(0, 100);
this.lineTo(100, 100);
this.lineTo(100, 0);
this.lineTo(0, 0);
this.endFill();
```

This example uses "pad" for the spread method, so the gradient fill looks like the following:

If you used "reflect" for the spread method, the gradient fill would look like the following:

If you used "repeat" for the spread method, the gradient fill would look like the following:

`interpolationMethod:String` [optional] - Added in Flash Player 8. Either "RGB" or "linearRGB". With "linearRGB", the colors are distributed linearly in the gradient. The default value is "RGB".

For example, consider a simple linear gradient between two colors (with the `spreadMethod` parameter set to "reflect"). The different interpolation methods affect the appearance as follows:

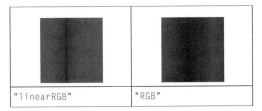

`focalPointRatio:Number` [optional] - Added in Flash Player 8. A number that controls the location of the focal point of the gradient. The value 0 means the focal point is in the center. The value 1 means the focal point is at one border of the gradient circle. The value -1 means the focal point is at the other border of the gradient circle. A value less than -1 or greater than 1 is rounded to -1 or 1. For example, the following image shows a `focalPointRatio` set to 0.75:

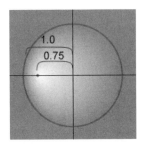

Example

The following code creates a spherical shade effect:

```
import flash.geom.*
this.createEmptyMovieClip("gradient_mc", this.getNextHighestDepth());
with (gradient_mc)
```

```
{
    fillType = "radial"
colors = [0x000000, 0xFFFFFF];
    alphas = [50, 90];
    ratios = [0, 0xFF];
    spreadMethod = "pad";
    interpolationMethod = "RGB";
focalPointRatio = 0.3;
matrix = new Matrix();
matrix.createGradientBox(100, 100, 0, 0, 0);
beginGradientFill(fillType, colors, alphas, ratios, matrix,
    spreadMethod, interpolationMethod, focalPointRatio);
moveTo(0, 0);
lineTo(0, 100);
lineTo(100, 100);
lineTo(100, 0);
lineTo(0, 0);
endFill();
}
```

This draws the following image (the image is scaled by 50%):

If your SWF file includes a version 2 component, use the version 2 components DepthManager class instead of the `MovieClip.getNextHighestDepth()` method, which is used in this example.

See also

createGradientBox (Matrix.createGradientBox method), beginFill (MovieClip.beginFill method), endFill (MovieClip.endFill method), lineStyle (MovieClip.lineStyle method), lineTo (MovieClip.lineTo method), moveTo (MovieClip.moveTo method)

blendMode (MovieClip.blendMode property)

`public blendMode : Object`

The blend mode for this movie clip. The blend mode affects the appearance of the movie clip when it is in a layer above another object onscreen.

Flash Player applies the `blendMode` property on each pixel of the movie clip. Each pixel is composed of three constituent colors (red, green, and blue), and each constituent color has a value between 0x00 and 0xFF. Flash Player compares each constituent color of one pixel in the movie clip with the corresponding color of the pixel in the background. For example, if `blendMode` is set to `"lighten"`, Flash Player compares the red value of the movie clip with the red value of the background, and uses the lighter of the two as the value for the red component of the displayed color.

The following table describes the `blendMode` settings. To set the `blendMode` property, you can use either an integer from 1 to 14 or a string. The illustrations in the table show `blendMode` values applied to a circular movie clip (2) superimposed on another onscreen object (1).

Integer value	String value	Illustration	Description
1	`"normal"`		The movie clip appears in front of the background. Pixel values of the movie clip override those of the background. Where the movie clip is transparent, the background is visible.
2	`"layer"`		Forces the creation of a temporary buffer for precomposition for the movie clip. This is done automatically if there is more than one child object in a movie clip and a `blendMode` setting other than `"normal"` is selected for the child.

Integer value	String value	Illustration	Description
3	`"multiply"`		Multiplies the values of the movie clip constituent colors by those of the background color, and then normalizes by dividing by 0xFF, resulting in darker colors. This setting is commonly used for shadows and depth effects. For example, if a constituent color (such as red) of one pixel in the movie clip and the corresponding color of the pixel in the background both have the value 0x88, the multiplied result is 0x4840. Dividing by 0xFF yields a value of 0x48 for that constituent color, which is a darker shade than that of the movie clip or that of the background.
4	`"screen"`		Multiplies the complement (inverse) of the movie clip color by the complement of the background color, resulting in a bleaching effect. This setting is commonly used for highlights or to remove black areas of the movie clip.
5	`"lighten"`		Selects the lighter of the constituent colors of the movie clip and those of the background (the ones with the larger values). This setting is commonly used for superimposing type. For example, if the movie clip has a pixel with an RGB value of 0xFFCC33, and the background pixel has an RGB value of 0xDDF800, then the resulting RGB value for the displayed pixel is 0xFFF833 (because 0xFF > 0xDD, 0xCC < 0xF8, and 0x33 > 0x00 = 33).

Integer value	String value	Illustration	Description
6	`"darken"`		Selects the darker of the constituent colors of the movie clip and those of the background (the ones with the smaller values). This setting is commonly used for superimposing type. For example, if the movie clip has a pixel with an RGB value of 0xFFCC33, and the background pixel has an RGB value of 0xDDF800, the resulting RGB value for the displayed pixel is 0xDDCC00 (because 0xFF › 0xDD, 0xCC ‹ 0xF8, and 0x33 › 0x00 = 33).
7	`"difference"`		Compares the constituent colors of the movie clip with those of its background, and subtracts the darker of the values of the two constituent colors from the lighter one. This setting is commonly used for more vibrant colors. For example, if the movie clip has a pixel with a RGB value of 0xFFCC33, and the background pixel has an RGB value of 0xDDF800, the resulting RGB value for the displayed pixel is 0x222C33 (because 0xFF - 0xDD = 0x22, 0xF8 - 0xCC = 0x2C, and 0x33 - 0x00 = 0x33).
8	`"add"`		Adds the values of the constituent colors of the movie clip to those of its background, applying a ceiling of 0xFF. This setting is commonly used for animating a lightening dissolve between two objects. For example, if the movie clip has a pixel with an RGB value of 0xAAA633, and the background pixel has an RGB value of 0xDD2200, the resulting RGB value for the displayed pixel is 0xFFC833 (because 0xAA + 0xDD › 0xFF, 0xA6 + 0x22 = 0xC8, and 0x33 + 0x00 = 0x33).

Integer value	String value	Illustration	Description
9	`"subtract"`		Subtracts the values of the constituent colors in the movie clip from those of the background, applying a floor of 0. This setting is commonly used for animating a darkening dissolve between two objects. For example, if the movie clip has a pixel with an RGB value of 0xAA2233, and the background pixel has an RGB value of 0xDDA600, the resulting RGB value for the displayed pixel is 0x338400 (because 0xDD - 0xAA = 0x33, 0xA6 - 0x22 = 0x84, and 0x00 - 0x33 < 0x00).
10	`"invert"`		Inverts the background.
11	`"alpha"`		Applies the alpha value of each pixel of the movie clip to the background. This requires the "layer" `blendMode` setting to be applied to a parent movie clip. For example, in the illustration, the parent movie clip, which is a white background, has `blendMode = "layer"`.
12	`"erase"`		Erases the background based on the alpha value of the movie clip. This requires the "layer" `blendMode` to be applied to a parent movie clip. For example, in the illustration, the parent movie clip, which is a white background, has `blendMode = "layer"`.

Integer value	String value	Illustration	Description
13	`"overlay"`		Adjusts the color of each bitmap based on the darkness of the background. If the background is lighter than 50% gray, the movie clip and background colors are screened, which results in a lighter color. If the background is darker than 50% gray, the colors are multiplied, which results in a darker color. This setting is commonly used for shading effects.
14	`"hardlight"`		Adjusts the color of each bitmap based on the darkness of the movie clip. If the movie clip is lighter than 50% gray, the movie clip and background colors are screened, which results in a lighter color. If the movie clip is darker than 50% gray, the colors are multiplied, which results in a darker color. This setting is commonly used for shading effects.

If you attempt to set the `blendMode` property to any other value, Flash Player sets it to `"normal"`.

However, if you set the property to an integer, Flash Player converts the value to the corresponding string version:

```
this.createEmptyMovieClip("mclip", this.getNextHighestDepth());
mclip.blendMode = 8;
trace (mclip.blendMode) // add
```

Availability: ActionScript 1.0; Flash Player 8

Example

The following example sets up two movie clips with gradient fills, and changes the blend mode of the one in the foreground every second. In order to have the `"alpha"` blend mode show up with an effect, the gradient for the mc2 movie clip includes a range of alpha ratios, and the `"layer"` blend mode is applied to the parent movie clip (`this.blendMode="layer"`).

```
this.createEmptyMovieClip("mc1", this.getNextHighestDepth());
this.createEmptyMovieClip("mc2", this.getNextHighestDepth());
this.blendMode="layer";
this.createTextField("blendLabel", this.getNextHighestDepth(), 50, 150,
100, 100)

fillClip(mc1, 0x00AA00, 0x22FFFF, 100, 100)
```

```
fillClip(mc2, 0xFF0000, 0x2211FF, 100, 50)
mc2._x = 33;
mc2._y = 33;

var blendModeIndex = 0;

setInterval(changeBlendMode, 1000);
function changeBlendMode()
{
   mc2.blendMode = blendModeIndex % 14 + 1 ;
      // values 1 - 14
blendLabel.text = (blendModeIndex% 14 + 1) + ": " + mc2.blendMode;
   blendModeIndex++;
}

function fillClip(mc:MovieClip, color1:Number, color2:Number,
      alpha1:Number, alpha2: Number)
{
   matrix = {a:100, b:0, c:0, d:0, e:100, f:0, g:50, h:20, i:1};
   mc.beginGradientFill("linear", [color1, color2], [alpha1, alpha2], [0,
0xFF], matrix);
   mc.lineStyle(8,0x888888,100)
   mc.moveTo(0, 0);
   mc.lineTo(0, 100);
   mc.lineTo(100, 100);
   mc.lineTo(100, 0);
   mc.lineTo(0, 0);
   mc.endFill();
}
```

If your SWF file includes a version 2 component, use the version 2 components DepthManager class instead of the `MovieClip.getNextHighestDepth()` method, which is used in the previous example.

cacheAsBitmap (MovieClip.cacheAsBitmap property)

`public cacheAsBitmap : Boolean`

If set to `true`, Flash Player caches an internal bitmap representation of the movie clip. This can increase performance for movie clips that contain complex vector content.

All vector data for a movie clip that has a cached bitmap is drawn to the bitmap instead of to the main Stage. The bitmap is then copied to the main Stage as unstretched, unrotated pixels snapped to the nearest pixel boundaries. Pixels are mapped one to one with the parent object. If the bounds of the bitmap change, the bitmap is recreated instead of being stretched.

No internal bitmap is created unless the `cacheAsBitmap` property is set to `true`.

After you set a movie clip's cacheAsBitmap property to true, the rendering does not change, however the movie clip performs pixel snapping automatically. The animation speed can be significantly faster, depending on the complexity of the vector content.

The cacheAsBitmap property is automatically set to true whenever you apply a filter to a movie clip (when its filter array is not empty). If a movie clip has a filter applied to it, cacheAsBitmap is reported as true for that movie clip, even if you set the property to false. If you clear all filters for a movie clip, the cacheAsBitmap setting changes to what it was last *set* to.

In the following cases a movie clip does not use a bitmap even if the cacheAsBitmap property is set to true, and instead renders the movie clip from vector data:

- The bitmap is too large: greater than 2880 pixels in either direction.
- The bitmap fails to allocate memory (due to an out of memory error).

The cacheAsBitmap property is best used with movie clips that have mostly static content and that do not scale and rotate frequently. With such movie clips, cacheAsBitmap can lead to performance increases when the movie clip is translated (when its *x* and *y* position is changed).

Availability: ActionScript 1.0; Flash Player 8

Example

The following example applies a drop shadow to a movie clip instance. It then traces the value of the `cacheAsBitmap` property which is set to `true` when a filter is applied.

```
import flash.filters.DropShadowFilter;

var container:MovieClip = setUpShape();
trace(container.cacheAsBitmap); // false
var dropShadow:DropShadowFilter = new DropShadowFilter(6, 45, 0x000000, 50,
  5, 5, 1, 2, false, false, false);
container.filters = new Array(dropShadow);
trace(container.cacheAsBitmap); // true

function setUpShape():MovieClip {
  var mc:MovieClip = this.createEmptyMovieClip("container",
  this.getNextHighestDepth());
  mc._x = 10;
  mc._y = 10;
  var w:Number = 50;
  var h:Number = 50;
  mc.beginFill(0xFFCC00);
  mc.lineTo(w, 0);
  mc.lineTo(w, h);
  mc.lineTo(0, h);
  mc.lineTo(0, 0);
  mc.endFill();
  return mc;
}
```

See also

opaqueBackground (MovieClip.opaqueBackground property), cacheAsBitmap (MovieClip.cacheAsBitmap property)

clear (MovieClip.clear method)

`public clear() : Void`

Removes all the graphics created during runtime by using the movie clip draw methods, including line styles specified with `MovieClip.lineStyle()`. Shapes and lines that are manually drawn during authoring time (with the Flash drawing tools) are unaffected.

Availability: ActionScript 1.0; Flash Player 6

Example

The following example draws a box on the Stage. When the user clicks the box graphic, it removes the graphic from the Stage.

```
this.createEmptyMovieClip("box_mc", this.getNextHighestDepth());
box_mc.onRelease = function() {
  this.clear();
};
drawBox(box_mc, 10, 10, 320, 240);
function drawBox(mc:MovieClip, x:Number, y:Number, w:Number, h:Number):Void
  {
  mc.lineStyle(0);
  mc.beginFill(0xEEEEEE);
  mc.moveTo(x, y);
  mc.lineTo(x+w, y);
  mc.lineTo(x+w, y+h);
  mc.lineTo(x, y+h);
  mc.lineTo(x, y);
  mc.endFill();
}
```

The `MovieClip.getNextHighestDepth()` method used in this example requires Flash Player 7 or later. If your SWF file includes a version 2 component, use the version 2 components DepthManager class instead of the `MovieClip.getNextHighestDepth()` method.

An example is also in the drawingapi.fla file in the Samples\ActionScript\DrawingAPI folder. The following list gives typical paths to this folder:

- Windows: \Program Files\Macromedia\Flash 8\Samples and Tutorials\Samples\ActionScript

- Macintosh: HD/Applications/Macromedia Flash 8/Samples and Tutorials/Samples/ActionScript

See also

`lineStyle (MovieClip.lineStyle method)`

createEmptyMovieClip (MovieClip.createEmptyMovieClip method)

`public createEmptyMovieClip(name:String, depth:Number) : MovieClip`

Creates an empty movie clip as a child of an existing movie clip. This method behaves similarly to the `attachMovie()` method, but you don't need to provide an external linkage identifier for the new movie clip. The registration point for a newly created empty movie clip is the upper-left corner. This method fails if any of the parameters are missing.

You can extend the methods and event handlers of the MovieClip class by creating a subclass.

Availability: ActionScript 1.0; Flash Player 6

Parameters

name:String - A string that identifies the instance name of the new movie clip.

depth:Number - An integer that specifies the depth of the new movie clip.

Returns

MovieClip - A reference to the newly created movie clip.

Example

The following example creates an empty MovieClip named container, creates a new TextField inside of it, and then sets the new TextField.text property.

```
var container:MovieClip = this.createEmptyMovieClip("container",
  this.getNextHighestDepth());
var label:TextField = container.createTextField("label", 1, 0, 0, 150, 20);
label.text = "Hello World";
```

The MovieClip.getNextHighestDepth() method used in this example requires Flash Player 7 or later. If your SWF file includes a version 2 component, use the version 2 components DepthManager class instead of the MovieClip.getNextHighestDepth() method.

See also

attachMovie (MovieClip.attachMovie method)

createTextField (MovieClip.createTextField method)

```
public createTextField(instanceName:String, depth:Number, x:Number,
  y:Number, width:Number, height:Number) : TextField
```

Creates a new, empty text field as a child of the movie clip on which you call this method. You can use the createTextField() method to create text fields while a SWF file plays. The depth parameter determines the new text field's depth level (z-order position) in the movie clip. Each depth level can contain only one object. If you create a new text field on a depth that already has a text field, the new text field replaces the existing text field. To avoid overwriting existing text fields, use MovieClip.getInstanceAtDepth() method to determine whether a specific depth is already occupied, or the MovieClip.getNextHighestDepth() method to determine the highest unoccupied depth. The text field is positioned at (x, y) with dimensions width by *height*. The x and y parameters are relative to the container movie clip; these parameters correspond to the _x and _y properties of the text field. The width and height parameters correspond to the _width and _height properties of the text field.

The default properties of a text field are as follows:

```
type = "dynamic"
border = false
background = false
password = false
multiline = false
html = false
embedFonts = false
selectable = true
wordWrap = false
mouseWheelEnabled = true
condenseWhite = false
restrict = null
variable = null
maxChars = null
styleSheet = undefined
tabInded = undefined
```

A text field created with `createTextField()` receives the following default TextFormat object settings:

```
font = "Times New Roman" // "Times" on Mac OS
size = 12
color = 0x000000
bold = false
italic = false
underline = false
url = ""
target = ""
align = "left"
leftMargin = 0
rightMargin = 0
indent = 0
leading = 0
blockIndent = 0
bullet = false
display = block
tabStops = [] // (empty array)
```

You can extend the methods and event handlers of the MovieClip class by creating a subclass.

Availability: ActionScript 1.0; Flash Player 6 - In Flash Player 8, this method returns a reference to the TextField object created, instead of void.

Parameters

`instanceName`:String - A string that identifies the instance name of the new text field.

`depth`:Number - A positive integer that specifies the depth of the new text field.

`x`:Number - An integer that specifies the *x* coordinate of the new text field.

y:Number - An integer that specifies the *y* coordinate of the new text field.

width:Number - A positive integer that specifies the width of the new text field.

height:Number - A positive integer that specifies the height of the new text field.

Returns

TextField - Flash Player 8 returns a reference to the TextField object that is created. Flash Player versions earlier than 8 return void.

Example

The following example creates a text field with a width of 300, a height of 100, an *x*coordinate of 100, a *y* coordinate of 100, no border, red, and underlined text:

```
this.createTextField("my_txt", 1, 100, 100, 300, 100);
my_txt.multiline = true;
my_txt.wordWrap = true;
var my_fmt:TextFormat = new TextFormat();
my_fmt.color = 0xFF0000;
my_fmt.underline = true;
my_txt.text = "This is my first test field object text.";
my_txt.setTextFormat(my_fmt);
```

An example is also in the animation.fla file in the Samples\ActionScriptAnimation folder. The following list gives typical paths to this folder:

- Windows: \Program Files\Macromedia\Flash 8\Samples and Tutorials\Samples\
- Macintosh: HD/Applications/Macromedia Flash 8/Samples and Tutorials/Samples/

See also

getInstanceAtDepth (MovieClip.getInstanceAtDepth method), getNextHighestDepth (MovieClip.getNextHighestDepth method), TextFormat

_currentframe (MovieClip._currentframe property)

public _currentframe : Number [read-only]

Returns the number of the frame in which the playhead is located in the movie clip's timeline.

Availability: ActionScript 1.0; Flash Player 4

Example

The following example uses the _currentframe property to direct the playhead of the actionClip_mc movie clip to advance five frames ahead of its current location:

actionClip_mc.gotoAndStop(actionClip_mc._currentframe + 5);

---

curveTo (MovieClip.curveTo method)

```
public curveTo(controlX:Number, controlY:Number, anchorX:Number,
  anchorY:Number) : Void
```

Draws a curve using the current line style from the current drawing position to (anchorX, anchorY) using the control point that ((controlX, controlY) specifies. The current drawing position is then set to (anchorX, anchorY). If the movie clip that you are drawing in contains content that was created with the Flash drawing tools, calls to the curveTo() method are drawn underneath this content. If you call the curveTo() method before any calls to the moveTo() method, the current drawing position is set to the default (0,0). If any of the parameters are missing, this method fails and the current drawing position is not changed.

You can extend the methods and event handlers of the MovieClip class by creating a subclass.

Availability: ActionScript 1.0; Flash Player 6

Parameters

controlX:Number - An integer that specifies the horizontal position of the control point relative to the registration point of the parent movie clip.

controlY:Number - An integer that specifies the vertical position of the control point relative to the registration point of the parent movie clip.

anchorX:Number - An integer that specifies the horizontal position of the next anchor point relative to the registration point of the parent movie clip.

anchorY:Number - An integer that specifies the vertical position of the next anchor point relative to the registration point of the parent movie clip.

Example

The following example draws a nearly circular curve with a solid blue hairline stroke and a solid red fill:

```
this.createEmptyMovieClip("circle_mc", 1);
with (circle_mc) {
  lineStyle(0, 0x0000FF, 100);
  beginFill(0xFF0000);
  moveTo(0, 100);
  curveTo(0,200,100,200);
  curveTo(200,200,200,100);
  curveTo(200,0,100,0);
  curveTo(0,0,0,100);
  endFill();
}
```

The curve drawn in this example is a quadratic Bezier curve. Quadratic Bezier curves consist of two anchor points and a control point. The curve interpolates the two anchor points, and curves toward the control point.

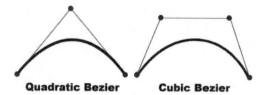

Quadratic Bezier   **Cubic Bezier**

The following script uses the curveTo() method and the Math class to create a circle:

```
this.createEmptyMovieClip("circle2_mc", 2);
circle2_mc.lineStyle(0, 0x000000);
drawCircle(circle2_mc, 100, 100, 100);
function drawCircle(mc:MovieClip, x:Number, y:Number, r:Number):Void {
  mc.moveTo(x+r, y);
  mc.curveTo(r+x, Math.tan(Math.PI/8)*r+y, Math.sin(Math.PI/4)*r+x,
Math.sin(Math.PI/4)*r+y);
  mc.curveTo(Math.tan(Math.PI/8)*r+x, r+y, x, r+y);
  mc.curveTo(-Math.tan(Math.PI/8)*r+x, r+y, -Math.sin(Math.PI/4)*r+x,
Math.sin(Math.PI/4)*r+y);
  mc.curveTo(-r+x, Math.tan(Math.PI/8)*r+y, -r+x, y);
  mc.curveTo(-r+x, -Math.tan(Math.PI/8)*r+y, -Math.sin(Math.PI/4)*r+x,
-Math.sin(Math.PI/4)*r+y);
  mc.curveTo(-Math.tan(Math.PI/8)*r+x, -r+y, x, -r+y);
  mc.curveTo(Math.tan(Math.PI/8)*r+x, -r+y, Math.sin(Math.PI/4)*r+x,
-Math.sin(Math.PI/4)*r+y);
  mc.curveTo(r+x, -Math.tan(Math.PI/8)*r+y, r+x, y);
}
```

An example is also in the drawingapi.fla file in the Samples\ActionScript\DrawingAPI. The following list gives typical paths to this folder:

- Windows: \Program Files\Macromedia\Flash 8\Samples and Tutorials\Samples\
- Macintosh: HD/Applications/Macromedia Flash 8/Samples and Tutorials/Samples/

See also

beginFill (MovieClip.beginFill method), createEmptyMovieClip
(MovieClip.createEmptyMovieClip method), endFill (MovieClip.endFill method),
lineStyle (MovieClip.lineStyle method), lineTo (MovieClip.lineTo method),
moveTo (MovieClip.moveTo method), Math

_droptarget (MovieClip._droptarget property)

`public _droptarget : String [read-only]`

Returns the absolute path in slash-syntax notation of the movie clip instance on which this movie clip was dropped. The _droptarget property always returns a path that starts with a slash (/). To compare the _droptarget property of an instance to a reference, use the `eval()` function to convert the returned value from slash syntax to a dot-syntax reference.

> **NOTE**
> You must perform this conversion if you are using ActionScript 2.0, which does not support slash syntax.

Availability: ActionScript 1.0; Flash Player 4

Example

The following example evaluates the _droptarget property of the `garbage_mc` movie clip instance and uses `eval()` to convert it from slash syntax to a dot syntax reference. The `garbage_mc` reference is then compared to the reference to the `trashcan_mc` movie clip instance. If the two references are equivalent, the visibility of `garbage_mc` is set to `false`. If they are not equivalent, the `garbage` instance resets to its original position.

```
origX = garbage_mc._x;
origY = garbage_mc._y;
garbage_mc.onPress = function() {
  this.startDrag();
};
garbage_mc.onRelease = function() {
  this.stopDrag();
  if (eval(this._droptarget) == trashcan_mc) {
  this._visible = false;
  } else {
  this._x = origX;
  this._y = origY;
  }
};
```

See also

`startDrag (MovieClip.startDrag method)`, `stopDrag (MovieClip.stopDrag method)`, `eval function`

duplicateMovieClip (MovieClip.duplicateMovieClip method)

`public duplicateMovieClip(name:String, depth:Number, [initObject:Object]) : MovieClip`

Creates an instance of the specified movie clip while the SWF file is playing. Duplicated movie clips always start playing at Frame 1, no matter what frame the original movie clip is on when the `duplicateMovieClip()` method is called. Variables in the parent movie clip are not copied into the duplicate movie clip. Movie clips that are created with the `duplicateMovieClip()` method are not duplicated if you call the `duplicateMovieClip()` method on their parent. If the parent movie clip is deleted, the duplicate movie clip is also deleted. If you used `MovieClip.loadMovie()` or the MovieClipLoader class to load a movie clip, the contents of the SWF file are not duplicated. This means that you cannot save bandwidth by loading a JPEG, GIF, PNG, or SWF file and then duplicating the movie clip.

Contrast this method with the global function version of `duplicateMovieClip()`. The global version of this method requires a parameter that specifies the target movie clip to duplicate. Such a parameter is unnecessary for the MovieClip class version, because the target of the method is the movie clip instance on which the method is invoked. Moreover, the global version of `duplicateMovieClip()` supports neither the `initobject` parameter nor the return value of a reference to the newly created MovieClip instance.

Availability: ActionScript 1.0; Flash Player 5

Parameters

`name:String` - A unique identifier for the duplicate movie clip.

`depth:Number` - A unique integer specifying the depth at which the new movie clip is placed. Use depth -16384 to place the new movie clip instance beneath all content that is created in the authoring environment. Values between -16383 and -1, inclusive, are reserved for use by the authoring environment and should not be used with this method. The remaining valid depth values range from 0 to 1048575, inclusive.

`initObject:Object` [optional] - (Supported for Flash Player 6 and later.) An object that contains properties with which to populate the duplicated movie clip. This parameter allows dynamically created movie clips to receive clip parameters. If `initObject` is not an object, it is ignored. All properties of `initObject` are copied into the new instance. The properties specified with `initObject` are available to the constructor function.

Returns

`MovieClip` - A reference to the duplicated movie clip (supported for Flash Player 6 and later).

Example

The following example duplicates a newly created MovieClip a number of times and traces the target for each duplicate.

```
var container:MovieClip = setUpContainer();
var ln:Number = 10;
```

```
var spacer:Number = 1;
var duplicate:MovieClip;
for(var i:Number = 1; i < ln; i++) {
  var newY:Number = i * (container._height + spacer);
  duplicate = container.duplicateMovieClip("clip-" + i, i, {_y:newY});
  trace(duplicate); // _level0.clip-[number]
}

function setUpContainer():MovieClip {
  var mc:MovieClip = this.createEmptyMovieClip("container",
  this.getNextHighestDepth());
  var w:Number = 100;
  var h:Number = 20;
  mc.beginFill(0x333333);
  mc.lineTo(w, 0);
  mc.lineTo(w, h);
  mc.lineTo(0, h);
  mc.lineTo(0, 0);
  mc.endFill();
  return mc;
}
```

The `MovieClip.getNextHighestDepth()` method used in this example requires Flash Player 7 or later. If your SWF file includes a version 2 component, use the version 2 components DepthManager class instead of the `MovieClip.getNextHighestDepth()` method.

See also

`loadMovie (MovieClip.loadMovie method)`, `removeMovieClip (MovieClip.removeMovieClip method)`, `duplicateMovieClip function`

enabled (MovieClip.enabled property)

`public enabled : Boolean`

A Boolean value that indicates whether a movie clip is enabled. The default value of `enabled` is `true`. If `enabled` is set to `false`, the movie clip's callback methods and `onaction` event handlers are no longer invoked, and the Over, Down, and Up frames are disabled. The `enabled` property does not affect the Timeline of the movie clip; if a movie clip is playing, it continues to play. The movie clip continues to receive movie clip events (for example, `mouseDown`, `mouseUp`, `keyDown`, and `keyUp`).

The `enabled` property only governs the button-like properties of a movie clip. You can change the `enabled` property at any time; the modified movie clip is immediately enabled or disabled. The `enabled` property can be read out of a prototype object. If `enabled` is set to `false`, the object is not included in automatic tab ordering.

Availability: ActionScript 1.0; Flash Player 6

Example

The following example disables the `circle_mc` movie clip when the user clicks it:

```
circle_mc.onRelease = function() {
  trace("disabling the "+this._name+" movie clip.");
  this.enabled = false;
};
```

endFill (MovieClip.endFill method)

```
public endFill() : Void
```

Applies a fill to the lines and curves that were since the last call to `beginFill()` or `beginGradientFill()`. Flash uses the fill that was specified in the previous call to `beginFill()` or `beginGradientFill()`. If the current drawing position does not equal the previous position specified in a `moveTo()` method and a fill is defined, the path is closed with a line and then filled.

Availability: ActionScript 1.0; Flash Player 6

Example

The following example creates a square with red fill on the Stage:

```
this.createEmptyMovieClip("square_mc", this.getNextHighestDepth());
square_mc.beginFill(0xFF0000);
square_mc.moveTo(10, 10);
square_mc.lineTo(100, 10);
square_mc.lineTo(100, 100);
square_mc.lineTo(10, 100);
square_mc.lineTo(10, 10);
square_mc.endFill();
```

The `MovieClip.getNextHighestDepth()` method used in this example requires Flash Player 7 or later. If your SWF file includes a version 2 component, use the version 2 components DepthManager class instead of the `MovieClip.getNextHighestDepth()` method.

An example is also in the drawingapi.fla file in the Samples\ActionScript\DrawingAPI. The following list gives typical paths to this folder:

- Windows: \Program Files\Macromedia\Flash 8\Samples and Tutorials\Samples\
- Macintosh: HD/Applications/Macromedia Flash 8/Samples and Tutorials/Samples/

See also

`beginFill (MovieClip.beginFill method)`, `beginGradientFill (MovieClip.beginGradientFill method)`, `moveTo (MovieClip.moveTo method)`

filters (MovieClip.filters property)

`public filters : Array`

An indexed array containing each filter object currently associated with the movie clip. The flash.filters package contains several classes that define specific filters you can use.

Filters can be applied in the Flash authoring tool at design-time, or at runtime using ActionScript code. To apply a filter using ActionScript, you must make a temporary copy of the entire `MovieClip.filters` array, modify the temporary array, and then assign the value of the temporary array back to the `MovieClip.filters` array. You cannot directly add a new filter object to the `MovieClip.filters` array. The following code has no effect on the target movie clip, named `myMC`:

`myMC.filters[0].push(myDropShadow);`

To add a filter using ActionScript, you must follow the following steps (assume that the target movie clip is named myMC):

- Create a new filter object using the constructor function of your chosen filter class.
- Assign the value of the `myMC.filters` array to a temporary array, such as one named `myFilters`.
- Add the new filter object to the temporary array, `myFilters`.
- Assign the value of the temporary array to the `myMC.filters` array.

If the `filters` array is empty, you need not use a temporary array. Instead, you can directly assign an array literal that contains one or more filter objects that you created.

To modify an existing filter object, whether it was created at design-time or at runtime, you must use the technique of modifying a copy of the `filters` array:

- Assign the value of the `myMC.filters` array to a temporary array, such as one named `myFilters`.

- Modify the property using the temporary array, `myFilters`. For example, if you want to set the quality property of the first filter in the array, you could use the following code: `myList[0].quality = 1;`

- Assign the value of the temporary array to the `myMC.filters` array.

To clear the filters for a movie clip, set `filters` to an empty array (`[]`).

At load time, if a movie clip has an associated filter, it is marked to cache itself as a transparent bitmap. From this point forward, as long as the movie clip has a valid filter list, the player caches the movie clip as a bitmap. This source bitmap is used as a source image for the filter effects. Each movie clip usually has two bitmaps: one with the original unfiltered source movie clip and another for the final image after filtering. The final image is used when rendering. As long as the movie clip does not change, the final image does not need updating.

If you are working with a `filters` array that contains multiple filters and you need to track the type of filter assigned to each array index, you can maintain your own `filters` array and use a separate data structure to track the type of filter associated with each array index. There is no simple way to determine the type of filter associated with each `filters` array index.

Availability: ActionScript 1.0; Flash Player 8

Example

The following example adds a drop shadow filter to a movie clip named `myMC`:

```
var myDropFilter = new flash.filters.DropShadowFilter();
var myFilters:Array = myMC.filters;
myFilters.push(myDropFilter);
myMC.filters = myFilters;
```

The following example changes the `quality` setting of the first filter in the array to 15 (this example works only if at least one filter object has been associated with the `myMC` movie clip):

```
var myList:Array = myMC.filters;
myList[0].quality = 15;
myMC.filters = myList;
```

See also

focusEnabled (MovieClip.focusEnabled property)

`public focusEnabled : Boolean`

If the value is `undefined` or `false`, a movie clip cannot receive input focus unless it is a button. If the `focusEnabled` property value is `true`, a movie clip can receive input focus even if it is not a button.

Availability: ActionScript 1.0; Flash Player 6

Example

The following example sets the `focusEnabled` property for the movie clip `my_mc` to `false`:

```
my_mc.focusEnabled = false;
```

_focusrect (MovieClip._focusrect property)

`public _focusrect : Boolean`

A Boolean value that specifies whether a movie clip has a yellow rectangle around it when it has keyboard focus. This property can override the global `_focusrect` property. The default value of the `_focusrect` property of a movie clip instance is `null`; this means that the movie clip instance does not override the global `_focusrect` property. If the `_focusrect` property of a movie clip instance is set to `true` or `false`, it overrides the setting of the global `_focusrect` property for the single movie clip instance.

In Flash Player 4 or Flash Player 5 SWF files, the `_focusrect` property controls the global `_focusrect` property. It is a Boolean value. This behavior was changed in Flash Player 6 and later to permit the customization of `_focusrect` on an individual movie-clip basis.

If the `_focusrect` property is set to `false`, keyboard navigation for that movie clip is limited to the Tab key. All other keys, including the Enter and arrow keys, are ignored. To restore full keyboard navigation, you must set `_focusrect` to `true`.

Availability: ActionScript 1.0; Flash Player 6

Example

This example demonstrates how to hide the yellow rectangle around a specified movie clip instance in a SWF file when it has focus in a browser window. Create three movie clips called `mc1_mc`, `mc2_mc`, and `mc3_mc`, and add the following ActionScript on Frame 1 of the Timeline:

```
mc1_mc._focusrect = true;
mc2_mc._focusrect = false;
mc3_mc._focusrect = true;

mc1_mc.onRelease = traceOnRelease;
```

```
mc3_mc.onRelease = traceOnRelease;

function traceOnRelease() {
  trace(this._name);
}
```

Test the SWF file in a browser window by selecting File > Publish Preview > HTML. Give the SWF focus by clicking it in the browser window, and press Tab to focus each instance. You cannot execute code for this movie clip in the browser by pressing Enter or the Spacebar when _focusrect is disabled.

Additionally, you can test your SWF file in the test environment. Select Control > Disable Keyboard Shortcuts from the main menu in the test environment. This allows you to view the focus rectangle around the instances in the SWF file.

See also

_focusrect property, _focusrect (Button._focusrect property)

_framesloaded (MovieClip._framesloaded property)

```
public _framesloaded : Number [read-only]
```

The number of frames that are loaded from a streaming SWF file. This property is useful for determining whether the contents of a specific frame, and all the frames before it, are loaded and are available locally in the browser. It is also useful for monitoring the downloading of large SWF files. For example, you might want to display a message to users indicating that the SWF file is loading until a specified frame in the SWF file has finished loading.

Availability: ActionScript 1.0; Flash Player 4

Example

The following example uses the _framesloaded property to start a SWF file when all the frames are loaded. If all the frames aren't loaded, the _xscale property of the bar_mc movie clip instance is increased proportionally to create a progress bar.

Enter the following ActionScript in Frame 1 of the Timeline:

```
var pctLoaded:Number = Math.round(this.getBytesLoaded()/
  this.getBytesTotal()*100);
bar_mc._xscale = pctLoaded;
```

Add the following code on Frame 2:

```
if (this._framesloaded < this._totalframes) {
  this.gotoAndPlay(1);
} else {
  this.gotoAndStop(3);
}
```

Place your content on or after Frame 3. Then add the following code on Frame 3:

```
stop();
```

See also

```
MovieClipLoader
```

getBounds (MovieClip.getBounds method)

```
public getBounds(bounds:Object) : Object
```

Returns properties that are the minimum and maximum *x* and *y* coordinate values of the movie clip, based on the `bounds` parameter.

> **NOTE**
>
> Use `MovieClip.localToGlobal()` and `MovieClip.globalToLocal()` methods to convert the movie clip's local coordinates, or Stage coordinates to local coordinates, respectively.

You can extend the methods and event handlers of the MovieClip class by creating a subclass.

Availability: ActionScript 1.0; Flash Player 5

Parameters

`bounds:Object` - The target path of the Timeline whose coordinate system you want to use as a reference point.

Returns

`Object` - An object with the properties `xMin`, `xMax`, `yMin`, and `yMax`.

Example

The following example creates a movie clip called `square_mc`. The code draws a square for that movie clip and uses `MovieClip.getBounds()` to display the coordinate values of the instance in the Output panel.

```
this.createEmptyMovieClip("square_mc", 1);
square_mc._x = 10;
square_mc._y = 10;
square_mc.beginFill(0xFF0000);
square_mc.moveTo(0, 0);
square_mc.lineTo(100, 0);
square_mc.lineTo(100, 100);
square_mc.lineTo(0, 100);
square_mc.lineTo(0, 0);
square_mc.endFill();

var bounds_obj:Object = square_mc.getBounds(this);
for (var i in bounds_obj) {
```

```
    trace(i+" --> "+bounds_obj[i]);
}
```

The following information appears in the Output panel:

```
yMax --> 110
yMin --> 10
xMax --> 110
xMin --> 10
```

See also

getRect (MovieClip.getRect method), globalToLocal (MovieClip.globalToLocal method), localToGlobal (MovieClip.localToGlobal method)

getBytesLoaded (MovieClip.getBytesLoaded method)

public getBytesLoaded() : Number

Returns the number of bytes that have already loaded (streamed) for the movie clip. You can compare this value with the value returned by MovieClip.getBytesTotal() to determine what percentage of a movie clip has loaded.

You can extend the methods and event handlers of the MovieClip class by creating a subclass.

Availability: ActionScript 1.0; Flash Player 5

Returns

Number - An integer that indicates the number of bytes loaded.

Example

The following example uses the _framesloaded property to start a SWF file when all the frames are loaded. If all the frames aren't loaded, the _xscale property of the loader movie clip instance is increased proportionally to create a progress bar.

Enter the following ActionScript on Frame 1 of the Timeline:

```
var pctLoaded:Number = Math.round(this.getBytesLoaded()/
  this.getBytesTotal() * 100);
bar_mc._xscale = pctLoaded;
```

Add the following code on Frame 2:

```
if (this._framesloaded<this._totalframes) {
  this.gotoAndPlay(1);
} else {
  this.gotoAndStop(3);
}
```

Place your content on or after Frame 3, and then add the following code on Frame 3:

```
stop();
```

See also

```
getBytesTotal (MovieClip.getBytesTotal method)
```

getBytesTotal (MovieClip.getBytesTotal method)

```
public getBytesTotal() : Number
```

Returns the size, in bytes, of the movie clip. For movie clips that are external (the root SWF file or a movie clip that is being loaded into a target or a level), the return value is the uncompressed size of the SWF file.

You can extend the methods and event handlers of the MovieClip class by creating a subclass.

Availability: ActionScript 1.0; Flash Player 5

Returns

`Number` - An integer that indicates the total size, in bytes, of the movie clip.

Example

The following example uses the `_framesloaded` property to start a SWF file when all the frames are loaded. If all the frames aren't loaded, the `_xscale` property of the movie clip instance `loader` is increased proportionally to create a progress bar.

Enter the following ActionScript on Frame 1 of the Timeline:

```
var pctLoaded:Number = Math.round(this.getBytesLoaded()/
  this.getBytesTotal()*100);
bar_mc._xscale = pctLoaded;
```

Add the following code on Frame 2:

```
if (this._framesloaded<this._totalframes) {
  this.gotoAndPlay(1);
} else {
  this.gotoAndStop(3);
}
```

Place your content on or after Frame 3. Then add the following code on Frame 3:

```
stop();
```

See also

getBytesLoaded (MovieClip.getBytesLoaded method)

getDepth (MovieClip.getDepth method)

`public getDepth() : Number`

Returns the depth of the movie clip instance.

Each movie clip, button, and text field has a unique depth associated with it that determines how the object appears in front of or in back of other objects. Objects with larger values for depths appear in front. Content created at design time (in the authoring tool) starts at depth -16383.

You can extend the methods and event handlers of the MovieClip class by creating a subclass.

Availability: ActionScript 1.0; Flash Player 6

Returns

`Number` - The depth of the movie clip.

Example

The following code traces the depth of all movie clip instances on the Stage:

```
for (var i in this) {
  if (typeof (this[i]) == "movieclip") {
    trace("movie clip '"+this[i]._name+"' is at depth "+this[i].getDepth());
  }
}
```

See also

getInstanceAtDepth (MovieClip.getInstanceAtDepth method), getNextHighestDepth (MovieClip.getNextHighestDepth method), swapDepths (MovieClip.swapDepths method), getDepth (TextField.getDepth method), getDepth (Button.getDepth method)

getInstanceAtDepth (MovieClip.getInstanceAtDepth method)

`public getInstanceAtDepth(depth:Number) : MovieClip`

Determines if a particular depth is already occupied by a movie clip. You can use this method before using `MovieClip.attachMovie()`, `MovieClip.duplicateMovieClip()`, or `MovieClip.createEmptyMovieClip()` to determine if the depth parameter you want to pass to any of these methods already contains a movie clip.

You can extend the methods and event handlers of the MovieClip class by creating a subclass.

Availability: ActionScript 1.0; Flash Player 7

Parameters

depth:Number - An integer that specifies the depth level to query.

Returns

MovieClip - A reference to the MovieClip instance located at the specified depth, or undefined if there is no movie clip at that depth.

Example

The following example displays the depth occupied by the triangle movie clip instance in the Output panel:

```
this.createEmptyMovieClip("triangle", 1);

triangle.beginFill(0x0000FF, 100);
triangle.moveTo(100, 100);
triangle.lineTo(100, 150);
triangle.lineTo(150, 100);
triangle.lineTo(100, 100);

trace(this.getInstanceAtDepth(1)); // output: _level0.triangle
```

See also

attachMovie (MovieClip.attachMovie method), duplicateMovieClip (MovieClip.duplicateMovieClip method), createEmptyMovieClip (MovieClip.createEmptyMovieClip method), getDepth (MovieClip.getDepth method), getNextHighestDepth (MovieClip.getNextHighestDepth method), swapDepths (MovieClip.swapDepths method)

getNextHighestDepth (MovieClip.getNextHighestDepth method)

```
public getNextHighestDepth() : Number
```

Determines a depth value that you can pass to MovieClip.attachMovie(), MovieClip.duplicateMovieClip(), or MovieClip.createEmptyMovieClip() to ensure that Flash renders the movie clip in front of all other objects on the same level and layer in the current movie clip. The value returned is 0 or larger (that is, negative numbers are not returned).

You can extend the methods and event handlers of the MovieClip class by creating a subclass.

> **NOTE**
>
> If you are using version 2 components, do not use this method. If you place a version 2 component either on the Stage or in the Library, the `getNextHighestDepth()` method can sometimes return depth 1048676, which is outside the valid range, If you are using version 2 components, you should always use the version 2 components DepthManager class.

Availability: ActionScript 1.0; Flash Player 7

Returns

`Number` - An integer that reflects the next available depth index that would render above all other objects on the same level and layer within the movie clip.

Example

The following example draws three movie clip instances, using the `getNextHighestDepth()` method as the `depth` parameter of the `createEmptyMovieClip()` method, and labels each movie clip them with its depth:

```
for (i = 0; i < 3; i++) {
  drawClip(i);
}

function drawClip(n:Number):Void {
  this.createEmptyMovieClip("triangle" + n, this.getNextHighestDepth());
  var mc:MovieClip = eval("triangle" + n);
  mc.beginFill(0x00aaFF, 100);
  mc.lineStyle(4, 0xFF0000, 100);
  mc.moveTo(0, 0);
  mc.lineTo(100, 100);
  mc.lineTo(0, 100);
  mc.lineTo(0, 0);
  mc._x = n * 30;
  mc._y = n * 50
  mc.createTextField("label", this.getNextHighestDepth(), 20, 50, 200, 200);
  mc.label.text = mc.getDepth();
}
```

See also

`getDepth (MovieClip.getDepth method)`, `getInstanceAtDepth (MovieClip.getInstanceAtDepth method)`, `swapDepths (MovieClip.swapDepths method)`, `attachMovie (MovieClip.attachMovie method)`, `duplicateMovieClip (MovieClip.duplicateMovieClip method)`, `createEmptyMovieClip (MovieClip.createEmptyMovieClip method)`

getRect (MovieClip.getRect method)

```
public getRect(bounds:Object) : Object
```

Returns properties that are the minimum and maximum *x* and *y* coordinate values of the movie clip, based on the `bounds` parameter, excluding any strokes on shapes. The values that `getRect()` returns are the same or smaller than those returned by `MovieClip.getBounds()`.

 NOTE Use `MovieClip.localToGlobal()` and `MovieClip.globalToLocal()` methods to convert the movie clip's local coordinates to Stage coordinates, or Stage coordinates to local coordinates, respectively.

You can extend the methods and event handlers of the MovieClip class by creating a subclass.

Availability: ActionScript 1.0; Flash Player 8

Parameters

`bounds:Object` - The target path of the timeline whose coordinate system you want to use as a reference point.

Returns

`Object` - An object with the properties `xMin`, `xMax`, `yMin`, and `yMax`.

Example

The following example creates a movie clip and draws inside of it a square with a stroke width of 4 pixels. The example then calls both the `MovieClip.getBounds()` and `MovieClip.getRect()` methods to show the difference between the two. The `getBounds()` method returns the minimum and maximum coordinate values of the entire movie clip, including the stroke width of the square. The `getRect()` method returns the minimum and maximum coordinate values excluding the stroke width of 4 pixels.

```
this.createEmptyMovieClip("square_mc", 1);
square_mc._x = 10;
square_mc._y = 10;
square_mc.beginFill(0xFF0000);
square_mc.lineStyle(4, 0xFF00FF, 100, true, "none", "round", "miter", 1);
square_mc.moveTo(0, 0);
square_mc.lineTo(100, 0);
square_mc.lineTo(100, 100);
square_mc.lineTo(0, 100);
square_mc.lineTo(0, 0);
square_mc.endFill();

var bounds_obj:Object = square_mc.getBounds(this);
trace("getBounds() output:");
for (var i in bounds_obj) {
   trace(i+" --> "+bounds_obj[i]);
}

var rect_obj:Object = square_mc.getRect(this);
trace("getRect() output:");
for (var i in rect_obj) {
   trace(i+" --> "+rect_obj[i]);
}
```

The `trace()` statement results in the following output.

```
getBounds() output:
yMax --> 112
yMin --> 8
xMax --> 112
xMin --> 8
getRect() output:
yMax --> 110
yMin --> 10
xMax --> 110
xMin --> 10
```

See also

getBounds (MovieClip.getBounds method), globalToLocal (MovieClip.globalToLocal method), localToGlobal (MovieClip.localToGlobal method)

getSWFVersion (MovieClip.getSWFVersion method)

`public getSWFVersion() : Number`

Returns an integer that indicates the Flash Player version for the movie clip was published. If the movie clip is a JPEG, GIF, or PNG file, or if an error occurs and Flash Player can't determine the SWF version of the movie clip, -1 is returned.

You can extend the methods and event handlers of the MovieClip class by creating a subclass.

Availability: ActionScript 1.0; Flash Player 7

Returns

`Number` - An integer that specifies the Flash Player version that was targeted when the SWF file loaded into the movie clip was published.

Example

The following example creates a new container and outputs the value of `getSWFVersion()`. It then uses MovieClipLoader to load an external SWF file that was published to Flash Player 7 and outputs the value of `getSWFVersion()` after the `onLoadInit` handler is triggered.

```
var container:MovieClip = this.createEmptyMovieClip("container",
  this.getUpperEmptyDepth());
var listener:Object = new Object();
listener.onLoadInit = function(target:MovieClip):Void {
  trace("target: " + target.getSWFVersion()); // target: 7
}
var mcLoader:MovieClipLoader = new MovieClipLoader();
mcLoader.addListener(listener);
trace("container: " + container.getSWFVersion()); // container: 8
mcLoader.loadClip("FlashPlayer7.swf", container);
```

getTextSnapshot (MovieClip.getTextSnapshot method)

```
public getTextSnapshot() : TextSnapshot
```

Returns a TextSnapshot object that contains the text in all the static text fields in the specified movie clip; text in child movie clips is not included. This method always returns a TextSnapshot object.

Flash concatenates text and places it in the TextSnapshot object in an order that reflects the tab index order of the static text fields in the movie clip. Text fields that don't have tab index values are placed in a random order in the object, and precede any text from fields that do have tab index values. No line breaks or formatting indicates where one field ends and the next begins.

> **NOTE**
> You can't specify a tab index value for static text in Flash. However, other products may do so (for example, Macromedia FlashPaper).

The contents of the TextSnapshot object aren't dynamic; that is, if the movie clip moves to a different frame, or is altered in some way (for example, objects in the movie clip are added or removed), the TextSnapshot object might not represent the current text in the movie clip. To ensure that the object's contents are current, reissue this command as needed.

You can extend the methods and event handlers of the MovieClip class by creating a subclass.

Availability: ActionScript 1.0; Flash Player 7 - SWF files published for Flash Player 6 or later, playing in Flash Player 7 or later.

Returns

`TextSnapshot` - A TextSnapshot object that contains the static text from the movie clip.

Example

The following example shows how to use this method. To use this code, place a static text field that contains the text "TextSnapshot Example" on the Stage.

```
var textSnap:TextSnapshot = this.getTextSnapshot();
trace(textSnap.getText(0, textSnap.getCount(), false));
```

See also

`TextSnapshot`

getURL (MovieClip.getURL method)

`public getURL(url:String, [window:String], [method:String]) : Void`

Loads a document from the specified URL into the specified window. You can also use the `getURL()` method to pass variables to another application that is defined at the URL by using a `GET` or `POST` method.

Web pages that host Flash content must explicitly set the `allowScriptAccess` attribute to allow or deny scripting for the Flash Player from the HTML code (in the `PARAM` tag for Internet Explorer or the `EMBED` tag for Netscape Navigator):

- When `allowScriptAccess` is `"never"`, outbound scripting always fails.
- When `allowScriptAccess` is `"always"`, outbound scripting always succeeds.
- When `allowScriptAccess` is `"sameDomain"` (supported by SWF files starting with version 8), outbound scripting is allowed if the SWF file is from the same domain as the hosting web page.
- If `allowScriptAccess` is not specified by an HTML page, the default value is `"sameDomain"` for version 8 SWF files, and the default value is `"always"` for earlier version SWF files.

When using this method, consider the Flash Player security model. For Flash Player 8, the method is not allowed if the calling SWF file is in the local-with-file-system sandbox and the resource is nonlocal.

For more information, see the following:

- Chapter 17, "Understanding Security," in *Learning ActionScript 2.0 in Flash*
- The Flash Player 8 Security white paper at http://www.macromedia.com/go/fp8_security
- The Flash Player 8 Security-Related API white paper at http://www.macromedia.com/go/fp8_security_apis

You can extend the methods and event handlers of the MovieClip class by creating a subclass.

Availability: ActionScript 1.0; Flash Player 5

Parameters

`url:String` - The URL from which to obtain the document.

`window:String` [optional] - A parameter specifying the name, frame, or expression that specifies the window or HTML frame that the document is loaded into. You can also use one of the following reserved target names: `_self` specifies the current frame in the current window, `_blank` specifies a new window, `_parent` specifies the parent of the current frame, and `_top` specifies the top-level frame in the current window.

method:String [optional] - A String (either "GET" or "POST") that specifies a method for sending variables associated with the SWF file to load. If no variables are present, omit this parameter; otherwise, specify whether to load variables using a GET or POST method. GET appends the variables to the end of the URL and is used for a small number of variables. POST sends the variables in a separate HTTP header and is used for long strings of variables.

Example

The following ActionScript creates a movie clip instance and opens the Macromedia website in a new browser window:

```
this.createEmptyMovieClip("loader_mc", this.getNextHighestDepth());
loader_mc.getURL("http://www.macromedia.com", "_blank");
```

The getURL() method also allows you to send variables to a remote server-side script, as seen in the following code:

```
this.createEmptyMovieClip("loader_mc", this.getNextHighestDepth());
loader_mc.username = "some user input";
loader_mc.password = "random string";
loader_mc.getURL("http://www.flash-mx.com/mm/viewscope.cfm", "_blank",
   "GET");
```

The MovieClip.getNextHighestDepth() method used in these examples requires Flash Player 7 or later. If your SWF file includes a version 2 component, use the version 2 components DepthManager class instead of the MovieClip.getNextHighestDepth() method.

When using this method, consider the Flash Player security model.

- For Flash Player 8, MovieClip.getURL() is not allowed if the calling SWF file is in the local-with-file-system sandbox and the resource is nonlocal.

For more information, see the following:

- Chapter 17, "Understanding Security," in *Learning ActionScript 2.0 in Flash*
- The Flash Player 8 Security white paper at http://www.macromedia.com/go/fp8_security
- The Flash Player 8 Security-Related API white paper at http://www.macromedia.com/go/fp8_security_apis

See also

getURL function, sendAndLoad (LoadVars.sendAndLoad method), send (LoadVars.send method)

globalToLocal (MovieClip.globalToLocal method)

```
public globalToLocal(pt:Object) : Void
```

Converts the pt object from Stage (global) coordinates to the movie clip's (local) coordinates.

The MovieClip.globalToLocal() method allows you to convert any given *x* and *y* coordinates from values that are relative to the top-left corner of the Stage to values that are relative to the top-left corner of a specific movie clip.

You must first create a generic object that has two properties, x and y. These x and y values (and they must be called x and y) are called the global coordinates because they relate to the top-left corner of the Stage. The x property represents the horizontal offset from the top-left corner. In other words, it represents how far to the right the point lies. For example, if x = 50, the point lies 50 pixels to the right of the top-left corner. The y property represents the vertical offset from the top-left corner. In other words, it represents how far down the point lies. For example, if y = 20, the point lies 20 pixels below the top-left corner. The following code creates a generic object with these coordinates:

```
var myPoint:Object = new Object();
myPoint.x = 50;
myPoint.y = 20;
```

Alternatively, you can create the object and assign the values at the same time with a literal Object value:

```
var myPoint:Object = {x:50, y:20};
```

After you create a point object with global coordinates, you can convert the coordinates to local coordinates. The globalToLocal() method doesn't return a value because it changes the values of x and y in the generic object that you send as the parameter. It changes them from values relative to the Stage (global coordinates) to values relative to a specific movie clip (local coordinates).

For example, if you create a movie clip that is positioned at the point (_x:100, _y:100), and you pass the global point representing the top-left corner of the Stage (x:0, y:0) to the globalToLocal() method, the method should convert the x and y values to the local coordinates, which in this case is (x:-100, y:-100). This is because the *x* and *y* coordinates are now expressed relative to the top-left corner of your movie clip rather than the top-left corner of the Stage. The values are negative because to get from the top-left corner of your movie clip to the top-left corner of the Stage you have to move 100 pixels to the left (negative *x*) and 100 pixels up (negative *y*).

The movie clip coordinates were expressed using _x and _y, because those are the MovieClip properties that you use to set the *x* and *y* values for MovieClips. However, your generic object uses x and y without the underscore. The following code converts the *x* and *y* values to the local coordinates:

```
var myPoint:Object = {x:0, y:0}; // Create your generic point object.
this.createEmptyMovieClip("myMovieClip", this.getNextHighestDepth());
myMovieClip._x = 100; // _x for movieclip x position
myMovieClip._y = 100; // _y for movieclip y position

myMovieClip.globalToLocal(myPoint);
trace ("x: " + myPoint.x); // output: -100
trace ("y: " + myPoint.y); // output: -100
```

You can extend the methods and event handlers of the MovieClip class by creating a subclass.

Availability: ActionScript 1.0; Flash Player 5

Parameters

pt:Object - The name or identifier of an object created with the generic Object class. The object specifies the *x* and *y* coordinates as properties.

Example

Add the following ActionScript to a FLA or AS file in the same directory as an image called photo1.jpg:

```
this.createTextField("coords_txt", this.getNextHighestDepth(), 10, 10, 100,
    22);
coords_txt.html = true;
coords_txt.multiline = true;
coords_txt.autoSize = true;
this.createEmptyMovieClip("target_mc", this.getNextHighestDepth());
target_mc._x = 100;
target_mc._y = 100;
target_mc.loadMovie("photo1.jpg");

var mouseListener:Object = new Object();
mouseListener.onMouseMove = function() {
   var point:Object = {x:_xmouse, y:_ymouse};
   target_mc.globalToLocal(point);
   var rowHeaders = "<b>   \t</b><b>_x\t</b><b>_y</b>";
   var row_1 = "_root\t"+_xmouse+"\t"+_ymouse;
   var row_2 = "target_mc\t"+point.x+"\t"+point.y;
   coords_txt.htmlText = "<textformat tabstops='[100, 150]'>";
   coords_txt.htmlText += rowHeaders;
   coords_txt.htmlText += row_1;
   coords_txt.htmlText += row_2;
   coords_txt.htmlText += "</textformat>";
};
```

```
Mouse.addListener(mouseListener);
```
The `MovieClip.getNextHighestDepth()` method used in this example requires Flash Player 7 or later. If your SWF file includes a version 2 component, use the version 2 components DepthManager class instead of the `MovieClip.getNextHighestDepth()` method.

See also

getBounds (MovieClip.getBounds method), localToGlobal (MovieClip.localToGlobal method), Object

gotoAndPlay (MovieClip.gotoAndPlay method)

```
public gotoAndPlay(frame:Object) : Void
```
Starts playing the SWF file at the specified frame. To specify a scene as well as a frame, use `gotoAndPlay()`.

You can extend the methods and event handlers of the MovieClip class by creating a subclass.

Availability: ActionScript 1.0; Flash Player 5

Parameters

`frame:Object` - A number representing the frame number, or a string representing the label of the frame, to which the playhead is sent.

Example

The following example uses the `_framesloaded` property to start a SWF file when all of the frames are loaded. If all of the frames aren't loaded, the `_xscale` property of the `loader` movie clip instance is increased proportionally to create a progress bar.

Enter the following ActionScript on Frame 1 of the Timeline:

```
var pctLoaded:Number = Math.round(this.getBytesLoaded()/
  this.getBytesTotal()*100);
bar_mc._xscale = pctLoaded;
```

Add the following code on Frame 2:

```
if (this._framesloaded<this._totalframes) {
  this.gotoAndPlay(1);
} else {
  this.gotoAndStop(3);
}
```

Place your content on or after Frame 3. Then add the following code on Frame 3:

```
stop();
```

See also

gotoAndPlay function, play function

gotoAndStop (MovieClip.gotoAndStop method)

`public gotoAndStop(frame:Object) : Void`

Brings the playhead to the specified frame of the movie clip and stops it there. To specify a scene in addition to a frame, use the `gotoAndStop()` method.

You can extend the methods and event handlers of the MovieClip class by creating a subclass.

Availability: ActionScript 1.0; Flash Player 5

Parameters

`frame:Object` - The frame number to which the playhead is sent.

Example

The following example uses the `_framesloaded` property to start a SWF file when all the frames are loaded. If all the frames aren't loaded, the `_xscale` property of the `loader` movie clip instance is increased proportionally to create a progress bar.

Enter the following ActionScript on Frame 1 of the Timeline:

```
var pctLoaded:Number = Math.round(this.getBytesLoaded()/
  this.getBytesTotal()*100);
bar_mc._xscale = pctLoaded;
```

Add the following code on Frame 2:

```
if (this._framesloaded<this._totalframes) {
  this.gotoAndPlay(1);
} else {
  this.gotoAndStop(3);
}
```

Place your content on or after Frame 3. Then add the following code on Frame 3:

```
stop();
```

See also

gotoAndStop function, stop function

_height (MovieClip._height property)

```
public _height : Number
```
The height of the movie clip, in pixels.

Availability: ActionScript 1.0; Flash Player 4

Example

The following code example displays the height and width of a movie clip in the Output panel:

```
this.createEmptyMovieClip("image_mc", this.getNextHighestDepth());
var image_mcl:MovieClipLoader = new MovieClipLoader();
var mclListener:Object = new Object();
mclListener.onLoadInit = function(target_mc:MovieClip) {
  trace(target_mc._name+" = "+target_mc._width+" X "+target_mc._height+"
  pixels");
};
image_mcl.addListener(mclListener);

image_mcl.loadClip("example.jpg", image_mc);
```

The `MovieClip.getNextHighestDepth()` method used in this example requires Flash Player 7 or later. If your SWF file includes a version 2 component, use the version 2 components DepthManager class instead of the `MovieClip.getNextHighestDepth()` method.

The MovieClipLoader class used in this example requires Flash Player 7 or later.

See also

```
_width (MovieClip._width property)
```

_highquality (MovieClip._highquality property)

```
public _highquality : Number
```
Deprecated since Flash Player 7. This property was deprecated in favor of `MovieClip._quality`.

Specifies the level of anti-aliasing applied to the current SWF file. Specify 2 (best quality) to apply high quality with bitmap smoothing always on. Specify 1 (high quality) to apply anti-aliasing; this smooths bitmaps if the SWF file does not contain animation. Specify 0 (low quality) to prevent anti-aliasing. This property can overwrite the global `_highquality` property.

Availability: ActionScript 1.0; Flash Player 6

Example

The following ActionScript specifies that best quality anti-aliasing should be applied to the SWF file.

```
my_mc._highquality = 2;
```

See also

`_quality (MovieClip._quality property)`, `_quality property`

hitArea (MovieClip.hitArea property)

`public hitArea : Object`

Designates another movie clip to serve as the hit area for a movie clip. If the `hitArea` property does not exist or the value is `null` or `undefined`, the movie clip itself is used as the hit area. The value of the `hitArea` property may be a reference to a movie clip object.

You can change the `hitArea` property at any time; the modified movie clip immediately uses the new hit area behavior. The movie clip designated as the hit area does not need to be visible; its graphical shape, although not visible, is still detected as the hit area.

Availability: ActionScript 1.0; Flash Player 6

Example

The following example sets the `circle_mc` movie clip as the hit area for the `square_mc` movie clip. Place these two movie clips on the Stage and test the document. When you click `circle_mc`, the `square_mc` movie clip traces that it was clicked.

```
square_mc.hitArea = circle_mc;
square_mc.onRelease = function() {
  trace("hit! "+this._name);
};
```

You can also set the `circle_mc` movie clip `visible` property to `false` to hide the hit area for `square_mc`.

```
circle_mc._visible = false;
```

See also

`hitTest (MovieClip.hitTest method)`

hitTest (MovieClip.hitTest method)

`public hitTest() : Boolean`

Evaluates the movie clip to see if it overlaps or intersects with the hit area that the `target` or x and y coordinate parameters identify.

Usage 1: Compares the *x* and *y* coordinates to the shape or bounding box of the specified instance, according to the `shapeFlag` setting. If `shapeFlag` is set to `true`, only the area actually occupied by the instance on the Stage is evaluated, and if *x* and *y* overlap at any point, a value of `true` is returned. This evaluation is useful for determining if the movie clip is within a specified hit or hotspot area.

Usage 2: Evaluates the bounding boxes of the `target` and specified instance, and returns `true` if they overlap or intersect at any point.

Parametersx : `Number` The *x* coordinate of the hit area on the Stage. y : `Number` The *y* coordinate of the hit area on the Stage. The *x* and *y* coordinates are defined in the global coordinate space. `shapeFlag`: `Boolean` A Boolean value specifying whether to evaluate the entire shape of the specified instance (`true`), or just the bounding box (`false`). This parameter can be specified only if the hit area is identified by using x and y coordinate parameters. `target`: `Object` The target path of the hit area that may intersect or overlap with the movie clip. The `target` parameter usually represents a button or text-entry field.

Availability: ActionScript 1.0; Flash Player 5

Returns

`Boolean` - A Boolean value of `true` if the movie clip overlaps with the specified hit area, `false` otherwise.

Example

The following example uses `hitTest()` to determine if the `circle_mc` movie clip overlaps or intersects the `square_mc` movie clip when the user releases the mouse button:

```
square_mc.onPress = function() {
  this.startDrag();
};
square_mc.onRelease = function() {
  this.stopDrag();
  if (this.hitTest(circle_mc)) {
  trace("you hit the circle");
  }
};
```

See also

getBounds (MovieClip.getBounds method), globalToLocal
(MovieClip.globalToLocal method), localToGlobal (MovieClip.localToGlobal
method)

lineGradientStyle (MovieClip.lineGradientStyle method)

```
public lineGradientStyle(fillType:String, colors:Array, alphas:Array,
   ratios:Array, matrix:Object, [spreadMethod:String],
   [interpolationMethod:String], [focalPointRatio:Number]) : Void
```

Specifies a line style that Flash uses for subsequent calls to the lineTo() and curveTo()
methods until you call the lineStyle() method or the lineGradientStyle() method with
different parameters. You can call the lineGradientStyle() method in the middle of
drawing a path to specify different styles for different line segments within a path.

 Call linestyle() before you call line GradientStyle() to enable a stroke, otherwise the
value of line style remains undefined.

 Calls to clear() set the line style back to undefined.

You can extend the methods and event handlers of the MovieClip class by creating a subclass.

Availability: ActionScript 1.0; Flash Player 8

Parameters

fillType:String - Valid values are "linear" or "radial".

colors:Array - An array of RGB hexadecimal color values that you use in the gradient (for
example, red is 0xFF0000, blue is 0x0000FF, and so on). You can specify up to 15 colors. For
each color, ensure that you specify a corresponding value in the alphas and ratios
parameters.

alphas:Array - An array of alpha values for the corresponding colors in the *colors* array;
valid values are 0 to 100. If the value is less than 0, Flash uses 0. If the value is greater than
100, Flash uses 100.

ratios:Array - An array of color distribution ratios; valid values are from 0 to 255. This
value defines the percentage of the width where the color is sampled at 100%. Specify a value
for each value in the *colors* parameter.

For example, for a linear gradient that includes two colors, blue and green, the following figure illustrates the placement of the colors in the gradient based on different values in the `ratios` array:

ratios	**Gradient**
[0, 127]	
[0, 255]	
[127, 255]	

The values in the array must increase, sequentially; for example, `[0, 63, 127, 190, 255]`.

`matrix:Object` - A transformation matrix that is an object with one of the following sets of properties:

- You can use the properties a, b, c, d, e, f, g, h, i to describe a 3 x 3 matrix of the following form:

```
a b c
d e f
g h i
```

The following example uses the `lineGradientFill()` method with a `matrix` parameter that is an object with the following properties:

```
this.createEmptyMovieClip("gradient_mc", 1);
with (gradient_mc) {
  colors = [0xFF0000, 0x0000FF];
    alphas = [100, 100];
    ratios = [0, 0xFF];
    matrix = {a:200, b:0, c:0, d:0, e:200, f:0, g:200, h:200, i:1};
    spreadMethod = "reflect";
    interpolationMethod = "linearRGB";
    focalPointRatio = 0.9;
  lineStyle(8);
    lineGradientStyle("linear", colors, alphas, ratios, matrix,
    spreadMethod, interpolationMethod, focalPointRatio);
    moveTo(100, 100);
    lineTo(100, 300);
    lineTo(300, 300);
    lineTo(300, 100);
    lineTo(100, 100);
    endFill();
}
```

This code draws the following image onscreen:

- matrixType, x, y, w, h, r.

    The properties indicate the following: matrixType is the string "box", x is the horizontal position relative to the registration point of the parent clip for the upper-left corner of the gradient, y is the vertical position relative to the registration point of the parent clip for the upper-left corner of the gradient, w is the width of the gradient, h is the height of the gradient, and r is the rotation in radians of the gradient.

    The following example uses the lineGradientFill() method with a matrix parameter that is an object with these properties:

```
this.createEmptyMovieClip("gradient_mc", 1);
with (gradient_mc) {
  colors = [0xFF0000, 0x0000FF];
  alphas = [100, 100];
  ratios = [0, 0xFF];
  matrix = {matrixType:"box", x:100, y:100, w:200, h:200, r:(45/
180)*Math.PI};
  spreadMethod = "reflect";
  interpolationMethod = "linearRGB";
  lineStyle(8);
  lineGradientStyle("linear", colors, alphas, ratios, matrix,
    spreadMethod, interpolationMethod);
  moveTo(100, 100);
  lineTo(100, 300);
  lineTo(300, 300);
  lineTo(300, 100);
  lineTo(100, 100);
  endFill();
}
```

spreadMethod:String [optional] - Valid values are "pad", "reflect," or "repeat," which controls the mode of the gradient fill.

interpolationMethod:String [optional] - Valid values are "RGB" or "linearRGB".

focalPointRatio:Number [optional] - A Number that controls the location of the focal point of the gradient. The value 0 means the focal point is in the center. The value 1 means the focal point is at one border of the gradient circle. The value -1 means that the focal point is at the other border of the gradient circle. Values less than -1 or greater than 1 are rounded to -1 or 1. The following image shows a gradient with a focalPointRatio of -0.75:

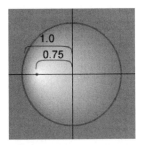

Example

The following code uses both methods to draw two stacked rectangles with a red-blue line gradient fill:

```
this.createEmptyMovieClip("gradient_mc", 1);
with (gradient_mc) {
  colors = [0xFF0000, 0x0000FF];
  alphas = [100, 100];
  ratios = [0, 0xFF];
  matrix = {a:500, b:0, c:0, d:0, e:200, f:0, g:350, h:200, i:1};
  lineStyle(16);
  lineGradientStyle("linear", colors, alphas, ratios, matrix);
  moveTo(100, 100);
  lineTo(100, 300);
  lineTo(600, 300);
  lineTo(600, 100);
  lineTo(100, 100);
  endFill();
  matrix2 = {matrixType:"box", x:100, y:310, w:500, h:200, r:(30/
180)*Math.PI};
  lineGradientStyle("linear", colors, alphas, ratios, matrix2);
  moveTo(100, 320);
  lineTo(100, 520);
  lineTo(600, 520);
  lineTo(600, 320);
  lineTo(100, 320);
  endFill();
}
```

This code draws the following image (the image is scaled by 50%):

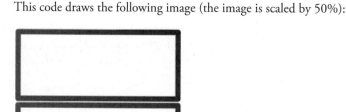

See also

beginGradientFill (MovieClip.beginGradientFill method), lineStyle
(MovieClip.lineStyle method), lineTo (MovieClip.lineTo method), moveTo
(MovieClip.moveTo method)

lineStyle (MovieClip.lineStyle method)

```
public lineStyle(thickness:Number, rgb:Number, alpha:Number,
    pixelHinting:Boolean, noScale:String, capsStyle:String,
    jointStyle:String, miterLimit:Number) : Void
```

Specifies a line style that Flash uses for subsequent calls to the lineTo() and curveTo()
methods until you call the lineStyle() method with different parameters. You can call
lineStyle() in the middle of drawing a path to specify different styles for different line
segments within a path.

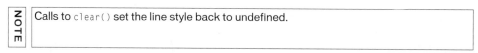

NOTE | Calls to clear() set the line style back to undefined.

You can extend the methods and event handlers of the MovieClip class by creating a subclass.

Availability: ActionScript 1.0; Flash Player 6 - Additional parameters pixelHinting, noScale,
capsStyle, jointStyle, and miterLimit are available in Flash Player 8.

Parameters

thickness:Number - An integer that indicates the thickness of the line in points; valid values
are 0 to 255. If a number is not specified, or if the parameter is undefined, a line is not
drawn. If a value of less than 0 is passed, Flash Player uses 0. The value 0 indicates hairline
thickness; the maximum thickness is 255. If a value greater than 255 is passed, the Flash
interpreter uses 255.

`rgb:Number` - A hexadecimal color value of the line; for example, red is 0xFF0000, blue is 0x0000FF, and so on. If a value isn't indicated, Flash uses 0x000000 (black).

`alpha:Number` - An integer that indicates the alpha value of the line's color; valid values are 0 to 100. If a value isn't indicated, Flash uses 100 (solid). If the value is less than 0, Flash uses 0; if the value is greater than 100, Flash uses 100.

`pixelHinting:Boolean` - Added in Flash Player 8. A Boolean value that specifies whether to hint strokes to full pixels. This value affects both the position of anchors of a curve and the line stroke size itself. If a value is not indicated, Flash Player does not use pixel hinting.

`noScale:String` - Added in Flash Player 8. A string that specifies how to scale a stroke. Valid values are as follows:

- `"normal"` Always scale the thickness (the default).
- `"none"` Never scale the thickness.
- `"vertical"` Do not scale thickness if object is scaled vertically only.
- `"horizontal"` Do not scale thickness if object is scaled horizontally only.

`capsStyle:String` - Added in Flash Player 8. A string that specifies the type of caps at the end of lines. Valid values are: `"round"`, `"square"`, and `"none"`. If a value is not indicated, Flash uses round caps.

For example, the following illustrations show the different `capsStyle` settings. For each setting, the illustration shows a blue line with a thickness of 30 (for which the `capsStyle` applies), and a superimposed black line with a thickness of 1 (for which no `capsStyle` applies):

"none"   "round"   "square"

`jointStyle:String` - Added in Flash Player 8. A string that specifies the type of joint appearance used at angles. Valid values are: `"round"`, `"miter"`, and `"bevel"`. If a value is not indicated, Flash uses round joints.

For example, the following illustrations show the different `capsStyle` settings. For each setting, the illustration shows an angled blue line with a thickness of 30 (for which the `jointStyle` applies), and a superimposed angled black line with a thickness of 1 (for which no `jointStyle` applies):

"miter"   "round"   "bevel"

Notice that for jointStyle set to "miter", you can limit the length of the miter point by using the miterLimit parameter.

miterLimit:Number - Added in Flash Player 8. A number that indicates the limit at which a miter is cut off. Valid values range from 1 to 255 (and values outside of that range are rounded to 1 or 255). This value is only used if the jointStyle is set to "miter". If a value is not indicated, Flash uses 3. The miterLimit value represents the length that a miter can extend beyond the point at which the lines meet to form a joint. The value expresses a factor of the line thickness. For example, with a miterLimit factor of 2.5 and a thickness of 10 pixels, the miter is cut off at 25 pixels.

For example, consider the following angled lines, each drawn with a thickness of 20, but with miterLimit set to 1, 2, and 4. Superimposed are black reference lines showing the meeting points of the joints:

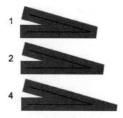

Notice that for a given miterLimit value, there is a specific maximum angle for which the miter is cut off. The following table lists some examples:

Value of miterLimit **value:**	**Angles smaller than this are cut off:**
1.414	90 degrees
2	60 degrees
4	30 degrees
8	15 degrees

Example

The following code draws a triangle with a 5-pixel, solid magenta line with no fill, with pixel hinting, no stroke scaling, no caps, and miter joints with miterLimit set to 1:

```
this.createEmptyMovieClip("triangle_mc", this.getNextHighestDepth());
triangle_mc.lineStyle(5, 0xff00ff, 100, true, "none", "round", "miter", 1);
triangle_mc.moveTo(200, 200);
triangle_mc.lineTo(300, 300);
triangle_mc.lineTo(100, 300);
triangle_mc.lineTo(200, 200);
```

If your SWF file includes a version 2 component, use the version 2 components DepthManager class instead of the `MovieClip.getNextHighestDepth()` method, which is used in this example.

See also

`beginFill` (`MovieClip.beginFill method`), `beginGradientFill` (`MovieClip.beginGradientFill method`), `clear` (`MovieClip.clear method`), `curveTo` (`MovieClip.curveTo method`), `lineTo` (`MovieClip.lineTo method`), `moveTo` (`MovieClip.moveTo method`)

lineTo (MovieClip.lineTo method)

`public lineTo(x:Number, y:Number) : Void`

Draws a line using the current line style from the current drawing position to (x, y); the current drawing position is then set to (x, y). If the movie clip that you are drawing in contains content that was created with the Flash drawing tools, calls to `lineTo()` are drawn underneath the content. If you call `lineTo()` before any calls to the `moveTo()` method, the current drawing position defaults to (0,0). If any of the parameters are missing, this method fails and the current drawing position is not changed.

You can extend the methods and event handlers of the MovieClip class by creating a subclass.

Availability: ActionScript 1.0; Flash Player 6

Parameters

`x:Number` - An integer that indicates the horizontal position relative to the registration point of the parent movie clip.

`y:Number` - An integer that indicates the vertical position relative to the registration point of the parent movie clip.

Example

The following example draws a triangle with a 5-pixel, solid magenta line and a partially transparent blue fill:

```
this.createEmptyMovieClip("triangle_mc", 1);
triangle_mc.beginFill(0x0000FF, 30);
triangle_mc.lineStyle(5, 0xFF00FF, 100);
triangle_mc.moveTo(200, 200);
triangle_mc.lineTo(300, 300);
triangle_mc.lineTo(100, 300);
triangle_mc.lineTo(200, 200);
triangle_mc.endFill();
```

See also

beginFill (MovieClip.beginFill method), createEmptyMovieClip
(MovieClip.createEmptyMovieClip method), endFill (MovieClip.endFill method),
lineStyle (MovieClip.lineStyle method), moveTo (MovieClip.moveTo method)

loadMovie (MovieClip.loadMovie method)

public loadMovie(url:String, [method:String]) : Void

Loads a SWF, JPEG, GIF, or PNG file into a movie clip in Flash Player while the original
SWF file is playing. Support for unanimated GIF files, PNG files, and progressive JPEG files
is added in Flash Player 8. If you load an animated GIF, only the first frame is displayed.

 To monitor the progress of the download, use the MovieClipLoader.loadClip() method
instead of the loadMovie() method.

Without the loadMovie() method, Flash Player displays a single SWF file and then closes.
The loadMovie() method lets you display several SWF files at once and switch between SWF
files without loading another HTML document.

A SWF file or image loaded into a movie clip inherits the position, rotation, and scale
properties of the movie clip. You can use the target path of the movie clip to target the loaded
SWF file.

When you call the loadMovie() method, set the MovieClip._lockroot property to true in
the loader movie, as the following code example shows. If you don't set _lockroot to true in
the loader movie, any references to _root in the loaded movie point to the _root of the
loader instead of the _root of the loaded movie:

myMovieClip._lockroot = true;

Use the MovieClip.unloadMovie() method to remove SWF files or images loaded with the
loadMovie() method.

Use the MovieClip.loadVariables() method, the XML object, Flash Remoting, or Runtime
Shared Objects to keep the active SWF file and load new data into it.

Using event handlers with MovieClip.loadMovie() can be unpredictable. If you attach an
event handler to a button by using on(), or if you create a dynamic handler by using an event
handler method such as MovieClip.onPress(), and then you call loadMovie(), the event
handler does not remain after the new content is loaded. However, if you attach an event
handler to a movie clip by using onClipEvent() or on(), and then call loadMovie() on that
movie clip, the event handler remains after the new content is loaded.

When using this method, consider the Flash Player security model.

For Flash Player 8:

- Loading is not allowed if the calling movie clip is in the local-with-file-system sandbox and the loaded movie clip is from a network sandbox.

- Loading is not allowed if the calling SWF file is in a network sandbox and the movie clip to be loaded is local.

- Network sandbox access from the local-trusted or local-with-networking sandbox requires permission from the website by means of a cross-domain policy file.

- Movie clips in the local-with-file-system sandbox may not script movie clips in the local-with-networking sandbox (and the reverse is also prevented).

For Flash Player 7 and later:

- Websites can permit cross-domain access to a resource by means of a cross-domain policy file.

- Scripting between SWF files is restricted based on the origin domain of the SWF files. Use the `System.security.allowDomain()` method to adjust these restrictions.

For more information, see the following:

- Chapter 17, "Understanding Security," in *Learning ActionScript 2.0 in Flash*
- The Flash Player 8 Security white paper at http://www.macromedia.com/go/fp8_security
- The Flash Player 8 Security-Related API white paper at http://www.macromedia.com/go/fp8_security_apis

You can extend the methods and event handlers of the MovieClip class by creating a subclass.

Availability: ActionScript 1.0; Flash Player 5 - The ability to load JPEG files is available as of Flash Player 6. The ability to load unanimated GIF files, PNG files, or progressive JPEG files is available as of Flash Player 8.

Parameters

`url:String` - The absolute or relative URL of the SWF, JPEG, GIF, and PNG file to be loaded. A relative path must be relative to the SWF file at level 0. Absolute URLs must include the protocol reference, such as `http://` or `file:///`.

`method:String` [optional] - Specifies an HTTP method for sending or loading variables. The parameter must be the string `GET` or `POST`. If no variables are to be sent, omit this parameter. The `GET` method appends the variables to the end of the URL and is used for small numbers of variables. The `POST` method sends the variables in a separate HTTP header and is used for long strings of variables.

Example

The following example creates a new movie clip, and then creates child inside of it and loads a PNG image into the child. This lets the parent retain any instance values that were assigned prior to the call to loadMovie.

```
var mc:MovieClip = this.createEmptyMovieClip("mc",
  this.getNextHighestDepth());
mc.onRelease = function():Void {
  trace(this.image._url); // http://www.w3.org/Icons/w3c_main.png
}
var image:MovieClip = mc.createEmptyMovieClip("image",
  mc.getNextHighestDepth());
image.loadMovie("http://www.w3.org/Icons/w3c_main.png");
```

The MovieClip.getNextHighestDepth() method used in this example requires Flash Player 7 or later. If your SWF file includes a version 2 component, use the version 2 components DepthManager class instead of the MovieClip.getNextHighestDepth() method.

See also

_lockroot (MovieClip._lockroot property), unloadMovie (MovieClip.unloadMovie method), loadVariables (MovieClip.loadVariables method), loadMovie (MovieClip.loadMovie method), onPress (MovieClip.onPress handler), MovieClipLoader, onClipEvent handler, on handler, loadMovieNum function, unloadMovie function, unloadMovieNum function

loadVariables (MovieClip.loadVariables method)

```
public loadVariables(url:String, [method:String]) : Void
```

Reads data from an external file and sets the values for variables in the movie clip. The external file can be a text file that Macromedia ColdFusion generates, a CGI script, an Active Server Page (ASP), a PHP script, or any other properly formatted text file. The file can contain any number of variables.

You can also use the loadVariables() method to update variables in the active movie clip with new values.

The loadVariables() method requires that the text of the URL be in the standard MIME format: *application/x-www-form-urlencoded* (CGI script format).

In SWF files running in a version earlier than Flash Player 7, url must be in the same superdomain as the SWF file that is issuing this call. A superdomain is derived by removing the left-most component of a file's URL. For example, a SWF file at www.someDomain.com can load data from a source at store.someDomain.com because both files are in the same superdomain of someDomain.com.

In SWF files of any version running in Flash Player 7 or later, url must be in exactly the same domain as the SWF file that is issuing this call. For example, a SWF file at www.someDomain.com can load data only from sources that are also at www.someDomain.com. To load data from a different domain, you can place a cross-domain policy file on the server hosting the data source that is being accessed.

To load variables into a specific level, use loadVariablesNum() instead of loadVariables().

You can extend the methods and event handlers of the MovieClip class by creating a subclass.

Availability: ActionScript 1.0; Flash Player 5 - Behavior changed in Flash Player 7.

Parameters

url:String - The absolute or relative URL for the external file that contains the variables to be loaded. If the SWF file issuing this call is running in a web browser, url must be in the same domain as the SWF file; for details, see the following description.

method:String [optional] - Specifies an HTTP method for sending variables. The parameter must be the string GET or POST. If no variables are sent, omit this parameter. The GET method appends the variables to the end of the URL and is used for small numbers of variables. The POST method sends the variables in a separate HTTP header and is used for long strings of variables.

Example

The following example loads information from a text file called params.txt into the target_mc movie clip that is created by using createEmptyMovieClip(). You use the setInterval() function to check the loading progress. The script checks for a variable named done in the params.txt file.

```
this.createEmptyMovieClip("target_mc", this.getNextHighestDepth());
target_mc.loadVariables("params.txt");
function checkParamsLoaded() {
  if (target_mc.done == undefined) {
  trace("not yet.");
  } else {
  trace("finished loading. killing interval.");
  trace("-------------");
  for (i in target_mc) {
    trace(i+": "+target_mc[i]);
  }
  trace("-------------");
  clearInterval(param_interval);
  }
}
var param_interval = setInterval(checkParamsLoaded, 100);
```

The params.txt file includes the following text:

```
var1="hello"&var2="goodbye"&done="done"
```

The `MovieClip.getNextHighestDepth()` method used in this example requires Flash Player 7 or later. If your SWF file includes a version 2 component, use the version 2 components DepthManager class instead of the `MovieClip.getNextHighestDepth()` method.

See also

`loadMovie (MovieClip.loadMovie method)`, `loadVariablesNum function`, `unloadMovie (MovieClip.unloadMovie method)`

localToGlobal (MovieClip.localToGlobal method)

```
public localToGlobal(pt:Object) : Void
```

Converts the `pt` object from the movie clip's (local) coordinates to the Stage (global) coordinates.

The `MovieClip.localToGlobal()` method allows you to convert any given *x* and *y* coordinates from values that are relative to the top-left corner of a specific movie clip to values that are relative to the top-left corner of the Stage.

You must first create a generic object that has two properties, x and y. These x and y values (and they must be called x and y) are called the local coordinates because they relate to the top-left corner of the movie clip. The x property represents the horizontal offset from the top-left corner of the movie clip. In other words, it represents how far to the right the point lies. For example, if x = 50, the point lies 50 pixels to the right of the top-left corner. The y property represents the vertical offset from the top-left corner of the movie clip. In other words, it represents how far down the point lies. For example, if y = 20, the point lies 20 pixels below the top-left corner. The following code creates a generic object with these coordinates.

```
var myPoint:Object = new Object();
myPoint.x = 50;
myPoint.y = 20;
```

Alternatively, you can create the object and assign the values at the same time with a literal Object value.

```
var myPoint:Object = {x:50, y:20};
```

After you create a point object with local coordinates, you can convert the coordinates to global coordinates. The `localToGlobal()` method doesn't return a value because it changes the values of x and y in the generic object that you send as the parameter. It changes them from values relative to a specific movie clip (local coordinates) to values relative to the Stage (global coordinates).

For example, if you create a movie clip that is positioned at the point (_x:100, _y:100), and you pass a local point representing a point near the top-left corner of the movie clip (x:10, y:10) to the localToGlobal() method, the method should convert the x and y values to global coordinates, which in this case is (x:110, y:110). This conversion occurs because the x and y coordinates are now expressed relative to the top-left corner of the Stage rather than the top-left corner of your movie clip.

The movie clip coordinates were expressed using _x and _y, because those are the MovieClip properties that you use to set the x and y values for MovieClips. However, your generic object uses x and y without the underscore. The following code converts the x and y coordinates to global coordinates:

```
var myPoint:Object = {x:10, y:10}; // create your generic point object
this.createEmptyMovieClip("myMovieClip", this.getNextHighestDepth());
myMovieClip._x = 100; // _x for movieclip x position
myMovieClip._y = 100; // _y for movieclip y position

myMovieClip.localToGlobal(myPoint);
trace ("x: " + myPoint.x); // output: 110
trace ("y: " + myPoint.y); // output: 110
```

You can extend the methods and event handlers of the MovieClip class by creating a subclass.

Availability: ActionScript 1.0; Flash Player 5

Parameters

pt:Object - The name or identifier of an object created with the Object class, specifying the x and y coordinates as properties.

Example

The following example converts x and y coordinates of the my_mc object, from the movie clip's (local) coordinates to the Stage (global) coordinates. The center point of the movie clip is reflected after you click and drag the instance.

```
this.createTextField("point_txt", this.getNextHighestDepth(), 0, 0, 100,
    22);
var mouseListener:Object = new Object();
mouseListener.onMouseMove = function() {
 var point:Object = {x:my_mc._width/2, y:my_mc._height/2};
 my_mc.localToGlobal(point);
 point_txt.text = "x:"+point.x+", y:"+point.y;
};
Mouse.addListener(mouseListener);
my_mc.onPress = function() {
 this.startDrag();
};
my_mc.onRelease = function() {
```

```
this.stopDrag();
};
```

The `MovieClip.getNextHighestDepth()` method used in this example requires Flash Player 7 or later. If your SWF file includes a version 2 component, use the version 2 components DepthManager class instead of the `MovieClip.getNextHighestDepth()` method.

See also

`globalToLocal (MovieClip.globalToLocal method)`

_lockroot (MovieClip._lockroot property)

`public _lockroot : Boolean`

A Boolean value that specifies what _root refers to when a SWF file is loaded into a movie clip. The `_lockroot` property is `undefined` by default. You can set this property within the SWF file that is being loaded or in the handler that is loading the movie clip.

For example, suppose you have a document called Games.fla that lets a user choose a game to play, and loads the game (for example, Chess.swf) into the `game_mc` movie clip. Make sure that, after being loaded into Games.swf, any use of _root in Chess.swf refers to _root in Chess.swf (not _root in Games.swf). If you have access to Chess.fla and publish it to Flash Player 7 or later, you can add this statement to Chess.fla on the main Timeline:

`this._lockroot = true;`

If you don't have access to Chess.fla (for example, if you are loading Chess.swf from someone else's site into `chess_mc`), you can set the Chess.swf `_lockroot` property when you load it. Place the following ActionScript on the main Timeline of Games.fla:

`chess_mc._lockroot = true;`

In this case, Chess.swf can be published for any version of Flash Player, as long as Games.swf is published for Flash Player 7 or later.

When calling `loadMovie()`, set the `MovieClip._lockroot` property to `true` in the loader movie, as the following code shows. If you don't set `_lockroot` to `true` in the loader movie, any references to _root in the loaded movie point to the _root of the loader instead of the _root of the loaded movie:

`myMovieClip._lockroot = true;`

Availability: ActionScript 1.0; Flash Player 7

Example

In the following example, lockroot.fla has _lockroot applied to the main SWF file. If the SWF file is loaded into another FLA document, _root always refers to the scope of lockroot.swf, which helps prevent conflicts. Place the following ActionScript on the main Timeline of lockroot.fla:

```
this._lockroot = true;
_root.myVar = 1;
_root.myOtherVar = 2;
trace("from lockroot.swf");
for (i in _root) {
  trace(" "+i+" -> "+_root[i]);
}
trace("");
```

which traces the following information:

```
from lockroot.swf
myOtherVar -> 2
myVar -> 1
_lockroot -> true
$version -> WIN 7,0,19,0
```

The following example loads two SWF files, lockroot.swf and nolockroot.swf. The lockroot.fla document contains the ActionScript from the preceding example. The nolockroot.fla file has the following code added to Frame 1 of the Timeline:

```
_root.myVar = 1;
_root.myOtherVar = 2;
trace("from nolockroot.swf");
for (i in _root) {
  trace(" "+i+" -> "+_root[i]);
}
trace("");
```

The lockroot.swf file has _lockroot applied to it, and nolockroot.swf does not. After the files are loaded, each file outputs the values variables from their _root scopes. Place the following ActionScript on the main Timeline of a FLA document:

```
this.createEmptyMovieClip("lockroot_mc", this.getNextHighestDepth());
lockroot_mc.loadMovie("lockroot.swf");
this.createEmptyMovieClip("nolockroot_mc", this.getNextHighestDepth());
nolockroot_mc.loadMovie("nolockroot.swf");
function dumpRoot() {
  trace("from current SWF file");
  for (i in _root) {
  trace(" "+i+" -> "+_root[i]);
  }
  trace("");
}
dumpRoot();
```

which traces the following information:

```
from current SWF file
dumpRoot -> [type Function]
$version -> WIN 7,0,19,0
nolockroot_mc -> _level0.nolockroot_mc
lockroot_mc -> _level0.lockroot_mc

from nolockroot.swf
myVar -> 1
i -> lockroot_mc
dumpRoot -> [type Function]
$version -> WIN 7,0,19,0
nolockroot_mc -> _level0.nolockroot_mc
lockroot_mc -> _level0.lockroot_mc

from lockroot.swf
myOtherVar -> 2
myVar -> 1
```

The file with no _lockroot applied also contains all of the other variables that the root SWF file contains. If you don't have access to the nolockroot.fla, you can use the following ActionScript added to the main Timeline to change the _lockroot in the preceding main FLA document:

```
this.createEmptyMovieClip("nolockroot_mc", this.getNextHighestDepth());
nolockroot_mc._lockroot = true;
nolockroot_mc.loadMovie("nolockroot.swf");
```

which then traces the following:

```
from current SWF file
dumpRoot -> [type Function]
$version -> WIN 7,0,19,0
nolockroot_mc -> _level0.nolockroot_mc
lockroot_mc -> _level0.lockroot_mc

from nolockroot.swf
myOtherVar -> 2
myVar -> 1

from lockroot.swf
myOtherVar -> 2
myVar -> 1
```

See also

_root property, _lockroot (MovieClip._lockroot property), attachMovie
(MovieClip.attachMovie method), loadMovie (MovieClip.loadMovie method),
onLoadInit (MovieClipLoader.onLoadInit event listener)

menu (MovieClip.menu property)

```
public menu : ContextMenu
```

Associates the specified ContextMenu object with the movie clip. The ContextMenu class lets
you modify the context menu that appears when the user right-clicks (Windows) or Control-
clicks (Macintosh) in Flash Player.

Availability: ActionScript 1.0; Flash Player 7

Example

The following example assigns the menu_cm ContextMenu object to the image_mc movie clip.
The ContextMenu object contains a custom menu item labeled "View Image in Browser" that
has an associated function named viewImage():

```
var menu_cm:ContextMenu = new ContextMenu();
menu_cm.customItems.push(new ContextMenuItem("View Image in Browser...",
  viewImage));
this.createEmptyMovieClip("image_mc", this.getNextHighestDepth());
var mclListener:Object = new Object();
mclListener.onLoadInit = function(target_mc:MovieClip) {
  target_mc.menu = menu_cm;
};
var image_mcl:MovieClipLoader = new MovieClipLoader();
image_mcl.addListener(mclListener);
image_mcl.loadClip("photo1.jpg", image_mc);

function viewImage(target_mc:MovieClip, obj:Object) {
  getURL(target_mc._url, "_blank");
}
```

When you right-click (Windows) or Control-click (Macintosh) the image at runtime, select
View Image in Browser from the context menu to open the image in a browser window.

See also

menu (Button.menu property), ContextMenu, ContextMenuItem, menu
(TextField.menu property)

moveTo (MovieClip.moveTo method)

```
public moveTo(x:Number, y:Number) : Void
```

Moves the current drawing position to (x, y). If any of the parameters are missing, this method fails and the current drawing position is not changed.

You can extend the methods and event handlers of the MovieClip class by creating a subclass.

Availability: ActionScript 1.0; Flash Player 6

Parameters

x:Number - An integer that indicates the horizontal position relative to the registration point of the parent movie clip.

y:Number - An integer that indicates the vertical position relative to the registration point of the parent movie clip.

Example

The following example draws a triangle with a 5-pixel, solid magenta line and a partially transparent blue fill:

```
this.createEmptyMovieClip("triangle_mc", 1);
triangle_mc.beginFill(0x0000FF, 30);
triangle_mc.lineStyle(5, 0xFF00FF, 100);
triangle_mc.moveTo(200, 200);
triangle_mc.lineTo(300, 300);
triangle_mc.lineTo(100, 300);
triangle_mc.lineTo(200, 200);
triangle_mc.endFill();
```

See also

createEmptyMovieClip (MovieClip.createEmptyMovieClip method), lineStyle (MovieClip.lineStyle method), lineTo (MovieClip.lineTo method)

_name (MovieClip._name property)

public _name : String

The instance name of the movie clip.

Availability: ActionScript 1.0; Flash Player 4

Example

The following example lets you right-click (Windows) or Control-click (Macintosh) a movie clip on the Stage and select Info from the context menu to view information about that instance. Add several movie clips with instance names, and then add the following ActionScript to your AS or FLA file:

```
var menu_cm:ContextMenu = new ContextMenu();
```

```
menu_cm.customItems.push(new ContextMenuItem("Info...", getMCInfo));
function getMCInfo(target_mc:MovieClip, obj:Object) {
  trace("You clicked on the movie clip '"+target_mc._name+"'.");
  trace("\t width:"+target_mc._width+", height:"+target_mc._height);
  trace("");
}
for (var i in this) {
  if (typeof (this[i]) == 'movieclip') {
  this[i].menu = menu_cm;
  }
}
```

See also

_name (Button._name property)

nextFrame (MovieClip.nextFrame method)

```
public nextFrame() : Void
```

Sends the playhead to the next frame and stops it.

You can extend the methods and event handlers of the MovieClip class by creating a subclass.

Availability: ActionScript 1.0; Flash Player 5

Example

The following example uses _framesloaded and nextFrame()to load content into a SWF file. Do not add any code on Frame 1, but add the following ActionScript on Frame 2 of the Timeline:

```
if (this._framesloaded >= 3) {
  this.nextFrame();
} else {
  this.gotoAndPlay(1);
}
```

Then, add the following code (and the content you want to load) on Frame 3:

```
stop();
```

See also

nextFrame function, prevFrame function, prevFrame (MovieClip.prevFrame method)

onData (MovieClip.onData handler)

```
onData = function() {}
```

Invoked when a movie clip receives data from a `MovieClip.loadVariables()` call or a `MovieClip.loadMovie()` call. You must define a function that executes when the event handler is invoked. You can define the function on the Timeline or in a class file that extends the MovieClip class and is linked to a symbol in the library.

You can use this handler only with the `MovieClip.loadVariables()` method or the `loadVariables()` global function. If you want an event handler to be invoked with `MovieClip.loadMovie()` method or the `loadMovie()` function, you must use `onClipEvent(data)` instead of this handler.

Availability: ActionScript 1.0; Flash Player 6

Example

The following example illustrates the correct use of `MovieClip.onData()`. It loads a file named *OnData.txt* from the same directory as the FLA. When the data from the file is loaded into the `MovieClip` object, `onData()` executes and we trace out the data.

```
var mc:MovieClip = this.createEmptyMovieClip("mc",
  this.getNextHighestDepth());

mc.onData = function() {
  for(var i in this) {
    trace(">> " + i + ": " + this[i]);
  }
}

mc.loadVariables("OnData.txt");
```

See also

`onClipEvent` handler, `loadVariables` (MovieClip.loadVariables method)

onDragOut (MovieClip.onDragOut handler)

`onDragOut = function() {}`

Invoked when the mouse button is pressed and the pointer rolls outside the object. You must define a function that executes when the event handler is invoked. You can define the function on the timeline or in a class file that extends the MovieClip class or is linked to a symbol in the library.

Availability: ActionScript 1.0; Flash Player 6

Example

The following example defines a function for the `onDragOut` method that sends a `trace()` action to the Output panel:

```
my_mc.onDragOut = function () {
   trace ("onDragOut called");
}
```

See also

onDragOver (MovieClip.onDragOver handler)

onDragOver (MovieClip.onDragOver handler)

`onDragOver = function() {}`

Invoked when the pointer is dragged outside and then over the movie clip. You must define a function that executes when the event handler is invoked. You can define the function on the timeline or in a class file that extends the MovieClip class or is linked to a symbol in the library.

Availability: ActionScript 1.0; Flash Player 6

Example

The following example defines a function for the `onDragOver` method that sends a `trace()` action to the Output panel:

```
my_mc.onDragOver = function () {
   trace ("onDragOver called");
}
```

See also

onDragOut (MovieClip.onDragOut handler)

onEnterFrame (MovieClip.onEnterFrame handler)

`onEnterFrame = function() {}`

Invoked repeatedly at the frame rate of the SWF file. The function that you assign to the `onEnterFrame` event handler is processed before any other ActionScript code that is attached to the affected frames.

You must define a function that executes when the event handler is invoked. You can define the function on the timeline or in a class file that extends the MovieClip class or that is linked to a symbol in the library.

Availability: ActionScript 1.0; Flash Player 6

Example

The following example defines a function for the onEnterFrame event handler that sends a trace() action to the Output panel:

```
my_mc.onEnterFrame = function () {
  trace ("onEnterFrame called");
}
```

onKeyDown (MovieClip.onKeyDown handler)

```
onKeyDown = function() {}
```

Invoked when a movie clip has input focus and user presses a key. The onKeyDown event handler is invoked with no parameters. You can use the Key.getAscii() and Key.getCode() methods to determine which key the user pressed. You must define a function that executes when the event handler is invoked. You can define the function on the timeline or in a class file that extends the MovieClip class or is linked to a symbol in the library.

The onKeyDown event handler works only if the movie clip has input focus enabled and set. First, the MovieClip.focusEnabled property must be set to true for the movie clip. Then, the clip must be given focus. You can do this by using Selection.setFocus() or by setting the Tab key to navigate to the movie clip.

If you use Selection.setFocus(), you must pass the path for the movie clip to Selection.setFocus(). It is very easy for other elements to take the focus back after a user moves the mouse.

Availability: ActionScript 1.0; Flash Player 6

Example

The following example defines a function for the onKeyDown() method that sends a trace() action to the Output panel. Create a movie clip called my_mc and add the following ActionScript to your FLA or AS file:

```
my_mc.onKeyDown = function () {
  trace ("key was pressed");
}
```

The movie clip must have focus for the onKeyDown event handler to work. Add the following ActionScript to set input focus:

```
my_mc.tabEnabled = true;
my_mc.focusEnabled = true;
Selection.setFocus(my_mc);
```

When the user presses a key, `key was pressed` displays in the Output panel. However, this does not occur after you move the mouse, because the movie clip loses focus. Therefore, you should use `Key.onKeyDown` in most cases.

See also

`getAscii (Key.getAscii method)`, `getCode (Key.getCode method)`, `onKeyDown (Key.onKeyDown event listener)`, `focusEnabled (MovieClip.focusEnabled property)`, `onKeyUp (MovieClip.onKeyUp handler)`, `setFocus (Selection.setFocus method)`

onKeyUp (MovieClip.onKeyUp handler)

`onKeyUp = function() {}`

Invoked when a key is released. The `onKeyUp` event handler is invoked with no parameters. You can use the `Key.getAscii()` and `Key.getCode()` methods to determine which key was pressed. You must define a function that executes when the event handler is invoked. You can define the function on the timeline or in a class file that extends the MovieClip class or is linked to a symbol in the library.

The `onKeyUp` event handler works only if the movie clip has input focus enabled and set. First, the `MovieClip.focusEnabled` property must be set to `true` for the movie clip. Then, the movie clip must be given focus. You can do this by using `Selection.setFocus()` or by setting the Tab key to navigate to the movie clip.

If you use `Selection.setFocus()`, you must pass the path for the movie clip to `Selection.setFocus()`. It is very easy for other elements to take the focus back after the user moves the mouse.

Availability: ActionScript 1.0; Flash Player 6

Example

The following example defines a function for the `onKeyUp` method that sends a `trace()` action to the Output panel:

```
my_mc.onKeyUp = function () {
  trace ("onKey called");
}
```

The following example sets input focus:

```
my_mc.focusEnabled = true;
Selection.setFocus(my_mc);
```

See also

`getAscii` (`Key.getAscii method`), `getCode` (`Key.getCode method`), `onKeyDown`
(`Key.onKeyDown event listener`), `focusEnabled` (`MovieClip.focusEnabled`
`property`), `onKeyDown` (`MovieClip.onKeyDown handler`), `setFocus`
(`Selection.setFocus method`)

onKillFocus (MovieClip.onKillFocus handler)

`onKillFocus = function(newFocus:Object) {}`

Invoked when a movie clip loses keyboard focus. The `onKillFocus` method receives one
parameter, `newFocus`, which is an object that represents the new object receiving the focus. If
no object receives the focus, `newFocus` contains the value `null`.

You must define a function that executes when the event handler is invoked. You can define
the function on the timeline or in a class file that extends the MovieClip class or is linked to a
symbol in the library.

Availability: ActionScript 1.0; Flash Player 6

Parameters

`newFocus:Object` - The object that is receiving the keyboard focus.

Example

The following example reports information about the movie clip that loses focus, and the
instance that currently has focus. Two movie clips, called `my_mc` and `other_mc`, are on the
Stage. Add the following ActionScript to your AS or FLA document:

```
my_mc.onRelease = Void;
other_mc.onRelease = Void;
my_mc.onKillFocus = function(newFocus) {
   trace("onKillFocus called, new focus is: "+newFocus);
};
```

Tab between the two instances, and information displays in the Output panel.

See also

`onSetFocus` (`MovieClip.onSetFocus handler`)

onLoad (MovieClip.onLoad handler)

`onLoad = function() {}`

Invoked when the movie clip is instantiated and appears in the timeline. You must define a function that executes when the event handler is invoked. You can define the function on the timeline or in a class file that extends the MovieClip class or is linked to a symbol in the library.

You use this handler only with movie clips for which you have a symbol in the library that is associated with a class. If you want an event handler to be invoked when a specific movie clip loads, you must use `onClipEvent(load)` or the MovieClipLoader class instead of this handlerl; for example, when you use `MovieClip.loadMovie()` to load a SWF file dynamically. Unlike `MovieClip.onLoad`, the other handlers are invoked when any movie clip loads.

Availability: ActionScript 1.0; Flash Player 6

Example

This example shows you how to use the `onLoad` event handler in an ActionScript 2.0 class definition that extends the MovieClip class. First, create a class file named Oval.as and define a class method named `onLoad()`. Then ensure that the class file is placed in the proper class path, as in the following example:

```
// contents of Oval.as
class Oval extends MovieClip{
  public function onLoad () {
    trace ("onLoad called");
  }
}
```

Second, create a movie clip symbol in your library and name it Oval. Context-click (usually right-click) on the symbol in the Library panel and select Linkage... from the pop-up menu. Click the Export for ActionScript option and enter `Oval` in the Identifier and ActionScript 2.0 Class fields. Leave the "Export in First Frame" option selected, and click OK.

Third, go to the first frame of your file and enter the following code in the Actions Panel:

```
var myOval:Oval = Oval(attachMovie("Oval","Oval_1",1));
```

Finally, do a test movie, and you should see the output text "onLoad called".

See also

`loadMovie (MovieClip.loadMovie method)`, `onClipEvent handler`, `MovieClipLoader`

onMouseDown (MovieClip.onMouseDown handler)

```
onMouseDown = function() {}
```

Invoked when the mouse button is pressed. You must define a function that executes when the event handler is invoked. You can define the function on the timeline or in a class file that extends the MovieClip class or is linked to a symbol in the library.

Availability: ActionScript 1.0; Flash Player 6

Example

The following example defines a function for the onMouseDown() method that sends a trace() action to the Output panel:

```
my_mc.onMouseDown = function () {
  trace ("onMouseDown called");
}
```

onMouseMove (MovieClip.onMouseMove handler)

```
onMouseMove = function() {}
```

Invoked when the mouse moves. You must define a function that executes when the event handler is invoked. You can define the function on the timeline or in a class file that extends the MovieClip class or is linked to a symbol in the library.

Availability: ActionScript 1.0; Flash Player 6

Example

The following example defines a function for the onMouseMove() method that sends a trace() action to the Output panel:

```
my_mc.onMouseMove = function () {
  trace ("onMouseMove called");
}
```

onMouseUp (MovieClip.onMouseUp handler)

```
onMouseUp = function() {}
```

Invoked when the mouse button is released. You must define a function that executes when the event handler is invoked. You can define the function on the timeline or in a class file that extends the MovieClip class or is linked to a symbol in the library.

Availability: ActionScript 1.0; Flash Player 6

Example

The following example defines a function for the onMouseUp() method that sends a trace() action to the Output panel:

```
my_mc.onMouseUp = function () {
```

```
    trace ("onMouseUp called");
}
```

onPress (MovieClip.onPress handler)

`onPress = function() {}`

Invoked when the user clicks the mouse while the pointer is over a movie clip. You must define a function that executes when the event handler is invoked. You can define the function in the library.

Availability: ActionScript 1.0; Flash Player 6

Example

The following example defines a function for the `onPress()` method that sends a `trace()` action to the Output panel:

```
my_mc.onPress = function () {
  trace ("onPress called");
}
```

onRelease (MovieClip.onRelease handler)

`onRelease = function() {}`

Invoked when a user releases the mouse button over a movie clip. You must define a function that executes when the event handler is invoked. You can define the function on the timeline or in a class file that extends the MovieClip class or is linked to a symbol in the library.

Availability: ActionScript 1.0; Flash Player 6

Example

The following example defines a function for the `onRelease()` method that sends a `trace()` action to the Output panel:

```
my_mc.onRelease = function () {
  trace ("onRelease called");
}
```

onReleaseOutside (MovieClip.onReleaseOutside handler)

`onReleaseOutside = function() {}`

Invoked after a user presses the mouse button inside the movie clip area and then releases it outside the movie clip area.

You must define a function that executes when the event handler is invoked. You can define the function on the timeline or in a class file that extends the MovieClip class or is linked to a symbol in the library.

Availability: ActionScript 1.0; Flash Player 6

Example

The following example defines a function for the `onReleaseOutside()` method that sends a `trace()` action to the Output panel:

```
my_mc.onReleaseOutside = function () {
  trace ("onReleaseOutside called");
}
```

onRollOut (MovieClip.onRollOut handler)

```
onRollOut = function() {}
```

Invoked when a user moves the pointer outside a movie clip area.

You must define a function that executes when the event handler is invoked. You can define the function on the timeline or in a class file that extends the MovieClip class or is linked to a symbol in the library.

Availability: ActionScript 1.0; Flash Player 6

Example

The following example defines a function for the `onRollOut()` method that sends a `trace()` action to the Output panel:

```
my_mc.onRollOut = function () {
  trace ("onRollOut called");
}
```

onRollOver (MovieClip.onRollOver handler)

```
onRollOver = function() {}
```

Invoked when user moves the pointer over a movie clip area.

You must define a function that executes when the event handler is invoked. You can define the function on the timeline or in a class file that extends the MovieClip class or is linked to a symbol in the library.

Availability: ActionScript 1.0; Flash Player 6

Example

The following example defines a function for the `onRollOver()` method that sends a `trace()` action to the Output panel:

```
my_mc.onRollOver = function () {
  trace ("onRollOver called");
}
```

onSetFocus (MovieClip.onSetFocus handler)

```
onSetFocus = function(oldFocus:Object) {}
```

Invoked when a movie clip receives keyboard focus. The `oldFocus` parameter is the object that loses the focus. For example, if the user presses the Tab key to move the input focus from a movie clip to a text field, `oldFocus` contains the movie clip instance.

If there is no previously focused object, `oldFocus` contains a null value.

You must define a function that executes when the event handler in invoked. You can define the function on the timeline or in a class file that extends the MovieClip class or is linked to a symbol in the library.

Availability: ActionScript 1.0; Flash Player 6

Parameters

`oldFocus:Object` - The object to lose focus.

Example

The following example displays information about the movie clip that receives keyboard focus, and the instance that previously had focus. Two movie clips, called `my_mc` and `other_mc` are on the Stage. Add the following ActionScript to your AS or FLA document:

```
my_mc.onRelease = Void;
other_mc.onRelease = Void;
my_mc.onSetFocus = function(oldFocus) {
  trace("onSetFocus called, previous focus was: "+oldFocus);
}
```

Tab between the two instances, and information displays in the Output panel.

See also

`onKillFocus (MovieClip.onKillFocus handler)`

onUnload (MovieClip.onUnload handler)

```
onUnload = function() {}
```

Invoked in the first frame after the movie clip is removed from the Timeline. Flash processes the actions associated with the `onUnload` event handler before attaching any actions to the affected frame. You must define a function that executes when the event handler is invoked. You can define the function on the Timeline or in a class file that extends the MovieClip class or is linked to a symbol in the library.

Availability: ActionScript 1.0; Flash Player 6

Example

The following example defines a function for the `MovieClip.onUnload()` method that sends a `trace()` action to the Output panel:

```
my_mc.onUnload = function () {
  trace ("onUnload called");
}
```

opaqueBackground (MovieClip.opaqueBackground property)

```
public opaqueBackground : Number
```

The color of the movie clip's opaque (not transparent) background of the color specified by the number (an RGB hexadecimal value). If the value is `null` or `undefined`, there is no opaque background. For movie clips in which the `cacheAsBitmap` property is set to `true`, setting `opaqueBackground` can improve rendering performance.

You recognize a greater performance benefit with a movie clip that would have many transparent regions if `opaqueBackground` were not set.

Note: The opaque background region is not matched in a `hitTest()` method that has the `shapeFlag` parameter set to `true`.

Availability: ActionScript 1.0; Flash Player 8

Example

The following example creates a triangle outline and sets the `opaqueBackground` property to a specific color:

```
var triangle:MovieClip = this.createEmptyMovieClip("triangle",
  this.getNextHighestDepth());
triangle._x = triangle._y = 50;
triangle.lineStyle(3, 0xFFCC00);
triangle.lineTo(0, 30);
triangle.lineTo(50, 0);
triangle.lineTo(0, 0);
triangle.endFill();
```

```
triangle.opaqueBackground = 0xCCCCCC;
```
If your SWF file includes a version 2 component, use the version 2 components DepthManager class instead of the `MovieClip.getNextHighestDepth()` method, which is used in this example.

See also

`cacheAsBitmap (MovieClip.cacheAsBitmap property)`, `hitTest (MovieClip.hitTest method)`

_parent (MovieClip._parent property)

```
public _parent : MovieClip
```
A reference to the movie clip or object that contains the current movie clip or object. The current object is the object that references the `_parent` property. Use the `_parent` property to specify a relative path to movie clips or objects that are above the current movie clip or object.

You can use `_parent` to move up multiple levels in the display list, as in the following code:
```
this._parent._parent._alpha = 20;
```
Availability: ActionScript 1.0; Flash Player 5

Example

The following example traces the reference to a movie clip and its parent timeline. Create a movie clip with the instance name `my_mc`, and add it to the main timeline. Add the following ActionScript to your FLA or AS file:
```
my_mc.onRelease = function() {
   trace("You clicked the movie clip: "+this);
   trace("The parent of "+this._name+" is: "+this._parent);
}
```
When you click the movie clip, the following information appears in the Output panel:
```
You clicked the movie clip: _level0.my_mc
The parent of my_mc is: _level0
```

See also

`_parent (Button._parent property)`, `_root property`, `targetPath function`, `_parent (TextField._parent property)`

play (MovieClip.play method)

```
public play() : Void
```

Moves the playhead in the timeline of the movie clip.

You can extend the methods and event handlers of the MovieClip class by creating a subclass.

Availability: ActionScript 1.0; Flash Player 5

Example

Use the following ActionScript to play the main timeline of a SWF file. This ActionScript is for a movie clip button called my_mc on the main Timeline:

```
stop();
my_mc.onRelease = function() {
  this._parent.play();
};
```

Use the following ActionScript to play the timeline of a movie clip in a SWF file. This ActionScript is for a button called my_btn on the main Timeline that plays a movie clip called animation_mc:

```
animation_mc.stop();
my_btn.onRelease = function(){
  animation_mc.play();
};
```

See also

play function, gotoAndPlay (MovieClip.gotoAndPlay method), gotoAndPlay function

prevFrame (MovieClip.prevFrame method)

```
public prevFrame() : Void
```

Sends the playhead to the previous frame and stops it.

You can extend the methods and event handlers of the MovieClip class by creating a subclass.

Availability: ActionScript 1.0; Flash Player 5

Example

In the following example, two movie clip buttons control the timeline. The prev_mc button moves the playhead to the previous frame, and the next_mc button moves the playhead to the next frame. Add content to a series of frames on the Timeline, and add the following ActionScript on Frame 1 of the Timeline:

```
stop();
prev_mc.onRelease = function() {
  var parent_mc:MovieClip = this._parent;
  if (parent_mc._currentframe>1) {
  parent_mc.prevFrame();
```

```
  } else {
  parent_mc.gotoAndStop(parent_mc._totalframes);
  }
};
next_mc.onRelease = function() {
  var parent_mc:MovieClip = this._parent;
  if (parent_mc._currentframe<parent_mc._totalframes) {
  parent_mc.nextFrame();
  } else {
  parent_mc.gotoAndStop(1);
  }
};
```

See also

prevFrame function

_quality (MovieClip._quality property)

`public _quality : String`

Sets or retrieves the rendering quality used for a SWF file. Device fonts are always aliased and therefore are unaffected by the `_quality` property.

You can set the `_quality` to the following values:

Value	Description	Graphic anti-aliasing	Bitmap smoothing
`"LOW"`	Low rendering quality.	Graphics are not anti-aliased.	Bitmaps are not smoothed.
`"MEDIUM"`	Medium rendering quality. This setting is suitable for movies that do not contain text.	Graphics are anti-aliased using a 2 x 2 pixel grid.	Flash Player 8: Bitmaps are smoothed based on the `smoothing` parameter used in `MovieClip.attachBitmap()` and `MovieClip.beginBitmapFill()` calls. Flash Player 6 and 7: Bitmaps are not smoothed.

Value	Description	Graphic anti-aliasing	Bitmap smoothing
`"HIGH"`	High rendering quality. This setting is the default rendering quality setting that Flash uses.	Graphics are anti-aliased using a 4 x 4 pixel grid.	Flash Player 8: Bitmaps are smoothed based on the `smoothing` parameter used in `MovieClip.attachBitmap()` and `MovieClip.beginBitmapFill()` calls. Flash Player 6 and 7: Bitmaps are smoothed if the movie clip is static.
`"BEST"`	Very high rendering quality.	Graphics are anti-aliased using a 4 x 4 pixel grid.	Flash Player 8: Bitmaps are smoothed based on the `smoothing` parameter used in `MovieClip.attachBitmap()` and `MovieClip.beginBitmapFill()` calls. When the `smoothing` is set, the result renders with higher quality when the movie clip is scaled down, by using an averaging algorithm. This can slow down rendering, but it allows for applications such as high-quality thumbnails of large images. Flash Player 6 and 7: Bitmaps are always smoothed.

> **NOTE**
> Although you can specify this property for a `MovieClip` object, it is also a global property, and you can specify its value simply as `_quality`.

Availability: ActionScript 1.0; Flash Player 6

Example

This example sets the rendering quality of a movie clip named `my_mc` to `LOW`:

```
my_mc._quality = "LOW";
```

`_quality property`

removeMovieClip (MovieClip.removeMovieClip method)

`public removeMovieClip() : Void`

Removes a movie clip instance created with `duplicateMovieClip()`, `MovieClip.duplicateMovieClip()`, `MovieClip.createEmptyMovieClip()`, or `MovieClip.attachMovie()`.

This method does not remove a movie clip assigned to a negative depth value. Movie clips created in the authoring tool are assigned negative depth values by default. To remove a movie clip that is assigned to a negative depth value, first use the `MovieClip.swapDepths()` method to move the movie clip to a positive depth value.

> **NOTE**
>
> If you are using version 2 components, do not use this method. If you place a version 2 component either on the Stage or in the Library, the `getNextHighestDepth()` method can sometimes return depth 1048676, which is outside the valid range. If you are using version 2 components, you should always use version 2 components DepthManager class.

> **NOTE**
>
> If you are using version 2 components, and use `MovieClip.getNextHighestDepth()` instead of the version 2 components DepthManager class to assign depth values, you may find that `removeMovieClip()` fails silently. When any version 2 component is used, the DepthManager class automatically reserves the highest (1048575) and lowest (-16383) available depths for cursors and tooltips. A subsequent call to `getNextHighestDepth()` returns 1048576, which is outside the valid range. The `removeMovieClip()` method fails silently if it encounters a depth value outside the valid range. If you must use `getNextHighestDepth()` with version 2 components, you can use `swapDepths()` to assign a valid depth value or use `MovieClip.unloadMovie()` to remove the contents of the movie clip. Alternatively, you can use the `DepthManager` class to assign depth values within the valid range.

You can extend the methods and event handlers of the MovieClip class by creating a subclass.

Availability: ActionScript 1.0; Flash Player 5

Example

Each time you click a button in the following example, you attach a movie clip instance to the Stage in a random position. When you click a movie clip instance, you remove that instance from the SWF file.

```
function randRange(min:Number, max:Number):Number {
```

```
    var randNum:Number = Math.round(Math.random()*(max-min))+min;
    return randNum;
}
var bugNum:Number = 0;
addBug_btn.onRelease = addBug;
function addBug() {
    var thisBug:MovieClip = this._parent.attachMovie("bug_id",
    "bug"+bugNum+"_mc", bugNum,
{_x:randRange(50, 500), _y:randRange(50, 350)});
    thisBug.onRelease = function() {
    this.removeMovieClip();
    };
    bugNum++;
}
```

See also

duplicateMovieClip function, createEmptyMovieClip
(MovieClip.createEmptyMovieClip method), duplicateMovieClip
(MovieClip.duplicateMovieClip method), attachMovie (MovieClip.attachMovie
method), swapDepths (MovieClip.swapDepths method)

_rotation (MovieClip._rotation property)

public _rotation : Number

Specifies the rotation of the movie clip, in degrees, from its original orientation. Values from 0 to 180 represent clockwise rotation; values from 0 to -180 represent counterclockwise rotation. Values outside this range are added to or subtracted from 360 to obtain a value within the range; for example, the statement my_mc._rotation = 450 is the same as my_mc._rotation = 90.

Availability: ActionScript 1.0; Flash Player 4

Example

The following example creates a `triangle` movie clip instance dynamically. When you run the SWF file, click the movie clip to rotate it.

```
this.createEmptyMovieClip("triangle", this.getNextHighestDepth());

triangle.beginFill(0x0000FF, 100);
triangle.moveTo(100, 100);
triangle.lineTo(100, 150);
triangle.lineTo(150, 100);
triangle.lineTo(100, 100);

triangle.onMouseUp= function() {
  this._rotation += 15;
};
```

The `MovieClip.getNextHighestDepth()` method used in this example requires Flash Player 7 or later. If your SWF file includes a version 2 component, use the version 2 components DepthManager class instead of the `MovieClip.getNextHighestDepth()` method.

See also

`_rotation` (Button._rotation property), `_rotation` (TextField._rotation property)

scale9Grid (MovieClip.scale9Grid property)

`public scale9Grid : Rectangle`

The rectangular region that defines the nine scaling regions for the movie clip. If set to `null`, the entire movie clip scales normally when any scale transformation is applied.

When a `scale9Grid` property is defined for a movie clip, the movie clip is divided into a grid with nine regions, based on the `scale9Grid` rectangle, which defines the center region of the grid. The grid has eight other regions:

- The area in the upper-left corner outside the rectangle
- The area above the rectangle
- The area in the upper-right corner outside the rectangle
- The area to the left of the rectangle
- The area to the right of the rectangle
- The area in the lower-left corner outside the rectangle
- The area below the rectangle
- The area in the lower-right corner outside the rectangle

You can think of the eight regions outside of the center (defined by the rectangle) as being like a picture frame that has special rules applied to it when the movie clip is scaled.

When the scale9Grid property is set and a movie clip is scaled, all text and child movie clips scale normally, regardless of which regions of the scale9 grid they are located in; however, for other types of objects the following rules apply:

- All content in the center region scales normally.
- Any content in the corners are only scaled when the center region is scaled to 0.
- Any content in the top and bottom regions scale only horizontally. Content in the left-hand and right-hand regions scale only vertically.
- All fills (including bitmaps, video, and gradients) are stretched to fit their shapes, and all fills (including bitmaps, video, and gradients) are stretched to fit their shapes.

If a movie clip is rotated, subsequent scaling is normal (and the scale9Grid property is ignored).

For example, consider the following movie clip and a rectangle that is applied as the movie clip's scale9Grid property:

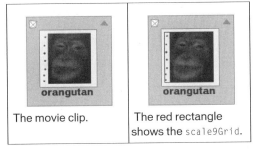

| The movie clip. | The red rectangle shows the scale9Grid. |

When the movie clip is scaled or stretched, the objects within the rectangle scale normally, but the objects outside of the rectangle scale according to the scale9Grid rules:

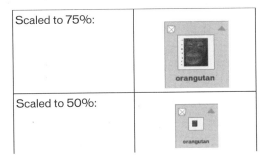

| Scaled to 75%: | |
| Scaled to 50%: | |

Scaled to 25%:	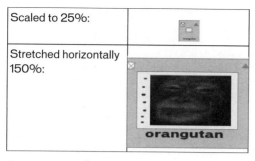
Stretched horizontally 150%:	

A common use for setting scale9Grid is to set up a component in which edge lines retain the same width when the component is scaled.

In the Macromedia Flash authoring environment, you can enable guides for *9-slice scaling* for a movie clip symbol in a library. This lets you graphically determine the scale9grid for the object. When you set 9-slice scaling for a symbol, the scale9grid property of any instance of that symbol is automatically set. For a symbol that has 9-slice scaling enabled, when you create the SWF file any curve that spans more than one region of the 9-slice scaling grid is divided into separate curves for each region of the grid. For instance, consider a curve in a movie clip symbol for which 9-slice scaling is enabled and the same curve in a movie clip symbol for which 9-slice scaling is *not* enabled:

Symbol with 9-slice scaling enabled:	
Symbol without 9-slice scaling enabled:	

When Flash creates the SWF file, the curve in first movie clip illustrated is divided into three curves. This is not the case for the second movie clip, for which the 9-slice scaling is not enabled. Even if you set scale9Grid for the second movie clip to a rectangle that matches the scale9Grid of the first movie clip, when you scale these movie clips the results differ because of the way Flash divides the curves in the first movie clip:

Symbol with 9-slice scaling enabled	
Symbol without 9-slice scaling enabled	

Availability: ActionScript 1.0; Flash Player 8

Example

The following creates a movie clip that contains a 20-pixel line (which forms a border) and a gradient fill. The movie clip scales based on the mouse position, and because of the scale9Grid set for the movie clip, the thickness of the 20-pixel line does not vary when the movie clip scales (although the gradient in the movie clip *does* scale):

```
import flash.geom.Rectangle;
import flash.geom.Matrix;

this.createEmptyMovieClip("my_mc", this.getNextHighestDepth());

var grid:Rectangle = new Rectangle(20, 20, 260, 260);
my_mc.scale9Grid = grid ;

my_mc._x = 50;
my_mc._y = 50;

function onMouseMove()
{
  my_mc._width = _xmouse;
  my_mc._height = _ymouse;
}

my_mc.lineStyle(20, 0xff3333, 100);
var gradient_matrix:Matrix = new Matrix();
gradient_matrix.createGradientBox(15, 15, Math.PI, 10, 10);
my_mc.beginGradientFill("radial", [0xffff00, 0x0000ff],
      [100, 100], [0, 0xFF], gradient_matrix,
      "reflect", "RGB", 0.9);
my_mc.moveTo(0, 0);
my_mc.lineTo(0, 300);
my_mc.lineTo(300, 300);
my_mc.lineTo(300, 0);
my_mc.lineTo(0, 0);
my_mc.endFill();
```

See also

```
Rectangle (flash.geom.Rectangle)
```

scrollRect (MovieClip.scrollRect property)

```
public scrollRect : Object
```

The scrollRect property allows you to quickly scroll movie clip content and have a window viewing larger content. Text fields and complex content scroll much faster, because pixel level copying is used to scroll data instead of regenerating the entire movie clip from vector data. To see the performance gain, use scrollRect in conjunction with a movie clip that has cacheAsBitmap set to true.

The movie clip is cropped and scrolled with a specific width, height, and scrolling offsets. The scrollRect properties are stored in the movie clip's coordinate space and are scaled just like the overall movie clip. The corner bounds of the cropped window on the scrolling movie clip are the origin of the movie clip (0, 0) and the (scrollWidth, scrollHeight) point. These points are not centered around the origin but use the origin at the upper-left corner. A scrolled movie clip always scrolls in whole pixel increments. If the movie clip is rotated 90 degrees and you scroll it left and right (by setting the scrollRect.x property), it scrolls up and down.

If set to a flash.geom.Rectangle object, the movie clip is cropped to a certain size and scrolled.

Availability: ActionScript 1.0; Flash Player 8

Example

The following example sets up a MovieClip hiearchy (by calling the setUpContainer() function) and then sets a new Rectangle as the scrollRect property.

```
import flash.geom.Rectangle;
var container:MovieClip = setUpContainer();
var window:Rectangle = new Rectangle(0, 0, 100, 40);
container.scrollRect = window;

function setUpContainer():MovieClip {
  var mc:MovieClip = this.createEmptyMovieClip("container",
  this.getNextHighestDepth());
  mc._x = 50;
  mc._y = 50;
  mc.opaqueBackground = 0xCCCCCC;

  var content:MovieClip = mc.createEmptyMovieClip("content",
  mc.getNextHighestDepth());
  var colors:Array = [0xFF0000, 0x0000FF];
  var alphas:Array = [100, 100];
  var ratios:Array = [0, 0xFF];
  var matrix:Object = {a:150, b:0, c:0, d:0, e:150, f:0, g:150, h:150,
  i:1};
  content.beginGradientFill("linear", colors, alphas, ratios, matrix);
  content.lineTo(300, 0);
  content.lineTo(300, 300);
```

```
content.lineTo(0, 300);
content.lineTo(0, 0);
content.endFill();
content._rotation = -90;

mc.onEnterFrame = function() {
  this.content._y += 1;
}

return mc;
}
```

The `setUpContainer()` function performs the following steps:

- Create a MovieClip named `container`
- Create a MovieClip named `content` inside of `container`
- Draw a gradient shape inside of the `content` MovieClip
- Return a reference to the `container` MovieClip

If your SWF file includes a version 2 component, use the version 2 components DepthManager class instead of the `MovieClip.getNextHighestDepth()` method, which is used in this example.

setMask (MovieClip.setMask method)

`public setMask(mc:Object) : Void`

Makes the movie clip in the parameter `mc` a mask that reveals the calling movie clip.

The `setMask()` method allows multiple-frame movie clips with complex, multilayered content to act as masks (which is possible by using mask layers). If you have device fonts in a masked movie clip, they are drawn but not masked. You can't set a movie clip to be its own mask; for example, `my_mc.setMask(my_mc)`.

If you create a mask layer that contains a movie clip, and then apply the `setMask()` method to it, the `setMask()` call takes priority and this is not reversible. For example, you could have a movie clip in a mask layer called `UIMask` that masks another layer that contains another movie clip called `UIMaskee`. If, as the SWF file plays, you call `UIMask.setMask(UIMaskee)`, from that point on, `UIMask` is masked by `UIMaskee`.

To cancel a mask created with ActionScript, pass the value `null` to the `setMask()` method. The following code cancels the mask without affecting the mask layer in the timeline.

`UIMask.setMask(null);`

You can extend the methods and event handlers of the MovieClip class by creating a subclass.

Availability: ActionScript 1.0; Flash Player 6

Parameters

`mc:Object` - The instance name of a movie clip to be a mask. This can be a String or a MovieClip.

Example

The following code uses the `circleMask_mc` movie clip to mask the `theMaskee_mc` movie clip:

```
theMaskee_mc.setMask(circleMask_mc);
```

_soundbuftime (MovieClip._soundbuftime property)

`public _soundbuftime : Number`

Specifies the number of seconds a sound prebuffers before it starts to stream.

Note: Although you can specify this property for a MovieClip object, it is actually a global property that applies to all sounds loaded, and you can specify its value simply as `_soundbuftime`. Setting this property for a MovieClip object actually sets the global property.

Availability: ActionScript 1.0; Flash Player 6

See also

`_soundbuftime property`

startDrag (MovieClip.startDrag method)

```
public startDrag([lockCenter:Boolean], [left:Number], [top:Number],
    [right:Number], [bottom:Number]) : Void
```

Lets the user drag the specified movie clip. The movie clip remains draggable until explicitly stopped through a call to `MovieClip.stopDrag()`, or until another movie clip is made draggable. Only one movie clip at a time is draggable.

You can extend the methods and event handlers of the MovieClip class by creating a subclass.

Availability: ActionScript 1.0; Flash Player 5

Parameters

`lockCenter:Boolean` [optional] - A Boolean value that specifies whether the draggable movie clip is locked to the center of the mouse position (`true`), or locked to the point where the user first clicked the movie clip (`false`).

`left:Number` [optional] - Value relative to the coordinates of the movie clip's parent that specify a constraint rectangle for the movie clip.

top:Number [optional] - Value relative to the coordinates of the movie clip's parent that specify a constraint rectangle for the movie clip.

right:Number [optional] - Value relative to the coordinates of the movie clip's parent that specify a constraint rectangle for the movie clip.

bottom:Number [optional] - Value relative to the coordinates of the movie clip's parent that specify a constraint rectangle for the movie clip.

Example

The following example creates a draggable movie clip instance called mc_1:

```
this.createEmptyMovieClip("mc_1", 1);

with (mc_1) {
  lineStyle(1, 0xCCCCCC);
  beginFill(0x4827CF);
  moveTo(0, 0);
  lineTo(80, 0);
  lineTo(80, 60);
  lineTo(0, 60);
  lineTo(0, 0);
  endFill();
}

mc_1.onPress = function() {
  this.startDrag();
};
mc_1.onRelease = function() {
  this.stopDrag();
};
```

See also

_droptarget (MovieClip._droptarget property), startDrag function, stopDrag (MovieClip.stopDrag method)

stop (MovieClip.stop method)

public stop() : Void

Stops the movie clip that is currently playing.

You can extend the methods and event handlers of the MovieClip class by creating a subclass.

Availability: ActionScript 1.0; Flash Player 5

Example

The following example shows how to stop a movie clip named `aMovieClip`:

```
aMovieClip.stop();
```

See also

```
stop function
```

stopDrag (MovieClip.stopDrag method)

```
public stopDrag() : Void
```

Ends a `MovieClip.startDrag()` method. A movie clip that was made draggable with that method remains draggable until a `stopDrag()` method is added, or until another movie clip becomes draggable. Only one movie clip is draggable at a time.

You can extend the methods and event handlers of the MovieClip class by creating a subclass.

Availability: ActionScript 1.0; Flash Player 5

Example

The following example creates a draggable movie clip instance called `mc_1`:

```
this.createEmptyMovieClip("mc_1", 1);

with (mc_1) {
  lineStyle(1, 0xCCCCCC);
  beginFill(0x4827CF);
  moveTo(0, 0);
  lineTo(80, 0);
  lineTo(80, 60);
  lineTo(0, 60);
  lineTo(0, 0);
  endFill();
}

mc_1.onPress = function() {
  this.startDrag();
};
mc_1.onRelease = function() {
  this.stopDrag();
};
```

See also

`_droptarget (MovieClip._droptarget property)`, `startDrag (MovieClip.startDrag method)`, `stopDrag function`

swapDepths (MovieClip.swapDepths method)

```
public swapDepths(target:Object) : Void
```

Swaps the stacking, or depth level (z-order), of this movie clip with the movie clip that is specified by the `target` parameter, or with the movie clip that currently occupies the depth level that is specified in the `target` parameter. Both movie clips must have the same parent movie clip. Swapping the depth level of movie clips has the effect of moving one movie clip in front of or behind the other. If a movie clip is tweening when this method is called, the tweening is stopped.

You can extend the methods and event handlers of the MovieClip class by creating a subclass.

Availability: ActionScript 1.0; Flash Player 5

Parameters

`target:Object` - This parameter can take one of two forms:

- A Number that specifies the depth level where the movie clip is to be placed.

- A String that specifies the movie clip instance whose depth is swapped with the movie clip for which the method is being applied. Both movie clips must have the same parent movie clip.

Example

The following example swaps the stacking order of two movie clip instances. Overlap two movie clip instances, called `myMC1_mc` and `myMC2_mc`, on the Stage and then add the following script to the parent Timeline:

```
myMC1_mc.onRelease = function() {
  this.swapDepths(myMC2_mc);
};
myMC2_mc.onRelease = function() {
  this.swapDepths(myMC1_mc);
};
```

See also

`_level` property, getDepth (MovieClip.getDepth method), getInstanceAtDepth (MovieClip.getInstanceAtDepth method), getNextHighestDepth (MovieClip.getNextHighestDepth method)

tabChildren (MovieClip.tabChildren property)

`public tabChildren : Boolean`

Determines whether the children of a movie clip are included in the automatic tab ordering. If the `tabChildren` property is `undefined` or `true`, the children of a movie clip are included in automatic tab ordering. If the value of `tabChildren` is `false`, the children of a movie clip are not included in automatic tab ordering. The default value is `undefined`.

Availability: ActionScript 1.0; Flash Player 6

Example

A list box user interface widget that is built as a movie clip contains several items. The user can click each item to select it, so each item is implemented as a button. However, only the list box itself should be a tab stop. The items inside the list box should be excluded from tab ordering. To do this, you set the `tabChildren` property of the list box to `false`.

The `tabChildren` property has no effect if the `tabIndex` property is used; the `tabChildren` property affects only automatic tab ordering.

The following example disables tabbing for all child movie clips inside a parent movie clip called `menu_mc`:

```
menu_mc.onRelease = function(){};
menu_mc.menu1_mc.onRelease = function(){};
menu_mc.menu2_mc.onRelease = function(){};
menu_mc.menu3_mc.onRelease = function(){};
menu_mc.menu4_mc.onRelease = function(){};

menu_mc.tabChildren = false;
```

Change the last line of code to the following to include the child movie clip instances of `menu_mc` in the automatic tab ordering:

```
menu_mc.tabChildren = true;
```

See also

`tabIndex (Button.tabIndex property)`, `tabEnabled (MovieClip.tabEnabled property)`, `tabIndex (MovieClip.tabIndex property)`, `tabIndex (TextField.tabIndex property)`

---

tabEnabled (MovieClip.tabEnabled property)

`public tabEnabled : Boolean`

Specifies whether the movie clip is included in automatic tab ordering. It is `undefined` by default.

If the `tabEnabled` property is `undefined`, the object is included in automatic tab ordering only if it defines at least one movie clip handler, such as `MovieClip.onRelease`. If `tabEnabled` is `true`, the object is included in automatic tab ordering. If the `tabIndex` property is also set to a value, the object is included in custom tab ordering as well.

If `tabEnabled` is `false`, the object is not included in automatic or custom tab ordering, even if the `tabIndex` property is set. However, if `MovieClip.tabChildren` is `true`, you can still include the movie clip's children in automatic tab ordering, even if `tabEnabled` is set to `false`.

Availability: ActionScript 1.0; Flash Player 6

Example

The following example does not include `myMC2_mc` in the automatic tab ordering:

```
myMC1_mc.onRelease = function() {};
myMC2_mc.onRelease = function() {};
myMC3_mc.onRelease = function() {};
myMC2_mc.tabEnabled = false;
```

See also

`onRelease (MovieClip.onRelease handler)`, `tabEnabled (Button.tabEnabled property)`, `tabChildren (MovieClip.tabChildren property)`, `tabIndex (MovieClip.tabIndex property)`, `tabEnabled (TextField.tabEnabled property)`

tabIndex (MovieClip.tabIndex property)

`public tabIndex : Number`

Lets you customize the tab ordering of objects in a movie. The `tabIndex` property is `undefined` by default. You can set the `tabIndex` property on a button, movie clip, or text field instance.

If an object in a SWF file contains a `tabIndex` property, automatic tab ordering is disabled, and the tab ordering is calculated from the `tabIndex` properties of objects in the SWF file. The custom tab ordering includes only objects that have `tabIndex` properties.

The tabIndex property must be a positive integer. The objects are ordered according to their tabIndex properties, in ascending order. An object with a tabIndex value of 1 precedes an object with a tabIndex value of 2. The custom tab ordering disregards the hierarchical relationships of objects in a SWF file. All objects in the SWF file with tabIndex properties are placed in the tab order. Do not use the same tabIndex value for multiple objects.

Availability: ActionScript 1.0; Flash Player 6

Example

The following ActionScript sets a custom tab order for three movie clip instances.

```
myMC1_mc.onRelease = function() {};
myMC2_mc.onRelease = function() {};
myMC3_mc.onRelease = function() {};
myMC1_mc.tabIndex = 2;
myMC2_mc.tabIndex = 1;
myMC3_mc.tabIndex = 3;
```

See also

tabIndex (Button.tabIndex property), tabIndex (TextField.tabIndex property)

_target (MovieClip._target property)

public _target : String [read-only]

Returns the target path of the movie clip instance, in slash notation. Use the eval() function to convert the target path to dot notation.

Availability: ActionScript 1.0; Flash Player 4

Example

The following example displays the target paths of movie clip instances in a SWF file, in both slash and dot notation.

```
for (var i in this) {
  if (typeof (this[i]) == "movieclip") {
  trace("name: " + this[i]._name + ",\t target: " + this[i]._target + ",\t
  target(2):"
     + eval(this[i]._target));
  }
}
```

_totalframes (MovieClip._totalframes property)

```
public _totalframes : Number [read-only]
```

Returns the total number of frames in the movie clip instance specified in the MovieClip parameter.

Availability: ActionScript 1.0; Flash Player 4

Example

In the following example, two movie clip buttons control the Timeline. The prev_mc button moves the playhead to the previous frame, and the next_mc button moves the playhead to the next frame. Add content to a series of frames on the Timeline, and add the following ActionScript on Frame 1 of the Timeline:

```
stop();
prev_mc.onRelease = function() {
   var parent_mc:MovieClip = this._parent;
   if (parent_mc._currentframe>1) {
   parent_mc.prevFrame();
   } else {
   parent_mc.gotoAndStop(parent_mc._totalframes);
   }
};
next_mc.onRelease = function() {
   var parent_mc:MovieClip = this._parent;
   if (parent_mc._currentframe<parent_mc._totalframes) {
   parent_mc.nextFrame();
   } else {
   parent_mc.gotoAndStop(1);
   }
};
```

trackAsMenu (MovieClip.trackAsMenu property)

```
public trackAsMenu : Boolean
```

A Boolean value that indicates whether other buttons or movie clips can receive mouse release events. The trackAsMenu property lets you create menus. You can set the trackAsMenu property on any button or movie clip object. If the trackAsMenu property does not exist, the default behavior is false.

You can change the trackAsMenu property at any time; the modified movie clip immediately uses the new behavior.

Availability: ActionScript 1.0; Flash Player 6

Example

The following example sets the `trackAsMenu` property for three movie clips on the Stage. Click a movie clip and release the mouse button on a second movie clip to see which instance receives the event.

```
myMC1_mc.trackAsMenu = true;
myMC2_mc.trackAsMenu = true;
myMC3_mc.trackAsMenu = false;

myMC1_mc.onRelease = clickMC;
myMC2_mc.onRelease = clickMC;
myMC3_mc.onRelease = clickMC;

function clickMC() {
  trace("you clicked the "+this._name+" movie clip.");
};
```

See also

`trackAsMenu (Button.trackAsMenu property)`

transform (MovieClip.transform property)

`public transform : Transform`

An object with properties pertaining to a movie clip's matrix, color transform, and pixel bounds. The specific properties matrix, colorTransform, and three read-only properties (`concatenatedMatrix`, `concatenatedColorTransform`, and `pixelBounds`) are described in the entry for the Transform class.

Each of the transform object's properties is itself an object. This is important because the only way to set new values for the matrix or colorTransform objects is to create an object and copy that object into the transform.matrix or transform.colorTransform property.

For example, to increase the `tx` value of a movie clip's matrix, you must make a copy of the entire matrix object, modify the `tx` property of the new object, and then copy the new object into the matrix property of the transform object:

```
var myMatrix:Object = myDisplayObject.transform.matrix;
myMatrix.tx += 10;
myDisplayObject.transform.matrix = myMatrix;
```

You cannot directly set the `tx` property. The following code has no effect on `myDisplayObject`: `myDisplayObject.transform.matrix.tx += 10;`

You can also copy an entire transform object and assign it to another movie clip's transform property. For example, the following code copies the entire transform object from `myOldDisplayObj` to `myNewDisplayObj`:

```
myNewDisplayObj.transform = myOldDisplayObj.transform;
```

The new movie clip, myNewDisplayObj, now has the same values for its matrix, color transform, and pixel bounds as the old movie clip, myOldDisplayObj.

Availability: ActionScript 1.0; Flash Player 8

Example

The following example shows how to use a movie clip's transform property to access and modify a movie clip's location by using Matix positioning.

```
import flash.geom.Matrix;

var rect:MovieClip = createRectangle(20, 80, 0xFF0000);

var translateMatrix:Matrix = new Matrix();
translateMatrix.translate(10, 0);

rect.onPress = function() {
  var tmpMatrix:Matrix = this.transform.matrix;
  tmpMatrix.concat(translateMatrix);
  this.transform.matrix = tmpMatrix;
}

function createRectangle(width:Number, height:Number, color:Number,
  scope:MovieClip):MovieClip {
  scope = (scope == undefined) ? this : scope;
  var depth:Number = scope.getNextHighestDepth();
  var mc:MovieClip = scope.createEmptyMovieClip("mc_" + depth, depth);
  mc.beginFill(color);
  mc.lineTo(0, height);
  mc.lineTo(width, height);
  mc.lineTo(width, 0);
  mc.lineTo(0, 0);
  return mc;
}
```

If your SWF file includes a version 2 component, use the version 2 components DepthManager class instead of the MovieClip.getNextHighestDepth() method, which is used in this example.

See also

Transform (flash.geom.Transform)

unloadMovie (MovieClip.unloadMovie method)

```
public unloadMovie() : Void
```

Removes the contents of a movie clip instance. The instance properties and clip handlers remain.

To remove the instance, including its properties and clip handlers, use `MovieClip.removeMovieClip()`.

You can extend the methods and event handlers of the MovieClip class by creating a subclass.

Availability: ActionScript 1.0; Flash Player 5

Example

The following example unloads a movie clip instance called `box` when a user clicks the `box` movie clip:

```
this.createEmptyMovieClip("box", 1);

with (box) {
  lineStyle(1, 0xCCCCCC);
  beginFill(0x4827CF);
  moveTo(0, 0);
  lineTo(80, 0);
  lineTo(80, 60);
  lineTo(0, 60);
  lineTo(0, 0);
  endFill();
}

box.onRelease = function() {
    box.unloadMovie();
};
```

See also

removeMovieClip (MovieClip.removeMovieClip method), attachMovie (MovieClip.attachMovie method), loadMovie (MovieClip.loadMovie method), unloadMovie function, unloadMovieNum function

_url (MovieClip._url property)

```
public _url : String [read-only]
```

Retrieves the URL of the SWF, JPEG, GIF, or PNG file from which the movie clip was downloaded.

Availability: ActionScript 1.0; Flash Player 4 - The ability to retrieve the URL of JPEG files from which the movie clip was downloaded is available as of Flash Player 6. The ability to retrieve the URL of GIF files and PNG files from which the movie clip was downloaded is available as of Flash Player 8.

Example

The following example displays the URL of the image that is loaded into the `image_mc` instance in the Output panel.

```
this.createEmptyMovieClip("image_mc", 1);
var mclListener:Object = new Object();
mclListener.onLoadInit = function(target_mc:MovieClip) {
  trace("_url: "+target_mc._url);
};
var image_mcl:MovieClipLoader = new MovieClipLoader();
image_mcl.addListener(mclListener);
image_mcl.loadClip("http://www.macromedia.com/images/shared/product_boxes/
  112x112/box_studio_112x112.jpg", image_mc);
```

The following example assigns the `menu_cm` ContextMenu object to the `image_mc` movie clip. The `menu_cm` object contains a custom menu item labeled `View Image in Browser` that has an associated function named `viewImage()`.

```
var menu_cm:ContextMenu = new ContextMenu();
menu_cm.customItems.push(new ContextMenuItem("View Image in Browser...",
  viewImage));
this.createEmptyMovieClip("image_mc", this.getNextHighestDepth());
var mclListener:Object = new Object();
mclListener.onLoadInit = function(target_mc:MovieClip) {
  target_mc.menu = menu_cm;
};
var image_mcl:MovieClipLoader = new MovieClipLoader();
image_mcl.addListener(mclListener);
image_mcl.loadClip("photo1.jpg", image_mc);

function viewImage(target_mc:MovieClip, obj:Object) {
  getURL(target_mc._url, "_blank");
}
```

When you right-click (Windows) or Control-click (Macintosh) the image at runtime, select View Image in Browser from the context menu to open the image in a browser window.

The MovieClipLoader class used in these examples requires Flash Player 7 or later. The `MovieClip.getNextHighestDepth()` method used in these examples requires Flash Player 7 or later. If your SWF file includes a version 2 component, use the version 2 components DepthManager class instead of the `MovieClip.getNextHighestDepth()` method.

useHandCursor (MovieClip.useHandCursor property)

`public useHandCursor : Boolean`

A Boolean value that indicates whether the pointing hand (hand cursor) appears when the mouse rolls over a movie clip. The default value of the `useHandCursor` property is `true`. If `useHandCursor` is set to `true`, the pointing hand used for buttons appears when the mouse rolls over a button movie clip. If `useHandCursor` is `false`, the arrow pointer is used instead.

You can change the `useHandCursor` property at any time; the modified movie clip immediately uses the new cursor behavior. The `useHandCursor` property can be read out of a prototype object.

Availability: ActionScript 1.0; Flash Player 6

Example

The following example sets the `useHandCursor` property for two movie clips called `myMC1_mc` and `myMC2_mc`. The property is set to `true` for one instance, and `false` for the other instance. Notice how both instances can still receive events.

```
myMC1_mc.onRelease = traceMC;
myMC2_mc.onRelease = traceMC;
myMC2_mc.useHandCursor = false;

function traceMC() {
  trace("you clicked: "+this._name);
};
```

_visible (MovieClip._visible property)

`public _visible : Boolean`

A Boolean value that indicates whether the movie clip is visible. Movie clips that are not visible (`_visible` property set to `false`) are disabled. For example, a button in a movie clip with `_visible` set to `false` cannot be clicked.

Availability: ActionScript 1.0; Flash Player 4

Example

The following example sets the _visible property for two movie clips called myMC1_mc and myMC2_mc. The property is set to true for one instance, and false for the other. Notice that myMC1_mc instance cannot be clicked after the _visible property is set to false.

```
myMC1_mc.onRelease = function() {
    trace(this._name+"._visible = false");
    this._visible = false;
};
myMC2_mc.onRelease = function() {
    trace(this._name+"._alpha = 0");
    this._alpha = 0;
};
```

See also

_visible (Button._visible property), _visible (TextField._visible property)

_width (MovieClip._width property)

```
public _width : Number
```

The width of the movie clip, in pixels.

Availability: ActionScript 1.0; Flash Player 4

Example

The following code example displays the height and width of a movie clip in the Output panel:

```
this.createEmptyMovieClip("triangle", this.getNextHighestDepth());

triangle.beginFill(0x0000FF, 100);
triangle.moveTo(100, 100);
triangle.lineTo(100, 150);
triangle.lineTo(150, 100);
triangle.lineTo(100, 100);

trace(triangle._name + " = " + triangle._width + " X " + triangle._height +
    " pixels");
```

The MovieClip.getNextHighestDepth() method used in this example requires Flash Player 7 or later. If your SWF file includes a version 2 component, use the version 2 components DepthManager class instead of the MovieClip.getNextHighestDepth() method.

See also

_height (MovieClip._height property)

_x (MovieClip._x property)

```
public _x : Number
```

An integer that sets the *x* coordinate of a movie clip relative to the local coordinates of the parent movie clip. If a movie clip is in the main Timeline, its coordinate system refers to the upper-left corner of the Stage as (0, 0). If the move clip is inside another movie clip that has transformations, the movie clip is in the local coordinate system of the enclosing movie clip. Thus, for a movie clip rotated 90° counterclockwise, the movie clip's children inherit a coordinate system that is rotated 90° counterclockwise. The movie clip's coordinates refer to the registration point position.

Availability: ActionScript 1.0; Flash Player 3

Example

The following example attaches a movie clip with the linkage identifier `cursor_id` to a SWF file. The movie clip is called `cursor_mc`, and it is used to replace the default mouse pointer. The following ActionScript sets the current coordinates of the movie clip instance to the position of the mouse pointer:

```
this.attachMovie("cursor_id", "cursor_mc", this.getNextHighestDepth(),
  {_x:_xmouse, _y:_ymouse});
Mouse.hide();
var mouseListener:Object = new Object();
mouseListener.onMouseMove = function() {
  cursor_mc._x = _xmouse;
  cursor_mc._y = _ymouse;
  updateAfterEvent();
};
Mouse.addListener(mouseListener);
```

The `MovieClip.getNextHighestDepth()` method used in this example requires Flash Player 7 or later. If your SWF file includes a version 2 component, use the version 2 components DepthManager class instead of the `MovieClip.getNextHighestDepth()` method.

See also

`_xscale (MovieClip._xscale property)`, `_y (MovieClip._y property)`, `_yscale (MovieClip._yscale property)`

_xmouse (MovieClip._xmouse property)

```
public _xmouse : Number [read-only]
```

Returns the *x* coordinate of the mouse position.

Availability: ActionScript 1.0; Flash Player 5

Example

The following example returns the current *x* and *y* coordinates of the mouse on the Stage (_level0) and in relation to a movie clip on the Stage called my_mc:

```
this.createTextField("mouse_txt", this.getNextHighestDepth(), 0, 0, 150,
   66);
mouse_txt.html = true;
mouse_txt.multiline = true;
var row1_str:String = " \t<b>_xmouse\t</b><b>_ymouse</b>";
my_mc.onMouseMove = function() {
   mouse_txt.htmlText = "<textformat tabStops='[50,100]'>";
   mouse_txt.htmlText += row1_str;
   mouse_txt.htmlText += "<b>_level0</b>\t"+_xmouse+"\t"+_ymouse;
   mouse_txt.htmlText += "<b>my_mc</b>\t"+this._xmouse+"\t"+this._ymouse;
   mouse_txt.htmlText += "</textformat>";
};
```

The MovieClip.getNextHighestDepth() method used in this example requires Flash Player 7 or later. If your SWF file includes a version 2 component, use the version 2 components DepthManager class instead of the MovieClip.getNextHighestDepth() method.

See also

Mouse, _ymouse (MovieClip._ymouse property)

_xscale (MovieClip._xscale property)

public _xscale : Number

Determines the horizontal scale (*percentage*) of the movie clip as applied from the registration point of the movie clip. The default registration point is (0,0).

Scaling the local coordinate system affects the _x and _y property settings, which are defined in whole pixels. For example, if the parent movie clip is scaled to 50%, setting the _x property moves an object in the movie clip by half the number of pixels as it would if the movie were set at 100%.

Availability: ActionScript 1.0; Flash Player 4

Example

The following example creates a movie clip called box_mc at runtime. The Drawing API is used to draw a box in this instance, and when the mouse rolls over the box, horizontal and vertical scaling is applied to the movie clip. When the mouse rolls off the instance, it returns to the previous scaling.

```
this.createEmptyMovieClip("box_mc", 1);
box_mc._x = 100;
box_mc._y = 100;
```

```
with (box_mc) {
  lineStyle(1, 0xCCCCCC);
  beginFill(0xEEEEEE);
  moveTo(0, 0);
  lineTo(80, 0);
  lineTo(80, 60);
  lineTo(0, 60);
  lineTo(0, 0);
  endFill();
};
box_mc.onRollOver = function() {
  this._x -= this._width/2;
  this._y -= this._height/2;
  this._xscale = 200;
  this._yscale = 200;
};
box_mc.onRollOut = function() {
  this._xscale = 100;
  this._yscale = 100;
  this._x += this._width/2;
  this._y += this._height/2;
};
```

See also

_width (MovieClip._width property), _x (MovieClip._x property), _y (MovieClip._y property), _yscale (MovieClip._yscale property)

_y (MovieClip._y property)

public _y : Number

Sets the *y* coordinate of a movie clip relative to the local coordinates of the parent movie clip. If a movie clip is in the main Timeline, then its coordinate system refers to the upper-left corner of the Stage as (0,0). If the movie clip is inside another movie clip that has transformations, the movie clip is in the local coordinate system of the enclosing movie clip. Thus, for a movie clip that is rotated 90° counterclockwise, the movie clip's children inherit a coordinate system that is rotated 90° counterclockwise. The movie clip's coordinates refer to the registration point position.

Availability: ActionScript 1.0; Flash Player 3

Example

The following example attaches a movie clip with the `cursor_id` linkage identifier to a SWF file. The movie clip is called `cursor_mc`, and it is used to replace the default mouse pointer. The following ActionScript sets the current coordinates of the movie clip instance to the position of the mouse pointer:

```
this.attachMovie("cursor_id", "cursor_mc", this.getNextHighestDepth(),
  {_x:_xmouse, _y:_ymouse});
Mouse.hide();
var mouseListener:Object = new Object();
mouseListener.onMouseMove = function() {
  cursor_mc._x = _xmouse;
  cursor_mc._y = _ymouse;
  updateAfterEvent();
};
Mouse.addListener(mouseListener);
```

The `MovieClip.getNextHighestDepth()` method used in this example requires Flash Player 7 or later. If your SWF file includes a version 2 component, use the version 2 components DepthManager class instead of the `MovieClip.getNextHighestDepth()` method.

See also

`_x (MovieClip._x property)`, `_xscale (MovieClip._xscale property)`, `_yscale (MovieClip._yscale property)`

_ymouse (MovieClip._ymouse property)

`public _ymouse : Number [read-only]`

Indicates the *y* coordinate of the mouse position.

Availability: ActionScript 1.0; Flash Player 5

Example

The following example returns the current *x* and *y* coordinates of the mouse on the Stage (`_level0`) and in relation to a movie clip on the Stage called `my_mc`.

```
this.createTextField("mouse_txt", this.getNextHighestDepth(), 0, 0, 150,
  66);
mouse_txt.html = true;
mouse_txt.multiline = true;
var row1_str:String = " \t<b>_xmouse\t</b><b>_ymouse</b>";
my_mc.onMouseMove = function() {
  mouse_txt.htmlText = "<textformat tabStops='[50,100]'>";
  mouse_txt.htmlText += row1_str;
  mouse_txt.htmlText += "<b>_level0</b>\t"+_xmouse+"\t"+_ymouse;
  mouse_txt.htmlText += "<b>my_mc</b>\t"+this._xmouse+"\t"+this._ymouse;
```

```
    mouse_txt.htmlText += "</textformat>";
};
```

The `MovieClip.getNextHighestDepth()` method used in this example requires Flash Player 7 or later. If your SWF file includes a version 2 component, use the version 2 components DepthManager class instead of the `MovieClip.getNextHighestDepth()` method.

See also

`Mouse, _xmouse (MovieClip._xmouse property)`

_yscale (MovieClip._yscale property)

`public _yscale : Number`

Sets the vertical scale (*percentage*) of the movie clip as applied from the registration point of the movie clip. The default registration point is (0,0).

Scaling the local coordinate system affects the _x and _y property settings, which are defined in whole pixels. For example, if the parent movie clip is scaled to 50%, setting the _x property moves an object in the movie clip by half the number of pixels as it would if the movie were at 100%.

Availability: ActionScript 1.0; Flash Player 4

Example

The following example creates a movie clip called `box_mc` at runtime. The Drawing API is used to draw a box in this instance, and when the mouse rolls over the box, horizontal and vertical scaling is applied to the movie clip. When the mouse rolls off the instance, it returns to the previous scaling.

```
this.createEmptyMovieClip("box_mc", 1);
box_mc._x = 100;
box_mc._y = 100;
with (box_mc) {
  lineStyle(1, 0xCCCCCC);
  beginFill(0xEEEEEE);
  moveTo(0, 0);
  lineTo(80, 0);
  lineTo(80, 60);
  lineTo(0, 60);
  lineTo(0, 0);
  endFill();
};
box_mc.onRollOver = function() {
  this._x -= this._width/2;
  this._y -= this._height/2;
  this._xscale = 200;
```

```
  this._yscale = 200;
};
box_mc.onRollOut = function() {
  this._xscale = 100;
  this._yscale = 100;
  this._x += this._width/2;
  this._y += this._height/2;
};
```

See also

_height (MovieClip._height property), _x (MovieClip._x property), _xscale
(MovieClip._xscale property), _y (MovieClip._y property)

MovieClipLoader

```
Object
  |
  +-MovieClipLoader
```

public class **MovieClipLoader**
extends Object

This class lets you implement listener callbacks that provide status information while SWF, JPEG, GIF, and PNG files are being loaded into movie clips. To use MovieClipLoader features, use MovieClipLoader.loadClip() instead of loadMovie() or MovieClip.loadMovie() to load SWF files.

After you issue the MovieClipLoader.loadClip() command, the following events take place in the order listed:

- When the first bytes of the downloaded file have been written to the hard disk, the MovieClipLoader.onLoadStart listener is invoked.

- If you have implemented the MovieClipLoader.onLoadProgress listener, it is invoked during the loading process.
  Note: You can call MovieClipLoader.getProgress() at any time during the load process.

- When the entire downloaded file has been written to the hard disk, the MovieClipLoader.onLoadComplete listener is invoked.

- When the downloaded file's first frame actions have been executed, the MovieClipLoader.onLoadInit listener is invoked.

When MovieClipLoader.onLoadInit has been invoked, you can set properties, use methods, and otherwise interact with the loaded movie.

If the file fails to load completely, the MovieClipLoader.onLoadError listener is invoked.

Availability: ActionScript 1.0; Flash Player 7

Property summary

Properties inherited from class Object

```
constructor (Object.constructor property),__proto__ (Object.__proto__
property),prototype (Object.prototype property),__resolve
(Object.__resolve property)
```

Event summary

Event	Description
`onLoadComplete = function([target _mc:MovieClip], [httpStatus:Numb er]) {}`	Invoked when a file that was loaded with `MovieClipLoader.loadClip()` is completely downloaded.
`onLoadError = function(target_ mc:MovieClip, errorCode:String , [httpStatus:Numb er]) {}`	Invoked when a file loaded with `MovieClipLoader.loadClip()` has failed to load.
`onLoadInit = function([target _mc:MovieClip]) {}`	Invoked when the actions on the first frame of the loaded clip have been executed.
`onLoadProgress = function([target _mc:MovieClip], loadedBytes:Numb er, totalBytes:Numbe r) {}`	Invoked every time the loading content is written to the hard disk during the loading process (that is, between `MovieClipLoader.onLoadStart` and `MovieClipLoader.onLoadComplete`).
`onLoadStart = function([target _mc:MovieClip]) {}`	Invoked when a call to `MovieClipLoader.loadClip()` has begun to download a file.

Constructor summary

Signature	Description
`MovieClipLoader()`	Creates a MovieClipLoader object that you can use to implement a number of listeners to respond to events while a SWF, JPEG, GIF, or PNG file is downloading.

Method summary

Modifiers	Signature	Description
	`addListener(listener :Object) : Boolean`	Registers an object to receive notification when a `MovieClipLoader` event handler is invoked.
	`getProgress(target:O bject) : Object`	Returns the number of bytes loaded and the total number of bytes of a file that is being loaded by using `MovieClipLoader.loadClip()`; for compressed movies, returns the number of compressed bytes.
	`loadClip(url:String, target:Object) : Boolean`	Loads a SWF, JPEG, progressive JPEG, unanimated GIF, or PNG file into a movie clip in Flash Player while the original movie is playing.
	`removeListener(liste ner:Object) : Boolean`	Removes the listener that was used to receive notification when a `MovieClipLoader` event handler was invoked.
	`unloadClip(target:Ob ject) : Boolean`	Removes a movie clip that was loaded by using `MovieClipLoader.loadClip()`.

Methods inherited from class Object

```
addProperty (Object.addProperty method), hasOwnProperty
(Object.hasOwnProperty method), isPropertyEnumerable
(Object.isPropertyEnumerable method), isPrototypeOf (Object.isPrototypeOf
method), registerClass (Object.registerClass method), toString
(Object.toString method), unwatch (Object.unwatch method), valueOf
(Object.valueOf method), watch (Object.watch method)
```

addListener (MovieClipLoader.addListener method)

`public addListener(listener:Object) : Boolean`

Registers an object to receive notification when a `MovieClipLoader` event handler is invoked.

Availability: ActionScript 1.0; Flash Player 7

Parameters

`listener:Object` - An object that listens for a callback notification from the `MovieClipLoader` event handlers.

Returns

`Boolean` - A Boolean value. Returns `true` if the listener was established successfully; otherwise `false`.

Example

The following example loads an image into a movie clip called `image_mc`. The movie clip instance is rotated and centered on the Stage, and both the Stage and movie clip have a stroke drawn around their perimeters.

```
this.createEmptyMovieClip("image_mc", this.getNextHighestDepth());
var mclListener:Object = new Object();
mclListener.onLoadInit = function(target_mc:MovieClip) {
   target_mc._x = Stage.width/2-target_mc._width/2;
   target_mc._y = Stage.height/2-target_mc._width/2;
   var w:Number = target_mc._width;
   var h:Number = target_mc._height;
   target_mc.lineStyle(4, 0x000000);
   target_mc.moveTo(0, 0);
   target_mc.lineTo(w, 0);
   target_mc.lineTo(w, h);
   target_mc.lineTo(0, h);
   target_mc.lineTo(0, 0);
   target_mc._rotation = 3;
};
var image_mcl:MovieClipLoader = new MovieClipLoader();
image_mcl.addListener(mclListener);
image_mcl.loadClip("http://www.helpexamples.com/flash/images/image1.jpg",
   image_mc);
```

If your SWF file includes a version 2 component, use the version 2 component's DepthManager class instead of the `MovieClip.getNextHighestDepth()` method, which is used in this example.

See also

`onLoadComplete` (MovieClipLoader.onLoadComplete event listener), `onLoadError` (MovieClipLoader.onLoadError event listener), `onLoadInit` (MovieClipLoader.onLoadInit event listener), `onLoadProgress` (MovieClipLoader.onLoadProgress event listener), `onLoadStart` (MovieClipLoader.onLoadStart event listener), `removeListener` (MovieClipLoader.removeListener method)

getProgress (MovieClipLoader.getProgress method)

`public getProgress(target:Object) : Object`

Returns the number of bytes loaded and the total number of bytes of a file that is being loaded by using `MovieClipLoader.loadClip()`; for compressed movies, returns the number of compressed bytes. The `getProgress` method lets you explicitly request this information, instead of (or in addition to) writing a `MovieClipLoader.onLoadProgress` listener function.

Availability: ActionScript 1.0; Flash Player 7

Parameters

`target:Object` - A SWF, JPEG, GIF, or PNG file that is loaded by using `MovieClipLoader.loadClip()`.

Returns

`Object` - An object that has two integer properties: `bytesLoaded` and `bytesTotal`.

Example

The following example demonstrates the use of the `getProgress()` method. Rather than using this method, you will usually create a listener object to listen for the `onLoadProgress` event. Also note that the first, synchronous call to `getProgress()` can return the number of bytes loaded and the total number of bytes of the *container* and not the values for the externally requested object.

```
var container:MovieClip = this.createEmptyMovieClip("container",
  this.getNextHighestDepth());
var image:MovieClip = container.createEmptyMovieClip("image",
  container.getNextHighestDepth());

var mcLoader:MovieClipLoader = new MovieClipLoader();
var listener:Object = new Object();
listener.onLoadProgress = function(target:MovieClip, bytesLoaded:Number,
  bytesTotal:Number):Void {
  trace(target + ".onLoadProgress with " + bytesLoaded + " bytes of " +
  bytesTotal);
}
mcLoader.addListener(listener);
mcLoader.loadClip("http://www.w3.org/Icons/w3c_main.png", image);

var interval:Object = new Object();
interval.id = setInterval(checkProgress, 100, mcLoader, image, interval);

function checkProgress(mcLoader:MovieClipLoader, image:MovieClip,
  interval:Object):Void {
  trace(">> checking progress now with : " + interval.id);
  var progress:Object = mcLoader.getProgress(image);
  trace("bytesLoaded: " + progress.bytesLoaded + " bytesTotal: " +
  progress.bytesTotal);
  if(progress.bytesLoaded == progress.bytesTotal) {
    clearInterval(interval.id);
  }
}
```

If your SWF file includes a version 2 component, use the version 2 component's DepthManager class instead of the `MovieClip.getNextHighestDepth()` method, which is used in this example.

See also

`loadClip (MovieClipLoader.loadClip method)`, `onLoadProgress` `(MovieClipLoader.onLoadProgress event listener)`

loadClip (MovieClipLoader.loadClip method)

`public loadClip(url:String, target:Object) : Boolean`

Loads a SWF, JPEG, progressive JPEG, unanimated GIF, or PNG file into a movie clip in Flash Player while the original movie is playing. If you load an animated GIF, only the first frame is displayed. Using this method you can display several SWF files at once and switch between SWF files without loading another HTML document.

Using the `loadClip()` method instead of `loadMovie()` or `MovieClip.loadMovie()` has a number of advantages. The following handlers are implemented by the use of a listener object. You activate the listener by registering it with the MovieClipLoader class by using `MovieClipLoader.addListener(listenerObject)`.

- The `MovieClipLoader.onLoadStart` handler is invoked when loading begins.
- The `MovieClipLoader.onLoadError` handler is invoked if the clip cannot be loaded.
- The `MovieClipLoader.onLoadProgress` handler is invoked as the loading process progresses.
- The `MovieClipLoader.onLoadComplete` handler is invoked when a file completes downloading, but before the loaded movie clip's methods and properties are available. This handler is called before the `onLoadInit` handler.
- The `MovieClipLoader.onLoadInit` handler is invoked after the actions in the first frame of the clip have executed, so you can begin manipulating the loaded clip. This handler is called after the `onLoadComplete` handler. For most purposes, use the `onLoadInit` handler.

A SWF file or image loaded into a movie clip inherits the position, rotation, and scale properties of the movie clip. You can use the target path of the movie clip to target the loaded movie.

You can use the `loadClip()` method to load one or more files into a single movie clip or level; MovieClipLoader listener objects are passed to the loading target movie clip instance as parameters. Alternatively, you can create a different MovieClipLoader object for each file that you load.

Use `MovieClipLoader.unloadClip()` to remove movies or images loaded with this method or to cancel a load operation that is in progress.

`MovieClipLoader.getProgress()` and `MovieClipLoaderListener.onLoadProgress` do not report the actual `bytesLoaded` and `bytesTotal` values in the authoring player when the files are local. When you use the Bandwidth Profiler feature in the authoring environment, `MovieClipLoader.getProgress()` and `MovieClipLoaderListener.onLoadProgress` report the download at the actual download rate, not at the reduced bandwidth rate that the Bandwidth Profiler provides.

When using this method, consider the Flash Player security model.

For Flash Player 8:

- Loading is not allowed if the calling movie clip is in the local-with-file-system sandbox and the loaded movie clip is from a network sandbox.
- Loading is not allowed if the calling SWF file is in a network sandbox and the movie clip to be loaded is local.
- Network sandbox access from the local-trusted or local-with-networking sandbox requires permission from the website by means of a cross-domain policy file.
- Movie clips in the local-with-file-system sandbox may not script movie clips in the local-with-networking sandbox (and the reverse is also prevented).

For Flash Player 7 and later:

- Websites can permit cross-domain access to a resource by means of a cross-domain policy file.
- Scripting between SWF files is restricted based on the origin domain of the SWF files. Use the `System.security.allowDomain()` method to adjust these restrictions.

For more information, see the following:

- Chapter 17, "Understanding Security," in *Learning ActionScript 2.0 in Flash*
- The Flash Player 8 Security white paper at http://www.macromedia.com/go/fp8_security
- The Flash Player 8 Security-Related API white paper at http://www.macromedia.com/go/fp8_security_apis

Availability: ActionScript 1.0; Flash Player 7 - Support for unanimated GIF files, PNG files, and progressive JPEG files is available as of Flash Player 8.

Parameters

`url:String` - The absolute or relative URL of the SWF, JPEG, GIF, or PNG file to be loaded. A relative path must be relative to the SWF file at level 0. Absolute URLs must include the protocol reference, such as http:// or file:///. Filenames cannot include disk drive specifications.

`target:Object` - The target path of a movie clip, or an integer specifying the level in Flash Player into which the movie will be loaded. The target movie clip is replaced by the loaded SWF file or image.

Returns

`Boolean` - A Boolean value. Returns `true` if the URL request was sent successfully; otherwise `false`.

Example

The following example shows how to use the `MovieClipLoader.loadClip()` method by creating a handler for the `onLoadInit` event and then making the request.

You should either place the following code directly into a frame action on a Timeline, or paste it into a class that extends MovieClip. This code also expects an image named YourImage.jpg to exist in the same directory as the compiled SWF file.

```
var container:MovieClip = createEmptyMovieClip("container",
  getNextHighestDepth());
var mcLoader:MovieClipLoader = new MovieClipLoader();
mcLoader.addListener(this);
mcLoader.loadClip("YourImage.jpg", container);

function onLoadInit(mc:MovieClip) {
  trace("onLoadInit: " + mc);
}
```

If your SWF file includes a version 2 component, use the version 2 component's DepthManager class instead of the `MovieClip.getNextHighestDepth()` method, which is used in this example.

See also

`onLoadInit (MovieClipLoader.onLoadInit event listener)`

MovieClipLoader constructor

`public MovieClipLoader()`

Creates a MovieClipLoader object that you can use to implement a number of listeners to respond to events while a SWF, JPEG, GIF, or PNG file is downloading.

Availability: ActionScript 1.0; Flash Player 7

Example

See `MovieClipLoader.loadClip()`.

See also

`addListener (MovieClipLoader.addListener method)`, `loadClip (MovieClipLoader.loadClip method)`

onLoadComplete (MovieClipLoader.onLoadComplete event listener)

`onLoadComplete = function([target_mc:MovieClip], [httpStatus:Number]) {}`
Invoked when a file that was loaded with `MovieClipLoader.loadClip()` is completely downloaded. Call this listener on a listener object that you add using `MovieClipLoader.addListener()`. The `onLoadComplete` event listener is passed by Flash Player to your code, but you do not have to implement all of the parameters in the listener function. The value for `target_mc` identifies the movie clip for which this call is being made. This identification is useful when multiple files are being loaded with the same set of listeners.

In Flash Player 8, this listener can return an HTTP status code. If Flash Player cannot get the status code from the server, or if Flash Player cannot communicate with the server, the default value of 0 is passed to your ActionScript code. A value of 0 can be generated in any player (for example, if a malformed URL is requested), and a value of 0 is always generated by the Flash Player plug-in when run in the following browsers, which cannot pass HTTP status codes from the server to Flash Player: Netscape, Mozilla, Safari, Opera, and Internet Explorer for the Macintosh.

It's important to understand the difference between `MovieClipLoader.onLoadComplete` and `MovieClipLoader.onLoadInit`. The `onLoadComplete` event is called after the SWF, JPEG, GIF, or PNG file loads, but before the application is initialized. At this point, it is impossible to access the loaded movie clip's methods and properties, and therefore you cannot call a function, move to a specific frame, and so on. In most situations, it's better to use the `onLoadInit` event instead, which is called after the content is loaded and fully initialized.

Availability: ActionScript 1.0; Flash Player 7 - Support for unanimated GIF files, PNG files, and progressive JPEG files is available as of Flash Player 8.

Parameters

`target_mc:MovieClip` [optional] - A movie clip loaded by the `MovieClipLoader.loadClip()` method.

---

httpStatus:Number [optional] - (Flash Player 8 only) The HTTP status code returned by the server. For example, a status code of 404 indicates that the server has not found anything matching the requested URI. For more information about HTTP status codes, see sections 10.4 and 10.5 of the HTTP specification at ftp://ftp.isi.edu/in-notes/rfc2616.txt.

Example

The following example creates a movie clip, a new MovieClipLoader instance, and an anonymous event listener which listens for the onLoadComplete event but waits for an onLoadInit event to interact with the loaded element properties.

```
var loadListener:Object = new Object();

loadListener.onLoadComplete = function(target_mc:MovieClip,
  httpStatus:Number):Void {
  trace(">> loadListener.onLoadComplete()");
  trace(">> =============================");
  trace(">> target_mc._width: " + target_mc._width); // 0
  trace(">> httpStatus: " + httpStatus);
}

loadListener.onLoadInit = function(target_mc:MovieClip):Void {
  trace(">> loadListener.onLoadInit()");
  trace(">> =============================");
  trace(">> target_mc._width: " + target_mc._width); // 315
}

var mcLoader:MovieClipLoader = new MovieClipLoader();
mcLoader.addListener(loadListener);

var mc:MovieClip = this.createEmptyMovieClip("mc",
  this.getNextHighestDepth());
mcLoader.loadClip("http://www.w3.org/Icons/w3c_main.png", mc);
```

If your SWF file includes a version 2 component, use the version 2 component's DepthManager class instead of the MovieClip.getNextHighestDepth() method, which is used in this example.

See also

addListener (MovieClipLoader.addListener method), loadClip (MovieClipLoader.loadClip method), onLoadStart (MovieClipLoader.onLoadStart event listener), onLoadError (MovieClipLoader.onLoadError event listener), onLoadInit (MovieClipLoader.onLoadInit event listener)

onLoadError (MovieClipLoader.onLoadError event listener)

```
onLoadError = function(target_mc:MovieClip, errorCode:String,
    [httpStatus:Number]) {}
```

Invoked when a file loaded with `MovieClipLoader.loadClip()` has failed to load. This listener can be invoked for various reasons; for example, if the server is down, the file is not found, or a security violation occurs.

Call this listener on a listener object that you add by using `MovieClipLoader.addListener()`.

The value of `target_mc` identifies the movie clip for which this call is being made. This parameter is useful if you are loading multiple files with the same set of listeners.

For the `errorCode` parameter, the string `"URLNotFound"` is returned if neither the `MovieClipLoader.onLoadStart` or `MovieClipLoader.onLoadComplete` listener has been called; for example, if a server is down or the file is not found. The string `"LoadNeverCompleted"` is returned if `MovieClipLoader.onLoadStart` was called but `MovieClipLoader.onLoadComplete` was not called; for example, if the download was interrupted because of server overload, server crash, and so on.

In Flash Player 8, this listener can return an HTTP status code in the `httpStatus` parameter. If Flash Player cannot get a status code from the server, or if Flash Player cannot communicate with the server, the default value of 0 is passed to your ActionScript code. A value of 0 can be generated in any player (for example, if a malformed URL is requested), and a value of 0 is always generated by the Flash Player plug-in when run in the following browsers, which cannot pass HTTP status codes from the server to Flash Player: Netscape, Mozilla, Safari, Opera, and Internet Explorer for the Macintosh. A value of 0 can also be generated if the player did not try to make the URL request to perform the load operation. This can happen because the request violates security sandbox rules for the SWF file.

Availability: ActionScript 1.0; Flash Player 7

Parameters

`target_mc:MovieClip` - A movie clip loaded by the `MovieClipLoader.loadClip()` method.

`errorCode:String` - A string that explains the reason for the failure, either `"URLNotFound"` or `"LoadNeverCompleted"`.

httpStatus:Number [optional] - (Flash Player 8 only) The HTTP status code returned by the server. For example, a status code of 404 indicates that the server has not found anything that matches the requested URI. For more information about HTTP status codes, see sections 10.4 and 10.5 of the HTTP specification at ftp://ftp.isi.edu/in-notes/rfc2616.txt.

Example

The following example displays information in the Output panel when an image fails to load. The URL used in this example is for demonstration purposes only; replace it with your own valid URL.

```
var loadListener:Object = new Object();

loadListener.onLoadError = function(target_mc:MovieClip, errorCode:String,
  httpStatus:Number) {
  trace(">> loadListener.onLoadError()");
  trace(">> ==========================");
  trace(">> errorCode: " + errorCode);
  trace(">> httpStatus: " + httpStatus);
}

var mcLoader:MovieClipLoader = new MovieClipLoader();
mcLoader.addListener(loadListener);

var mc:MovieClip = this.createEmptyMovieClip("mc",
  this.getNextHighestDepth());
mcLoader.loadClip("http://www.fakedomain.com/images/bad_hair_day.jpg", mc);
```

If your SWF file includes a version 2 component, use the version 2 component's DepthManager class instead of the MovieClip.getNextHighestDepth() method, which is used in this example.

See also

addListener (MovieClipLoader.addListener method), loadClip (MovieClipLoader.loadClip method), onLoadStart (MovieClipLoader.onLoadStart event listener), onLoadComplete (MovieClipLoader.onLoadComplete event listener)

onLoadInit (MovieClipLoader.onLoadInit event listener)

```
onLoadInit = function([target_mc:MovieClip]) {}
```

Invoked when the actions on the first frame of the loaded clip have been executed. When this listener has been invoked, you can set properties, use methods, and otherwise interact with the loaded movie. Call this listener on a listener object that you add by using `MovieClipLoader.addListener()`.

The value for `target_mc` identifies the movie clip for which this call is being made. This parameter is useful if you are loading multiple files with the same set of listeners.

Availability: ActionScript 1.0; Flash Player 7

Parameters

`target_mc:MovieClip` [optional] - A movie clip loaded by the `MovieClipLoader.loadClip()` method.

Example

The following example loads an image into a movie clip instance called `image_mc`. The `onLoadInit` and `onLoadComplete` events are used to determine how long it takes to load the image. This information is displayed in a text field called `timer_txt`.

```
this.createEmptyMovieClip("image_mc", this.getNextHighestDepth());
var mclListener:Object = new Object();
mclListener.onLoadStart = function(target_mc:MovieClip) {
   target_mc.startTimer = getTimer();
};
mclListener.onLoadComplete = function(target_mc:MovieClip) {
   target_mc.completeTimer = getTimer();
};
mclListener.onLoadInit = function(target_mc:MovieClip) {
   var timerMS:Number = target_mc.completeTimer-target_mc.startTimer;
   target_mc.createTextField("timer_txt", target_mc.getNextHighestDepth(),
   0, target_mc._height,
target_mc._width, 22);
   target_mc.timer_txt.text = "loaded in "+timerMS+" ms.";
};
var image_mcl:MovieClipLoader = new MovieClipLoader();
image_mcl.addListener(mclListener);
image_mcl.loadClip("http://www.helpexamples.com/flash/images/image1.jpg",
   image_mc);
```

The following example checks whether a movie has loaded into a movie clip created at runtime. The URL used in this example is for demonstration purposes only; replace it with your own valid URL.

```
this.createEmptyMovieClip("tester_mc", 1);
var mclListener:Object = new Object();
mclListener.onLoadInit = function(target_mc:MovieClip) {
   trace("movie loaded");
}
```

```
var image_mcl:MovieClipLoader = new MovieClipLoader();
image_mcl.addListener(mclListener);
image_mcl.loadClip("http://www.yourserver.com/your_movie.swf", tester_mc);
```

If your SWF file includes a version 2 component, use the version 2 component's DepthManager class instead of the `MovieClip.getNextHighestDepth()` method, which is used in this example.

See also

`addListener (MovieClipLoader.addListener method)`, `loadClip (MovieClipLoader.loadClip method)`, `onLoadStart (MovieClipLoader.onLoadStart event listener)`

onLoadProgress (MovieClipLoader.onLoadProgress event listener)

```
onLoadProgress = function([target_mc:MovieClip], loadedBytes:Number,
    totalBytes:Number) {}
```

Invoked every time the loading content is written to the hard disk during the loading process (that is, between `MovieClipLoader.onLoadStart` and `MovieClipLoader.onLoadComplete`). Call this listener on a listener object that you add by using `MovieClipLoader.addListener()`. You can use this method to display information about the progress of the download, by using the `loadedBytes` and `totalBytes` parameters.

The value for `target_mc` identifies the movie clip for which this call is being made. This is useful when you are loading multiple files with the same set of listeners.

 If you attempt to use onloadProgress in test mode with a local file that resides on your hard disk, it does not work properly because, in test mode, Flash Player loads local files in their entirety.

Availability: ActionScript 1.0; Flash Player 7

Parameters

`target_mc:MovieClip` [optional] - A movie clip loaded by the `MovieClipLoader.loadClip()` method.

`loadedBytes:Number` - The number of bytes that had been loaded when the listener was invoked.

`totalBytes:Number` - The total number of bytes in the file being loaded.

Example

The following example creates a movie clip, a new `MovieClipLoader` instance, and an anonymous event listener. It periodically outputs the progress of a load and finally provides notification when the load is complete and the asset is available to ActionScript.

```
var container:MovieClip = this.createEmptyMovieClip("container",
  this.getNextHighestDepth());
var mcLoader:MovieClipLoader = new MovieClipLoader();
var listener:Object = new Object();
listener.onLoadProgress = function(target:MovieClip, bytesLoaded:Number,
  bytesTotal:Number):Void {
    trace(target + ".onLoadProgress with " + bytesLoaded + " bytes of " +
    bytesTotal);
}
listener.onLoadInit = function(target:MovieClip):Void {
    trace(target + ".onLoadInit");
}
mcLoader.addListener(listener);
mcLoader.loadClip("http://www.w3.org/Icons/w3c_main.png", container);
```

If your SWF file includes a version 2 component, use the version 2 component's DepthManager class instead of the `MovieClip.getNextHighestDepth()` method, which is used in this example.

See also

`addListener (MovieClipLoader.addListener method)`, `loadClip (MovieClipLoader.loadClip method)`, `getProgress (MovieClipLoader.getProgress method)`

onLoadStart (MovieClipLoader.onLoadStart event listener)

```
onLoadStart = function([target_mc:MovieClip]) {}
```

Invoked when a call to `MovieClipLoader.loadClip()` has begun to download a file. Call this listener on a listener object that you add by using `MovieClipLoader.addListener()`.

The value for `target_mc` identifies the movie clip for which this call is being made. This parameter is useful if you are loading multiple files with the same set of listeners.

Availability: ActionScript 1.0; Flash Player 7

Parameters

`target_mc:MovieClip` [optional] - A movie clip loaded by the `MovieClipLoader.loadClip()` method.

Example

The following example loads an image into a movie clip instance called `image_mc`. The `onLoadInit` and `onLoadComplete` events are used to determine how long it takes to load the image. This information is displayed in a text field called `timer_txt`.

```
this.createEmptyMovieClip("image_mc", this.getNextHighestDepth());
var mclListener:Object = new Object();
mclListener.onLoadStart = function(target_mc:MovieClip) {
  target_mc.startTimer = getTimer();
};
mclListener.onLoadComplete = function(target_mc:MovieClip) {
  target_mc.completeTimer = getTimer();
};
mclListener.onLoadInit = function(target_mc:MovieClip) {
  var timerMS:Number = target_mc.completeTimer-target_mc.startTimer;
  target_mc.createTextField("timer_txt", target_mc.getNextHighestDepth(),
  0, target_mc._height,
target_mc._width, 22);
  target_mc.timer_txt.text = "loaded in "+timerMS+" ms.";
};
var image_mcl:MovieClipLoader = new MovieClipLoader();
image_mcl.addListener(mclListener);
image_mcl.loadClip("http://www.helpexamples.com/flash/images/image1.jpg",
  image_mc);
```

If your SWF file includes a version 2 component, use the version 2 component's DepthManager class instead of the `MovieClip.getNextHighestDepth()` method, which is used in this example.

See also

addListener (MovieClipLoader.addListener method), loadClip (MovieClipLoader.loadClip method), onLoadError (MovieClipLoader.onLoadError event listener), onLoadInit (MovieClipLoader.onLoadInit event listener), onLoadComplete (MovieClipLoader.onLoadComplete event listener)

removeListener (MovieClipLoader.removeListener method)

```
public removeListener(listener:Object) : Boolean
```

Removes the listener that was used to receive notification when a `MovieClipLoader` event handler was invoked. No further loading messages will be received.

Availability: ActionScript 1.0; Flash Player 7

Parameters

`listener:Object` - A listener object that was added by using
`MovieClipLoader.addListener()`.

Returns

`Boolean` - A Boolean value. Returns `true` if the listener was removed successfully; otherwise
`false`.

Example

The following example loads an image into a movie clip, and enables the user to start and stop
the loading process using two buttons called `start_button` and `stop_button`. When the
user starts or stops the progress, information is displayed in the Output panel.

```
this.createEmptyMovieClip("image_mc", this.getNextHighestDepth());
var mclListener:Object = new Object();
mclListener.onLoadStart = function(target_mc:MovieClip) {
  trace("\t onLoadStart");
};
mclListener.onLoadComplete = function(target_mc:MovieClip) {
  trace("\t onLoadComplete");
};
mclListener.onLoadError = function(target_mc:MovieClip, errorCode:String) {
  trace("\t onLoadError: "+errorCode);
};
mclListener.onLoadInit = function(target_mc:MovieClip) {
  trace("\t onLoadInit");
  start_button.enabled = true;
  stop_button.enabled = false;
};
var image_mcl:MovieClipLoader = new MovieClipLoader();
//
start_button.clickHandler = function() {
  trace("Starting...");
  start_button.enabled = false;
  stop_button.enabled = true;
  //
  image_mcl.addListener(mclListener);
  image_mcl.loadClip("http://www.helpexamples.com/flash/images/
  image1.jpg", image_mc);
};
stop_button.clickHandler = function() {
  trace("Stopping...");
  start_button.enabled = true;
  stop_button.enabled = false;
  //
  image_mcl.removeListener(mclListener);
};
```

```
stop_button.enabled = false;
```
If your SWF file includes a version 2 component, use the version 2 component's DepthManager class instead of the `MovieClip.getNextHighestDepth()` method, which is used in this example.

See also

addListener (MovieClipLoader.addListener method)

unloadClip (MovieClipLoader.unloadClip method)

public unloadClip(target:Object) : Boolean

Removes a movie clip that was loaded by using `MovieClipLoader.loadClip()`. If you issue this command while a movie is loading, `MovieClipLoader.onLoadError` is invoked.

Availability: ActionScript 1.0; Flash Player 7

Parameters

target:Object - The string or integer that is passed to the corresponding call to my_mcl.loadClip().

Returns

Boolean - A Boolean value. Returns true if the movie clip was removed successfully; otherwise false.

Example

The following example loads an image into a movie clip called image_mc. When you click the movie clip, the movie clip is removed and information is displayed in the Output panel.

```
this.createEmptyMovieClip("image_mc", this.getNextHighestDepth());
var mclListener:Object = new Object();
mclListener.onLoadInit = function(target_mc:MovieClip) {
    target_mc._x = 100;
    target_mc._y = 100;
    target_mc.onRelease = function() {
    trace("Unloading clip...");
    trace("\t name: "+target_mc._name);
    trace("\t url: "+target_mc._url);
    image_mcl.unloadClip(target_mc);
    };
};
var image_mcl:MovieClipLoader = new MovieClipLoader();
image_mcl.addListener(mclListener);
image_mcl.loadClip("http://www.helpexamples.com/flash/images/image1.jpg",
    image_mc);
```

If your SWF file includes a version 2 component, use the version 2 component's DepthManager class instead of the `MovieClip.getNextHighestDepth()` method, which is used in this example.

See also

`loadClip (MovieClipLoader.loadClip method)`, `onLoadError (MovieClipLoader.onLoadError event listener)`

NetConnection

```
Object
  |
  +-NetConnection
```

```
public dynamic class NetConnection
extends Object
```

| | This class is also supported in Flash Player 6 when used with Flash Communication Server. For more information, see your Flash Communication Server documentation. |

Availability: ActionScript 1.0; Flash Player 7

Property summary

Properties inherited from class Object

```
constructor (Object.constructor property), __proto__ (Object.__proto__
property), prototype (Object.prototype property), __resolve
(Object.__resolve property)
```

Constructor summary

Signature	Description
`NetConnection()`	Creates a NetConnection object that you can use in conjunction with a NetStream object to play back local streaming video (FLV) files.

Method summary

Modifiers	Signature	Description
	`connect(targetURI:St ring) : Boolean`	Opens a local connection through which you can play back video (FLV) files from an HTTP address or from the local file system.

Methods inherited from class Object

```
addProperty (Object.addProperty method),hasOwnProperty
(Object.hasOwnProperty method),isPropertyEnumerable
(Object.isPropertyEnumerable method),isPrototypeOf (Object.isPrototypeOf
method),registerClass (Object.registerClass method),toString
(Object.toString method),unwatch (Object.unwatch method),valueOf
(Object.valueOf method),watch (Object.watch method)
```

connect (NetConnection.connect method)

`public connect(targetURI:String) : Boolean`

Opens a local connection through which you can play back video (FLV) files from an HTTP address or from the local file system.

When using this method, consider the Flash Player security model and the following security considerations:

- The default is to deny access between sandboxes. The website can enable access to a resource via a cross-domain policy file.

- A website can deny access to a resource by adding server-side ActionScript application logic in Flash Communication Server.

- For Flash Player 8, NetConnection.connect() is not allowed if the calling SWF file is in the local-with-file-system sandbox.

For more information, see the following:

- Chapter 17, "Understanding Security," in *Learning ActionScript 2.0 in Flash*
- The Flash Player 8 Security white paper at http://www.macromedia.com/go/fp8_security
- The Flash Player 8 Security-Related API white paper at http://www.macromedia.com/go/fp8_security_apis

Availability: ActionScript 1.0; Flash Player 7 - Note: This method is also supported in Flash Player 6 when used with Flash Communication Server. For more information, see the Flash Communication Server documentation.

Parameters

targetURI:String - For this parameter, you must pass null.

Returns

Boolean - If false, the connection failed and is not usable. If true, the connection has not failed at the time the connect() method is called, but this does not guarantee success.

Example

The following example opens a connection to play the video2.flv file. Select New Video from the Library panel's options menu to create a new video object, and give it the instance name my_video.

```
var connection_nc:NetConnection = new NetConnection();
connection_nc.connect(null);
var stream_ns:NetStream = new NetStream(connection_nc);
my_video.attachVideo(stream_ns);
stream_ns.play("video2.flv");
```

See also

NetStream

NetConnection constructor

public NetConnection()

Creates a NetConnection object that you can use in conjunction with a NetStream object to play back local streaming video (FLV) files. After creating the NetConnection object, use NetConnection.connect() to make the actual connection.

Playing external FLV files provides several advantages over embedding video in a Flash document, such as better performance and memory management, and independent video and Flash frame rates. The NetConnection class provides the means to play back streaming FLV files from a local drive or HTTP address.

Availability: ActionScript 1.0; Flash Player 7 - Note: This class is also supported in Flash Player 6 when used with Flash Communication Server. For more information, see your Flash Communication Server documentation.

Example

See the example for NetConnection.connect().

See also

connect (NetConnection.connect method), attachVideo (Video.attachVideo method), NetStream

NetStream

```
Object
  |
  +-NetStream
```

public dynamic class **NetStream**
extends Object

The NetStream class provides methods and properties for playing Flash Video (FLV) files from the local file system or an HTTP address. You use a NetStream object to stream video through a NetConnection object. Playing external FLV files provides several advantages over embedding video in a Flash document, such as better performance and memory management, and independent video and Flash frame rates. This class provides a number of methods and properties you can use to track the progress of the file as it loads and plays, and to give the user control over playback (stopping, pausing, and so on).

Availability: ActionScript 1.0; Flash Player 7

Property summary

Modifiers	Property	Description
	`bufferLength:Number` [read-only]	The number of seconds of data currently in the buffer.
	`bufferTime:Number` [read-only]	The number of seconds assigned to the buffer by `NetStream.setBufferTime()`.
	`bytesLoaded:Number` [read-only]	The number of bytes of data that have been loaded into the player.
	`bytesTotal:Number` [read-only]	The total size in bytes of the file being loaded into the player.
	`currentFps:Number` [read-only]	The number of frames per second being displayed.
	`time:Number` [read-only]	The position of the playhead, in seconds.

Properties inherited from class Object

```
constructor (Object.constructor property),__proto__ (Object.__proto__
property),prototype (Object.prototype property),__resolve
(Object.__resolve property)
```

Event summary

Event	Description
`onCuePoint = function(infoObject:Object) {}`	Invoked when an embedded cue point is reached while playing an FLV file.
`onMetaData = function(infoObject:Object) {}`	Invoked when the Flash Player receives descriptive information embedded in the FLV file being played.
`onStatus = function(infoObject:Object) {}`	Invoked every time a status change or error is posted for the NetStream object.

Constructor summary

Signature	Description
`NetStream(connection :NetConnection)`	Creates a stream that can be used for playing FLV files through the specified NetConnection object.

Method summary

Modifiers	Signature	Description
	`close() : Void`	Stops playing all data on the stream, sets the `NetStream.time` property to 0, and makes the stream available for another use.
	`pause([flag:Boolean]) : Void`	Pauses or resumes playback of a stream.
	`play(name:Object, start:Number, len:Number, reset:Object) : Void`	Begins playback of an external video (FLV) file.
	`seek(offset:Number) : Void`	Seeks the keyframe closest to the specified number of seconds from the beginning of the stream.
	`setBufferTime(bufferTime:Number) : Void`	Specifies how long to buffer messages before starting to display the stream.

Methods inherited from class Object

```
addProperty (Object.addProperty method), hasOwnProperty
(Object.hasOwnProperty method), isPropertyEnumerable
(Object.isPropertyEnumerable method), isPrototypeOf (Object.isPrototypeOf
method), registerClass (Object.registerClass method), toString
(Object.toString method), unwatch (Object.unwatch method), valueOf
(Object.valueOf method), watch (Object.watch method)
```

bufferLength (NetStream.bufferLength property)

`public bufferLength : Number [read-only]`

The number of seconds of data currently in the buffer. You can use this property in conjunction with `NetStream.bufferTime` to estimate how close the buffer is to being full-- for example, to display feedback to a user who is waiting for data to be loaded into the buffer.

Availability: ActionScript 1.0; Flash Player 7 - Note: This property is also supported in Flash Player 6 when used with Flash Communication Server. For more information, see the Flash Communication Server documentation.

Example

The following example dynamically creates a text field that displays information about the number of seconds that are currently in the buffer. The text field also displays the buffer length that the video is set to, and percentage of buffer that is filled.

```
this.createTextField("buffer_txt", this.getNextHighestDepth(), 10, 10, 300,
    22);
buffer_txt.html = true;

var connection_nc:NetConnection = new NetConnection();
connection_nc.connect(null);
var stream_ns:NetStream = new NetStream(connection_nc);
stream_ns.setBufferTime(3);
my_video.attachVideo(stream_ns);
stream_ns.play("video1.flv");

var buffer_interval:Number = setInterval(checkBufferTime, 100, stream_ns);
function checkBufferTime(my_ns:NetStream):Void {
    var bufferPct:Number = Math.min(Math.round(my_ns.bufferLength/
    my_ns.bufferTime 100), 100);
    var output_str:String = "<textformat tabStops='[100,200]'>";
    output_str += "Length: "+my_ns.bufferLength+"\t"+"Time:
    "+my_ns.bufferTime+"\t"+"Buffer:"+bufferPct+"%";
    output_str += "</textformat>";
    buffer_txt.htmlText = output_str;
}
```

If your SWF file includes a version 2 component, use the version 2 components
DepthManager class instead of the `MovieClip.getNextHighestDepth()` method, which is
used in this example.

See also

`bufferTime (NetStream.bufferTime property)`, `bytesLoaded`
`(NetStream.bytesLoaded property)`

bufferTime (NetStream.bufferTime property)

`public bufferTime : Number [read-only]`

The number of seconds assigned to the buffer by `NetStream.setBufferTime()`. The default
value is .1(one-tenth of a second). To determine the number of seconds currently in the
buffer, use `NetStream.bufferLength`.

Availability: ActionScript 1.0; Flash Player 7 - Note: This property is also supported in Flash
Player 6 when used with Flash Communication Server. For more information, see the Flash
Communication Server documentation.

Example

The following example dynamically creates a text field that displays information about the
number of seconds that are currently in the buffer. The text field also displays the buffer
length that the video is set to, and percentage of buffer that is filled.

```
this.createTextField("buffer_txt", this.getNextHighestDepth(), 10, 10, 300,
  22);
buffer_txt.html = true;

var connection_nc:NetConnection = new NetConnection();
connection_nc.connect(null);
var stream_ns:NetStream = new NetStream(connection_nc);
stream_ns.setBufferTime(3);
my_video.attachVideo(stream_ns);
stream_ns.play("video1.flv");

var buffer_interval:Number = setInterval(checkBufferTime, 100, stream_ns);
function checkBufferTime(my_ns:NetStream):Void {
  var bufferPct:Number = Math.min(Math.round(my_ns.bufferLength/
  my_ns.bufferTime 100), 100);
  var output_str:String = "<textformat tabStops='[100,200]'>";
  output_str += "Length: "+my_ns.bufferLength+"\t"+"Time:
  "+my_ns.bufferTime+"\t"+"Buffer:"+bufferPct+"%";
  output_str += "</textformat>";
  buffer_txt.htmlText = output_str;
}
```

If your SWF file includes a version 2 component, use the version 2 components
DepthManager class instead of the `MovieClip.getNextHighestDepth()` method, which is
used in this example.

See also

`setBufferTime` (NetStream.setBufferTime method), `time` (NetStream.time
property), `bufferLength` (NetStream.bufferLength property)

bytesLoaded (NetStream.bytesLoaded property)

`public bytesLoaded : Number [read-only]`

The number of bytes of data that have been loaded into the player. You can use this method in
conjunction with `NetStream.bytesTotal` to estimate how close the buffer is to being full--
for example, to display feedback to a user who is waiting for data to be loaded into the buffer.

Availability: ActionScript 1.0; Flash Player 7

Example

The following example creates a progress bar using the Drawing API and the `bytesLoaded`
and `bytesTotal` properties that displays the loading progress of video1.flv into the video
object instance called `my_video`. A text field called `loaded_txt` is dynamically created to
display information about the loading progress as well.

```
var connection_nc:NetConnection = new NetConnection();
```

```
connection_nc.connect(null);
var stream_ns:NetStream = new NetStream(connection_nc);
my_video.attachVideo(stream_ns);
stream_ns.play("video1.flv");

this.createTextField("loaded_txt", this.getNextHighestDepth(), 10, 10, 160,
    22);
this.createEmptyMovieClip("progressBar_mc", this.getNextHighestDepth());
progressBar_mc.createEmptyMovieClip("bar_mc",
    progressBar_mc.getNextHighestDepth());
with (progressBar_mc.bar_mc) {
    beginFill(0xFF0000);
    moveTo(0, 0);
    lineTo(100, 0);
    lineTo(100, 10);
    lineTo(0, 10);
    lineTo(0, 0);
    endFill();
    _xscale = 0;
}
progressBar_mc.createEmptyMovieClip("stroke_mc",
    progressBar_mc.getNextHighestDepth());
with (progressBar_mc.stroke_mc) {
    lineStyle(0, 0x000000);
    moveTo(0, 0);
    lineTo(100, 0);
    lineTo(100, 10);
    lineTo(0, 10);
    lineTo(0, 0);
}

var loaded_interval:Number = setInterval(checkBytesLoaded, 500, stream_ns);
function checkBytesLoaded(my_ns:NetStream) {
    var pctLoaded:Number = Math.round(my_ns.bytesLoaded/my_ns.bytesTotal
    100);
    loaded_txt.text = Math.round(my_ns.bytesLoaded/1000)+" of
    "+Math.round(my_ns.bytesTotal/1000)+" KB loaded ("+pctLoaded+"%)";
    progressBar_mc.bar_mc._xscale = pctLoaded;
    if (pctLoaded>=100) {
    clearInterval(loaded_interval);
    }
}
```

If your SWF file includes a version 2 component, use the version 2 components
DepthManager class instead of the MovieClip.getNextHighestDepth() method, which is
used in this example.

See also

bytesTotal (NetStream.bytesTotal property), bufferLength
(NetStream.bufferLength property)

bytesTotal (NetStream.bytesTotal property)

`public bytesTotal : Number [read-only]`

The total size in bytes of the file being loaded into the player.

Availability: ActionScript 1.0; Flash Player 7

Example

The following example creates a progress bar using the Drawing API and the `bytesLoaded` and `bytesTotal` properties that displays the loading progress of video1.flv into the video object instance called `my_video`. A text field called `loaded_txt` is dynamically created to display information about the loading progress as well.

```
var connection_nc:NetConnection = new NetConnection();
connection_nc.connect(null);
var stream_ns:NetStream = new NetStream(connection_nc);
my_video.attachVideo(stream_ns);
stream_ns.play("video1.flv");

this.createTextField("loaded_txt", this.getNextHighestDepth(), 10, 10, 160,
    22);
this.createEmptyMovieClip("progressBar_mc", this.getNextHighestDepth());
progressBar_mc.createEmptyMovieClip("bar_mc",
    progressBar_mc.getNextHighestDepth());
with (progressBar_mc.bar_mc) {
    beginFill(0xFF0000);
    moveTo(0, 0);
    lineTo(100, 0);
    lineTo(100, 10);
    lineTo(0, 10);
    lineTo(0, 0);
    endFill();
    _xscale = 0;
}
progressBar_mc.createEmptyMovieClip("stroke_mc",
    progressBar_mc.getNextHighestDepth());
with (progressBar_mc.stroke_mc) {
    lineStyle(0, 0x000000);
    moveTo(0, 0);
    lineTo(100, 0);
    lineTo(100, 10);
    lineTo(0, 10);
    lineTo(0, 0);
```

```
}
var loaded_interval:Number = setInterval(checkBytesLoaded, 500, stream_ns);
function checkBytesLoaded(my_ns:NetStream) {
  var pctLoaded:Number = Math.round(my_ns.bytesLoaded/my_ns.bytesTotal
  100);
  loaded_txt.text = Math.round(my_ns.bytesLoaded/1000)+" of
  "+Math.round(my_ns.bytesTotal/1000)+" KB loaded ("+pctLoaded+"%)";
  progressBar_mc.bar_mc._xscale = pctLoaded;
  if (pctLoaded>=100) {
  clearInterval(loaded_interval);
  }
}
```

If your SWF file includes a version 2 component, use the version 2 components
DepthManager class instead of the `MovieClip.getNextHighestDepth()` method, which is
used in this example.

See also

`bytesLoaded (NetStream.bytesLoaded property)`, `bufferTime`
`(NetStream.bufferTime property)`

close (NetStream.close method)

`public close() : Void`

Stops playing all data on the stream, sets the `NetStream.time` property to 0, and makes the
stream available for another use. This command also deletes the local copy of an FLV file that
was downloaded using HTTP. Although Flash Player will delete the local copy of the FLV file
that it creates, a copy of the video may persist in the browser's cache directory. If complete
prevention of caching or local storage of the FLV file is required, use Flash Communication
Server MX.

Availability: ActionScript 1.0; Flash Player 7 - Note: This method is also supported in Flash
Player 6 when used with Flash Communication Server. For more information, see the Flash
Communication Server documentation.

Example

The following `onDisconnect()` function closes a connection and deletes the temporary copy
of video1.flv that was stored on the local disk when you click the button called `close_btn`:

```
var connection_nc:NetConnection = new NetConnection();
connection_nc.connect(null);
var stream_ns:NetStream = new NetStream(connection_nc);
my_video.attachVideo(stream_ns);
stream_ns.play("video1.flv");
```

```
close_btn.onRelease = function(){
  stream_ns.close();
};
```

See also

`pause (NetStream.pause method)`, `play (NetStream.play method)`

currentFps (NetStream.currentFps property)

`public currentFps : Number [read-only]`

The number of frames per second being displayed. If you are exporting FLV files to be played back on a number of systems, you can check this value during testing to help you determine how much compression to apply when exporting the file.

Availability: ActionScript 1.0; Flash Player 7 - Note: This property is also supported in Flash Player 6 when used with Flash Communication Server. For more information, see the Flash Communication Server documentation.

Example

The following example creates a text field that displays the current number of frames per second that video1.flv displays.

```
var connection_nc:NetConnection = new NetConnection();
connection_nc.connect(null);
var stream_ns:NetStream = new NetStream(connection_nc);
my_video.attachVideo(stream_ns);
stream_ns.play("video1.flv");

this.createTextField("fps_txt", this.getNextHighestDepth(), 10, 10, 50,
  22);
fps_txt.autoSize = true;
var fps_interval:Number = setInterval(displayFPS, 500, stream_ns);
function displayFPS(my_ns:NetStream) {
  fps_txt.text = "currentFps (frames per second):
  "+Math.floor(my_ns.currentFps);
}
```

If your SWF file includes a version 2 component, use the version 2 components DepthManager class instead of the `MovieClip.getNextHighestDepth()` method, which is used in this example.

NetStream constructor

```
public NetStream(connection:NetConnection)
```

Creates a stream that can be used for playing FLV files through the specified NetConnection object.

Availability: ActionScript 1.0; Flash Player 7 - Note: This class is also supported in Flash Player 6 when used with Flash Communication Server. For more information, see the Flash Communication Server documentation.

Parameters

`connection:NetConnection` - A NetConnection object.

Example

The following code first constructs a new NetConnection object, `connection_nc`, and uses it to construct a new NetStream object called `stream_ns`. Select New Video from the Library options menu to create a video object instance, and give it an instance name `my_video`.

```
var connection_nc:NetConnection = new NetConnection();
connection_nc.connect(null);
var stream_ns:NetStream = new NetStream(connection_nc);
my_video.attachVideo(stream_ns);
stream_ns.play("video1.flv");
```

See also

`NetConnection, attachVideo (Video.attachVideo method)`

onCuePoint (NetStream.onCuePoint handler)

```
onCuePoint = function(infoObject:Object) {}
```

Invoked when an embedded cue point is reached while playing an FLV file. You can use this handler to trigger actions in your code when the video reaches a specific cue point. This lets you synchronize other actions in your application with video playback events.

There are two types of cue points that can be embedded in an FLV file.

- A "navigation" cue point specifies a keyframe within the FLV file and the cue point's `time` property corresponds to that exact keyframe. Navigation cue points are often used as bookmarks or entry points to let users navigate through the video file.

- An "event" cue point is specified by time, whether or not that time corresponds to a specific keyframe. An event cue point usually represents a time in the video when something happens that could be used to trigger other application events.

The `onCuePoint()` event handler receives an object with these properties:

Property	Description
name	The name given to the cue point when it was embedded in the FLV file.
time	The time in seconds at which the cue point occurred in the video file during playback.
type	The type of cue point that was reached, either "navigation" or "event".
parameters	A associative array of name/value pair strings specified for this cue point. Any valid string can be used for the parameter name or value.

You can define cue points in an FLV file when you first encode the file, or when you import a video clip in the Flash Authoring tool by using the Video Import wizard.

The `onMetaData()` event handler also retrieves information about the cue points in a video file. However the `onMetaData()` event handler gets information about all of the cue points before the video begins playing. The `onCuePoint()` event handler receives information about a single cue point at the time specified for that cue point during playback.

Generally if you want your code to respond to a specific cue point at the time it occurs you should use the `onCuePoint()` event handler to trigger some action in your code.

You can use the list of cue points provided to the `onMetaData()` event handler to let your user start playing the video at predefined points along the video stream. Pass the value of the cue point's `time` property to the `NetStream.seek()` method to play the video from that cue point.

Availability: ActionScript 1.0; Flash Player 8

Parameters

`infoObject:Object` - An object containing the `name`, `time`, `type`, and `parameters` for the cue point.

Example

The code in this example starts by creating new NetConnection and NetStream objects. Then it defines the `onCuePoint()` handler for the NetStream object. The handler cycles through each named property in the `infoObject` object and prints the property's name and value. When it finds the property named `parameters` it cycles through each parameter name in the list and prints the parameter name and value.

```
var nc:NetConnection = new NetConnection();
nc.connect(null);
```

```
var ns:NetStream = new NetStream(nc);

ns.onCuePoint = function(infoObject:Object)
{
    trace("onCuePoint:");
    for (var propName:String in infoObject) {
        if (propName != "parameters")
        {
            trace(propName + " = " + infoObject[propName]);
        }
        else
        {
            trace("parameters =");
            if (infoObject.parameters != undefined) {
                for (var paramName:String in infoObject.parameters)
                {
                    trace("  " + paramName + ": " +
infoObject.parameters[paramName]);
                }
            }
            else
            {
                trace("undefined");
            }
        }
    }
    trace("---------");
}

ns.play("http://www.helpexamples.com/flash/video/cuepoints.flv");
```

This causes the following information to be displayed:

```
onCuePoint:
parameters =
lights: beginning
type = navigation
time = 0.418
name = point1
---------
onCuePoint:
parameters =
lights: middle
type = navigation
time = 7.748
name = point2
---------
onCuePoint:
parameters =
lights: end
type = navigation
```

```
time = 16.02
name = point3
- - - - - - - - -
```

The parameter name "lights" is an arbitrary name used by the author of the example video. You can give cue point parameters any name you want.

See also

onMetaData (NetStream.onMetaData handler)

onMetaData (NetStream.onMetaData handler)

```
onMetaData = function(infoObject:Object) {}
```

Invoked when the Flash Player receives descriptive information embedded in the FLV file being played.

The Flash Video Exporter utility (version 1.1 or greater) embeds a video's duration, creation date, data rates, and other information into the video file itself. Different video encoders embed different sets of metadata.

This handler is triggered after a call to the NetStream.play() method, but before the video playhead has advanced.

In many cases the duration value embedded in FLV metadata approximates the actual duration but is not exact. In other words it will not always match the value of the NetStream.time property when the playhead is at the end of the video stream.

Availability: ActionScript 1.0; Flash Player 7

Parameters

infoObject:Object - An object containing one property for each metadata item.

Example

The code in this example starts by creating new NetConnection and NetStream objects. Then it defines the onMetaData() handler for the NetStream object. The handler cycles through each named property in the infoObject object and prints the property's name and value.

```
var nc:NetConnection = new NetConnection();
nc.connect(null);
var ns:NetStream = new NetStream(nc);

ns.onMetaData = function(infoObject:Object) {
  for (var propName:String in infoObject) {
    trace(propName + " = " + infoObject[propName]);
  }
};
```

```
ns.play("http://www.helpexamples.com/flash/video/water.flv");
```
This causes the following information to be displayed:
```
canSeekToEnd = true
videocodecid = 4
framerate = 15
videodatarate = 400
height = 215
width = 320
duration = 7.347
```
The list of properties will vary depending on the software that was used to encode the FLV file.

See also

time (NetStream.time property), play (NetStream.play method), NetConnection

onStatus (NetStream.onStatus handler)

```
onStatus = function(infoObject:Object) {}
```
Invoked every time a status change or error is posted for the NetStream object. If you want to respond to this event handler, you must create a function to process the information object.

The information object has a code property containing a string that describes the result of the onStatus handler, and a level property containing a string that is either status or error.

In addition to this onStatus handler, Flash also provides a "super" function called System.onStatus. If onStatus is invoked for a particular object and there is no function assigned to respond to it, Flash processes a function assigned to System.onStatus if it exists.

The following events notify you when certain NetStream activities occur.

Code property	Level property	Meaning
NetStream.Buffer.Empty	status	Data is not being received quickly enough to fill the buffer. Data flow will be interrupted until the buffer refills, at which time a NetStream.Buffer.Full message will be sent and the stream will begin playing again.
NetStream.Buffer.Full	status	The buffer is full and the stream will begin playing.
NetStream.Buffer.Flush	status	Data has finished streaming, and the remaining buffer will be emptied.
NetStream.Play.Start	status	Playback has started.

Code property	Level property	Meaning
NetStream.Play.Stop	status	Playback has stopped.
NetStream.Play.Stream NotFound	error	The FLV passed to the play() method can't be found.
NetStream.Seek.Invali dTime	error	For video downloaded with progressive download, the user has tried to seek or play past the end of the video data that has downloaded thus far, or past the end of the video once the entire file has downloaded. The message.details property contains a time code that indicates the last valid position to which the user can seek.
NetStream.Seek.Notify	status	The seek operation is complete.

If you consistently see errors regarding buffer, you should try changing the buffer using the NetStream.setBufferTime() method.

Availability: ActionScript 1.0; Flash Player 6

Parameters

infoObject:Object - A parameter defined according to the status message or error message.

Example

The following example displays data about the stream in the Output panel:

```
var connection_nc:NetConnection = new NetConnection();
connection_nc.connect(null);
var stream_ns:NetStream = new NetStream(connection_nc);
my_video.attachVideo(stream_ns);
stream_ns.play("video1.flv");
stream_ns.onStatus = function(infoObject:Object) {
    trace("NetStream.onStatus called: ("+getTimer()+" ms)");
    for (var prop in infoObject) {
      trace("\t"+prop+":\t"+infoObject[prop]);
    }
    trace("");
};
```

See also

setBufferTime (NetStream.setBufferTime method), onStatus (System.onStatus handler)

pause (NetStream.pause method)

`public pause([flag:Boolean]) : Void`

Pauses or resumes playback of a stream.

The first time you call this method (without sending a parameter), it pauses play; the next time, it resumes play. You might want to attach this method to a button that the user presses to pause or resume playback.

Availability: ActionScript 1.0; Flash Player 7 - Note: This method is also supported in Flash Player 6 when used with Flash Communication Server. For more information, see the Flash Communication Server documentation.

Parameters

`flag:Boolean` [optional] - A Boolean value specifying whether to pause play (`true`) or resume play (`false`). If you omit this parameter, `NetStream.pause()` acts as a toggle: the first time it is called on a specified stream, it pauses play, and the next time it is called, it resumes play.

Example

The following examples illustrate some uses of this method:

```
my_ns.pause(); // pauses play first time issued
my_ns.pause(); // resumes play
my_ns.pause(false); // no effect, play continues
my_ns.pause(); // pauses play
```

See also

`close (NetStream.close method)`, `play (NetStream.play method)`

play (NetStream.play method)

`public play(name:Object, start:Number, len:Number, reset:Object) : Void`

Begins playback of an external video (FLV) file. To view video data, you must call a `Video.attachVideo()` method; audio being streamed with the video, or an FLV file that contains only audio, is played automatically.

If you want to control the audio associated with an FLV file, you can use `MovieClip.attachAudio()` to route the audio to a movie clip; you can then create a Sound object to control some aspects of the audio. For more information, see `MovieClip.attachAudio()`.

If the FLV file can't be found, the `NetStream.onStatus` event handler is invoked. If you want to stop a stream that is currently playing, use `NetStream.close()`.

You can play local FLV files that are stored in the same directory as the SWF file or in a subdirectory; you can't navigate to a higher-level directory. For example, if the SWF file is located in a directory named /training, and you want to play a video stored in the /training/ videos directory, you would use the following syntax:

```
my_ns.play("videos/videoName.flv");
```

To play a video stored in the /training directory, you would use the following syntax:

```
my_ns.play("videoName.flv");
```

When using this method, consider the Flash Player security model.

For Flash Player 8:

- NetStream.play() is not allowed if the calling SWF file is in the local-with-file-system sandbox and the resource is in a non-local sandbox.

- Network sandbox access from the local-trusted or local-with-networking sandbox requires permission from the website via a cross-domain policy file.

For more information, see the following:

- Chapter 17, "Understanding Security," in *Learning ActionScript 2.0 in Flash*
- The Flash Player 8 Security white paper at http://www.macromedia.com/go/fp8_security
- The Flash Player 8 Security-Related API white paper at http://www.macromedia.com/go/ fp8_security_apis

Availability: ActionScript 1.0; Flash Player 7 - Note: This method is also supported in Flash Player 6 when used with Flash Communication Server. For more information, see the Flash Communication Server documentation.

Parameters

`name:Object` - The name of an FLV file to play, in quotation marks. Both http:// and file:// formats are supported; the file:// location is always relative to the location of the SWF file.

`start:Number` -

`len:Number` -

`reset:Object` -

Example

The following example illustrates some ways to use the `NetStream.play()` command. You can play a file that is on a user's computer. The joe_user directory is a subdirectory of the directory where the SWF is stored. And, you can play a file on a server:

```
// Play a file that is on the user's computer.
my_ns.play("file://joe_user/flash/videos/lectureJune26.flv");
```

```
// Play a file on a server.
my_ns.play("http://someServer.someDomain.com/flash/video/orientation.flv");
```

See also

```
attachAudio (MovieClip.attachAudio method), close (NetStream.close method),
onStatus (NetStream.onStatus handler), pause (NetStream.pause method),
attachVideo (Video.attachVideo method)
```

seek (NetStream.seek method)

```
public seek(offset:Number) : Void
```

Seeks the keyframe closest to the specified number of seconds from the beginning of the stream. The stream resumes playing when it reaches the specified location in the stream.

Availability: ActionScript 1.0; Flash Player 7 - Note: This method is also supported in Flash Player 6 when used with Flash Communication Server. For more information, see the Flash Communication Server documentation.

Parameters

`offset:Number` - The approximate time value, in seconds, to move to in an FLV file. The playhead moves to the keyframe of the video that's closest to *numberOfSeconds*.

- To return to the beginning of the stream, pass 0 for *numberOfSeconds*.
- To seek forward from the beginning of the stream, pass the number of seconds you want to advance. For example, to position the playhead at 15 seconds from the beginning, use `my_ns.seek(15)`.
- To seek relative to the current position, pass `my_ns.time + n` or `my_ns.time - n` to seek *n* seconds forward or backward, respectively, from the current position. For example, to rewind 20 seconds from the current position, use `my_ns.seek(my_ns.time - 20)`.

The precise location to which a video seeks will differ depending on the frames per second setting at which it was exported. Therefore, if the same video is exported at 6 fps and 30 fps, it will seek to two different locations if you use, for example, `my_ns.seek(15)` for both video objects.

Example

The following example illustrates some ways to use the `NetStream.seek()` command. You can return to the beginning of the stream, move to a location 30 seconds from the beginning of the stream, and move backwards three minutes from the current location:

```
// Return to the beginning of the stream
my_ns.seek(0);
```

```
// Move to a location 30 seconds from the beginning of the stream
my_ns.seek(30);

// Move backwards three minutes from current location
my_ns.seek(my_ns.time - 180);
```

See also

```
, time (NetStream.time property)
```

setBufferTime (NetStream.setBufferTime method)

```
public setBufferTime(bufferTime:Number) : Void
```

Specifies how long to buffer messages before starting to display the stream. For example, if you want to make sure that the first 15 seconds of the stream play without interruption, set *numberOfSeconds* to 15; Flash begins playing the stream only after 15 seconds of data are buffered.

Availability: ActionScript 1.0; Flash Player 7 - Note: This method is also supported in Flash Player 6 when used with Flash Communication Server. For more information, see the Flash Communication Server documentation.

Parameters

`bufferTime:Number` - The number of seconds of data to be buffered before Flash begins displaying data. The default value is 0.1 (one-tenth of a second).

Example

See the example for `NetStream.bufferLength`.

See also

```
bufferLength (NetStream.bufferLength property), bufferTime
(NetStream.bufferTime property)
```

time (NetStream.time property)

```
public time : Number [read-only]
```

The position of the playhead, in seconds.

Availability: ActionScript 1.0; Flash Player 7 - Note: This property is also supported in Flash Player 6 when used with Flash Communication Server. For more information, see the Flash Communication Server documentation.

Example

The following example displays the current position of the playhead in a dynamically created text field called `time_txt`. Select New Video from the Library options menu to create a video object instance, and give it an instance name `my_video`. Create a new video object called my_video. Add the following ActionScript to your FLA or AS file:

```
var connection_nc:NetConnection = new NetConnection();
connection_nc.connect(null);
var stream_ns:NetStream = new NetStream(connection_nc);
my_video.attachVideo(stream_ns);
stream_ns.play("video1.flv");
//
stream_ns.onStatus = function(infoObject:Object) {
  statusCode_txt.text = infoObject.code;
};

this.createTextField("time_txt", this.getNextHighestDepth(), 10, 10, 100,
  22);
time_txt.text = "LOADING";

var time_interval:Number = setInterval(checkTime, 500, stream_ns);
function checkTime(my_ns:NetStream) {
  var ns_seconds:Number = my_ns.time;
  var minutes:Number = Math.floor(ns_seconds/60);
  var seconds = Math.floor(ns_seconds%60);
  if (seconds<10) {
  seconds = "0"+seconds;
  }
  time_txt.text = minutes+":"+seconds;
}
```

If your SWF file includes a version 2 component, use the version 2 components DepthManager class instead of the `MovieClip.getNextHighestDepth()` method, which is used in this example.

See also

`bufferLength (NetStream.bufferLength property)`, `bytesLoaded (NetStream.bytesLoaded property)`

Number

```
Object
   |
   +-Number
```

```
public class Number
extends Object
```

The Number class is a simple wrapper object for the Number data type. You can manipulate primitive numeric values by using the methods and properties associated with the Number class. This class is identical to the JavaScript Number class.

The properties of the Number class are static, which means you do not need an object to use them, so you do not need to use the constructor.

The following example calls the `toString()` method of the Number class, which returns the string `1234`:

```
var myNumber:Number = new Number(1234);
myNumber.toString();
```

The following example assigns the value of the `MIN_VALUE` property to a variable declared without the use of the constructor:

```
var smallest:Number = Number.MIN_VALUE;
```

Availability: ActionScript 1.0; Flash Player 5 - (became a native object in Flash Player 6, which improved performance significantly).

Property summary

Modifiers	Property	Description
static	MAX_VALUE:Number	The largest representable number (double-precision IEEE-754).
static	MIN_VALUE:Number	The smallest representable number (double-precision IEEE-754).
static	NaN:Number	The IEEE-754 value representing Not A Number (NaN).
static	NEGATIVE_INFINITY:Number	Specifies the IEEE-754 value representing negative infinity.
static	POSITIVE_INFINITY:Number	Specifies the IEEE-754 value representing positive infinity.

Properties inherited from class Object

```
constructor (Object.constructor property), __proto__ (Object.__proto__
property), prototype (Object.prototype property), __resolve
(Object.__resolve property)
```

Constructor summary

Signature	Description
Number(num:Object)	Creates a new Number object.

Method summary

Modifiers	Signature	Description
	toString(radix:Number) : String	Returns the string representation of the specified Number object (*myNumber*).
	valueOf() : Number	Returns the primitive value type of the specified Number object.

Methods inherited from class Object

```
addProperty (Object.addProperty method), hasOwnProperty
(Object.hasOwnProperty method), isPropertyEnumerable
(Object.isPropertyEnumerable method), isPrototypeOf (Object.isPrototypeOf
method), registerClass (Object.registerClass method), toString
(Object.toString method), unwatch (Object.unwatch method), valueOf
(Object.valueOf method), watch (Object.watch method)
```

MAX_VALUE (Number.MAX_VALUE property)

```
public static MAX_VALUE : Number
```

The largest representable number (double-precision IEEE-754). This number is approximately 1.79e+308.

Availability: ActionScript 1.0; Flash Player 5

Example

The following ActionScript displays the largest and smallest representable numbers to the Output panel.

```
trace("Number.MIN_VALUE = "+Number.MIN_VALUE);
trace("Number.MAX_VALUE = "+Number.MAX_VALUE);
```

This code displays the following values:

```
Number.MIN_VALUE = 4.94065645841247e-324
Number.MAX_VALUE = 1.79769313486232e+308
```

MIN_VALUE (Number.MIN_VALUE property)

`public static MIN_VALUE : Number`

The smallest representable number (double-precision IEEE-754). This number is approximately 5e-324.

Availability: ActionScript 1.0; Flash Player 5

Example

The following ActionScript displays the largest and smallest representable numbers to the Output panel.

```
trace("Number.MIN_VALUE = "+Number.MIN_VALUE);
trace("Number.MAX_VALUE = "+Number.MAX_VALUE);
```

This code displays the following values:

```
Number.MIN_VALUE = 4.94065645841247e-324
Number.MAX_VALUE = 1.79769313486232e+308
```

NaN (Number.NaN property)

`public static NaN : Number`

The IEEE-754 value representing Not A Number (`NaN`).

Availability: ActionScript 1.0; Flash Player 5

See also

`isNaN function`

NEGATIVE_INFINITY (Number.NEGATIVE_INFINITY property)

`public static NEGATIVE_INFINITY : Number`

Specifies the IEEE-754 value representing negative infinity. The value of this property is the same as that of the constant `-Infinity`.

Negative infinity is a special numeric value that is returned when a mathematical operation or function returns a negative value larger than can be represented.

Availability: ActionScript 1.0; Flash Player 5

Example

This example compares the result of dividing the following values.

```
var posResult:Number = 1/0;
if (posResult == Number.POSITIVE_INFINITY) {
  trace("posResult = "+posResult); // output: posResult = Infinity
}
var negResult:Number = -1/0;
if (negResult == Number.NEGATIVE_INFINITY) {
  trace("negResult = "+negResult); // output: negResult = -Infinity
```

Number constructor

`public Number(num:Object)`

Creates a new Number object. The `new Number` constructor is primarily used as a placeholder. A Number object is not the same as the `Number()` function that converts a parameter to a primitive value.

Availability: ActionScript 1.0; Flash Player 5

Parameters

`num:Object` - The numeric value of the Number object being created or a value to be converted to a number. The default value is 0 if `value` is not provided.

Example

The following code constructs new Number objects:

```
var n1:Number = new Number(3.4);
var n2:Number = new Number(-10);
```

See also

`toString` (Number.toString method), `valueOf` (Number.valueOf method)

POSITIVE_INFINITY (Number.POSITIVE_INFINITY property)

`public static POSITIVE_INFINITY : Number`

Specifies the IEEE-754 value representing positive infinity. The value of this property is the same as that of the constant `Infinity`.

Positive infinity is a special numeric value that is returned when a mathematical operation or function returns a value larger than can be represented.

Availability: ActionScript 1.0; Flash Player 5

Example

This example compares the result of dividing the following values.

```
var posResult:Number = 1/0;
if (posResult == Number.POSITIVE_INFINITY) {
  trace("posResult = "+posResult); // output: posResult = Infinity
}
var negResult:Number = -1/0;
if (negResult == Number.NEGATIVE_INFINITY) {
  trace("negResult = "+negResult); // output: negResult = -Infinity
```

toString (Number.toString method)

```
public toString(radix:Number) : String
```

Returns the string representation of the specified Number object (*myNumber*).

Availability: ActionScript 1.0; Flash Player 5

Parameters

`radix:Number` - Specifies the numeric base (from 2 to 36) to use for the number-to-string conversion. If you do not specify the `radix` parameter, the default value is 10.

Returns

`String` - A string.

Example

The following example uses 2 and 8 for the `radix` parameter and returns a string that contains the corresponding representation of the number 9:

```
var myNumber:Number = new Number(9);
trace(myNumber.toString(2)); // output: 1001
trace(myNumber.toString(8)); // output: 11
```

The following example results in a hexadecimal value.

```
var r:Number = new Number(250);
var g:Number = new Number(128);
var b:Number = new Number(114);
var rgb:String = "0x"+ r.toString(16)+g.toString(16)+b.toString(16);
trace(rgb);
// output: rgb:0xFA8072 (Hexadecimal equivalent of the color 'salmon')
```

valueOf (Number.valueOf method)

```
public valueOf() : Number
```

Returns the primitive value type of the specified Number object.

Availability: ActionScript 1.0; Flash Player 5

Returns

`Number` - A string.

Example

The following example results in the primative value of the `numSocks` object.

```
var numSocks = new Number(2);
trace(numSocks.valueOf()); // output: 2
```

Object

```
Object
```

```
public class Object
```

The Object class is at the root of the ActionScript class hierarchy. This class contains a small subset of the features provided by the JavaScript Object class.

Availability: ActionScript 1.0; Flash Player 5 - (became a native object in Flash Player 6, which improved performance significantly).

Property summary

Modifiers	Property	Description
	`constructor:Object`	Reference to the constructor function for a given object instance.
	`__proto__:Object`	Refers to the `prototype` property of the class (ActionScript 2.0) or constructor function (ActionScript 1.0) used to create the object.
static	`prototype:Object`	A reference to the superclass of a class or function object.
	`__resolve:Object`	A reference to a user-defined function that is invoked if ActionScript code refers to an undefined property or method.

Constructor summary

Signature	Description
Object()	Creates an Object object and stores a reference to the object's constructor method in the object's constructor property.

Method summary

Modifiers	Signature	Description
	addProperty(name:String, getter:Function, setter:Function) : Boolean	Creates a getter/setter property.
	hasOwnProperty(name: String) : Boolean	Indicates whether an object has a specified property defined.
	isPropertyEnumerable (name:String) : Boolean	Indicates whether the specified property exists and is enumerable.
	isPrototypeOf(theClass:Object) : Boolean	Indicates whether an instance of the Object class is in the prototype chain of the object specified as an argument.
static	registerClass(name:String, theClass:Function) : Boolean	Associates a movie clip symbol with an ActionScript object class.
	toString() : String	Converts the specified object to a string and returns it.
	unwatch(name:String) : Boolean	Removes a watchpoint that Object.watch() created.
	valueOf() : Object	Returns the primitive value of the specified object.
	watch(name:String, callback:Function, [userData:Object]) : Boolean	Registers an event handler to be invoked when a specified property of an ActionScript object changes.

addProperty (Object.addProperty method)

public addProperty(name:String, getter:Function, setter:Function) : Boolean

Creates a getter/setter property. When Flash reads a getter/setter property, it invokes the get function, and the function's return value becomes the value of name. When Flash writes a getter/setter property, it invokes the set function and passes it the new value as a parameter. If a property with the given name already exists, the new property overwrites it.

A "get" function is a function with no parameters. Its return value can be of any type. Its type can change between invocations. The return value is treated as the current value of the property.

A "set" function is a function that takes one parameter, which is the new value of the property. For example, if property x is assigned by the statement x = 1, the set function is passed the parameter 1 of type number. The return value of the set function is ignored.

You can add getter/setter properties to prototype objects. If you add a getter/setter property to a prototype object, all object instances that inherit the prototype object inherit the getter/setter property. This makes it possible to add a getter/setter property in one location, the prototype object, and have it propagate to all instances of a class (similar to adding methods to prototype objects). If a get/set function is invoked for a getter/setter property in an inherited prototype object, the reference passed to the get/set function is the originally referenced object--not the prototype object.

If invoked incorrectly, `Object.addProperty()` can fail with an error. The following table describes errors that can occur:

Error condition	What happens
`name` is not a valid property name; for example, an empty string.	Returns `false` and the property is not added.
`getter` is not a valid function object.	Returns `false` and the property is not added.
`setter` is not a valid function object.	Returns `false` and the property is not added.

Availability: ActionScript 1.0; Flash Player 6 - In ActionScript 2.0 classes, you can use get or set instead of this method.

Parameters

`name:String` - A string; the name of the object property to create.

`getter:Function` - The function that is invoked to retrieve the value of the property; this parameter is a Function object.

`setter:Function` - The function that is invoked to set the value of the property; this parameter is a Function object. If you pass the value `null` for this parameter, the property is read-only.

Returns

`Boolean` - A Boolean value: `true` if the property is successfully created; `false` otherwise.

Example

In the following example, an object has two internal methods, setQuantity() and getQuantity(). A property, bookcount, can be used to invoke these methods when it is either set or retrieved. A third internal method, getTitle(), returns a read-only value that is associated with the property bookname. When a script retrieves the value of myBook.bookcount, the ActionScript interpreter automatically invokes myBook.getQuantity(). When a script modifies the value of myBook.bookcount, the interpreter invokes myObject.setQuantity(). The bookname property does not specify a set function, so attempts to modify bookname are ignored.

```
function Book() {
    this.setQuantity = function(numBooks:Number):Void {
    this.books = numBooks;
    };
    this.getQuantity = function():Number {
    return this.books;
    };
    this.getTitle = function():String {
    return "Catcher in the Rye";
    };
    this.addProperty("bookcount", this.getQuantity, this.setQuantity);
    this.addProperty("bookname", this.getTitle, null);
}
var myBook = new Book();
myBook.bookcount = 5;
trace("You ordered "+myBook.bookcount+" copies of "+myBook.bookname);
// output: You ordered 5 copies of Catcher in the Rye
```

The previous example works, but the properties bookcount and bookname are added to every instance of the Book object, which requires having two properties for every instance of the object. If there are many properties, such as bookcount and bookname, in a class, they could consume a great deal of memory. Instead, you can add the properties to Book.prototype so that the bookcount and bookname properties exist only in one place. The effect, however, is the same as that of the code in the example that added bookcount and bookname directly to every instance. If an attempt is made to access either property in a Book instance, the property's absence will cause the prototype chain to be ascended until the versions defined in Book.prototype are encountered. The following example shows how to add the properties to Book.prototype:

```
function Book() {}
Book.prototype.setQuantity = function(numBooks:Number):Void {
    this.books = numBooks;
};
Book.prototype.getQuantity = function():Number {
    return this.books;
};
```

```
Book.prototype.getTitle = function():String {
  return "Catcher in the Rye";
};
Book.prototype.addProperty("bookcount", Book.prototype.getQuantity,
  Book.prototype.setQuantity);
Book.prototype.addProperty("bookname", Book.prototype.getTitle, null);
var myBook = new Book();
myBook.bookcount = 5;
trace("You ordered "+myBook.bookcount+" copies of "+myBook.bookname);
```

The following example shows how to use the implicit getter and setter functions available in ActionScript 2.0. Rather than defining the `Book` function and editing `Book.prototype`, you define the `Book` class in an external file named Book.as. The following code must be in a separate external file named Book.as that contains only this class definition and resides within the Flash application's classpath:

```
class Book {
  var books:Number;
  function set bookcount(numBooks:Number):Void {
  this.books = numBooks;
  }
  function get bookcount():Number {
  return this.books;
  }
  function get bookname():String {
  return "Catcher in the Rye";
  }
}
```

The following code can then be placed in a FLA file and will function the same way as it does in the previous examples:

```
var myBook:Book = new Book();
myBook.bookcount = 5;
trace("You ordered "+myBook.bookcount+" copies of "+myBook.bookname);
```

See also

`get statement`, `set statement`

constructor (Object.constructor property)

`public constructor : Object`

Reference to the constructor function for a given object instance. The `constructor` property is automatically assigned to all objects when they are created using the constructor for the Object class.

Availability: ActionScript 1.0; Flash Player 5

Example

The following example is a reference to the constructor function for the myObject object.

```
var my_str:String = new String("sven");
trace(my_str.constructor == String); //output: true
```

If you use the instanceof operator, you can also determine if an object belongs to a specified class:

```
var my_str:String = new String("sven");
trace(my_str instanceof String); //output: true
```

However, in the following example the Object.constructor property converts primitive data types (such as the string literal seen here) into wrapper objects. The instanceof operator does not perform any conversion, as seen in the following example:

```
var my_str:String = "sven";
trace(my_str.constructor == String); //output: true
trace(my_str instanceof String); //output: false
```

See also

instanceof operator

hasOwnProperty (Object.hasOwnProperty method)

public hasOwnProperty(name:String) : Boolean

Indicates whether an object has a specified property defined. This method returns true if the target object has a property that matches the string specified by the name parameter, and false otherwise. This method does not check the object's prototype chain and returns true only if the property exists on the object itself.

Availability: ActionScript 1.0; Flash Player 6

Parameters

name:String -

Returns

Boolean - A Boolean value: true if the target object has the property specified by the name parameter, false otherwise.

isPropertyEnumerable (Object.isPropertyEnumerable method)

public isPropertyEnumerable(name:String) : Boolean

Indicates whether the specified property exists and is enumerable. If true, then the property exists and can be enumerated in a for..in loop. The property must exist on the target object because this method does not check the target object's prototype chain.

Properties that you create are enumerable, but built-in properties are generally not enumerable.

Availability: ActionScript 1.0; Flash Player 6

Parameters

`name:String` -

Returns

`Boolean` - A Boolean value: `true` if the property specified by the `name` parameter is enumerable.

Example

The following example creates a generic object, adds a property to the object, then checks whether the object is enumerable. By way of contrast, the example also shows that a built-in property, the `Array.length` property, is not enumerable.

```
var myObj:Object = new Object();
myObj.prop1 = "hello";
trace(myObj.isPropertyEnumerable("prop1")); // Output: true

var myArray = new Array();
trace(myArray.isPropertyEnumerable("length")); // Output: false
```

See also

`for..in statement`

isPrototypeOf (Object.isPrototypeOf method)

`public isPrototypeOf(theClass:Object) : Boolean`

Indicates whether an instance of the Object class is in the prototype chain of the object specified as an argument. This method returns `true` if the object is in the prototype chain of the object specified by the `theClass` parameter. The method returns `false` not only if the target object is absent from the prototype chain of the `theClass` object, but also if the `theClass` argument is not an object.

Availability: ActionScript 1.0; Flash Player 6

Parameters

`theClass:Object` -

Returns

`Boolean` - A Boolean value: `true` if the object is in the prototype chain of the object specified by the `theClass` parameter; `false` otherwise.

Object constructor

`public Object()`

Creates an Object object and stores a reference to the object's constructor method in the object's `constructor` property.

Availability: ActionScript 1.0; Flash Player 5

Example

The following example creates a generic object named myObject:

`var myObject:Object = new Object();`

__proto__ (Object.__proto__ property)

`public __proto__ : Object`

Refers to the `prototype` property of the class (ActionScript 2.0) or constructor function (ActionScript 1.0) used to create the object. The __proto__ property is automatically assigned to all objects when they are created. The ActionScript interpreter uses the __proto__ property to access the `prototype` property of the object's class or constructor function to find out what properties and methods the object inherits from its superclass.

Availability: ActionScript 1.0; Flash Player 5

Example

The following example creates a class named Shape and a subclass of Shape named Circle.

```
// Shape class defined in external file named Shape.as
class Shape {
  function Shape() {}
}

// Circle class defined in external file named Circle.as
class Circle extends Shape{
  function Circle() {}
}
```

The Circle class can be used to create two instances of Circle:

```
var oneCircle:Circle = new Circle();
var twoCircle:Circle = new Circle();
```
The following trace statements show that the __proto_ property of both instances refers to the prototype property of the Circle class.
```
trace(Circle.prototype == oneCircle.__proto__); // Output: true
trace(Circle.prototype == twoCircle.__proto__); // Output: true
```

See also

prototype (Object.prototype property)

prototype (Object.prototype property)

public static prototype : Object

A reference to the superclass of a class or function object. The prototype property is automatically created and attached to any class or function object you create. This property is static in that it is specific to the class or function you create. For example, if you create a custom class, the value of the prototype property is shared by all instances of the class, and is accessible only as a class property. Instances of your custom class cannot directly access the prototype property, but can access it through the __proto__ property.

Availability: ActionScript 1.0; Flash Player 6

Example

The following example creates a class named Shape and a subclass of Shape named Circle.
```
// Shape class defined in external file named Shape.as
class Shape {
   function Shape() {}
}

// Circle class defined in external file named Circle.as
class Circle extends Shape{
   function Circle() {}
}
```
The Circle class can be used to create two instances of Circle:
```
var oneCircle:Circle = new Circle();
var twoCircle:Circle = new Circle();
```
The following trace statement shows that the prototype property of the Circle class points to its superclass Shape. The identifier Shape refers to the constructor function of the Shape class.
```
trace(Circle.prototype.constructor == Shape); // Output: true
```

The following trace statement shows how you can use the `prototype` property and the `__proto__` property together to move two levels up the inheritance hierarchy (or prototype chain). The `Circle.prototype.__proto__` property contains a reference to the superclass of the Shape class.

```
trace(Circle.prototype.__proto__ == Shape.prototype); // Output: true
```

See also

`__proto__` (Object.__proto__ property)

registerClass (Object.registerClass method)

`public static registerClass(name:String, theClass:Function) : Boolean`

Associates a movie clip symbol with an ActionScript object class. If a symbol doesn't exist, Flash creates an association between a string identifier and an object class.

When an instance of the specified movie clip symbol is placed on the Timeline, it is registered to the class specified by the `theClass` parameter rather than to the class MovieClip.

When an instance of the specified movie clip symbol is created by using `MovieClip.attachMovie()` or `MovieClip.duplicateMovieClip()`, it is registered to the class specified by `theClass` rather than to the MovieClip class. If `theClass` is `null`, this method removes any ActionScript class definition associated with the specified movie clip symbol or class identifier. For movie clip symbols, any existing instances of the movie clip remain unchanged, but new instances of the symbol are associated with the default class MovieClip.

If a symbol is already registered to a class, this method replaces it with the new registration.

When a movie clip instance is placed by the Timeline or created using `attachMovie()` or `duplicateMovieClip()`, ActionScript invokes the constructor for the appropriate class with the keyword `this` pointing to the object. The constructor function is invoked with no parameters.

If you use this method to register a movie clip with an ActionScript class other than MovieClip, the movie clip symbol doesn't inherit the methods, properties, and events of the built-in MovieClip class unless you include the MovieClip class in the prototype chain of the new class. The following code creates a new ActionScript class called `theClass` that inherits the properties of the MovieClip class:

```
theClass.prototype = new MovieClip();
```

Availability: ActionScript 1.0; Flash Player 6 - If you are using ActionScript 2.0 classes, you can use the ActionScript 2.0 Class field in the Linkage Properties or Symbol Properties dialog box to associate an object with a class instead of using this method.

Parameters

`name:String` - String; the linkage identifier of the movie clip symbol or the string identifier for the ActionScript class.

`theClass:Function` - A reference to the constructor function of the ActionScript class or `null` to unregister the symbol.

Returns

`Boolean` - A Boolean value: if the class registration succeeds, a value of `true` is returned; `false` otherwise.

See also

`attachMovie (MovieClip.attachMovie method)`, `duplicateMovieClip (MovieClip.duplicateMovieClip method)`

__resolve (Object.__resolve property)

`public __resolve : Object`

A reference to a user-defined function that is invoked if ActionScript code refers to an undefined property or method. If ActionScript code refers to an undefined property or method of an object, Flash Player determines whether the object's `__resolve` property is defined. If `__resolve` is defined, the function to which it refers is executed and passed the name of the undefined property or method. This lets you programmatically supply values for undefined properties and statements for undefined methods and make it seem as if the properties or methods are actually defined. This property is useful for enabling highly transparent client/server communication, and is the recommended way of invoking server-side methods.

Availability: ActionScript 1.0; Flash Player 6

Example

The following examples progressively build upon the first example and illustrate five different usages of the `__resolve` property. To aid understanding, key statements that differ from the previous usage are in bold typeface.

Usage 1: the following example uses `__resolve` to build an object where every undefined property returns the value `"Hello, world!"`.

```
// instantiate a new object
var myObject:Object = new Object();

// define the __resolve function
myObject.__resolve = function (name) {
```

```
  return "Hello, world!";
};
trace (myObject.property1); // output: Hello, world!
trace (myObject.property2); // output: Hello, world!
```

Usage 2: the following example uses __resolve as a *functor*, which is a function that generates functions. Using __resolve redirects undefined method calls to a generic function named myFunction.

```
// instantiate a new object
var myObject:Object = new Object();

// define a function for __resolve to call
myObject.myFunction = function (name) {
  trace("Method " + name + " was called");
};

// define the __resolve function
myObject.__resolve = function (name) {
    return function () { this.myFunction(name); };
};

// test __resolve using undefined method names
myObject.someMethod(); // output: Method someMethod was called
myObject.someOtherMethod(); //output: Method someOtherMethod was called
```

Usage 3: The following example builds on the previous example by adding the ability to cache resolved methods. By caching methods, __resolve is called only once for each method of interest. This allows *lazy construction* of object methods. Lazy construction is an optimization technique that defers the creation, or *construction*, of methods until the time at which a method is first used.

```
// instantiate a new object
var myObject:Object = new Object();
// define a function for __resolve to call
myObject.myFunction = function(name) {
  trace("Method "+name+" was called");
};
// define the __resolve function
myObject.__resolve = function(name) {
  trace("Resolve called for "+name); // to check when __resolve is called
  // Not only call the function, but also save a reference to it
  var f:Function = function () {
    this.myFunction(name);
  };
  // create a new object method and assign it the reference
  this[name] = f;
  // return the reference
  return f;
};
// test __resolve using undefined method names
```

```
// __resolve will only be called once for each method name
myObject.someMethod(); // calls __resolve
myObject.someMethod(); // does not call __resolve because it is now defined
myObject.someOtherMethod(); // calls __resolve
myObject.someOtherMethod(); // does not call __resolve, no longer undefined
```

Usage 4: The following example builds on the previous example by reserving a method name, onStatus(), for local use so that it is not resolved in the same way as other undefined properties. Added code is in bold typeface.

```
// instantiate a new object
var myObject:Object = new Object();
// define a function for __resolve to call
myObject.myFunction = function(name) {
  trace("Method "+name+" was called");
};
// define the __resolve function
myObject.__resolve = function(name) {
  // reserve the name "onStatus" for local use
  if (name == "onStatus") {
    return undefined;
  }
  trace("Resolve called for "+name); // to check when __resolve is called
  // Not only call the function, but also save a reference to it
  var f:Function = function () {
    this.myFunction(name);
  };
  // create a new object method and assign it the reference
  this[name] = f;
  // return the reference
  return f;
};
// test __resolve using the method name "onStatus"
trace(myObject.onStatus("hello"));
// output: undefined
```

Usage 5: The following example builds on the previous example by creating a functor that accepts parameters. This example makes extensive use of the arguments object, and uses several methods of the Array class.

```
// instantiate a new object
var myObject:Object = new Object();

// define a generic function for __resolve to call
myObject.myFunction = function (name) {
  arguments.shift();
  trace("Method " + name + " was called with arguments: " +
  arguments.join(','));
};

// define the __resolve function
```

```
myObject.__resolve = function (name) {
  // reserve the name "onStatus" for local use
  if (name == "onStatus") {
    return undefined;
  }
  var f:Function = function () {
    arguments.unshift(name);
    this.myFunction.apply(this, arguments);
  };
  // create a new object method and assign it the reference
  this[name] = f;
  // return the reference to the function
  return f;
};

// test __resolve using undefined method names with parameters
myObject.someMethod("hello");
// output: Method someMethod was called with arguments: hello

myObject.someOtherMethod("hello","world");
// output: Method someOtherMethod was called with arguments: hello,world
```

See also

`arguments, Array`

toString (Object.toString method)

`public toString() : String`

Converts the specified object to a string and returns it.

Availability: ActionScript 1.0; Flash Player 5

Returns

`String` - A string.

Example

This example shows the return value for toString() on a generic object:

```
var myObject:Object = new Object();
trace(myObject.toString()); // output: [object Object]
```

This method can be overridden to return a more meaningful value. The following examples show that this method has been overridden for the built-in classes Date, Array, and Number:

```
// Date.toString() returns the current date and time
var myDate:Date = new Date();
trace(myDate.toString()); // output: [current date and time]
```

```
// Array.toString() returns the array contents as a comma-delimited string
var myArray:Array = new Array("one", "two");
trace(myArray.toString()); // output: one,two

// Number.toString() returns the number value as a string
// Because trace() won't tell us whether the value is a string or number
// we will also use typeof() to test whether toString() works.
var myNumber:Number = 5;
trace(typeof (myNumber)); // output: number
trace(myNumber.toString()); // output: 5
trace(typeof (myNumber.toString())); // output: string
```

The following example shows how to override `toString()` in a custom class. First create a
text file named *Vehicle.as* that contains only the Vehicle class definition and place it into your
Classes folder inside your Configuration folder.

```
// contents of Vehicle.as
class Vehicle {
  var numDoors:Number;
  var color:String;
  function Vehicle(param_numDoors:Number, param_color:String) {
  this.numDoors = param_numDoors;
  this.color = param_color;
  }
  function toString():String {
  var doors:String = "door";
  if (this.numDoors > 1) {
    doors += "s";
  }
  return ("A vehicle that is " + this.color + " and has " + this.numDoors +
  " " + doors);
  }
}

// code to place into a FLA file
var myVehicle:Vehicle = new Vehicle(2, "red");
trace(myVehicle.toString());
// output: A vehicle that is red and has 2 doors

// for comparison purposes, this is a call to valueOf()
// there is no primitive value of myVehicle, so the object is returned
// giving the same output as toString().
trace(myVehicle.valueOf());
// output: A vehicle that is red and has 2 doors
```

unwatch (Object.unwatch method)

`public unwatch(name:String) : Boolean`

Removes a watchpoint that `Object.watch()` created. This method returns a value of `true` if the watchpoint is successfully removed, `false` otherwise.

Availability: ActionScript 1.0; Flash Player 6

Parameters

`name:String` - A string; the name of the object property that should no longer be watched.

Returns

`Boolean` - A Boolean value: `true` if the watchpoint is successfully removed, `false` otherwise.

Example

See the example for `Object.watch()`.

See also

`watch (Object.watch method)`, `addProperty (Object.addProperty method)`

valueOf (Object.valueOf method)

`public valueOf() : Object`

Returns the primitive value of the specified object. If the object does not have a primitive value, the object is returned.

Availability: ActionScript 1.0; Flash Player 5

Returns

`Object` - The primitive value of the specified object or the object itself.

Example

The following example shows the return value of valueOf() for a generic object (which does not have a primitive value) and compares it to the return value of toString(). First, create a generic object. Second, create a new Date object set to February 1, 2004, 8:15 AM. The toString() method returns the current time in human-readable form. The valueOf() method returns the primitive value in milliseconds. Third, create a new Array object containing two simple elements. Both toString() and valueOf() return the same value: one,two:

```
// Create a generic object
var myObject:Object = new Object();
```

```
trace(myObject.valueOf()); // output: [object Object]
trace(myObject.toString()); // output: [object Object]
```

The following examples show the return values for the built-in classes Date and Array, and compares them to the return values of `Object.toString()`:

```
// Create a new Date object set to February 1, 2004, 8:15 AM
// The toString() method returns the current time in human-readable form
// The valueOf() method returns the primitive value in milliseconds
var myDate:Date = new Date(2004,01,01,8,15);
trace(myDate.toString()); // output: Sun Feb 1 08:15:00 GMT-0800 2004
trace(myDate.valueOf()); // output: 1075652100000

// Create a new Array object containing two simple elements
// In this case both toString() and valueOf() return the same value: one,two
var myArray:Array = new Array("one", "two");
trace(myArray.toString()); // output: one,two
trace(myArray.valueOf()); // output: one,two
```

See the example for `Object.toString()` for an example of the return value of `Object.valueOf()` for a custom class that overrides `toString()`.

See also

toString (Object.toString method)

watch (Object.watch method)

`public watch(name:String, callback:Function, [userData:Object]) : Boolean`

Registers an event handler to be invoked when a specified property of an ActionScript object changes. When the property changes, the event handler is invoked with `myObject` as the containing object.

You can use the `return` statement in your `callback` method definition to affect the value of the property you are watching. The value returned by your `callback` method is assigned to the watched object property. The value you choose to return depends on whether you wish to monitor, modify or prevent changes to the property:

- If you are merely monitoring the property, return the `newVal` parameter.
- If you are modifying the value of the property, return your own value.
- If you want to prevent changes to the property, return the `oldVal` parameter.

If the `callback` method you define does not have a `return` statement, then the watched object property is assigned a value of `undefined`.

A watchpoint can filter (or nullify) the value assignment, by returning a modified newval (or oldval). If you delete a property for which a watchpoint has been set, that watchpoint does not disappear. If you later recreate the property, the watchpoint is still in effect. To remove a watchpoint, use the Object.unwatch method.

Only a single watchpoint can be registered on a property. Subsequent calls to Object.watch() on the same property replace the original watchpoint.

The Object.watch() method behaves similarly to the Object.watch() function in JavaScript 1.2 and later. The primary difference is the userData parameter, which is a Flash addition to Object.watch() that Netscape Navigator does not support. You can pass the userData parameter to the event handler and use it in the event handler.

The Object.watch() method cannot watch getter/setter properties. Getter/setter properties operate through *lazy evaluation*-- the value of the property is not determined until the property is actually queried. Lazy evaluation is often efficient because the property is not constantly updated; it is, rather, evaluated when needed. However, Object.watch() needs to evaluate a property to determine whether to invoke the callback function. To work with a getter/setter property, Object.watch() needs to evaluate the property constantly, which is inefficient.

Generally, predefined ActionScript properties, such as _x, _y, _width, and _height, are getter/setter properties and cannot be watched with Object.watch().

Availability: ActionScript 1.0; Flash Player 6

Parameters

name:String - A string; the name of the object property to watch.

callback:Function - The function to invoke when the watched property changes. This parameter is a function object, not a function name as a string. The form of callback is callback(prop, oldVal, newVal, userData).

userData:Object [optional] - An arbitrary piece of ActionScript data that is passed to the callback method. If the userData parameter is omitted, undefined is passed to the callback method.

Returns

Boolean - A Boolean value: true if the watchpoint is created successfully, false otherwise.

Example

The following example uses watch() to check whether the speed property exceeds the speed limit:

```
// Create a new object
```

```
var myObject:Object = new Object();

// Add a property that tracks speed
myObject.speed = 0;

// Write the callback function to be executed if the speed property changes
var speedWatcher:Function = function(prop, oldVal, newVal, speedLimit) {
  // Check whether speed is above the limit
  if (newVal > speedLimit) {
  trace ("You are speeding.");
  }
  else {
  trace ("You are not speeding.");
  }

  // Return the value of newVal.
  return newVal;
}
// Use watch() to register the event handler, passing as parameters:
// - the name of the property to watch: "speed"
// - a reference to the callback function speedWatcher
// - the speedLimit of 55 as the userData parameter
myObject.watch("speed", speedWatcher, 55);

// set the speed property to 54, then to 57
myObject.speed = 54; // output: You are not speeding
myObject.speed = 57; // output: You are speeding

// unwatch the object
myObject.unwatch("speed");
myObject.speed = 54; // there should be no output
```

See also

`addProperty` (Object.addProperty method), `unwatch` (Object.unwatch method)

Point (flash.geom.Point)

```
Object
  |
  +-flash.geom.Point
```

```
public class Point
extends Object
```

The Point class represents a location in a two-dimensional coordinate system, where x represents the horizontal axis and y represents the vertical axis.

The following code creates a point at (0,0):

```
var myPoint:Point = new Point();
```
Availability: ActionScript 1.0; Flash Player 8

Property summary

Modifiers	Property	Description
	length:Number	The length of the line segment from (0,0) to this point.
	x:Number	The horizontal coordinate of the point.
	y:Number	The vertical coordinate of the point.

Properties inherited from class Object

```
constructor (Object.constructor property), __proto__ (Object.__proto__
property), prototype (Object.prototype property), __resolve
(Object.__resolve property)
```

Constructor summary

Signature	Description
Point(x:Number, y:Number)	Creates a new point.

Method summary

Modifiers	Signature	Description
	add(v:Point) : Point	Adds the coordinates of another point to the coordinates of this point to create a new point.
	clone() : Point	Creates a copy of this Point object.
static	distance(pt1:Point, pt2:Point) : Number	Returns the distance between pt1 and pt2.
	equals(toCompare:Object) : Boolean	Determines whether two points are equal.
static	interpolate(pt1:Point, pt2:Point, f:Number) : Point	Determines a point between two specified points.
	normalize(length:Number) : Void	Scales the line segment between (0,0) and the current point to a set length.
	offset(dx:Number, dy:Number) : Void	Offsets the Point object by the specified amount.

Modifiers	Signature	Description
`static`	`polar(len:Number, angle:Number) : Point`	Converts a pair of polar coordinates to a cartesian point coordinate.
	`subtract(v:Point) : Point`	Subtracts the coordinates of another point from the coordinates of this point to create a new point.
	`toString() : String`	Returns a string that contains the values of the x and y coordinates.

Methods inherited from class Object

```
addProperty (Object.addProperty method), hasOwnProperty
(Object.hasOwnProperty method), isPropertyEnumerable
(Object.isPropertyEnumerable method), isPrototypeOf (Object.isPrototypeOf
method), registerClass (Object.registerClass method), toString
(Object.toString method), unwatch (Object.unwatch method), valueOf
(Object.valueOf method), watch (Object.watch method)
```

add (Point.add method)

`public add(v:Point) : Point`

Adds the coordinates of another point to the coordinates of this point to create a new point.

Availability: ActionScript 1.0; Flash Player 8

Parameters

`v:flash.geom.Point` - The point to be added.

Returns

`flash.geom.Point` - The new point.

Example

The following example creates a Point object `resultPoint` by adding `point_2` to `point_1`.

```
import flash.geom.Point;
var point_1:Point = new Point(4, 8);
var point_2:Point = new Point(1, 2);
var resultPoint:Point = point_1.add(point_2);
trace(resultPoint.toString()); // (x=5, y=10)
```

clone (Point.clone method)

`public clone() : Point`

Creates a copy of this Point object.

Availability: ActionScript 1.0; Flash Player 8

Returns

`flash.geom.Point` - The new Point object.

Example

The following example creates a copy of the Point object called `clonedPoint` from the values found in the `myPoint` object. The `clonedPoint` object contains all of the values from `myPoint`, but it is not the same object.

```
import flash.geom.Point;
var myPoint:Point = new Point(1, 2);
var clonedPoint:Point = myPoint.clone();
trace(clonedPoint.x); // 1
trace(clonedPoint.y); // 2
trace(myPoint.equals(clonedPoint)); // true
trace(myPoint === clonedPoint); // false
```

distance (Point.distance method)

```
public static distance(pt1:Point, pt2:Point) : Number
```

Returns the distance between pt1 and pt2.

Availability: ActionScript 1.0; Flash Player 8

Parameters

`pt1:flash.geom.Point` - The first point.

`pt2:flash.geom.Point` - The second point.

Returns

`Number` - The distance between the first and second points.

Example

The following example creates `point_1` and `point_2`, then determines the distance between them (`distanceBetween`).

```
import flash.geom.Point;
var point_1:Point = new Point(-5, 0);
var point_2:Point = new Point(5, 0);
var distanceBetween:Number = Point.distance(point_1, point_2);
trace(distanceBetween); // 10
```

equals (Point.equals method)

```
public equals(toCompare:Object) : Boolean
```

Determines whether two points are equal. Two points are equal if they have the same *x* and *y* values.

Availability: ActionScript 1.0; Flash Player 8

Parameters

`toCompare:Object` - The point to be compared.

Returns

`Boolean` - If the object is equal to this Point object, `true`; if it is not equal, `false`.

Example

The following example determines whether the values of one point are equal to the values of another point. If the objects are the same, `equals()` does not return the same result that the strict equality operator (`===`) does.

```
import flash.geom.Point;
var point_1:Point = new Point(1, 2);
var point_2:Point = new Point(1, 2);
var point_3:Point = new Point(4, 8);
trace(point_1.equals(point_2)); // true
trace(point_1.equals(point_3)); // false
trace(point_1 === point_2); // false
trace(point_1 === point_3); // false
```

interpolate (Point.interpolate method)

```
public static interpolate(pt1:Point, pt2:Point, f:Number) : Point
```

Determines a point between two specified points.

Availability: ActionScript 1.0; Flash Player 8

Parameters

`pt1:flash.geom.Point` - The first point.

`pt2:flash.geom.Point` - The second point.

`f:Number` - The level of interpolation between the two points. Indicates where the new point will be, along the line between pt1 and pt2. If f=0, pt1 is returned; if f=1, pt2 is returned.

Returns

`flash.geom.Point` - The new, interpolated point.

Example

The following example locates the interpolated point (`interpolatedPoint`) half way (50%) between `point_1` and `point_2`.

```
import flash.geom.Point;
var point_1:Point = new Point(-100, -100);
var point_2:Point = new Point(50, 50);
var interpolatedPoint:Point = Point.interpolate(point_1, point_2, .5);
trace(interpolatedPoint.toString()); // (x=-25, y=-25)
```

length (Point.length property)

`public length : Number`

The length of the line segment from (0,0) to this point.

Availability: ActionScript 1.0; Flash Player 8

Example

The following example creates a Point object, `myPoint`, and determines the length of a line from (0, 0) to that Point.

```
import flash.geom.Point;
var myPoint:Point = new Point(3,4);
trace(myPoint.length); // 5
```

See also

`polar (Point.polar method)`

normalize (Point.normalize method)

`public normalize(length:Number) : Void`

Scales the line segment between (0,0) and the current point to a set length.

Availability: ActionScript 1.0; Flash Player 8

Parameters

`length:Number` - The scaling value. For example, if the current point is (0,5), and you normalize it to 1, the point returned is at (0,1).

Example

The following example extends the length of the `normalizedPoint` object from 5 to 10.

```
import flash.geom.Point;
var normalizedPoint:Point = new Point(3, 4);
trace(normalizedPoint.length); // 5
```

```
trace(normalizedPoint.toString()); // (x=3, y=4)
normalizedPoint.normalize(10);
trace(normalizedPoint.length); // 10
trace(normalizedPoint.toString()); // (x=6, y=8)
```

See also

```
length (Point.length property)
```

offset (Point.offset method)

```
public offset(dx:Number, dy:Number) : Void
```

Offsets the Point object by the specified amount. The value of dx is added to the original value of *x* to create the new *x* value. The value of dy is added to the original value of *y* to create the new *y* value.

Availability: ActionScript 1.0; Flash Player 8

Parameters

dx : Number - The amount by which to offset the horizontal coordinate, *x*.

dy : Number - The amount by which to offset the vertical coordinate, *y*.

Example

The following example offsets a point's position by specified *x* and *y* amounts.

```
import flash.geom.Point;
var myPoint:Point = new Point(1, 2);
trace(myPoint.toString()); // (x=1, y=2)
myPoint.offset(4, 8);
trace(myPoint.toString()); // (x=5, y=10)
```

See also

```
add (Point.add method)
```

Point constructor

```
public Point(x:Number, y:Number)
```

Creates a new point. If you pass no parameters to this method, a point is created at (0,0).

Availability: ActionScript 1.0; Flash Player 8

Parameters

x : Number - The horizontal coordinate. The default value is 0.

y : Number - The vertical coordinate. The default value is 0.

Example

The first example creates a Point object `point_1` with the default constructor.

```
import flash.geom.Point;
var point_1:Point = new Point();
trace(point_1.x); // 0
trace(point_1.y); // 0
```

The second example creates a Point object `point_2` with the coordinates $x = 1$ and $y = 2$.

```
import flash.geom.Point;
var point_2:Point = new Point(1, 2);
trace(point_2.x); // 1
trace(point_2.y); // 2
```

polar (Point.polar method)

```
public static polar(len:Number, angle:Number) : Point
```

Converts a pair of polar coordinates to a cartesian point coordinate.

Availability: ActionScript 1.0; Flash Player 8

Parameters

`len:Number` - The length coordinate of the polar pair.

`angle:Number` - The angle, in radians, of the polar pair.

Returns

`flash.geom.Point` - The cartesian point.

Example

The following example creates a Point object `cartesianPoint` from the value of `angleInRadians` and a line length of 5. The `angleInRadians` value equal to Math.atan(3/4) is used because of the characteristics of right triangles with sides that have ratios of 3:4:5.

```
import flash.geom.Point;
var len:Number = 5;
var angleInRadians:Number = Math.atan(3/4);
var cartesianPoint:Point = Point.polar(len, angleInRadians);
trace(cartesianPoint.toString()); // (x=4, y=3)
```

When computers work with transcendental numbers such as pi, some round-off error occurs because floating-point arithmetic has only finite precision. When you use `Math.PI`, consider using the `Math.round()` function, as shown in the following example.

```
import flash.geom.Point;
var len:Number = 10;
var angleInRadians:Number = Math.PI;
var cartesianPoint:Point = Point.polar(len, angleInRadians);
trace(cartesianPoint.toString()); // should be (x=-10, y=0), but is (x=-10,
    y=1.22460635382238e-15)
trace(Math.round(cartesianPoint.y)); // 0
```

See also

`length (Point.length property)`, `round (Math.round method)`

subtract (Point.subtract method)

`public subtract(v:Point) : Point`

Subtracts the coordinates of another point from the coordinates of this point to create a new point.

Availability: ActionScript 1.0; Flash Player 8

Parameters

`v:flash.geom.Point` - The point to be subtracted.

Returns

`flash.geom.Point` - The new point.

Example

The following example creates `point_3` by subtracting `point_2` from `point_1`.

```
import flash.geom.Point;
var point_1:Point = new Point(4, 8);
var point_2:Point = new Point(1, 2);
var resultPoint:Point = point_1.subtract(point_2);
trace(resultPoint.toString()); // (x=3, y=6)
```

toString (Point.toString method)

`public toString() : String`

Returns a string that contains the values of the x and y coordinates. It has the form (x, y), so a Point at 23,17 would report "$(x=23, y=17)$".

Availability: ActionScript 1.0; Flash Player 8

Returns

`String` - A string.

Example

The following example creates a point and converts its values to a string in the format (x=x, y=y).

```
import flash.geom.Point;
var myPoint:Point = new Point(1, 2);
trace("myPoint: " + myPoint.toString()); // (x=1, y=2)
```

x (Point.x property)

`public x : Number`

The horizontal coordinate of the point. The default value is 0.

Availability: ActionScript 1.0; Flash Player 8

Example

The following example creates a Point object `myPoint` and sets the *x* coordinate value.

```
import flash.geom.Point;
var myPoint:Point = new Point();
trace(myPoint.x); // 0
myPoint.x = 5;
trace(myPoint.x); // 5
```

y (Point.y property)

`public y : Number`

The vertical coordinate of the point. The default value is 0.

Availability: ActionScript 1.0; Flash Player 8

Example

The following example creates a Point object `myPoint` and sets the *y* coordinate value.

```
import flash.geom.Point;
var myPoint:Point = new Point();
trace(myPoint.y); // 0
myPoint.y = 5;
trace(myPoint.y); // 5
```

PrintJob

```
Object
  |
  +-PrintJob
```

```
public class PrintJob
extends Object
```

The PrintJob class lets you create content and print it to one or more pages. This class, in addition to offering improvements to print functionality provided by the `print()` method, lets you render dynamic content offscreen, prompt users with a single Print dialog box, and print an unscaled document with proportions that map to the proportions of the content. This capability is especially useful for rendering and printing dynamic content, such as database content and dynamic text.

Additionally, with properties populated by `PrintJob.start()`, your document can read your user's printer settings, such as page height, width, and orientation, and you can configure your document to dynamically format Flash content that is appropriate for the printer settings. These user layout properties are read-only and cannot be changed by Flash Player.

Availability: ActionScript 1.0; Flash Player 7

Property summary

Modifiers	Property	Description
	orientation:String [read-only]	The image orientation for printing.
	pageHeight:Number [read-only]	The height of the actual printable area on the page, in points.
	pageWidth:Number [read-only]	The width of the actual printable area on the page, in points.
	paperHeight:Number [read-only]	The overall paper height, in points.
	paperWidth:Number [read-only]	The overall paper width, in points.

Properties inherited from class Object

```
constructor (Object.constructor property), __proto__ (Object.__proto__
property), prototype (Object.prototype property), __resolve
(Object.__resolve property)
```

Constructor summary

Signature	Description
`PrintJob()`	Creates a PrintJob object that you can use to print one or more pages.

Method summary

Modifiers	Signature	Description
	`addPage(target:Objec t, [printArea:Object], [options:Object], [frameNum:Number]) : Boolean`	Sends the specified level or movie clip as a single page to the print spooler.
	`send() : Void`	Used following the `PrintJob.start()` and `PrintJob.addPage()` methods to send spooled pages to the printer.
	`start() : Boolean`	Displays the operating system's print dialog boxes and starts spooling.

Methods inherited from class Object

```
addProperty (Object.addProperty method), hasOwnProperty
(Object.hasOwnProperty method), isPropertyEnumerable
(Object.isPropertyEnumerable method), isPrototypeOf (Object.isPrototypeOf
method), registerClass (Object.registerClass method), toString
(Object.toString method), unwatch (Object.unwatch method), valueOf
(Object.valueOf method), watch (Object.watch method)
```

addPage (PrintJob.addPage method)

`public addPage(target:Object, [printArea:Object], [options:Object], [frameNum:Number]) : Boolean`

Sends the specified level or movie clip as a single page to the print spooler. Before using this method, you must use `PrintJob.start()`; after calling `PrintJob.addPage()` one or more times for a print job, you must use `PrintJob.send()` to send the spooled pages to the printer.

If this method returns `false` (for example, if you haven't called `PrintJob.start()` or the user canceled the print job), any subsequent calls to `PrintJob.addPage()` will fail. However, if previous calls to `PrintJob.addPage()` were successful, the concluding `PrintJob.send()` command sends the successfully spooled pages to the printer.

If you passed a value for `printArea`, the `xMin` and `yMin` coordinates map to the upper left corner (0,0 coordinates) of the printable area on the page. The user's printable area is described by the read-only `pageHeight` and `pageWidth` properties set by `PrintJob.start()`. Because the printout aligns with the upper left corner of the printable area on the page, the printout is clipped to the right and/or bottom if the area defined in `printArea` is bigger than the printable area on the page. If you haven't passed a value for `printArea` and the Stage is larger than the printable area, the same type of clipping takes place.

If you want to scale a movie clip before you print it, set its `MovieClip._xscale` and `MovieClip._yscale` properties before calling this method, and set them back to their original values afterward. The scale of a movie clip has no relation to `printArea`. That is, if you specify that you print an area that is 50 x 50 pixels in size, 2500 pixels are printed. If you have scaled the movie clip, the same 2500 pixels are printed, but the movie clip is printed at the scaled size.

The Flash Player printing feature supports PostScript and non-PostScript printers. Non-PostScript printers convert vectors to bitmaps.

Availability: ActionScript 1.0; Flash Player 7

Parameters

`target:Object` - A number or string; the level or instance name of the movie clip to print. Pass a number to specify a level (for example, 0 is the _root movie), or a string (in quotation marks [""]) to specify the instance name of a movie clip.

`printArea:Object` [optional] - An object that specifies the area to print, in the following format:

{xMin:*topLeft*, xMax:*topRight*, yMin:*bottomLeft*, yMax:*bottomRight*}

The coordinates you specify for `printArea` represent screen pixels relative to the registration point of the _root movie clip (if `target` = 0) or of the level or movie clip specified by `target`. You must provide all four coordinates. The width (`xMax`-`xMin`) and height (`yMax`-`yMin`) must each be greater than 0.

Points are print units of measurement, and pixels are screen units of measurement; points are a fixed physical size (1/72 inch), but the size of a pixel depends on the resolution of the particular screen. You can use the following equivalencies to convert inches or centimeters to twips or points (a twip is 1/20 of a point):

- 1 point = 1/72 inch = 20 twips

- 1 inch = 72 points = 1440 twips

- 1 cm = 567 twips

You can't reliably convert between pixels and points; the conversion rate depends on the screen and its resolution. If the screen is set to display 72 pixels per inch, for example, one point is equal to one pixel.

> **NOTE**
> If you have previously used `print()`, `printAsBitmap()`, `printAsBitmapNum()`, or `printNum()` to print from Flash, you might have used a #b frame label to specify the area to print. When using the `addPage()` method, you must use the `printArea` parameter to specify the print area; #b frame labels are ignored.

If you omit the `printArea` parameter, or if it is passed incorrectly, the full Stage area of `target` is printed. If you don't want to specify a value for `printArea` but want to specify a value for `options` or `frameNumber`, pass `null` for `printArea`.

`options:Object` [optional] - A parameter that specifies whether to print as vector or bitmap, in the following format:

`{printAsBitmap:`*`Boolean`*`}`

The default value is `false`, which represents a request for vector printing. To print `target` as a bitmap, pass `true` for printAsBitmap. Remember the following suggestions when determining which value to use:

- If the content that you're printing includes a bitmap image, use `{printAsBitmap:true}` to include any transparency and color effects.
- If the content does not include bitmap images, omit this parameter or use `{printAsBitmap:false}` to print the content in higher quality vector format.

If `options` is omitted or is passed incorrectly, vector printing is used. If you don't want to specify a value for `options` but want to specify a value for `frameNumber`, pass `null` for `options`.

`frameNum:Number` [optional] - A number that lets you specify which frame to print; passing a `frameNumber` does not cause the ActionScript on that frame to be invoked. If you omit this parameter, the current frame in `target` is printed.

> **NOTE**
> If you have previously used `print()`, `printAsBitmap()`, `printAsBitmapNum()`, or `printNum()` to print from Flash, you might have used a #p frame label on multiple frames to specify which pages to print. To use `PrintJob.addPage()` to print multiple frames, you must issue a `PrintJob.addPage()` command for each frame; #p frame labels are ignored. For one way to do this programmatically, see the Example section.

Returns

`Boolean` - A Boolean value: `true` if the page is successfully sent to the print spooler; `false` otherwise.

Example

The following example shows several ways to issue the addPage() command:

```
my_btn.onRelease = function()
{
  var pageCount:Number = 0;

  var my_pj:PrintJob = new PrintJob();

  if (my_pj.start())
  {
// Print entire current frame of the _root movie in vector format
  if (my_pj.addPage(0)){
    pageCount++;

    // Starting at 0,0, print an area 400 pixels wide and 500 pixels high
    // of the current frame of the _root movie in vector format
    if (my_pj.addPage(0, {xMin:0,xMax:400,yMin:0,yMax:500})){
    pageCount++;

    // Starting at 0,0, print an area 400 pixels wide and 500 pixels high
    // of frame 1 of the _root movie in bitmap format
    if (my_pj.addPage(0, {xMin:0,xMax:400,yMin:0,yMax:500},
      {printAsBitmap:true}, 1)){
      pageCount++;

    // Starting 50 pixels to the right of 0,0 and 70 pixels down,
    // print an area 500 pixels wide and 600 pixels high
    // of frame 4 of level 5 in vector format
    if (my_pj.addPage(5, {xMin:50,xMax:550,yMin:70,yMax:670},null, 4)){
    pageCount++;

    // Starting at 0,0, print an area 400 pixels wide
    // and 400 pixels high of frame 3 of the "dance_mc" movie clip
    // in bitmap format
    if (my_pj.addPage("dance_mc",
      {xMin:0,xMax:400,yMin:0,yMax:400},{printAsBitmap:true}, 3)){
      pageCount++;

      // Starting at 0,0, print an area 400 pixels wide
      // and 600 pixels high of frame 3 of the "dance_mc" movie clip
      // in vector format at 50% of its actual size
      var x:Number = dance_mc._xscale;
      var y:Number = dance_mc._yscale;
      dance_mc._xscale = 50;
      dance_mc._yscale = 50;

      if (my_pj.addPage("dance_mc",
        {xMin:0,xMax:400,yMin:0,yMax:600},null, 3)){
      pageCount++;
```

```
      }
      dance_mc._xscale = x;
      dance_mc._yscale = y;
    }
    }
  }
  }
 }
 }

 // If addPage() was successful at least once, print the spooled pages.
 if (pageCount > 0){
 my_pj.send();
 }
 delete my_pj;
}
```

See also

send (PrintJob.send method), start (PrintJob.start method)

orientation (PrintJob.orientation property)

public orientation : String [read-only]

The image orientation for printing. This property can be either "landscape" or "portrait".
Note that this property is only available after a call to the PrintJob.start() method.

Availability: ActionScript 1.0; Flash Player 7

pageHeight (PrintJob.pageHeight property)

public pageHeight : Number [read-only]

The height of the actual printable area on the page, in points. Any user-set margins are
ignored. Note that this property is only available after a call to the PrintJob.start()
method.

Availability: ActionScript 1.0; Flash Player 7

pageWidth (PrintJob.pageWidth property)

public pageWidth : Number [read-only]

The width of the actual printable area on the page, in points. Any user-set margins are
ignored. Note that this property is only available after a call to the PrintJob.start()
method.

Availability: ActionScript 1.0; Flash Player 7

paperHeight (PrintJob.paperHeight property)

```
public paperHeight : Number [read-only]
```

The overall paper height, in points. Note that this property is only available after a call to the `PrintJob.start()` method.

Availability: ActionScript 1.0; Flash Player 7

paperWidth (PrintJob.paperWidth property)

```
public paperWidth : Number [read-only]
```

The overall paper width, in points. Note that this property is only available after a call to the `PrintJob.start()` method.

Availability: ActionScript 1.0; Flash Player 7

PrintJob constructor

```
public PrintJob()
```

Creates a PrintJob object that you can use to print one or more pages.

To implement a print job, use the following methods in sequence. You must place all commands relating to a specific print job in the same frame, from the constructor through `PrintJob.send()` and delete. Replace the `[params]` to the `my_pj.addPage()` method calls with your custom parameters.

```
// create PrintJob object
var my_pj:PrintJob = new PrintJob();

// display print dialog box, but only initiate the print job
// if start returns successfully.
if (my_pj.start()) {

  // use a variable to track successful calls to addPage
  var pagesToPrint:Number = 0;

  // add specified area to print job
  // repeat once for each page to be printed
  if (my_pj.addPage([params])) {
  pagesToPrint++;
  }
  if (my_pj.addPage([params])) {
  pagesToPrint++;
  }
  if (my_pj.addPage([params])) {
  pagesToPrint++;
  }
```

```
// send pages from the spooler to the printer, but only if one or more
// calls to addPage() was successful. You should always check for
successful
// calls to start() and addPage() before calling send().
if (pagesToPrint > 0) {
my_pj.send();  // print page(s)
}
}

// clean up
delete my_pj;  // delete object
```

You cannot create a second PrintJob object while the first one is still active. You cannot create a second PrintJob object (by calling new PrintJob()) while the first PrintJob object is still active, the second PrintJob object will not be created.

Availability: ActionScript 1.0; Flash Player 7

Example

See PrintJob.addPage().

See also

addPage (PrintJob.addPage method), send (PrintJob.send method), start (PrintJob.start method)

send (PrintJob.send method)

```
public send() : Void
```

Used following the PrintJob.start() and PrintJob.addPage() methods to send spooled pages to the printer. Because calls to PrintJob.send() will not be successful if related calls to PrintJob.start() and PrintJob.addpage() failed, you should check that calls to PrintJob.addpage() and PrintJob.start() were successful before calling PrintJob.send():

```
var my_pj:PrintJob = new PrintJob();
if (my_pj.start()) {
   if (my_pj.addPage(this)) {
   my_pj.send();
   }
}
delete my_pj;
```

Availability: ActionScript 1.0; Flash Player 7

Example

See `PrintJob.addPage()` and `PrintJob.start()`.

See also

addPage (PrintJob.addPage method), start (PrintJob.start method)

start (PrintJob.start method)

`public start() : Boolean`

Displays the operating system's print dialog boxes and starts spooling. The print dialog boxes let the user change print settings. When the `PrintJob.start()` method returns successfully, the following read-only properties are populated, representing the user's print settings:

Property	Type	Units	Notes
PrintJob.paperHeight	Number	Points	Overall paper height.
PrintJob.paperWidth	Number	Points	Overall paper width.
PrintJob.pageHeight	Number	Points	Height of actual printable area on the page; any user-set margins are ignored.
PrintJob.pageWidth	Number	Points	Width of actual printable area on the page; any user-set margins are ignored.
PrintJob.orientation	Number	Points	"Portrait" or "landscape."

After the user clicks OK in the Print dialog box, the player begins spooling a print job to the operating system. You should issue any ActionScript commands that affect the printout, and you can use `PrintJob.addPage()` commands to send pages to the spooler. You can use the read-only height, width, and orientation properties this method populates to format the printout.

Because the user sees information such as "Printing page 1" immediately after clicking OK, you should call the `PrintJob.addPage()` and `PrintJob.send()` commands as soon as possible.

If this method returns `false` (for example, if the user clicks Cancel instead of OK in the operating system's Print dialog box), any subsequent calls to `PrintJob.addPage()` and `PrintJob.send()` will fail. However, if you test for this return value and don't send `PrintJob.addPage()` commands as a result, you should still delete the PrintJob object to make sure the print spooler is cleared, as shown in the following example:

```
var my_pj:PrintJob = new PrintJob();
var myResult:Boolean = my_pj.start();
  if(myResult) {
  // addPage() and send() statements here
  }
delete my_pj;
```

Availability: ActionScript 1.0; Flash Player 7

Returns

`Boolean` - A Boolean value: `true` if the user clicks OK when the print dialog boxes appear; `false` if the user clicks Cancel or if an error occurs.

Example

The following example shows how you might use the value of the orientation property to adjust the printout:

```
// create PrintJob object
var my_pj:PrintJob = new PrintJob();

// display print dialog box
if (my_pj.start()) {
  // boolean to track whether addPage succeeded, change this to a counter
  // if more than one call to addPage is possible
  var pageAdded:Boolean = false;

  // check the user's printer orientation setting
  // and add appropriate print area to print job
  if (my_pj.orientation == "portrait") {
  // Here, the printArea measurements are appropriate for an 8.5" x 11"
  // portrait page.
  pageAdded = my_pj.addPage(this,{xMin:0,xMax:600,yMin:0,yMax:800});
  }
  else {
  // my_pj.orientation is "landscape".
  // Now, the printArea measurements are appropriate for an 11" x 8.5"
  // landscape page.
  pageAdded = my_pj.addPage(this,{xMin:0,xMax:750,yMin:0,yMax:600});
  }

  // send pages from the spooler to the printer
  if (pageAdded) {
  my_pj.send();
  }
}

// clean up
delete my_pj;
```

See also

addPage (PrintJob.addPage method), send (PrintJob.send method)

Rectangle (flash.geom.Rectangle)

```
Object
  |
  +-flash.geom.Rectangle
```

public class **Rectangle**
extends Object

The Rectangle class is used to create and modify Rectangle objects. A Rectangle object is an area defined by its position, as indicated by its top-left corner point (*x, y*), and by its width and its height. Be careful when you design these areas—if a rectangle is described as having its upper-left corner at 0,0 and has a height of 10 and a width of 20, the lower-right corner is at 9,19, because the count of width and height began at 0,0.

The x, y, width, and height properties of the Rectangle class are independent of each other; changing the value of one property has no effect on the others. However, the right and bottom properties are integrally related to those four—if you change right, you are changing width; if you change bottom, you are changing height, and so on. And you must have the left or *x* property established before you set width or right property.

Rectangle objects are used to support the BitmapData class filters. They are also used in the MovieClip.scrollRect property to support the ability to crop and scroll a MovieClip instance with specific width, height and scrolling offsets.

Availability: ActionScript 1.0; Flash Player 8

See also

scrollRect (MovieClip.scrollRect property)

Property summary

Modifiers	Property	Description
	bottom:Number	The sum of the y and height properties.
	bottomRight:Point	The location of the Rectangle object's bottom-right corner, determined by the values of the x and y properties.
	height:Number	The height of the rectangle in pixels.
	left:Number	The *x* coordinate of the top-left corner of the rectangle.
	right:Number	The sum of the x and width properties.

Modifiers	Property	Description
	`size:Point`	The size of the Rectangle object, expressed as a Point object with the values of the `width` and `height` properties.
	`top:Number`	The y coordinate of the top-left corner of the rectangle.
	`topLeft:Point`	The location of the Rectangle object's top-left corner determined by the x and y values of the point.
	`width:Number`	The width of the rectangle in pixels.
	`x:Number`	The x coordinate of the top-left corner of the rectangle.
	`y:Number`	The y coordinate of the top-left corner of the rectangle.

Properties inherited from class Object

```
constructor (Object.constructor property), __proto__ (Object.__proto__
property), prototype (Object.prototype property), __resolve
(Object.__resolve property)
```

Constructor summary

Signature	Description
`Rectangle(x:Number, y:Number, width:Number, height:Number)`	Creates a new Rectangle object whose top-left corner is specified by the x and y parameters.

Method summary

Modifiers	Signature	Description
	`clone() : Rectangle`	Returns a new Rectangle object with the same values for the x, y, `width`, and `height` properties as the original Rectangle object.
	`contains(x:Number, y:Number) : Boolean`	Determines whether the specified point is contained within the rectangular region defined by this Rectangle object.
	`containsPoint(pt:Point) : Boolean`	Determines whether the specified point is contained within the rectangular region defined by this Rectangle object.

Modifiers	Signature	Description
	`containsRectangle(re ct:Rectangle) : Boolean`	Determines whether the Rectangle object specified by the `rect` parameter is contained within this Rectangle object.
	`equals(toCompare:Obj ect) : Boolean`	Determines whether the object specified in the `toCompare` parameter is equal to this Rectangle object.
	`inflate(dx:Number, dy:Number) : Void`	Increases the size of the Rectangle object by the specified amounts.
	`inflatePoint(pt:Poin t) : Void`	Increases the size of the Rectangle object.
	`intersection(toInter sect:Rectangle) : Rectangle`	If the Rectangle object specified in the `toIntersect` parameter intersects with this Rectangle object, the `intersection()` method returns the area of intersection as a Rectangle object.
	`intersects(toInterse ct:Rectangle) : Boolean`	Determines whether the object specified in the `toIntersect` parameter intersects with this Rectangle object.
	`isEmpty() : Boolean`	Determines whether or not this Rectangle object is empty.
	`offset(dx:Number, dy:Number) : Void`	Adjusts the location of the Rectangle object, as determined by its top-left corner, by the specified amounts.
	`offsetPoint(pt:Point ) : Void`	Adjusts the location of the Rectangle object using a Point object as a parameter.
	`setEmpty() : Void`	Sets all of the Rectangle object's properties to 0.
	`toString() : String`	Builds and returns a string that lists the horizontal and vertical positions and the width and height of the Rectangle object.
	`union(toUnion:Rectan gle) : Rectangle`	Adds two rectangles together to create a new Rectangle object, by filling in the horizontal and vertical space between the two rectangles.

Methods inherited from class Object

addProperty (Object.addProperty method), hasOwnProperty
(Object.hasOwnProperty method), isPropertyEnumerable
(Object.isPropertyEnumerable method), isPrototypeOf (Object.isPrototypeOf
method), registerClass (Object.registerClass method), toString
(Object.toString method), unwatch (Object.unwatch method), valueOf
(Object.valueOf method), watch (Object.watch method)

bottom (Rectangle.bottom property)

public bottom : Number

The sum of the y and height properties.

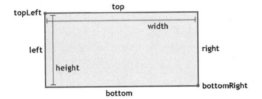

Availability: ActionScript 1.0; Flash Player 8

Example

The following example creates a Rectangle object and changes the value of its bottom property from 15 to 30. Notice that the value of rect.height is also changed, from 10 to 25.

```
import flash.geom.Rectangle;

var rect:Rectangle = new Rectangle(5, 5, 10, 10);
trace(rect.height); // 10
trace(rect.bottom); // 15

rect.bottom = 30;
trace(rect.height); // 25
trace(rect.bottom); // 30
```

See also

y (Rectangle.y property), height (Rectangle.height property)

bottomRight (Rectangle.bottomRight property)

`public bottomRight : Point`

The location of the Rectangle object's bottom-right corner, determined by the values of the x and y properties.

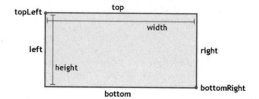

Availability: ActionScript 1.0; Flash Player 8

Example

The following example sets the Rectangle object's `bottomRight` property using the values of the Point object. Notice that `rect.width` and `rect.height` are changed.

```
import flash.geom.Rectangle;
import flash.geom.Point;

var rect:Rectangle = new Rectangle(1, 2, 4, 8);
trace(rect.bottom); // 10
trace(rect.right); // 5
trace(rect.height); // 8
trace(rect.width); // 4

var myBottomRight:Point = new Point(16, 32);
rect.bottomRight = myBottomRight;
trace(rect.bottom); // 32
trace(rect.right); // 16
trace(rect.height); // 30
trace(rect.width); // 15
```

See also

`Point (flash.geom.Point)`

clone (Rectangle.clone method)

`public clone() : Rectangle`

Returns a new Rectangle object with the same values for the x, y, `width`, and `height` properties as the original Rectangle object.

Availability: ActionScript 1.0; Flash Player 8

Returns

flash.geom.Rectangle - A new Rectangle object with the same values for the x, y, width, and height properties as the original Rectangle object.

Example

The following example creates three Rectangle objects and compares them. rect_1 is created using the Rectangle constructor. rect_2 is created by setting it equal to rect_1. And, clonedRect is created by cloning rect_1. Notice that while rect_2 evaluates as being equal to rect_1, clonedRect, even though it contains the same values as rect_1, does not.

```
import flash.geom.Rectangle;

var rect_1:Rectangle = new Rectangle(1, 2, 4, 8);
var rect_2:Rectangle = rect_1;
var clonedRect:Rectangle = rect_1.clone();

trace(rect_1 == rect_2); // true
trace(rect_1 == clonedFilter); // false

for(var i in rect_1) {
   trace(">> " + i + ": " + rect_1[i]);
   >> toString: [type Function]
   >> equals: [type Function]
   >> union: [type Function]
   >> intersects: [type Function]
   >> intersection: [type Function]
   >> containsRectangle: [type Function]
   >> containsPoint: [type Function]
   >> contains: [type Function]
   >> offsetPoint: [type Function]
   >> offset: [type Function]
   >> inflatePoint: [type Function]
   >> inflate: [type Function]
   >> size: (x=4, y=8)
   >> bottomRight: (x=5, y=10)
   >> topLeft: (x=1, y=2)
   >> bottom: 10
   >> top: 2
   >> right: 5
   >> left: 1
   >> isEmpty: [type Function]
   >> setEmpty: [type Function]
   >> clone: [type Function]
   >> height: 8
   >> width: 4
   >> y: 2
   >> x: 1
}
```

```
for(var i in clonedRect) {
  trace(">> " + i + ": " + clonedRect[i]);
  >> toString: [type Function]
  >> equals: [type Function]
  >> union: [type Function]
  >> intersects: [type Function]
  >> intersection: [type Function]
  >> containsRectangle: [type Function]
  >> containsPoint: [type Function]
  >> contains: [type Function]
  >> offsetPoint: [type Function]
  >> offset: [type Function]
  >> inflatePoint: [type Function]
  >> inflate: [type Function]
  >> size: (x=4, y=8)
  >> bottomRight: (x=5, y=10)
  >> topLeft: (x=1, y=2)
  >> bottom: 10
  >> top: 2
  >> right: 5
  >> left: 1
  >> isEmpty: [type Function]
  >> setEmpty: [type Function]
  >> clone: [type Function]
  >> height: 8
  >> width: 4
  >> y: 2
  >> x: 1
}
```

To further demonstrate the relationships between rect_1, rect_2, and clonedRect the example below modifies the x property of rect_1. Modifying x demonstrates that the clone() method creates a new instance based on values of the rect_1 instead of pointing to them in reference.

```
import flash.geom.Rectangle;

var rect_1:Rectangle = new Rectangle(1, 2, 4, 8);
var rect_2:Rectangle = rect_1;
var clonedRect:Rectangle = rect_1.clone();

trace(rect_1.x); // 1
trace(rect_2.x); // 1
trace(clonedRect.x); // 1

rect_1.x = 10;

trace(rect_1.x); // 10
trace(rect_2.x); // 10
```

```
trace(clonedRect.x); // 1
```

See also

x (Rectangle.x property), y (Rectangle.y property), width (Rectangle.width
property), height (Rectangle.height property)

contains (Rectangle.contains method)

```
public contains(x:Number, y:Number) : Boolean
```
Determines whether the specified point is contained within the rectangular region defined by
this Rectangle object.

Availability: ActionScript 1.0; Flash Player 8

Parameters

x:Number - The *x*-value (horizontal position) of the point.

y:Number - The *y*-value (vertical position) of the point.

Returns

Boolean - If the specified point is contained in the Rectangle object, returns true; otherwise
false.

Example

The following example creates a Rectangle object and tests whether each of three coordinate
pairs falls within its boundaries.

```
import flash.geom.Rectangle;

var rect:Rectangle = new Rectangle(10, 10, 50, 50);
trace(rect.contains(59, 59)); // true
trace(rect.contains(10, 10)); // true
trace(rect.contains(60, 60)); // false
```

See also

Point (flash.geom.Point)

containsPoint (Rectangle.containsPoint method)

```
public containsPoint(pt:Point) : Boolean
```
Determines whether the specified point is contained within the rectangular region defined by
this Rectangle object. This method is similar to the Rectangle.contains() method, except
that it takes a Point object as a parameter.

Availability: ActionScript 1.0; Flash Player 8

Parameters

`pt:flash.geom.Point` - The point, as represented by its *x,y* values.

Returns

`Boolean` - If the specified point is contained within this Rectangle object, returns `true`; otherwise `false`.

Example

The following example creates a Rectangle object and three Point objects, and tests whether each of the points falls within the boundaries of the rectangle.

```
import flash.geom.Rectangle;
import flash.geom.Point;

var rect:Rectangle = new Rectangle(10, 10, 50, 50);
trace(rect.containsPoint(new Point(10, 10))); // true
trace(rect.containsPoint(new Point(59, 59))); // true
trace(rect.containsPoint(new Point(60, 60))); // false
```

See also

`contains (Rectangle.contains method)`, `Point (flash.geom.Point)`

containsRectangle (Rectangle.containsRectangle method)

`public containsRectangle(rect:Rectangle) : Boolean`

Determines whether the Rectangle object specified by the `rect` parameter is contained within this Rectangle object. A Rectangle object is said to contain another if the second Rectangle object falls entirely within the boundaries of the first.

Availability: ActionScript 1.0; Flash Player 8

Parameters

`rect:flash.geom.Rectangle` - The Rectangle object being checked.

Returns

`Boolean` - If the Rectangle object that you specify is contained by this Rectangle object, returns `true`; otherwise `false`.

Example

The following example creates four new Rectangle objects and determines whether rectangle A contains rectangle B, C, or D.

```
import flash.geom.Rectangle;

var rectA:Rectangle = new Rectangle(10, 10, 50, 50);
var rectB:Rectangle = new Rectangle(10, 10, 50, 50);
var rectC:Rectangle = new Rectangle(10, 10, 51, 51);
var rectD:Rectangle = new Rectangle(15, 15, 45, 45);

trace(rectA.containsRectangle(rectB)); // true
trace(rectA.containsRectangle(rectC)); // false
trace(rectA.containsRectangle(rectD)); // true
```

equals (Rectangle.equals method)

```
public equals(toCompare:Object) : Boolean
```

Determines whether the object specified in the toCompare parameter is equal to this Rectangle object. This method compares the x, y, width, and height properties of an object against the same properties of this Rectangle object.

Availability: ActionScript 1.0; Flash Player 8

Parameters

toCompare:Object - The rectangle to compare to this Rectangle object.

Returns

Boolean - If the object has exactly the same values for the x, y, width, and height properties as this Rectangle object, returns true; otherwise false.

Example

In the following example, rect_1 and rect_2 are equal, but rect_3 is not equal to the other two objects because its x, y, width, and height properties are not equal to those of rect_1 and rect_2.

```
import flash.geom.Rectangle;

var rect_1:Rectangle = new Rectangle(0, 0, 50, 100);
var rect_2:Rectangle = new Rectangle(0, 0, 50, 100);
var rect_3:Rectangle = new Rectangle(10, 10, 60, 110);

trace(rect_1.equals(rect_2)); // true;
trace(rect_1.equals(rect_3)); // false;
```

Even though the method signature expects only an abstract object, only other Rectangle instances are treated as equal.

```
import flash.geom.Rectangle;

var rect_1:Rectangle = new Rectangle(0, 0, 50, 100);
var nonRect:Object = new Object();
nonRect.x = 0;
nonRect.y = 0;
nonRect.width = 50;
nonRect.height = 100;
trace(rect_1.equals(nonRect));
```

See also

x (Rectangle.x property), y (Rectangle.y property), width (Rectangle.width property), height (Rectangle.height property)

height (Rectangle.height property)

```
public height : Number
```

The height of the rectangle in pixels. Changing the height value of a Rectangle object has no effect on the x, y, and width properties.

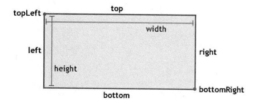

Availability: ActionScript 1.0; Flash Player 8

Example

The following example creates a Rectangle object and changes its height property from 10 to 20. Notice that rect.bottom is also changed.

```
import flash.geom.Rectangle;

var rect:Rectangle = new Rectangle(5, 5, 10, 10);
trace(rect.height); // 10
trace(rect.bottom); // 15

rect.height = 20;
trace(rect.height); // 20
trace(rect.bottom); // 25
```

See also

x (Rectangle.x property), y (Rectangle.y property), width (Rectangle.width property)

inflate (Rectangle.inflate method)

```
public inflate(dx:Number, dy:Number) : Void
```

Increases the size of the Rectangle object by the specified amounts. The center point of the Rectangle object stays the same, and its size increases to the left and right by the dx value, and to the top and the bottom by the dy value.

Availability: ActionScript 1.0; Flash Player 8

Parameters

dx:Number - The value to be added to the left and the right of the Rectangle object. The following equation is used to calculate the new width and position of the rectangle:

```
x  -= dx;
width += 2 * dx;
```

dy:Number - The value to be added to the top and the bottom of the Rectangle object. The following equation is used to calculate the new height and position of the rectangle.

```
y  -= dy;
height += 2 * dy;
```

Example

The following example creates a Rectangle object and increases the value of its width property by 16 * 2 (32) and of its height property by 32 * 2 (64)

```
import flash.geom.Rectangle;

var rect:Rectangle = new Rectangle(1, 2, 4, 8);
trace(rect.toString()); // (x=1, y=2, w=4, h=8)

rect.inflate(16, 32);
trace(rect.toString()); // (x=-15, y=-30, w=36, h=72)
```

See also

x (Rectangle.x property), y (Rectangle.y property)

inflatePoint (Rectangle.inflatePoint method)

```
public inflatePoint(pt:Point) : Void
```

Increases the size of the Rectangle object. This method is similar to the `Rectangle.inflate()` method, except that it takes a Point object as a parameter.

The following two code examples give the same result:

```
rect1 = new flash.geom.Rectangle(0,0,2,5);
rect1.inflate(2,2)
rect1 = new flash.geom.Rectangle(0,0,2,5);
pt1 = new flash.geom.Point(2,2);
rect1.inflatePoint(pt1)
```

Availability: ActionScript 1.0; Flash Player 8

Parameters

`pt`:`flash.geom.Point` - Increases the rectangle by the x and y coordinate values of the point.

Example

The following example creates a Rectangle object and inflates it by the x (horizontal) and y (vertical) amounts found in a point.

```
import flash.geom.Rectangle;
import flash.geom.Point;

var rect:Rectangle = new Rectangle(0, 0, 2, 5);
trace(rect.toString()); // (x=0, y=0, w=2, h=5

var myPoint:Point = new Point(2, 2);
rect.inflatePoint(myPoint);
trace(rect.toString()); // (x=-2, y=-2, w=6, h=9)
```

See also

Point (flash.geom.Point)

intersection (Rectangle.intersection method)

`public intersection(toIntersect:Rectangle) : Rectangle`

If the Rectangle object specified in the `toIntersect` parameter intersects with this Rectangle object, the `intersection()` method returns the area of intersection as a Rectangle object. If the rectangles do not intersect, this method returns an empty Rectangle object with its properties set to 0.

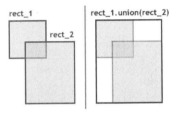

Availability: ActionScript 1.0; Flash Player 8

Parameters

`toIntersect:flash.geom.Rectangle` - The Rectangle object to compare against to see if it intersects with this Rectangle object.

Returns

`flash.geom.Rectangle` - A Rectangle object that equals the area of intersection. If the rectangles do not intersect, this method returns an empty Rectangle object; that is, a rectangle with its `x`, `y`, `width`, and `height` properties set to 0.

Example

The following example determines the area where `rect_1` intersects `rect_2`.

```
import flash.geom.Rectangle;

var rect_1:Rectangle = new Rectangle(0, 0, 50, 50);
var rect_2:Rectangle = new Rectangle(25, 25, 100, 100);
var intersectingArea:Rectangle = rect_1.intersection(rect_2);
trace(intersectingArea.toString()); // (x=25, y=25, w=25, h=25)
```

intersects (Rectangle.intersects method)

`public intersects(toIntersect:Rectangle) : Boolean`

Determines whether the object specified in the `toIntersect` parameter intersects with this Rectangle object. This method checks the `x`, `y`, `width`, and `height` properties of the specified Rectangle object to see if it intersects with this Rectangle object.

Availability: ActionScript 1.0; Flash Player 8

Parameters

`toIntersect:flash.geom.Rectangle` - The Rectangle object to compare against this Rectangle object.

Returns

`Boolean` - If the specified object intersects with this Rectangle object, returns `true`; otherwise `false`.

Example

The following example determines whether `rectA` intersects with `rectB` or `rectC`.

```
import flash.geom.Rectangle;
var rectA:Rectangle = new Rectangle(10, 10, 50, 50);
var rectB:Rectangle = new Rectangle(59, 59, 50, 50);
var rectC:Rectangle = new Rectangle(60, 60, 50, 50);
var rectAIntersectsB:Boolean = rectA.intersects(rectB);
var rectAIntersectsC:Boolean = rectA.intersects(rectC);
trace(rectAIntersectsB); // true
trace(rectAIntersectsC); // false

var firstPixel:Rectangle = new Rectangle(0, 0, 1, 1);
var adjacentPixel:Rectangle = new Rectangle(1, 1, 1, 1);
var pixelsIntersect:Boolean = firstPixel.intersects(adjacentPixel);
trace(pixelsIntersect); // false
```

See also

`x (Rectangle.x property)`, `y (Rectangle.y property)`, `width (Rectangle.width property)`, `height (Rectangle.height property)`

isEmpty (Rectangle.isEmpty method)

`public isEmpty() : Boolean`

Determines whether or not this Rectangle object is empty.

Availability: ActionScript 1.0; Flash Player 8

Returns

`Boolean` - If the Rectangle object's width or height is less than or equal to 0, returns `true`; otherwise `false`.

Example

The following example creates an empty Rectangle object and verifies that it is empty.

```
import flash.geom.*;
var rect:Rectangle = new Rectangle(1, 2, 0, 0);
trace(rect.toString()); // (x=1, y=2, w=0, h=0)
trace(rect.isEmpty()); // true
```

The following example creates a non-empty Rectangle and makes it become empty.

```
import flash.geom.Rectangle;

var rect:Rectangle = new Rectangle(1, 2, 4, 8);
trace(rect.isEmpty()); // false
rect.width = 0;
trace(rect.isEmpty()); // true
rect.width = 4;
trace(rect.isEmpty()); // false
rect.height = 0;
trace(rect.isEmpty()); // true
```

left (Rectangle.left property)

```
public left : Number
```

The x coordinate of the top-left corner of the rectangle. Changing the x value of a Rectangle object has no effect on the y, width, and height properties.

The left property is equal to the x property.

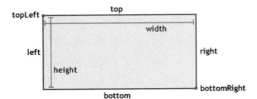

Availability: ActionScript 1.0; Flash Player 8

Example

The following example changes the left property from 0 to 10. Notice that rect.x also changes.

```
import flash.geom.Rectangle;

var rect:Rectangle = new Rectangle();
trace(rect.left); // 0
trace(rect.x); // 0
```

```
rect.left = 10;
trace(rect.left); // 10
trace(rect.x); // 10
```

See also

```
x (Rectangle.x property), y (Rectangle.y property), width (Rectangle.width
property), height (Rectangle.height property)
```

offset (Rectangle.offset method)

```
public offset(dx:Number, dy:Number) : Void
```
Adjusts the location of the Rectangle object, as determined by its top-left corner, by the specified amounts.

Availability: ActionScript 1.0; Flash Player 8

Parameters

`dx:Number` - Moves the x value of the Rectangle object by this amount.

`dy:Number` - Moves the y value of the Rectangle object by this amount.

Example

The following example creates a Rectangle object and offsets its x and y values by 5 and 10 respectively

```
import flash.geom.Rectangle;

var rect:Rectangle = new Rectangle(1, 2, 4, 8);
trace(rect.toString()); // (x=1, y=2, w=4, h=8)

rect.offset(16, 32);
trace(rect.toString()); // (x=17, y=34, w=4, h=8)
```

offsetPoint (Rectangle.offsetPoint method)

```
public offsetPoint(pt:Point) : Void
```
Adjusts the location of the Rectangle object using a Point object as a parameter. This method is similar to the `Rectangle.offset()` method, except that it takes a Point object as a parameter.

Availability: ActionScript 1.0; Flash Player 8

Parameters

`pt:flash.geom.Point` - A Point object to use to offset this Rectangle object.

Example

The following example offsets a Rectangle by using the values found in a point.

```
import flash.geom.Rectangle;
import flash.geom.Point;

var rect:Rectangle = new Rectangle(1, 2, 4, 8);
trace(rect.toString()); // (x=1, y=2, w=4, h=8)

var myPoint:Point = new Point(16, 32);
rect.offsetPoint(myPoint);
trace(rect.toString()); // (x=17, y=34, w=4, h=8)
```

See also

Point (flash.geom.Point)

Rectangle constructor

```
public Rectangle(x:Number, y:Number, width:Number, height:Number)
```

Creates a new Rectangle object whose top-left corner is specified by the x and y parameters. If you call this constructor function without parameters, a rectangle with x, y, width, and height properties set to 0 is created.

Availability: ActionScript 1.0; Flash Player 8

Parameters

x:Number - The *x* coordinate of the top-left corner of the rectangle.

y:Number - The *y* coordinate of the top-left corner of the rectangle.

width:Number - The width of the rectangle in pixels.

height:Number - The height of the rectangle in pixels.

Example

The following example creates a Rectangle object with the specified parameters.

```
import flash.geom.Rectangle;

var rect:Rectangle = new Rectangle(5, 10, 50, 100);
trace(rect.toString()); // (x=5, y=10, w=50, h=100)
```

See also

x (Rectangle.x property), y (Rectangle.y property), width (Rectangle.width property), height (Rectangle.height property)

right (Rectangle.right property)

`public right : Number`

The sum of the x and `width` properties.

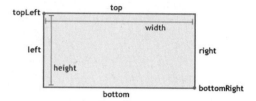

Availability: ActionScript 1.0; Flash Player 8

Example

The following example creates a Rectangle object and changes its `right` property from 15 to 30. Notice that `rect.width` also changes.

```
import flash.geom.Rectangle;

var rect:Rectangle = new Rectangle(5, 5, 10, 10);
trace(rect.width); // 10
trace(rect.right); // 15

rect.right = 30;
trace(rect.width); // 25
trace(rect.right); // 30
```

See also

`x (Rectangle.x property)`, `width (Rectangle.width property)`

setEmpty (Rectangle.setEmpty method)

`public setEmpty() : Void`

Sets all of the Rectangle object's properties to 0. A Rectangle object is empty if its width or height is less than or equal to 0.

This method sets the values of the x, y, `width`, and `height` properties to 0.

Availability: ActionScript 1.0; Flash Player 8

Example

The following example creates a non-empty Rectangle object and makes it empty.

```
import flash.geom.Rectangle;
```

```
var rect:Rectangle = new Rectangle(5, 10, 50, 100);
trace(rect.isEmpty()); // false
rect.setEmpty();
trace(rect.isEmpty()); // true
```

See also

`x (Rectangle.x property)`, `y (Rectangle.y property)`, `width (Rectangle.width property)`, `height (Rectangle.height property)`

size (Rectangle.size property)

`public size : Point`

The size of the Rectangle object, expressed as a Point object with the values of the `width` and `height` properties.

Availability: ActionScript 1.0; Flash Player 8

Example

The following example creates a Rectangle object, retrieves its size (`size`), changes its size (`size`), and sets the new values on the Rectangle object. It is important to remember that the `Point` object used by the `size` property uses *x* and *y* values to represent the `width` and `height` properties of the Rectangle object.

```
import flash.geom.Rectangle;
import flash.geom.Point;

var rect:Rectangle = new Rectangle(1, 2, 4, 8);
var size:Point = rect.size;
trace(size.x); // 4;
trace(size.y); // 8;

size.x = 16;
size.y = 32;
rect.size = size;
trace(rect.x); // 1
trace(rect.y); // 2
trace(rect.width); // 16
trace(rect.height); // 32
```

See also

`Point (flash.geom.Point)`

top (Rectangle.top property)

```
public top : Number
```

The *y* coordinate of the top-left corner of the rectangle. Changing the value of the `top` property of a Rectangle object has no effect on the x, `width`, and `height` properties. The value of the `top` property is equal to the value of the y property.

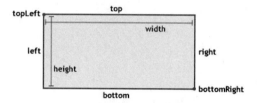

Availability: ActionScript 1.0; Flash Player 8

Example

This example changes the value of the `top` property from 0 to 10. Notice that `rect.y` also changes.

```
import flash.geom.Rectangle;

var rect:Rectangle = new Rectangle();
trace(rect.top); // 0
trace(rect.y); // 0

rect.top = 10;
trace(rect.top); // 10
trace(rect.y); // 10
```

See also

x (Rectangle.x property), y (Rectangle.y property), width (Rectangle.width property), height (Rectangle.height property)

topLeft (Rectangle.topLeft property)

`public topLeft : Point`

The location of the Rectangle object's top-left corner determined by the *x* and *y* values of the point.

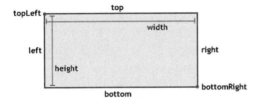

Availability: ActionScript 1.0; Flash Player 8

Example

The following example sets the Rectangle object's `topLeft` property using the values in a Point object. Notice that `rect.x` and `rect.y` are changed.

```
import flash.geom.Rectangle;
import flash.geom.Point;

var rect:Rectangle = new Rectangle();
trace(rect.left); // 0
trace(rect.top); // 0
trace(rect.x); // 0
trace(rect.y); // 0

var myTopLeft:Point = new Point(5, 15);
rect.topLeft = myTopLeft;
trace(rect.left); // 5
trace(rect.top); // 15
trace(rect.x); // 5
trace(rect.y); // 15
```

See also

`Point (flash.geom.Point)`, `x (Rectangle.x property)`, `y (Rectangle.y property)`

toString (Rectangle.toString method)

`public toString() : String`

Builds and returns a string that lists the horizontal and vertical positions and the width and height of the Rectangle object.

Availability: ActionScript 1.0; Flash Player 8

Returns

`String` - A string that lists the value of each of the following properties of the Rectangle object: `x`, `y`, `width`, and `height`.

Example

The following example concatenates a string representation of `rect_1` with some helpful debugging text.

```
import flash.geom.Rectangle;

var rect_1:Rectangle = new Rectangle(0, 0, 50, 100);
trace("Rectangle 1 : " + rect_1.toString()); // Rectangle 1 : (x=0, y=0,
    w=50, h=100)
```

See also

`x` (`Rectangle.x` property), `y` (`Rectangle.y` property), `width` (`Rectangle.width` property), `height` (`Rectangle.height` property)

union (Rectangle.union method)

`public union(toUnion:Rectangle) : Rectangle`

Adds two rectangles together to create a new Rectangle object, by filling in the horizontal and vertical space between the two rectangles.

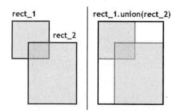

Availability: ActionScript 1.0; Flash Player 8

Parameters

`toUnion:flash.geom.Rectangle` - A Rectangle object to add to this Rectangle object.

Returns

`flash.geom.Rectangle` - A new Rectangle object that is the union of the two rectangles.

Example

The following example creates a Rectangle object out of the union of two others.

For example, consider a rectangle with properties x=20, y=50, width=60, and height=30 (20, 50, 60, 30), and a second rectangle with properties (150, 130, 50, 30). The union of these two rectangles is a larger rectangle that encompasses the two rectangles with the properties (20, 50, 180, 110).

```
import flash.geom.Rectangle;

var rect_1:Rectangle = new Rectangle(20, 50, 60, 30);
var rect_2:Rectangle = new Rectangle(150, 130, 50, 30);
var combined:Rectangle = rect_1.union(rect_2);
trace(combined.toString()); // (x=20, y=50, w=180, h=110)
```

width (Rectangle.width property)

```
public width : Number
```

The width of the rectangle in pixels. Changing the value of the width property of a Rectangle object has no effect on the x, y, and height properties.

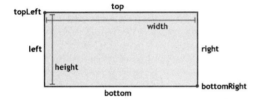

Availability: ActionScript 1.0; Flash Player 8

Example

The following example creates a Rectangle object and change its width property from 10 to 20. Notice that rect.right also changes.

```
import flash.geom.Rectangle;

var rect:Rectangle = new Rectangle(5, 5, 10, 10);
trace(rect.width); // 10
trace(rect.right); // 15

rect.width = 20;
trace(rect.width); // 20
trace(rect.right); // 25
```

See also

x (Rectangle.x property), y (Rectangle.y property), height (Rectangle.height property)

x (Rectangle.x property)

`public x : Number`

The *x* coordinate of the top-left corner of the rectangle. Changing the value of the *x* property of a Rectangle object has no effect on the `y`, `width`, and `height` properties.

The `x` property is equal to the `left` property.

Availability: ActionScript 1.0; Flash Player 8

Example

The following example creates an empty Rectangle and sets its `x` property to 10. Notice that `rect.left` is also changed.

```
import flash.geom.Rectangle;

var rect:Rectangle = new Rectangle();
trace(rect.x); // 0
trace(rect.left); // 0

rect.x = 10;
trace(rect.x); // 10
trace(rect.left); // 10
```

See also

`left (Rectangle.left property)`

y (Rectangle.y property)

`public y : Number`

The *y* coordinate of the top-left corner of the rectangle. Changing the value of the `y` property of a Rectangle object has no effect on the `x`, `width`, and `height` properties.

The `y` property is equal to the `top` property.

Availability: ActionScript 1.0; Flash Player 8

Example

The following example creates an empty Rectangle and sets its `y` property to 10. Notice that `rect.top` is also changed.

```
import flash.geom.Rectangle;

var rect:Rectangle = new Rectangle();
trace(rect.y); // 0
trace(rect.top); // 0
```

```
rect.y = 10;
trace(rect.y); // 10
trace(rect.top); // 10
```

See also

x (Rectangle.x property), width (Rectangle.width property), height
(Rectangle.height property), top (Rectangle.top property)

security (System.security)

```
Object
  |
  +-System.security
```

```
public class security
extends Object
```

The System.security class contains methods that specify how SWF files in different domains
can communicate with each other.

For more information, see the following:

- Chapter 17, "Understanding Security," in *Learning ActionScript 2.0 in Flash*
- The Flash Player 8 Security white paper at http://www.macromedia.com/go/fp8_security
- The Flash Player 8 Security-Related API white paper at http://www.macromedia.com/go/
  fp8_security_apis

Availability: ActionScript 1.0; Flash Player 6

Property summary

Modifiers	Property	Description
static	sandboxType:String [read-only]	Indicates the type of security sandbox in which the calling SWF file is operating.

Properties inherited from class Object

constructor (Object.constructor property), __proto__ (Object.__proto__
property), prototype (Object.prototype property), __resolve
(Object.__resolve property)

Method summary

Modifiers	Signature	Description
static	`allowDomain(domain1: String) : Void`	Lets SWF files and HTML files in the identified domains access objects and variables in the SWF file that contains the `allowDomain()` call.
static	`allowInsecureDomain( domain:String) : Void`	Lets SWF files and HTML files in the identified domains access objects and variables in the calling SWF file, which is hosted by means of the HTTPS protocol.
static	`loadPolicyFile(url:S tring) : Void`	Loads a cross-domain policy file from a location specified by the `url` parameter.

Methods inherited from class Object

```
addProperty (Object.addProperty method), hasOwnProperty
(Object.hasOwnProperty method), isPropertyEnumerable
(Object.isPropertyEnumerable method), isPrototypeOf (Object.isPrototypeOf
method), registerClass (Object.registerClass method), toString
(Object.toString method), unwatch (Object.unwatch method), valueOf
(Object.valueOf method), watch (Object.watch method)
```

allowDomain (security.allowDomain method)

`public static allowDomain(domain1:String) : Void`

Lets SWF files and HTML files in the identified domains access objects and variables in the SWF file that contains the `allowDomain()` call.

If two SWF files are served from the same domain — for example, http://mysite.com/movieA.swf and http://mysite.com/movieB.swf — then movieA.swf can examine and modify variables, objects, properties, methods, and so on in movieB.swf, and movieB.swf can do the same for movieA.swf. This is called *cross-movie scripting* or simply *cross-scripting*.

If two SWF files are served from different domains — for example, http://mysite.com/movieA.swf and http://othersite.com/movieB.swf — then, by default, Flash Player does not allow movieA.swf to script movieB.swf, nor movieB.swf to script movieA.swf. A SWF file gives SWF files from other domains permission to script it by calling `System.security.allowDomain()`. This is called *cross-domain scripting*. By calling `System.security.allowDomain("mysite.com")`, movieB.swf gives movieA.swf permission to script movieB.swf.

In any cross-domain situation, two parties are involved, and it's important to be clear about which side is which. For the purposes of this discussion, the side performing the cross-scripting is called the *accessing party* (usually the accessing SWF), and the other side is called *the party being accessed* (usually the SWF being accessed). To continue the example, when movieA.swf scripts movieB.swf, movieA.swf is the accessing party, and movieB.swf is the party being accessed.

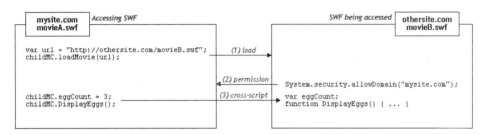

Cross-domain permissions that are established with System.security.allowDomain() are asymmetrical. In the previous example, movieA.swf can script movieB.swf, but movieB.swf cannot script movieA.swf, because movieA.swf has not called System.security.allowDomain() to give othersite.com permission to script movieA.swf. You can set up symmetrical permissions by having both SWF files call System.security.allowDomain().

In addition to protecting SWF files from cross-domain scripting originated by other SWF files, Flash Player protects SWF files from cross-domain scripting originated by HTML files. HTML-to-SWF scripting can be performed with older Flash browser functions such as SetVariable or callbacks established by using ExternalInterface.addCallback(). When HTML-to-SWF scripting crosses domain boundaries, the SWF file being accessed must call System.security.allowDomain(), just as when the accessing party is a SWF file, or the operation will fail.

Specifying an IP address as a parameter to System.security.allowDomain() does not permit access by all parties that originate at the specified IP address. Instead, it permits access only by parties that were loaded by explicitly specifying that IP address in their URLs, rather than by a domain name that maps to that IP address.

Version-specific differences Flash Player's cross-domain security rules have evolved from version to version. The following table summarizes the differences.

Latest SWF version involved in the cross-scripting operation.	allowDomain() needed?	allowInsecureDomain() needed?	Which SWF must call allowDomain() or allowInsecureDomain()?	What can be specified in allowDomain() or allowInsecureDomain()?
5 or earlier	No	No	N/A	
6	Yes, if superdomains don't match		The SWF file being accessed, or any SWF file with the same superdomain as the SWF file being accessed	• Text-based domain (mysite.com) • IP address (192.168.1.1)
7	Yes, if domains don't match exactly	Yes, if performing HTTP-to-HTTPS access (even if domains match exactly)	The SWF file being accessed, or any SWF file with exactly the same domain as the SWF file being accessed	
8 or later			SWF being accessed	• Text-based domain (mysite.com) • IP address (192.168.1.1) • Wildcard (*)

The versions that control the behavior of Flash Player are *SWF versions* (the published version of a SWF file), not the version of Flash Player itself. For example, when Flash Player 8 is playing a SWF file published for version 7, it applies behavior that is consistent with version 7. This practice ensures that player upgrades do not change the behavior of `System.security.allowDomain()` in deployed SWF files.

The version column in the previous table shows the latest SWF version involved in a cross-scripting operation. Flash Player determines its behavior according to either the accessing SWF file's version or the version of the SWF file that is being accessed, whichever is later.

The following paragraphs provide more detail about Flash Player security changes involving `System.security.allowDomain()`.

Version 5. No cross-domain scripting restrictions.

Version 6. Cross-domain scripting security is introduced. By default, Flash Player forbids cross-domain scripting; `System.security.allowDomain()` can permit it. To determine whether two files are in the same domain, Flash Player uses each file's superdomain, which is the exact host name from the file's URL, minus the first segment, down to a minimum of two segments. For example, the superdomain of www.mysite.com is mysite.com. This example would permit SWF files from www.mysite.com and store.mysite.com to script each other without calling `System.security.allowDomain()`.

Version 7. Superdomain matching is changed to exact domain matching. Two files are permitted to script each other only if the host names in their URLs are identical; otherwise, a call to `System.security.allowDomain()` is required. By default, files loaded from non-HTTPS URLs are no longer permitted to script files loaded from HTTPS URLs, even if the files are loaded from the exactly same domain. This restriction helps protect HTTPS files, because a non-HTTPS file is vulnerable to modification during download, and a maliciously modified non-HTTPS file could corrupt an HTTPS file, which is otherwise immune to such tampering. `System.security.allowInsecureDomain()` is introduced to allow HTTPS SWF files that are being accessed to voluntarily disable this restriction, but Macromedia recommends against using `System.security.allowInsecureDomain()`.

Version 8. Two major areas of change:

- Calling `System.security.allowDomain()` now permits cross-scripting operations only if the SWF file being accessed is the SWF file that called `System.security.allowDomain()`. In other words, a SWF file that calls `System.security.allowDomain()` now permits access only to itself. In previous versions, calling `System.security.allowDomain()` permitted cross-scripting operations where the SWF file being accessed could be any SWF file in the same domain as the SWF file that called `System.security.allowDomain()`. Calling `System.security.allowDomain()` previously opened up the entire domain of the calling SWF file.

- Support has been added for wildcard values with `System.security.allowDomain("*")` and `System.security.allowInsecureDomain("*")`. The wildcard (*) value permits cross-scripting operations where the accessing file is any file at all, loaded from anywhere. Think of the wildcard as a global permission. Wildcard permissions can be useful in general, and in particular they are required to enable certain kinds of operations under the new local file security rules in Flash Player 8. Specifically, for a local SWF file with network-access permissions to script a SWF file on the Internet, the Internet SWF file being accessed must call `System.security.allowDomain("*")`, reflecting that the origin of a local SWF file is unknown. (If the Internet SWF file being accessed is loaded from an HTTPS URL, the Internet SWF file must instead call `System.security.allowInsecureDomain("*")`.)

Occasionally, you may encounter the following situation: You load a child SWF file from a different domain and want to allow the child SWF file to script the parent SWF file, but you don't know the final domain from which the child SWF file will come. This can happen, for example, when you use load-balancing redirects or third-party servers.

In this situation, you can use the `MovieClip._url` property as a parameter to this method. For example, if you load a SWF file into the movie clip `my_mc`, you can call `System.security.allowDomain(my_mc._url)`. If you do this, be sure to wait until the SWF file in `my_mc` begins loading, because the `_url` property does not have its final, correct value until this time. The best way to determine when a child SWF file has begun loading is to use `MovieClipLoader.onLoadStart`.

The opposite situation can also occur; that is, you might create a child SWF file that wants to allow its parent to script it, but doesn't know what the domain of its parent will be. In this situation, call `System.security.allowDomain(_parent._url)` from the child SWF. You don't have to wait for the parent SWF file to load; the parent will already be loaded by the time the child loads.

If you are publishing for Flash Player 8, you can also handle these situations by calling `System.security.allowDomain("*")`. However, this can sometimes be a dangerous shortcut, because it allows the calling SWF file to be accessed by any other SWF file from any domain. It is usually safer to use the `_url` property.

For more information, see the following:

- Chapter 17, "Understanding Security," in *Learning ActionScript 2.0 in Flash*
- The Flash Player 8 Security white paper at http://www.macromedia.com/go/fp8_security
- The Flash Player 8 Security-Related API white paper at http://www.macromedia.com/go/fp8_security_apis

Availability: ActionScript 1.0; Flash Player 6 - Behavior changed in Flash Player 7; behavior changed in Flash Player 8.

Parameters

`domain1:String` - One or more strings that specify domains that can access objects and variables in the SWF file that contains the `System.Security.allowDomain()` call. The domains can be formatted in the following ways:

- `"domain.com"`
- `"http://domain.com"`
- `"http://IPaddress"`

- (Flash Player 8 only) "*"
  You can pass a wildcard ("*") to `System.security.allowDomain()` to allow all domains, including local hosts, access to the calling SWF file. Before using the wildcard, be sure that you want to provide such broad access to the calling SWF file. See the discussion in the main description of this method.

Example

The SWF file located at www.macromedia.com/MovieA.swf contains the following lines:

```
System.security.allowDomain("www.shockwave.com");
loadMovie("http://www.shockwave.com/MovieB.swf", my_mc);
```

Because MovieA contains the `allowDomain()` call, MovieB can access the objects and variables in MovieA. If MovieA didn't contain this call, the Flash Player security implementation would prevent MovieB from accessing MovieA's objects and variables.

See also

`addCallback (ExternalInterface.addCallback method)`, `onLoadComplete (MovieClipLoader.onLoadComplete event listener)`, `_parent (MovieClip._parent property)`, `_url (MovieClip._url property)`, `allowInsecureDomain (security.allowInsecureDomain method)`

allowInsecureDomain (security.allowInsecureDomain method)

`public static allowInsecureDomain(domain:String) : Void`

Lets SWF files and HTML files in the identified domains access objects and variables in the calling SWF file, which is hosted by means of the HTTPS protocol. Macromedia does not recommend using this method; see "Security considerations," later in this entry.

This method works in the same way as `System.security.allowDomain()`, but it also permits operations in which the accessing party is loaded with a non-HTTPS protocol, and the party being accessed is loaded with HTTPS. In Flash Player 7 and later, non-HTTPS files are not allowed to script HTTPS files. The `allowInsecureDomain()` method lifts this restriction when the HTTPS SWF file being accessed uses it.

Use `allowInsecureDomain()` only to enable scripting from non-HTTPS files to HTTPS files. Use it to enable scripting when the accessing non-HTTPS file and the HTTPS file being accessed are served from the same domain, for example, if a SWF file at http://mysite.com wants to script a SWF file at https://mysite.com. Do not use this method to enable scripting between non-HTTPS files, between HTTPS files, or from HTTPS files to non-HTTPS files. For those situations, use `allowDomain()` instead.

Security considerations: Flash Player provides `allowInsecureDomain()` to maximize flexibility, but Macromedia recommends against calling this method. Serving a file over HTTPS provides several protections for you and your users, and calling `allowInsecureDomain` weakens one of those protections. The following scenario illustrates how `allowInsecureDomain()` can compromise security, if it is not used with careful consideration.

> **NOTE** The following information is only one possible scenario, designed to help you understand `allowInsecureDomain()` through a real-world example of cross-scripting. It does not cover all issues with security architecture and should be used for background information only. The Macromedia Developer Center contains extensive information on Flash Player and security. For more information, see http://www.macromedia.com/devnet/security/..

Imagine that you are building an e-commerce site that consists of two components: a catalog, which does not need to be secure, because it contains only public information; and a shopping cart/checkout component, which must be secure to protect users' financial and personal information. Suppose that you are considering serving the catalog from http://mysite.com/catalog.swf and the cart from https://mysite.com/cart.swf. One requirement for your site is that a third party should not be able to steal your users' credit card numbers by taking advantage of a weakness in your security architecture.

Suppose that a middle-party attacker intervenes between your server and your users, attempting to steal the credit card numbers that your users enter into your shopping cart application. A middle party might, for example, be an unscrupulous ISP used by some of your users, or a malicious administrator at a user's workplace — anyone who has the ability to view or alter network packets transmitted over the public Internet between your users and your servers. This situation is not uncommon.

If cart.swf uses HTTPS to transmit credit card information to your servers, then the middle-party attacker can't directly steal this information from network packets, because the HTTPS transmission is encrypted. However, the attacker can use a different technique: altering the contents of one of your SWF files as it is delivered to the user, replacing your SWF file with an altered version that transmits the user's information to a different server, owned by the attacker.

The HTTPS protocol, among other things, prevents this "modification" attack from working, because, in addition to being encrypted, HTTPS transmissions are tamper-resistant. If a middle-party attacker alters a packet, the receiving side detects the alteration and discards the packet. So the attacker in this situation can't alter cart.swf, because it is delivered over HTTPS.

However, suppose that you want to allow buttons in catalog.swf, served over HTTP, to add items to the shopping cart in cart.swf, served over HTTPS. To accomplish this, cart.swf calls `allowInsecureDomain()`, which allows catalog.swf to script cart.swf. This action has an unintended consequence: Now the hypothetical attacker can alter catalog.swf as it is initially being downloaded by the user, because catalog.swf is delivered with HTTP and is not tamper-resistant. The attacker's altered catalog.swf can now script cart.swf, because cart.swf contains a call to `allowInsecureDomain()`. The altered catalog.swf file can use ActionScript to access the variables in cart.swf, thus reading the user's credit card information and other sensitive data. The altered catalog.swf can then send this data to an attacker's server.

Obviously, this implementation is not desired, but you still want to allow cross-scripting between the two SWF files on your site. Here are two possible ways to redesign this hypothetical e-commerce site to avoid `allowInsecureDomain()`:

- Serve all SWF files in the application over HTTPS. This is by far the simplest and most reliable solution. In the scenario described, you would serve both catalog.swf and cart.swf over HTTPS. You might experience slightly higher bandwidth consumption and server CPU load when switching a file such as catalog.swf from HTTP to HTTPS, and your users might experience slightly longer application load times. You need to experiment with real servers to determine the severity of these effects; usually they are no worse than 10-20% each, and sometimes they are not present at all. You can usually improve results by using HTTPS-accelerating hardware or software on your servers. A major benefit of serving all cooperating SWF files over HTTPS is that you can use an HTTPS URL as the main URL in the user's browser without generating any mixed-content warnings from the browser. Also, the browser's padlock icon becomes visible, providing your users with a common and trusted indicator of security.

- Use HTTPS-to-HTTP scripting, rather than HTTP-to-HTTPS scripting. In the scenario described, you could store the contents of the user's shopping cart in catalog.swf, and have cart.swf manage only the checkout process. At checkout time, cart.swf could retrieve the cart contents from ActionScript variables in catalog.swf. The restriction on HTTP-to-HTTPS scripting is asymmetrical; although an HTTP-delivered catalog.swf file cannot safely be allowed to script an HTTPS-delivered cart.swf file, an HTTPS cart.swf file may script the HTTP catalog.swf file. This approach is more delicate than the all-HTTPS approach; you must be careful not to trust any SWF file delivered over HTTP, because of its vulnerability to tampering. For example, when cart.swf retrieves the ActionScript variable that describes the cart contents, the ActionScript code in cart.swf cannot trust that the value of this variable is in the format that you expect. You must carefully validate that the cart contents do not contain invalid data that might lead cart.swf to take an undesired action. You must also accept the risk that a middle party, by altering catalog.swf, could supply valid but inaccurate data to cart.swf; for example, by placing items in the user's cart. The usual checkout process mitigates this risk somewhat by displaying the cart contents and total cost for final approval by the user, but the risk remains present.

Web browsers have enforced separation between HTTPS and non-HTTPS files for years, and the scenario described illustrates one good reason for this restriction. Flash Player gives you the ability to work around this security restriction when you absolutely must, but be sure to consider the consequences carefully before doing so.

For more information, see the following:

- Chapter 17, "Understanding Security," in *Learning ActionScript 2.0 in Flash*
- The Flash Player 8 Security white paper at http://www.macromedia.com/go/fp8_security
- The Flash Player 8 Security-Related API white paper at http://www.macromedia.com/go/fp8_security_apis

Availability: ActionScript 1.0; Flash Player 7

Parameters

`domain:String` - An exact domain name, such as www.myDomainName.com or store.myDomainName.com. In Flash Player 8, you can pass a wildcard ("*") to `System.security.allowInsecureDomain()` to allow all domains, including local hosts, access to the calling SWF file. Do not use the wildcard unless you are certain that you want to allow *all* domains, including local hosts, to access the HTTPS SWF file.

Example

In the following example, you host a math test on a secure domain so that only registered students can access it. You have also developed a number of SWF files that illustrate certain concepts, which you host on an insecure domain. You want students to access the test from the SWF file that contains information about a concept.

```
// This SWF file is at https://myEducationSite.somewhere.com/mathTest.swf
// Concept files are at http://myEducationSite.somewhere.com
System.security.allowInsecureDomain("myEducationSite.somewhere.com");
```

See also

```
allowDomain (security.allowDomain method), exactSettings
(System.exactSettings property)
```

loadPolicyFile (security.loadPolicyFile method)

```
public static loadPolicyFile(url:String) : Void
```

Loads a cross-domain policy file from a location specified by the `url` parameter. Flash Player uses policy files as a permission mechanism to permit Flash movies to load data from servers other than their own.

Flash Player 7.0.14.0 looked for policy files in only one location: /crossdomain.xml on the server to which a data-loading request was being made. For an XMLSocket connection attempt, Flash Player 7.0.14.0 looked for /crossdomain.xml on an HTTP server on port 80 in the subdomain to which the XMLSocket connection attempt was being made. Flash Player 7.0.14.0 (and all earlier players) also restricted XMLSocket connections to ports 1024 and later.

With the addition of `System.security.loadPolicyFile()`, Flash Player 7.0.19.0 can load policy files from arbitrary locations, as shown in the following example:

```
System.security.loadPolicyFile("http://foo.com/sub/dir/pf.xml");
```

This causes Flash Player to retrieve a policy file from the specified URL. Any permissions granted by the policy file at that location will apply to all content at the same level or lower in the virtual directory hierarchy of the server. The following code continues the previous example:

```
loadVariables("http://foo.com/sub/dir/vars.txt") // allowed
loadVariables("http://foo.com/sub/dir/deep/vars2.txt") // allowed
loadVariables("http://foo.com/elsewhere/vars3.txt") // not allowed
```

You can use loadPolicyFile() to load any number of policy files. When considering a request that requires a policy file, Flash Player always waits for the completion of any policy file downloads before denying a request. As a final fallback, if no policy file specified with loadPolicyFile() authorizes a request, Flash Player consults the original default location, /crossdomain.xml.

Using the xmlsocket protocol along with a specific port number, lets you retrieve policy files directly from an XMLSocket server, as shown in the following example:

```
System.security.loadPolicyFile("xmlsocket://foo.com:414");
```

This causes Flash Player to attempt to retrieve a policy file from the specified host and port. Any port can be used, not only ports 1024 and higher. Upon establishing a connection with the specified port, Flash Player transmits <policy-file-request />, terminated by a null byte. An XMLSocket server can be configured to serve both policy files and normal XMLSocket connections over the same port, in which case the server should wait for <policy-file-request /> before transmitting a policy file. A server can also be set up to serve policy files over a separate port from standard connections, in which case it can send a policy file as soon as a connection is established on the dedicated policy file port. The server must send a null byte to terminate a policy file, and may thereafter close the connection; if the server does not close the connection, Flash Player does so upon receiving the terminating null byte.

A policy file served by an XMLSocket server has the same syntax as any other policy file, except that it must also specify the ports to which access is granted. When a policy file comes from a port lower than 1024, it can grant access to any ports; when a policy file comes from port 1024 or higher, it can grant access only to other ports 1024 and higher. The allowed ports are specified in a "to-ports" attribute in the <allow-access-from> tag. Single port numbers, port ranges, and wildcards are all allowed. The following example shows an XMLSocket policy file:

```
<cross-domain-policy>
<allow-access-from domain="*" to-ports="507" />
<allow-access-from domain="*.foo.com" to-ports="507,516" />
<allow-access-from domain="*.bar.com" to-ports="516-523" />
<allow-access-from domain="www.foo.com" to-ports="507,516-523" />
<allow-access-from domain="www.bar.com" to-ports="*" />
</cross-domain-policy>
```

A policy file obtained from the old default location--/crossdomain.xml on an HTTP server on port 80—implicitly authorizes access to all ports 1024 and above. There is no way to retrieve a policy file to authorize XMLSocket operations from any other location on an HTTP server; any custom locations for XMLSocket policy files must be on an XMLSocket server.

Because the ability to connect to ports lower than 1024 is new, a policy file loaded with `loadPolicyFile()` must always authorize this connection, even when a movie clip is connecting to its own subdomain.

For more information, see the following:

- Chapter 17, "Understanding Security," in *Learning ActionScript 2.0 in Flash*
- The Flash Player 8 Security white paper at http://www.macromedia.com/go/fp8_security
- The Flash Player 8 Security-Related API white paper at http://www.macromedia.com/go/fp8_security_apis

Availability: ActionScript 1.0; Flash Player 7,0,19,0

Parameters

`url:String` - A string; the URL where the cross-domain policy file to be loaded is located.

sandboxType (security.sandboxType property)

`public static sandboxType : String [read-only]`

Indicates the type of security sandbox in which the calling SWF file is operating.

`System.security.sandboxType` has one of the following values:

- `remote`: This SWF file is from an Internet URL, and will operate under domain-based sandbox rules.
- `localWithFile`: This SWF file is a local file, and has not been trusted by the user, and was not published with a networking designation. This SWF file may read from local data sources, but may not communicate with the Internet.
- `localWithNetwork`: This SWF file is a local file, and has not been trusted by the user, and was published with a networking designation. This SWF may communicate with the Internet, but may not read from local data sources.
- `localTrusted`: This SWF file is a local file, and has been trusted by the user, using either the Settings Manager or a FlashPlayerTrust configuration file. This SWF file may both read from local data sources and communicate with the Internet.

Note that this property may be examined from a SWF file of any version, but is only supported in Flash Player 8 or greater. This unusual arrangement means that you can examine this property, for example, from a version 7 SWF file playing in Flash Player 8. This all-versions support means that, if you publish for a version earlier than 8, you will not know at publish time whether this property will be supported or not at playback time. Thus, in a SWF file of version 7 or lower, you may find that this property has an undefined value; that should only happen when the player version (indicated by `System.capabilities.version`) is less than 8. In that situation, you can determine the sandbox type according to whether your SWF file's URL is a local file or not. If so, you can assume Flash Player will classify your SWF as `"localTrusted"` (prior to Flash Player 8, this was how all local content was treated). If not, you can assume Flash Player will classify your SWF file as `"remote"`.

For more information, see the following:

- Chapter 17, "Understanding Security," in *Learning ActionScript 2.0 in Flash*
- The Flash Player 8 Security white paper at http://www.macromedia.com/go/fp8_security
- The Flash Player 8 Security-Related API white paper at http://www.macromedia.com/go/fp8_security_apis

Availability: ActionScript 1.0; Flash Player 8 - See the description for version-specific details.

Selection

```
Object
  |
  +-Selection
```

```
public class Selection
extends Object
```

The Selection class lets you set and control the text field in which the insertion point is located (that is, the field that has focus). Selection-span indexes are zero-based (for example, the first position is 0, the second position is 1, and so on).

There is no constructor function for the Selection class, because there can be only one currently focused field at a time.

Availability: ActionScript 1.0; Flash Player 5

Property summary

Properties inherited from class Object

```
constructor (Object.constructor property),__proto__ (Object.__proto__
property),prototype (Object.prototype property),__resolve
(Object.__resolve·property)
```

Event summary

Event	Description
`onSetFocus = function([oldfoc us:Object], [newfocus:Object ]) {}`	Notified when the input focus changes.

Method summary

Modifiers	Signature	Description
`static`	`addListener(listener :Object) : Void`	Registers an object to receive keyboard focus change notifications.
`static`	`getBeginIndex() : Number`	Returns the index at the beginning of the selection span.
`static`	`getCaretIndex() : Number`	Returns the index of the blinking insertion point (caret) position.
`static`	`getEndIndex() : Number`	Returns the ending index of the currently focused selection span.
`static`	`getFocus() : String`	Returns a string specifying the target path of the object that has focus.
`static`	`removeListener(liste ner:Object) : Boolean`	Removes an object previously registered with `Selection.addListener()`.
`static`	`setFocus(newFocus:Ob ject) : Boolean`	Gives focus to the selectable (editable) text field, button, or movie clip, specified by the `newFocus` parameter.
`static`	`setSelection(beginIn dex:Number, endIndex:Number) : Void`	Sets the selection span of the currently focused text field.

```
addProperty (Object.addProperty method), hasOwnProperty
(Object.hasOwnProperty method), isPropertyEnumerable
(Object.isPropertyEnumerable method), isPrototypeOf (Object.isPrototypeOf
method), registerClass (Object.registerClass method), toString
(Object.toString method), unwatch (Object.unwatch method), valueOf
(Object.valueOf method), watch (Object.watch method)
```

addListener (Selection.addListener method)

```
public static addListener(listener:Object) : Void
```

Registers an object to receive keyboard focus change notifications. When the focus changes (for example, whenever `Selection.setFocus()` is invoked), all listening objects registered with `addListener()` have their `onSetFocus` method invoked. Multiple objects may listen for focus change notifications. If the specified listener is already registered, no change occurs.

Availability: ActionScript 1.0; Flash Player 6

Parameters

`listener:Object` - A new object with an `onSetFocus` method.

Example

In the following example, you create two input text fields at runtime, setting the borders for each text field to `true`. This code creates a new (generic) ActionScript object named `focusListener`. This object defines for itself an `onSetFocus` property, to which it assigns a function. The function takes two parameters: a reference to the text field that lost focus, and one to the text field that gained focus. The function sets the `border` property of the text field that lost focus to `false`, and sets the border property of the text field that gained focus to `true`:

```
this.createTextField("one_txt", 99, 10, 10, 200, 20);
this.createTextField("two_txt", 100, 10, 50, 200, 20);
one_txt.border = true;
one_txt.type = "input";
two_txt.border = true;
two_txt.type = "input";

var focusListener:Object = new Object();
focusListener.onSetFocus = function(oldFocus_txt, newFocus_txt) {
  oldFocus_txt.border = false;
  newFocus_txt.border = true;
};
Selection.addListener(focusListener);
```

When you test the SWF file, try using Tab to move between the two text fields. Make sure that you select Control > Disable Keyboard Shortcuts so you can change focus between the two fields using Tab.

See also

setFocus (Selection.setFocus method)

getBeginIndex (Selection.getBeginIndex method)

public static getBeginIndex() : Number

Returns the index at the beginning of the selection span. If no index exists or no text field currently has focus, the method returns -1. Selection span indexes are zero-based (for example, the first position is 0, the second position is 1, and so on).

Availability: ActionScript 1.0; Flash Player 5

Returns

Number - An integer.

Example

The following example creates a text field at runtime, and sets its properties. A context menu item is added that can be used to change the currently selected text to uppercase characters.

```
this.createTextField("output_txt", this.getNextHighestDepth(), 0, 0, 300,
    200);
output_txt.multiline = true;
output_txt.wordWrap = true;
output_txt.border = true;
output_txt.type = "input";
output_txt.text = "Enter your text here";
var my_cm:ContextMenu = new ContextMenu();
my_cm.customItems.push(new ContextMenuItem("Uppercase...", doUppercase));
function doUppercase():Void {
   var startIndex:Number = Selection.getBeginIndex();
   var endIndex:Number = Selection.getEndIndex();
   var stringToUppercase:String = output_txt.text.substring(startIndex,
   endIndex);
   output_txt.replaceText(startIndex, endIndex,
   stringToUppercase.toUpperCase());
}
output_txt.menu = my_cm;
```

The MovieClip.getNextHighestDepth() method used in this example requires Flash Player 7 or later. If your SWF file includes a version 2 component, use the version 2 components DepthManager class instead of the MovieClip.getNextHighestDepth() method.

An example can also be found in the Strings.fla file in the ActionScript samples Folder. Typical paths to this folder are:

- Windows: *boot drive*\Program Files\Macromedia\Flash 8\Samples and Tutorials\Samples\ActionScript
- Macintosh: *Macintosh HD*/Applications/Macromedia Flash 8/Samples and Tutorials/ Samples/ActionScript

See also

getEndIndex (Selection.getEndIndex method)

getCaretIndex (Selection.getCaretIndex method)

public static getCaretIndex() : Number

Returns the index of the blinking insertion point (caret) position. If there is no blinking insertion point displayed, the method returns -1. Selection span indexes are zero-based (for example, the first position is 0, the second position is 1, and so on).

Availability: ActionScript 1.0; Flash Player 5

Returns

Number - An integer.

Example

The following example creates and sets the properties of a text field at runtime. The getCaretIndex() method is used to return the index of the caret and display its value in another text field.

```
this.createTextField("pos_txt", this.getNextHighestDepth(), 50, 20, 100,
    22);
this.createTextField("content_txt", this.getNextHighestDepth(), 50, 50,
    400, 300);
content_txt.border = true;
content_txt.type = "input";
content_txt.wordWrap = true;
content_txt.multiline = true;
content_txt.onChanged = getCaretPos;

var keyListener:Object = new Object();
keyListener.onKeyUp = getCaretPos;
Key.addListener(keyListener);

var mouseListener:Object = new Object();
mouseListener.onMouseUp = getCaretPos;
Mouse.addListener(mouseListener);
```

```
function getCaretPos() {
  pos_txt.text = Selection.getCaretIndex();
}
```

The `MovieClip.getNextHighestDepth()` method used in this example requires Flash Player 7 or later. If your SWF file includes a version 2 component, use the version 2 components DepthManager class instead of the `MovieClip.getNextHighestDepth()` method.

An example can also be found in the Strings.fla file in the ActionScript samples Folder. Typical paths to this folder are:

- Windows: *boot drive*\Program Files\Macromedia\Flash 8\Samples and Tutorials\Samples\ActionScript
- Macintosh: *Macintosh HD*/Applications/Macromedia Flash 8/Samples and Tutorials/ Samples/ActionScript

getEndIndex (Selection.getEndIndex method)

`public static getEndIndex() : Number`

Returns the ending index of the currently focused selection span. If no index exists, or if there is no currently focused selection span, the method returns -1. Selection span indexes are zero-based (for example, the first position is 0, the second position is 1, and so on).

Availability: ActionScript 1.0; Flash Player 5

Returns

`Number` - An integer.

Example

This example is excerpted from the Strings.fla file in the ActionScript samples folder.

```
// define the function which converts the selected text in an instance,
// and convert the string to upper or lower case.
function convertCase(target, menuItem) {
  var beginIndex:Number = Selection.getBeginIndex();
  var endIndex:Number = Selection.getEndIndex();
  var tempString:String;
  // make sure that text is actually selected.
  if (beginIndex>-1 && endIndex>-1) {
  // set the temporary string to the text before the selected text.
  tempString = target.text.slice(0, beginIndex);
  switch (menuItem.caption) {
  case 'Uppercase...' :
    // if the user selects the "Uppercase..." context menu item,
    // convert the selected text to upper case.
```

```
    tempString += target.text.substring(beginIndex,
endIndex).toUpperCase();
    break;
  case 'Lowercase...' :
    tempString += target.text.substring(beginIndex,
endIndex).toLowerCase();
    break;
  }
  // append the text after the selected text to the temporary string.
  tempString += target.text.slice(endIndex);
  // set the text in the target text field to the contents of the temporary
string.
  target.text = tempString;
  }
}
```

See the Strings.fla file for the entire script. Typical paths to the ActionScript samples folder are:

- Windows: *boot drive*\Program Files\Macromedia\Flash 8\Samples and Tutorials\Samples\ActionScript

- Macintosh: *Macintosh HD*/Applications/Macromedia Flash 8/Samples and Tutorials/Samples/ActionScript

See also

`getBeginIndex (Selection.getBeginIndex method)`

getFocus (Selection.getFocus method)

`public static getFocus() : String`

Returns a string specifying the target path of the object that has focus.

- If a TextField object has focus, and the object has an instance name, this method returns the target path of the TextField object. Otherwise, it returns the TextField's variable name.

- If a Button object or button movie clip has focus, this method returns the target path of the Button object or button movie clip.

- If neither a TextField object, Button object, Component instance, nor button movie clip has focus, this method returns `null`.

Availability: ActionScript 1.0; Flash Player 5 - Instance names for buttons and text fields work in Flash Player 6 and later.

Returns

`String` - A string or `null`.

Example

The following example displays the currently focused selection's target path in a TextArea component instance. Add several component instances or button, text field and movie clip instances to the Stage. Add several component instances or button, text field and movie clip instances to your SWF file. Then add the following ActionScript to your AS or FLA file.

```
var focus_ta:mx.controls.TextArea;
my_mc.onRelease = function() {};
my_btn.onRelease = function() {};

var keyListener:Object = new Object();
keyListener.onKeyDown = function() {
  if (Key.isDown(Key.SPACE)) {
  focus_ta.text = Selection.getFocus()+newline+focus_ta.text;
  }
};
Key.addListener(keyListener);
```

Test the SWF file, and use Tab to move between the instances on the Stage. Make sure you have Control > Disable Keyboard Shortcuts selected in the test environment.

See also

onSetFocus (Selection.onSetFocus event listener), setFocus (Selection.setFocus method)

onSetFocus (Selection.onSetFocus event listener)

```
onSetFocus = function([oldfocus:Object], [newfocus:Object]) {}
```

Notified when the input focus changes. To use this listener, you must create a listener object. You can then define a function for this listener and use Selection.addListener() to register the listener with the Selection object, as in the following code:

```
var someListener:Object = new Object();
someListener.onSetFocus = function () {
  // statements
}
Selection.addListener(someListener);
```

Listeners enable different pieces of code to cooperate because multiple listeners can receive notification about a single event.

Availability: ActionScript 1.0; Flash Player 6

Parameters

oldfocus:Object [optional] - The object losing focus.

newfocus:Object [optional] - The object receiving focus.

Example

The following example demonstrates how to determine when input focus changes in a SWF file between several dynamically created text fields. Enter the following ActionScript into a FLA or AS file and then test the document:

```
this.createTextField("one_txt", 1, 0, 0, 100, 22);
this.createTextField("two_txt", 2, 0, 25, 100, 22);
this.createTextField("three_txt", 3, 0, 50, 100, 22);
this.createTextField("four_txt", 4, 0, 75, 100, 22);

for (var i in this) {
  if (this[i] instanceof TextField) {
  this[i].border = true;
  this[i].type = "input";
  }
}

this.createTextField("status_txt", this.getNextHighestDepth(), 200, 10,
  300, 100);
status_txt.html = true;
status_txt.multiline = true;

var someListener:Object = new Object();
someListener.onSetFocus = function(oldFocus, newFocus) {
  status_txt.htmlText = "<b>setFocus triggered</b>";
  status_txt.htmlText += "<textformat tabStops='[20,80]'>";
  status_txt.htmlText += " \toldFocus:\t"+oldFocus;
  status_txt.htmlText += " \tnewFocus:\t"+newFocus;
  status_txt.htmlText += " \tgetFocus:\t"+Selection.getFocus();
  status_txt.htmlText += "</textformat>";
};
Selection.addListener(someListener);
```

The `MovieClip.getNextHighestDepth()` method used in this example requires Flash Player 7 or later. If your SWF file includes a version 2 component, use the version 2 components DepthManager class instead of the `MovieClip.getNextHighestDepth()` method.

See also

`addListener` (`Selection.addListener` method), `setFocus` (`Selection.setFocus` method)

removeListener (Selection.removeListener method)

`public static removeListener(listener:Object) : Boolean`

Removes an object previously registered with `Selection.addListener()`.

Availability: ActionScript 1.0; Flash Player 6

Parameters

listener:Object - The object that will no longer receive focus notifications.

Returns

Boolean - If listener was successfully removed, the method returns a true value. If listener was not successfully removed--for example, if listener was not on the Selection object's listener list--the method returns a value of false.

Example

The following ActionScript dynamically creates several text field instances. When you select a text field, information displays in the Output panel. When you click the remove_btn instance, the listener is removed and information no longer displays in the Output panel.

```
this.createTextField("one_txt", 1, 0, 0, 100, 22);
this.createTextField("two_txt", 2, 0, 25, 100, 22);
this.createTextField("three_txt", 3, 0, 50, 100, 22);
this.createTextField("four_txt", 4, 0, 75, 100, 22);

for (var i in this) {
  if (this[i] instanceof TextField) {
  this[i].border = true;
  this[i].type = "input";
  }
}

var selectionListener:Object = new Object();
selectionListener.onSetFocus = function(oldFocus, newFocus) {
  trace("Focus shifted from "+oldFocus+" to "+newFocus);
};
Selection.addListener(selectionListener);

remove_btn.onRelease = function() {
  trace("removeListener invoked");
  Selection.removeListener(selectionListener);
};
```

See also

addListener (Selection.addListener method)

setFocus (Selection.setFocus method)

public static setFocus(newFocus:Object) : Boolean

Gives focus to the selectable (editable) text field, button, or movie clip, specified by the newFocus parameter. If null or undefined is passed, the current focus is removed.

Availability: ActionScript 1.0; Flash Player 5 - Instance names for buttons and movie clips work only in Flash Player 6 and later.

Parameters

`newFocus:Object` - An object such as a button, movie clip or text field instance, or a string specifying the path to a button, movie clip, or text field instance. If you pass a string literal specifying a path, enclose the path in quotation marks (" "). You can use dot or slash notation to specify the path. If you are using ActionScript 2.0, you must use dot notation. You can use a relative or absolute path.

Returns

`Boolean` - A Boolean value; `true` if the focus attempt is successful, `false` if it fails.

Example

In the following example, the text field focuses on the `username_txt` text field when it is running in a browser window. If the user does not fill in one of the required text fields (`username_txt` and `password_txt`), the cursor automatically focuses in the text field that's missing data. For example, if the user does not type anything into the `username_txt` text field and clicks the submit button, an error message appears and the cursor focuses in the `username_txt` text field.

```
this.createTextField("status_txt", this.getNextHighestDepth(), 100, 70,
    100, 22);
this.createTextField("username_txt", this.getNextHighestDepth(), 100, 100,
    100, 22);
this.createTextField("password_txt", this.getNextHighestDepth(), 100, 130,
    100, 22);
this.createEmptyMovieClip("submit_mc", this.getNextHighestDepth());
submit_mc.createTextField("submit_txt", this.getNextHighestDepth(), 100,
    160, 100, 22);
submit_mc.submit_txt.autoSize = "center";
submit_mc.submit_txt.text = "Submit";
submit_mc.submit_txt.border = true;
submit_mc.onRelease = checkForm;
username_txt.border = true;
password_txt.border = true;
username_txt.type = "input";
password_txt.type = "input";
password_txt.password = true;
Selection.setFocus("username_txt");
//
function checkForm():Boolean {
    if (username_txt.text.length == 0) {
        status_txt.text = "fill in username";
        Selection.setFocus("username_txt");
```

```
  return false;
  }
  if (password_txt.text.length == 0) {
  status_txt.text = "fill in password";
  Selection.setFocus("password_txt");
  return false;
  }
  status_txt.text = "success!";
  Selection.setFocus(null);
  return true;
}
```

The MovieClip.getNextHighestDepth() method used in this example requires Flash Player 7 or later. If your SWF file includes a version 2 component, use the version 2 components DepthManager class instead of the MovieClip.getNextHighestDepth() method.

See also

getFocus (Selection.getFocus method)

setSelection (Selection.setSelection method)

public static setSelection(beginIndex:Number, endIndex:Number) : Void

Sets the selection span of the currently focused text field. The new selection span will begin at the index specified in the beginIndex parameter, and end at the index specified in the endIndex parameter. Selection span indexes are zero-based (for example, the first position is 0, the second position is 1, and so on). This method has no effect if there is no currently focused text field.

Availability: ActionScript 1.0; Flash Player 5

Parameters

beginIndex:Number - The beginning index of the selection span.

endIndex:Number - The ending index of the selection span.

Example

In the following ActionScript, you create a text field at runtime and add a string to it. Then you focus the text field and select a span of characters in the focused text field.

```
this.createTextField("myText_txt", 99, 10, 10, 200, 30);
myText_txt.text = "this is my text";
this.onEnterFrame = function () {
  Selection.setFocus("myText_txt");
  Selection.setSelection(0, 3);
  delete this.onEnterFrame;
}
```

The following example illustrates how the `endIndex` parameter is not inclusive. In order to select the first character, you must use an `endIndex` of 1, not 0. If you change the `endIndex` parameter to 0, nothing will be selected.

```
this.createTextField("myText_txt", 99, 10, 10, 200, 30);
myText_txt.text = "this is my text";
this.onEnterFrame = function () {
  Selection.setFocus("myText_txt");
  Selection.setSelection(0, 1);
  delete this.onEnterFrame;
}
```

SharedObject

```
Object
  |
  +-SharedObject
```

```
public dynamic class SharedObject
extends Object
```

The SharedObject class is used to read and store limited amounts of data on a user's computer. Shared objects offer real-time data sharing between objects that are persistent on the user's computer. Local shared objects are similar to browser cookies.

Here are three possible uses of shared objects:

- A game that stores a user's high scores. The game could provide personalized data for users, such as user name and high score, without dedicating storage on the server.

- A phone book application that can work either online or offline. The phone book, delivered as a projector application, could contain a local data cache with a list of names and phone numbers entered by the user. When an Internet connection is available, the application would retrieve up-to-date information from a server. When no connection is available, the application would use the latest data saved in shared objects.

- User preferences or tracking data for a complex website, such as a record of which articles a user read on a news site. Tracking this information would allow you to display articles that have already been read differently from new, unread articles. Storing this information on the user's computer reduces server load.

Local shared objects maintain local persistence. For example, you can call SharedObject.getLocal() to create a shared object that contains the high score in a game. Because the shared object is locally persistent, Flash saves its data attributes on the user's computer when the game is closed. The next time the game is opened, the high score from the previous session is displayed. Alternatively, you could set the shared object's properties to null before the game is closed. The next time the SWF file runs, the game opens without the previous high score.

To create a local shared object, use the following syntax:

```
var so:SharedObject = SharedObject.getLocal("userHighScore");
so.data.highScore = new Number();
so.flush();
```

In the example, the shared object is explicitly *flushed*, or written to a disk. When an application closes, shared objects are automatically flushed; however, it is shown here to demonstrate the step of writing data to a disk.

Local disk space considerations: Local shared objects can be very useful, but they have some limitations that are important to consider as you design your application. Sometimes your SWF files may not be allowed to write local shared objects, and sometimes the data stored in local shared objects can be deleted without your knowledge. Flash Player users can manage the disk space that is available to individual domains or to all domains. When users lower the amount of disk space available, some local shared objects may be deleted. Flash Player users also have privacy controls that can prevent third-party domains (domains other than the domain in the current browser address bar) from reading or writing local shared objects.

> **NOTE**
> Local content can always write third-party shared objects to disk, even if writing of shared objects to disk by third-party domains is disallowed.

Macromedia recommends that you check for failures that are related to the amount of disk space available and to user privacy controls. Perform these checks when you call getLocal() and flush():

SharedObject.getLocal() — This method returns null when the user has disabled third-party shared objects and the domain of your SWF file does not match the domain in the browser address bar.

SharedObject.flush() — This method returns false when the user has disabled shared objects for your domain or for all domains. It returns "pending" when additional storage space is needed and the user must interactively decide whether to allow an increase.

If your SWF file attempts to create or modify local shared objects, make sure that your SWF file is at least 215 pixels wide and at least 138 pixels high (the minimum dimensions for displaying the dialog box that prompts users to increase their local shared object storage limit). If your SWF file is smaller than these dimensions and an increase in the storage limit is required, `SharedObject.flush()` fails, returning `"pending"` but then calling your `SharedObject.onStatus` handler with a result of `"SharedObject.Flush.Failed"`.

Availability: ActionScript 1.0; Flash Player 6

See also

`getLocal (SharedObject.getLocal method)`, `flush (SharedObject.flush method)`, `onStatus (SharedObject.onStatus handler)`

Property summary

Modifiers	Property	Description
	`data:Object`	The collection of attributes assigned to the `data` property of the object; these attributes can be shared and/or stored.

Properties inherited from class Object

`constructor (Object.constructor property)`, `__proto__ (Object.__proto__ property)`, `prototype (Object.prototype property)`, `__resolve (Object.__resolve property)`

Event summary

Event	Description
`onStatus = function(infoObject:Object) {}`	Invoked every time an error, warning, or informational note is posted for a shared object.

Method summary

Modifiers	Signature	Description
	`clear() : Void`	Purges all the data from the shared object and deletes the shared object from the disk.
	`flush([minDiskSpace: Number]) : Object`	Immediately writes a locally persistent shared object to a local file.
static	`getLocal(name:String , [localPath:String], [secure:Boolean]) : SharedObject`	Returns a reference to a locally persistent shared object that is available only to the current client.
	`getSize() : Number`	Gets the current size of the shared object, in bytes.

Methods inherited from class Object

```
addProperty (Object.addProperty method),hasOwnProperty
(Object.hasOwnProperty method),isPropertyEnumerable
(Object.isPropertyEnumerable method),isPrototypeOf (Object.isPrototypeOf
method),registerClass (Object.registerClass method),toString
(Object.toString method),unwatch (Object.unwatch method),valueOf
(Object.valueOf method),watch (Object.watch method)
```

clear (SharedObject.clear method)

`public clear() : Void`

Purges all the data from the shared object and deletes the shared object from the disk. The reference to `my_so` is still active, and `my_so` is now empty.

Availability: ActionScript 1.0; Flash Player 7

Example

The following example sets data in the shared object, and then empties all of the data from the shared object.

```
var my_so:SharedObject = SharedObject.getLocal("superfoo");
my_so.data.name = "Hector";
trace("before my_so.clear():");
for (var prop in my_so.data) {
   trace("\t"+prop);
}
trace("");
my_so.clear();
trace("after my_so.clear():");
for (var prop in my_so.data) {
```

```
    trace("\t"+prop);
}
```

This ActionScript displays the following message in the Output panel:

```
before my_so.clear():
  name

after my_so.clear():
```

data (SharedObject.data property)

```
public data : Object
```

The collection of attributes assigned to the data property of the object; these attributes can be shared and/or stored. Each attribute can be an object of any basic ActionScript or JavaScript type—Array, Number, Boolean, and so on. For example, the following lines assign values to various aspects of a shared object:

```
var items_array:Array = new Array(101, 346, 483);
var currentUserIsAdmin:Boolean = true;
var currentUserName:String = "Ramona";

var my_so:SharedObject = SharedObject.getLocal("superfoo");
my_so.data.itemNumbers = items_array;
my_so.data.adminPrivileges = currentUserIsAdmin;
my_so.data.userName = currentUserName;

for (var prop in my_so.data) {
   trace(prop+": "+my_so.data[prop]);
}
```

All attributes of a shared object's data property are saved if the object is persistent, and the shared object contains the following information:

```
userName: Ramona
adminPrivileges: true
itemNumbers: 101,346,483
```

 NOTE | Do not assign values directly to the data property of a shared object, as in so.data=someValue ; Flash ignores these assignments.

To delete attributes for local shared objects, use code such as delete so.data.attributeName; setting an attribute to null or undefined for a local shared object does not delete the attribute.

To create *private* values for a shared object--values that are available only to the client instance while the object is in use and are not stored with the object when it is closed--create properties that are not named data to store them, as shown in the following example:

```
var my_so:SharedObject = SharedObject.getLocal("superfoo");
```

```
my_so.favoriteColor = "blue";
my_so.favoriteNightClub = "The Bluenote Tavern";
my_so.favoriteSong = "My World is Blue";

for (var prop in my_so) {
  trace(prop+": "+my_so[prop]);
}
```

The shared object contains the following data:

```
favoriteSong: My World is Blue
favoriteNightClub: The Bluenote Tavern
favoriteColor: blue
data: [object Object]
```

Availability: ActionScript 1.0; Flash Player 6

Example

The following example saves text from a TextInput component instance to a shared object named my_so (for the complete example, see SharedObject.getLocal()):

```
// Create a listener object and function for the <enter> event.
var textListener:Object = new Object();
textListener.enter = function(eventObj:Object) {
  my_so.data.myTextSaved = eventObj.target.text;
  my_so.flush();
};
```

See also

flush (SharedObject.flush method)

```
public flush([minDiskSpace:Number]) : Object
```

Immediately writes a locally persistent shared object to a local file. If you don't use this method, Flash writes the shared object to a file when the shared object session ends—that is, when the SWF file is closed, that is when the shared object is garbage-collected because it no longer has any references to it or you call SharedObject.clear().

If this method returns "pending", Flash Player shows a dialog box asking the user to increase the amount of disk space available to objects from this domain. To allow space for the shared object to grow when it is saved in the future, which avoids return values of "pending", pass a value for minimumDiskSpace. When Flash tries to write the file, it looks for the number of bytes passed to minimumDiskSpace, instead of looking for enough space to save the shared object at its current size.

For example, if you expect a shared object to grow to a maximum size of 500 bytes, even though it might start out much smaller, pass 500 for `minimumDiskSpace`. If Flash asks the user to allot disk space for the shared object, it asks for 500 bytes. After the user allots the requested amount of space, Flash won't have to ask for more space on future attempts to flush the object (as long as its size doesn't exceed 500 bytes).

After the user responds to the dialog box, this method is called again and returns either `true` or `false`; `SharedObject.onStatus` is also invoked with a `code` property of `SharedObject.Flush.Success` or `SharedObject.Flush.Failed`.

For more information, see "Local disk space considerations" in the SharedObject class overview.

Availability: ActionScript 1.0; Flash Player 6

Parameters

`minDiskSpace:Number` [optional] - An integer specifying the number of bytes that must be allotted for this object. The default value is 0.

Returns

`Object` - A Boolean value: `true` or `false`; or a string value of `"pending"`, as described in the following list:

■ If the user has permitted local information storage for objects from this domain, and the amount of space allotted is sufficient to store the object, this method returns `true`. (If you have passed a value for `minimumDiskSpace`, the amount of space allotted must be at least equal to that value for `true` to be returned).

■ If the user has permitted local information storage for objects from this domain, but the amount of space allotted is not sufficient to store the object, this method returns `"pending"`.

■ If the user has permanently denied local information storage for objects from this domain, or if Flash cannot save the object for any reason, this method returns `false`.

Note: Local content can always write shared objects from third-party domains (domains other than the domain in the current browser address bar) to disk, even if writing of third-party shared objects to disk is disallowed.

Example

The following function gets a shared object, `my_so`, and fills writable properties with user-provided settings. Finally, `flush()` is called to save the settings and allot a minimum of 1000 bytes of disk space.

```
this.syncSettingsCore = function(soName:String, override:Boolean,
  settings:Object) {
  var my_so:SharedObject = SharedObject.getLocal(soName, "http://
www.mydomain.com/app/sys");
  // settings list index
  var i;
  // For each specified value in settings:
  // If override is true, set the persistent setting to the provided value.
  // If override is false, fetch the persistent setting, unless there
  // isn't one, in which case, set it to the provided value.
  for (i in settings) {
  if (override || (my_so.data[i] == null)) {
    my_so.data[i] = settings[i];
  } else {
    settings[i] = my_so.data[i];
  }
  }
  my_so.flush(1000);
};
```

See also

clear (SharedObject.clear method), onStatus (SharedObject.onStatus handler)

getLocal (SharedObject.getLocal method)

```
public static getLocal(name:String, [localPath:String], [secure:Boolean]) :
  SharedObject
```

Returns a reference to a locally persistent shared object that is available only to the current client. If the shared object does not already exist, this method creates one. This method is a static method of the SharedObject class. To assign the object to a variable, use syntax like the following:

```
var so:SharedObject = SharedObject.getLocal("savedData")
```

> **NOTE**
>
> If the user has selected to never allow local storage for this domain, the object is not saved locally, even if a value for localPath is specified. The exception to this rule is local content. Local content can always write shared objects from third-party domains (domains other than the domain in the current browser address bar) to disk, even if writing of third-party shared objects to disk is disallowed. .

To avoid name collisions, Flash looks at the location of the SWF file that is creating the shared object. For example, if a SWF file at www.myCompany.com/apps/stockwatcher.swf creates a shared object named portfolio, that shared object does not conflict with another object named portfolio that was created by a SWF file at www.yourCompany.com/photoshoot.swf because the SWF files originate from different directories.

Although the `localPath` parameter is optional, you should give some thought to its use, especially if other SWF files need to access the shared object. If the data in the shared object is specific to one SWF file that will not be moved to another location, then use of the default value makes sense. If other SWF files need access to the shared object, or if the SWF file that creates the shared object will later be moved, then the value of this parameter affects whether any SWF files are able to access the shared object. For example, if you create a shared object with `localPath` set to the default value of the full path to the SWF file, then no other SWF file can access that shared object. If you later move the original SWF file to another location, then not even that SWF file can access the data already stored in the shared object.

You can reduce the likelihood that you will inadvertently restrict access to a shared object by using the `localpath` parameter. The most permissive option is to set the `localPath` parameter to "/", which makes the shared object available to all SWF files in the domain, but increases the likelihood of name collisions with other shared objects in the domain. More restrictive options are available to the extent that you can append the `localPath` parameter with folder names that are contained in the full path to the SWF file; for example, your `localPath` parameter options for the `portfolio` shared object created by the SWF file at www.myCompany.com/apps/stockwatcher.swf are: "/"; "/apps"; and "/apps/stockwatcher.swf". You need to determine which option provides optimal flexibility for your application.

When using this method, consider the Flash Player security model:

- You cannot access shared objects across sandbox boundaries.
- Users can restrict shared object access via the Flash Player Settings dialog box, or the Settings Manager. By default, shared objects can be created up to a maximum of 100K of data per domain. Administrative users and users can also place restrictions on the ability to write to the file system.

If you publish SWF file content to be played back as local files (either locally installed SWF files or projectors [EXE]), and you need to access a specific shared object from more than one local SWF file, be aware that for local files, two different locations may be used to store shared objects. The domain that is used depends on the security permissions granted to the local file that created the shared object. Local files can have three different levels of permissions: 1) access to the local filesystem only, 2) access to the network only, or 3) access to both the network and the local filesystem. Local files with access to the local filesystem (either 1 or 3) store their shared objects in one location. Local files with no access to the local filesystem (2) store their shared objects in another location. For more information, see the following:

- Chapter 17, "Understanding Security," in *Learning ActionScript 2.0 in Flash*
- The Flash Player 8 Security white paper at http://www.macromedia.com/go/fp8_security

- The Flash Player 8 Security-Related API white paper at http://www.macromedia.com/go/fp8_security_apis

Availability: ActionScript 1.0; Flash Player 6

Parameters

`name:String` - A string that represents the name of the object. The name can include forward slashes (/); for example, `work/addresses` is a legal name. Spaces are not allowed in a shared object name, nor are the following characters:

```
~ % & \ ; : " ' , < > ? #
```

`localPath:String` [optional] - A string that specifies the full or partial path to the SWF file that created the shared object, and that determines where the shared object is stored locally. The default value is the full path.

`secure:Boolean` [optional] - (Flash Player 8 only) Determines whether access to this shared object is restricted to SWF files that are delivered over an HTTPS connection. Assuming that your SWF file is delivered over HTTPS:

- If this parameter is set to `true`, Flash Player creates a new secure shared object or gets a reference to an existing secure shared object. This secure shared object can be read from or written to only by SWF files delivered over HTTPS that call `SharedObject.getLocal()` with the `secure` parameter set to `true`.

- If this parameter is set to `false`, Flash Player creates a new shared object or gets a reference to an existing shared object. This shared object can be read from or written to by SWF files delivered over non-HTTPS connections.

If your SWF file is delivered over a non-HTTPS connection and you try to set this parameter to `true`, the creation of a new shared object (or the access of a previously created secure shared object) fails and `null` is returned. Regardless of the value of this parameter, the created shared objects count toward the total amount of disk space allowed for a domain. The default value is `false`.

The following diagram shows the use of the secure parameter:

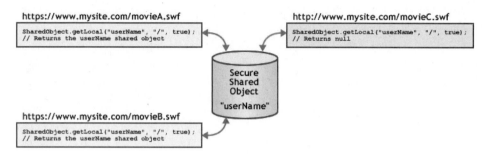

Returns

SharedObject - A reference to a shared object that is persistent locally and is available only to the current client. If Flash Player can't create or find the shared object (for example, if localPath was specified but no such directory exists, or if the secure parameter is used incorrectly) this method returns null.

This method fails and returns null if persistent shared object creation and storage by third-party Flash content is prohibited (does not apply to local content). Users can prohibit third-party persistent shared objects on the Global Storage Settings panel of the Settings Manager, located at http://www.macromedia.com/support/documentation/en/flashplayer/help/settings_manager03.html.

Example

The following example creates a shared object that stores text that is typed into a TextInput component instance. The resulting SWF file loads the saved text from the shared object when it starts playing. Every time the user presses Enter, the text in the text field is written to the shared object. To use this example, drag a TextInput component onto the Stage, and name the instance myText_ti. Copy the following code into the main Timeline (click in an empty area of the Stage or press Escape to remove focus from the component):

```
// Create the shared object and set localpath to server root.
var my_so:SharedObject = SharedObject.getLocal("savedText", "/");
// Load saved text from the shared object into the myText_ti TextInput
   component.
myText_ti.text = my_so.data.myTextSaved;
// Assign an empty string to myText_ti if the shared object is undefined
// to prevent the text input box from displaying "undefined" when
// this script is first run.
if (myText_ti.text == undefined) {
  myText_ti.text = "";
}
// Create a listener object and function for <enter> event
```

```
var textListener:Object = new Object();
textListener.enter = function(eventObj:Object) {
  my_so.data.myTextSaved = eventObj.target.text;
  my_so.flush();
};
// Register the listener with the TextInput component instance
myText_ti.addEventListener("enter", textListener);
```

The following example saves the last frame that a user entered to a local shared object kookie:

```
// Get the kookie
var my_so:SharedObject = SharedObject.getLocal("kookie");

// Get the user of the kookie and go to the frame number saved for this
  user.
if (my_so.data.user != undefined) {
  this.user = my_so.data.user;
  this.gotoAndStop(my_so.data.frame);
}
```

The following code block is placed on each SWF file frame:

```
// On each frame, call the rememberme function to save the frame number.
function rememberme() {
  my_so.data.frame=this._currentframe;
  my_so.data.user="John";
}
```

getSize (SharedObject.getSize method)

```
public getSize() : Number
```

Gets the current size of the shared object, in bytes.

Flash calculates the size of a shared object by stepping through all of its data properties; the more data properties the object has, the longer it takes to estimate its size. Estimating object size can take significant processing time, so you may want to avoid using this method unless you have a specific need for it.

Availability: ActionScript 1.0; Flash Player 6

Returns

Number - A numeric value specifying the size of the shared object, in bytes.

Example

The following example gets the size of the shared object my_so:

```
var items_array:Array = new Array(101, 346, 483);
var currentUserIsAdmin:Boolean = true;
var currentUserName:String = "Ramona";
```

```
var my_so:SharedObject = SharedObject.getLocal("superfoo");
my_so.data.itemNumbers = items_array;
my_so.data.adminPrivileges = currentUserIsAdmin;
my_so.data.userName = currentUserName;

var soSize:Number = my_so.getSize();
trace(soSize);
```

onStatus (SharedObject.onStatus handler)

```
onStatus = function(infoObject:Object) {}
```

Invoked every time an error, warning, or informational note is posted for a shared object. If you want to respond to this event handler, you must create a function to process the information object that is generated by the shared object.

The information object has a code property containing a string that describes the result of the onStatus handler, and a level property containing a string that is either "Status" or "Error".

In addition to this onStatus handler, Flash also provides a super function called System.onStatus. If onStatus is invoked for a particular object and no function is assigned to respond to it, Flash processes a function assigned to System.onStatus, if it exists.

The following events notify you when certain SharedObject activities occur:

Code property	Level property	Meaning
SharedObject.Flush.Failed	Error	SharedObject.flush() command that returned "pending" has failed (the user did not allot additional disk space for the shared object when Flash Player showed the Local Storage Settings dialog box).
SharedObject.Flush.Success	Status	SharedObject.flush() command that returned "pending" has been successfully completed (the user allotted additional disk space for the shared object).

Availability: ActionScript 1.0; Flash Player 6

Parameters

infoObject:Object - A parameter defined according to the status message.

Example

The following example displays different messages based on whether the user chooses to allow or deny the SharedObject object instance to write to the disk.

```
var message_str:String;
this.createTextField("message_txt", this.getNextHighestDepth(), 0, 0, 300,
    22);
message_txt.html = true;
this.createTextField("status_txt", this.getNextHighestDepth(), 10, 30, 300,
    100);
status_txt.multiline = true;
status_txt.html = true;

var items_array:Array = new Array(101, 346, 483);
var currentUserIsAdmin:Boolean = true;
var currentUserName:String = "Ramona";
var my_so:SharedObject = SharedObject.getLocal("superfoo");
my_so.data.itemNumbers = items_array;
my_so.data.adminPrivileges = currentUserIsAdmin;
my_so.data.userName = currentUserName;

my_so.onStatus = function(infoObject:Object) {
    status_txt.htmlText = "<textformat tabStops='[50]'>";
    for (var i in infoObject) {
        status_txt.htmlText += "<b>"+i+"</b>"+"\t"+infoObject[i];
    }
    status_txt.htmlText += "</textformat>";
};

var flushResult = my_so.flush(1000001);
switch (flushResult) {
case 'pending' :
    message_str = "flush is pending, waiting on user interaction.";
    break;
case true :
    message_str = "flush was successful. Requested storage space approved.";
    break;
case false :
    message_str = "flush failed. User denied request for additional
    storage.";
    break;
}
message_txt.htmlText = "<a href=\"asfunction:System.showSettings,1\
"><u>"+message_str+"</u></a>";
```

The `MovieClip.getNextHighestDepth()` method used in this example requires Flash Player 7 or later. If your SWF file includes a version 2 component, use the version 2 components DepthManager class instead of the `MovieClip.getNextHighestDepth()` method.

See also

`getLocal (SharedObject.getLocal method)`, `onStatus (System.onStatus handler)`

Sound

```
Object
   |
   +-Sound
```

```
public class Sound
extends Object
```

The Sound class lets you control sound in a movie. You can add sounds to a movie clip from the library while the movie is playing and control those sounds. If you do not specify a target when you create a new Sound object, you can use the methods to control sound for the whole movie.

You must use the constructor `new Sound` to create a Sound object before calling the methods of the Sound class.

Availability: ActionScript 1.0; Flash Player 5

Property summary

Modifiers	Property	Description
	`duration:Number` [read-only]	The duration of a sound, in milliseconds.
	`id3:Object` [read-only]	Provides access to the metadata that is part of an MP3 file.
	`position:Number` [read-only]	The number of milliseconds a sound has been playing.

Properties inherited from class Object

```
constructor (Object.constructor property), __proto__ (Object.__proto__
property), prototype (Object.prototype property), __resolve
(Object.__resolve property)
```

Event summary

Event	Description
`onID3 = function() {}`	Invoked each time new ID3 data is available for an MP3 file that you load using `Sound.attachSound()` or `Sound.loadSound()`.

Event	Description
`onLoad = function(success :Boolean) {}`	Invoked automatically when a sound loads.
`onSoundComplete = function() {}`	Invoked automatically when a sound finishes playing.

Constructor summary

Signature	Description
`Sound([target:Object ])`	Creates a new Sound object for a specified movie clip.

Method summary

Modifiers	Signature	Description
	`attachSound(id:String) : Void`	Attaches the sound specified in the `id` parameter to the specified Sound object.
	`getBytesLoaded() : Number`	Returns the number of bytes loaded (streamed) for the specified Sound object.
	`getBytesTotal() : Number`	Returns the size, in bytes, of the specified Sound object.
	`getPan() : Number`	Returns the pan level set in the last `setPan()` call as an integer from -100 (left) to +100 (right).
	`getTransform() : Object`	Returns the sound transform information for the specified Sound object set with the last `Sound.setTransform()` call.
	`getVolume() : Number`	Returns the sound volume level as an integer from 0 to 100, where 0 is off and 100 is full volume.
	`loadSound(url:String , isStreaming:Boolean) : Void`	Loads an MP3 file into a Sound object.
	`setPan(value:Number) : Void`	Determines how the sound is played in the left and right channels (speakers).
	`setTransform(transfo rmObject:Object) : Void`	Sets the sound transform (or balance) information, for a Sound object.
	`setVolume(value:Numb er) : Void`	Sets the volume for the Sound object.

Modifiers	Signature	Description

	`start([secondOffset:`
	`Number],`
	`[loops:Number]) :`
	`Void`
		Starts playing the last attached sound from the beginning if no parameter is specified, or starting at the point in the sound specified by the `secondOffset` parameter.

	`stop([linkageID:Stri` `ng]) : Void`	Stops all sounds currently playing if no parameter is specified, or just the sound specified in the `idName` parameter.

Methods inherited from class Object

```
addProperty (Object.addProperty method), hasOwnProperty
(Object.hasOwnProperty method), isPropertyEnumerable
(Object.isPropertyEnumerable method), isPrototypeOf (Object.isPrototypeOf
method), registerClass (Object.registerClass method), toString
(Object.toString method), unwatch (Object.unwatch method), valueOf
(Object.valueOf method), watch (Object.watch method)
```

attachSound (Sound.attachSound method)

`public attachSound(id:String) : Void`

Attaches the sound specified in the `id` parameter to the specified Sound object. The sound must be in the library of the current SWF file and specified for export in the Linkage Properties dialog box. You must call `Sound.start()` to start playing the sound.

To make sure that the sound can be controlled from any scene in the SWF file, place the sound on the main Timeline of the SWF file.

Availability: ActionScript 1.0; Flash Player 5

Parameters

`id:String` - The identifier of an exported sound in the library. The identifier is located in the Linkage Properties dialog box.

Example

The following example attaches the sound `logoff_id` to `my_sound`. A sound in the library has the linkage identifier `logoff_id`.

```
var my_sound:Sound = new Sound();
my_sound.attachSound("logoff_id");
my_sound.start();
```

duration (Sound.duration property)

```
public duration : Number [read-only]
```

The duration of a sound, in milliseconds.

Availability: ActionScript 1.0; Flash Player 6

Example

The following example loads a sound and displays the duration of the sound file in the Output panel. Add the following ActionScript to your FLA or AS file.

```
var my_sound:Sound = new Sound();
my_sound.onLoad = function(success:Boolean) {
  var totalSeconds:Number = this.duration/1000;
  trace(this.duration+" ms ("+Math.round(totalSeconds)+" seconds)");
  var minutes:Number = Math.floor(totalSeconds/60);
  var seconds = Math.floor(totalSeconds)%60;
  if (seconds<10) {
  seconds = "0"+seconds;
  }
  trace(minutes+":"+seconds);
};
my_sound.loadSound("song1.mp3", true);
```

The following example loads several songs into a SWF file. A progress bar, created using the Drawing API, displays the loading progress. When the music starts and completes loading, information displays in the Output panel. Add the following ActionScript to your FLA or AS file.

```
var pb_height:Number = 10;
var pb_width:Number = 100;
var pb:MovieClip = this.createEmptyMovieClip("progressBar_mc",
  this.getNextHighestDepth());
pb.createEmptyMovieClip("bar_mc", pb.getNextHighestDepth());
pb.createEmptyMovieClip("vBar_mc", pb.getNextHighestDepth());
pb.createEmptyMovieClip("stroke_mc", pb.getNextHighestDepth());
pb.createTextField("pos_txt", pb.getNextHighestDepth(), 0, pb_height,
  pb_width, 22);

pb._x = 100;
pb._y = 100;

with (pb.bar_mc) {
  beginFill(0x00FF00);
  moveTo(0, 0);
  lineTo(pb_width, 0);
  lineTo(pb_width, pb_height);
  lineTo(0, pb_height);
  lineTo(0, 0);
```

```
    endFill();
    _xscale = 0;
}
with (pb.vBar_mc) {
  lineStyle(1, 0x000000);
  moveTo(0, 0);
  lineTo(0, pb_height);
}
with (pb.stroke_mc) {
  lineStyle(3, 0x000000);
  moveTo(0, 0);
  lineTo(pb_width, 0);
  lineTo(pb_width, pb_height);
  lineTo(0, pb_height);
  lineTo(0, 0);
}

var my_interval:Number;
var my_sound:Sound = new Sound();
my_sound.onLoad = function(success:Boolean) {
  if (success) {
  trace("sound loaded");
  }
};
my_sound.onSoundComplete = function() {
  clearInterval(my_interval);
  trace("Cleared interval");
}
my_sound.loadSound("song3.mp3", true);
my_interval = setInterval(updateProgressBar, 100, my_sound);

function updateProgressBar(the_sound:Sound):Void {
  var pos:Number = Math.round(the_sound.position/the_sound.duration 100);
  pb.bar_mc._xscale = pos;
  pb.vBar_mc._x = pb.bar_mc._width;
  pb.pos_txt.text = pos+"%";
}
```

The MovieClip.getNextHighestDepth() method used in this example requires Flash Player 7 or later. If your SWF file includes a version 2 component, use the version 2 components DepthManager class instead of the MovieClip.getNextHighestDepth() method.

See also

position (Sound.position property)

getBytesLoaded (Sound.getBytesLoaded method)

```
public getBytesLoaded() : Number
```

Returns the number of bytes loaded (streamed) for the specified Sound object. You can compare the value of getBytesLoaded() with the value of getBytesTotal() to determine what percentage of a sound has loaded.

Availability: ActionScript 1.0; Flash Player 6

Returns

Number - An integer indicating the number of bytes loaded.

Example

The following example dynamically creates two text fields that display the bytes that are loaded and the total number of bytes for a sound file that loads into the SWF file. A text field also displays a message when the file finishes loading. Add the following ActionScript to your FLA or AS file:

```
this.createTextField("message_txt", this.getNextHighestDepth(),
  10,10,300,22)
this.createTextField("status_txt", this.getNextHighestDepth(), 10, 50, 300,
  40);
status_txt.autoSize = true;
status_txt.multiline = true;
status_txt.border = false;

var my_sound:Sound = new Sound();
my_sound.onLoad = function(success:Boolean) {
  if (success) {
  this.start();
  message_txt.text = "Finished loading";
  }
};
my_sound.onSoundComplete = function() {
  message_txt.text = "Clearing interval";
  clearInterval(my_interval);
};
my_sound.loadSound("song2.mp3", true);
var my_interval:Number;
my_interval = setInterval(checkProgress, 100, my_sound);
function checkProgress(the_sound:Sound):Void {
  var pct:Number = Math.round(the_sound.getBytesLoaded()/
  the_sound.getBytesTotal() 100);
  var pos:Number = Math.round(the_sound.position/the_sound.duration 100);
  status_txt.text = the_sound.getBytesLoaded()+" of
  "+the_sound.getBytesTotal()+" bytes ("+pct+"%)"+newline;
  status_txt.text += the_sound.position+" of "+the_sound.duration+"
  milliseconds ("+pos+"%)"+newline;
}
```

The `MovieClip.getNextHighestDepth()` method used in this example requires Flash Player 7 or later. If your SWF file includes a version 2 component, use the version 2 components DepthManager class instead of the `MovieClip.getNextHighestDepth()` method.

See also

getBytesTotal (Sound.getBytesTotal method)

getBytesTotal (Sound.getBytesTotal method)

`public getBytesTotal() : Number`

Returns the size, in bytes, of the specified Sound object.

Availability: ActionScript 1.0; Flash Player 6

Returns

`Number` - An integer indicating the total size, in bytes, of the specified Sound object.

Example

See `Sound.getBytesLoaded()` for a sample usage of this method.

See also

getBytesLoaded (Sound.getBytesLoaded method)

getPan (Sound.getPan method)

`public getPan() : Number`

Returns the pan level set in the last `setPan()` call as an integer from -100 (left) to +100 (right). (0 sets the left and right channels equally.) The pan setting controls the left-right balance of the current and future sounds in a SWF file.

This method is cumulative with `setVolume()` or `setTransform()`.

Availability: ActionScript 1.0; Flash Player 5

Returns

`Number` - An integer.

Example

The following example creates a slider bar using the Drawing API. When the user drags the slider bar, the pan level of the loaded sound changes. The current pan level is displayed in a dynamically created text field. Add the following ActionScript to your FLA or AS file:

```
var bar_width:Number = 200;
this.createEmptyMovieClip("bar_mc", this.getNextHighestDepth());
with (bar_mc) {
  lineStyle(4, 0x000000);
  moveTo(0, 0);
  lineTo(bar_width+4, 0);
  lineStyle(0, 0x000000);
  moveTo((bar_width/2)+2, -8);
  lineTo((bar_width/2)+2, 8);
}
bar_mc._x = 100;
bar_mc._y = 100;

this.createEmptyMovieClip("knob_mc", this.getNextHighestDepth());
with (knob_mc) {
  lineStyle(0, 0x000000);
  beginFill(0xCCCCCC);
  moveTo(0, 0);
  lineTo(4, 0);
  lineTo(4, 10);
  lineTo(0, 10);
  lineTo(0, 0);
  endFill();
}
knob_mc._x = bar_mc._x+(bar_width/2);
knob_mc._y = bar_mc._y-(knob_mc._height/2);

knob_mc.left = knob_mc._x-(bar_width/2);
knob_mc.right = knob_mc._x+(bar_width/2);
knob_mc.top = knob_mc._y;
knob_mc.bottom = knob_mc._y;

knob_mc.onPress = function() {
  this.startDrag(false, this.left, this.top, this.right, this.bottom);
};
knob_mc.onRelease = function() {
  this.stopDrag();
  var multiplier:Number = 100/(this.right-this.left) 2;
  var pan:Number = (this._x-this.left-(bar_width/2)) multiplier;
  my_sound.setPan(pan);
  pan_txt.text = my_sound.getPan();
};

var my_sound:Sound = new Sound();
my_sound.loadSound("song2.mp3", true);
this.createTextField("pan_txt", this.getNextHighestDepth(), knob_mc._x,
  knob_mc._y+knob_mc._height, 20, 22);
pan_txt.selectable = false;
pan_txt.autoSize = "center";
pan_txt.text = my_sound.getPan();
```

The `MovieClip.getNextHighestDepth()` method used in this example requires Flash Player 7 or later. If your SWF file includes a version 2 component, use the version 2 components DepthManager class instead of the `MovieClip.getNextHighestDepth()` method.

See also

`setPan (Sound.setPan method)`

getTransform (Sound.getTransform method)

`public getTransform() : Object`

Returns the sound transform information for the specified Sound object set with the last `Sound.setTransform()` call.

Availability: ActionScript 1.0; Flash Player 5

Returns

`Object` - An object with properties that contain the channel percentage values for the specified sound object.

Example

The following example attaches four movie clips from a symbol in the library (linkage identifier: knob_id) that are used as sliders (or knobs) to control the sound file that loads into the SWF file. These sliders control the transform object, or balance, of the sound file. For more information, see the entry for `Sound.setTransform()`. Add the following ActionScript to your FLA or AS file:

```
var my_sound:Sound = new Sound();
my_sound.loadSound("song1.mp3", true);
var transform_obj:Object = my_sound.getTransform();

this.createEmptyMovieClip("transform_mc", this.getNextHighestDepth());
transform_mc.createTextField("transform_txt",
   transform_mc.getNextHighestDepth, 0, 8, 120, 22);
transform_mc.transform_txt.html = true;

var knob_ll:MovieClip = transform_mc.attachMovie("knob_id", "ll_mc",
   transform_mc.getNextHighestDepth(), {_x:0, _y:30});
var knob_lr:MovieClip = transform_mc.attachMovie("knob_id", "lr_mc",
   transform_mc.getNextHighestDepth(), {_x:30, _y:30});
var knob_rl:MovieClip = transform_mc.attachMovie("knob_id", "rl_mc",
   transform_mc.getNextHighestDepth(), {_x:60, _y:30});
var knob_rr:MovieClip = transform_mc.attachMovie("knob_id", "rr_mc",
   transform_mc.getNextHighestDepth(), {_x:90, _y:30});

knob_ll.top = knob_ll._y;
```

```
knob_ll.bottom = knob_ll._y+100;
knob_ll.left = knob_ll._x;
knob_ll.right = knob_ll._x;
knob_ll._y = knob_ll._y+(100-transform_obj['ll']);
knob_ll.onPress = pressKnob;
knob_ll.onRelease = releaseKnob;
knob_ll.onReleaseOutside = releaseKnob;

knob_lr.top = knob_lr._y;
knob_lr.bottom = knob_lr._y+100;
knob_lr.left = knob_lr._x;
knob_lr.right = knob_lr._x;
knob_lr._y = knob_lr._y+(100-transform_obj['lr']);
knob_lr.onPress = pressKnob;
knob_lr.onRelease = releaseKnob;
knob_lr.onReleaseOutside = releaseKnob;

knob_rl.top = knob_rl._y;
knob_rl.bottom = knob_rl._y+100;
knob_rl.left = knob_rl._x;
knob_rl.right = knob_rl._x;
knob_rl._y = knob_rl._y+(100-transform_obj['rl']);
knob_rl.onPress = pressKnob;
knob_rl.onRelease = releaseKnob;
knob_rl.onReleaseOutside = releaseKnob;

knob_rr.top = knob_rr._y;
knob_rr.bottom = knob_rr._y+100;
knob_rr.left = knob_rr._x;
knob_rr.right = knob_rr._x;
knob_rr._y = knob_rr._y+(100-transform_obj['rr']);
knob_rr.onPress = pressKnob;
knob_rr.onRelease = releaseKnob;

knob_rr.onReleaseOutside = releaseKnob;

updateTransformTxt();

function pressKnob() {
  this.startDrag(false, this.left, this.top, this.right, this.bottom);
}
function releaseKnob() {
  this.stopDrag();
  updateTransformTxt();
}
function updateTransformTxt() {
  var ll_num:Number = 30+100-knob_ll._y;
  var lr_num:Number = 30+100-knob_lr._y;
  var rl_num:Number = 30+100-knob_rl._y;
  var rr_num:Number = 30+100-knob_rr._y;
```

```
my_sound.setTransform({ll:ll_num, lr:lr_num, rl:rl_num, rr:rr_num});
transform_mc.transform_txt.htmlText = "<textformat
tabStops='[0,30,60,90]'>";
transform_mc.transform_txt.htmlText +=
ll_num+"\t"+lr_num+"\t"+rl_num+"\t"+rr_num;
transform_mc.transform_txt.htmlText += "</textformat>";
}
```

The `MovieClip.getNextHighestDepth()` method used in this example requires Flash Player 7 or later. If your SWF file includes a version 2 component, use the version 2 components DepthManager class instead of the `MovieClip.getNextHighestDepth()` method.

See also

`setTransform (Sound.setTransform method)`

getVolume (Sound.getVolume method)

`public getVolume() : Number`

Returns the sound volume level as an integer from 0 to 100, where 0 is off and 100 is full volume. The default setting is 100.

Availability: ActionScript 1.0; Flash Player 5

Returns

`Number` - An integer.

Example

The following example creates a slider using the Drawing API and a movie clip that is created at runtime. A dynamically created text field displays the current volume level of the sound playing in the SWF file. Add the following ActionScript to your AS or FLA file:

```
var my_sound:Sound = new Sound();
my_sound.loadSound("song3.mp3", true);

this.createEmptyMovieClip("knob_mc", this.getNextHighestDepth());

knob_mc.left = knob_mc._x;
knob_mc.right = knob_mc.left+100;
knob_mc.top = knob_mc._y;
knob_mc.bottom = knob_mc._y;

knob_mc._x = my_sound.getVolume();

with (knob_mc) {
  lineStyle(0, 0x000000);
  beginFill(0xCCCCCC);
```

```
moveTo(0, 0);
lineTo(4, 0);
lineTo(4, 18);
lineTo(0, 18);
lineTo(0, 0);
endFill();
}

knob_mc.createTextField("volume_txt", knob_mc.getNextHighestDepth(),
    knob_mc._width+4, 0, 30, 22);
knob_mc.volume_txt.text = my_sound.getVolume();

knob_mc.onPress = function() {
    this.startDrag(false, this.left, this.top, this.right, this.bottom);
    this.isDragging = true;
};
knob_mc.onMouseMove = function() {
    if (this.isDragging) {
    this.volume_txt.text = this._x;
    }
}
knob_mc.onRelease = function() {
    this.stopDrag();
    this.isDragging = false;
    my_sound.setVolume(this._x);

};
```

The `MovieClip.getNextHighestDepth()` method used in this example requires Flash Player 7 or later. If your SWF file includes a version 2 component, use the version 2 components DepthManager class instead of the `MovieClip.getNextHighestDepth()` method.

See also

`setVolume (Sound.setVolume method)`

id3 (Sound.id3 property)

`public id3 : Object [read-only]`

Provides access to the metadata that is part of an MP3 file.

MP3 sound files can contain ID3 tags, which provide metadata about the file. If an MP3 sound that you load using `Sound.attachSound()` or `Sound.loadSound()` contains ID3 tags, you can query these properties. Only ID3 tags that use the UTF-8 character set are supported.

Flash Player 6 (6.0.40.0) and later use the Sound.id3 property to support ID3 1.0 and ID3 1.1 tags. Flash Player 7 adds support for ID3 2.0 tags, specifically 2.3 and 2.4. The following table lists the standard ID3 2.0 tags and the type of content the tags represent; you query them in the format *my_sound*.id3.COMM, *my_sound*.id3.TIME, and so on. MP3 files can contain tags other than those in this table; Sound.id3 provides access to those tags as well.

Property	Description
TFLT	File type
TIME	Time
TIT1	Content group description
TIT2	Title/song name/content description
TIT3	Subtitle/description refinement
TKEY	Initial key
TLAN	Languages
TLEN	Length
TMED	Media type
TOAL	Original album/movie/show title
TOFN	Original filename
TOLY	Original lyricists/text writers
TOPE	Original artists/performers
TORY	Original release year
TOWN	File owner/licensee
TPE1	Lead performers/soloists
TPE2	Band/orchestra/accompaniment
TPE3	Conductor/performer refinement
TPE4	Interpreted, remixed, or otherwise modified by
TPOS	Part of a set
TPUB	Publisher

Property	Description
TRCK	Track number/position in set
TRDA	Recording dates
TRSN	Internet radio station name
TRSO	Internet radio station owner
TSIZ	Size
TSRC	ISRC (international standard recording code)
TSSE	Software/hardware and settings used for encoding
TYER	Year
WXXX	URL link frame

Flash Player 6 supported several ID31.0 tags. If these tags are in not in the MP3 file, but corresponding ID3 2.0 tags are, the ID3 2.0 tags are copied into the ID3 1.0 properties, as shown in the following table. This process provides backward compatibility with scripts that you may have written already that read ID3 1.0 properties.

ID3 2.0 tag	Corresponding ID3 1.0 property
COMM	Sound.id3.comment
TALB	Sound.id3.album
TCON	Sound.id3.genre
TIT2	Sound.id3.songname
TPE1	Sound.id3.artist
TRCK	Sound.id3.track
TYER	Sound.id3.year

Availability: ActionScript 1.0; Flash Player 6 - Behavior updated in Flash Player 7.

Example

The following example traces the ID3 properties of song.mp3 to the Output panel:

```
var my_sound:Sound = new Sound();
my_sound.onID3 = function(){
   for( var prop in my_sound.id3 ){
   trace( prop + " : "+ my_sound.id3[prop] );
   }
```

```
}
my_sound.loadSound("song.mp3", false);
```

See also

```
attachSound (Sound.attachSound method), loadSound (Sound.loadSound method)
```

loadSound (Sound.loadSound method)

```
public loadSound(url:String, isStreaming:Boolean) : Void
```

Loads an MP3 file into a Sound object. You can use the `isStreaming` parameter to indicate whether the sound is an event or a streaming sound.

Event sounds are completely loaded before they play. They are managed by the ActionScript Sound class and respond to all methods and properties of this class.

Streaming sounds play while they are downloading. Playback begins when sufficient data has been received to start the decompressor.

All MP3s (event or streaming) loaded with this method are saved in the browser's file cache on the user's system.

When using this method, consider the Flash Player security model.

For Flash Player 8:

- `Sound.loadSound()` is not allowed if the calling SWF file is in the local-with-file-system sandbox and the sound is in a network sandbox.
- Access from the local-trusted or local-with-networking sandbox requires permission from website via a cross-domain policy file.

For Flash Player 7 and later:

- Websites can permit access to a resource from requesters in different domains via a cross-domain policy file.

For more information, see the following:

- Chapter 17, "Understanding Security," in *Learning ActionScript 2.0 in Flash*
- The Flash Player 8 Security white paper at http://www.macromedia.com/go/fp8_security
- The Flash Player 8 Security-Related API white paper at http://www.macromedia.com/go/fp8_security_apis

Availability: ActionScript 1.0; Flash Player 6

Parameters

`url:String` - The location on a server of an MP3 sound file.

`isStreaming:Boolean` - A Boolean value that indicates whether the sound is a streaming sound (`true`) or an event sound (`false`).

Example

The following example loads an event sound, which cannot play until it is fully loaded:

```
var my_sound:Sound = new Sound();
my_sound.loadSound("song1.mp3", false);
```

The following example loads a streaming sound:

```
var my_sound:Sound = new Sound();
my_sound.loadSound("song1.mp3", true);
```

See also

`onLoad (Sound.onLoad handler)`

onID3 (Sound.onID3 handler)

`onID3 = function() {}`

Invoked each time new ID3 data is available for an MP3 file that you load using `Sound.attachSound()` or `Sound.loadSound()`. This handler provides access to ID3 data without polling. If both ID3 1.0 and ID3 2.0 tags are present in a file, this handler is called twice.

Availability: ActionScript 1.0; Flash Player 7

Example

The following example displays the ID3 properties of `song1.mp3` to an instance of the DataGrid component. Add a DataGrid with the instance name `id3_dg` to your document, and add the following ActionScript to your FLA or AS file:

```
import mx.controls.gridclasses.DataGridColumn;
var id3_dg:mx.controls.DataGrid;
id3_dg.move(0, 0);
id3_dg.setSize(Stage.width, Stage.height);
var property_dgc:DataGridColumn = id3_dg.addColumn(new
  DataGridColumn("property"));
property_dgc.width = 100;
property_dgc.headerText = "ID3 Property";
var value_dgc:DataGridColumn = id3_dg.addColumn(new
  DataGridColumn("value"));
value_dgc.width = id3_dg._width-property_dgc.width;
value_dgc.headerText = "ID3 Value";
```

```
var my_sound:Sound = new Sound();
my_sound.onID3 = function() {
trace("onID3 called at "+getTimer()+" ms.");
for (var prop in this.id3) {
id3_dg.addItem({property:prop, value:this.id3[prop]});
}
};
my_sound.loadSound("song1.mp3", true);
```

See also

`attachSound` (Sound.attachSound method), `id3` (Sound.id3 property), `loadSound`
(Sound.loadSound method)

onLoad (Sound.onLoad handler)

`onLoad = function(success:Boolean) {}`

Invoked automatically when a sound loads. You must create a function that executes when the
this handler is invoked. You can use either an anonymous function or a named function (for
an example of each, see `Sound.onSoundComplete`). You should define this handler before you
call `mySound.loadSound()`.

Availability: ActionScript 1.0; Flash Player 6

Parameters

`success:Boolean` - A Boolean value of `true` if `my_sound` has been loaded successfully, `false`
otherwise.

Example

The following example creates a new Sound object, and loads a sound. Loading the sound is
handled by the `onLoad` handler, which allows you to start the song after it is successfully
loaded. Create a new FLA file, and add the following ActionScript to your FLA or AS file. For
this example to work, you must have an MP3 called `song1.mp3` in the same directory as your
FLA or AS file.

```
this.createTextField("status_txt", this.getNextHighestDepth(), 0,0,100,22);

// create a new Sound object
var my_sound:Sound = new Sound();
// if the sound loads, play it; if not, trace failure loading
my_sound.onLoad = function(success:Boolean) {
if (success) {
my_sound.start();
status_txt.text = "Sound loaded";
```

```
} else (
status_txt.text = "Sound failed";
}
};
// load the sound
my_sound.loadSound("song1.mp3", true);
```

The `MovieClip.getNextHighestDepth()` method used in this example requires Flash Player 7 or later. If your SWF file includes a version 2 component, use the version 2 components DepthManager class instead of the `MovieClip.getNextHighestDepth()` method.

See also

loadSound (Sound.loadSound method)

onSoundComplete (Sound.onSoundComplete handler)

```
onSoundComplete = function() {}
```

Invoked automatically when a sound finishes playing. You can use this handler to trigger events in a SWF file when a sound finishes playing.

You must create a function that executes when this handler is invoked. You can use either an anonymous function or a named function.

Availability: ActionScript 1.0; Flash Player 6

Example

Usage 1: The following example uses an anonymous function:

```
var my_sound:Sound = new Sound();
my_sound.attachSound("mySoundID");
my_sound.onSoundComplete = function() {
trace("mySoundID completed");
};
my_sound.start();
```

Usage 2: The following example uses a named function:

```
function callback1() {
trace("mySoundID completed");
}
var my_sound:Sound = new Sound();
my_sound.attachSound("mySoundID");
my_sound.onSoundComplete = callback1;
my_sound.start();
```

See also

onLoad (Sound.onLoad handler)

position (Sound.position property)

`public position : Number [read-only]`

The number of milliseconds a sound has been playing. If the sound is looped, the position is reset to 0 at the beginning of each loop.

Availability: ActionScript 1.0; Flash Player 6

Example

See `Sound.duration` for a sample usage of this property.

See also

`duration (Sound.duration property)`

setPan (Sound.setPan method)

`public setPan(value:Number) : Void`

Determines how the sound is played in the left and right channels (speakers). For mono sounds, *pan* determines which speaker (left or right) the sound plays through.

Availability: ActionScript 1.0; Flash Player 5

Parameters

`value:Number` - An integer specifying the left-right balance for a sound. The range of valid values is -100 to 100, where -100 uses only the left channel, 100 uses only the right channel, and 0 balances the sound evenly between the two channels.

Example

See `Sound.getPan()` for a sample usage of this method.

See also

`attachSound (Sound.attachSound method)`, `getPan (Sound.getPan method)`, `setTransform (Sound.setTransform method)`, `setVolume (Sound.setVolume method)`, `start (Sound.start method)`

setTransform (Sound.setTransform method)

`public setTransform(transformObject:Object) : Void`

Sets the sound transform (or balance) information, for a Sound object.

The soundTransformObject parameter is an object that you create using the constructor method of the generic Object class with parameters specifying how the sound is distributed to the left and right channels (speakers).

Sounds use a considerable amount of disk space and memory. Because stereo sounds use twice as much data as mono sounds, it is generally best to use 22-KHz 6-bit mono sounds. You can use setTransform() to play mono sounds as stereo, play stereo sounds as mono, and to add interesting effects to sounds.

The properties for the soundTransformObject are as follows:

ll - A percentage value specifying how much of the left input to play in the left speaker (0-100).

lr - A percentage value specifying how much of the right input to play in the left speaker (0-100).

rr - A percentage value specifying how much of the right input to play in the right speaker (0-100).

rl - A percentage value specifying how much of the left input to play in the right speaker (0-100).

The net result of the parameters is represented by the following formula:

```
leftOutput = left_input ~ ll + right_input ~ lr
rightOutput = right_input ~ rr + left_input ~ rl
```

The values for left_input or right_input are determined by the type (stereo or mono) of sound in your SWF file.

Stereo sounds divide the sound input evenly between the left and right speakers and have the following transform settings by default:

```
ll = 100
lr = 0
rr = 100
rl = 0
```

Mono sounds play all sound input in the left speaker and have the following transform settings by default:

```
ll = 100
lr = 100
rr = 0
rl = 0
```

Availability: ActionScript 1.0; Flash Player 5

Parameters

transformObject:Object - An object created with the constructor for the generic Object class.

Example

The following example illustrates a setting that can be achieved by using setTransform(), but cannot be achieved by using setVolume() or setPan(), even if they are combined.

The following code creates a new soundTransformObject object and sets its properties so that sound from both channels will play only in the left channel.

```
var mySoundTransformObject:Object = new Object();
mySoundTransformObject.ll = 100;
mySoundTransformObject.lr = 100;
mySoundTransformObject.rr = 0;
mySoundTransformObject.rl = 0;
```

To apply the soundTransformObject object to a Sound object, you then need to pass the object to the Sound object using setTransform() as follows:

```
my_sound.setTransform(mySoundTransformObject);
```

The following example plays a stereo sound as mono; the soundTransformObjectMono object has the following parameters:

```
var mySoundTransformObjectMono:Object = new Object();
mySoundTransformObjectMono.ll = 50;
mySoundTransformObjectMono.lr = 50;
mySoundTransformObjectMono.rr = 50;
mySoundTransformObjectMono.rl = 50;
my_sound.setTransform(mySoundTransformObjectMono);
```

This example plays the left channel at half capacity and adds the rest of the left channel to the right channel; the soundTransformObjectHalf object has the following parameters:

```
var mySoundTransformObjectHalf:Object = new Object();
mySoundTransformObjectHalf.ll = 50;
mySoundTransformObjectHalf.lr = 0;
mySoundTransformObjectHalf.rr = 100;
mySoundTransformObjectHalf.rl = 50;
my_sound.setTransform(mySoundTransformObjectHalf);

var mySoundTransformObjectHalf:Object = {ll:50, lr:0, rr:100, rl:50};
```

Also see the example for Sound.getTransform().

See also

Object, getTransform (Sound.getTransform method)

setVolume (Sound.setVolume method)

```
public setVolume(value:Number) : Void
```

Sets the volume for the Sound object.

Availability: ActionScript 1.0; Flash Player 5

Parameters

`value:Number` - A number from 0 to 100 representing a volume level. 100 is full volume and 0 is no volume. The default setting is 100.

Example

See `Sound.getVolume()` for a sample usage of this method.

See also

`setPan (Sound.setPan method)`, `setTransform (Sound.setTransform method)`

Sound constructor

`public Sound([target:Object])`

Creates a new Sound object for a specified movie clip. If you do not specify a target instance, the Sound object controls all of the sounds in the movie.

Availability: ActionScript 1.0; Flash Player 5

Parameters

`target:Object` [optional] - The movie clip instance on which the Sound object operates.

Example

The following example creates a new Sound object called `global_sound`. The second line calls `setVolume()` and adjusts the volume on all sounds in the movie to 50%.

```
var global_sound:Sound = new Sound();
global_sound.setVolume(50);
```

The following example creates a new Sound object, passes it the target movie clip *my_mc*, and calls the `start` method, which starts any sound in *my_mc*.

```
var movie_sound:Sound = new Sound(my_mc);
movie_sound.start();
```

start (Sound.start method)

`public start([secondOffset:Number], [loops:Number]) : Void`

Starts playing the last attached sound from the beginning if no parameter is specified, or starting at the point in the sound specified by the `secondOffset` parameter.

Availability: ActionScript 1.0; Flash Player 5

Parameters

`secondOffset:Number` [optional] - A parameter that lets you start playing the sound at a specific point. For example, if you have a 30-second sound and want the sound to start playing in the middle, specify 15 for the `secondOffset` parameter. The sound is not delayed 15 seconds, but rather starts playing at the 15-second mark.

`loops:Number` [optional] - A parameter that lets you specify the number of times the sound should play consecutively. This parameter is not available if the sound is a streaming sound.

Example

The following example creates a new Sound object, and loads a sound. Loading the sound is handled by the `onLoad` handler, which allows you to start the song after it is successfully loaded. Then the sound starts playing using the `start()` method. Create a new FLA file, and add the following ActionScript to your FLA or AS file. For this example to work, you must have an MP3 called song1.mp3 in the same directory as your FLA or AS file.

```
this.createTextField("status_txt", this.getNextHighestDepth(), 0,0,100,22);

// create a new Sound object
var my_sound:Sound = new Sound();
// if the sound loads, play it; if not, trace failure loading
my_sound.onLoad = function(success:Boolean) {
  if (success) {
  my_sound.start();
  status_txt.text = "Sound loaded";
  } else {
  status_txt.text = "Sound failed";
  }
};
// load the sound
my_sound.loadSound("song1.mp3", true);
```

The `MovieClip.getNextHighestDepth()` method used in this example requires Flash Player 7 or later. If your SWF file includes a version 2 component, use the version 2 components DepthManager class instead of the `MovieClip.getNextHighestDepth()` method.

See also

stop (Sound.stop method)

stop (Sound.stop method)

`public stop([linkageID:String]) : Void`

Stops all sounds currently playing if no parameter is specified, or just the sound specified in the `idName` parameter.

Availability: ActionScript 1.0; Flash Player 5

Parameters

`linkageID:String` [optional] - A parameter specifying a specific sound to stop playing. The `idName` parameter must be enclosed in quotation marks (" ").

Example

The following example uses two buttons, `stop_btn` and `play_btn`, to control the playback of a sound that loads into a SWF file. Add two buttons to your document and add the following ActionScript to your FLA or AS file:

```
var my_sound:Sound = new Sound();
my_sound.loadSound("song1.mp3", true);

stop_btn.onRelease = function() {
  trace("sound stopped");
  my_sound.stop();
};
play_btn.onRelease = function() {
  trace("sound started");
  my_sound.start();
};
```

See also

`start (Sound.start method)`

Stage

```
Object
  |
  +-Stage
```

```
public class Stage
extends Object
```

The Stage class is a top-level class whose methods, properties, and handlers you can access without using a constructor. Use the methods and properties of this class to access and manipulate information about the boundaries of a SWF file.

Availability: ActionScript 1.0; Flash Player 5 - (became a native object in Flash Player 6, which improved performance significantly).

Property summary

Modifiers	Property	Description
static	align:String	Indicates the current alignment of the SWF file in the player or browser.
static	height:Number	Property (read-only); indicates the current height, in pixels, of the Stage.
static	scaleMode:String	Indicates the current scaling of the SWF file within Flash Player.
static	showMenu:Boolean	Specifies whether to show or hide the default items in the Flash Player context menu.
static	width:Number	Property (read-only); indicates the current width, in pixels, of the Stage.

Properties inherited from class Object

constructor (Object.constructor property), __proto__ (Object.__proto__ property), prototype (Object.prototype property), __resolve (Object.__resolve property)

Event summary

Event	Description
onResize = function() {}	Invoked when Stage.scaleMode is set to noScale and the SWF file is resized.

Method summary

Modifiers	Signature	Description
static	`addListener(listener :Object) : Void`	Detects when a SWF file is resized (but only if `Stage.scaleMode = "noScale"`).
static	`removeListener(listener:Object) : Boolean`	Removes a listener object created with addListener().

Methods inherited from class Object

```
addProperty (Object.addProperty method),hasOwnProperty
(Object.hasOwnProperty method),isPropertyEnumerable
(Object.isPropertyEnumerable method),isPrototypeOf (Object.isPrototypeOf
method),registerClass (Object.registerClass method),toString
(Object.toString method),unwatch (Object.unwatch method),valueOf
(Object.valueOf method),watch (Object.watch method)
```

addListener (Stage.addListener method)

```
public static addListener(listener:Object) : Void
```

Detects when a SWF file is resized (but only if `Stage.scaleMode = "noScale"`). The `addListener()` method doesn't work with the default movie clip scaling setting (`showAll`) or other scaling settings (`exactFit` and `noBorder`).

To use `addListener()`, you must first create a *listener object*. Stage listener objects receive notification from `Stage.onResize`.

Availability: ActionScript 1.0; Flash Player 6

Parameters

`listener:Object` - An object that listens for a callback notification from the `Stage.onResize` event.

Example

This example creates a new listener object called `stageListener`. It then uses `stageListener` to call `onResize` and define a function that will be called when `onResize` is triggered. Finally, the code adds the `stageListener` object to the callback list of the Stage object. Listener objects allow multiple objects to listen for resize notifications.

```
this.createTextField("stageSize_txt", this.getNextHighestDepth(), 10, 10,
    100, 22);
var stageListener:Object = new Object();
stageListener.onResize = function() {
```

```
    stageSize_txt.text = "w:"+Stage.width+", h:"+Stage.height;
};
Stage.scaleMode = "noScale";
Stage.addListener(stageListener);
```

See also

onResize (Stage.onResize event listener), removeListener
(Stage.removeListener method)

align (Stage.align property)

public static align : String

Indicates the current alignment of the SWF file in the player or browser.

The following table lists the values for the align property. Any value not listed here centers the SWF file in Flash player or browser area, which is the default setting.

Value	Vertical	Horizontal
"T"	top	center
"B"	bottom	center
"L"	center	left
"R"	center	right
"TL"	top	left
"TR"	top	right
"BL"	bottom	left
"BR"	bottom	right

Availability: ActionScript 1.0; Flash Player 6

Example

The following example demonstrates different alignments of the SWF file. Add a ComboBox instance to your document with the instance name `stageAlign_cb`. Add the following ActionScript to your FLA or AS file:

```
var stageAlign_cb:mx.controls.ComboBox;
stageAlign_cb.dataProvider = ['T', 'B', 'L', 'R', 'TL', 'TR', 'BL', 'BR'];
var cbListener:Object = new Object();
cbListener.change = function(evt:Object) {
  var align:String = evt.target.selectedItem;
  Stage.align = align;
};
stageAlign_cb.addEventListener("change", cbListener);
Stage.scaleMode = "noScale";
```

Select different alignment settings from the ComboBox.

height (Stage.height property)

```
public static height : Number
```

Property (read-only); indicates the current height, in pixels, of the Stage. When the value of `Stage.scaleMode` is noScale, the height property represents the height of Flash Player. When the value of `Stage.scaleMode` is not noScale, height represents the height of the SWF file.

Availability: ActionScript 1.0; Flash Player 6

Example

This example creates a new listener object called `stageListener`. It then uses `myListener` to call `onResize` and define a function that will be called when `onResize` is triggered. Finally, the code adds the `myListener` object to the callback list of the Stage object. Listener objects allow multiple objects to listen for resize notifications.

```
this.createTextField("stageSize_txt", this.getNextHighestDepth(), 10, 10,
  100, 22);
var stageListener:Object = new Object();
stageListener.onResize = function() {
  stageSize_txt.text = "w:"+Stage.width+", h:"+Stage.height;
};
Stage.scaleMode = "noScale";
Stage.addListener(stageListener);
```

See also

align (Stage.align property), scaleMode (Stage.scaleMode property), width (Stage.width property)

onResize (Stage.onResize event listener)

```
onResize = function() {}
```

Invoked when `Stage.scaleMode` is set to noScale and the SWF file is resized. You can use this event handler to write a function that lays out the objects on the Stage when a SWF file is resized.

```
myListener.onResize = function()[
 // your statements here
 }
```

Availability: ActionScript 1.0; Flash Player 6

Example

The following example displays a message in the Output panel when the Stage is resized:

```
Stage.scaleMode = "noScale"
var myListener:Object = new Object();
myListener.onResize = function () {
   trace("Stage size is now " + Stage.width + " by " + Stage.height);
}
Stage.addListener(myListener);
// later, call Stage.removeListener(myListener)
```

See also

scaleMode (Stage.scaleMode property), addListener (Stage.addListener method), removeListener (Stage.removeListener method)

removeListener (Stage.removeListener method)

```
public static removeListener(listener:Object) : Boolean
```

Removes a listener object created with addListener().

Availability: ActionScript 1.0; Flash Player 6

Parameters

listener:Object - An object added to an object's callback list with addListener().

Returns

Boolean - A Boolean value.

Example

The following example displays the Stage dimensions in a dynamically created text field. When you resize the Stage, the values in the text field update. Create a button with an instance name remove_btn. Add the following ActionScript to Frame 1 of the Timeline.

```
this.createTextField("stageSize_txt", this.getNextHighestDepth(), 10, 10,
  100, 22);
stageSize_txt.autoSize = true;
stageSize_txt.border = true;
var stageListener:Object = new Object();
stageListener.onResize = function() {
  stageSize_txt.text = "w:"+Stage.width+", h:"+Stage.height;
};
Stage.addListener(stageListener);

remove_btn.onRelease = function() {
  stageSize_txt.text = "Removing Stage listener...";
  Stage.removeListener(stageListener);
}
```

Select Control > Test Movie to test this example. The values you see in the text field are updated when you resize the testing environment. When you click remove_btn, the listener is removed and the values are no longer updated in the text field.

See also

addListener (Stage.addListener method)

scaleMode (Stage.scaleMode property)

public static scaleMode : String

Indicates the current scaling of the SWF file within Flash Player. The scaleMode property forces the SWF file into a specific scaling mode. By default, the SWF file uses the HTML parameters set in the Publish Settings dialog box.

The scaleMode property can use the values "exactFit", "showAll", "noBorder", and "noScale". Any other value sets the scaleMode property to the default "showAll".

- showAll (Default) makes the entire Flash content visible in the specified area without distortion while maintaining the original aspect ratio of the. Borders can appear on two sides of the application.

- noBorder scales the Flash content to fill the specified area, without distortion but possibly with some cropping, while maintaining the original aspect ratio of the application.

- exactFit makes the entire Flash content visible in the specified area without trying to preserve the original aspect ratio. Distortion can occur.

- noScale makes the size of the Flash content fixed, so that it remains unchanged even as the size of the player window changes. Cropping may occur if the player window is smaller than the Flash content.

> **NOTE** The default setting is showAll, except when in test movie mode, where the default setting is noScale.

Availability: ActionScript 1.0; Flash Player 6

Example

The following example demonstrates various scale settings for the SWF file. Add a ComboBox instance to your document with the instance name scaleMode_cb. Add the following ActionScript to your FLA or AS file:

```
var scaleMode_cb:mx.controls.ComboBox;
scaleMode_cb.dataProvider = ["showAll", "exactFit", "noBorder", "noScale"];
var cbListener:Object = new Object();
cbListener.change = function(evt:Object) {
  var scaleMode_str:String = evt.target.selectedItem;
  Stage.scaleMode = scaleMode_str;
};
scaleMode_cb.addEventListener("change", cbListener);
```

To view another example, see the stagesize.fla file in the ActionScript samples Folder. The following list provides typical paths to the ActionScript samples Folder:

- Windows: *boot drive*\Program Files\Macromedia\Flash 8\Samples and Tutorials\Samples\ActionScript
- Macintosh: *Macintosh HD*/Applications/Macromedia Flash 8/Samples and Tutorials/Samples/ActionScript

showMenu (Stage.showMenu property)

```
public static showMenu : Boolean
```

Specifies whether to show or hide the default items in the Flash Player context menu. If showMenu is set to true (the default), all context menu items appear. If showMenu is set to false, only Settings and About Macromedia Flash Player items appear.

Availability: ActionScript 1.0; Flash Player 6

Example

The following example creates a clickable text link that lets the user enable and disable the Flash Player context menu.

```
this.createTextField("showMenu_txt", this.getNextHighestDepth(), 10, 10,
    100, 22);
showMenu_txt.html = true;
showMenu_txt.autoSize = true;
showMenu_txt.htmlText = "<a
    href=\"asfunction:toggleMenu\"><u>Stage.showMenu = "+Stage.showMenu+"</
    u></a>";
function toggleMenu() {
    Stage.showMenu = !Stage.showMenu;
    showMenu_txt.htmlText = "<a
    href=\"asfunction:toggleMenu\"><u>Stage.showMenu = "+Stage.showMenu+"</
    u></a>";
}
```

See also

`ContextMenu, ContextMenuItem`

width (Stage.width property)

`public static width : Number`

Property (read-only); indicates the current width, in pixels, of the Stage. When the value of `Stage.scaleMode` is `"noScale"`, the `width` property represents the width of Flash Player. This means that `Stage.width` will vary as you resize the player window. When the value of `Stage.scaleMode` is not `"noScale"`, `width` represents the width of the SWF file as set at author-time in the Document Properties dialog box. This means that the value of `width` will stay constant as you resize the player window.

Availability: ActionScript 1.0; Flash Player 6

Example

This example creates a new listener object called `stageListener`. It then uses `stageListener` to call `onResize` and define a function that will be called when `onResize` is triggered. Finally, the code adds the `stageListener` object to the callback list of the Stage object. Listener objects allow multiple objects to listen for resize notifications.

```
this.createTextField("stageSize_txt", this.getNextHighestDepth(), 10, 10,
    100, 22);
var stageListener:Object = new Object();
stageListener.onResize = function() {
    stageSize_txt.text = "w:"+Stage.width+", h:"+Stage.height;
};
```

```
Stage.scaleMode = "noScale";
Stage.addListener(stageListener);
```

See also

align (Stage.align property), height (Stage.height property), scaleMode
(Stage.scaleMode property)

String

```
Object
  |
  +-String
```

```
public class String
extends Object
```

The String class is a wrapper for the string primitive data type, and provides methods and
properties that let you manipulate primitive string value types. You can convert the value of
any object into a string using the String() function.

All the methods of the String class, except for concat(), fromCharCode(), slice(), and
substr(), are generic, which means the methods call toString() before performing their
operations, and you can use these methods with other non-String objects.

Because all string indexes are zero-based, the index of the last character for any string x is
x.length - 1.

You can call any of the methods of the String class using the constructor method new String
or using a string literal value. If you specify a string literal, the ActionScript interpreter
automatically converts it to a temporary String object, calls the method, and then discards the
temporary String object. You can also use the String.length property with a string literal.

Do not confuse a string literal with a String object. In the following example, the first line of
code creates the string literal first_string, and the second line of code creates the String
object second_string:

```
var first_string:String = "foo"
var second_string:String = new String("foo")
```

Use string literals unless you specifically need to use a String object.

Availability: ActionScript 1.0; Flash Player 5 - (became a native object in Flash Player 6,
which improved performance significantly).

Property summary

Modifiers	Property	Description
	`length:Number`	An integer specifying the number of characters in the specified String object.

Properties inherited from class Object

```
constructor (Object.constructor property), __proto__ (Object.__proto__
property), prototype (Object.prototype property), __resolve
(Object.__resolve property)
```

Constructor summary

Signature	Description
`String(value:String)`	Creates a new String object.

Method summary

Modifiers	Signature	Description
	`charAt(index:Number) : String`	Returns the character in the position specified by the parameter `index`.
	`charCodeAt(index:Number) : Number`	Returns a 16-bit integer from 0 to 65535 that represents the character specified by `index`.
	`concat(value:Object) : String`	Combines the value of the String object with the parameters and returns the newly formed string; the original value, `my_str`, is unchanged.
`static`	`fromCharCode() : String`	Returns a string comprising the characters represented by the Unicode values in the parameters.
	`indexOf(value:String , [startIndex:Number]) : Number`	Searches the string and returns the position of the first occurrence of `value` found at or after `startIndex` within the calling string.
	`lastIndexOf(value:String, [startIndex:Number]) : Number`	Searches the string from right to left and returns the index of the last occurrence of `value` found before `startIndex` within the calling string.
	`slice(start:Number, end:Number) : String`	Returns a string that includes the `start` character and all characters up to, but not including, the `end` character.

Modifiers	Signature	Description
	`split(delimiter:Stri ng, [limit:Number]) : Array`	Splits a String object into substrings by breaking it wherever the specified `delimiter` parameter occurs and returns the substrings in an array.
	`substr(start:Number, length:Number) : String`	Returns the characters in a string from the index specified in the `start` parameter through the number of characters specified in the `length` parameter.
	`substring(start:Numb er, end:Number) : String`	Returns a string comprising the characters between the points specified by the `start` and `end` parameters.
	`toLowerCase() : String`	Returns a copy of the `String` object, with all uppercase characters converted to lowercase.
	`toString() : String`	Returns an object's properties as strings regardless of whether the properties are strings.
	`toUpperCase() : String`	Returns a copy of the String object, with all lowercase characters converted to uppercase.
	`valueOf() : String`	Returns the primitive value of a String instance.

Methods inherited from class Object

```
addProperty (Object.addProperty method), hasOwnProperty
(Object.hasOwnProperty method), isPropertyEnumerable
(Object.isPropertyEnumerable method), isPrototypeOf (Object.isPrototypeOf
method), registerClass (Object.registerClass method), toString
(Object.toString method), unwatch (Object.unwatch method), valueOf
(Object.valueOf method), watch (Object.watch method)
```

charAt (String.charAt method)

`public charAt(index:Number) : String`

Returns the character in the position specified by the parameter `index`. If `index` is not a number from 0 to `string.length - 1`, an empty string is returned.

This method is similar to `String.charCodeAt()` except that the returned value is a character, not a 16-bit integer character code.

Availability: ActionScript 1.0; Flash Player 5

Parameters

`index:Number` - An integer specifying the position of a character in the string. The first character is indicated by 0, and the last character is indicated by `my_str.length-1`.

Returns

String - The character at the specified index. Or an empty String if the specified index is outside the range of this String's indeces.

Example

In the following example, this method is called on the first letter of the string "Chris":

```
var my_str:String = "Chris";
var firstChar_str:String = my_str.charAt(0);
trace(firstChar_str); // output: C
```

See also

charCodeAt (String.charCodeAt method)

charCodeAt (String.charCodeAt method)

```
public charCodeAt(index:Number) : Number
```

Returns a 16-bit integer from 0 to 65535 that represents the character specified by index. If index is not a number from 0 to string.length - 1, NaN is returned.

This method is similar to String.charAt() except that the returned value is a 16-bit integer character code, not a character.

Availability: ActionScript 1.0; Flash Player 5

Parameters

index:Number - An integer that specifies the position of a character in the string. The first character is indicated by 0, and the last character is indicated by my_str.length - 1.

Returns

Number - An integer that represents the character specified by index.

Example

In the following example, this method is called on the first letter of the string "Chris":

```
var my_str:String = "Chris";
var firstChar_num:Number = my_str.charCodeAt(0);
trace(firstChar_num); // output: 67
```

See also

charAt (String.charAt method)

concat (String.concat method)

```
public concat(value:Object) : String
```

Combines the value of the String object with the parameters and returns the newly formed string; the original value, my_str, is unchanged.

Availability: ActionScript 1.0; Flash Player 5

Parameters

`value:Object` - value1[,...valueN] Zero or more values to be concatenated.

Returns

`String` - A string.

Example

The following example creates two strings and combines them using `String.concat()`:

```
var stringA:String = "Hello";
var stringB:String = "World";
var combinedAB:String = stringA.concat(" ", stringB);
trace(combinedAB); // output: Hello World
```

fromCharCode (String.fromCharCode method)

```
public static fromCharCode() : String
```

Returns a string comprising the characters represented by the Unicode values in the parameters.

Availability: ActionScript 1.0; Flash Player 5

Returns

`String` - A string value of the specified Unicode character codes.

Example

The following example uses `fromCharCode()` to insert an @ character in the e-mail address:

```
var address_str:String = "dog"+String.fromCharCode(64)+"house.net";
trace(address_str); // output: dog@house.net
```

indexOf (String.indexOf method)

```
public indexOf(value:String, [startIndex:Number]) : Number
```

Searches the string and returns the position of the first occurrence of `value` found at or after `startIndex` within the calling string. This index is zero-based, meaning that the first character in a string is considered to be at index 0--not index 1. If `value` is not found, the method returns -1.

Availability: ActionScript 1.0; Flash Player 5

Parameters

`value:String` - A string; the substring to search for.

`startIndex:Number` [optional] - An integer specifying the starting index of the search.

Returns

`Number` - The position of the first occurrence of the specified substring or -1.

Example

The following examples use `indexOf()` to return the index of characters and substrings:

```
var searchString:String = "Lorem ipsum dolor sit amet.";
var index:Number;

index = searchString.indexOf("L");
trace(index); // output: 0

index = searchString.indexOf("l");
trace(index); // output: 14

index = searchString.indexOf("i");
trace(index); // output: 6

index = searchString.indexOf("ipsum");
trace(index); // output: 6

index = searchString.indexOf("i", 7);
trace(index); // output: 19

index = searchString.indexOf("z");
trace(index); // output: -1
```

See also

```
lastIndexOf (String.lastIndexOf method)
```

lastIndexOf (String.lastIndexOf method)

```
public lastIndexOf(value:String, [startIndex:Number]) : Number
```

Searches the string from right to left and returns the index of the last occurrence of `value` found before `startIndex` within the calling string. This index is zero-based, meaning that the first character in a string is considered to be at index 0--not index 1. If `value` is not found, the method returns -1.

Availability: ActionScript 1.0; Flash Player 5

Parameters

`value:String` - The string for which to search.

`startIndex:Number` [optional] - An integer specifying the starting point from which to search for `value`.

Returns

`Number` - The position of the last occurrence of the specified substring or -1.

Example

The following example shows how to use `lastIndexOf()` to return the index of a certain character:

```
var searchString:String = "Lorem ipsum dolor sit amet.";
var index:Number;

index = searchString.lastIndexOf("L");
trace(index); // output: 0

index = searchString.lastIndexOf("l");
trace(index); // output: 14

index = searchString.lastIndexOf("i");
trace(index); // output: 19

index = searchString.lastIndexOf("ipsum");
trace(index); // output: 6

index = searchString.lastIndexOf("i", 18);
trace(index); // output: 6

index = searchString.lastIndexOf("z");
trace(index); // output: -1
```

See also

`indexOf (String.indexOf method)`

---

length (String.length property)

```
public length : Number
```

An integer specifying the number of characters in the specified String object.

Because all string indexes are zero-based, the index of the last character for any string x is `x.length - 1`.

Availability: ActionScript 1.0; Flash Player 5

Example

The following example creates a new String object and uses `String.length` to count the number of characters:

```
var my_str:String = "Hello world!";
trace(my_str.length); // output: 12
```

The following example loops from 0 to `my_str.length`. The code checks the characters within a string, and if the string contains the @ character, `true` displays in the Output panel. If it does not contain the @ character, then `false` displays in the Output panel.

```
function checkAtSymbol(my_str:String):Boolean {
  for (var i = 0; i<my_str.length; i++) {
  if (my_str.charAt(i) == "@") {
    return true;
  }
  }
  return false;
}

trace(checkAtSymbol("dog@house.net")); // output: true
trace(checkAtSymbol("Chris")); // output: false
```

An example is also in the Strings.fla file in the ActionScript samples folder. The following list gives typical paths to this folder:

- Windows: *boot drive*\Program Files\Macromedia\Flash 8\Samples and Tutorials\Samples\ActionScript
- Macintosh: *Macintosh HD*/Applications/Macromedia Flash 8/Samples and Tutorials/Samples/ActionScript

slice (String.slice method)

```
public slice(start:Number, end:Number) : String
```

Returns a string that includes the start character and all characters up to, but not including, the end character. The original String object is not modified. If the end parameter is not specified, the end of the substring is the end of the string. If the character indexed by start is the same as or to the right of the character indexed by end, the method returns an empty string.

Availability: ActionScript 1.0; Flash Player 5

Parameters

start:Number - The zero-based index of the starting point for the slice. If start is a negative number, the starting point is determined from the end of the string, where -1 is the last character.

end:Number - An integer that is one greater than the index of the ending point for the slice. The character indexed by the end parameter is not included in the extracted string. If this parameter is omitted, String.length is used. If end is a negative number, the ending point is determined by counting back from the end of the string, where -1 is the last character.

Returns

String - A substring of the specified string.

Example

The following example creates a variable, my_str, assigns it a String value, and then calls the slice() method using a variety of values for both the start and end parameters. Each call to slice() is wrapped in a trace() statement that displays the output in the Output panel.

```
// Index values for the string literal
// positive index: 0 1 2 3 4
// string: L o r e m
// negative index: -5 -4 -3 -2 -1

var my_str:String = "Lorem";

// slice the first character
trace("slice(0,1): "+my_str.slice(0, 1)); // output: slice(0,1): L
trace("slice(-5,1): "+my_str.slice(-5, 1)); // output: slice(-5,1): L

// slice the middle three characters
trace("slice(1,4): "+my_str.slice(1, 4)); // slice(1,4): ore
trace("slice(1,-1): "+my_str.slice(1, -1)); // slice(1,-1): ore

// slices that return empty strings because start is not to the left of end
```

```
trace("slice(1,1): "+my_str.slice(1, 1)); // slice(1,1):
trace("slice(3,2): "+my_str.slice(3, 2)); // slice(3,2):
trace("slice(-2,2): "+my_str.slice(-2, 2)); // slice(-2,2):

// slices that omit the end parameter use String.length, which equals 5
trace("slice(0): "+my_str.slice(0)); // slice(0): Lorem
trace("slice(3): "+my_str.slice(3)); // slice(3): em
```

An example is also in the Strings.fla file in the ActionScript samples folder. The following list gives typical paths to this folder:

- Windows: *boot drive*\Program Files\Macromedia\Flash 8\Samples and Tutorials\Samples\ActionScript
- Macintosh: *Macintosh HD*/Applications/Macromedia Flash 8/Samples and Tutorials/Samples/ActionScript

See also

`substr` (String.substr method), `substring` (String.substring method)

split (String.split method)

`public split(delimiter:String, [limit:Number]) : Array`

Splits a String object into substrings by breaking it wherever the specified `delimiter` parameter occurs and returns the substrings in an array. If you use an empty string ("") as a delimiter, each character in the string is placed as an element in the array.

If the `delimiter` parameter is undefined, the entire string is placed into the first element of the returned array.

Availability: ActionScript 1.0; Flash Player 5

Parameters

`delimiter:String` - A string; the character or string at which `my_str` splits.

`limit:Number` [optional] - The number of items to place into the array.

Returns

`Array` - An array containing the substrings of `my_str`.

Example

The following example returns an array with five elements:

```
var my_str:String = "P,A,T,S,Y";
var my_array:Array = my_str.split(",");
for (var i = 0; i<my_array.length; i++) {
```

```
  trace(my_array[i]);
}
// output:
  P
  A
  T
  S
  Y
```

The following example returns an array with two elements, "P" and "A":

```
var my_str:String = "P,A,T,S,Y";
var my_array:Array = my_str.split(",", 2);
trace(my_array); // output: P,A
```

The following example shows that if you use an empty string ("") for the delimiter parameter, each character in the string is placed as an element in the array:

```
var my_str:String = new String("Joe");
var my_array:Array = my_str.split("");
for (var i = 0; i<my_array.length; i++) {
  trace(my_array[i]);
}
// output:
  J
  o
  e
```

An example is also in the Strings.fla file in the ActionScript samples folder. The following list gives typical paths to this folder:

- Windows: *boot drive*\Program Files\Macromedia\Flash 8\Samples and Tutorials\Samples\ActionScript
- Macintosh: *Macintosh HD*/Applications/Macromedia Flash 8/Samples and Tutorials/ Samples/ActionScript

See also

join (Array.join method)

String constructor

public String(value:String)

Creates a new String object.

 Because string literals use less overhead than String objects and are generally easier to use, you should use string literals instead of the constructor for the String class unless you have a good reason to use a String object rather than a string literal.

Availability: ActionScript 1.0; Flash Player 5

Parameters

`value:String` - The initial value of the new String object.

substr (String.substr method)

`public substr(start:Number, length:Number) : String`

Returns the characters in a string from the index specified in the `start` parameter through the number of characters specified in the `length` parameter. The `substr` method does not change the string specified by `my_str`; it returns a new string.

Availability: ActionScript 1.0; Flash Player 5

Parameters

`start:Number` - An integer that indicates the position of the first character in `my_str` to be used to create the substring. If `start` is a negative number, the starting position is determined from the end of the string, where the -1 is the last character.

`length:Number` - The number of characters in the substring being created. If `length` is not specified, the substring includes all the characters from the start to the end of the string.

Returns

`String` - A substring of the specified string.

Example

The following example creates a new string, `my_str` and uses `substr()` to return the second word in the string; first, using a positive `start` parameter, and then using a negative `start` parameter:

```
var my_str:String = new String("Hello world");
var mySubstring:String = new String();
mySubstring = my_str.substr(6,5);
trace(mySubstring); // output: world

mySubstring = my_str.substr(-5,5);
trace(mySubstring); // output: world
```

An example is also in the Strings.fla file in the ActionScript samples folder. The following list gives typical paths to this folder:

- Windows: *boot drive*\Program Files\Macromedia\Flash 8\Samples and Tutorials\Samples\ActionScript
- Macintosh: *Macintosh HD*/Applications/Macromedia Flash 8/Samples and Tutorials/Samples/ActionScript

substring (String.substring method)

```
public substring(start:Number, end:Number) : String
```

Returns a string comprising the characters between the points specified by the `start` and `end` parameters. If the `end` parameter is not specified, the end of the substring is the end of the string. If the value of `start` equals the value of `end`, the method returns an empty string. If the value of `start` is greater than the value of `end`, the parameters are automatically swapped before the function executes and the original value is unchanged.

Availability: ActionScript 1.0; Flash Player 5

Parameters

`start:Number` - An integer that indicates the position of the first character of `my_str` used to create the substring. Valid values for `start` are 0 through `String.length` - 1. If `start` is a negative value, 0 is used.

`end:Number` - An integer that is 1+ the index of the last character in `my_str` to be extracted. Valid values for `end` are 1 through `String.length`. The character indexed by the `end` parameter is not included in the extracted string. If this parameter is omitted, `String.length` is used. If this parameter is a negative value, 0 is used.

Returns

`String` - A substring of the specified string.

Example

The following example shows how to use `substring()`:

```
var my_str:String = "Hello world";
var mySubstring:String = my_str.substring(6,11);
trace(mySubstring); // output: world
```

The following example shows what happens if a negative `start` parameter is used:

```
var my_str:String = "Hello world";
var mySubstring:String = my_str.substring(-5,5);
trace(mySubstring); // output: Hello
```

An example is also in the Strings.fla file in the ActionScript samples folder. The following list gives typical paths to this folder:

- Windows: *boot drive*\Program Files\Macromedia\Flash 8\Samples and Tutorials\Samples\ActionScript

- Macintosh: *Macintosh HD*/Applications/Macromedia Flash 8/Samples and Tutorials/ Samples/ActionScript

toLowerCase (String.toLowerCase method)

```
public toLowerCase() : String
```

Returns a copy of the `String` object, with all uppercase characters converted to lowercase. The original value is unchanged.

Availability: ActionScript 1.0; Flash Player 5

Returns

`String` - A string.

Example

The following example creates a string with all uppercase characters and then creates a copy of that string using `toLowerCase()` to convert all uppercase characters to lowercase characters:

```
var upperCase:String = "LOREM IPSUM DOLOR";
var lowerCase:String = upperCase.toLowerCase();
trace("upperCase: " + upperCase); // output: upperCase: LOREM IPSUM DOLOR
trace("lowerCase: " + lowerCase); // output: lowerCase: lorem ipsum dolor
```

An example is also in the Strings.fla file in the ActionScript samples folder. The following list gives typical paths to this folder:

- Windows: *boot drive*\Program Files\Macromedia\Flash 8\Samples and Tutorials\Samples\ActionScript

- Macintosh: *Macintosh HD*/Applications/Macromedia Flash 8/Samples and Tutorials/ Samples/ActionScript

See also

`toUpperCase (String.toUpperCase method)`

toString (String.toString method)

```
public toString() : String
```

Returns an object's properties as strings regardless of whether the properties are strings.

Availability: ActionScript 1.0; Flash Player 5

Returns

`String` - The string.

Example

The following example outputs an uppercase string that lists all of an object's properties, regardless of whether the properties are strings:

```
var employee:Object = new Object();
employee.name = "bob";
employee.salary = 60000;
employee.id = 284759021;

var employeeData:String = new String();
for (prop in employee)
{
   employeeData += employee[prop].toString().toUpperCase() + " ";
}
trace(employeeData);
```

If the `toString()` method were not included in this code, and the line in the `for` loop used `employee[prop].toUpperCase()`, the output would be "undefined undefined BOB". Including the `toString()` method produces the desired output: "284759021 60000 BOB".

toUpperCase (String.toUpperCase method)

```
public toUpperCase() : String
```

Returns a copy of the String object, with all lowercase characters converted to uppercase. The original value is unchanged.

Availability: ActionScript 1.0; Flash Player 5

Returns

`String` - A string.

Example

The following example creates a string with all lowercase characters and then creates a copy of that string using `toUpperCase()`:

```
var lowerCase:String = "lorem ipsum dolor";
var upperCase:String = lowerCase.toUpperCase();
trace("lowerCase: " + lowerCase); // output: lowerCase: lorem ipsum dolor
trace("upperCase: " + upperCase); // output: upperCase: LOREM IPSUM DOLOR
```

An example is also found in the Strings.fla file in the ActionScript samples folder. The following list gives typical paths to this folder:

- Windows: *boot drive*\Program Files\Macromedia\Flash 8\Samples and Tutorials\Samples\ActionScript
- Macintosh: *Macintosh HD*/Applications/Macromedia Flash 8/Samples and Tutorials/ Samples/ActionScript

See also

`toLowerCase (String.toLowerCase method)`

valueOf (String.valueOf method)

`public valueOf() : String`

Returns the primitive value of a String instance. This method is designed to convert a String object into a primitive string value. Because Flash Player automatically calls `valueOf()` when necessary, you rarely need to explicitly call this method.

Availability: ActionScript 1.0; Flash Player 5

Returns

`String` - The value of the string.

Example

The following example creates a new instance of the String class and then shows that the `valueOf` method returns the *primitive* value, rather than a reference to the new instance.

```
var str:String = new String("Hello World");
var value:String = str.valueOf();
trace(str instanceof String); // true
trace(value instanceof String); // false
trace(str === value); // false
```

StyleSheet (TextField.StyleSheet)

```
Object
  |
  +-TextField.StyleSheet
```

```
public class StyleSheet
extends Object
```

The StyleSheet class lets you create a StyleSheet object that contains text formatting rules for font size, color, and other styles. You can then apply styles defined by a style sheet to a TextField object that contains HTML- or XML-formatted text. The text in the TextField object is automatically formatted according to the tag styles defined by the StyleSheet object. You can use text styles to define new formatting tags, redefine built-in HTML tags, or create style classes that you can apply to certain HTML tags.

To apply styles to a TextField object, assign the StyleSheet object to a TextField object's `styleSheet` property.

Flash Player supports a subset of properties in the original CSS1 specification (www.w3.org/TR/REC-CSS1). The following table shows the supported Cascading Style Sheet (CSS) properties and values, as well as their corresponding ActionScript property names. (Each ActionScript property name is derived from the corresponding CSS property name; if the name contains a hyphen, the hyphen is omitted and the subsequent character is capitalized.)

CSS property	ActionScript property	Usage and supported values
color	color	Only hexadecimal color values are supported. Named colors (such as `blue`) are not supported. Colors are written in the following format: `#FF0000`.
display	display	Supported values are `inline`, `block`, and `none`.
font-family	fontFamily	A comma-separated list of fonts to use, in descending order of desirability. Any font family name can be used. If you specify a generic font name, it is converted to an appropriate device font. The following font conversions are available: `mono` is converted to `_typewriter`, `sans-serif` is converted to `_sans`, and `serif` is converted to `_serif`.

CSS property	ActionScript property	Usage and supported values
font-size	fontSize	Only the numeric part of the value is used. Units (px, pt) are not parsed; pixels and points are equivalent.
font-style	fontStyle	Recognized values are normal and italic.
font-weight	fontWeight	Recognized values are normal and bold.
kerning	kerning	Recognized values are true and false. Kerning is supported for embedded fonts only. Certain fonts, such as Courier New, do not support kerning. The kerning property is only supported in SWF files created in Windows, not in SWF files created on the Macintosh. However, these SWF files can be played in non-Windows versions of Flash Player and the kerning still applies.
letter-spacing	letterSpacing	The amount of space that is uniformly distributed between characters. The value specifies the number of pixels that are added to the advance after each character. A negative value condenses the space between characters. Only the numeric part of the value is used. Units (px, pt) are not parsed; pixels and points are equivalent.
margin-left	marginLeft	Only the numeric part of the value is used. Units (px, pt) are not parsed; pixels and points are equivalent.
margin-right	marginRight	Only the numeric part of the value is used. Units (px, pt) are not parsed; pixels and points are equivalent.
text-align	textAlign	Recognized values are left, center, right, and justify.
text-decoration	textDecoration	Recognized values are none and underline.
text-indent	textIndent	Only the numeric part of the value is used. Units (px, pt) are not parsed; pixels and points are equivalent.

Availability: ActionScript 1.0; Flash Player 7

Property summary

Properties inherited from class Object

```
constructor (Object.constructor property), __proto__ (Object.__proto__
property), prototype (Object.prototype property), __resolve
(Object.__resolve property)
```

Event summary

Event	Description
`onLoad = function(success :Boolean) {}`	Invoked when a `load()` operation has completed.

Constructor summary

Signature	Description
`StyleSheet()`	Creates a StyleSheet object.

Method summary

Modifiers	Signature	Description
	`clear() : Void`	Removes all styles from the specified StyleSheet object.
	`getStyle(name:String ) : Object`	Returns a copy of the style object associated with the specified style (`name`).
	`getStyleNames() : Array`	Returns an array that contains the names (as strings) of all of the styles registered in this style sheet.
	`load(url:String) : Boolean`	Starts loading the CSS file into the StyleSheet.
	`parseCSS(cssText:Str ing) : Boolean`	Parses the CSS in `cssText` and loads the StyleSheet with it.
	`setStyle(name:String , style:Object) : Void`	Adds a new style with the specified name to the StyleSheet object.
	`transform(style:Obje ct) : TextFormat`	Extends the CSS parsing capability.

```
addProperty (Object.addProperty method), hasOwnProperty
(Object.hasOwnProperty method), isPropertyEnumerable
(Object.isPropertyEnumerable method), isPrototypeOf (Object.isPrototypeOf
method), registerClass (Object.registerClass method), toString
(Object.toString method), unwatch (Object.unwatch method), valueOf
(Object.valueOf method), watch (Object.watch method)
```

clear (StyleSheet.clear method)

```
public clear() : Void
```

Removes all styles from the specified StyleSheet object.

Availability: ActionScript 1.0; Flash Player 7

Example

The following example loads a StyleSheet called styles.css into a SWF file, and displays the styles that are loaded in the Output panel. When you click `clear_btn`, all styles from the `my_styleSheet` object are removed.

```
// Create a new StyleSheet object
import TextField.StyleSheet;
var my_styleSheet:StyleSheet = new StyleSheet();

my_styleSheet.onLoad = function(success:Boolean) {
  if (success) {
    trace("Styles loaded.");
    var styles_array:Array = my_styleSheet.getStyleNames();
    for (var i = 0; I < styles_array.length; i++) {
      trace("\t"+styles_array[i]);
    }
    trace("");
  } else {
    trace("Error loading CSS");
  }
};

// Start the loading operation
my_styleSheet.load("styles.css");

clear_btn.onRelease = function() {
  my_styleSheet.clear();
  trace("Styles cleared.");
  var styles_array:Array = my_styleSheet.getStyleNames();
  for (var i = 0; i<styles_array.length; i++) {
    trace("\t"+styles_array[i]);
```

```
  }
  trace("");
};
```

getStyle (StyleSheet.getStyle method)

```
public getStyle(name:String) : Object
```

Returns a copy of the style object associated with the specified style (name). If there is no style object associated with name, the method returns null.

Availability: ActionScript 1.0; Flash Player 7

Parameters

name:String - The name of the style to retrieve.

Returns

Object - A style object; otherwise null.

Example

The following example loads styles from a CSS file, parses the StyleSheet and displays style names and property values in the Output panel. Create a ActionScript file called StyleSheetTracer.as and enter the following code in the file:

```
import TextField.StyleSheet;
class StyleSheetTracer {
  // StyleSheetTracer.displayFromURL
  // This method displays the CSS style sheet at
  // the specified URL in the Output panel.
  static function displayFromURL(url:String):Void {
    // Create a new StyleSheet object
    var my_styleSheet:StyleSheet = new StyleSheet();
    // The load operation is asynchronous, so set up
    // a callback function to display the loaded StyleSheet.
    my_styleSheet.onLoad = function(success:Boolean) {
      if (success) {
        StyleSheetTracer.display(this);
      } else {
        trace("Error loading style sheet "+url);
      }
    };
    // Start the loading operation.
    my_styleSheet.load(url);
  }
  static function display(my_styleSheet:StyleSheet):Void {
    var styleNames:Array = my_styleSheet.getStyleNames();
    if (!styleNames.length) {
```

```
      trace("This is an empty style sheet.");
  } else {
    for (var i = 0; i<styleNames.length; i++) {
      var styleName:String = styleNames[i];
      trace("Style "+styleName+":");
      var styleObject:Object = my_styleSheet.getStyle(styleName);
      for (var propName in styleObject) {
        var propValue = styleObject[propName];
        trace("\t"+propName+": "+propValue);
      }
      trace("");
    }
  }
}
```

Create a CSS document called styles.css, which has two styles called .heading and
.mainBody that define properties for font-family, font-size and font-weight. Enter the
following code in the CSS document:

```
/~ In styles.css ~/
.heading {
font-family: Arial, Helvetica, sans-serif;
font-size: 24px;
font-weight: bold;
}
.mainBody {
font-family: Arial, Helvetica, sans-serif;
font-size: 12px;
font-weight: normal;
}
```

Finally, in a FLA or ActionScript file, enter the following ActionScript to load the external
style sheet, styles.css:

```
StyleSheetTracer.displayFromURL("styles.css");
```

This displays the following in the Output panel:

```
Style .heading:
fontWeight: bold
fontSize: 24px
fontFamily: Arial, Helvetica, sans-serif

Style .mainBody:
fontWeight: normal
fontSize: 12px
fontFamily: Arial, Helvetica, sans-serif
```

See also

getStyleNames (StyleSheet.getStyleNames method)

`public getStyleNames() : Array`

Returns an array that contains the names (as strings) of all of the styles registered in this style sheet.

Availability: ActionScript 1.0; Flash Player 7

Returns

`Array` - An array of style names (as strings).

Example

This example creates a StyleSheet object named `styleSheet` that contains two styles, `heading` and `bodyText`. It then invokes the StyleSheet object's `getStyleNames()` method, assigns the results to the array `names_array`, and displays the contents of the array in the Output panel.

```
import TextField.StyleSheet;
var my_styleSheet:StyleSheet = new StyleSheet();
my_styleSheet.setStyle("heading", {fontsize:'24px'});
my_styleSheet.setStyle("bodyText", {fontsize:'12px'});
var names_array:Array = my_styleSheet.getStyleNames();
trace(names_array.join("\n"));
```

The following information appears in the Output panel:

```
bodyText
heading
```

See also

`getStyle (StyleSheet.getStyle method)`

load (StyleSheet.load method)

`public load(url:String) : Boolean`

Starts loading the CSS file into the StyleSheet. The load operation is asynchronous; use the `onLoad()` callback handler to determine when the file has finished loading. The CSS file must reside in the same domain as the SWF file that is loading it.

Availability: ActionScript 1.0; Flash Player 7

Parameters

`url:String` - The URL of a CSS file to load. The URL must be in the same domain as the URL where the SWF file currently resides.

Returns

Boolean - `false` if no parameter (`null`) is passed; `true` otherwise. Use the `onLoad()` callback handler to check the success of a loaded StyleSheet.

Example

For an example of asynchronously loading style sheets using ActionScript 2.0, see the example for `getStyle()`.

The following example loads the CSS file named styles.css into the StyleSheet object `my_styleSheet`. When the file has loaded successfully, the StyleSheet object is applied to a TextField object named `news_txt`.

```
import TextField.StyleSheet;
this.createTextField("news_txt", 999, 10, 10, 320, 240);
news_txt.multiline = true;
news_txt.wordWrap = true;
news_txt.html = true;

var my_styleSheet:StyleSheet = new StyleSheet();
my_styleSheet.onLoad = function(success:Boolean) {
  if (success) {
  news_txt.styleSheet = my_styleSheet;
  news_txt.htmlText = "<p class=\"heading\">Heading goes here!</p>"
    + "<p class=\"mainBody\">Lorem ipsum dolor sit amet, consectetuer "
    + "adipiscing elit, sed diam nonummy nibh euismod tincidunt ut laoreet
"
    + "dolore magna aliquam erat volutpat.</p>";
  }
};
my_styleSheet.load("styles.css");
```

For the complete code for styles.css, see the example for `getStyle()`.

See also

onLoad (StyleSheet.onLoad handler), getStyle (StyleSheet.getStyle method)

onLoad (StyleSheet.onLoad handler)

`onLoad = function(success:Boolean) {}`

Invoked when a `load()` operation has completed. If the StyleSheet loaded successfully, the `success` parameter is `true`. If the document was not received, or if an error occurred in receiving the response from the server, the `success` parameter is `false`.

Availability: ActionScript 1.0; Flash Player 7

Parameters

`success:Boolean` - A Boolean value that indicates whether the CSS file loaded successfully (`true`) or not (`false`).

Example

The following example loads the CSS file named styles.css into the StyleSheet object `my_styleSheet`. When the file has finished loading successfully, the StyleSheet object is applied to a TextField object named `news_txt`.

```
import TextField.StyleSheet;
this.createTextField("news_txt", 999, 10, 10, 320, 240);
news_txt.multiline = true;
news_txt.wordWrap = true;
news_txt.html = true;

var my_styleSheet:StyleSheet = new StyleSheet();
my_styleSheet.onLoad = function(success:Boolean) {
  if (success) {
    news_txt.styleSheet = my_styleSheet;
    news_txt.htmlText = "<p class=\"heading\">Heading goes here!"
      + "</p><p class=\"mainBody\">Lorem ipsum dolor "
      + "sit amet, consectetuer adipiscing elit, sed diam nonummy "
      + "nibh euismod tincidunt ut laoreet dolore magna aliquam "
      + "erat volutpat.</p>";
  }
};
my_styleSheet.load("styles.css");
```

For the complete code for styles.css, see the example for `getStyle()`. For an example of asynchronously loading style sheets using ActionScript 2.0, see the example for `getStyle()`.

See also

`load` (StyleSheet.load method), `getStyle` (StyleSheet.getStyle method)

parseCSS (StyleSheet.parseCSS method)

`public parseCSS(cssText:String) : Boolean`

Parses the CSS in `cssText` and loads the StyleSheet with it. If a style in `cssText` is already in the StyleSheet, the StyleSheet retains its properties, and only the ones in `cssText` are added or changed.

To extend the native CSS parsing capability, you can override this method by creating a subclass of the StyleSheet class.

Availability: ActionScript 1.0; Flash Player 7

Parameters

`cssText:String` - The CSS text to parse.

Returns

`Boolean` - A Boolean value that indicates whether the text was parsed successfully (`true`) or not (`false`).

Example

The following example parses the CSS in `css_str`. The script displays information about whether it parsed the CSS successfully, and then displays the parsed CSS in the Output panel.

```
import TextField.StyleSheet;
var css_str:String = ".heading {font-family: Arial, Helvetica, sans-serif;
  font-size: 24px; font-weight: bold; }";
var my_styleSheet:StyleSheet = new StyleSheet();
if (my_styleSheet.parseCSS(css_str)) {
  trace("parsed successfully");
  dumpStyles(my_styleSheet);
} else {
  trace("unable to parse CSS");
}
//
function dumpStyles(styles:StyleSheet):Void {
  var styleNames_array:Array = styles.getStyleNames();
  for (var i = 0; i<styleNames_array.length; i++) {
    var styleName_str:String = styleNames_array[i];
    var styleObject:Object = styles.getStyle(styleName_str);
    trace(styleName_str);
    for (var prop in styleObject) {
      trace("\t"+prop+": "+styleObject[prop]);
    }
    trace("");
  }
}
```

setStyle (StyleSheet.setStyle method)

`public setStyle(name:String, style:Object) : Void`

Adds a new style with the specified name to the StyleSheet object. If the named style does not already exist in the StyleSheet, it is added. If the named style already exists in the StyleSheet, it is replaced. If the `style` parameter is `null`, the named style is removed.

Flash Player creates a copy of the style object that you pass to this method.

For a list of supported styles, see the table in the description for the StyleSheet class.

Availability: ActionScript 1.0; Flash Player 7

Parameters

`name:String` - The name of the style to add to the StyleSheet.

`style:Object` - An object that describes the style, or `null`.

Example

The following example adds a style named `emphasized` to the StyleSheet `myStyleSheet`. The style includes two style properties: `color` and `fontWeight`. The style object is defined with the `{}` operator.

```
myStyleSheet.setStyle("emphasized", {color:'#000000',fontWeight:'bold'});
```

You could also create a style object using an instance of the Object class, and then pass that object (`styleObj`) as the `style` parameter, as the next example shows:

```
import TextField.StyleSheet;
var my_styleSheet:StyleSheet = new StyleSheet();

var styleObj:Object = new Object();
styleObj.color = "#000000";
styleObj.fontWeight = "bold";
my_styleSheet.setStyle("emphasized", styleObj);
delete styleObj;

var styleNames_array:Array = my_styleSheet.getStyleNames();
for (var i=0;i<styleNames_array.length;i++) {
  var styleName:String = styleNames_array[i];
  var thisStyle:Object = my_styleSheet.getStyle(styleName);
  trace(styleName);
  for (var prop in thisStyle) {
    trace("\t"+prop+": "+thisStyle[prop]);
  }
  trace("");
}
```

The following information appears in the Output panel:

```
emphasized
fontWeight: bold
color: #000000
```

 NOTE Because Flash Player creates a copy of the style object you pass to `setStyle()`, the `delete styleObj` command in the code example reduces memory usage by deleting the original style object passed to `setStyle()`.

See also

`{} object initializer operator`, `StyleSheet (TextField.StyleSheet)`

StyleSheet constructor

```
public StyleSheet()
```

Creates a StyleSheet object.

Availability: ActionScript 1.0; Flash Player 7

Example

The following example loads in a style sheet and traces the styles that load into the document. Add the following ActionScript to your ActionScript or FLA file:

```
import TextField.StyleSheet;
var my_styleSheet:StyleSheet = new StyleSheet();
my_styleSheet.onLoad = function(success:Boolean) {
  if (success) {
    trace("Styles loaded:");
    var styles_array:Array = my_styleSheet.getStyleNames();
    trace(styles_array.join(newline));
  } else {
    trace("Error loading CSS");
  }
};
my_styleSheet.load("styles.css");
```

The styles.css file contains two styles, called `.heading` and `.mainbody`, so the following information is displayed in the Output panel:

```
Styles loaded:
.heading
.mainBody
```

The complete code for styles.css is found in the example for `getStyle()`.

See also

`getStyle (StyleSheet.getStyle method)`

transform (StyleSheet.transform method)

```
public transform(style:Object) : TextFormat
```

Extends the CSS parsing capability. Advanced developers can override this method by extending the StyleSheet class.

Availability: ActionScript 1.0; Flash Player 7

Parameters

`style:Object` - An object that describes the style, containing style rules as properties of the object, or `null`.

Returns

`TextFormat` - A TextFormat object containing the result of the mapping of CSS rules to text format properties.

Example

The following example extends the `transform()` method:

```
import TextField.StyleSheet;
class AdvancedCSS extends StyleSheet {
  public function AdvancedCSS() {
    trace("AdvancedCSS instantiated");
  }

  public function transform(styleObject):TextFormat {
    trace("tranform called");
  }
}
```

System

```
Object
  |
  +-System
```

```
public class System
extends Object
```

The System class contains properties related to certain operations that take place on the user's computer, such as operations with shared objects, local settings for cameras and microphones, and use of the Clipboard. The following additional properties and methods are in specific classes within the System package: the capabilities class, the security class, and the IME class.

Availability: ActionScript 1.0; Flash Player 6

See also

`capabilities (System.capabilities)`, `security (System.security)`, IME
`(System.IME)`

Property summary

Modifiers	Property	Description
static	exactSettings:Boolean	A Boolean value that specifies whether to use superdomain (false) or exact domain (true) matching rules when accessing local settings (such as camera or microphone access permissions) or locally persistent data (shared objects).
static	useCodepage:Boolean	A Boolean value that tells Flash Player whether to use Unicode or the traditional code page of the operating system running the player to interpret external text files.

Properties inherited from class Object

```
constructor (Object.constructor property), __proto__ (Object.__proto__
property), prototype (Object.prototype property), __resolve
(Object.__resolve property)
```

Event summary

Event	Description
onStatus = function(infoObject:Object) {}	Event handler: provides a super event handler for certain objects.

Method summary

Modifiers	Signature	Description
static	setClipboard(text:String) : Void	Replaces the contents of the Clipboard with a specified text string.
static	showSettings([tabID: Number]) : Void	Shows the specified Flash Player Settings panel.

Methods inherited from class Object

```
addProperty (Object.addProperty method), hasOwnProperty
(Object.hasOwnProperty method), isPropertyEnumerable
(Object.isPropertyEnumerable method), isPrototypeOf (Object.isPrototypeOf
method), registerClass (Object.registerClass method), toString
(Object.toString method), unwatch (Object.unwatch method), valueOf
(Object.valueOf method), watch (Object.watch method)
```

exactSettings (System.exactSettings property)

```
public static exactSettings : Boolean
```

A Boolean value that specifies whether to use superdomain (false) or exact domain (true) matching rules when accessing local settings (such as camera or microphone access permissions) or locally persistent data (shared objects). The default value is true for files published for Flash Player 7 or later, and false for files published for Flash Player 6.

If this value is true, the settings and data for a SWF file hosted at here.xyz.com are stored in a directory called here.xyz.com, the settings and data for a SWF file hosted at there.xyz.com are stored in a directory called there.xyz.com, and so on. If this value is false, the settings and data for SWF files hosted at here.xyz.com, there.xyz.com, and xyz.com are shared, and are all stored in a directory called xyz.com.

If some of your files set this property to false and others set it to true, you might find that SWF files in different subdomains share settings and data. For example, if this property is false in a SWF file hosted at here.xyz.com and true in a SWF file hosted at xyz.com, both files will use the same settings and data--namely, those in the xyz.com directory. If this isn't the behavior you want, ensure that you set this property in each file to correctly represent where you want to store settings and data.

If you want to change this property from its default value, do so in the first frame of your document. If you want to change this property from its default value, do so near the beginning of your script. The property can't be changed after any activity that requires access to local settings, such as System.showSettings() or SharedObject.getLocal().

If you use loadMovie(), MovieClip.loadMovie(), or MovieClipLoader.loadClip() to load one SWF file into another, all the files published for Flash Player 7 share a single value for System.exactSettings, and all the files published for Flash Player 6 share a single value for System.exactSettings. If you use MovieClip.loadMovie() or MovieClipLoader.loadClip() to load one SWF file into another, all of the files share a single value for System.exactSettings. Therefore, if you specify a value for this property in one file published for a particular Player version, you should do so in all the files that you plan to load. If you load multiple files, the setting specified in the last file that's loaded overwrites any previously specified setting.

Usually you should find that the default value of `System.exactSettings` is fine. Often your only requirement is that when a SWF file saves a shared object in one session, the same SWF file can retrieve the same shared object in a later session. This situation will always be true, regardless of the value of `System.exactSettings`. But you might want to change `System.exactSettings` from its default so that a SWF file published for Flash Player 7 or later can retrieve shared objects originally created by a SWF file published for Flash Player 6. Because the player has stored the shared objects created by the Flash Player 6 SWF file in a folder that's specific to the superdomain of that SWF file, you should use superdomain rules for shared object retrieval in your Flash Player 7 SWF file. This step requires specifying `System.exactSettings = false` in your Flash Player 7 SWF file. It is also possible that you might have SWF files that are published for Flash Player 6 and Flash Player 7 SWF files that share the same shared object data. In this case, simply pick a value for `System.exactSettings` (either `true` or `false`) and use it consistently in your Flash Player 6 and Flash Player 7 SWF files.

Availability: ActionScript 1.0; Flash Player 7

Example

The following example shows how to specify superdomain matching rules:

See also

`loadMovie (MovieClip.loadMovie method)`, `loadClip (MovieClipLoader.loadClip method)`, `getLocal (SharedObject.getLocal method)`, `exactSettings (System.exactSettings property)`

onStatus (System.onStatus handler)

`onStatus = function(infoObject:Object) {}`

Event handler: provides a super event handler for certain objects.

The LocalConnection, NetStream, and SharedObject classes provide an onStatus event handler that uses an information object for providing information, status, or error messages. To respond to this event handler, you must create a function to process the information object, and you must know the format and contents of the returned information object.

In addition to these specific onStatus methods, Flash also provides a super function called System.onStatus, which serves as a secondary error message handler. If an instance of the LocalConnection, NetStream, or SharedObject class passes an information object with a level property of "error", but you have not defined an onStatus function for that particular instance, then Flash uses the function you define for System.onStatus instead.

> **NOTE** The Camera and Microphone classes also have onStatus handlers but do not pass information objects with a level property of "error". Therefore, System.onStatus is not called if you don't specify a function for these handlers.

Availability: ActionScript 1.0; Flash Player 6

Parameters

infoObject:Object - A parameter defined according to the status message.

Example

The following example shows how to create a System.onStatus function to process information objects when a class-specific onStatus function does not exist:

```
// Create generic function
System.onStatus = function(genericError:Object){
    // Your script would do something more meaningful here
    trace("An error has occurred. Please try again.");
}
```

The following example shows how to create an onStatus function for an instance of the NetStream class:

```
// Create function for NetStream object

videoStream_ns.onStatus = function(infoObject:Object) {
    if (infoObject.code == "NetStream.Play.StreamNotFound") {
        trace("Could not find video file.");
    }
}
```

See also

onStatus (Camera.onStatus handler), onStatus (LocalConnection.onStatus handler), onStatus (Microphone.onStatus handler), onStatus (NetStream.onStatus handler), onStatus (SharedObject.onStatus handler)

setClipboard (System.setClipboard method)

```
public static setClipboard(text:String) : Void
```

Replaces the contents of the Clipboard with a specified text string.

 NOTE Because of security concerns, it is not possible to read the contents of the system Clipboard. In other words, there is no corresponding `System.getClipboard()` method.

Availability: ActionScript 1.0; Flash Player 7 - SWF files published for Flash Player 6 or later, playing in Flash Player 7 or later.

Parameters

`text:String` - A plain-text string of characters to place on the system Clipboard, replacing its current contents (if any).

Example

The following example places the phrase `"Hello World"` onto the system Clipboard:

```
System.setClipboard("Hello world");
```

The following example creates two text fields at runtime, called `in_txt` and `out_txt`. When you select text in the `in_txt` field, you can click the `copy_btn` to copy the data to the Clipboard. Then you can paste the text into the `out_txt` field.

```
this.createTextField("in_txt", this.getNextHighestDepth(), 10, 10, 160,
    120);
in_txt.multiline = true;
in_txt.border = true;
in_txt.text = "lorum ipsum...";
this.createTextField("out_txt", this.getNextHighestDepth(), 10, 140, 160,
    120);
out_txt.multiline = true;
out_txt.border = true;
out_txt.type = "input";

copy_btn.onRelease = function() {
   System.setClipboard(in_txt.text);
   Selection.setFocus("out_txt");
};
```

If your SWF file includes a version 2 component, use the version 2 components DepthManager class instead of the `MovieClip.getNextHighestDepth()` method, which is used in this example.

showSettings (System.showSettings method)

```
public static showSettings([tabID:Number]) : Void
```

Shows the specified Flash Player Settings panel. The panel lets users do any of the following actions:

- Allow or deny access to the camera and microphone
- Specify the local disk space available for shared objects
- Select a default camera and microphone
- Specify microphone gain and echo suppression settings

For example, if your application requires the use of a camera, you can tell the user to select Allow in the Privacy Settings panel and then issue a `System.showSettings(0)` command. (Ensure that your Stage size is at least 215 x 138 pixels)

Availability: ActionScript 1.0; Flash Player 6

Parameters

`tabID:Number` [optional] - A number; a number that specifies which Flash Player Settings panel to display, as shown in the following table:

Value passed for panel	Settings panel displayed
None (parameter is omitted) or an unsupported value	The panel that was open the last time the user closed the Player Settings panel.
0	Privacy
1	Local Storage
2	Microphone
3	Camera

Example

The following example shows how to display the Flash Player Settings Local Storage panel:

```
System.showSettings(1);
```

See also

```
get (Camera.get method), get (Microphone.get method), getLocal
(SharedObject.getLocal method)
```

useCodepage (System.useCodepage property)

```
public static useCodepage : Boolean
```

A Boolean value that tells Flash Player whether to use Unicode or the traditional code page of the operating system running the player to interpret external text files. The default value of `System.useCodepage` is false.

- When the property is set to false, Flash Player interprets external text files as Unicode. (These files must be encoded as Unicode when you save them.)
- When the property is set to true, Flash Player interprets external text files using the traditional code page of the operating system running the player.

Text that you load as an external file (using the `loadVariables()` or `getURL()` statements, or the LoadVars class or XML class) must be encoded as Unicode when you save the text file in order for Flash Player to recognize it as Unicode. To encode external files as Unicode, save the files in an application that supports Unicode, such as Notepad on Windows 2000.

If you load external text files that are not Unicode-encoded, you should set `System.useCodepage` to true. Add the following code as the first line of code in the first frame of the SWF file that is loading the data:

```
System.useCodepage = true;
```

When this code is present, Flash Player interprets external text using the traditional code page of the operating system running Flash Player. This is generally CP1252 for an English Windows operating system and Shift-JIS for a Japanese operating system. If you set `System.useCodepage` to true, Flash Player 6 and later treat text as Flash Player 5 does. (Flash Player 5 treated all text as if it were in the traditional code page of the operating system running the player.)

If you set `System.useCodepage` to true, remember that the traditional code page of the operating system running the player must include the characters used in your external text file in order for the text to display. For example, if you load an external text file that contains Chinese characters, those characters cannot display on a system that uses the CP1252 code page because that code page does not include Chinese characters.

To ensure that users on all platforms can view external text files used in your SWF files, you should encode all external text files as Unicode and leave `System.useCodepage` set to false by default. This way, Flash Player 6 and later interprets the text as Unicode.

Availability: ActionScript 1.0; Flash Player 6

TextField

```
Object
  |
  +-TextField
```

```
public dynamic class TextField
extends Object
```

The TextField class is used to create areas for text display and input. All dynamic and input text fields in a SWF file are instances of the TextField class. You can give a text field an instance name in the Property inspector and use the methods and properties of the TextField class to manipulate it with ActionScript. TextField instance names are displayed in the Movie Explorer and in the Insert Target Path dialog box in the Actions panel.

To create a text field dynamically, you do not use the `new` operator. Instead, you use `MovieClip.createTextField()`.

The methods of the TextField class let you set, select, and manipulate text in a dynamic or input text field that you create during authoring or at runtime.

ActionScript provides several ways to format your text at runtime. The TextFormat class lets you set character and paragraph formatting for TextField objects. In Flash Player 7 and later, you can apply Cascading Style Sheets (CSS) styles to text fields using the TextField.styleSheet property and the StyleSheet class. You can use CSS to style built-in HTML tags, define new formatting tags, or apply styles. You can assign HTML formatted text, which might optionally use CSS styles, directly to a text field. In Flash Player 7 and later, HTML text that you assign to a text field can contain embedded media (movie clips, SWF files, JPEG files, GIF files, PNG files). The text wraps around the embedded media in the same way that a web browser wraps text around media embedded in an HTML document.

Flash Player supports a subset of HTML tags that you can use to format text.

Availability: ActionScript 1.0; Flash Player 6

See also

Object, createTextField (MovieClip.createTextField method)

Property summary

Modifiers	Property	Description
	_alpha:Number	Sets or retrieves the alpha transparency value of the text field.
~	antiAliasType:String	The type of anti-aliasing used for this TextField instance.

Modifiers	Property	Description
	`autoSize:Object`	Controls automatic sizing and alignment of text fields.
	`background:Boolean`	Specifies if the text field has a background fill.
	`backgroundColor:Number`	The color of the text field background.
	`border:Boolean`	Specifies if the text field has a border.
	`borderColor:Number`	The color of the text field border.
	`bottomScroll:Number` [read-only]	An integer (one-based index) that indicates the bottommost line that is currently visible the text field.
	`condenseWhite:Boolean`	A Boolean value that specifies whether extra white space (spaces, line breaks, and so on) in an HTML text field should be removed when the field is rendered in a browser.
	`embedFonts:Boolean`	Specifies whether to render using embedded font outlines.
	`filters:Array`	An indexed array containing each filter object currently associated with the text field.
	`gridFitType:String`	The type of grid fitting used for this TextField instance.
	`_height:Number`	The height of the text field in pixels.
	`_highquality:Number`	**Deprecated** since Flash Player 7. This property was deprecated in favor of `TextField._quality`. Specifies the level of anti-aliasing applied to the current SWF file.
	`hscroll:Number`	Indicates the current horizontal scrolling position.
	`html:Boolean`	A flag that indicates whether the text field contains an HTML representation.
	`htmlText:String`	If the text field is an HTML text field, this property contains the HTML representation of the text field's contents.
	`length:Number [read-only]`	Indicates the number of characters in a text field.
	`maxChars:Number`	Indicates the maximum number of characters that the text field can contain.
	`maxhscroll:Number` [read-only]	Indicates the maximum value of `TextField.hscroll`.

Modifiers	Property	Description
	maxscroll:Number [read-only]	Indicates the maximum value of TextField.scroll.
	menu:ContextMenu	Associates the ContextMenu object *contextMenu* with the text field *my_txt*.
	mouseWheelEnabled:Boolean	A Boolean value that indicates whether Flash Player should automatically scroll multiline text fields when the mouse pointer clicks a text field and the user rolls the mouse wheel.
	multiline:Boolean	Indicates whether the text field is a multiline text field.
	_name:String	The instance name of the text field.
	_parent:MovieClip	A reference to the movie clip or object that contains the current text field or object.
	password:Boolean	Specifies whether the text field is a password text field.
	_quality:String	The rendering quality used for a SWF file.
	restrict:String	Indicates the set of characters that a user may enter into the text field.
	_rotation:Number	The rotation of the text field, in degrees, from its original orientation.
	scroll:Number	The vertical position of text in a text field.
	selectable:Boolean	A Boolean value that indicates whether the text field is selectable.
	sharpness:Number	The sharpness of the glyph edges in this TextField instance.
	_soundbuftime:Number	The number of seconds a sound prebuffers before it starts to stream.
	styleSheet:StyleSheet	Attaches a style sheet to the text field.
	tabEnabled:Boolean	Specifies whether the text field is included in automatic tab ordering.
	tabIndex:Number	Lets you customize the tab ordering of objects in a SWF file.
	_target:String [read-only]	The target path of the text field instance.
	text:String	Indicates the current text in the text field.

Modifiers	Property	Description
	`textColor:Number`	Indicates the color of the text in a text field.
	`textHeight:Number`	Indicates the height of the text.
	`textWidth:Number`	Indicates the width of the text.
	`thickness:Number`	The thickness of the glyph edges in this TextField instance.
	`type:String`	Specifies the type of text field.
	`_url:String` [read-only]	Retrieves the URL of the SWF file that created the text field.
	`variable:String`	The name of the variable that the text field is associated with.
	`_visible:Boolean`	A Boolean value that indicates whether the text field *my_txt* is visible.
	`_width:Number`	The width of the text field, in pixels.
	`wordWrap:Boolean`	A Boolean value that indicates if the text field has word wrap.
	`_x:Number`	An integer that sets the x coordinate of a text field relative to the local coordinates of the parent movie clip.
	`_xmouse:Number` [read-only]	Returns the x coordinate of the mouse position relative to the text field.
	`_xscale:Number`	Determines the horizontal scale of the text field as applied from the registration point of the text field, expressed as a percentage.
	`_y:Number`	The y coordinate of a text field relative to the local coordinates of the parent movie clip.
	`_ymouse:Number` [read-only]	Indicates the y coordinate of the mouse position relative to the text field.
	`_yscale:Number`	The vertical scale of the text field as applied from the registration point of the text field, expressed as a percentage.

Properties inherited from class Object

```
constructor (Object.constructor property),__proto__ (Object.__proto__
property),prototype (Object.prototype property),__resolve
(Object.__resolve property)
```

Event summary

Event	Description
onChanged = function(changed Field:TextField) {}	Event handler/listener; invoked when the content of a text field changes.
onKillFocus = function(newFocu s:Object) {}	Invoked when a text field loses keyboard focus.
onScroller = function(scrolle dField:TextField) {}	Event handler/listener; invoked when one of the text field scroll properties changes.
onSetFocus = function(oldFocu s:Object) {}	Invoked when a text field receives keyboard focus.

Method summary

Modifiers	Signature	Description
	addListener(listener :Object) : Boolean	Registers an object to receive TextField event notifications.
	getDepth() : Number	Returns the depth of a text field.
static	getFontList() : Array	Returns the names of fonts on the player's host system as an array.
	getNewTextFormat() : TextFormat	Returns a TextFormat object containing a copy of the text field's text format object.
	getTextFormat([begin Index:Number], [endIndex:Number]) : TextFormat	Returns a TextFormat object for a character, a range of characters, or an entire TextField object.
	removeListener(liste ner:Object) : Boolean	Removes a listener object previously registered to a text field instance with TextField.addListener().
	removeTextField() : Void	Removes the text field.

Modifiers	Signature	Description
	`replaceSel(newText:String) : Void`	Replaces the current selection with the contents of the `newText` parameter.
	`replaceText(beginIndex:Number, endIndex:Number, newText:String) : Void`	Replaces a range of characters, specified by the `beginIndex` and `endIndex` parameters, in the specified text field with the contents of the `newText` parameter.
	`setNewTextFormat(tf:TextFormat) : Void`	Sets the default new text format of a text field.
	`setTextFormat([beginIndex:Number], [endIndex:Number], textFormat:TextFormat) : Void`	Applies the text formatting specified by the `textFormat` parameter to some or all of the text in a text field.

Methods inherited from class Object

```
addProperty (Object.addProperty method),hasOwnProperty
(Object.hasOwnProperty method),isPropertyEnumerable
(Object.isPropertyEnumerable method),isPrototypeOf (Object.isPrototypeOf
method),registerClass (Object.registerClass method),toString
(Object.toString method),unwatch (Object.unwatch method),valueOf
(Object.valueOf method),watch (Object.watch method)
```

addListener (TextField.addListener method)

`public addListener(listener:Object) : Boolean`

Registers an object to receive TextField event notifications. The object will receive event notifications whenever the `onChanged` and `onScroller` event handlers have been invoked. When a text field changes or is scrolled, the `TextField.onChanged` and `TextField.onScroller` event handlers are invoked, followed by the `onChanged` and `onScroller` event handlers of any objects registered as listeners. Multiple objects can be registered as listeners.

To remove a listener object from a text field, call `TextField.removeListener()`.

A reference to the text field instance is passed as a parameter to the `onScroller` and `onChanged` handlers by the event source. You can capture this data by putting a parameter in the event handler method. For example, the following code uses `txt` as the parameter that is passed to the `onScroller` event handler. The parameter is then used in a `trace` statement to send the instance name of the text field to the Output panel.

```
my_txt.onScroller = function(textfield_txt:TextField) {
```

```
   trace(textfield_txt._name+" scrolled");
};
```
Availability: ActionScript 1.0; Flash Player 6

Parameters

`listener:Object` - An object with an `onChanged` or `onScroller` event handler.

Returns

`Boolean -`

Example

The following example defines an `onChanged` handler for the input text field `my_txt`. It then defines a new listener object, `txtListener`, and defines an `onChanged` handler for that object. This handler will be invoked when the text field `my_txt` is changed. The final line of code calls `TextField.addListener` to register the listener object `txtListener` with the text field `my_txt` so that it will be notified when `my_txt` changes.

```
this.createTextField("my_txt", this.getNextHighestDepth(), 10, 10, 100,
    22);
my_txt.border = true;
my_txt.type = "input";

my_txt.onChanged = function(textfield_txt:TextField) {
   trace(textfield_txt._name+" changed");
};
var txtListener:Object = new Object();
txtListener.onChanged = function(textfield_txt:TextField) {
   trace(textfield_txt._name+" changed and notified myListener");
};
my_txt.addListener(txtListener);
```

The `MovieClip.getNextHighestDepth()` method used in this example requires Flash Player 7 or later. If your SWF file includes a version 2 component, use the version 2 components DepthManager class instead of the `MovieClip.getNextHighestDepth()` method.

See also

`onChanged` (TextField.onChanged handler), `onScroller` (TextField.onScroller handler), `removeListener` (TextField.removeListener method)

_alpha (TextField._alpha property)

`public _alpha : Number`

Sets or retrieves the alpha transparency value of the text field. Valid values are 0 (fully transparent) to 100 (fully opaque). The default value is 100. Transparency values are not supported for text fields that use device fonts. You must use embedded fonts to use the `_alpha` transparency property with a text field.

Availability: ActionScript 1.0; Flash Player 6

Example

The following code sets the `_alpha` property of a text field named `my_txt` to 20%. Create a new font symbol in the library by selecting New Font from the Library options menu. Then set the linkage of the font to `my font`. Set the linkage for a font symbol to `my font`. Add the following ActionScript code to your FLA or AS file.

```
var my_fmt:TextFormat = new TextFormat();
my_fmt.font = "my font";
// where 'my font' is the linkage name of a font in the Library
this.createTextField("my_txt", this.getNextHighestDepth(), 10, 10, 100,
    22);
my_txt.border = true;
my_txt.embedFonts = true;
my_txt.text = "Hello World";
my_txt.setTextFormat(my_fmt);
my_txt._alpha = 20;
```

The `MovieClip.getNextHighestDepth()` method used in this example requires Flash Player 7 or later. If your SWF file includes a version 2 component, use the version 2 components DepthManager class instead of the `MovieClip.getNextHighestDepth()` method.

See also

`_alpha` (`Button._alpha` property), `_alpha` (`MovieClip._alpha` property)

antiAliasType (TextField.antiAliasType property)

`public antiAliasType : String`

The type of anti-aliasing used for this TextField instance. Advanced anti-aliasing is available only in Flash Player 8 and later. You can control this setting only if the font is embedded (with the `embedFonts` property set to `true`). For Flash Player 8, the default setting is `"advanced"`.

To set values for this property, use the following string values:

String value	Description
"normal"	Applies the regular text anti-aliasing. This matches the type of anti-aliasing that Flash Player used in version 7 and earlier.
"advanced"	Applies advanced anti-aliasing, which makes text more legible. (This feature is available as of Flash Player 8.) Advanced anti-aliasing allows for high-quality rendering of font faces at small sizes. It is best used with applications that have a lot of small text. Advanced anti-aliasing is not recommended for fonts that are larger than 48 points.

Availability: ActionScript 1.0; Flash Player 8

Example

This example creates two text fields and applies advanced anti-aliasing to the first one only. It assumes that you have a font embedded in the Library with the linkage identifier set to "Times-12". To embed the font, follow these steps:

- Open your Library
- Click the Library options menu in the upper right corner of the Library
- Select "New Font" from the dropdown list
- Name the font "Times-12"
- Select "Times New Roman" from the font dropdown list
- Press the "OK" button
- Right-click on the newly created font and select "Linkage..."
- Check the "Export for ActionScript" box
- Accept the default identifier "Times-12" by pressing the "OK" button

```
var my_format:TextFormat = new TextFormat();
my_format.font = "Times-12";

var my_text1:TextField = this.createTextField("my_text1",
  this.getNextHighestDepth(), 10, 10, 300, 30);
my_text1.text = "This text uses advanced anti-aliasing.";
my_text1.antiAliasType = "advanced";
my_text1.border = true;
my_text1.embedFonts = true;
my_text1.setTextFormat(my_format);

var my_text2:TextField = this.createTextField("my_text2",
  this.getNextHighestDepth(), 10, 50, 300, 30);
my_text2.text = "This text uses normal anti-aliasing."
my_text2.antiAliasType = "normal";
```

```
my_text2.border = true;
my_text2.embedFonts = true;
my_text2.setTextFormat(my_format);
```

If your SWF file includes a version 2 component, use the version 2 components DepthManager class instead of the `MovieClip.getNextHighestDepth()` method, which is used in this example.

See also

`TextRenderer (flash.text.TextRenderer)`, `gridFitType (TextField.gridFitType property)`, `thickness (TextField.thickness property)`, `sharpness (TextField.sharpness property)`

autoSize (TextField.autoSize property)

`public autoSize : Object`

Controls automatic sizing and alignment of text fields. Acceptable values for autoSize are `"none"` (the default), `"left"`, `"right"`, and `"center"`. When you set the `autoSize` property, `true` is a synonym for `"left"` and `false` is a synonym for `"none"`.

The values of `autoSize` and `TextField.wordWrap` determine whether a text field expands or contracts to the left side, right side, or bottom side. The default value for each of these properties is `false`.

If `autoSize` is set to `"none"` (the default) or `false`, then no resizing will occur.

If `autoSize` is set to `"left"` or `true`, then the text is treated as left-justified text, meaning the left side of the text field will remain fixed and any resizing of a single line text field will be on the right side. If the text includes a line break (for example, `"\n"` or `"\r"`), then the bottom side will also be resized to fit the next line of text. If `wordWrap` is also set to `true`, then only the bottom side of the text field will be resized and the right side will remain fixed.

If `autoSize` is set to `"right"`, then the text is treated as right-justified text, meaning the right side of the text field will remain fixed and any resizing of a single line text field will be on the left side. If the text includes a line break (for example, `"\n"` or `"\r"`), then the bottom side will also be resized to fit the next line of text. If `wordWrap` is also set to `true`, then only the bottom side of the text field will be resized and the left side will remain fixed.

If `autoSize` is set to `"center"`, then the text is treated as center-justified text, meaning any resizing of a single line text field will be equally distributed to both the right and left sides. If the text includes a line break (for example, `"\n"` or `"\r"`), then the bottom side will also be resized to fit the next line of text. If `wordWrap` is also set to `true`, then only the bottom side of the text field will be resized and the left and right sides will remain fixed.

Availability: ActionScript 1.0; Flash Player 6

Example

You can use the following code and enter different values for `autoSize` to see how the field resizes when these values change. A mouse click while the SWF file is playing will replace each text field's `"short text"` string with longer text using several different settings for `autoSize`.

```
this.createTextField("left_txt", 997, 10, 10, 70, 30);
this.createTextField("center_txt", 998, 10, 50, 70, 30);
this.createTextField("right_txt", 999, 10, 100, 70, 30);
this.createTextField("true_txt", 1000, 10, 150, 70, 30);
this.createTextField("false_txt", 1001, 10, 200, 70, 30);

left_txt.text = "short text";
left_txt.border = true;

center_txt.text = "short text";
center_txt.border = true;

right_txt.text = "short text";
right_txt.border = true;

true_txt.text = "short text";
true_txt.border = true;

false_txt.text = "short text";
false_txt.border = true;

// create a mouse listener object to detect mouse clicks
var myMouseListener:Object = new Object();
// define a function that executes when a user clicks the mouse
myMouseListener.onMouseDown = function() {
  left_txt.autoSize = "left";
  left_txt.text = "This is much longer text";
  center_txt.autoSize = "center";
  center_txt.text = "This is much longer text";
  right_txt.autoSize = "right";
  right_txt.text = "This is much longer text";
  true_txt.autoSize = true;
  true_txt.text = "This is much longer text";
  false_txt.autoSize = false;
  false_txt.text = "This is much longer text";
};
// register the listener object with the Mouse object
Mouse.addListener(myMouseListener);
```

background (TextField.background property)

```
public background : Boolean
```

Specifies if the text field has a background fill. If `true`, the text field has a background fill. If `false`, the text field has no background fill.

Availability: ActionScript 1.0; Flash Player 6

Example

The following example creates a text field with a background color that toggles on and off when nearly any key on the keyboard is pressed.

```
this.createTextField("my_txt", this.getNextHighestDepth(), 10, 10, 320,
   240);
my_txt.border = true;
my_txt.text = "Lorum ipsum";
my_txt.backgroundColor = 0xFF0000;

var keyListener:Object = new Object();
keyListener.onKeyDown = function() {
  my_txt.background = !my_txt.background;
};
Key.addListener(keyListener);
```

The `MovieClip.getNextHighestDepth()` method used in this example requires Flash Player 7 or later. If your SWF file includes a version 2 component, use the version 2 components DepthManager class instead of the `MovieClip.getNextHighestDepth()` method.

backgroundColor (TextField.backgroundColor property)

`public backgroundColor : Number`

The color of the text field background. Default is `0xFFFFFF` (white). This property may be retrieved or set, even if there currently is no background, but the color is only visible if the text field has a border.

Availability: ActionScript 1.0; Flash Player 6

Example

See the example for `TextField.background`.

See also

`background (TextField.background property)`

border (TextField.border property)

`public border : Boolean`

Specifies if the text field has a border. If `true`, the text field has a border. If `false`, the text field has no border.

Availability: ActionScript 1.0; Flash Player 6

Example

The following example creates a text field called `my_txt`, sets the border property to `true`, and displays some text in the field.

```
this.createTextField("my_txt", this.getNextHighestDepth(), 10, 10, 320,
    240);
my_txt.border = true;
my_txt.text = "Lorum ipsum";
```

The `MovieClip.getNextHighestDepth()` method used in this example requires Flash Player 7 or later. If your SWF file includes a version 2 component, use the version 2 components DepthManager class instead of the `MovieClip.getNextHighestDepth()` method.

borderColor (TextField.borderColor property)

`public borderColor : Number`

The color of the text field border. The default is `0x000000` (black). This property may be retrieved or set, even if there is currently no border.

Availability: ActionScript 1.0; Flash Player 6

Example

The following example creates a text field called `my_txt`, sets the border property to `true`, and displays some text in the field.

```
this.createTextField("my_txt", this.getNextHighestDepth(), 10, 10, 320,
    240);
my_txt.border = true;
my_txt.borderColor = 0x00FF00;
my_txt.text = "Lorum ipsum";
```

The `MovieClip.getNextHighestDepth()` method used in this example requires Flash Player 7 or later. If your SWF file includes a version 2 component, use the version 2 components DepthManager class instead of the `MovieClip.getNextHighestDepth()` method.

See also

`border (TextField.border property)`

bottomScroll (TextField.bottomScroll property)

```
public bottomScroll : Number [read-only]
```

An integer (one-based index) that indicates the bottommost line that is currently visible the text field. Think of the text field as a window onto a block of text. The property `TextField.scroll` is the one-based index of the topmost visible line in the window.

All the text between lines `TextField.scroll` and `TextField.bottomScroll` is currently visible in the text field.

Availability: ActionScript 1.0; Flash Player 6

Example

The following example creates a text field and fills it with text. You must insert a button (with the instance name "my_btn"), and when you click it, the `scroll` and `bottomScroll` properties for the text field are then traced for the `comment_txt` field.

```
this.createTextField("comment_txt", this.getNextHighestDepth(), 0, 0, 160,
   120);
comment_txt.html = true;
comment_txt.selectable = true;
comment_txt.multiline = true;
comment_txt.wordWrap = true;
comment_txt.htmlText = "<b>What is hexadecimal?</b><br>"
   + "The hexadecimal color system uses six digits to represent color
   values. "
   + "Each digit has sixteen possible values or characters. The characters
   range"
   + " from 0 to 9 and then A to F. Black is represented by (#000000) and
   white, "
   + "at the opposite end of the color system, is (#FFFFFF).";
my_btn.onRelease = function() {
   trace("scroll: "+comment_txt.scroll);
   trace("bottomScroll: "+comment_txt.bottomScroll);
};
```

The `MovieClip.getNextHighestDepth()` method used in this example requires Flash Player 7 or later. If your SWF file includes a version 2 component, use the version 2 components DepthManager class instead of the `MovieClip.getNextHighestDepth()` method.

condenseWhite (TextField.condenseWhite property)

```
public condenseWhite : Boolean
```

A Boolean value that specifies whether extra white space (spaces, line breaks, and so on) in an HTML text field should be removed when the field is rendered in a browser. The default value is `false`.

If you set this value to `true`, you must use standard HTML commands such as `<BR>` and `<P>` to place line breaks in the text field.

If the text field's `.html` is `false`, this property is ignored.

Availability: ActionScript 1.0; Flash Player 6

Example

The following example creates two text fields, called `first_txt` and `second_txt`. The white space is removed from the second text field. Add the following ActionScript to your FLA or AS file:

```
var my_str:String = "Hello\tWorld\nHow are you?\t\t\tEnd";

this.createTextField("first_txt", this.getNextHighestDepth(), 10, 10, 160,
    120);
first_txt.html = true;
first_txt.multiline = true;
first_txt.wordWrap = true;
first_txt.condenseWhite = false;
first_txt.border = true;
first_txt.htmlText = my_str;

this.createTextField("second_txt", this.getNextHighestDepth(), 180, 10,
    160, 120);
second_txt.html = true;
second_txt.multiline = true;
second_txt.wordWrap = true;
second_txt.condenseWhite = true;
second_txt.border = true;
second_txt.htmlText = my_str;
```

The `MovieClip.getNextHighestDepth()` method used in this example requires Flash Player 7 or later. If your SWF file includes a version 2 component, use the version 2 components DepthManager class instead of the `MovieClip.getNextHighestDepth()` method.

See also

`html (TextField.html property)`

embedFonts (TextField.embedFonts property)

`public embedFonts : Boolean`

Specifies whether to render using embedded font outlines. A Boolean value that, when `true`, renders the text field using embedded font outlines. If `false`, it renders the text field using device fonts.

If you set embedFonts to true for a text field, then you must specify a font for that text via the font property of a TextFormat object applied to the text field. If the specified font does *not* exist in the library (with the corresponding Linkage Instance name), then the text will not be displayed.

Availability: ActionScript 1.0; Flash Player 6

Example

In this example, you need to create a dynamic text field called my_txt, and then use the following ActionScript to embed fonts and rotate the text field. The reference to my font refers to a Font symbol in the library, with linkage set to my font. The example assumes that you have a Font symbol in the library called my font, with linkage properties set as follows: the identifier set to my font and Export for ActionScript and Export in First Frame selected.

```
var my_fmt:TextFormat = new TextFormat();
my_fmt.font = "my font";

this.createTextField("my_txt", this.getNextHighestDepth(), 10, 10, 160,
    120);
my_txt.wordWrap = true;
my_txt.embedFonts = true;
my_txt.text = "Hello world";
my_txt.setTextFormat(my_fmt);
my_txt._rotation = 45;
```

The MovieClip.getNextHighestDepth() method used in this example requires Flash Player 7 or later. If your SWF file includes a version 2 component, use the version 2 components DepthManager class instead of the MovieClip.getNextHighestDepth() method.

filters (TextField.filters property)

```
public filters : Array
```

An indexed array containing each filter object currently associated with the text field. The flash.filters package contains several classes that define specific filters that you can use.

Filters can be applied in the Flash authoring tool at design-time, or at runtime using ActionScript code. To apply a filter using ActionScript, you must make a temporary copy of the entire TextField.filters array, modify the temporary array, and then assign the value of the temporary array back to the TextField.filters array. You cannot directly add a new filter object to the TextField.filters array. The following code has no effect on the target text field, named myTextField:

```
myTextField.filters[0].push(myDropShadow);
```

To add a filter using ActionScript, you must follow these steps (assume that the target movie clip is named myTextField):

- Create a new filter object using the constructor function of your chosen filter class.
- Assign the value of the `myTextField.filters` array to a temporary array, such as one named `myFilters`.
- Add the new filter object to the temporary array, `myFilters`.
- Assign the value of the temporary array to the `myTextField.filters` array.

If the `filters` array is empty, you need not use a temporary array. Instead, you can directly assign an array literal that contains one or more filter objects that you have created.

To modify an existing filter object, whether it was created at design-time or at runtime, you must use the technique of modifying a copy of the `filters` array, as follows:

- Assign the value of the `myTextField.filters` array to a temporary array, such as one named `myFilters`.
- Modify the property using the temporary array, `myFilters`. For example, if you want to set the `quality` property of the first filter in the array, you could use the following code: `myList[0].quality = 1;`
- Assign the value of the temporary array to the `myTextField.filters` array.

To clear the filters for a text field, set `filters` to an empty array (`[]`).

If you are working with a `filters` array that contains multiple filters and you need to track the type of filter assigned to each array index, you can maintain your own `filters` array and use a separate data structure to track the type of filter associated with each array index. There is no simple way to determine the type of filter associated with each `filters` array index.

Availability: ActionScript 1.0; Flash Player 8

Example

The following example adds a drop shadow filter to a text field named `myTextField`.

```
var myDropFilter = new flash.filters.DropShadowFilter();
var myFilters:Array = myTextField.filters;
myFilters.push(myDropFilter);
myTextField.filters = myFilters;
```

The following example changes the `quality` setting of the first filter in the array to 15 (this example works only if at least one filter object has been associated with the `myTextField` text field).

```
var myList:Array = myTextField.filters;
myList[0].quality = 15;
myTextField.filters = myList;
```

See also

getDepth (TextField.getDepth method)

```
public getDepth() : Number
```

Returns the depth of a text field.

Availability: ActionScript 1.0; Flash Player 6

Returns

`Number` - An integer that represents the depth of the text field.

Example

The following example demonstrates text fields that reside at different depths. Create a dynamic text field on the Stage and add the following ActionScript code to your FLA or AS file. The code dynamically creates two text fields at runtime and outputs their depths.

```
this.createTextField("first_mc", this.getNextHighestDepth(), 10, 10, 100,
    22);
this.createTextField("second_mc", this.getNextHighestDepth(), 10, 10, 100,
    22);
for (var prop in this) {
    if (this[prop] instanceof TextField) {
    var this_txt:TextField = this[prop];
    trace(this_txt._name+" is a TextField at depth: "+this_txt.getDepth());
    }
}
```

The `MovieClip.getNextHighestDepth()` method used in this example requires Flash Player 7 or later. If your SWF file includes a version 2 component, use the version 2 components DepthManager class instead of the `MovieClip.getNextHighestDepth()` method.

getFontList (TextField.getFontList method)

```
public static getFontList() : Array
```

Returns the names of fonts on the player's host system as an array. (This method does not return names of all fonts in currently loaded SWF files.) The names are of type `String`. This method is a static method of the global TextField class. You cannot specify a text field instance when you call this method.

Availability: ActionScript 1.0; Flash Player 6

Returns

`Array` - An array of font names.

Example

The following code displays a font list returned by `getFontList()`:

```
var font_array:Array = TextField.getFontList();
font_array.sort();
trace("You have "+font_array.length+" fonts currently installed");
trace("----------------------------------------");
for (var i = 0; i<font_array.length; i++) {
   trace("Font #"+(i+1)+":\t"+font_array[i]);
}
```

getNewTextFormat (TextField.getNewTextFormat method)

`public getNewTextFormat() : TextFormat`

Returns a TextFormat object containing a copy of the text field's text format object. The text format object is the format that newly inserted text, such as text inserted with the `replaceSel()` method or text entered by a user, receives. When `getNewTextFormat()` is invoked, the TextFormat object returned has all of its properties defined. No property is `null`.

Availability: ActionScript 1.0; Flash Player 6

Returns

`TextFormat` - A TextFormat object.

Example

The following example displays the specified text field's (`my_txt`) text format object.

```
this.createTextField("my_txt", this.getNextHighestDepth(), 10, 10, 160,
   120);
var my_fmt:TextFormat = my_txt.getNewTextFormat();
trace("TextFormat has the following properties:");
for (var prop in my_fmt) {
   trace(prop+": "+my_fmt[prop]);
}
```

The `MovieClip.getNextHighestDepth()` method used in this example requires Flash Player 7 or later. If your SWF file includes a version 2 component, use the version 2 components DepthManager class instead of the `MovieClip.getNextHighestDepth()` method.

getTextFormat (TextField.getTextFormat method)

```
public getTextFormat([beginIndex:Number], [endIndex:Number]) : TextFormat
```

Returns a TextFormat object for a character, a range of characters, or an entire TextField object.

The following table describes three possible usages:

Usage	Description
my_textField.getTextForm at()	Returns a TextFormat object containing formatting information for all text in a text field. Only properties that are common to all text in the text field are set in the resulting TextFormat object. Any property that is *mixed*, meaning that it has different values at different points in the text, has a value of null.
my_textField.getTextForm at(beginIndex:Number)	Returns a TextFormat object containing a copy of the text field's text format at the beginIndex position.
my_textField.getTextForm at(beginIndex:Number,end Index:Number)	Returns a TextFormat object containing formatting information for the span of text from beginIndex to endIndex. Only properties that are common to all of the text in the specified range are set in the resulting TextFormat object. Any property that is mixed (that is, has different values at different points in the range) has its value set to null.

Availability: ActionScript 1.0; Flash Player 6

Parameters

beginIndex:Number [optional] - An integer that specifies a character in a string. If you do not specify beginIndex and endIndex, the TextFormat object returned is for the entire TextField.

endIndex:Number [optional] - An integer that specifies the end position of a span of text. If you specify beginIndex but do not specify endIndex, the TextFormat returned is for the single character specified by beginIndex.

Returns

TextFormat - The TextFormat object that represents the formatting properties for the specified text.

Example

The following ActionScript code traces all of the formatting information for a text field that is created at runtime.

```
this.createTextField("dyn_txt", this.getNextHighestDepth(), 0, 0, 100,
   200);
dyn_txt.text = "Frank";
dyn_txt.setTextFormat(new TextFormat());
var my_fmt:TextFormat = dyn_txt.getTextFormat();
for (var prop in my_fmt) {
  trace(prop+": "+my_fmt[prop]);
}
```

The `MovieClip.getNextHighestDepth()` method used in this example requires Flash Player 7 or later. If your SWF file includes a version 2 component, use the version 2 components DepthManager class instead of the `MovieClip.getNextHighestDepth()` method.

See also

getNewTextFormat (TextField.getNewTextFormat method), setNewTextFormat (TextField.setNewTextFormat method), setTextFormat (TextField.setTextFormat method)

gridFitType (TextField.gridFitType property)

`public gridFitType : String`

The type of grid fitting used for this TextField instance. This property applies only if the `antiAliasType` property of the text field is set to `"advanced"`.

For the `gridFitType` property, you can use the following string values:

String value	Description
`"none"`	Specifies no grid fitting. Horizontal and vertical lines in the glyphs are not forced to the pixel grid. This setting is usually good for animation or for large font sizes.
`"pixel"`	Specifies that strong horizontal and vertical lines are fit to the pixel grid. This setting works only for left-aligned text fields. To use this setting, the `antiAliasType` property of the text field must be set to `"advanced"`. This setting generally provides the best legibility for left-aligned text.
`"subpixel"`	Specifies that strong horizontal and vertical lines are fit to the subpixel grid on an LCD monitor. To use this setting, the `antiAliasType` property of the text field must be set to `"advanced"`. The `"subpixel"` setting is often good for right-aligned or centered dynamic text, and it is sometimes a useful trade-off for animation versus text quality.

Availability: ActionScript 1.0; Flash Player 8

Example

This example shows three text fields that use the different `gridFitType` settings. It assumes that you have a font embedded in the Library with the linkage identifier set to `"Times-12"`. To embed the font, follow these steps:

- Open your Library
- Click the Library options menu in the upper right corner of the Library
- Select "New Font" from the dropdown list
- Name the font "Times-12"
- Select "Times New Roman" from the font dropdown list
- Press the "OK" button
- Right-click on the newly created font and select "Linkage..."
- Check the "Export for ActionScript" box
- Accept the default identifier "Times-12" by pressing the "OK" button

```
var my_format:TextFormat = new TextFormat();
my_format.font = "Times-12";

var my_text1:TextField = this.createTextField("my_text1",
  this.getNextHighestDepth(), 9.5, 10, 400, 100);
my_text1.text = "this.gridFitType = none";
my_text1.embedFonts = true;
my_text1.antiAliasType = "advanced";
my_text1.gridFitType = "none";
my_text1.setTextFormat(my_format);

var my_text2:TextField = this.createTextField("my_text2",
  this.getNextHighestDepth(), 9.5, 40, 400, 100);
my_text2.text = "this.gridFitType = advanced";
my_text2.embedFonts = true;
my_text2.antiAliasType = "advanced";
my_text2.gridFitType = "pixel";
my_text2.setTextFormat(my_format);

var my_text3:TextField = this.createTextField("my_text3",
  this.getNextHighestDepth(), 9.5, 70, 400, 100);
my_text3.text = "this.gridFitType = subpixel";
my_text3.embedFonts = true;
my_text3.antiAliasType = "advanced";
my_text3.gridFitType = "subpixel";
my_text3.setTextFormat(my_format);
```

If your SWF file includes a version 2 component, use the version 2 components DepthManager class instead of the `MovieClip.getNextHighestDepth()` method, which is used in this example.

TextRenderer (flash.text.TextRenderer), antiAliasType
(TextField.antiAliasType property), sharpness (TextField.sharpness property)

_height (TextField._height property)

`public _height : Number`

The height of the text field in pixels.

Availability: ActionScript 1.0; Flash Player 6

Example

The following code example sets the height and width of a text field:

```
my_txt._width = 200;
my_txt._height = 200;
```

_highquality (TextField._highquality property)

`public _highquality : Number`

Deprecated since Flash Player 7. This property was deprecated in favor of
`TextField._quality`.

Specifies the level of anti-aliasing applied to the current SWF file. Specify 2 (best quality) to
apply high quality with bitmap smoothing always on. Specify 1 (high quality) to apply anti-
aliasing; this smoothes bitmaps if the SWF file does not contain animation and is the default
value. Specify 0 (low quality) to prevent anti-aliasing.

Availability: ActionScript 1.0; Flash Player 6

See also

`_quality (TextField._quality property)`

hscroll (TextField.hscroll property)

`public hscroll : Number`

Indicates the current horizontal scrolling position. If the `hscroll` property is 0, the text is not horizontally scrolled.

The units of horizontal scrolling are pixels, while the units of vertical scrolling are lines. Horizontal scrolling is measured in pixels because most fonts you typically use are proportionally spaced; meaning, the characters can have different widths. Flash performs vertical scrolling by line because users usually want to see a line of text in its entirety, as opposed to seeing a partial line. Even if there are multiple fonts on a line, the height of the line adjusts to fit the largest font in use.

Note: The hscroll property is zero-based not one-based like the vertical scrolling property `TextField.scroll`.

Availability: ActionScript 1.0; Flash Player 6

Example

The following example scrolls the `my_txt` text field horizontally using two buttons called `scrollLeft_btn` and `scrollRight_btn`. The amount of scroll displays in a text field called `scroll_txt`. Add the following ActionScript to your FLA or AS file:

```
this.createTextField("scroll_txt", this.getNextHighestDepth(), 10, 10, 160,
    20);
this.createTextField("my_txt", this.getNextHighestDepth(), 10, 30, 160,
    22);
my_txt.border = true;
my_txt.multiline = false;
my_txt.wordWrap = false;
my_txt.text = "Lorem ipsum dolor sit amet, consectetuer adipiscing...";

scrollLeft_btn.onRelease = function() {
  my_txt.hscroll -= 10;
  scroll_txt.text = my_txt.hscroll+" of "+my_txt.maxhscroll;
};
scrollRight_btn.onRelease = function() {
  my_txt.hscroll += 10;
  scroll_txt.text = my_txt.hscroll+" of "+my_txt.maxhscroll;
};
```

The `MovieClip.getNextHighestDepth()` method used in this example requires Flash Player 7 or later. If your SWF file includes a version 2 component, use the version 2 components DepthManager class instead of the `MovieClip.getNextHighestDepth()` method.

See also

maxhscroll (TextField.maxhscroll property), scroll (TextField.scroll property)

html (TextField.html property)

`public html : Boolean`

A flag that indicates whether the text field contains an HTML representation. If the `html` property is `true`, the text field is an HTML text field. If `html` is `false`, the text field is a non-HTML text field.

Availability: ActionScript 1.0; Flash Player 6

Example

The following example creates a text field that sets the `html` property to `true`. HTML-formatted text displays in the text field.

```
this.createTextField("my_txt", this.getNextHighestDepth(), 10, 10, 160,
    22);
my_txt.html = true;
my_txt.htmlText = "<b> this is bold text </b>";
```

The `MovieClip.getNextHighestDepth()` method used in this example requires Flash Player 7 or later. If your SWF file includes a version 2 component, use the version 2 components DepthManager class instead of the `MovieClip.getNextHighestDepth()` method.

See also

htmlText (TextField.htmlText property)

htmlText (TextField.htmlText property)

`public htmlText : String`

If the text field is an HTML text field, this property contains the HTML representation of the text field's contents. If the text field is not an HTML text field, it behaves identically to the `text` property. You can indicate that a text field is an HTML text field in the Property inspector, or by setting the text field's `html` property to `true`.

Availability: ActionScript 1.0; Flash Player 6

Example

The following example creates a text field that sets the `html` property to `true`. HTML-formatted text displays in the text field.

```
this.createTextField("my_txt", this.getNextHighestDepth(), 10, 10, 160,
    22);
my_txt.html = true;
my_txt.htmlText = "<b> this is bold text </b>";
```

The `MovieClip.getNextHighestDepth()` method used in this example requires Flash Player 7 or later. If your SWF file includes a version 2 component, use the version 2 components DepthManager class instead of the `MovieClip.getNextHighestDepth()` method.

See also

`html (TextField.html property)`, `asfunction protocol`

length (TextField.length property)

```
public length : Number [read-only]
```

Indicates the number of characters in a text field. This property returns the same value as `text.length`, but is faster. A character such as tab (`\t`) counts as one character.

Availability: ActionScript 1.0; Flash Player 6

Example

The following example outputs the number of characters in the `date_txt` text field, which displays the current date.

```
var today:Date = new Date();
this.createTextField("date_txt", this.getNextHighestDepth(), 10, 10, 100,
    22);
date_txt.autoSize = true;
date_txt.text = today.toString();
trace(date_txt.length);
```

The `MovieClip.getNextHighestDepth()` method used in this example requires Flash Player 7 or later. If your SWF file includes a version 2 component, use the version 2 components DepthManager class instead of the `MovieClip.getNextHighestDepth()` method.

maxChars (TextField.maxChars property)

`public maxChars : Number`

Indicates the maximum number of characters that the text field can contain. A script may insert more text than `maxChars` allows; the `maxChars` property indicates only how much text a user can enter. If the value of this property is `null`, there is no limit on the amount of text a user can enter.

Availability: ActionScript 1.0; Flash Player 6

Example

The following example creates a text field called `age_txt` that only lets users enter up to two numbers in the field.

```
this.createTextField("age_txt", this.getNextHighestDepth(), 10, 10, 30,
    22);
age_txt.type = "input";
age_txt.border = true;
age_txt.maxChars = 2;
age_txt.restrict = "0-9";
```

The `MovieClip.getNextHighestDepth()` method used in this example requires Flash Player 7 or later. If your SWF file includes a version 2 component, use the version 2 components DepthManager class instead of the `MovieClip.getNextHighestDepth()` method.

maxhscroll (TextField.maxhscroll property)

`public maxhscroll : Number [read-only]`

Indicates the maximum value of `TextField.hscroll`.

Availability: ActionScript 1.0; Flash Player 6

Example

See the example for `TextField.hscroll`.

maxscroll (TextField.maxscroll property)

`public maxscroll : Number [read-only]`

Indicates the maximum value of `TextField.scroll`.

Availability: ActionScript 1.0; Flash Player 6

Example

The following example sets the maximum value for the scrolling text field `my_txt`. Create two buttons, `scrollUp_btn` and `scrollDown_btn`, to scroll the text field. Add the following ActionScript to your FLA or AS file.

```
this.createTextField("scroll_txt", this.getNextHighestDepth(), 10, 10, 160,
    20);
this.createTextField("my_txt", this.getNextHighestDepth(), 10, 30, 320,
    240);
my_txt.multiline = true;
my_txt.wordWrap = true;
for (var i = 0; i<10; i++) {
   my_txt.text += "Lorem ipsum dolor sit amet, consectetuer adipiscing elit,
   sed diam nonummy nibh "
       + "euismod tincidunt ut laoreet dolore magna aliquam erat volutpat.";
}
scrollUp_btn.onRelease = function() {
   my_txt.scroll--;
   scroll_txt.text = my_txt.scroll+" of "+my_txt.maxscroll;
};
scrollDown_btn.onRelease = function() {
   my_txt.scroll++;
   scroll_txt.text = my_txt.scroll+" of "+my_txt.maxscroll;
};
```

The `MovieClip.getNextHighestDepth()` method used in this example requires Flash Player 7 or later. If your SWF file includes a version 2 component, use the version 2 components DepthManager class instead of the `MovieClip.getNextHighestDepth()` method.

menu (TextField.menu property)

`public menu : ContextMenu`

Associates the ContextMenu object *contextMenu* with the text field *my_txt*. The ContextMenu class lets you modify the context menu that appears when the user right-clicks (Windows) or Control-clicks (Macintosh) in Flash Player.

This property works only with selectable (editable) text fields; it has no effect on nonselectable text fields.

Availability: ActionScript 1.0; Flash Player 7

Example

The following example assigns the ContextMenu object `menu_cm` to the text field `news_txt`. The ContextMenu object contains a custom menu item labeled "Resize" with an associated callback handler named `doResize()`, which could be used to add resizing functionality (not shown):

```
this.createTextField("news_txt", this.getNextHighestDepth(), 10, 10, 320,
    240);
news_txt.border = true;
news_txt.wordWrap = true;
news_txt.multiline = true;
news_txt.text = "To see the custom context menu item, right click (PC) or ";
news_txt.text += "control click (Mac) within the text field.";
var menu_cm:ContextMenu = new ContextMenu();
menu_cm.customItems.push(new ContextMenuItem("Resize", doResize));

function doResize(obj:TextField, item:ContextMenuItem):Void {
  // "Resize" code here
  trace("you selected: "+item.caption);
}
news_txt.menu = menu_cm;
```

When you right-click or Control-click within the area of the text field, you see the custom menu item.

> **NOTE** You cannot use a menu item that is already used by Flash. For example, Print... (with three dots) is reserved by Flash, so you cannot use this menu item; however, you could use Print... (with two dots) or any menu item not already used by Flash.

If your SWF file includes a version 2 component, use the version 2 components DepthManager class instead of the `MovieClip.getNextHighestDepth()` method, which is used in this example.

See also

Button, ContextMenu, ContextMenuItem, MovieClip

mouseWheelEnabled (TextField.mouseWheelEnabled property)

`public mouseWheelEnabled : Boolean`

A Boolean value that indicates whether Flash Player should automatically scroll multiline text fields when the mouse pointer clicks a text field and the user rolls the mouse wheel. By default, this value is `true`. This property is useful if you want to prevent mouse wheel scrolling of text fields, or implement your own text field scrolling.

Availability: ActionScript 1.0; Flash Player 7

Example

The following example creates two text fields. The `scrollable_txt` field has the `mouseWheelEnabled` property set to true, so `scrollable_txt` scrolls when you click the field and roll the mouse wheel. The `nonscrollable_txt` field does not scroll if you click the field and roll the mouse wheel.

```
var font_array:Array = TextField.getFontList().sort();

this.createTextField("scrollable_txt", this.getNextHighestDepth(), 10, 10,
  240, 320);
scrollable_txt.border = true;
scrollable_txt.wordWrap = true;
scrollable_txt.multiline = true;
scrollable_txt.text = font_array.join("\n");

this.createTextField("nonscrollable_txt", this.getNextHighestDepth(), 260,
  10, 240, 320);
nonscrollable_txt.border = true;
nonscrollable_txt.wordWrap = true;
nonscrollable_txt.multiline = true;
nonscrollable_txt.mouseWheelEnabled = false;
nonscrollable_txt.text = font_array.join("\n");
```

`Mouse.onMouseWheel`

If your SWF file includes a version 2 component, use the version 2 components DepthManager class instead of the `MovieClip.getNextHighestDepth()` method, which is used in this example.

See also

`mouseWheelEnabled (TextField.mouseWheelEnabled property)`

multiline (TextField.multiline property)

`public multiline : Boolean`

Indicates whether the text field is a multiline text field. If the value is `true`, the text field is multiline; if the value is `false`, the text field is a single-line text field.

Availability: ActionScript 1.0; Flash Player 6

Example

The following example creates a multiline text field called `fontList_txt` that displays a long, multiline list of fonts.

```
var font_array:Array = TextField.getFontList().sort();

this.createTextField("fontList_txt", this.getNextHighestDepth(), 10, 10,
    240, 320);
fontList_txt.border = true;
fontList_txt.wordWrap = true;
fontList_txt.multiline = true;
fontList_txt.text = font_array.join("\n");
```

The `MovieClip.getNextHighestDepth()` method used in this example requires Flash Player 7 or later. If your SWF file includes a version 2 component, use the version 2 components DepthManager class instead of the `MovieClip.getNextHighestDepth()` method.

_name (TextField._name property)

```
public _name : String
```

The instance name of the text field.

Availability: ActionScript 1.0; Flash Player 6

Example

The following example demonstrates text fields residing at different depths. Create a dynamic text field on the Stage. Add the following ActionScript to your FLA or AS file, which dynamically creates two text fields at runtime and displays their depths in the Output panel.

```
this.createTextField("first_mc", this.getNextHighestDepth(), 10, 10, 100,
    22);
this.createTextField("second_mc", this.getNextHighestDepth(), 10, 10, 100,
    22);
for (var prop in this) {
  if (this[prop] instanceof TextField) {
  var this_txt:TextField = this[prop];
  trace(this_txt._name+" is a TextField at depth: "+this_txt.getDepth());
  }
}
```

When you test the document, the instance name and depth is displayed in the Output panel.

The `MovieClip.getNextHighestDepth()` method used in this example requires Flash Player 7 or later. If your SWF file includes a version 2 component, use the version 2 components DepthManager class instead of the `MovieClip.getNextHighestDepth()` method.

onChanged (TextField.onChanged handler)

```
onChanged = function(changedField:TextField) {}
```

Event handler/listener; invoked when the content of a text field changes. By default, it is undefined; you can define it in a script.

A reference to the text field instance is passed as a parameter to the `onChanged` handler. You can capture this data by putting a parameter in the event handler method. For example, the following code uses `textfield_txt` as the parameter that is passed to the `onChanged` event handler. The parameter is then used in a `trace()` statement to send the instance name of the text field to the Output panel:

```
this.createTextField("myInputText_txt", 99, 10, 10, 300, 20);
myInputText_txt.border = true;
myInputText_txt.type = "input";

myInputText_txt.onChanged = function(textfield_txt:TextField) {
trace("the value of "+textfield_txt._name+" was changed. New value is:
   "+textfield_txt.text);
};
```

The `onChanged` handler is called only when the change results from user interaction; for example, when the user is typing something on the keyboard, changing something in the text field using the mouse, or selecting a menu item. Programmatic changes to the text field do not trigger the `onChanged` event because the code recognizes changes that are made to the text field.

Availability: ActionScript 1.0; Flash Player 6

Parameters

`changedField:TextField` - The field triggering the event.

See also

`TextFormat`, `setNewTextFormat (TextField.setNewTextFormat method)`

onKillFocus (TextField.onKillFocus handler)

```
onKillFocus = function(newFocus:Object) {}
```

Invoked when a text field loses keyboard focus. The `onKillFocus` method receives one parameter, `newFocus`, which is an object representing the new object receiving the focus. If no object receives the focus, `newFocus` contains the value `null`.

Availability: ActionScript 1.0; Flash Player 6

Parameters

`newFocus:Object` - The object that is receiving the focus.

Example

The following example creates two text fields called `first_txt` and `second_txt`. When you give focus to a text field, information about the text field with current focus and the text field that lost focus is displayed in the Output panel.

```
this.createTextField("first_txt", 1, 10, 10, 300, 20);
first_txt.border = true;
first_txt.type = "input";
this.createTextField("second_txt", 2, 10, 40, 300, 20);
second_txt.border = true;
second_txt.type = "input";
first_txt.onKillFocus = function(newFocus:Object) {
   trace(this._name+" lost focus. New focus changed to: "+newFocus._name);
};
first_txt.onSetFocus = function(oldFocus:Object) {
   trace(this._name+" gained focus. Old focus changed from:
   "+oldFocus._name);
}
```

See also

`onSetFocus (TextField.onSetFocus handler)`

onScroller (TextField.onScroller handler)

`onScroller = function(scrolledField:TextField) {}`

Event handler/listener; invoked when one of the text field scroll properties changes.

A reference to the text field instance is passed as a parameter to the `onScroller` handler. You can capture this data by putting a parameter in the event handler method. For example, the following code uses `my_txt` as the parameter that is passed to the `onScroller` event handler. The parameter is then used in a `trace()` statement to send the instance name of the text field to the Output panel.

```
myTextField.onScroller = function (my_txt:TextField) {
   trace (my_txt._name + " scrolled");
};
```

The `TextField.onScroller` event handler is commonly used to implement scroll bars. Scroll bars typically have a thumb or other indicator that shows the current horizontal or vertical scrolling position in a text field. Text fields can be navigated using the mouse and keyboard, which causes the scroll position to change. The scroll bar code needs to be notified if the scroll position changes because of such user interaction, which is what `TextField.onScroller` is used for.

`onScroller` is called whether the scroll position changed because of a users interaction with the text field, or programmatic changes. The `onChanged` handler fires only if a user interaction causes the change. These two options are necessary because often one piece of code changes the scrolling position, while the scroll bar code is unrelated and won't know that the scroll position changed without being notified.

Availability: ActionScript 1.0; Flash Player 6

Parameters

`scrolledField:TextField` - A reference to the TextField object whose scroll position was changed.

Example

The following example creates a text field called `my_txt`, and uses two buttons called `scrollUp_btn` and `scrollDown_btn` to scroll the contents of the text field. When the `onScroller` event handler is called, a trace statement is used to display information in the Output panel. Create two buttons with instance names `scrollUp_btn` and `scrollDown_btn`, and add the following ActionScript to your FLA or AS file:

```
this.createTextField("scroll_txt", this.getNextHighestDepth(), 10, 10, 160,
    20);
this.createTextField("my_txt", this.getNextHighestDepth(), 10, 30, 320,
    240);
my_txt.multiline = true;
my_txt.wordWrap = true;

for (var i = 0; i<10; i++) {
    my_txt.text += "Lorem ipsum dolor sit amet, consectetuer adipiscing elit,
    sed diam "
        + "nonummy nibh euismod tincidunt ut laoreet dolore magna aliquam erat
    volutpat.";
}
scrollUp_btn.onRelease = function() {
    my_txt.scroll--;
};
scrollDown_btn.onRelease = function() {
    my_txt.scroll++;
};
```

```
my_txt.onScroller = function() {
    trace("onScroller called");
  scroll_txt.text = my_txt.scroll+" of "+my_txt.maxscroll;
};
```

The `MovieClip.getNextHighestDepth()` method used in this example requires Flash Player 7 or later. If your SWF file includes a version 2 component, use the version 2 components DepthManager class instead of the `MovieClip.getNextHighestDepth()` method.

See also

`hscroll (TextField.hscroll property)`, `maxhscroll (TextField.maxhscroll property)`, `maxscroll (TextField.maxscroll property)`, `scroll (TextField.scroll property)`

onSetFocus (TextField.onSetFocus handler)

`onSetFocus = function(oldFocus:Object) {}`

Invoked when a text field receives keyboard focus. The `oldFocus` parameter is the object that loses the focus. For example, if the user presses the Tab key to move the input focus from a button to a text field, oldFocus contains the button instance. If there is no previously focused object, `oldFocus` contains a null value.

Availability: ActionScript 1.0; Flash Player 6

Parameters

`oldFocus:Object` - The object to lose focus.

Example

See the example for `TextField.onKillFocus`.

See also

`onKillFocus (TextField.onKillFocus handler)`

_parent (TextField._parent property)

`public _parent : MovieClip`

A reference to the movie clip or object that contains the current text field or object. The current object is the one containing the ActionScript code that references _parent.

Use _parent to specify a relative path to movie clips or objects that are above the current text field. You can use _parent to climb up multiple levels in the display list as in the following:

`_parent._parent._alpha = 20;`

Availability: ActionScript 1.0; Flash Player 6

Example

The following ActionScript creates two text fields and outputs information about the
_parent of each object. The first text field, `first_txt`, is created on the main Timeline. The
second text field, `second_txt`, is created inside the movie clip called `holder_mc`.

```
this.createTextField("first_txt", this.getNextHighestDepth(), 10, 10, 160,
    22);
first_txt.border = true;
trace(first_txt._name+"'s _parent is: "+first_txt._parent);

this.createEmptyMovieClip("holder_mc", this.getNextHighestDepth());
holder_mc.createTextField("second_txt", holder_mc.getNextHighestDepth(),
    10, 40, 160, 22);
holder_mc.second_txt.border = true;
trace(holder_mc.second_txt._name+"'s _parent is:
    "+holder_mc.second_txt._parent);
```

The following information is displayed in the Output panel:

```
first_txt's _parent is: _level0
second_txt's _parent is: _level0.holder_mc
```

The `MovieClip.getNextHighestDepth()` method used in this example requires Flash Player
7 or later. If your SWF file includes a version 2 component, use the version 2 components
DepthManager class instead of the `MovieClip.getNextHighestDepth()` method.

See also

`_parent (Button._parent property)`, `_parent (MovieClip._parent property)`,
`_root property`, `targetPath function`

password (TextField.password property)

`public password : Boolean`

Specifies whether the text field is a password text field. If the value of password is `true`, the
text field is a password text field and hides the input characters using asterisks instead of the
actual characters. If `false`, the text field is not a password text field. When password mode is
enabled, the *Cut* and *Copy* commands and their corresponding keyboard accelerators will not
function. This security mechanism prevents an unscrupulous user from using the shortcuts to
discover a password on an unattended computer.

Availability: ActionScript 1.0; Flash Player 6

Example

The following example creates two text fields: username_txt and password_txt. Text is entered into both text fields; however, password_txt has the password property set to true. Therefore, the characters display as asterisks instead of as characters in the password_txt field.

```
this.createTextField("username_txt", this.getNextHighestDepth(), 10, 10,
    100, 22);
username_txt.border = true;
username_txt.type = "input";
username_txt.maxChars = 16;
username_txt.text = "hello";

this.createTextField("password_txt", this.getNextHighestDepth(), 10, 40,
    100, 22);
password_txt.border = true;
password_txt.type = "input";
password_txt.maxChars = 16;
password_txt.password = true;
password_txt.text = "world";
```

The MovieClip.getNextHighestDepth() method used in this example requires Flash Player 7 or later. If your SWF file includes a version 2 component, use the version 2 components DepthManager class instead of the MovieClip.getNextHighestDepth() method.

_quality (TextField._quality property)

`public _quality : String`

The rendering quality used for a SWF file. Device fonts are always aliased and, therefore, are unaffected by the _quality property.

 NOTE Although you can specify this property for a TextField object, it is actually a global property, and you can specify its value simply as _quality. For more information, see the _quality global property.

The _quality property can be set to the following values:

- "LOW" Low rendering quality. Graphics are not anti-aliased, and bitmaps are not smoothed.

- "MEDIUM" Medium rendering quality. Graphics are anti-aliased using a 2 x 2 pixel grid, but bitmaps are not smoothed. Suitable for movies that do not contain text.

- "HIGH" High rendering quality. Graphics are anti-aliased using a 4 x 4 pixel grid, and bitmaps are smoothed if the movie is static. This is the default rendering quality setting used by Flash.
- "BEST" Very high rendering quality. Graphics are anti-aliased using a 4 x 4 pixel grid and bitmaps are always smoothed.

Availability: ActionScript 1.0; Flash Player 6

Example

The following example sets the rendering quality to LOW:

```
my_txt._quality = "LOW";
```

See also

`_quality property`

removeListener (TextField.removeListener method)

```
public removeListener(listener:Object) : Boolean
```

Removes a listener object previously registered to a text field instance with `TextField.addListener()`.

Availability: ActionScript 1.0; Flash Player 6

Parameters

`listener:Object` - The object that will no longer receive notifications from `TextField.onChanged` or `TextField.onScroller`.

Returns

`Boolean` - If `listener` was successfully removed, the method returns a `true` value. If `listener` was not successfully removed (for example, if `listener` was not on the TextField object's listener list), the method returns a value of `false`.

Example

The following example creates an input text field called `my_txt`. When the user types into the field, information about the number of characters in the text field is displayed in the Output panel. If the user clicks the `removeListener_btn` instance, then the listener is removed and information is no longer displayed.

```
this.createTextField("my_txt", this.getNextHighestDepth(), 10, 10, 160,
    20);
my_txt.border = true;
my_txt.type = "input";
```

```
var txtListener:Object = new Object();
txtListener.onChanged = function(textfield_txt:TextField) {
  trace(textfield_txt+" changed. Current length is:
  "+textfield_txt.length);
};
my_txt.addListener(txtListener);

removeListener_btn.onRelease = function() {
  trace("Removing listener...");
  if (!my_txt.removeListener(txtListener)) {
  trace("Error! Unable to remove listener");
  }
};
```

The `MovieClip.getNextHighestDepth()` method used in this example requires Flash Player 7 or later. If your SWF file includes a version 2 component, use the version 2 components DepthManager class instead of the `MovieClip.getNextHighestDepth()` method.

removeTextField (TextField.removeTextField method)

```
public removeTextField() : Void
```

Removes the text field. This operation can only be performed on a text field that was created with `MovieClip.createTextField()`. When you call this method, the text field is removed. This method is similar to `MovieClip.removeMovieClip()`.

Availability: ActionScript 1.0; Flash Player 6

Example

The following example creates a text field that you can remove from the Stage when you click the remove_btn instance. Create a button and call it `remove_btn`, and then add the following ActionScript to your FLA or AS file.

```
this.createTextField("my_txt", this.getNextHighestDepth(), 10, 10, 300,
  22);
my_txt.text = new Date().toString();
my_txt.border = true;

remove_btn.onRelease = function() {
  my_txt.removeTextField();
};
```

The `MovieClip.getNextHighestDepth()` method used in this example requires Flash Player 7 or later. If your SWF file includes a version 2 component, use the version 2 components DepthManager class instead of the `MovieClip.getNextHighestDepth()` method.

replaceSel (TextField.replaceSel method)

`public replaceSel(newText:String) : Void`

Replaces the current selection with the contents of the `newText` parameter. The text is inserted at the position of the current selection, using the current default character format and default paragraph format. The text is not treated as HTML, even if the text field is an HTML text field.

You can use the `replaceSel()` method to insert and delete text without disrupting the character and paragraph formatting of the rest of the text.

You must use `Selection.setFocus()` to focus the field before issuing this command.

Availability: ActionScript 1.0; Flash Player 6

Parameters

`newText:String` - A string.

Example

The following example code creates a multiline text field with text on the Stage. When you select some text and then right-click or Control-click over the text field, you can select `Enter current date` from the context menu. This selection calls a function that replaces the selected text with the current date.

```
this.createTextField("my_txt", this.getNextHighestDepth(), 10, 10, 320,
    240);
my_txt.border = true;
my_txt.wordWrap = true;
my_txt.multiline = true;
my_txt.type = "input";
my_txt.text = "Select some sample text from the text field and then right-
    click/control click "
    + "and select 'Enter current date' from the context menu to replace the
    "
    + "currently selected text with the current date.";

var my_cm:ContextMenu = new ContextMenu();
my_cm.customItems.push(new ContextMenuItem("Enter current date",
    enterDate));
function enterDate(obj:Object, menuItem:ContextMenuItem) {
    var today_str:String = new Date().toString();
    var date_str:String = today_str.split(" ", 3).join(" ");
    my_txt.replaceSel(date_str);
}
my_txt.menu = my_cm;
```

The `MovieClip.getNextHighestDepth()` method used in this example requires Flash Player 7 or later. If your SWF file includes a version 2 component, use the version 2 components DepthManager class instead of the `MovieClip.getNextHighestDepth()` method.

See also

setFocus (Selection.setFocus method)

replaceText (TextField.replaceText method)

```
public replaceText(beginIndex:Number, endIndex:Number, newText:String) :
  Void
```

Replaces a range of characters, specified by the `beginIndex` and `endIndex` parameters, in the specified text field with the contents of the `newText` parameter.

Availability: ActionScript 1.0; Flash Player 7

Parameters

`beginIndex:Number` - The start index value for the replacement range.

`endIndex:Number` - The end index value for the replacement range.

`newText:String` - The text to use to replace the specified range of characters.

Example

The following example creates a text field called `my_txt` and assigns the text `dog@house.net` to the field. The `indexOf()` method is used to find the first occurrence of the specified symbol (@). If the symbol is found, the specified text (between the index of 0 and the symbol) replaces with the string `bird`. If the symbol is not found, an error message is displayed in the Output panel.

```
this.createTextField("my_txt", this.getNextHighestDepth(), 10, 10, 320,
  22);
my_txt.autoSize = true;
my_txt.text = "dog@house.net";

var symbol:String = "@";
var symbolPos:Number = my_txt.text.indexOf(symbol);
if (symbolPos>-1) {
  my_txt.replaceText(0, symbolPos, "bird");
} else {
  trace("symbol '"+symbol+"' not found.");
}
```

If your SWF file includes a version 2 component, use the version 2 components DepthManager class instead of the `MovieClip.getNextHighestDepth()` method, which is used in this example.

---

restrict (TextField.restrict property)

```
public restrict : String
```

Indicates the set of characters that a user may enter into the text field. If the value of the restrict property is null, you can enter any character. If the value of the restrict property is an empty string, you cannot enter any character. If the value of the restrict property is a string of characters, you can enter only characters in the string into the text field. The string is scanned from left to right. A range may be specified using the dash (-). This only restricts user interaction; a script may put any text into the text field. This property does not synchronize with the Embed Font Outlines check boxes in the Property inspector.

If the string begins with ^, all characters are initially accepted and succeeding characters in the string are excluded from the set of accepted characters. If the string does not begin with ^, no characters are initially accepted and succeeding characters in the string are included in the set of accepted characters.

Availability: ActionScript 1.0; Flash Player 6

Example

The following example allows only uppercase characters, spaces, and numbers to be entered into a text field:

```
my_txt.restrict = "A-Z 0-9";
```

The following example includes all characters, but excludes lowercase letters:

```
my_txt.restrict = "^a-z";
```

You can use a backslash to enter a ^ or - verbatim. The accepted backslash sequences are \-, \^ or \\. The backslash must be an actual character in the string, so when specified in ActionScript, a double backslash must be used. For example, the following code includes only the dash (-) and caret (^):

```
my_txt.restrict = "\\-\\^";
```

The ^ may be used anywhere in the string to toggle between including characters and excluding characters. The following code includes only uppercase letters, but excludes the uppercase letter Q:

```
my_txt.restrict = "A-Z^Q";
```

You can use the \u escape sequence to construct restrict strings. The following code includes only the characters from ASCII 32 (space) to ASCII 126 (tilde).

```
my_txt.restrict = "\u0020-\u007E";
```

_rotation (TextField._rotation property)

```
public _rotation : Number
```

The rotation of the text field, in degrees, from its original orientation. Values from 0 to 180 represent clockwise rotation; values from 0 to -180 represent counterclockwise rotation. Values outside this range are added to or subtracted from 360 to obtain a value within the range. For example, the statement my_txt._rotation = 450 is the same as my_txt._rotation = 90.

Rotation values are not supported for text fields that use device fonts. You must use embedded fonts to use _rotation with a text field.

Availability: ActionScript 1.0; Flash Player 6

Example

In this example, you need to create a dynamic text field called my_txt, and then use the following ActionScript to embed fonts and rotate the text field. The reference to my font refers to a Font symbol in the library, with linkage set to my font.

```
var my_fmt:TextFormat = new TextFormat();
my_fmt.font = "my font";

this.createTextField("my_txt", this.getNextHighestDepth(), 10, 10, 160,
    120);
my_txt.wordWrap = true;
my_txt.embedFonts = true;
my_txt.text = "Hello world";
my_txt.setTextFormat(my_fmt);
my_txt._rotation = 45;
```

Apply additional formatting for the text field using the TextFormat class.

The MovieClip.getNextHighestDepth() method used in this example requires Flash Player 7 or later. If your SWF file includes a version 2 component, use the version 2 components DepthManager class instead of the MovieClip.getNextHighestDepth() method.

See also

_rotation (Button._rotation property), _rotation (MovieClip._rotation property), TextFormat

scroll (TextField.scroll property)

```
public scroll : Number
```

The vertical position of text in a text field. The scroll property is useful for directing users to a specific paragraph in a long passage, or for creating scrolling text fields. This property can be retrieved and modified.

The units of horizontal scrolling are pixels and the units of vertical scrolling are lines. Horizontal scrolling is measured in pixels because most fonts that you typically use are proportionally spaced, meaning that the characters can have different widths. Flash performs vertical scrolling by line because users usually want to see a line of text in its entirety, as opposed to seeing a partial line. Even if there are multiple fonts on a line, the height of the line adjusts to fit the largest font in use.

Availability: ActionScript 1.0; Flash Player 6

Example

The following example sets the maximum value for the scrolling text field `my_txt`. Create two buttons, `scrollUp_btn` and `scrollDown_btn`, to scroll through the text field. Add the following ActionScript code to your FLA or AS file.

```
this.createTextField("scroll_txt", this.getNextHighestDepth(), 10, 10, 160,
   20);
this.createTextField("my_txt", this.getNextHighestDepth(), 10, 30, 320,
   240);
my_txt.multiline = true;
my_txt.wordWrap = true;
for (var i = 0; i<10; i++) {
   my_txt.text += "Lorem ipsum dolor sit amet, consectetuer adipiscing elit,
   sed diam nonummy "
      + "nibh euismod tincidunt ut laoreet dolore magna aliquam erat
   volutpat.";
}
scrollUp_btn.onRelease = function() {
   my_txt.scroll--;
   scroll_txt.text = my_txt.scroll+" of "+my_txt.maxscroll;
};
scrollDown_btn.onRelease = function() {
   my_txt.scroll++;
   scroll_txt.text = my_txt.scroll+" of "+my_txt.maxscroll;
};
```

The `MovieClip.getNextHighestDepth()` method used in this example requires Flash Player 7 or later. If your SWF file includes a version 2 component, use the version 2 components DepthManager class instead of the `MovieClip.getNextHighestDepth()` method.

See also

hscroll (TextField.hscroll property), maxscroll (TextField.maxscroll property)

selectable (TextField.selectable property)

```
public selectable : Boolean
```

A Boolean value that indicates whether the text field is selectable. The value `true` indicates that the text is selectable. The `selectable` property controls whether a text field is selectable, and not whether a text field is editable. A dynamic text field can be selectable even if it is not editable. If a dynamic text field is not selectable, that means you cannot select its text.

If selectable is set to `false`, the text in the text field does not respond to selection commands from the mouse or keyboard, and the text cannot be copied using the Copy command. If selectable is set to `true`, the text in the text field can be selected using the mouse or keyboard. You can select text this way even if the text field is a dynamic text field instead of an input text field. The text can be copied using the Copy command.

Availability: ActionScript 1.0; Flash Player 6

Example

The following example creates a selectable text field that constantly updates with the current date and time.

```
this.createTextField("date_txt", this.getNextHighestDepth(), 10, 10, 100,
    22);
date_txt.autoSize = true;
date_txt.selectable = true;

var date_interval:Number = setInterval(updateTime, 500, date_txt);
function updateTime(my_txt:TextField) {
  my_txt.text = new Date().toString();
}
```

The `MovieClip.getNextHighestDepth()` method used in this example requires Flash Player 7 or later. If your SWF file includes a version 2 component, use the version 2 components DepthManager class instead of the `MovieClip.getNextHighestDepth()` method.

setNewTextFormat (TextField.setNewTextFormat method)

`public setNewTextFormat(tf:TextFormat) : Void`

Sets the default new text format of a text field. The default new text format is the new text format used for newly inserted text such as text inserted with the `replaceSel()` method or text entered by a user. When text is inserted, the newly inserted text is assigned the default new text format.

The new default text format is specified by `textFormat`, which is a TextFormat object.

Availability: ActionScript 1.0; Flash Player 6

Parameters

`tf`:`TextFormat` - A TextFormat object.

Example

In the following example, a new text field (called `my_txt`) is created at runtime and several properties are set. The format of the newly inserted text is applied.

```
var my_fmt:TextFormat = new TextFormat();
my_fmt.bold = true;
my_fmt.font = "Arial";
my_fmt.color = 0xFF9900;

this.createTextField("my_txt", 999, 0, 0, 400, 300);
my_txt.wordWrap = true;.
my_txt.multiline = true;
my_txt.border = true;
my_txt.type = "input";
my_txt.setNewTextFormat(my_fmt);
my_txt.text = "Oranges are a good source of vitamin C";
```

See also

`getNewTextFormat` (TextField.getNewTextFormat method), `getTextFormat` (TextField.getTextFormat method), `setTextFormat` (TextField.setTextFormat method)

setTextFormat (TextField.setTextFormat method)

```
public setTextFormat([beginIndex:Number], [endIndex:Number],
    textFormat:TextFormat) : Void
```

Applies the text formatting specified by the `textFormat` parameter to some or all of the text in a text field. `textFormat` must be a TextFormat object that specifies the text formatting changes desired. Only the non-null properties of textFormat are applied to the text field. Any property of `textFormat` that is set to null will not be applied. By default, all of the properties of a newly created TextFormat object are set to `null`.

There are two types of formatting information in a TextFormat object: character level, and paragraph level formatting. Each character in a text field might have its own character formatting settings, such as font name, font size, bold, and italic.

For paragraphs, the first character of the paragraph is examined for the paragraph formatting settings for the entire paragraph. Examples of paragraph formatting settings are left margin, right margin, and indentation.

The setTextFormat() method changes the text formatting applied to an individual character, to a range of characters, or to the entire body of text in a text field. These usages are shown in the following table:

Usage	Description
my_textField.setTextFor mat(textFormat:TextForm at)	Applies the properties of textFormat to all text in the text field.
my_textField.setTextFor mat(beginIndex:Number, textFormat:TextFormat)	Applies the properties of textFormat to the character at the beginIndex position.
my_textField.setTextFor mat(beginIndex:Number, endIndex:Number, textFormat:TextFormat)	Applies the properties of the textFormat parameter to the span of text from the beginIndex position to the endIndex position.

Notice that any text inserted manually by the user, or replaced by means of TextField.replaceSel(), receives the text field's default formatting for new text, and not the formatting specified for the text insertion point. To set a text field's default formatting for new text, use TextField.setNewTextFormat().

Availability: ActionScript 1.0; Flash Player 6

Parameters

beginIndex:Number [optional] - An integer that specifies the first character of the desired text span. If you do not specify beginIndex and endIndex, the TextFormat is applied to the entire TextField.

endIndex:Number [optional] - An integer that specifies the first character after the desired text span. If you specify beginIndex but do not specify endIndex, the TextFormat is applied to the single character specified by beginIndex.

textFormat:TextFormat - A TextFormat object, which contains character and paragraph formatting information.

Example

The following example sets the text format for two different strings of text. The setTextFormat() method is called and applied to the my_txt text field.

```
var format1_fmt:TextFormat = new TextFormat();
format1_fmt.font = "Arial";
var format2_fmt:TextFormat = new TextFormat();
format2_fmt.font = "Courier";

var string1:String = "Sample string number one."+newline;
```

```
var string2:String = "Sample string number two."+newline;

this.createTextField("my_txt", this.getNextHighestDepth(), 0, 0, 300, 200);
my_txt.multiline = true;
my_txt.wordWrap = true;
my_txt.text = string1;
var firstIndex:Number = my_txt.length;
my_txt.text += string2;
var secondIndex:Number = my_txt.length;

my_txt.setTextFormat(0, firstIndex, format1_fmt);
my_txt.setTextFormat(firstIndex, secondIndex, format2_fmt);
```

The `MovieClip.getNextHighestDepth()` method used in this example requires Flash Player 7 or later. If your SWF file includes a version 2 component, use the version 2 components DepthManager class instead of the `MovieClip.getNextHighestDepth()` method.

See also

TextFormat, setNewTextFormat (TextField.setNewTextFormat method)

sharpness (TextField.sharpness property)

public sharpness : Number

The sharpness of the glyph edges in this TextField instance. This property applies only if the `antiAliasType` property of the text field is set to `"advanced"`. The range for `sharpness` is a number from -400 to 400. If you attempt to set `sharpness` to a value outside that range, Flash sets the property to the nearest value in the range (either -400 or 400).

Availability: ActionScript 1.0; Flash Player 8

Example

This example creates three text fields with `sharpness` set to 400, 0, and -400. It assumes that you have a font embedded in the Library with the linkage identifier set to `"Times-12"`. To embed the font, follow these steps:

- Open your Library
- Click the Library options menu in the upper right corner of the Library
- Select "New Font" from the dropdown list
- Name the font "Times-12"
- Select "Times New Roman" from the font dropdown list
- Press the "OK" button
- Right-click on the newly created font and select "Linkage..."

- Check the "Export for ActionScript" box
- Accept the default identifier "Times-12" by pressing the "OK" button

```
var my_format:TextFormat = new TextFormat();
my_format.font = "Times-12";

var my_text1:TextField = this.createTextField("my_text1",
    this.getNextHighestDepth(), 10, 10, 400, 100);
my_text1.text = "This text has sharpness set to 400.";
my_text1.embedFonts = true;
my_text1.antiAliasType = "advanced";
my_text1.gridFitType = "pixel";
my_text1.sharpness = 400;
my_text1.setTextFormat(my_format);

var my_text2:TextField = this.createTextField("my_text2",
    this.getNextHighestDepth(), 10, 40, 400, 100);
my_text2.text = "This text has sharpness set to 0.";
my_text2.embedFonts = true;
my_text2.antiAliasType = "advanced";
my_text2.gridFitType = "pixel";
my_text2.sharpness = 0;
my_text2.setTextFormat(my_format);

var my_text3:TextField = this.createTextField("my_text3",
    this.getNextHighestDepth(), 10, 70, 400, 100);
my_text3.text = "This text has sharpness set to -400.";
my_text3.embedFonts = true;
my_text3.antiAliasType = "advanced";
my_text3.gridFitType = "pixel";
my_text3.sharpness = -400;
my_text3.setTextFormat(my_format);
```

If your SWF file includes a version 2 component, use the version 2 components DepthManager class instead of the `MovieClip.getNextHighestDepth()` method, which is used in this example.

See also

`gridFitType` (TextField.gridFitType property), `antiAliasType` (TextField.antiAliasType property)

_soundbuftime (TextField._soundbuftime property)

```
public _soundbuftime : Number
```

The number of seconds a sound prebuffers before it starts to stream.

Although you can specify this property for a `TextField` object, it is actually a global property that applies to all sounds loaded, and you can specify its value simply as `_soundbuftime`. Setting this property for a `TextField` object actually sets the global property

For more information and an example, see the `_soundbuftime` global property.

Availability: ActionScript 1.0; Flash Player 6

See also
`_soundbuftime` property

styleSheet (TextField.styleSheet property)

`public styleSheet : StyleSheet`

Attaches a style sheet to the text field. For information on creating style sheets, see the TextField.StyleSheet class entry.

The style sheet associated with a text field may be changed at any time. If the style sheet in use is changed, the text field is redrawn using the new style sheet. The style sheet may be set to `null` or `undefined` to remove the style sheet. If the style sheet in use is removed, the text field is redrawn without a style sheet. The formatting done by a style sheet is not retained if the style sheet is removed.

Availability: ActionScript 1.0; Flash Player 7

Example

The following example creates a new text field at runtime, called `news_txt`. Three buttons on the Stage, `css1_btn`, `css2_btn` and `clearCss_btn`, are used to change the style sheet that is applied to `news_txt`, or clear the style sheet from the text field. Add the following ActionScript to your FLA or AS file:

```
this.createTextField("news_txt", this.getNextHighestDepth(), 0, 0, 300,
    200);
news_txt.wordWrap = true;
news_txt.multiline = true;
news_txt.html = true;
var newsText:String = "<p class='headline'>Description</p> Method; "
    + "starts loading the CSS file into styleSheet. The load operation is
    asynchronous; "
    + "use the <span class='bold'>TextField.StyleSheet.onLoad</span> "
    + "callback handler to determine when the file has finished loading. "
    + "<span class='important'>The CSS file must reside in exactly the same "
```

```
    + "domain as the SWF file that is loading it.</span> For more information
    about "
    + "restrictions on loading data across domains, see Flash Player security
    features.";

news_txt.htmlText = newsText;

css1_btn.onRelease = function() {
  var styleObj:TextField.StyleSheet = new TextField.StyleSheet();
  styleObj.onLoad = function(success:Boolean) {
    if (success) {
      news_txt.styleSheet = styleObj;
      news_txt.htmlText = newsText;
    }
  };
  styleObj.load("styles.css");
};

css2_btn.onRelease = function() {
  var styleObj:TextField.StyleSheet = new TextField.StyleSheet();
  styleObj.onLoad = function(success:Boolean) {
    if (success) {
      news_txt.styleSheet = styleObj;
      news_txt.htmlText = newsText;
    }
  };
  styleObj.load("styles2.css");
};

clearCss_btn.onRelease = function() {
  news_txt.styleSheet = undefined;
  news_txt.htmlText = newsText;
};
```

The following styles are applied to the text field. Save the following two CSS files in the same directory as the FLA or AS file you created previously:

```
// in styles.css
.important {
  color: #FF0000;
}
.bold {
  font-weight: bold;
}
.headline {
  color: #000000;
  font-family: Arial,Helvetica,sans-serif;
  font-size: 18px;
  font-weight: bold;
  display: block;
}
```

```
// in styles2.css
.important {
  color: #FF00FF;
}
.bold {
  font-weight: bold;
}
.headline {
  color: #00FF00;
  font-family: Arial,Helvetica,sans-serif;
  font-size: 18px;
  font-weight: bold;
  display: block;
}
```

If your SWF file includes a version 2 component, use the version 2 components DepthManager class instead of the `MovieClip.getNextHighestDepth()` method, which is used in this example.

See also

StyleSheet (TextField.StyleSheet)

tabEnabled (TextField.tabEnabled property)

`public tabEnabled : Boolean`

Specifies whether the text field is included in automatic tab ordering. It is `undefined` by default.

If the `tabEnabled` property is `undefined` or `true`, the object is included in automatic tab ordering. If the `tabIndex` property is also set to a value, the object is included in custom tab ordering as well. If `tabEnabled` is `false`, the object is not included in automatic or custom tab ordering, even if the `tabIndex` property is set.

Availability: ActionScript 1.0; Flash Player 6

Example

The following example creates several text fields, called one_txt, two_txt, three_txt and four_txt. The three_txt text field has the `tabEnabled` property set to `false`, so it is excluded from the automatic tab ordering.

```
this.createTextField("one_txt", this.getNextHighestDepth(), 10, 10, 100,
  22);
one_txt.border = true;
one_txt.type = "input";
this.createTextField("two_txt", this.getNextHighestDepth(), 10, 40, 100,
  22);
two_txt.border = true;
```

```
two_txt.type = "input";
this.createTextField("three_txt", this.getNextHighestDepth(), 10, 70, 100,
    22);
three_txt.border = true;
three_txt.type = "input";
this.createTextField("four_txt", this.getNextHighestDepth(), 10, 100, 100,
    22);
four_txt.border = true;
four_txt.type = "input";

three_txt.tabEnabled = false;
three_txt.text = "tabEnabled = false;";
```

The `MovieClip.getNextHighestDepth()` method used in this example requires Flash Player 7 or later. If your SWF file includes a version 2 component, use the version 2 components DepthManager class instead of the `MovieClip.getNextHighestDepth()` method.

See also

`tabEnabled (Button.tabEnabled property)`, `tabEnabled (MovieClip.tabEnabled property)`

tabIndex (TextField.tabIndex property)

`public tabIndex : Number`

Lets you customize the tab ordering of objects in a SWF file. You can set the `tabIndex` property on a button, movie clip, or text field instance; it is `undefined` by default.

If any currently displayed object in the SWF file contains a `tabIndex` property, automatic tab ordering is disabled, and the tab ordering is calculated from the `tabIndex` properties of objects in the SWF file. The custom tab ordering only includes objects that have `tabIndex` properties.

The `tabIndex` property must be a positive integer. The objects are ordered according to their `tabIndex` properties, in ascending order. An object with a `tabIndex` value of 1 precedes an object with a `tabIndex` value of 2. If two objects have the same `tabIndex` value, the one that precedes the other in the tab ordering is `undefined`.

The custom tab ordering defined by the `tabIndex` property is *flat*. This means that no attention is paid to the hierarchical relationships of objects in the SWF file. All objects in the SWF file with `tabIndex` properties are placed in the tab order, and the tab order is determined by the order of the `tabIndex` values. If two objects have the same `tabIndex` value, the one that goes first is `undefined`. You should not use the same `tabIndex` value for multiple objects.

Availability: ActionScript 1.0; Flash Player 6

Example

The following ActionScript dynamically creates four text fields and assigns them to a custom tab order. Add the following ActionScript to your FLA or AS file:

```
this.createTextField("one_txt", this.getNextHighestDepth(), 10, 10, 100,
    22);
one_txt.border = true;
one_txt.type = "input";
this.createTextField("two_txt", this.getNextHighestDepth(), 10, 40, 100,
    22);
two_txt.border = true;
two_txt.type = "input";
this.createTextField("three_txt", this.getNextHighestDepth(), 10, 70, 100,
    22);
three_txt.border = true;
three_txt.type = "input";
this.createTextField("four_txt", this.getNextHighestDepth(), 10, 100, 100,
    22);
four_txt.border = true;
four_txt.type = "input";

one_txt.tabIndex = 3;
two_txt.tabIndex = 1;
three_txt.tabIndex = 2;
four_txt.tabIndex = 4;
```

The `MovieClip.getNextHighestDepth()` method used in this example requires Flash Player 7 or later. If your SWF file includes a version 2 component, use the version 2 components DepthManager class instead of the `MovieClip.getNextHighestDepth()` method.

See also

`tabIndex (Button.tabIndex property)`, `tabIndex (MovieClip.tabIndex property)`

_target (TextField._target property)

`public _target : String [read-only]`

The target path of the text field instance. The `_self` target specifies the current frame in the current window, `_blank` specifies a new window, `_parent` specifies the parent of the current frame, and `_top` specifies the top-level frame in the current window.

Availability: ActionScript 1.0; Flash Player 6

Example

The following ActionScript creates a text field called `my_txt` and outputs the target path of the new field, in both slash and dot notation.

```
this.createTextField("my_txt", this.getNextHighestDepth(), 10, 10, 100,
    22);
trace(my_txt._target); // output: /my_txt
trace(eval(my_txt._target)); // output: _level0.my_txt
```

The `MovieClip.getNextHighestDepth()` method used in this example requires Flash Player 7 or later. If your SWF file includes a version 2 component, use the version 2 components DepthManager class instead of the `MovieClip.getNextHighestDepth()` method.

text (TextField.text property)

```
public text : String
```

Indicates the current text in the text field. Lines are separated by the carriage return character ("\r", ASCII 13). This property contains the normal, unformatted text in the text field, without HTML tags, even if the text field is HTML.

Availability: ActionScript 1.0; Flash Player 6

Example

The following example creates an HTML text field called `my_txt`, and assigns an HTML-formatted string of text to the field. When you trace the `htmlText` property, the Output panel displays the HTML-formatted string. When you trace the value of the `text` property, the unformatted string with HTML tags displays in the Output panel.

```
this.createTextField("my_txt", this.getNextHighestDepth(), 10, 10, 400,
    22);
my_txt.html = true;
my_txt.htmlText = "<B>Lorem ipsum dolor sit amet.</B>";

trace("htmlText: "+my_txt.htmlText);
trace("text: "+my_txt.text);
```

This generates the following output:

```
htmlText: <P ALIGN="LEFT"><FONT FACE="Times New Roman" SIZE="12"
  COLOR="#000000" KERNING="0">
<B>Lorem ipsum dolor sit amet.</B></FONT></P>
text: Lorem ipsum dolor sit amet.
```

The `MovieClip.getNextHighestDepth()` method used in this example requires Flash Player 7 or later. If your SWF file includes a version 2 component, use the version 2 components DepthManager class instead of the `MovieClip.getNextHighestDepth()` method.

See also

```
htmlText (TextField.htmlText property)
```

textColor (TextField.textColor property)

```
public textColor : Number
```

Indicates the color of the text in a text field. The hexadecimal color system uses six digits to represent color values. Each digit has sixteen possible values or characters. The characters range from 0 to 9 and then A to F. Black is represented by (#000000) and white, at the opposite end of the color system, is (#FFFFFF).

Availability: ActionScript 1.0; Flash Player 6

Example

The following ActionScript creates a text field and changes its color property to red.

```
this.createTextField("my_txt", 99, 10, 10, 100, 300);
my_txt.text = "this will be red text";
my_txt.textColor = 0xFF0000;
```

The `MovieClip.getNextHighestDepth()` method used in this example requires Flash Player 7 or later. If your SWF file includes a version 2 component, use the version 2 components DepthManager class instead of the `MovieClip.getNextHighestDepth()` method.

textHeight (TextField.textHeight property)

```
public textHeight : Number
```

Indicates the height of the text.

Availability: ActionScript 1.0; Flash Player 6

Example

The following example creates a text field, and assigns a string of text to the field. A trace statement is used to display the text height and width in the Output panel. The `autoSize` property is then used to resize the text field, and the new height and width will also be displayed in the Output panel.

```
this.createTextField("my_txt", 99, 10, 10, 100, 300);
my_txt.text = "Sample text";
trace("textHeight: "+my_txt.textHeight+", textWidth: "+my_txt.textWidth);
trace("_height: "+my_txt._height+", _width: "+my_txt._width+"\n");
my_txt.autoSize = true;
trace("after my_txt.autoSize = true;");
trace("_height: "+my_txt._height+", _width: "+my_txt._width);
```

Which outputs the following information:

```
textHeight: 15, textWidth: 56
_height: 300, _width: 100
```

```
after my_txt.autoSize = true;
_height: 19, _width: 60
```

See also

textWidth (TextField.textWidth property)

textWidth (TextField.textWidth property)

`public textWidth : Number`

Indicates the width of the text.

Availability: ActionScript 1.0; Flash Player 6

Example

See the example for `TextField.textHeight`.

See also

textHeight (TextField.textHeight property)

thickness (TextField.thickness property)

`public thickness : Number`

The thickness of the glyph edges in this TextField instance. This property applies only when `antiAliasType()` is set to `"advanced"`.

The range for `thickness` is a number from -200 to 200. If you attempt to set `thickness` to a value outside that range, the property is set to the nearest value in the range (either -200 or 200).

Availability: ActionScript 1.0; Flash Player 8

Example

This example creates two text fields and applies a `thickness` of -200 to one and 200 to the other. It assumes that you have a font embedded in the Library with the linkage identifier set to `"Times-12"`. To embed the font, follow these steps:

- Open your Library
- Click the Library options menu in the upper right corner of the Library
- Select "New Font" from the dropdown list
- Name the font "Times-12"
- Select "Times New Roman" from the font dropdown list
- Press the "OK" button

- Right-click on the newly created font and select "Linkage..."
- Check the "Export for ActionScript" box
- Accept the default identifier "Times-12" by pressing the "OK" button

```
var my_format:TextFormat = new TextFormat();
my_format.font = "Times-12";

var my_text1:TextField = this.createTextField("my_text1",
  this.getNextHighestDepth(), 10, 10, 300, 30);
my_text1.text = "thickness = 200";
my_text1.antiAliasType = "advanced";
my_text1.border = true;
my_text1.thickness = 200;
my_text1.embedFonts = true;
my_text1.setTextFormat(my_format);

var my_text2:TextField = this.createTextField("my_text2",
  this.getNextHighestDepth(), 10, 50, 300, 30);
my_text2.text = "thickness = -200."
my_text2.antiAliasType = "advanced";
my_text2.thickness = -200;
my_text2.border = true;
my_text2.embedFonts = true;
my_text2.setTextFormat(my_format);
```

If your SWF file includes a version 2 component, use the version 2 components
DepthManager class instead of the `MovieClip.getNextHighestDepth()` method, which is
used in this example.

See also

`antiAliasType (TextField.antiAliasType property)`

type (TextField.type property)

`public type : String`

Specifies the type of text field. There are two values: `"dynamic"`, which specifies a dynamic
text field that cannot be edited by the user, and `"input"`, which specifies an input text field.

Availability: ActionScript 1.0; ActionScript 1.0; Flash Player 6

Example

The following example creates two text fields: username_txt and password_txt. Text is entered into both text fields; however, password_txt has the password property set to true. Therefore, the characters display as asterisks instead of as characters in the password_txt field.

```
this.createTextField("username_txt", this.getNextHighestDepth(), 10, 10,
    100, 22);
username_txt.border = true;
username_txt.type = "input";
username_txt.maxChars = 16;
username_txt.text = "hello";

this.createTextField("password_txt", this.getNextHighestDepth(), 10, 40,
    100, 22);
password_txt.border = true;
password_txt.type = "input";
password_txt.maxChars = 16;
password_txt.password = true;
password_txt.text = "world";
```

The MovieClip.getNextHighestDepth() method used in this example requires Flash Player 7 or later. If your SWF file includes a version 2 component, use the version 2 components DepthManager class instead of the MovieClip.getNextHighestDepth() method.

_url (TextField._url property)

```
public _url : String [read-only]
```

Retrieves the URL of the SWF file that created the text field.

Availability: ActionScript 1.0; Flash Player 6

Example

The following example retrieves the URL of the SWF file that created the text field, and a SWF file that loads into it.

```
this.createTextField("my_txt", 1, 10, 10, 100, 22);
trace(my_txt._url);

var mclListener:Object = new Object();
mclListener.onLoadInit = function(target_mc:MovieClip) {
    trace(target_mc._url);
};
var holder_mcl:MovieClipLoader = new MovieClipLoader();
holder_mcl.addListener(mclListener);
holder_mcl.loadClip("best_flash_ever.swf",
    this.createEmptyMovieClip("holder_mc", 2));
```

When you test this example, the URL of the SWF file you are testing, and the file called best_flash_ever.swf are displayed in the Output panel.

The MovieClipLoader class used in this example requires Flash Player 7 or later.

variable (TextField.variable property)

```
public variable : String
```

The name of the variable that the text field is associated with. The type of this property is String.

Availability: ActionScript 1.0; Flash Player 6

Example

The following example creates a text field called `my_txt` and associates the variable `today_date` with the text field. When you change the variable `today_date`, then the text that displays in `my_txt` updates.

```
this.createTextField("my_txt", 1, 10, 10, 200, 22);
my_txt.variable = "today_date";
var today_date:Date = new Date();

var date_interval:Number = setInterval(updateDate, 500);
function updateDate():Void {
   today_date = new Date();
}
```

_visible (TextField._visible property)

```
public _visible : Boolean
```

A Boolean value that indicates whether the text field *my_txt* is visible. Text fields that are not visible (`_visible` property set to `false`) are disabled.

Availability: ActionScript 1.0; Flash Player 6

Example

The following example creates a text field called `my_txt`. A button called `visible_btn` toggles the visibility of `my_txt`.

```
this.createTextField("my_txt", 1, 10, 10, 200, 22);
my_txt.background = true;
my_txt.backgroundColor = 0xDFDFDF;
my_txt.border = true;
my_txt.type = "input";

visible_btn.onRelease = function() {
```

```
    my_txt._visible = !my_txt._visible;
};
```

See also

`_visible (Button._visible property)`, `_visible (MovieClip._visible property)`

_width (TextField._width property)

`public _width : Number`

The width of the text field, in pixels.

Availability: ActionScript 1.0; Flash Player 6

Example

The following example creates two text fields that you can use to change the width and height of a third text field on the Stage. Add the following ActionScript to a FLA or AS file.

```
this.createTextField("my_txt", this.getNextHighestDepth(), 10, 40, 160,
    120);
my_txt.background = true;
my_txt.backgroundColor = 0xFF0000;
my_txt.border = true;
my_txt.multiline = true;
my_txt.type = "input";
my_txt.wordWrap = true;

this.createTextField("width_txt", this.getNextHighestDepth(), 10, 10, 30,
    20);
width_txt.border = true;
width_txt.maxChars = 3;
width_txt.restrict = "0-9";
width_txt.type = "input";
width_txt.text = my_txt._width;
width_txt.onChanged = function() {
    my_txt._width = this.text;
}

this.createTextField("height_txt", this.getNextHighestDepth(), 70, 10, 30,
    20);
height_txt.border = true;
height_txt.maxChars = 3;
height_txt.restrict = "0-9";
height_txt.type = "input";
height_txt.text = my_txt._height;
height_txt.onChanged = function() {
    my_txt._height = this.text;
}
```

When you test the example, try entering new values into `width_txt` and `height_txt` to change the dimensions of `my_txt`.

The `MovieClip.getNextHighestDepth()` method used in this example requires Flash Player 7 or later. If your SWF file includes a version 2 component, use the version 2 components DepthManager class instead of the `MovieClip.getNextHighestDepth()` method.

See also

`_height (TextField._height property)`

wordWrap (TextField.wordWrap property)

`public wordWrap : Boolean`

A Boolean value that indicates if the text field has word wrap. If the value of `wordWrap` is `true`, the text field has word wrap; if the value is `false`, the text field does not have word wrap.

Availability: ActionScript 1.0; Flash Player 6

Example

The following example demonstrates how `wordWrap` affects long text in a text field that is created at runtime.

```
this.createTextField("my_txt", 99, 10, 10, 100, 200);
my_txt.text = "This is very long text that will certainly extend beyond the
    width of this text field";
my_txt.border = true;
```

Test the SWF file in Flash Player by selecting Control > Test Movie. Then return to your ActionScript and add the following line to the code and test the SWF file again:

```
my_txt.wordWrap = true;
```

_x (TextField._x property)

`public _x : Number`

An integer that sets the x coordinate of a text field relative to the local coordinates of the parent movie clip. If a text field is on the main Timeline, then its coordinate system refers to the upper left corner of the Stage as (0, 0). If the text field is inside a movie clip that has transformations, the text field is in the local coordinate system of the enclosing movie clip. Thus, for a movie clip rotated 90 degrees counterclockwise, the enclosed text field inherits a coordinate system that is rotated 90 degrees counterclockwise. The text field's coordinates refer to the registration point position.

Availability: ActionScript 1.0; Flash Player 6

Example

The following example creates a text field wherever you click the mouse. When it creates a text field, that field displays the current *x* and *y* coordinates of the text field.

```
this.createTextField("coords_txt", this.getNextHighestDepth(), 0, 0, 60,
    22);
coords_txt.autoSize = true;
coords_txt.selectable = false;
coords_txt.border = true;

var mouseListener:Object = new Object();
mouseListener.onMouseDown = function() {
    coords_txt.text = "X:"+Math.round(_xmouse)+", Y:"+Math.round(_ymouse);
    coords_txt._x = _xmouse;
    coords_txt._y = _ymouse;
};
Mouse.addListener(mouseListener);
```

The `MovieClip.getNextHighestDepth()` method used in this example requires Flash Player 7 or later. If your SWF file includes a version 2 component, use the version 2 components DepthManager class instead of the `MovieClip.getNextHighestDepth()` method.

See also

`_xscale` (TextField._xscale property), `_y` (TextField._y property), `_yscale` (TextField._yscale property)

_xmouse (TextField._xmouse property)

`public _xmouse : Number [read-only]`

Returns the x coordinate of the mouse position relative to the text field.

Availability: ActionScript 1.0; Flash Player 6

Example

The following example creates three text fields on the Stage. The `mouse_txt` instance displays the current position of the mouse in relation to the Stage. The `textfield_txt` instance displays the current position of the mouse pointer in relation to the `my_txt` instance. Add the following ActionScript to a FLA or AS file:

```
this.createTextField("mouse_txt", this.getNextHighestDepth(), 10, 10, 200,
    22);
mouse_txt.border = true;
this.createTextField("textfield_txt", this.getNextHighestDepth(), 220, 10,
    200, 22);
textfield_txt.border = true;
```

```
this.createTextField("my_txt", this.getNextHighestDepth(), 100, 100, 160,
    120);
my_txt.border = true;

var mouseListener:Object = new Object();
mouseListener.onMouseMove = function() {
    mouse_txt.text = "MOUSE ... X:" + Math.round(_xmouse) + ",\tY:" +
    Math.round(_ymouse);
    textfield_txt.text = "TEXTFIELD ... X:" + Math.round(my_txt._xmouse) +
    ",\tY:" +
    Math.round(my_txt._ymouse);
}

Mouse.addListener(mouseListener);
```

The `MovieClip.getNextHighestDepth()` method used in this example requires Flash Player 7 or later. If your SWF file includes a version 2 component, use the version 2 components DepthManager class instead of the `MovieClip.getNextHighestDepth()` method.

See also

`_ymouse (TextField._ymouse property)`

_xscale (TextField._xscale property)

`public _xscale : Number`

Determines the horizontal scale of the text field as applied from the registration point of the text field, expressed as a percentage. The default registration point is (0,0).

Availability: ActionScript 1.0; Flash Player 6

Example

The following example scales the `my_txt` instance when you click the `scaleUp_btn` and `scaleDown_btn` instances.

```
this.createTextField("my_txt", 99, 10, 40, 100, 22);
my_txt.autoSize = true;
my_txt.border = true;
my_txt.selectable = false;
my_txt.text = "Sample text goes here.";

scaleUp_btn.onRelease = function() {
    my_txt._xscale = 2;
    my_txt._yscale = 2;
}
scaleDown_btn.onRelease = function() {
    my_txt._xscale /= 2;
    my_txt._yscale /= 2;
```

}

See also

_x (TextField._x property), _y (TextField._y property), _yscale (TextField._yscale property)

_y (TextField._y property)

public _y : Number

The y coordinate of a text field relative to the local coordinates of the parent movie clip. If a text field is in the main Timeline, then its coordinate system refers to the upper left corner of the Stage as (0, 0). If the text field is inside another movie clip that has transformations, the text field is in the local coordinate system of the enclosing movie clip. Thus, for a movie clip rotated 90 degrees counterclockwise, the enclosed text field inherits a coordinate system that is rotated 90 degrees counterclockwise. The text field's coordinates refer to the registration point position.

Availability: ActionScript 1.0; Flash Player 6

Example

See the example for TextField._x.

See also

_x (TextField._x property), _xscale (TextField._xscale property), _yscale (TextField._yscale property)

_ymouse (TextField._ymouse property)

public _ymouse : Number [read-only]

Indicates the y coordinate of the mouse position relative to the text field.

Availability: ActionScript 1.0; Flash Player 6

Example

See the example for TextField._xmouse.

See also

_xmouse (TextField._xmouse property)

_yscale (TextField._yscale property)

`public _yscale : Number`

The vertical scale of the text field as applied from the registration point of the text field, expressed as a percentage. The default registration point is (0,0).

Availability: ActionScript 1.0; Flash Player 6

Example

See the example for `TextField._xscale`.

See also

`_x (TextField._x property)`, `_xscale (TextField._xscale property)`, `_y (TextField._y property)`

TextFormat

```
Object
  |
  +-TextFormat
```

`public class TextFormat`
`extends Object`

The TextFormat class represents character formatting information. Use the TextFormat class to create specific text formatting for text fields. You can apply text formatting to both static and dynamic text fields. Some properties of the TextFormat class are not available for both embedded and device fonts.

You must use the constructor `new TextFormat()` to create a TextFormat object before calling its methods.

You can set TextFormat parameters to `null` to indicate that they are undefined. When you apply a TextFormat object to a text field using `TextField.setTextFormat()`, only its defined properties are applied, as in the following example:

```
this.createTextField("my_txt", this.getNextHighestDepth(), 0, 0, 100, 22);
my_txt.autoSize = true;
my_txt.text = "Lorem ipsum dolor sit amet...";

var my_fmt:TextFormat = new TextFormat();
my_fmt.bold = true;
my_txt.setTextFormat(my_fmt);
```

This code first creates an empty TextFormat object with all of its properties `null`, and then sets the `bold` property to a defined value. The `MovieClip.getNextHighestDepth()` method used in this example requires Flash Player 7 or later. If your SWF file includes a version 2 component, use the version 2 components DepthManager class instead of the `MovieClip.getNextHighestDepth()` method.

The code `my_txt.setTextFormat(my_fmt)` only changes the `bold` property of the text field's default text format, because the `bold` property is the only one defined in `my_fmt`. All other aspects of the text field's default text format remain unchanged.

When `TextField.getTextFormat()` is invoked, a TextFormat object is returned with all of its properties defined; no property is `null`.

Availability: ActionScript 1.0; Flash Player 6

See also

setTextFormat (TextField.setTextFormat method), getTextFormat (TextField.getTextFormat method)

Property summary

Modifiers	Property	Description
	align:String	A string that indicates the alignment of the paragraph.
	blockIndent:Number	A number that indicates the block indentation in points.
	bold:Boolean	A Boolean value that specifies whether the text is boldface.
	bullet:Boolean	A Boolean value that indicates that the text is part of a bulleted list.
	color:Number	Indicates the color of text.
	font:String	The name of the font for text in this text format, as a string.
	indent:Number	An integer that indicates the indentation from the left margin to the first character in the paragraph.
	italic:Boolean	A Boolean value that indicates whether text in this text format is italicized.
	kerning:Boolean	A Boolean value that indicates whether kerning is enabled or disabled.
	leading:Number	An integer that represents the amount of vertical space in pixels (called *leading*) between lines.

Modifiers	Property	Description
	`leftMargin:Number`	The left margin of the paragraph, in points.
	`letterSpacing:Number`	The amount of space that is uniformly distributed between characters.
	`rightMargin:Number`	The right margin of the paragraph, in points.
	`size:Number`	The point size of text in this text format.
	`tabStops:Array`	Specifies custom tab stops as an array of non-negative integers.
	`target:String`	Indicates the target window where the hyperlink is displayed.
	`underline:Boolean`	A Boolean value that indicates whether the text that uses this text format is underlined (`true`) or not (`false`).
	`url:String`	Indicates the URL that text in this text format hyperlinks to.

Properties inherited from class Object

```
constructor (Object.constructor property),__proto__ (Object.__proto__
property),prototype (Object.prototype property),__resolve
(Object.__resolve property)
```

Constructor summary

Signature	Description
`TextFormat([font:String], [size:Number], [color:Number], [bold:Boolean], [italic:Boolean], [underline:Boolean], [url:String], [target:String], [align:String], [leftMargin:Number], [rightMargin:Number], [indent:Number], [leading:Number])`	Creates a TextFormat object with the specified properties.

Method summary

Modifiers	Signature	Description
	`getTextExtent(text:S tring, [width:Number]) : Object`	**Deprecated** since Flash Player 8. There is no replacement. Returns text measurement information for the text string `text` in the format specified by `my_fmt`.

Methods inherited from class Object

```
addProperty (Object.addProperty method),hasOwnProperty
(Object.hasOwnProperty method),isPropertyEnumerable
(Object.isPropertyEnumerable method),isPrototypeOf (Object.isPrototypeOf
method),registerClass (Object.registerClass method),toString
(Object.toString method),unwatch (Object.unwatch method),valueOf
(Object.valueOf method),watch (Object.watch method)
```

align (TextFormat.align property)

`public align : String`

A string that indicates the alignment of the paragraph. You can apply this property to static and dynamic text. The following list shows possible values for this property:

- `"left"`—The paragraph is left-aligned.

- `"center"`—The paragraph is centered.

- `"right"`—The paragraph is right-aligned.

- `"justify"`—The paragraph is justified. (This value was added in Flash Player 8.)

The default value is `null`, which indicates that the property is undefined.

Availability: ActionScript 1.0; Flash Player 6 - The "justify" value is available beginning with Flash Player 8.

Example

The following example shows the `align` property being set to justify, which causes the characters on each line to be spread out so that the text looks more evenly spaced horizontally.

```
var format:TextFormat = new TextFormat();
format.align = "justify";

var txtField:TextField = this.createTextField("txtField",
  this.getNextHighestDepth(), 100, 100, 300, 100);
txtField.multiline = true;
txtField.wordWrap = true;
txtField.border = true;
```

```
txtField.text = "When this text is justified, it will be "
    + "spread out to more cleanly fill the horizontal "
    + "space for each line. This can be considered an "
    + "improvement over regular left-aligned text that "
    + "will simply wrap and do no more.";
txtField.setTextFormat(format);
```

The `MovieClip.getNextHighestDepth()` method used in this example requires Flash Player 7 or later. If your SWF file includes a version 2 component, use the version 2 components DepthManager class instead of the `MovieClip.getNextHighestDepth()` method.

blockIndent (TextFormat.blockIndent property)

```
public blockIndent : Number
```

A number that indicates the block indentation in points. Block indentation is applied to an entire block of text; that is, to all lines of the text. In contrast, normal indentation (`TextFormat.indent`) affects only the first line of each paragraph. If this property is `null`, the TextFormat object does not specify block indentation.

Availability: ActionScript 1.0; Flash Player 6

Example

This example creates a text field with a border and sets the blockIndent to 20.

```
this.createTextField("mytext",1,100,100,100,100);
mytext.multiline = true;
mytext.wordWrap = true;
mytext.border = true;

var myformat:TextFormat = new TextFormat();
myformat.blockIndent = 20;

mytext.text = "This is my first test field object text";
mytext.setTextFormat(myformat);
```

bold (TextFormat.bold property)

```
public bold : Boolean
```

A Boolean value that specifies whether the text is boldface. The default value is `null`, which indicates that the property is undefined. If the value is `true`, then the text is boldface.

Availability: ActionScript 1.0; Flash Player 6

Example

The following example creates a text field that includes characters in boldface.

```
var my_fmt:TextFormat = new TextFormat();
my_fmt.bold = true;

this.createTextField("my_txt", 1, 100, 100, 300, 100);
my_txt.multiline = true;
my_txt.wordWrap = true;
my_txt.border = true;
my_txt.text = "This is my test field object text";
my_txt.setTextFormat(my_fmt);
```

bullet (TextFormat.bullet property)

```
public bullet : Boolean
```

A Boolean value that indicates that the text is part of a bulleted list. In a bulleted list, each paragraph of text is indented. To the left of the first line of each paragraph, a bullet symbol is displayed. The default value is `null`.

Availability: ActionScript 1.0; Flash Player 6

Example

The following example creates a new text field at runtime, and enters a string with a line break into the field. The TextFormat class is used to format the characters by adding bullets to each line in the text field. This is demonstrated in the following ActionScript:

```
var my_fmt:TextFormat = new TextFormat();
my_fmt.bullet = true;

this.createTextField("my_txt", 1, 100, 100, 300, 100);
my_txt.multiline = true;
my_txt.wordWrap = true;
my_txt.border = true;
my_txt.text = "this is my text"+newline;
my_txt.text += "this is more text"+newline;
my_txt.setTextFormat(my_fmt);
```

color (TextFormat.color property)

```
public color : Number
```

Indicates the color of text. A number containing three 8-bit RGB components; for example, 0xFF0000 is red, and 0x00FF00 is green.

Availability: ActionScript 1.0; Flash Player 6

Example

The following example creates a text field and sets the text color to red.

```
var my_fmt:TextFormat = new TextFormat();
my_fmt.blockIndent = 20;
my_fmt.color = 0xFF0000; // hex value for red

this.createTextField("my_txt", 1, 100, 100, 300, 100);
my_txt.multiline = true;
my_txt.wordWrap = true;
my_txt.border = true;
my_txt.text = "this is my first test field object text";
my_txt.setTextFormat(my_fmt);
```

font (TextFormat.font property)

`public font : String`

The name of the font for text in this text format, as a string. The default value is `null`, which indicates that the property is undefined.

Availability: ActionScript 1.0; Flash Player 6

Example

The following example creates a text field and sets the font to Courier.

```
this.createTextField("mytext",1,100,100,100,100);
mytext.multiline = true;
mytext.wordWrap = true;
mytext.border = true;

var myformat:TextFormat = new TextFormat();
myformat.font = "Courier";

mytext.text = "this is my first test field object text";
mytext.setTextFormat(myformat);
```

getTextExtent (TextFormat.getTextExtent method)

`public getTextExtent(text:String, [width:Number]) : Object`

Deprecated since Flash Player 8. There is no replacement.

Returns text measurement information for the text string `text` in the format specified by `my_fmt`. The text string is treated as plain text (not HTML).

The method returns an object with six properties: `ascent`, `descent`, `width`, `height`, `textFieldHeight`, and `textFieldWidth`. All measurements are in pixels.

If a `width` parameter is specified, word wrapping is applied to the specified text. This lets you determine the height at which a text box shows all of the specified text.

The `ascent` and `descent` measurements provide, respectively, the distance above and below the baseline for a line of text. The baseline for the first line of text is positioned at the text field's origin plus its `ascent` measurement.

The `width` and `height` measurements provide the width and height of the text string. The `textFieldHeight` and `textFieldWidth` measurements provide the height and width required for a text field object to display the entire text string. Text fields have a 2-pixel-wide gutter around them, so the value of `textFieldHeight` is equal the value of `height` + 4; likewise, the value of `textFieldWidth` is always equal to the value of `width` + 4.

If you are creating a text field based on the text metrics, use `textFieldHeight` rather than `height` and `textFieldWidth` rather than `width`.

The following figure illustrates these measurements.

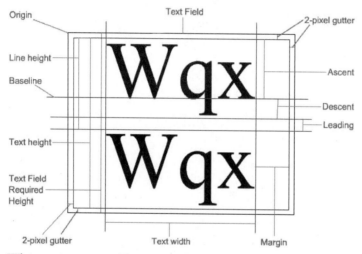

When setting up your TextFormat object, set all the attributes exactly as they will be set for the creation of the text field, including font name, font size, and leading. The default value for leading is 2.

Availability: ActionScript 1.0; Flash Player 6 - The width parameter is supported in Flash Player 7.

Parameters

`text`:`String` - A string.

`width`:`Number` [optional] - A number that represents the width, in pixels, at which the specified text should wrap.

Returns

`Object` - An object with the properties `width`, `height`, `ascent`, `descent`, `textFieldHeight`, `textFieldWidth`.

Example

This example creates a single-line text field that's just big enough to display a text string using the specified formatting.

```
var my_str:String = "Small string";

// Create a TextFormat object,
// and apply its properties.
var my_fmt:TextFormat = new TextFormat();
with (my_fmt) {
   font = "Arial";
   bold = true;
}

// Obtain metrics information for the text string
// with the specified formatting.
var metrics:Object = my_fmt.getTextExtent(my_str);

// Create a text field just large enough to display the text.
this.createTextField("my_txt", this.getNextHighestDepth(), 100, 100,
   metrics.textFieldWidth,
metrics.textFieldHeight);
my_txt.border = true;
my_txt.wordWrap = true;
// Assign the same text string and TextFormat object to the my_txt object.
my_txt.text = my_str;
my_txt.setTextFormat(my_fmt);
```

The following example creates a multiline, 100-pixel-wide text field that's high enough to display a string with the specified formatting.

```
// Create a TextFormat object.
var my_fmt:TextFormat = new TextFormat();
// Specify formatting properties for the TextFormat object:
my_fmt.font = "Arial";
my_fmt.bold = true;
my_fmt.leading = 4;

// The string of text to be displayed
var textToDisplay:String = "Macromedia Flash Player 7, now with improved
   text metrics.";

// Obtain text measurement information for the string,
// wrapped at 100 pixels.
var metrics:Object = my_fmt.getTextExtent(textToDisplay, 100);
```

```
// Create a new TextField object using the metric
// information just obtained.
this.createTextField("my_txt", this.getNextHighestDepth(), 50, 50-
    metrics.ascent, 100,
metrics.textFieldHeight);
my_txt.wordWrap = true;
my_txt.border = true;
// Assign the text and the TextFormat object to the TextObject:
my_txt.text = textToDisplay;
my_txt.setTextFormat(my_fmt);
```

indent (TextFormat.indent property)

```
public indent : Number
```

An integer that indicates the indentation from the left margin to the first character in the paragraph. A positive value indicates normal indentation. You can use a negative value, but the negative indentation only applies if the left margin is greater than 0. To set the margin greater than 0, use the indent property or the blockIndent property of the TextFormat object. The default value is null, which indicates that the property is undefined.

Availability: ActionScript 1.0; Flash Player 6 - The ability to use negative values is available as of Flash Player 8.

Example

The following example creates a text field and sets the indentation to 10:

```
this.createTextField("mytext",1,100,100,100,100);
mytext.multiline = true;
mytext.wordWrap = true;
mytext.border = true;

var myformat:TextFormat = new TextFormat();
myformat.indent = 10;

mytext.text = "this is my first test field object text";
mytext.setTextFormat(myformat);
```

See also

```
blockIndent (TextFormat.blockIndent property)
```

italic (TextFormat.italic property)

```
public italic : Boolean
```

A Boolean value that indicates whether text in this text format is italicized. The default value is `null`, which indicates that the property is undefined.

Availability: ActionScript 1.0; Flash Player 6

Example

The following example creates a text field and sets the text style to italic.

```
this.createTextField("mytext",1,100,100,100,100);
mytext.multiline = true;
mytext.wordWrap = true;
mytext.border = true;

var myformat:TextFormat = new TextFormat();
myformat.italic = true;

mytext.text = "This is my first text field object text";
mytext.setTextFormat(myformat);
```

kerning (TextFormat.kerning property)

```
public kerning : Boolean
```

A Boolean value that indicates whether kerning is enabled or disabled. Kerning puts a predetermined amount of space between certain character pairs to improve readability. The default value is `false`, which indicates that kerning is disabled.

Kerning is supported for embedded fonts only. Certain fonts, such as Courier New, do not support kerning.

The `kerning` property is only supported in SWF files created in Windows, not in SWF files created on the Macintosh. However, Windows SWF files *can* be played in non-Windows versions of Flash Player, and the kerning will still apply.

Use kerning only when necessary, such as with headings in large fonts.

Availability: ActionScript 1.0; Flash Player 8

Example

The following example shows two text fields: The format of the first uses red text with kerning set to `false`, and the format of the second uses blue text with kerning set to `true`. To use this example, you add a font symbol to the Library, and then select Arial as the font. In the Linkage Properties dialog box for the font, you set the Identifier name to "`Font 1`", select Export for ActionScript, and then select Export in First Frame.

```
var fmt1:TextFormat = new TextFormat();
fmt1.font = "Font 1";
fmt1.size = 50;
```

```
fmt1.color = 0xFF0000;
fmt1.kerning = false;

var fmt2:TextFormat = new TextFormat();
fmt2.font = "Font 1";
fmt2.size = 50;
fmt2.color = 0x0000FF;
fmt2.kerning = true;

this.createTextField("tf1", this.getNextHighestDepth(), 10, 10, 400, 100);
tf1.embedFonts = true;
tf1.text = "Text 7AVA-7AVA";
tf1.setTextFormat(fmt1);

this.createTextField("tf2", this.getNextHighestDepth(), 10, 40, 400, 100);
tf2.embedFonts = true;
tf2.text = tf1.text;
tf2.setTextFormat(fmt2);
```

If your SWF file includes a version 2 component, use the version 2 components DepthManager class instead of the `MovieClip.getNextHighestDepth()` method, which is used in this example.

leading (TextFormat.leading property)

`public leading : Number`

An integer that represents the amount of vertical space in pixels (called *leading*) between lines. The default value is `null`, which indicates that the property is undefined.

Flash Player 8 supports *negative leading*, meaning that the amount of space between lines is less than the text height. Negative leading can be useful when you want to put lines of text, such as headings, very close together. To prevent the overlap of text, you use negative leading for lines of text that do not contain descenders, such as text that is all uppercase.

Availability: ActionScript 1.0; Flash Player 6

Example

The following example creates a text field and sets the leading to 10.

```
var my_fmt:TextFormat = new TextFormat();
my_fmt.leading = 10;

this.createTextField("my_txt", 1, 100, 100, 100, 100);
my_txt.multiline = true;
my_txt.wordWrap = true;
my_txt.border = true;
my_txt.text = "This is my first text field object text";
my_txt.setTextFormat(my_fmt);
```

leftMargin (TextFormat.leftMargin property)

`public leftMargin : Number`

The left margin of the paragraph, in points. The default value is `null`, which indicates that the property is undefined.

Availability: ActionScript 1.0; Flash Player 6

Example

The following example creates a text field and sets the left margin to 20 points.

```
this.createTextField("mytext",1,100,100,100,100);
mytext.multiline = true;
mytext.wordWrap = true;
mytext.border = true;

var myformat:TextFormat = new TextFormat();
myformat.leftMargin = 20;

mytext.text = "this is my first test field object text";
mytext.setTextFormat(myformat);
```

letterSpacing (TextFormat.letterSpacing property)

`public letterSpacing : Number`

The amount of space that is uniformly distributed between characters. The Number value specifies the number of pixels that are added to the space after each character. A negative value condenses the space between characters.

System fonts support integer values only; however, for embedded fonts, you can specify floating point (noninteger) values (such as 2.6).

Availability: ActionScript 1.0; Flash Player 8

Example

The following code example uses two TextFormat objects to apply positive and negative values of `letterSpacing` to different ranges of text in a text field.

```
this.createTextField("mytext", this.getNextHighestDepth(), 10, 10, 200,
   100);
mytext.multiline = true;
mytext.wordWrap = true;
mytext.border = true;

var format1:TextFormat = new TextFormat();
format1.letterSpacing = -1;
```

```
var format2:TextFormat = new TextFormat();
format2.letterSpacing = 10;

mytext.text = "Eat at \nJOE'S.";
mytext.setTextFormat(0, 7, format1);
mytext.setTextFormat(8, 12, format2);
```

If your SWF file includes a version 2 component, use the version 2 components
DepthManager class instead of the `MovieClip.getNextHighestDepth()` method, which is
used in this example.

rightMargin (TextFormat.rightMargin property)

`public rightMargin : Number`

The right margin of the paragraph, in points. The default value is `null`, which indicates that
the property is undefined.

Availability: ActionScript 1.0; Flash Player 6

Example

The following example creates a text field and sets the right margin to 20 points.

```
this.createTextField("mytext",1,100,100,100,100);
mytext.multiline = true;
mytext.wordWrap = true;
mytext.border = true;

var myformat:TextFormat = new TextFormat();
myformat.rightMargin = 20;

mytext.text = "this is my first test field object text";
mytext.setTextFormat(myformat);
```

size (TextFormat.size property)

`public size : Number`

The point size of text in this text format. The default value is `null`, which indicates that the
property is undefined.

Availability: ActionScript 1.0; Flash Player 6

Example

The following example creates a text field and sets the text size to 20 points.

```
this.createTextField("mytext",1,100,100,100,100);
mytext.multiline = true;
mytext.wordWrap = true;
mytext.border = true;
```

```
var myformat:TextFormat = new TextFormat();
myformat.size = 20;

mytext.text = "This is my first text field object text";
mytext.setTextFormat(myformat);
```

tabStops (TextFormat.tabStops property)

`public tabStops : Array`

Specifies custom tab stops as an array of non-negative integers. Each tab stop is specified in pixels. If custom tab stops are not specified (`null`), the default tab stop is 4 (average character width).

Availability: ActionScript 1.0; Flash Player 6

Example

The following example creates two text fields, one with tab stops every 40 pixels, and the other with tab stops every 75 pixels.

```
this.createTextField("mytext",1,100,100,400,100);
mytext.border = true;
var myformat:TextFormat = new TextFormat();
myformat.tabStops = [40,80,120,160];
mytext.text = "A\tB\tC\tD"; // \t is the tab stop character
mytext.setTextFormat(myformat);

this.createTextField("mytext2",2,100,220,400,100);
mytext2.border = true;
var myformat2:TextFormat = new TextFormat();
myformat2.tabStops = [75,150,225,300];
mytext2.text ="A\tB\tC\tD";
mytext2.setTextFormat(myformat2);
```

target (TextFormat.target property)

`public target : String`

Indicates the target window where the hyperlink is displayed. If the target window is an empty string, the text is displayed in the default target window _self. You can choose a custom name or one of the following four names: _self specifies the current frame in the current window, _blank specifies a new window, _parent specifies the parent of the current frame, and _top specifies the top-level frame in the current window. If the `TextFormat.url` property is an empty string or `null`, you can get or set this property, but the property will have no effect.

Availability: ActionScript 1.0; Flash Player 6

Example

The following example creates a text field with a hyperlink to the Macromedia website. The example uses `TextFormat.target` to display the Macromedia website in a new browser window.

```
var myformat:TextFormat = new TextFormat();
myformat.url = "http://www.macromedia.com";
myformat.target = "_blank";

this.createTextField("mytext",1,100,100,200,100);
mytext.multiline = true;
mytext.wordWrap = true;
mytext.border = true;
mytext.html = true;
mytext.text = "Go to Macromedia.com";
mytext.setTextFormat(myformat);
```

See also

`url (TextFormat.url property)`

TextFormat constructor

```
public TextFormat([font:String], [size:Number], [color:Number],
    [bold:Boolean], [italic:Boolean], [underline:Boolean], [url:String],
    [target:String], [align:String], [leftMargin:Number],
    [rightMargin:Number], [indent:Number], [leading:Number])
```

Creates a TextFormat object with the specified properties. You can then change the properties of the TextFormat object to change the formatting of text fields.

Any parameter may be set to `null` to indicate that it is not defined. All of the parameters are optional; any omitted parameters are treated as `null`.

Availability: ActionScript 1.0; Flash Player 6

Parameters

`font:String` [optional] - The name of a font for text as a string.

`size:Number` [optional] - An integer that indicates the point size.

`color:Number` [optional] - The color of text using this text format. A number containing three 8-bit RGB components; for example, 0xFF0000 is red, and 0x00FF00 is green.

`bold:Boolean` [optional] - A Boolean value that indicates whether the text is boldface.

`italic:Boolean` [optional] - A Boolean value that indicates whether the text is italicized.

`underline:Boolean` [optional] - A Boolean value that indicates whether the text is underlined.

`url:String` [optional] - The URL to which the text in this text format hyperlinks. If `url` is an empty string, the text does not have a hyperlink.

`target:String` [optional] - The target window where the hyperlink is displayed. If the target window is an empty string, the text is displayed in the default target window `_self`. If the `url` parameter is set to an empty string or to the value `null`, you can get or set this property, but the property will have no effect.

`align:String` [optional] - The alignment of the paragraph, represented as a string. If `"left"`, the paragraph is left-aligned. If `"center"`, the paragraph is centered. If `"right"`, the paragraph is right-aligned.

`leftMargin:Number` [optional] - Indicates the left margin of the paragraph, in points.

`rightMargin:Number` [optional] - Indicates the right margin of the paragraph, in points.

`indent:Number` [optional] - An integer that indicates the indentation from the left margin to the first character in the paragraph.

`leading:Number` [optional] - A number that indicates the amount of leading vertical space between lines.

Example

The following example creates a TextFormat object, formats the `stats_txt` text field, and creates a new text field to display the text in:

```
// Define a TextFormat which is used to format the stats_txt text field.
var my_fmt:TextFormat = new TextFormat();
my_fmt.bold = true;
my_fmt.font = "Arial";
my_fmt.size = 12;
my_fmt.color = 0xFF0000;
// Create a text field to display the player's statistics.
this.createTextField("stats_txt", 5000, 10, 0, 530, 22);
// Apply the TextFormat to the text field.
stats_txt.setNewTextFormat(my_fmt);
stats_txt.selectable = false;
stats_txt.text = "Lorem ipsum dolor sit amet...";
```

To view another example, see the animations.fla file in the ActionScript samples Folder. The following list provides typical paths to the ActionScript samples Folder:

- Windows: *boot drive*\Program Files\Macromedia\Flash 8\Samples and Tutorials\Samples\ActionScript

- Macintosh: *Macintosh HD*/Applications/Macromedia Flash 8/Samples and Tutorials/Samples/ActionScript

underline (TextFormat.underline property)

```
public underline : Boolean
```

A Boolean value that indicates whether the text that uses this text format is underlined (`true`) or not (`false`). This underlining is similar to that produced by the `<U>` tag, but the latter is not true underlining, because it does not skip descenders correctly. The default value is `null`, which indicates that the property is undefined.

Availability: ActionScript 1.0; Flash Player 6

Example

The following example creates a text field and sets the text style to underline.

```
this.createTextField("mytext",1,100,100,200,100);
mytext.multiline = true;
mytext.wordWrap = true;
mytext.border = true;

var myformat:TextFormat = new TextFormat();
myformat.underline = true;
mytext.text = "This is my first text field object text";
mytext.setTextFormat(myformat);
```

url (TextFormat.url property)

```
public url : String
```

Indicates the URL that text in this text format hyperlinks to. If the `url` property is an empty string, the text does not have a hyperlink. The default value is `null`, which indicates that the property is undefined.

Availability: ActionScript 1.0; Flash Player 6

Example

This example creates a text field that is a hyperlink to the Macromedia website.

```
var myformat:TextFormat = new TextFormat();
myformat.url = "http://www.macromedia.com";

this.createTextField("mytext",1,100,100,200,100);
mytext.multiline = true;
mytext.wordWrap = true;
mytext.border = true;
mytext.html = true;
mytext.text = "Go to Macromedia.com";
mytext.setTextFormat(myformat);
```

TextRenderer (flash.text.TextRenderer)

```
Object
  |
  +-flash.text.TextRenderer
```

```
public class TextRenderer
extends Object
```

The TextRenderer class provides functionality for the advanced anti-aliasing capability of embedded fonts. Advanced anti-aliasing allows font faces to render at very high quality at small sizes. Use advanced anti-aliasing with applications that have a lot of small text. Macromedia does not recommend using advanced anti-aliasing for very large fonts (larger than 48 points). Advanced anti-aliasing is available in Flash Player 8 only.

To set advanced anti-aliasing on a text field, set the `antiAliasType` property of the TextField instance. The following example requires a shared font in the library with a linkage identifier named, "CustomFont".

```
var txtFormat:TextFormat = new TextFormat();
txtFormat.font = "CustomFont";

var label:TextField = this.createTextField("label",
   this.getNextHighestDepth(), 10, 10, 200, 20);
label.setNewTextFormat(txtFormat);
label.text = "Hello World";
label.embedFonts = true;
label.antiAliasType = "advanced";
```

Advanced anti-aliasing provides continuous stroke modulation (CSM), which is continuous modulation of both stroke weight and edge sharpness. As an advanced feature, you can use the `setAdvancedAntialiasingTable()` method to define settings for specific typefaces and font sizes.

Availability: ActionScript 1.0; Flash Player 8

See also

`antiAliasType (TextField.antiAliasType property)`

Property summary

Modifiers	Property	Description
static	maxLevel:Number	The adaptively sampled distance fields (ADFs) quality level for advanced anti-aliasing.

Properties inherited from class Object

```
constructor (Object.constructor property),__proto__ (Object.__proto__
property),prototype (Object.prototype property),__resolve
(Object.__resolve property)
```

Method summary

Modifiers	Signature	Description
static	setAdvancedAntialias ingTable(fontName:St ring, fontStyle:String, colorType:String, advancedAntialiasing Table:Array) : Void	Sets a custom continuous stroke modulation (CSM) lookup table for a font.

Methods inherited from class Object

```
addProperty (Object.addProperty method),hasOwnProperty
(Object.hasOwnProperty method),isPropertyEnumerable
(Object.isPropertyEnumerable method),isPrototypeOf (Object.isPrototypeOf
method),registerClass (Object.registerClass method),toString
(Object.toString method),unwatch (Object.unwatch method),valueOf
(Object.valueOf method),watch (Object.watch method)
```

maxLevel (TextRenderer.maxLevel property)

```
public static maxLevel : Number
```

The adaptively sampled distance fields (ADFs) quality level for advanced anti-aliasing. The only acceptable values are 3, 4, and 7.

Advanced anti-aliasing uses ADFs to represent the outlines that determine a glyph. The higher the quality, the more cache space is required for ADF structures. A value of 3 takes the least amount of memory and provides the lowest quality. Larger fonts require more cache space; at a font size of 64 pixels, the quality level increases from 3 to 4 or from 4 to 7 unless, the level is already set to 7.

Availability: ActionScript 1.0; Flash Player 8

Example

The following example specifies the `maxLevel` value for the entire SWF file, and then displays a text field with the value set. For the text in this example to display correctly, there must be a font symbol available with a linkage identifier of `"CustomFont"`.

```
import flash.text.TextRenderer;
TextRenderer.maxLevel = 3;

var txtFormat:TextFormat = new TextFormat();
txtFormat.font = "CustomFont";
txtFormat.size = 64;

var label:TextField = this.createTextField("label",
    this.getNextHighestDepth(), 10, 10, 500, 100);
label.setNewTextFormat(txtFormat);
label.text = "Hello World";
label.embedFonts = true;
trace("TextRenderer.maxLevel: " + TextRenderer.maxLevel);
```

setAdvancedAntialiasingTable (TextRenderer.setAdvancedAntialiasingTable method)

```
public static setAdvancedAntialiasingTable(fontName:String,
    fontStyle:String, colorType:String, advancedAntialiasingTable:Array) :
    Void
```

Sets a custom continuous stroke modulation (CSM) lookup table for a font. This is an advanced method.

Flash Player only includes advanced anti-aliasing settings for 10 basic fonts; and for these fonts, advanced anti-aliasing settings are only provided for the font sizes from 6 to 20. For these fonts, all sizes below 6 use the settings for 6; all sizes above 20 use the settings for 20. Other fonts map to the supplied font data. The `setAdvancedAntialiasingTable()` method lets you set custom anti-aliasing data for other fonts and font sizes, or override the default settings for the provided fonts.

Availability: ActionScript 1.0; Flash Player 8

Parameters

`fontName:String` - The name of the font for which you are applying settings.

`fontStyle:String` - The font style can be `"bold"`, `"bolditalic"`, `"italic"`, and `"none"`.

`colorType:String` - This value can be either `"dark"` or `"light"`.

`advancedAntialiasingTable:Array` - An array of CSM settings for the specified font. Each setting is an object with the following properties:

- `fontSize`
- `insideCutOff`
- `outsideCutOff`

The `advancedAntialiasingTable` array can contain multiple entries that specify CSM settings for different font sizes. (See example.)

The `fontSize` is the size, in pixels, for which the settings apply.

Advanced anti-aliasing uses adaptively sampled distance fields (ADFs) to represent the outlines that determine a glyph. Macromedia Flash uses an outside cutoff value (`outsideCutOff`), below which densities are set to zero, and an inside cutoff value (`insideCutOff`), above which densities are set to a maximum density value (such as 255). Between these two cutoff values, the mapping function is a linear curve ranging from zero at the outside cutoff to the maximum density at the inside cutoff.

Adjusting the outside and inside cutoff values affects stroke weight and edge sharpness. The spacing between these two parameters is comparable to twice the filter radius of classic anti-aliasing methods; a narrow spacing provides a sharper edge, while a wider spacing provides a softer, more filtered edge. When the spacing is zero, the resulting density image is a bilevel bitmap. When the spacing is very wide, the resulting density image has a watercolor-like edge.

Typically, users prefer sharp, high-contrast edges at small point sizes, and softer edges for animated text and larger point sizes.

The outside cutoff typically has a negative value, and the inside cutoff typically has a positive value, and their midpoint typically lies near zero. Adjusting these parameters to shift the midpoint toward negative infinity increases the stroke weight; shifting the midpoint toward positive infinity decreases the stroke weight. Make sure that the outside cutoff value is always less than or equal to the inside cutoff value.

Under most circumstances, a gamma exponent equal to 1 is adequate. However, when subpixel rendering [Liquid Crystal Display mode (LCD)], you use the gamma exponent to mitigate color fringing artifacts that occur when rendering typefaces with thin strokes (for example, Times Roman) and small point sizes. You can also use the gamma exponent to enhance contrast in both Cathode Ray Tube (CRT) and LCD modes.

Example

The following example creates two anti-alias entries and two text fields to illustrate them. For this example to work, the SWF file must have a shared font embedded with a linkage identifier of `"myArial"`. To embed the font, follow these steps:

- Open your Library.
- Click the Library options menu in the upper-right corner of the Library.
- Select New Font from the pop-up menu.
- Name the font **myArial**.
- Select Arial from the font pop-up menu.
- Click OK.
- Right-click the newly created font, and select Linkage.
- Select the Export for ActionScript check box.
- Click OK to accept the default identifier, myArial.

```
import flash.text.TextRenderer;

var antiAliasEntry_1 = {fontSize:24, insideCutoff:1.61, outsideCutoff:-
   3.43};
var antiAliasEntry_2 = {fontSize:48, insideCutoff:0.8, outsideCutoff:-0.8};
var arialTable:Array = new Array(antiAliasEntry_1, antiAliasEntry_2);

var lbl_1:TextField = createLabel(0, 0, 300, 100, 24);
var lbl_2:TextField = createLabel(0, 100, 300, 100, 48);

TextRenderer.setAdvancedAntialiasingTable("Arial", "none", "dark",
   arialTable);

function createLabel(x:Number, y:Number, width:Number, height:Number,
   fontSize:Number):TextField {
   var depth:Number = this.getNextHighestDepth();

   var tmpTxt = this.createTextField("txt_" + depth, depth, x, y, width,
   height);
   tmpTxt.antiAliasType = "advanced";
   tmpTxt.gridFitType = "pixel";
   tmpTxt.border = true;
   tmpTxt.text = "Hello World";
   tmpTxt.embedFonts = true;
   tmpTxt.setTextFormat(getTextFormat(fontSize));
   return tmpTxt;
}
```

```
function getTextFormat(fontSize:Number):TextFormat {
  var tf:TextFormat = new TextFormat();
  tf.align = "center";
  tf.size = fontSize;
  tf.font = "myArial";
  return tf;
}
```

TextSnapshot

```
Object
  |
  +-TextSnapshot
```

public class **TextSnapshot**
extends Object

TextSnapshot objects let you work with static text in a movie clip. You can use TextSnapshot objects, for example, to layout text with greater precision than that allowed by dynamic text, but still access the text as read-only.

You don't use a constructor to create a TextSnapshot object; it is returned by the `MovieClip.getTextSnapshot()` method.

Availability: ActionScript 1.0; Flash Player 7 - The SWF file must be published for Flash Player 6 or later, and must be played in Flash Player 7 or later.

See also

getTextSnapshot (MovieClip.getTextSnapshot method)

Property summary
Properties inherited from class Object

```
constructor (Object.constructor property),__proto__ (Object.__proto__
property),prototype (Object.prototype property),__resolve
(Object.__resolve property)
```

Method summary

Modifiers	Signature	Description
	`findText(startIndex: Number, textToFind:String, caseSensitive:Boolea n) : Number`	Searches the specified TextSnapshot object and returns the position of the first occurrence of `textToFind` found at or after `startIndex`.
	`getCount() : Number`	Returns the number of characters in a TextSnapshot object.
	`getSelected(start:Nu mber, [end:Number]) : Boolean`	Returns a Boolean value that specifies whether a TextSnapshot object contains selected text in the specified range.
	`getSelectedText([inc ludeLineEndings:Bool ean]) : String`	Returns a string that contains all the characters specified by the corresponding `TextSnapshot.setSelected()` method.
	`getText(start:Number , end:Number, [includeLineEndings: Boolean]) : String`	Returns a string that contains all the characters specified by the `start` and `end` parameters.
	`getTextRunInfo(begin Index:Number, endIndex:Number) : Array`	Returns an array of objects that contains information about a run of text.
	`hitTestTextNearPos(x :Number, y:Number, [closeDist:Number]) : Number`	Lets you determine which character within a TextSnapshot object is on or near the specified *x*, *y* coordinates of the movie clip containing the text in the TextSnapshot object.
	`setSelectColor(color :Number) : Void`	Specifies the color to use when highlighting characters that were selected with the `TextSnapshot.setSelected()` method.
	`setSelected(start:Nu mber, end:Number, select:Boolean) : Void`	Specifies a range of characters in a TextSnapshot object to be selected or not.

Methods inherited from class Object

```
addProperty (Object.addProperty method), hasOwnProperty
(Object.hasOwnProperty method), isPropertyEnumerable
(Object.isPropertyEnumerable method), isPrototypeOf (Object.isPrototypeOf
method), registerClass (Object.registerClass method), toString
(Object.toString method), unwatch (Object.unwatch method), valueOf
(Object.valueOf method), watch (Object.watch method)
```

findText (TextSnapshot.findText method)

```
public findText(startIndex:Number, textToFind:String,
  caseSensitive:Boolean) : Number
```

Searches the specified TextSnapshot object and returns the position of the first occurrence of textToFind found at or after startIndex. If textToFind is not found, the method returns -1.

Availability: ActionScript 1.0; Flash Player 7 - The SWF file must be published for Flash Player 6 or later, and must be played in Flash Player 7 or later.

Parameters

startIndex:Number - Specifies the starting index point in the TextSnapshot text at which to search for the specified text.

textToFind:String - The text to search for. Specify either a String literal (enclosed in quotation marks) or a variable.

caseSensitive:Boolean - Boolean value that specifies whether the found text must match the case of the string in textToFind (true); otherwise false.

Returns

Number - The zero-based index position of the first occurrence of the specified text, or -1 if no text matched.

Example

The following example illustrates how to use this method. To use this code, place a static text field that contains the text "TextSnapshot Example" on the Stage.

```
var my_mc:MovieClip = this;
var my_snap:TextSnapshot = my_mc.getTextSnapshot();
var index1:Number = my_snap.findText(0, "Snap", true);
var index2:Number = my_snap.findText(0, "snap", true);
var index3:Number = my_snap.findText(0, "snap", false);
trace(index1); // 4
trace(index2); // -1
trace(index3); // 4
```

See also

getText (TextSnapshot.getText method)

getCount (TextSnapshot.getCount method)

```
public getCount() : Number
```

Returns the number of characters in a TextSnapshot object.

Availability: ActionScript 1.0; Flash Player 7 - The SWF file must be published for Flash Player 6 or later, and must be played in Flash Player 7 or later.

Returns

`Number` - The number of characters in the TextSnapshot object.

Example

The following example illustrates how you can return the number of characters in a TextSnapshot object. To use this code, place one static text field that contains the text "TextSnapshot Example" (and only that text) on the Stage.

```
var my_mc:MovieClip = this;
var my_snap:TextSnapshot = my_mc.getTextSnapshot();
var count:Number = my_snap.getCount();
var theText:String = my_snap.getText(0, count, false);
trace(count); // 20
trace(theText); // TextSnapshot Example
```

See also

`getText (TextSnapshot.getText method)`

getSelected (TextSnapshot.getSelected method)

`public getSelected(start:Number, [end:Number]) : Boolean`

Returns a Boolean value that specifies whether a TextSnapshot object contains selected text in the specified range.

To search all characters, pass a value of 0 for `start`, and `TextSnapshot.getCount()` (or any very large number) for `end`. To search a single character, pass the end parameter a value that is one greater than the `start` parameter.

Availability: ActionScript 1.0; Flash Player 7 - The SWF file must be published for Flash Player 6 or later, and must be played in Flash Player 7 or later.

Parameters

`start:Number` - The index position of the first character to be examined. Valid values for `start` are 0 through `TextSnapshot.getCount()` - 1. If `start` is a negative value, 0 is used.

end:Number [optional] - The index position that is one greater than the last character to be examined. Valid values for end are 0 through TextSnapshot.getCount(). The character indexed by the end parameter is not included in the extracted string. If you omit this parameter, TextSnapshot.getCount() is used. If the value of end is less than or equal to the value of start, start + 1 is used.

Returns

Boolean - A Boolean value that indicates whether at least one character in the given range has been selected by the corresponding TextSnapshot.setSelected() method (true); otherwise, false.

Example

The following example illustrates how to use this method. To use this code, place a static text field that contains the text "TextSnapshot Example" on the Stage. In the library, include the font used by the static text field, and in Linkage options for the font, select Export for ActionScript. Add the following ActionScript to Frame 1 of the Timeline:

```
var my_snap:TextSnapshot = this.getTextSnapshot();
var count:Number = my_snap.getCount();
my_snap.setSelected(0, 4, true);
my_snap.setSelected(1, 2, false);

var firstCharIsSelected:Boolean = my_snap.getSelected(0, 1);
var secondCharIsSelected:Boolean = my_snap.getSelected(1, 2);
trace(firstCharIsSelected); // true
trace(secondCharIsSelected); // false
```

See also

getCount (TextSnapshot.getCount method), getText (TextSnapshot.getText method), getSelectedText (TextSnapshot.getSelectedText method), setSelected (TextSnapshot.setSelected method)

getSelectedText (TextSnapshot.getSelectedText method)

public getSelectedText([includeLineEndings:Boolean]) : String

Returns a string that contains all the characters specified by the corresponding TextSnapshot.setSelected() method. If no characters are specified (by the TextSnapshot.setSelected() method), an empty string is returned.

If you pass `true` for `includeLineEndings`, newline characters are inserted in the return string, and the return string might be longer than the input range. If `includeLineEndings` is `false` or omitted, the method returns the selected text without adding any characters.

Availability: ActionScript 1.0; Flash Player 7 - The SWF file must be published for Flash Player 6 or later, and must be played in Flash Player 7 or later.

Parameters

`includeLineEndings:Boolean` [optional] - A Boolean value that specifies whether newline characters are inserted (`true`) or are not inserted (`false`) into the returned string. The default value is `false`.

Returns

`String` - A string that contains all the characters specified by the corresponding `TextSnapshot.setSelected()` method.

Example

The following example illustrates how to use this method. To use this code, place a static text field that contains the text "TextSnapshot Example" on the Stage. Then in the Library, include the font used by the static text field, and in Linkage options for the font, select Export for ActionScript. Add the following ActionScript to Frame 1 of the Timeline:

```
var my_snap:TextSnapshot = this.getTextSnapshot();
var count:Number = my_snap.getCount();
my_snap.setSelected(0, 4, true);
my_snap.setSelected(1, 2, false);

var theText:String = my_snap.getSelectedText(false);
trace(theText); // Text
```

When you test the SWF file, a colored rectangle surrounds the specified characters.

See also

`getSelected (TextSnapshot.getSelected method)`, `setSelected (TextSnapshot.setSelected method)`

getText (TextSnapshot.getText method)

```
public getText(start:Number, end:Number, [includeLineEndings:Boolean]) :
  String
```

Returns a string that contains all the characters specified by the `start` and `end` parameters. If no characters are specified, the method returns an empty string.

To return all characters, pass a value of 0 for `start`, and `TextSnapshot.getCount()` (or any very large number) for `end`. To return a single character, pass a value of `start +1` for `end`.

If you pass `true` for `includeLineEndings`, newline characters are inserted in the return string where deemed appropriate, and the return string might be longer than the input range. If `includeLineEndings` is `false` or omitted, the method returns the selected text without adding any characters.

Availability: ActionScript 1.0; Flash Player 7 - The SWF file must be published for Flash Player 6 or later, and must be played in Flash Player 7 or later.

Parameters

`start:Number` - An integer that indicates the position of the first character to be included in the returned string. Valid values for `start` are 0 through `TextSnapshot.getCount()` - 1. If `start` is a negative value, 0 is used.

`end:Number` - An integer that is 1 + the index of the last character to be examined in the TextSnapshot object. Valid values for `end` are 0 through `TextSnapshot.getCount()`. The character indexed by the `end` parameter is not included in the extracted string. If you omit this parameter, `TextSnapshot.getCount()` is used. If the value of `end` is less than or equal to the value of `start`, `start + 1` is used.

`includeLineEndings:Boolean` [optional] - A Boolean value that specifies whether newline characters are inserted (`true`) or are not inserted (`false`) into the returned string. The default value is `false`.

Returns

`String` - A string that contains the characters in the specified range, or an empty string if no characters are found in the specified range.

Example

The following example illustrates how you can return the number of characters in a specified TextSnapshot object. To use this code, place a static text field that contains the text "TextSnapshot Example" on the Stage.

```
var my_mc:MovieClip = this;
var my_snap:TextSnapshot = my_mc.getTextSnapshot();
var count:Number = my_snap.getCount();
var theText:String = my_snap.getText(0, count, false);
trace(count); // 20
trace(theText); // TextSnapshot Example
```

See also

getCount (TextSnapshot.getCount method), getSelectedText
(TextSnapshot.getSelectedText method)

getTextRunInfo (TextSnapshot.getTextRunInfo method)

public getTextRunInfo(beginIndex:Number, endIndex:Number) : Array

Returns an array of objects that contains information about a run of text. Each object corresponds to one character in the range of characters specified by the two method parameters.

| NOTE | Using the getTextRunInfo() method for a large range of text can return a large object. Macromedia recommends limiting the text range defined by the beginIndex and endIndex parameters. |

Availability: ActionScript 1.0; Flash Player 7 - The SWF file must be published for Flash Player 6 or later, and must be played in Flash Player 7r19 or later.

Parameters

beginIndex:Number - The index value of the first character in the range of characters.

endIndex:Number - The index value of the last character in the range of characters.

Returns

`Array` - An array of objects in which each object contains information about a specific character in the specified range. Each object contains the following properties:

- `indexInRun` A zero-based integer index of the character (relative to the entire string rather than the selected run of text).

- `selected` A Boolean value that indicates whether the character is selected `true`; `false` otherwise.

- `font` The name of the character's font.

- `color` The combined alpha and color value of the character. The first two hexidecimal digits represent the alpha value, and the remaining digits represent the color value. (The example includes a method for converting decimal values to hexidecimal values.)

- `height` The height of the character, in pixels.

- `matrix_a`, `matrix_b`, `matrix_c`, `matrix_d`, `matrix_tx`, and `matrix_ty` The values of a matrix that define the geometric transformation on the character. Normal, upright text always has a matrix of the form [1 0 0 1 x y], where x and y are the position of the character within the parent movie clip, regardless of the height of the text. The matrix is in the parent movie clip coordinate system, and does not include any transformations that may be on that movie clip itself (or its parent).

- `corner0x`, `corner0y`, `corner1x`, `corner1y`, `corner2x`, `corner2y`, `corner3x`, and `corner3y` The corners of the bounding box of the character, based on the coordinate system of the parent movie clip. These values are only available if the font used by the character is embedded in the SWF file.

Example

The following example illustrates how to use this method. To use this code, on the Stage create a static text field that contains the text "AB". Rotate the text field by 45 degrees, and set the second character to be superscript with a color of 0xFFFFFF with a 50% alpha, as the following figure shows:

The following script lists the `getTextRunInfo()` properties of each character in the text field:

```
var myTS:TextSnapshot = this.getTextSnapshot();
var myArray:Array = myTS["getTextRunInfo"](0, myTS.getCount());
for (var i = 0; i < myTS.getCount(); i++) {
  trace("indexInRun: " + myArray[i].indexInRun);
  trace("selected: " + myArray[i].selected);
  trace("font: " + myArray[i].font);
  trace("color: " + decToHex(myArray[i].color));
  trace("height: " + myArray[i].height);
```

```
    trace("matrix_a: " + myArray[i].matrix_a);
    trace("matrix_b: " + myArray[i].matrix_b);
    trace("matrix_c: " + myArray[i].matrix_c);
    trace("matrix_d: " + myArray[i].matrix_d);
    trace("matrix_ty: " + myArray[i].matrix_tx);
    trace("matrix_tx: " + myArray[i].matrix_ty);
    trace(" ");
}

function decToHex(dec:Number) {
  var hexString:String = "";
  if (dec > 15) {
    hexString = decToHex(Math.floor(dec / 16));
  }
  var hexDigit = dec - 16 * (Math.floor(dec / 16));
    if (hexDigit > 9) {
      hexDigit = String.fromCharCode(hexDigit + 55);
    }
    hexString = hexString + hexDigit;
    return hexString;
}
```

This creates the following output:

```
indexInRun: 0
selected: false
font: Times New Roman
color: FF000000
height: 28,6
matrix_a: 0.0316612236983293
matrix_b: 0.0385940558426864
matrix_c: -0.0385940558426864
matrix_d: 0.0316612236983293
matrix_ty: 22.75
matrix_tx: 40.35

indexInRun: 0
selected: false
font: Times New Roman
color: 80000000
height: 28.6
matrix_a: 0.0316612236983293
matrix_b: 0.0385940558426864
matrix_c: -0.0385940558426864
matrix_d: 0.0316612236983293
matrix_ty: 49
matrix_tx: 45.5
```

This example uses a decToHex() method to convert the decimal value of the color property
to a hexidecimal value.

See also

Matrix (flash.geom.Matrix)

hitTestTextNearPos
(TextSnapshot.hitTestTextNearPos method)

public hitTestTextNearPos(x:Number, y:Number, [closeDist:Number]) : Number

Lets you determine which character within a TextSnapshot object is on or near the specified *x*, *y* coordinates of the movie clip containing the text in the TextSnapshot object.

If you omit or pass a value of 0 for closeDist, the location specified by the *x*, *y* coordinates must lie inside the bounding box of the TextSnapshot object.

This method works correctly only with fonts that include character metric information; however, by default, Macromedia Flash does not include this information for static text fields. Therefore, the method might return -1 instead of an index value. To ensure that an index value is returned, you can force the Flash authoring tool to include the character metric information for a font. To do this, add a dynamic text field that uses that font, select Character Options for that dynamic text field, and then specify that font outlines should be embedded for at least one character. (It doesn't matter which characters you specify, nor whether they are the characters used in the static text fields.)

Availability: ActionScript 1.0; Flash Player 7 - The SWF file must be published for Flash Player 6 or later, and must be played in Flash Player 7 or later.

Parameters

x:Number - The *x* coordinate of the movie clip that contains the text in the TextSnapshot object.

y:Number - The *y* coordinate of the movie clip that contains the text in the TextSnapshot object.

closeDist:Number [optional] - The maximum distance from *x*, *y* that can be searched for text. The distance is measured from the centerpoint of each character. The default value is 0.

Returns

Number - The index value of the character in the TextSnapshot object that is nearest to the specified *x*, *y* coordinate. The method returns -1 if no character is found, or if the font doesn't contain character metric information.

Example

The following example illustrates how to use this method. To use this code, place a static text field that contains the text "TextSnapshot Example" on the Stage. In the library, include the font used by the static text field, and in Linkage options for the font, select Export for ActionScript. To test the code, run the SWF file and point the mouse pointer to the onscreen text.

```
var my_ts:TextSnapshot = getTextSnapshot();
this.onMouseMove = function() {
  var hitIndex:Number = my_ts.hitTestTextNearPos(_xmouse, _ymouse, 0);
  my_ts.setSelected(0, my_ts.getCount(), false);
  if (hitIndex >= 0) {
    my_ts.setSelected(hitIndex, hitIndex + 1, true);
  }
};
```

See also

getTextSnapshot (MovieClip.getTextSnapshot method), _x (MovieClip._x property), _y (MovieClip._y property)

setSelectColor (TextSnapshot.setSelectColor method)

```
public setSelectColor(color:Number) : Void
```

Specifies the color to use when highlighting characters that were selected with the TextSnapshot.setSelected() method. The color is always opaque; you can't specify a transparency value.

This method works correctly only with fonts that include character metric information; however, by default, Macromedia Flash does not include this information for static text fields. Therefore, the method might return -1 instead of an index value. To ensure that an index value is returned, you can force the Flash authoring tool to include the character metric information for a font. To do this, add a dynamic text field that uses that font, select Character Options for that dynamic text field, and then specify that font outlines should be embedded for at least one character. (It doesn't matter which characters you specify, nor if they are the characters used in the static text fields.)

Availability: ActionScript 1.0; Flash Player 7 - The SWF file must be published for Flash Player 6 or later, and must be played in Flash Player 7 or later.

Parameters

`color:Number` - The color used for the border placed around characters that have been selected by the corresponding `TextSnapshot.setSelected()` method, expressed in 0x*RRGGBB* format.

Example

The following example illustrates how to use this method. To use this code, place a static text field that contains the text "TextSnapshot Example" on the Stage. In the library, include the font used by the static text field, and in Linkage options for the font, select Export for ActionScript. Add the following ActionScript to Frame 1 of the Timeline:

```
var my_snap:TextSnapshot = this.getTextSnapshot();
var count:Number = my_snap.getCount();
my_snap.setSelectColor(0xFF0000);
my_snap.setSelected(0, 4, true);
my_snap.setSelected(1, 2, false);

var theText:String = my_snap.getSelectedText(false); // get the selected
    text
trace(theText); // Text
```

When you test the SWF file, you see a colored rectangle surrounds the specified characters.

See also

setSelected (TextSnapshot.setSelected method)

setSelected (TextSnapshot.setSelected method)

`public setSelected(start:Number, end:Number, select:Boolean) : Void`

Specifies a range of characters in a TextSnapshot object to be selected or not. Characters that are selected are drawn with a colored rectangle behind them, matching the bounding box of the character. The color of the bounding box is defined by `TextSnapshot.setSelectColor()`.

To select or deselect all characters, pass a value of 0 for `start` and `TextSnapshot.getCount()` (or any very large number) for `end`. To specify a single character, pass a value of `start + 1` for `end`.

Because characters are individually marked as selected, you can call this method multiple times to select multiple characters; that is, using this method does not deselect other characters that have been set by this method.

This method works correctly only with fonts that include character metric information; by default, Flash does not include this information for static text fields. Therefore, text that is selected might not appear to be selected onscreen. To ensure that all selected text appears to be selected, you can force the Flash authoring tool to include the character metric information for a font. To do this, in the library, include the font used by the static text field, and in Linkage options for the font, select Export for ActionScript.

Availability: ActionScript 1.0; Flash Player 7 - The SWF file must be published for Flash Player 6 or later, and must be played in Flash Player 7 or later.

Parameters

`start:Number` - The position of the first character to select. Valid values for `start` are 0 through `TextSnapshot.getCount()` - 1. If `start` is a negative value, 0 is used.

`end:Number` - An integer that is 1+ the index of the last character to be examined. Valid values for `end` are 0 through `TextSnapshot.getCount()`. The character indexed by the `end` parameter is not included in the extracted string. If you omit this parameter, `TextSnapshot.getCount()` is used. If the value of `end` is less than or equal to the value of `start`, `start` + 1 is used.

`select:Boolean` - A Boolean value that specifies whether the text should be selected (`true`) or not (`false`).

Example

The following example illustrates how to use this method. To use this code, place a static text field that contains the text "TextSnapshot Example" on the Stage. In the library, include the font used by the static text field, and in Linkage options for the font, select Export for ActionScript. Add the following ActionScript to Frame 1 of the Timssseline:

```
var my_snap:TextSnapshot = this.getTextSnapshot();
var count:Number = my_snap.getCount();
my_snap.setSelected(0, 4, true);
my_snap.setSelected(1, 2, false);

var theText:String = my_snap.getSelectedText(false);
trace(theText); // Text
```

See also

`getCount (TextSnapshot.getCount method)`

Transform (flash.geom.Transform)

```
Object
  |
  +-flash.geom.Transform
```

public class **Transform**
extends Object

The Transform class collects data about color transformations and coordinate manipulations that are applied to a MovieClip object.

A Transform object is normally obtained by getting the value of the transform property from a MovieClip object.

Availability: ActionScript 1.0; Flash Player 8

See also

transform (MovieClip.transform property), ColorTransform (flash.geom.ColorTransform), Matrix (flash.geom.Matrix)

Property summary

Modifiers	Property	Description
	colorTransform:Color Transform	A ColorTransform object containing values that universally adjust the colors in the movie clip.
	concatenatedColorTra nsform:ColorTransfor m [read-only]	A ColorTransform object representing the combined color transformations applied to this object and all of its parent objects, back to the root level.
	concatenatedMatrix:M atrix [read-only]	A Matrix object representing the combined transformation matrixes of this object and all of its parent objects, back to the root level.
	matrix:Matrix	A transformation Matrix object containing values that affect the scaling, rotation, and translation of the movie clip.
	pixelBounds:Rectangl e	A Rectangle object that defines the bounding rectangle of the MovieClip object on the Stage.

Properties inherited from class Object

```
constructor (Object.constructor property), __proto__ (Object.__proto__
property), prototype (Object.prototype property), __resolve
(Object.__resolve property)
```

Constructor summary

Signature	Description
`Transform(mc:MovieCl` `ip)`	Creates a new Transform object attached to the given MovieClip object.

Method summary
Methods inherited from class Object

```
addProperty (Object.addProperty method), hasOwnProperty
(Object.hasOwnProperty method), isPropertyEnumerable
(Object.isPropertyEnumerable method), isPrototypeOf (Object.isPrototypeOf
method), registerClass (Object.registerClass method), toString
(Object.toString method), unwatch (Object.unwatch method), valueOf
(Object.valueOf method), watch (Object.watch method)
```

colorTransform (Transform.colorTransform property)

`public colorTransform : ColorTransform`

A ColorTransform object containing values that universally adjust the colors in the movie clip.

Availability: ActionScript 1.0; Flash Player 8

Example

The following example applies the ColorTransform object `blueColorTransform` to the Transform object `trans`. This ColorTransform converts the color of the MovieClip `rect` from red to blue.

```
import flash.geom.Transform;
import flash.geom.ColorTransform;

var rect:MovieClip = createRectangle(20, 80, 0xFF0000);

var trans:Transform = new Transform(rect);
trace(trans.colorTransform);
// (redMultiplier=1, greenMultiplier=1, blueMultiplier=1,
   alphaMultiplier=1, redOffset=0, greenOffset=0, blueOffset=0,
   alphaOffset=0)

var blueColorTransform:ColorTransform = new ColorTransform(0, 1, 1, 1, 0,
   0, 255, 0);

rect.onPress = function() {
   trans.colorTransform = blueColorTransform;
   trace(trans.colorTransform);
```

```
// (redMultiplier=0, greenMultiplier=1, blueMultiplier=1,
alphaMultiplier=1, redOffset=0, greenOffset=0, blueOffset=255,
alphaOffset=0)
}

function createRectangle(width:Number, height:Number, color:Number,
   scope:MovieClip):MovieClip {
   scope = (scope == undefined) ? this : scope;
   var depth:Number = scope.getNextHighestDepth();
   var mc:MovieClip = scope.createEmptyMovieClip("mc_" + depth, depth);
     mc.beginFill(color);
   mc.lineTo(0, height);
   mc.lineTo(width, height);
   mc.lineTo(width, 0);
   mc.lineTo(0, 0);
   return mc;
}
```

See also

```
ColorTransform (flash.geom.ColorTransform)
```

concatenatedColorTransform (Transform.concatenatedColorTransform property)

```
public concatenatedColorTransform : ColorTransform [read-only]
```

A ColorTransform object representing the combined color transformations applied to this object and all of its parent objects, back to the root level. If different color transformations have been applied at different levels, each of those transformations will be concatenated into one ColorTransform object for this property.

Availability: ActionScript 1.0; Flash Player 8

Example

The following example applies two Transform objects to both a parent and child MovieClip object. A blueColorTransform variable is then applied to the Transform object parentTrans, which adjusts the color of both parent and child MovieClip objects toward blue. You can see how child.concatenatedColorTransform is the combination of parentTrans and childTrans.

```
import flash.geom.Transform;
import flash.geom.ColorTransform;

var parentRect:MovieClip = createRectangle(20, 80, 0xFF0000);
var childRect:MovieClip = createRectangle(10, 40, 0x00FF00, parentRect);
```

```
var parentTrans:Transform = new Transform(parentRect);
var childTrans:Transform = new Transform(childRect);

var blueColorTransform:ColorTransform = new ColorTransform(0, 1, 1, 1, 0,
  0, 255, 0);

parentTrans.colorTransform = blueColorTransform;

trace(childTrans.concatenatedColorTransform);
// (redMultiplier=0, greenMultiplier=1, blueMultiplier=1,
  alphaMultiplier=1, redOffset=0, greenOffset=0, blueOffset=255,
  alphaOffset=0)
trace(childTrans.colorTransform);
// (redMultiplier=1, greenMultiplier=1, blueMultiplier=1,
  alphaMultiplier=1, redOffset=0, greenOffset=0, blueOffset=0,
  alphaOffset=0)
trace(parentTrans.concatenatedColorTransform);
// (redMultiplier=0, greenMultiplier=1, blueMultiplier=1,
  alphaMultiplier=1, redOffset=0, greenOffset=0, blueOffset=255,
  alphaOffset=0)

function createRectangle(width:Number, height:Number, color:Number,
  scope:MovieClip):MovieClip {
  scope = (scope == undefined) ? this : scope;
  var depth:Number = scope.getNextHighestDepth();
  var mc:MovieClip = scope.createEmptyMovieClip("mc_" + depth, depth);
  mc.beginFill(color);
  mc.lineTo(0, height);
  mc.lineTo(width, height);
  mc.lineTo(width, 0);
  mc.lineTo(0, 0);
  return mc;
}
```

See also

ColorTransform (flash.geom.ColorTransform)

concatenatedMatrix (Transform.concatenatedMatrix property)

`public concatenatedMatrix : Matrix [read-only]`

A Matrix object representing the combined transformation matrixes of this object and all of its parent objects, back to the root level. If different transformation matrixes have been applied at different levels, each of those matrixes will be concatenated into one matrix for this property.

Availability: ActionScript 1.0; Flash Player 8

Example

The following example applies two Transform objects to both a child and parent MovieClip object. A `scaleMatrix` is then applied to the Transform object `parentTrans`, which scales both parent and child MovieClip objects. You can see how `child.concatenatedMatrix` is the combination of `parentTrans` and `childTrans`.

```
import flash.geom.Transform;
import flash.geom.Matrix;

var parentRect:MovieClip = createRectangle(20, 80, 0xFF0000);
var childRect:MovieClip = createRectangle(10, 40, 0x00FF00, parentRect);

var parentTrans:Transform = new Transform(parentRect);
var childTrans:Transform = new Transform(childRect);

var scaleMatrix:Matrix = new Matrix();
scaleMatrix.scale(2, 2);

parentTrans.matrix = scaleMatrix;

trace(childTrans.concatenatedMatrix); // (a=2, b=0, c=0, d=2, tx=0, ty=0)
trace(childTrans.matrix); // (a=1, b=0, c=0, d=1, tx=0, ty=0)
trace(parentTrans.concatenatedMatrix); // (a=2, b=0, c=0, d=2, tx=0, ty=0)

function createRectangle(width:Number, height:Number, color:Number,
  scope:MovieClip):MovieClip {
  scope = (scope == undefined) ? this : scope;
  var depth:Number = scope.getNextHighestDepth();
  var mc:MovieClip = scope.createEmptyMovieClip("mc_" + depth, depth);
  mc.beginFill(color);
  mc.lineTo(0, height);
  mc.lineTo(width, height);
  mc.lineTo(width, 0);
  mc.lineTo(0, 0);
  return mc;
}
```

matrix (Transform.matrix property)

```
public matrix : Matrix
```

A transformation Matrix object containing values that affect the scaling, rotation, and translation of the movie clip.

Availability: ActionScript 1.0; Flash Player 8

Example

The following example applies the Matrix object `scaleMatrix` to the Transform object `trans`. This Matrix scales the MovieClip `rect` by a factor of two.

```
import flash.geom.Transform;
import flash.geom.Matrix;

var rect:MovieClip = createRectangle(20, 80, 0xFF0000);

var trans:Transform = new Transform(rect);
trace(trans.matrix); // (a=1, b=0, c=0, d=1, tx=0, ty=0)

var scaleMatrix:Matrix = new Matrix();
scaleMatrix.scale(2, 2);

rect.onPress() = function() {
  trans.matrix = scaleMatrix;
  trace(trans.matrix); // (a=2, b=0, c=0, d=2, tx=0, ty=0)
}

function createRectangle(width:Number, height:Number, color:Number,
  scope:MovieClip):MovieClip {
  scope = (scope == undefined) ? this : scope;
  var depth:Number = scope.getNextHighestDepth();
  var mc:MovieClip = scope.createEmptyMovieClip("mc_" + depth, depth);
  mc.beginFill(color);
  mc.lineTo(0, height);
  mc.lineTo(width, height);
  mc.lineTo(width, 0);
  mc.lineTo(0, 0);
  return mc;
}
```

See also

Matrix (flash.geom.Matrix)

pixelBounds (Transform.pixelBounds property)

`public pixelBounds : Rectangle`

A Rectangle object that defines the bounding rectangle of the MovieClip object on the Stage.

Availability: ActionScript 1.0; Flash Player 8

Example

The following example creates a Transform object `trans` and traces out its `pixelBounds` property. Notice that `pixelBounds` returns a bounding box with values equal to the MovieClip object's `getBounds()` and `getRect()` methods.

```
import flash.geom.Transform;

var rect:MovieClip = createRectangle(20, 80, 0xFF0000);
var trans:Transform = new Transform(rect);
trace(trans.pixelBounds); // (x=0, y=0, w=20, h=80)

var boundsObj:Object = rect.getBounds();
trace(boundsObj.xMin); // 0
trace(boundsObj.yMin); // 0
trace(boundsObj.xMax); // 20
trace(boundsObj.yMax); // 80

var rectObj:Object = rect.getRect();
trace(rectObj.xMin); // 0
trace(rectObj.yMin); // 0
trace(rectObj.xMax); // 20
trace(rectObj.yMax); // 80

function createRectangle(width:Number, height:Number, color:Number,
  scope:MovieClip):MovieClip {
  scope = (scope == undefined) ? this : scope;
  var depth:Number = scope.getNextHighestDepth();
  var mc:MovieClip = scope.createEmptyMovieClip("mc_" + depth, depth);
  mc.beginFill(color);
  mc.lineTo(0, height);
  mc.lineTo(width, height);
  mc.lineTo(width, 0);
  mc.lineTo(0, 0);
  return mc;
}
```

Transform constructor

`public Transform(mc:MovieClip)`

Creates a new Transform object attached to the given MovieClip object.

When it is created the new Transform object can be retrieved by getting the `transform` property of the given MovieClip object.

Availability: ActionScript 1.0; Flash Player 8

Parameters

`mc:MovieClip` - The MovieClip object to which the new Transform object is applied.

Example

The following example creates the Transform `trans` and applies it to the MovieClip `rect`. You can see that the Transform object's `trans` and `rect.transform` do not evaluate as equals even though they contain the same values.

```
import flash.geom.Transform;

var rect:MovieClip = createRectangle(20, 80, 0xFF0000);

var trans:Transform = new Transform(rect);

trace(rect.transform == trans); // false

for(var i in trans) {
    trace(">> " + i + ": " + trans[i]);
    // >> pixelBounds: (x=0, y=0, w=20, h=80)
    // >> concatenatedColorTransform: (redMultiplier=1, greenMultiplier=1,
    blueMultiplier=1, alphaMultiplier=1, redOffset=0, greenOffset=0,
    blueOffset=0, alphaOffset=0)
    // >> colorTransform: (redMultiplier=1, greenMultiplier=1,
    blueMultiplier=1, alphaMultiplier=1, redOffset=0, greenOffset=0,
    blueOffset=0, alphaOffset=0)
    // >> concatenatedMatrix: (a=1, b=0, c=0, d=1, tx=0, ty=0)
    // >> matrix: (a=1, b=0, c=0, d=1, tx=0, ty=0)
}

for(var i in rect.transform) {
    trace(">> " + i + ": " + rect.transform[i]);
    // >> pixelBounds: (x=0, y=0, w=20, h=80)
    // >> concatenatedColorTransform: (redMultiplier=1, greenMultiplier=1,
    blueMultiplier=1, alphaMultiplier=1, redOffset=0, greenOffset=0,
    blueOffset=0, alphaOffset=0)
    // >> colorTransform: (redMultiplier=1, greenMultiplier=1,
    blueMultiplier=1, alphaMultiplier=1, redOffset=0, greenOffset=0,
    blueOffset=0, alphaOffset=0)
    // >> concatenatedMatrix: (a=1, b=0, c=0, d=1, tx=0, ty=0)
    // >> matrix: (a=1, b=0, c=0, d=1, tx=0, ty=0)
}

function createRectangle(width:Number, height:Number, color:Number,
    scope:MovieClip):MovieClip {
    scope = (scope == undefined) ? this : scope;
    var depth:Number = scope.getNextHighestDepth();
    var mc:MovieClip = scope.createEmptyMovieClip("mc_" + depth, depth);
    mc.beginFill(color);
    mc.lineTo(0, height);
    mc.lineTo(width, height);
    mc.lineTo(width, 0);
    mc.lineTo(0, 0);
```

```
    return mc;
}
```

Video

```
Object
  |
  +-Video
```

```
public class Video
extends Object
```

The Video class enables you to display live streaming video on the Stage without embedding it in your SWF file. You capture the video by using `Camera.get()`. In files published for Flash Player 7 and later, you can also use the Video class to play back Flash Video (FLV) files over HTTP or from the local file system. For more information, see the NetConnection class and NetStream class entries.

Flash Player 7 supports Flash video (FLV) encoded with the Sorenson Spark video codec. Flash Player 8 supports Flash video (FLV) encoded with either the Sorenson or the On2 VP6 codec and also supports an alpha channel. The On2 VP6 video codec uses less bandwidth than older technologies, and offers additional deblocking and deringing filters.

If your Flash content dynamically loads Flash video (using either progressive download or Flash Communication Server), you can use On2 VP6 video without having to republish your SWF for Flash Player 8, as long as users view your content through Flash Player 8. By streaming or downloading On2 VP6 video into Flash SWF version 6 or 7, and playing the content using Flash Player 8, you avoid having to recreate your SWF files for use with Flash Player 8.

Codec	Content (SWF)Version(publish version)	Flash PlayerVersion(version required for playback)
Sorenson Spark	6	6, 7, 8
	7	7, 8
On2 VP6	6	8*
	7	8
	8	8

* If your Flash content dynamically loads Flash video (FLV), you can use On2 VP6 video without having to republish your SWF for Flash Player 8, as long as users use Flash Player 8 to view your content. Only Flash Player 8 supports both publish and playback of On2 VP6 video.

A Video object can be used like a movie clip. As with other objects you place on the Stage, you can control various properties of Video objects. For example, you can move the Video object around on the Stage by using its _x and _y properties, you can change its size using its _height and _width properties, and so on.

To display the video stream, first place a Video object on the Stage. Then use Video.attachVideo() to attach the video stream to the Video object.

- If the Library panel isn't visible, select Window > Library to display it.

- Add an embedded Video object to the library by clicking the Options menu on the right side of the Library panel title bar and selecting New Video.

- Drag the Video object to the Stage and use the Property inspector to give it a unique instance name, such as my_video. (Do not name it Video.)

Availability: ActionScript 1.0; Flash Player 6 - The ability to play Flash Video (FLV) files was added in Flash Player 7. The ability to use the On2 VP6 codec and to use an alpha channel was added in Flash Player 8.

See also

NetConnection, NetStream

Property summary

Modifiers	Property	Description
	_alpha:Number	Indicates the alpha transparency value of the Video object specified.
	deblocking:Number	Indicates the type of deblocking filter applied to decoded video as part of postprocessing.
	_height:Number	Indicates the height of the Video object, in pixels.
	height:Number [read-only]	An integer specifying the height of the video stream, in pixels.
	_name:String	Indicates the instance name of the Video object specified.
	_parent:MovieClip	Indicates the movie clip or object that contains the current Video object.

Modifiers	Property	Description
	`_rotation:Number`	Indicates the rotation of the Video object, in degrees, from its original orientation.
	`smoothing:Boolean`	Specifies whether the video should be smoothed (interpolated) when it is scaled.
	`_visible:Boolean`	Indicates whether the Video object specified by *my_video* is visible.
	`_width:Number`	Indicates the width of the Video object, in pixels.
	`width:Number` [read-only]	An integer specifying the width of the video stream, in pixels.
	`_x:Number`	Indicates the x coordinate of a Video object relative to the local coordinates of the parent movie clip.
	`_xmouse:Number` [read-only]	Indicates the x coordinate of the mouse position.
	`_xscale:Number`	Indicates the horizontal scale (*percentage*) of the Video object as applied from the registration point of the Video object.
	`_y:Number`	Indicates the y coordinate of a Video object relative to the local coordinates of the parent movie clip.
	`_ymouse:Number` [read-only]	Indicates the y coordinate of the mouse position.
	`_yscale:Number`	Indicates the vertical scale (*percentage*) of the Video object as applied from the registration point of the Video object.

Properties inherited from class Object

```
constructor (Object.constructor property),__proto__ (Object.__proto__
property),prototype (Object.prototype property),__resolve
(Object.__resolve property)
```

Method summary

Modifiers	Signature	Description
	`attachVideo(source:O bject) : Void`	Specifies a video stream (*source*) to be displayed within the boundaries of the Video object on the Stage.
	`clear() : Void`	Clears the image currently displayed in the Video object.

```
addProperty (Object.addProperty method),hasOwnProperty
(Object.hasOwnProperty method),isPropertyEnumerable
(Object.isPropertyEnumerable method),isPrototypeOf (Object.isPrototypeOf
method),registerClass (Object.registerClass method),toString
(Object.toString method),unwatch (Object.unwatch method),valueOf
(Object.valueOf method),watch (Object.watch method)
```

_alpha (Video._alpha property)

`public _alpha : Number`

Indicates the alpha transparency value of the Video object specified. Valid values are 0 (fully transparent) to 100 (fully opaque). The default value is 100. Objects in a movie clip with _alpha set to 0 are active, even though they are invisible.

Availability: ActionScript 1.0; Flash Player 8

See also

`_visible (Video._visible property)`

attachVideo (Video.attachVideo method)

`public attachVideo(source:Object) : Void`

Specifies a video stream (*source*) to be displayed within the boundaries of the Video object on the Stage. The video stream is either an FLV file being displayed by means of the `NetStream.play()` command, a Camera object, or `null`. If *source* is `null`, video is no longer played within the Video object.

You don't have to use this method if the FLV file contains only audio; the audio portion of an FLV files is played automatically when the `NetStream.play()` command is issued.

If you want to control the audio associated with an FLV file, you can use `MovieClip.attachAudio()` to route the audio to a movie clip; you can then create a Sound object to control some aspects of the audio. For more information, see `MovieClip.attachAudio()`.

Availability: ActionScript 1.0; Flash Player 6 - The ability to work with Flash Video (FLV) files was added in Flash Player 7.

Parameters

`source:Object` - A Camera object that is capturing video data or a NetStream object. To drop the connection to the Video object, pass `null` for *source*.

Example

The following example plays live video locally:

```
var my_video:Video; //my_video is a Video object on the Stage
var active_cam:Camera = Camera.get();
my_video.attachVideo(active_cam);
```

The following example plays a previously recorded file named myVideo.flv that is stored in the same directory as the SWF file.

```
var my_video:Video; // my_video is a Video object on the Stage
var my_nc:NetConnection = new NetConnection();
my_nc.connect(null);
var my_ns:NetStream = new NetStream(my_nc);
my_video.attachVideo(my_ns);
my_ns.play("video1.flv");
```

See also

Camera, NetStream

clear (Video.clear method)

```
public clear() : Void
```

Clears the image currently displayed in the Video object. This is useful when, for example, you want to display standby information without having to hide the Video object.

Availability: ActionScript 1.0; Flash Player 6

Example

The following example pauses and clears video1.flv that is playing in a Video object (called my_video) when the user clicks the pause_btn instance.

```
var pause_btn:Button;
var my_video:Video; // my_video is a Video object on the Stage
var my_nc:NetConnection = new NetConnection();
my_nc.connect(null);
var my_ns:NetStream = new NetStream(my_nc);
my_video.attachVideo(my_ns);
my_ns.play("video1.flv");
pause_btn.onRelease = function() {
  my_ns.pause();
  my_video.clear();
};
```

See also

attachVideo (Video.attachVideo method)

deblocking (Video.deblocking property)

```
public deblocking : Number
```

Indicates the type of deblocking filter applied to decoded video as part of postprocessing. Two deblocking filters are available: one in the Sorenson codec and one in the On2 VP6 codec. The following values are acceptable:

- 0 (the default)—Let the video compressor apply the deblocking filter as needed.
- 1—Do not use any deblocking filter.
- 2—Use the Sorenson deblocking filter.
- 3—Use the On2 deblocking filter and no deringing filter.
- 4—Use the On2 deblocking and the fast On2 deringing filter.
- 5—Use the On2 deblocking and the better On2 deringing filter.
- 6—Same as 5.
- 7—Same as 5.

If a mode greater than 2 is selected for video when you are using the Sorenson codec, the Sorenson decoder defaults to mode 2 internally.

Use of a deblocking filter has an effect on overall playback performance, and it is usually not necessary for high-bandwidth video. If your system is not powerful enough, you may experience difficulties playing back video with this filter enabled.

Availability: ActionScript 1.0; Flash Player 6

Example

The following example plays video1.flv in the `my_video` video object, and lets the user change the deblocking filter behavior on video1.flv. Add a video object called `my_video` and a ComboBox instance called `deblocking_cb` to your file, and then add the following ActionScript to your FLA or AS file.

```
var deblocking_cb:mx.controls.ComboBox;
var my_video:Video; // my_video is a Video object on the Stage
var my_nc:NetConnection = new NetConnection();
my_nc.connect(null);
var my_ns:NetStream = new NetStream(my_nc);
my_video.attachVideo(my_ns);
my_ns.play("video1.flv");

deblocking_cb.addItem({data:0, label:'Auto'});
deblocking_cb.addItem({data:1, label:'No'});
deblocking_cb.addItem({data:2, label:'Yes'});

var cbListener:Object = new Object();
cbListener.change = function(evt:Object) {
```

```
    my_video.deblocking = evt.target.selectedItem.data;
};
deblocking_cb.addEventListener("change", cbListener);
```
Use the ComboBox instance to change the deblocking filter behavior on video1.flv.

_height (Video._height property)

```
public _height : Number
```
Indicates the height of the Video object, in pixels.

Availability: ActionScript 1.0; Flash Player 8

See also
```
_width (Video._width property)
```

height (Video.height property)

```
public height : Number [read-only]
```
An integer specifying the height of the video stream, in pixels. For live streams, this value is the same as the `Camera.height` property of the Camera object that is capturing the video stream. For FLV files, this value is the height of the file that was exported as FLV.

You may want to use this property, for example, to ensure that the user is seeing the video at the same size at which it was captured, regardless of the actual size of the Video object on the Stage.

Availability: ActionScript 1.0; Flash Player 6

Example
The following example sets the `_height` and `_width` properties of the Video Symbol instance equal to the `height` and `width` of the loaded FLV file.

To use this example, first create a new Video symbol with an instance name of "myVideo" and place it in the same context as this script. The `height` and `width` properties will be zero when the `NetStream.Play.Start` status code is triggered. By resizing the video when the status of `NetStream.Buffer.Full` is received you make sure that its size is correct before the first frame of video is shown.

```
var netConn:NetConnection = new NetConnection();
netConn.connect(null);
var netStrm:NetStream = new NetStream(netConn);

myVideo.attachVideo(netStrm);
netStrm.play("Video.flv");

netStrm.onStatus = function(infoObject:Object) {
```

```
switch (infoObject.code) {
  case 'NetStream.Play.Start' :
  case 'NetStream.Buffer.Full' :
    myVideo._width = myVideo.width;
    myVideo._height = myVideo.height;
    break;
  }
}
```

See also

`_height (MovieClip._height property), width (Video.width property)`

_name (Video._name property)

`public _name : String`

Indicates the instance name of the Video object specified.

Availability: ActionScript 1.0; Flash Player 8

_parent (Video._parent property)

`public _parent : MovieClip`

Indicates the movie clip or object that contains the current Video object. The current object is the object containing the ActionScript code that references _parent. Use the _parent property to specify a relative path to movie clips or objects that are above the current object.

You can use _parent to move up multiple levels in the display list as in the following:

`this._parent._parent._alpha = 20;`

Availability: ActionScript 1.0; Flash Player 8

See also

`_root property, _target (MovieClip._target property)`

_rotation (Video._rotation property)

`public _rotation : Number`

Indicates the rotation of the Video object, in degrees, from its original orientation. Values from 0 to 180 represent clockwise rotation; values from 0 to -180 represent counterclockwise rotation. Values outside this range are added to or subtracted from 360 to obtain a value within the range. For example, the statement `my_video._rotation = 450` is the same as `my_video._rotation = 90`.

Availability: ActionScript 1.0; Flash Player 8

smoothing (Video.smoothing property)

`public smoothing : Boolean`

Specifies whether the video should be smoothed (interpolated) when it is scaled. For smoothing to work, the player must be in high-quality mode. The default value is `false` (no smoothing).

Availability: ActionScript 1.0; Flash Player 6

Example

The following example uses a button (called `smoothing_btn`) to toggle the smoothing property that is applied to the video `my_video` when it plays in a SWF file. Create a button called `smoothing_btn` and add the following ActionScript to your FLA or AS file:

```
this.createTextField("smoothing_txt", this.getNextHighestDepth(), 0, 0,
   100, 22);
smoothing_txt.autoSize = true;

var my_nc:NetConnection = new NetConnection();
my_nc.connect(null);
var my_ns:NetStream = new NetStream(my_nc);
my_video.attachVideo(my_ns);
my_ns.play("video1.flv");
my_ns.onStatus = function(infoObject:Object) {
   updateSmoothing();
};
smoothing_btn.onRelease = function() {
   my_video.smoothing = !my_video.smoothing;
   updateSmoothing();
};
function updateSmoothing():Void {
   smoothing_txt.text = "smoothing = "+my_video.smoothing;
}
```

The `MovieClip.getNextHighestDepth()` method used in this example requires Flash Player 7 or later. If your SWF file includes a version 2 component, use the version 2 components DepthManager class instead of the `MovieClip.getNextHighestDepth()` method.

_visible (Video._visible property)

`public _visible : Boolean`

Indicates whether the Video object specified by *my_video* is visible.

Availability: ActionScript 1.0; Flash Player 8

_width (Video._width property)

`public _width : Number`

Indicates the width of the Video object, in pixels.

Availability: ActionScript 1.0; Flash Player 8 - as a read-only property.

See also

`_height (Video._height property)`

width (Video.width property)

`public width : Number [read-only]`

An integer specifying the width of the video stream, in pixels. For live streams, this value is the same as the `Camera.width` property of the Camera object that is capturing the video stream. For FLV files, this value is the width of the file that was exported as an FLV file.

You may want to use this property, for example, to ensure that the user is seeing the video at the same size at which it was captured, regardless of the actual size of the Video object on the Stage.

Availability: ActionScript 1.0; Flash Player 6

Example

See the examples for `Video.height`.

_x (Video._x property)

`public _x : Number`

Indicates the x coordinate of a Video object relative to the local coordinates of the parent movie clip. If a Video object is in the main Timeline, then its coordinate system refers to the upper left corner of the Stage as (0, 0). If the Video object is inside a movie clip that has transformations, the Video object is in the local coordinate system of the enclosing movie clip. Thus, for a movie clip rotated 90° counterclockwise, the movie clip's children inherit a coordinate system that is rotated 90° counterclockwise. The Video object's coordinates refer to the registration point position.

Availability: ActionScript 1.0; Flash Player 8

See also

`_xscale (Video._xscale property)`, `_y (Video._y property)`, `_yscale (Video._yscale property)`

_xmouse (Video._xmouse property)

`public _xmouse : Number [read-only]`

Indicates the *x* coordinate of the mouse position.

Availability: ActionScript 1.0; Flash Player 8

See also

`Mouse, _ymouse (Video._ymouse property)`

_xscale (Video._xscale property)

`public _xscale : Number`

Indicates the horizontal scale (*percentage*) of the Video object as applied from the registration point of the Video object. The default registration point is (0,0).

Scaling the local coordinate system affects the _x and _y property settings, which are defined in whole pixels.

Availability: ActionScript 1.0; Flash Player 8

See also

`_x (Video._x property), _y (Video._y property), _yscale (Video._yscale property), _width (Video._width property)`

_y (Video._y property)

`public _y : Number`

Indicates the *y* coordinate of a Video object relative to the local coordinates of the parent movie clip. If a Video object is in the main Timeline, then its coordinate system refers to the upper left corner of the Stage as (0, 0). If the Video object is inside a movie clip that has transformations, the Video object is in the local coordinate system of the enclosing movie clip. Thus, for a movie clip rotated 90° counterclockwise, the movie clip's children inherit a coordinate system that is rotated 90° counterclockwise. The Video object's coordinates refer to the registration point position.

Availability: ActionScript 1.0; Flash Player 8

See also

`_x (Video._x property), _xscale (Video._xscale property), _yscale (Video._yscale property)`

_ymouse (Video._ymouse property)

`public _ymouse : Number [read-only]`

Indicates the *y* coordinate of the mouse position.

Availability: ActionScript 1.0; Flash Player 8

See also

`Mouse, _xmouse (Video._xmouse property)`

_yscale (Video._yscale property)

`public _yscale : Number`

Indicates the vertical scale (`percentage`) of the Video object as applied from the registration point of the Video object. The default registration point is (0,0).

Scaling the local coordinate system affects the _x and _y property settings, which are defined in whole pixels.

Availability: ActionScript 1.0; Flash Player 8

See also

`_x (Video._x property), _xscale (Video._xscale property), _y (Video._y property), _height (Video._height property)`

XML

```
Object
  |
  +-XMLNode
    |
    +-XML
```

`public class XML`
`extends XMLNode`

Use the methods and properties of the XML class to load, parse, send, build, and manipulate XML document trees.

You must use the constructor `new XML()` to create an XML object before calling any method of the XML class.

An XML document is represented in Flash by the XML class. Each element of the hierarchical document is represented by an XMLNode object.

For information on the following methods and properties, you can see the XMLNode class, specifically `appendChild()`, `attributes`, `childNodes`, `cloneNode()`, `firstChild`, `hasChildNodes()`, `insertBefore()`, `lastChild`, `nextSibling`, `nodeName`, `nodeType`, `nodeValue`, `parentNode`, `previousSibling`, `removeNode()`, and `toString()`.

In earlier versions of the ActionScript Language Reference, the previous methods and properties were documented in the XML class. They are now documented in the XMLNode class.

> **NOTE** The XML and XMLNode objects are modeled after the W3C DOM Level 1 recommendation, which you can find at: http://www.w3.org/tr/1998/REC-DOM-Level-1-19981001/level-one-core.html. That recommendation specifies a Node interface and a Document interface. The Document interface inherits from the Node interface, and adds methods such as `createElement()` and `createTextNode()`. In ActionScript, the XML and XMLNode objects are designed to divide functionality along similar lines.

Availability: ActionScript 1.0; Flash Player 5 - (became a native object in Flash Player 6, which improved performance significantly).

See also

`appendChild` (XMLNode.appendChild method), `attributes` (XMLNode.attributes property), `childNodes` (XMLNode.childNodes property), `cloneNode` (XMLNode.cloneNode method), `firstChild` (XMLNode.firstChild property), `hasChildNodes` (XMLNode.hasChildNodes method), `insertBefore` (XMLNode.insertBefore method), `lastChild` (XMLNode.lastChild property), `nextSibling` (XMLNode.nextSibling property), `nodeName` (XMLNode.nodeName property), `nodeType` (XMLNode.nodeType property), `nodeValue` (XMLNode.nodeValue property), `parentNode` (XMLNode.parentNode property), `previousSibling` (XMLNode.previousSibling property), `removeNode` (XMLNode.removeNode method), `toString` (XMLNode.toString method)

Property summary

Modifiers	Property	Description
	contentType:String	The MIME content type that is sent to the server when you call the XML.send() or XML.sendAndLoad() method.
	docTypeDecl:String	Specifies information about the XML document's DOCTYPE declaration.
	idMap:Object	An object containing the XML file's nodes that have an id attribute assigned.

Modifiers	Property	Description
	`ignoreWhite:Boolean`	Default setting is `false`.
	`loaded:Boolean`	The property that indicates whether the XML document has successfully loaded.
	`status:Number`	Automatically sets and returns a numeric value that indicates whether an XML document was successfully parsed into an XML object.
	`xmlDecl:String`	A string that specifies information about a document's XML declaration.

Properties inherited from class XMLNode

```
attributes (XMLNode.attributes property), childNodes (XMLNode.childNodes
property), firstChild (XMLNode.firstChild property), lastChild
(XMLNode.lastChild property), localName (XMLNode.localName property),
namespaceURI (XMLNode.namespaceURI property), nextSibling
(XMLNode.nextSibling property), nodeName (XMLNode.nodeName property),
nodeType (XMLNode.nodeType property), nodeValue (XMLNode.nodeValue
property), parentNode (XMLNode.parentNode property), prefix (XMLNode.prefix
property), previousSibling (XMLNode.previousSibling property)
```

Properties inherited from class Object

```
constructor (Object.constructor property), __proto__ (Object.__proto__
property), prototype (Object.prototype property), __resolve
(Object.__resolve property)
```

Event summary

Event	Description
`onData = function(src:String) {}`	Invoked when XML text has been completely downloaded from the server, or when an error occurs downloading XML text from a server.
`onHTTPStatus = function(httpStatus:Number) {}`	Invoked when Flash Player receives an HTTP status code from the server.
`onLoad = function(success:Boolean) {}`	Invoked by Flash Player when an XML document is received from the server.

Constructor summary

Signature	Description
`XML(text:String)`	Creates a new XML object.

Method summary

Modifiers	Signature	Description
	`addRequestHeader(hea der:Object, headerValue:String) : Void`	Adds or changes HTTP request headers (such as `Content-Type` or `SOAPAction`) sent with `POST` actions.
	`createElement(name:S tring) : XMLNode`	Creates a new XML element with the name specified in the parameter.
	`createTextNode(value :String) : XMLNode`	Creates a new XML text node with the specified text.
	`getBytesLoaded() : Number`	Returns the number of bytes loaded (streamed) for the XML document.
	`getBytesTotal() : Number`	Returns the size, in bytes, of the XML document.
	`load(url:String) : Boolean`	Loads an XML document from the specified URL, and replaces the contents of the specified XML object with the downloaded XML data.
	`parseXML(value:Strin g) : Void`	Parses the XML text specified in the `value` parameter, and populates the specified XML object with the resulting XML tree.
	`send(url:String, [target:String], [method:String]) : Boolean`	Encodes the specified XML object into an XML document and sends it to the specified `target` URL.
	`sendAndLoad(url:Stri ng, resultXML:XML) : Void`	Encodes the specified XML object into an XML document, sends it to the specified URL using the `POST` method, downloads the server's response, and loads it into the `resultXMLobject` specified in the parameters.

```
appendChild (XMLNode.appendChild method), cloneNode (XMLNode.cloneNode
method), getNamespaceForPrefix (XMLNode.getNamespaceForPrefix method),
getPrefixForNamespace (XMLNode.getPrefixForNamespace method), hasChildNodes
(XMLNode.hasChildNodes method), insertBefore (XMLNode.insertBefore method),
removeNode (XMLNode.removeNode method), toString (XMLNode.toString method)
```

Methods inherited from class Object

```
addProperty (Object.addProperty method), hasOwnProperty
(Object.hasOwnProperty method), isPropertyEnumerable
(Object.isPropertyEnumerable method), isPrototypeOf (Object.isPrototypeOf
method), registerClass (Object.registerClass method), toString
(Object.toString method), unwatch (Object.unwatch method), valueOf
(Object.valueOf method), watch (Object.watch method)
```

addRequestHeader (XML.addRequestHeader method)

```
public addRequestHeader(header:Object, headerValue:String) : Void
```

Adds or changes HTTP request headers (such as `Content-Type` or `SOAPAction`) sent with `POST` actions. In the first usage, you pass two strings to the method: `header` and `headerValue`. In the second usage, you pass an array of strings, alternating header names and header values.

If multiple calls are made to set the same header name, each successive value replaces the value set in the previous call.

You cannot add or change the following standard HTTP headers using this method: `Accept-Ranges`, `Age`, `Allow`, `Allowed`, `Connection`, `Content-Length`, `Content-Location`, `Content-Range`, `ETag`, `Host`, `Last-Modified`, `Locations`, `Max-Forwards`, `Proxy-Authenticate`, `Proxy-Authorization`, `Public`, `Range`, `Retry-After`, `Server`, `TE`, `Trailer`, `Transfer-Encoding`, `Upgrade`, `URI`, `Vary`, `Via`, `Warning`, and `WWW-Authenticate`.

Availability: ActionScript 1.0; Flash Player 6

Parameters

`header:Object` - A string that represents an HTTP request header name.

`headerValue:String` - A string that represents the value associated with `header`.

Example

The following example adds a custom HTTP header named `SOAPAction` with a value of `Foo` to an XML object named `my_xml`:

```
my_xml.addRequestHeader("SOAPAction", "'Foo'");
```

The following example creates an array named `headers` that contains two alternating HTTP headers and their associated values. The array is passed as a parameter to the `addRequestHeader()` method.

```
var headers:Array = new Array("Content-Type", "text/plain", "X-
    ClientAppVersion", "2.0");
my_xml.addRequestHeader(headers);
```

See also

addRequestHeader (LoadVars.addRequestHeader method)

contentType (XML.contentType property)

```
public contentType : String
```

The MIME content type that is sent to the server when you call the `XML.send()` or `XML.sendAndLoad()` method. The default is `application/x-www-form-urlencoded`, which is the standard MIME content type used for most HTML forms.

Availability: ActionScript 1.0; Flash Player 6

Example

The following example creates a new XML document and checks its default content type:

```
// create a new XML document
var doc:XML = new XML();

// trace the default content type
trace(doc.contentType); // output: application/x-www-form-urlencoded
```

The following example defines an XML packet, and sets the content type for the XML object. The data is then sent to a server and shows a result in a browser window.

```
var my_xml:XML = new XML("<highscore><name>Ernie</name><score>13045</
    score></highscore>");
my_xml.contentType = "text/xml";
my_xml.send("http://www.flash-mx.com/mm/highscore.cfm", "_blank");
```

Press F12 to test this example in a browser.

See also

send (XML.send method), sendAndLoad (XML.sendAndLoad method)

createElement (XML.createElement method)

```
public createElement(name:String) : XMLNode
```

Creates a new XML element with the name specified in the parameter. The new element initially has no parent, no children, and no siblings. The method returns a reference to the newly created XML object that represents the element. This method and the `XML.createTextNode()` method are the constructor methods for creating nodes for an XML object.

Availability: ActionScript 1.0; Flash Player 5

Parameters

`name:String` - The tag name of the XML element being created.

Returns

`XMLNode` - An XMLNode object; an XML element.

Example

The following example creates three XML nodes using the `createElement()` method:

```
// create an XML document
var doc:XML = new XML();

// create three XML nodes using createElement()
var element1:XMLNode = doc.createElement("element1");
var element2:XMLNode = doc.createElement("element2");
var element3:XMLNode = doc.createElement("element3");

// place the new nodes into the XML tree
doc.appendChild(element1);
element1.appendChild(element2);
element1.appendChild(element3);

trace(doc);
// output: <element1><element2 /><element3 /></element1>
```

See also

createTextNode (XML.createTextNode method)

createTextNode (XML.createTextNode method)

```
public createTextNode(value:String) : XMLNode
```

Creates a new XML text node with the specified text. The new node initially has no parent, and text nodes cannot have children or siblings. This method returns a reference to the XML object that represents the new text node. This method and the `XML.createElement()` method are the constructor methods for creating nodes for an XML object.

Availability: ActionScript 1.0; Flash Player 5

Parameters

`value:String` - A string; the text used to create the new text node.

Returns

`XMLNode` - An XMLNode object.

Example

The following example creates two XML text nodes using the `createTextNode()` method, and places them into existing XML nodes:

```
// create an XML document
var doc:XML = new XML();

// create three XML nodes using createElement()
var element1:XMLNode = doc.createElement("element1");
var element2:XMLNode = doc.createElement("element2");
var element3:XMLNode = doc.createElement("element3");

// place the new nodes into the XML tree
doc.appendChild(element1);
element1.appendChild(element2);
element1.appendChild(element3);

// create two XML text nodes using createTextNode()
var textNode1:XMLNode = doc.createTextNode("textNode1 String value");
var textNode2:XMLNode = doc.createTextNode("textNode2 String value");

// place the new nodes into the XML tree
element2.appendChild(textNode1);
element3.appendChild(textNode2);
```

```
trace(doc);
// output (with line breaks added between tags):
// <element1>
// <element2>textNode1 String value</element2>
// <element3>textNode2 String value</element3>
// </element1>
```

See also

createElement (XML.createElement method)

docTypeDecl (XML.docTypeDecl property)

`public docTypeDecl : String`

Specifies information about the XML document's DOCTYPE declaration. After the XML text has been parsed into an XML object, the XML.docTypeDecl property of the XML object is set to the text of the XML document's DOCTYPE declaration (for example, <!DOCTYPEgreeting SYSTEM "hello.dtd">). This property is set using a string representation of the DOCTYPE declaration, not an XML node object.

The ActionScript XML parser is not a validating parser. The DOCTYPE declaration is read by the parser and stored in the XML.docTypeDecl property, but no Dtd validation is performed.

If no DOCTYPE declaration was encountered during a parse operation, the XML.docTypeDecl property is set to undefined. The XML.toString() method outputs the contents of XML.docTypeDecl immediately after the XML declaration stored in XML.xmlDecl, and before any other text in the XML object. If XML.docTypeDecl is undefined, no DOCTYPE declaration is output.

Availability: ActionScript 1.0; Flash Player 5

Example

The following example uses the XML.docTypeDecl property to set the DOCTYPE declaration for an XML object:

```
my_xml.docTypeDecl = "<!DOCTYPE greeting SYSTEM \"hello.dtd\">";
```

See also

xmlDecl (XML.xmlDecl property)

getBytesLoaded (XML.getBytesLoaded method)

`public getBytesLoaded() : Number`

Returns the number of bytes loaded (streamed) for the XML document. You can compare the value of `getBytesLoaded()` with the value of `getBytesTotal()` to determine what percentage of an XML document has loaded.

Availability: ActionScript 1.0; Flash Player 6

Returns

`Number` - An integer that indicates the number of bytes loaded.

Example

The following example shows how to use the `XML.getBytesLoaded()` method with the `XML.getBytesTotal()` method to trace the progress of an `XML.load()` command. You must replace the URL parameter of the `XML.load()` command so that the parameter refers to a valid XML file using HTTP. If you attempt to use this example to load a local file that resides on your hard disk, this example will not work properly because in test movie mode Flash Player loads local files in their entirety.

```
// create a new XML document
var doc:XML = new XML();

var checkProgress = function(xmlObj:XML) {
  var bytesLoaded:Number = xmlObj.getBytesLoaded();
  var bytesTotal:Number = xmlObj.getBytesTotal();
  var percentLoaded:Number = Math.floor((bytesLoaded / bytesTotal ) 100);
  trace ("milliseconds elapsed: " + getTimer());
  trace ("bytesLoaded: " + bytesLoaded);
  trace ("bytesTotal: " + bytesTotal);
  trace ("percent loaded: " + percentLoaded);
  trace ("-------------------------------");
}

doc.onLoad = function(success:Boolean) {
  clearInterval(intervalID);
  trace("intervalID: " + intervalID);
}
doc.load("[place a valid URL pointing to an XML file here]");
var intervalID:Number = setInterval(checkProgress, 100, doc);
```

See also

`getBytesTotal (XML.getBytesTotal method)`

getBytesTotal (XML.getBytesTotal method)

```
public getBytesTotal() : Number
```

Returns the size, in bytes, of the XML document.

Availability: ActionScript 1.0; Flash Player 6

Returns

`Number` - An integer.

Example

See example for `XML.getBytesLoaded()`.

See also

`getBytesLoaded (XML.getBytesLoaded method)`

idMap (XML.idMap property)

```
public idMap : Object
```

An object containing the XML file's nodes that have an `id` attribute assigned. The names of the properties of the object (each containing a node) match the values of the `id` attributes.

Consider the following XML object:

```
<employee id='41'>
<name>
John Doe
</name>
<address>
601 Townsend St.
</address>
</employee>

<employee id='42'>
<name>
Jane Q. Public
</name>
</employee>
<department id="IT">
Information Technology
</department>
```

In this example, the `idMap` property for this XML object is an Object with three properties: 41, 42, and `IT`. Each of these properties is an XMLNode that has the matching `id` value. For example, the `IT` property of the `idMap` object is this node:

```
<department id="IT">
Information Technology
</department>
```

You must use the `parseXML()` method on the XML object for the `idMap` property to be instantiated.

If there is more than one XMLNode with the same `id` value, the matching property of the `idNode` object is that of the last node parsed, as follows:

```
var x1:XML = new XML("<a id='1'><b id='2' /><c id='1' /></a>");
x2 = new XML();
x2.parseXML(x1);
trace (x2.idMap['1']);
```

The following will output the `<c>` node:

```
<c id='1' />
```

Availability: ActionScript 1.0; Flash Player 8

Example

You can create a text file named `idMapTest.xml` that contains the following text.

```
<?xml version="1.0"?>
<doc xml:base="http://example.org/today/" xmlns:xlink="http://www.w3.org/
 1999/xlink">
<head>
<title>Virtual Library</title>
</head>
<body>
<paragraph id="linkP1">See <link xlink:type="simple"
 xlink:href="new.xml">what's
new</link>!</paragraph>
<paragraph>Check out the hot picks of the day!</paragraph>
<olist xml:base="/hotpicks/">
<item>
<link id="foo" xlink:type="simple" xlink:href="pick1.xml">Hot Pick #1</
 link>
</item>
<item>
<link id="bar" xlink:type="simple" xlink:href="pick2.xml">Hot Pick #2</
 link>
</item>
<item>
<link xlink:type="simple" xlink:href="pick3.xml">Hot Pick #3</link>
</item>
</olist>
</body>
</doc>
```

Then you can create a SWF file in the same directory as the XML file. You can include the following script in the SWF.

```
var readXML = new XML();
readXML.load("idMapTest.xml");
readXML.onLoad = function(success) {
  myXML = new XML();
  myXML.parseXML(readXML);
  for (var x in myXML.idMap){
    trace('idMap.' + x + " = " + newline + myXML.idMap[x]);
    trace('_____' + newline);
  }
}
```

When you test the SWF file, the following output is generated.

```
idMap.bar =
<link id="bar" xlink:type="simple" xlink:href="pick2.xml">Hot Pick #2</
  link>

  _____

idMap.foo =
<link id="foo" xlink:type="simple" xlink:href="pick1.xml">Hot Pick #1</
  link>

  _____

idMap.linkP1 =
<paragraph id="linkP1">See <link xlink:type="simple"
  xlink:href="new.xml">what's

new</link>!</paragraph>

  _____
```

ignoreWhite (XML.ignoreWhite property)

```
public ignoreWhite : Boolean
```

Default setting is `false`. When set to `true`, text nodes that contain only white space are discarded during the parsing process. Text nodes with leading or trailing white space are unaffected.

Usage 1: You can set the `ignoreWhite` property for individual XML objects, as the following code shows:

```
my_xml.ignoreWhite = true;
```

Usage 2: You can set the default `ignoreWhite` property for XML objects, as the following code shows:

```
XML.prototype.ignoreWhite = true;
```

Availability: ActionScript 1.0; Flash Player 5

Example

The following example loads an XML file with a text node that contains only white space; the foyer tag comprises fourteen space characters. To run this example, create a text file named *flooring.xml*, and copy the following tags into it:

```
<house>
<kitchen> ceramic tile </kitchen>
<bathroom>linoleum</bathroom>
<foyer> </foyer>
</house>
```

Create a new Flash document named *flooring.fla* and save it to the same directory as the XML file. Place the following code into the main Timeline:

```
// Create a new XML object.
var flooring:XML = new XML();

// Set the ignoreWhite property to true (default value is false)
flooring.ignoreWhite = true;

// After loading is complete, trace the XML object.
flooring.onLoad = function(success:Boolean) {
  trace(flooring);
}

// Load the XML into the flooring object.
flooring.load("flooring.xml");

// Output (line breaks added for clarity):
<house>
  <kitchen> ceramic tile </kitchen>
  <bathroom>linoleum</bathroom>
  <foyer />
</house>
```

If you then change the setting of flooring.ignoreWhite to false, or simply remove that line of code entirely, the fourteen space characters in the foyer tag will be preserved:

```
...
// Set the ignoreWhite property to false (default value).
flooring.ignoreWhite = false;
...
// Output (line breaks added for clarity):
```

```
<house>
  <kitchen> ceramic tile </kitchen>
  <bathroom>linoleum</bathroom>
  <foyer> </foyer>
</house>
```

The XML_blogTracker.fla and XML_languagePicker.fla files in the ActionScript samples folder also contain a code example. The following are typical paths to this folder:

- Windows: *boot drive*\Program Files\Macromedia\Flash 8\Samples and Tutorials\Samples\ActionScript
- Macintosh: *Macintosh HD*/Applications/Macromedia Flash 8/Samples and Tutorials/ Samples/ActionScript

load (XML.load method)

```
public load(url:String) : Boolean
```
Loads an XML document from the specified URL, and replaces the contents of the specified XML object with the downloaded XML data. The URL is relative and is called using HTTP. The load process is asynchronous; it does not finish immediately after the `load()` method is executed.

When the `load()` method is executed, the XML object property `loaded` is set to `false`. When the XML data finishes downloading, the `loaded` property is set to `true`, and the `onLoad` event handler is invoked. The XML data is not parsed until it is completely downloaded. If the XML object previously contained any XML trees, they are discarded.

You can define a custom function that executes when the `onLoad` event handler of the XML object is invoked.

 If a file being loaded contains non-ASCII characters (as found in many non-English languages), it is recommended that you save the file with UTF-8 or UTF-16 encoding as opposed to a non-Unicode format like ASCII.

When using this method, consider the Flash Player security model:

For Flash Player 8:

- Data loading is not allowed if the calling SWF file is in the local-with-file-system sandbox and the target resource is from a network sandbox.
- Data loading is also not allowed if the calling SWF file is from a network sandbox and the target resource is local.

For more information, see the following:

- Chapter 17, "Understanding Security," in *Learning ActionScript 2.0 in Flash*
- The Flash Player 8 Security white paper at http://www.macromedia.com/go/fp8_security
- The Flash Player 8 Security-Related API white paper at http://www.macromedia.com/go/fp8_security_apis

For Flash Player 7 and later websites can permit cross-domain access to a resource via a cross-domain policy file. In SWF files of any version running in Flash Player 7 and later, the `url` parameter must be in exactly the same domain. For example, a SWF file at www.someDomain.com can load data only from sources that are also at www.someDomain.com.

In SWF files running in a version of the player earlier than Flash Player 7, the `url` parameter must be in the same superdomain as the SWF file that issues this call. A *superdomain* is derived by removing the leftmost component of a file's URL. For example, a SWF file at www.someDomain.com can load data from sources at store.someDomain.com, because both files are in the same superdomain of someDomain.com.

Availability: ActionScript 1.0; Flash Player 5 - The behavior changed in Flash Player 7.

Parameters

`url:String` - A string that represents the URL where the XML document to be loaded is located. If the SWF file that issues this call is running in a web browser, `url` must be in the same domain as the SWF file.

Returns

`Boolean` - A Boolean value of `false` if no parameter (null) is passed; `true` otherwise. Use the `onLoad()` event handler to check the success of a loaded XML document.

Example

The following code example uses the XML.load() method:

```
// Create a new XML object.
var flooring:XML = new XML();

// Set the ignoreWhite property to true (default value is false).
flooring.ignoreWhite = true;

// After loading is complete, trace the XML object.
flooring.onLoad = function(success) {
  trace(flooring);
};

// Load the XML into the flooring object.
flooring.load("flooring.xml");
```

For the contents of the flooring.xml file, and the output that this example produces, see the example for the XML.ignoreWhite property.

See also

ignoreWhite (XML.ignoreWhite property), loaded (XML.loaded property), onLoad (XML.onLoad handler), useCodepage (System.useCodepage property)

loaded (XML.loaded property)

```
public loaded : Boolean
```

The property that indicates whether the XML document has successfully loaded. If there is no custom onLoad() event handler defined for the XML object, Flash Player sets this property to true when the document-loading process initiated by the XML.load() call has completed successfully; otherwise, it is false. However, if you define a custom behavior for the onLoad() event handler for the XML object, you must be sure to set onload in that function.

Availability: ActionScript 1.0; Flash Player 5

Example

The following example uses the XML.loaded property in a simple script.

```
var my_xml:XML = new XML();
my_xml.ignoreWhite = true;
my_xml.onLoad = function(success:Boolean) {
  trace("success: "+success);
  trace("loaded: "+my_xml.loaded);
  trace("status: "+my_xml.status);
};
my_xml.load("http://www.flash-mx.com/mm/problems/products.xml");
```

Information is displayed in the Output panel when Flash invokes the onLoad() handler. If the call completes successfully, true is displayed for the loaded status in the Output panel.

```
success: true
loaded: true
status: 0
```

See also

`load (XML.load method)`, `onLoad (XML.onLoad handler)`

onData (XML.onData handler)

`onData = function(src:String) {}`

Invoked when XML text has been completely downloaded from the server, or when an error occurs downloading XML text from a server. This handler is invoked before the XML is parsed, and you can use it to call a custom parsing routine instead of using the Flash XML parser. The src parameter is a string that contains XML text downloaded from the server, unless an error occurs during the download, in which case the src parameter is undefined.

By default, the XML.onData event handler invokes XML.onLoad. You can override the XML.onData event handler with custom behavior, but XML.onLoad is not called unless you call it in your implementation of XML.onData.

Availability: ActionScript 1.0; Flash Player 5

Parameters

`src:String` - A string or undefined; the raw data, usually in XML format, that is sent by the server.

Example

The following example shows what the XML.onData event handler looks like by default:

```
XML.prototype.onData = function (src:String) {
  if (src == undefined) {
    this.onLoad(false);
  } else {
    this.parseXML(src);
    this.loaded = true;
    this.onLoad(true);
  }
}
```

You can override the XML.onData event handler to intercept the XML text without parsing it.

onLoad (XML.onLoad handler)

onHTTPStatus (XML.onHTTPStatus handler)

`onHTTPStatus = function(httpStatus:Number) {}`

Invoked when Flash Player receives an HTTP status code from the server. This handler lets you capture and act on HTTP status codes.

The `onHTTPStatus` handler is invoked before `onData`, which triggers calls to `onLoad` with a value of `undefined` if the load fails. It's important to note that after `onHTTPStatus` is triggered, `onData` is always subsequently triggered, regardless of whether or not you override `onHTTPStatus`. To best use the `onHTTPStatus` handler, write an appropriate function to catch the result of the `onHTTPStatus` call; you can then use the result in your `onData` or `onLoad` handler functions. If `onHTTPStatus` is not invoked, this indicates that the player did not try to make the URL request. This can happen because the request violates security sandbox rules for the SWF.

If Flash Player cannot get a status code from the server or if Flash Player cannot communicate with the server, the default value of 0 is passed to your ActionScript code. A value of 0 can be generated in any player, such as if a malformed URL is requested, and is always generated by the Flash Player plug-in when run in the following browsers, which do not pass HTTP status codes to the player: Netscape, Mozilla, Safari, Opera, or Internet Explorer for the Macintosh.

Availability: ActionScript 1.0; Flash Player 8

Parameters

`httpStatus:Number` - The HTTP status code returned by the server. For example, a value of 404 indicates that the server has not found anything matching the requested URI. HTTP status codes can be found in sections 10.4 and 10.5 of the HTTP specification at ftp://ftp.isi.edu/in-notes/rfc2616.txt.

Example

The following example shows how to use the `onHTTPStatus` method to help with debugging. The example collects HTTP status codes and assigns their value and type to an instance of the `XML` object (notice that this example creates the instance members `this.httpStatus` and `this.httpStatusType` at runtime). The `onData` method uses these to trace information about the HTTP response that could be useful when debugging.

```
var myXml:XML = new XML();

myXml.onHTTPStatus = function(httpStatus:Number) {
    this.httpStatus = httpStatus;
```

```
      if(httpStatus < 100) {
        this.httpStatusType = "flashError";
      }
      else if(httpStatus < 200) {
        this.httpStatusType = "informational";
      }
      else if(httpStatus < 300) {
        this.httpStatusType = "successful";
      }
      else if(httpStatus < 400) {
        this.httpStatusType = "redirection";
      }
      else if(httpStatus < 500) {
        this.httpStatusType = "clientError";
      }
      else if(httpStatus < 600) {
        this.httpStatusType = "serverError";
      }
    }

myXml.onData = function(src:String) {
    trace(">> " + this.httpStatusType + ": " + this.httpStatus);
    if(src != undefined) {
      this.parseXML(src);
      this.loaded = true;
      this.onLoad(true);
    }
    else {
      this.onLoad(false);
    }
  }

myXml.onLoad = function(success:Boolean) {
}

myXml.load("http://weblogs.macromedia.com/mxna/xml/
    rss.cfm?query=byMostRecent&languages=1");
```

See also

onHTTPStatus (LoadVars.onHTTPStatus handler), load (XML.load method),
sendAndLoad (XML.sendAndLoad method)

onLoad (XML.onLoad handler)

```
onLoad = function(success:Boolean) {}
```

Invoked by Flash Player when an XML document is received from the server. If the XML document is received successfully, the `success` parameter is `true`. If the document was not received, or if an error occurred in receiving the response from the server, the `success` parameter is `false`. The default, implementation of this method is not active. To override the default implementation, you must assign a function that contains custom actions.

Availability: ActionScript 1.0; Flash Player 5

Parameters

`success:Boolean` - A Boolean value that evaluates to `true` if the XML object is successfully loaded with a `XML.load()` or `XML.sendAndLoad()` operation; otherwise, it is `false`.

Example

The following example includes ActionScript for a simple e-commerce storefront application. The `sendAndLoad()` method transmits an XML element that contains the user's name and password, and uses an `XML.onLoad` handler to process the reply from the server.

```
var login_str:String = "<login username=\""+username_txt.text+"\"
  password=\""+password_txt.text+"\" />";
var my_xml:XML = new XML(login_str);
var myLoginReply_xml:XML = new XML();

myLoginReply_xml.ignoreWhite = true;

myLoginReply_xml.onLoad = function(success:Boolean){

  if (success) {

    if ((myLoginReply_xml.firstChild.nodeName == "packet") &&
      (myLoginReply_xml.firstChild.attributes.success == "true")) {
      gotoAndStop("loggedIn");
    } else {
      gotoAndStop("loginFailed");
    }

  } else {
    gotoAndStop("connectionFailed");
  }

};

my_xml.sendAndLoad("http://www.flash-mx.com/mm/login_xml.cfm",
  myLoginReply_xml);
```

load (XML.load method), sendAndLoad (XML.sendAndLoad method), function statement

parseXML (XML.parseXML method)

public parseXML(value:String) : Void

Parses the XML text specified in the value parameter, and populates the specified XML object with the resulting XML tree. Any existing trees in the XML object are discarded.

Availability: ActionScript 1.0; Flash Player 5

Parameters

value:String - A string that represents the XML text to be parsed and passed to the specified XML object.

Example

The following example creates and parses an XML packet:

```
var xml_str:String = "<state name=\"California\">
<city>San Francisco</city></state>"

// defining the XML source within the XML constructor:
var my1_xml:XML = new XML(xml_str);
trace(my1_xml.firstChild.attributes.name); // output: California

// defining the XML source using the XML.parseXML method:
var my2_xml:XML = new XML();
my2_xml.parseXML(xml_str);
trace(my2_xml.firstChild.attributes.name); // output: California
```

send (XML.send method)

public send(url:String, [target:String], [method:String]) : Boolean

Encodes the specified XML object into an XML document and sends it to the specified target URL.

When using this method, consider the Flash Player security model:

- For Flash Player 8, the method is not allowed if the calling SWF file is in an untrusted local sandbox.

- For Flash Player 7 and later, the method is not allowed if the calling SWF file is a local file.

For more information, see the following:

- Chapter 17, "Understanding Security," in *Learning ActionScript 2.0 in Flash*

- The Flash Player 8 Security white paper at http://www.macromedia.com/go/fp8_security
- The Flash Player 8 Security-Related API white paper at http://www.macromedia.com/go/fp8_security_apis

Availability: ActionScript 1.0; Flash Player 5

Parameters

url:String - The destination URL for the specified XML object.

target:String [optional] - The browser window to show data that the server returns:

- _self specifies the current frame in the current window.
- _blank specifies a new window.
- _parent specifies the parent of the current frame.
- _top specifies the top-level frame in the current window.

If you do not specify a target parameter, it is the same as specifying _self.

method:String [optional] - the method of the HTTP protocol used: either "GET" or "POST". In a browser, the default value is "POST". In the Flash test environment, the default value is "GET".

Returns

Boolean - false if no parameters are specified, true otherwise.

Example

The following example defines an XML packet and sets the content type for the XML object. The data is then sent to a server and shows a result in a browser window.

```
var my_xml:XML = new XML("<highscore><name>Ernie</name><score>13045</
  score></highscore>");
my_xml.contentType = "text/xml";
my_xml.send("http://www.flash-mx.com/mm/highscore.cfm", "_blank");
```

Press F12 to test this example in a browser.

See also

sendAndLoad (XML.sendAndLoad method)

sendAndLoad (XML.sendAndLoad method)

`public sendAndLoad(url:String, resultXML:XML) : Void`

Encodes the specified XML object into an XML document, sends it to the specified URL using the `POST` method, downloads the server's response, and loads it into the `resultXMLobject` specified in the parameters. The server response loads in the same manner used by the `XML.load()` method.

When the `sendAndLoad()` method is executed, the XML object property `loaded` is set to `false`. When the XML data finishes downloading, the `loaded` property is set to `true` if the data successfully loaded, and the `onLoad` event handler is invoked. The XML data is not parsed until it is completely downloaded. If the XML object previously contained any XML trees, those trees are discarded.

When using this method, consider the Flash Player security model:

For Flash Player 8:

- Data loading is not allowed if the calling SWF file is in the local-with-file-system sandbox and the target resource is from a network sandbox.

- Data loading is also not allowed if the calling SWF file is from a network sandbox and the target resource is local.

For more information, see the following:

- Chapter 17, "Understanding Security," in *Learning ActionScript 2.0 in Flash*
- The Flash Player 8 Security white paper at http://www.macromedia.com/go/fp8_security
- The Flash Player 8 Security-Related API white paper at http://www.macromedia.com/go/fp8_security_apis

For Flash Player 7 and later websites can permit cross-domain access to a resource via a cross-domain policy file. In SWF files of any version running in Flash Player 7 and later, the `url` parameter must be in exactly the same domain. For example, a SWF file at www.someDomain.com can load data only from sources that are also at www.someDomain.com.

In SWF files running in a version of the player earlier than Flash Player 7, the `url` parameter must be in the same superdomain as the SWF file that is issuing this call. A *superdomain* is derived by removing the left-most component of a file's URL. For example, a SWF file at www.someDomain.com can load data from sources at store.someDomain.com, because both files are in the same superdomain of someDomain.com.

Availability: ActionScript 1.0; Flash Player 5 - Behavior changed in Flash Player 7.

Parameters

`url:String` - A string; the destination URL for the specified XML object. If the SWF file issuing this call is running in a web browser, `url` must be in the same domain as the SWF file; for details, see the Description section.

`resultXML:XML` - A target XML object created with the XML constructor method that will receive the return information from the server.

Example

The following example includes ActionScript for a simple e-commerce storefront application. The `XML.sendAndLoad()` method transmits an XML element that contains the user's name and password, and uses an `onLoad` handler to process the reply from the server.

```
var login_str:String = "<login username=\""+username_txt.text+"\"
  password=\""+password_txt.text+"\" />";
var my_xml:XML = new XML(login_str);
var myLoginReply_xml:XML = new XML();
myLoginReply_xml.ignoreWhite = true;
myLoginReply_xml.onLoad = myOnLoad;
my_xml.sendAndLoad("http://www.flash-mx.com/mm/login_xml.cfm",
  myLoginReply_xml);
function myOnLoad(success:Boolean) {
  if (success) {
    if ((myLoginReply_xml.firstChild.nodeName == "packet") &&
      (myLoginReply_xml.firstChild.attributes.success == "true")) {
      gotoAndStop("loggedIn");
    } else {
      gotoAndStop("loginFailed");
    }
  } else {
    gotoAndStop("connectionFailed");
  }
}
```

See also

`send (XML.send method)`, `load (XML.load method)`, `loaded (XML.loaded property)`, `onLoad (XML.onLoad handler)`

status (XML.status property)

```
public status : Number
```

Automatically sets and returns a numeric value that indicates whether an XML document was successfully parsed into an XML object. The following are the numeric status codes, with descriptions:

- 0 No error; parse was completed successfully.
- -2 A CDATA section was not properly terminated.
- -3 The XML declaration was not properly terminated.
- -4 The DOCTYPE declaration was not properly terminated.
- -5 A comment was not properly terminated.
- -6 An XML element was malformed.
- -7 Out of memory.
- -8 An attribute value was not properly terminated.
- -9 A start-tag was not matched with an end-tag.
- -10 An end-tag was encountered without a matching start-tag.

Availability: ActionScript 1.0; Flash Player 5

Example

The following example loads an XML packet into a SWF file. A status message displays, depending on whether the XML loads and parses successfully. Add the following ActionScript to your FLA or AS file:

```
var my_xml:XML = new XML();
my_xml.onLoad = function(success:Boolean) {
  if (success) {
  if (my_xml.status == 0) {
    trace("XML was loaded and parsed successfully");
  } else {
    trace("XML was loaded successfully, but was unable to be parsed.");
  }
  var errorMessage:String;
  switch (my_xml.status) {
  case 0 :
    errorMessage = "No error; parse was completed successfully.";
    break;
  case -2 :
    errorMessage = "A CDATA section was not properly terminated.";
    break;
  case -3 :
    errorMessage = "The XML declaration was not properly terminated.";
    break;
```

```
  case -4 :
    errorMessage = "The DOCTYPE declaration was not properly terminated.";
    break;
  case -5 :
    errorMessage = "A comment was not properly terminated.";
    break;
  case -6 :
    errorMessage = "An XML element was malformed.";
    break;
  case -7 :
    errorMessage = "Out of memory.";
    break;
  case -8 :
    errorMessage = "An attribute value was not properly terminated.";
    break;
  case -9 :
    errorMessage = "A start-tag was not matched with an end-tag.";
    break;
  case -10 :
    errorMessage = "An end-tag was encountered without a matching
    start-tag.";
    break;
  default :
    errorMessage = "An unknown error has occurred.";
    break;
  }
  trace("status: "+my_xml.status+" ("+errorMessage+")");
  } else {
  trace("Unable to load/parse XML. (status: "+my_xml.status+")");
  }
};
my_xml.load("http://www.helpexamples.com/flash/badxml.xml");
```

XML constructor

`public XML(text:String)`

Creates a new XML object. You must use the constructor to create an XML object before you call any of the methods of the XML class.

 NOTE Use the `createElement()` and `createTextNode()` methods to add elements and text nodes to an XML document tree.

Availability: ActionScript 1.0; Flash Player 5

Parameters

`text:String` - A string; the XML text parsed to create the new XML object.

Example

The following example creates a new, empty XML object:

```
var my_xml:XML = new XML();
```

The following example creates an XML object by parsing the XML text specified in the source parameter, and populates the newly created XML object with the resulting XML document tree:

```
var other_xml:XML = new XML("<state name=\"California\"><city>San
  Francisco</city></state>");
```

See also

createElement (XML.createElement method), createTextNode (XML.createTextNode method)

xmlDecl (XML.xmlDecl property)

```
public xmlDecl : String
```

A string that specifies information about a document's XML declaration. After the XML document is parsed into an XML object, this property is set to the text of the document's XML declaration. This property is set using a string representation of the XML declaration, not an XML node object. If no XML declaration is encountered during a parse operation, the property is set to undefined. The XML.toString() method outputs the contents of the XML.xmlDecl property before any other text in the XML object. If the XML.xmlDecl property contains the undefined type, no XML declaration is output.

Availability: ActionScript 1.0; Flash Player 5

Example

The following example creates a text field called my_txt that has the same dimensions as the Stage. The text field displays properties of the XML packet that loads into the SWF file. The doc type declaration displays in my_txt. Add the following ActionScript to your FLA or AS file:

```
var my_fmt:TextFormat = new TextFormat();
my_fmt.font = "_typewriter";
my_fmt.size = 12;
my_fmt.leftMargin = 10;

this.createTextField("my_txt", this.getNextHighestDepth(), 0, 0,
  Stage.width, Stage.height);
my_txt.border = true;
my_txt.multiline = true;
my_txt.wordWrap = true;
```

```
my_txt.setNewTextFormat(my_fmt);

var my_xml:XML = new XML();
my_xml.ignoreWhite = true;
my_xml.onLoad = function(success:Boolean) {
  var endTime:Number = getTimer();
  var elapsedTime:Number = endTime-startTime;
  if (success) {
    my_txt.text = "xmlDecl:"+newline+my_xml.xmlDecl+newline+newline;
    my_txt.text +=
  "contentType:"+newline+my_xml.contentType+newline+newline;
    my_txt.text +=
  "docTypeDecl:"+newline+my_xml.docTypeDecl+newline+newline;
    my_txt.text += "packet:"+newline+my_xml.toString()+newline+newline;
  } else {
    my_txt.text = "Unable to load remote XML."+newline+newline;
  }
  my_txt.text += "loaded in: "+elapsedTime+" ms.";
};
my_xml.load("http://www.helpexamples.com/crossdomain.xml");
var startTime:Number = getTimer();
```

The `MovieClip.getNextHighestDepth()` method used in this example requires Flash Player 7 or later. If your SWF file includes a version 2 component, use the version 2 components DepthManager class instead of the `MovieClip.getNextHighestDepth()` method.

See also

`docTypeDecl (XML.docTypeDecl property)`

XMLNode

```
Object
  |
  +-XMLNode
```

```
public class XMLNode
extends Object
```

An XML document is represented in Flash by the XML class. Each element of the hierarchical document is represented by an XMLNode object.

Availability: ActionScript 1.0; Flash Player 5

See also

`XML`

Property summary

Modifiers	Property	Description
	attributes:Object	An object containing all of the attributes of the specified XML instance.
	childNodes:Array [read-only]	An array of the specified XML object's children.
	firstChild:XMLNode [read-only]	Evaluates the specified XML object and references the first child in the parent node's child list.
	lastChild:XMLNode [read-only]	An XMLNode value that references the last child in the node's child list.
	localName:String [read-only]	The local name portion of the XML node's name.
	namespaceURI:String [read-only]	If the XML node has a prefix, namespaceURI is the value of the xmlns declaration for that prefix (the URI), which is typically called the namespace URI.
	nextSibling:XMLNode [read-only]	An XMLNode value that references the next sibling in the parent node's child list.
	nodeName:String	A string representing the node name of the XML object.
	nodeType:Number [read-only]	A nodeType value, either 1 for an XML element or 3 for a text node.
	nodeValue:String	The node value of the XML object.
	parentNode:XMLNode [read-only]	An XMLNode value that references the parent node of the specified XML object, or returns null if the node has no parent.
	prefix:String [read-only]	The prefix portion of the XML node name.
	previousSibling:XMLNode [read-only]	An XMLNode value that references the previous sibling in the parent node's child list.

Properties inherited from class Object

```
constructor (Object.constructor property),__proto__ (Object.__proto__
property),prototype (Object.prototype property),__resolve
(Object.__resolve property)
```

Constructor summary

Signature	Description
`XMLNode(type:Number, value:String)`	The XMLNode constructor lets you instantiate an XML node based on a string specifying its contents and on a number representing its node type.

Method summary

Modifiers	Signature	Description
	`appendChild(newChild :XMLNode) : Void`	Appends the specified node to the XML object's child list.
	`cloneNode(deep:Boole an) : XMLNode`	Constructs and returns a new XML node of the same type, name, value, and attributes as the specified XML object.
	`getNamespaceForPrefi x(prefix:String) : String`	Returns the namespace URI that is associated with the specified prefix for the node.
	`getPrefixForNamespac e(nsURI:String) : String`	Returns the prefix that is associated with the specified namespace URI for the node.
	`hasChildNodes() : Boolean`	Specifies whether or not the XML object has child nodes.
	`insertBefore(newChil d:XMLNode, insertPoint:XMLNode) : Void`	Inserts a `newChild` node into the XML object's child list, before the `insertPoint` node.
	`removeNode() : Void`	Removes the specified XML object from its parent.
	`toString() : String`	Evaluates the specified XML object, constructs a textual representation of the XML structure, including the node, children, and attributes, and returns the result as a string.

Methods inherited from class Object

```
addProperty (Object.addProperty method), hasOwnProperty
(Object.hasOwnProperty method), isPropertyEnumerable
(Object.isPropertyEnumerable method), isPrototypeOf (Object.isPrototypeOf
method), registerClass (Object.registerClass method), toString
(Object.toString method), unwatch (Object.unwatch method), valueOf
(Object.valueOf method), watch (Object.watch method)
```

appendChild (XMLNode.appendChild method)

```
public appendChild(newChild:XMLNode) : Void
```

Appends the specified node to the XML object's child list. This method operates directly on the node referenced by the childNode parameter; it does not append a copy of the node. If the node to be appended already exists in another tree structure, appending the node to the new location will remove it from its current location. If the childNode parameter refers to a node that already exists in another XML tree structure, the appended child node is placed in the new tree structure after it is removed from its existing parent node.

Availability: ActionScript 1.0; Flash Player 5

Parameters

newChild:XMLNode - An XMLNode that represents the node to be moved from its current location to the child list of the *my_xml* object.

Example

This example does the following things in the order shown:

- Creates two empty XML documents, doc1 and doc2.
- Creates a new node using the createElement() method, and appends it, using the appendChild() method, to the XML document named doc1.
- Shows how to move a node using the appendChild() method, by moving the root node from doc1 to doc2.
- Clones the root node from doc2 and appends it to doc1.
- Creates a new node and appends it to the root node of the XML document doc1.

```
var doc1:XML = new XML();
var doc2:XML = new XML();

// create a root node and add it to doc1
var rootnode:XMLNode = doc1.createElement("root");
doc1.appendChild(rootnode);
trace ("doc1: " + doc1); // output: doc1: <root />
trace ("doc2: " + doc2); // output: doc2:

// move the root node to doc2
doc2.appendChild(rootnode);
trace ("doc1: " + doc1); // output: doc1:
trace ("doc2: " + doc2); // output: doc2: <root />

// clone the root node and append it to doc1
var clone:XMLNode = doc2.firstChild.cloneNode(true);
doc1.appendChild(clone);
trace ("doc1: " + doc1); // output: doc1: <root />
```

```
trace ("doc2: " + doc2); // output: doc2: <root />

// create a new node to append to root node (named clone) of doc1
var newNode:XMLNode = doc1.createElement("newbie");
clone.appendChild(newNode);
trace ("doc1: " + doc1); // output: doc1: <root><newbie /></root>
```

attributes (XMLNode.attributes property)

```
public attributes : Object
```

An object containing all of the attributes of the specified XML instance. The XML.attributes object contains one variable for each attribute of the XML instance. Because these variables are defined as part of the object, they are generally referred to as properties of the object. The value of each attribute is stored in the corresponding property as a string. For example, if you have an attribute named color, you would retrieve that attribute's value by specifying color as the property name, as the following code shows:

```
var myColor:String = doc.firstChild.attributes.color;
```

Availability: ActionScript 1.0; Flash Player 5

Example

The following example shows how to read and write the attributes of an XML node:

```
var doc:XML = new XML("<mytag name='Val'> item </mytag>");
trace(doc.firstChild.attributes.name); // Val

doc.firstChild.attributes.order = "first";
trace (doc.firstChild); // <mytag order="first" name="Val"> item </mytag>

for (attr in doc.firstChild.attributes) {
   trace (attr + " = " + doc.firstChild.attributes[attr]);
}

// order = first
// name = Val
```

childNodes (XMLNode.childNodes property)

```
public childNodes : Array [read-only]
```

An array of the specified XML object's children. Each element in the array is a reference to an XML object that represents a child node. This is a read-only property and cannot be used to manipulate child nodes. Use the appendChild(), insertBefore(), and removeNode() methods to manipulate child nodes.

This property is undefined for text nodes (nodeType == 3).

Availability: ActionScript 1.0; Flash Player 5

Example

The following example shows how to use the XML.childNodes property to return an array of child nodes:

```
// create a new XML document
var doc:XML = new XML();

// create a root node
var rootNode:XMLNode = doc.createElement("rootNode");

// create three child nodes
var oldest:XMLNode = doc.createElement("oldest");
var middle:XMLNode = doc.createElement("middle");
var youngest:XMLNode = doc.createElement("youngest");

// add the rootNode as the root of the XML document tree
doc.appendChild(rootNode);

// add each of the child nodes as children of rootNode
rootNode.appendChild(oldest);
rootNode.appendChild(middle);
rootNode.appendChild(youngest);

// create an array and use rootNode to populate it
var firstArray:Array = doc.childNodes;
trace (firstArray);
// output: <rootNode><oldest /><middle /><youngest /></rootNode>

// create another array and use the child nodes to populate it
var secondArray:Array = rootNode.childNodes;
trace(secondArray);
// output: <oldest />,<middle />,<youngest />
```

See also

nodeType (XMLNode.nodeType property), appendChild (XMLNode.appendChild method), insertBefore (XMLNode.insertBefore method), removeNode (XMLNode.removeNode method)

cloneNode (XMLNode.cloneNode method)

```
public cloneNode(deep:Boolean) : XMLNode
```

Constructs and returns a new XML node of the same type, name, value, and attributes as the specified XML object. If deep is set to true, all child nodes are recursively cloned, resulting in an exact copy of the original object's document tree.

The clone of the node that is returned is no longer associated with the tree of the cloned item. Consequently, nextSibling, parentNode, and previousSibling all have a value of null. If the deep parameter is set to false, or the *my_xml* node has no child nodes, firstChild and lastChild are also null.

Availability: ActionScript 1.0; Flash Player 5

Parameters

deep:Boolean - A Boolean value; if set to true, the children of the specified XML object will be recursively cloned.

Returns

XMLNode - An XMLNode Object.

Example

The following example shows how to use the XML.cloneNode() method to create a copy of a node:

```
// create a new XML document
var doc:XML = new XML();

// create a root node
var rootNode:XMLNode = doc.createElement("rootNode");

// create three child nodes
var oldest:XMLNode = doc.createElement("oldest");
var middle:XMLNode = doc.createElement("middle");
var youngest:XMLNode = doc.createElement("youngest");

// add the rootNode as the root of the XML document tree
doc.appendChild(rootNode);

// add each of the child nodes as children of rootNode
rootNode.appendChild(oldest);
rootNode.appendChild(middle);
rootNode.appendChild(youngest);

// create a copy of the middle node using cloneNode()
var middle2:XMLNode = middle.cloneNode(false);

// insert the clone node into rootNode between the middle and youngest nodes
rootNode.insertBefore(middle2, youngest);
trace(rootNode);
// output (with line breaks added):
// <rootNode>
// <oldest />
```

```
// <middle />
// <middle />
// <youngest />
// </rootNode>

// create a copy of rootNode using cloneNode() to demonstrate a deep copy
var rootClone:XMLNode = rootNode.cloneNode(true);

// insert the clone, which contains all child nodes, to rootNode
rootNode.appendChild(rootClone);
trace(rootNode);
// output (with line breaks added):
// <rootNode>
// <oldest />
// <middle />
// <middle />
// <youngest />
// <rootNode>
// <oldest />
// <middle />
// <middle />
// <youngest />
// </rootNode>
// </rootNode>
```

firstChild (XMLNode.firstChild property)

```
public firstChild : XMLNode [read-only]
```

Evaluates the specified XML object and references the first child in the parent node's child list. This property is null if the node does not have children. This property is undefined if the node is a text node. This is a read-only property and cannot be used to manipulate child nodes; use the appendChild(), insertBefore(), and removeNode() methods to manipulate child nodes.

Availability: ActionScript 1.0; Flash Player 5

Example

The following example shows how to use XML.firstChild to loop through a node's child nodes:

```
// create a new XML document
var doc:XML = new XML();

// create a root node
var rootNode:XMLNode = doc.createElement("rootNode");

// create three child nodes
```

```
var oldest:XMLNode = doc.createElement("oldest");
var middle:XMLNode = doc.createElement("middle");
var youngest:XMLNode = doc.createElement("youngest");

// add the rootNode as the root of the XML document tree
doc.appendChild(rootNode);

// add each of the child nodes as children of rootNode
rootNode.appendChild(oldest);
rootNode.appendChild(middle);
rootNode.appendChild(youngest);

// use firstChild to iterate through the child nodes of rootNode
for (var aNode:XMLNode = rootNode.firstChild; aNode != null; aNode =
  aNode.nextSibling) {
  trace(aNode);
}

// output:
// <oldest />
// <middle />
// <youngest />
```

The following example is from the XML_languagePicker FLA file in the Examples directory and can be found in the languageXML.onLoad event handler function definition:

```
// loop through the strings in each language node
// adding each string as a new element in the language array
for (var stringNode:XMLNode = childNode.firstChild; stringNode != null;
  stringNode = stringNode.nextSibling, j++) {
  masterArray[i][j] = stringNode.firstChild.nodeValue;
}
```

To view the entire script, see XML_languagePicker.fla in the ActionScript samples folder:

- Windows: *boot drive*\Program Files\Macromedia\Flash 8\Samples and Tutorials\Samples\ActionScript

- Macintosh: *Macintosh HD*/Applications/Macromedia Flash 8/Samples and Tutorials/Samples/ActionScript

See also

appendChild (XMLNode.appendChild method), insertBefore (XMLNode.insertBefore method), removeNode (XMLNode.removeNode method)

getNamespaceForPrefix
(XMLNode.getNamespaceForPrefix method)

```
public getNamespaceForPrefix(prefix:String) : String
```

Returns the namespace URI that is associated with the specified prefix for the node. To determine the URI, `getPrefixForNamespace()` searches up the XML hierarchy from the node, as necessary, and returns the namespace URI of the first `xmlns` declaration for the given `prefix`.

If no namespace is defined for the specified prefix, the method returns `null`.

If you specify an empty string (`""`) as the `prefix` and there is a default namespace defined for the node (as in `xmlns="http://www.example.com/"`), the method returns that default namespace URI.

Availability: ActionScript 1.0; Flash Player 8

Parameters

`prefix:String` - The prefix for which the method returns the associated namespace.

Returns

`String` - The namespace that is associated with the specified prefix.

Example

The following example creates a very simple XML object and outputs the result of a call to `getNamespaceForPrefix()`

```
function createXML():XMLNode {
   var str:String = "<Outer xmlns:exu=\"http://www.example.com/util\">"
      + "<exu:Child id='1' />"
      + "<exu:Child id='2' />"
      + "<exu:Child id='3' />"
      + "</Outer>";
   return new XML(str).firstChild;
}

var xml:XMLNode = createXML();
trace(xml.getNamespaceForPrefix("exu")); // output: http://www.example.com/
   util
trace(xml.getNamespaceForPrefix("")); // output: null
```

See also

`getPrefixForNamespace` (XMLNode.getPrefixForNamespace method), `namespaceURI` (XMLNode.namespaceURI property)

---

getPrefixForNamespace
(XMLNode.getPrefixForNamespace method)

`public getPrefixForNamespace(nsURI:String) : String`

Returns the prefix that is associated with the specified namespace URI for the node. To determine the prefix, `getPrefixForNamespace()` searches up the XML hierarchy from the node, as necessary, and returns the prefix of the first `xmlns` declaration with a namespace URI that matches `nsURI`.

If there is no `xmlns` assignment for the given URI, the method returns `null`. If there is an `xmlns` assignment for the given URI but no prefix is associated with the assignment, the method returns an empty string (`""`).

Availability: ActionScript 1.0; Flash Player 8

Parameters

`nsURI:String` - The namespace URI for which the method returns the associated prefix.

Returns

`String` - The prefix associated with the specified namespace.

Example

The following example creates a very simple XML object and outputs the result of a call to the `getPrefixForNamespace()` method. The `Outer` XML node, which is represented by the `xmlDoc` variable, defines a namespace URI and assigns it to the `exu` prefix. Calling the `getPrefixForNamespace()` method with the defined namespace URI ("http://www.example.com/util") returns the prefix `exu`, but calling this method with an undefined URI ("http://www.example.com/other") returns `null`. The first `exu:Child` node, which is represented by the `child1` variable, also defines a namespace URI ("http://www.example.com/child"), but does not assign it to a prefix. Calling this method on the defined, but unassigned, namespace URI returns an empty string.

```
function createXML():XMLNode {
  var str:String = "<Outer xmlns:exu=\"http://www.example.com/util\">"
    + "<exu:Child id='1' xmlns=\"http://www.example.com/child\"/>"
    + "<exu:Child id='2' />"
    + "<exu:Child id='3' />"
    + "</Outer>";
  return new XML(str).firstChild;
}

var xmlDoc:XMLNode = createXML();
```

```
trace(xmlDoc.getPrefixForNamespace("http://www.example.com/util")); //
   output: exu
trace(xmlDoc.getPrefixForNamespace("http://www.example.com/other")); //
   output: null

var child1:XMLNode = xmlDoc.firstChild;
trace(child1.getPrefixForNamespace("http://www.example.com/child")); //
   output: [empty string]
trace(child1.getPrefixForNamespace("http://www.example.com/other")); //
   output: null
```

See also

getNamespaceForPrefix (XMLNode.getNamespaceForPrefix method), namespaceURI
(XMLNode.namespaceURI property)

hasChildNodes (XMLNode.hasChildNodes method)

`public hasChildNodes() : Boolean`

Specifies whether or not the XML object has child nodes.

Availability: ActionScript 1.0; Flash Player 5

Returns

`Boolean` - `true` if the specified XMLNode has one or more child nodes; otherwise `false`.

Example

The following example creates a new XML packet. If the root node has child nodes, the code
loops over each child node to display the name and value of the node. Add the following
ActionScript to your FLA or AS file:

```
var my_xml:XML = new XML("hankrudolph");
if (my_xml.firstChild.hasChildNodes()) {
// use firstChild to iterate through the child nodes of rootNode
   for (var aNode:XMLNode = my_xml.firstChild.firstChild; aNode != null;
   aNode=aNode.nextSibling) {
      if (aNode.nodeType == 1) {
         trace(aNode.nodeName+":\t"+aNode.firstChild.nodeValue);
      }
   }
}
```

The following is displayed in the Output panel:

```
output:
username: hank
password: rudolph
```

insertBefore (XMLNode.insertBefore method)

```
public insertBefore(newChild:XMLNode, insertPoint:XMLNode) : Void
```
Inserts a `newChild` node into the XML object's child list, before the `insertPoint` node. If `insertPoint` is *not* a child of the XMLNode object, the insertion fails.

Availability: ActionScript 1.0; Flash Player 5

Parameters

`newChild:XMLNode` - The XMLNode object to be inserted.

`insertPoint:XMLNode` - The XMLNode object that will follow the `newChild` node after the method is invoked.

Example

The following inserts a new XML node between two existing nodes:

```
var my_xml:XML = new XML("<a>1</a>\n<c>3</c>");
var insertPoint:XMLNode = my_xml.lastChild;
var newNode:XML = new XML("<b>2</b>\n");
my_xml.insertBefore(newNode, insertPoint);
trace(my_xml);
```

See also

XML, cloneNode (XMLNode.cloneNode method)

lastChild (XMLNode.lastChild property)

```
public lastChild : XMLNode [read-only]
```
An XMLNode value that references the last child in the node's child list. The `XML.lastChild` property is `null` if the node does not have children. This property cannot be used to manipulate child nodes; use the `appendChild()`, `insertBefore()`, and `removeNode()` methods to manipulate child nodes.

Availability: ActionScript 1.0; Flash Player 5

Example

The following example uses the `XML.lastChild` property to iterate through the child nodes of an XML node, beginning with the last item in the node's child list and ending with the first child of the node's child list:

```
// create a new XML document
var doc:XML = new XML();
```

```
// create a root node
var rootNode:XMLNode = doc.createElement("rootNode");

// create three child nodes
var oldest:XMLNode = doc.createElement("oldest");
var middle:XMLNode = doc.createElement("middle");
var youngest:XMLNode = doc.createElement("youngest");

// add the rootNode as the root of the XML document tree
doc.appendChild(rootNode);

// add each of the child nodes as children of rootNode
rootNode.appendChild(oldest);
rootNode.appendChild(middle);
rootNode.appendChild(youngest);

// use lastChild to iterate through the child nodes of rootNode
for (var aNode:XMLNode = rootNode.lastChild; aNode != null; aNode =
  aNode.previousSibling) {
  trace(aNode);
}

// output:
// <youngest />
// <middle />
// <oldest />
```

The following example creates a new XML packet and uses the XML.lastChild property to iterate through the child nodes of the root node:

```
// create a new XML document
var doc:XML = new XML("");

var rootNode:XMLNode = doc.firstChild;

// use lastChild to iterate through the child nodes of rootNode
for (var aNode:XMLNode = rootNode.lastChild; aNode != null;
  aNode=aNode.previousSibling) {
  trace(aNode);
}

// output:
// <youngest />
// <middle />
// <oldest />
```

See also

appendChild (XMLNode.appendChild method), insertBefore (XMLNode.insertBefore method), removeNode (XMLNode.removeNode method), XML

---

localName (XMLNode.localName property)

```
public localName : String [read-only]
```

The local name portion of the XML node's name. This is the element name without the namespace prefix. For example, the node `<contact:mailbox/>bob@example.com</contact:mailbox>` has the local name "mailbox", and the prefix "contact", which comprise the full element name "contact.mailbox".

You can access the namespace prefix via the `prefix` property of the XML node object. The `nodeName` property returns the full name (including the prefix and the local name).

Availability: ActionScript 1.0; Flash Player 8

Example

This example uses a SWF file and an XML file located in the same directory. The XML file, named "SoapSample.xml" contains the following:

```
<?xml version="1.0"?>
<soap:Envelope xmlns:soap="http://www.w3.org/2001/12/soap-envelope">
<soap:Body xmlns:w="http://www.example.com/weather">
<w:GetTemperature>
<w:City>San Francisco</w:City>
</w:GetTemperature>
</soap:Body>
</soap:Envelope>
```

The source for the SWF file contains the following script (note the comments for the Output strings):

```
var xmlDoc:XML = new XML()
xmlDoc.ignoreWhite = true;
xmlDoc.load("SoapSample.xml")
xmlDoc.onLoad = function(success:Boolean)
{
  var tempNode:XMLNode = xmlDoc.childNodes[0].childNodes[0].childNodes[0];
  trace("w:GetTemperature localname: " + tempNode.localName); // Output:
  ... GetTemperature
  var soapEnvNode:XMLNode = xmlDoc.childNodes[0];
  trace("soap:Envelope localname: " + soapEnvNode.localName); // Output:
  ... Envelope
}
```

namespaceURI (XMLNode.namespaceURI property)

```
public namespaceURI : String [read-only]
```

If the XML node has a prefix, `namespaceURI` is the value of the `xmlns` declaration for that prefix (the URI), which is typically called the namespace URI. The `xmlns` declaration is in the current node or in a node higher in the XML hierarchy.

If the XML node does not have a prefix, the value of the `namespaceURI` property depends on whether there is a default namespace defined (as in `xmlns="http://www.example.com/"`). If there is a default namespace, the value of the `namespaceURI` property is the value of the default namespace. If there is no default namespace, the `namespaceURI` property for that node is an empty string ("").

You can use the `getNamespaceForPrefix()` method to identify the namespace associated with a specific prefix. The `namespaceURI` property returns the prefix associated with the node name.

Availability: ActionScript 1.0; Flash Player 8

Example

The following example shows how the `namespaceURI` property is affected by the use of prefixes. A directory contains a SWF file and an XML file. The XML file, named `SoapSample.xml` contains the following tags.

```
<?xml version="1.0"?>
<soap:Envelope xmlns:soap="http://www.w3.org/2001/12/soap-envelope">
<soap:Body xmlns:w="http://www.example.com/weather">
<w:GetTemperature>
<w:City>San Francisco</w:City>
</w:GetTemperature>
</soap:Body>
</soap:Envelope>
```

The source for the SWF file contains the following script (note the comments for the Output strings). For `tempNode`, which represents the `w:GetTemperature` node, the value of `namespaceURI` is defined in the `soap:Body` tag. For `soapBodyNode`, which represents the `soap:Body` node, the value of `namespaceURI` is determined by the definition of the `soap` prefix in the node above it, rather than the definition of the `w` prefix that the `soap:Body` node contains.

```
var xmlDoc:XML = new XML();
xmlDoc.load("SoapSample.xml");
xmlDoc.ignoreWhite = true;
xmlDoc.onLoad = function(success:Boolean)
{
    var tempNode:XMLNode = xmlDoc.childNodes[0].childNodes[0].childNodes[0];
```

```
trace("w:GetTemperature namespaceURI: " + tempNode.namespaceURI);
  // Output: ... http://www.example.com/weather

trace("w:GetTemperature soap namespace: " +
tempNode.getNamespaceForPrefix("soap"));
  // Output: ... http://www.w3.org/2001/12/soap-envelope

var soapBodyNode:XMLNode = xmlDoc.childNodes[0].childNodes[0];
trace("soap:Envelope namespaceURI: " + soapBodyNode.namespaceURI);
  // Output: ... http://www.w3.org/2001/12/soap-envelope
}
```

The following example uses XML tags without prefixes. It uses a SWF file and an XML file located in the same directory. The XML file, named `NoPrefix.xml` contains the following tags.

```
<?xml version="1.0"?>
<rootnode>
<simplenode xmlns="http://www.w3.org/2001/12/soap-envelope">
<innernode />
</simplenode>
</rootnode>
```

The source for the SWF file contains the following script (note the comments for the Output strings). The `rootNode` does not have a default namespace, so its `namespaceURI` value is an empty string. The `simpleNode` defines a default namespace, so its `namespaceURI` value is the default namespace. The `innerNode` does not define a default namespace, but uses the default namespace defined by `simpleNode`, so its `namespaceURI` value is the same as that of `simpleNode`.

```
var xmlDoc:XML = new XML()
xmlDoc.load("NoPrefix.xml");
xmlDoc.ignoreWhite = true;
xmlDoc.onLoad = function(success:Boolean)
{
  var rootNode:XMLNode = xmlDoc.childNodes[0];
  trace("rootNode Node namespaceURI: " + rootNode.namespaceURI);
    // Output: [empty string]

  var simpleNode:XMLNode = xmlDoc.childNodes[0].childNodes[0];
  trace("simpleNode Node namespaceURI: " + simpleNode.namespaceURI);
    // Output: ... http://www.w3.org/2001/12/soap-envelope

  var innerNode:XMLNode = xmlDoc.childNodes[0].childNodes[0].childNodes[0];
  trace("innerNode Node namespaceURI: " + innerNode.namespaceURI);
    // Output: ... http://www.w3.org/2001/12/soap-envelope
}
```

getNamespaceForPrefix (XMLNode.getNamespaceForPrefix method),
getPrefixForNamespace (XMLNode.getPrefixForNamespace method)

nextSibling (XMLNode.nextSibling property)

public nextSibling : XMLNode [read-only]

An XMLNode value that references the next sibling in the parent node's child list. This property is null if the node does not have a next sibling node. This property cannot be used to manipulate child nodes; use the appendChild(), insertBefore(), and removeNode() methods to manipulate child nodes.

Availability: ActionScript 1.0; Flash Player 5

Example

The following example is an excerpt from the example for the XML.firstChild property, and shows how you can use the XML.nextSibling property to loop through an XML node's child nodes:

```
for (var aNode:XMLNode = rootNode.firstChild; aNode != null; aNode =
  aNode.nextSibling) {
  trace(aNode);
}
```

See also

firstChild (XMLNode.firstChild property), appendChild (XMLNode.appendChild method), insertBefore (XMLNode.insertBefore method), removeNode (XMLNode.removeNode method), XML

nodeName (XMLNode.nodeName property)

public nodeName : String

A string representing the node name of the XML object. If the XML object is an XML element (nodeType == 1), nodeName is the name of the tag that represents the node in the XML file. For example, TITLE is the nodeName of an HTML TITLE tag. If the XML object is a text node (nodeType == 3), nodeName is null.

Availability: ActionScript 1.0; Flash Player 5

Example

The following example creates an element node and a text node, and checks the node name of each:

```
// create an XML document
var doc:XML = new XML();

// create an XML node using createElement()
var myNode:XMLNode = doc.createElement("rootNode");

// place the new node into the XML tree
doc.appendChild(myNode);

// create an XML text node using createTextNode()
var myTextNode:XMLNode = doc.createTextNode("textNode");

// place the new node into the XML tree
myNode.appendChild(myTextNode);

trace(myNode.nodeName);
trace(myTextNode.nodeName);

// output:
// rootNode
// null
```

The following example creates a new XML packet. If the root node has child nodes, the code loops over each child node to display the name and value of the node. Add the following ActionScript to your FLA or AS file:

```
var my_xml:XML = new XML("hankrudolph");
if (my_xml.firstChild.hasChildNodes()) {
  // use firstChild to iterate through the child nodes of rootNode
  for (var aNode:XMLNode = my_xml.firstChild.firstChild; aNode != null;
  aNode=aNode.nextSibling) {
    if (aNode.nodeType == 1) {
      trace(aNode.nodeName+":\t"+aNode.firstChild.nodeValue);
    }
  }
}
```

The following node names are displayed in the Output panel:

```
output:
username: hank
password: rudolph
```

See also

nodeType (XMLNode.nodeType property)

nodeType (XMLNode.nodeType property)

`public nodeType : Number [read-only]`

A `nodeType` value, either 1 for an XML element or 3 for a text node.

The `nodeType` is a numeric value from the NodeType enumeration in the W3C DOM Level 1 recommendation: www.w3.org/tr/1998/REC-DOM-Level-1-19981001/level-one-core.html. The following table lists the values:

Integer value	Defined constant
1	ELEMENT_NODE
2	ATTRIBUTE_NODE
3	TEXT_NODE
4	CDATA_SECTION_NODE
5	ENTITY_REFERENCE_NODE
6	ENTITY_NODE
7	PROCESSING_INSTRUCTION_NODE
8	COMMENT_NODE
9	DOCUMENT_NODE
10	DOCUMENT_TYPE_NODE
11	DOCUMENT_FRAGMENT_NODE
12	NOTATION_NODE

In Flash Player, the built-in XML class only supports 1 (`ELEMENT_NODE`) and 3 (`TEXT_NODE`).

Availability: ActionScript 1.0; Flash Player 5

Example

The following example creates an element node and a text node, and checks the node type of each:

```
// create an XML document
var doc:XML = new XML();

// create an XML node using createElement()
var myNode:XMLNode = doc.createElement("rootNode");

// place the new node into the XML tree
doc.appendChild(myNode);

// create an XML text node using createTextNode()
var myTextNode:XMLNode = doc.createTextNode("textNode");

// place the new node into the XML tree
myNode.appendChild(myTextNode);

trace(myNode.nodeType);
trace(myTextNode.nodeType);

// output:
// 1
// 3
```

See also

nodeValue (XMLNode.nodeValue property)

nodeValue (XMLNode.nodeValue property)

`public nodeValue : String`

The node value of the XML object. If the XML object is a text node, the `nodeType` is 3, and the `nodeValue` is the text of the node. If the XML object is an XML element (`nodeType` is 1), `nodeValue` is `null` and read-only

Availability: ActionScript 1.0; Flash Player 5

Example

The following example creates an element node and a text node, and checks the node value of each:

```
// create an XML document
var doc:XML = new XML();

// create an XML node using createElement()
var myNode:XMLNode = doc.createElement("rootNode");
```

```
// place the new node into the XML tree
doc.appendChild(myNode);

// create an XML text node using createTextNode()
var myTextNode:XMLNode = doc.createTextNode("textNode");

// place the new node into the XML tree
myNode.appendChild(myTextNode);

trace(myNode.nodeValue);
trace(myTextNode.nodeValue);

// output:
// null
// myTextNode
```

The following example creates and parses an XML packet. The code loops through each child node, and displays the node value using the firstChild property and firstChild.nodeValue. When you use firstChild to display contents of the node, it maintains the & entity. However, when you explicitly use nodeValue, it converts to the ampersand character (&).

```
var my_xml:XML = new XML("mortongood&evil");
trace("using firstChild:");
for (var i = 0; i<my_xml.firstChild.childNodes.length; i++) {
  trace("\t"+my_xml.firstChild.childNodes[i].firstChild);
}
trace("");
trace("using firstChild.nodeValue:");
for (var i = 0; i<my_xml.firstChild.childNodes.length; i++) {
  trace("\t"+my_xml.firstChild.childNodes[i].firstChild.nodeValue);
}
```

The following information is displayed in the Output panel:

```
using firstChild:
morton
good&evil

using firstChild.nodeValue:
morton
good&evil
```

See also

nodeType (XMLNode.nodeType property)

parentNode (XMLNode.parentNode property)

`public parentNode : XMLNode [read-only]`

An XMLNode value that references the parent node of the specified XML object, or returns `null` if the node has no parent. This is a read-only property and cannot be used to manipulate child nodes; use the `appendChild()`, `insertBefore()`, and `removeNode()` methods to manipulate child nodes.

Availability: ActionScript 1.0; Flash Player 5

Example

The following example creates an XML packet and displays the parent node of the username node in the Output panel:

```
var my_xml:XML = new XML("mortongood&evil");

// first child is the <login /> node
var rootNode:XMLNode = my_xml.firstChild;

// first child of the root is the <username /> node
var targetNode:XMLNode = rootNode.firstChild;
trace("the parent node of '"+targetNode.nodeName+"' is:
  "+targetNode.parentNode.nodeName);
trace("contents of the parent node are:\n"+targetNode.parentNode);
```

Output (line breaks added for clarity):

```
the parent node of 'username' is: login
contents of the parent node are:
morton
good&evil
```

See also

`appendChild` (XMLNode.appendChild method), `insertBefore` (XMLNode.insertBefore method), `removeNode` (XMLNode.removeNode method), XML

prefix (XMLNode.prefix property)

`public prefix : String [read-only]`

The prefix portion of the XML node name. For example, the node `<contact:mailbox/>bob@example.com</contact:mailbox>` prefix "contact" and the local name "mailbox", which comprise the full element name "contact.mailbox".

The `nodeName` property of an XML node object returns the full name (including the prefix and the local name). You can access the local name portion of the element's name via the `localName` property.

Availability: ActionScript 1.0; Flash Player 8

Example

A directory contains a SWF file and an XML file. The XML file, named "SoapSample.xml" contains the following:

```
<?xml version="1.0"?>
<soap:Envelope xmlns:soap="http://www.w3.org/2001/12/soap-envelope">
<soap:Body xmlns:w="http://www.example.com/weather">
<w:GetTemperature>
<w:City>San Francisco</w:City>
</w:GetTemperature>
</soap:Body>
</soap:Envelope>
```

The source for the SWF file contains the following script (note the comments for the Output strings):

```
var xmlDoc:XML = new XML();
xmlDoc.ignoreWhite = true;
xmlDoc.load("SoapSample.xml");
xmlDoc.onLoad = function(success:Boolean)
{
   var tempNode:XMLNode = xmlDoc.childNodes[0].childNodes[0].childNodes[0];
   trace("w:GetTemperature prefix: " + tempNode.prefix); // Output: ... w
   var soapEnvNode:XMLNode = xmlDoc.childNodes[0];
   trace("soap:Envelope prefix: " + soapEnvNode.prefix); // Output: ... soap
}
```

previousSibling (XMLNode.previousSibling property)

`public previousSibling : XMLNode [read-only]`

An XMLNode value that references the previous sibling in the parent node's child list. The property has a value of null if the node does not have a previous sibling node. This property cannot be used to manipulate child nodes; use the `appendChild()`, `insertBefore()`, and `removeNode()` methods to manipulate child nodes.

Availability: ActionScript 1.0; Flash Player 5

Example

The following example is an excerpt from the example for the `XML.lastChild` property, and shows how you can use the `XML.previousSibling` property to loop through an XML node's child nodes:

```
for (var aNode:XMLNode = rootNode.lastChild; aNode != null; aNode =
  aNode.previousSibling) {
  trace(aNode);
}
```

See also

`lastChild (XMLNode.lastChild property)`, `appendChild (XMLNode.appendChild method)`, `insertBefore (XMLNode.insertBefore method)`, `removeNode (XMLNode.removeNode method)`, XML

removeNode (XMLNode.removeNode method)

`public removeNode() : Void`

Removes the specified XML object from its parent. Also deletes all descendants of the node.

Availability: ActionScript 1.0; Flash Player 5

Example

The following example creates an XML packet, and then deletes the specified XML object and its descendant nodes:

```
var xml_str:String = "<state name=\"California\"><city>San Francisco</
  city></state>";

var my_xml:XML = new XML(xml_str);
var cityNode:XMLNode = my_xml.firstChild.firstChild;
trace("before XML.removeNode():\n"+my_xml);
cityNode.removeNode();
trace("");
trace("after XML.removeNode():\n"+my_xml);

// output (line breaks added for clarity):
//
// before XML.removeNode():
// <state name="California">
// <city>San Francisco</city>
// </state>
//
// after XML.removeNode():
// <state name="California" />
```

toString (XMLNode.toString method)

`public toString() : String`

Evaluates the specified XML object, constructs a textual representation of the XML structure, including the node, children, and attributes, and returns the result as a string.

For top-level XML objects (those created with the constructor), the `XML.toString()` method outputs the document's XML declaration (stored in the `XML.xmlDecl` property), followed by the document's `DOCTYPE` declaration (stored in the `XML.docTypeDecl` property), followed by the text representation of all XML nodes in the object. The XML declaration is not output if the `XML.xmlDecl` property is undefined. The `DOCTYPE` declaration is not output if the `XML.docTypeDecl` property is `undefined`.

Availability: ActionScript 1.0; Flash Player 5

Returns

`String` - String.

Example

The following code uses the `toString()` method to convert an XMLNode object to a String, and then uses the `toUpperCase()` method of the String class:

```
var xString = "<first>Mary</first>"
    + "<last>Ng</last>"
var my_xml:XML = new XML(xString);
var my_node:XMLNode = my_xml.childNodes[1];
trace(my_node.toString().toUpperCase());
    // output: <LAST>NG</LAST>
```

See also

`docTypeDecl (XML.docTypeDecl property)`, `xmlDecl (XML.xmlDecl property)`

XMLNode constructor

`public XMLNode(type:Number, value:String)`

The XMLNode constructor lets you instantiate an XML node based on a string specifying its contents and on a number representing its node type.

Availability: ActionScript 1.0; Flash Player 8

Parameters

`type:Number` - An integer representing the node type:

Integer value	Defined constant
1	ELEMENT_NODE
2	ATTRIBUTE_NODE
3	TEXT_NODE
4	CDATA_SECTION_NODE
5	NTITY_REFERENCE_NODE
6	ENTITY_NODE
7	PROCESSING_INSTRUCTION_NODE
8	COMMENT_NODE
9	DOCUMENT_NODE
10	DOCUMENT_TYPE_NODE
11	DOCUMENT_FRAGMENT_NODE
12	NOTATION_NODE

In Flash Player, the XML class only supports node types 1 (ELEMENT_NODE) and 3 (TEXT_NODE).

`value:String` - For a text node, this is the text of the node; for an element node, this is the contents of the tag.

Example

```
var ELEMENT_NODE:Number = 1;
var node1:XMLNode = new XMLNode(ELEMENT_NODE, "fullName");

var TEXT_NODE:Number = 3;
var node2:XMLNode = new XMLNode(TEXT_NODE, "Justin Case");

// Create a new XML document
var doc:XML = new XML();

// Create a root node
var rootNode:XMLNode = doc.createElement("root");

// Add the rootNode as the root of the XML document tree
doc.appendChild(rootNode);

// Build the rest of the document:
```

```
rootNode.appendChild(node1);
node1.appendChild(node2);

trace(doc);

// Output: Justin Case
```

XMLSocket

```
Object
  |
  +-XMLSocket
```

public class **XMLSocket**
extends Object

The XMLSocket class implements client sockets that let the computer running Flash Player communicate with a server computer identified by an IP address or domain name. The XMLSocket class is useful for client-server applications that require low latency, such as real-time chat systems. A traditional HTTP-based chat solution frequently polls the server and downloads new messages using an HTTP request. In contrast, an XMLSocket chat solution maintains an open connection to the server, which lets the server immediately send incoming messages without a request from the client. To use the XMLSocket class, the server computer must run a daemon that understands the protocol used by the XMLSocket class. The protocol is described in the following list:

- XML messages are sent over a full-duplex TCP/IP stream socket connection.

- Each XML message is a complete XML document, terminated by a zero (0) byte.

- An unlimited number of XML messages can be sent and received over a single XMLSocket connection.

The following restrictions apply to how and where an XMLSocket object can connect to the server:

- The XMLSocket.connect() method can connect only to TCP port numbers greater than or equal to 1024. One consequence of this restriction is that the server daemons that communicate with the XMLSocket object must also be assigned to port numbers greater than or equal to 1024. Port numbers below 1024 are often used by system services such as FTP, Telnet, and HTTP, so XMLSocket objects are barred from these ports for security reasons. The port number restriction limits the possibility that these resources will be inappropriately accessed and abused.

- The XMLSocket.connect() method can connect only to computers in the same domain where the SWF file resides. This restriction does not apply to SWF files running off a local disk. (This restriction is identical to the security rules for loadVariables(), XML.sendAndLoad(), and XML.load().) To connect to a server daemon running in a domain other than the one where the SWF resides, you can create a security policy file on the server that allows access from specific domains.

Setting up a server to communicate with the XMLSocket object can be challenging. If your application does not require real-time interactivity, use the loadVariables() function, or Flash HTTP-based XML server connectivity (XML.load(), XML.sendAndLoad(), XML.send()), instead of the XMLSocket class. To use the methods of the XMLSocket class, you must first use the constructor, new XMLSocket, to create an XMLSocket object.

Availability: ActionScript 1.0; Flash Player 5

Property summary
Properties inherited from class Object

```
constructor (Object.constructor property), __proto__ (Object.__proto__
property), prototype (Object.prototype property), __resolve
(Object.__resolve property)
```

Event summary

Event	Description
`onClose = function() {}`	Invoked only when an open connection is closed by the server.
`onConnect = function(success :Boolean) {}`	Invoked by Flash Player when a connection request initiated through `XMLSocket.connect()` has succeeded or failed.

Event	Description
`onData = function(src:String) {}`	Invoked when a message has been downloaded from the server, terminated by a zero (0) byte.
`onXML = function(src:XML) {}`	Invoked by Flash Player when the specified XML object containing an XML document arrives over an open XMLSocket connection.

Constructor summary

Signature	Description
`XMLSocket()`	Creates a new XMLSocket object.

Method summary

Modifiers	Signature	Description
	`close() : Void`	Closes the connection specified by XMLSocket object.
	`connect(url:String, port:Number) : Boolean`	Establishes a connection to the specified Internet host using the specified TCP port (must be 1024 or higher), and returns `true` or `false`, depending on whether a connection is successfully established.
	`send(data:Object) : Void`	Converts the XML object or data specified in the `object` parameter to a string and transmits it to the server, followed by a zero (0) byte.

Methods inherited from class Object

```
addProperty (Object.addProperty method), hasOwnProperty
(Object.hasOwnProperty method), isPropertyEnumerable
(Object.isPropertyEnumerable method), isPrototypeOf (Object.isPrototypeOf
method), registerClass (Object.registerClass method), toString
(Object.toString method), unwatch (Object.unwatch method), valueOf
(Object.valueOf method), watch (Object.watch method)
```

close (XMLSocket.close method)

```
public close() : Void
```

Closes the connection specified by XMLSocket object.

Availability: ActionScript 1.0; Flash Player 5

Example

The following simple example creates an XMLSocket object, attempts to connect to the server, and then closes the connection.

```
var socket:XMLSocket = new XMLSocket();
socket.connect(null, 2000);
socket.close();
```

See also

```
connect (XMLSocket.connect method)
```

connect (XMLSocket.connect method)

```
public connect(url:String, port:Number) : Boolean
```

Establishes a connection to the specified Internet host using the specified TCP port (must be 1024 or higher), and returns `true` or `false`, depending on whether a connection is successfully established. If you do not know the port number of your Internet host computer, contact your network administrator.

If you specify `null` for the `host` parameter, the host contacted is the one where the SWF file calling `XMLSocket.connect()` resides. For example, if the SWF file was downloaded from www.yoursite.com, specifying `null` for the host parameter is the same as entering the IP address for www.yoursite.com.

In SWF files running in a version of the player earlier than Flash Player 7, `host` must be in the same superdomain as the SWF file that is issuing this call. For example, a SWF file at www.someDomain.com can load variables from a SWF file at store.someDomain.com because both files are in the same superdomain of someDomain.com.

In SWF files of any version running in Flash Player 7 or later, `host` must be in exactly the same domain. For example, a SWF file at www.someDomain.com that is published for Flash Player 5, but is running in Flash Player 7 or later can load variables only from SWF files that are also at www.someDomain.com. If you want to load variables from a different domain, you can place a *cross-domain policy file* on the server hosting the SWF file that is being accessed.

When load() is executed, the XML object property loaded is set to false. When the XML data finishes downloading, the loaded property is set to true, and the onLoad event handler is invoked. The XML data is not parsed until it is completely downloaded. If the XML object previously contained any XML trees, they are discarded.

If XMLSocket.connect() returns a value of true, the initial stage of the connection process is successful; later, the XMLSocket.onConnect method is invoked to determine whether the final connection succeeded or failed. If XMLSocket.connect() returns false, a connection could not be established.

When using this method, consider the Flash Player security model.

- For Flash Player 8, the XMLSocket.connect() method is not allowed if the calling SWF file is in the local-with-file-system sandbox.

- For Flash Player 7 and later, websites can permit access to a resource from requesters in different domains by deploying a cross-domain policy file.

For more information, see the following:

- Chapter 17, "Understanding Security," in *Learning ActionScript 2.0 in Flash*
- The Flash Player 8 Security white paper at http://www.macromedia.com/go/fp8_security
- The Flash Player 8 Security-Related API white paper at http://www.macromedia.com/go/fp8_security_apis

Availability: ActionScript 1.0; Flash Player 5 - Behavior changed in Flash Player 7.

Parameters

url:String - String; a fully qualified DNS domain name or an IP address in the form *aaa.bbb.ccc.ddd*. You can also specify null to connect to the host server on which the SWF file resides. If the SWF file issuing this call is running in a web browser, host must be in the same domain as the SWF file; for details, see the information about domain restrictions for SWF files in the main description of this method.

port:Number - A number; the TCP port number on the host used to establish a connection. The port number must be 1024 or greater.

Returns

Boolean - true if the connection is successful; false otherwise.

Example

The following example uses `XMLSocket.connect()` to connect to the host where the SWF file resides and uses `trace` to display the return value indicating the success or failure of the connection:

```
var socket:XMLSocket = new XMLSocket()
socket.onConnect = function (success:Boolean) {
  if (success) {
  trace ("Connection succeeded!")
  } else {
  trace ("Connection failed!")
  }
}
if (!socket.connect(null, 2000)) {
  trace ("Connection failed!")
}
```

See also

`onConnect (XMLSocket.onConnect handler)`, `function statement`

onClose (XMLSocket.onClose handler)

```
onClose = function() {}
```

Invoked only when an open connection is closed by the server. The default implementation of this method performs no actions. To override the default implementation, you must assign a function containing custom actions.

Availability: ActionScript 1.0; Flash Player 5

Example

The following example executes a trace statement if an open connection is closed by the server:

```
var socket:XMLSocket = new XMLSocket();
socket.connect(null, 2000);
socket.onClose = function () {
  trace("Connection to server lost.");
}
```

See also

`onConnect (XMLSocket.onConnect handler)`, `function statement`

onConnect (XMLSocket.onConnect handler)

```
onConnect = function(success:Boolean) {}
```

Invoked by Flash Player when a connection request initiated through `XMLSocket.connect()` has succeeded or failed. If the connection succeeded, the `success` parameter is `true`; otherwise the `success` parameter is `false`.

The default implementation of this method performs no actions. To override the default implementation, you must assign a function containing custom actions.

Availability: ActionScript 1.0; Flash Player 5

Parameters

`success:Boolean` - A Boolean value indicating whether a socket connection is successfully established (`true` or `false`).

Example

The following example illustrates the process of specifying a replacement function for the `onConnect` method in a simple chat application.

After creating the XMLSocket object using the constructor method, the script defines the custom function to be executed when the onConnect event handler is invoked. The function controls the screen to which users are taken, depending on whether a connection is successfully established. If the connection is successfully made, users are taken to the main chat screen on the frame labeled `startChat`. If the connection is not successful, users go to a screen with troubleshooting information on the frame labeled `connectionFailed`.

```
var socket:XMLSocket = new XMLSocket();
socket.onConnect = function (success) {
  if (success) {
    gotoAndPlay("startChat");
  } else {
    gotoAndStop("connectionFailed");
  }
}
```

Finally, the connection is initiated. If `connect()` returns `false`, the SWF file is sent directly to the frame labeled `connectionFailed`, and `onConnect` is never invoked. If `connect()` returns `true`, the SWF file jumps to a frame labeled `waitForConnection`, which is the "Please wait" screen. The SWF file remains on the `waitForConnection` frame until the `onConnect` handler is invoked, which happens at some point in the future depending on network latency.

```
if (!socket.connect(null, 2000)) {
  gotoAndStop("connectionFailed");
} else {
```

```
    gotoAndStop("waitForConnection");
}
```

See also

connect (XMLSocket.connect method), function statement

onData (XMLSocket.onData handler)

onData = function(src:String) {}

Invoked when a message has been downloaded from the server, terminated by a zero (0) byte. You can override XMLSocket.onData to intercept the data sent by the server without parsing it as XML. This is a useful if you're transmitting arbitrarily formatted data packets, and you'd prefer to manipulate the data directly when it arrives, rather than have Flash Player parse the data as XML.

By default, the XMLSocket.onData method invokes the XMLSocket.onXML method. If you override XMLSocket.onData with custom behavior, XMLSocket.onXML is not called unless you call it in your implementation of XMLSocket.onData.

Availability: ActionScript 1.0; Flash Player 5

Parameters

src:String - A string containing the data sent by the server.

Example

In this example, the src parameter is a string containing XML text downloaded from the server. The zero (0) byte terminator is not included in the string.

```
XMLSocket.prototype.onData = function (src) {
  this.onXML(new XML(src));
}
```

onXML (XMLSocket.onXML handler)

onXML = function(src:XML) {}

Invoked by Flash Player when the specified XML object containing an XML document arrives over an open XMLSocket connection. An XMLSocket connection can be used to transfer an unlimited number of XML documents between the client and the server. Each document is terminated with a zero (0) byte. When Flash Player receives the zero byte, it parses all the XML received since the previous zero byte or since the connection was established if this is the first message received. Each batch of parsed XML is treated as a single XML document and passed to the onXML method.

The default implementation of this method performs no actions. To override the default implementation, you must assign a function containing actions that you define.

Availability: ActionScript 1.0; Flash Player 5

Parameters

`src:XML` - An XML object that contains a parsed XML document received from a server.

Example

The following function overrides the default implementation of the `onXML` method in a simple chat application. The function `myOnXML` instructs the chat application to recognize a single XML element, `MESSAGE`, in the following format.

```
<MESSAGE USER="John" TEXT="Hello, my name is John!" />.
```

The following function `displayMessage()` is assumed to be a user-defined function that displays the message received by the user:

```
var socket:XMLSocket = new XMLSocket();
socket.onXML = function (doc) {
  var e = doc.firstChild;
  if (e != null && e.nodeName == "MESSAGE") {
    displayMessage(e.attributes.user, e.attributes.text);
  }
}
```

See also

`function statement`

send (XMLSocket.send method)

`public send(data:Object) : Void`

Converts the XML object or data specified in the `object` parameter to a string and transmits it to the server, followed by a zero (0) byte. If `object` is an XML object, the string is the XML textual representation of the XML object. The send operation is asynchronous; it returns immediately, but the data may be transmitted at a later time. The `XMLSocket.send()` method does not return a value indicating whether the data was successfully transmitted.

If the *myXMLSocket* object is not connected to the server (using XMLSocket.connect()), the `XMLSocket.send()` operation will fail.

Availability: ActionScript 1.0; Flash Player 5

Parameters

`data:Object` - An XML object or other data to transmit to the server.

Example

The following example shows how you could specify a user name and password to send the XML object `my_xml` to the server:

```
var myXMLSocket:XMLSocket = new XMLSocket();
var my_xml:XML = new XML();
var myLogin:XMLNode = my_xml.createElement("login");
myLogin.attributes.username = usernameTextField;
myLogin.attributes.password = passwordTextField;
my_xml.appendChild(myLogin);
myXMLSocket.send(my_xml);
```

See also

`connect (XMLSocket.connect method)`

XMLSocket constructor

`public XMLSocket()`

Creates a new XMLSocket object. The XMLSocket object is not initially connected to any server. You must call XMLSocket.connect() to connect the object to a server.

Availability: ActionScript 1.0; Flash Player 5

Example

The following example creates an XMLSocket object:

```
var socket:XMLSocket = new XMLSocket();
```

XMLUI

```
Object
  |
  +-XMLUI
```

```
public class XMLUI
extends Object
```

The XMLUI object enables communication with SWF files that are used as custom user interfaces for the flash authoring tool's extensibility features (such as Behaviors, Commands, Effects, and Tools).

Macromedia Flash comes with several extensibility features including Behaviors, Commands (JavaScript API), Effects, and Tools. With these features, advanced users can extend or automate the authoring tool's functionality. The XML to UI engine works with each of these extensibility features to create dialog boxes that the user sees if the extension either requires or accepts parameters. Dialog boxes can be defined using XML tags or by creating a SWF file to display. The XMLUI object provides a mechanism by which an advanced user can communicate with a SWF file used in such a manner.

Availability: ActionScript 1.0; Flash Player 7

Property summary

Properties inherited from class Object

```
constructor (Object.constructor property), __proto__ (Object.__proto__
property), prototype (Object.prototype property), __resolve
(Object.__resolve property)
```

Method summary

Modifiers	Signature	Description
static	accept() : Void	Makes the current XMLUI dialog exit with an "accept" state.
static	cancel() : Void	Makes the current XMLUI dialog exit with a "cancel" state.
static	get(name:String) : String	Retrieves the value of the specified property of the current XMLUI dialog.
static	set(name:String, value:String) : Void	Modifies the value of the specified property of the current XMLUI dialog.

Methods inherited from class Object

```
addProperty (Object.addProperty method), hasOwnProperty
(Object.hasOwnProperty method), isPropertyEnumerable
(Object.isPropertyEnumerable method), isPrototypeOf (Object.isPrototypeOf
method), registerClass (Object.registerClass method), toString
(Object.toString method), unwatch (Object.unwatch method), valueOf
(Object.valueOf method), watch (Object.watch method)
```

accept (XMLUI.accept method)

`public static accept() : Void`

Makes the current XMLUI dialog exit with an "accept" state. Identical to the user clicking the OK button.

Availability: ActionScript 1.0; Flash Player 7

cancel (XMLUI.cancel method)

`public static cancel() : Void`

Makes the current XMLUI dialog exit with a "cancel" state. Identical to the user clicking the Cancel button.

Availability: ActionScript 1.0; Flash Player 7

get (XMLUI.get method)

`public static get(name:String) : String`

Retrieves the value of the specified property of the current XMLUI dialog.

Availability: ActionScript 1.0; Flash Player 7

Parameters

`name:String` - The name of the XMLUI property to retrieve.

Returns

`String` - Returns the value of the property as a String.

set (XMLUI.set method)

`public static set(name:String, value:String) : Void`

Modifies the value of the specified property of the current XMLUI dialog.

Availability: ActionScript 1.0; Flash Player 7

Parameters

`name:String` - The name of the XMLUI property to modify.

`value:String` - The value to which the specified property will be set.

CHAPTER 3

Deprecated ActionScript

The evolution of ActionScript has deprecated many elements of the language. This section lists the deprecated items and suggests alternatives when available. While deprecated elements still work in Flash Player 8, Macromedia recommends that you do not continue using deprecated elements in your code. Support of deprecated elements in the future is not guaranteed.

Deprecated Class summary

Modifiers	Class Name	Description
	Color	**Deprecated** since Flash Player 8. The Color class has been deprecated in favor of the flash.geom.ColorTransform class.

Deprecated Function summary

Modifiers	Function Name	Description
	call(frame:Object)	**Deprecated** since Flash Player 5. This action was deprecated in favor of the `function` statement.
	chr(number:Number)	**Deprecated** since Flash Player 5. This function was deprecated in favor of `String.fromCharCode()`.
	TextFormat.getTextExtent(text:String, [width:Number])	**Deprecated** since Flash Player 8. There is no replacement.
	ifFrameLoaded([scene:String], frame:Object)	**Deprecated** since Flash Player 5. This function has been deprecated. Macromedia recommends that you use the `MovieClip._framesloaded` property.
	int(value:Number)	**Deprecated** since Flash Player 5. This function was deprecated in favor of `Math.round()`.

Modifiers	Function Name	Description
	length(expression:String, variable:Object)	**Deprecated** since Flash Player 5. This function, along with all the string functions, has been deprecated. Macromedia recommends that you use the methods of the String class and the `String.length` property to perform the same operations.
	mbchr(number:Number)	**Deprecated** since Flash Player 5. This function was deprecated in favor of the `String.fromCharCode()` method.
	mblength(string:String)	**Deprecated** since Flash Player 5. This function was deprecated in favor of the methods and properties of the String class.
	mbord(character:String)	**Deprecated** since Flash Player 5. This function was deprecated in favor of `String.charCodeAt()`.
	mbsubstring(value:String, index:Number, count:Number)	**Deprecated** since Flash Player 5. This function was deprecated in favor of `String.substr()`.
	ord(character:String)	**Deprecated** since Flash Player 5. This function was deprecated in favor of the methods and properties of the String class.
	random(value:Number)	**Deprecated** since Flash Player 5. This function was deprecated in favor of `Math.random()`.
	substring(string:String, index:Number, count:Number)	**Deprecated** since Flash Player 5. This function was deprecated in favor of `String.substr()`.
	tellTarget(target:String, statement(s))	**Deprecated** since Flash Player 5. Macromedia recommends that you use dot (.) notation and the `with` statement.
	toggleHighQuality()	**Deprecated** since Flash Player 5. This function was deprecated in favor of `_quality`.

Deprecated Property summary

Modifiers	Property Name	Description
	Button._highquality	**Deprecated** since Flash Player 7. This property was deprecated in favor of `Button._quality`.
	MovieClip._highqualit y	**Deprecated** since Flash Player 7. This property was deprecated in favor of `MovieClip._quality`.
	TextField._highquality	**Deprecated** since Flash Player 7. This property was deprecated in favor of `TextField._quality`.
	_highquality	**Deprecated** since Flash Player 5. This property was deprecated in favor of `_quality`.
	maxscroll	**Deprecated** since Flash Player 5. This property was deprecated in favor of `TextField.maxscroll`.
	scroll	**Deprecated** since Flash Player 5. This property was deprecated in favor of `TextField.scroll`.

Deprecated Operator summary

Operator	Description
<> (inequality)	**Deprecated** since Flash Player 5. This operator has been deprecated. Macromedia recommends that you use the `!= (inequality)` operator.
add (concatenation (strings))	**Deprecated** since Flash Player 5. Macromedia recommends that you use the add (+) operator when creating content for Flash Player 5 or later. This operator is not supported in Flash Player 8 or later.
and (logical AND)	**Deprecated** since Flash Player 5. Macromedia recommends that you use the logical AND (`&&`) operator.
eq (equality (strings))	**Deprecated** since Flash Player 5. This operator was deprecated in favor of the `== (equality)` operator.
ge (greater than or equal to (strings))	**Deprecated** since Flash Player 5. This operator was deprecated in favor of the >= (greater than or equal to) operator.
gt (greater than (strings))	**Deprecated** since Flash Player 5. This operator was deprecated in favor of the > (greater than) operator.

Operator	Description
le (less than or equal to (strings))	**Deprecated** since Flash Player 5. This operator was deprecated in Flash 5 in favor of the <= (less than or equal to) operator.
lt (less than (strings))	**Deprecated** since Flash Player 5. This operator was deprecated in favor of the < (less than) operator.
ne (not equal (strings))	**Deprecated** since Flash Player 5. This operator was deprecated in favor of the != (inequality) operator.
not (logical NOT)	**Deprecated** since Flash Player 5. This operator was deprecated in favor of the ! (logical NOT) operator.
or (logical OR)	**Deprecated** since Flash Player 5. This operator was deprecated in favor of the || (logical OR) operator.

Index

Symbols

B

Training from the Source

Macromedia's *Training from the Source* series is one of the best-selling series on the market. This series offers you a unique self-paced approach that introduces you to the major features of the software and guides you step by step through the development of real-world projects.

Each book is divided into a series of lessons. Each lesson begins with an overview of the lesson's content and learning objectives and is divided into short tasks that break the skills into bite-size units. All the files you need for the lessons are included on the CD that comes with the book.

**Macromedia Flash 8:
Training from the Source**
ISBN 0-321-33629-1

**Macromedia Flash
Professional 8: Training
from the Source**
ISBN 0-321-38403-2

**Macromedia Flash 8
ActionScript: Training
from the Source**
ISBN 0-321-33619-4

**Macromedia Studio 8:
Training from the Source**
ISBN 0-321-33620-8

**Macromedia Dreamweaver 8:
Training from the Source**
ISBN 0-321-33626-7

**Macromedia Dreamweaver 8
with ASP, PHP and ColdFusion:
Training from the Source**
ISBN 0-321-33625-9

**Macromedia Fireworks 8:
Training from the Source**
ISBN 0-321-33591-0

macromedia®
PRESS

www.macromediapress.com